Business Ethics

A foundational text for the modern business student and an essential instructor resource, this book presents a thorough and comprehensive introduction to business ethics. Taking a strategic stakeholder approach—one that emphasizes how important it is to balance multiple stakeholders' needs—students will develop the critical skills they need to analyze and solve complex ethical issues, while ensuring overall business success.

The second edition retains *Business Ethics'* strong balance of theory and practice, but incorporates several new features, including:

- Fresh cases ensuring students are exposed to the most topical real-world examples
- A global view, with examples from international and emerging markets, and coverage of ethical standards from around the world
- An expanded chapter on individual ethical decision-making, as well as a new chapter devoted to ethical theory
- A renewed emphasis on the popular boxed features with more integration of newer case studies, and the addition of "Emerging Market Business Ethics Insights"
- The latest data on business ethics and ethics related issues from a variety of reputable sources

A comprehensive set of lecture slides, test questions, and instructor notes provide additional material for the classroom.

K. Praveen Parboteeah is the inaugural COBE Distinguished Professor of Management and Director of the Doctorate of Business Administration program in the College of Business & Economics at the University of Wisconsin–Whitewater, USA.

John B. Cullen is Professor of Management and former Huber Chair of Entrepreneurial Studies and Associate Dean for Graduate Programs at Washington State University, USA. He received his PhD from Columbia University.

"*Business Ethics, second edition* is a rare combination of both impressive scholarship together with accessibility for the non-specialist reader. It covers the emerging ground of CSR effectively and impressively. The authors have taken the opportunity of the second edition not to just update the text but to enhance it. *Business Ethics* remains a welcome addition to reading lists for post and undergraduate courses in the subject area."

John Bateman, *Sussex Business School, UK*

"The second edition of Parboteeah and Cullen's *Business Ethics* retains the strong pedagogical foundations of stakeholder management and ethics theory while providing new, timely cases, many with a global perspective, and other enhancements throughout the book."

James Weber, *Palumbo Donahue School of Business, USA*

"By using a stakeholder focus as the foundation for examining ethical issues facing today's managers, *Business Ethics, second edition* gives readers a decision making model which they will find both highly relevant as students and extremely useful as they move into careers."

Robert Letovsky, *St. Michael's College, USA*

Business Ethics

Second Edition

K. Praveen Parboteeah

and

John B. Cullen

NEW YORK AND LONDON

First published 2019
by Routledge
711 Third Avenue, New York, NY 10017

and by Routledge
2 Park Square, Milton Park, Abingdon, Oxon, OX14 4RN

Routledge is an imprint of the Taylor & Francis Group, an informa business

Library of Congress Cataloging in Publication Data
A catalog record for this book has been requested

ISBN: 978-1-138-74533-9 (hbk)
ISBN: 978-1-138-74534-6 (pbk)
ISBN: 978-1-315-18066-3 (ebk)

Typeset in Perpetua and Bell Gothic
by Florence Production Ltd, Stoodleigh, Devon, UK

Printed and bound by CPI Group (UK) Ltd, Croydon, CR0 4YY

Visit the companion website: www.routledge.com/cw/parboteeah

To
Kyong, Alisha and Davin
and
Jean and Jaye

Brief Contents

Contents

Preface

Despite several well-known ethical scandals in the 1980s and more recent incidents and scandals, frequent ethical transgressions continue to characterize the business world. The latest crises involving global corporations suggest that business ethics continue to be extremely important today. No companies are immune from such forces. To cope adequately with such needs for ethical behavior, managers of global and domestic companies will need to be able to develop and implement successful strategies to encourage ethical behavior. *Business Ethics* continues its strong tradition of providing students with the latest insights into managing companies to become more ethical and to build an ethical culture. *Business Ethics* was originally written to provide students with the necessary theoretical background and subsequent practical applications to understand the complexities of business ethics in the workplace. The text continues this approach by using a strategic stakeholder approach to emphasize these core issues. Furthermore, the text also recognizes key forces such as globalization of business, increased reliance on information technology and increased pressure for environmental sustainability as key drivers of business ethics today.

With the success of the first edition, this second edition improves on many of the strong features of the previous edition. Among many changes, the following are the most crucial:

- This text represents one of the more global centric business ethics texts on the market. Students will read about many examples of companies located worldwide. They will also have the chance to read specific examples of companies in emerging markets.
- Based on reviewer feedback, the previous chapter on individual ethics has now been divided into two chapters. Students will now get a more in-depth look into the individual factors influencing ethical behavior. Students will also have the opportunity to read a chapter solely devoted to ethical theories and their implications for companies. Furthermore, the importance of individual ethical behavior is recognized as these two chapters are now discussed ahead of stakeholders.

- All end-of-chapter cases have been replaced. Students will have the opportunity to read cases about global companies such as Volkswagen, GlaxoSmithKline, IKEA and emerging market cases such as IKEA in Russia and the now defunct Satyam Computers. The text also includes a number of new cases about well-known U.S.-based companies such as Apple and Starbucks.
- All chapters have been thoroughly updated with fresh data and research on the area. Whenever possible, the latest frameworks or approaches have also been discussed.
- The textbook retains its strong balance between theory and real-life examples. The many popular boxed features have been emphasized in the second edition with the addition of a new feature termed Emerging Market Business Ethics Insight.
- Most reviewer feedback has been incorporated. Changes include a more extensive discussion of executive compensation, addition of virtue ethics as an additional ethical theory, more extensive discussion of other frameworks to combat bribery among many others.

PEDAGOGICAL APPROACH

Business Ethics provides a thorough review and analysis of business ethics issues using several learning tools.

Strategic stakeholder management as the theme: All chapters use a strategic stakeholder approach as a unifying theme. The text is thus the first text that continues this approach. Most business ethics scholars and practitioners agree that successful ethical companies are the ones that can strategically balance the needs of their various stakeholders. By adopting this approach, students will be able to see how the various aspects of business ethics are connected.

Theory-based and application-based: All chapters have important applicable theories integrated with discussion of how such theories apply in practice. Unlike other texts that are either too theoretical or too practical, this text provides the appropriate blend of theory and practice to provide deeper insights into the concepts covered in the chapter. Furthermore, each chapter includes many opportunities for readers to apply the knowledge gained from reading, an internet activity, a "What Would You Do?" scenario, and an end-of-chapter case study. All three activities help students apply the concepts to real-life situations.

Integrating: Chapters build on each other in a logical way in contrast to many texts that have stand-alone chapters. The stakeholder approach presented in the text provides a good integrating mechanism and the last chapter brings it all together.

Current: The text includes many of the most recent examples pertaining to business ethics issues. Furthermore, discussion of most current trends was not limited to U.S.-only examples. The authors took great effort to ensure that the examples pertain to multinationals worldwide.

More global perspective: Unlike most other texts, this text provides a global perspective on business ethics. Most chapters include material pertaining to ethics in global contexts. Included are cases about companies in a wide range of countries including

Japan, the UK, the USA, Germany etc. However, the text also recognizes the critical role played by emerging markets and emerging market multinationals. The text therefore includes ample coverage of issues from countries such as Russia, China, and India and regions such as Africa and Latin America.

KEY FEATURES

Chapter case studies, internet activities, and "What Would You Do?": Each chapter provides several opportunities to apply text material to real-life business ethics problems. Short cases provide the instructor with the ability to assign an activity that students can read and discuss within 30 minutes. The "What Would You Do?" feature provides students with scenarios to confront potential personal ethical dilemmas and how they would react to such decisions. Chapter case studies are longer cases that provide students with the opportunity to examine case material in much more depth. Internet activities acknowledge the growing importance of the internet as a learning tool and allow students to explore business ethics issues in that environment. We have also included interesting comprehensive cases that can be used to discuss issues pertaining to the different parts of the book.

Extensive examples: Throughout the text, many examples enhance the text material by showing actual business ethics situations. The text uses several different formats to illustrate the environment driving business ethics today:

- *Preview Business Ethics Insight* discusses how a multinational or other entity has dealt with ethical situations pertaining to the chapter.
- *Business Ethics Insight* pertains to specific examples of companies dealing with the general business ethics issues discussed in the text.
- *Strategic Business Ethics Insight* provides information regarding the strategic implications of the ethical issues discussed in the chapter.
- *Ethics Sustainability Insight* where we discuss the environmental or sustainability implications of the ethical issues discussed in the chapter.
- *Global Business Ethics Insight* provides information on the global nature and implications of the ethical issues in the chapter.

In response to the feedback we received from reviews of the first edition, we have also added the following boxed features:

- *Emerging Market Business Ethics Insight* where we discuss ethical issues with the specific context of emerging markets.
- *Business Ethics Brief* provides information on the ethical issues more succinctly.
- *Learning Aids*: The companion website continues the strong tradition of providing additional material that complements (and does not repeat) the text. The website includes an extensive selection of regularly updated internet links to resources and information.

CONTENTS

This book includes four major sections. Each section contains chapters that provide information on essential topics of international business. The intent is to give you an overview of the complex and exciting world of business ethics.

In Part I, we present a general introduction to business ethics. Chapter 1 presents the readers with a general introduction to business ethics. The main aim of the chapter is to discuss the prevalence of unethical behaviors worldwide and to discuss the main benefits of being ethical. In response to the feedback we got from reviewers, we emphasize aspects of individual ethics next. As such, in Chapter 2, we explore the many facets of individual ethics. Recognizing that the ethical orientation of a company often subsumes the ethical orientations of individuals within the company, we discuss some of the most important determinants of individual ethics. Furthermore, reviewers also wanted to see a more balanced discussion of ethical theories. Chapter 3 is therefore devoted to some of the major theories or frameworks that can explain ethical behavior. Chapters 2 and 3 therefore present a more comprehensive understanding of the determinants of individual ethical behavior. Furthermore, as we saw earlier, a strategic business ethics approach means that a company is properly balancing the needs of its various stakeholders. In Chapter 4, we discuss the many core stakeholder issues such as the types of stakeholders, the characteristics of stakeholders, etc. We conclude that chapter with a tool to assess stakeholder needs.

In Part II, we examine certain stakeholders. Specifically, we argue that there are four critical organizational stakeholders; namely, employees, customers, investors and the media/special interest groups. These stakeholders are conveniently categorized as primary and secondary stakeholders. Because primary stakeholders are more likely to affect companies, Part II devotes three chapters to such stakeholders. In Chapter 5, we consider the role of employees as stakeholders and the many obligations companies have with respect to employees. In that chapter, we consider key aspects of the relationship between a company and its employees such as compensation practices and policies, discrimination, and sexual harassment. Furthermore, given the current business environment focused on reducing sexual harassment, we conclude the chapter with a case on sexual harassment in India. In Chapter 6, we consider another important stakeholder; namely, the customer. In this chapter, we consider the many responsibilities a company has with respect to its customers. We also consider customer rights and what companies do to respect such rights. Finally, we discuss some of the proactive approaches companies use today to keep this stakeholder group happy. Chapter 7 discusses the role of shareholders as stakeholders of a company. As we discussed earlier, shareholders are typically the owners of a public company. However, managers are the ones running the company. This poses special issues that reflect the unique relationships between shareholders and companies. We will also consider corporate governance issues as they relate to the mechanisms available to shareholders to control management. Corporate governance is a key aspect of how any company manages ethics. Additionally, we also expanded the section on board diversity and performance as well as executive compensation. Finally, in Chapter 8, we examine a number of other stakeholders; namely, the government, the media, and non-governmental organizations.

While these stakeholders may not always have direct impact on the organization like employees or customers, they are nevertheless very influential stakeholders. We will therefore consider the roles played by these three stakeholders and the influences they have on companies.

In Part III, we examine the environment that most companies are facing today. Each chapter is dedicated to important driving forces that are shaping business environments in most countries. Chapter 9 examines the role of information technologies and their impact on ethics. As the use of information technologies continues to explode, more companies are facing unexpected ethical issues. In Chapter 10, we discuss another important aspect of any company's setting; namely, the environment and environmental sustainability. In this chapter, we discuss the growing pressure companies are facing to become more environmentally sensitive. We consider the various approaches to managing the environment and best practices of the world's most environmental multinationals. Finally, Chapter 11 considers another critical aspect of the environment: the global environment. In this chapter, we consider why countries view business ethics issues differently. We also learn about the major international ethics issues with a special focus on corruption and bribery. The chapter also includes discussion of some of the latest regulatory frameworks to reduce bribery and corruption.

Finally, Part IV is dedicated to understanding how managers can build an ethical company. Chapter 12 considers the company's ethical culture and how the culture affects ethical behaviors. We will discuss the most popular way of characterizing ethical culture; namely, through ethical climates. Finally, Chapter 13 integrates the various chapters to present a strategic approach to managing business ethics; namely, through corporate social responsibility. We also cover in detail the important trend of increased formal reporting of ethical and sustainability reporting such as the Global Reporting Initiative.

SUPPORT MATERIALS

Business Ethics: A Strategic Stakeholder Perspective offers a website for both students and instructors at www.routledge.com/cw/parboteeah. This site contains supplements to the text that give students and instructors many more options for learning and teaching the text content.

For Instructors

Web support is available with the following features:

- *Instructor's Manual.* Chapter-by-chapter outlines with teaching tips, web and in-class exercises, relevant YouTube videos and other video resources.
- *Test bank.* A full test bank for each chapter including both multiple choice and true/false questions. These are available both as Word documents and in formats compatible with uploading to Blackboard or WebCT.

- *PowerPoint slide presentations.* Instructors have access to more than 40 slides that complement the main points of each chapter.
- *Weblinks.* Useful links to instructional resources including all links in the Instructor's Manual.

For Students

Web support is available with the following features:

- *Practice quizzes.* The website provides practice quizzes to students with instant feedback on their answers.
- *Flashcards.* Interactive flashcards allow students to test their knowledge of the book's key concepts.
- *Weblinks.* Informational links give students easy access to online resources.

Acknowledgments

This textbook follows on the revisions of two other jointly authored texts on other management topics. This is therefore almost the third textbook revision in a row. Such activity is not possible without the support of numerous individuals. We thank our families for giving us the time and quiet to accomplish this task:

- Kyong Pyun, Praveen's wife, accurately deserves the moniker "best wife." She enabled uninterrupted blocks of time to finish this new project and provided expertise when needed. Alisha, Praveen's daughter, is now a confident teenager finishing high school. She remains curious about Daddy's projects and continues to inquire about progress. She is Daddy's favorite daughter. Davin, Praveen's son, has also been through many text revisions. He is also curious now but is still trying to figure out what Daddy does. And he keeps the title "Best Son in the World!"
- Jean Johnson, John's wife, and also an academic, provided council, support and occasional goal-setting to keep John on schedule.

The inspiration for this text comes from Praveen's parents. They raised him with a strong work ethic while also emphasizing honesty and integrity. Praveen's foray and interest in business ethics is only natural. However, the text would not have been possible without the support and inspiration of many of Praveen's colleagues. John Cullen provided the inspiration by encouraging Praveen to work on the concept of ethical climates. Former chair of the Management Department Yezdi Godiwalla initially assigned Praveen his first business ethics course. This led to sustained interest in business ethics issues. Subsequent chair, James Bronson, continues such teaching assignments. Praveen is also grateful to his colleagues Jerry Gosenpud and Lois Smith for intellectual discussions that helped refine his teaching. Praveen is also very grateful to former dean Christine Clements and current dean John Chenoweth for supporting all business ethics endeavors, including a faculty workshop and many other activities. All of these contributions helped Praveen keep his focus.

This text would have been impossible without the support of a professional editorial team. In particular, we thank Routledge editor Alston Slatton, who supported the project. He came in at the end of the project but continued supporting the effort while also learning quickly about the publishing process. He helped us navigate the many challenges that we faced as we went along the process. Developmental editor Jill D'Urso kept us on track for a very tight writing schedule. She was also very patient with us. Our thanks go to several other professionals who contributed to this project, including the individuals who contributed cases in the book. We also appreciate the efforts of individuals involved in the marketing and production.

Finally, the authors would also like to thank the many reviewers from a wide array of universities and countries, including James Weber, Professor at Duquesne University. The authors would like to thank the feedback from the anonymous reviewers. The feedback helped improve the manuscript for this second edition.

K. Praveen Parboteeah
John B. Cullen

About the Authors

K. Praveen Parboteeah is the inaugural COBE Distinguished Professor of Management and Director of the Doctorate of Business Administration program in the College of Business and Economics, University of Wisconsin–Whitewater. He received his PhD from Washington State University, holds an MBA from California State University–Chico and a BSc (Honors) in Management Studies from the University of Mauritius.

Although Parboteeah used to regularly teach international management, business ethics and strategic management at both undergraduate and graduate levels, he now exclusively teaches doctoral level classes. He has received numerous teaching awards and is included in multiple editions of *Who's Who Among America's Teachers* and is a University of Wisconsin–Whitewater Master Teacher and Teaching Scholar. He is one of two faculties who received the University of Wisconsin–Whitewater Research Award in 2007–2008 and 2015–2016.

Parboteeah's research interests include business ethics, international management, and technology and innovation management. He has published over 45 articles in leading journals such as the *Academy of Management Journal*, *Organization Science*, *Decision Sciences*, *Journal of Business Ethics*, *Human Relations*, *Journal of International Business Studies*, *Journal of Business Research* and *Management International Review*.

Parboteeah has been involved in many aspects of business ethics at the University of Wisconsin–Whitewater. He initiated a faculty workshop where faculty members met and discussed business ethics issues. He is among a handful of judges for Wisconsin's only business ethics award; namely, the Better Business Bureau Torch Award. He also lectures on the matter worldwide. His research in business ethics was recently ranked 8th in the world for publications in top-tier journals. He has also been consulted by the media numerous times including most recently an interview on Wisconsin Public Radio on the Volkswagen Diesel scandal.

Of Indian ancestry, Parboteeah grew up on the African island of Mauritius and speaks Creole, French and English. He currently lives in Whitewater with his South Korean wife, Kyong, and children, Alisha and Davin.

John B. Cullen is Professor of Management now on half time appointment and former Huber Chair of Entrepreneurial Studies and Associate Dean of Graduate Programs at Washington State University. He received his PhD from Columbia University.

Professor Cullen is the author or co-author of five books and over 70 journal articles, most of which appeared in major business journals such as *Administrative Science Quarterly*, *Journal of International Business Studies*, *Academy of Management Journal*, *Organization Science*, *Journal of Management*, *Organizational Studies*, *Journal of Vocational Behavior*, *American Journal of Sociology*, *Organizational Dynamics* and the *Journal of World Business*. In the area of business ethics, he is known primarily for his groundbreaking work on ethical climates. Most recently, his work examines business ethics in the international context.

Professor Cullen is currently Senior Editor for the *Journal of World Business*. He is also a past president of the Western Academy of Management and a former Fulbright Scholar. He lives with his wife, Jean Johnson, with whom he has co-authored one child and numerous academic publications.

Part I

Introduction

Chapter 1

Introduction to Business Ethics

LEARNING OBJECTIVES

After reading this chapter you should be able to:

- Understand what business ethics is
- Appreciate the global nature of business ethics
- Be aware of the prevalence of unethical behavior around the world
- Appreciate the benefits of ethical companies
- Understand the types of business ethics issues
- Understand the stakeholder approach discussed in this book

PREVIEW BUSINESS ETHICS INSIGHT

Ethical Challenges Worldwide

Companies such as Enron and WorldCom are well known for their ethical scandals. Both companies engaged in fraud and used questionable accounting practices to inflate their financial records. Both companies had senior executives and top management involved in such unethical transactions. Consequently, both companies suffered, resulting in tremendous losses for a substantial number of people. Employees lost their jobs and years of retirement savings. Investors lost billions of U.S. dollars after their shares became worthless. Both companies also led to the demise of their accounting auditors. These auditors were blamed for turning a blind eye to these accounting improprieties and for not doing their job properly.

Although most people have heard about these well-publicized cases, other companies worldwide were also embroiled in similar scandals. Consider the following examples. Satyam used to be India's fourth largest information technology services exporter alongside other Indian IT giants such as WIPRO and Infosys. In January 2009, the news broke that the company had been engaged in one of India's biggest frauds. The chairman of the company and nine other top executives had manipulated the company's accounting records over the previous years to inflate revenues. Fake customers and invoices were created to generate fictitious revenue. Furthermore, these individuals forged board decisions in order to obtain unauthorized loans to buy property and land. The company's founder, Ramalinga Raju, admitted to overstating company profits resulting in the creation of a fake cash balance of over $1 billion. These activities also resulted in similar disastrous consequences for people. Investors lost significant amounts of money as shares in the company tumbled. However, the industry also feared losing lucrative customers such as GE and IBM. While the Indian IT sector was generally seen as clean, the Satyam incident could potentially result in the loss of trust and billions of dollars outsourcing loss.

The above represent well-known cases that occurred in the early 2000s. However, multinationals continue to engage in ethically suspect behaviors. Consider the recent case of H&M, the Swedish retail company. They recently posted an advertisement on their website for a children's 'hoodie' reading 'coolest monkey in the jungle' using a black child model. The advertisement was immediately criticized as being racist and insensitive and H&M had to quickly apologize for their mistake. Tech companies such as Uber, Facebook, Alibaba etc. are all facing increasing scrutiny because of their power and the amount of data they are collecting on individuals. As an example, Uber is facing a backlash in many markets for their operations as well as their male-dominated organizational culture. Well-established companies are also facing ethical issues in the new markets they are operating. Consider that McDonald's in India is currently engaged in a court battle with Mr. Bakshi, the individual who brought McDonald's in India. When McDonald's tried to buy Mr. Bakshi's share, he refused and has been suing the company on many different fronts. Such lawsuits have the real potential of closing down McDonald's in India.

Based on *The Economist*. 2017. "McDonald's in India; Not loving it." September 30, 60; *The Economist*. 2017. "Tech's toughest job; From Uber to kinder." October 7, 65–66; Fontanella-Khan, James. 2009. "Satyam shares tumble over fresh charges." *Financial Times*, 24; Guha, Romit. 2009. "Wider fraud is seen at India's Satyam." *Wall Street Journal*, B1; Kottasova, I. 2018. "H&M apologizes for using black child to sell 'coolest monkey' top. *CNN Money*, January 8 http://money.cnn.com/2018/01/08/news/companies/hm-apologizes-monkey-hoodie/index.html.

The Preview Business Ethics Insight above shows the prevalence of unethical behavior worldwide. While attention in the U.S. has been mostly focused on companies such as Enron, WorldCom, and Arthur Andersen, there are many examples of companies worldwide that have been involved in fraud and other deceptive and unethical behaviors. In addition, as the H&M case shows, even if companies are not intentionally engaged in questionable actions, they need to be very vigilant as to their actions globally. What may be perceived as acceptable for a marketing team may be seen as incredibly insensitive by others. Additionally, the case of McDonald's shows that operating globally is fraught with ethical challenges.[1] They are facing a significant battle as they continue battling in the Indian court system.

Given the above, it is therefore imperative for any business student to have a solid foundation in understanding business ethics globally. As the public and the media grow warier or suspicious of the motives of companies, large and small, it is becoming ever more critical for companies to become more ethical. Additionally, the dangers of operating globally have to be recognized. What is considered acceptable at home may be viewed very negatively in other societies.

WHAT IS BUSINESS ETHICS?

To understand the meaning of business ethics, we must first understand the meaning of ethics. **Ethics** refer to society's perception of what is right or wrong. Consider, for example, that some people consider abortion as unethical as they believe abortion is wrong. Others believe that abortion pertains to a woman's ability to decide and is therefore right. This simple example shows the complexity involved in understanding ethics. As you see, ethics may not be viewed similarly by all. Furthermore, ethics do change over time.

When applied to the business context, **business ethics** refer to the principles and standards that guide business. For instance, consider the real situation of a corporation that was created to trade in blood. The entrepreneur who created the company saw a market for blood. The company purchased blood from African nations and sold to hospitals in the U.S. The blood was purchased at very low prices in Africa and sold at what would be considered exorbitant prices in the U.S. There was significant controversy around the entrepreneur and his actions. Many questions relating to business ethics were asked. Should that corporation be allowed to continue business? Is it ethical to trade in blood? Or is the company simply satisfying a market need and should thus be allowed to operate? Is it appropriate for the company to buy blood at very low prices and sell to U.S. hospitals at much higher prices? The views on these subjects varied. Some people felt that a market existed and that the entrepreneur was simply satisfying that need. Others could not understand how someone could actually trade in blood and charge very high prices for something acquired very cheaply.

As you can see from the above example, business ethics is a very complex subject and decisions are seldom black and white. Often, ethical dilemmas have shades of gray that require intense consideration before a resolution can be achieved. Similar to individual ethics, people may have different perceptions of what is considered ethical or not. For instance, some argue that the high level of compensation given to top executives is fair as it reflects the forces of demand and supply. Others see executive compensation as exaggerated given how much lower level workers may be paid.

This book will therefore prepare you to first understand the complexity inherent in business ethics dilemmas. It will also provide solutions to these dilemmas and situations. The framework in the book will allow you to systematically understand business ethics and to learn about tools and techniques that can help resolve these ethical dilemmas.

To help drive the concepts, this text has several boxed features. The **Preview Business Ethics Insight** discusses how a multinational or other entity has dealt with ethical situations pertaining to the chapter. The **Business Ethics Insight** pertains to specific examples of companies dealing with the general business ethics issues discussed in the text. In contrast, the **Strategic Business Ethics Insight** provides information regarding the strategic implications of the ethical issues discussed in the chapter. Furthermore, given the current emphasis on the environment and sustainability, each chapter also contains an **Ethics Sustainability Insight** where we discuss the environmental or sustainability implications of the ethical issues discussed in the chapter. Additionally, in some cases, we discuss ethical implications briefly in a **Business Ethics Brief** boxed feature.

Finally, this book is among the first to provide a global orientation toward understanding business ethics. While most other business ethics texts have considered ethics mostly from a U.S. perspective, trade has never before crossed international borders so much and it is necessary to integrate this international dimension. This book therefore also includes **Global Business Ethics Insight** providing information on the global nature and implications of the ethical issues in the chapter. Why this global focus? Consider the Global Business Ethics Insight below.

GLOBAL BUSINESS ETHICS INSIGHT

Global Ethical Issues

Siemens, based in Germany and operating for more than 160 years, is Europe's biggest engineering firm. It operates in the industry, energy, and healthcare industries and manufactures electronic and electrical engineering products. As of 2018, it had 372,000 employees in more than 200 countries. But despite Siemens' prominence in Europe and worldwide, it was embroiled in an embarrassing and widespread bribery scandal. For over a decade, Siemens would readily pay foreign officials to win contracts. Siemens would also engage in the routine practice of claiming the bribes as tax deductions for "useful expenditures." However, what surprised investigators was the candor with which these bribes were taking place. Siemens created three "cash desks" where employees could stop by with empty suitcases to be filled with cash. More surprisingly, these cash desks operated on an honor system and employees were allowed to take as much as 1 million euros without filling out any documents. As reported, employees carried over $67 million between 2001 and 2004.

However, in 1999, Germany made bribery illegal. Siemens also listed its shares on the New York Stock Exchange in 2001. While these activities should have stopped bribery, because of a strong culture of permitting bribes, bribery continued. Siemens created special accounts that were not included in the corporate books. Managers could still get easy access to millions of dollars for bribery purposes and over $805 million was paid out to win contracts worldwide. As the company was operating at a global level and it is listed on the New York Stock Exchange, Siemens had to abide by strict worldwide bribery laws. When investigators found about the extent of bribery, Siemens faced legal action. As such, in 2008, Siemens agreed to pay $800 million to U.S. authorities and over $540 million in Germany. It pleaded guilty to the charges of bribery and corruption and vowed to turn over a new leaf. Today, bribery and corruption is a distant past for Siemens.

Another multinational giant, McKinsey is currently facing an ethical scandal for its operations in South Africa. It is a global management firm with over 14,000 consultants in over 120 cities worldwide. It recently faced a significant backlash for its work in South Africa. The ethical scandal revolves around the Indian business group led by the Guptas who moved to South Africa in the 1990s and developed a computer parts business into a global conglomerate. Many anti-corruption groups assert that the Guptas got rich because of their connections with South Africa's president, Jacob Zuma. Evidence reveals that McKinsey was lavishly compensated for its work with a local consulting firm that has ties to the Guptas. The local company won many local contracts from a state-owned electricity monopoly. Additionally, McKinsey is also accused of charging outrageous fees for work done for a local public entity. Experts agree that such fees are very unusual for the industry.

Based on *The Economist.* 2008. "Business: Bavarian baksheesh; The Siemens scandal." 389: 8611, 112; *The Economist. 2017.* "McKinsey in South Africa; In the eye of the storm." October 14, 58; McKinsey. 2018. www.mckinsey.com; Siemens. 2018. www.siemens.com

As the Global Business Ethics Insight shows, business ethics has a decidedly global flavor. Although Siemens is a German company, it is also listed on the New York Stock Exchange and is therefore liable under U.S. laws. Furthermore, any unethical behavior on its part could have repercussions for people beyond German borders. For instance, holders of Siemens shares could lose money. Employees in its foreign plants could lose their jobs because of poor ethical practices. For McKinsey, a global consulting firm, unethical behavior in South Africa can have damaging effects worldwide. Customers in other countries may decide they no longer want to work with McKinsey. Although the company has weathered many scandals so far, South African politicians want to investigate this issue in more depth. This could therefore be a public relations nightmare for a while.

This text therefore acknowledges the global nature of business ethics and adopts this perspective. However, we also acknowledge that emerging markets present unique challenges and opportunities for multinationals. As such, we also include **Emerging Market Business Ethics Insight** to discuss ethical dilemmas and challenges specific to emerging markets.

Given the above, next we discuss the prevalence of unethical behavior worldwide.

How Prevalent Are Unethical Behaviors Worldwide?

This text presupposes that unethical behavior is very frequent. But how prevalent is unethical behavior worldwide? Fortunately, there are many organizations undertaking business ethics surveys worldwide. Most societies want their companies to behave ethically and there is an understandable focus on assessing the degree of ethicality in societies.

One of the most well-known organizations promoting ethical behavior worldwide is Transparency International (TI; www.transparency.org). Created in 1993, TI is actively engaged in eradicating corruption worldwide. It is now made up of a network of around 90 local chapters leading campaigns to lobby governments to put in practice anti-corruption efforts. Transparency International sees corruption as the abuse of power by public officials for private gains. It also sees corruption as having many negative side effects such as being a barrier to democracy and costing people their lives, health and freedom.

Annually, Transparency International computes a Corruption Perception Index (CPI) that provides an indication of the degree of corruption in the public sector. In its latest survey (please see www.transparency.org/), TI reports the following:

- No country gets a perfect score of 100 on the CPI.
- Over 66% of the 176 countries listed falls below the midpoint of the 1 to 100 index. This indicates that corruption is a significant problem worldwide.
- The average CPI score is 43 indicating that corruption is decidedly an endemic problem.
- The latest TI CPI index also shows that countries that have the highest level of corruption also have the highest level of social inequality. This indicates that there is some sort of vicious circle between social inequality and corruption. Where people feel that the environment is not fair, they are more likely to engage and condone corruption.
- Finally, countries that have the highest levels of corruption tend to be the ones with weak public institutions such as the government and the police. Although these countries may have anti-corruption laws, these laws are often ignored.
- Corruption hurts all countries indiscriminately. Although corruption is lower in some countries, the release of the Panama papers and many other scandals indicate that corruption is a challenge worldwide.

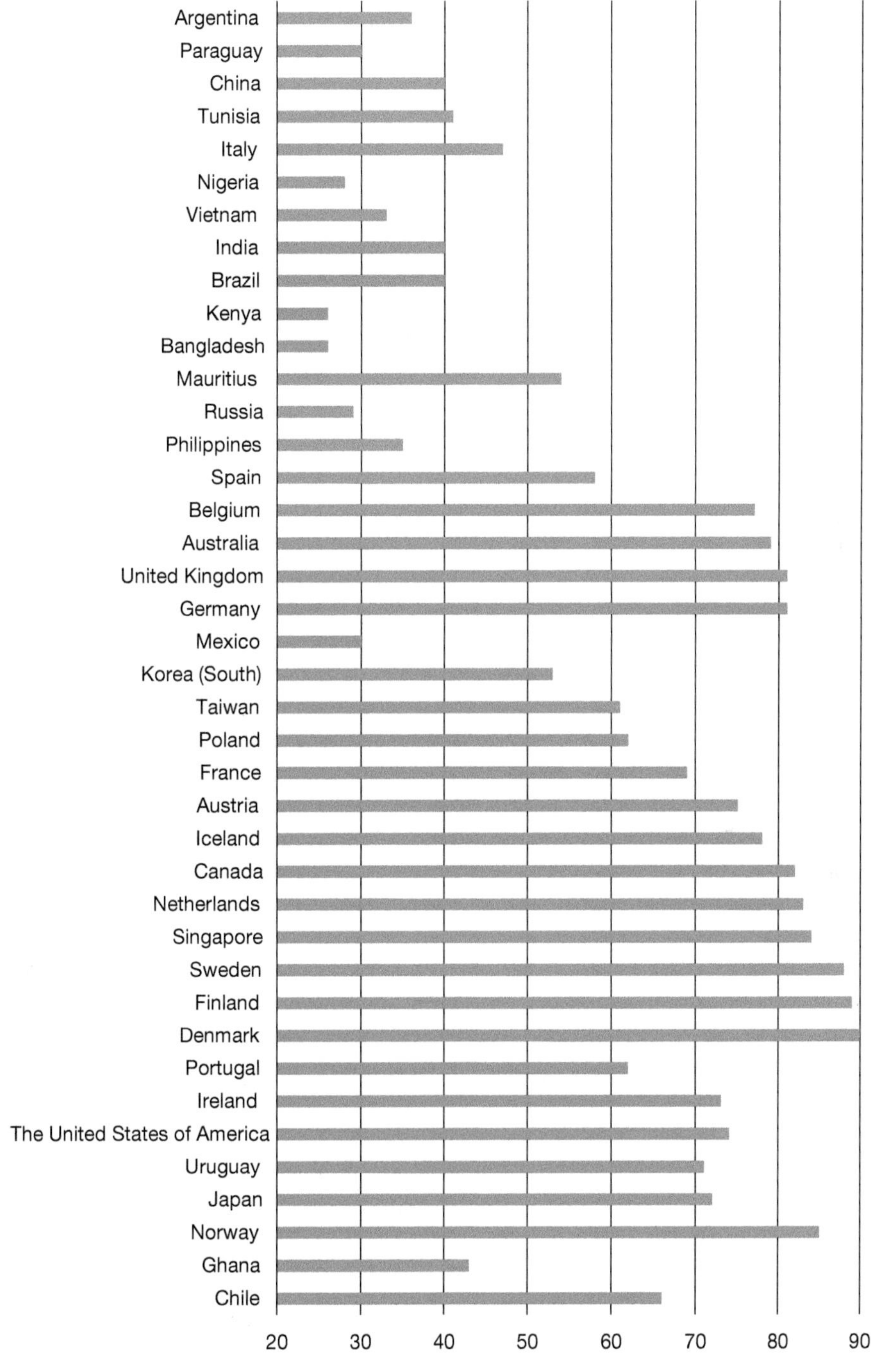

EXHIBIT 1.1—CPI by Country

Based on Transparency International, 2018. www.transparency.org/news/feature/corruption_perceptions_index_2016.

To give you further insights into the latest CPI, Exhibit 1.1 shows the CPI for selected 40 countries. This index ranges from 0 (highest level of perceived corruption to 100 (lowest perceived level of corruption).

As Exhibit 1.1 shows, perceived corruption is much more prevalent in emerging markets such as Russia, China, India and Mexico. Such findings are not surprising given the acknowledged level of corruption in some of these countries. Additionally, some other economies such as Kenya, Nigeria and Paraguay also show high levels of perceived CPI. In contrast, Scandinavian societies such as Denmark, Finland and Sweden tend to show some of the lowest levels of perceived corruption. However, what is troubling is that corruption is not limited only to some societies. Most countries see some level of corruption as no country has a perfect score of 100.

BUSINESS ETHICS INSIGHT

United Nations Global Compact

The extent of unethical behaviors worldwide is so widespread that even the United Nations got involved in helping curb such unethical actions. In 2000, it created the United Nations Global Compact. However, rather than focus on unethical behavior, the Global Compact encourages companies to voluntarily abide by ten key principles. These principles include human rights (companies should respect international human rights and should not participate in human rights abuses), labor rights (companies should allow workers to unionize, companies should not force compulsory labor and should not employ child labor, companies should eliminate discrimination), environment (companies should support environmental causes and greater environmental responsibility, companies should encourage environmentally friendly technologies) and anti-corruption (businesses should work against corruption).

The Global Compact message of ethical behavior and social responsibility has been very successful. The Global Compact has over 9670 signatories based in over 161 countries. Furthermore, the signatories come from both developed and emerging economies. The signatories also represent an even split between small and medium companies with fewer than 250 employees and large companies.

To be listed on the Global Compact list of signatories, companies must submit yearly reports on how they are abiding by and making progress on the ten principles. If companies do not submit the yearly reports, they can be delisted from the Global Compact. Additionally, the process includes a number of integrity measures that need to be communicated regularly to stakeholders. The United Nations ensures that companies that are listed are not simply engaging in window dressing but have established genuine sustainability and integrity goals.

Based on United Nations. 2018. United Nations Global Compact 2018. www.un.org.

Although Exhibit 1.1 paints a very bleak picture of ethics worldwide, not all organizations are focused on unethical behavior. Consider the Business Ethics Insight above.

As Exhibit 1.1 shows, unethical behavior in the form of corruption is very prevalent worldwide. However, unethical behavior is not necessarily limited to corruption. In that context, another international association that examines business ethics issues worldwide is the Ethics and Compliance Initiative (ECI).[2] Created in 1992, the ECI brings together business ethics practitioners as well as business ethics scholars to promote business ethics. Similar to TI, the aim of ECI is to find ways to reduce forms of unethical behaviors.

It recently conducted a Global Business Ethics Survey in 13 countries including Brazil, China, France, Germany, India, Italy, Japan, Mexico, Russia, South Korea, Spain, the United Kingdom and the USA. It surveyed workers in these countries on four key metrics beyond corruption. These include 1) the pressure to violate or compromise organizational standards pertaining to ethics, 2) whether these employees observed misconduct at work, 3) the proportion of employees who decided to report such misconduct rather than just being silent and 4) the percentage of workers who reported retaliation. Results of the study suggest the following:

- Twenty-two percent of employees surveyed reported that they perceived some form of pressure to compromise or violate organizational standards of business ethics
- A third of employees reported that they observed misconduct at work

To give you more insights on this study by country, Exhibit 1.2 shows the results of the above two metrics for the 13 countries surveyed.

Similar to the earlier results conducted by TI, emerging markets such as Russia, India and Brazil have the highest levels on the two metrics reported. However, Exhibit 1.2 also shows that even in more developed markets such as Germany, France and the UK, there is still a high level of misconduct reported. This suggests that misconduct is fairly pervasive worldwide. The ECI also surveys specific forms of misconduct. Among many other forms of misconduct, the ECI found that employees reported lying and abusive behaviors as the most frequent forms of misconduct. Exhibit 1.3 shows the data for the workers from the 13 countries.

As Exhibit 1.3 shows, lying and abusive behaviors are observed in all 13 countries surveyed. The lowest levels are in Japan while 37% of surveyed workers observed both lying and abusive behaviors in Brazil. Similarly, Russia also observed high levels of both. More than a fifth of workers surveyed observed misconduct in all countries except Japan.

In addition to the above, the ECI also revealed the following findings:

- Fortunately, 59% of employees surveyed mentioned that they reported the misconduct to management. This is very positive as it indicates that a significant percentage of employees reported misconduct rather than accept such misconduct by being silent.

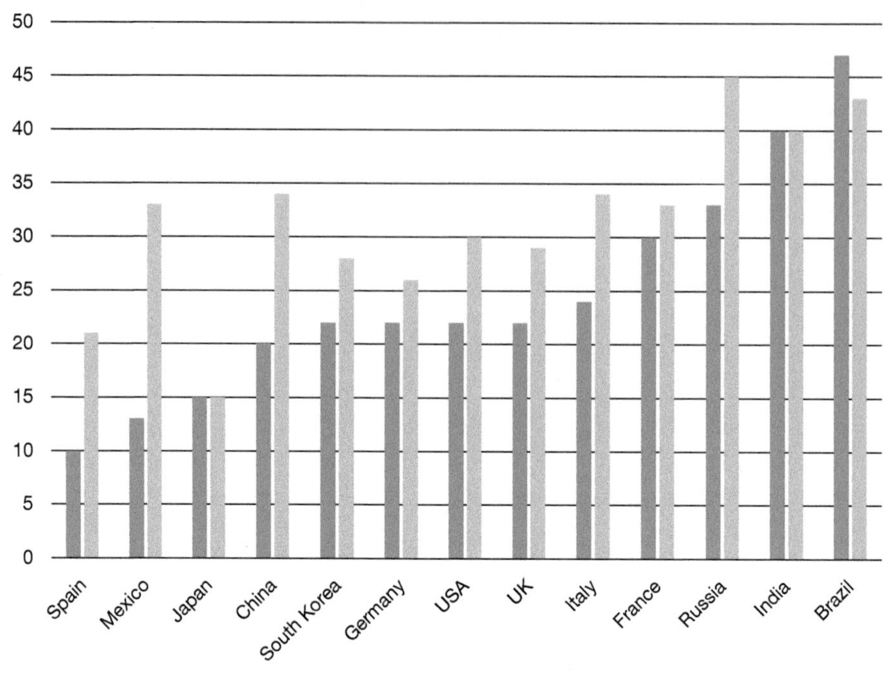

EXHIBIT 1.2—Pressured to Compromise and Observed Misconduct

Based on Ethics and Compliance Initiative, 2018. www.ethics.org/home.

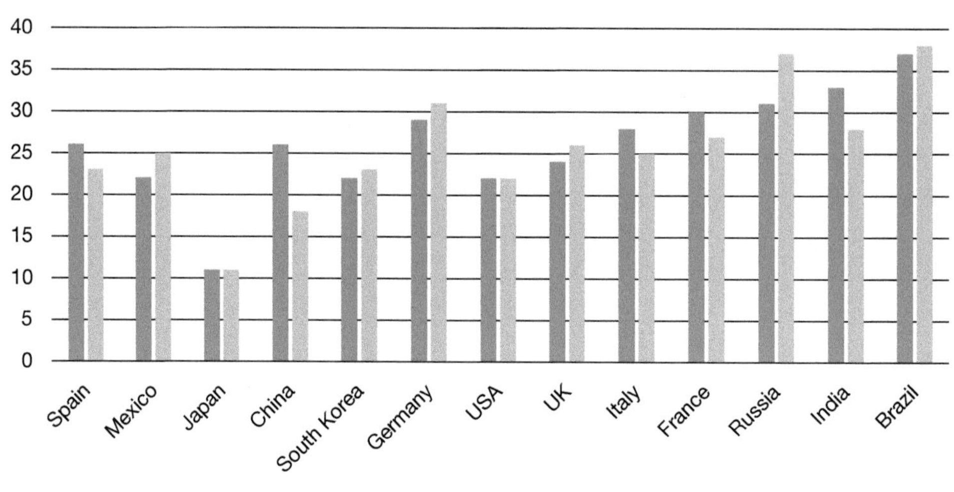

EXHIBIT 1.3—Lying and Abusive Behaviors

Based on Ethics and Compliance Initiative, 2018. www.ethics.org/home.

- Unfortunately, 36% of employees report that they suffered some form of retaliation because of such misconduct reporting. According to ECI, retaliation can include behaviors such as silent treatment, demotions and even harassment. In some extreme cases, workers also experienced violence as a form of retaliation.

Taken together, the ECI notes that the results of their study provide insights to help organizations develop better ethics programs. They note that unethical behavior is fairly pervasive and that multinationals need to invest the resources to develop compliance programs worldwide. They also suggest that because retaliation is so widespread, multinationals are well advised to protect whistle-blowers while also implementing mechanisms to ensure that there are other forms of reporting mechanisms.

Another reputed organization that studies unethical behavior is the Association of Certified Fraud Examiners (ACFE). They release an annual "Report to the Nation" on incidences of occupational fraud and abuse. The ACFE defines **occupational fraud** as "the use of one's occupation for personal enrichment through the deliberate misuse or misapplication of the employing organization's resources or assets."[3] Examples of occupational fraud include such activities such as skimming (cash is stolen from the company before the cash is recorded), billing (submission of fictitious invoices to the company), expense reimbursement (submission of fictitious business expenses for reimbursement), and payroll (false claims for compensation).

In 2016, the ACFE based its survey on over 2410 cases of occupational fraud in 114 countries worldwide. Major findings include:

- Participants report that their companies lose approximately $6.3 billion.
- The typical company loses 5% of their revenues to occupational fraud.
- More than 23% of occupational fraud resulted in losses over $1 million.
- Not surprisingly, companies that lack anti-fraud controls were more likely to experience fraud. Because smaller companies are less likely to have such controls, they are also more likely to be susceptible to fraud.
- People committing occupational fraud were often first-time offenders with no prior criminal conviction.
- Most cases were committed by members of the accounting department.
- Occupational frauds occur in a wide range of industries, with most cases occurring in banking and financial services, government and manufacturing.
- Most cases of occupational fraud were discovered as a result of tips rather than audits and controls.

To give you further insights on this study, Exhibit 1.4 shows the media loss as a result of occupational fraud by region.

As the above reviews of the reported survey results from worldwide fraud reveal, occupational fraud can be very costly to the average company worldwide. Companies are therefore well-advised to implement anti-fraud measures to ensure compliance.

In sum, the various surveys reported in this section suggest that unethical behavior and associated aspects are extremely prevalent in most societies. Even in countries that score highly on the Transparency International CPI, there are still incidences of such

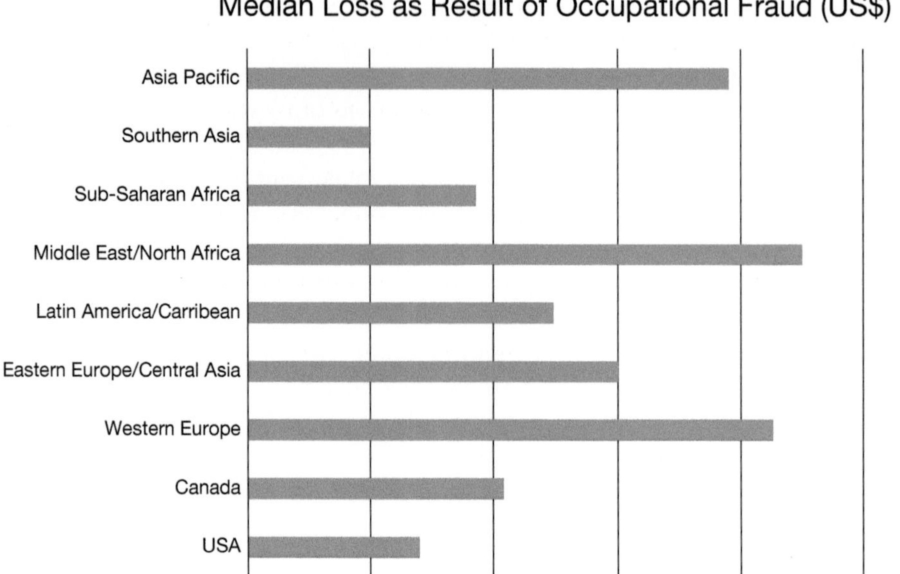

EXHIBIT 1.4—Median Loss by Region

Based on Association of Certified Fraud Examiners, 2018. Available at www.acfe.com.

behaviors in these countries. Furthermore, the fact that the United Nations got involved implies that business ethics need to be taken seriously. This book therefore argues that it is critical for companies to be more ethical. To further build the case for the crucial need for companies to be ethical, we next discuss some of the benefits of being ethical.

WHAT ARE THE BENEFITS OF BEING ETHICAL?

As the previous section demonstrated, unethical behaviors occur with some regularity in corporations around the world. Such unwanted behaviors can take many shapes and forms. However, an important question is to ascertain why companies should be ethical. Any serious ethics program is costly both in terms of human and capital resources. It is therefore critical to demonstrate that being ethical has important benefits for any corporation. In this section, we examine the many benefits accruing to corporations for their ethical actions.

At a fundamental level, an organization can only exist if it has the ability to build and sustain competitive advantage to make profits. Without profits, a company will eventually cease to exist. A basic defense of business ethics should therefore pertain to financial performance. In other words, we need to determine whether ethical companies perform better financially than unethical companies. A review of the literature by van Beurden and Gossling[4] provides some answers to this important question. In this review, the authors examine a very large number of studies linking corporate social responsibility and many aspects of performance. As you will see in Chapter 13, **corporate social responsibility** represents a strategic approach to managing ethics in an organization.

Results reviewed in the study show that corporate social responsibility has many positive benefits for organizations. The authors show that having strong corporate social responsibility programs has positive effects on many performance aspects such as 1) firm financial performance, 2) firm market value, 3) stock market value, 4) stock market returns, and 5) perceived future financial performance. Perhaps, most importantly, the authors reviewed many different dimensions of business ethics such as adherence to global environmental standards, environmental purchasing, corporate reputation for social performance, strong environmental management, philanthropy,

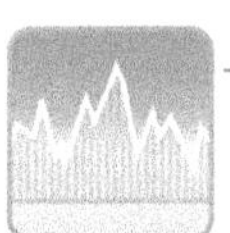

EMERGING MARKET BUSINESS ETHICS INSIGHT

Being Ethical in a Corrupt Environment

Research shows that it is indeed beneficial to be ethical. But is it worth it to be ethical in an environment that is corrupt? Is it worthwhile to do the right thing if anti-corruption laws are not very effective and the cost of corruption is low as a multinational rarely gets punished for unethical behavior? As the saying goes "if everybody else is doing it, should we do it too?"

A recent study of organizations in India, Egypt and Zimbabwe provides some insight. These three countries have accepted corrupt environments. However, the study shows that being ethical has clear advantages. First, in an environment where all companies are corrupt, it is helpful to be ethical and to stand out. Ethics can thus be a differentiator that leads to competitive advantage. In more corrupt environments, stakeholders such as customers and shareholders tend to prefer more ethical companies. As an example, Sekem in Egypt was able to get support from the country and international community for its efforts to give back to the community because of its strong emphasis on ethics. Such values have confirmed the company as genuine in its goal of helping the community rather than a Non-governmental corrupt organization window dressing noble goals.

Second, it is frequently assumed that because stakeholders are generally silent about corruption, they accept corruption. The research also shows that not all stakeholders are indifferent. There are many critical stakeholders who value ethical companies. For example, India's technology giant Infosys has been able to attract the brightest young university-educated workforce because of their emphasis on ethics.

The above therefore suggests that it is beneficial to be ethical even in highly corrupt environments. This is powerful given that most of the research on ethics has been done in less corrupt societies.

Based on Velamuri, S.R., Harvey, W.S. and Venkataraman, S. 2017. "Being an ethical business in a corrupt environment." *Harvard Business Review*, March 23, 2–5.

social programs and voluntary disclosure regarding matters of social concern. While there were few studies that showed that business ethics programs do not have any benefits, the overwhelming majority of the studies reviewed show that having various aspects of a business ethics program has significant financial benefits for the organization.

Does this relationship hold worldwide? A number of studies have been done in various countries showing similar findings. For instance, Peinado-Vara uses two case studies to show that corporate actions such as philanthropy and other corporate business ethics programs resulted in higher levels of accounting-based performance measurements in Latin America.[5] Choi and Jung find that South Korean companies that displayed ethical commitment (level of commitment to ethics) had higher stock valuation on the Korean stock market.[6] Donker, Poff, and Zahir also find that Canadian companies with strong ethical corporate values had higher levels of performance.[7] Additionally, ethical companies in more corrupt environments may send strong signals that contribute to competitive advantage. Consider the Emerging Market Business Ethics Insight on page 15.

As the reviews show, clearly business ethics have positive benefits for companies worldwide in all environments. However, it is important to also see the effects of unethical behavior. In that context, Sims argues that company reputation is a key aspect that any company is eager to protect.[8] Reputation represents the belief people have about a company based on their experiences and knowledge of the company. Ethical scandals can seriously damage a company's reputation and its future. Furthermore, the process of rebuilding reputation can take years. It is therefore critical for any company to be ethical to enhance its reputation and to minimize the risk of damaging such reputation.

In addition to the costs associated with companies behaving unethically, our earlier discussion of incidences of fraud and other employee unethical behaviors are also costly to the organization.[9] Consider the case of employee theft that has been estimated to be in the $20 to $50 billion range in the U.S. Clearly, multinationals have to bear the costs of such theft as well as the legal aspects of recovering the stolen aspects. Furthermore, research also suggests that companies that have a high level of theft are likely to have cultures that promote such theft. This becomes an added cost as such cultures are unlikely to be beneficial. To give you more insights into such costs, Exhibit 1.5 shows the media costs by type of organization based on the same data collected by the ACFE.

According to Exhibit 1.5, it is clear that fraud and theft have a high cost to any type of organization. In that respect, it is not surprising to see both public and private companies getting severely impacted. However, it is surprising to see that both government and non-profits also suffer consequences of theft and fraud globally. Such data provide evidence of the pervasiveness of costs to any type of company.

It is clear how good ethics can be beneficial to a multinational. An examination of the processes suggests that good ethics benefit the organization through employees, customers, suppliers and investors among others. However, the company itself has a lot to gain from being ethical. As we saw with the example of Siemens, unethical behavior can result in significant fines that can appreciably impair a company's ability

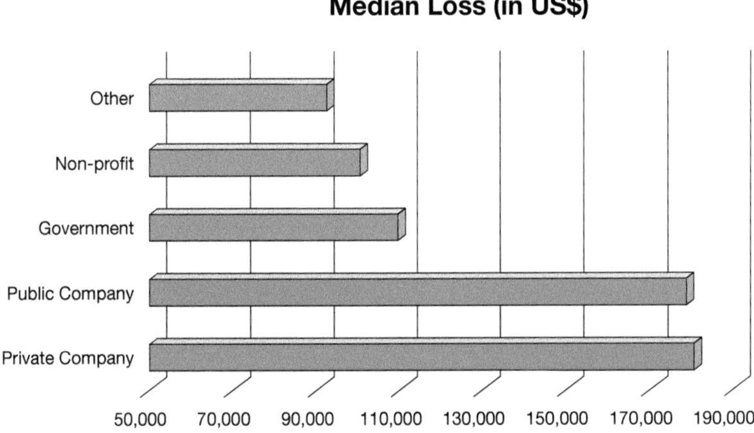

EXHIBIT 1.5—Median Loss by Type of Victim Organization

Based on Association of Certified Fraud Examiners, 2018. Available at www.acfe.com.

to survive. Because of its size and clout, Siemens was able to weather a fine of over $800 million to the U.S. and a fine of over $540 million paid to the German authorities. Other companies such as Food Lion or individuals such as Martha Stewart were not as fortunate and suffered serious consequences after unethical behaviors occurred. The legal woes and other associated fines may prove very unsettling for any organization involved in ethical scandals. Additionally, if a company has a strong culture discouraging unethical behavior, it is also less likely to suffer fraud and theft that contributes to the costs to the organization.[10]

Beyond the benefits of minimizing the chances of fines and other legal woes, organizations can enjoy other benefits from being ethical. Vilanova, Lozano and Arenas argue that a strategic approach to business ethics (i.e., corporate social responsibility) can also make a company more innovative.[11] They argue that implementing a corporate social responsibility program typically results in new corporate values, policies and practices that are being constantly defined and re-defined. During that process, the company also starts focusing on new groups that may not have mattered to the company before. For instance, there is more concern to satisfy the needs of employees, customers, suppliers, etc. This new focus can also result in innovative practices that help the company become more competitive. Thus, business ethics can help a company become competitive.

In addition to direct benefits to companies, business ethics can have important benefits for employees. Sharma, Borna, and Stearns (2009) review the recent literature to discuss some of these benefits.[12] First, employees who identify with the ethics of his or her organization are more likely to be intrinsically motivated at work. It is more probable that employees identify with more ethical companies and are thus more likely to be motivated. In fact, recent research suggests that the connection between an ethical work environment and meaningful work is very strong. In other words, if a company provides an ethical environment, employees should also be more likely to see meaning, purpose and identity in what they do.[13] Second, because of the compatibility of values, employees working in companies with stronger ethical values are also more likely to be committed to these organizations. Higher levels of commitment may result in additional benefits for the company. Third, research also shows that this high congruity in ethical values between the employee and the company should also result in higher job performance. Thus, more ethical companies tend to have employees with higher levels of motivation, commitment, and performance.

Companies also enjoy significant benefits as strong ethics programs cultivate customer trust and satisfaction. For instance, the earlier Emerging Market Business Ethics Insight showed how customers in the corrupt markets of India, Egypt and Zimbabwe were more likely to prefer more ethical companies. However, previous research has shown that consumers expect companies to be ethical while also being prepared to punish those companies that are unethical. Specifically, Trudel and Cotte note the asymmetric way people react to positive and negative information.[14] They argue that consumers tend to react more to negative information than positive information. As such, it is critical for companies to properly manage their ethics to avoid any unethical behaviors. It is also critical to consider whether consumers are willing to reward companies for being ethical. Consider the Ethics Sustainability Insight below.

ETHICS SUSTAINABILITY INSIGHT

Are Consumers Willing to Pay More for More Ethical Products?

Do consumers care if a company is more ethical? Are they willing to pay higher prices if they feel that a company is being more ethical? If consumers reward ethical companies, how far do these companies have to go to gain such rewards? Two different studies address this issue. First, Trudel and Cotte set out to test[15] these questions in several separate experiments. In the first experiment, coffee-drinking adult consumers were assigned to three groups. All three groups were told that they were helping a local grocery store evaluate a specific coffee brand. The first group was told that the coffee was sourced from fair trade organizations dedicated to better trading and working conditions for the coffee bean farmers. The second group was told that the coffee was being sourced from a company that had been criticized for unsustainable farming practices, unfair trade practices, and employing children. The third group was told that they were evaluating a typical coffee and were not provided any ethical or unethical information.

Results showed that consumers from the first group were willing to pay a premium of $1.40 over those from the second group. However, most importantly, the results showed that consumers who evaluated the more unethical coffee brand were more willing to punish the company by wanting to pay $2.40 less than the control group. In other words, consumers were willing to punish unethical companies at more than double the rate of rewarding ethical companies.

In a second experiment, the authors wanted to determine how ethical a company has to be to get rewarded. In this experiment, participants were divided into five groups. They were all told that they had to evaluate cotton t-shirts that were manufactured according to varying degrees of environmental standards. Participants were informed about conventionally grown cotton and the resulting environmental damage due to widespread use of harmful insecticides. They were told that the t-shirt they were evaluating was made by a company that only used natural fertilizers and that the company was 100% organic (Group 1), 50% organic (Group 2), 25% organic (Group 3), control where no ethical information was provided (Group 4), and the unethical group where the company used harmful pesticides (Group 5).

Results were similar to the first experiment, where it was found that consumers were willing to pay more for the ethical situations (Groups 1, 2, and 3) than the unethical situations (Group 5). However, the results showed that consumers responded fairly similarly to the different levels of ethicalness. Once a level of ethicalness is achieved, the results show that consumers will not reward the company more for higher levels of ethics.

In a more recent study, Nielsen, the global performance management company that provides data on what customers watch and buy, surveyed 30,000 consumers in 60 countries. They found that 66% of the surveyed customers are willing to pay more for sustainable brands. This is significantly higher than the 2014 levels of 55%. Additionally, these consumers were not only from urban areas but from all areas worldwide. Additionally, although the millennials have been through some of the toughest times in history, 73% of this customer group is willing to pay more for sustainable products.

Based on McSkill, A. 2015. "Consumer-good brands that demonstrate commitment to sustainability outperform those who don't." Nielsen, www.nielsen.com/us/en/press-room/2015/consumer-goods-brands-that-demonstrate-commitment-to-sustainability-outperform.html; Trudel, Remi and Cotte, June. 2009. "Does it pay to be good?" *MIT Sloan Management Review*, 50:2, 61–68.

The Ethics Sustainability Insight clearly shows that consumers are willing not only to reward more ethical companies but also to punish unethical companies. In fact, research reviewed by Bhattacharya, Korschun, and Sen also shows that consumers who perceived that a company is involved in corporate social responsibility are more inclined to positively evaluate such companies as well as to purchase the company's products.[16] Furthermore, companies can build trust through good ethics. Through good ethics, a company can provide evidence of its caring for various aspects of its environment. This display of caring is likely to result in higher levels of customer trust thereby enhancing the company's chances of building market share.

Worthington proposes that being ethical can have benefits for both suppliers and the organization.[17] One manifestation of responsible ethics is socially responsible purchasing. In such cases, large purchasing organizations provide opportunities to suppliers that are usually underrepresented in the typical supplier chains. Examples of underrepresented suppliers are smaller firms, ethnic minority firms and women-owned firms. Through purchases with these suppliers, an organization can show its effort to build supplier diversity. While U.S. companies have been involved in such efforts, Worthington contends that companies in the UK and Europe are now also implementing initiatives to engage in responsible purchasing.

Worthington argues that many benefits accrue to companies involved in responsible purchasing.[18] The suppliers benefit through the additional sales opportunities. However, responsible purchasing through increased supplier diversity can also have many benefits for the participating companies. By interacting with an ethnic minority supplier, a company can get access to new ethnic minority market knowledge. Such markets are important to companies worldwide. Furthermore, by providing opportunities to smaller suppliers, a company can reduce its dependence on its more traditional suppliers. These actions can also result in enhanced reputation for the company as it engages with a larger group of stakeholders.

More ethical companies also benefit through increased interest from investors. As Petersen and Vredenburg suggest, business ethics and corporate social responsibility efforts signal that the company is taking into consideration the needs of its various stakeholders.[19] Such efforts signal the potential to add value to the company in the long term. Investors tend to look for such factors and are therefore more likely to invest in such companies. In fact, many investors see the link between corporate social responsibility and profits as we discussed earlier. In contrast, examples of companies

BENEFITS OF BEING ETHICAL

- Positive effects on many performance aspects such as firm financial performance, firm market value, stock market value and returns, and perceived future financial performance
- Minimization of loss of reputation and financial losses due to legal costs and fines
- Increased potential to achieve sustainable competitive advantage through the consideration of various stakeholders inherent in an ethical approach
- Many employee benefits such as higher organizational commitment, better identification with company values, and higher job satisfaction
- Higher customer trust and satisfaction
- Potential willingness for consumers to pay higher prices
- Potential to increase supplier diversity and benefit from these partnerships
- Increased interest from investors

EXHIBIT 1.6—Benefits of Business Ethics

such as Martha Stewart and others show that unethical behavior may result in damages to the company. As investors hear about investigations or the potential for ethical scandals, they are more inclined to sell their shares, thereby hurting the company's market valuation.

Clearly, being ethical presents many benefits to any organization. Such benefits range from stronger financial performance to more committed employees to more loyal customers. It is therefore in the best interest of any organization to behave ethically. Exhibit 1.6 summarizes the many benefits discussed in this section.

However, beyond these benefits, many companies have realized that being ethical is the strategic approach to managing their businesses. In the face of constant criticisms from both the media and the public, most multinationals view a strong business ethics program as a way to manage their relationship with these groups.

Next we discuss the two major approaches to business ethics and finally the approach adopted in this text.

APPROACHES TO BUSINESS ETHICS

To understand the current approach to business ethics, it is necessary to examine the evolution of business ethics over the past decades. Being ethical was not always an important aspect of any corporation. In fact, in 1970, Milton Friedman, a Nobel Prize winner in economics, argued that the sole responsibility of any corporation is to make profits. Friedman argued that companies are not people but entities and therefore cannot have social responsibilities. Furthermore, he asserts that in a free enterprise economy, managers are employees of the owners of the business. Thus, managers should operate businesses in the best interests of the owners. This often means that managers should run the organization to make more money for shareholders. Additionally, Friedman posits that if a company is being socially responsible, then it is diverting money away from the owners of the company (i.e., shareholders). Shareholders are then double taxed, as their money is being taken away on top of all taxes that they already paid. Friedman thus argues that the company should only strive to achieve shareholder goals.

The best articulation of this approach to business is probably Boatright's (2002) **stockholder theory**.[20] According to Boatright, shareholders or owners have the right to control and earn residual earnings (or profits). However, Boatright's arguments are somewhat different than Friedman's. Specifically, Boatright argues that there are costs associated with any owners whether they are employees, customers, or shareholders. However, one of the most pertinent costs related to the role of shareholders is the cost of decision-making. Specifically, if a company was owned by different entities such as customers, employees, or shareholders, each of these groups could have conflicting interests regarding the goals of the company. However, Boatright suggests that the suppliers of equity capital or shareholders are the ones that have the least cost of decision-making because they are the ones with the least conflicting interests. Thus, the most efficient arrangement is ownership by suppliers of equity capital or shareholders and they have the right and control of profits. Boatright therefore argues that the best way to organize a company is through the stockholder model whereby managers are hired to achieve shareholders' goals.

As this chapter shows, the approach adopted in this book is that any company has to go beyond just shareholders. The many examples we have discussed show that any successful company has to take into consideration the needs of other groups such as employees, customers, suppliers, the community, etc. Any company that ignores the needs of these various groups does so at its own risk. Next we discuss the contrasting theory to stockholder theory.

Edward Freeman (2010) presents the **stakeholder theory** of the modern corporation, basically arguing that companies need to go beyond satisfying the needs

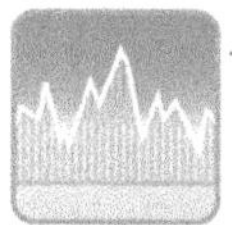

EMERGING MARKET **BUSINESS ETHICS INSIGHT**

Benefits of a Stakeholder Approach

Stakeholder theory is based on the assumption that it is beneficial for multinationals to balance and respond to various stakeholder needs. But is this approach beneficial for the multinational? A recent case study of several projects provides some valuable insights. In that study, the researchers examined Rio Tinto, a major international mining company, and how the company took steps to address stakeholder concerns regarding the opening of a new aluminum smelter project in the Samalaju Industrial Park in Malaysia. They first had to deal with public outcries about the project given the surrounding communities' concerns about pollution and cancer that could be brought by the plant. The company was very transparent about the environmental impact of their plant and shared the environmental impact assessment report with the public. Once concerns were satisfied, the company could move ahead with the project. However, because of a fall in aluminum price, the company decided not to proceed with the project.

In a review of another case, Aznerl Holding, a Malaysian company was investigating the construction of a beach resort in Bintulu. The company demonstrated the benefit that could accrue to the town as a result of becoming a resort city. Additionally, much of the construction was to take place on land that contained swamps. Furthermore, although the project was delayed at times, the developers ensured that they worked diligently to address the concerns of customers who had already paid for their units.

The two cases above show that addressing stakeholder needs is very critical. In both cases, the companies could have gone with the stockholder approach and simply satisfied the needs of owners. However, the efforts to go beyond just satisfying owners helped the companies address concerns and led to successful completion of the projects.

Based on Loi, T.H. 2016. "Stakeholder management: A case of its related capability and performance." *Management Decision*, 54, 148–173.

of shareholders only.[21] Freeman bases his theory on a few arguments. First, he asserts that although any company should operate in the interests of stockholders, the company also has to operate within the boundaries imposed by the legal system. Many new laws have been implemented over time worldwide and such laws suggest that companies need to take into consideration the needs of stakeholders governed by these laws. For instance, laws protecting employees imply that companies need to take into consideration the needs of employees. Such principles apply to most other stakeholders such as consumers, suppliers, and the community.

Second, Freeman defends his stakeholder theory based on economic arguments. He asserts that pure capitalism suggests that companies will operate according to the invisible hand argument, producing the greatest good for the greatest number. However, the invisible hand may not always function properly, especially in the presence of externalities and monopoly power. Consider, for example, air or water pollution. Often, companies have no incentive to engage in cleanups, as these costs may only create marginal benefits for them. Thus, letting the company operate only in shareholders' interests may result in other stakeholders' needs being ignored (i.e., in this case, pollution can be detrimental to society). A second facet of the economic argument is in cases where a company has monopoly power. In these cases, it is very easy for any company to abuse its market power. Thus, in these cases, it is also critical to consider the needs of all stakeholders. Clearly, the current environment demands that stakeholder needs be satisfied. Is this view shared worldwide? But is such an approach worthwhile? Consider the above Emerging Market Business Ethics Insight.

This Emerging Market Business Ethics Insight clearly shows that a stakeholder approach is the preferred way to approach business ethics. This is the approach adopted in this book. Next, we discuss the many ethical issues any corporation faces. We also frame the various chapters of this book within this context.

WHAT BUSINESS ETHICS ISSUES DO COMPANIES FACE? PLAN OF THE BOOK

In the previous sections, you have already read about the many ethical issues facing any company. How can a systematic approach be used to determine the key ethical issues? In that context, it is important to understand that a company's actions have consequences for many different groups or individuals. For instance, in an earlier Global Business Ethics Insight, we saw how Siemens' bribery had damaging consequences for its employees (some were fired, others were hurt by the illegal activities), the societies in which it operates (illegally getting contracts by bribing individuals in these societies and affecting free market forces in these societies), investors (hurting their chances of future earnings), and for the company itself (hurting chances of survival given the fines imposed on the company). As such, these various groups are known as stakeholders. This stakeholder approach provides the framework around which the various parts of the book are organized.

In Part I, we present a general introduction to business ethics. Specifically, Part I includes Chapters 1, 2, 3 and 4. The ethics of any company starts with individual employees. As such, Chapter 2 explores the many facets of individual ethics. Recognizing that the ethical orientation of a company often subsumes the ethical orientations of individuals within the company, we discuss some of the most important determinants of individual ethics. However, understanding how individuals approach ethics also means understanding their approaches to morality. Chapter 3 is thus a new addition to this second edition and discusses the various approaches to ethical theories. This chapter also discusses the various forms of moral development and the critical need for organizations to understand such levels.

As we saw earlier, a strategic business ethics approach means that a company is properly balancing the needs of its various stakeholders. As such, in Chapter 4, we will discuss stakeholders in much more depth. A stakeholder approach provides a systematic framework to understand the key ethical issues facing any corporation. In that chapter, we will discuss the many core stakeholder issues such as the types of stakeholders, the characteristics of stakeholders, etc. We conclude that chapter with a tool to properly assess stakeholder needs.

In Part II, we examine specific stakeholders. In particular, we argue that there are four critical stakeholders that any organization has to deal with; namely, employees, customers, investors, and the media/special interest groups. In Chapter 5, we consider the role of employees as stakeholders and the many obligations companies have with respect to employees. In that chapter, we look at key aspects of the relationship between a company and its employees such as compensation practices and policies, discrimination, and sexual harassment.

In Chapter 6, we consider another important stakeholder; namely, the customer. In earlier parts of the chapter, we discuss the benefits that accrue to companies as they deal with their employees in an ethical fashion. Furthermore, in this current age of information technology, it is easy for unhappy customers to vent their frustration globally simply through a blog or uploaded video. It is now much harder to manage one's reputation reactively. As such, in Chapter 6, we consider the many responsibilities a company has with respect to its customers. We also consider customer rights and what companies do to respect such rights. Finally, we discuss some of the proactive approaches companies use today to keep this stakeholder group happy.

Chapter 7 discusses the role of shareholders as stakeholders of a company. As we discussed earlier, shareholders are typically the owners of a public company. However, managers are the ones running the company. This poses special issues that reflect the unique relationships between shareholders and companies. We consider corporate governance issues as they relate to the mechanisms available to shareholders to control management. Corporate governance is also a key aspect of how ethics are managed in any company.

In Chapter 8, we examine a number of other stakeholders; namely, the government, the media, and non-governmental organizations. While these stakeholders may not always have direct impact on the organization like employees or customers, they are nevertheless very influential stakeholders. We will therefore consider the roles played by these three stakeholders and the influences they have on companies. We will also consider how companies can proactively manage these groups. To give you examples of ethical issues emanating from each of the above stakeholder groups, consider Exhibit 1.7.

STAKEHOLDERS AND ETHICAL ISSUES

Employees

- Employee conflict of interest
- Honesty and integrity
- Discrimination, diversity, and sexual harassment
- Compensation and benefits
- Employee screening and privacy

Customers

- Fairness in pricing and marketing
- Advertising content and truth in advertising
- Customer privacy
- Dealing with customer complaints
- Product safety and quality

Shareholders

- Shareholder interests
- Transparency in accounting
- Transparency in shareholder communications
- Executive salaries and compensation
- Corporate governance

Suppliers

- Enforcing contracts
- Supplier diversity in terms of country, gender, and race
- Appropriation of supplier ideas

Government

- Respecting rules and regulations
- Practices in foreign nations with weak governments
- Lobbying

Community

- Corporate social responsibility
- Pollution and environmental degradation issues
- Donation to local community charities and organizations

EXHIBIT 1.7—Stakeholder Ethical Issues

GLOBAL BUSINESS ETHICS INSIGHT

Government and Business

How influential are governments in shaping the business environment? While governments are considered less influential in more laissez-faire countries such as the U.S. and the UK, governments in other countries play a much more active role. Consider the case of China. The Chinese government routinely implements new regulations that have significant consequences for companies operating there. Both Google and Microsoft have changed their operations to accommodate Chinese governmental demands. Specifically, when Google started operations, it agreed to censor search results that could be seen as detrimental to the Chinese government. However, Google may change its policy as recent claims of hacking have emerged. In contrast, Microsoft has agreed to abide by these censorship requests to take advantage of a soaring market.

However, government intervention does not occur only in emerging markets such as China. Consider the case of the European Union and Ms. Margrethe Vestager, the commissioner in charge of competition policy. As the regulator of anti-competition efforts, Ms. Vestager sees her role as the defender of public interest. She has therefore gone after many of the U.S. high tech firms. For instance, Apple was fined $14.5 billion in back taxes to Ireland. Additionally, Goggle has also been fined 2.4 billion euros because it used its search engine to encourage customers to use its own shopping comparison service. As such, Ms Vestager sees her role at the European Union as the regulator providing a necessary counterbalance to the enormous power the giant tech firms have in shaping politics and the economy.

Based on Chao, Loretta. 2009. "World news: China firms defend tech-purchase rules." *Wall Street Journal*, A10; *The Economist*. 2017. "Europe's chief trustbuster; Big Tech's nemesis." September 16, 5758; Vascellaro, Jessica. 2010. "Google says it is committed to China as net soars." *Wall Street Journal*, B1.

Chapter 8 also devotes a significant part to the role of governments. How critical are governments in other societies? Consider the above Global Business Ethics Insight on the role of the government with respect to business ethics.

In Part III, we start examining the environment that most companies are facing today. Our decision to dedicate three chapters to understanding the environment is based on the fact that any company has to consider these issues as they implement their business ethics initiatives. Each chapter is dedicated to important driving forces that are shaping business environments in most countries.

Chapter 9 examines the role of information technologies and their impact on ethics. As the use of information technologies continues to explode, more companies are facing unexpected ethical issues. This chapter will therefore examine the many aspects of information technologies and the ease of collecting data and the consequent ethical issues associated with these new aspects.

Chapter 10 discusses another important aspect of any company's setting; namely, the environment and environmental sustainability. As discussions regarding climate change and the contributions of companies to carbon emissions continue, more companies are implementing environmental programs to be proactive. In this chapter, we discuss the growing pressure companies are facing to become more environmentally sensitive. We consider the various approaches to managing the environment and best practices of the world's most environmental multinationals. We conclude with the need for companies to actively integrate their environmental efforts in their business ethics programs.

Finally, Chapter 11 considers another critical aspect of the environment: the global environment. Although this book is among the first business ethics texts to adopt a global perspective on business ethics, we believe it is critical to have a chapter dedicated to global ethics. In this chapter, we consider why countries view business ethics issues differently. We also learn about the major international ethics issues with a special focus on corruption and bribery. Finally, we look at the many efforts and regulations that have been implemented worldwide to encourage multinationals to eliminate bribery and be more ethical.

Part IV is dedicated to understanding how an ethical company can be built. In Part IV, we first discuss some of the major factors contributing to unethical behavior by considering both the individual and the corporate culture. Both factors have been recognized as major determining factors regarding unethical behavior. We also discuss the steps a company needs to take to become more socially responsible.

Chapter 12 considers the ethical culture of any company and how that culture contributes to ethical behavior within the company. We discuss the most popular way of characterizing ethical culture; namely, through ethical climates. We review the three major forms of ethical climates and the consequences of these different types for any company. Lastly, we discuss how a company can encourage some forms of ethical climates. The chapter will also discuss such issues within the context of emerging markets. Consider the following Emerging Market Business Ethics Insight.

Finally, Chapter 13 integrates the various chapters to present a strategic approach to managing business ethics. As mentioned earlier, this book adopts a strategic approach to business ethics. Why a strategic approach? To succeed in today's chaotic and constantly changing environment, companies have to devise strategies to outmaneuver competitors in order to enjoy a sustainable competitive advantage. A **strategic approach to business ethics** means that a company will integrate business ethics issues across all of its operations and activities. All decisions are guided by what is known as the triple bottom line: do the decisions contribute to economic, social, and environmental goals? In contrast, a less holistic approach to business ethics will not provide the strategic approaches compared to a more integrated business ethics approach.

Chapter 13 therefore discusses corporate social responsibility as a strategic approach to business ethics. We explore the various approaches to corporate social responsibility, and look at the key aspects of a corporate social responsibility program. In doing so, you learn how a company can strive to balance the needs of its various stakeholders.

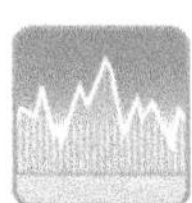

EMERGING MARKET BUSINESS ETHICS INSIGHT

Ethics in Small and Medium-sized Businesses in South Africa

What ethical practices are in place in companies in emerging markets? Such insights can be very helpful in terms of understanding the current situation in order to determine how to build ethical climates and culture. Fortunately, a recent study conducted across small and medium-sized businesses in that context provides some insights within the context of South Africa. The researchers surveyed a number of business leaders across a wide range of ethical practices. These business leaders were asked the degree to which specific ethical practices were adopted (frequency of adoption) as well as the degree to which the business leaders perceived such systems as being useful.

Exhibit 1.8 below shows the results of the study across the various types of ethical practices.

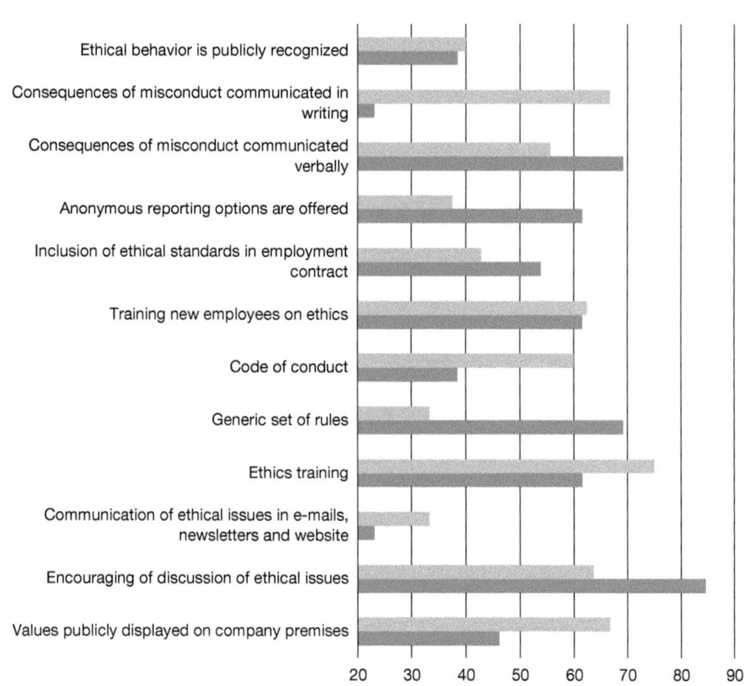

EXHIBIT 1.8—Business Ethics Practices in South African Small and Medium-sized Firms

Based on Robinson, B.M. 2017. "Inculcating ethics in small and medium-sized business enterprises: A South African leadership perspective." *African Journal of Business Ethics,* 11, 63–81

The Exhibit 1.8 findings are very encouraging. As you will learn in Chapter 12, building an ethical climate takes effort and dedication. Simply having a code of conduct is not sufficient. It is therefore insightful to see that a very large percentage of the South African firms surveyed encourage discussion of ethical issues. Additionally, a larger percentage of the firms see the utility of the approach. Additionally, many of the other ethics activities associated with a more ethical climate (rewarding of ethical behavior, ethics training, discouraging of unethical behaviors) are in place in the majority of the companies surveyed.

Based on Robinson, B.M. 2017. "Inculcating ethics in small and medium-sized business enterprises: A South African leadership perspective." *African Journal of Business Ethics,* 11, 63–81.

CHAPTER SUMMARY

This chapter provides some introductory background business ethics information. We first defined business ethics and considered some examples of current ethical dilemmas. We then presented the case for business ethics. You read about the many benefits pertaining to any company for its ethical efforts. For instance, you learned that more ethical companies tend to perform better than less ethical ones on many measures, including financial performance. You also read about many other benefits that accrue to companies through their employees (more satisfied, happier, and more committed employees), customers (more trusting, more loyal, and willing to pay more for ethical products), and investors (more loyalty).

The chapter then provides some insights into the two main approaches to business ethics. You first read about the stockholder approach where the needs of stockholders have strong influences on decisions. However, you also learned about the stakeholder approach where the stakeholder needs are balanced.

The final part of the chapter presents an overview of the chapters that you will be reading throughout the text. We frame these chapters within a strategic approach and argue that these chapters all converge in Chapter 13 on corporate social responsibility.

NOTES

1 *The Economist*. 2017. "McDonald's in India; Not loving it." September 30, 60.
2 Ethics and Compliance Initiative. 2018. www.ethics.org/home.
3 ACFE, 2018. Available at www.acfe.com.
4 Beurden, P. van & Gossling, T. 2008. "The worth of values—A literature review on the relation between corporate social and financial performance." *Journal of Business Ethics*, 82, 407–424.
5 Peinado-Vara, E. 2006. "Corporate social responsibility in Latin America." *Journal of Corporate Citizenship*, Spring, 61–69.

6 Choi, T.H. & Jung, J. 2008. "Ethical commitment, financial performance, and valuation: An empirical investigation of Korean companies." *Journal of Business Ethics*, 81, 447–463.
7 Donker, H., Poff, D. & Zahir, S. 2008. "Corporate values, codes of ethics, and firm performance: A look at the Canadian context." *Journal of Business Ethics*, 82, 527–537.
8 Sims, R.R. 2009. "Toward a better understanding of organizational efforts to rebuild reputation following an ethical scandal." *Journal of Business Ethics*, 90, 453–472.
9 Peters, S. & Maniam, B. 2016. "Corporate fraud and employee theft: Impacts and costs of business." *Journal of Business and Behavioral Sciences*, 28, 104–117.
10 Peters, S. & Maniam, B. 2016. "Corporate fraud and employee theft: Impacts and costs of business." *Journal of Business and Behavioral Sciences*, 28, 104–117.
11 Vilanova, M., Lozano, J.M. & Arenas, D. 2009. "Exploring the nature of the relationship between CSR and competitiveness." *Journal of Business Ethics*, 87, 57–69.
12 Sharma, D., Borna, S. & Stearns, J.M. 2009. "An investigation of the effects of corporate ethical values on employee commitment and performance: Examining the moderating role of perceived fairness." *Journal of Business Ethics*, 89, 251–260.
13 Michaelson, C., Pratt, M.G., Grant, A.M. & Dunn, P. "Meaningful work: Connecting business ethics and organization studies." *Journal of Business Ethics,* 121, 77–90.
14 Trudel, R. & Cotte, J. 2009. "Does it pay to be good?" *MIT Sloan Management Review*, 50, 2, 61–68.
15 Trudel & Cotte, "Does it pay to be good?"
16 Bhattacharya, C.B., Korschun, D. & Sen, S. 2009. "Strengthening stakeholder–company relationships through mutually beneficial corporate social responsibility initiatives." *Journal of Business Ethics*, 85, 257–272.
17 Worthington, I. 2009. "Corporate perceptions of the business case for supplier diversity: How socially responsible purchasing can 'pay'." *Journal of Business Ethics*, 90, 4.
18 Worthington, "Corporate perceptions."
19 Petersen, H.L. & Harrie Vredenburg, H. 2009. "Morals or economics? Institutional preferences for corporate social responsibility." *Journal of Business Ethics*, 90, 1, 1–14.
20 Boatright, J.R. 2002. "Ethics and corporate governance: Justifying the role of shareholder." In N.E. Bowie (Ed.), *The Blackwell guide to business ethics*. Malden, MA: Blackwell, pp. 38–60.
21 Freeman, E. 2010. "Managing for stakeholders." In T.L. Beauchamp, N.E. Bowie & D.G. Arnold (Eds.), *Ethical theory and business*, Upper Saddle River, NJ: Prentice Hall, pp. 56–68.

KEY TERMS

Bribe Payers Index: the degree to which executives expect companies to engage in bribery with their own companies in specific countries.

Bribery: the degree to which individuals have to be provided with some compensation (e.g., money, gifts, etc.) to influence the individual.

Business ethics: refer to the principles and standards that guide business.

Business Ethics Brief: brief discussion of ethical implications of business ethics issues.

Business Ethics Insight: pertains to specific examples of companies dealing with the general business ethics issues discussed in the text.

Corporate social responsibility: a strategic approach to managing ethics in an organization.

Emerging Market Business Ethics Insight: discussion of ethical dilemmas and challenges specific to emerging markets.

Ethics: refer to society's perception of what is right or wrong.

Ethics Sustainability Insight: discussion of the environmental or sustainability implications of the ethical issues discussed in the chapter.

Global Business Ethics Insight: provides information on the global nature and implications of the ethical issues in the chapter.

Occupational fraud: use of one's occupation for personal enrichment through the deliberate misuse or misapplication of the employing organization's resources or assets.

Preview Business Ethics Insight: discusses how a multinational or other entity has dealt with ethical situations pertaining to the chapter.

Stakeholder theory: approach that assumes that companies need to go beyond satisfying the needs of shareholders only.

Stockholder theory: approach that assumes that shareholders or owners have the right to control and earn residual earnings (or profits).

Strategic approach to business ethics: a company will integrate business ethics issues across all of its operations and activities.

Strategic Business Ethics Insight: provides information regarding the strategic implications of the ethical issues discussed in the chapter.

DISCUSSION QUESTIONS

1. What is business ethics? Give some examples of business ethics dilemmas.
2. What do the various surveys of business ethics worldwide reveal? What are some of the common unethical behaviors?
3. Discuss specific findings of any of the business ethics surveys mentioned in this chapter. What are the implications of these findings?
4. What are some of the benefits companies enjoy for their ethics program? Be specific.
5. What are the benefits of good ethics for employees?
6. Why do investors prefer to invest in companies with good ethics?
7. How do customers react to companies with good ethics? Be specific.
8. Describe stockholder theory. What are the main arguments supporting stockholder theory?
9. What is stakeholder theory? Why is the stakeholder theory approach the way companies should manage their ethics?
10. Compare and contrast stakeholder and stockholder theory.

INTERNET ACTIVITY

1. Access the website of one of the organizations, assessing ethical behavior (e.g., Transparency International, United Nations Global Compact, etc.) mentioned in the text.
2. How does that organization define ethics? Which aspects of ethics are they most concerned with?
3. What are some of the major findings of recent surveys? Prepare a presentation and share with the class.
4. What lessons do you learn regarding ethics?

For more Internet Activities and resources, please visit the Companion Website at www.routledge.com/cw/parboteeah.

WHAT WOULD YOU DO?

Facebook and Cheating

You are currently taking an online section of the Business Ethics course as part of your undergraduate program. The course is now a permanent part of your school's business curriculum. Because the course is being taught online, you never meet your classmates in person. Rather, you have "befriended" many of the students on Facebook. Occasionally, you discuss the course on Facebook.

For this week's lessons, you will be assessed primarily through a quiz conducted in an online environment. The quiz will cover a third of the semester's chapters and you will have a fairly short period of time to answer a relatively large number of questions. Because the quiz is an open book, you therefore realize that you will need to read the chapters a few times to make sure to know where information is located in the text. Once you start taking the quiz, you won't have much time to look for relevant information in the text for the questions.

When you logged into your Facebook account this morning, you see that one of your classmates (who also happens to be a very close friend) has decided to post the questions he had to attempt on the quiz. While each student gets a random list of questions from a test bank, most students will still get a significant overlap among questions. Studying the posted questions could thus be helpful.

What would you do? Did you do anything wrong by simply looking at the questions? Would you report your close friend to the teacher?

BRIEF CASE: BUSINESS ETHICS INSIGHT

Anna Hazare and Corruption in India

Vishal is a typical New Delhi resident and owns a fried chicken stall on the streets of New Delhi. However, he faces a range of petty corruption as he operates his fried chicken stand. He has to bribe the senior police officers to stay open late while the more junior police officers routinely take free lunches. He also pays local officials to make sure that he does not have any problems with health and safety inspections. He gets stopped by the police almost every other week and is asked to pay so that he is not "bothered." He also has to pay the headmaster of the best local school to ensure that his son has access to the best local school. Altogether, Vishal spends almost a third of his restaurant earnings as bribes. Many of the emerging middle-class Indians seem to have similar experiences on a daily basis.

In the face of such growing frustration, it is not surprising to see that India is experiencing the emergence of the anti-corruption social activist Anna Hazare. Hazare, a retired army driver from the state of Maharashtra, has become the voice of people frustrated with corruption. He has held a number of hunger strikes to force the local government to enact laws to combat corruption. However, he is now campaigning at the national level and wants the Indian government to adopt a version of his own Jan Lokpal Bill, a bill that most see as very weak. In his own version, the bill would call for the creation of a powerful ombudsperson to investigate top officials for corruption.

In August 2011, Anna Hazare was arrested by the Indian government for refusing to accept police restrictions on his proposed anti-corruption protests. His arrest immediately sparked demonstrations across India. Thousands of middle-class individuals frustrated with corruption marched in cities around India to protest at his arrest. Furthermore, as hundreds gathered outside the jail where he was housed, the government quickly capitulated and gave him permission for a 15-day public protest. He triumphantly left the jail and has renewed his demand that his version of the anti-corruption bill be passed. While some see his efforts as likely to bring changes to Indian corruption, others believe that business as usual will be back as the protests subside.

Mr. Hazare remains a thorn in the government's side. He is planning to launch a Martyr's day in 2018 to raise awareness about Indian farmers' issues. At least 12 farmers committed suicide in the last 22 years because of economic difficulties.

Based on Anonymous, 2011. "Indian activist leads Delhi protest." *Wall Street Journal*, August 19, online version; Associated Press. 2011. "Anna Hazare leaves jail to begin public hunger strike." *Economic Times*. 2018. "Anna Hazare to launch Jan Lokpal stir from March 23rd next year" https://economictimes.indiatimes.com/news/politics-and-nation/anna-hazare-to-launch-jan-lokpal-stir-from-march-23-next-year/articleshow/61847792.cms; *The Guardian*, August 19, online version http://guardian.co.uk; Burke, J. 2011. "Corruption in India: 'All your life you pay for things that should be free'." *The Guardian*, August 19, online version http://guardian.co.uk.

BRIEF CASE QUESTIONS

1. Research Transparency International's website and find India's ranking on the Corruption Index. Is India's ranking consistent with the Business Ethics Insight? Why or why not?
2. Why is corruption so rampant in India? Who should be blamed for such corruption?
3. How effective is social activism like Anna Hazare's actions? Do you share optimism that things will change in India? Or do you believe that "business will be back to usual"?
4. What roles do multinationals have to play to combat corruption in societies like India? What can multinationals do to combat such corruption?
5. What can be done at the societal level to combat corruption?

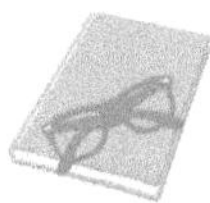

LONG CASE: BUSINESS ETHICS

THE VOLKSWAGEN EMISSIONS SCANDAL

In October 2015, Mathias Müller became CEO of Volkswagen (VW), the 78-year-old economic jewel of Germany. His predecessor, Martin Winterkorn, who had led VW for eight years, had resigned suddenly in the midst of one of the biggest scandals to ever hit VW and the auto industry. In September, VW had admitted to United States regulators that it had deliberately installed "defeat devices" in many of its diesel cars, which enabled the cars to cheat on federal and state emissions tests, making them able to pass the tests and hit ambitious mileage and performance targets while actually emitting up to 40 times more hazardous gases into the atmosphere than legally allowed. The discovery had prompted the U.S. Environmental Protection Agency (EPA) to halt final certification of VW's 2016 diesel models, and VW itself had halted sales of its 2015 models. As fallout from the defeat devices developed, VW posted its first quarterly loss in more than 15 years, and its stock plummeted. Winterkorn and several other top executives were replaced, and VW abandoned its goal of becoming the world's largest automaker. In addition to significant financial implications, VW was rapidly losing its prized reputation as a trustworthy company capable of outstanding engineering feats.

Sitting in his new office, Müller must have asked himself the question stakeholders around the world had been asking since the scandal broke: "How could this have happened at Volkswagen?"

Volkswagen Background: The Power of German Engineering[1]

In 1937, VW was founded in Germany under the Nazi regime by the labor unions with the help of Ferdinand Porsche, the inventor of the Beetle (the people's car). Tasked with making a car that was affordable for all consumers, VW's flagship car, the compact and iconic Beetle, first rolled off the manufacturing floor in 1945, and by 1949, half of all passenger cars produced in West Germany were built by VW. The company began exporting cars in the late 1940s, and by 1955, the company had sold over 1 million Beetles worldwide. The Beetle would eventually surpass Ford's Model T as the highest-selling model ever built, reaching sales of more than 15 million by 1972. When sales of the Beetle began to decline in the late 1970s, VW branched into other models, including the Passat, Jetta, Golf, and Polo. The VW brand eventually folded into a broader public holding company, Volkswagen AG, which by 2014 owned 12 subsidiaries, including VW passenger cars, Audi, Porsche, and Bentley.

By 2014 (**Exhibit 1**), VW was one of the biggest firms in the world. It had factories in 31 countries, employed almost 600,000 people worldwide, and sold its cars around the world. In 2014, it sold 10.2 million vehicles, a 5% growth over 2013, and reached its goal of taking over the title of "world's largest auto manufacturer" from Toyota. Sales revenue in 2014 was EUR202 billion, with an operating profit of EUR12 billion (**Exhibit 2**).[2]

The shareholders of Volkswagen AG were largely made up of descendants of Porsche (50% ownership), but VW also had significant ownership from the German state of Lower Saxony (20% ownership) and Qatar's sovereign wealth fund (17% ownership), as well as independent shareholders who made up 10% ownership.[3] Per German corporate law, Volkswagen AG had a 20-member supervisory board responsible for corporate governance, rather than a board of directors. As required by law, 50% of the seats were allocated to VW's labor force (union representatives and employees that are elected representatives of the union), leaving the other 10 seats to be divvied up among the shareholders. As of 2015, only one of these seats was held by an outsider (Annika Falkengren, the CEO of a Swedish bank); the other nine were as follows: five to members of the Porsche and Piëch (relatives of the Porsche) families, two to Lower Saxony, and two to Qatar.[4]

At a time when Europe was continuing to recover from the global financial crisis, VW was one of the most significant engines in the German economy. In May 2015, it was listed by *Forbes* as the largest public company in Germany by revenue, surpassing its nearest competitor, Daimler, by almost USD100 billion.[5] It was also one of Germany's largest employers.[6] Wolfsburg, Germany, the town in Lower Saxony where VW was headquartered, owed its existence to the company: it was created out of farmland to be the original site for manufacturing the VW Beetle. By the mid-2000s, the company owned the town's professional soccer team, its major hotels, and even an automotive theme park that attracted millions of visitors per year.[7]

The company's stated values included "customer focus, superior performance, creating value, renewability, respect, responsibility, and sustainability."[8] These values were intended to guide decisions made by employees throughout the company and were accompanied by a 25-page Code of Conduct on which every employee was trained after joining VW. This Code of Conduct was written in 2009 and systematically rolled out to employees across the globe in 2010. It addressed topics such as management culture and collaboration, anticorruption, and fair competition, and it was intended to be a "guidepost that combines the essential basic principles of our activities and supports our employees in mastering the legal and ethical challenges in their daily work."[9] In addition, all VW employees received compliance training; 185,000 were trained on compliance in 2014.[10]

Throughout its history, VW had been widely admired for its innovation in design and engineering. It was one of the first companies to introduce the three-way catalytic converter, prompting it to boast on its website that it was a "pioneer of low-emission monitoring."[11] The company experienced its first brush with U.S. emissions standards in the 1970s, however, when the EPA caught it installing defeat devices that would allow it to cheat on newly enacted emissions standards. At the time, it paid a USD120,000 fine.[12]

VW had also been known for its quirky advertising highlighting its unique products and top-notch engineering. The company made advertising history with its "Think Small" campaign in the United States in the 1950s, which encouraged Americans to consider smaller vehicles like the Beetle. In recent years, it stressed its virtue through advertisements proclaiming "the power of German engineering," with commercials featuring engineers sprouting angel wings. At a time when most major U.S. automakers were still struggling to recover from the global financial crisis and both Toyota and General Motors were reeling from major safety recalls, VW was perceived as reliable, successful, and innovative. In his 2014 annual letter to shareholders, CEO Martin Winterkorn wrote: "We stand for strength, reliability, and long-term success—even under less favorable conditions."[13]

"The power of German engineering" was more than just a marketing tagline for VW; it was a motto, a way of doing business, and a symbol of national pride. Germany had become a country that prided itself on its world-class engineering and precision manufacturing.[14] In part due to the country's engineering prowess, the automobile industry had become a powerhouse in Germany, and VW had become the leader in that industry. This dominance in manufacturing helped Germany weather the 2008 global financial crisis and kept unemployment low. Germany was able to boost employment and its economy largely through its ability to export products; automobiles made up a full one-fifth of this market. The strength of VW and much of the German economy depended on the growth of its engineering exports, making German engineering more than a just a point of national pride—it was an economic necessity.[15]

VW Leadership and Strategy 2018

Winterkorn, who took over as CEO in 2007, was focused on leading VW through its Strategy 2018, an ambitious plan to position the company as a global and environmental leader. The overarching goal of the strategy was to transform VW into the world's largest automaker. Said Winterkorn, "Our pursuit of innovation and perfection and our responsible approach will help to make us the world's largest automaker by 2018—both economically and ecologically." Strategy 2018 had four primary goals:

(1) to sell 10 million+ vehicles per year (thus making VW the world's largest automaker); (2) to become the world leader in customer satisfaction and quality; (3) to achieve an 8% return on sales; and (4) to be the most attractive employer in the automotive industry.[16] Throughout Winterkorn's tenure, VW made steady progress on each of these goals.

Under the leadership of Winterkorn and his mentor, VW Chairman Ferdinand Piëch (a grandson of VW founder Porsche and himself VW CEO from 1993 until 2002), VW became a tightly controlled, highly centralized company. Its corporate culture was one of command-and-control, with leadership setting aggressive goals and senior executives involved in even relatively minor decisions.[17] The company gained a reputation for being hard-charging and brutally competitive, and former employees described an environment in which subordinates were fearful of ever admitting failure or contradicting their superiors.

Both Piëch and Winterkorn came from engineering backgrounds and kept a close eye on product development. Piëch, who recruited Winterkorn to Audi in 1981 and became his mentor for more than 25 years, would boast that he elicited superior performance by "terrifying his engineers."[18] It was well known that VW executives and engineers would be "shaking in their boots prior to presentations before Piëch, knowing that if he was displeased, they might be fired instantly."[19] By the time he became CEO in 2007, Winterkorn was considered "a cold, distant figure . . . known for obsessive attention to detail."[20] Unlike other contemporary auto industry CEOs who were experts in financial management and turnarounds, Winterkorn was considered a "classic car guy."[21] He was known for carrying a gauge with him at all times to measure flaws in vehicles as they came off the production line and for publicly disparaging subordinates. Said an industry analyst, "He doesn't like bad news. Before anyone reports to him, they make sure they have good news."[22]

Winterkorn was relentless in his pursuit of becoming the world's largest automaker. Speaking at the opening of VW's new factory in Chattanooga, Tennessee, in 2011, he promised that "by 2018, we want to take our group to the very top of the global car industry."[23] Although VW was growing, these promises were still considered ambitious, especially in the United States, a market that VW had previously neglected and where it held a reputation for selling expensive and undesirable cars.[24] In order to meet Winterkorn's goals, the U.S. market would be a critical component to success. The company would need to sell 1 million vehicles (800,000 Volkswagens and 200,000 Audis) annually, tripling its 2007 sales.[25]

Achieving Ambitious Goals While Meeting Regulations[26]

In the mid-2000s, when Winterkorn began his tenure as CEO and announced VW's goal of becoming the world's largest automaker within the next decade, the auto industry in the United States and around the world was facing significant engineering challenges. Persistently high prices at the gas pump and toughening mileage standards put pressure on automakers to design more fuel-efficient vehicles, while growing concerns about climate change spurred increasingly stringent emissions regulations. In order to drive sales, automakers needed to find ways to optimize fuel efficiency and emissions while still designing the high-performing vehicles that Americans had become accustomed to driving. The market for hybrid-electric cars, notably Toyota's Prius, was growing rapidly.[27]

Rather than compete with Toyota and other automakers in the hybrid market, VW had opted for a strategy of diesel, viewing it as a huge growth opportunity within the U.S. car market and a viable eco-friendly alternative. While diesel made up almost half of new car sales in Europe, it held just 5% of the U.S. auto market in 2007,[28] and Winterkorn believed it was an opportune time to expand diesel sales in the United States. Diesel offered a cheaper, more powerful alternative to hybrid vehicles, promising high fuel efficiency without sacrificing powerful performance. But before it could market fuel-efficient diesel in the United States, VW had to overcome one major roadblock: diesel cars generated significantly more nitrogen oxide (NOx) than gasoline-powered engines, making it difficult for them to clear the stringent American emissions standards without sacrificing fuel efficiency or performance. In order to sell its cars in the U.S. market, a critical part of the company's goal of becoming the world's largest car manufacturer, VW would have to engineer a way to strip its cars of these pollutants to meet U.S. regulations (**Exhibit 3**).

In 2005, Wolfgang Bernhard, VW's head of brand, was in charge of designing the next-generation diesel engine for consumer cars that would provide both fuel efficiency and meet low U.S. emission standards. Bernhard chose a strategy seen as controversial within the VW management team. Rather than develop an in-house solution, he instead adopted a competitor's technology, a Daimler invention called BlueTec. BlueTec used a substance called urea—essentially cat urine—to neutralize NOx. It required that VW install an extra pump and tank of urea in each vehicle, at a cost of EUR300 per vehicle. But just two years later, in 2007, boardroom battles within VW led to the appointment of Winterkorn as CEO, who promptly ousted Bernhard and cancelled the BlueTec deal. VW leadership stressed that BlueTec was too expensive, took up too much space in small cars, would hamper fuel efficiency, and that VW did not need to partner with an archrival to achieve its engineering goals.

VW engineers were suddenly on their own to find a way to meet stringent U.S. emissions standards on diesel without sacrificing mileage or performance, and they needed to find it quickly. As it struggled to come up with a solution, the company was forced to delay for six months the release of the new diesel Jetta that was to be at the center of its new marketing push.

Whatever solution was devised, software was likely to be at the center of it. Modern cars contained approximately 100 million lines of software code that controlled everything from basic operations to media to safety. Software could also help a car control the amount of pollutants it emitted, by monitoring carbon monoxide and NOx emissions and then diverting pollutants to special systems that converted them into less harmful substances. Around the time that VW engineers were struggling to determine the right solution, auto industry-supplier Bosch gave VW diesel engine-management software for use during testing. This software could detect when a vehicle was in a testing environment and activated emissions-controlling devices. Bosch believed VW was only using this software during its internal testing, and sold the software to VW with the understanding that utilizing the software in publicly sold vehicles was illegal.[29]

Clean Diesel Sales Take Off

By 2008, it appeared that "the power of German engineering" had once again pulled through. VW announced the rollout of a new clean diesel technology called the Lean NOx Trap, which it claimed had solved the problem of delivering high fuel efficiency while still meeting emissions standards. The new technology garnered considerable attention for VW. Its 2009 clean diesel Jetta TDI won the Green Car of the Year award, beating out hybrids and electric vehicles. It hosted a multiweek "dieselution tour" to "change any outdated perceptions about diesel technology" and prove its environmental virtue.[30] Some of its vehicles were reportedly getting almost 60 mpg, which was unheard of for a nonelectric or hybrid car. At a conference on diesel emissions the same year, a VW executive boasted that "you don't have to sacrifice power to be environmentally conscious."[31] Clean diesel became the centerpiece of VW's U.S. marketing strategy, and sales took off. Diesel sales grew by 20% in 2010, 26% in 2011, and 25% in 2012, though they began to taper off slightly in 2013 and 2014.[32] By 2014, VW's diesel cars accounted for 21% of the company's U.S. sales.[33]

In 2011, VW's goal of selling 1 million vehicles in the United States was beginning to look achievable. U.S. domestic companies struggled under the weight of economic crises and bailouts, and Toyota and Honda had yet to fully recover from the impact on production of the 2011 Japanese earthquake. By 2012, VW claimed 3% market share in the United States,[34] up from 2.5% in 2011 and 2.2% in 2010.[35] VW sales in the United States hit 440,000 in 2014, more than double 2009 sales.[36]

By 2014, VW was well on its way to achieving all four Strategy 2018 goals. Worldwide sales grew steadily at approximately 7.2% CAGR from 2007, when Winterkorn took over, to 2014.[37] Most notably, the company reached its sales goal in 2014, selling more than 10 million vehicles and surpassing Toyota in sales volume, thereby becoming the world's largest automaker four years ahead of the deadline it had set for itself (**Exhibit 4**).[38]

Sales were particularly strong for VW vehicles in China, growing 10% since 2013.[39] Yet sales in the United States were causing concern. U.S. consumers' tastes had shifted toward midsized SUVs, an area in which VW had very few offerings. By 2014, VW held only 2.2% market share in the United States,[40] and VW sales dipped down to just around 370,000, far short of the 800,000 projected and just barely above the company's 2011 numbers.

While VW invested in its U.S. diesel strategy, EPA officials in the Obama administration announced in 2011 a plan to require automakers to increase fleet-wide fuel efficiency from an average of 35.5 mpg to 54.5 mpg by 2025, while also further reducing emissions. To help car manufacturers offset the business implications of these ambitious new standards, companies were able to earn credits for utilizing groundbreaking technology that improved the environmental effects of their fleets, such as hybrids and electric cars. Credits could be used to lower the average fleet miles per gallon or emissions rating of the manufacturer that would otherwise be over the EPA limits. But credits were not offered to diesel manufacturers, as diesel technology was not viewed as the future of environmental car manufacturing. Automakers that had invested in diesel, such as VW and Mercedes-Benz, lobbied for diesel cars to be eligible to earn credits due to the technology's superior fuel efficiency. These firms had made the decision to invest in diesel on the basis that it was environmentally conscious, but the EPA argued that diesel traditionally emitted much higher levels of NOx than gasoline-powered vehicles, and therefore would not allow diesel cars to earn the credits. This left VW with a fleet that did not meet the EPA's new standards, and unlike its competitors, the company had no credit-earning hybrid cars.

Scandal Unfolds[41]

In 2013, a nonprofit group called the International Council on Clean Transportation (ICCT) noticed something strange: diesel technologies appeared cleaner in the United States than in Europe. The ICCT hoped to identify what made diesel technologies superior in the United States in order to improve emissions in Europe. The traditional in-lab emissions tests had not provided any clues to the engineering differences, which were producing lower-emission vehicles in the United States, so the researchers proposed on-road (as opposed to in-lab) testing of diesel cars in order to better understand these differences. They partnered with West Virginia University's Center for Alternative Fuels, Engines, and Emissions and California environmental regulators to perform tests on several types of diesel vehicles, starting with a BMW X5, a VW Jetta, and a VW Passat (all three selected by chance; they were models conveniently available to the researchers). The researchers compared in-lab and on-road emissions and mileage performance.

Almost immediately, the two VW vehicles stood out. They performed flawlessly in the lab, but once on the open road, their emissions were significantly higher, as shown in **Table 1**. What the researchers unexpectedly uncovered was that these differences were perhaps not the result of superior engineering, but rather the result of cars specifically designed to take advantage of testing environments.

In early 2014, the researchers turned over the surprising results of the study to the U.S. EPA, which questioned VW about the findings. VW flatly denied any accusations of wrongdoing. The West Virginia University researcher who led the tests said VW "tried to poke holes in our study and its methods, saying we didn't know what we were doing."[42] The researchers eventually conducted an in-depth examination of VW's software, reviewing millions of lines of code for something to explain the strange

Table 1. Emissions test results.

	EPA Limit	2015 Jetta In-Lab Testing	2015 Jetta On-Road Testing
Emissions level (grams of NOx emitted per mile)	0.07	0.07	2.45 (~35× higher than legal limit)

Data sources: *Bloomberg Businessweek*, www.bloomberg.com/news/articles/2015-10-21/how-could-volkswagen-s-top-engineers-not-have-known; EPA, www3.epa.gov/otaq/consumer/f99017.pdf.

discrepancy in emissions. They discovered an unusual set of instructions that was sent to emissions controls whenever the vehicle was only utilizing two of its four wheels (as it would during in-lab testing). In essence, the vehicle recognized whether it was in a test lab or on the road. The defeat device limited emissions in the lab (therefore hindering performance), but once out on the road, emissions returned to levels far above federal regulations and performance did not suffer.

Armed with this information, EPA officials threatened to withhold certification of VW and Audi's 2016 diesel models, which forced VW's hand. On September 18, 2015—one week after being named the world's "most sustainable automaker"[43]—the company publicly admitted that it had installed defeat devices on nearly 500,000 diesel vehicles across 14 models sold in the United States since 2009, when the clean diesel technology launched (**Exhibit 5**). This number was later scaled up to 11 million vehicles worldwide. It was discovered that the vehicles were emitting up to 40 times the U.S. legal limit of pollution into the atmosphere.[44]

VW officials apologized but vehemently denied widespread knowledge of the defeat devices within the company, blaming a few engineers for the error and claiming that senior management had no knowledge of wrongdoing. They claimed that the millions of lines of software code made it impossible for anyone to know every line, particularly upper management, meaning that engineers could have included the emissions-defeating protocol without management knowing.[45] Michael Horn, VW's CEO of American operations, testified before Congress in October 2015, stressing that the defeat devices were "not a corporate decision" and were instead the work of "a couple of software engineers."[46] As members of Congress expressed disbelief that VW's senior leadership did not know about the devices, Horn admitted, "I agree, that's very hard to believe."[47]

Despite denying any wrongdoing, CEO Martin Winterkorn resigned five days after the scandal became public, stating that "I am stunned that misconduct on such a scale was possible in the Volkswagen Group. As CEO I accept responsibility for the irregularities that have been found in the diesel engines . . . even though I am not aware of any wrong doing on my part." (See **Exhibit 6** for Winterkorn's full statement.)

Fallout[48]

The fallout of the scandal was swift and far-reaching. Regulators across the United States and across the globe opened investigations. In the United States, the EPA stated that VW could face up to USD18 billion in fines—USD37,500 per car for each of the estimated 500,000 cars impacted.[49] The FBI opened a criminal probe, as did the attorneys general of all 50 states, and the Justice Department opened a civil lawsuit against the company over the deception. Outside of the United States, Germany and the European Union also opened criminal investigations, and German officials raided VW's headquarters days after the scandal came to light.[50]

The scandal had considerable immediate effects on VW's business. In the wake of VW's admission, the EPA withheld final certification on VW's 2016 diesel models, and VW voluntarily halted sales of its 2015 models still in inventory. As diesel vehicles composed approximately 20% of VW's U.S. sales, this significantly affected VW's performance. In October, VW reported its first quarterly loss in 15 years. Furthermore, its market cap shrunk by one-third in the month after the scandal went public (**Exhibit 7**), and the company quickly abandoned its goal of remaining the world's largest automaker.[51] In addition to Winterkorn's resignation, at least nine senior managers were quickly suspended or put on leave, and Matthias Müller, formerly the Porsche brand chief, was appointed VW's new CEO.

VW's American operations and dealers were severely hurt by the scandal they claimed to have known nothing about. VW America said in a statement to American customers, "The recent TDI (Turbocharged Direct Injection) news is a disappointment to the entire VW of America family. We sincerely apologize, and we recognize this matter has jeopardized the strong relationship between our loyal owners and the brand."[52] The scandal had a considerable effect on independent VW dealers, who were crippled by the sudden drop in sales. VW paid dealers up to USD1,000 per car and wired cash to dealers to handle the crisis locally.[53] In November, American consumers who had purchased the vehicles that were affected received a goodwill package in the mail, which included USD1,000 and 24-hour roadside assistance and did not require the consumer to release VW of any liability.

The German economy expected to see a substantial change as a result of VW's actions. The German auto industry, led by VW, accounted for 20% of German exports and 3% of German GDP. One in seven jobs were directly or indirectly linked to the industry, and the country was steeling itself for potential job losses.[54] The city of Wolfsburg, Germany, where VW was headquartered, issued an immediate budget and hiring freeze and halted all infrastructure projects in anticipation of substantially reduced corporate taxes coming from its hometown company.[55] "While the German economy defied Greece, the euro crisis and the Chinese slowdown, it could now be facing the biggest downside risk in a long while," Carsten Brzeski, chief economist at Germany's ING-DiBa bank, wrote. "The irony of all of this is that the threat could now come from the inside, rather than from the outside."[56]

The long-term environmental and health repercussions of VW's defeat devices were not yet known. Researchers from MIT and Harvard estimated that excess NOx emissions from VW diesels would cause 59 deaths in the United States. They also suspected that these excess emissions were responsible for more than 30 cases of chronic bronchitis and hospital admissions, about 120,000 days of restricted activity, about 210,000 days of lower respiratory symptoms, and about 33,000 days of increased use of bronchodilators, which increased airflow to the lungs.[57]

In June 2016, VW agreed to a USD14.7 billion settlement in the emissions scandal. The settlement was estimated to provide USD10 billion to fund buybacks of vehicles from approximately 475,000 vehicle owners and additional cash compensation of USD2.7 billion was to assist in environmental clean-up and USD2 billion to fund programs by the EPA and California that focused on cleaner vehicles. The company could still face additional civil penalties or charges in other countries, and the company and some of its executives could face criminal charges as well.[58]

How Could This Have Happened?

As Müller began his new role as CEO of VW, he must have wondered how such a scandal could have happened at VW and how such scandals could be prevented in the future. Was it really possible that Winterkorn and other top management officials really didn't know about the defeat devices? Engineers had run VW for its entire history, and Winterkorn was famous for his involvement in even minute details of his products and processes. Regardless of who knew about the devices, was the scandal the result of a few bad actors, or was there something more systemic going on? More importantly, how could Müller help VW regain the trust of the public, and how could he prevent something like this from happening to VW in the future?

* * *

Exhibit 1

The Volkswagen Emissions Scandal

Timeline of Events

2007
Martin Winterkorn becomes CEO of VW and through his Strategy 2018 sets ambitious goals for vehicle sales.

2008
After canceling deal with BlueTec technology, VW announces new clean diesel technology called Lean NOx Trap and designed to meet regulations.

2009
VW's Jetta wins Green Car of the Year award.

2011
In reaction to growing public concern, the EPA announces plans to further regulate U.S. emissions by offering "credits" to companies for using new technology, such as hybrid or electric cars, to improve the environmental effects of their fleets. Credits were not offered to diesel manufacturers.

2013
A nonprofit group, the ICCT, notices that diesel technology in the United States appears to be cleaner—begins road testing of diesel vehicles.

2014
Researchers turn over the results of the study to the U.S. EPA. The EPA opens investigation and questions VW about the findings. VW denies accusations of wrongdoing.

VW reaches its Strategy 2018 sales goal early, selling over 10 million vehicles and surpassing Toyota in sales volume, thereby becoming the world's largest automaker.

2015
The EPA and the state of California prepare for further testing and confirm that initial test findings are consistent.

September 18, 2015
VW publicly admits that it had installed defeat devices on nearly 500,000 diesel vehicles across 14 models sold in the United States since 2009.

September 23–25, 2015
Martin Winterkorn resigns as CEO, and Mathias Müller becomes new CEO.

Source: Created by author based on the order of events as portrayed in the case.

* * *

Exhibit 2

The Volkswagen Emissions Scandal

Volkswagen Group Key Financials, Prescandal

	Vehicles Sold	Revenue (EUR millions)	Operating Profit (EUR millions)
2007	6,191,618	108,897	6,151
2008	6,271,724	113,808	6,333
2009	6,309,743	105,187	1,855
2010	7,278,440	126,875	7,141
2011	8,361,294	159,337	11,271
2012	9,344,559	192,676	11,498
2013	9,728,250	197,007	11,671
2014	10,217,003	202,458	12,697

Exhibit 3

The Volkswagen Emissions Scandal

Background on U.S. Emissions Regulations[1]

The EPA both sets minimum standards for fuel efficiency for a company's fleet of vehicles and regulates emissions according to the Clean Air Act. The Clean Air Act, passed by the United States Congress in 1970, was designed to combat a number of air pollution problems threatening environmental safety and public health. As the country had grown more industrialized and urban, dense smog was visible in many of the nation's cities and prompted a public outcry for government action. The Clean Air Act required the EPA to "establish national ambient air quality standards for certain common and widespread pollutants based on the latest science."[2] One of the key provisions emphasized minimizing pollution from motor vehicles, focusing on emissions of carbon monoxide, volatile organic compounds, and NOx. Emissions standards were gradually tightened over time.

The Clean Air Act requires that the EPA certify that all motor vehicles sold in the United States meet federal emissions standards. Without this certification, a vehicle cannot be sold in the United States. For decades, tests on new models to be released in the United States have been conducted at indoor laboratories as opposed to performing actual driving tests on the road. The tests use dynamometers—essentially car treadmills—which simulate driving and measure the exhaust emissions of a stationary car. The tests are conducted in laboratories rather than on the road to achieve cost efficiency and ensure standardization of the test from vehicle to vehicle within a fleet.[3]

Source: Created by author.

Notes

1 Most of the information in this section is from the EPA's "Clean Air Act Overview," www.epa.gov/clean-air-act-overview; "Clean Air Act Text," www.epa.gov/clean-air-act-overview/clean-air-act-text; "Clean Air Act Requirements and History," www.epa.gov/clean-air-act-overview/clean-air-act-requirements-and-history; and "Progress Cleaning the Air and Improving People's Health," www.epa.gov/clean-air-act-overview/progress-cleaning-air-and-improving-peoples-health (all accessed Jan. 16, 2015); as well as www.bloomberg.com/news/articles/2015-10-21/how-could-volkswagen-s-top-engineers-not-have-known.

2 www.epa.gov/clean-air-act-overview/clean-air-act-requirements-and-history.

3 "EPA Should Do More Road Emissions Tests, Critics Say," *Automotive News*, September 29, 2015, www.autonews.com/article/20150929/OEM11/150929807/epa-should-do-more-road-emissions-tests-critics-say (accessed Jun. 20, 2016).

* * *

Exhibit 4

The Volkswagen Emissions Scandal

Worldwide Annual Car and Light Truck Sales by Manufacturer, 2005–2015

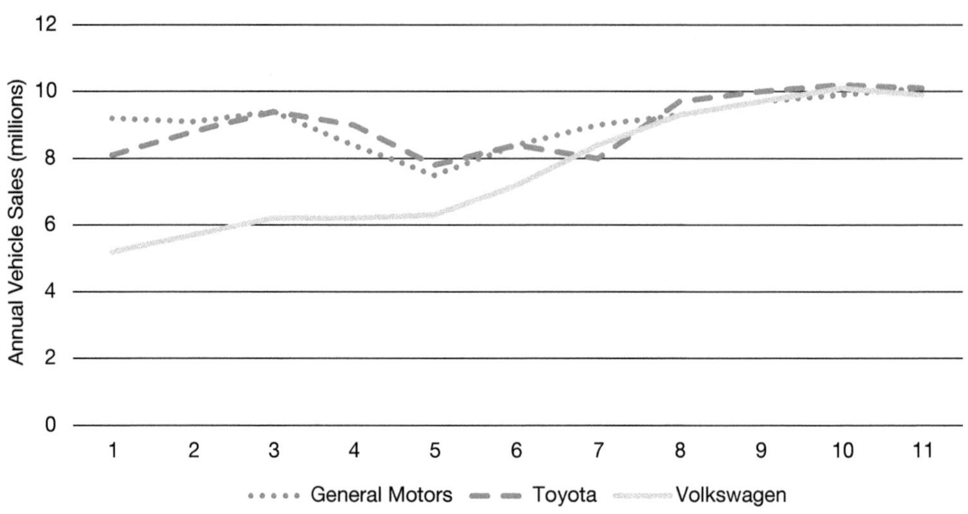

Data source: Created by author using data obtained from Bloomberg.

Exhibit 5

The Volkswagen Emissions Scandal

U.S. Models with Defeat Device

Affected 2.0-Liter Diesel Models:

- Jetta (2009–2015)
- Jetta Sportwagen (2009–2014)
- Beetle (2012–2015)
- Beetle Convertible (2012–2015)
- Audi A3 (2010–2015)
- Golf (2010–2015)
- Golf Sportwagen (2015)
- Passat (2012–2015)

Affected 3.0-Liter Diesel Models:

- Volkswagen Touareg (2014)
- Porsche Cayenne (2015)
- Audi A6 Quattro (2016)
- Audi A7 Quattro (2016)
- Audi A8 (2016)
- Audi A8L (2016)
- Audi Q5 (2016)

Data source: EPA, "Volkswagen Light Duty Diesel Vehicle Violations for Model Years 2009–2016," www.epa.gov/vw (accessed Feb. 28, 2016).

Exhibit 6

The Volkswagen Emissions Scandal

Postscandal Statement by Martin Winterkorn, September 23, 2015

"I am shocked by the events of the past few days. Above all, I am stunned that misconduct on such a scale was possible in the Volkswagen Group.

"As CEO I accept responsibility for the irregularities that have been found in diesel engines and have therefore requested the Supervisory Board to agree on terminating my function as CEO of the Volkswagen Group. I am doing this in the interests of the company even though I am not aware of any wrong doing on my part.

"Volkswagen needs a fresh start—also in terms of personnel. I am clearing the way for this fresh start with my resignation.

"I have always been driven by my desire to serve this company, especially our customers and employees. Volkswagen has been, is, and will always be my life.

"The process of clarification and transparency must continue. This is the only way to win back trust. I am convinced that the Volkswagen Group and its team will overcome this grave crisis."

Source: "Statement by Prof. Dr. Winterkorn," Volkswagen U.S. Media Newsroom, September 23, 2015, http://media.vw.com/release/1070/ (accessed Jun. 20, 2016).

* * *

Exhibit 7

The Volkswagen Emissions Scandal

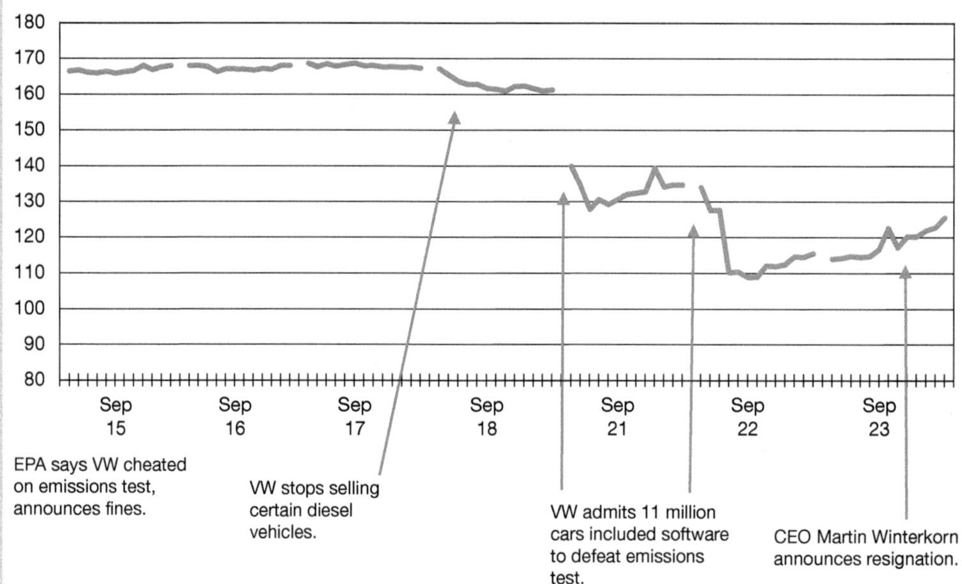

Data source: Created by author with stock price data from Bloomberg.

Source for announcements: *New York Times.*

Chapter 1: Long Case Notes

This public-sourced case was prepared by Luann J. Lynch, Almand R. Coleman Professor of Business Administration, Cameron Cutro (MBA '16), and Elizabeth Bird (MBA '16). It was written as a basis for class discussion rather than to illustrate effective or ineffective handling of an administrative situation. Our goal is to publish materials of the highest quality, so please submit any errata to editorial@dardenbusinesspublishing.com.

1 Most of the material in the first paragraph of this section comes from Tim Bowler, "Volkswagen: From the Third Reich to Emissions Scandal," BBC, October 2, 2015, www.bbc.com/news/business-34358783; and from Volkswagen's own company history and annual reports, available at www.volkswagenag.com/content/vwcorp/content/en/the_group/history.html and www.volkswagenag.com/content/vwcorp/info_center/en/publications/publications.acq.html/archive-on/icr-financial_publications!annual_reports/index.html (accessed Jan. 17, 2016).

2 EUR = euros.

3 Richard Milne, "Volkswagen: System Failure," *Financial Times*, November 4, 2015, www.ft.com/cms/s/2/47f233f0-816b-11e5-a01c-8650859a4767.html?siteedition=uk#axzz4BTTrG0FY (accessed Feb. 28, 2016).

4 Hans Dieter Pötsch, the company's former finance director who was close to the Porsche and Piëch families, became chairman of the supervisory board in 2015, replacing Ferdinand Piëch, who was the company's CEO from 1993 to 2002 and chairman of the supervisory board from 2002 to 2015.

5 Steve Schaefer and Andrea Murphy, "The World's Biggest Public Companies," *Forbes*, May 2015, www.forbes.com/global2000/ (accessed Feb. 27, 2016; USD = U.S. dollars).

6 www.forbes.com/global2000/.

7 Joann Muller, "How Volkswagen Will Rule the World," *Forbes*, May 6, 2013, www.forbes.com/sites/joannmuller/2013/04/17/volkswagens-mission-to-dominate-global-auto-industry-gets-noticeably-harder/#52b13a501ab6 (accessed Feb. 28, 2016).

8 Volkswagen annual report, 2016.

9 The Volkswagen Group Code of Conduct, September 2015, www.volkswagenag.com/content/vwcorp/info_center/en/publications/2015/09/Verhaltensgrundsaetze_des_Volkswagen_Konzerns.bin.html/binarystorageitem/file/20150930_Verhaltensgrunds%C3%A4tze+-+update_coc_englisch_digital.pdf (accessed Feb. 27, 2016).

10 The Volkswagen Group Code of Conduct, 2010, http://en.volkswagen.com/content/medialib/vwd4/de/Volkswagen/Nachhaltigkeit/service/download/corporate_governance/Code_of_Conduct/_jcr_content/renditions/rendition.file/the-volkswagen-group-code-of-conduct.pdf; www.volkswagenag.com/content/vwcorp/info_center/en/publications/2015/09/Verhaltensgrundsaetze_des_Volkswagen_Konzerns.bin.html/binarystorageitem/file/20150930_Verhaltensgrunds%C3%A4tze+-+update_coc_englisch_digital.pdf. Although the two versions are similar, the earlier one contains signatures from VW CEO Martin Winterkorn and other top executives; the newer version, republished after the scandal, omits these signatures.

11 Danny Hakim, Aaron M. Kessler, and Jack Ewin, "As Volkswagen Pushed to Be No. 1, Ambitions Fueled a Scandal," *New York Times*, September 26, 2015, www.nytimes.com/2015/09/27/business/as-vw-pushed-to-be-no-1-ambitions-fueled-a-scandal.html?action=click&contentCollection=International%20Business®ion=Footer&module=WhatsNext&version=WhatsNext&contentID=WhatsNext&moduleDetail=undefined&pgtype=Multimedia&_r=1 (accessed Jan. 25, 2016).

12 www.nytimes.com/2015/09/27/business/as-vw-pushed-to-be-no-1-ambitions-fueled-a-scandal.html?action=click&contentCollection=International%20Business®ion=Footer&module=WhatsNext&version=WhatsNext&contentID=WhatsNext&moduleDetail=undefined&pgtype=Multimedia&_r=1.

13 Volkswagen annual report, 2014.

14 Chiyo Robertson, "The Best Engineers Come from Germany," *BBC News*, September 18, 2013, www.bbc.com/news/business-24131534 (accessed Jan. 25, 2016).

15 Rick Noack, "For Germans, VW Scandal is a National Embarrassment," *Washington Post*, September 23, 2015, www.washingtonpost.com/news/worldviews/wp/2015/09/23/for-germans-the-volkswagen-scandal-is-a-national-embarrassment/ (accessed Feb. 27, 2016).

16 Volkswagen's Strategy 2018, www.volkswagenag.com/content/vwcorp/content/de/homepage.html (accessed Jan. 25, 2016).

17 Jack Ewing and Graham Bowley, "The Engineering of Volkswagen's Aggressive Ambition," *New York Times*, December 13, 2015, www.nytimes.com/2015/12/14/business/the-engineering-of-volkswagens-aggressive-ambition.html (accessed Jan. 25, 2016).

18 Doran Levin, "The Man who Created VW's Toxic Culture Still Looms Large," *Fortune*, October 16, 2015, http://fortune.com/2015/10/16/vw-ferdinand-piech-culture/ (accessed Feb. 23, 2016).

19 http://fortune.com/2015/10/16/vw-ferdinand-piech-culture/.

20 http://fortune.com/2015/10/16/vw-ferdinand-piech-culture/.

21 www.forbes.com/sites/joannmuller/2013/04/17/volkswagens-mission-to-dominate-global-auto-industry-gets-noticeably-harder/#52b13a501ab6.

22 www.forbes.com/sites/joannmuller/2013/04/17/volkswagens-mission-to-dominate-global-auto-industry-gets-noticeably-harder/#52b13a501ab6.

23 www.nytimes.com/2015/09/27/business/as-vw-pushed-to-be-no-1-ambitions-fueled-a-scandal.html.

24 www.forbes.com/sites/joannmuller/2013/04/17/volkswagens-mission-to-dominate-global-auto-industry-gets-noticeably-harder/#52b13a501ab6.

25 www.forbes.com/sites/joannmuller/2013/04/17/volkswagens-mission-to-dominate-global-auto-industry-gets-noticeably-harder/#52b13a501ab6.

26 Most of the information in this section is from Dune Lawrence, Benjamin Elgin, and Vernon Silver, "How Could Volkswagen's Top Engineers Not Have Known?," *Bloomberg Businessweek*, October 21, 2015, www.bloomberg.com/news/articles/2015-10-21/how-could-volkswagen-s-top-engineers-not-have-known- (accessed Jan. 25, 2016).

27 "U.S. HEV Sales by Model," U.S. Department of Energy Alternative Fuels Data Center, January 2016, www.afdc.energy.gov/data/ (accessed Apr. 1, 2016).

28 William Boston, "Volkswagen Emissions Investigation Zeroes In on Two Engineers," *Wall Street Journal*, October 5, 2015, www.wsj.com/articles/vw-emissions-probe-zeroes-in-on-two-engineers-1444011602 (accessed Jan. 25, 2016).

29 Bob Sorokanich, "Report: Bosch Warned VW About Diesel Emissions Cheating in 2007," *Car and Driver*, September 28, 2015, http://blog.caranddriver.com/report-bosch-warned-vw-about-diesel-emissions-cheating-in-2007/ (accessed Jan. 25, 2016).

30 Volkswagen Group of America press release, September 26, 2007.

31 www.bloomberg.com/news/articles/2015-10-21/how-could-volkswagen-s-top-engineers-not-have-known-.

32 Angelo Young, "Volkswagen Diesel Scandal: Here's How Bad Volkswagen Sales Were Before the Company Was Caught Cheating," *International Business Times*, September 25, 2015, www.ibtimes.com/volkswagen-diesel-scandal-heres-how-bad-volkswagen-sales-were-company-was-caught-2114603 (accessed Feb. 27, 2016).

33 Volkswagen of America earnings report, 2014, http://media.vw.com/release/907/.

34 "Volkswagen's U.S. Market Share from 2012 to 2014," Statista, www.statista.com/statistics/343189/market-share-of-volkswagen-in-the-us/ (accessed Mar. 3, 2016).

35 "Volkswagen in the U.S.: An Evolving Growth Story," Volkswagen Group of America presentation, January 10, 2012, www.volkswagenag.com/content/vwcorp/info_center/en/talks_and_presentations/2012/01/Global_Auto_Industry_Conference.bin.html/binarystorageitem/file/Volkswagen+in+the+US+-+An+Evolving+Growth+Story.pdf (accessed Mar. 3, 2016).

36 Neal E. Boudette, "How VW Veered Off Target," *Automotive News*, January 26, 2016, www.autonews.com/article/20150126/RETAIL01/301269949/how-vw-veered--off-target (accessed Feb. 28, 2016).

37 Bloomberg Intelligence, Automobiles Dashboard, Annual Unit Sales by Manufacturer (accessed Mar. 31, 2016).

38 www.nytimes.com/2015/09/27/business/as-vw-pushed-to-be-no-1-ambitions-fueled-a-scandal.html.

39 Henk Bekker, "2014 (Full Year) China and Worldwide German Luxury Car Sales," Best Selling Cars, January 9, 2015, www.best-selling-cars.com/china/2014-full-year-china-worldwide-german-luxury-car-sales/ (accessed Feb. 28, 2016).

40 www.statista.com/statistics/343189/market-share-of-volkswagen-in-the-us/.

41 www.bloomberg.com/news/articles/2015-10-21/how-could-volkswagen-s-top-engineers-not-have-known-; www.nytimes.com/2015/09/27/business/as-vw-pushed-to-be-no-1-ambitions-fueled-a-scandal.html.

42 www.nytimes.com/2015/09/27/business/as-vw-pushed-to-be-no-1-ambitions-fueled-a-scandal.html.

43 Richard Hardyment, "CSR after Volkswagen Scandal," TriplePundit, October 28, 2015, www.triplepundit.com/2015/10/csr-volkswagen-scandal/ (accessed Jun. 20, 2016).

44 Guilbert Gates, Jack Ewing, Karl Russell, and Derek Watkins, "Explaining Volkswagen's Emissions Scandal," *New York Times*, June 1, 2016, www.nytimes.com/interactive/2015/business/international/vw-diesel-emissions-scandal-explained.html?_r=0 (accessed Jun. 20, 2016).

45 Paul Kedrosky, "An Engineering Theory of the Volkswagen Scandal," *New Yorker*, October 16, 2015, www.newyorker.com/business/currency/an-engineering-theory-of-the-volkswagen-scandal (accessed Jan. 15, 2016).

46 "'It Was Installed For This Purpose,' VW's U.S. CEO Tells Congress About Defeat Device," NPR, October 8, 2015, www.npr.org/sections/thetwo-way/2015/10/08/446861855/volkswagen-u-s-ceo-faces-questions-on-capitol-hill (accessed Jan. 25, 2016).

47 www.npr.org/sections/thetwo-way/2015/10/08/446861855/volkswagen-u-s-ceo-faces-questions-on-capitol-hill.

48 Most of this section comes from www.nytimes.com/interactive/2015/business/international/vw-diesel-emissions-scandal-explained.html?_r=0.

49 Chris Isidore, "Volkswagen Could Be Hit with $18 Billion in U.S. Fines," CNN, January 4, 2016, http://money.cnn.com/2016/01/04/news/companies/volkswagen-emissions-cheating-suit-fine/ (accessed Jan. 25, 2016).

50 www.npr.org/sections/thetwo-way/2015/10/08/446861855/volkswagen-u-s-ceo-faces-questions-on-capitol-hill.

51 Clifford Atiyeh, "Everything You Need to Know About the VW Diesel-Emissions Scandal," *Car and Driver*, May 11, 2016, http://blog.caranddriver.com/everything-you-need-to-know-about-the-vw-diesel-emissions-scandal/ (accessed Jun. 20, 2016).

52 "We're Working to Make Things Right," Volkswagen website, www.vwdieselinfo.com (accessed Feb. 27, 2016).

53 www.npr.org/sections/thetwo-way/2015/10/08/446861855/volkswagen-u-s-ceo-faces-questions-on-capitol-hill.

54 Ruth Bender, "Town that VW Built Views Future with Caution," *Wall Street Journal*, October 2, 2015, www.wsj.com/articles/town-that-vw-built-views-future-with-caution-1443797584 (accessed Jan. 25, 2016).

55 www.wsj.com/articles/town-that-vw-built-views-future-with-caution-1443797584.

56 Jack Ewing, "Volkswagen CEO Martin Winterkorn Resigns amid Emissions Scandal," *New York Times*, September 23, 2015, www.nytimes.com/2015/09/24/business/international/volkswagen-chief-martin-winterkorn-resigns-amid-emissions-scandal.html (accessed Jan. 25, 2016).

57 Tonya Garcia, "Scientists Say Volkswagen Deception Will Kill 59 People Unless Company Does This," MarketWatch, October 31, 2015, www.marketwatch.com/story/how-volkswagen-could-save-lives-after-its-emissions-scandal-2015-10-30 (accessed Jan. 25, 2016).

58 Chris Isidore and David Goldman,"Volkswagon Agrees to Record $14.7 Billion Settlement over Emissions Cheating," *CNN Money*, June 28, 2016, http://money.cnn.com/2016/06/28/news/companies/volkswagen-fine/ (accessed Jul. 15, 2016); David Shepardson and Joel Schectman, "VW Agrees to Buy Back Diesel Vehicles, Fund Clean Air Efforts," Reuters, June 28, 2016, www.reuters.com/article/us-volkswagen-emissions-settlement-idUSKCN0ZD2S5 (accessed Jul. 15, 2016); Jack Ewing and Hiroko Tabuchi, "VW's U.S. Diesel Settlement Clears Just One Financial Hurdle," *New York Times*, June 28, 2016, www.nytimes.com/2016/06/29/business/vw-diesel-emissions-us-settlement.html (accessed Jul. 15, 2016).

LONG CASE QUESTIONS

1. What factors might have contributed to the actions taken to install defeat devices on VW cars so that they would cheat on and pass emissions test?
2. What have been negative consequences of such actions for VW?
3. How important is it for multinationals like VW to behave ethically today?
4. What should Müller do to prevent similar actions in the future?

Chapter 2

Building Ethics at the Individual Level

LEARNING OBJECTIVES

After reading this chapter you should be able to:

- Understand what individual ethics is
- Learn about the many aspects and factors that contribute to individual ethics including an emphasis on Rest's ethical decision-making process
- Become aware of the concept of moral awareness to understand how individuals assess the ethical nature of situations
- Understand what moral judgment is and how conscious and unconscious biases can influence moral judgment
- Become aware of moral intentions and moral behaviors and how moral intensity and moral disengagement can affect moral intentions and behaviors
- Learn about the many steps companies can take to better prepare employees to be ethical

PREVIEW BUSINESS ETHICS INSIGHT

Individuals and Ethics

Examples of people behaving unethically and engaging in corruption are plenty. Consider the classic case of Enron, which occurred during the 2000s. Although the Enron case tends to be used frequently to illustrate individual unethical behavior, it is important to appreciate how the company went from one of the most admired companies to oblivion. Enron collapsed in 2001 under a mountain of debt. Over time, several high-ranking officials in the company, including CEO Jeffrey Skilling, Chairman Ken Lay, and Chief Financial Officer Andrew Fastow, condoned a number of practices that concealed the debt. For instance, they created special-purpose entities to move its assets and losses, thereby showing cash flow in the company. Skilling was also instrumental in creating a rank and yank system that basically ranked employees every six months, whereby the bottom 20% of employees were fired. This also created an atmosphere where employees were ready to lie to keep their jobs. Furthermore, many accounting improprieties occurred whereby investors were being misled. This all came to a crash in 2001.

The case of Enron is not unique. Other companies in the 2000s such as WorldCom and Arthur Andersen also suffered considerable damage mainly due to individual misbehavior. These companies also had individuals who devised schemes for personal gains that ultimately led to the downfall of the companies. However, more recently, Volkswagen was also involved in a scandal whereby the company was fitting its diesel cars with software that would provide lower readings of carbon emissions when the car was being tested. This software made the diesel emissions less polluting than reality. Recent evidence suggests that top managers were aware of this software but did not do much to stop it. Additionally, it was also found that Volkswagen was fitting Audi cars (it also owns Audi) with other cheating software the same day the crisis began.

However, although there are many examples of individuals perpetrating unethical behavior, there are others who are willing to take the risk and expose such practice. Consider the case of Enron Vice President Sherron Watkins. When she was given the task of finding more assets to sell by the CEO, she was troubled to find the many accounting irregularities at Enron. She then confronted CEO Skilling. However, Skilling decided to quit and Watkins then wrote a memo to the newly appointed CEO Ken Lay. Rather than investigate her suspicions, Ms. Watkins was demoted and moved from her plush executive office in the top floors of Enron headquarters to a more ordinary office in the basement of the building. Her hard drive was also confiscated, while the new tasks she was assigned became rather meaningless relative to the high-level projects she used to work on. Her testimonies eventually helped convict the high-ranking officials at Enron. Similar cases of whistle-blowers exist in many other companies.

Based on *The Economist*. 2017. "Volkswagen; A long road to recovery." November 12, 58; Herndon, N. 2011. "Enron: Questionable accounting lead to collapse." In Thorne, D.M., Ferrell, O.C. and Ferrell, L. 2010. *Business and society. A strategic approach to social responsibility*. Boston, MA: Houghton Mifflin.

The Preview Business Ethics Insight above highlights the importance of individual actions with regards to unethical behavior. In the many examples discussed, single individuals or groups of individuals conspired and engaged in actions that resulted in major losses for large groups of people. For example, the fall of Enron resulted in tens of billions of losses for investors as well as employees. Volkswagen may experience similar losses as it grapples with the consequences of such an ethical scandal. Fortunately, the examples also show that there were concerned individuals who eventually decided to blow the whistle. These individuals often felt that what they were observing went against their own principles and beliefs. Unlike others who either turned a blind eye or supported the unethical behavior, they decided to find ways to stop such unethical behaviors.

The Preview Business Ethics Insight provides evidence that unethical behavior starts with employees within a company. Consistent with accepted practices, we define **unethical behavior** as any actions that violate accepted societal norms.[1] While many argue that the organizational culture can play an important role in promoting unethical behavior, the culture can partly be blamed on individuals supporting and enforcing the unethical norms of the culture. It therefore becomes very important to understand how and why individuals behave unethically. Furthermore, the examples show that some other individuals are less likely to conform to pressures around them and are more inclined to follow their own beliefs and principles. It also becomes crucial to understand why some behave unethically while others are more prone to follow their own ethical principles.

Why should companies attempt to understand individual ethics to reduce unethical behavior? Chapter 1 discussed the many benefits of ethical behavior for companies. Companies enjoy better financial results and many other side benefits. However, Giacalone and Promislo provide further evidence of the need of reducing unethical behavior.[2] They argue that unethical behavior can lead to a decrease in general well-being as a result of the trauma and stress associated with either being victimized or committing unethical behavior. Understanding individual ethics can thus help a company ensure its employees' well-being. Thus, from a strategic standpoint, reducing unethical behavior should result in more productive and happier employees.

In this part of the book, we therefore consider the many critical aspects of ethics as they apply to individuals. To provide a systematic coverage of individual ethics, we first consider the individual ethical decision-making process and the many factors that affect such decision-making. We also provide some guidelines that companies can follow to ensure employees behave ethically. Additionally, to comprehensively understand ethical decision-making, we also need to consider ethical theories and how they influence employees to make choices that have ethical ramifications. We consider such theories in Chapter 3.

To comprehensively understand individual ethical decision-making, we frame our discussion within Rest's stages of ethical decision-making.[3] Although there are other ways to examine ethical decision-making, Rest's framework has received significant attention.[4] Rest argues that individuals go through four stages before they decide to commit an unethical behavior. These stages include 1) moral awareness (the recognition of whether a situation has a moral component or presents an ethical dilemma), 2) moral judgment (the determination of how to respond to the ethical dilemma with choices), 3) moral intention (deciding how one should act) and 4) moral behavior (how one acts). Rest argues that people go through these stages when confronted with issues related to ethical dilemmas. If they fail at any stage of the ethical decision-making process, they are likely to engage in unethical behaviors.

Below, we therefore discuss these four stages and how individuals approach each stage. We then discuss what companies can do to ensure that the right decisions and choices are made to behave ethically.

MORAL AWARENESS

One of the most important phases of understanding individual ethics is moral awareness. **Moral awareness** refers to the ability of an individual to understand the ethicality of a situation or behavior. It is considered as one of the most important aspects of ethical decision-making, since the ability to identify a situation as being ethical suggests that steps may be taken to ensure that consequent behavior is ethical.[5] Although appreciating the ethicality of a decision seems obvious, evidence suggests that people do not always properly understand such ethicality.

Consider the case of applicants to some of the U.S.'s most prestigious MBA programs. While visiting a *Businessweek* online messaging board, some applicants came across hacking instructions posted by an anonymous hacker. The hacking instructions basically gave access to the decision page to MBA programs at Harvard, Dartmouth, Duke, Carnegie Mellon, MIT, and Stanford. By the time it took the company running the program to apply a patch, around 200 students were able to access the page. The universities were quickly given the names of those who hacked into the system. Harvard immediately took a stance reporting that they would deny admission to those 119 applicants who hacked into the system.

However, reaction to the dismissal was swift. Many felt that the universities were at fault because they didn't have the appropriate safeguards. Interviews with applicants who hacked into the system were also fascinating. Many applicants felt offended, as their ethics were being called into question. They did not necessarily find any ethical aspect around the behavior, as they felt that they were only accessing their information and were not harming others.

The above clearly shows that what many would perceive as unethical was clearly not seen as such by the applicants. Accessing the decision web page is equivalent to getting unauthorized access to restricted pages. Such a behavior is clearly unethical. However, many of the applicants failed to understand the unethical nature of their actions. Why did these applicants not see the ethics of their actions? Was it simply because they grew up in the internet age and do not see web snooping as an ethical issue? The case nevertheless suggests that companies need to work hard to train their employees to be able to properly identify the ethics of their behaviors.

How critical is moral awareness? Consider the following additional Emerging Market Business Ethics Insight.

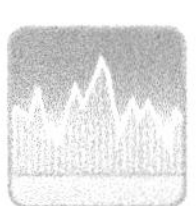

EMERGING MARKET BUSINESS ETHICS INSIGHT

Moral Awareness and Ethical Leadership in Turkey

In Chapter 1, you read about the importance of ethical leadership. Ethical leaders are seen as those who can inspire employees to be more ethical and to not engage in workplace deviance. Ethical leadership is therefore seen as a way that could have prevented the likes of Enron and Worldcom from collapsing. In the presence of an ethical leader, even Volkswagen was less likely to experience the diesel scandal.

Although research has shown the importance of ethical leadership, a recent and interesting study of working professionals in Turkey provides evidence of the power of moral awareness. Researchers found that when employees were already morally aware, the impact of ethical leadership in reducing unethical behaviors was actually weak. In other words, if employees are already morally aware of specific ethical issues in the organization, they are less likely to need ethical leadership to behave ethically.

The researchers offer two practical recommendations based on the findings of the study. First, they recommend that company leaders take a more customized approach in terms of exercising ethical leadership. Not all employees benefit from ethical leadership and managers are therefore well-advised to gauge the level of moral awareness to exercise ethical leadership. Such approaches will enhance the effectiveness of being an ethical leader and also not subject employees to unnecessary approaches.

Second, it is critical for employers to select employees with moral awareness. In fact, if moral awareness becomes a critical selection criterion, the company is less likely to hire employees who may behave unethically. Additionally, if companies can hire morally aware employees, these employees are still likely to behave ethically even when facing a leader who does not necessarily display ethical leadership qualities.

Based on Gok, K., Sumanth, J.J., Bommer, W.H., Demirtas, O., Arslan, A., Eberhard, J., Ozdemir, A.I. and Yigit, A. 2017. "You may not reap what you sow: How employees' moral awareness minimizes ethical leadership's positive impact on workplace deviance." *Journal of Business Ethics,* 146, 257–277.

Given the above importance, understanding the factors that determine moral awareness becomes critical. Current research suggests that the way situations are framed will have an impact on how the morality of a situation is viewed. This framing can be dependent on company level factors as well as individual level factors. One of the most important company factors is the organizational culture. For instance, as the Enron case showed earlier, the organizational culture an individual is in can play a big role in desensitizing employees as to the ethics of situations. Because of the rank and yank system whereby the weakest employees were being fired, Enron's leadership created a culture where moral awareness decreased as financial performance became the main focus. Employees were willing to ignore morality in their actions because such actions were discouraged.

In Chapter 12, you will also learn about ethical climates that represent the dominant way people base decisions when confronted with ethical dilemmas. Research suggests that the ethical climate can also impact moral awareness[6]. A survey of employees across seven different companies suggest that companies that encourage ethical climates that show caring for others (benevolent ethical climates) and follow rules and regulations (principled ethical climates) had employees with higher moral awareness. In contrast and not surprisingly, employees who were in ethical climates that promote self-interested behaviors had lower moral awareness.

Other determinants of moral awareness come from more personal factors. For example, recent research suggests that ethical predispositions can play an important role. Specifically, **ethical predispositions** refer to the "cognitive framework individuals prefer to use in moral decision making."[7] For instance, in Chapter 3, you will learn about utilitarianism and Kantian ethics. Both are approaches that individuals use to consider situations with moral implications. As you will see later, it is possible for those who follow the utilitarianism framework where the moral awareness of situations is based on looking at cost and benefits of the situation. In this case, individuals may not necessarily perceive a situation as having moral consequences if they feel that the benefits of making a decision outweigh the cost. You will learn about ethical predispositions in more depth in Chapter 3.

Another important factor contributing to moral awareness is moral attentiveness. **Moral attentiveness** refers to the ability of individuals to access and interpret the moral content of information and stimuli they are presented with.[8] When dealing with any situation, an individual will interpret the information based on prior experiences and decisions. Those with higher moral attentiveness are more likely to recognize the moral aspects of everyday situations. According to extant research, moral attentiveness is a relatively stable trait of individuals and represents the lens through which levels of attention is dedicated to moral aspects of any information.

Recent research suggests that higher levels of moral attentiveness do indeed increase moral awareness. Using a study of over 200 individuals, researchers asked these individuals seven questions measuring moral attentiveness.[9] Examples of these questions include "my life has been filled with one moral predicament after another" and "I regularly think about the ethical implications of my decisions." The researchers found that those individuals with higher moral attentiveness also had higher moral awareness. This suggests that companies can also use moral attentiveness as a way to recruit individuals with stronger moral awareness.

What is the level of moral awareness of individuals around the world? In that context, the World Values Survey is a global project of researchers examining many societal aspects worldwide. These researchers also examine matters related to business ethics. For example, they asked respondents worldwide the degree to which they felt that "cheating on their taxes" was justifiable. It is feasible to argue that those individuals who rated cheating on their taxes as never justifiable have higher levels of moral

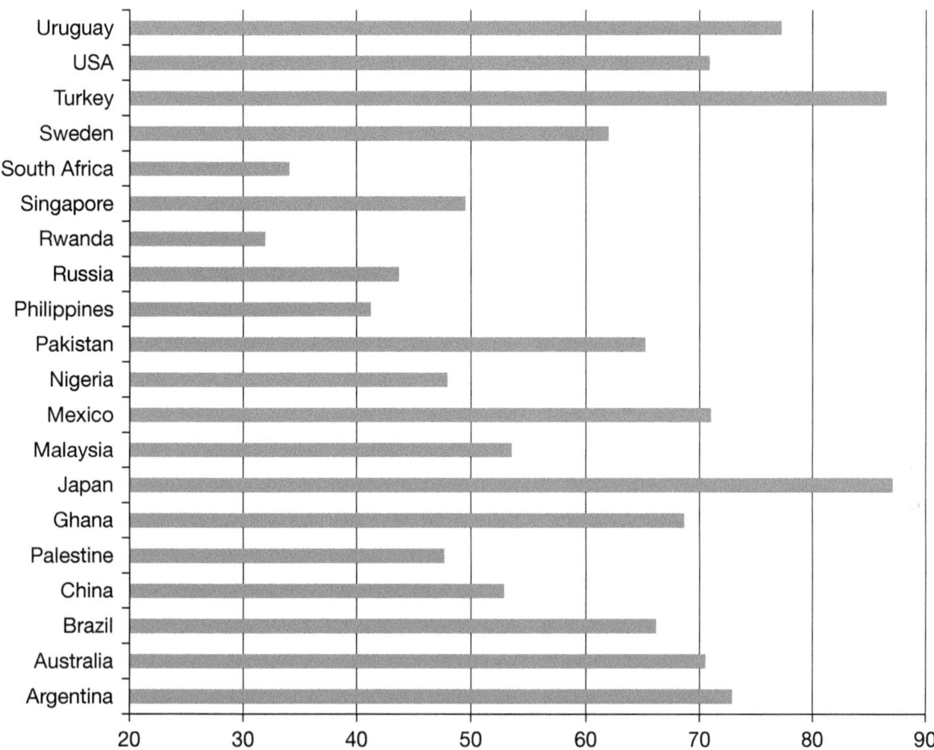

EXHIBIT 2.1—Moral Awareness Worldwide

Based on World Values Survey, 2018. www.worldvaluessurvey.org/wvs.jsp.

awareness. Exhibit 2.1 shows the percentage of individuals in each country who felt that they could never justify cheating on their taxes.

Exhibit 2.1 therefore provides some insights on the level of awareness worldwide. Furthermore, the overwhelming evidence suggests that moral awareness is something that should be encouraged by managers. Taking steps to make employees aware of the ethicality of situations therefore becomes critical. For example, training employees on what is considered unethical is a very important aspect of moral awareness. Companies can also encourage their employees to become involved in projects aimed at addressing societal concerns. Consider the following Business Ethics Insight.

The following Business Ethics Brief provides some insights into the potential of civic engagement projects to increase moral awareness. Additionally, given the importance of organizational cultures in terms of encouraging moral awareness, companies are strongly encouraged to develop processes to ensure that employees are aware of the potential consequences of different decisions. Simply having codes of conduct clarifying the ethical aspects associated with operations is also very helpful.

BUSINESS ETHICS INSIGHT

Importance of Training

A recent study of efforts to infuse civic engagement within business ethics courses at a university provides some insights as to the utility of training to enhance moral awareness. Faculty members of that university incorporated civic engagement projects across the curriculum by encouraging teams of students to become engaged in projects tackling key issues such as focusing on the well-being of children, the elderly and other socially responsible projects such as working with animal shelters and environmental organizations. Students' projects were then assessed based on a number of criteria such as the lessons they learned and the impact they made.

The results of the study showed that being involved in such programs made them more interested in working in careers that helped improve the lives of people. Most importantly, the project helped raise the moral awareness of these students by showing them the importance of being involved in the community. Additionally, the projects also improved the sensitivity and empathy of these students in terms of the needs of those who are less fortunate. Ultimately, the students became aware of many key societal problems that require attention. To give you more insights into these projects, Exhibit 2.2 shows the number of students who were involved in each of these areas.

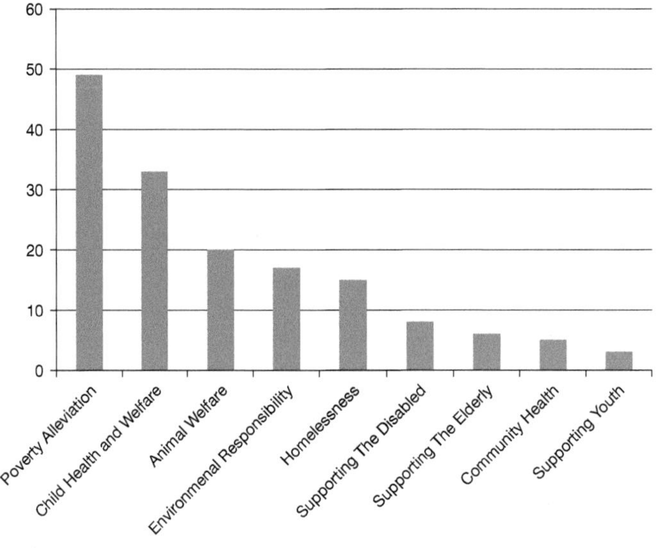

EXHIBIT 2.2—Number of Students Involved in Moral and Social Awareness Projects

What are the implications of this study for companies? Providing the time and support for employees to become involved in projects that support community projects may help employees become more morally aware. In fact, when employees have a chance to be involved in such projects, they may become more aware of their own good fortune relative to others. Additionally, they are likely to also become more sensitized to the many ethical issues confronting society. Finally, allowing employees to volunteer in community programs is also likely to make them more ethical by making them become more aware of the social and ethical implications of their actions and decisions at work.

Based on Marques, J. 2017. "Shaping morally responsible leaders: Infusing civic engagement into business ethics courses." *Journal of Business Ethics,* 135, 279–291.

Next, we consider the second step of Rest's ethical decision-making framework, namely moral judgment.

MORAL JUDGMENT

According to Rest, the likelihood of someone behaving ethically is enhanced when someone properly identifies a situation as having ethical implications. However, this does not necessarily guarantee that the individual will behave ethically. The second step involves how an individual assesses the situation and makes a proper moral judgment. **Moral judgment** therefore refers to the process by which someone reasons about how to deal with an ethical situation. The more accurate the moral judgment of a situation, the more likely the individual will behave ethically.

Moral judgment is an extremely critical element of the ethical decision-making process. The more accurate the moral judgment an individual makes, the more likely the person will behave ethically. Specifically, accurately judging the morality of any situation allows the employee to make the appropriate choices to behave ethically.

In addition to the role of moral judgment in helping employees make moral judgments, recent research also shows that importance of moral judgment for leaders. Examining a large sample of purchasing professionals in Taiwan and China,[10] researchers found that supervisors with high levels of moral judgment had a positive influence on their subordinates' moral judgment level. Such findings are not surprising as employees look up to their leaders when faced with issues that have moral implications. If they see that their supervisors are good role models who also make morally sound judgment, subordinates are more likely to have strong moral judgment.

To properly judge the morality of any situation, employees need to be rational and logical. However, research indicates that many biases and other factors can interfere with an employee's ability to make correct moral judgment. Because of our limitations, we often fall prey to biases that result in unethical behaviors. Biases can be **conscious** whereby the employee intentionally relies on biases to make unethical choices. In contrast, **unconscious biases** occur when the "most well-meaning person unwittingly allows unconscious thoughts and feelings to influence seemingly objective decisions."[11]

What types of biases can employees experience? According to Banaji et al. and Bazerman and Tenbrunsel, managers can engage in unethical behaviors through several potential biases.[12] **Implicit prejudice** occurs when people rely on unconscious biases and prejudice when people judge others. This occurs because people tend to make associations between employee characteristics and organizational outcomes that may not be accurate. For instance, consider the case of *Price Waterhouse v. Hopkins*, where a woman employee sued the company for not being appointed as a partner although she was a great employee. The court case revealed that many of the evaluators had serious implicit prejudice based on gender stereotypes. For example, the evaluators felt that she was being overcompensated for being a woman and that she needed training in charm school. Implicit prejudice can thus be very costly, as Price Waterhouse had to pay $25 million to Ms. Ann Hopkins.

Another unconscious bias that may affect employees is in-group favoritism. According to Banaji et al. (2003), **in-group favoritism** occurs because people tend to favor those individuals who share similar characteristics to their own, such as being from the same school, social class, or religion. For instance, a company executive may unconsciously prefer a job applicant who also holds an MBA from the same school that the executive went to. Thus, rather than objectively considering all candidates for the job opening, in-group favoritism may give an unfair advantage to another person because that person possesses certain characteristics.

Another important bias is termed motivated blindness. **Motivated blindness** takes place when people turn a blind eye to unethical behavior because such behavior is beneficial to them.[13] For example, a manager may turn a blind eye to a salesperson filing a fraudulent expense claim as the salesperson is one of the best performers in the company. In such cases, the manager may unconsciously ignore the unethical behavior and focus more on desired sales results.

Another unconscious bias that may affect decision-making is conflict of interest. **Conflict of interest** occurs when decision-making can be unconsciously affected because the decision-maker may benefit from the chosen decision. As Banaji et al. discuss, although Nasdaq fell by almost 60% in 2000, most brokerage firms advised their clients to buy or hold their stocks.[14] Why did this occur? Most of the brokers were compensated based on the extent of the relationship with customers. A sell recommendation would end the relationship. As a consequence, the broker may unconsciously recommend a buy or hold in order to prolong the relationship to get compensated.

In addition to the above biases discussed in Banaji et al.,[15] other types of more conscious biases can also lead to unethical behavior.[16] Employees can fall prone to **obedience to authority** whereby they justify unethical behavior as orders that came from their managers or CEO. Companies such as both Enron and Volkswagen had CEOs that placed impossible demands on their employees thereby leading to unethical behavior on their part. For example, at Volkswagen, the CEO set unrealistic carbon dioxide targets for its diesel cars. This may have led to the Volkswagen engineers' decision to install software to cheat emissions tests.

Employees are also likely to succumb to the **conformity bias** whereby the employee has the "tendency of imitating or accepting the values of others" (page 501) as a way to justify one's actions.[17] Rather than be willing to question one's judgment, this bias provides the means by which someone can find a questionable action as morally permissible. Cases of insider trading, minor theft and even surfing the web on company time can become judged as morally permissible because "everyone is doing it."

Finally, another bias that employees can be prone to is **incrementalism** whereby employees engage in minor unethical behaviors that eventually leads to major ethical infractions. Analysis of many ethical scandals shows that unethical behaviors do not always occur suddenly. Rather, such ethical scandals start with small infractions that can gradually escalate into major ethical transgressions.

To give you further insights into the above biases, consider the following Global Business Ethics Insight.

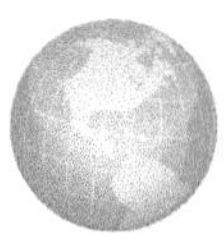

GLOBAL BUSINESS ETHICS INSIGHT

Nick Leeson and the Barings Bank Collapse

Barings Bank, England's oldest merchant bank, collapsed as a result of rogue trading. At the time of the collapse, Nick Leeson was a Barings Bank trader in his 20s. His trading decisions led to the bank losing USD1.3 billion and eventually bankrupted the company. What led to this spectacular collapse? An analysis of the events leading to the downfall of Barings Bank reveals that Nick Leeson was influenced by many factors that clouded both his moral awareness and judgment. For example, his moral awareness was severely affected because the culture at Barings Bank was simply to make profits. In fact, the young trader was seen as a rising star as he made significant profits for the bank. Although there were many red flags, his supervisors ignored such information and instead praised him for his trades.

Mr. Leeson was also affected by many other biases. For instance, he was affected by motivated blindness because he was engaged in actions that would be of benefit to himself. As an example, when one of his subordinates made a wrong order by doing the opposite of what the client wanted, Leeson did not report the mistake to his supervisors. Rather, Barings Bank had an error account where traders could "warehouse" the losses while they tried to fix such losses. As such, rather than report the losses, Mr. Leeson wanted to protect his reputation.

Although he made many unauthorized trades, Mr. Leeson's moral judgment was also affected by obedience to authority. As mentioned earlier, managers only wanted traders to make profits. In an attempt to satisfy his supervisors and to make sure he survived, Mr. Leeson continued to make many trades meant to increase profits. Unfortunately, such actions backfired.

Mr. Leeson's moral judgment was also affected by incrementalism. The final rogue trade started with smaller actions where losses were being set inside in an error loss account while Mr. Leeson was trying to correct the situation. After trying to protect others from mistakes and losses, soon he was also covering up his own losses using the loss accounts. This gave him the opportunity to bet the bank's entire equity to make up for larger losses.

Analysis of the actions leading to the downfall also shows that Mr. Leeson was subject to conformity bias. While he explicitly acknowledged that he knew what he was doing was wrong, he also noted that many of his colleagues were also engaging in similar activities. The pervasiveness of loss warehousing made the practice more morally permissible.

In the end, Mr. Leeson's final trade was unauthorized bets of £827 million (British pounds) on the Japanese Nikkei index. Unfortunately, the Japanese earthquake of 1995 led to the collapse of the Nikkei index and the collapse of the bank. Singlehandedly, Mr. Leeson's actions led to the downfall of the Queen of England's personal bank. Mr. Leeson was eventually arrested and sentenced to 6.5 years in jail.

Based on Schwartz, M. 2017. "Teaching behavioral ethics: Overcoming the key impediments to ethical behavior." *Journal of Management Education,* 41, 497–513; Seijts, G. 2016. "Rogue learnings." *Ivey Business Journal,* July/August, 2–8.

It shows how these biases led Mr. Leeson to engage in actions that led to the downfall of England's oldest bank. Given the dangers of being affected by both conscious and unconscious biases, it is important that companies take steps to reduce the likelihood of occurrences. It is therefore important for companies to consider the following steps:[18]

- First, it is important for companies to collect data to determine whether employees are engaging in implicit prejudice. If patterns of decision-making seem consistent with implicit prejudice, the necessary training must be given to employees to encourage them to abandon such biases. It is critical that employees be made aware of how these biases may be influencing them so that they can take a more deliberate look at future decisions. Furthermore, experts suggest that employees take the Implicit Association Tests to determine the presence of such biases (see Internet Activity, p. 79).
- Companies can also train their employees to be empathetic. When decisions are to be made, it is important to visualize how minorities or other disadvantaged groups might be affected by the decision. It is important for employees to realize how they may make different decisions if they belonged to a different group. Additionally, employees can participate in exercises where they are asked to discuss personal ethical dilemmas they have faced at work. They can then discuss potential options

to resolve such dilemmas. Trainers can provide insights when it is clear that decisions are being made based on biases.

- Rather than focus on outcomes or ignore unethical behavior, employees should be trained to understand the process behind decision-making. Systems should be implemented so that employees do not ignore unethical behavior for the sake of performance outcomes. Companies thus need to sensitize employees to the importance of ethical behavior.
- Employees should also be trained to understand the presence of conflicts of interest. While decision-makers may be unconsciously influenced by such conflicts, companies can emphasize the presence of such conflicts by exposing workers to potential work dilemmas and sensitizing them to avoid such conflicts. Making employees aware of such conflicts of interest will push these issues into the conscious.
- A recent interview with Mr. Leeson, the rogue trader at Barings Bank, also provides some suggestions. Companies need to create a culture that allows employees to make mistakes and not be punished for it. Pressures to perform need to be alleviated and a culture of doing the right thing should be encouraged. This will then ensure that employees make the correct judgment.

BUSINESS ETHICS BRIEF

Algorithms and Reducing Unconscious Bias

As more companies make use of large data, experts predict that companies will start integrating data analytics in order to reduce unconscious bias in the many functions related to employee management. Specifically, many Human Resource Management departments are now using algorithms to scan their data to determine if biases are creeping in across all HR functions. Such practice called "talent analytics" is gathering momentum in many companies worldwide.

What is the nature of such talent analytics? Companies are relying on a tool called "Blendoor" whereby irrelevant data such as photos and names are hidden from recruiting teams. In contrast, the program will highlight critical information such as skills and experiences, key aspects of the hiring process. Another program known as "Indexio" can quickly scan job advertisements to determine if bias is present in the language used. Other programs can scan blog posts in companies to see whether sexist of racist language is being used.

According to experts, the success of such "talent analytics" will depend on the algorithms being used. For instance, early software simply relied on basic criteria such as whether someone attended a prestigious school as a way to reduce bias. However, experts also agree that the quality of talent analytics programs is quickly improving.

Based on Bishop, M. 2017. "Working for the algorithm; Machines will help employers overcome bias." *The Economist: The World in 2018*, 131.

Companies can therefore implement many practices to ensure that their employees do not engage in biases. Many companies are now also relying on the power of computers to determine if bias is occurring. Consider the above Business Ethics Brief.

Next, we consider the final two steps of Rest's ethical decision-making framework.

MORAL INTENTION AND BEHAVIORS

The various issues discussed earlier provide some insights into what factors affect individual ethics. Companies routinely design ethics training and programs to address these factors and ensure that employees behave ethically by being morally aware and making the correct moral judgment. However, despite the training and despite people's best intentions, unethical behavior still occurs to a very large extent. Why do such unethical behaviors still occur? Why do people consider themselves as being ethical while having intentions in engaging in unethical behaviors?

The final part of the chapter examines Rest's third and fourth step of the ethical decision-making process. **Moral intention and behaviors** refers to the employees' choices and decisions when confronting moral situations. An important aspect of understanding moral intention and behaviors is to understand the factors that interfere with such processes. Understanding the ethicality of situations and how employees can morally disengage from ethical situations provides important insights. Specifically, here we consider how individuals who consider themselves very ethical may end up rationalizing unethical behaviors.

Jones' Ethical Decision-Making Aspects

How do individuals examine ethical situations and decide how to act? According to Jones, people evaluate the moral intensity of any situation and behave accordingly. If they perceive that the situation has high moral intensity, they are more likely to have intentions to or behave ethically.

According to Jones, the moral intensity is dependent on six elements.[19] These elements include: 1) **magnitude of consequences**—refers to the degree of harm that the victims of an unethical choice will have to endure; 2) **social consensus**—the degree to which others agree that a specific behavior is wrong; 3) **probability of effect**—the probability that any action will result in harm to victims of the action; 4) **temporal immediacy**—the length of time between the action and the harmful consequences of such actions; 5) **proximity**—the psychological or cultural nearness to the victim; and 6) **concentration of effect**—the number of people affected by the act.

To gain better insights into the theory, Jones' six elements can be applied in the case of Mr. Leeson and the Barings Bank disaster. Mr. Leeson likely felt that his actions did not really harm anyone as all he wanted to do was to correct errors. Thus, the magnitude of consequences was negligible and the action not perceived as unethical. Social consensus was low for what he was doing. At Barings Bank, the focus was on making profits and rogue traders were expected to make money. Mr. Leeson could therefore rationalize his actions. Furthermore, probability of effect, concentration of effect, and proximity were low simply because Mr. Leeson did not perceive that anyone was being harmed by his actions. Finally, temporal immediacy was low because no harm was necessarily perceived. To give you even further insights into Jones' six elements, consider the following Emerging Market Business Ethics Insight.

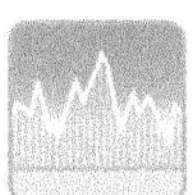

EMERGING MARKET BUSINESS ETHICS INSIGHT

Bank Heist in Bangladesh

Bangladesh is still reeling from one of the most spectacular bank heists in its history. Cyber criminals were able to hack into the country's central bank and order the transfer of $101 million dollars into private accounts in Sri Lanka and Philippines through the New York Federal Reserve. While these cyber criminals do not necessarily need any justification for their actions, an examination through the lens of Jones' many aspects shows how the moral intensity of the robbery may have been low.

The fact that the criminals were targeting the central bank of Bangladesh means that it is easy to dissociate from any actual victims of the crime. As such, the magnitude of consequences is very low because the victim in this case is not individuals but a bank. It is much easier to rationalize unethical behaviors because companies or other institutions can't really be hurt. Additionally, probability of effect, temporal immediacy, proximity and concentration of effect are also all very low. The criminals are not necessarily close to their victims and do not likely see any major negative consequences for their victim. Furthermore, they likely do not associate a large number of victims with the heist because they only robbed a single bank. All of these issues probably reduce the moral intensity of the action.

Despite intense investigations, the heist remains unresolved at the time of writing. The heist shows how sophisticated cyber criminals are in today's globally connected world.

Based on *The Economist*. 2017. "The Bangladesh bank heist; Still on the trail." March 25, 63.

As mentioned earlier, people will perceive moral intensity if any of the six elements is perceived at a high level. In the case of the Bangladesh bank heist, most of the six elements were low. However, if all six elements are perceived as high, the employee is likely to have moral intentions and behave morally. In fact, a recent review of published studies provides support for Jones' assertions.[20] Specifically, the review showed that all six elements were indeed negatively related to unethical choices. Such results are consistent with the main assertions that low levels of each of the six components should result in less unethical choices. Furthermore, the authors of the review also created a combined measure for all six elements. They found that the combined elements also resulted in reduced unethical choices.

Given the above, companies can take the necessary steps to promote ethical behavior. First, it becomes critical for companies to provide training regarding proper identification of issues with moral implications.[21] For example, training can be provided to help employees see the harm they can inflict on victims (i.e., magnitude of consequences) or their closeness to potential victims (i.e., proximity). Second, companies can highlight issues with moral implications so as to create a norm that such issues are wrong. Most companies, whether domestic or international, experience misconduct. Such misconduct can range from employee issues, such as discrimination and sexual harassment, to information technology issues, such as internet abuse. Companies can provide training to employees, sensitizing them to these many examples of unethical behavior. By providing such training, employees can be made aware of the unethical nature of such activities. By equipping workers to better identify behaviors with unethical consequences, it is more likely that employees will take the necessary steps to reduce the likelihood that the behavior occurs. Furthermore, for each of the misconducts discussed, the moral intensity of the actions can be clarified. Each of the six elements can be discussed within the context of each of the misconducts.

Moral Disengagement

Despite strong training programs, people will often engage in unethical behavior despite overwhelming evidence that the behaviors are wrong. Consider the following Business Ethics Insight about the tobacco industry.

How could the tobacco executives deny the link between smoking and cancer despite decades of evidence suggesting such a link? How could they belong to an industry that was clearly selling a harmful product? How could they deny that cigarettes are addictive? Despite strong internal ethical codes, these individuals willingly altered their own ethical values to justify their unethical actions. Thus, a big question for this part of the chapter is to understand why individuals engage repeatedly in unethical behavior despite clearly knowing that such activities are unethical. Why would tobacco executives engage in clearly unethical behavior and strongly believe that their actions are morally right? To understand why these situations occur, we consider moral disengagement.

Moral disengagement was developed to explain how individuals can behave unethically despite having moral standards.[22] However, to understand moral disengagement, it is necessary to first understand social cognitive theory. Specifically, Bandura developed social cognitive theory, arguing that most people have developed "personal standards of moral behavior . . . that guide good behavior and deter bad behavior."[23] As individuals consider how to behave, they use these personal standards to monitor the morality of their actions. If they feel that their actions are against their personal standards, they will likely not engage in the behavior.

BUSINESS ETHICS INSIGHT

Tobacco Industry Executives and the Ethics of Cigarettes

While some industries receive frequent scrutiny, no industry has received more attention than the tobacco industry. For decades, people have examined the actions of the companies and their behaviors. Tobacco executives have also been subject to the same intense scrutiny. Examination of years of executive decision-making in the industry shows a pattern of deception and dishonesty. For decades, tobacco executives have defended the industry and its products under oath. These executives have publicly argued that tobacco is not addictive and not harmful to health if used properly. These executives engaged in many other behaviors that showed that they had cognitively justified these unethical behaviors. In other words, these executives developed mechanisms to justify their unethical behavior.

According to experts, the pattern of deceit started in December 1953, when the CEOs of five tobacco companies met and discussed a strategy to defend themselves against scientific research that linked cigarette smoking with lung cancer. Because various stakeholders such as the government, consumers, and other tobacco control advocates were starting to demand tobacco control, the executives knew that the industry was in danger. They therefore decided to present evidence suggesting that the statistical link does not necessarily mean that smoking causes lung cancer. From a research standpoint, the only way to conclusively prove causation is through experiments where smokers and non-smokers were compared in controlled experiments. Such experiments are clearly impossible to conduct. Thus, the executives argued that, in the absence of such experiments, the statistical link should be discounted.

In addition to the denial that there is a link between smoking and lung cancer, tobacco executives engaged in many other clearly unethical behaviors. For instance, they argued that smokers have a choice and that they choose to smoke. Thus, rather than admit that the industry was responsible, the executives shifted the responsibility to the smoker's decision to smoke when justifying the product. In another case, tobacco executives were asked at a social reception why they chose not to smoke. The reply was, "We don't smoke the s. . ., we just sell it. We reserve that for the young, poor, the black, and the stupid."

Based on Armenakis, A. and Wigand, J. 2010. "Stakeholder actions and their impact on the organizational cultures of two tobacco companies." *Business and Society Review*, 115, 2, 147–171.

Bandura, however, argues that individuals have the ability to activate and deactivate this form of moral regulation.[24] **Moral disengagement** refers to this deactivation process where, when faced with potential behavior counter to their own personal standards, a person may choose to deactivate the standard and still engage in the behavior. Thus, moral disengagement helps individuals justify behaviors that may go against their moral standards.

Bandura argues that moral disengagement can occur through eight mechanisms categorized under three forms of justification of immoral behavior. The first type refers to cognitive reconstruction of behavior whereby people reconstruct behaviors cognitively to make them acceptable. Cognitive reconstruction includes three forms of moral disengagement; namely, moral justification, euphemistic labeling, and advantageous comparison. **Moral justification** occurs when individuals justify certain actions to make them seem more morally acceptable. For instance, a company CEO may justify employing child labor in a foreign plant on the basis that these children would otherwise engage in other more degrading forms of behavior to help their poor families.[25] **Euphemistic labeling** refers to the use of morally neutral language to make something seem less immoral. For instance, accidentally killing your own in a war is now called "friendly fire," while the killing of civilians is referred to as "collateral damage." In the mind of the decision-maker, this use of different terminology lessens the unethical nature of the action. **Advantageous comparison** occurs when someone compares a worse behavior with another behavior and rationalizes the behavior on that basis. As Detert et al. suggest, a student may ask about general content of an exam to a student who has inappropriately obtained the exam with the justification that it is less problematic to ask about the exam generally than it is to ask for an actual review of the specific exam questions.[26]

The second set of moral disengagement refers to mechanisms that minimizes one's responsibility for unethical behavior, and includes displacement of responsibility, diffusion of responsibility, and distorting consequences of the unethical behavior. **Displacement of responsibility** occurs when the perpetrator of an unethical behavior can attribute the behavior to other factors. For example, a person can blame the misreporting of sales figures for a quarter because the boss wanted the behavior. In such cases, the employee can attribute the action to his/her boss. Furthermore, **diffusion of responsibility** can occur if decisions are being made by a group. For instance, a specific member of a board of directors can attribute the decision to close a plant to the group rather than an individual decision. **Distortion of consequences** occurs when an individual can disconnect the actions from the harmful connections of the action. For example, a customer may return a used product by justifying that the unethical behavior will clearly not impact the large company from which the product was purchased.

The third and final set of moral disengagement mechanisms focus on the target's unfavorable acts and includes dehumanization and attribution of blame. **Dehumanization** occurs when the target of the decision is derogated or is seen as lacking in human qualities. For instance, a company may justify dumping toxic pollutants in a river because the wildlife destroyed by the act may not be seen as worth saving because they are seen as subhuman. Finally, **attribution of blame** occurs when the decision-maker ascribes the blame for the decision to the target. As Detert et al. discuss, some have argued that torturing terrorists is acceptable, as they have brought such actions to themselves.[27] Exhibit 2.3 summarizes the types of moral disengagement and its application as executives of the tobacco industry justified their actions.

Moral Disengagement Mechanisms	Examples from the Tobacco Industry
Moral Justification	Employees of the tobacco industry focused on redefining their jobs as working in a rewarding environment rather than selling cigarettes. This quote is indicative: "I must tell you, the people you have around you everyday and the kind of environment you live in everyday, become an incredibly important part of the quality of your life . . . you deny the problems . . . It's the question of being very happy at doing what you are doing."
Euphemistic Labeling	Review of tobacco industry documents showed that there was strong effort to attract consumers younger than 18 years old. However, the documents showed that the industry used code words such as "new smoker," "presmoker," and "beginning smoker" instead of "underage smokers."
Advantageous Comparison	Tobacco executives from one company justifying their actions by arguing that others are also engaging in such behaviors.
Displacement of Responsibility	Tobacco executives using the argument that their actions are generally permissible as they do not break any rules or regulations. Fault is placed on regulators for not having the appropriate laws in place.
Diffusion of Responsibility	Scene of seven CEOs of the top tobacco companies appearing before the U.S. Congress and swearing that tobacco is not addictive.
Distortion of Consequences	Open questioning of the "causation" hypothesis. Tobacco executives sought to sow seeds of doubt regarding the link between smoking and lung cancer, although statistics showed a strong link.
Dehumanization	Tobacco executives arguing that they do not smoke but that they leave the choice to the "poor, the black, and the stupid." A husband suing after his wife died was also told that he should not get any money as his wife admitted to enjoying smoking and that smoking made her feel glamorous.
Attribution of Blame	Blame smokers for making the choice, for enjoying smoking, for enjoying smoking as it made the smoker feel glamorous.

EXHIBIT 2.3—Moral Disengagement and the Tobacco Industry

As Exhibit 2.3 shows, moral disengagement can be dangerous when carried to the extreme. As the exhibit shows and as discussed earlier in the Business Ethics Insight, tobacco executives relied on moral disengagement to justify their unethical decisions. For instance, the executives frequently used distortion of consequences to argue that the effects of smoking are not harmful to individuals. By arguing that statistical correlation (higher incidences of smoking is linked to more harmful health effects) is not necessarily causation (one leads to the other), the tobacco executives brought into question decades of evidence of the harmful effects of smoking.

Research by Claybourn provides further evidence of the disastrous consequences of moral disengagement on workplace harassment.[28] Workplace harassment refers to problematic interpersonal relationships in organizations that lead to employees feeling victimized. Such harassment seems to be fairly prevalent. Claybourn finds that organizations that allow their employees to be harassed are also more likely to have these employees use moral disengagement to justify harming and harassing others. Thus, it seems like the feeling of being victimized can engender justification for harming others.

Another study provides more evidence of the damaging effects of moral disengagement.[29] Examining a wide sample of individuals from five different studies, the researchers find that moral disengagement results in a host of negative outcomes. Moral disengagement is a significant predictor of unethical behavior, decision to commit fraud, and co-worker reported unethical work behaviors.

Taken together, the current research on moral disengagement suggests the latter can have very disastrous consequences for companies. It therefore becomes important for the company to find ways to limit the occurrence of moral disengagement. How can this be done? The following is suggested:[30]

- A company needs to create an ethical culture where employees do not feel harassed. As Claybourn argues, employees in an unhealthy culture are more likely to resort to moral disengagement in hurting others. You will read more about creating the ethical culture in Chapter 12.[31]
- Companies need to carefully screen new applicants to ensure that only those who are low on moral disengagement are hired. How can that be done? Exhibit 2.4 shows the typical questions that can be asked to assess the different moral disengagement mechanisms. Companies can thus assess their new hires.

Furthermore, Detert et al. (2008) show that people high on empathy and low on cynicism are less likely to adopt moral disengagement tactics.[32] Care must be taken to emphasize hiring of such individuals.

- Training can be given to those who are more prone to use moral disengagement tactics. Specific training can be developed to tailor one's own workplace environment. Examples pinpointing the various moral disengagement mechanisms can be provided to employees so as to make the training more relevant to their workplace. Employees should also be trained on the dangers of moral disengagement and the need for workers to guard themselves against such actions.

Moral Disengagement Mechanism	Moral Disengagement Questions
Moral Justification	• It is alright to fight to protect your friends • It's OK to steal to take care of your family's needs • It's OK to attack someone who threatens your family's honor • It is alright to lie to keep your friends out of trouble
Euphemistic Labeling	• Sharing test questions is just a way of helping your friends • Talking about people behind their back is just part of the game • Looking at a friend's homework without permission is just "borrowing it" • It is not bad to "get high" once in a while
Advantageous Comparison	• Not working very hard in school is really no big deal when you consider that other people are probably cheating • Compared to other illegal things people do, taking things from a store without paying for them is not very serious
Displacement of Responsibility	• If people are living in bad conditions, they cannot be blamed for behaving aggressively • If the professor doesn't discipline cheaters, students should not be blamed for cheating • If someone is pressured into doing something, they should not be blamed for it • People cannot be blamed for misbehaving if their friends pressured them to do it
Diffusion of Responsibility	• A member of a group or team should not be blamed for the trouble the team caused • A student who only suggests breaking the rules should not be blamed if other students go ahead and do it • If a group decides together to do something harmful, it is unfair to blame any one member of the group • You can't blame a person who plays only a small part in the harm caused by a group
Distortion of Consequences	• It is OK to tell small lies, because they really don't do any harm • People don't mind being teased because it shows interest in them • Teasing someone does not really hurt them • Insults really don't hurt anyone
Dehumanization	• Some people deserve to be treated like animals • It is OK to treat badly someone who behaved like a "worm" • Someone who is obnoxious does not deserve to be treated like a human being • Some people have to be treated roughly because they lack feelings that can be hurt
Attribution of Blame	• If someone leaves something lying around, it is their own fault if it gets stolen • People who are mistreated have usually done things to deserve it • People are not at fault for misbehaving at work if their managers mistreat them • If students misbehave in class, it is their teacher's fault

EXHIBIT 2.4—Moral Disengagement Questions

- Ethics officers can be appointed so that they can review decision-making processes across projects in the organization. The officer should have the ability to examine projects with potential ethical implications and determine whether moral disengagement is being used. Warnings such as “everybody is doing it” or “it doesn’t really hurt anyone” should be carefully scrutinized to ensure that project members are not engaging in moral disengagement mechanisms.

CONCLUSION

This chapter considered one of the most popular approaches to understand individual ethics, namely Rest’s ethical decision-making model. We do acknowledge that there are other models available, although we do consider most of them in this chapter.[33] Additionally, although the chapter presented the model as a series of steps, reality suggests that these steps don’t necessarily have to occur in the order discussed. Additionally, as research has shown, it is possible for some steps to have an impact on other steps. Consider, as an example, the study conducted in India showing that the moral disengagement of 160 young adults had a significant effect on moral judgment.[34] It is important to appreciate the connection among the four aspects discussed above.

Nevertheless, the chapter presents a very comprehensive understanding of the many factors that contribute to individual ethics. Unethical behaviors start with the individual employee and understanding what contributes to ethical behavior is important. Additionally, one of the common suggestions for all four areas was to build an ethical culture. An ethical culture starts with the leader setting a vision for the organization. Consider the following Global Business Ethics Insight.

GLOBAL BUSINESS ETHICS INSIGHT

DSM and CEO Feike Sijbesma’s Vision

DSM is a Dutch nutrition and materials multinational and although the company is not well known, it manufactures many of the ingredients that go into many products. For instance, it manufactures the ingredients that go into many food and beverage products as well as into animal feed and many personal cosmetics products. It also produces the lighter plastics that go into cars as well as paints and coatings. It is also the first company to produce a fully recyclable carpet.

Although the company was in the bulk chemistry business, the CEO Feike Sijbesma decided to set the company’s vision as "improving the planet and the lives of people on it." It is now one of the most environmentally friendly companies in the world and this push for sustainability has resulted in many innovations for the company. Mr. Sijbesma has taken every step to build a culture emphasizing the planet and people over profits. For example, the company rewards its executives with short- and long-term incentives tied to sustainability initiatives. It incentivizes its plant operators to make use of renewable energy. And the CEO has remained committed to working with institutions such as the World Food Programme despite opposition from some shareholders.

This culture has been very beneficial to the company. Such a focus has enabled the company to be innovative in many areas. For example, DSM has developed a process to convert corn waste into ethanol, a much more environmentally friendly process than using corn. DSM has also developed a low-cost micronutrient powder that has been used to fight malnutrition at a refugee camp in Kenya. In partnership with the World Food Programme, the company has fed over 31 million individuals worldwide. Additionally, the company recently developed a product that reduces flatulence in cows. Cattle flatulence is an important contributor to global warming as it contributes to around 10% of methane emissions. Additionally, the company has benefitted from higher employee motivation and retention as employees are proud to work for such a company.

It is also likely that DSM's vision and approach has enhanced all of the decision-making aspects discussed in this chapter. By focusing on improving the planet, DSM has increased moral awareness by emphasizing key areas of importance. Additionally, through its incentives program and focus, the company provides the necessary guidance encouraging employees to make the appropriate moral judgment. The CEO has remained an important advocate of the power of companies to do good and it is likely that such focus guides employees to make the right moral judgment. Finally, it is clear that the many innovative products that the company has discovered have been the result of the employees having moral intentions.

Based on Fry, E. 2017. "$E=MC^2$; Earth friendly—manufacturing X Conscientiousness." *Fortune,* September, 120–123; Lemonick, S. 2017. "Scientists underestimated how bad cow farts are." *Forbes,* www.forbes.com/sites/samlemonick/2017/09/29/scientists-underestimated-how-bad-cow-farts-are/#18ec0f0078a9

CHAPTER SUMMARY

In this chapter, you read about the many factors contributing to an understanding of individual ethics through Rest's ethical decision-making framework. Rest argues that individuals go through four stages before they decide to commit an unethical behavior. These stages include 1) moral awareness (the recognition of whether a situation has a moral component or presents an ethical dilemma), 2) moral judgment (the determination of how to respond to the ethical dilemma with choices), 3) moral intention (deciding how one should act) and 4) moral behavior (how one acts). We therefore consider individual decision-making along these lines.

The first set of factors considered is moral awareness. Research shows that people may not always readily understand the ethical implications of situations. To better understand such implications, you read about many elements contributing to moral awareness. Relevant steps companies can take to increase moral awareness were also discussed.

The second set of factors pertains to moral judgment. Specifically, moral judgment deals with the process behind how people make decisions with ethical implications. You read about the many conscious and unconscious biases that may interfere with moral judgment. You also read about what multinationals can do to reduce such biases.

The third and final aspect of this chapter dealt with moral intention and behaviors (stages 3 and 4). Here you read about how people can evaluate the moral intensity of a situation based on Jones' factors. Additionally, this part of the chapter is concerned with how people may believe they are ethical and deliberately engage in unethical behavior. Moral disengagement is concerned with how people can cognitively justify unethical behavior through several mechanisms. You also learned about the many factors and processes that companies can implement to encourage moral intention and moral behaviors.

Taken together, the chapter discusses the most important factors determining unethical behavior. Companies that take the time and effort to properly understand these individual aspects of ethics can then implement the appropriate steps to ensure ethical behavior. However, how individuals approach decision-making and the theories they rely on can also be a critical determinant of ethical behavior. We consider these issues in the next chapter.

NOTES

1 Kish-Gephart, J.J., Harrison, D.A. & Treviño, L.K. 2010. "Bad apples, bad cases, and bad barrels: Meta-analytic evidence about sources of unethical decisions at work." *Journal of Applied Social Psychology*, 95, 1, 1–31.
2 Giacalone, R.A. & Promislo, M.D. 2010. "Unethical and unwell: Decrements in well-being and unethical activity at work." *Journal of Business Ethics*, 91, 275–297.
3 Rest, J. 1986. *Development in judging moral issues*. Minneapolis, MN: University of Minnesota Press.
4 Schwartz, M. 2017. "Teaching behavioral ethics: Overcoming the key impediments to ethical behavior." *Journal of Management Education*, 41, 497–513.
5 Treviño, L.K., Weaver, G.R. & Reynolds, S.J. 2006. "Behavioral ethics in organizations: A review." *Journal of Management*, 32, 6, 951–990.
6 VanSandt, C.V., Shepard, J.M. & Zappe, S.M. 2006. "An examination of the relationship between ethical work climate and moral awareness." *Journal of Business Ethics*, 68, 409–432.
7 Ishida, C., Chang, W. & Taylor, S. 2016. "Moral intensity, moral awareness and ethical predispositions: The case of insurance fraud." *Journal of Financial Services Marketing*, 21, 4–18.
8 Sturm, R.E. 2017. "Decreasing unethical decisions: The role of morality-based individual differences." *Journal of Business Ethics*, 142, 37–57.
9 Sturm, R.E. 2017. "Decreasing unethical decision."
10 Ho, Y. & Lin, C. 2016. "The moral judgment relationship between leaders and followers: A comparative study across the Taiwan Strait." *Journal of Business Ethics*, 134, 299–310.

11 Banaji, M., Bazerman, M.H. & Chugh, D. 2003. "How (un) ethical are you?" *Harvard Business Review*, November, 56–64 (at 56).
12 Banaji et al., "How (un) ethical are you?"; Bazerman, M.H. & Tenbrunsel, A.E. 2011. "Good people often let bad things happen. Why?" *Harvard Business Review*, April, 58–65.
13 Bazerman & Tenbrunsel, "Good people often let bad things happen. Why?"
14 Banaji et al., "How (un) ethical are you?"
15 Banaji et al., "How (un) ethical are you?"
16 Schwartz, M. 2017. "Teaching behavioral ethics."
17 Schwartz, M. 2017. "Teaching behavioral ethics."
18 Banaji et al., "How (un) ethical are you?"; Bazerman & Tenbrunsel, "Good people often let bad things happen. Why?"; Seijts, G. 2016. "Rogue learnings." *Ivey Business Journal*, July/August, 2–8.
19 Jones, "Ethical decision making by individuals in organizations."
20 Kish-Gephart et al., "Bad apples, bad cases, and bad barrels."
21 Kish-Gephart et al., "Bad apples, bad cases, and bad barrels."
22 Bandura, A. 1999. "Moral disengagement in the preparations of inhumanities." *Personal and Social Psychology Review*, 3, 193–209.
23 Bandura, A. 1986. *Social foundations of thought and action: A social cognitive theory*. Englewoods Cliffs, NJ: Prentice Hall; Detert, J.E., Treviño, L.K. & Sweitzer, V.L. 2008. "Moral disengagement in ethical decision making: A study of antecedents and outcomes." *Journal of Applied Psychology*, 93, 2, 374–391 (at 375).
24 Bandura, "Moral disengagement in the preparations of inhumanities."
25 Detert et al., "Moral disengagement in ethical decision making."
26 Detert et al., "Moral disengagement in ethical decision making."
27 Detert et al., "Moral disengagement in ethical decision making."
28 Claybourn, M. 2011. "Relationships between moral disengagement, work characteristics and workplace harassment." *Journal of Business Ethics*, 100, 283–301.
29 Moore, C., Detert, J.S., Treviño, L.K., Baker, V.L. & Mayer, D.M. 2002. "Why employees do bad things: Moral disengagement and unethical organizational behavior." *Personnel Psychology*, 65, 1–48.
30 Claybourn, "Relationships between moral disengagement"; Detert et al., "Moral disengagement in ethical decision making."
31 Claybourn, "Relationships between moral disengagement."
32 Detert et al., "Moral disengagement in ethical decision making."
33 Schwartz, M.S. 2016. "Ethical decision-making theory: An integrated approach." *Journal of Business Ethics*, 139, 755–776.
34 Bhattacharyya, J. & Ray, D. 2017. "Exploring the moral factor: The influence of locus of control and moral disengagement on moral judgment." *Indian Journal of Positive Psychology*, 8, 291–296.

KEY TERMS

Advantageous comparison: occurs when someone compares a worse behavior with another behavior and rationalizes the behavior on that basis.

Attribution of blame: occurs when the decision-maker ascribes the blame for the decision to the target.

Authority/fear of punishment stage: the person defines right or wrong based on the obedience to rules from those in power.

Concentration of effect: the number of people affected by the act.

Conflict of interest: occurs when decision-making can be unconsciously affected because the decision-maker may benefit from the chosen decision.

Conformity bias: employees have the tendency to imitate or merely accept the values of other people.

Conscious biases: employee intentionally relies on biases to make unethical choices.

Dehumanization: occurs when the target of the decision is derogated or is seen as lacking in human qualities.

Diffusion of responsibility: can occur if decisions are being made by a group.

Displacement of responsibility: occurs when the perpetrator of an unethical behavior can attribute the behavior to other factors.

Distortion of consequences: occurs when an individual can disconnect the actions from the harmful connections of the action.

Ethical predisposition: cognitive framework used when making decisions with ethical consequences.

Euphemistic labeling: refers to the use of morally neutral language to make something seem less immoral.

Incrementalism: employees engaging in minor unethical behaviors that eventually leads to major ethical infractions.

Implicit prejudice: occurs when people rely on unconscious biases and prejudice when people judge others.

In-group favoritism: occurs because people tend to favor those individuals who share similar characteristics to their own, such as being from the same school, social class, or religion.

Magnitude of consequences: refers to the degree of harm that the victims of an unethical choice will have to endure.

Moral attentiveness refers to the ability of individuals to access and interpret the moral content of information and stimuli they are presented with.

Moral awareness: refers to the ability of an individual to understand the ethicality of a situation or behavior.

Moral disengagement: refers to the process where, when faced with potential behavior counter to their own personal standards, a person may choose to deactivate the standard and still engage in the behavior.

Moral intention and behaviors: employees' choices and decisions when confronting moral situations.

Moral judgment: refers to the process by which someone reasons about how to deal with an ethical situation.

Moral justification: occurs when individuals justify certain actions to make them seem more morally acceptable.

Motivated blindness: takes place when people turn a blind eye to unethical behavior because such behavior is beneficial to them.

Obedience to authority: whereby individuals justify unethical behavior as orders that came from their managers or CEO.

Probability of effect: the probability that any action will result in harm to victims of the action.

Proximity: the psychological or cultural nearness to the victim.

Social consensus: the degree to which others agree that a specific behavior is wrong.

Temporal immediacy: the length of time between the action and the harmful consequences of such actions.

Unconscious biases: occur when the most well-meaning person unwittingly allows unconscious thoughts and feelings to influence seemingly objective decisions.

Unethical behavior: actions that violate accepted societal norms.

DISCUSSION QUESTIONS

1. What is moral awareness? Discuss main factors determining moral awareness.
2. What is moral judgment? Discuss some of the critical factors affecting moral judgment.
3. What are biases? What are the key differences between conscious and unconscious biases?
4. What are the main types of unconscious biases? How can companies protect themselves against biases?
5. Discuss Rest's moral intention and behaviors stages of ethical decision-making.
6. Discuss Jones' ethical decision-making theory. What are the main factors determining whether someone behaves unethically?
7. What is moral disengagement? Briefly describe three moral disengagement mechanisms.
8. Discuss moral disengagement through the cognitive reconstruction mechanisms. Describe the three mechanisms pertaining to cognitive reconstruction. Provide some examples to illustrate your answers.
9. What are unconscious biases? Discuss four of the most popular unconscious biases.
10. Describe how companies can build individual ethics based on what you read in the chapter. Use at least two major factors to illustrate your answer.

INTERNET ACTIVITY

1. Go to the Harvard University Implicit Association Test at https://implicit.harvard.edu/implicit/demo/.
2. Review the background information and share that information with the class.
3. Take one of the tests such as Disability–IAT, Religion–IAT, Arab–Muslim IAT.
4. What are the results of your test? What does it reveal about your biases?
5. Share your findings with others.

For more Internet Activities and resources, please visit the Companion Website at www.routledge.com/cw/parboteeah.

WHAT WOULD YOU DO?

The Salesperson

You have been recently hired as a salesperson by a well-known company that provides many services including uniforms, laundry services, document shredding and a large number of other business services. Your job requires you to continue developing relationships with existing customers while also developing new customers. You realize that your district manager likes you much more than other salespersons hired with you. He wants to make sure that you succeed and provides you with many tips on how to develop new customers and what to do to keep existing ones.

After working for the company for several months, you realize that many of the tips that the district manager gives you are not ethical. For example, you find that some customers require that you report some products as being defective so that they can get reimbursed. However, you know that these products are not defective. Furthermore, you find that you can get new customers through existing customers. You discover that your predecessor would often take existing customers and their referrals for new customers to the local strip clubs. Moreover, you find that your predecessor would also often take existing customers and their family members to expensive restaurants if they happened to be at the same conference.

You realize that many of these practices are against company policy. However, at the same time, you also realize that your district manager/mentor condones such practices. What would you do? Do you report your district manager? Or do you do nothing? Why?

BRIEF CASE: BUSINESS ETHICS INSIGHT

Raj Rajaratnam and Insider Trading

Until recently, Raj Rajaratnam was considered to be a very successful hedge-fund manager. He founded the Galleon Group in 1997 and grew the company to an impressive $7 billion. He was considered a hero in his native Sri Lanka and also one of his native country's richest sons. However, the reason behind Rajaratnam's success unraveled after a lengthy government investigation. These investigations showed that Rajaratnam developed extensive contacts in many prominent companies. He provided benefits to these contacts in exchange for valuable company information that he used for investment purposes.

According to Mr. Kumar, one of Mr. Rajaratnam's classmates at the Wharton School of Business and a former McKinsey director, it all started when he saw Mr. Rajaratnam at a gala. During the gala, Mr. Rajaratnam pulled him aside and offered to pay him for his insights. Over time, he developed useful contacts with senior officials at many of the world's biggest companies including IBM, Goldman Sachs, McKinsey and Akamai. While it is not illegal to have a network of contacts, Mr. Rajaratnam's actions regarding how he used his network is what sparked the investigation. Investors routinely use company information to make investment decisions. However, Mr. Rajaratnam used substantial and non-private information to trade and profit from the information. For example, through wiretaps of his phone conversations, the federal government showed that he was able to get confidential Goldman Sachs earnings information from Mr. Gupta, a board member of the company. He then used the information to trade and made a profit. The investigations revealed similar insider trading based on information provided by insiders from many of the U.S.'s largest corporations, such as Advanced Micro Devices, Moody's, IBM, Intel, etc.

After a lengthy seven-week trial, Mr. Rajaratnam was convicted of insider trading in May 2011. He was sentenced to 11 years in jail. Furthermore, although experts believed that it would be difficult to prove insider trading, the government wiretaps of his phone conversations proved invaluable. However, many are still wondering why Mr. Rajaratnam was the only one who was prosecuted. Many of the company officials who provided such insider information also broke the law. Additionally, Mr. Rajaratnam recently tried to get his sentence overturned and the judge upheld the sentence.

Based on Anonymous. 2011. "The fall of Raj." *Wall Street Journal*, May 12, A14; Scannell, K. 2011a. "Big names drawn into Galleon web." *Financial Times*, May 12, online version; Scannell, K. 2011b. "Rajaratnam found guilty." *Financial Times*, May 12, online version; Scannell, K. 2011c. "Insider trading was a drama worthy of Hollywood." *Financial Times*, May 12, online version. Stempel, J. 2017. "Galleon's Rajaratnam loses bid to cut insider trading sentence." *Reuters*, www.reuters.com/article/us-usa-crime-rajaratnam/galleons-rajaratnam-loses-bid-to-cut-insider-trading-sentence-idUSKBN16A2DX; Rothfield, M., Pulliam, S. and Bray, C. 2011. "Fund titan found guilty." *Wall Street Journal*, May 12, online version.

BRIEF CASE QUESTIONS

1. Given what you know after reading this chapter, what are some of the reasons why Mr. Rajaratnam may have engaged in such widespread unethical behavior? Why were so many others accomplices in the schemes?
2. Looking at moral awareness, how likely did the people involved in the scandal see the moral aspect of the scandal? Be specific about each aspect of moral awareness.
3. How is moral disengagement relevant in this situation? Discuss how each of the moral disengagement aspects may have been activated to justify the behavior.
4. What can be done to ensure that such behaviors do not occur again?

Which *Kaptein* to Choose? The Havøysund Fleet Question

> *The way you continue to be a successful business is you don't wait for the car to go off the cliff. You have to manage yourself. And make sure you do it in the right way so you are not making decisions in crisis.*

Olaf Tryggvason looked at the quotation, his own, that sat on his desk. It was, for him, more than a passing inspirational comment. Tryggvason sat in his office in Havøysund, a small fishing village of just 1,000 inhabitants on the northern Norwegian island of Havøya. From his window, he could see tourists disembarking from a cruise ship, and he knew very soon they would make their way through his hometown, swelling the streets and clogging the stores. If you were able to share some aquavit with him,[1] Tryggvason would confess that he found the tourists an irritating yet necessary evil. Tourism and entertainment had become critical to the economies of a number of port towns in Norway. Historically, Havøysund had been an important fishing village at least since the late Middle Ages, and there was even evidence of early fishing settlements dating back to the Neolithic era. Years ago, the city had leveraged this heritage into a revenue-generating asset. The citizens had converted an old religious rectory into the Måsøy Museum. The museum featured a collection of historic fishing and whaling equipment. Tryggvason begrudgingly acknowledged that for some in the village, becoming an entertainment hub had "cheapened" their culture. He looked at the quote again. It gave him resolve for the decisions ahead.

Specifically, Tryggvason, who operated a fleet of fishing vessels, had accepted a reality television deal that he'd been offered by a producer from Oslo, Arvid Strømstad. He needed to make recommendations about which ships and their skippers, or *kapteiner*,[2] should have a shot at becoming the "stars" of the show; however, this responsibility would come with increased risks and rewards. As he diversified his lines of business, Tryggvason wondered how his quote should shape his obligations to his employees.

Small Fishing Towns and the Global Marketplace

Tryggvason was the owner of Gudrun Fiskeri, a fleet of ships that sought out *skrei*—migrating cod. Gudrun ships sought their quarry over the expansive Norwegian coastline—southern Norway through Fjord Norway on the west coast, and even as far into the Arctic Circle as Kirkenes. What had started as a small fleet that plied only local coasts was now quite large and expansive. At the same time, returns from fishing were flat. There was a lot of talk in Havøysund of increasing revenues through tourism.

Tryggvason had come to accept the reality of tourism and a global economy but was not willing to make himself or his people subservient to these trends. If the visiting public desired relaxation and entertainment, he could turn this to his people's advantage. He had steered toward an intriguing opportunity that would place a select few of his firm's fleet of ships and their *kapteiner* as leading players in the new reality television show, and he hoped that the deal would create considerable increases in Norwegian kroner, certainly for the village and also for some lucky fishing *kapteiner* and their crews.

On this morning, his task was to review the performance of the fleet along a number of indicators. The show producer's request was that he choose five ship *kapteiner* from among the 32 in the fleet who could be featured in the program.

To do this, Tryggvason intended to look beyond the obvious—big, heroic personalities that would evoke "camera appeal." He had to decide which factors determined efficiency across the fleet of vessels, all of which were named after Norse gods (see **Exhibit 1** for the Havøysund fleet performance for the year 2011). He recalled that during his studies at the University of Tromsø, Norwegian College of Fishery Science, there were many opinions about what mattered, but few key guideposts on how to approach this analytical task.

The Norwegian Fisheries Industry

Fishing the oceans had been a central element of the history of the Norwegian people. In terms of the national diet, Norwegians consumed large amounts of seafood. Annual per capita fish consumption amounted to an estimated 53.4 kilograms in 2011, the 6th highest in the world (for comparison, U.S. residents consumed only 21.7 kilograms, the 33rd highest amount in the world).[3] Over time, other industries, including technology and oil production, also became critical to Norway's economy. As the percentage of Norwegians working in fisheries declined, the industry innovated, primarily in fish farming.

The Norwegian coastline was vast, stretching over 103,000 kilometers. The North Sea, the Barents Sea, and the Norwegian Sea polar front were among the most productive in the world, and contained globally important fish breeding areas.[4] In 1946, Norway became the first country in the world to establish a Ministry of Fisheries and Coastal Affairs.[5] In addition to being prolific, the stocks of seafood caught by Norwegian fisheries were of greater value than those of competing nations. By 2011, Norway was the world's second-largest exporter of fish and fish products by value (11th in global fisheries tonnage, 2.63 million).[6] Norway's fish were well received in the European Union, Eastern Europe (Russia, Ukraine), Japan, China, and the United States. By the late 2010s, global per capita consumption had grown to higher than 20 kilograms, double the level in the 1960s.[7] Aquaculture and sustainable management enabled the global seafood industry to grow supply for human consumption faster than population growth overall; this created an uncertainty about the prices those fishing the oceans could command. Efficiency became the resulting need, and Tryggvason's company constantly instituted improvements to the fleet to offset price variability.

The *Kaptein* Effect: Powerful Myth or Important Reality?

Over centuries in Norwegian fishing and up to the present day, there was a powerful belief that the man Norwegians knew as *kaptein* made a dramatic difference in a ship's success. *Kapteiner* were the undisputed authority on their ships, and deference to their commands was an absolute when on board. They decided when to leave port, where to navigate to find the most valuable stocks, and what methods to use once they reached the desired location. The economic fate of the crew was reliant on a *kaptein*'s ability to somehow "find the fish," which legend held was based less on science than on some mystical intuition. Some said that *kapteiner* were able to find fish through their dreams, or through their ancestors speaking to them from the great beyond. *Kapteiner* developed reputations in the field, and there were legendary stories about how, when a ship and crew had a change of *kaptein*, the tonnage that a ship could return in a season changed dramatically. In short, the *Kaptein* was a revered and heroic cultural folklore figure.[8]

Of course, Tryggvason was deeply familiar with these beliefs, starting with stories that dated from his childhood. However, as he grew up and his understanding of science developed, he began to question the "mystical" basis for the legends. Perhaps there were individual factors that influenced the skills of a given *kaptein*: photographic memory, scientific knowledge of fish, better management of the crew, and the machinery on the ships. For example, Tryggvason had a strong belief that when pursuing cod, choices made by *kapteiner* mattered. His logic was that an individual *kaptein* could choose when to use nets versus longlines, and there were differences in the facility various *kapteiner* had with one method or the other. The underlying scientific connection was that when fish were taking bait, longlines are more effective; and when they were less likely to take bait, gill nets were more productive. It nagged at him that he could not determine which underlying scientific factors might matter, and yet, even if he could isolate them, there was the strong cultural belief that the *kaptein*'s instincts mattered to a large degree. Whether based in fact or not, these beliefs had genuine impact. Crews followed legendary *kapteiner* to successive ships, and residents of the village treated the successful ones as local legends.

The Opportunity in Hazards

As other industrial sectors took hold, many left fishing as a career choice. At least one reason was the occupational hazard rates. Fishing extracted a toll from those who chose it as a career. Those working on ships faced long hours, and few were able to work year round. When valuable fish were in season, workers were at sea for weeks or months at a time, without a return to home port. The work could be grueling, including standing on deck waiting for hours, with intermittent sparks of activity. Many worked while sleep deprived, raising risks of injury.[9] Mikkel Eggen, a long-term hand on one of the leading ships, was passionate about the matter. "Just like our forefathers," Eggen said, "we understand this is a dangerous profession with consequences not just in the short term, but for the rest of our lives. All of us who go to sea, from deckhands to spotters, chose this profession."

On the water, *kapteiner* and their crews were at the mercy of Ægir, the sea *jötunn*, a giant that governed and ruled the seas. Storms were an expected part of the job. When fish were in season, only the most dangerous storm would keep a crew in port. An integral part of a crewmember's experience involved gaining "sea legs": becoming accustomed to working under harsh winds, getting soaked from head to toe, being cold, and needing to make sure one did not slip on wet decks. Workers were frequently injured on the job, and since, when at sea, there were no medical facilities nearby, they had to make do with the emergency or prescriptive care available from their crewmates.

It was relatively common for crewmembers to sustain life-altering injuries on the water. To some degree, this danger was a part of the appeal. Eggen acknowledged this reality: "Sometimes I can tell when a guy is injured during a trip—there are tells that something's not quite right—but I'm not going to take his health into my hands and tell anybody, because fishing with injuries is a risk that guys are willing to take." Additionally, some vessels had reputations for violating regulatory strictures when on water. The fishing industry was heavily monitored in the capital, Oslo, and some *kapteiner* violated the rules about when, where, and how to fish. If these resulted in better catches, who really cared?

Typically fishermen on Nordic fishing boats had short careers. The average tenure of a fisherman actively working on a boat was a mere three to four years. But the draw was inescapable; by mid-2011, the 1,696 fishermen employed by the *kapteiner* earned a median salary of NOK460,513[10] (equivalent to USD55,000). Now, with the reality television deal, the fishermen would be able to enjoy a salary that would be the equivalent of a six-to-eight-times multiple of the otherwise average income level for workers of the same backgrounds and education levels. That said, the brutality of the work was also inescapable: for instance, the three to four years an average fisherman was able to work on a crew was not enough time to advance and become *kapteiner* themselves. The *kapteiner* typically came from a different background altogether, in terms of nationality as well as college education and affluence to begin with. Occasionally, there were rumblings from activists about crews being treated as expendable human resources. These critics focused on the health and safety issues. The Oslo *Daily Prophet* had recently suggested that fishermen, though handsomely paid, were being used up and discarded, while the *kapteiner* and fleet owners benefitted from long and lucrative returns. The predominantly immigrant base of workers didn't help the optics on this matter. Tryggvason wondered if there was any merit to these criticisms, and how the reality show would impact these concerns.

Additionally, there had been some recent controversy in the industry around safety equipment. Recent innovations could provide more safety features on vessels at a higher cost, something he'd like to be able to afford but that could make the television show less appealing.

The New Opportunity: Reality Television

Recently, Tryggvason had agreed to a new source of revenue—television production. He had consummated a deal with Arvid Strømstad, managing director of Nobel

Productions, based in Oslo. Strømstad was attempting to create a reality television show, not unlike ones popular in the United States—*Deadliest Catch*; *Hook, Line & Sisters*; *Wicked Tuna*; *Big Shrimpin'*; and *Toughest Tribes*. Far from being a deterrent, Strømstad pointed out that on these shows, the danger of the work was central to the drama on the screen. Producers sought out content that could illustrate the competition between *kapteiner* as they pursued the elusive schools of fish, avoided the storms, and dealt with water on their faces (and it was nice if it also splashed on the camera lens). The risks of physical danger provided an additional sense of mystery.

In his pitch, Strømstad explained that successful shows also played up the rivalry between *kapteiner*, and, to a certain degree, ethnic and gender stereotypes. Strømstad pulled out his iPad, and shared with Tryggvason clips of *Ragin' Cajuns*, which had recently aired on the U.S.-based Discovery Channel. "Look at the titles of the shows," Strømstad said excitedly. "They tell the viewer what she's getting: *Shrimping, Storming, and Stabbing*; *Man Overboard*; and *One Last Shove*. They want the macho. This is how you build excitement."[11]

Strømstad handed Tryggvason a copy of a review from the *Hollywood Reporter*. "You'll see," he said. "The reviewer's opening paragraphs set the stage."

> A lumbering, 400-pound monster lurks in the Bayou waters of the Louisiana gulf coast. Largely unintelligible, missing many of his front teeth, his weathered face framed by long, greasy brown hair, this rather astounding human specimen goes by the name of Blimp, and he's the star of Discovery's latest realty fishing expedition, *Ragin' Cajuns*.
>
> The skipper of a ramshackle shrimping trawler dubbed the Mo De Girls, Blimp is described as the heart of Venice, Louisiana, a town that has seen its share of hardship due to the double blows of Hurricane Katrina and the BP oil spill.[12]

"We have all the elements to pull this off here, and on a grander, Nordic stage. First, we have the place. Norway controls the world's best fishing waters. We can showcase scenes on the cold and swelling sea. Second, we have fish that make for good copy, large fish like *skrei*. Third, we have the rich culture and diversity of our people."

On average, each of the ships generated NOK37.39 million each year from fishing. The reality television package could contribute as much as an additional 43% in revenues for each *kaptein* and crew featured. The notion to diversify the fleet's revenue stream presented a very enticing possibility, but Tryggvason also had to consider the risks. Among these, Tryggvason worried that the heightened publicity from television viewership—while providing additional kroner—could also shine a brighter light on what was now only a view among leftists and academics: that the work involved excessive risk to life and limb.

Demography of the Norwegian Fishing Industry

Tryggvason knew well the path to working in fisheries. Being from an upper-income family, he had chosen to attend the best of Norway's 11 fisheries colleges (the first fisherman's school had been founded in 1939). His attendance at Tromsø, where he was able to attend with a large number of foreign students, had helped him secure an office on the decks. He briefly considered pursuing a doctorate, but he recognized the salary discount he would be taking.

Those who could not attend a fisheries college might be able to get a degree from one of Norway's 32 secondary schools, in which career seekers could pursue an occupational fishing certificate (the equivalent of a high school degree in the United States). This certification often helped secure a middle-management supervisory job, perhaps on the docks or in the offices of a large fisheries company. Eggen had a strong opinion about this as well: "People are always going to fish the seas," he said. "And if higher-income families choose to pull their kids out of the business, it will only broaden the talent pool, giving the underprivileged more opportunities to make vessels. Most of the top guys in this business come from underprivileged situations anyway." Tryggvason thought Eggen would certainly be one of the deckhands to be featured on the reality television show.

Jobs on fleet ships, on which the proposed show would focus, were generally filled by those from lower-income families (in terms of gender, the crews and *kapteiner* were all male). Ethnically speaking, the residents of Norway were predominantly of North Germanic and Nordic descent (approximately 94%). Since the 1990s, Norway had seen a rising influx of immigrants from the Asian continent (e.g., Pakistanis, Sri Lankans, Chinese, Filipinos), and the Middle East (e.g., Somalis, Turks, Moroccans). The country was also home to the indigenous Sami and Lapps, who were said to have settled the area almost 11,000 years ago.[13] Lapps and Sami had traditionally survived as coastal fishermen for centuries, and a number also lived as seminomadic reindeer herders. There was a much greater representation of these non-Nordic workers on the docks and on the ships than in the general Norwegian population; indeed, although the ships were filled in the early years by Nordics, now nearly 70% of the fishing crews were composed of members of other ethnic groups or immigrants. Strømstad perceived this as a benefit. "Reality television is misnomer," he said. "A great amount ends up on the cutting floor and relatively little is edited into the shows. Our experience from shows in the West is that conflict and danger drive ratings." Tryggvason wondered whether television production might also bring to larger light realities of the industry that many overlooked. The public mostly focused on the prices they paid for North Atlantic fish and not much else.

Strømstad leaned forward, almost whispering: "Let's face it, the world thinks we're just a group of tall, blonde Nordics. With the diversity on your ships, we can have differences work for us. Imagine that we can feature one *kaptein* and his Pakistani crew on one episode, the Arabs on another, and they're all competing against each other." Strømstad went further with this idea: "Like the other shows, we play up the fishing season for all that it is worth. The drama. The danger. The ethnicity. And yes, the fish." He got excited as he offered the differentiator. "They will compete against each other to hunt as they've done for centuries. Now, taking us into the virtual age, I have also created an app so that folks across the globe can follow the hunt. They can download images, follow the crews out on the water. And here's the ultimate: They can bid for some of the fish stock that has actually been caught on the show."

Where to Navigate?

It was clear to Tryggvason that this deal had the potential to create uncommon value for his company, his town, and his employees. The additional revenue from the television rights could provide individual *kapteiner* millions of kroner, and those on the decks would become the best-paid fishermen on the planet, enjoying salaries beyond their wildest dreams. Some would become famous celebrities. For Gudrun Fiskeri, the deal could provide his company a means of diversifying revenues. On the other hand, the increased exposure might draw the attention of protestors or NGOs interested in highlighting the risks to the fishermen.

Tryggvason needed to think carefully about which *kapteiner* to feature and how he felt about profiting from the increased risks (and rewards) that the *kapteiner* would face.

During his visit, Strømstad had indicated that the *kaptein*'s ethnicity could positively influence viewership, but Tryggvason wanted to know on this day which *kapteiner* and ships were the most productive from a purely fishing perspective. This wasn't exactly a straightforward task. Of course, tonnage was an obvious differentiating factor, but he knew that was insufficient. He wanted to better understand the *how* of the tonnage. Were there other ways of determining efficiency? One central problem in determining this was the level of variability across the fleet. Although the ships themselves were basically the same, and each had crews of comparable size, each *kaptein* developed his own strategy to bring the optimal tonnage: when and where a *kaptein* chose to venture out, the fish that were being sought, and the methods for catching them. And each of these choices posed different economic and injury risks to fishing crews. How could these data help him choose? On which variables should he focus?

Tryggvason had a set of decisions to make, and his eyes were glued to his computer screen and the volumes of data. Just then, Kjetil Bjorvatn, one of the fleet's *kapteiner*, came into the office, so Tryggvason asked Bjorvatn about safety on the ships.

"My wife worries about it a little more than I do," Bjorvatn replied.

* * *

EXHIBIT 1 Which *Kaptein* to Choose? The Havøysund Fleet Question

Havøysund Fleet Performance by Vessel, 2011

Vessel	Tons/ Trip	Total Tonnage	Lines Used	Nets Used	Regulatory Warnings	Days on Water	"Port" Days	Avg. Lost Days from Injury
Baduhenna	19.1	306	1,009	327.4	116	31:44:00	12	101.8
Balder	30.1	482	1,067	402.9	120	30:46:00	5	36.9
Bragi	25.6	409	1,021	364.9	111	29:40:00	8	52.6
Forsetti	18.8	301	1,006	358.6	120	30:47:00	13	89.5
Freyr	23.8	381	1,035	378.2	97	29:28:00	8	93.8
Frigg	27.2	436	1,068	411.1	103	32:24:00	11	42.8
Gerðr	19.9	319	1,005	327.1	113	30:13:00	10	101.6
Gersemi	15.8	253	994	282.2	116	28:20:00	13	103.6
Heimdall	24.2	388	1,040	350.1	81	30:08:00	11	79.5
Höðr	21.2	339	1,060	346.7	83	32:17:00	11	51.4
Hretha	17.7	283	1,052	326.6	109	31:01:00	9	41.5
Irpa	15.6	249	988	289.6	73	27:11:00	8	77.8
Lofn	17.3	277	936	292	118	27:17:00	13	87.2
Nanna	18.7	299	1,010	324.6	116	28:13:00	7	67
Nerthus	19.4	310	993	319.8	91	29:48:00	5	72.8
Nilfheim	24.6	394	1,021	375.8	130	32:22:00	7	74.8

EXHIBIT 1 *continued*

Havøysund Fleet Performance by Vessel, 2011

Vessel	Tons/ Trip	Total Tonnage	Lines Used	Nets Used	Regulatory Warnings	Days on Water	"Port" Days	Avg. Lost Days from Injury
Njord	29.2	467	1,014	383.6	105	32:51:00	14	76.1
Njörðr	23.2	372	1,062	344.6	94	31:07:00	9	59.9
Odin	25.1	401	1,095	411.4	80	30:35:00	13	58
Ragnarok	23.8	380	1,086	367.2	101	30:44:00	14	137.1
Rindr	22.1	353	962	318.8	88	30:00:00	11	98.8
Sif	29.2	468	1,073	365.5	120	29:37:00	4	62
Skaði	21.4	343	1,020	318.5	124	29:45:00	10	59
Sunna	15.9	254	919	303.7	111	27:31:00	10	79.7
Tanfana	20.3	325	981	315.5	100	28:52:00	2	56.1
Thornssen	28.6	458	1,105	406.6	105	31:54:00	15	104.7
Tyr	29.6	474	1,127	396.8	115	26:40:00	15	48.6
Ullr	21.8	348	1,009	341.6	111	30:58:00	5	119.1
Vanir	30.4	486	1,001	386.1	92	30:32:00	7	41.9
Ve	22.8	365	1,018	348	102	30:32:00	9	71.7
Vili	20.1	321	1,045	340.8	118	31:41:00	8	67.6
Zisa	20.2	324	957	314.7	123	29:13:00	11	64.1

Source: Created by author, based on disguised, publicly available data.

Chapter 2: Long Case Notes

This fictional case was prepared by Gregory B. Fairchild, Isidore Horween Research Associate Professor of Business Administration; Bidhan L. Parmar, Associate Professor of Business Administration; Jared D. Harris, Samuel L. Slover Research Chair in Business Administration; and Jenny Mead, Senior Researcher. It was written as a basis for class discussion rather than to illustrate effective or ineffective handling of an administrative situation. Our goal is to publish materials of the highest quality, so please submit any errata to editorial@dardenbusinesspublishing.com.

1 Aquavit was Norway's traditional distilled spirit.
2 *Kapteiner* was the plural form of *kaptein.*
3 "List of Countries by Fish Consumption per Capita," Stats Monkey, 2011, www.statsmonkey.com/table/20598-list-of-countries-by-fish-consumption-per-capita.php (accessed Jan. 3, 2018).
4 "Fishery and Aquaculture Country Profiles: The Kingdom of Norway," Food and Agricultural Organization of the United Nations, Fisheries and Aquaculture Department, 2011, www.fao.org/fishery/facp/NOR/en#CountrySector-SectorSocioEcoContribution (accessed Jan. 3, 2018).
5 www.fao.org/fishery/facp/NOR/en.
6 www.fao.org/fishery/facp/NOR/en.
7 "Global per Capita Fish Consumption Rises above 20 Kilograms a Year," Food and Agricultural Organization of the United Nations, www.fao.org/news/story/en/item/421871/icode/ (accessed Jan. 3, 2018).
8 For more on the skipper in Scandinavian culture, see Gísli Pálsson and Paul Durrenberger, "To Dream of Fish: The Causes of Icelandic Skippers' Fishing Success," *Journal of Anthropological Research* 38, no. 2 (1982): 227–242.
9 Jill Janocha, "Facts of the Catch: Occupational Injuries, Illnesses, and Fatalities to Fishing Workers, 2003–2009," United States Department of Labor, Bureau of Labor Statistics, *Workplace Injuries* 1, no. 9 (2012), www.bls.gov/opub/btn/volume-1/facts-of-the-catch-occupational-injuries-illnesses-and-fatalities-to-fishing-workers-2003-2009.htm (accessed Jan. 3, 2018).
10 NOK = Norwegian kroner; USD = U.S. dollars.
11 "*Ragin' Cajuns* Episode Guide," Internet Movie Database (IMDb), http://m.imdb.com/title/tt2157887/episodes/?season=1 (accessed Jan. 3, 2018).
12 David Knowles, "Ragin' Cajuns: TV Review," *Hollywood Reporter*, January 17, 2012, www.hollywoodreporter.com/review/ragin-cajuns-review-discovery-channel-282641 (accessed Jan. 3, 2018).
13 Jonathan Snatic, "Hunting and Gathering by the Sami," *Sami Culture* (blog), University of Texas at Austin College of Liberal Arts, www.laits.utexas.edu/sami/diehtu/siida/hunting/jonsa.htm (accessed Jan. 3, 2018).

* * *

LONG CASE QUESTIONS

1. What are some of the major issues facing Tryggvason as he ponders on the decision?
2. Which of the individual level factors discussed in this chapter are relevant for the case? For instance, how could biases affect who he decides to choose?
3. Do you believe that the dangers associated with the fishing profession justify the potential for large incomes? Why or why not? How do your own views of ethics influence your reasoning?
4. What should Tryggvason do? Why?

Chapter 3

Ethical Theories

LEARNING OBJECTIVES

After reading this chapter you should be able to:

- Understand the importance of ethical theories and their applications to business ethics dilemmas
- Learn about the stages of Kohlberg's cognitive moral development theory
- Understand the three most critical normative ethical theories, namely utilitarianism, Kantian and virtue ethics
- Become aware of moral philosophies
- Understand Institutional Anomie Theory and how the theory can be used to better understand unethical behaviors
- Learn about the many steps companies can take to apply the above theories to better prepare employees to be ethical

PREVIEW BUSINESS ETHICS INSIGHT

Ethical Challenges Worldwide

Mr. Sang-jo Kim, the *Chaebol* Sniper

As we saw in Chapter 2 on individual ethics, there are many cases of people behaving unethically and bringing down companies. However, companies also have to contend with individuals who are always willing to do the "right thing." Consider the case of Mr. Sang-jo Kim, officially known as the "*chaebol* sniper" among members of the public in South Korea. Over the years, Mr. Kim has been a thorn in the sides of South Korea's *chaebols* or the large family empires that control a significant percentage of economic activity in the country. Many of these companies have been accused of numerous unethical activities including, most recently, contributions to a charitable fund controlled by Ms. Choi, the former South Korean president's confidante. These family empires, which include major companies such as Hyundai, LG and Samsung, also violated fair trade principles by colluding to keep prices high and hurting consumer rights.

Mr. Kim was recently appointed as South Korea's fair trade commissioner and is vowing to implement many changes to improve corporate governance in South Korea. However, even before he was appointed as the fair trade commissioner, Mr. Kim had a history of forcing the *chaebols* to stop engaging in unethical behavior. Consider that many of these companies have strong business activities but barely return dividends to shareholders. As an activist shareholder, Mr. Kim forced attention on these companies' reluctance to return dividends to smaller shareholders as controlling family members hoard cash. Samsung has now promised to return half of its cash flow to shareholders.

Mr. Kim has a lot to do as the fair trade commissioner. He will need to encourage these South Korean giants to abandon complex structures and hierarchies that mask family control of these companies. Additionally, many of these family conglomerates also bully suppliers and give preference to other suppliers that are often owned by individuals connected to the family. Additionally, these *chaebols* will also now be fined if they do not abide by fair trade principles. Consider that Lotte, an entertainment empire, was found guilty of violating rules of competition and will likely be fined. Hyundai was also fined $US74 million for violating the fair trade regulations.

Based on *The Economist*. 2018. "Business in South Korea; Diary of a sniper." January, 45–47.

In Chapter 2 we discussed the many individual aspects that contribute to unethical behavior. However, as the Preview Business Ethics Insight above highlights, unethical or ethical behavior sometimes persist even in the face of intense pressures. Why is Mr. Kim so intent on forcing the South Korean *chaebols* to engage in ethical behavior? Consider also the case of Ms. Watkins, the whistle-blower that led to the exposure of the accounting and other ethical scandals at Enron. Why do some individuals choose to engage in ethical behaviors when the majority of participants are unethical?

While many of the concepts and approaches discussed in Chapter 2 may help explain Mr. Kim's behaviors, there are other business ethics factors that explain unethical behaviors that fall outside of the range of individual factors discussed in Chapter 2. These explanations are often provided by theories. As such, Chapter 3 will discuss these additional theories or approaches that can help explain unethical (or lack of ethical) behaviors. Chapter 3 is a new addition to this textbook and will contribute to a more comprehensive understanding of ethical behavior.

The chapter will discuss ethical theories and their applications to understand business ethics. **Theories** are frameworks that allow researchers to predict or explain some phenomena. Recent research suggests that most business ethics textbooks have ignored ethics theories as "ethics theory is accorded a low profile in the teaching of business ethics"[1] (page 79). Many believe that ethics theories are not as useful as they are not as relevant to practice. Additionally, others believe that application of ethical theories often results in conflicting conclusions. Such experts therefore believe we should not emphasize theories.

However, theories are useful as they help us organize a chaotic world. Theories help us organize as they "are a way to organize and package information; they are a kind of compacting"[2] (page 21). Furthermore, many of the theories or frameworks we will discuss in this chapter have been tested using data. This therefore means that these theories have been verified and some parts of such theories hold in reality.

As such, through the examination of ethical theories, you will learn new mechanisms that can explain ethical behavior. Additionally, theories have important relevance for practice and you will also learn how these theories can be applied in organizations to improve ethics. This chapter will therefore discuss several important business ethics theories. First, we discuss Kohlberg's moral cognitive theory. Kohlberg's theory of moral development remains one of the most important theories of ethical judgment[3] assuming that individuals are at different stages of cognitive moral development. Understanding these stages becomes important to explain ethical behaviors.

A second important aspect of this chapter is a discussion of normative ethical theories. Specifically, normative ethical theories provide some guidance about what ought to be done or the "reasons for adopting a whole system of moral principles or virtues"[4] (page 7). The text will discuss three of the most important normative ethical theories, namely utilitarianism, Kantian and virtue ethics.

Third, the chapter will also devote some attention to moral philosophies. Moral philosophies are underlying cognitive approaches that individuals use when making decisions with moral implications. We will focus on relativism and idealism.

Finally, the chapter will also discuss one of the most important theories used to explain unethical behavior or deviance. In that context, research in sociology has made extensive use of Institutional Anomie Theory (IAT). The business ethics field has also applied this theory to understand many unethical business behaviors and you will learn about such applications. You will see how the theory can also provide important recommendations to reduce or prevent unethical behavior.

COGNITIVE MORAL DEVELOPMENT

As mentioned earlier, Kohlberg's theory of moral development remains one of the most important theories of ethical judgment. To develop the theory, Kohlberg presented males in middle childhood to young adulthood with hypothetical moral dilemmas.[5] He then analyzed how his subjects responded spontaneously to these moral dilemmas. After collecting responses to these ethical dilemmas from hundreds of students, Kolberg found that individuals move through six stages of moral reasoning over time. The theory assumes that as individuals move at higher levels, their ethical reasoning becomes more sophisticated and they are thus less likely to behave unethically.

Kohlberg's first stage is known as the obedience to **authority/fear of punishment stage** whereby the person defines right or wrong based on the obedience to rules from those in power. The primary rationale for someone at this stage is to avoid punishment by behaving consistent with expectations of those who have power. Kohlberg observed this mostly in the young children he studied. When applied to the organization, someone at this stage would decide not to bribe a foreign official because that person fears the potential punishment he/she may have to endure if his/her boss finds out.

The second stage of Kohlberg's theory is known as the **self-interest stage** where the person chooses the action that satisfies the person's self-interest the most. Instead of basing decisions on those who are in power, here the decision-maker makes the choice that is based on personal gains. As such, someone might decide to bribe in a foreign country because of the possibility of getting an order that will ultimately boost the person's income. This stage is therefore motivated primarily by personal gains.

People who are at the third stage, known as **expectations of others** stage, now make their judgment about right or wrong based on the expectations of significant others and peers.[6] At this stage, rather than simply consider personal gains, an individual determines right or wrong based on the impact of the consequences of their actions on significant others. For instance, someone may decide not to bribe a foreign official because that action may eventually harm the organization through fines and the consequent loss of reputation. Such consequences may result in job losses for many.

At stage four of Kohlberg's theory, known as the **rules and laws stage**, an individual's moral judgment is externally oriented and based on whether the action respects rules and policies. At this stage, the decision-maker judges an action as right or wrong depending on whether such actions violate rules and regulations. For instance, an employee may decide not to bribe a foreign official because doing so would violate the company's code of conduct or other code of ethics.

Individuals at stage five, or the **principled** stage, base their decisions on ethical principles of right and wrong and consider good to society. At this stage, the individual considers the impact of his/her actions based on the consequences for society and whether the action respects basic societal expectations. For instance, an individual may decide against bribing because such an action may violate local cultural norms.

The **universal ethical principles stage** is the last stage of Kohlberg's cognitive moral development theory. At this stage, the decision-maker determines whether an action is right based on universal ethical principles that everyone should follow. This stage is different from stage five in that the principles considered should apply to everyone rather than be specific to a country or culture. For instance, an individual may decide not to bribe because bribes are considered universally wrong.

According to the theory, people progress through these six stages as they mature and get ethics training. Furthermore, the higher the stage, the more sophisticated an individual's reasoning is about issues with moral implications. Research shows that most adults are at stages three or four.[7] However, only about 20% of adults are believed to reach the higher level stages (i.e., stages five or six). Additionally, it is believed that stage six is more of a theoretical stage, as very little empirical evidence has been found for that stage. How useful is the theory? Consider the following Business Ethics Insight.

BUSINESS ETHICS INSIGHT

Academic Cheating and Kohlberg's Stages of Moral Development

Academic dishonesty or cheating is an unfortunate factor of college life. However, this issue is even more pronounced for business schools where prior research suggests that not only is cheating more prevalent but also more accepted. Furthermore, such research also suggests that there is a strong correlation between cheating at school and unethical behaviors at work. Finding

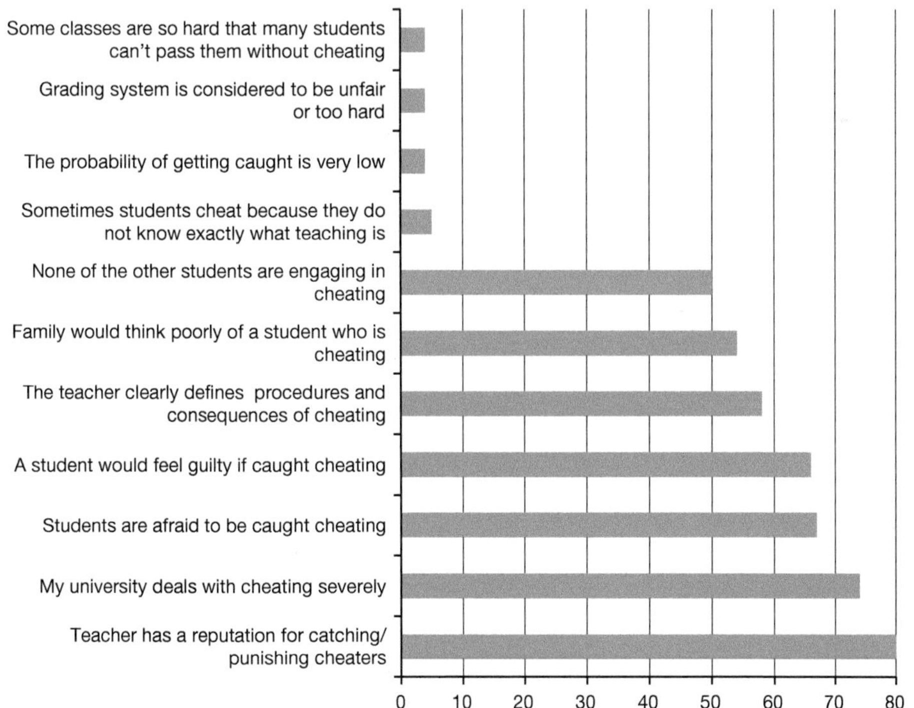

EXHIBIT 3.1—Percentage of Students Perceiving Factors as Contributing to Cheating

ways to better understand academic dishonesty and cheating is therefore important as it will help devise better ways to reduce cheating.

In an interesting study of 317 students, the researcher surveyed the perception of students' understanding of factors that inhibited cheating in the classroom. Students were presented with a number of statements that could be construed as either reducing or encouraging cheating. To give you some insights into the results, Exhibit 3.1 shows selected statements and the percentage of students who felt that these factors encouraged cheating.

The researcher also categorized the many factors along Kohlberg's moral development stage. This categorization revealed interesting findings. The research shows that most students categorize factors inhibiting cheating along the first two stages of Kohlberg's moral development theory. Additionally, the researchers also examined the same factors above to see which ones were contributing to cheating. They found that factors that contributed to cheating were mostly categorized at the third and fourth stages.

The researcher therefore concludes that such results are not surprising. Most college students should be operating at the stages 3 and 4 of Kohlberg's moral development stages. However, the researcher also suggests that universities take steps to move students along the stages of moral development to make them see not cheating as the right thing to do. The author suggests that character and virtue training may be very useful to help students progress along the stages of moral development.

Based on Forsha, S.K. 2017. "Virtue and moral development, changing ethics instruction in business school education." *College Student Journal,* 51, 429–443.

As you can see above, Kohlberg has received significant research attention. The essence of such research has been to understand what stages individuals are at and how they respond to ethical dilemmas. In general, such research has shown that those at lower levels are more likely to engage in unethical behavior. However, despite the popularity of Kohlberg's theory, it has still received significant criticism. Critics have argued that people do not necessarily go through the rigid hierarchy as originally proposed.[8] Furthermore, some criticize Kohlberg's data collection methods arguing that he relied on self-reported data as the primary source for his study. Self-reports tend to be problematic as respondents may not always reveal their true details. In other cases, respondents may exaggerate or respond in ways consistent with the interviewer's expectations. In such cases, the data collected may have been flawed. Furthermore, Kohlberg only studied males in crafting his theory, and questions arise as to whether the theory is generalizable to females.

In response to such critics, Rest, a former student of Kohlberg, developed an alternative to Kohlberg's theory.[9] Rest et al. suggest that the six stages can be conveniently collapsed into three levels.[10] Each of Kohlberg's two stages are combined to form one stage in Rest's application. These are then classified as levels of moral development whereby individuals are considered to be at higher levels of moral development if they can be categorized at higher levels.

At the **pre-conventional level** (stage one and two), decisions are typically driven internally by either reward or punishment. According to recent research, this level reflects the moral development of children of the age of nine or younger.[11] At this level, the individual is said to obey these external rules as they cannot change such rules.

At the **conventional level** (stage three and four), decisions are made based on external rules and norms coming from family, friends, peers and society.[12] According to current research, most adults and adolescents tend to be at this level. In this case, the generally accepted social rules and conduct are seen as reflection of years of knowledge and tradition. Individuals thus respect such rules and codes of conduct as respect for accumulated societal knowledge.

Finally, at the **post-conventional level**, individuals are driven by consideration of universal principles and values. Here, most individuals are less concerned about the impact of their actions on themselves. Rather, at this level, individuals are more about respect of universal ethical principles. This is also the highest stage that individuals can achieve.

Kohlberg (1969)	Rest (1986)	Examples
Stage 1: Authority/fear of punishment—You do what you are told to avoid punishment	Level 1: Pre-conventional level—Focus is on the self	Decision not to bribe foreign officials for fear of punishment if supervisor finds out
Stage 2: Self-interest—You scratch my back, I scratch yours		Decision to bribe because bribe results in personal gains
Stage 3: Expectations of others—Decisions are made to please other people and society	Level 2: Conventional level—Focus is on relationships and others' well-being	Decision not to bribe as bribe may hurt organization if sued
Stage 4: Rules and laws stage—Follow the laws and regulations		Decision not to bribe so as not to break company code of conduct
Stage 5: Principled stage—Base decisions on ethical principles of right and wrong	Level 3: Post-conventional level—Focus is on universal rules and regulations	Decision not to bribe as bribe breaks local cultural norms
Stage 6: Universal ethical principles—Follow universal ethical principles		Decision not to bribe as bribing is against universal ethical principles

EXHIBIT 3.2—Kohlberg's Cognitive Moral Development, Rest's Conceptualization, and Examples

To give you further insights into Rest's conceptualization, Exhibit 3.2 shows the various levels, features and examples when applied to organizational situations.

Rest et al.'s adaptation of Kohlberg's theory has received empirical validation.[13] Consider the following Emerging Market Business Ethics Insight.

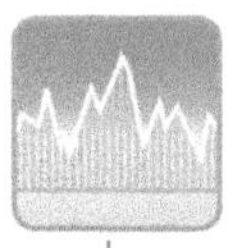

EMERGING MARKET BUSINESS ETHICS INSIGHT

Software Piracy in South Africa

Software piracy, the unauthorized distribution or copying of software for use in computers or other devices without explicit permission from or payment to the authors, is an important issue that affects most societies. Software piracy is especially relevant for companies whose products are digital. Such companies are often producers of movies, software and music. Furthermore, as most countries become more dependent on information technologies, it is becoming imperative to understand what factors encourage or discourage software piracy.

In a recent interesting study, researchers examined software piracy in the South African context. Software piracy is an even more urgent problem for emerging markets because of the disadvantageous impact it can have on economic development. Specifically, the researchers argue that piracy rates in South Africa are around 35%. This results in significant economic losses for companies and estimates suggest that the loss is around half a billion US$. Additionally, such losses can have a domino effect whereby companies producing software lose revenue while also acting as a disincentive for others to produce innovative technologies. As a consequence, software piracy can also affect production of wealth as the software industry can be an economic driver.

To get some insights on how Rest's three levels are related to attitudes towards software piracy, the researchers studied 402 respondents in a wide variety of South African companies from a variety of industries. The research showed that there was a strong and negative relationship between levels and attitudes towards software piracy. In other words, the higher the employee was on the level of moral development, the more negative their attitudes towards software piracy. Such results are not surprising and provide strong empirical validation of Kohlberg's work and Rest's extension.

Based on King, B. and Thatcher, A. 2014. "Attitudes towards software piracy in South Africa: Knowledge of intellectual property laws as a moderator." *Behavior and Information Technology*, 33, 209–223; Machado, F.S., Raghu, T.S., Sainam, P. and Sinha, R. 2017. "Software piracy in the presence of open source alternatives." *Journal of the Association for Information Systems*, 18, 1–21.

As the above shows, Rest's extension of Kohlberg's work is also useful. The findings suggest that training employees to reach higher levels of moral development may be advantageous. Additionally, it has also been shown to be generalizable to different populations and cultures. In addition, higher levels of cognitive moral development have been shown to be related to less ethical choices.[14] Furthermore, studies over time have indeed shown that people progress through the various levels. Most importantly, studies have shown that people can be helped to progress to higher levels through ethics training.

How can companies benefit from using the theory? The development of the Defining Issues Test provides the best way to measure the level of cognitive moral development for organizational use.[15] The approach asks respondents to activate their moral line of reasoning by presenting them with ethical dilemmas and potential solutions.[16]

In the test, respondents are presented with six hypothetical ethical dilemmas. For example, in one dilemma, respondents are presented with the case of a husband who has to buy a drug that has been recently developed and that has the best chances of saving his wife from dying from cancer. However, the druggist is charging ten times more than the cost of making the drug. The husband can only borrow half of the cost of the drug and asks the druggist to let him get the drug for half the price or allow him to pay later. The druggist refuses arguing that he needs to make as much money as possible, as he developed the drug. The husband then considers breaking into the pharmacy to steal the drug. Respondents are then presented three options: steal, do not steal, or cannot decide. They are then presented with considerations and are asked to rate and rank these considerations when making their decision. For instance, considerations such as whether it is right to steal for one's dying wife, or whether the druggist deserves to be robbed because he is greedy, or whether the law should be upheld are presented.

Based on the ratings and rankings of the various considerations, the cognitive moral development level of an individual can be determined. For example, people at the post-conventional level may decide not to steal because the person believes the druggist's rights to his inventions have to be respected (potentially a universal principle).

Companies can use the Defining Issues Test to gauge the moral development of their employees. The utility of assessing cognitive moral development stems from the fact that research shows that ethics training can help individuals to progress along the cognitive moral development levels. As such, understanding the cognitive moral development level can be useful on many levels, including:[17]

- Companies can gauge the level of cognitive moral development prior to hiring. They can potentially eliminate those applicants who are at lower levels and who may be of lower integrity. These individuals may be more likely to behave unethically. In fact, research by Venezia et al. shows that surveyed students who were at the pre-conventional level in their study were more likely to cheat than other students at higher levels.[18] This also provides support for the notion that those at the lower end of Rest et al.'s levels are more likely to engage in unethical behavior.
- Cognitive moral development of existing employees can be assessed. Those at lower levels can be provided with more extensive ethics training. Current research suggests that business ethics training provided over only a few weeks improved the cognitive moral development of students.[19] In both cases, students were simply presented

with information pertaining to a typical business course. Both samples of students experienced improvements in cognitive moral reasoning. Similar types of ethics training can also be provided to employees and levels of cognitive moral development can be assessed regularly to determine progress.

- Companies can also provide very explicit training by having employees consider actual ethical dilemmas and assess how employees react to these dilemmas. Companies can then provide employees with the preferred way to react to such dilemmas by also discussing the considerations that need to be taken.
- The cognitive moral development theory has also received cross-cultural validation. This suggests that training in multinationals may also be useful and can be approached uniformly worldwide.

ETHICAL THEORIES

Another important aspect of understanding ethical behavior is to understand the moral philosophy behind ethical decisions. As such, moral philosophies or ethical theory refers to concerns regarding acceptable ways to solve ethical dilemmas. As managers face ethical issues, ethical theories provide insights into the processes behind ethical decision-making. By understanding how managers approach these decisions, companies can take steps to understand decision outcomes and ways to improve the decision-making process. We consider three of the more prominent ethical theories; namely, utilitarian theories, Kantian and virtue ethics in depth.

The basic premise of **utilitarian ethics** is that the moral worth of an action is based on the consequences of the action.[20] Specifically, when deciding among many potential options, an individual will consider the benefits and harm caused by the action. The individual will then choose the option that maximizes good and minimizes harm. For instance, if a CEO is considering closing a plant in Germany and moving operations to China, the utilitarian CEO will consider the many gains and losses incurred by options of closing the plant and moving to China or keeping the plant in Germany. For the closing the plant option, gains may be the efficiency the company can achieve in China while losses would be the damaged reputation in Germany because of the plant closing. If the CEO considers keeping the plant, losses are the potential long run loss of competitive advantage while gains are the improved relations with workers. Thus, the utilitarian ethics CEO will choose the option that provides the most net gains. Utilitarian ethics is based on the premise of maximization of benefits and minimization of harm. Furthermore, the theory accepts that harm can occur in any decision and focuses on the greatest good based on consequences of actions. Furthermore, utilitarian ethics accept that it is possible to measure everything.

Given the above, utilitarian ethics has many advantageous uses for organizational decision-making. It provides a simple way of gauging the impact of organizational decisions. By forcing decision-makers to consider the costs and benefits of various decisions, utilitarian ethics provide a convenient way to consider various alternatives. Furthermore, utilitarian ethics do not provide any special preference to any specific groups affected by decisions. This suggests a more objective way of making decisions.

However, despite these benefits, the basic premises of utilitarian ethics provide some of utilitarian ethics strongest criticisms. First, many argue that it is not always possible to precisely measure gains and losses.[21] Often, estimates are made based on different assumptions. However, making accurate estimations may not always be possible. For instance, going back to the earlier example, how can the CEO accurately gauge the reputational losses if the company moves the plant to China? How can the gains of improved relationship with employees be assessed?

Another important criticism of utilitarian ethics is that in the calculation of gains and losses, the needs of minorities are typically ignored. Justice is typically ignored. For instance, it is possible that the German company operates the plants mostly using German immigrants. In calculating the gains and losses from opening the plant in China, all considerations are considered equal. However, the losses associated with loss of jobs may be disproportionately higher if the German immigrants were to lose their jobs. However, they are considered as merely a number in the equation.

Finally, the most serious criticism of utilitarian ethics is that the rights of people are ignored.[22] To a utilitarian ethicist, violating someone's rights is irrelevant. The most important consideration is whether the good from the decision outweighs the bad.

As you will see at the end of the chapter with the case of the Ford Pinto, pushing utilitarian ethics to the limit can be dangerous. In trying to face competition and achieving its strategic objectives, Ford's employees made a number of assumptions and calculations that were ultimately very damaging. However, is this criticism warranted? More recent research suggests that many have criticized utilitarianism because they have equated the theory with profit maximization.[23] However, when applied properly, utilitarianism is not simply concerned about maximizing gains for individual benefits.

At a very fundamental level, utilitarianism is concerned about the well-being and happiness of humanity as a whole rather than concern with a single individual. When considering utilitarianism, a proper analysis using John Stuart Mill's (one of the leading utilitarian philosophers) principles of classical utilitarianism involves considering common good as well as the greatest amount of happiness. Simply considering economic cost and benefit calculation is not necessarily consistent with utilitarianism. Thus, despite the criticisms, utilitarianism has many benefits to offer.

Nevertheless, extant evidence suggests that there are other alternatives to utilitarian thinking. In that context, **Kantian ethics** "is about following universal norms that prescribe what people ought to do, how they should behave, and what is right or wrong" (page 22).[24] Unlike utilitarian ethics, Kantian ethics see the consequences of an action as irrelevant. The moral worth of any action is the action itself and whether the action respects universal rules and norms.

Kant argues that universal rules and norms (or what he terms "categorical imperatives") should be based on pure reasoning and logic free from situational influences.[25] The notion of categorical imperatives suggests that they take the form of "do this" and that there are no exceptions to the rule. Kantian ethics thus argue that situations or consequences of actions have no relevance to the moral worth of a decision.

In making decisions, Kantian ethics suggest several categorical imperatives that should be followed. First, the decision should have universal acceptability. According to Kant, a person should "act according to that maxim whereby you can at the same time will that it should become a universal law."[26] In other words, if a person can act a certain way and is confident that such an action can become universally accepted, then Kant sees the action as moral. For instance, one would refrain from lying as lying can never become a universal law. If lying were to become universal, trust and other critical aspects of societal functioning would break down.

Second, a decision should respect the dignity of human beings such that a person acts "in a way that you treat humanity, whether in your own person or in the person of another, always at the same time as an end and never simply as a means."[27] Specifically, Kantian ethics believe that every human being has an inherent worth that should be respected and treated with dignity.

If we examine the earlier scenario regarding the decision to close a plant in Germany and move it to China, Kantian ethics would suggest that the plant remain open. Both categorical imperatives would suggest against closing the plant. A plant closure can never be considered a universal act and employees losing their jobs mean that they are not being treated with respect and dignity.

Kantian ethics offers many benefits for organizational decision-making. First, by forcing decision-makers to only consider universal rules, Kantian ethics fosters universal decisions that are not guided by specific situations. Second, unlike utilitarian ethics, Kantian ethics emphasize treating human beings with dignity and respect. This humanistic aspect is a very valued aspect of the theory. Finally, Kantian ethics focus on principles rather than consequences of actions. Decisions are thus considered to be superior. Consider the following Emerging Market Business Ethics Insight.

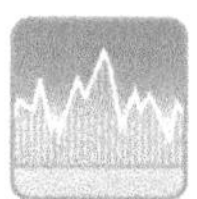

EMERGING MARKET BUSINESS ETHICS INSIGHT

Heineken and Kantian Ethics

Heineken is an independent global brewer that was established in 1864. It has a global portfolio of more than 250 international and regional beers and ciders. Today, it has over 73,500 employees operating more than 165 breweries globally. It also has operations in Sub-Saharan South Africa. However, Heineken is also guided by principles of social responsibility. While governments in most developed nations provide for their population's health needs, that is not always the case for more emerging markets. Heineken has therefore decided to address healthcare issues in such markets.

To do so, Heineken set up the Heineken Africa Foundation (HAF) in June 2012. HAF's primary mission is to improve the healthcare of the communities close to its subsidiaries in Sub-Saharan Africa. As a result, HAF's first scheme was provision of healthcare to its employees as well as surrounding communities. Among many other healthcare initiatives, HAF also set up the 'Mister Sister' health program with the main objective of providing healthcare in rural areas.

In most cases, HAF provided the initial funding with the understanding that NGOs and others will work together to make the programs self-sustaining.

An examination of HAF's programs show Kantian ethics at work. Specifically, when examining the principles that guided many of the programs, it is clear that Heineken was guided by Kantian principles rather than the consequences of their actions. For instance, the decision to provide healthcare to the employees and surrounding communities was motivated by Heineken expatriates feeling that the difference between access to healthcare between them and the surrounding communities was in conflict with their own principles. They therefore decided to take action and set up the "Workplace Health Provision Program" as a result of their own convictions rather than consideration of external pressures emanating from NGOs or other outside pressures.

Based on Heineken. 2018. www.theheinekencompany.com/; Van Cranenburgh, K.C. and Arenas, D. 2014. "Strategic and moral dilemmas of corporate philanthropy in developing countries: Heineken in Sub-Saharan Africa." *Journal of Business Ethics,* 122, 523–536.

As the above Emerging Market Business Ethics Insight shows, there are significant benefits approaching ethics from a Kantian perspective. However, despite the benefits, Kantian ethics has also been criticized. Kantian ethics do not provide as useful guidelines as utilitarian ethics. For instance, what does it mean not to treat people as means to an end? If we consider the case of the German plant, what about the location of the new plant and the potential new Chinese workers who are being denied a job. Furthermore, the neglect of situations may not always be practical. For instance, consider the case of a company that may decide to provide additional benefits or preferential treatment to regular customers. Examining the situation purely from a Kantian perspective would suggest that the company is being unethical. Preferential treatment does not necessarily reflect a universal moral code. Thus, in such cases, including the situation in the decision may be helpful. Finally, Kantian ethics place the responsibility on each individual to make the moral choice. This places responsibility only on the self and does not take into consideration social consensus and dynamics.

Nevertheless, as the above shows, utilitarian ethics and Kantian ethics provide different foci on which decisions can be made. Understanding which theory people adopt when making decisions is very useful. From an organizational standpoint, employees can be trained in both approaches and encouraged to combine these approaches when making decisions. As shown above, both approaches have strong benefits and these benefits need to be emphasized. Specifically:

- Employees can be trained in utilitarian ethics where the strengths of utilitarian ethics can be emphasized. Cost and benefit analysis is a very useful tool and can often provide very precise decision-making. By carefully considering the costs and benefits of any decision, the decision-maker can uncover unexpected issues that may also need addressing. Furthermore, utilitarian ethics encourages the decision-maker to think of all those affected by a decision.

- Employees can also be trained to use Kantian ethics, especially when decisions involve significant human costs. Specifically, Kantian ethics emphasize following universal rules and training can be undertaken through the adoption of universal rules as part of the code of conduct. For instance, Kantian ethics can help provide answers to questions when a decision may harm someone in a foreign country. The categorical imperative of treating human beings with respect can be useful in cases where there are human costs associated with decisions.

Both utilitarian and Kantian ethics place the emphasis on the behavior and whether characteristics or consequences of the behavior make the behavior ethical. More recently, several philosophers have suggested that we should focus our attention on the persons committing the behaviors. In that context, **virtue ethics** emphasizes the decisions made by individuals of good moral character and integrity. It is widely believed that the earliest thinker of virtue ethics is Aristotle.[28] The essence of virtue ethics is that one can live the good life by working to cultivate a virtuous character. This "character was understood to correspond with right behaviors as the challenges of life were confronted"[29] (page 446). As such, this approach is concerned with the cultivation of virtue, one of the highest forms that a human being can attain. Virtue indicates achievement of both moral and intellectual excellence. Additionally, for thousands of years, various philosophers and civilizations have seen the attainment of virtue as one of the critical factors that allow both humans and societies to develop and flourish.

Recent research suggests that virtue ethics were mostly non-existent in the English-speaking world as both utilitarian and Kantian ethics dominated discussions of ethics in general. However, as a recent review shows, virtue ethics became more popular in the 1980s. Furthermore, while virtue ethics may seem irrelevant for multinationals given the focus on individuals, it has still been extensively studied in the business areas. Exhibit 3.3 shows the themes of research on virtue ethics within the business and management journals.

As Exhibit 3.3 shows, although virtue ethics may not be seen as readily applicable to business ethics situations as utilitarian and Kantian ethics, the focus on character and other aspects of the human condition provides some potential utility for stronger ethical behavior. Virtue ethics is therefore seen as having many advantages. Compared to other ethical philosophies, experts believe that employees who do things out of their moral ideals and virtue are more likely to be trusted than those who are simply following rules. Furthermore, a manager with virtue is also more likely to understand what ethical behavior should be performed and will be more likely to be motivated to engage in such behaviors.[30] Additionally, some experts believe virtue ethics is much more developmental than both utilitarian and Kantian ethics.[31] Furthermore, research also shows that virtue ethics may also be generalizable across culture.[32] With the emphasis on individuals, virtue ethics provide a more integrative and balanced framework to understand how morality can be developed and cultivated.

How useful is this perspective? Consider the following Strategic Business Ethics Insight.

Main Theme	Number of Articles	Overall Findings
Virtues in relationships between multinationals as moral institutions and individuals	36	This theme rejected the individualistic view of human beings. Rather, the focus is on collectives such as organizations and markets and how such participation affects individual morality. Through this theme, the focus is on cultivation of virtue in companies and human beings.
Model to study and teach business ethics	33	Comparison of virtue ethics with utilitarianism and Kantian ethics in terms of strengths and weaknesses.
Virtues in ethical decision-making and leadership	29	Focus on how virtues in terms of habits and character influence choices and decisions with a particular emphasis on how such choices are made. Discussion of the characteristics categorizing virtuous individuals including integrity and ethical leadership.
Quantitative and empirical studies of virtue ethics	10	Examination of the influence of virtue and virtue ethics on many organizational outcomes.

EXHIBIT 3.3—Themes of Virtue Ethics Research in Business Ethics and Management Journals

Based on Ferrero, I. and Sison, A.J.G. 2014. "A quantitative analysis of authors, schools and themes in virtue ethics in business ethics and management journals (1980–2011)." *Business Ethics: A European Review*, 23, 375–400.

STRATEGIC BUSINESS ETHICS INSIGHT

Benefits of Virtue Ethics

Two recent studies provide evidence of the power of virtue ethics in promoting more ethical behavior. In the first one, the concept of organizational virtue was examined. Specifically, six characteristics of organizational virtue (empathy, warmth, integrity, conscientiousness, courage and zeal) were assessed using 2,548 questionnaires administered to both customers and employees of 7 companies in the UK. Results showed that companies that were perceived as having higher levels of the six virtues were also more likely to have both employees and customers seeing the organizations as being more distinctive. Given the importance of differentiation and being unique to achieve competitive advantage, such results provide evidence of the importance of virtues at a company level. Additionally, companies that were perceived as having the highest levels of organizational virtues were also seen as more satisfying for both customers and employees. Finally, both customers and employees were also more likely to identify with companies that displayed the highest levels of virtue.

A second study provides further evidence of virtue ethics theory. In that study, researchers were interested in the reasons why a number of New Zealand wineries adopted ethical behaviors, specifically sustainable practices. As such, in this case, the focus was on virtues of individuals rather than the companies. While the interviews of 15 individuals from 14 important wineries revealed that some wineries adopted such practices for market reasons, many of the interviewees revealed that their motivations were guided by their own personal morality. In fact, many of the participants mentioned that such a rationale made them provide a stronger reason for sustainability practices rather than merely responding to market forces. Many mentioned that being sustainable is the "right" thing to do while others mentioned the personal and sentimental values guiding their decisions. When viewed through the lens of virtue ethics theory, the study revealed that the virtues of many of the winery owners and managers were much stronger reasons for the adoption of sustainable practices. Such findings also provide support for the virtue ethics perspective.

Based on Chun, R. 2017. "Organizational virtue and performance: An empirical study of customers and employees." *Journal of Business Ethics*, 146, 869–881; Wang, Y., Cheney, G. and Roper, J. 2016. "Virtue ethics and the practice-institution schema: An ethical case of excellent business practices." *Journal of Business Ethics*, 138, 67–77.

As the Strategic Business Ethics Insight above shows, virtue ethics can be very beneficial for multinationals to use to cultivate a more ethical environment. However, it is not without any criticisms. First, it is difficult to know what virtue is. The traditional view has seen virtues as those characteristics that represents the best of human condition and also mentions the idea of "flourishing."[33] Nevertheless, such views do not necessarily provide clear guidance as to what should be cultivated. Many see the abstract universal principles proposed by virtue ethics as less relevant for moral situations as compared to other theories such as utilitarianism.[34] Second, virtues are acquired after significant and long-term habitual training.[35] This also means that multinationals may need to be very deliberate and take a long-term orientation if they develop virtue in their employees.

Nevertheless, despite these criticisms, companies can take the following steps to take advantage of the benefits of virtue ethics:[36]

- According to experts, virtue ethics cannot be cultivated overnight. In fact, many believe that acquisition of virtue starts within the family through education and socialization. However, companies can take the steps to train employees to develop the values of honesty, integrity and not lying. Such values and principles are likely to lead to stronger ethics.
- Experts also suggest that the experiences and work environment can also be shaped to train employees in the importance of developing virtues. For example, if a company adopts ethical policies because of their values rather than rules or the marketplace dictates such values, employees are more likely to see such companies as virtuous and embrace such values themselves.

- Companies can also provide meaningful work that enables employees to developing virtues. Work that allows employees to contribute to bettering of the human condition (i.e., corporate social responsibility initiatives or time off to volunteer) will also allow employees to see the value of such activities and potentially develop virtues.

MORAL PHILOSOPHIES: IDEALISM AND RELATIVISM

Beyond making a moral judgment based on cognitive moral development level, others argue that people's ethical decision-making is also influenced by their approaches to making ethical decisions.[37] In that respect, **moral philosophies** refer to the preferred way for individuals to approach ethical decision-making. In other words, the moral philosophy "refers to a system of ethics . . . which provides guidelines for judging and resolving behavior that may be ethically questionable."[38] Although there are many aspects of moral philosophies, two have received significant attention in the business ethics literature. We therefore consider idealism and relativism in this section. Forsyth argues that most people can be classified along these two continua.[39]

Idealism refers the degree to which an individual will minimize harm and maximize gain to others when making a decision. The more idealistic an individual is, the higher the concern for the welfare of others and the higher desire to minimize harm to others. For example, a manager high on idealism is less likely to give raises to high-performing employees if such raises mean that some employees will get laid off.[40] In contrast, less idealistic individuals believe that some decisions may unavoidably cause harm to some. These individuals are more likely to believe that they must sometimes choose between the lesser of two evils.[41] For example, such individuals are more likely to accept laying off employees if they are concerned about increasing profits.

Relativism, in contrast, refers to the degree to which individuals adhere to universal rules regardless of the situation when making decisions with ethical consequences. People highest on the relativism scale believe that there are no universal rules, codes, or norms that need to be followed.[42] The higher an individual is on the relativism scale, the more likely they will reject the existence of universal laws and codes. Relativists, for instance, may believe that sweatshops are acceptable because the pursuit of profits for shareholder gain is a situation that justifies employing workers in such conditions. In contrast, people who have low relativism believe that all situations should be guided by universal moral principles. Morality for such individuals implies the application of principles, rules and norms regardless of the situation.

To give you further insights into idealism and relativism, Exhibit 3.4 shows the typical questions respondents are asked when assessing these two dimensions.

Moral philosophies are also very relevant to understand individual ethics. For example, a review of research shows that, consistent with expectations, people with high relativism are more likely to make unethical choices at work.[43] This suggests that such individuals are more likely to use the situation to justify the unethical choices. Furthermore, the same review of a very large number of studies also shows that more idealistic individuals are less likely to make unethical choices at work. More idealistic individuals are more likely to be cognizant of the negative impact of their actions on others. As a consequence, idealists are more likely to make ethical choices when confronted with situations that have ethical implications.

Other research also provides evidence of the utility of understanding relativism and idealism. Henle, Giacalone, and Jurkiewicz examined how idealism and relativism impacts workplace deviance.[44] Workplace deviance simply refers to behaviors that are in violation of company norms and policies that have the potential to threaten the organization or employee well-being. In a study of working individuals, Henle

Relativism Questions	Idealism Questions
1. A person should make certain that their actions never intentionally harm another, even to a small degree 2. Risks to another should never be tolerated, irrespective of how small the risks might be 3. One should never psychologically or physically harm another person 4. One should not perform an action that might in any way threaten the dignity and welfare of another individual 5. If an action could harm an innocent other, then it should not be done 6. Deciding whether or not to perform an act by balancing the positive consequences of the act against the negative consequences of the act is immoral 7. The dignity and welfare of people should be the most important concern in any society 8. It is never necessary to sacrifice the welfare of others	1. Moral actions are those that closely match ideals of the "perfect" action 2. There are no ethical principles that are so important that they should be part of any code of ethics 3. What is ethical varies from one situation and society to another 4. Moral standards should be seen as being individualistic; what one person considers to be moral may be judged to be immoral by another person 5. Different types of moralities cannot be compared to "rightness" 6. Questions of what is ethical for everyone can never be resolved, since what is moral or immoral is up to the individual 7. Moral standards are simply personal rules that indicate how a person should behave, and are not to be applied in making judgments of others 8. Ethical considerations in interpersonal relations are so complex that individuals should be allowed to formulate their own individual codes 9. Rigidly codifying an ethical position that prevents certain types of actions could stand in the way of better human relations and adjustment 10. No rule concerning lying can be formulated; whether a lie is permissible or not "permissible" totally depends on the situation 11. Whether a lie is judged to be moral or immoral depends upon the circumstances surrounding the action

EXHIBIT 3.4—Relativism and Idealism Questions

et al. show that idealism negatively affects workplace deviance. Furthermore, the study shows that relativism is also positively related to workplace deviance. The study again shows that people with high idealism and low relativism are less likely to behave unethically and commit workplace deviance. But how is idealism and relativism relevant for business? Consider the Emerging Market Business Ethics Insight below.

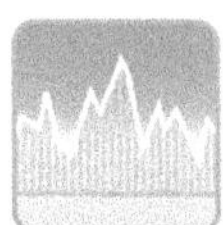

EMERGING MARKET BUSINESS ETHICS INSIGHT

Idealism and Relativism in China and Lebanon

According to the current practitioner literature, bribery and gift giving is a very common phenomenon in China. In fact, current research suggests that bribers are now offering officials not only money or other expensive home appliances but also stocks, houses, overseas travel and even sexual services. However, the Chinese government has begun to crack down on bribery and there are now severe penalties for those caught bribing.

It is undeniable that a person's propensity to bribe will be dependent on that person's moral philosophy. In that context, a recent study examined how idealism and relativism affect 224 Mainland Chinese managers' perception of bribery and gift giving. Bribery is usually a gift large enough to affect the recipient's decision. In contrast, gift giving refers to gifts that reflect people's friendship with others. Results of the study show that relativism positively affects bribery, while idealism negatively affects perceptions of bribery. In other words, people who are rated high on relativism are more likely to have a favorable perception of bribery. Furthermore, consistent with expectations, those managers who have high idealism scores were more likely to have a negative perception of bribery. This provides further support for the utility of understanding relativism and idealism.

A second study examined the impact of moral philosophies on individuals' attitudes towards tax evasion in Lebanon. Using surveys completed by 207 Lebanese employees in the sales, manufacturing and trade sectors, the researchers examined the personal moral philosophies of these individuals and their attitudes towards tax evasion, a clearly unethical behavior. As expected, they find that relativism is positively related to attitudes towards tax evasion. Not surprisingly, those who let the situation influence the morality of a situation are more likely to support tax evasion. However, the study also found that those high on idealism were also more likely to support tax evasion. The authors suggest that people in Lebanon feel that the taxation system is not fair. As such, even those high on the idealism concept feel that it is fine to support tax evasion.

Based on Sidani, Y.M., Ghanem, A.J. and Rawwas, M.Y.A. 2014. "When idealists evade taxes: The influence of personal moral philosophy on attitudes to tax evasion – a Lebanese study." *Business Ethics: A European Review*, 23, 183–196; Tian, Q. 2008. "Perception of business bribery in China: The impact of moral philosophy." *Journal of Business Ethics*, 80, 437–445.

Despite the unexpected results for the Lebanese study, clearly, the above shows that the idealism and relativism aspects are relevant in a cross-cultural environment. Further research provides support for the relevance of idealism and relativism in a cross-cultural environment. In a review of 139 samples drawn from 29 different countries with 30,230 respondents, Forsyth et al. find that both relativism and idealism exist worldwide and that there are predictable variations in these concepts worldwide.[45]

Given the utility of both relativism and idealism, companies are well advised to do the following:

- At a fundamental level, research provides overwhelming evidence of the propensity for individuals with low levels of idealism and high levels of relativism to behave unethically. A company can therefore assess the level of relativism and idealism of potential new employees and consider only those who display higher levels of idealism and lower levels of relativism using the items shown in Exhibit 3.4. This will ensure that new employees are less likely to have attributes that lead to deviance.
- Although relativism and idealism are relatively stable in people, recent research showed that business ethics training in as little as a week altered relativism and idealism. In a study of around 100 German students taking a business ethics course conducted by the main author, comparison of relativism and idealism before and after a business ethics course showed a significant increase in idealism and a significant decrease in relativism.
- As shown in Exhibit 3.5, both relativism and idealism changed significantly after students took the business ethics course. These students were surveyed when they started the course (pre-test) and after they completed the course (post-test).

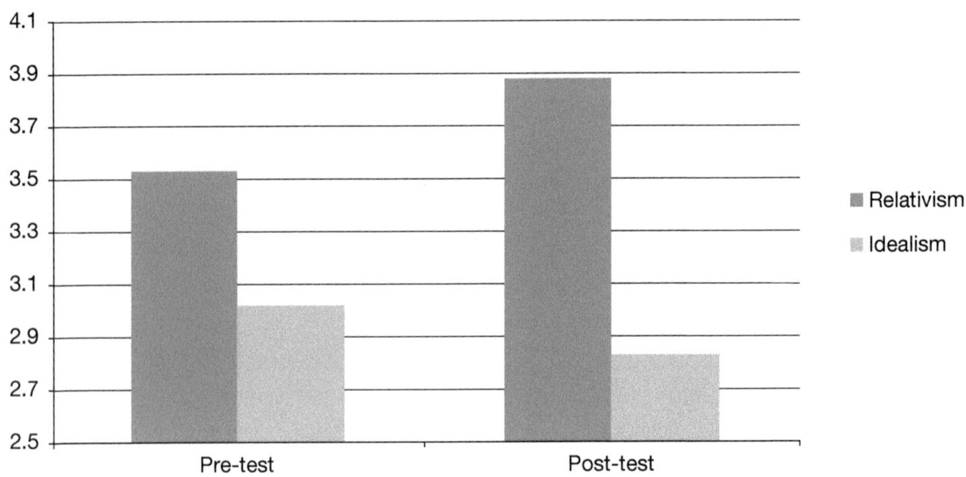

EXHIBIT 3.5—Relativism and Idealism Change after Business Ethics Course

Idealism went up while relativism came down as a result of the course. While it still needs to be determined whether such changes are permanent, this provides support for the assertion that business ethics training may be useful. Specifically, if companies provide training to emphasize the need to follow universal moral codes or the company codes and the need to not harm people in any circumstance, the company can potentially increase idealism and decrease relativism, at least in the short term.

INSTITUTIONAL ANOMIE THEORY

The above approaches and theories focused on frameworks and factors that help explain why individuals cognitively decide to make ethical or unethical choices. However, the ethics field also includes theories that explain the environment that induces individuals to behave unethically. One of the more prominent approaches is **institutional anomie theory (IAT)**, the focus of the final part of this chapter. When originally proposed, the basic premise of institutional anomie theory was that conflicts between the social structure of a society and the goals of that society will result in deviance whereby the members of that society will resort to any means to achieve the societal goals. For example, while U.S. society emphasizes the American Dream, the social structures in place (high levels of social inequality and income disparities) may not always support such goals. As a result, individuals within American society experience **anomie** or a sense of disconnect from society. Because of this disconnect, they are willing to break social norms to reach the American dream. They are willing to break the law to reach their goals. Institutional anomie theory has a strong tradition in the field of sociology and has been used extensively to explain rates of crime and other forms of deviance both in the U.S. and worldwide.

More recent extensions of IAT have proposed that this between societal goals and the means to achieve those are not as critical. What is more important is the predominance of the market. In other words, in U.S. society, we see a focus on of the economy at the expense of other institutions. As such, when the economy starts dominating a society, other non-economic institutions weaken. In turn, other non-economic institutions of the family and education become less critical as the economy grows. This therefore means that the focus on the economy encourages people to strive for materialistic pursuits. In such pursuit, they are willing to achieve the American Dream at all costs.

Although IAT was originally proposed to explain differences in crime rates between and within countries, it has also been applied to explain unethical behaviors both at a country level and within companies. To provide more evidence of the utility of IAT to understanding individual ethics, consider the following Strategic Business Ethics Insight.

STRATEGIC BUSINESS ETHICS INSIGHT

IAT and Data Breach

According to current research and as you will see in Chapter 9 on IT and ethics, data breach is becoming an increasingly difficult problem for companies. Data breach involves the unauthorized access to sensitive or confidential information that can then be used against the holders of such data. Sensitive data includes health information or other important information such as trade secrets or credit card information that can then be used by criminals for personal gains. An important aspect of data breach is identity theft and it is estimated that approximately $16 billion were stolen as a result of identity theft from 12.7 individuals. Understanding the factors that explain identity theft is therefore critical.

A recent study provides some evidence of the utility of IAT in terms of understanding data breaches. The study examined the factors predicting the extent of data breaches at the state level. The authors argue that IAT predicts that the focus on materialism as a result of the dominance of markets forces in the U.S. should explain higher levels of data breaches in states where the strength of the market dominates. The author's logic is that a focus on a strong market signifies that hackers have more of an incentive to achieve higher riches. They therefore hypothesize that wealthier states in the U.S. should have the highest levels of data breaches.

Using data from a number of sources about state level economic indicators such as state gross domestic product in areas such as retail, financial services, government and other services, the authors find support for their contention. Specifically, the authors' overall findings are that for every increase of $1 billion in state GDP, the risks of data breaches increase by 10%. As suggested by IAT, the wealthier the states, the more likely there are pressures for others to fulfill materialistic goals. As a result, hackers are more likely to engage in data breaches, an unethical behavior, to reach such goals.

Based on Sen, R. and Borle, S. 2015. "Estimating the contextual risk of data breach: An empirical approach." *Journal of Management Information Systems*, 32, 314–341.

As the above Strategic Business Ethics Insight shows, IAT is also very relevant to understanding the factors that lead individuals to commit unethical behaviors. While most work has been done in the field of sociology, more recent studies have been done within the field of business ethics that shows the relevance of IAT to understanding individual unethical behavior. For instance, as you will see in Chapter 11 on global ethics, IAT has been used to explain the differences between countries in terms of justification of ethically suspect behaviors. Specifically, research has shown that there are differences between countries in terms of how much individuals justify ethically suspect behaviors such as cheating on taxes and accepting bribes. The use of IAT showed that cultural variables as well as institutions such as the education level and the degree of family strength affect how much individuals justify ethically suspect behaviors.

More recent research has also shown that IAT can be used to predict the level of company tax evasion.[46] In that research, the authors asked employees from 10,032 in 31 countries "what percentage of total sales would you estimate the typical firm in your area of activity kept off the books?" They then examined the degree to which national culture variables such as the level of achievement and the level of individualism were related to the degree of firm tax evasion. Findings show, consistent with IAT, firms in high achievement societies and more assertive cultures were more likely to engage in tax evasion. To give you more insights on the variables considered in IAT studies, Exhibit 3.6 shows many of the variables considered in IAT studies and findings.

Variables	Definition	Findings
Achievement Orientation	Degree to which society emphasizes goal achievement at the expense of reasonable expectations	Achievement orientation encourages tax evasion
Family Strength	Degree to which families are important institutions in society	Family strength is related to lower justification of ethically suspect behaviors
Industrialization	Degree to which society is industrialized	Industrialization encourages justification of ethically suspect behaviors
Pecuniary Materialism	The degree to which society is focused on monetary rewards or material pursuits	Pecuniary materialism encourages stronger justification of ethically suspect behaviors
Universalism	Degree to which societies judge everyone on similar criteria	Universalism encourages lower justification of ethically suspect behaviors

EXHIBIT 3.6—IAT and Tax Evasion

Based on Bame-Aldred, C.W., Cullen, J.B., Martin, K.D. & Parboteeah, K.P. 2013. "National culture and firm-level tax evasion." *Journal of Business Research*, 66, 390–396; Cullen, J.B., Parboteeah, K.P. and Hoegl, M. 2004. "Cross-national differences in managers; willingness to justify ethically suspect behaviors: A test of institutional anomie theory." *Academy of Management Journal*, 47, 411–421.

As Exhibit 3.6 shows, IAT has been very useful in explaining cross-national differences in various types of unethical behavior and deviance in general. As a result of these and other findings, IAT provided the following guidelines:

- Multinationals can review the findings of the cross-national IAT studies to better understand the ethical propensity of their employees in the society they want to operate in. For example, if they are opening a plant in a society where IAT findings suggest that factors may encourage unethical behavior, multinationals can implement policies and practices to counter such propensity to behave unethically. Multinationals can implement stronger practices such as codes of conduct or ethics training and hold employees accountable. Later in the book you will read about many such practices.

- A critical lesson from IAT research is that individuals will likely engage in unethical behavior if there is an emphasis on achievement outcomes such as profits or commissions and if there are barriers to achieve such goals. A company can therefore create an ethical culture that emphasizes more than just materialistic pursuits. If there is focus on such outcomes, the company should ensure that employees are given the means to achieve such outcomes. Furthermore, IAT also emphasizes a fair system where everyone has the same opportunities to succeed as opposed to making opportunities available to a select few. Companies therefore also need to devise systems that emphasize fairness. In Chapter 12, you will read about the many steps multinationals can take to create a more ethical culture.

CHAPTER SUMMARY

In this chapter, you read about the many theories that can contribute to an additional understanding of individual ethics beyond what we discussed in Chapter 2. You learned about the importance of theories and their role in organizing phenomena in order.

You first read about Kohlberg's stages of moral development. Specifically, Kohlberg argues that people go through various stages of moral development in life. Higher stages typically imply superior ethical decision-making. Another important aspect of this chapter is a discussion of normative ethical theories. The text thus discussed three of the most important normative ethical theories, namely utilitarianism, Kantian and virtue ethics.

You also read about moral philosophies and how people approach decisions with moral implications. You learned about both relativism and idealism and the implications of higher ratings on these dimensions. Finally, you also learned about institutional anomie theory (IAT). You read about the application of the theory to business and how the theory can also provide important recommendations to reduce or prevent unethical behavior.

Taken together, the chapter discusses other key theories or frameworks determining unethical behavior. Companies that take the time and effort to properly understand these theories (in addition to the individual aspects of ethics discussed in Chapter 2) and implement the appropriate steps to ensure ethical behavior are likely to have more ethical employees. Combined with Chapter 2, Chapter 3 therefore provides you with a very thorough understanding of the determinants of unethical behavior.

NOTES

1 Fryer, M. 2016. “A role for ethics theory in speculative business ethics teaching.” *Journal of Business Ethics*, 138, 79–90.
2 Devlin, A.S. 2018. *The research experience*. Thousand Oaks, CA: Sage Publishing.
3 Kohlberg, L. 1969. “Stage and sequence: The cognitive-developmental approach to socialization.” In Goslin, D.A. (Ed.), *Handbook of socialization theory and research*. Chicago, IL: Rand McNally.
4 Beauchamp, T.L., Bowie, N.E. & Arnold, D.G. 2009. *Ethical theory and business*. Upper Saddle River, NJ: Pearson-Prentice Hall.
5 Treviño, L.K., Weaver, G.R. & Reynolds, S.J. 2006. “Behavioral ethics in organizations: A review.”
6 Kish-Gephart, J.J., Harrison, D.A. & Treviño, L.K. 2010. “Bad apples, bad cases, and bad barrels: Meta-analytic evidence about sources of unethical decisions at work.” *Journal of Applied Social Psychology*, 95, 1, 1–31.
7 Treviño et al., “Behavioral ethics in organizations: A review.”
8 Treviño et al., “Behavioral ethics in organizations: A review.”
9 Rest, J., Narvaez, D., Bebeau, M.J. & Thoma, S.J. 1999. *Postconventional moral thinking: A neo-Kolhbergian approach*. Mahwah, NJ: Lawrence Erlbaum.
10 Rest et al., *Postconventional moral thinking*.
11 King, B. & Thatcher, A. 2014. “Attitudes towards software piracy in South Africa: Knowledge of intellectual property laws as a moderator.” *Behavior and Information Technology*, 33, 209–223.
12 Narvaez, D. & Bock, T. 2002. “Moral schemas and tacit judgment or how the Defining Issues Test is supported by cognitive science.” *Journal of Moral Education*, 31, 3, 297–341.
13 Rest et al., *Postconventional moral thinking*.
14 Kish-Gephart et al., “Bad apples, bad cases, and bad barrels.”
15 Rest et al., *Postconventional moral thinking*.
16 Kish-Gephart, J.J., Harrison, D.A. & Treviño, L.K. 2010. “Bad apples, bad cases, and bad barrels.”; Narvaez, D. and Bock. T. 2002. “Moral schemas and tacit judgment.”
17 Jones, D.A. 2009. “A novel approach to business ethics training: Improving moral reasoning in just a few weeks.” *Journal of Business Ethics*, 88, 367–379; Jordan, J. 2009. “A social cognition framework for examining moral awareness in managers and academics.” *Journal of Business Ethics*, 84, 237–258.
18 Venezia, C.C., Venezia, G., Cavico, F.J. & Mujtaba, B.G. 2011. “Is ethics education necessary? A comparative study of moral cognizance in Taiwan and the United States.” *International Business & Economics Research Journal*, 10, 3, 17–28.
19 Jones, “A novel approach to business ethics training”; Ritter, B.A. 2006. “Can business ethics be trained? A study of the ethical decision-making process in business students.” *Journal of Business Ethics*, 68, 153–164.
20 Bentham, J. 1781/1988. *The principles of morals and legislation*. Amherst, NY: Prometheus Books; Mill, J.S. 1861/1979. *Utilitarianism*. Cambridge, UK: Hackett Publishing Company; McGee, R.W. 2009. “Analyzing insider trading from the perspective of utilitarian ethics and rights theory.” *Journal of Business Ethics*, 91, 65–82.
21 McGee, “Analyzing insider trading.”
22 McGee, “Analyzing insider trading.”
23 Gustafson, A. 2013. “In defense of a utilitarian business ethic.” *Business and Society Review*, 118, 325–360.
24 Van Staveren, I. 2007. “Beyond utilitarianism and deontology: Ethics in economics.” *Review of Political Economy*, 19, 1, 21–35.
25 Kant, I. 1785/1988. *Groundwork of the metaphysics of morals*. New York: Cambridge University Press.
26 Kant, *Groundwork of the metaphysics of morals*, p. 421.
27 Kant, *Groundwork of the metaphysics of morals*, p. 429.

28 MacIntyre, A. 2007. *After virtue: A study in moral theory.*" (3rd edition). Notre Dame, IN: University of Notre Dame Press.
29 Bright, D.S., Winn, B.A. & Kanov, J. 2014. "Reconsidering virtue: Differences of perspective in virtue ethics and the positive social sciences." *Journal of Business Ethics*, 119, 445–460.
30 Arnold, D.G., Beauchamp, T.L. & Bowie, N.E. 2012. *Ethical Theory and Business.* (9th edition). Upper Saddle River, NJ: Pearson.
31 Ferrero, I. & Sison, A.J.G. 2014. "A quantitative analysis of authors, schools and themes in virtue ethics in business ethics and management journals (1980–2011)." *Business Ethics: A European Review*, 23, 375–400.
32 Fernando, M. & Moore, G. 2015. "MacIntyrean virtue ethics in business: A cross-cultural comparison." *Journal of Business Ethics*, 132, 185–202.
33 Ferrero, I. & Sison, A.J.G. 2014. "A quantitative analysis of authors, schools and themes."
34 Demuijnck, G. 2015. "Universal values and virtues in management versus cross-cultural moral relativism: An educational strategy to clear the ground for business ethics." *Journal of Business Ethics*, 128, 817–835.
35 Arnold, D.G., Beauchamp, T.L. & Bowie, N.E. 2012. *Ethical theory and business.*
36 Wang, Y., Cheney, G. & Roper, J. 2016. "Virtue ethics and the practice-institution schema: An ethical case of excellent business practices." *Journal of Business Ethics*, 138, 67–77.
37 Forsyth, D.R., O'Boyle, E.H., Jr. & McDaniel, M.A. "East meets West: A meta-analytic investigation of cultural variations in idealism and relativism." *Journal of Business Ethics*, 83, 813–833.
38 Henle, C.A., Giacalone, R.A. & Jurkiewicz, C.L. 2005. "The role of ethical ideology in workplace deviance." *Journal of Business Ethics*, 56, 219–230.
39 Forsyth, D.R. 1980. "A taxonomy of ethical ideologies." *Journal of Personality and Social Psychology*, 39, 175–184.
40 Neubaum, D.O., Pagell, M., Drexler J.A., Jr., McKee-Ryan, F.M. & Larson, E. 2009. "Business education and its relationship to student personal moral philosophies and attitudes toward profits: An empirical response to critics." *Academy of Management Learning and Education*, 8, 1, 9–24.
41 Forsyth et al., "East meets West."
42 Neubaum et al., "Business education."
43 Kish-Gephart et al., "Bad apples, bad cases, and bad barrels."
44 Henle et al., "The role of ethical ideology in workplace deviance."
45 Forsyth et al., "East meets West."
46 Bame-Aldred, C.W., Cullen, J.B., Martin, K.D. & Parboteeah, K.P. 2013. "National culture and firm-level tax evasion." *Journal of Business Research*, 66, 390–396.

KEY TERMS

Authority/fear of punishment stage: the person defines right or wrong based on the obedience to rules from those in power.

Conventional level: decisions are made based on external rules and norms coming from family, friends, peers and society.

Expectations of others stage: judgment about right or wrong is based on the expectations of significant others and peers.

Idealism: degree to which an individual will minimize harm and maximize gain to others when making a decision.

Institutional anomie theory: basic premise is that conflicts between the social structure of a society and the goals of that society will result in deviance whereby the members of that society will resort to any means to achieve the societal goals.

Kantian ethics: basic premise is about following universal norms that prescribe what people ought to do, how they should behave, and what is right or wrong.

Moral philosophies: the preferred way for individuals to approach ethical decision-making.

Post-conventional level: individuals are driven by consideration of universal principles and values.

Pre-conventional level: decisions are typically driven internally by either reward or punishment.

Principled stage: decisions based on ethical principles of right and wrong and consider what is good to society.

Relativism: refers to the degree to which individuals adhere to universal rules regardless of the situation when making decisions with ethical consequences.

Rules and laws stage: moral judgment is externally oriented and based on whether the action respects rules and policies.

Self-interest stage: person chooses the action that satisfies the person's self-interest the most.

Theories: frameworks that allow researchers to predict or explain some phenomena.

Universal ethical principles stage: the decision-maker determines whether an action is right based on universal ethical principles that everyone should follow.

Utilitarian ethics: basic premise is that the moral worth of an action is based on the consequences of the action.

Virtue ethics: Emphasis of decisions made by individuals of good moral character and integrity.

DISCUSSION QUESTIONS

1. What are theories? Why are theories important?
2. Briefly discuss Kohlberg's theory of moral development. How can companies use Kohlberg's theory to better train their employees?
3. Discuss the first and second stages of Kohlberg's theory of moral development. How are the two stages different?
4. What are relativism and idealism? Discuss why it is important for companies to understand the relativism and idealism of their employees.
5. What is utilitarian ethics? What are some of the assumptions of utilitarian theory? Discuss some advantages and disadvantages of the approach.
6. Discuss the basic assumptions of Kantian ethics. What are the advantages and weaknesses of the theory?
7. What is virtue ethics? Briefly describe the focus of virtue ethics.
8. Compare and contrast the three types of ethical theories discussed in this chapter. How can these three theories be used to encourage ethical behaviors?
9. What is institutional anomie theory (IAT)? How does IAT explain unethical behaviors?

10. Describe how companies can build individual ethics based on what you read in the chapter. Use at least two major factors to illustrate your answer.

INTERNET ACTIVITY

1. Using access to articles from your university library, identify an article that uses institutional anomie theory in management or business administration. Share that article with your class.
2. What aspects of unethical behavior does the article seek to explain?
3. What are the findings of the study? Which variables does the article use?
4. What are the practical implications of the article?
5. Share your findings with your class.

For more Internet Activities and resources, please visit the Companion Website at www.routledge.com/cw/parboteeah.

WHAT WOULD YOU DO?

The Salesperson

You have been recently hired as an ethics officer by an international manufacturing company. Your job is to assess the ethical readiness of your employees. As more multinationals see their ethical activities being scrutinized, you know that having ethical employees is critical. Your first task is to examine recent decisions with ethical implications. To do so, you organize a meeting with all of the department heads. You also send out surveys to a selected group of employees.

Your surveys and interviews show a pattern whereby employees make decisions that either benefit themselves or their departments. For example, the customer complaints department is usually not willing to carefully consider customer complaints to avoid hurting the sales commissions of their departmental members. Production plant managers are not willing to admit their fault when product defects often at substantial cost to the company. Most importantly, you find that employees are often discussing best practices with competitors.

You soon realize that employees blatantly disregard many rules and policies governing many of the actions discussed above. What would you do? How do you use Kohlberg's stages of moral development to change the culture in the company? In other words, how do you move employees from being self-interested to being principled?

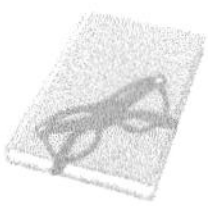

BRIEF CASE: BUSINESS ETHICS INSIGHT

The Ford Pinto

Ford is a global automotive company with a rich history of car making worldwide. It is currently based in Dearborn, Michigan, USA, and employs over 203,000 individuals in the world. Despite an impressive list of achievements in the industry, the case of the Ford Pinto provides one of the best examples of what can happen when individuals rely solely on utilitarian ethics when making decisions.

In 1968, facing severe competition, Ford decided to start producing the Ford Pinto. The Ford Pinto was a subcompact car that was then retailing for around $2,000. To have the model ready by 1971, Ford hastened the design to make it to production. However, any changes to the design would have to be made during the production tooling process. During the design process, Ford was required to respect the new safety standard proposed by the National Highway Traffic Safety Administration (NHTSA) whereby cars could safely withstand rear impact without fuel loss at 20 mph. The Pinto failed and, although the problem could have been fixed with a rubber bladder in the gas tank for an additional $11, Ford decided against it. Engineers at the company engaged in utilitarian ethics to justify not adding the rubber bladder.

To make the decision, Ford engaged in the practical application of utilitarian ethics; namely, cost and benefit analysis. It estimated that the cost of adding the safety improvement would be around $137.5 million (11 million cars and 1.5 million trucks equipped at $11 per vehicle).

To estimate the benefits, Ford calculated the cost it would have to incur by not implementing the safety device. As such, it relied on the NHTSA estimation that the value of a life is $200,725, as society loses that amount when someone is killed in an accident. It also estimated that it would have to pay $67,000 per serious injury and $700 per burned vehicle. Assuming that 180 individuals would die from burn deaths (180 x $200,725), 180 (180 x $67,000) would have serious burns and 2,100 vehicles (2,100 x $700) would get burned, Ford estimated that the benefit would only amount to $49.5 million.

As the costs to Ford far outweighed the benefits, Ford decided not to implement the rubber bladder safety device. The decision proved very costly to Ford, as many of their assumptions were flawed. Many lawsuits were brought, with substantial damages given to the victims. Furthermore, Ford was even charged with criminal homicide in one case, when three teenagers died when the gas tank of their Pinto exploded on impact in an accident.

Based on Ford. 2018. www.ford.com/; Shaw, W.H. and Barry, V. 2011. "The Ford Pinto." In *Moral issues in business*, Florence, KY: Thomson-Wadsworth, p. 79.

BRIEF CASE QUESTIONS

1. What are some of the factors that led Ford to use utilitarian ethics to make the decision about the Ford Pinto?
2. How does this case illustrate some of the dangers of using utilitarian ethics?
3. What can be done to ensure that such decisions do not occur again? How can Kantian ethics be used to improve the decision-making process?

LONG CASE: BUSINESS ETHICS

PHILOSOPHICAL FOUNDATIONS OF IMPACT INVESTING

September 30, 2017

By: Georgette Fernandez Laris

As pointed in our earlier piece, Impact investing is about good profits: making money while doing good. Impact investing reminds us sound monetary returns and positive socio-environmental impact returns are not mutually exclusive, but can be complementary and even mutually enhancing. Here are the philosophical reasons why.

1. Context: where the impact investment market stands

While financial initiatives in favor of investments for social good emerged in the 1980s, the impact investing label gathered momentum in the early 2000s, especially from the onset of the 2008 global financial crisis. Some analysts attribute the rising interest in impact investing to a generational shift in values. Generation X and Millennials hold business corporations and the financial sector more accountable for their role in society. Emerging generations of investors will likely see social justice and environmental objectives as parallel with financial returns (World Economic Forum & Deloitte, 2013). Others ascribe impact investment's increasing popularity to the broad disappointment with traditional financial service providers arising from the latest crisis. Younger investors need to find instruments with a renewed purpose to fund shared collective social and environmental challenges.

Recently, a concerted international effort has accelerated the development of a high-functioning impact investing market. For example, the Global Impact Investment

Network (GIIN) was founded in 2007. Since 2009, GIIN has deployed its **Impact Reporting and Investment Standards (IRIS)** initiative to support transparency, credibility, and accountability in impact measurement practices. The initiative increases the scale and effectiveness of the market. Impact investing was the core topic of discussion at the 2013 World Economic Forum Annual Meeting in Davos, Switzerland. Similarly, it was a key area of focus for David Cameron, Prime Minister of the United Kingdom, at the G8 meetings throughout 2013. Despite ongoing growth in the impact investment sector, the CEO of GIIN, Amit Bouri, recognizes it is still a young market. The available supply of impact capital and the existing demands are not clearing into deals efficiently yet. To date, niche players such as family offices, high-net-worth individuals (HNWIs) and development finance institutions (DFIs) are driving the capital development of the impact investment sector. These groups' share of global asset ownership is relatively small. Hence, to fully develop into a mature investment sector, impact investing will rely on the collaboration between: mainstream liability-constrained investors (pension funds, insurance firms, etc.), asset-based investors (private equity firms, mutual funds, sovereign wealth funds, endowments), social impact enterprises, philanthropists and foundations, governments and financial intermediaries.

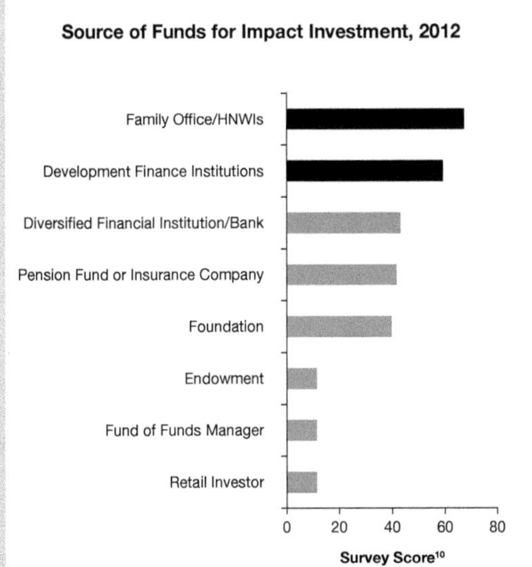

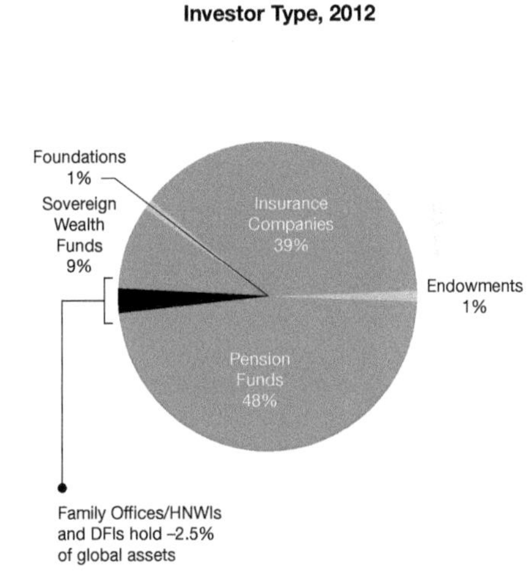

2. Clarifying the terminology

To understand the evolution of the impact investment sector, it is worthwhile clarifying the confusion over related concepts. The terms **socially responsible investing**, sustainable investing, and impact investing are often used interchangeably. Although the three are all *responsible investing* practices, they don't refer to the same thing. Differences between them can be couched in terms of the motivations to invest, reliance on asset classes, degree of control, and range of expected returns. The extent to which elements such as control and expected returns are guaranteed can influence diverse growth dynamics across these three related, but different, types of investment practices.

As the figure shows, **socially responsible investing** (SRI) involves negative screening, that is, opting out of investments with a negative impact on society and the environment or avoiding companies judged to be doing harm. SRI is a soft ethical approach due to the inherent, subjective, moral relativism of evaluating what constitutes harm. For example, an investor committed to revitalizing urban neighborhoods plagued with unemployment might not exclude companies or enterprises within the casino industry from the portfolio of potential capital recipients. Without consideration of any other ethical prerogative to guide the investment decision, the investor could deem that the *ancillary benefits* (creation of jobs, tourism revenue) of casinos suffice to make them better or less harmful than the status quo of the impoverished neighborhoods.

Sustainable investing takes a step forward towards strengthening ethical considerations. It does more than shy away from companies and stocks engaged in "sin" activities (alcohol, tobacco, gambling, sex-related industries, arms industry, etc.). Rather, sustainable investing pro-actively incorporates environmental, social, and governance criteria into the analysis of the investment decision and aims to positively

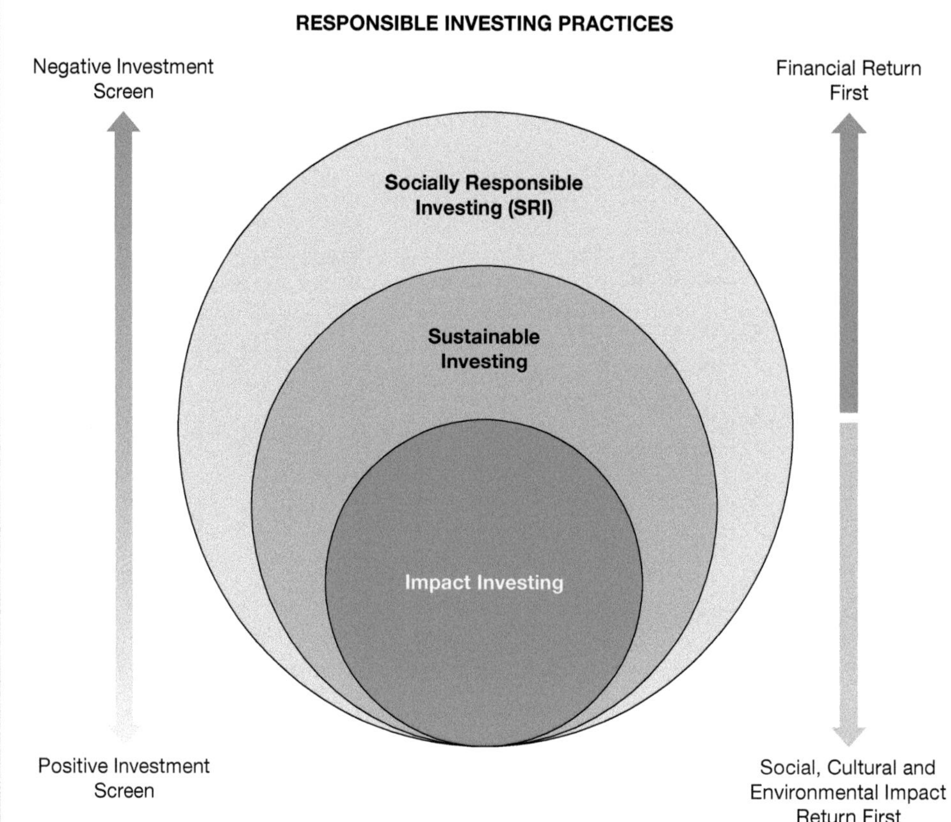

screen for companies that can demonstrate affirmative leadership in these areas. While certainly impactful, sustainable investing gives priority to financial returns over social and/or environmental returns.

Impact investment, the focus of this article, goes even further along the ethical screening ladder by explicitly integrating intentionality into the positive screening of investments. From the onset (before the investment is made), impact investing deliberately and clearly sets out to deliver the dual objective of attaining specific social/environmental outcomes and financial returns simultaneously.

Impact investing is not a stand-alone asset class. It is not solely philanthropy either. It is an investment approach across a range of asset classes with a clear, transparent and distinctive intentionality.

Impact investing is a lens through which investment decisions are made deontologically, that is, responding to a moral sense of duty to give our capital resources a greater purpose. It is a teleological investment practice that invites us to redirect the use of our monetary resources so that the funds sustainably function as levers for social, humanitarian, and environmental transformation.

Results from the GIIN 2016 Annual Impact Investor Survey defy sceptics who contend that impact investments always generate below-market returns. According to the GIIN survey, more than 70% of their 2016 respondents observed that impact performance and financial returns were at least as high as expected.

In these surveys, as in its 2017 GIIN edition, half of respondents engaged in impact investing had both social and environmental impact objectives, about 41% of respondents primarily targeted social justice impact objectives and roughly 9% focused on environmental objectives exclusively. Respondents from developed countries tended to target environmental outcomes much more than those in emerging markets. The best-performing impact investing recipients or investees (normally social enterprises,

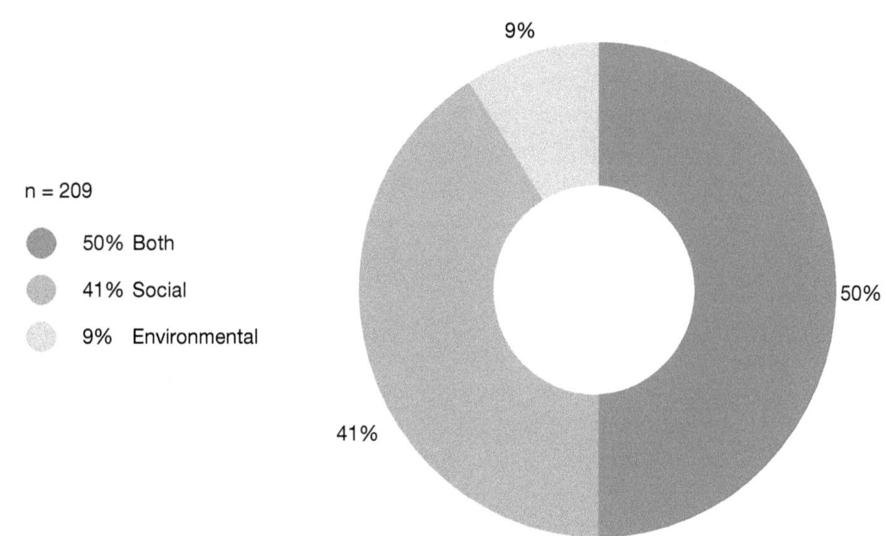

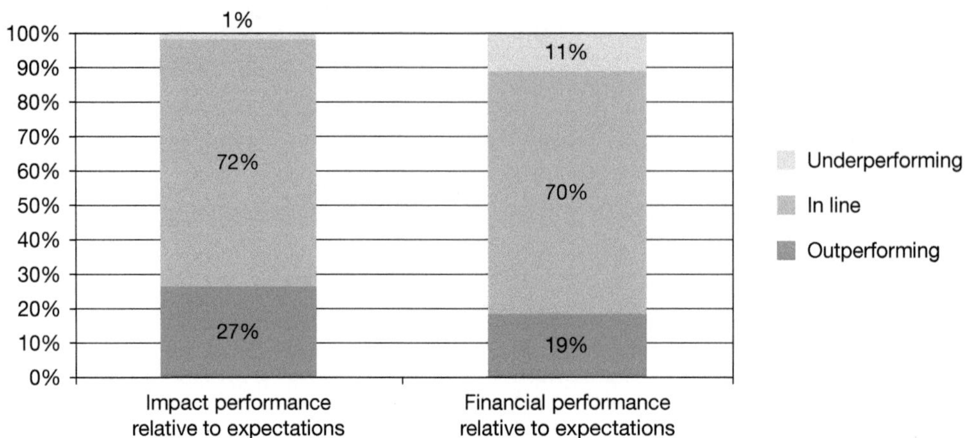

start-ups, or public initiatives), are those who make their social justice or environmental objectives intrinsic to their business model.

This type of business model allows them to avoid conflicts of interest between socio-environmental and financial returns because their business indicators coincide with their impact indicators. Ultimately, this strategy fosters a harmonious balance through which specific economic activity drives socio-environmental impact.

Many analysts still consider the impact investment market an early-stage ecosystem. The market has sustained year-over-year growth with, for example, impact investing organizations repeatedly reporting to GIIN a 15% increase in the total amount of capital invested and a 3% increase in the number of investments made. But a couple of challenges discourage larger institutionalized investors from entering the market. These include: the ambiguity with which investors differentiate impact investing from other forms of responsible investing, and the lack of widely agreed-upon standards to measure and report social and environmental outcomes so as to compare the impact and performance of investment portfolios. The improvement of impact measurement practices has been a top priority for institutions such as the GIIN, the World Economic Forum (WEF), the Organisation for Economic Co-operation and Development (OECD), the Global Association for Banking on Values (GABV), and several non-profits. However, the absence of commonly accepted measurement standards across regions and participants in the impact investing ecosystem constrains its evolution into a more mature system. The market is currently segmented in terms of financial return philosophies, motivations for engaging in the sector, and impact themes pursued. Uncertainty regarding uniformity and comparability of impact evaluations maintains this segmentation.

The consensus is that for impact investing to mature, investors need to be able to categorize and compare the social and financial impacts of diverse investments. This leads us to one of the most natural hesitations regarding impact investing, namely the acknowledgement of the (at times instrumental) wide range of ultimately relativist opinions of what constitutes "impact".

3. Philosophical foundations of impact investing

A categorization of impact investment as yet another investing possibility with a benevolent slant is simplistic. As a subset of investment opportunities within the universe of responsible investing practices, impact investing entails an endogenous, self-reinforcing vision regarding the purposeful use and allocation of capital resources. It is more than a benign investment asset class. Impact investing involves a process of scrutinizing the motivations to invest, the nature of the funded project, the choice of the investment instrument used, its expected return, and its guarantees. Impact investment's emphasis on a double-bottom line of measurable impact and financial returns aligns it with aspects of utilitarian and deontological **moral philosophies.**

Utilitarian review

Impact investing, sustainable investing, and SRI follow the consequentialist moral tradition. All three, either via negative or positive screening of corporations and social enterprises in which to invest, gauge their moral character based on the consequences of the main activities, services, and products of targeted capital recipients. Moreover, these three types of responsible investing approaches are utilitarian, the most widespread form of consequentialism. In making investment decisions, all three deem the investment opportunities that maximize welfare (understood as monetary utility or any other measure of social value) for the greatest number as the most morally right options.

Although "sin" activities are dealt with via negative investment screening, under utilitarianism rogue corporate and governance behaviours can still be justified as long as the resulting aggregate social welfare is maximized. Thus, it is perfectly possible for asset managers of socially responsible funds to include in a positively screened portfolio the stocks of companies considered best-in-class under a highly profitable leadership criterion while failing other non-pecuniary, social well-being norms. For example, an ethical investor would be disappointed to learn his money goes to support companies such as Volkswagen. In 2014, the car company deliberately set out strategies to circumvent emissions control, giving it an unfair advantage over competitors. It became the world's number one carmaker, on the basis of its "environmentally friendly" cars (*Forbes*, 2015). The utilitarian objective to maximize the sum-total of utilities (welfare) irrespective of distribution tends to incentivize this and other corporate and financial responsibility problems. Under utilitarian logic, even the smallest gain in the total utility sum can outweigh the most blatant distributional welfare and social inequalities.

Of the three responsible investing practices, impact investing is the least susceptible to the pitfalls of utilitarianism. Impact investing associations such as GIIN, supranational bodies including the ONU, OECD and WEF, and other impact investing market participants including ethical banks have devised thorough metrics and standards of impact that help represent the multidimensionality of investment portfolios claiming to be socially responsible. The detailed and more encompassing measures (which track a company's impact on its workers, community, and the environment) enhance the transparency of the sector to guide more ethical investing decisions. Some impact investing associations are starting to include stipulations on the full disclosure of the range of corporate activities conducted. Enforcement of these disclosures also keeps the sector transparent and aids ethical investments.

Utilitarian viewpoints also encourage companies and potential investees to use corporate social responsibility, social justice, and environmental sustainability labels as marketing and public relations tools. An investor seeking "good profits" would hence be surprised to learn his capital was allocated to giants such as Unilever. Even though its CEO declared it was his "*personal mission to galvanize the company to be an effective force for good,*" under his leadership Unilever has been implicated in numerous environmental and sexual harassment controversies in Africa and India (*Forbes*, 2017). Appearing good sells roughly as well as actually being good. The stronger ethical criteria of impact investing cannot change that unfortunate maxim until shared metrics of impact evaluation are uniformly understood and used.

Deontological review

Some critics believe that impact investing's dual-bottom-line objective dilutes its "good-investing side." They argue the selfless, virtuous value of altruistic social justice and environmental conservation is corrupted when integrated with financial profit motives. Some investment managers hesitate to fully disclose the financial performance of portfolios, fearing it would be interpreted as a promotional gimmick using other's misfortune. This reveals they indirectly rely on **Kantian deontological ethics**, by trying to respect the categorical imperative of "*treating others never merely as a means to an end but always at the same time as an end.*"

Impact investing practices not only follow utilitarian ethics but they also respond to a sense of duty (deontological view). For example, niche impact investors might be willing to provide seed capital to launch a social initiative out of their desire to support an enterprise, which conforms to their values and norms, even if it entails financial uncertainty and could lead to financial loss. These impact-first investors rely on the alignment of investment options with their personal moral code when judging ventures, rather than on the expected financial consequences. *Ceteris paribus*, under this specific aspect of impact investment, an altruistic investor may decide to finance research and development (R&D) of affordable treatments that improve the life-quality of people with incurable diseases that receive little attention and funding because of fatal prognoses and the rarity of cases. The investor might not expect to recoup any financial gain from this endeavor and perhaps she acknowledges the spread of its impact would be highly localized. However, her decision to invest in this way is founded on the intrinsic belief that everyone deserves an equal, fair, and enabling life-quality regardless of diagnosis.

Impact investing's characteristic double-bottom-line prerogative, consisting of rendering both financial returns and tangible positive impacts, allows it to bypass some of the criticisms faced by responsible investing practices solely relying on deontological ethics or on utilitarianism. The dual objective helps investors and advisers to consider simultaneously the intrinsic morality of the activities financed as well as the magnitude and spread of their consequences. Thus, considering maximization of social welfare (utilitarian motive) as well as the intrinsic value of life (deontological motive), an investor would decide to place her capital in an impact investment fund specializing in pooling resources to finding the most efficient allocation of funds to support the R&D of treatments for multiple serious diseases that can reach the most individuals.

Skepticism & cultural relativism

Confusion over the terminology of impact investing, sustainable investing, and SRI partly emerges from culturally relativistic interpretations of what constitutes harm (in the case of negative screening of investments) or of what constitutes impact (in the case of positive screening). Above, we used casinos to exemplify relativism regarding negative screening. However, critics analyzing the limitations of the responsible investing marketplace also argue there are no objective standards by which to define positive ethical investments. For moral skeptics, what is "impactful" is a matter of perception, not a matter of objective universal truth. Similarly, for moral relativists, parameters determining what is (or is not) of significant social or environmental benefit (impact) are not only considered lacking universal objectivity but they are understood as conventions shaped by context and subjected to evolving socio-historical, cultural and psychological frameworks. Defenders of cultural relativism warn us that our preferences over investees and choice of investing instruments can reflect the values, priorities and prejudices of our society. Thus, whether impact investors of a certain area or geopolitical region focus more on social justice, cultural, or environmental issues when allocating capital across investees could be partly culturally conditioned.

For moral relativists, all investors' judgments and observations (and those of their advisors) regarding the degree of impact generated through invested capital are equally valid. Thus, how can we ascertain whether an investment leading to increased schooling in rural, indigenous, Latin American communities outperforms an investment that helps supply green energy and reduce emissions in Asian cities? Likewise, through utilitarian welfare maximization considerations, how would we establish whether an investment with a significant direct impact on the lives of a few individuals is more valuable than a slight indirect impact on the lives of many more?

Relativism does more than question the nature of what normatively is the most beneficial social justice, cultural, or environmental imprint of a project in need of capital. Since metrics can be value-laden, the choice of impact measure used in investments' evaluation can leave room for relativism regarding the scope of impact of social enterprises and initiatives[i]. Different metrics used to monitor the impact of the same social enterprise could yield diverse depictions of its impact return.

Moreover, the impact investment marketplace has tried to start harmonizing the set of metrics suitable to assess enterprises' social or environmental performance through the Global Impact Investment Network's Rating System (GIIRS) and its Impact Reporting and Investment Standards (IRIS). For cultural relativists, both fall short of providing absolute objectivity in measurement. For one, these initiatives focus more on measuring outputs of impact investments (product or service produced by the investee enterprise) rather than on outcomes (specific effect of the output in improving people's lives). For example, GIIRS and IRIS help to measure the reach of invested capital (how many social or environmental interventions are achieved with impact investing capital flows) but fail to provide in-depth, comparable descriptions of the social value of the specific interventions.

Challenges to the continued growth of impact investing vary according to investment practices, regulatory environments, and culture. Nonetheless, investors still have an imperfectly met need to categorize and compare the social impact of diverse investments. This imperfection is a core constraint to the growth of the sector across the globe.

Metrics must help establish the causation between invested capital and the socio-environmental outcomes generated with it. Metrics that can show this link are essential in aiding investment managers to compare the true impact of portfolio options. Analysts seem to agree that steps towards building broadly accepted systems of investments' impact evaluation would attract more mainstream institutional investors and allow impact investing to grow by making the understanding of what is (or is not) significantly impactful more objectively reliable.

The role of agency

From its beginning, the core impact investing capital providers have been asset owners with a relatively small share of global asset holdings (family offices, HNWIs, and some diversified financial institutions and development banks). Analysts and current impact investment landscape participants concur that, to mature, a greater involvement of mainstream investors is needed, including liability-constrained asset owners such as pension funds, and insurance firms as well as of asset managers such as private equity firms and mutual funds. A variety of impact investment funds have provided a route for mainstream investors to become more engaged in impact investing. Differentiated by their target investee sector or geography, institutional structure as non-profits, use of subsidies and diverse return expectations; impact investment funds pool individual investor capital resources to make, primarily, debt and equity investments into impact enterprises.

Some critics argue that reliance on impact investment fund managers (or other wealth advisors) dilutes the moral agency of the *principal* investor who hires the services of such intermediaries. The rationale behind this critique is that, given the relativism found across guidelines that define what an affirmative ethical investment consists of, fund managers or wealth advisors' (agents) evaluations of an ethically positive investment may be different from those of the asset owners providing the capital (principal).

Agency theory, which explains the relationship between a party hired to act on behalf of another during business and financial transactions, assumes that both the financial wealth managers (agents) and their investor clients (principals) are self-interested.

Impact Investment Ecosystem

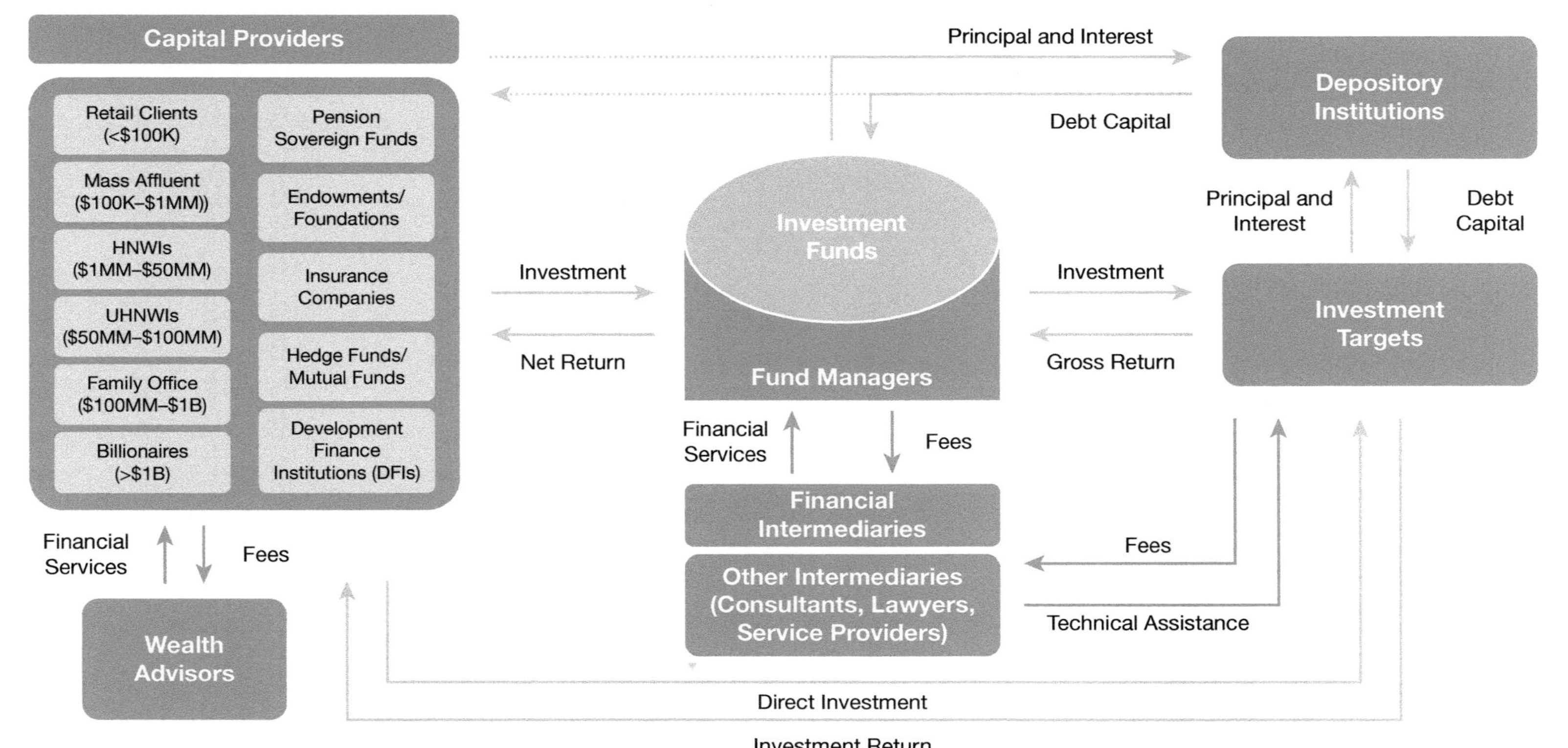

Even if the double bottom line motivates both sides, it is possible for conflicts of interest to emerge. Whenever investment managers do not place the impact priority over and above financial returns, but their clients do, the strength of the ultimate social impact attained could be less than the one initially sought by principal capital providers. For example, a certain principal could be interested in investing her capital to alleviate one consequence of poverty in a specific region, but she relinquishes control of her capital resources to an investment fund manager. The latter could decide to go after much more profitable humanitarian organizations in more affluent markets, arguing that she will try to move down-market, to the real target population, when the numbers are right, and yet never do so. The demands of the investment manager pull the funds away from the principal's target population toward those able to guarantee a larger financial return while the principal's initial intentionality is eroded through its concession of agency.

Therefore, to minimize any type of loss due to the principal-agent problem, it is useful to ensure the fund managers (or other wealth advisor intermediaries) share the same commitment to impact generation and intentionality as their asset-owning clients. It is also very helpful to create frameworks of disclosure and transparency that make the principal knowledgeable about the consequences of the agent's activities, motivations, and whether these factors ultimately serve the principal's best interests.

Some ethical banks pursue these principal-agent loss-minimizer conditions in their practices. For example, the French ethical bank La Nef (Nouvelle Economie Fraternelle—the New Fraternal Economy) only finances social justice and environmental impact projects by allocating the funds of its depositors. Moreover, it reports precisely on all the companies it finances and why it does so. La Nef presents its transparency as a means for savers and depositors to exercise their own responsibility over the use of their money, strengthening the moral agency of both La Nef and its clients. The pioneer Netherlands-based Triodos Bank (also active in the UK, Belgium, Spain and Denmark) likewise follows full transparency practices with its clients that help counteract claims on the diminished moral agency of capital providers using financial intermediaries to engage in impact investing.

4. Future directions and concluding thoughts

Recognizing the need to continue improving measurement standards of impact enterprises, in 2016 the OECD launched a working group dedicated to set out agreed-upon impact investing principles and create a roadmap for a comprehensive global reporting system. Likewise, the GIIN is perfecting its rating and impact reporting standards (IRIS and GIIRS). Of course, none of these efforts seek to establish absolutist metric standards. Rather, the goal is to spur the objectivity, precision, transparency, and comparability of measures to better inform impact investing decisions and help the sector grow. Better measures are expected to attract large-scale financial firms and to expand the horizon of impact investing instruments, fueling much more capital into a sector ripe for growth.

Bibliography/references

Born, Kelly & Paul Brest. (2013). *Unpacking the Impact in Impact Investing.* Stanford Social Innovation Review.

Emerson, Jed & Lindsay Smalling. (2016). *Understanding Impact: The Current and Future State of Impact Investing Research.* Impact Assets Issue Brief (No. 14).

Global Impact Investing Network (GIIN). (2016). *2016 Annual Impact Investor Survey.*

Global Impact Investing Network (GIIN). (2017). *2017 Annual Impact Investor Survey.*

Hart, Oliver & Luigi Zingales. (2017). *Companies Should Maximize Shareholder Welfare Not Market Value.* University of Chicago Booth School of Business and Stigler Center Working Paper Series (No. 12).

Monitor Institute. (2009). *Investing for Social & Environmental Impact. A Design for Catalyzing an Emerging Industry.*

Staskevicius, Alina & Ivy So. (2014). M*easuring the "Impact" in Impact Investing.* Harvard Business School Social Enterprise Initiative Report.

World Economic Forum (WEF) Investors Industries & Deloitte Touche Tohmatsu. (2013). *From the Margins to the Mainstream: Assessment of the Impact Investment Sector and Opportunities to Engage Mainstream Investors.* Industry Agenda Report.

Press Articles

Unilever and the Failure of Corporate Social Responsibility. Forbes (2017). Retrieved in June, 2017 from: www.forbes.com/sites/econostats/2017/03/15/unilever-and-the-failure-of-corporate-social-responsibility/#13385a84498d

Volkswagen and the Failure of Corporate Social Responsibility. Forbes (2015). Retrieved in June, 2017 from: www.forbes.com/sites/enriquedans/2015/09/27/volkswagen-and-the-failure-of-corporate-social-responsibility/#67a8531b4405

Chapter 3: Long Case Notes

[i] Metrics are also driven by the demands of institutional investors. Their level and type of interest, concern for comparability, and willingness to pay for measurement and assurance tends to determine the choice of specific metrics.

Editor: Eric Witmer

LONG CASE QUESTIONS

1. What is impact investing? How is impact investing different from traditional investing based on financial returns?
2. How is impact investing different from socially responsible investing or sustainable investing?
3. Why is consideration of Kantian ethics more likely in impact investing compared to other forms of investing?
4. Are you willing to consider impact investing? Why or why not? In your reasoning, integrate any of the ethical theories discussed in this chapter.

Chapter 4

Stakeholders

LEARNING OBJECTIVES

After reading this chapter you should be able to:

- Understand what stakeholders are and the strategic need to properly manage stakeholders
- Be aware of stakeholder categories and attributes
- Appreciate the many steps to appropriate stakeholder analysis and management
- Become aware of the importance of different stakeholders worldwide

PREVIEW BUSINESS ETHICS INSIGHT

BP and the Oil Spill in Louisiana

In April 2010, a British Petroleum (BP) oil rig experienced a massive explosion that killed 11 workers. After the rig caught fire and sank, oil from the BP well started spilling into the Gulf of Mexico. Initial estimates suggest that around 10,000 to 15,000 barrels of oil were spewing into the sea. Experts suggest that over 3 million gallons of oil spilled into the Gulf of Mexico over a three-month period.

The federal government's reaction was swift as they criticized BP's reaction to the scandal. At federal hearings, many BP officials admitted that the company was aware of the potential for this accident. BP ignored many warnings from its own engineers and proceeded with plans that seemed to ignore potential safety concerns. The hearings also revealed the massive lobbying resources BP invests in to influence the government.

The oil spill has had a tremendous impact on many levels. Many groups dependent on tourism in Louisiana and surrounding states have been affected as oil started appearing on the coastlines. Hundreds of individuals involved in the seafood industries in the Gulf region have been out of work. Furthermore, hundreds of other restaurants in the area have lost money as fewer tourists visit the area. Additionally, it is predicted that the price of seafood may rise as more and more restaurants avoid buying seafood from the Gulf. Restaurant owners report that customers are now becoming increasingly reluctant to eat seafood from the Gulf region because of the oil spill.

The disaster also seems to have had a severe impact on the ecological landscape. Many forms of wildlife have been severely affected, as the Louisiana marshes are crucial to many species including shrimp. Even a pelican species that had been rescued from the brink of extinction is now in catastrophic trouble. Recent anecdotal evidence from fishermen in the area suggests that the fish that fed the industry have yet to come back.

The public and communities worldwide have also expressed anger at BP and its operations. Many groups are building boycott campaigns worldwide. Many consumer groups have also been appalled at BP's lack of preparation in the face of the spill. While no specific actions against BP have yet been taken by consumers, BP is well aware of the difficulties it faces ahead.

Minimizing and stopping the oil spill has also mobilized scientists' and countless individuals' solutions. For instance, a federally assembled group of scientists were the ones to recommend that a toxic chemical be sprayed (a dispersant) in the Gulf of Mexico to prevent the spilled oil reaching the coastal areas. BP engineers and scientists also proposed and tried many different solutions to stop the oil spill.

BP's share prices have also suffered from the oil spill. A month after the spill, BP's shares plunged over 12%. Many investors were panicking and feared that the oil spill could irreparably harm BP's chances of survival. These investors believed that the costs of the cleanup, as well as the mounting litigation and compensation claims, may become too much for BP to handle.

Almost eight years later, the scandal has not subsided for BP. Although it had agreed to a settlement of $7.8 billion to reimburse victims of the oil spill, BP has started stalling the reimbursements. It is estimated that over 74% of small business owners who were affected by the spill will likely never get paid.

Based on Ball, J. 2010. "Scientists to back dispersant use, despite concerns." *Wall Street Journal* online; British Petroleum. 2018. www.bp.com; Chazan, G. 2010a. "BP shares under deeper pressure." *Wall Street Journal* online; Chazan, G. 2010b. "The Gulf oil spill: BP wasn't prepared for leak, CEO says." *Wall Street Journal*, A.5; Hughes, S. and Boles, C. 2010. "BP, regulators are grilled on hill over key decisions." *Wall Street Journal* online; Isikoff, M. and Hirsh, M. 2010. "Slick operator: How British oil giant BP used all the political muscle money can buy to fend off regulators and influence investigations into corporate neglect." *Newsweek*, 155, 20; Reckdahl, K. 2015. "Slimed: BP's forgotten victims." *The Nation*, May 4, 24–29.

The above Preview Business Ethics Insight shows the impact that the BP oil spill has had. The spill is turning out to be an even worse disaster than the *Exxon Valdez* oil spill. The *Exxon Valdez*, an oil tanker owned by Exxon, ran aground on Alaska's coast in March 1989. The accident resulted in millions of gallons of crude oil being spilled along Alaska's coasts. The effect of the spill is still being felt today. Although a jury awarded $5 billion to victims in 1994, Exxon kept appealing the judgment for over 20 years.[1] When the payments finally started in 2009, 6,000 of the original 32,000 victims were already dead.

Both accidents show the extent to which different groups and entities can be affected by a company's actions. These groups or entities are commonly known as stakeholders. Most companies have to contend with more direct stakeholders such as customers or employees. However, the BP case described in the Preview Business Ethics Insight shows that stakeholders do not necessarily have to be directly linked to a company. Seemingly indirect groups such as restaurants and hotel owners are being affected by the spill. In fact, many small business owners went bankrupt because the oil spill killed the source of their livelihood.

Any attempt by BP to deal adequately with the spill will be dependent on its ability to fully satisfy the needs and concerns of all stakeholders affected by the spill. This incident shows the critical need for companies to properly manage their stakeholders. However, as the Preview Business Ethics Insight shows, BP is not necessarily managing all of its stakeholders well. BP's decision to slow down reimbursement to small business owners for their losses will likely affect the company.

The BP spill also revealed an added complication of today's business environment. The spill was 2010's most micro-blogged topic of the year.[2] Anyone with access to the internet was able to voice their views about the spill to the public. Additionally, the power of social media also gave participants the ability to organize a collective response to the crisis. This also ended up being a challenge for BP to manage.

In Chapters 2 and 3, you learned about the important individual aspects contributing to ethical behavior. In this part of the text, you will start reading about how companies can build ethical organizations. One of the major components of the ethical organization is understanding and balancing the needs of stakeholders. Therefore, in this chapter, you will learn about stakeholders and their implications for a company's strategic success. You will first read about the strategic need to understand and manage stakeholders. You will also learn about the various types of stakeholders and critical stakeholder attributes. In this chapter, you will also be exposed to stakeholder management and the many practical tools and techniques that are used for such purposes.

WHAT ARE STAKEHOLDERS AND WHY DO THEY MATTER?

The most accepted definition of a **stakeholder** is any group or individual that "can affect or is affected by the achievement of an organization's objectives."[3] Freeman, in his classic book *Strategic Management: A Stakeholder Approach*, is widely credited for introducing the business ethics and management field to the concept of the stakeholder.[4] As we saw in Chapter 1, stakeholder theory was introduced as an alternative to the then popular notion of stockholder theory. Rather than manage the organization solely in the interests of stockholders/shareholders, Freeman argues that a company should be managed taking into consideration the interests of all constituents or stakeholders.

Who are stakeholders? Exhibit 4.1 shows some of the more important stakeholders and the typical needs they have over a company.

Stakeholder	Ethical Issue
Customers	• Product safety • Truth in advertising • Fair price
Shareholders	• Fair return on investment • Adequate management of company • Accurate financial reporting
Employees	• Discrimination • Sexual harassment • Child labor and sweatshops • Employee safety
Suppliers	• Impact of suppliers on environment • Exploitation of labor • Supply chain management
NGOs	• Environmental performance • Labor relations • Supplier sourcing issues
Host country	• Following local laws • Respecting local environment • Use of local labor
Government	• Lobbying • Regulation

EXHIBIT 4.1—Typical Stakeholders and their Needs

As Exhibit 4.1 shows, there are many different types of stakeholders. But why should a company be concerned about properly managing relationships with stakeholders? From a strategic management perspective, a strong stakeholder management approach is likely to help a company achieve and maintain strategic competitive advantage. For instance, a strong stakeholder management system means that a company has good relationships with its various stakeholders. Previous research suggests that such good relationships can increase a company's financial performance.[5] Furthermore, other research shows that a company's strong relationships with its stakeholders suggest that it has access to valuable, rare, inimitable and non-substitutable resources that contribute to sustainable competitive advantage.[6] In other words, if a company is to maintain competitive advantage, it needs access to resources that others cannot easily copy or imitate. A company's strong relationship with its stakeholders is something that is hard to replicate and can lead to success over the long term. Consider the following Strategic Business Ethics Insight.

STRATEGIC BUSINESS ETHICS INSIGHT

Unilever and Stakeholders

Unilever, a multinational based in the Netherlands, is a market leader in industries such as the food, home, and personal care brands. Its brands include well-known products such as Bertolli, Lipton, Slim-Fast, Axe, Dove, and Pond's among others. It enjoys a strong reputation among its many stakeholders for being committed to sustainability. Furthermore, Unilever works hard to engage and develop relationships with its stakeholders. Such efforts have paid off, as the company has enjoyed sustainable competitive advantage.

An important component of Unilever's stakeholder management aspects is to engage and listen to stakeholders. For example, when Unilever was presented with a damning report that raised serious concerns about its sourcing and working practices in its foreign operations, it took these allegations seriously and investigated the matter. Since this report, Unilever has implemented many new measures to address these concerns. As another example, Greenpeace issued a report detailing how Unilever's suppliers in Borneo were clearing land without permits in order to be able to grow palm trees. The cleared lands were often orangutan habitats, thus damaging many species' habitat. Unilever again responded to the report by commissioning its own report. Its own independent report found that the Greenpeace allegations were indeed accurate. Unilever has since been working with its suppliers to ensure that these practices end.

Unilever's stakeholder strategy has not been simply reactive to reports. It also actively engages with its suppliers to help these suppliers. Consider, for instance, Unilever's partnership with Ghana-based environmental and non-governmental organizations. It is working closely with these organizations to develop a way to accelerate the growth of the allanblackia tree. The allanblackia tree produces seeds that can be converted to oil. However, this oil is stable at room temperature and thus provides an important commercial advantage as the seeds do not need to be chemically processed. Furthermore, the oils in the allanblackia tree can make soaps harder, thus making these soaps more economical than the use of palm oil. Unilever's efforts have paid off and it has successfully developed a tree that grows faster. Such trees can provide new sources of income for farmers in Ghana. Furthermore, the program is being expanded to other African nations such as Tanzania and Nigeria.

Paul Polman, the company's CEO, believes that any company's role should be to balance the needs of all stakeholders rather than just shareholders. He believes that if a company is sustainable, profits will follow. So far, he has been able to lower emissions, water usage and waste by 43%, 38% and 96% respectively. However, there are some concerns about how employees are treated as income for employees has not risen. Nevertheless, Mr. Polman believes that sustainability and balancing stakeholder needs is superior to a focus on shareholders because sustainability practices tend to attract investors and customers. This may be working as Unilver's market share has risen globally and it has offered good returns to investors.

Based on *The Economist*. 2017. "Unilever is the world's biggest experiment in corporate do-gooding." September 2, 58; *Financial Times*. 2008. "Unilever's success with palm oil." September 25; Mahajan, V. 2016. "How Unilever reaches rural consumers in emerging markets." *Harvard Business Review*, December 14, 2–6; Unilever 2018, www.unilever.com.

As the Strategic Business Ethics Insight shows, companies can benefit greatly from properly managing the relationship with their stakeholders. Strong relationships with various stakeholders can provide valuable information for companies. In fact, Unilever is very aware of the potential of rural consumers. While its efforts to develop these markets have been very positively received by a generally ignored group of customers, Unilever is well aware that the rural consumers it currently serves in the ten countries in Asia and Africa represent two-thirds of the world's population. Although the group may not necessarily have the buying power of more developed world consumers, because of increased standards of living, this group presents tremendous opportunity. Unilever is therefore hoping that its efforts will develop brand awareness among these consumers and that they will become lifelong consumers.

But is a strong relationship with stakeholders necessarily beneficial? Choi and Wang provide some insights into this question. They use large-scale data collected by a research firm on companies from the S&P 500 over an 11-year period ranging from 1991 to 2001. They found that good stakeholder relations are indeed related to superior company performance measured in terms of return on assets. However, most importantly, Choi and Wang found that positive stakeholder relations are even more critical for companies performing poorly. They found evidence that positive stakeholder relations can actually help such poorly performing companies recover.[7]

The above clearly shows that good stakeholder relationship management is critical. Next we consider key aspects of stakeholders in terms of categories and attributes.

STAKEHOLDER CATEGORIZATION AND ATTRIBUTES

One of the critical aspects of properly managing stakeholders is the ability to identify these stakeholders. Being able to adequately identify critical stakeholders plays an important role in terms of how such relationships are managed and what impact such relationships have on any company. Furthermore, in such identification, critical attributes of these stakeholders have to be acknowledged. In this section, we discuss some of these key issues.

One of the most popular categorizations of stakeholders is to classify them either as primary or secondary stakeholders. **Primary stakeholders** are typically directly linked to a company's survival and are either impacted by or impact companies directly. Examples of primary stakeholders include customers, suppliers, employees and shareholders. These groups have a very strong and direct connection with a company. We will discuss some of these primary stakeholders in more detail in later chapters.

Ignoring primary stakeholders can be very disastrous for any company. Consider the case of oil companies in the Delta region in Nigeria.[8] Despite the lucrative nature of oil extraction, most of these oil companies have ignored the host communities, resulting in very tense relationships and hostilities. Oil companies have been accused of engaging in collusion with the government to appropriate ancestral lands for the purpose of oil extraction. Many of these companies have also been accused of damaging the environment irreversibly. Furthermore, there are allegations of human rights abuses and other discriminatory practices. To protest these practices, host communities in the Delta region have resorted to communal protests, hijacking of oil workers and even sabotage of oil equipment to protest against these companies. Most experts do agree that these oil-producing companies would have had smoother relationships if they had listened to these stakeholders.

Another important stakeholder group is **secondary stakeholders**. In contrast to primary stakeholders, secondary stakeholders tend to be less directly linked to the company's survival and include the media, trade associations, and special-interest groups. We will discuss examples of key secondary stakeholders in more detail in Chapter 8.

Although it may seem that secondary stakeholders have less impact for multinational companies, recent examples show that secondary stakeholders are as important as primary stakeholders in terms of impact. Consider, for example, how the agricultural giant Monsanto has been forced to deal with secondary stakeholders such as Greenpeace and Friends of the Earth as it tries to develop agricultural biotechnology products. Similarly, the tobacco industry worldwide has been affected disproportionately by government and communities in an effort to lower smoking levels. Such examples show that, depending on the industry, secondary stakeholders may have critical influence on any company. Exhibit 4.2 gives some examples of primary and secondary stakeholders for a typical multinational.

Primary Stakeholders	Secondary Stakeholders
Shareholders and investors	Media
Employees	Special-interest groups
Suppliers	Non-governmental organizations
Local community	Labor unions

EXHIBIT 4.2—Primary and Secondary Shareholders for a Typical Multinational

Although categorizing stakeholders as primary or secondary is one way to look at stakeholders, it is not the only approach. Lawrence and Weber propose that companies can also look at stakeholders as market or nonmarket stakeholders. **Market stakeholders** are those entities that have economic relationships with the company as the latter achieves its mission. Examples of market stakeholders are employees, suppliers, stockholders etc. as they all have some form of economic transaction with the company. Companies also have to contend with **nonmarket stakeholders** whereby such entities have a direct impact on companies although they do not have direct economic transaction with the company. Examples of nonmarket stakeholders include the community, the government, competitors, the public and any other groups that have an impact on any company.

Although the above approach provides for a different perspective on stakeholders, it is complementary with the earlier discussed approach. And the key lesson is that it is important to be able to clearly identify stakeholders. Any attempt to adequately manage stakeholders begins with proper identification. Consider the following Ethics Sustainability Insight.

ETHICS SUSTAINABILITY INSIGHT

Infrastructure Projects and China

Countries such as China are experiencing many large-scale infrastructure projects. However, successfully managing such projects is critical as such projects have the potential to impact many different types of stakeholders. Additionally, sustainability is a key goal given the impact of such projects on the environment and the current focus on sustainability goals. Understanding which stakeholders are affected and how they view sustainability is therefore very critical in order to manage any conflicts among stakeholders and to get their commitment to such infrastructure projects.

In an interesting study conducted in China pertaining to a railway construction project, stakeholders were first identified. Because of the nature of such projects and the impact such projects can have (both positive and negative), careful review of other similar projects revealed who are typically affected by such projects. These stakeholders were classified along four categories, namely secondary stakeholders such as government agencies, environmental protection entities and primary stakeholders such as contractors/clients and the general public.

Two hundred and twenty-six of these four types of stakeholders were then surveyed to determine their views of sustainability. Specifically, they were surveyed on many different dimensions of economic, environmental and societal aspects of sustainability along a five-point scale. Exhibit 4.3 below shows the most important concerns of the different stakeholders along these elements of sustainability.

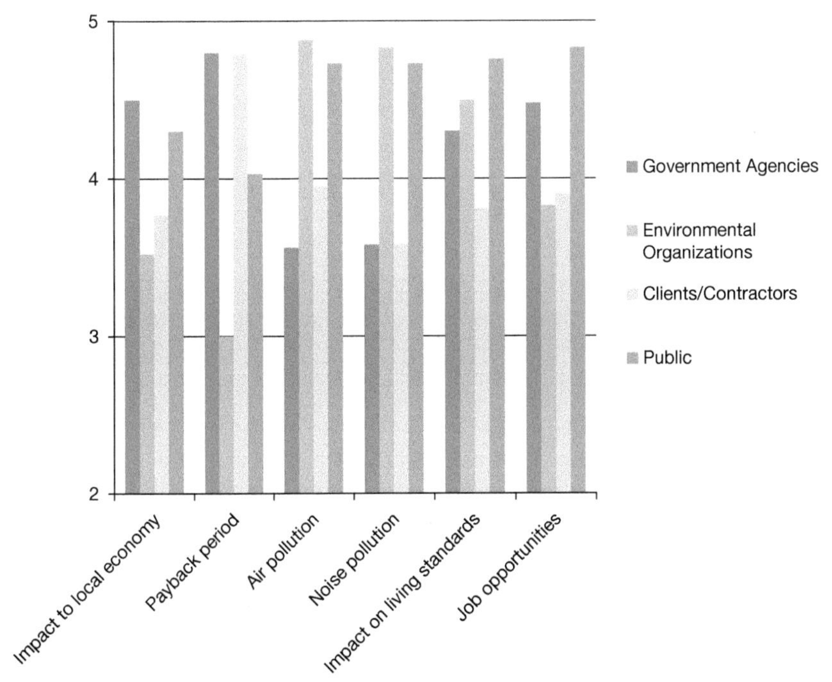

EXHIBIT 4.3—Ranking of Sustainability Issues

As Exhibit 4.3 shows, for government agencies, the most critical aspects were the economic aspects such as impact on local economy and payback period as well as the societal issues such as impact on living standards and job opportunities. In contrast, for the general public, environmental issues aspects of sustainability (air pollution and noise pollution) were deemed much more important. Similarly and not surprisingly, environmental organizations were mostly concerned about environmental aspects of sustainability. Contractors were also most concerned about economic aspects and less so about the environmental and societal implications. Finally, contractors rated most of these aspects lower than others because their focus is on project completion.

Based on Yuan, H. 2017. "Achieving sustainability in railway projects: Major stakeholder concerns. *Project Management Journal*, October/November, 115–132.

The above Ethics Sustainability Insight shows that different stakeholders have different views of sustainability. Successful completion of any projects requires proper identification of stakeholders and appropriate assessment of their needs. The construction company then needs to determine how to manage such competing needs to ensure that the project moves smoothly. An important part of this exercise is to determine the critical attributes of stakeholders. We therefore examine stakeholder attributes next.

Stakeholder Attributes: Power, Legitimacy, and Urgency

In addition to proper categorization of stakeholders in terms of the primary versus secondary types, it is important to examine the attributes of these stakeholders. In this section, we discuss three critical stakeholder attributes; namely, power, legitimacy, urgency and salience.[9] Each stakeholder attribute has the ability to influence an organization.

The first stakeholder attribute we consider is power. **Stakeholder power** refers to the ability of a stakeholder to exert pressures to force a company to make changes to accommodate such pressures. According to Mitchell, Agle and Wood, power can take different forms.[10] Power can be of coercive, utilitarian, or normative forms.

Coercive power involves the use of force, violence, or other restraint to force a company to accommodate or respond to stakeholder needs. For instance, in the earlier discussed example of oil companies and their presence in the Delta region, host communities frequently resorted to coercive means to force oil companies to halt their exploitative practices. As these oil companies have colluded with the state to appropriate land and have been more concerned about oil production at the expense of the environment, militant groups have mushroomed and have resorted to coercive power to force these oil companies to re-examine their practices.[11]

A second form of power is **utilitarian power**. Utilitarian power refers to the use of financial or other monetary means to force a company to accommodate a particular stakeholder need. Common manifestations of utilitarian power are use of money or boycott. Consider, for example, tobacco companies. For decades, they defended their products, arguing that the claims that tobacco can result in negative health effects were not true.[12] Many stakeholders, such as the government and states, used their utilitarian power to force tobacco companies to acknowledge the nature of their products and provide the means to start addressing problems associated with tobacco. Actions such as long lawsuits were only possible because the government has access to the necessary financial resources to face the tobacco industry. Yet another example of utilitarian power is manifested in boycotts whereby stakeholders may decide to stop buying a company's specific products.

Finally, a third form of power is normative power. **Normative power** refers to the use of symbolic and other resources to force a company to accommodate stakeholder needs. As argued by Thorne, Ferrell and Ferrell, actions such as letter writing campaigns and other advertising messages are examples of the use of normative power.[13] The advent of the internet also means that people can now easily vent about a company publicly. The internet and social media have therefore provided an important source of normative power.

It is critical for companies to properly assess the power of their stakeholders in order to adequately address their needs. If the extent of the power is not fully acknowledged, it can signal disaster for the company. Consider the following Strategic Business Ethics Insight.

As the Strategic Business Ethics Insight shows, Uber will have to address many stakeholder concerns. For example, Mr. Khosrowshahi has already taken away voting

STRATEGIC **BUSINESS ETHICS INSIGHT**

Uber and Stakeholder Power

Uber, the revolutionary ride hailing company, is facing opposition for its app worldwide. Many of its stakeholders are actively opposed to its methods and are showing their power to force Uber to change its approaches. Local regulators are using their utilitarian power by taking Uber to court and trying to force Uber out of business in their towns. Other regulators are also using their utilitarian power by forcing Uber to provide benefits to its full-time employees. These regulators are arguing that Uber is a regular employer and should therefore provide similar benefits. In fact, the European Court of Justice will soon consider whether Uber is a technology or transport firm. Many of the regulators want to treat Uber as a transport company and force them to provide a minimum wage and benefits to its taxi drivers.

Many investors are also making use of their power against Uber. Benchmark, one of the initial investors in Uber, has agreed to drop a lawsuit against Mr. Kalanick, the founder and early investor of Uber. Mr. Kalanick was seen as having too much power and investors are using their utilitarian power to limit use of this power. These investors see Mr. Kalanick as the main reason behind Uber's toxic culture and have stripped Mr. Kalanick's super voting rights.

Taxi drivers in cities are also using their power to show their displeasure with Uber. Many feel that Uber is unfairly operating in their territory and is running them out of business. They have staged protests in many cities. However, in Africa, taxi drivers are resorting to coercive power to drive away Uber. In the South African city of Johannesburg, taxi drivers have been manhandling customers who seem to be getting into Uber cabs. In some cases, shots have even been fired. In the other African cities of Cape Town and Nairobi, taxi drivers have attacked Uber drivers and torched their taxis.

Uber's new CEO, Mr. Dara Khosrowshahi, is actively working to end dissatisfaction of stakeholders against Uber. Uber's future is heavily dependent on his efforts.

Based on *The Economist*. 2017. "Tech's toughest job; From Uber to kinder." October 7, 65–66; *The Economist*. 2017. "Taxis take on Uber; African potholes." November 12, 60.

rights from the initial investors thereby satisfying current investors. Many other steps will have to be taken to address other stakeholder concerns.

A second key stakeholder attribute we consider is **legitimacy**. A company behaves legitimately if it conducts itself in such a way that is consistent with widely held values and beliefs.[14] When a company behaves legitimately, it is more likely to be supported by society. Similarly, a stakeholder is considered to have a legitimate need if the actions of the stakeholder are considered reasonable and acceptable within a certain context.

A company is well advised to carefully consider the legitimacy of its various stakeholders. Ignorance of the legitimacy of some stakeholders can be disastrous. Consider the case of the public-sector healthcare reforms in Canada.[15] In 1994, the Canadian healthcare industry had to respond to the needs of the government-initiated efficiency reforms. The Canadian healthcare providers perceived the government as the only legitimate stakeholder. However, this focus on the government led to an important decline in quality and patient satisfaction. The Canadian companies simply ignored the legitimate demands of other stakeholders such as the employees and patients. The legitimacy of these other stakeholders had to be recognized as the companies also started addressing their needs.

A third critical attribute is urgency. **Urgency** refers to the degree to which a company needs to respond to stakeholder needs. The more urgent a stakeholder's needs are, the more quickly a company has to respond to such needs. Similar to the other attributes, response to urgency is also critical.

One of the most urgent stakeholder claims that have emerged over the past decade is pressure on companies to be more environmentally sensitive. However, other urgent claims such as fair trade, human rights and labor rights have also become very prevalent.[16] Many of these claims have resulted from the perceived growing power of large multinationals. This has also led to a number of non-governmental organizations making more urgent claims to counterbalance such power. These issues will be explored in depth in Chapter 11 on global ethics.

As the above shows, it is extremely critical to properly assess stakeholder attributes. This points to the importance of adequately addressing stakeholder needs. Next, we discuss stakeholder management.

STAKEHOLDER MANAGEMENT

Stakeholder management refers to the deliberate and purposeful process a company has devised to work with its stakeholders. As we saw in the many examples earlier, stakeholders often have disparate needs when they relate to companies. Companies have found that ignoring such needs can be very detrimental to their health. Having a systematic process to anticipate and address such needs is therefore critical.

Why is stakeholder management critical? As we saw earlier in this chapter, adequately dealing with stakeholders can be financially beneficial for a company. Having a strong stakeholder management system implies that a company has strong relationships with its stakeholders. Such relationships can provide the company with valuable, rare, and difficult to imitate resources. Such resources can thus lead to competitive advantage whereby companies have access to skills and capabilities that other companies do not have access to. Consider, for instance, the example of Uber discussed in this chapter and how they are facing troubles with their stakeholders. If they had a stakeholder management system in place, they would have likely been able to anticipate such trouble.

Choi and Wang's study provides further evidence of the strong link between stakeholder management and competitive advantage.[17] Companies that have superior relationships with their workers tend to have employees that will work harder to help the company achieve its goals. Strong relationships with suppliers often result in greater willingness of suppliers to share knowledge with the firm. Furthermore, strong relationships with communities often mean that the communities may provide better terms for the use of local infrastructure. Thus, strong stakeholder management programs are likely to provide a company with resources that contribute to strategic competitive advantage.

How useful are strategic stakeholder management systems? Consider the following Strategic Business Ethics Insight.

STRATEGIC **BUSINESS ETHICS INSIGHT**

Stakeholder Management in China and Sweden

How critical are stakeholder management systems? Consider the earlier discussed example of railway construction projects in China. Clearly, the builders are taking every steps they can to make sure that they address stakeholder concerns. However, a study comparison of railway construction projects in Sweden provides even more evidence of the importance of the stakeholder management process. The first case involved the construction of 18 km of tracks around the city of Malmö in Sweden. The project was necessary to take into consideration the large increase in traffic that was placing increased pressure on the Malmö tracks. The project involved the construction of two parallel tunnels under the city. The second case involved the expansion and improvement of tracks in the city of Lund. Because of projected traffic growth, there was a crucial need to expand and improve the tracks to cope with such growth.

An analysis of both projects shows the importance of stakeholder management practices. For example, surveys of the public and others affected by the Malmö project showed that around 68% of respondents had a very positive attitude toward the project and around 17% were neutral. Furthermore, of the 15% who had a negative perception of the project, 88% of them were comfortable with the project being built. In contrast, the Lund project ran into significant opposition and a delay before the project was completed.

The two projects were perceived very differently because the stakeholder management process was done differently. For the Malmö project, the project management team regarded stakeholder acceptance as extremely critical for successful completion of the project. Through surveys and other processes, the construction team identified six major critical stakeholder groups that could potentially influence the project. Using many of the methods described later, the construction company was able to proactively identify relevant stakeholder needs and respond to such needs. For example, project managers for the project met with members of the public on numerous occasions to provide open communication regarding seven critical areas where the project would most likely affect the public. Furthermore, the group communicated openly with the media to address any lingering issues. Members of the media then became the strongest advocates for the project.

The Lund project was conducted in an almost opposite manner. No stakeholder management process was established and the construction company chose to ignore stakeholders. For instance, although the public is an external stakeholder, they had tremendous informal power on the projects. By ignoring the public, the company encouraged opposition, and politicians and the media soon formed coalitions with the public to oppose the project. While the public was considered as a legitimate stakeholder in the first project, it was completely ignored in the second project. This lack of a stakeholder management process resulted in a six-year delay, which added significant costs to the project. Furthermore, the project managers in the Lund project chose not to respond to negative criticisms from the media. This also resulted in negative articles promoting the views of opponents of the project only.

Sweden continues to be involved in efforts to modernize its rail system. Stronger stakeholder management has helped projects become reality. Researchers have also spent time understanding the factors that encourage affected citizens to eventually use the new railway system.

Based on Nordlund, A. and Westin. K. 2013. "Influence of values, beliefs, and age on intention to travel by a new railway line under construction in northern Sweden." *Transportation Research A: Policy and Practice*, 48, 86–95; Olander, S. and Landin, A. 2008. "A comparative study of factors affecting the external stakeholder management process." *Construction Management and Economics*, 26, 553–561; Yuan, H. 2017. "Achieving sustainability in railway projects: Major stakeholder concerns. *Project Management Journal*, October/November, 115–132.

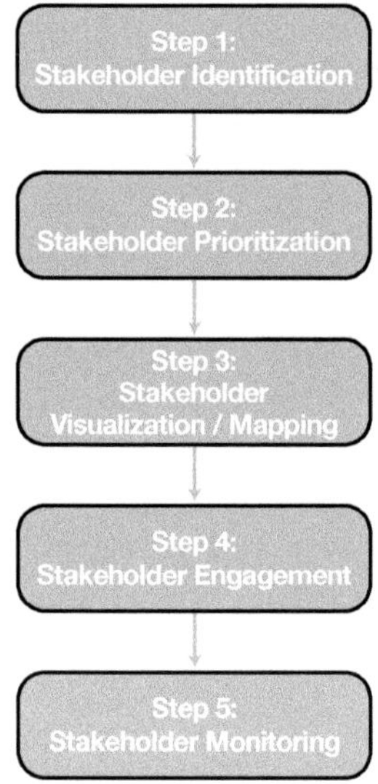

EXHIBIT 4.4—Steps of the Stakeholder Management Process

Next, we consider the various steps in the stakeholder management process. Exhibit 4.4 on page 148 shows the five steps of the process.

Step 1: Stakeholder Identification

A critical first step in the stakeholder management process is **stakeholder identification**, where the main focus is to properly identify stakeholders.[18] A company needs to determine and understand which stakeholders have the ability to affect the organization. In that context, the earlier categorization of primary and secondary stakeholders is helpful. Companies can identify stakeholders based on the stakeholders' ability to directly (primary stakeholders) or indirectly affect (secondary stakeholders).

However, while the primary versus secondary classification may work for most industries, it may not be necessarily useful for all industries. For some industries, the primary versus secondary categorization may pose peculiar challenges. Consider, for example, the construction industry where most projects are undertaken regularly on a contract level for a defined time period. In such instances, the industry has found it more useful to classify stakeholders in four categories based on the nature of the contract. Moodley, Smith and Preece provide some insights for that industry.[19] They argue that those stakeholders that relate to construction firms directly on a contract basis are explicit stakeholders. Examples of explicit stakeholders include shareholders, alliance partners, and other contractors. However, although a construction firm may not have explicit contracts with other groups such as regulators, they still need to abide by the demands of such groups. Such groups form part of the implicit stakeholder group and include regulators, employees of the company and the consumers. Furthermore, construction firms have to contend with groups that may have no contracts but are interested in the company's projects. Such groups are the implicit recognized group and include activists, charities and non-governmental organizations. These groups may not have a contract with the company but may have concerns about the construction project and its impact on the local community. Finally, the construction industry also recognizes "unknowns," which are groups whose interests or influence is unknown. Examples of the "unknown" stakeholders include trade associations, overseas regulators, etc. Exhibit 4.5 shows examples of stakeholders for the construction industry.

As the Exhibit shows, it is important for companies to determine appropriate categorization of their stakeholders. Next, we discuss stakeholder prioritization and mapping.

Step 2: Stakeholder Prioritization

After the company has identified its stakeholders, it needs to assess the attributes of these stakeholders. It is critical for any company to be concerned about the influence any stakeholder can have on its operations. This influence, also termed **salience**, will provide information on the degree to which managers need to give priority to

Explicit stakeholders
Project financiers
Equity holders
Sponsors

Implicit stakeholders
Suppliers
Regulators
Users
Consumers

Implicit recognized stakeholders
Community
Government
Local government
NGOs
Unions

Unknown stakeholders
Trade associations
Overseas government
Public-interest groups

EXHIBIT 4.5—Stakeholder Categorization for the Construction Industry

competing stakeholder demands and claims.[20] The more salient a stakeholder is, the more likely the stakeholder has a potential to affect the company and the more priority the stakeholder needs. How critical is it to properly identify the salience of stakeholders? Consider the following Emerging Market Business Ethics Insight.

According to Mitchell et al., stakeholder salience is based on a combination of the three attributes we discussed earlier.[21] Each combination of attribute strength results in a specific type of stakeholder demanding specific actions from the company. Exhibit 4.7 shows a combination of the various stakeholders' attributes.

The first groups of stakeholders we discuss are latent stakeholders. **Latent** stakeholders are those that possess only one of the three attributes and thus represent low salience. There are three types of latent stakeholders. The **dormant** stakeholders are those that possess power but have no legitimate claims or urgency. For instance, non-governmental organizations such as Greenpeace and others tend to have power. In such cases, it is advisable for companies to carefully monitor these stakeholders. The potential for dormant stakeholders to acquire another attribute is possible and careful attention needs to be paid to such stakeholders. A second form of latent stakeholder is the **discretionary** stakeholder, which has legitimacy but no power or urgency. Examples of discretionary stakeholders are philanthropic organizations such as the Red Cross and others. While a manager may not necessarily engage with such stakeholders,

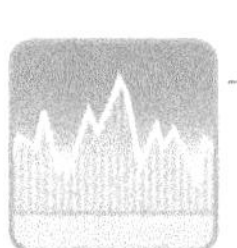

EMERGING MARKET BUSINESS ETHICS INSIGHT

Stakeholder Management at SAB Miller

Stakeholder management is seen as a critical process that helps a multinational build corporate reputation. In that context, the reputation of any company is a function of how its various stakeholders see it. If stakeholders have positive interactions with companies, they will likely develop a more positive perception of reputation. This is even more critical for multinationals like SAB Miller, the world's second largest beer brewer. Companies in the alcohol industry are often negatively perceived because their products have the potential to harm society. As a consequence, it is very critical for such companies to have strong stakeholder management processes in place to ensure that it has a good reputation among its stakeholders.

A recent survey of senior executives at SAB Miller in South Africa reveals some challenges that should be of concern to the brewer. These executives were asked to first identify stakeholders and then rate these stakeholders on importance ranging from 1 (least important) to 10 (most important). Exhibit 4.6 shows the rankings of these executives.

Senior Executive Rankings

Shareholders
Customers
Suppliers
Government
Media
Employees
Competitors
Unions
Police
Social bodies

0 1 2 3 4 5 6 7 8 9 10

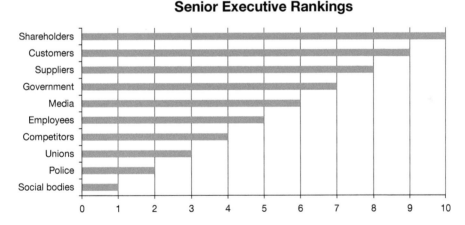

EXHIBIT 4.6—Senior Executive Rankings

Why are the above rankings problematic? Many senior executives at the company felt that shareholders should be the most important stakeholder. Additionally, they did not see the importance of social bodies such as Alcoholics Anonymous, the police or even labor unions. One of the interviewed senior executives argued that accepting that stakeholders such as the police and Alcoholics Anonymous are important would mean accepting the premise that alcohol is a problem in society. However, that senior executive further implied that other alcohol companies could also be blamed.

The implications of this research are that these senior executives need to be trained to understand stakeholder management. Many stakeholders such as Alcoholics Anonymous, the police and the media are important entities that can have significant influence on the company's activities. Social media posts or an article on the company's products consequences can have damaging effects on the company.

Based on Govender, D. and Abratt. R. 2016. "Multiple stakeholder management and corporate reputation in South Africa." *International Studies of Management & Organization*, 46, 235–246.

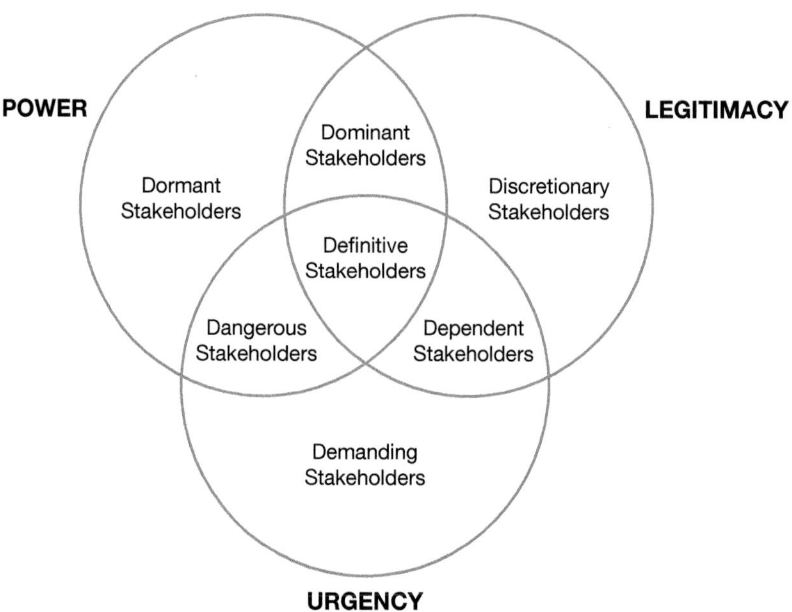

EXHIBIT 4.7—Combination of Stakeholder Attributes

they may do so for strategic reasons to gain goodwill. In the earlier discussed example, Alcoholics Anonymous would be another example of a stakeholder that has legitimacy but no power necessarily. The final form of latent stakeholders is the **demanding** stakeholders. Demanding stakeholders have urgency but do not have power or legitimacy. Companies are well advised to also monitor such stakeholders, as they are likely to generate much attention for their cause.

While the above categories of stakeholders only require monitoring on the part of the company, the next category requires much closer attention and sometimes responses. The **expectant** stakeholders are those that possess two of the attributes discussed earlier. Such stakeholders are considered to have moderate salience.

Similar to latent stakeholders, there are three types of expectant stakeholders. The first type, known as **dominant** stakeholders, represents stakeholders that are both powerful and legitimate. Such stakeholders require formal actions as they are not only legitimate but they also have the ability to exercise power on a company. Examples of dominant stakeholders are employees or investors and most companies have formal structures (e.g., human resource department or investor relations) to tackle such stakeholders. **Dependent** stakeholders are those stakeholders that have urgency and legitimacy. For example, many stakeholders such as restaurant owners or fishermen or community residents are considered as dependent stakeholders in the BP oil spill as discussed in the Preview Business Ethics Insight. Much of BP's response has been to cater to the needs of these stakeholders. Finally, the third form of latent stakeholders is **dangerous** stakeholders. Dangerous stakeholders have power and urgency but no legitimacy. An example of a dangerous stakeholder is the case of the fringe organizations in the Niger Delta involved in oil employee kidnappings. While such groups may not be legitimate, they have been able to get Shell's and the world's attention because of their power and urgency.

The stakeholder that is most salient for any company is the definitive stakeholder. **Definitive stakeholders** have power, urgency and are legitimate. For instance, consider the case of Nestlé and its use of palm oil in its products. Most of the palm oil comes from countries like Indonesia and Malaysia. Greenpeace published a report blaming Sinar Mas, an Indonesian palm oil supplier, for severely contributing to deforestation. Sinar Mas was accused of clearing protected forests to make room for plantations. Furthermore, Greenpeace also released a YouTube video parodying one of Nestlé's KitKat chocolate commercials. In that commercial, an employee opens a KitKat bar and finds an orangutan finger. Greenpeace's commercial was intended to show the connection between the use of palm oil in Nestlé KitKat bars and the resulting deforestation of orangutan habitat.

Nestle's reaction showed disregard for the power, urgency and legitimacy of Greenpeace. When the video was released, Nestlé immediately emailed YouTube administrators to have the video removed because of copyright issues. The video was quickly removed. However, Greenpeace re-posted the video on other video-sharing websites and shared the censorship on Twitter. This resulted in increased attention to the video, which quickly went viral. However, this also initiated discussions on various social networks and some individuals even started discussing the issue on Nestlé's own Facebook page. Someone from the company started responding to the posts with very arrogant and angry rebuttals. This resulted in further consumers getting enraged as the issue was also discussed on Twitter

As such, it is clear that Nestlé failed to recognize Greenpeace as a stakeholder with power (it has access to resources and can force companies to make changes), urgency (it sees deforestation as a critical issue that needs to be addressed) and legitimacy (it is recognized as a credible environmental force). Thus, rather than address Greenpeace's concerns, Nestlé's ridicule of the Greenpeace report resulted in a major public relations nightmare for them. Not all companies react similarly. Consider the following Strategic Business Ethics Insight.

As the Strategic Business Ethics Insight shows, Nokia's actions show that it recognized the European Union as a definitive stakeholder. The European Union has power (through legislations and other actions), legitimacy (it is regarded as a credible stakeholder), and urgency (environmental issues require quick actions). By addressing the European Union's concerns and being proactive, Nokia has considerably strengthened its environmental image and credibility. After the stakeholder salience is determined, the next step is to visualize and map the stakeholders.

STRATEGIC BUSINESS ETHICS INSIGHT

Nokia and the European Union

Mobile communications equipment, such as mobile phones, contributes significantly to electronic scrap worldwide. In fact, the end of 2015 saw around 7 billion mobile phones in the world. This means that there are likely more phones than individuals in the world. Furthermore, companies such as Nokia involved in manufacturing these products have a fairly large environmental impact by making these products. Such companies have had to respond to voluntary calls and legislative actions to minimize the impact of their actions on the environment worldwide. And scrapped mobile phones will become an even larger challenge as many of these phones end in landfills.

The European Union has been very proactive in encouraging and enforcing actions to encourage companies to improve their environmental records. In that context, the Integrated Product Policy was adopted with the aim of reducing the environmental impacts of products at various stages of their lifecycles. More recent legislations such as the Waste Electrical and Electronic Equipment (WEEE) encourage companies to think of as many ways as possible of minimizing environmental harm. For instance, companies are required to manage the end of life of the product by taking back and recycling such equipment.

Nokia is an important player in the mobile phone industry. Rather than wait for new legislations or try to fight new legislations, as is typical of many corporations, Nokia has taken a leadership role. They have worked hard to implement policies aimed at reducing environmental waste as well as minimizing use of toxic chemicals. Furthermore, they even piloted a project bringing the industry and non-governmental organizations to discuss ideas and actions dedicated to environmental issues. This project has resulted in a large group of corporations voluntarily committing to reducing waste and encouraging recycling.

Based on European Union. 2018. "Waste Electrical and Electronic Equipment." http://ec.europa.eu/environment/waste/weee/index_en.htm; Nokia. 2018. www.nokia.com/en_int/about-us/sustainability; Paloviita, A. and Luoma-aho, V. 2010. "Recognizing definitive stakeholders in corporate environmental management." *Management Research Review*, 33, 4, 306–316; Welfens, M.J., Nordmann, J. and Seibt, A. 2016. "Drivers and barriers to return and recycling of mobile phones. Case studies of communication and collection campaigns." *Journal of Cleaner Production*, 132, 108–121.

Step 3: Stakeholder Visualization and Mapping

After the stakeholder salience is determined, the next step is to **visualize and map** the stakeholders. This step is necessary to determine the extent of claims, rights, and expectations stakeholders have and the appropriate response to these needs. Unmet stakeholders needs and expectations can be very disastrous and properly assessing these needs through visualization and mapping can be very helpful.

A simple way to visualize stakeholders to determine appropriate responses is to construct the power and urgency matrix. Rather than use all three attributes discussed earlier, most companies rely on a simpler consideration of only two attributes. Exhibit 4.8 displays the matrix with the corresponding company responses.

As Exhibit 4.8 shows, the attributes of power and urgency are often used to assess stakeholder influence.[22] The consideration of high and low levels of both power and urgency results in a four-quadrant matrix. Each quadrant recommends a specific action for the company. The quadrant that needs the most attention is the quadrant representing stakeholders with high power and high urgency. Such stakeholders need to be managed constantly to ensure that their needs are being met. In contrast, stakeholders with low power and low urgency do not place the same immediate need for concern for the company. Such stakeholders need to be monitored and their needs addressed when necessary. Furthermore, the appropriate response to those stakeholders that have high power and low interest is for the company to keep them satisfied. Finally, those stakeholders that have high urgency but low power should also be monitored and informed regularly of what is being done.

Once the stakeholder positions are visualized, a company can devise more complex matrices to gauge the degree to which they systematically need to respond to stakeholder needs. One example is the Stakeholder Ethical Responsibility Matrix as shown in Exhibit 4.8.[23]

Exhibit 4.8 shows the potential Stakeholder Ethical Responsibility Matrix (SERM) for a shoe manufacturing company such as the German Puma. Along the vertical axis are the many ethical issues that a company like Puma has to face. Along the horizontal axis are the stakeholders that were identified earlier. A company can then assess these various stakeholders based on 1) the importance of the stakeholder based on a rating of 1–5 obtained from the earlier matrix, 2) whether the stakeholder poses an ethical risk (ER), 3) whether the stakeholder will support the company (ES), and finally 4) whether the stakeholder will need to be consulted.

A well-constructed SERM serves many purposes for the company.[24] It should help a company identify the potential for ethical risks. However, it can also help the company identify areas for opportunities to enhance the company's ethics. For example, in the case of Puma, the potential to consult non-governmental organizations to develop better labor practices may be useful in improving ethical reputation. As a company strives to properly manage its stakeholders, the SERM can also help devise better training and policy to address stakeholder needs and expectations. Next, we consider stakeholder engagement.

Stakeholders		Shareholders	Employees	Customers	Unions	Governments	Suppliers	NGOs
Ethical Issues								
Product	Product safety	5ER	5ES	5ER	2	5ER	2	5ER
	Safety of materials	2	5ES	5ER	2	5ER	3	5ER
	Pricing	2	3ES	5ER	2	3	2	3
Environment	Compliance with local laws	5	3ES	3ER	2	5ER	5ES	5ER
	Carbon footprint	5	3ES	4ER	2	5ER	5ES	5ER
	Pollution	2	3ES	5ER	2	4ER	5ES	5ER
	Waste	2	3ES	3ER	2	4ER	5ES	5ER
	Water usage	2	3ES	4ER	2	5ER	5ES	5ER
	Habitat destruction	2	3ES	5ER	2	5ER	5ES	5ER
Labor and Human Rights	Collective bargaining	2	5ES	2	5ER	2	3ER	2
	Forced labor	2	5ES	2	5ER	3	3ER	2
	Child labor	2	5ES	3ER	5ER	5ER	4ER	2
	Gender equality	2	5ES	3	5ER	3	4ER	2
	Fair wage	2	5ES	3	5ER	4ER	5ER	2
Community	Local causes	2	5ES	4ER	2	2	2	2
	Charity	2	5ES	3ER	2	2	2	2
	Employment	3	5ES	2	3ER	2	2	2
	Social and economic impact	2	3ES	2	2	4ER	2	2
Supply chain	Labor practice	2	5ES	3	5ER	3ER	5ES	2
	Use of sustainable materials	2	3ES	3	2	2	5ES	5ER
	Health and safety	2	5ES	3	2	4ER	5ES	5ER
Conduct	Compliance with local codes	5ER	3ES	3	2	5ER	2	2
	Corrupt practices	5ER	3ES	2	2	5ER	2	2
	Competitive practices	5ER	4ES	2	2	5ER	2	2
Suppliers	Use of sweatshops	2	5ES	3	5ER	5ER	5ES	5ER
	Labor exploitation	2	5ES	3	5ER	5ER	5ES	5ER
	Working conditions	2	5ES	3	5ER	5ER	5ES	5ER

KEY
Ranking 1 to 5 (Importance to stakeholder)
ER: Ethical risk from stakeholder
ES: Ethical support from stakeholder

EXHIBIT 4.8—Stakeholder Ethical Responsibility Matrix for Puma

Step 4: Stakeholder Engagement

Stakeholders often have different claims, rights and expectations of organizations. As we saw in many instances earlier, such demands often influence a company's operations. In extreme cases, such stakeholder demands can even pose severe threats to a company's survival. However, companies that engage their stakeholders are less likely to experience such threats. The next step in the stakeholder management process is **stakeholder engagement**. Stakeholder engagement refers to the deliberate attempt of a company to actively seek its stakeholders' inputs to better deal with their needs and also improve their operations. As we saw in the case of stakeholder management in Sweden, the project that actively engaged key stakeholders such as the media and the public were the ones that were perceived more positively.

According to Chinyio and Akintoye, companies that engage their shareholders enjoy significant advantages.[25] For instance, stakeholder management systems can provide companies with a broad idea of potential stakeholder problematic areas. However, by engaging these stakeholders, a company can find ways to alleviate such problems. Companies discover that stakeholder management not only develops a better ability for them to relate to their stakeholders but also results in significant reputational advantages. Such efforts help the company develop a better public and community image.

Recent research also underlies the low levels of trust the public generally have in companies.[26] This problem is relevant for companies worldwide. Low levels of trust may be driven by the perception that companies have low levels of ethics. As such, stakeholder engagement may also be the means by which companies build trust. By engaging with the various stakeholders, companies are afforded with the opportunity to learn about the various stakeholder needs. This can then help the company satisfy such needs to build trust. Stronger trust can also be a source of competitive advantage.

Exhibit 4.9 lists the many advantages companies can reap from stakeholder engagement.

To develop an appropriate stakeholder management program, any company must actively engage with its stakeholders. The earlier steps discussed should provide

Advantages of Stakeholder Engagement
• Increased relationships with stakeholders
• Increase in process and organizational efficiency
• Stronger market positioning
• Reduced conflict with stakeholders and smaller risk of getting sued
• Better service to customers and other end-users
• Increased ability to identify new business potential
• Better ability to forecast future stakeholder demands
• Better organizational learning

EXHIBIT 4.9—Advantages of Stakeholder Engagement

important information about who the key stakeholders are. Depending on the company's mission and vision, the company should then devise an appropriate system to develop an ongoing dialogue with these stakeholders. Such systems can occur through a variety of methods and media. Consider the following Ethics Sustainability Insight.

As the Ethics Sustainability Insight shows, stakeholder engagement involves deliberate efforts on a company's part to involve stakeholders in uncovering problematic

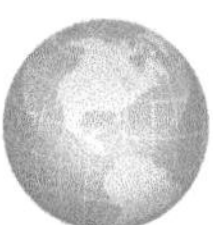

ETHICS SUSTAINABILITY INSIGHT

Stakeholder Management Process in New Zealand

Several New Zealand companies have developed different stakeholder management approaches to address specific needs. Consider the case of Vodafone. It typically runs stakeholder engagement workshops to engage with its stakeholders. However, most recently, it has been concerned about the role of telecommunications in a more sustainable future for New Zealand. To do so, it has invited its key stakeholders and organized their sessions around key questions such as what a sustainable New Zealand looks like, what the barriers to such a future are, and what telecommunications companies can do to overcome such barriers. This exercise has the potential not only to reveal new business opportunities to Vodafone but also to engage stakeholders in such discussions.

Urgent Courier is New Zealand's leading delivery services company. Recently, it engaged in a number of stakeholder engagement exercises as it continues its sustainability efforts. One of the most surprising results was that one of the biggest problem areas for its business was the earnings of its contracted drivers. They found that although drivers are extremely critical for their business, these drivers were not earning enough for them to attract and retain the best. Urgent Courier then embarked on a new pricing strategy to ensure that its prices would provide better earnings to its drivers while also remaining competitive. Urgent Couriers has now received workplace awards in an industry that is not often concerned about its drivers.

Another area that Urgent Couriers has worked on is its carbon emissions. Through stakeholder engagement, it has emphasized the importance of sustainability to its contractors and all other major stakeholders. Urgent Courier is now one of New Zealand's only delivery service that is carbon neutral. They were able to achieve this goal by encouraging contractors to use only low-emission vehicles. More than 75% of their fleet are now low-emission vehicles. They also use GPS technology to encourage their contractors to use the most efficient routes possible.

Based on Brown, R. 2010. "Engaging your stakeholders." *NZ Business*, July, 24, 6; Urgent Couriers. 2018. www.urgent.co.nz/Public/.

issues and opportunities in running the company. What are some of the key success factors in developing stakeholder management systems? Chinyio and Akintoye provide some insight in the process.[27] They argue that successful stakeholder engagement systems should be systematic, involve top-level support, and should be proactive. In practice, effective stakeholder engagement systems make heavy use of frequent and effective communication with stakeholders through meetings, workshops, and other communication methods. Effective stakeholder management systems also rely heavily on use of people skills to work with stakeholders.

Step 5: Stakeholder Monitoring

The final step in the stakeholder management process is that of **stakeholder monitoring**. At this stage, a company is interested in finding out how stakeholders are responding to stakeholder management issues and if further actions are necessary. A company can also determine the effectiveness of its communication strategies to gauge whether the appropriate message is being delivered to stakeholders.

An effective way to monitor stakeholders is to have regular meetings with critical stakeholders. Through the meetings, a company can determine whether stakeholder needs are continuously being met. Furthermore, a company can continue communicating its efforts to address stakeholder concerns. Finally, these meetings can reveal other new problematic areas where new stakeholders are identified and/or new visualization and prioritization is needed.

Consider the case of the rail track construction project in Sweden discussed earlier in this chapter. The Malmö project was extremely successful because the construction company continuously monitored its stakeholders (the public and the media) and devised ways to proactively address their needs. This regular monitoring showed stakeholders that their views are valued. Through these efforts, the construction company was able to change these stakeholders' perceptions and encourage them to embrace the project. In contrast, the Lund project was conducted without any stakeholder input or monitoring. It is therefore not surprising to find that this project met with significant resistance and delays.

STAKEHOLDER IMPORTANCE WORLDWIDE

Most experts agree that the key to stakeholder management is to properly assess stakeholder needs and find appropriate ways to satisfy these needs. However, it may not always be possible for a company to satisfy all stakeholder needs. In such cases, it becomes more important to balance needs and to satisfy those needs that are most critical to the company's survival. Many companies develop missions and visions that suggest that some stakeholders are more critical than others. For instance, Starbucks considers its employees as important, if not more important, than customers.

Which stakeholders are considered most important? In this final section, we examine how stakeholders are viewed worldwide.

In a recent piece in the *Harvard Business Review*, Martin traces the evolution of stakeholder importance over time in the U.S. Martin argues that the U.S. business environment saw the birth of managerial capitalism around 1932.[28] Instead of having owner-CEOs run their companies, experts at the time suggested that there should be a separation between owners and managers. However, in 1976, another influential article suggested that owners were getting duped by managers. In "Theory of the firm: Managerial behavior, agency costs and ownership structure," Jensen and Meckling argued that managers were running companies for their own financial interest. Instead, Jensen and Meckling suggested that managers should run companies by focusing on the needs of shareholders.[29] This led to the age of shareholder capitalism where shareholder needs became the most important focus of any company.

Is this preference for shareholders warranted? Martin rightly argues that a focus on shareholders may not always be beneficial for the company.[30] He argues that shareholder value maximization is not always within the control of managers. Managers may find ways to increase the value of shares by raising expectations about the future performance of the company. However, such expectations inevitably decline as it is impossible to continuously increase such expectations. In the light of such reality, managers may often resort to short-term and other misguided strategies to keep shareholder expectations up. Unfortunately, this goal of putting shareholders first may end up hurting the firm. In the end, this focus on the short term ends up hurting the long-term viability of the firm while also damaging the overall economy of a society.[31]

Martin thus argues that a better way to benefit the company and shareholders is to put customers first.[32] By focusing on customer value, managers become free to manage and grow the business rather than manage shareholder expectations. Examples of companies such as Procter & Gamble and Johnson & Johnson are all provided to support this notion. Furthermore, even Unilever, mentioned earlier in this chapter, is known for its focus on customers. In fact, some companies have taken this focus on customers even further. Consider the following Business Ethics Insight.

BUSINESS ETHICS INSIGHT

Focusing on Emerging Markets' Poor Customer Needs

While some companies focus on putting customers first, other companies are taking this focus to the next level. Companies such as Nokia, Tata and Unilever are all taking into consideration the needs of poor customers in emerging markets. Emerging markets represent tremendous potential and even poor customers are expected to eventually reach the middle class.

Consider some of the products that have been targeted for this segment. Nokia, for example, has developed a cheap handset that includes a flashlight (because of frequent power interruptions), multiple phone books to accommodate several users, and menus in different languages. Tata has developed a water filter that uses rice husks to purify the water. Because of the need for water purification, this very low-tech device can provide bacteria-free water to users. Finally, consider the case of General Electric, which has developed a portable electrocardiogram machine that can run on both batteries and power. This small device is very useful for the Indian market, where heart disease is prevalent and most patients cannot afford the costs associated with traditional electrocardiogram machines. In another example, GE discovered that infant mortality in India is high because incubators cost $2,000 and many hospitals cannot afford such incubators. When it found that a social enterprise named Embrace had created a $200 incubator, it partnered with the company to distribute the product.

Unilever's efforts with rural customers provide another example of its engagement with this segment. Through its market research in Pakistan, Unilever found that women in rural areas were interested in beauty products without much access to such products. It launched the Guddi Bajis (or good sisters) program and trained hundreds of village women on how to apply makeup, shampoo hair and sell other Unilever products. Through these efforts, Unilever has been able to provide rural consumers access to a desired product. However, this effort has also provided money-making opportunities to women who can work from home. As another example, in Thailand, Unilver has developed the Platinum store to give rural consumers an urban shopping feeling. It helped local stores develop displays and other services to provide a more varied and pleasant experience to rural consumers while also requiring these stores to carry its own products. Additionally, it also provided other services such as community washing machines. Such efforts have endeared the company to a segment that is generally ignored by multinationals.

This focus on poor customers is termed "frugal innovation." Rather than add new features to products, companies are working backwards to produce robust products that can satisfy customer demands.

Based on *The Economist*. 2010. "First break all of the rules." A special report on innovation in emerging markets. April 17, 6–8; Mahajan, V. 2016. "How Unilever reaches rural consumers in emerging markets." *Harvard Business Review*, December 14, 2–6; Pfitzer, M., Bockstette, V. and Stamp, M. 2013. "Innovating for shared value." *Harvard Business Review*, September, 100–107.

Although the above provides further proof of the importance of customers as stakeholders, this view is not necessarily shared by all societies. Although there are no recent studies that have investigated stakeholder preference worldwide, many societies are now embracing sustainability as the most important goal. Because of global warming and other potentially negative effects of companies on the environment, companies are also becoming more proactive and adopting corporate sustainability as a key goal. Other companies such as TOMS, Patagonia etc. have made it a point to integrate social purpose in their mission and the reason for existence. Such companies see their main purpose as providing products that bring societal benefits. For instance, TOMS is well known as the company that will donate a pair of shoes to the needy for every pair that is sold in developed markets.

While the environment or societal purpose may potentially be the most important stakeholder, it is necessary to also note that that importance varies for companies. Depending on their mission, some companies will consider key stakeholders such as customers, employees and the environment as equally important. The major lesson in this chapter therefore is that, no matter which stakeholder or stakeholders a company holds as most important, these stakeholders need to be managed. The various steps discussed in this chapter should provide you with the many things companies can do to manage and engage with their stakeholders.

CHAPTER SUMMARY

In this chapter, you learned about the many key issues facing companies as they deal with stakeholders. Stakeholders are groups or individuals that can affect or be influenced by a company's goals. You read about the various classifications of stakeholders such as the primary and secondary classifications. You also learned that both secondary and primary stakeholders can have important influences on companies.

In the second part of the chapter, you learned about stakeholder attributes. You read about three important attributes; namely, power (the degree to which stakeholders can exert pressure on a company), legitimacy (the degree to which a stakeholder's needs are consistent with societal values and beliefs) and urgency (the degree to which stakeholder needs have to be prioritized). Each attribute's importance to the company was discussed and practical examples were provided.

An important message in this chapter is that stakeholders need to be managed. In the third section, key aspects of the stakeholder management process were discussed. The first step expanded on the adequate identification of stakeholders by discussing other available categorizations. In this step, the company needed to properly identify all of the stakeholders that have the potential to influence or be influenced. In the second step, the attributes of stakeholders discussed earlier could then be combined to provide the company with stakeholder prioritization. In other words, the combination of attributes revealed which stakeholders need to be catered to immediately and which other ones can receive attention later. The third step, namely stakeholder visualization and mapping, involved listing all identified stakeholders and corresponding issues associated with the stakeholder. The concept of the Stakeholder Ethical Responsibility Matrix was discussed in that context. In the fourth step, stakeholder engagement, you learned about the many efforts companies expend to involve their stakeholders in the company's operations and survival. By engaging stakeholders, a company can proactively gauge stakeholder needs and assess such needs before they become problematic. Finally, in the fifth and final step, a monitoring system was put in place to assess the degree of success of the stakeholder management program.

In the final part of the chapter, you read about stakeholder preferences worldwide. You learned about the importance of customers as the most important stakeholder. However, you also learned that customers may not be viewed as the most important stakeholder worldwide. Many examples discussed in the chapter point to the environment. Nevertheless, the important lesson of the chapter is that stakeholders need to be adequately managed.

NOTES

1 Reckdahl, K. 2015. "Slimed: BP's forgotten victims." *The Nation*, May 4, 24–29.
2 Vaast, E., Safadi, H., Lapointe, L. & Negoita, B. 2017. "Social media affordances for collective action: An examination of microblogging use during the Gulf of Mexico oil spill." *MIS Quarterly*, 41, 1179–1205.
3 Freeman, R.E. 1984. *Strategic management: A stakeholder approach*. Boston, MA: Pitman, p. 3.
4 Freeman, *Strategic management*.
5 Orlitzy, M., Schmidt, F. & Rynes, S.L. 2003. "Corporate social and financial performance: A meta-analysis." *Organization Studies*, 24, 403–441.
6 Hillman, A.J. & Keim, G.D. 2001. "Stakeholder value, stakeholder management, and social issues: What's the bottom line?" *Strategic Management Journal*, 22, 2, 125–139.
7 Choi, J. & Wang, H. 2009. "Stakeholder relations and the persistence of corporate financial performance." *Strategic Management Journal*, 30, 895–907.
8 Ako, R.T., Obokoh, L.O. & Okonmah, P. 2009. "Forging peaceful relationships between oil companies and host-communities in Nigeria's Delta region." *Journal of Enterprising Communities: People and Practice in the Global Economy*, 3, 2, 205–216.
9 Mitchell, R., Agle, B. & Wood, D.J. 1997. "Toward a theory of stakeholder identification and salience: Defining the principle of who and what really counts." *Academy of Management Review*, 22, 4, 853–886.
10 Mitchell et al., "Toward a theory of stakeholder identification and salience."
11 Ako, R.T., Obokoh, L.O. & Okonmah, P. 2009. "Forging peaceful relationships between oil companies and host-communities in Nigeria's Delta region." *Journal of Enterprising Communities: People and Practice in the Global Economy*, 3, 2, 205–216.
12 Armenakis, A. & Wigand, J. 2010. "Stakeholder actions and their impact on the organizational cultures of two tobacco companies." *Business and Society Review*, 115, 2, 147–171.
13 Thorne, D.M., Ferrell, O.C. & Ferrell, L. 2010. *Business and society. A strategic approach to social responsibility*. Boston, MA: Houghton Mifflin.
14 Sonpar, K., Pazzaglia, F. & Kornijenko, J. 2010. "The paradox and constraints of legitimacy." *Journal of Business Ethics*, 95, 1–21.
15 Sonpar et al., "The paradox and constraints of legitimacy."
16 Fassin, Y. 2009. "Inconsistencies in activists' behaviours and the ethics of NGOs." *Journal of Business Ethics*, 90, 503–521.
17 Choi & Wang, "Stakeholder relations."
18 Perrault, E. 2017. "A 'names-and-faces approach' to stakeholder identification and salience: A matter of status." *Journal of Business Ethics*, 146, 25–38.
19 Moodley, K., Smith, N. & Preece, C. 2008. "Stakeholder matrix for ethical relationships in the construction industry." *Construction Management and Economics*, 26, 625–632.
20 Mitchell et al., "Toward a theory of stakeholder identification and salience."
21 Mitchell et al., "Toward a theory of stakeholder identification and salience."
22 Chinyio, E. & Akintoye, A. 2008. "Practical approaches for engaging stakeholders: Findings from the U.K." *Construction Management and Economics*, 26, 591–599.

23 Moodley et al., "Stakeholder matrix for ethical relationships in the construction industry."
24 Moodley et al., "Stakeholder matrix for ethical relationships in the construction industry."
25 Chinyio & Akintoye, "Practical approaches for engaging stakeholders."
26 Pirson, M., Martin, K. & Parmar, B. 2017. "Formation of stakeholder trust in business and the role of personal values." *Journal of Business Ethics*, 145, 1–20.
27 Chinyio & Akintoye, "Practical approaches for engaging stakeholders."
28 Martin, R. 2010. "The age of customer capitalism." *Harvard Business Review*, January, 58–66.
29 Jensen, Michael C. & Meckling, William H. 1976. "Theory of the firm: Managerial behavior, agency costs and ownership structure." *Journal of Financial Economics*, 3, 4.
30 Martin, "The age of customer capitalism."
31 Ignatius, A. 2017. "Are we giving shareholders too much power?" *Harvard Business Review*, May–June, 8.
32 Martin, "The age of customer capitalism."

KEY TERMS

Coercive power: use of force, violence, or other restraint to force a company to accommodate or respond to their needs.
Dangerous stakeholders: have power and urgency but no legitimacy.
Definitive stakeholders: have power, urgency, and are legitimate.
Demanding stakeholders: have urgency but do not have power or legitimacy.
Dependent stakeholders: are those stakeholders that have urgency and legitimacy.
Discretionary stakeholder: stakeholder that has legitimacy but no power or urgency.
Dominant stakeholders: represents stakeholders that are both powerful and legitimate.
Dormant stakeholders: stakeholders that possess power but have no legitimate claims or urgency.
Expectant stakeholders: are those that possess two of the attributes.
Latent stakeholders: are those that possess only one of the three attributes and thus represent low salience.
Legitimacy: company conducts itself in such a way that is consistent with widely held values and beliefs.
Market stakeholders: entities that have economic relationships with the company as the latter achieves its mission.
Nonmarket stakeholders: entities that have a direct impact on companies, although they do not have direct economic transactions with the company.
Normative power: refers to the use of symbolic and other resources to force a company to accommodate stakeholder needs.
Primary stakeholders: stakeholders directly linked to a company's survival and are either impacted by or impact companies directly.
Salience: influence any stakeholder can have on a company's operations.
Secondary stakeholders: stakeholders that tend to be less directly linked to the company's survival and include the media, trade associations, and special-interest groups.
Stakeholder: any group or individual that can affect or is affected by the achievement of an organization's objectives.

Stakeholder engagement: deliberate attempt of a company to actively seek its stakeholders' inputs to better deal with their needs and also improve their operations.

Stakeholder identification: main focus is to properly identify stakeholders.

Stakeholder management: refers to the deliberate and purposeful process a company has devised to work with its stakeholders.

Stakeholder monitoring: determines how stakeholders are responding to stakeholder management issues and if further actions are necessary.

Stakeholder power: ability of a stakeholder to exert pressures to force a company to make changes to accommodate such pressures.

Urgency: refers to the degree to which a company needs to respond to stakeholder needs.

Utilitarian power: refers to the use of financial or other monetary means to force a company to accommodate a particular stakeholder need.

Visualizing and mapping stakeholders: necessary step to determine the extent of claims, rights and expectations stakeholders have and the appropriate response to these needs.

DISCUSSION QUESTIONS

1. What are stakeholders? Why do stakeholders matter to companies?
2. What are primary stakeholders? How are primary stakeholders different from secondary stakeholders? Discuss your answer with examples.
3. What are the three types of stakeholder attributes? Illustrate your answer with one example for each stakeholder attribute.
4. What are the three different types of stakeholder power? How do these forms of power impact a company differently?
5. Compare and contrast stakeholder legitimacy and stakeholder urgency.
6. Briefly discuss the five steps of the stakeholder management process. Illustrate each step with examples.
7. What is stakeholder prioritization? How can companies identify which stakeholders need to be attended to quickly?
8. What are latent stakeholders? How are they different from expectant stakeholders?
9. What is stakeholder engagement? What are the steps companies can take to engage their stakeholders?
10. What is stakeholder monitoring? What steps can companies take to monitor their stakeholders?

INTERNET ACTIVITY

1. Go to the Unilever website: www.unilever.com.
2. Review the company's vision and goals. Discuss their purposes and principles and how they relate to the issues discussed in this chapter.
3. What do you learn about who Unilever's most important stakeholders are?
4. Describe in detail each of Unilever's important stakeholders. How do they address the needs of each stakeholder?
5. What are some of the codes that Unilever abides by as they deal with suppliers?

For more Internet Activities and resources, please visit the Companion Website at www.routledge.com/cw/parboteeah.

WHAT WOULD YOU DO?

Plant Closing in Wisconsin

You are the owner of a plant producing automotive parts in a small town in Wisconsin. Your plant is the main employer of the small town. You have lived in the town for your whole life. Your father operated the plant until you took over. Your family is well established in the town. You are involved in many charities in the town. Your children also attend the local schools.

The recent economic downturn has been very disastrous for your company, as you have suffered a significant decline in revenues. Despite these losses, you have not yet terminated any employee. You have been able to survive mostly because of your strong relationships with your customers. You are very reliable and have operated a very ethical company and most customers have stuck with you.

When you showed up to your office today, your assistant mentioned that the Chief Executive Officer of a German competitor called you. You call him back and he proposes to buy your plant for a very attractive price. However, you also learn that, if you sell, the German company will likely try to consolidate operations with another plant they bought in Pennsylvania. You find that all of your employees will be offered the option to move to the Pennsylvanian plant.

What would you do? Do you go ahead with the sale? Who is affected by such sale? How do you take into consideration the impact of your actions on the town if you sell?

BRIEF CASE: BUSINESS ETHICS INSIGHT

Taiwan's Sun Moon Lake

Taiwan's Sun Moon Lake is considered one of Taiwan's vacation spots. The lake, which originated as a Japanese era reservoir, is surrounded by beautiful mountain scenery. It is a preferred spot for both local and foreign tourists. The lake is also popular with the Chinese, as it is described in Chinese literature. Furthermore, the lake acquired even more mystique as legal barriers prevented the Chinese from visiting the lake. Now that such barriers are slowly being removed, there is strong desire for Chinese tourists to visit the lake as its beauty is perceived as unmatched on the Chinese mainland.

Recent indicators suggest that the popularity of Sun Moon Lake is indeed growing. For instance, the Sun Moon Lake International Fireworks Festival that was started in 2003 now draws hordes of people interested in both music and fireworks. Furthermore, recent official figures show that the number of Chinese tourists during the first week of October (a holiday to celebrate China's national day) of 2010 nearly doubled compared to the previous year. The Taiwanese government is continuing its sustained effort to advertise the lake in many nearby Asian countries such as South Korea and Japan.

However, not everyone is happy with the growing popularity of Sun Moon Lake. Many locals and environmentalists suspect that the continuing development will spoil the lake's natural beauty. Many hotels are being built at a very quick pace in anticipation of more affluent Chinese making visits to the lake. However, such construction is taking place without much planning. In fact, one of the hotels under construction will be 30 floors high, greatly exceeding the seven-floor limit. Furthermore, it is anticipated that more hotels will be built.

Locals are thus worried that such a construction boom will affect the region environmentally. The influx of tourists has already started to create traffic jams and other ills associated with more people. However, locals are also very worried that the growth of hotels and customers will cause increased pollution to the lake. With more tourists, local tourism officials believe that the lake water quality may go down. In 2007, four hotels were fined for improper waste treatment. However, as more hotels go up, it becomes very unlikely that local officials will still be able to properly manage the environmental impact of these hotels.

Sun Moon Lake officials thus have to properly manage the growth of the region. While increased tourism will bring in additional profits (it is estimated that tourists spent an average of $232 per day during the first "golden" week of October 2010), the impact on the environment will also need to be assessed.

Based on Anonymous. 2010. "Chinese visitors to Taiwan double in first October Week." *Asia Pulse*, October 8; *Business Wire*, 2010. "Sun Moon Lake International Fireworks music festival." *Business Wire*, August 19; Jennings, R. 2008. "Tourism brightens, darkens Taiwan's Sun Moon Lake." *Reuters*, online edition.

BRIEF CASE QUESTIONS

1. Who are the primary stakeholders in this case? Identify secondary stakeholders.
2. Who are most affected by the changes at Sun Moon Lake? How are they affected?
3. How would you compare the benefits of higher tourism profits with the environmental impact of increased tourism? What would you do if you were a local tourism official at Sun Moon Lake?
4. Assume that you are hired as a consultant by a hotel chain interested in building a hotel at Sun Moon Lake. What would you advise them? Describe the methodology you will use to provide advice.

LONG CASE: BUSINESS ETHICS

STARBUCKS CORPORATION (A)

Tax Avoidance Controversies in the United Kingdom

"Starbucks' coffee menu famously baffles some people. In Britain, it's their accounts that are confusing. Starbucks has been telling investors the business was profitable, even as it consistently reported losses." [1]

Introduction

On October 15, 2012, Reuters released a special report titled "*How Starbucks avoids UK Taxes.*" The investigative reporters at Reuters compared legal filings in the English company register, *Companies House*, with Starbucks' own group reports and 46 transcripts of conference calls with investors and analysts over a 12 year period. What they turned up were stark differences in how Starbucks viewed its UK subsidiary internally and how it was portrayed to the UK government, specifically the tax authority, Her Majesty's Revenue and Customs.

Starbucks officials internally gushed praise on their UK business unit. On multiple occasions it was referred to as "profitable" and a model for other regions to follow. In November 2007, the Chief Operating Officer Martin Coles told analysts that the UK unit's profits were funding Starbucks' expansion in other overseas markets. However, the unit's accounts showed a tenth consecutive annual loss. The Reuters report went on to cite multiple instances when Starbucks provided positive news to analysts yet showed operating losses to the UK government:

"For 2008, Starbucks filed a 26 million pounds loss in the UK. Yet CEO Schultz told an analysts' call that the UK business had been so successful he planned to take the lessons he had learnt there and apply them to the company's largest market—the United States. He also promoted Cliff Burrows, former head of the UK and Europe, to head the U.S. business."[2]

As soon as the newspaper hit newsstands and the Reuters website, there was an immediate public and political outcry. UK Uncut, an activist organization, planned boycotts and sit-ins. Several Members of Parliament (MPs) voiced outrage and quickly summoned Starbucks Chief Financial Officer Troy Alstead to testify before committee.

Starbucks History and Image

Starbucks Corporation

In 1971, Starbucks was founded in Seattle as a coffee bean roaster and retailer. The location sold high-quality coffee beans and equipment. The company started serving espresso coffee, the first drink that Starbucks sold, in 1986. The next year, the original owners sold the fledgling chain to former employee and current CEO Howard Schultz, who began an aggressive expansion campaign. Since 1986, the company has opened, on average, two stores per day.

Starbucks performed its Initial Public Offering in June 1992. At the time the company owned or licensed 140 outlets and booked annual revenue of $75 million. In 2012, the total number of stores in operation numbered more than 18,000 and were spread over 60 countries.

For the fiscal year, Starbucks' consolidated revenues reached a record $13.3 billion. Company-operated stores accounted for 79 percent of total net revenues during the 2012 fiscal year.[3]

Coffee is no longer the only item sold through Starbucks locations. This excerpt from the 2012 10-K filing with the United States Securities and Exchange Commission summarizes the extent of their offerings:

"Starbucks stores offer a choice of coffee and tea beverages, distinctively packaged roasted whole bean and ground coffees, a variety of premium single serve products, juices and bottled water. Starbucks stores also offer an assortment of fresh food offerings, including selections focusing on high-quality ingredients, nutritional value and great flavor. A focused selection of beverage-making equipment and accessories are also sold in our stores."[4]

Starbucks has also spun off a unique tea bar concept called Teavana Fine Teas and Tea Bar. They are expanding their juice line, Evolution Fresh, with an aggressive growth strategy with the goal of further increasing their market share in the super-premium juice category. The company has also begun exploring handcrafted carbonated beverages to offer for sale in its existing locations.

Howard Schultz

Howard Schultz is the Chairman, President, and Chief Executive Officer of Starbucks. Before joining the company he was the general manager for a Swedish drip coffee maker manufacturer called Hammarplast.[5] Starbucks was a client of Hammarplast and Schultz was impressed by the company's knowledge of coffee and the amount of business that they were conducting, even as a small outfit. A couple of years after his first encounter with Starbucks, Schultz joined the company in 1983 as the Director of Marketing.

While visiting Milan on a buying trip, Schultz was struck by the presence of a coffee bar on virtually every street corner. Not only were they serving countless espresso drinks, they also acted as meeting places or public squares, providing a sense of community and belongingness. He took this newfound knowledge back with him and tried to convince the owners to start offering hot brewed beverages in addition to the coffee beans and leaf teas that they already offered. The owners resisted and, after a brief stint trying to start his own coffee company, Schultz bought the retail unit of Starbucks for $3.8 million.[6]

Social Responsibility

Howard Schultz is considered the "soul" of the company. His passion and business savvy have made the company into what it is today. He also brought to the company "a distinctive set of values that has and continually shapes how the company engages their customers, their employees, and the communities where they do business."[7] The company continually monitors with social responsibility and has . . .

> ". . . *been building a company with a conscience for more than four decades, intent on the fair and humane treatment of our people as well as the communities where we do business, and the global environment we all share.*"
>
> – CEO Howard Schultz, 2012 Global Responsibility Report Message[8]

Starbucks provides full benefits for all of its employees, which it refers to as "partners." They also have a goal: All of their coffee will be "ethically sourced" by 2015. The cornerstone of this approach is Coffee and Farmer Equity (C.A.F.E.) Practices, "a comprehensive coffee buying program that ensures coffee quality while promoting social, economic and environmental standards." Through 2012, the company purchased 93 percent of its coffee in this manner.[9]

International Taxation

Typical International Tax Methods

Most governments tax individuals and/or corporations on income or profits, respectively. These taxes are used to pay for everything from national defense and transportation infrastructure to food stamps and farm subsidies. These taxation systems vary widely by government and there are few broad, general rules. However, it is possible to understand the general corporate tax environment by understanding a few choices that each government must make when it comes to its corporate tax policy.

Nations usually choose between two systems: territorial or residential. In a territorial system, only the income from a source inside the country is taxed. For example, an American company with locations in Canada would only have to pay Canadian taxes on the portion of sales that are within Canadian borders. In a residential system, the residents of a country are taxed on their worldwide income, not just local income. The residential system is geared more toward personal income tax and does not affect corporations.

Corporate tax rates also vary widely by country. Every country has different funding needs based on their size, the extent to which the government operates social welfare programs, and numerous other factors. Those looking to increase investment within their borders may offer lower tax rates and those with large infrastructures to maintain may have higher tax rates. These varied tax rates provide an unintended incentive for companies to attempt to transfer revenues and profits from countries with higher tax rates to those with lower tax rates, thereby retaining more net income for shareholders and managers.

Several tax avoidance strategies exist to achieve such goals. Some companies charge subsidiaries for the use of "intellectual property" such as the brand name and their business practices. These types of arrangements typically charge 4% of revenue. Other companies that are vertically integrated upstream and downstream charge units in high tax jurisdictions higher prices in order to move money to lower-taxed countries. Transfer-pricing regulations allow this practice and companies can then allocate profits to high-charging subsidiaries in low tax rate areas.

Starbucks Money Trail

Starbucks employs various legal methods in order to minimize their tax liability within the UK. The corporate tax rate in the UK in 2011 was 26%. Each step along the money trail is designed so that in the end, the Starbucks subsidiary in the UK shows no profits on paper. This effectively reduces their tax bill in that jurisdiction to zero even though that market may be very profitable for them.

The Starbucks subsidiary in the UK is heavily debt-financed. Even for a company with positive net cash flows, the UK subsidiary still has large amounts of debt and large interest bills. All of these loans are from the Starbucks headquarters in Seattle. The interest on these loans is higher than the interest rate on the average Starbucks bond, at the LIBOR rate plus 4% versus the LIBOR rate plus 1.3%. While this moves profits to the United States where there is a relatively high tax rate, the interest stays within the company instead of being paid out to banks or investors who purchase their bonds.

Starbucks also charges the UK unit a royalty and licensing fee of 6%. This is higher than the 4% that a typical arrangement of this sort would charge. Starbucks claims that it has some independent licensees who also pay 6%, so they are within their legal right to charge their own subsidiary the higher rate, as well.[10]

The final method that Starbucks employs is how it pays for its main product and largest source of revenue: coffee. A Starbucks entity is set up in Switzerland which is responsible for all coffee bean purchases. The Switzerland location then has those beans sent to roasters throughout Europe, which turn the raw beans into product suitable for making coffee products. The beans are then sold to the UK Starbucks with a 20% markup. The beans never physically enter Switzerland. Switzerland has an approximate 5% corporate tax rate on profits tied to international trade in commodities, a category under which coffee falls.[11]

Coffee Shop Market

Starbucks' growth plan and business model have been widely successful, allowing it to become the second largest restaurant chain globally after McDonald's with a market capitalization of $40 billion.[12] Starbucks' 2012 SEC annual filings reports revenues of $13.3 billion, with revenues in the EMEA region, including the United Kingdom, of $1.14 billion. The EMEA revenues represent a 9% growth over the previous fiscal year. Within the United Kingdom specifically, the coffee shop market has remained strong despite a recession. A 2009 study from Allegra Strategies shows that the coffee shop market in the UK has seen 15 consecutive years of either flat sales or growth, with the market reaching £2 billion in consumer spending in 2012.[13]

Within the United Kingdom, Starbucks faces a fierce competitor in Costa Coffee. Founded in London in 1971, Costa Coffee has grown from a wholesale roasted coffee supplier to become the UK's largest coffee chain, supplanting Starbucks in 2010.[14] In 2012, Costa saw an increase in profits of nearly 30%, reaching £90.1 million. In contrast to Starbucks, Costa paid a tax bill of £15 million during the 2011–12 reporting period. While the UK coffee bar market appears strong and close competitor Costa Coffee reports growing profits, Starbucks claims that it is not generating profits within the UK. Global CFO Troy Alstead reports that Starbucks have recorded profits in only three years since they entered the UK in 1998 and that 25% of their UK stores run at a loss.[15] High rents and space costs within UK cities were proposed as reasons for Starbucks' failure to generate profits; however, Costa Coffee has been able to achieve an operating margin of 14.3% with a similar retail footprint and comparable labor costs.[16] Chief executive of Costa Coffee, Andy Harrison, appeared to enjoy Starbucks' tax avoidance controversy, commenting "Costa has been the UK's favourite coffee shop for quite some time and we remain the taxman's favourite coffee shop, too."[17]

HMRC, Parliament & Public Opinion

The taxman within the United Kingdom is Her Majesty's Revenue and Customs (HMRC), which is responsible for the collection of both personal and corporate income taxes, among other duties. Formed in 2005 as a merger of two previous tax entities, HMRC outlined its purpose and vision by stating "We make sure that the money is available to fund the UK's public services" and "We will close the tax gap, our customers will feel that the tax system is simple for them and even-handed, and we will be seen as a highly professional organisation."[18] In the HMRC charter, it is further laid out that the public can expect HMRC to "tackle people who deliberately break the rules and challenge those who bend the rules."[19]

HMRC received help in its mission from Reuters in publishing their special report on Starbucks, as well as from several other media investigations in 2012. A *Guardian* report on Amazon showed the online retail giant paid no corporation tax on more than £7 billion in sales within the United Kingdom,[20] while *The Telegraph* reported that Google paid just £6 million in tax on £395 million of UK turnover.[21] Following these reports, representatives from all of the firms were summoned to Parliament to speak to the Public Accounts Committee. Corporate tax avoidance had become a hot button issue for both the media and government, with Michael Meacher, an MP for the Labour Party, stating specifically that Starbucks' tax behaviour "is certainly profoundly against the interests of the countries where they operate and is extremely unfair . . . they are trying to play the taxman, game him. It is disgraceful."[22]

While several corporations were the subject of media tax avoidance investigations and summoned to Parliament, Starbucks faced the brunt of the public uproar. According to the YouGov BrandIndex, which measures the strength of a company's brand perception, Starbucks dropped to a record low score of –28.6 following the release of the Reuters special report. In the month leading up to the Parliament summons, Starbucks' score remained around –16.7, which is in sharp contrast to its score from 2011 of +3.1.[23] In contrast, the BrandIndex scores for Google and Amazon barely dropped due to their media reports and Parliament summons. The UK director for BrandIndex, Sarah Murphy commented:

> "*A brand's buzz score typically recovers following a spate of bad press, but we aren't seeing that with Starbucks, which is quite unusual. Its scores started to level out around the end of last month, but whatever modest recovery Starbucks has made could well be in jeopardy if this story flares up again in the media.*"[24]

UK Uncut

The continued negative public backlash against Starbucks could have something to do with the actions of the organization UK Uncut. While it started as a simple hashtag, UK Uncut grew during the recession into an organized movement with protests and boycotts in over fifty UK cities.[25]

UK Uncut campaigned against the government's austerity plans to cut public services and reduce the deficit, claiming the deficit could be reduced and welfare services maintained if the government collected all the tax revenue it was due. A UK Uncut FAQ says, "It is estimated that £25bn a year is lost through tax avoidance—money that could fund the refuges, rape crisis centres, sure start centres and child benefit payments that are currently being axed by the government." [26]

One of the first UK Uncut targets, Vodafone, was forced to close nearly thirty stores around the country due to protests and sit-ins.[27] Since 2010, banks such as Barclays, RBS and HSBC, and retailers like Boots and Tesco have come under fire from UK Uncut.

Following the release of the Reuters report in October 2012, UK Uncut began to target Starbucks with protests and boycotts. On November 11, 2012, the date that Starbucks CFO Troy Alstead was scheduled to meet with Parliament, UK Uncut announced a new campaign against Starbucks, titled "Refuge from the Cuts." The intent of the campaign was to turn dozens of Starbucks locations on a Saturday in December 2012 into services that were being cut by the government, such as refuges, homeless shelters and crèches.[28] A UK Uncut activist was quoted as saying "Starbucks is a really great target because it is on every high street across the country and that's what UK Uncut finds really important: people can take action in their local areas."[29]

What Next?

In November 2012, Starbucks finds itself in an untenable situation with the British government summoning CFO Troy Alstead to hearings in Parliament, and public protests and demonstrations against the company escalating. Starbucks has not been accused of illegal activities, but has followed common international tax procedures to minimize payments within the United Kingdom.

References

1 Bergin, Tom. "Special Report: How Starbucks avoids UK taxes," Reuters, 15 Oct 2012. <http://uk.reuters.com/article/2012/10/15/us-britain-starbucks-tax-idUKBRE89E0EX20121015>
2 Ibid.
3 Starbucks 2012 Form 10-K. United States Securities and Exchange Commission. <www.sec.gov/Archives/edgar/data/829224/000082922412000007/sbux-9302012x10k.htm>
4 Ibid.
5 "Starbucks' Howard Schultz on how he became coffee king," *Mirror News*, 5 Aug 2010. <www.mirror.co.uk/news/uk-news/starbucks-howard-schultz-on-how-he-became-239790>
6 Ibid.
7 "2012 Global Responsibility Report Message From Howard Schultz," Starbucks.com. <www.starbucks.com/responsibility/global-report/leadership-letter>
8 Ibid.
9 "Ethically Sourced Coffee Goals and Progress," Starbucks.com. <www.starbucks.com/responsibility/sourcing/coffee>
10 Pollock, Lisa. "How Starbucks stirs things up to pay no UK tax," *Financial Times.* 15 Dec 2012.
11 Bergin, Tom. "Special Report: How Starbucks avoids UK taxes," Reuters, 15 Oct. 2012. <http://uk.reuters.com/article/2012/10/15/us-britain-starbucks-tax-idUKBRE89E0EX20121015>
12 Ibid.
13 Weston, Shaun. "UK coffee bar market still growing despite recession," FoodBev.com, 2 Mar 2010. <www.foodbev.com/news/uk-coffee-bar-market-still-growing-despite-recessi#.Uw3-soWSaMh>
14 Poulter, Sean. "Costa, the coffee chain that keeps on growing: Brand to open hundreds more stores across the UK and around the world," *Daily Mail*, 30 April 2013. <www.dailymail.co.uk/news/article-2317419/Costa-coffee-chain-keeps-growing-Chain-open-hundreds-stores-UK-world.html>
15 Houlder, Vanessa, Jopson, Barney & Lucas, Louise. "Starbucks ground down: Taxation; Public anger over tax avoidance by corporate giants is spreading around the globe, as the US coffee chain found to its cost," *Financial Times*, 8 Dec 2012.
16 Ibid.

17 Poulter, Sean. "Costa, the coffee chain that keeps on growing: Brand to open hundreds more stores across the UK and around the world," *Daily Mail*, 30 April 2013. <www.dailymail.co.uk/news/article-2317419/Costa-coffee-chain-keeps-growing-Chain-open-hundreds-stores-UK-world.html>

18 "HM Revenue & Customs:The HMRC Vision," Her Majesty's Revenue and Customs, The National Archives. <http://webarchive.nationalarchives.gov.uk/+/http://www.hmrc.gov.uk/governance/vision.htm>

19 "Your Charter," Her Majesty's Revenue and Customs. <www.gov.uk/government/uploads/system/uploads/attachment_data/file/91888/charter.pdf>

20 Griffiths, Ian. "Amazon: £7bn sales, no corporation tax," *The Guardian*, 4 April 2012. <www.theguardian.com/technology/2012/apr/04/amazon-british-operation-corporation-tax>

21 Warman, Matt. "Google pays just £6m UK tax," *The Telegraph*, 8 Aug 2012. <www.telegraph.co.uk/technology/google/9460950/Google-pays-just-6m-UK-tax.html>

22 Bergin, Tom. "Special Report: How Starbucks avoids UK taxes," Reuters, 15 Oct. 2012. <http://uk.reuters.com/article/2012/10/15/us-britain-starbucks-tax-idUKBRE89E0EX20121015>

23 Neville, Simon & Malik, Shiv. "Starbucks wakes up and smells the stench of tax avoidance and controversy," *The Guardian*, 11 Nov 2012. <www.theguardian.com/business/2012/nov/12/starbucks-tax-avoidance-controversy>

24 Ibid.

25 "UK Uncut," UK Uncut. <www.ukuncut.org.uk/about/ukuncut>

26 "Starbucks tax dodging FAQs," UK Uncut. <www.ukuncut.org.uk/media/W1siZiIsIjUxM2NiZmJhYjAxOTFmMDAwMzAwMDE1MyJdXQ/starbucks-tax-dodging-faqs.pdf>

27 "UK Uncut," UK Uncut. <www.ukuncut.org.uk/about/ukuncut>

28 Neville, Simon & Malik, Shiv. "Starbucks wakes up and smells the stench of tax avoidance and controversy," *The Guardian*, 11 Nov 2012. <www.theguardian.com/business/2012/nov/12/starbucks-tax-avoidance-controversy>

29 Ibid.

* * *

STARBUCKS CORPORATION (B)

Tax Avoidance Controversies in the United Kingdom

Starbucks Response

Starbucks Chief Financial Officer Troy Alstead was called to testify before Parliament on November 15, 2012. Mr. Alstead, despite being asked multiple direct and pointed questions, repeatedly stood by his assertion that Starbucks does nothing illegal and pays every cent of taxes that it owes. As the questioning continued, Mr. Alstead denied funneling money into tax havens in order to reduce the company's tax liability. The interrogation concluded with Mr. Alstead proclaiming:

> *We sincerely believe that we are doing everything to an ethical standard—not just the legal standard, but exactly what we should be doing. We will continue to do our best to communicate that both here and with our customers.*[1]

Public outcry persisted and UK Uncut planned an even larger number of sit-ins and boycotts. On December 6th, Starbucks posted an open letter on its website (Attachment 1) discussing how they plan to remedy the tax avoidance claims. The letter was signed by the Managing Director of Starbucks Coffee Company UK, Kris Engskov. At the same time, they published a "Starbucks commitment to the UK" section on their UK corporate website. The new page not only has a Tax FAQ section but links to a video showing Mr. Engskov delivering a speech to the London Chamber of Commerce and Industry.

The open letter and new web page indicated that while Starbucks did nothing illegal, it wished to be in good standing with its customers:

> *In 2013 and 2014 Starbucks will not claim the tax deductions for royalties or payments related to our intercompany charges for interest and mark-up on the coffee we buy . . . . In addition, we have committed to paying a significant amount of corporation tax during 2013 and 2014 regardless of whether our company is profitable during these years. We are still working through some of the calculations, but we believe we could pay or prepay somewhere in the range of £10 million in each of the next two years in addition to the variety of taxes we already pay.*[2]

An Open Letter from Kris Engskov

06 December 2012

Posted by Kris Engskov, Managing Director, Starbucks Coffee Company UK

Today, we're taking action to pay corporation tax in the United Kingdom– above what is currently required by tax law. Since Starbucks was founded in 1971, we've learned it is vital to listen closely to our customers—and that acting responsibly makes good business sense.

Over the more than 14 years we've been in business here in the UK, the most important asset we have built is trust. Trust with our partners (employees), our customers and the wider society in which we operate.

The fact remains that Starbucks has found making a profit in the UK to be difficult. This is a hugely competitive market and we have not performed to our expectations over the many years we've been in business here.

It has always been our plan to become sustainably profitable in the UK. We annually inject nearly £300 million into the UK economy and are exploring additional initiatives to expand our growth and speed our way to profitability in future.

And while Starbucks has complied with all UK tax laws, today we are announcing changes that will result in the company paying higher corporation tax in the UK. Specifically, Starbucks will not claim tax deductions for royalties and standard intercompany charges. Furthermore, Starbucks will commit to paying a significant amount of tax during 2013 and 2014 regardless of whether the company is profitable during these years.

Starbucks will continue to open our books to HM Treasury and HM Revenue and Customs on an ongoing basis to ensure our financial performance and tax structure is transparent and appropriate.

The commitments Starbucks is making today are intended to begin a process of enhancing trust with customers and the communities that we have been honoured to serve for the past 14 years. And we will do even more. Our contribution will increase as we train over 1,000 apprentices over the next two years and pursue a series of initiatives that will increase employment and investment.

We know we are not perfect. But we have listened over the past few months and are committed to the UK for the long term. We hope that over time, through our actions and our contribution, you will give us an opportunity to build on your trust and custom.

Yours sincerely,

Kris Engskov, managing director, Starbucks Coffee Company UK[3]

References

1 "Public Accounts Committee—Minutes of Evidence HC 716" www.parliament.uk, 12 Nov 2012. <www.publications.parliament.uk/pa/cm201213/cmselect/cmpubacc/716/121112.htm>

2 "Starbucks commitment to the UK," www.starbucks.co.uk. <www.starbucks.co.uk/our-commitment>

3 "An Open Letter from Kris Engskov," www.starbucks.co.uk, 06 Dec 1012. <www.starbucks.co.uk/blog/an-open-letter-from-kris-engskov/1249>

* * *

LONG CASE QUESTIONS

1. How should CFO Troy Alstead testify at the Parliament hearings? Should he continue Starbucks' claims of an unprofitable UK market, or admit to tax avoidance practices?
2. What actions, if any, should Starbucks take in order to minimize the impact of the public outcry and actions planned by UK Uncut? What strategies discussed in the chapter can be used here?
3. Does Starbucks have a responsibility to the community to obey the spirit of corporate tax laws, or an obligation to shareholders to legally minimize tax expenses? Why?
4. How can Starbucks, or other companies, avoid such situations in the future?

Part I: Comprehensive Case

CHINA AND CORRUPTION: THE CASE OF GLAXOSMITHKLINE

July 14, 2015

By: Conner Lee

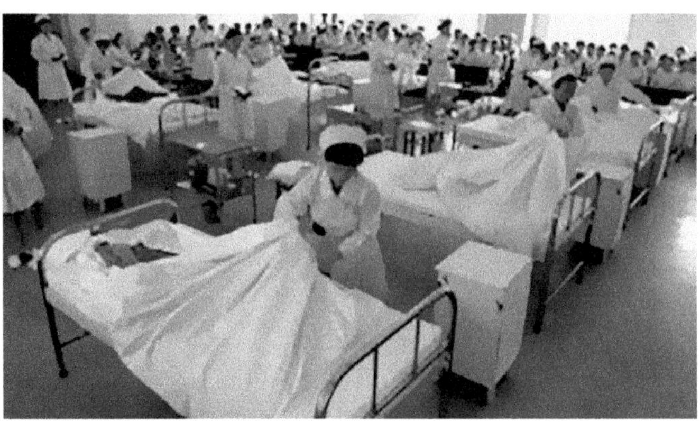

GlaxoSmithKline (GSK) is Britain's biggest drug maker. Chinese authorities found GSK guilty of bribing both hospitals and doctors to help promote their products in China, using a network of nearly seven hundred travel agencies to pay medical professionals, health-related organizations, and government officials. According to Chinese authorities, GSK funneled about 3 billion yuan, or US$482 million, through this network to recipients. Receipts were forged for purchases and transactions that never took place, including fake conferences. At first, GSK denied any involvement in the bribes. Then, after an internal investigation, GSK admitted that certain executives acted independently in ways that broke Chinese law (Rajagopalan). Chinese television even went so far as to air an alleged confession of one of the four senior GSK executives under investigation of how the scheme relied on "fake conferences and travel agencies to create receipts for services that were never performed" (Thompson). GSK denies the sums of money are as high as Chinese officials suggest.

The Chinese officials also seemed to emphasize how the cost of the bribes was passed directly to Chinese consumers. In other words, doctors and other medical staff were bribed to sell their products and the cost of those bribes was added to the price of the products that consumers paid for. In some cases, the final price of the product was several times the cost in other countries (*BBC News*). Chinese officials also claim GSK bribed officials to obstruct Chinese investigations, according to a security ministry official (Bloomberg).

Five senior executives of GSK were arrested and subsequently found guilty of bribery. Mark Reilly, the chief executive of GlaxoSmithKline operations in China, received a suspended prison sentence. Four other GSK managers in China received similar suspended sentences. GSK's local subsidiary in China was found guilty of bribery and fined nearly US$500 million, the largest corporate fine in China, according to the official Chinese news agency Xinhua. While the total fine is large, it is dwarfed by GSK's annual free cash flow of about £4 billion. The company is also being investigated in other countries, and faces allegations that it bribed doctors in "Poland, Iraq, Jordan, and Lebanon" (Rajagopalan). GSK wants to be the "The first company in the drugs industry to stop paying outside doctors to promote its products" (Rajagopalan). It also claims to want to stop company policies that incentivize sales representatives to bribe doctors, and end payments for medical professionals to attend conferences (Rajagopalan). In addition, since GSK was accused of bribery, its sales in China have taken a hit as well, and may be down permanently. In 2013, GSK's sales dropped 30% after it was accused of corruption (*Financial Times*). Once one of GSK's fastest-growing markets, GSK's medicine and vaccine sales dropped 61% in the country, and sales of its consumer health products dropped by 29% (Jack).

Corruption in China

China is in the middle of a growing anti-corruption program, a program initiated by Chinese President Xi Jinping (Shobert). Cases of corruption used to be rare; however, due to public discontent with corruption in the Chinese Communist Party, the government was forced to respond. Announcements of investigations of party officials and businesses are now constantly in China's headlines (First Source from Hatton).

Corruption is a serious problem in China; even low-level officials can easily make small fortunes. Party officials can make millions of dollars a year in bribes and blackmail. The family of the official who launched the anti-corruption campaign, according to Bloomberg, holds an estimated $376 million (Second Source from Hatton). In 2013, China was ranked 80th out of 178 countries in Transparency International's Corruption Perceptions Index. Corruption is widely believed to be one of the major barriers to China's social and economic development; some analysts warn that corruption threatens the country's future and the popularity (and power) of the Communist Party. The Chinese public views corruption as a major problem. Many citizens in surveys say it is the biggest problem the country faces. Citizens describe corruption as unrestricted and rapidly growing. According to some estimates, approximately 10 percent of Chinese government funding is used as bribes, kickbacks, or is stolen. Even when investigations take place, the likelihood of corrupt officials going to jail is less than three percent (Pei).

Anticorruption attempts have largely been failures in China. It is hard to enforce laws and regulations when everyone is breaking them. However, it is also possible the Western media has a false perception of how bad corruption is in China. As one source notes, "Between 1979 and 2000, over 700,000 cases for investigation were filed against officials by investigators." Of these, approximately 56 percent of such cases were embezzlement, 28 percent bribery, and misuse of public funds 16 percent. If this is true, then it is possible the Chinese government may be doing more than it seems to confront corruption (Manion, 87).

Corruption in China increased dramatically after 1978, and has grown hand-in-hand with the economy. As one source notes, "The Chinese economy has, it would seem, flourished even as corruption worsened" (Wedeman, 4). Some nations are able to succeed despite high levels of corruption, and China seems to be one such country (Wedeman, 4). Many authors seem to agree that while corruption and rapid growth may coexist together in the short term, they are essentially contradictory. While the steps the Chinese government has taken to curtail corruption may have been ineffective, it is possible these efforts have prevented corruption from spiraling out of control (Wedeman, 8).

China's Healthcare System

China is in the midst of reforming its healthcare system, which is being expanded at a rapid pace. This includes a new national health insurance plan, which covers basic health needs. Unfortunately, these additions are "Being built on a top of a very weak foundation." "Doctors are chronically over-worked and under-paid" (Shobert), working long hours and earning far too little. In addition, hospitals are stuck between fund shortages and rising healthcare costs. Consequently, alternative means of revenue have been found. In this case, doctors seem to be making up for low salaries with bribes, as seen in cases such as the GSK scandal. In addition, Chinese citizens often bribe healthcare professionals to ensure that they receive good treatment when needed (Shobert).

There are several major forms of corruption in the Chinese healthcare system. The first is the pricing system. The government has laws on how much hospitals can charge for various products and services, but hospitals often simply ignore these laws, setting their own prices or simply overbilling patients (Tam, 267). There have been several cases in which hospitals have charged patients for care they did not receive. Hospital staff at all levels were found to be accepting bribes, from patients that expect better medical services to medical equipment and pharmaceutical firms hoping to sell their products. Doctors, especially, accept bribes often (Tam, 268). Hospitals have been documented to sell patients cheaper fake and substandard medications, illegally charging them the cost of the real medication and then pocketing the difference. Hospitals reap vast profits this way, especially in medical departments that treat serious illness, such as oncology (Tam, 269).

The medical industry is stuck between rising expenses and declining budgets. China has a desperately underfunded public healthcare system. Between 1985 and 2005, government spending as a percentage of total healthcare spending dropped from an estimated 38.6% to 17.9%. Health expenditure by private organizations declined as well. Meanwhile, personal spending on healthcare increased, from 20.4% in 1978 to 52.2% in 2005. Hospitals are forced to make up for the difference using illicit income to cover their expenses (Tam, 270, 272).

Many healthcare professionals use corruption as a means for personal gains. Loopholes and lax enforcement of law worsen the problem. One way in which physicians gain personal profit is by prescribing drugs and medical procedures that patients do not need. Sometimes part of the money paid for the medicine is kicked back to the physician (Tam, 273). Doctors who are found accepting bribes are rarely penalized (Tam, 274), authorities who are aware of the budgetary problems the healthcare system faces are often unwilling to confront corruption.

Competition in the Chinese healthcare system is intense, and many pharmaceutical firms resort to bribery and corruption as a means of selling their products. Chinese firms typically spend twenty to thirty percent of the price of their products on bribing doctors and hospitals, and customers are forced to pay the costs of these bribes (Tam, 274).

The problems in the health industry have diminished public trust in the hospital systems. Various surveys indicate that many patients feel they must bribe doctors to ensure they receive good care. Otherwise, they fear poor treatment within the healthcare system. This sentiment cannot be understated (Tam, 277).

Many foreign companies complain that, "China is broadly becoming a less hospitable place for multinational companies to operate" (Shobert). Many foreign firms are convinced they are being scrutinized by regulatory oversight, and they are being held to higher regulatory standards than their domestic counterparts. If these suspicions are in fact true, then domestic firms in China are likely behaving far worse than their foreign competitors (Shobert).

Public pressure for reform in the healthcare industry is growing. A backlash threatens to undermine the Chinese government, and public resentment regarding corrupt officials in the industry is growing. While past attempts to deal with corruption in the industry have fallen short, it is possible the government may eventually be forced to deal with the problem. For instance, in 2006, 2,000 people rioted outside a hospital after a three-year old boy died of ingesting pesticide. The doctors there had refused to treat the boy because the parents did not have cash on hand when they arrived at the hospital. According to some estimates, there were about 17,000 such incidents in 2010. Officials have good reason to fear a public backlash. It is also possible that reform attempts will fall apart as in the past.

Since the scandal, China has passed several bills aimed at dealing with corruption in the healthcare industry. The National Health and Family Planning Commission issued two bills with "anti-corruption compliance requirements" (Ross and Zhou), as well as a "blacklist" of certain medical-device firms and pharmaceutical companies that have violated the law. Chapter 49 establishes "Nine prohibitions" aimed at preventing bribery in the healthcare sector. These prohibitions are aimed at preventing institutions and individuals from accepting various types of bribes and kickbacks, including preventing medical personnel from accepting commissions or kickbacks of any kind from medical institutions other than the one they work at. Chapter 50, however, establishes a blacklist system that shuts firms and individuals who have participated in bribery out of the healthcare system. The last attempt at doing this was a 2007 law that was ineffective, and this new law aims to be much more effective. These bills are now law (Ross and Zhou).

The GlaxoSmithKline Case

The case that GlaxoKlineSmith bribed Chinese officials does have merit. The company itself has acknowledged that there seems to have been some misconduct by certain executives, so it is almost undeniable the bribery took place. There is another side to this case, however. Bribery and other forms of corruption are not just common in China, companies are actually expected to bribe simply as a way of business. In many hospitals, all of the staff can be expected to be involved in the bribery system. It is so common there are literally systems in some hospitals to divide the profits from the bribes.

GSK was wrong in participating in the bribery schemes. It also was wrong in participating in corruption even if it was following expected industry norms in the country. It is never ethical to do a wrong act (in this case bribery) even if everyone else is doing the same act.

Given that large numbers of foreign companies complain of being unfairly scrutinized by Chinese authorities, it is likely the Chinese government unfairly investigated GSK because it was a large, foreign company with rapid market share growth that threatened domestic industry. Because bribery is so common, and because everyone does it, the Chinese government has the power to pick winners and losers. The government can arrest and press charges against any company it does not like, and rightfully claim the company was in violation of the law. GSK, in particular, was targeted for being a big, foreign firm with high market share growth in China.

Ultimately the consequences of the bribery scandal had a net negative impact on many people especially patients who carried most of the cost of corruption. The bribes caused many doctors to prescribe certain medications when they should have prescribed others, and it's caused certain patients to receive better treatment than others. Corruption also vastly undermined public trust in the Chinese healthcare system, with most of the public deeply skeptical of hospitals and physicians. Unfortunately, bribery and corruption are the only ways that the Chinese healthcare system gets the funding it needs. Without bribery and other such forms of illegal funding, the Chinese healthcare system would either go bankrupt or go into debt. But bribery doesn't just affect the people who have direct association with the act. It affects the behavior of a large segment of society. Even when everyone else is doing something bad, doing the action yourself only makes the problem worse. In the case of GlaxoSmithKline, the consequences of bribery actually contribute in undermining society, making the act unethical.

Works Cited

"Glaxo's Former China Head Accused of Ordering Bribes." Bloomberg.com. Bloomberg, 14 May 2014. Web. 25 June 2014.

(First Source from) Hatton, Celia. "How Real Is China's Anti-corruption Campaign?" *BBC News*. BBC, 4 Sept. 2013. Web. 25 June 2014.

(Second Source from) Hatton, Celia. "How Serious Is China on Corruption?" *BBC News*. BBC, 28 Jan. 2013. Web. 25 June 2014.

Insider, The. "The Glaxo-China Bribery Scandal: A New Policeman Walks The Beat." *Forbes*. Forbes Magazine, 25 July 2013. Web. 25 June 2014.

Jack, Andrew. "GSK China Sales Plummet 60% since Scandal—FT.com." *Financial Times*. The Financial Times LTD, 23 Oct. 2013. Web. 25 June 2014.

Jack, Andrew, Patrick Jenkins, and David Oakley. "GlaxoSmithKline China Sales Face Growing Pressure—FT.com." *Financial Times*. Financial Times LTD, 23 Sept. 2013. Web. 18 July 2014.

Manion, Melanie. *Corruption by Design: Building Clean Government in Mainland China and Hong Kong*. Cambridge, MA: Harvard University Press, 2004. Print.

Pei, Minxin. "Corruption Threatens China's Future." *Carnegie Endowment for International Peace*. Carnegie Endowment, 9 Oct. 2007. Web. 25 June 2014.

Rajagopalan, Megha, and Kazunori Takada. "Chinese Police Charge British Former Head of GSK in China with Bribery." *Reuters*. Thomson Reuters, 14 May 2014. Web. 24 June 2014.

Ross, Lester, and Kenneth Zhou. "China's New Anti-Corruption Policies in the Health Care Industry." *Wilmerhale*. Wilmer Cutler Pickering Hale and Dorr LLP, 9 Jan. 2014. Web. 25 June 2014.

Shobert, Benjamin. "Three Ways To Understand GSK's China Scandal." *Forbes*. Forbes Magazine, 04 Sept. 2013. Web. 25 June 2014.

Tam, W. "Organizational Corruption By Public Hospitals In China." *Crime Law And Social Change*, 56, 3 (n.d.): 265–282. *Social Sciences Citation Index*. Web. 25 June 2014.

Thompson, Mark. "Bribery Scandal Will Hit Glaxo's China Growth." *CNN Money*. Cable News Network, 24 July 2013. Web. 25 June 2014.

"UK Executive Accused in GlaxoSmithKline China Probe." *BBC News*. BBC, 14 May 2014. Web. 25 June 2014.

Wedeman, Andrew Hall. *Double Paradox: Rapid Growth and Rising Corruption in China*. Ithaca, NY: Cornell University Press, 2012. Print.

COMPREHENSIVE CASE QUESTIONS

1. Who are the stakeholders affected by the bribery scandal?
2. Should multinationals be held responsible for actions committed by its executives? Why or why not?
3. What can the company do to ensure that such scandals do not occur in the future?

Part II

Stakeholders

Chapter 5

Primary Stakeholders: Employees

LEARNING OBJECTIVES

After reading this chapter you should be able to:

- Understand employees as stakeholders and the role of the company in terms of the hiring and firing of employees
- Be aware of diversity and affirmative action programs and the roles they play
- Understand what constitutes sexual harassment and the ways sexual harassment can be minimized in companies
- Become aware of the importance of whistle-blowing
- Examine the critical role of the human resource management department in ensuring ethical programs are in place

PREVIEW BUSINESS ETHICS INSIGHT

The Japanese Salaryman

Japanese corporations have largely employed "salarymen," employees that devoted their lives to the company. These employees would be rewarded more for their hard work and loyalty to the company rather than their skills. In return, the salaryman was expected to give himself fully to the company. The salarymen were not allowed to refuse transfers and were often posted in locations that could be 100 miles away from their homes. Children would therefore often grow in families without fathers as they would move to new locations. Such salarymen would often work long grueling hours adding to 400 more than their German or French counterparts. Work thus became the most critical aspect of the salaryman's life.

Japan is currently experiencing many changes that are making the salaryman unnecessary. During times when workers lived up to 70, Japanese corporations were able to support these employees in retirement. However, many Japanese corporations are finding that such retirement support for a workforce that lives in their 80s and 90s is very expensive and makes them less competitive globally. Additionally, many corporations are finding that these employees are not as valuable in declining industries such as consumer electronics as most of them are hard to retrain. As a result, many Japanese companies are offering early retirement packages for these employees.

These changes have been very difficult for these workers. Shedding decades of work practices based on titles and office hierarchies is challenging. Additionally, trying to acquire new skills is also taxing as these employees have been used to years of monotonous work. It is therefore not surprising that Japan has seen the emergence of new training programs such as those at the Institute of Social Capital where the aim is to retrain the salarymen. Such programs often require months of retraining so that these salarymen can shed their old habits to take on new jobs such as teachers.

Based on *The Economist*. 2016. "White-collar blues; Retraining the salarymen isn't easy". December 24, 86–87.

The salarymen discussed in the Preview Business Ethics Insight above indicates one of the major ethical challenges facing Japanese employees today. As evidence mounts that Japan is also experiencing an ageing population, the pressures on corporations to deal with such challenges are increasing. There is no doubt that societies and top performing companies that have exceptional working conditions tend to attract and retain the best employees. **Employees** represent the human resources available to a company dedicated to achieving its goals. However, to attract and retain the best employees, ethical challenges need to be addressed.

The challenges facing Japan today are not unique. Most countries in the world are facing other employee ethical challenges. For instance, more developed societies such as Germany and emerging markets such as China are also facing ageing populations.[1] This has meant that companies in these countries have had to develop stronger policies to better manage older workers while also combating age discrimination. At the same time, societies such as India, Turkey and countries in the African continent are seeing a younger workforce. Emerging markets such as China are faced with a paradoxical situation where they are also seeing a younger, ambitious and increasingly impatient workforce. Tackling the needs of a younger population has been key to avoiding social unrest and promoting social cohesion. In addition to these challenges, most multinationals are also seeing their human resource practices scrutinized for aspects such as sexual harassment, wages, sweatshop conditions etc. Understanding business ethics aspects of the employee is therefore critical.

Given the above ethical employee challenges, many companies also put their employees at the top of their priorities. From a strategy standpoint, most experts suggest that having the right types of employees is critical to build sustainable competitive advantage. As we saw in Chapter 1, sustainable competitive advantage relates to the ability of a company to create the right conditions where the company has access to critical competencies and skills to be able to succeed and be profitable over the long term. Employees provide such means and are influential in helping the company achieve its vision and mission. In the absence of employees who are supportive of the mission and vision of the company, the company will likely fail.

This chapter will therefore discuss employees as critical stakeholders. While there are many potential issues that can be discussed (e.g., occupational risk, workforce reduction, work–life balance), we focus on those issues that seem to be most relevant to multinationals today. In the next few sections, you will learn about hiring/firing of employees, diversity and affirmative action, sexual harassment, whistle-blowing, and unions. We note that critical employee issues such as gender equality and child labor, related to the hiring of cheap labor, will be discussed later in Chapter 11. Finally, we also discuss the role of the human resource management department in addressing employee business ethics issues.

Next we discuss the hiring/terminating of employees.

HIRING AND TERMINATING OF EMPLOYEES

Hiring, Recruitment, and Selection

One of the most critical ways companies relate to employees as stakeholders is through the **hiring process**. Collins argues that the key to developing an ethical organization is by carefully selecting employees that display high ethics.[2] Potential employees who display the propensity to be unethical may eventually affect other employees and corrupt a culture of integrity. Care must therefore be taken to maximize the chances of hiring employees who are ethical. In that respect, Collins suggests the use of combination of integrity tests (asking employees whether they have committed unethical workplace behavior or whether they condone unethical behavior, personality tests, interviews, and other diagnostics to ensure that new employees display the highest level of ethics).

The process of hiring is even more critical when one considers the effects of hiring the wrong employee. Recent research suggests that hiring a toxic employee (someone who is rude and does not display norms of civility and hence ethics) can have devastating effects on a company's culture.[3] In fact, research suggests that hiring a toxic employee can eliminate the gains of two super-performing employees. Carefully managing the hiring process through the asking of adequate interview questions emphasizing civility becomes very important. Representative examples include asking the references and subordinates questions such as 1) what negative things can former employers say about the candidate? 2) how did the candidate deal with conflict? and 3) how did subordinates like working for the candidate and can the candidate carefully manage his/her emotions? The recruitment and selection process therefore becomes very important.

Recruitment refers to the process of identifying and attracting qualified people to apply for vacant positions in an organization. For all types of positions, U.S. companies use a variety of methods to recruit. These include, among others, applications and advertisements placed in newspapers or on the internet, internal job postings where companies post a list of vacancies on their websites or internally, use of private or public agencies, and use of recommendations from current employees. Nevertheless, in an age of a tight labor market, some companies are resorting to lateral hiring. Consider the Business Ethics Insight below.

As we see from this, recruitment methods in the U.S. tend to be open or may take the form of lateral hiring. However, this preference for open forms of recruitment is not shared worldwide. For many of the collectivist societies such as Japan, South Korea,

BUSINESS ETHICS INSIGHT

Lateral Hiring

In an age where companies are aggressively competing for prized employees to build competitive advantage, the practice of **lateral hiring** is gathering steam. Lateral hiring refers to the process by which companies actively search and solicit competitors' employees to apply for jobs. In fact, Michael Homula, the director of talent acquisition at First Merit bank has gone as far as sending employment letters to top performers at other banks with a cover letter explaining that they can start in two weeks. A U.S.-based law firm wishing to get established in the Ukraine recently hired seven local employees from a Kiev law practice.

Not surprisingly, lateral hiring is controversial. On one hand, employers abhor the practice because they believe that it goes against the norms of fair competition. Many employers feel that they have invested significantly in their employees' training and that lateral hiring is a form of stealing. Additionally, others feel that lateral hiring is more likely to disrupt internal cultures and promote disloyalty. Finally, some employers feel that the practice is a way to gain competitive advantage through the disruption of business operations.

In addition to the above controversies, lateral hiring can also result in significant legal trouble for companies because departing employees take trade secrets with them. Move Inc., which operates Realtor.com successfully sued competitor Zillow for allegedly stealing former top executives who took trade secrets with them. Companies therefore need to make sure that they take the necessary steps to avoid legal challenges if they engage in lateral hiring.

To protect themselves against lateral hiring, some companies have implemented policies to prevent employees from leaving and working for direct competitors for a period of time after leaving the employer. However, some experts argue that this is also a form of domination by employers. By preventing lateral hiring, companies can exert their domination on what is then considered their "property." Some business ethics experts therefore argue that it should be the employee's privilege to have the ability to evaluate a lateral hire offer and decide whether they want to accept or reject such offers.

Based on Gardner, T.M., Stansbury, J., and Hart, D. 2010. "The ethics of lateral hiring," *Business Ethics Quarterly*, 20, 3, 341–349; Richmond, R., Morrison, K.M. and Pillikyan, N.K. 2017. "Hiring lateral employees? Consider how to minimize the risk of trade secret litigation." *Employee Relations Law Journal*, 43, 2, 45–49.

and Taiwan, referrals from friends or family tend to be much more important. Collectivistic societies place heavy emphasis on the family and friends compared to more individualistic societies like the U.S. where the focus is on the individual. Such practices are not surprising, as collectivist societies place emphasis on harmony and loyalty.

Does the practice of employee referral work? In an interesting study in three U.S. industries (call centers, trucking, and high technology), the authors find varying support for the use of employee referrals.[4] Referred workers tend to have similar productivity across all three industries. However, the researchers found that referred workers tended to have fewer trucking accidents in the trucking industry while also producing more patents in the high technology industry. Additionally, compared to non-referred workers, referred workers tended to produce higher profits. Thus while the practice is not as prevalent in the U.S., it does seem to bring benefits in some industries.

Selection also varies by country. While recruitment is concerned with attracting people to apply for jobs, **selection** is the process by which a company chooses a person to fill a vacant position. The U.S. selection process is guided by legal considerations, as employers need to ensure that they do not discriminate against job candidates based on race, color, religion, gender, national origin, age, or disability.[5] In the U.S., selection practices are focused on gathering credible information on a candidate's job qualifications. Previous work experience, performance on tests, and perceptions of qualifications from interviews help inform human resource managers about the applicant's qualifications.

Selection is also affected by cultural practices. One of the most critical differences pertains again to more collectivist countries. As Hofstede notes,

> the hiring process in a collectivist society always takes the in-group into account. Usually preference is given to hiring relatives, first of the employer, but also of other persons already employed by the company. Hiring persons from a family one already knows reduces risks. Also relatives will be concerned about the reputation of the family and help correct misbehavior of a family member.[6]

Thus, in selecting employees, collectivist cultural norms value trustworthiness, reliability, and loyalty over performance-related background characteristics. Personal traits such as loyalty to the company, loyalty to the boss, and trustworthiness are the traits that family members can provide. As such, in smaller companies, preference is given to family members.

The hiring process is thus extremely critical for any multinational intent on building an ethical organization. Careful attention has to be paid to assessing the ethical potential of employees. Exhibit 5.1 shows the five-step job screening process suggested by Collins.[7]

Steps	Type	Activities
Step 1	Set legal ground rules	• Make sure that information gathered does not discriminate against job candidates based on protected classes (race, gender, etc.) • Respect all laws and regulations concerning recruitment
Step 2	Seek behavioral information	• Get as much review information from résumés and reference checks • Conduct background checks • Conduct integrity tests or other honesty tests
Step 3	Determine personality traits	• Conduct conscientiousness tests, as more conscientious employees are more likely to be ethical and perform at a high level • Evaluate organization citizenship behavior traits
Step 4	Conduct interview	• Interview candidates regarding ethics from previous jobs • Ask questions such as whether candidate saw unethical behavior (saw colleague steal, saw sexual harassment, etc.) and how candidate responded • Ask candidate about their response to potential ethical dilemmas • Interview about how candidate managed ethical dilemma
Step 5	Conduct other tests	Conduct other tests to determine ethics of candidate • Alcohol test • Drug test • Final integrity tests

EXHIBIT 5.1—Five-step Job Screening Process

However, the multinational must also pay close attention to the recruitment and selection practices in the country. While the U.S. recruitment and selection process is heavily guided by legal considerations, other societies may present additional considerations. Careful attention must be paid to such issues. Additionally, as you saw in Chapter 2, we are all particularly prone to biases when engaging in business activities. Multinationals should also take special steps to reduce biases. Consider the following Strategic Business Ethics Insight.

STRATEGIC BUSINESS ETHICS INSIGHT

Reducing Bias in Hiring Process

As you saw in Chapter 2, we are all prone to engaging in biases. Biases are unconscious practices that end up benefitting one group at the expense of another. This is especially prevalent in the hiring process where recruiters can overlook candidates because of their age or race. In the long run, such biases can end up shaping an industry's culture. Consider, for instance, Silicon Valley and the companies that have endured backlash in their treatment of minorities. One of the companies involved in such biased decisions is Google, which has been the subject of a lawsuit by the U.S. Department of Labor. The latter accuses Google of underpaying its female employees.

Given the above, what can multinationals do to reduce the probability of biases? Experts advise that companies first examine potential biases their employees could be committing. Training and education can be provided to eliminate the potential of such biases. However, multinationals are also advised to reword job descriptions to make the jobs more appropriate for all employees. Consider that words such as aggressive and competitive tend to discourage women while words such as collaborative tend to attract women. Multinationals are therefore advised to use more neutral words. Additionally, to prevent biases from entering evaluation of résumés, experts advise blind résumé reviews. Removing the names of applicants ensures that familiarity with names does not add biases.

A critical aspect of elimination of biases is through the use of standardized interviews. Asking every candidate the same set of questions and having a similar scoring system ensures that biases do not interfere with hiring. In contrast, research has shown that unstructured interviews may allow biases and that such approaches do not always correlate well with job success.

Finally, as we will see later, diversity is an important goal for many companies. Setting diversity goals can therefore also help in reducing biases by encouraging hiring committees to give second looks at qualified minorities who may not have been given the appropriate assessment in the hiring process.

Based on *The Economist,* 2017. "Women in tech; Bits and bias." April 15, 54–56; Knight, R. 2017. "7 practical ways to reduce bias in your hiring process." *Harvard Business Review,* June 12, 2–7.

TERMINATING EMPLOYEES

Another critical issue related to employees is the **termination** of these employees. Bird and Charters (2004: 205) argue that such involuntary separation likely "represents one of the most dramatic events that can happen to an individual in his or her lifetime."[8] Terminations, in any form, affect the worker's well-being and the people in their families. There is strong evidence of the devastating effects of layoffs on those who survive such layoffs.[9] In a representative sample of 13,683 workers, they find that survivors of layoffs tend to have lower organizational performance and lower perception of job security. Not surprisingly, such survivors also tend to feel less attached to their company and have higher desires to look for jobs elsewhere. Evidence of the negative impact of layoffs on companies is also provided by Thurm.[10] Companies that tend to have the deepest cuts tend to be the ones that suffer the most. For example, Honeywell International lost most of its industrial base when it laid off a fourth of its workforce.

U.S. workers have seen extensive layoffs over the past few years. The 2007 recession forced many companies to reduce costs. One of the ways that such costs reduction can occur is through layoffs. However, layoffs have dramatic consequences for both survivors and those who are fired. Understanding the ethical implications of the firing process is therefore very important.

In that context, U.S. companies have the legal ability to terminate employees at short notice. Such ease of firing is not the same in all countries. We therefore look at the employment environment in the U.S. and worldwide.

In the U.S., terminations are regulated by the employment-at-will doctrine. **Employment-at-will** means that "an employer may terminate its employee for a good reason, bad reason, or no reason at all."[11] As such, except for a number of reasons deemed illegitimate by the law (firing on the basis of race, religion, age, etc.) companies have significant discretion regarding the procedures and the reasons why employees are fired.[12] In fact, a recent case suggests that at-will employers do not have to provide any legitimate reasons as to why they fired an employee.[13] Additionally, companies do not have any responsibility to undertake a full investigation before they fire employees. Werhane and Radin (2010) further argue that over 60% of employees in the private sector are at-will employees.[14]

This legal environment is one of the major reasons why the U.S. work environment sees regular mass layoffs. Furthermore, employment-at-will also favors employers in that if an employee feels that he/she has been terminated unlawfully, it is his/her responsibility and burden to show that the termination was unlawful. Thus, while employees can win millions of dollars for unlawful termination, they also face significant upfront costs to fight any charges.

Proponents of employment-at-will provide a number of reasons to justify its use.[15] First, employment-at-will has been rooted in U.S. law since 1871 and is seen as being central to the free market economy where both employers and employees have the freedom to choose.[16] As much as employers have freedom to terminate employees, employees also have the right to freely choose who they work for. Employees can quit their jobs for any or no reason and do not have to give notice to their employers. Second, companies have the proprietary rights to be able to employ and fire whomever they want. Employees willingly choose jobs where they know that they can be fired at any time. Third, proponents also argue that due process (i.e., giving employees the opportunity to contest their termination) can often negatively impact a company's efficiency and productivity. Finally, some proponents also advance that the U.S. economy is already overregulated and there is no need for further regulation.

Despite the support, employment-at-will has an equal share of critics. By arguing that employers have proprietary rights to hire and fire employees as they see fit, employers are treating employees as inanimate property. However, many argue that employees should be treated with respect and dignity and be provided reasons for their termination.[17] Furthermore, it is routinely assumed that employment-at-will is desirable because both companies and employees have equal freedom. However, it is undeniable that most employees have more to lose when they are fired. An employment relationship also demands loyalty, trust, and respect from the employee. Employers thus have reciprocal obligations and should treat their employees similarly. Finally, Dannin also argues that employment-at-will is not always efficient for companies.[18] Employment litigation is now a major cost for many corporations as more employees file termination lawsuits.

While employment-at-will is widely practiced in the U.S., many other countries such as those found in the European Union and Canada use the **just-cause dismissal** approach.[19] Unlike employment-at-will where employees can be dismissed for "any reason or no reason," in just-cause dismissal, employers must provide reasonable notice of termination of an employee.[20] In other words, employers must have legitimate reasons to terminate an employee. Justifiable reasons include employee misconduct that negatively affects the employer's business. Such misconduct can include "habitual neglect of duty, incompetence, willful disobedience, insubordination, dishonesty or intoxication."[21]

To fulfill just-cause dismissal provisions, employers typically give reasonable notice to employees.[22] Reasonable notice is based on the premise that the employer must give enough time for the employee to find a new job. Just-cause requirements can be satisfied with two options. Either the employer gives notice to employees for a reasonable amount of time and allows them to work during that time. However, most employers prefer the second option whereby employees can be terminated immediately and provided for an amount of pay equivalent to the amount of time equivalent to the reasonable notice. To give you further insights on the notice needed and amount of time given to workers worldwide, Exhibit 5.2 on page 196 shows where various countries rank.

As Exhibit 5.2 shows, there is wide variation in terms of the notice period or severance pay worldwide. Based on the data provided by the World Bank's Doing Business Project, countries such as the U.S. that have employment-at-will do not need to provide any notice or severance pay when they terminate employees. In contrast, other countries such as Argentina, China, Brazil etc. do provide significant advance notice and severance pay if they fire employees. According to Bird and Charters, the reasonable notice time is determined based on factors such as length of service, the character of the employee, the age, and availability of similar employment, as well as general environmental factors such as the general economic climate and industry custom.[23]

An interesting aspect of just-cause dismissal is that if employees are terminated, it is the employer's responsibility to provide adequate justification for such termination. The burden of proof thus rests with the employer. Most employers are therefore required to have a system of regular feedback in place to let employees know the level of their performance. If employees are performing poorly, they need to have the chance to show improvement by being given feedback on how to improve. Failure to show improvement then becomes ground for fair dismissal.

As the above shows, just-cause dismissal seems more ethical as the burden is on the employer to provide the justification for firing. But such features may actually discourage multinationals from hiring in some countries specially when also considering severance pay and advance notice. Consider the following Global Business Ethics Insight.

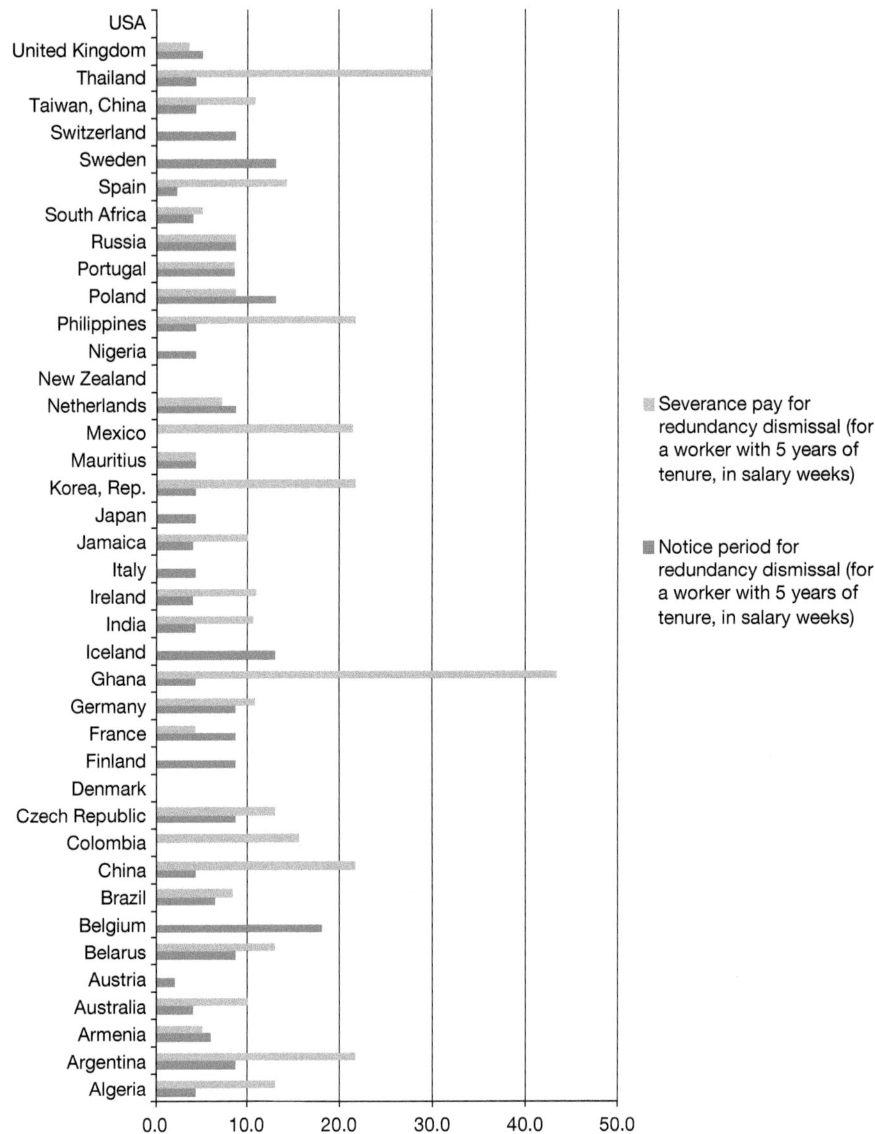

EXHIBIT 5.2—Severance Pay and Notice Period based on World Bank, 2016

Doing Business—Labor Market Regulation, www.doingbusiness.org/data/exploretopics/labor-market-regulation

GLOBAL BUSINESS ETHICS INSIGHT

Hiring and Firing in France

According to the World Bank's Doing Business project, France has a labor environment that is very beneficial to employees. When examining the Labor Market Regulation, data collected by the World Bank shows that workers who have worked for a French company for a year are legally required to get 30 work days off annually. Additionally, after a French employee has worked for a company for a year, the employee has unemployment protection. Furthermore, workers need to be given adequate notice if they are to be fired. With a just-cause dismissal approach, employees with at least one year tenure are guaranteed one month of severance salary.

Although the labor market regulations are in favor of employees, many experts have argued that the regulations have created headaches for entrepreneurs willing to hire workers. Consider the case of Mr. Veneau, a barber in Paris. Although he turns away many customers, he has been unwilling to hire new employees. He feels that the labor market system in France is too chaotic to allow him to hire. A major reason for his reluctance is that he once had an employee who sued him for allegedly getting injured because of the repetitive movement of the scissors. The French labor court ordered Mr. Veneau to pay 17,000 euros to the worker and he vowed never to hire employees again.

Mr. Macron, France's new president, is taking steps to reform the labor market. He has implemented laws to allow firms to negotiate directly with unions rather than accept wider national agreements. Furthermore, he has also made unfair dismissal processes more predictable. Additionally, he wants to reform the apprenticeship system that will provide vocational training to workers to acquire the skills companies want. But experts agree that such moves will be very challenging given the power of unions and people's expectations of generous unemployment benefits.

Based on *The Economist*. 2017. "France's next reforms; Just a trim". 53; World Bank. 2017. Labor Market Regulation, www.doingbusiness.org/data/exploretopics/labor-market-regulation

The contrasting termination modes discussed above thus present different ethical dilemmas for companies. It therefore becomes imperative to decide which system to adopt to conform to ethical norms. Some argue that employment-at-will is necessary in order to provide companies with the means to freely participate in a capitalist system.[24] However, others argue that employment-at-will has many disadvantages that should encourage companies to adopt more of a just-cause dismissal approach.[25] Treating employees humanely and fairly, a reflection of ethical companies, seems more likely with a just-cause system. It is also important to note that many factors now prevent companies from adopting a strict employment-at-will policy. We discuss some of these factors next.

DIVERSITY AND AFFIRMATIVE ACTION

While employment-at-will remains the dominant firing method in the U.S., recent regulations have made certain grounds illegal for dismissal. Thus, companies can no longer fire on the basis of race, gender, age, or even if a potential employee is handicapped.[26] The relevant regulation enforcing prohibition of discrimination is Title VII of the 1964 Civil Rights Act prohibiting discrimination that was due to race, color, religion, sex, or national origin.[27] These new regulations have encouraged some companies to strive for more **diversity** in their workforce. Diversity thus refers to hiring of workers who are different in race, color, or religion compared to the traditional Caucasian male workforce. However, as the Emerging Market Business Ethics Insight below shows, achieving diversity is not necessarily a U.S.-only phenomenon.

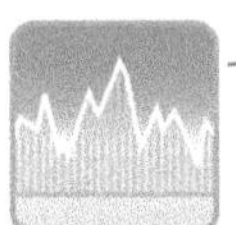

EMERGING MARKET BUSINESS ETHICS INSIGHT

Affirmative Action around Emerging Markets

Brazil is among the most multiracial societies in the world. Around 44% of the population describe themselves as mixed. However, with a racially diverse population with descent from countries such as Italy, Germany, and Lebanon, Brazil's black population faces significant discrimination. Afro-Brazilians tend to earn almost half that of white people and have fewer years of schooling compared to their white counterparts. This has led to some Brazilian universities implementing quota-based admission policies to allow black students to gain admission. However, as the country continues to experience a significant economic boom, it is investigating affirmative action models worldwide to decide which model to adopt.

India's caste system has for centuries sustained a stratified society where success is heavily dependent on what caste one is born into. Those from the lower castes (about 100 million untouchables) are only allowed to do the most demeaning jobs and face considerable challenges in improving their lot. The Indian government thus embarked on an affirmative action program to give preferential treatment to those from lower castes. Lower caste individuals were reserved seats in the parliament, admission in universities, and jobs in the public sector. Through legislation, the government has reserved a percentage of public sector jobs for the lower castes. However, while this program was originally created to last ten years, it still remains a controversial aspect of Indian society today.

The apartheid system in South Africa encouraged an environment where black people were discriminated against at all levels. When apartheid was abolished, the ruling African National Congress (ANC) brought in some new laws to eradicate such discrimination. However, the ANC has strived especially hard to improve women's rights. In a traditionally patriarchal society, the ANC decided that it was necessary to introduce numerous legislations to provide wider opportunities for women to succeed. Through such affirmative action programs, South Africa has progressed considerably and presents a significantly improved environment for women. For example, women hold around 44% of parliamentary seats, ranking South Africa third in the world in terms of gender parliamentary representation. However, progress in companies has been much slower.

In Malaysia, the indigenous population known as *bumiputras* suffered under British colonial rule as preference was given to ethnic Chinese and Indian citizens. As a consequence, although half of the population were *bumiputras,* they owned only a small fraction of the wealth. This resulted in resentment and riots in 1969. The government therefore implemented a number of affirmative action programs to give *bumiputras* preferential access to loans and government jobs and contracts.

Based on Axman, N., Swanson, K., Contreras, V.C. 2016. "Caste and religion-based wage discrimination in the Indian private sector: Evidence from the Indian human development survey." *Review of Black Political Economy,* 43, 165–175; Brown, G. and Langer, A. 2015. "Does affirmative action work?" *Foreign Affairs,* 94, 2, 49–56; *The Economist.* 2010. "Walking several paces behind; Women in South Africa". 397, 8703, 68; Dalmia, S. 2010. "India's government by quota; The affirmative-action plan to eliminate caste discrimination was supposed to last 10 years. Instead it has become a permanent, and divisive, fact of life." *Wall Street Journal* online, April 30; Stillman, A. 2010. "Wealth is still unevenly distributed." *Financial Times,* November 15.

The Emerging Market Business Ethics Insight shows that achieving diversity is not confined to U.S. multinationals. Fearfull and Kamenou argue that reduction of inequality of all forms is an area of crucial importance for most societies.[28] In fact, a recent study examining 41,544 households in India found that lower castes experienced significant discrimination in the private sector compared to other workers.[29] This provides support for India's efforts to combat such discrimination. Furthermore, even the European Union has drafted numerous legislations aimed at reducing discrimination based on gender, religious belief, sexual orientation, and age. However, such factors also represent "protected classes" that U.S. companies cannot discriminate against. In this section, we therefore look at diversity and the consequent affirmative action programs.

Diversity can take many shapes and forms. However, most U.S. companies have focused on increasing diversity on the basis of gender and race. These two groups of employees have been traditionally discriminated against and diversity efforts are necessary to provide more opportunities to these groups to succeed. However, as mentioned earlier, in other parts of the world, discrimination has occurred against people because of their castes (India) and race (South Africa) and because they are indigenous (Malaysia).

Why should companies be concerned about diversity? Consider the Strategic Business Ethics Insight below.

STRATEGIC BUSINESS ETHICS INSIGHT

Diversity and Benefits of Diversity

Proponents of diversity argue that diversity can be very beneficial to the organization. Diversity enriches the workplace whereby employees of different perspectives can interact to work on problems, thus offering more creative solutions to problems. The conflicting ideas inherent in diverse organizations can lead to broadening of perspectives and to a more complex environment that provides significant resources as companies craft strategies. Strategically, this can allow companies to find superior ways to address problems, thus outcompeting the opponents.

The benefits of diversity are even more apparent considering recent research on competitive firms. Herring used large-scale data from the National Organizations Survey of for-profit organizations.[30] His results show that greater racial diversity is "increased sales revenue, more customers, greater market share, and greater relative profit," while gender diversity is associated with "increased sales revenue, more customers, and greater relative profits."[31] To provide further insights into these advantages, Exhibit 5.3 shows the differing levels of profits based on the level of diversity in companies.

Why is diversity associated with greater profits? More diverse companies tend to have broader perspectives that can help find better solutions to organizational problems. This not only helps employees feel more engaged but also helps

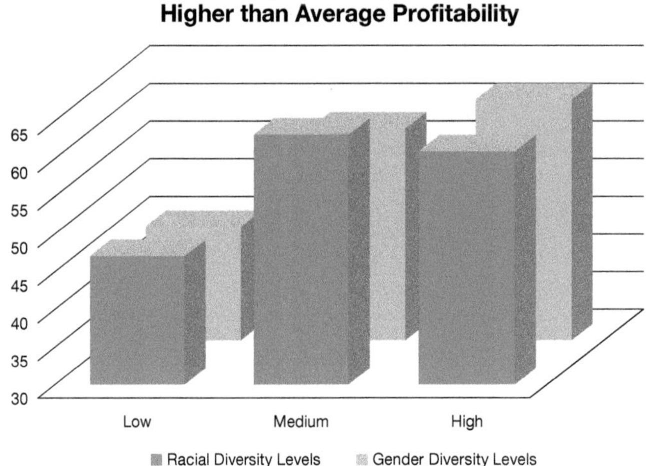

EXHIBIT 5.3—Diversity and Profits

companies better understand their markets. Consider that products such as Guacamole Burritos and Mountain Dew Code Red all come from Pepsi's diversity initiatives. These initiatives have paid off for them, as they found that around 8% of their revenue growth came from such initiatives. However, diversity also helps better understand the market. Consider that in the U.S. the African-American sector is growing 34% faster than any other sectors. Furthermore, the growth of African-American households with an income over $75,000 has grown over 47% in the past five years. Taking advantage of this $860 billion purchasing power is only possible if employees mirror the demographics. Such employees are more likely to be able to understand the needs of such customers.

In addition to the company benefits, diversity has been shown to be beneficial at a societal level. Diversity programs typically imply that countries are finding ways to reduce inequalities and injustices. For instance, in Malaysia, the indigenous *bumiputra* population has seen increases in wealth thereby reducing the potential for social conflict. In India, members of the lower castes have seen increases in representation in various public sectors. Such efforts are helping pave the way for a more just society. Additionally, a recent study also showed that having higher representation of minorities in the Indian railway sector was linked to higher productivity in some cases.

As such, diversity is also very beneficial for multinationals. As most companies enter foreign markets and engage in trade with such markets, a diverse workforce provides them with better ability to understand diverse cultures and global markets. However, these multinationals can also make a contribution to societal equality and justice.

Based on Axman, N., Swanson, K. and Contreras, V.C. 2016. "Caste and religion-based wage discrimination in the Indian private sector: Evidence from the Indian human development survey." *Review of Black Political Economy*, 43, 165–175; Brown, G. and Langer, A. 2015. "Does affirmative action work?" *Foreign Affairs*, 94, 2, 49–56; Despande, A. and Weisskopf, T.E. 2014. "Does affirmative action reduce productivity? A case study of the Indian railways." *World Development*, 64, 169–180; Lencioni, P., 2010. "Power of diversity." *Leadership Excellence*, 27, 1, 15; Toland, S. "The diversity payoff." *Fortune*, November 1, 58; *Stanford Social Innovation Review*. 2010. "Diversity brings the dollars." Fall, 9–10.

Given the benefits of diversity and the legal requirements to encourage diversity, most companies have embarked on affirmative action programs. **Affirmative action** programs refer to "laws, policies, or guidelines that specify positive steps to be taken to hire and promote persons from groups previously and presently discriminated against."[32] Specifically, companies endeavor to proactively recruit employees from groups that have traditionally been discriminated against. For example, many U.S.-based companies such as IBM and Johnson Controls focus their attention on recruiting, developing, and promoting women, minorities, and people with disability.

In India, the government legislated the 1950 Constitution of independent India to provide preferential treatment to groups that had been discriminated against—traditionally scheduled castes, scheduled tribes and other backward classes. In terms of policy, this has meant providing more education and job opportunities to these groups.[33] Recent research suggests that the Indian public sector has been very successful implementing such policies.[34] With the growth of the discriminated group members in the government, there is now strong pressure for these protections to be extended to the private sector. Additionally, while these affirmative action programs had been designed to reserve positions and opportunities to the lower castes, there is now extensive debate about extending such preferential treatment to women and people with disabilities.[35]

In contrast, to help companies implement affirmative action in the U.S., the U.S. Equal Employment Opportunity Commission has issued various "Uniform Guidelines on Employee Selection Procedures." The major aspects of these guidelines are that companies need to publish an affirmative action policy to show their commitment. High-level employees need to be appointed to show the importance of affirmative action. Companies also need to assess the degree of diversity in the company and determine programs to address problematic areas represented by gender or racial diversity.

Proponents of affirmative action argue that the latter is necessary to counteract ingrained discriminatory practices. Furthermore, affirmative action is seen as necessary as compensation for the damages caused by discrimination over the past. Additionally, both minorities and women face glass ceilings and other barriers that keep them in lower paid and less prestigious jobs. Affirmative action is seen as a way to alleviate such barriers and having more of such groups in the workforce can result in benefits accruing to a more diverse workforce. Furthermore, as we saw earlier, affirmative action is also meant to create a more just society. With minorities and other disadvantaged groups getting better treatment, they can get access to more opportunities and play a bigger role in the society's affairs.

Despite the above reasoning behind affirmative action programs, such programs have encountered significant criticisms. Because specific races or gender are given preference, some critics see affirmative action as violating the principle of equality. In India, critics argue that because those with lower qualifications are hired over those with better qualifications, it is expected that the quality of work and academic performance is poorer. This thus results in less productivity and efficiency.[36] Furthermore, others argue that white males tend to be discriminated against in what is termed "reverse discrimination." Finally, some argue that all should be viewed and seen equally if we want to have an equal and fair society.

While affirmative action has its critics, some argue that many companies have actually not gone far enough in their programs.[37] In the case of India, the programs have been very successful in the public sector. However, the private sector has been much more reluctant to adopt such practices.[38] Additionally, a recent study of attitudes towards affirmative action programs in India shows that Indian multinationals have been more focused on hiring women at the expense of the other lower castes and classes. The Indian government is therefore working hard to encourage more private sector adoption of affirmative action programs.

The situation is also very dire in the U.S. Consider that although the Bank of America has a well-known diversity program, it was recently given a $60 million fine because it was found that the program was keeping black employees away from rich

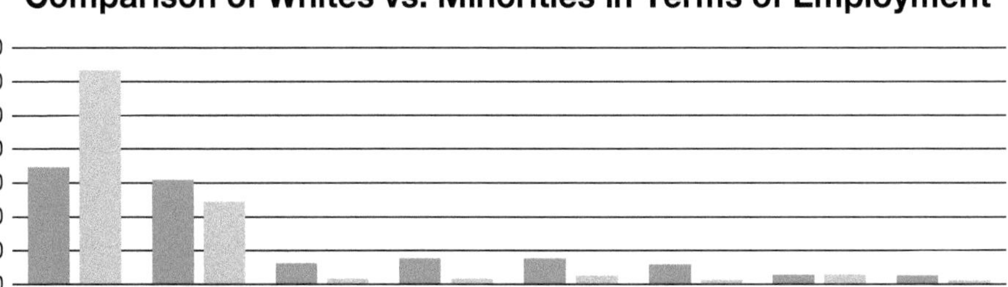

EXHIBIT 5.4—Comparison of Whites and Minorities

white customers. Similarly, KPMG's statistics show that its new hires include around 28% of minorities, while around 27% of promoted managers are also minorities. However, at the higher partner level, diversity metrics show that 93% of all KPMG partners are white. Examination of data from the U.S. Bureau of Labor Statistics shows the wide racial and gender disparity in the workforce. As Exhibit 5.4 shows, although white employees account for around two-thirds of all employment, they hold 90% of executive/senior level positions in companies.

Given the bleak picture painted by Exhibit 5.4, it becomes imperative for companies to implement strong affirmative action programs. In fact, Combs, Nadkarni and Combs go as far as suggesting that multinationals need to implement affirmative action programs in their global operations.[39] Such recommendations are necessary given that vulnerable groups such as women or minorities tend to be discriminated against worldwide. Furthermore, as the earlier Global Business Ethics Insight showed, many other countries such as the UK, Malaysia, India, Nigeria, South Africa, and Canada have all embarked on affirmative action legislation. Implementing affirmative action and diversity programs allow multinationals to be proactive by staying ahead of potential new regulations. Furthermore, global affirmative action programs allow these multinationals to reap the benefits of a more diverse and creative workforce while also projecting a socially responsible image.

While implementing affirmative action programs for domestic companies involves following the Equal Opportunity Uniform Guidelines and investing in other efforts such as 1) having a diversity advisory board and diversity officer, 2) establishing diversity networks for mentoring, 3) providing diversity training, 4) active diversity recruiting, and 5) establishing diversity scorecards for accountability and to gauge progress, most experts agree that multinationals face additional challenges when implementing such programs.[40] For instance, not all cultures readily accept implementation of affirmative action programs. As an example, the cultural dimension of power distance suggests that countries with high power distance have societal members who are more likely to accept and submit to authority. Previous research suggests that it is easier to implement programs in such countries. Additionally, legal frameworks may constrain the types of affirmative action programs that are implemented. Consider that both India and Malaysia have programs that require quotas in certain jobs. This suggests that multinationals will need to clearly understand the local requirements before implementing such programs.

Given the above constraints, Combs et al. and others suggest that the following be kept in mind when implementing global affirmative action programs:[41]

- The local requirements should dictate the appropriate form of affirmative action programs. Such programs fall within two categories: 1) opportunity enhancement plans whereby multinationals proactively hire and promote minorities and women without focus on rigid quotas; and 2) preferential treatment plans where multinationals adhere to strict quotas and hire on the basis of race, ethnicity, or caste. For instance, India has passed legislation to encourage companies to encourage more of a preferential treatment program.
- Multinationals should also make sure to understand the importance of having diversity. Many companies tend to shy away from diverse candidates because they believe that the diverse candidate will not fit in the company's culture and within teams. However, multinationals should acknowledge that diversity can and does create conflict. It is the appropriate management of such conflict that will result in stronger gains based on diversity of ideas and perspectives.
- Multinationals need to clearly define the target groups of affirmative action program beneficiaries. For example, in Canada, affirmative action programs target four groups: women, racial minorities, aboriginal groups, and people with disabilities. In India, while affirmative action programs in multinationals have focused on the lowest caste, namely untouchables, they should be extended to women and employees with disability.
- While customization to local needs is necessary, multinationals must also actively integrate the various affirmative action programs. Top management should play a key role in supporting such efforts. Liaison units should be created to coordinate the various efforts. Finally, networks should be established to help mentor disadvantaged groups worldwide. For instance, it is well known that women expatriates (employees who decide to take employment in a foreign subsidiary of a multinational) are rare and face significant barriers. Multinationals can thus work to establish female expatriate networks.

SEXUAL HARASSMENT

Sexual harassment is another critical issue most companies have to face as they relate to employees. **Sexual harassment** is defined by the Equal Employment Opportunity Commission as:

> Unwelcome sexual advances, requests for sexual favors, and other verbal or physical conduct of a sexual nature constitute sexual harassment when a) submission to such conduct is made either explicitly or implicitly a term or condition of an individual's

employment, b) submission to or rejection of such conduct by an individual is used as the basis for employment decisions affecting such individual, and c) such conduct has the purpose or effect of unreasonably interfering with an individual's work performance, or creating an intimidating, hostile or offensive work environment.[42]

Given the above definition, sexual harassment is usually categorized in two forms. Sexual harassment can be seen as **quid pro quo** (i.e., this for that) where a person makes explicit requests for sexual favors in exchange for a workplace benefit such as a raise or a promotion. Often, the person making the request is in a position of power and has authority over the victim.[43] The second form of sexual harassment is referred to as the **hostile/poisoned work environment**, where sex-related behaviors and mores make individuals feel uncomfortable and abused in the workplace. Hostile environment sexual harassment can take the form of sexual jokes being told in the workplace, derogatory name calling where the victim is labeled with a sexual nickname, rubbing of buttocks or breasts, and other forms of more subtle harassment. Exhibit 5.5 lists the most frequent forms of harassment.

Most Common Forms of Sexual Harassment
1. Sexual teasing, jokes, or remarks
2. Pressure for dating
3. Letters, phone calls, or other materials of sexual nature
4. Sexual gestures or looks
5. Deliberate touching, leaning, or cornering
6. Pressure for sexual favors
7. Actual or attempted rape or sexual assault

EXHIBIT 5.5—Most Common Forms of Sexual Harassment

The U.S. is currently seeing a large wave of sexual harassment claims against well-known personalities. Consider the case of Harvey Weinstein, the former CEO of Miramax, who has been accused of sexual harassment and assault by a large number of women. Sexual harassment is also a global issue. Consider the Emerging Market Business Ethics Insight below, which provides some understanding of the prevalence of sexual harassment in Mexico and Nigeria. However, recent surveys published by the International Labor Organization and others[44] reveal that sexual harassment is a worldwide phenomenon. Exhibit 5.6 summarizes worldwide surveys.

While sexual harassment has traditionally been viewed as men harassing women, the evidence suggests that sexual harassment is also prevalent. In fact, a review of data provided by the U.S. based Equal Employment Opportunity Commission in charge of enforcing sexual harassment laws, shows around 16 to 18% of sexual harassment cases between 2010 and 2016 were filed by men.[45] Additionally, recent court cases also

Country	Prevalence of Sexual Harassment
Hong Kong	Survey of employees in 2007 revealed that nearly 25% of workers were sexually harassed. One third of those harassed were men.
Italy	A 2004 report suggests that 55.4% of women in the 14–59 age group reported being sexually harassed.
European Union	Around 40–50% of women reported sexual harassment.
Australia	According to a survey carried out in 2004, 18% of interviewees reported being victims of sexual harassment.
Netherlands	Study published in 1986 reported that 58% of women interviewed had experienced sexual harassment.
United Kingdom	A 1987 study shows that 73% of women respondents felt sexually harassed during their occupational life. A 2017 study undertaken by the BBC revealed that 63% of women had experienced sexual harassment. However, 20% of men also revealed that they had experienced sexual harassment.
Germany	In a study conducted in 1991, 93% of women reported sexual harassment.
Japan	In a large-scale study conducted among 6,762 employees, a third reported being sexually harassed at work.
South Korea	Two separate studies conducted found that between 64% and 70% of women reported being subject to sexual harassment at work.
Philippines	A survey of women workers revealed that at least 17% of the companies surveyed had sexual harassment cases.
Malaysia	Between 83% and 88% of women responding to a survey experienced some form of sexual harassment.

EXHIBIT 5.6—Prevalence of Sexual Harassment Worldwide

EMERGING MARKET BUSINESS ETHICS INSIGHT

Sexual Harassment in Mexico and Nigeria

Maquiladoras are factories owned by corporations in foreign countries. In Mexico, many of these maquiladoras often have women form large proportions of their workforce. While the maquiladoras have provided women with the opportunity to work outside the home and to be financially independent, they are often discriminated against and sexually harassed. These women are often hired based on gender stereotypes. While men are generally viewed as primary wage earners, women are often seen as docile, passive human beings who are easy to train. Owners thus frequently subject these women to sexual harassment. Supervisors use sexual harassment as a means to control and manipulate women employees. For example, they are often encouraged to attend company parties and dinners and to give in to the sexual advances of their supervisors in exchange for job benefits such as additional pay or vacation days. Furthermore, supervisors will also harass women employees to encourage them to compete against each other for affection and to lessen the likelihood of the formation of unions. Because these women are often expected to also fulfill female gender roles such as caring for children and cooking, they often do not have time to pursue sexual harassment claims.

In a field survey of employees in Nigeria, Johnson found that women are being sexually harassed on a regular basis.[46] Additionally, Johnson reported that many women were unwilling to complete the survey because of the lack of education regarding sexual harassment. More educated women were more likely to complete the survey and indicated that sexual harassment is pervasive in the Nigerian workplace. Many women mentioned that they were afraid to report the harassment for fear of losing their jobs. Sexual harassment included perpetrators asking for sexual favors, making sexual comments, grabbing the victim's buttocks, or kissing the victim. Additionally, a recent study also shows that sexual harassment is also very prevalent in Nigerian tertiary institutions. Male lecturers who are often wealthier and older are likely to harass the young women students.

Why is sexual harassment so prevalent in Mexico and Nigeria? Both societies embrace traditional gender roles where men are expected to be dominant providers while women are seen as submissive caregivers. Furthermore, attitudes toward sexuality are very different for males and females in Nigeria. Young men and men in general are encouraged to sexuality, while women are stigmatized if they engage in similar behaviors. This has also reinforced male sexual aggressiveness as normal and not worth reporting.

Based on Akpotor, J. 2016. "Sexism and sexual harassment in tertiary institutions." *Gender and Behavior*, 11, 1, 5237–5243; Johnson, K. 2010. "Sexual harassment in the workplace: A case study of Nigeria." *Gender and Behaviour*, 8, 1, 2903–2918; Tanner-Rosati, C. 2010. "Is there a remedy to sex discrimination in maquiladoras?" *Law and Business Review of the Americas*, 16, 3, 533–557.

suggest that sexual harassment can also occur between same sexes. While sexual harassment between males has often been seen as mere horseplay, the recent case of *Smith v. Rock-Tenn. Services* suggests that the law also protects victims of same sex harassment.[47] In this case, the victim complained several times about unwanted touching and harassment by other male employees. The court agreed that such practices constitute sexual harassment that created a hostile work environment and not typical male socializing.

Clearly, sexual harassment is an issue that confronts most multinationals. Furthermore, the consequences of sexual harassment can be very devastating. A recent review of sexual harassment studies shows the extent to which sexual harassment can be destructive.[48] First, sexual harassment can have job-related consequences. For example, the review found that sexual harassment tends to negatively affect job satisfaction (the degree to which an employee is satisfied with his/her job) and organizational commitment (the degree to which an employee identifies with his/her employer company).

Additionally, an international study done by Merkin in Argentina, Brazil, and Chile shows that the more sexually harassed employees feel, the more likely they were to look for other jobs.[49] Furthermore, more harassed workers were more likely to be late or absent. Given the high costs associated with both tardiness and absence, sexual harassment can thus be very costly for any multinational.

Merkin also found that worker productivity can be greatly affected by sexual harassment.[50] Because employees feel abused or disempowered, they may develop personal animosities against other co-workers. Such an environment can be very hard for an employee to be productive. Roumeliotis and Kleiner (2005) also report that sometimes employees can become distracted from their task as a way to escape the harassment.[51] Furthermore, teamwork can suffer especially if an employee is being sexually harassed by another member of the team.

Beyond such work-related problems, sexual harassment can also be very disastrous for the harassed individual. Willness et al. argue that sexually harassed employees often suffer consequential poor mental health.[52] Some forms of sexual harassment can also be so traumatic that employees suffer from post-traumatic stress disorder. A recent study involving in-depth interviews of Australian workers showed that the victims of sexual harassment faced deep emotional scars, mental health problems as well as negative consequences for their personal relationships.[53] Additionally, a recent survey in Asia and the Pacific showed that those that are sexually harassed can suffer from physical symptoms (nausea, loss of appetite, anger, fear, and anxiety) as well as emotional and physiological effects (humiliation, anger, powerlessness, depression, and loss of motivation). Furthermore, the survey reveals that women who are sexually harassed also face the possibility of unwanted pregnancies and sexually transmitted diseases as well as HIV. The most extreme consequence is suicide. The International Labor Organization report suggests that women who are sexually harassed in some societies are seen as "tainted" or morally reprehensible women. There are therefore reports of such women attempting suicide in countries such as Bangladesh, Nepal, and Sri Lanka.

While employees suffer considerably from sexual harassment, research shows that the companies involved also suffer from the consequences of rampant sexual harassment. Companies with cultures supporting sexual harassment tend to have employees with poorer productivity. Such companies may also have trouble retaining employees. Furthermore, the costs of litigation can be very high. According to statistics published by the Equal Employment Opportunity Commission, they received 6758 complaints in 2016 and resolved 7433 of those cases. In the process, the EEOC collected $40.7 million in damages.

Given the many negatives associated with sexual harassment, it is critical for multinationals to implement steps to reduce such incidences. Such steps must include the following:[54,55]

- *Determine the extent to which the problem currently exists.* Employees can be surveyed to determine the incidence of sexual harassment. The company should carefully look at gray areas where issues such as jokes are exceeding reasonable boundaries.

Are employees too affectionate with each other? Carefully determining the extent of inappropriate behavior will enable the company to determine the extent of the problem and the degree to which sexual harassment needs to be addressed.

- *Employee education.* Extant evidence suggests that people do not always view sexual harassment in the same light as the victim of the harassment. Employees may think that something is not offensive or that sexual harassment behaviors are acceptable because it is expected. As such, multinationals can implement preventative measures focused on awareness. It therefore becomes critical that employees be made aware of what constitutes sexual harassment and be given the means to end such abuses. Abusers can determine whether their behavior is appropriate by asking questions such as "Would you say it in front of your spouse or parents?," "How would you feel if your mother, sister, wife or daughter were subjected to the same behaviors or words?," or "Do such things really need to be said?" Making employees aware of what constitutes sexual harassment and the negative effects of sexual harassment is a good start to a healthy workplace environment.
- *Employee training.* In addition to finding what sexual harassment issues exist and making workers aware of sexual harassment, multinationals should also train their employees. Extant research suggests that training regularly for all employees works best. Using the information garnered earlier about the extent of sexual harassment, companies can devise programs to target problem areas. Additionally, managers and others should be trained to be effective listeners and communicators. Programs dedicated to conflict management are also highly advisable.
- *Having the right sexual harassment officer.* A sexual harassment program is effective if a company chooses the right person to implement sexual harassment policies. This individual should be provided with ongoing training in harassment issues. The person should be able to listen, investigate, mediate, and counsel. Victims in a multinational should feel comfortable to talk to the officer without fear of retaliation. The officer should also have the appropriate training to be able to propose effective solutions to sexual harassment problems.
- *Having and communicating the right procedures.* The multinational should set up clear reporting procedures if employees feel sexually harassed. Managers and supervisors should be familiar with these procedures. Such procedures should also be clearly communicated to employees. Such policies should be regularly communicated to employees so that they feel that there is an outlet if they are sexually harassed. The worst outcome for a multinational is if the victim steps out of the company outlets to make such complaints.
- *Strong disciplinary action.* For the sexual harassment program to be effective, employees must perceive the program to be protecting them from sexual harassment while also punishing harassers. It therefore becomes critical for the multinational to take strong disciplinary action against the harasser if the sexual harassment incidences do not stop after training. This is especially critical in societies where strong gender roles exist and where women have been traditionally harassed.
- *Enforce and support national regulations and laws.* Multinationals have a critical role to play in enforcing sexual harassment laws and regulations worldwide. Most societies

view sexual harassment negatively, although there are varying levels of support for the behavior. Multinationals can thus play important roles in enforcing healthy workplace environments in their foreign subsidiaries by clearly enforcing such policies.

The pervasiveness of social media has added another challenging dimension to sexual harassment prevention. Consider the following Strategic Business Ethics Insight.

STRATEGIC BUSINESS ETHICS INSIGHT

Social Media and Sexual Harassment Prevention

New social media technologies such as Facebook, LinkedIn, Twitter, Foursquare etc. have created new challenges with respect to sexual harassment. Consider the case of two employees who are posted on a short international assignment. Through conversations at work, they decide to book plane tickets together and eventually develop a romantic relationship in the remote location. However, after they come back to the U.S., they decide to break up. Nevertheless, the male employee continues to text his female co-worker and makes demeaning posts on her Facebook page. Even when she "unfriends" him on Facebook, he continues to send texts asking where she is and who she is having lunch with. The female worker thus feels constantly stalked and sexually harassed. Use of social media allows access to private aspects of one's life that was not possible before.

How can multinationals deal with such new challenges? One overarching method has been for companies to simply prevent romance at work. Such practices ensure that workers do not get into positions where sexual harassment can occur through the use of social media or other means. Romantic relationships at work can quickly turn sour and enhance the likelihood of sexual harassment.

However, many companies are also adopting specific social media policies to prevent sexual harassment. For instance, companies can have policies where employees are allowed to trade work-related texts during working hours. Furthermore, if companies are providing mobile phones, they can train their employees to use texting during work times but prevent texting after work hours. Additionally, employees can also be trained on the appropriate and inappropriate use of social media. The consequences of inappropriate use of social media can be discussed through the use of hypothetical scenarios. Finally, multinationals should also have systems in place to properly investigate and punish sexual harassment due to social media.

Based on Mainiero, L.A. and Jones, K.J. 2013. "Workplace romance 2.0: Developing a communication ethics model to address potential sexual harassment from inappropriate social media contacts between coworkers." *Journal of Business Ethics*, 114, 367–379.

As the above shows, sexual harassment is a key issue that affects most companies. Dealing appropriately with employees as stakeholders means providing a workplace environment free of sexual harassment. Next we discuss whistle-blowing.

WHISTLE-BLOWING

The final key employee issue we will examine in this chapter is whistle-blowing. **Whistle-blowing** refers to the activities involved "when current or former employees disclose illegal, immoral or illegitimate organizational activities to parties that they believe may be able to stop it."[56] Many recent high-profile ethical scandals at Enron and WorldCom came to light because of whistle-blowers who decided to publicize ethical wrongdoing. Consider, for instance, the case of Mr. Birkenfeld who was a wealth manager at Credit Suisse. He disclosed information about many unethical activities at the Swiss bank including money laundering, accounting fraud and violation of U.S. anti-bribery laws.[57] This led to the successful prosecution of the bank. Whistle-blowing is therefore a key element of an ethical organization and its relationship to employees.

Is whistle-blowing a beneficial activity? Many argue that whistle-blowing has several advantages for society as well as the participating company. For example, whistle-blowing can benefit society as it can prevent faulty or dangerous products from reaching the marketplace. Furthermore, Verschoor reports that the U.S. Food and Drug Administration has received significant settlement from many pharmaceuticals companies for fraud.[58] For instance, Pfizer was involved in the illegal marketing of several drugs for unapproved uses. Additionally, government whistle-blowers such as Chelsea Manning who leaked 75,000 documents to reveal the massive U.S. domestic and international surveillance programs, are seen as playing critical roles in revealing information about government action.[59] Such whistle-blowing has clearly benefited society in general.

However, whistle-blowing can also be beneficial to the organizations. At an individual level, whistle-blowing is often seen as the moral thing to do.[60] However, as you read in Chapter 1, fraud is a significant problem for many companies. Whistle-blowing tips are often the primary way fraud can be detected and losses curbed. Furthermore, a good internal whistle-blowing program can enable a company to address some ethical problems before such problems escalate and cause significant losses and reputational damages to the company. Research reported in Miceli et al. also suggests that a strong whistle-blowing program should result in a workplace environment free of ethical wrongdoing.[61] Such an environment can lead to a very healthy culture that makes employees feel more committed to and satisfied with their employing organization. Finally, addressing whistle-blowing programs is now a legal requirement in the U.S. The Sarbanes-Oxley Act provides legal protection from retaliation to employees who whistle-blow.

Despite these advantages, many see whistle-blowing as an unethical behavior on the part of the employee. A company expects that its employees will be loyal and behave in ways that will protect the employing company's interests. For example, by exposing the fraudulent reporting at Enron, Sherron Watkins was perceived as being disloyal to Enron. However, recent arguments by Varelius suggest that whistle-blowing is not necessarily incompatible with being loyal to one's company.[62] In fact, whistle-blowing is beneficial to the company as it prevents further unethical wrongdoing that can hurt the company. For instance, whistle-blowing can also be the means by which an employee prevents the release of dangerous products that can end up hurting the public.[63] Whistle-blowing becomes a way for the employee to prevent future harm to the company through lawsuits etc. Thus, it is possible to be loyal to a company and to whistle-blow on unethical wrongdoings.

While whistle-blowing is a key aspect of most U.S. companies' ethical programs, it is also practiced worldwide. Research documents whistle-blowing programs in countries such as Australia, Canada, China, Croatia, France, Hong Kong, India, Iceland, Jamaica, Japan, Peru, South Africa, South Korea, and New Zealand among many others.[64] However, although whistle-blowing may be practiced in many countries, it is not necessarily as embraced as sexual harassment policies. In fact, the European Union has been problematic, as U.S. multinationals enforce whistle-blowing programs in their European subsidiaries. Many countries in the European Union have strict laws and regulations that ban whistle-blowing. Such bans stem from the fact that the European Union has different views regarding data privacy protection rights and individual rights. For instance, the collection, registration, and storage of personal data related to an individual may fall foul of European Union laws governing privacy of personal data.[65]

However, whistle-blowing has not been a failure in all countries of the European Union. For instance, a recent study of the Norwegian public sector showed that a very large proportion of employees blew the whistle when they observed misconduct.[66] Surprisingly, a majority of these employees received positive reactions and helped improve the conduct that was whistle-blown. Authors of the study argue that the model of labor relations in Norway and the strong emphasis on collective arrangements provide for a healthy environment where employees are free to voice their opinions on misconduct and not fear retaliation.

Given the varying rules and regulations, it becomes difficult for any multinational to establish uniform worldwide codes of conduct for whistle-blowing. Astute multinationals will have to scan local laws and establish whistle-blowing programs in compliance with such rules and regulations. In some parts of the world, whistle-blowing may not be viewed as favorably. However, another key area of interest as it relates to employees as stakeholders is the consequences of whistle-blowing. Dasgupta and Kesharwani argue that one of the most damaging consequences of whistle-blowing has been retaliation against the whistle-blower.[67] Consider that Lee informed both the CEO and the chief financial officer of Lehman Brothers of senior management's violation of the company's code of conduct and the tens of billions of dollars that could not be substantiated on the balance sheet. Instead of taking Lee's report seriously, Lehman Brothers concluded that his report was unfounded and allegations baseless.[68] Mr. Lee was also fired. Retaliation can thus range from the employer attacking the whistle-blower on the basis of his/her credibility and sources, to subsequent poor performance evaluations, to eventually losing their job. Research also suggests that

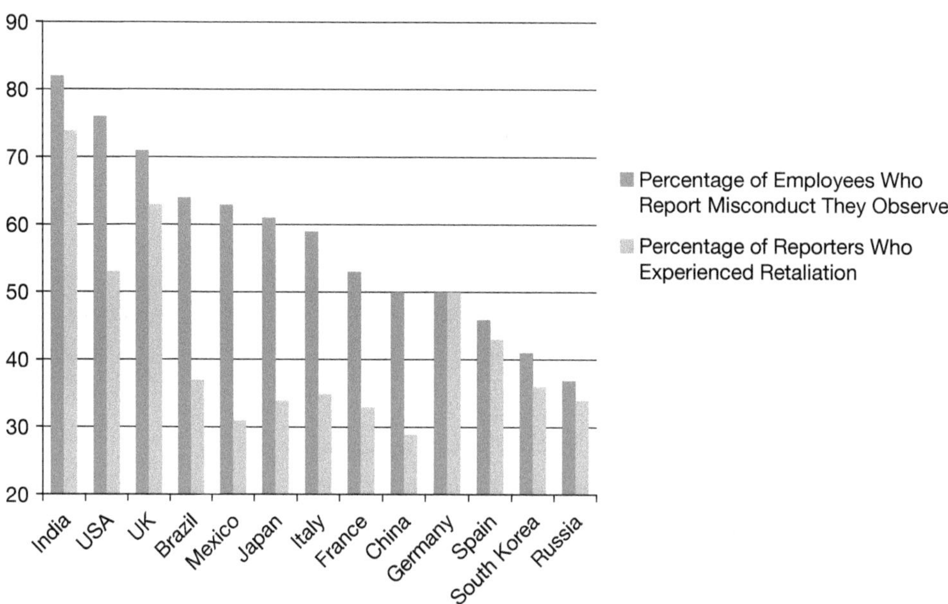

EXHIBIT 5.7—Misconduct Reporting and Retaliation

Based on Ethics Resource Center—Global Business Ethics Survey, www.ethics.org/research/gbes

whistle-blowers suffer in their non-work lives though depression, divorce, and other personal life difficulties.

Such retaliation is not limited to U.S. companies. Consider the results of the most recent survey undertaken by the Ethics Research Center on whether employees reported misconduct if they observed it and whether they experienced retaliation after the report. As Exhibit 5.7 shows, the good news is that a large percentage of employees do report misconduct if they see such misconduct. However, it is important to note that over 1/3 of those surveyed experienced some form of retaliation. This data suggests that multinationals need to implement aggressive policies to protect their employees from retaliation.

Given the importance of whistle-blowing to companies, recent regulation has been promulgated in the U.S. to protect whistle-blowers from retaliation. Specifically, the Sarbanes-Oxley Act was passed to provide protection to whistle-blowers. A company is in violation if it takes wrongful action against an employee who whistle-blows about activities that the employee reasonably thinks are in violation of laws or accounting practices. Furthermore, the law protects employees of public companies who whistle-blow about activities related to financial securities or shareholder fraud. Such legal protection has been shown to make whistle-blowing more effective in countries such as Peru and South Korea.[69]

As whistle-blowing becomes a global phenomenon, more multinationals will be encouraged to establish whistle-blowing programs. As such, multinationals need to first establish some in-house mechanism for employees to whistle-blow. One of the popular ways to allow whistle-blowing is through the implementation of hotlines.[70] Employees should be made aware of such mechanisms, while new employees should be trained and informed of the existence of such mechanisms. Employees should also be aware that they will not be punished or retaliated against if they decide to whistle-blow. Some experts even argue for reward systems for those who whistle-blow.

The process by which multinationals deal with complaints is also an important factor in determining the effectiveness of a whistle-blowing program. Employees should have some reasonable assurance that their complaints will be dealt with seriously with no fear of retaliation. Managers and other supervisors should be properly trained in how to handle complaints. Furthermore, those participating in the violating activities should be punished. Employees need to know that their attempts to whistle-blow are taken seriously.

STRATEGIC ROLE OF HUMAN RESOURCE MANAGEMENT ENFORCING ETHICS

The **human resource management (HRM) department** has a strategic role in ensuring an ethical organization, as the organization deals with employees as stakeholders. Sloan and Gavin argue that around one-third of ethics programs in *Fortune* 500 companies are housed in the human resource management department.[71] The HRM department is the critical link between a company and its employees. The department is in charge of ensuring the welfare of employees while also ensuring that the rights of these employees are being respected. For instance, as you read in the opening paragraphs of this chapter, a company can maximize its chances of hiring employees with higher ethical dispositions by paying careful attention to the recruitment and selection process. Making sure that potential new employees are more likely to be ethical is a critical component of the ethical organization. In the final section of this chapter, we therefore look very briefly at the relevant HRM functions and how they contribute to ethics in any organization.

At a basic level, the HRM functions can be instrumental in developing an ethical culture in the organization. As you will see in Chapter 12, the ethical culture is what employees believe is the appropriate way to deal with ethical issues. If properly implemented, the many aspects discussed below will contribute to a culture where employees will do the right thing. For instance, L'Oreal, the French cosmetics multinational, appointed a high-level HR person as the director of ethics.[72] That person is responsible for preparing ethics reports for the CEO and the executive board. Additionally, the company implemented many policies and practices to cultivate employee ethical "fluency." Additionally, a recent study of 6000 employees from six European countries showed that the adoption of ethical practices in all HRM functions led to synergistic effects that contributed to more ethical cultures.[73]

What are the ways an HR department can contribute to a more ethical company? As you read earlier, if properly implemented, the HRM functions of recruitment and selection allows the company to hire only those employees who have a higher likelihood of behaving ethically. However, the HRM recruitment and selection process can also play a critical role in ensuring that diversity and affirmative actions are met. The HRM department can take steps to encourage a multinational to pay attention to reaching out to potential candidates of prejudiced groups. The HRM department can find locally appropriate ways to recruit employees from these groups (e.g., advertising in different outlets). The HRM department can also ensure that there is fit between the potential new employee and the ethical values of the company.[74] Applicants should be surveyed to gauge their level of agreement with the ethical values espoused by the company. New employees should be committed to both enforcing ethics and discussing ethics issues. Additionally, the use of hiring algorithms may also introduce biases. Consider the following Business Ethics Insight.

BUSINESS ETHICS INSIGHT

Use of Hiring Algorithms

Because so many companies are now receiving large numbers of résumés for open positions, many more HR managers are relying on hiring algorithms to eliminate applicants who may not fit the ideal profile for these openings. Hiring algorithms are criteria that can be specified to examine résumés to weed out candidates based on previous success. Such practices are becoming important ways that companies can quickly assess thousands of résumés and select those that are deserving of consideration.

Although hiring algorithms can be a way for companies to save cost by effectively sifting through large amounts of résumés, the hiring criteria in the algorithm may inadvertently introduce biases. Hiring algorithms are often based on what has worked in the past. However, such decision criteria may end up discriminating against specific groups. For example, hiring software may be based on criteria such as participation in extra-curricular activities while in college. However, such criteria may end up disadvantaging particular groups because these minority groups may not have been able to participate in these activities because they had to work. As a result, a hiring algorithm may not be necessarily neutral.

To eliminate the potential of bias, experts suggest that HR departments work with individuals affected by bias to develop better algorithms. Decisions made by the software can also be checked at random to ensure that biases are not entering the selection process. Additionally, the HR department can also introduce rigorous observation and control systems to make sure that selection processes are free of bias.

Based on Mann, G. and O'Neil, C. 2016. "Hiring algorithms are not neutral." *Harvard Business Review*, December 9, 2–4.

The Business Ethics Insight suggests that companies need to be careful about biases entering the hiring process. However, another critical function undertaken by a HRM department is performance appraisals. Performance appraisals relate to how employees' productivity and other performance components are assessed. For the ethical organization, the process by which performance takes place needs to embody ethical values.[75] The system should be transparent and provide for objective ways to assess how employees are doing.

The compensation area is also a critical area that embodies the ethical values of an organization. As Sloan and Gavin argue, this is an area that received considerable

BUSINESS ETHICS INSIGHT

Should Multinationals be Transparent About Salary?

As mentioned earlier in this chapter, women face significant pay inequities in the technology fields. For example, Google was recently sued by several women as they felt underpaid compared with their male counterparts. This situation is no different in other parts of the world. Reports in a recent study suggested that women in the information technology and engineering fields reported gender-based segregation based on pay and promotion opportunities. Despite their high education and equivalent skills, Indian women were paid less than Indian men and were placed in more routine jobs. This was also the case in the case of Indian women working in factories.

How can multinationals promote pay equity? A recent article suggests that pay transparency can become an important way to fight pay inequity. Through pay transparency, employees can quickly see what others are getting paid for and find ways to address inequity. For example, when hackers published salary data for Sony Pictures, the public was horrified to see blatant pay differences between male and female star actors. Nevertheless, such information has provided the basis for other women actors to negotiate more equitable pay. Additionally, supporters for this position argue that pay transparency also plays an important market function. When people are aware of prices (or salaries), the market (labor) works better.

Despite the benefits of pay transparency, it seems unlikely that most multinationals' HR departments will publish such data soon. Companies usually count on knowing more about salaries when negotiating with potential new employees. Additionally, recent studies also suggest that pay transparency can reduce morale and job satisfaction as employees are more aware of what their peers make.

Based on *The Economist*, 2017. "Women in tech; Bits and bias." April 15, 54–56; *The Economist*, 2017. "Too tight to mention; Firms should make more information about salaries public." October 28, 74; Haq, R. 2012. "The managing diversity mindset in public versus private organizations in India." *International Journal of Human Resource Management*, 23, 5, 892–914.

attention from both employees and society.[76] A multinational must therefore ensure that compensation and benefits are distributed in a fair and equitable manner. As you will see later in Chapter 11, the low wages paid in developing nations has always been a source of ethical controversy. Through compensation and benefits programs, a multinational must be ready and willing to address such controversies. Additionally, another source of ethical frustration for companies is pay inequity. Companies need to therefore decide how they can address such inequity. Consider the Business Ethics Insight on the facing page.

Although all multinationals may not necessarily make salaries public, such transparency may play an important role in furthering the ethics function of the HRM department. In that context, a final critical HRM function that we consider is **training**. This refers to the efforts by a multinational to impart new skills and capabilities in employees. However, many aspects of enforcing ethics in an organization involve training. Consider the case of Auchan, a French multinational, started in 1961 as a single supermarket and which now runs supermarkets and hypermarkets in over 12 countries with sales of 35 billion Euros. In 2004, when the Charte de la Diversité (Diversity Charter) passed in France, Auchan decided to examine diversity in its operations. The diversity team found evidence of implicit discrimination based on stereotypes. To address these problems, Auchan spent around 1 million Euros to provide 130 half-day training sessions to 5500 of its employees. A major emphasis was placed on training employees to become more sensitive to unconscious discrimination. Employees had to confront their stereotypes through role-playing, and people from immigrant backgrounds, gays, and people with disabilities discussed how they cope with such discrimination.

Training is thus a critical function that HRM departments have to offer. For instance, consider that Howard suggests that while many companies offer training to their employees on how to detect sexual harassment, they often do not train workers to know how to stop such harassment or even deal with sexual harassment when it occurs.[77] Recent discussions suggest that sexual harassment victims are often reluctant to report such instances.[78] As such, companies can train and make all employees aware of appropriate complaints handling procedures, availability of several reporting channels, the timeliness of handling of complaints and the application of the appropriate punishment for sexual harassment violations. Such training will ensure that employees perceive the system to be fair.

Training is thus necessary to ensure that the many activities discussed in this chapter (affirmative action, sexual harassment, whistle-blowing) occur in ways that are consistent with the values of an ethical organization. In fact, merely having ethics policies and codes and communicating such aspects to employees may not always be effective. The HRM function has a critical role to play in training employees to see how organizational values are translated into daily life in the company.[79] Furthermore, training for the job must be offered in an equitable manner while also taking into consideration individual differences in abilities and learning styles.[80]

Finally, the HRM department is also responsible for implementing ethics metrics and conducting ethics audits.[81] Ethics improvement is not possible without actual benchmarks. A multinational can therefore set tangible ethics measures such as use of ethics hotlines, number of code of conduct violations, and other checks and balances to gauge the level of ethics.[82] Together with such metrics, ethics audits can also ensure that prohibited behaviors and actions within the realm of ethics are not occurring in the organization. A recent report suggests that the most common ethics audits involve examining "conflicts of interest, access to personal information, bidding and award practices, giving and receiving gifts and employee discrimination issues."[83] Thus, the HRM department may be responsible for setting up mechanisms to gauge the level of behavior consistent with the espoused values of the organization.

Exhibit 5.8 summarizes the HRM functions and the critical role these functions play in enforcing ethics.

Human Resource Management Function	Ethics Activity
Recruitment and Selection	• Abide by all laws and regulations when soliciting candidates to ensure good representation in terms of traditionally prejudiced groups (race, gender) to meet all diversity and affirmative action goals • Respect local laws regarding recruitment and selection • Conduct extensive tests (integrity tests, interviews, honesty tests) to ensure that potential new employees are ethical • Ensure that potential new employees' values match those of the organization
Performance Appraisal	• Design systems that embody the multinational's ethical norms and values • Ensure that systems can objectively (as far as possible) assess performance and provide feedback • Ensure that performance appraisal is conducted in a fair and objective manner
Compensation and Benefits	• Compensation and benefits must be distributed in a fair and equitable manner • Wage levels should be reasonable, taking into consideration local laws and norms • Address controversies surrounding low wages given in developing nations
Training	• Provide adequate training to ensure that employees can grow professionally • Provide sexual harassment, whistle-blowing, and other forms of needed training • Provide training in equitable manner while also taking into consideration personal needs and capabilities • Ensure that employees are trained to recognize prejudiced behaviors and/or use of stereotypes against protected classes (race, gender, etc.)
Other Activities	• Conduct ethics audit • Collect data regarding all ethics aspects in the organization (e.g., data regarding incidence of sexual harassment, data regarding discrimination, etc.)

EXHIBIT 5.8—HRM Functions and Ethics

CHAPTER SUMMARY

In this chapter, you learned about the many key issues facing companies as they deal with employees. While it is debatable, employees may still be the most important stakeholder. Employees help implement the company's strategy. It therefore becomes critical to address such employee issues. You therefore read about four key aspects of the organization's relationship with employees; namely, hiring and firing, diversity and affirmative action, sexual harassment, and whistle-blowing.

The hiring process is a critical aspect of how any organization relates to employees. It represents the first point of contact between the company and a potential employee. Multinationals thus need to be sensitive to the cultural needs of the countries they operate in. However, the firing process also represents one of the most traumatic aspects of any employee's life. You therefore learned about the employment-at-will environment common in the U.S. and the contrasting just-cause employment system in countries such as Canada and those in the European Union.

As most multinationals strive for some form of diversity (race, gender, etc.), you read about the importance of diversity. You also learned about affirmative action and the importance of such programs in companies. You also read about the many issues to keep in mind when establishing such programs.

Sexual harassment remains one of the most critical issues facing multinationals as they relate to employees. You read about the types of sexual harassment and the potentially devastating consequences of sexual harassment for the victim, the employer, and society. You also learned about the steps multinationals can take to address sexual harassment problems.

You also learned about whistle-blowing and the critical role played by whistle-blowing. Unlike the other employee issues, you read about the need for multinationals to be sensitive to local rules and regulations. You also read about the steps a multinational can take to implement a strong whistle-blowing program.

Finally, the text concludes with a discussion of the role that the HRD department plays in implementing and enforcing ethics in the company. The HRD department can play a critical role furthering an ethical culture and bringing to life the ethical values of the company. As such, the various HRM functions such as hiring and firing, training and performance appraisal were discussed and the implications of these functions for the ethical company were emphasized.

NOTES

1 Jackson, K. & Debroux, P. 2016. "HRM responses to ageing societies in Germany and Japan: Contexts for comparison." *Management Revue*, 27, 1–2, 5–13.
2 Collins, D. 2009. *Essentials of business ethics*. Hoboken, NJ: John Wiley and Sons.
3 Porath, C. 2016. "How to avoid hiring toxic employees." *Harvard Business Review*, February 3, 2–5.
4 Burks, S.V., Cowgill, B., Hoffman, M., Housman, M. 2015. "The value of hiring through employee referrals." *Quarterly Journal of Economics*, 130, 2, 805–839.

5 Collins, *Essentials of business ethics*.
6 Hofstede, G. 1997. *Cultures and organizations: Software of the mind*. New York: McGraw-Hill, pp. 64–65.
7 Collins, *Essentials of business ethics*.
8 Bird, R.B. & Charters, D. 2004. "Good faith and wrongful termination in Canada and the United States: A comparative and relational inquiry." *American Business Law Journal*, 41, 2/3, 205–250 (at 205).
9 Maertz, C.P., Wiley, J.W., Lerouge, C. & Campion, M.A. 2010. "Downsizing effects on survivors: Layoffs, offshoring, and outsourcing." *International Relations*, 49, 2, 275–285; Thurm, S. 2010. "Recalculating the cost of big layoffs." *Wall Street Journal Online*, May 4.
10 Thurm, S. 2010. "Recalculating the cost of big layoffs."
11 Bird & Charters, "Good faith and wrongful termination," 205.
12 McCall, J.J. 2003. "A defense of just cause dismissal rule." *Business Ethics Quarterly*, 12, 2, 151–175.
13 *The HR Specialist*. 2017. "Are you obligated to investigate before firing? For at-will employees, you have discretion." October 2, www.thehrspecialist.com/
14 Werhane, P.H & Radin, T.J. 2009. "Employment at will and due process." In Beauchamp, T.L., Bowie, N.L. & Arnold, D.G. (Eds.), *Ethical theory and business*, Harlow, UK: Pearson Publishing, pp. 113–120.
15 Werhane & Radin, "Employment at will and due process."
16 Dannin, E. 2007. "Why at-will employment is bad for employers and just cause is good for them." *Labor Law Journal*, 58, 1, 5–16.
17 Werhane & Radin, "Employment at will and due process."
18 Dannin, "Why at-will employment is bad for employers."
19 McCall, "A defense of just cause dismissal rule."
20 Dannin, "Why at-will employment is bad for employers," 5.
21 Kaiser, D.M. 2005. "The implications of at-will versus just-cause employment." *Proceedings of the Academy of Organizational Culture, Communications and Conflict*, 10, 2 (at 34).
22 Bird & Charters, "Good faith and wrongful termination."
23 Bird & Charters, "Good faith and wrongful termination."
24 Werhane & Radin, "Employment at will and due process."
25 Dannin, "Why at-will employment is bad for employers."
26 Beauchamp, T.L., Bowie, N.L. & Arnold, D.G. 2010. *Ethical theory and business*. Harlow, UK: Pearson Publishing.
27 Owens, J.M., Gomes, G.M. & Morgan, J.F. 2008. "Broadening the definition of unlawful retaliation under Title VII." *Employee Responsibility and Rights Journal*, 20, 249–260.
28 Fearfull, A. & Kamenou, N. 2010. "Work and career experiences of ethnic minority men and women." Introductory chapter for special issue, *Quality, Diversity and Inclusion: An International Journal*, 29, 4, 325–331.
29 Haq, R. 2012. "The managing diversity mindset in public versus private organizations in India." *International Journal of Human Resource Management*, 23, 5, 892–914.
30 Herring, C. 2009. "Does diversity pay? Race, gender, and the business case for diversity."*American Sociology Review*, 74, 2, 208–222.
31 Herring, "Does diversity pay?" 208.
32 Beauchamp et al., *Ethical theory and business*, p. 185.
33 Haq "The managing diversity mindset."
34 Brown, G. & Langer, A. 2015. "Does affirmative action work?" *Foreign Affairs*, 94, 2, 49–56
35 Haq, "The managing diversity mindset."
36 Despande, A. & Weisskopf, T.E. 2014. "Does affirmative action reduce productivity? A case study of the Indian railways." *World Development*, 64, 169–180
37 Hansen, F. 2010. "Diversity of a different color." *Workforce Management*, 89, 6, 23–26.
38 Haq, "The managing diversity mindset."
39 Combs, M.G., Nadkarni, S. & Combs, M.W. 2005. "Implementing affirmative action plans in multinational corporations." *Organizational Dynamics*, 34, 4, 346–360.

40 Combs et al., "Implementing affirmative action plans."
41 Combs et al., "Implementing affirmative action plans."; Haq, "The managing diversity mindset."; de Anca, C. 2016. "Why hiring for cultural fit can thwart your diversity efforts." *Harvard Business Review*, April 25, 2–4.
42 Willness, C.R., Steel, P. & Lee, K. 2007. "A meta-analysis of the antecedents and consequences of workplace sexual harrasment." *Personnel Psychology*, 60, 1, 127–162 (at 131).
43 Smolensky, E. & Kleiner, B.H. 2003. "How to prevent sexual harassment in the workplace." *Equal Opportunities International*, 22, 2, 59–65.
44 *BBC News*. 2017. "Half of women sexually harassed at work says BBC Survey." October 25, www.bbc.com/news/uk-41741615
45 Equal Employment Opportunity Commission, www.eeoc.gov/eeoc/statistics/enforcement/sexual_harassment_new.cfm
46 Johnson, K. 2010. "Sexual harassment in the workplace: A case study of Nigeria." *Gender and Behaviour*, 8, 1, 2903–2918.
47 Dean, K. 2016. "Employment law – *Smith v. Rock Tenn. Services* – Employer held liable for same-sex sexual harassment in the workplace." *Tennessee Journal of Law and Policy*, 11, 2, 154–157.
48 Willness et al., "A meta-analysis."
49 Merkin, R.S. 2008. "The impact of sexual harassment on turnover intentions, absenteeism, and job satisfaction: Findings from Argentina, Brazil and Chile." *Journal of International Women's Studies*, 10, 2, 73–91.
50 Merkin, "The impact of sexual harassment."
51 Roumeliotis, B.D. & Kleiner, B.H. 2005. "Individual response strategies to sexual harassment." *Equal Opportunities International*, 24, 5/6, 41–48.
52 Willness et al., "A meta-analysis."
53 Birinxhikaj, M. & Guggisberg, M. 2017. "The wide ranging impact of sexual harassment in the workplace: An Australian pilot study." *International Journal of Employment Studies*, 25, 1, 6–26.
54 Hunt, C.M., Davidson, M.J., Fielden, S.L. & Hoel, H. 2010. "Reviewing sexual harassment in the workplace—An intervention model." *Personnel Review*, 39, 5, 655–668; Johnson, "Sexual harassment in the workplace."; Smolensky & Kleiner, "How to prevent sexual harassment in the workplace."
55 McDonald, P., Charlesworth, S. & Graham, T. 2015. "Developing a framework of effective prevention and response strategies in workplace sexual harassment." *Asia Pacific Journal of Human Resources*, 53, 41–58.
56 Miceli, M.P., Near, J.P. & Dworkin, M.T. 2009. "A word to the wise: How managers and policy-makers can encourage employees to report wrongdoing." *Journal of Business Ethics*, 86, 379–392.
57 Delmas, C. 2015. "The ethics of government whistleblowing." *Social Theory and Practice*, 41, 1, 77–105.
58 Verschoor, C. 2010. "Increased motivation for whistleblowing." *Ethics*, 16, 18, 61.
59 Delmas, C. 2015. "The ethics of government whistleblowing." *Social Theory and Practice*, 41, 1, 77–105.
60 Hoffman, W.M. & Schwartz, M.S. 2015. "The morality of whistleblowing: A commentary on Richard T. De George." *Journal of Business Ethics*, 127, 771–781.
61 Miceli et al., "A word to the wise."
62 Varelius, J. 2009. "Is whistle–blowing compatible with employee loyalty?" *Journal of Business Ethics*, 85, 263–275.
63 Hoffman & Schwartz "The morality of whistleblowing."
64 Miceli et al., "A word to the wise."; Apaza, C.R. & Chang, Y. 2011. "What makes whistleblowing effective." *Public Integrity*, 13, 2, 113–129.
65 *Oprisk and Compliance*. 2009. "Global whistleblowing systems could fall foul of local rules." April, 11.
66 Skivenes, M. & Trygstad, C.S. 2010. "When whistle-blowing works: The Norwegian case." *Human Relations*, 63, 7, 1072–1092
67 Dasgupta, S. & Kesharwani A. 2010. "Whistleblowing: A survey of literature." *IUP Journal of Corporate Governance*, 9, 4, 57–70.

68 Jennings, M. 2010. "The employee we ignore, the signs we miss and the reality we avoid." *Corporate Finance Review*, 14, 6, 42–46.
69 Apaza, C.R. & Chang, Y. 2011. "What makes whistleblowing effective." *Public Integrity*, 13, 2, 113–129.
70 Sweeney, P. 2008. "Hotlines helpful for blowing the whistle." *Financial Executive*, May 24, 28–31.
71 Sloan, K.A. & Gavin, J.H. 2010. "Human resources management: Meeting the ethical obligations of the function." *Business and Society Review*, 115, 1, 57–74.
72 Berenbeim, R.E. 2010. "Utilizing HR and ethics and compliance collaboration to promote an ethical culture." *Employment Relations Today*, Spring, 17–26.
73 Guerci, M., Radaelli, G., De Battistis, F. & Siletti, E. 2017. "Empirical insights on the nature of synergies among HRM policies – an analysis of an ethics-oriented HRM system." *Journal of Business Research*, 71, 66–73.
74 Sloan & Gavin, "Human resources management."
75 Sloan & Gavin, "Human resources management."
76 Sloan & Gavin, "Human resources management."
77 Howard, L.G. 2007. "Employees poorly equipped to deal with sexual harassment." *Canadian HR Reporter*, 20, 6, 31.
78 McDonald, P., Charlesworth, S. & Graham, T. 2015. "Developing a framework of effective prevention and response strategies in workplace sexual harassment." *Asia Pacific Journal of Human Resources*, 53, 41–58.
79 Khandelwal, L.A. 2015. "To do or not to do – ethics in question!" *Human Capital*, September, 14–17.
80 Sloan & Gavin, "Human resources management."
81 Krell, E. 2010. "How to conduct an ethics audit." *HR Magazine*, 55, 4, 48–51.
82 Khandelwal, L.A. 2015. "HR – the enabler for ethics" *Human Capital*, September, 19.
83 Krell, "How to conduct an ethics audit," 49.

KEY TERMS

Affirmative action: laws, policies, or guidelines that specify positive steps to be taken to hire and promote persons from groups previously and presently discriminated against.

Diversity: hiring of workers who are different in race, color, or religion compared to the traditional Caucasian male workforce.

Employees: human resources available to a company dedicated to achieving its goals.

Employment-at-will: company may terminate its employee for a good reason, bad reason, or no reason at all.

Hiring: one of the critical ways that companies relate to employees as stakeholders.

Hostile/poisoned work environment: where sex-related behaviors and mores make women feel uncomfortable and abused in the workplace.

Human resource management (HRM) department: critical link between employees and company.

Just-cause dismissal: employers must provide reasonable notice of termination of an employee.

Quid pro quo sexual harassment: where a person makes explicit requests for sexual favors in exchange for a workplace benefit such as a raise or a promotion.

Recruitment: process of identifying and attracting qualified people to apply for vacant positions in an organization.
Selection: process by which a company chooses a person to fill a vacant position.
Sexual harassment: unwelcome sexual advances, requests for sexual favors, and other verbal or physical conduct of a sexual nature.
Termination: involuntary separation of company from employee.
Training: efforts by a multinational to impart new skills and capabilities in its employees.
Whistle-blowing: disclosure by current or former employees of illegal, immoral, or illegitimate organizational activities to parties that they believe may be able to stop it.

DISCUSSION QUESTIONS

1. What are recruitment and selection? How do recruitment and selection differ by countries?
2. What are the main features of employment-at-will? Discuss arguments to support employment-at-will.
3. Discuss the just-cause dismissal approach. How is this approach different from employment-at-will?
4. What is diversity? How is diversity beneficial for a multinational?
5. What is affirmative action? How can companies implement affirmative action programs?
6. What is sexual harassment? Discuss the types of sexual harassment and provide examples.
7. What can companies do to implement effective sexual harassment programs?
8. What is whistle-blowing? What are the benefits of whistle-blowing? How can companies implement effective whistle-blowing programs?
9. Discuss the human resource management functions. How can each function help enforce ethics in a company?
10. Why is the human resource management department so critical to build an ethical organization? Defend your answer with specific examples.

INTERNET ACTIVITY

1. Go to the International Labor Organization (ILO) website: www.ilo.org.
2. Read about the organization and its many functions. Discuss these functions and the critical role played by the ILO.
3. Go to the "Topics" area. List the many activities the ILO is involved in.
4. Pick four of these topics. Read the latest reports on these four topics. What are some of the major areas of concern for each of the four topics you read about?

5. Read about "Child Labor." How prevalent is the problem worldwide? What solutions do the ILO suggest to address child labor issues?

For more Internet Activities and resources, visit the Companion Website at www.routledge.com/cw/parboteeah.

WHAT WOULD YOU DO?

Competitor's Products

You recently graduated from a prestigious university with a degree in marketing. You apply for several marketing jobs and eventually get the job that you wanted the most. You will be a salesperson in a pharmaceuticals company that has had several breakthrough drugs recently. You know that this job will give you significant experience but you are also aware that the job will require hard work and long days ahead. During the interview, you impressed many of the top executives in the company.

After several weeks at work, you are approached by the vice president of marketing, who invites you for drinks after work. You realize that several new employees who were hired at the same time as you often get invited for such events. However, you are unsure whether you should go or not. After giving the idea some thought, you decide to accept the invitation.

The event at the local pub starts out well. You are having a good time with your co-workers and several top executives of the company. During the conversation, you also reveal that your best friend works for a competitor. However, soon you find that some individuals are getting drunk and making uncomfortable sexual advances to you. The vice president (VP) of marketing also makes some advances to you and mentions that you will go far in the company. During the conversation, the VP also starts questioning you about information you gleaned from your best friend. The VP seems interested in new products being developed by the competitor.

What would you do? Do you leave the party and forget that anything happened? Or do you report the offending individuals the next day and run the risk of ruining your new career?

* * *

BRIEF CASE: BUSINESS ETHICS INSIGHT

WalMart and Healthcare Benefits

On Friday October 20, 2011, WalMart made some shocking announcements during a press conference. It announced that all employees who worked less than 24 hours per week for the company would no longer qualify for any of the company's health plans. This was a surprising turnaround from a few years ago when WalMart decided to become an advocate for larger companies providing healthcare to all of its employees, and to part-time employees in 1996. Under strong pressure from labor unions and many states, WalMart had agreed to provide healthcare to its part-time employees after these employees had worked one year on the job. WalMart's decision was praised, as more than half of larger employers did not provide any healthcare to part-time employees at that time.

WalMart claims that rising healthcare costs and declining profitability are some of the main reasons they have decided to reduce health benefits. Reports suggest that employer-sponsored health premiums are predicted to go up by 9% over the 2011–2012 time period. However, some WalMart employees will see premium growth of around 40% in 2012. Despite this growth, WalMart employees will still be paying less than plans offered by other employers.

One of the other controversial aspects of WalMart's new health offerings is that employees who smoke will be required to pay a significant penalty. Specifically, smoking employees will likely have to pay around $10 to $90 extra per pay period. For some employees, this premium increase will mean that they can no longer afford the health insurance from the company.

Based on Greenhouse, S. and Abelson, R. 2011. "WalMart cuts some healthcare benefits." *New York Times*, online edition, October 20; Kliff, S. 2011. "The health insurance plight of part-time workers." *Washington Post*, online edition, October 23.

BRIEF CASE QUESTIONS

1. Is it a moral obligation for companies to provide healthcare for their employees? Why or why not?
2. Is WalMart justified in cutting healthcare benefits for part-time workers?
3. Is it ethical for companies to ask employees who smoke to pay higher health premiums? Or are the companies infringing on an employee's right to privacy?
4. How should WalMart respond to critics who say that the company does not cover its fair share of healthcare costs?

LONG CASE: BUSINESS ETHICS

IBS Center for Management Research

A SEXUAL HARASSMENT COMPLAINT AND THE FALLOUT

This case was written by Syeda Maseeha Qumer, Debapratim Purkayastha (IBS Hyderabad), and Vijaya Narapareddy (Daniels College of Business, University of Denver). It was compiled from published sources, and is intended to be used as a basis for class discussion rather than to illustrate either effective or ineffective handling of a management situation.

Won the **2017 Dark Side Case Award** organized by Critical Management Studies division of the Academy of Management, Atlanta, Georgia, USA.

On November 18, 2013, managing editor of Indian weekly news magazine *Tehelka*, Shoma Chaudhury (Shoma), received an e-mail from a woman journalist on her staff at *Tehelka*. In that e-mail, the journalist, Nina[a] accused Tarun Tejpal (Tarun), founder and Editor-in-Chief of *Tehelka*, of sexually assaulting her on two occasions during THiNK Fest 2013, an annual conference organized by the magazine in Goa. The victim provided a detailed and graphic account of the alleged sexual assault and demanded an official written apology from Tarun, an acknowledgement of the assault to be circulated among the staff and bureau of *Tehelka*, and the setting up of an anti-sexual harassment cell at *Tehelka* to probe the matter.

Shocked and distraught, Shoma was caught in a dilemma over her possible future course of action. *Tehelka* did not have any internal complaints committee as mandated under the Vishaka guidelines to prevent sexual harassment at the workplace (*see Exhibits I and II*).

About *Tehelka* and its Founder

In 2000, Tarun Tejpal co-founded *Tehelka* as an investigative news portal tehelka.com. After its launch, *Tehelka* broke new ground with its first sting operation called "Operation Fallen Heroes", which exposed match-fixing and betting in Indian cricket. In 2001, *Tehelka* was again in the spotlight when its "Operation West End" exposed

www.icmrindia.org

a The name of the victim is disguised in the case as under Indian law, the identity of a rape victim cannot be disclosed and those guilty of doing so face prosecution under Section 228-A of the Indian Penal Code.

corruption in the Indian Defense ministry and how several Defense officials and politicians from the then-ruling coalition government had accepted bribes. The sting operation carried out by *Tehelka,* in which some of its journalists posed as arms dealers, secretly captured senior army officials and bureaucrats accepting bribes in a fake arms deal. This scandal pushed the Indian government to the brink of a crisis and caused the resignations of several officials including the then Defense Minister and the presidents of two of the parties of the ruling coalition. According to media analysts, this exposé gave *Tehelka* and Tarun a larger than life image.

The aftermath of the scandal saw the Indian government launching an inquiry into the exposé as it questioned the methods adopted by *Tehelka* while making this exposé. Some reports alleged that *Tehelka* had resorted to unethical means such as using its women staff as prostitutes to lure army officials in the sting operation. It was also rumored that as a backlash, the Indian government had subjected *Tehelka* to tax raids and judicial investigations and filed cases against it. *Tehelka* was forced to lay off all but four of its 120 staff. The magazine's main financial backer and the reporters who carried out the sting were jailed. The website became virtually defunct and was forced to shut down in 2003.

However, with public funding, Tarun relaunched *Tehelka* in January 2004 as a weekly newspaper in the tabloid format. He reportedly raised Rs.[b] 20 million through 220 individual donations from his contacts in the business, political, art, and literary worlds.[1] He began to call the magazine the "People's Paper"—one committed to crusading and fearless journalism. The magazine lived up to its "Free, Fair, and Fearless" slogan by publishing news reports which often went unreported in the mainstream media. Since its inception, *Tehelka* had broken some of India's biggest stories including the match-fixing scandal, the Gujarat riots[c], the Jessica Lal case[d], and several corruption scandals. However, the magazine suffered a high rate of attrition, which Tarun attributed to its inability to match big media salaries.

In September 2007, Tarun rebranded *Tehelka* from a tabloid format newspaper to a national weekly magazine to attract more advertisers. That same year, he also set up the *Tehelka* Foundation, a non-profit group that worked with youngsters on governance and social issues. The magazine received a major boost in 2009 when an Indian politician and industrialist invested about Rs. 250 million in *Tehelka*'s holding company, Anant Media Private Limited, in which Tarun's family members were shareholders. By 2013, Tarun owned 19% of *Tehelka*. In partnership with close friends and family members, he set up a network of eight firms which were involved in organizing events and running tourist resorts.

---

b Rs. is the short form for Indian rupees or INR. As on April 2015, US$1 was approximately equal to Rs.62.

c *Tehelka*'s investigative report about the 2002 Gujarat riots published in the November 17, 2007, issue exposed the role of Hindu right-wing parties in carrying out the genocide of Muslims with the alleged support of the then chief minister of Gujarat, Narendra Modi.

d *Tehelka* helped expose witnesses who turned hostile in a famous murder case involving a model in Delhi.

Over the years, Tarun projected himself as a crusader for the underprivileged. He fought for those who had been wronged in society, from taking on corrupt politicians to advocating women's rights. He was outspoken against the abuse of women, sexual violence, and the state of rape victims in Indian society. In fact, one of his favorite areas of journalistic interest was the condition of women in India. In cases where women were victimized, such as the Delhi gang rape case[e] and the Soni Sori Case[f], *Tehelka* led the coverage, provided an in-depth analysis, and supported the victims.

But, according to some in the media, Tarun was domineering himself toward his employees and tried to flirt with interns and juniors, taking advantage of his official position. It was reported that many of his employees had left the publication over what they described as his volatile, hypocritical, and unethical behavior.[g]

Shoma Chaudhury

Shoma was a senior journalist and a prolific writer and columnist and political commentator in India. In 2000, she joined *Tehelka* and was part of the team that started tehelka.com. When *Tehelka* was forced to shut down in 2003, Shoma was one of the four people who stayed on to fight, reposition, and relaunch it as a national weekly. After that, she worked as Director of Special Projects and Features Editor at *Tehelka,* later becoming the Managing Editor of the magazine. Shoma wrote extensively on critical issues of economic and social development, including state, caste, and gender politics, and issues related to Muslim identity; Maoist insurgency and terrorism; corruption of the state, and issues of capitalist development and land grab. Her creative writing and independent thinking catapulted her into the league of the finest and most powerful journalists in India.

An ardent supporter of women's rights, Shoma was vocal about issues concerning sexual abuse and assault. People saw a fearless feminist in her who used her profession to champion the rights of women, underline the cultural misogyny in India, and demand prompt and harsh punishment for brutal crimes and sexual violence against women. For instance, as a panelist at the "Women in the World Summit 2013"[h] in New York, Shoma occupied center stage in a discussion on the topic "Outcry in India" that focused on what was driving the sexual abuse of women in India after the infamous Delhi gang rape incident. As a fearless activist, Shoma who had reported

e On the night of December 16, 2012, a paramedical student was brutally gang raped by six men on a moving bus in Delhi. The incident led to widespread anguish and protests across the country for the brutality and torture inflicted on the girl who eventually died.

f Soni Sori is a tribal woman who was subjected to physical torture, including sexual violence by the police. However, *Tehelka* caught some police officers on tape confessing that Sori and her nephew had been falsely implicated.

g Paranjoy Guha Thakurta, The Rise and "Fall" of Tarun Tejpal, www.aljazeera.com, November 26, 2013.

h Sponsored by *Newsweek* and the *Daily Beast,* the Women in the World Summit 2013 invited inspirational women pioneers from disparate cultures who were fighting for the rights of women to discuss global issues and engage in first-person storytelling.

widely on the incident, was outspoken about social prejudice against women in India and called for a change in the psychological view of rape in the country.

Shoma was an award-winning journalist and in 2011, American news magazine *Newsweek* named her among the "150 Women Who Shake the World." She was one of the minority shareholders of Anant Media Pvt Ltd, the publishing company of *Tehelka*. She was also the director of Thinkworks Pvt Ltd[i] and owned 10% shares of the company.

Nina's Complaint

On November 18, 2013, Shoma received an e-mail from Nina alleging that Tarun had sexually assaulted her on two occasions in the elevator of a five-star hotel in Goa. Nina was a young promising journalist in her twenties who had been working for *Tehelka* since January 2010. A native of Delhi, Nina joined the group as an intern at *Tehelka*'s Delhi office and was confirmed as a trainee journalist in February 2010. In May 2012, after her promotion as Principal Correspondent, she was transferred to *Tehelka*'s office in Mumbai. As of end 2013, she was a Senior Correspondent with *Tehelka* in Mumbai.

In the e-mail, Nina provided a detailed and graphic account of the alleged sexual assault. According to her, on November 7, at THiNK Fest, 2013, she was specifically assigned to chaperone well-known Hollywood actor Robert De Niro (De Niro) and his daughter Drena De Niro (Drena), who were among the guests invited for the fest at the Grand Hyatt Hotel in Goa. In the evening, Tarun accompanied De Niro, Drena, and Nina to De Niro's suite situated in Block 7 on the 2nd floor of the hotel to wish them goodnight. After taking leave of them, Nina and Tarun left the suite and came out of the lobby of Block 7 on the ground floor. According to Nina, Tarun then put an arm around her shoulders and told her, *"Let's go wake up Bob [De Niro]."* Though she asked him why he wanted to go back, she trusted Tarun's intentions completely and entered the elevator with him. Nina said she had known Tarun since her childhood. Tarun was like a father figure to her as he had worked closely with her own father, who was also a senior journalist. After her father met with an accident, Tarun supported Nina and offered her her first job.

Giving an account of the incident that followed, Nina said as soon as the doors of the elevator closed, Tarun began to kiss her. She was shocked and asked him to stop, reminding him that he was her boss, that her family had implicit faith in him, and that she was a friend of Tiya (Tarun's daughter). But, according to her, it was like talking to a deaf person determined to do exactly what he wanted. *"Mr Tejpal lifted my dress up, went down on his knees and pulled my underwear down. He attempted to perform oral sex on me as I continued to struggle and hysterically asked him to stop. At that moment he began to try and penetrate me with his fingers, I became scared and pushed him hard and asked him to stop the lift. He would not listen,"*[2] she wrote.

i Established in 2010, Thinkworks Pvt. Ltd. is a media and advertising company. It is co-owned by Tarun Tejpal, his sister Neena Tejpal, and *Tehelka*'s then managing editor Shoma Chaudhary.

When Nina walked out of the elevator, Tarun followed her, asking her what the matter was to which she replied that what he was doing was wrong as she was his employee. Justifying his behavior, he then supposedly told her, "*Well, this is the easiest way for you to keep your job.*"[3]

Back at her hotel, Nina informed some of her colleagues about the incident and sought their advice. She was apprehensive about lodging a complaint with the Goa police as she was unsure how her complaint of sexual assault would be received given the fact that Tarun was a powerful and influential man. While they were engrossed in this discussion, Nina received a text message on her mobile phone from Tarun which read "*The fingertips,*" which according to her, pointed to the extent he had managed to penetrate her before she had pushed him and run out of the elevator.

Despite the shocking incident, Nina wrote that she decided to remain calm and collected and that she had gone about her duties the following day as she feared losing her job. The next morning—on November 8, 2013—she left for work. "*I was confused, hurt, and really, really scared. At that point I did not want to lose my job. And so the next morning, I went about my work determined not to give Mr Tejpal or* Tehelka *a reason to fire me, as I was sure they would do once this story got out,*"[4] That evening, Tarun allegedly came to her and asked her to accompany him to fetch something from De Niro's room. Scared of getting into the elevator with him again and not wanting a replay of the previous day's incidents, she told Tarun that she herself would go and get the things from De Niro's room. However, Tarun did not pay any heed to her; he held her by the wrist and took her into the lift and sexually assaulted her again.[5]

Nina wrote that despite the ordeal, she did not abandon her duties for fear of losing her job. She said that as she was to accompany De Niro to the dining area, she somehow composed herself and took De Niro from the main garden to the Capiz Bar for dinner. Tarun's daughter, Tiya, also joined them at the Capiz Bar. Nina then told Tiya about her father's sexual advances toward her. After half an hour, Nina escorted De Niro and Drena back to their rooms. De Niro, who had been mobbed by fans at the dinner table, was extremely upset at the day's events as was Drena, and De Niro asked Nina to convey this to Tarun. When she went to convey the message to Tarun, he allegedly brushed aside the incident and instead questioned her, "*How could you tell Tiya what happened? She's my daughter. Do you even understand what the word means? Just get away from me, I'm so f***ing pissed off with you right now.*"[6] Nina wrote that she left the place in tears.

According to Nina, she was scared of being alone at the Grand Hyatt because she knew Tarun could call her at any moment and reprimand her. The next day, she received a text message from Tarun that read, "*I hope you told Tiya that it was just drunken banter, and nothing else.*"[7] She then replied to Tarun that she had indeed told Tiya that they'd had a few drinks on the first night. However, Nina stated that she did not reply to his second message ("*And just banter, nothing else*") as she knew that when he assaulted her the second time, they were not drunk and the whole episode, according to her, could not just be described as "*banter.*"

According to Nina, Tarun, in an attempt to downplay the incident, sent her a third message ("*Why?? What's happened??*"), followed by a fourth one, pretending that he saw absolutely nothing wrong with what he had done. She wrote that he was in fact trying to disgrace her for informing Tiya. He reportedly messaged her again, saying, "*I can't believe u went and mentioned even the smallest thing to her. What an absence of any understanding of a parent-child relationship.*"[8] Nina stated that after this message, she stayed away from Tarun, except when they were in public situations.

Nina further reported that on November 16, Tarun sent some messages to her to establish his innocence. The conversations verbatim between Tarun and her were as follows:

Tarun: "*Have you spoken to Tee? Is she Ok?*"
Nina: "*Why would she be ok about the fact that you sexually assaulted her best friend, that is me?*"
Tarun: "*What's with saying this awful stuff??*"
Nina: "*Do not send me any messages. You are lying and you know that.*"
Tarun: "*Oh is that so? I cherished you like one of my best kids always, all these years; and because of one drunken banter you so easily say these awful things.*"
Nina: "*It was twice Tarun, not once and it was no banter. You did the most horrible things to me and I certainly was not drunk. I asked you to stop repeatedly.*"
Tarun: "*Oh so that's what you told Tee. No wonder she's so madly upset. It's ok. Am not going to contest anything with her. Will let time and my love heal what it can.*"
Tarun: "*Don't think I've been more saddened in the longest time.*"[9]

Nina wrote that as a journalist who in all her writings, had always urged women to speak out and break the silence that surrounded sexual crime, she found herself at a crossroads. She had two options: to remain silent or to formally report the incident to her seniors and file charges against her boss. After a series of discussions with her mother and friends, Nina finally made up her mind that she would talk about what had happened regardless of the consequences. In her letter to Shoma, Nina demanded an official written apology from Tarun, an acknowledgement of the assault to be circulated among the staff and bureau of *Tehelka*, and the setting up of an anti-sexual harassment cell at *Tehelka* to probe the matter.

Shoma's Response

Immediately after receiving the complaint from Nina, Shoma consulted a lawyer-friend who directed her to seek an apology from Tarun as demanded by the victim. She then confronted Tarun and asked for an unconditional apology to the victim. Shoma said that Tarun had presented a different version of the incident to her saying that it was consensual. But, she overruled his version and told him that as a leader of the organization he had misbehaved and betrayed the faith of other journalists. According to Shoma, she gave credence to the victim's version of events and neither questioned her nor cross-checked it with the colleagues mentioned in the complaint. On November 19, 2013, the very next day of receiving the complaint, Shoma pressed

Tarun to send a letter containing an unconditional apology to the victim and acknowledged that she had drafted the letter on Tarun's behalf in accordance with what the victim wanted. In the letter sent to Nina, Tarun reportedly wrote: "*It wrenches me beyond describing, therefore, to accept that I have violated that long-standing relationship of trust and respect between us and I apologise unconditionally for the shameful lapse of judgement that led me to attempt a sexual liaison with you on two occasions on 7 November and 8 November 2013, despite your clear reluctance that you did not want such attention from me [. . .].*"[10]

Shoma said that in addition to the apology, Tarun had also sent a personal mail to Nina saying that he had no idea that she was upset or that he had imposed upon her. According to him, that evening the conversation between them was heavily loaded and they were flirtatiously talking about desire and sex. Tarun had also asked Nina to forgive him and was even willing to apologize to her mother and boyfriend. However, Nina rebutted his claims and replied that the moment Tarun had laid his hand on her she had begged him to stop and reminded him that he was her employer and a father figure to her. But, according to her, he refused to listen and in fact attempted to molest her the following night as well. "*Tarun, I can't believe you think molesting an employee your daughter's age, who is also your daughter's friend, is something you'd describe as "the smallest thing." What an absence of understanding of what* Tehelka *stands for. Unfortunately, your desire to apologise to (the male friend) only reeks of your own patriarchal notion that men own and possess female bodies. ... The only people you owe an apology to are your employees at* Tehelka*, for desecrating their and my faith in you. Please do not attempt any further personal correspondence with me—you lost that privilege when you violated my trust and body,*"[11] she wrote back.

On November 20, 2013, Shoma received an e-mail titled "Atonement" from Tarun where he confessed to his misconduct and apologized for what he felt was a situation that he had utterly misunderstood. In the letter, he admitted that a bad lapse of judgment and a misreading of the situation had led to an unfortunate incident. He wrote that he was going to "recuse" himself as the editor of *Tehelka* for the next six months as a penance for his misbehavior. On the same day, Shoma circulated a letter among the *Tehelka* staff appending Tarun's letter of recusal. She added a short note saying what had occurred was an untoward incident and the organization had dealt with it with the right thought and action. However, according to some reports, the words "sexual harassment" were used nowhere, neither in Tarun's apology to the victim or in Shoma's letter to the staff. Rather, the entire episode was presented as an attempt to form a "sexual liaison" proposing an offer made and rejected. Reacting to the media outcry that followed, Shoma told media journalists that Nina as well as other staffers at *Tehelka* were satisfied with the action taken and therefore had not filed a criminal complaint. She said that the incident was an internal matter and that they would not approach the police.

On November 21, 2013, Shoma again received an e-mail from Nina rebutting and contesting Tarun's claims in his letter of recusal. Nina wrote that Tarun was fudging facts and that the incident was not an attempt at a sexual liaison. She also confronted Shoma about her media statements that she or other *Tehelka* journalists were satisfied with the action taken. Nina wrote that she was deeply hurt as Shoma, whom she considered as her mentor, had termed the blatant misrepresentation of facts as satisfactory action. The victim also alleged that Shoma had told her colleagues that she did not see the need to set up an anti-sexual harassment cell, because she did not contest the victim's version of what had occurred. Nina asked Shoma to publicly withdraw her statement and set up an anti-sexual harassment cell at *Tehelka* to investigate the matter at the earliest. Sensing that the matter was turning serious, on November 22, 2013, Shoma announced the setting up of a formal sexual harassment committee at *Tehelka* in accordance with the Vishaka guidelines. She said the committee would be presided over by Urvashi Butalia, an eminent feminist and publisher, to investigate the matter.

Tarun's Retort

The victim's e-mail with the details of the alleged sexual assault, Tarun's apology, and Shoma's letter to her staff were leaked online although they were never intended to be in the public domain. With the matter having gone public, there was a huge media outcry. The incident led to an uproar in the Indian media, sparking a widespread debate on social networking sites such as Facebook and Twitter, dominating headlines in newspapers, and leading conversations on prime-time television. The sexual assault allegations by Nina led to outrage among women activists who condemned Tarun's actions and demanded criminal proceedings against him. Some women's groups felt that Tarun was no God to decide his own course of punishment and that the rule of law must prevail and the perpetrator be brought to justice. According to Brinda Karat, a member of the Politbureau of the Communist Party of India (Marxist), "Tehelka *has often advocated the rights of women and other sections of the marginalised and therefore its admirers are shocked and angered at the ethical and moral collapse of the organisation as soon as it was called upon to use the same standards for itself as it had rightly demanded of others.*"[12]

With public pressure mounting, a criminal enquiry seemed inevitable. The Goa Police was instructed by the state government to investigate the matter. On November 22, 2013, a formal First Information Report (FIR) was lodged with the Goa Police by the National Commission for Women (NCW)[j]. The charges filed against Tarun included rape, which meant that if found guilty under the new Sexual Harassment of Women in Workplace Act, 2013, Tarun could be jailed for 10 years at the very minimum. The statements of the victim and the witnesses were recorded, and all the relevant material such as e-mails and other messages were attached.

Meanwhile, Tarun issued statements in the media saying that the victim's versions of events were concocted and that the complaint was motivated and false. He denigrated Nina and called her a liar. According to Tarun, the encounter with her was just light-hearted banter and that she was completely normal and friendly throughout

j The National Commission for Women (NCW) is a statutory body of the Government of India constituted under the National Commission for Women Act, 1990, to protect, promote, and safeguard the interests and rights of women.

her stay in Goa. He urged the police to check the CCTV footage of the hotel to get an accurate version of events. However, according to sources, there were no CCTV cameras inside the elevators of the hotel.

Tarun also blamed Shoma saying that his apology had been sent on the terms desired by Nina on Shoma's insistence and that the words used were not his own. He said the initial internal letters had been drafted by Shoma and that she had pressured him to close the issue with the apology that had been sought. He said he had apologized to Nina out of honor and respect for someone who had worked for him and who wanted him to apologize for what he thought had been consensual. In a statement sent to his friends on November 22, 2013, Tarun wrote: "*All my actions so far were out of an attempt to preserve the girl's dignity and on Chaudhury's adamantine feminist-principle insistence that I keep correct form by apologising. The truth is it was a fleeting, totally consensual encounter of less than a minute in a lift (of a two-storey building!) Now that a committee has been announced the truth will come out. As will the cctv footage. My life and work have been trashed on a total lie.*"[13]

Pointing to the delay in reporting the incident (Nina complained nearly 11 days after the incident) and the subsequent conduct of the victim, Tarun said it was a conspiracy hatched by some political parties as he opposed their ideology. He added that the FIR had been filed at the behest of some politicians to malign his reputation. However, author Arundhati Roy whose Booker Prize-winning novel was published by India Ink, a publishing house set up by Tarun, said, "*Outrageously, it is being suggested that Tarun is being 'framed' for political reasons — presumably by the right-wing Hindutva brigade. So now a young woman who he very recently saw fit to employ, is not just a loose woman, but an agent of fascists? This is Rape Number Two: the rape of the values and politics that* Tehelka *claims it stands for, and an affront to those who work there who have supported it in the past. It is the hollowing out of the last vestiges of integrity, political as well as personal. Free, fair, fearless. That is* Tehelka's *definition of itself. Where is courage now?*"[14]

Nina Resigns

Nina was deeply distressed by rumors that her complaint had been politically motivated and the assertions that the institution had suffered due to the crisis as she had chosen to speak out. She said that Tarun was trying to vilify her character. On November 25, 2013, Shoma received a resignation letter from Nina expressing unhappiness over the way the organization had handled the case. Nina wrote that she was deeply disturbed by the lack of support from the organization and that it was untenable for her to continue to work for *Tehelka.* She blamed Shoma for ignoring her rebuttals to Tarun's e-mails, while insisting in public that the victim was satisfied with the course of action. In her resignation letter, Nina stated, "*Over the past years, we have collectively defended the rights of women, written about custodial rape, sexual molestation at the workplace, spoken out harshly against the culture of victim blame and the tactical emotional intimidation and character assassination of those who dare to speak out against sexual violence. At a time when I find myself victim to such a crime, I am shattered to find the Editor in Chief of* Tehelka, *and you—in your capacity as*

Managing Editor—resorting to precisely these tactics of intimidation, character assassination and slander. Given the sequence of events since the 7th of November, it is not just Mr Tejpal who has failed me as an employer—but Tehelka *that has failed women, employees, journalists and feminists collectively."*[15]

Nina said she had faced a traumatic time when efforts were made to pressure and influence her family members. She said she feared further intimidation and harassment from family members of Tarun. According to her, by coming out into the open about the incident, she had not just lost a job that she liked, but much-needed financial security and independence. She felt she had also opened herself up to personal and slanderous attacks. What troubled Nina even more was the fact that there were some people including women who gave Tarun the benefit of the doubt by questioning her motives. As journalist Nirupama Sekhri commented, *"In the case that the first time you were totally paralysed with shock and an overwhelming sense of betrayal by your "boss", your "father figure" misbehaving with you, surely the second time round you had had enough time to see him for the lecherous lout he was, and should have gathered enough courage to hit out. Why did you choose only to plead and beg and not do something more drastic? [. . .] You were in a swanky hotel in Goa, why didn't you go and report it immediately to the security, the hotel manager, the police? Why did it take a savvy girl like you so long to make an official record of the violation? So far your case has displayed the most classic attributes of bubblegum feminism. What you have done is not a leg up for women's freedom and rights, it is reverse female chauvinism."*[16]

According to Nina, what Tarun did was a clear case of rape under the law and she was more determined to get him punished. She admitted that it was a difficult decision for her as she really needed the job after her father's demise.

Shoma's Departure

Shoma drew flak from the media and feminists for her decisions and comments in the case. Her feminist principles were questioned and she came under heavy criticism for taking the in-house probe route instead of seeking a police investigation into the matter. According to some analysts, the new Sexual Harassment law[k] stated that an employer needed to report incidents which fell under the rape law to the authorities, while offering support to the victim. Hence, Shoma had been legally obliged to report to the police. Instead, she had acted on her own, they said. Some critics slammed her for violating the law by not having a legally mandated sexual harassment committee in place at *Tehelka*. They pointed that if an internal policy and mechanism had been in place at *Tehelka* as required by the law, the victim would have been directed to the in-house complaints committee, which would then have taken a careful

k The Sexual Harassment of Women in Workplace Act, 2013 was passed in February 2013 and it was notified in the official gazette on April 23, 2013. The Act aimed to provide protection against sexual harassment of women at the workplace and for the prevention and redressal of complaints of sexual harassment and for matters concerned hitherto.

and collective decision about action to be taken in accordance with the law. They questioned Shoma's reasoning that sexual assault was simply an internal matter.

Shoma felt that she had become a punching bag for the social media, politicians, and women's activist groups for her alleged irresponsible actions. She said she was being blamed for not doing enough for Nina and for her apparent attempts of cover-up. However, defending her decision, Shoma said instead of following the law, she had sought to resolve the complaint internally as it was what the victim wanted. She said she had respected Nina's privacy as she had hesitated to file a police complaint at the beginning: "*I am driven by what she wants. This is an internal matter. My understanding is she wanted an apology and it was given to her. He [Tarun] stepped down. It was something she had not asked for. It was much more than what she wanted.*"[17]

Critics accused Shoma of resorting to double standards. She was also charged by some critics of allegedly blackmailing Nina about how a different version of the events would be out, and that she would no longer be able to protect her. They labeled Shoma as a convenient feminist, who voiced outrage for others but resorted to self-defense for herself. According to Pratyasha Rath, a former consultant at the National Centre for Advocacy Studies[I], "*And as a responsible feminist and as the managing editor of* Tehelka *how were you not stringent about a sexual harassment committee at your office according to the Vishakha guidelines? You talk about systemic changes in your multiple lectures as a feminist. You talk about constitutionally available spaces, about the law being biased against women. Your magazine has broken amazing stories about female safety amidst rising sexism. Then why the apathy, in your own front yard?*"[18]

Shoma was also indicted by the Goa State Police Chief of indulging in a cover-up and for delaying the investigation. The Goa Police said she was un-cooperative and did not respond to their requests for information and had to be reminded repeatedly. The Goa State Women Commission even demanded the arrest of Shoma, calling her an accomplice of Tarun.

Criticizing Shoma's actions, some observers said as a superior at *Tehelka*, it was her job to resolve the issue to the satisfaction of the victim. Instead, she chose to whitewash Tarun's crime by accepting the apology and his self-imposed atonement, they added. "*Indeed Ms Chaudhury has let down those who see a fearless feminist in her and failed as a professional who could not live up to the standards she set for others. I have always resisted the phrase 'woman is the enemy of woman' but the fast developing urbanscapes where social reality is constructed by media big shots, one may assume that in fact it is the powerful women who, in order to retain their own influence, turn into an enemy of the women living on the margins. It appears if this case brings an end to Shoma Chauhdury's stellar career it might be a beginning of an end to the lounge feministas,*"[19] commented Duriyya Hashmi (Hashmi), an activist and blogger.

I The National Centre for Advocacy Studies (NCAS) is a social change resource organization that works on issues of justice and governance in South Asia through people-centered and rights-based advocacy tools.

On November 28, 2013, Shoma tendered her resignation after facing allegations of a cover-up in the case. Refuting the accusations hurled at her, Shoma said the moment she received the complaint, in the absence of an official grievance redressal mechanism at *Tehelka,* she had acted absolutely and solely driven by solidarity for the victim as a woman and a colleague. She believed that she had tried to do what Nina wanted and her sole concern was to address the victim's sense of injury and to act in her interests. According to Shoma, "*Over the past week, I have been accused of an attempt to 'cover-up' and for not standing by my feminist positions. While I accept that I could have done many things differently and in a more measured way, I reject the allegations of a cover-up because in no way could the first actions that were taken be deemed suppression of any kind. As for my feminist positions, I believe I acted in consonance with them by giving my colleague's account precedence over everything else. However, despite this, as a result of what's transpired over the past few days my integrity has repeatedly been questioned by people from our fraternity and, in fact, by the public at large.*"[20]

Shoma said that Tarun's apology was also forwarded to three close journalist friends of Nina, and rejected the claims made in the media that she had indulged in intimidation or character assassination of Nina. On being asked why she did not approach the police immediately, she indicated that Nina wanted redressal from the institution in a way that would recognize the seriousness of her complaint, yet protect her privacy. Shoma said that in a phone conversation with Nina, she had even discussed the possibility of going to the police, but Nina refused to take that route and she had respected Nina's decision. Nina reportedly told her that she was satisfied with the actions and felt no further need for action. Moreover, Shoma said that it was not her (Shoma's) prerogative to go to the police and it was up to Nina as the victim to decide if she wanted to do so. She added that Nina had already spoken to her colleagues about the sexual assault, and if they wanted they could have approached the police in the ten days that had transpired before the incident was brought to her notice.

On the use of words such as "untoward incident" or "satisfied" in the letter circulated to *Tehelka* staff, Shoma admitted that the vocabulary she had used was mild and insufficient and apologized for it. She said she had even urged Nina to continue working at *Tehelka,* if she wanted to. Defending her, some analysts said that despite doing whatever she could within the given space, Shoma had been made a scapegoat. According to Nishtha Gautam, an equal rights activist, "*The trend takes a more appalling form when women are made to bear the brunt of the blunders and crimes of men. The biggest example is that of Shoma Chaudhury, who has been on the receiving end for the misdoings of her boss. With Tarun Tejpal's alleged sexual assault dominating the headlines, Chaudhury has metamorphosed into an apologist, willingly or by force. And this seems to be the most unfortunate fallout of the entire episode. The crusader of justice that Chaudhury was once seen to be now appears silenced by corporate loyalty. Oddly, her alleged attempts to trivialise the matter have deflected the anger and disgust that should have met Tejpal in face. One can't help but feel sorry for a situation wherein the woman's job is to make the erring man appear better.*"[21]

Shoma said that her decision to quit was painful and it had never been a part of her character to give up midway through a challenge. She said she would have liked to continue at *Tehelka* and steer the organization through the dark times, but owing to the allegations leveled against her she was unsure whether her presence was harming or helping *Tehelka*.[22]

Exhibit I

Sexual Harassment Law in India

Sexual harassment at the workplace has been one of the prime concerns of women's empowerment in India. During the 1990s, a brutal gang rape at the workplace was reported involving a Rajasthan (a state in India) state government employee who tried to prevent child marriage as part of her duties as a worker of the Women Development Program. Infuriated by her boldness, the feudal patriarchs decided to take revenge and repeatedly raped her. Even after going through a harrowing legal battle in the Rajasthan High Court, the rape victim did not get justice and the rapists who were affluent men from the upper caste went scot free. This incensed a women's rights group called Vishakha that filed a public interest litigation in the Supreme Court of India. In 1997, the Supreme Court passed a landmark judgment in the Vishakha case laying down guidelines and norms to be followed by establishments in dealing with complaints and redressal of sexual harassment cases at the workplace. The Supreme Court ruled that freedom from sexual harassment was a fundamental right, and that every workplace should have a committee to deal with such complaints.

With the passage of time, it was felt that the Vishakha guidelines and norms were insufficient to deal with the incidents of sexual harassment of women at workplaces and a stronger law was the need of the hour. It was only after some very serious incidents of sexual harassment that jolted the country such as the brutal gang rape of a paramedical student on the night of December 16, 2012, on a moving bus in Delhi, that two new laws were brought in. The first was the Sexual Harassment of Women at Workplace (Prevention, Prohibition and Redressal) Act, 2013, and the other was the Criminal Law (Amendment) Act, 2013. The Sexual Harassment of Women at Workplace (Prevention, Prohibition and Redressal) Act, 2013, received Presidential assent on April 22, 2013, and came into force on December 9, 2013. Based on the Vishakha guidelines, the Act passed by the Indian Parliament went one step ahead and included various issues which had not been addressed in the past such as extension of the definition of workplace to include almost all types of establishments including private sector organizations, houses, inclusion of the term domestic worker and unorganized sector in order to address the issue of sexual harassment of women.

The Act is meant to provide protection against sexual harassment of women at the workplace; prevention; redressal of complaints of sexual harassment.

The Act makes it mandatory for all offices with 10 or more employees to have an internal complaints committee to address grievances within a stipulated time frame or face penalty. If an employer fails to set up an internal complaints committee or does not comply with the requirements prescribed under the Sexual Harassment Act, a monetary penalty of up to US$1,000 would be levied. Repeated non-compliance with the provisions of the law could result in the penalty being doubled or could even lead to cancellation of the license or registration of the organization.

Sexual harassment cases at the workplace will have to be disposed of by in-house committees within 90 days failing which a penalty will be charged. If proved, sexual harassment at the workplace may lead to termination of the service of the accused, withholding of promotions and increments, and payment of suitable compensation to the complainant. If the charges against the accused turn out to be false and are found to have been made with malicious intent, the complainant may face similar penalty provisions as mentioned for the accused. The law allows the victim to request for conciliation for the matter to be settled but adds that a monetary settlement should not be made the basis of conciliation. As per the new law, in case the victim is unable to make a complaint on account of her physical incapacity, a complaint may be filed on her behalf by a relative, friend, or co-worker or an officer of the National Commission for Woman or State Women's Commission or any person who has knowledge of the incident, with the written consent of the victim *(See the flowchart for the process to be followed for complaint and inquiry).*

Flowchart: Process for Complaint and Inquiry under the New Sexual Harassment Law at the Work Place

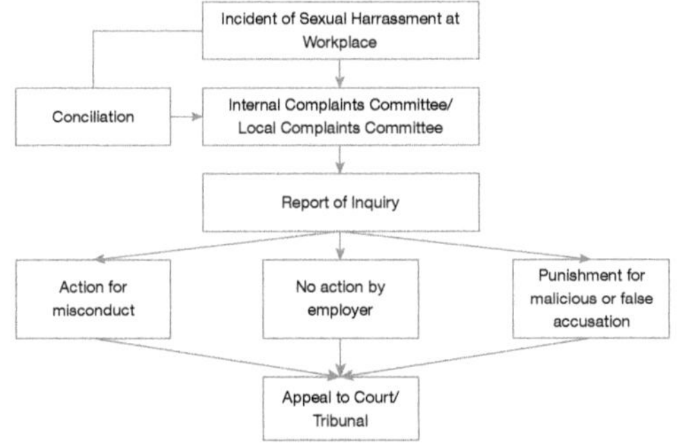

Timelines

A written complaint (6 copies) along with supporting documents and names and addresses of witnesses have to be filed by the aggrieved woman within 3 months of the date of the incident.

Upon receipt of the complaint, 1copy of the complaint is to be sent to the respondent within 7 days.

Upon receipt of the copy of complaint, the respondent should file his reply to the complaint along with his list of documents, and names and addresses of witnesses within 10 working days.

The inquiry has to be completed within a total of 90 days from the receipt of the complaint. The inquiry report has to be issued within 10 days from the date of completion of inquiry.

The employer is required to act on the recommendations of the committee within 60 days of receipt of the inquiry report.

Appeal against the decision of the committee is allowed within 90 days of the date of recommendations.

Source: www.nishithdesai.com/fileadmin/user_upload/pdfs/Research%20Articles/India_s_New_Law_on_ Prohibition_of_sexual_harassment_at_the_work_place.pdf

Exhibit II

Regulations under the New Criminal Law (Amendment) Act, 2013

Offense	Existing Law	The Criminal Law (Amendment) Act, 2013
Touching inappropriately	Maximum 2 years' imprisonment and fine	1–5 years' imprisonment and fine
Disrobing forcibly	Maximum 2 years' jail and fine	3–7 years' jail and fine
Stalking	Not a legal offence	1–5 years' imprisonment and fine
Sexual word and gesture	1 year imprisonment and/or fine	Up to 3 years' imprisonment and fine
Consensual sex by a person in authority	5 years' imprisonment. Applicable to public servants only	5–10 years' rigorous imprisonment. Covers all fiduciary relationships
Rape (being in a position of control or dominance over a woman, commits rape on such woman)	Imprisonment of not less than 7 years but which may be for life or for a term which may extend to 10 years and shall also be liable to a fine	Rigorous imprisonment for a term which shall not be less than 10 years, but which may extend to imprisonment for life, and shall also be liable to a fine

Sources: PRS Legislative Research, http://indiacode.nic.in/acts-in-pdf/132013.pdf

Chapter 5: Long Case Notes

1 "Tarun Tejpal | The Man in the Mirror," www.livemint.com, December 2, 2013.
2 "The Complete E-mail Trail of the Tarun Tejpal Sexual Assault Case," http://ibnlive.in.com, November 28, 2013.
3 http://upcpri.blogspot.in/2014/02/chargesheet-against-tarun-tejpal-read_18.html.
4 "The Complete E-mail Trail of the Tarun Tejpal Sexual Assault Case," http://ibnlive.in.com, November 28, 2013.
5 "The Victim's Letter to Shoma Chaudhuri," www.newindianexpress.com, November 24, 2013.
6 Ibid.
7 Ibid.
8 "The Complete E-mail Trail of the Tarun Tejpal Sexual Assault Case," http://ibnlive.in.com, November 28, 2013.
9 "Sexual Assault Victim's E-mail Against Tarun Tejpal, Editor in Chief, *Tehelka*," www.expresstoday.in, November 21, 2013.
10 "*Tehelka* case: Read Tarun Tejpal's Letter to the Victim," http://indianexpress.com, February 6, 2014,
11 Himanshi Dhawan, "In fresh Communications Leak, Tarun Tejpal Explains Why He Did It," http://timesofindia.indiatimes.com, November 28, 2013.
12 "Issues of Sexual Assault: The *Tehelka* Case," www.thehindu.com, November 25, 2013.
13 Sandeep Dougal, "Tarun Tejpal's 'Unconditional Apology'," www.outlookindia.com, November 22, 2013.

14 Arundhati Roy, "'This is Rape Number Two'," www.outlookindia.com, November 25, 2013.
15 "Full Text: Tejpal Sexual Assault Victim's Resignation Letter," www.firstpost.com, November 26, 2013.
16 Nirupama Sekhri, "Letter to Ms *Tehelka*-Assault-Victim," www.newslaundry.com, February 14, 2014.
17 "Tejpal's Resignation More Than the Apology Woman Wanted: *Tehelka*'s Shoma Chaudhury," www.hindustantimes.com, November 22, 2013.
18 Pratyasha Rath, "Shoma Chaudhury and Tales of Selective Feminism," http://centreright.in, November 24, 2013.
19 Duriyya Hashmi, "Why Shoma Chaudhury Got More Flak than Tarun Tejpal?" www.viewpoint online.net, November 29, 2013.
20 "Full text: Managing Editor Shoma Chaudhury Resigns from *Tehelka*," www.firstpost.com, November 28, 2013.
21 Nishtha Gautam, "Dear Men, Women Don't Exist Merely to Make you Look Grand," www.dna india.com, November 29, 2013.
22 Duriyya Hashmi, "Why Shoma Chaudhury Got More Flak than Tarun Tejpal?" www.viewpoint online.net, November 29, 2013.

LONG CASE QUESTIONS

1. What do the incidents in this case say about the resources and strategies adopted by offenders in sexual offending?
2. What was at stake for all parties involved in the case?
3. What is your assessment of how Shoma handled the situation? What could Shoma have done differently?
4. What issues does the case raise? What can companies do to make sure that such incidents don't happen again?

Chapter 6

Primary Stakeholders:

Customers

LEARNING OBJECTIVES

After reading this chapter you should be able to:

- Understand the general relationship of marketing's 4Ps for the ethical interface with customers
- Be aware of the ethical issues in pricing your products or services
- Understand what constitutes deception in advertising and be able to identify techniques used in deception
- Become aware of ethically sensitive issues in advertising such as the use of sexuality and advertising to children
- Understand a company's obligations to provide safe products in terms of buyer beware and the contract, due care, and strict liability views of product liability
- Become aware of the increasingly complex issues regarding consumer privacy

PREVIEW BUSINESS ETHICS INSIGHT

Determining Product Liability: It's Not Always Easy

Claiming that the talcum in Johnson & Johnson's classic baby powder caused their ovarian cancer, nearly 5000 women are suing or have sued the company. The first to go to trial in 2013, Deane Berg of Sioux Falls, SD, received a favorable jury ruling but the jury did not award her any damages.

Since many of the patients are very ill, the cases generate very emotional reactions. Ms. Berg, for example, developed ovarian cancer in 2006 after using the baby powder for 40 years. Ms. Berg called her chemotherapy "brutal." The chemotherapy resulted in nerve damage, permanent hearing loss, depression, and anemia.

As such, these suits can not only cause Johnson & Johnson hundreds of millions of dollars in court judgments but also, they can damage Johnson & Johnson's reputation as an ethical company.

However, there is inconclusive scientific evidence regarding the link between the baby powder and cancer. Because the scientific evidence varies, the dangers of talcum powder remain a subject of debate among medical field researchers.

Plaintiffs in the talc cases argue that a women's reproductive system can absorb the talc in baby powder, which leads to inflammation in the ovaries. One study found an increased risk of ovarian cancer among women who used the genital powder. In contrast, other studies that followed a group of women over a sustained period of time found no evidence of higher levels of ovarian cancer. The National Cancer Institute position is that "the weight of evidence does not support an association between perineal talc exposure and an increased risk of ovarian cancer." However, they still call for more research and have not offered a final conclusion.

Johnson & Johnson lost several of the initial cases. It was costly. They reported $806 million in net litigation expenses for 2016 and at least $400 million in expenses in the first half of 2017. Later in that year, a Los Angeles County Superior Court awarded Eva Echeverria, 63, of California, $417 million. Ms. Echeverria used Johnson's Baby Powder for more than 40 years and was diagnosed with ovarian cancer in 2007. Although Ms. Echeverria died in late 2017, a judge later tossed out the $417 million citing the "insufficiency of the evidence award" and ordered a new trial. Her lawyer appealed.

Hsu, Tiffany. 2017. "Risk on all sides as 4,800 women sue over Johnson's Baby Powder and cancer." www.nytimes.com/2017/09/28/business/johnson-and-johnson-baby-talcum-powder-lawsuits.html?action=click&contentCollection=Business%20Day&module=RelatedCoverage®ion=EndOfArticle&pgtype=article. Caron, Christian. 2017. "Courts reverse Johnson's Baby Powder judgments for nearly $500 million." www.nytimes.com/2017/10/23/business/johnson-talc-cancer.html?rref=collection%2Ftimestopic%2FLiability%20For%20Products&action=click&contentCollection=timestopics®ion=stream&module=stream_unit&version=latest&contentPlacement=2&pgtype=collection

This chapter considers customers as stakeholders. Some might argue that customers are the primary stakeholders because, without customers, a business could not exist. That is, by purchasing products or services, customers are the stakeholders that provide the money necessary for the organization to exist and to serve other stakeholders.

In this chapter, we focus on points of contact between the company and the customer that raise the most important ethical issues for today's companies. The Preview Business Ethics Insight above shows one area of concern, product liability, where companies are often challenged to confront situations where their products might do harm to people. The preview insight also shows that it is not always clear if a product is harmful and often it is left up to the legal system to make the final call.

In the next few sections, you will learn about three important points of contact between the company and the consumer. The first relates to marketing and issues such as truthful advertising and fair pricing. The second relates to product safety and issues such as who is responsible when a product has a defect. The third section relates to privacy and issues such as the legal and ethical obligations for getting and protecting your customers' personal information. The correct ethical choice for how companies deal with customers as stakeholders is not always apparent and different perspectives are open to debate.

MARKETING

In this section, we are interested in how the marketing function affects customers as stakeholders. **Marketing** is the first level where the organization interacts with customers. There are various ways of looking at marketing, but most focus on how we communicate the nature of our product, how we identify what the customer values, and how we deliver the product to create an exchange between the customer and the company.[1] Formal definitions of marketing include:

> Marketing is the activity, set of institutions, and processes for creating, communicating, delivering, and exchanging offerings that have value for customers, clients, partners, and society at large.[2]

And:

> Marketing is the management process that identifies, anticipates, and satisfies customer requirements profitably.[3]

The functions of marketing are usually divided into the marketing mix, which is sometimes called the **4Ps**: product, price, promotion, and place. Each of these has different ethical challenges when considering the customer as a stakeholder. The 4Ps are:

- *Product*: the product or services offered by the company that meet the requirements of the customers.
- *Price*: the process of setting the prices for the products/services.
- *Promotion*: this includes the tools used by marketers to make potential customers aware of the company's products or services and the benefits to the customers of buying these products or services.
- *Place*: this refers to the geographic areas to sell in and the channels selected to reach the market. For example, companies may sell directly to the end users or use distributors to get their product to the users.

THE AMERICAN MARKETING ASSOCIATION'S PERSPECTIVE ON MARKETING ETHICS
Honesty—to be forthright in dealings with customers and stakeholders. To this end, we will: • Strive to be truthful in all situations and at all times. • Offer products of value that do what we claim in our communications. • Stand behind our products if they fail to deliver their claimed benefits. • Honor our explicit and implicit commitments and promises.
Responsibility—to accept the consequences of our marketing decisions and strategies. To this end, we will: • Strive to serve the needs of customers. • Avoid using coercion with all stakeholders. • Acknowledge the social obligations to stakeholders that come with increased marketing and economic power. • Recognize our special commitments to vulnerable market segments such as children, seniors, the economically impoverished, market illiterates and others who may be substantially disadvantaged. • Consider environmental stewardship in our decision-making.
Fairness—to balance justly the needs of the buyer with the interests of the seller. To this end, we will: • Represent products in a clear way in selling, advertising and other forms of communication; this includes the avoidance of false, misleading and deceptive promotion. • Reject manipulations and sales tactics that harm customer trust. • Refuse to engage in price fixing, predatory pricing, price gouging, or "bait-and-switch" tactics. • Avoid knowing participation in conflicts of interest. • Seek to protect the private information of customers, employees, and partners.
Respect—to acknowledge the basic human dignity of all stakeholders. To this end, we will: • Value individual differences and avoid stereotyping customers or depicting demographic groups (e.g., gender, race, sexual orientation) in a negative or dehumanizing way. • Listen to the needs of customers and make all reasonable efforts to monitor and improve their satisfaction on an ongoing basis. • Make every effort to understand and respectfully treat buyers, suppliers, intermediaries, and distributors from all cultures. • Acknowledge the contributions of others, such as consultants, employees, and coworkers, to marketing endeavors. • Treat everyone, including our competitors, as we would wish to be treated.
Transparency—to create a spirit of openness in marketing operations. To this end, we will: • Strive to communicate clearly with all constituencies. • Accept constructive criticism from customers and other stakeholders. • Explain and take appropriate action regarding significant product or service risks, component substitutions or other foreseeable eventualities that could affect customers or their perception of the purchase decision. • Disclose list prices and terms of financing as well as available price deals and adjustments.
Citizenship—to fulfill the economic, legal, philanthropic and societal responsibilities that serve stakeholders. To this end, we will: • Strive to protect the ecological environment in the execution of marketing campaigns. • Give back to the community through volunteerism and charitable donations. • Contribute to the overall betterment of marketing and its reputation. • Urge supply chain members to ensure that trade is fair for all participants, including producers in developing countries.

EXHIBIT 6.1—The American Marketing Association's Perspective on Marketing Ethics

Quoted from: www.ama.org/AboutAMA/Pages/Statement-of-Ethics.aspx

A general view, proposed by the American Marketing Association, of what is considered ethical in the marketing function is shown in Exhibit 6.1. We will consider some specific issues from the 4Ps that are most important for the customers as stakeholders. Because most of the "place" decisions relate to businesses dealings with other businesses, these aspects of marketing are not as important when considering the customer as a stakeholder.

Customer stakeholder issues regarding products tend to focus on issues related to product safety, which we will deal with in a separate section later in this chapter. However, two other important issues regarding products raise ethical concerns.

The first deals with the issue of whether the product meets a legitimate customer need. Many criticize controversial products such as casinos, tobacco, low mileage SUVs, and fast food as unethical because they do not satisfy legitimate needs but just customer wants. Such products have questionable value to the consumer and are particularly questionable if they appeal to vulnerable customer groups.

One classic example comes from Nestlé and its marketing of infant formula to mothers in Third World countries. Using free samples and paid workers looking like medical personnel, mothers were convinced to use the formula rather than breastfeed. For the target market, the formula was expensive and many mothers stretched the use by using more water than recommended. Additionally, local water supplies were often unsanitary and unfit for infant use and this unsanitary water was mixed with the formula. Although Nestlé profited greatly from this product, babies starved and often died, leaving a legacy that Nestlé has never fully overcome. How do you think Nestlé might have avoided this problem in the first place?

A second issue regarding products is that managers just ensure that the products they sell actually perform as claimed. There is an ethical obligation not to deceive the customer.[4] One type of product for which the evidence provides little support is the fitness device that proposes to reduce fat in specific areas. There is little scientific support for this claim, although many products purport to achieve fat loss in different parts of the body.[5] Ethical issues regarding deception of the customer often show up in advertising, which is covered in more detail below.

Ethical Issues in Pricing

Pricing is of concern to ethical marketers because we want to sell our products to consumers at a "**just price**." The concept of the just price is usually attributed to St. Thomas Aquinas. Following Aquinas' reasoning, a seller should not raise prices simply because a buyer has a strong need for a product.[6] Thus, for example, the high interest rate charged by payday loan companies would be unethical from Aquinas' point of view because the sellers (the lenders) are taking advantage of the short-term needs for cash of their customers. In a capitalistic market, there is always some ambiguity over what constitutes a just price. However, several aspects surrounding pricing raise ethical concerns when dealing with the customer as a stakeholder.

These include:

- **Price gouging**. This occurs when sellers take advantage of situations like national disasters or shortages to raise prices during that situation. After Hurricane Katrina, WalMart, Home Depot, and Lowes took an opposite position by not only decreasing prices of high-demand products, but also giving some away free and using their distribution system to get people-needed goods. However, some might argue that companies should maximize their profits when they can, regardless of the reasons why. How can you argue for this point of view?
- **Predatory pricing**. Predatory pricing occurs when a company lowers its prices so far below competitors' that it drives the competitors out of the market. As a stakeholder, the consumer will later feel the effects because the predatory pricing company gains a more monopolistic power to set the prices.
- **Price fixing**. One type of price fixing, called horizontal, also has the effect of creating a monopoly effect when sellers agree with each other to sell at one price that is often above what they would have to do in a competitive market. Another type of price fixing is called vertical and occurs when sellers force the retailers to sell their products to consumers at specific prices. Horizontal price fixing is illegal in most countries but vertical price fixing has a more ambitious legal standard. In most cases, however, the consumer will pay more when competitive pricing is restricted.
- **Price discrimination**. This occurs when different groups are charged different prices. Youth or senior discounts or "ladies' nights" in nightclubs are types of price discrimination. Although most forms of price discrimination are considered ethical and legal, there are areas when the practice has a more ambivalent ethical foundation. For example, in upscale men's clothing stores the tailoring of suits is often considered as a service without charge, whereas for women's clothes there is a much greater chance of being charged for similar tailoring. Is this ethical? Is this fair?
- **Failure to disclose the full price**. This often occurs when listed prices do not include other fees or charges that the consumer will have to pay. For example, U.S. Airways was fined $40,000 because when "consumers searched the carrier's website for one-way flights sorted by schedule, U.S. Airways provided a set of fares that did not include additional applicable taxes and fees, or any notice on that page that these additional charges would be required." This violated U.S. statutes on pricing.[7]
- **Bait-and-switch**. This is a sales tactic where a product is advertised at a low price, but when the consumer comes in he or she finds that the product is sold out (often there was only one in the store) or is pressured by sales people to look at higher-priced versions of the product.

Ethical Issues in Promotion

The objective of **promotion** is to make the customer aware of your product. Promotion involves an array of tools including, for example, advertising, sponsorships, coupons, and point-of-sale displays. Of most importance in dealing with ethical issues related to the consumer is the advertising function. The objective of advertising is to make customers aware of the product and to persuade them to purchase the product or service. The approach can appeal to rational self-interest (e.g., if you use this product you will be healthier or more physically attractive) or subtly to create an emotional tie to the product (e.g., Calvin Klein's controversial jeans advertisement that showed a 15-year-old in Calvin Klein jeans, with her saying: "Want to know what gets between me and my Calvin's? Nothing"). Can you think of any reasons why a company should not use beauty to sell?

Below, we will discuss several issues regarding the nature and management of ethical advertising.

Ethical advertisements must be truthful and not deceptive. The U.S. Federal Trade Commission (FTC)[8] identifies criteria by which we can decide if an advertisement is not deceptive. To make this judgment one needs to consider the ad from the point of view of the typical person looking at the ad. One should ask what the words, phrases, and pictures convey to consumers. In making judgments about the legality of an advertisement, the FTC considers both **express** and **implied claims**. An express claim is stated directly in the ad. For example, "ABC tablets will reduce your weight by two pounds a week" is an express claim that you will lose weight if you take the pills. Implied claims for a product are made indirectly or by inference. "XYZ tablets reduce your appetite for fatty foods, a major contributor to weight gain" contains an implied claim that taking the pills results in your losing weight. Although the ad in this example does not claim directly that the pills cause weight loss, most reasonable consumers would conclude from the statement "reduce your appetite for fatty foods, a major contributor to weight gain" that the product will lead to weight loss.

Under U.S. law, advertisers must have evidence that supports both express *and* implied claims that advertisements make to consumers. If an advertisement makes health or safety claims, the company must support the claims with scientific evidence from studies evaluated by other professionals or scientists in the field.

For an international view on marketing communications look at Exhibit 6.2, which contains excerpts from the International Chamber of Commerce's Advertising and Marketing Practice Consolidated Code.[9] Exhibit 6.2 provides only a fraction of the detail in the Code so you should go to the original for more detail: https://cdn.iccwbo.org/content/uploads/sites/3/2011/08/ICC-Consolidated-Code-of-Advertising-and-Marketing-2011-English.pdf.

Techniques for deceptive advertising include:[10]

- **Ambiguity in advertisements**. In ambiguous ads, the wording is sufficiently confusing and leads the consumer to make erroneous conclusions about the nature of the product. A classic example is Sara Lee's Light Classic desserts. Most consumers interpreted the word "light" to mean fewer calories. However, the State of Iowa confronted Sara Lee on the meaning of "light" when they found that the light products have almost the same calorie content as their regular desserts. When pressed under the requirement to provide evidence of the reduced calories, Sara Lee noted that this referred only to the texture of the products.

Truthfulness Marketing communications should be truthful and not misleading. **Use of technical/scientific data and terminology** Marketing communications should not misuse technical data, e.g. research results or quotations from technical and scientific publications. **Use of "free" and "guarantee"** The term "free", e.g. "free gift" or "free offer", should be used only where the offer involves no obligation. Marketing communications should not state or imply that a "guarantee", "warranty" or other expression having substantially the same meaning,offers the consumer rights additional to those provided by law when it does not. **Substantiation** Descriptions, claims or illustrations relating to verifiable facts in marketing communication should be capable of substantiation. **Identification** Marketing communications should be clearly distinguishable as such, whatever they are for and whatever the medium used. **Identity** The identity of the marketer should be apparent. **Comparisons** Marketing communications containing comparisons should be so designed that the comparison is not likely to mislead, and should comply with the principles of fair competition. **Denigration** Marketing communications should not denigrate any person or group of persons, firm, organization, industrial or commercial activity, profession or product, or seek to bring it or them into public contempt or ridicule. **Testimonials** Marketing communications should not contain or refer to any testimonial, endorsement or supportive documentation unless it is genuine, verifiable and relevant.	**Exploitation of goodwill** Marketing communications should not in any way take undue advantage of another firms, individual's or institution's goodwill in its name, brands or other intellectual property, or take advantage of the goodwill earned by other marketing campaigns without prior consent. **Imitation** Marketing communications should not imitate those of another marketer in any way likely to mislead or confuse the consumer, for example through the general layout, text, slogan, visual treatment, music or sound effects. **Safety and health** Marketing communications should not, without justification on educational or social grounds, contain any visual portrayal or any description of potentially dangerous practices, or situations. **Children and young people** Special care should be taken in marketing communications directed to or featuring children or young people. **Inexperience and credulity** Marketing communications should not exploit inexperience or credulity. **Avoidance of harm** Marketing communications should not contain any statement or visual treatment that could have the effect of harming children or young people mentally, morally or physically. **Social values** Marketing communications should not suggest that possession or use of the promoted product will give a child or young person physical, psychological or social advantages over other children or young people, or that not possessing the product will have the opposite effect. **Data protection and privacy** When collecting personal data from individuals, care should be taken to respect and protect their privacy by complying with relevant rules and regulations.

EXHIBIT 6.2—The ICC Advertising and Marketing Practice Consolidated Code

Source: https://cdn.iccwbo.org/content/uploads/sites/3/2011/08/ICC-Consolidated-Code-of-Advertising-and-Marketing-2011-English.pdf

Collection of data and notice When personal information is collected from consumers, it is essential to ensure that the individuals concerned are aware of the purpose of the collection and of any intention to transfer the data to a third party for that third party's marketing purposes. Use of data Personal data collected in accordance with this code should be collected for specified and legitimate purposes and not used in any manner incompatible with those purposes. Security of processing Adequate security measures should be in place, having regard to the sensitivity of the information, in order to prevent unauthorized access to, or disclosure of, the personal data. Children's personal information When personal information is collected from individuals known or reasonably believed to be children 12 and younger, guidance should be provided to parents or legal guardians about protecting children's privacy if feasible. Privacy policy Those who collect data in connection with marketing communication activities should have a privacy policy	Rights of the consumer Appropriate measures should be taken to ensure that consumers understand and exercise their rights to opt out of marketing lists. Cross-border transactions Particular care should be taken to maintain the data protection rights of the consumer when personal data are transferred from the country to another country. Unsolicited products and undisclosed costs Marketing communications associated with the practice of sending unsolicited products to consumers who are then asked for should be avoided. Environmental behavior Marketing communications should not appear to condone or encourage actions that contravene the law, self-regulatory codes or generally accepted standards of environmentally responsible behavior. Responsibility These general rules on responsibility apply to all forms of marketing communications. Implementation The Code and the principles enshrined in it, should be adopted and implemented, nationally and internationally, by the relevant local, national or regional self-regulatory bodies.

EXHIBIT 6.2—*continued*

- **Concealing facts**. Advertisements that conceal facts often begin with truthful statements regarding the positive attributes of a product. For example, a company might state, "the ingredients in this car polish will result in a beautiful shine for your car." What the advertisement fails to note is that the car polish manufacturer uses the same ingredients as the other manufacturers. Consider Bayer Aspirin's scientifically factual claim that their aspirin "contains an ingredient doctors recommend most." This advertisement, which ran for years, was designed to convince the consumer that Bayer Aspirin is preferable to other brands of aspirin. What Bayer did not say is that the ingredient doctors recommend most is aspirin.
- **Exaggeration**. Trident chewing gum is one example of an exaggeration in advertising. Described as a cavity fighting "dental instrument," this is a clear exaggeration of the benefits of Trident. Not only does the sugar substitutive used in Trident promote tooth decay, but all forms of sugarless chewing gum also help to prevent plaque formation by increasing salivary flow and prompting continuous

chewing action. A step away from exaggeration is called "puffery." **Puffery** is an exaggeration so extreme that the assumption is that no reasonable person would believe the statement such as that BMW is unambiguously "the ultimate driving machine." As such, most government policymakers allow advertisers to use *puffery*. However, studies[11] show that, while consumers are able to identify exaggerated claims, continued exposure to puffed claims still increases the positive evaluation of the advertised brand.

Ethical advertisements should also not be manipulative. That is, they should not take advantage of giving false or misleading cues to manipulate the consumer psychologically. One ad that some might say used this tactic was employed by Michelin tires for many years. The visual presented by the advertisement shows a baby sitting on a Michelin tire. The quite simple slogan was "Because so much is riding on your tires." Of course, the implication was that if you do not buy Michelin tires, you are endangering your baby. Another insurance company ad showed a family in a dire economic situation because the chief breadwinner had not purchased life insurance, with the implication being you will fail your family if you do not buy our insurance.

Advertisements based on such emotional appeals are often not considered unethical and praised as effective advertising. However, they fall into a gray area between advertisements that provide consumers with the information to determine if they should purchase this product and the other extreme of coercion.[12] From the perspective of Kantian ethical philosophy, such manipulations are ethically questionable because they are a means to achieve the seller's ends and treat the consumer as an object. How would you respond to a Kantian objection to your company's advertisements that appeal to emotions?

Exhibit 6.3 gives examples of potential exaggeration or perhaps manipulation in advertisements for weight loss products.

Other Ethically Sensitive Issues: Sexual Appeals and Marketing to Children

Reichart et al. defined **sexual appeals** as "messages, as brand information in advertising contexts . . . that are associated with sexual information."[13] As anyone who watches TV or reads magazines knows, sexual innuendo in advertising content is quite common. Yet, to some people, it is considered immoral or a form of sexual harassment. Mark Levit,[14] managing partner of Partners & Levit Advertising and a professor of marketing at New York University, agrees that sexual content of ads can increase their effectiveness because they attract the customer's attention. It is just human nature. However, when misused, sex appeal can be costly to companies. For example, nude or seminude pictures in Abercrombie & Fitch catalogues have led to customer boycotts.

According to Levit,[15] ads that, for example, show an attractive model endorsing a product can lead to positive responses from consumers. However, more graphic sexual content often fails to do more than attract attention. Research[16] suggests that strong

A claim is too good to be true if it says the product will . . .	Example Claims
Cause weight loss of two pounds or more a week for a month or more without dieting or exercise	• "I lost 30 pounds in 30 days even though I ate all my favorite foods." • "Lose up to two pounds daily without diet or exercise."
Cause substantial weight loss no matter what or how much the consumer eats	• "My 'formula for living' lets you eat: hamburgers, hot dogs, fries, steak, ice cream, sausage, bacon, eggs, and cheeses! And STILL LOSE WEIGHT!" • "Eat all the foods you love, and still lose weight (pill does all the work)."
Cause permanent weight loss (even when the consumer stops using product)	• "Thousands of dieters are already using it and losing weight faster than they have before . . . and keeping the weight off." • "For 15 years, Mary yo-yo dieted without success. Fed up and desperate, she discovered a new miracle product to lose weight easily and permanently."
Block the absorption of fat or calories to enable consumers to lose substantial weight	• "Lose up to two pounds daily . . . Apple Pectin is an energized enzyme that can absorb up to 900 times its own weight in fat. That's why it's a fantastic FAT BLOCKER." • "Brindall berries cause very rapid and substantial weight loss by reducing fat absorption by 76%."
Safely enable consumers to lose more than three pounds per week for more than four weeks	• "Lose 30–40–50 pounds. Yes! You can lose three pounds per week, naturally and without side effects." • "Neptune's Potion is safe and effective," with customer testimonials claiming more than 12 pounds of weight loss per month.
Cause substantial weight loss for all users	• "Lose excess body fat. You cannot fail, because no will power is required." • "Lose 10–15–20 pounds. Works for everyone, no matter how many times you've tried and failed before."

EXHIBIT 6.3—Suspect Advertisements for Weight Loss

sexual messages, like strong violence content, tend to attract attention but reduce the consumers' intention to buy the product.

One successful approach used by Heineken in "It's All About the Beer" campaign called "The Premature Pour," shows a man responding to a seductive woman by nervously pouring his beer so fast that it spills and dumps foam over him and the table. The sexual innuendo is clear but the ad worked. Targeted at young men, Heineken's beer sales jumped by over 10% in the U.S.

One strategic issue in the use of sexual innuendo in advertisements is the cross-cultural transferability of such ads. The following Emerging Market Business Ethics Insight looks at how sex appeal advertising may be changing in China. One question in how the ads work concerns whether the models are domestic or foreign.

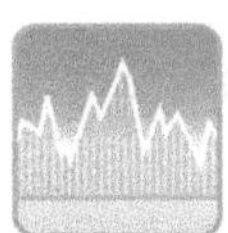

EMERGING MARKET BUSINESS ETHICS INSIGHT

Does Sex Appeal Advertising Work in China?

With the increased liberalization of China and access to Western media such as MTV, the use of sexual appeals has increased in print and television advertisements in China. This reflects, in part, the attempt by multinational companies to gain the efficiency of having similar promotional activities in all the countries in which they operate. However, the assumption that even mild forms of sexual innuendo that seem to work in the West with Heineken will work in an emerging market economy with an Eastern cultural tradition is not a sure thing.

One study in 2009 by two marketing professors from Hong Kong casts doubt on the efficacy of using sexual innuendo in Mainland Chinese advertisements. They found that Chinese consumers responded more favorably to ads with no sex appeal in terms of both their attitudes toward the advertisements and their intentions to buy the advertised products. They also found that Chinese consumers preferred Chinese models rather than Caucasian models, regardless of whether the ads contained high levels of sex appeal. The researchers recommended "caution" in using sexual messages to Chinese consumers as their findings suggest that Chinese consumers perceive such ads ethically less acceptable.

However, things may be changing. The U.S. company Tyson has recently had success using ads with partially clothed Asian models in 2016 ad campaigns.

Based on Cui, Geng and Yang, Xiaoyan. 2009. "Responses of Chinese consumers to sex appeals in international advertising: A test of congruency theory." *Journal of Global Marketing*, 22, 229–245. Clode, Jerry. 2016. "Sex sells in China – More and more than it used to." *brandinginasia*. https://brandinginasia.com/sex-sells-in-china/

Advertising to Vulnerable Groups: Children

One of the most sensitive ethical topics in advertising is advertising to children. Gunilla Jarlbro[17] identifies four recurring themes in the literature on children's advertising. The first issue is the ability of children to recognize a marketing communication as advertising. Research on the issue at which age children can distinguish between advertisements and regular programs has mixed results. However, there seems to be agreement that a majority of children, by the age of eight, have developed the ability to distinguish commercials from programs. By the age of 10–12, nearly all children can make this distinction. One caveat for advertisers is that development of this ability varies by individuals and perhaps by cultural settings, as the research seems to find different abilities in different countries.

The second issue of concern for advertising to children relates to the age children develop the perceptual skills to understand the intent of the advertisement. However, for this issue, the level of the child's cognitive development seems most important and it is not clear that science can identify a specific age. Experts generally agree that the older the child, the more likely the child grasps the intent behind advertising.

The third issue concerns the extent that children influence their family's purchases, sometimes called "pester power." One recent review of the existing research[18] concluded, at least in the area of food advertising, that advertising does result in pestering, leading to parents buying less healthy products that are higher in calories and often associated with obesity. They note that this conflicts with industry arguments that "pester power" is minimal in its effects.

The fourth issue concerns how advertisements to children work indirectly by influencing children as a group. Experts[19] agree that family, friends, and siblings have more influence over children's views on products than do advertisements. However, TV commercials can be a common source of conversation among school children, suggesting that age-group-targeted ads may work indirectly by stimulating peer group interest. In addition, promotions such as Barbie Clubs encourage peer groups to discuss and potentially purchase products associated with the clubs.

Issue	Recommendation
Harm	• Children should not be shown in unsafe situations or behaving dangerously except for advertisements that promote safety • Children should not be shown using or in close proximity to dangerous substances or equipment without direct adult supervision • Children should be discouraged from copying potentially hazardous activities that may be displayed in ads
Credulity and Unfair Pressure	• Children should not be encouraged to feel inferior or unpopular if they do not buy the advertised product • Children should not be encouraged to feel that they are lacking in courage, duty, or loyalty if they do not buy the advertised product • Should be possible for children of the target age group to judge the size, characteristics, and performance of advertised products and to distinguish between real-life situations and fantasy • For complex or costly products, adult permission should be obtained before purchasing • Should not exaggerate what an ordinary child can do using the product being marketed
Price	• Should not lead children to an unrealistic perception of the product's value • Should not be presented that the price of the product is in the reach of every family
Parental Authority	• Should not undermine the authority and judgment of parents • Should not include appeals to children to persuade their parents to buy the advertised product
Skills and Age Levels	• Should not underestimate the degree of skill and age level needed to assemble or operate the products as shown
Social Values	• Should not suggest that the use of product will give a child physical or psychological superiority over other children

EXHIBIT 6.4—Example Standards for Advertisements to Children

REGULATION OF BROADCAST MEDIA

Ireland

- Advertising at children <13 yrs. must not include nutrient or health claims or licensed characters.
- Food advertising to children <18 yrs. must not feature celebrities, and for children <15 yrs. must not include characters and personalities from children's programs.

Sweden

- General prohibition of TV advertising during programs appealing to children under 12 (WHO 2016).
- Programs addressed at children below 12 may not be preceded or followed by advertising.

United Kingdom

- Licensed characters and celebrities popular with children, as well as health or nutrition claims, may not be used in product advertisements for pre-school or primary school children. Advertisements "must not directly advise or ask children to buy or to ask their parents or other adults to make enquiries or purchases for them".
- The Code also contains rules on advertising of weight control, slimming and low-calorie products.

Norway

- General advertising, including foods and beverages, in children's programs on TV, radio and teletext is prohibited in broadcast media originating in Norway.
- Advertising cannot include persons or figures that had a prominent role in radio and TV programs for children or young adults in Norway in the previous 12 months.

Iran

- Broadcast advertising of soft drinks has been prohibited since 2004, while a list of 24 food items to be prohibited from advertising in all media is pending approval.

Mexico

- Restricted advertising of foods and sweetened beverages within the times of 2.30–7.30pm on weekdays and 7.00am–7.30pm on weekends, where over 35% of the audience are <13 yrs.

South Korea

- TV advertising to children <18 years of age is prohibited for specific categories of food before, during and after programs shown between 5–7 pm; also applies to advertising on TV, radio and internet that includes gratuitous incentives to purchase e.g. free toys.

Taiwan

- Restricted food products are banned from being advertised on dedicated TV channels for children between 5–9 pm.
- Restricted food products include snacks, candies, drinks, ice products and food products with fats >30% of total calorie content, saturated fat >10% of total calorie count, foods with >400mg of sodium per serving and foods where added sugars account for >10% of total calorie count.

REGULATION OF ANY MEDIUM

Brazil

- Established criteria for publicity and marketing, aimed at children ≤11 yrs. and adolescents 12–18 yrs. and prohibits any kind of abusive publicity. Applies also to food marketing.
- Promotions where a food product is advertised alongside a toy or another object that a child would like to acquire, but which can only be obtained if a certain quantity of the food is purchased, are prohibited.

Canada

- Prohibition of advertising, including food and beverage products directed at children <13 on TV, radio, print, internet, mobile phones as well as through using promotional items.

Chile

- Limits advertising directed to children <14 yrs. for foods and beverages high in calories, saturated fat, sugar and sodium content.

Peru

- Range of provisions designed to discourage unhealthy diets, including restrictions for advertising aimed at children and adolescents <16 yrs. through any medium.
- Includes not using age inappropriate portion sizes, gifts, prizes or any other benefit to encourage purchase or consumption of food or drinks, not using real or fictional characters known to children.

EXHIBIT 6.5—National Differences in Regulations Concerning Advertisements to Children

Source: European Commission's science and knowledge service 2017. *Food and non-alcoholic beverage marketing to children and adolescents* https://ec.europa.eu/jrc/en/health-knowledge-gateway/promotion-prevention/other-policies/marketing#_Toc479324900

REGULATION OF MARKETING IN SCHOOLS	
Poland • Legislation includes rules for sales, advertising and promotion of foods (based on a list of food categories) • Advertising and promotion of foods in schools that do not meet government nutrition standards is banned. **Spain** • No advertising in schools and kindergartens. **Chile** • Promotion, marketing, or advertising of foods in the "high in" category products in pre-school, primary and secondary schools banned (since 1 July 2016).	**Uruguay** • Prohibited advertising and marketing of foods and drinks that don't meet nutrition standards. • Applies to all forms of advertising, including posters, billboards, use of logos/brands on school supplies, sponsorship, distribution of prizes, free samples to schools and the display and visibility of food.

EXHIBIT 6.5—*continued*

Exhibit 6.4 shows some general standards for advertising to children. These come from various codes of professional groups from around the world. In the next section, we will consider issues regarding product safety.

Some countries have additional restrictions regarding advertising to children that multinational companies need to be aware of. Exhibit 6.5 shows some examples.

PRODUCT SAFETY

Many products we purchase have some risks associated with their use. Whether it is the automobiles we drive, or the fertilizer we use on our lawns, harm will befall some users when using products, especially if the products are misused. A dilemma is that, even with improved safety for a product such as the automobile, can it be done at prices that consumers can afford? Thus, since many if not most products we use can potentially cause harm, the basic question is: who has the responsibility for this harm?

There are several areas of concern regarding how defective products can cause harm to users. There can be design defects, material defects, manufacturing defects, the failure to warn with appropriate labels and warnings regarding potential product dangers, and notifications to users if faults are found in the future. Failure to warn is sometimes called a marketing failure.

One example of an apparent **design defect** was the sticking accelerator pedal that plagued a variety of Toyota models. This defect resulted in Toyota recalling millions of cars worldwide. In the U.S., courts assessed penalties totaling $48.8 million. Toyota was forced to pay $16.4 million to settle claims for fatal accidents caused by the defects based on allegations that the company hid the accelerator pedal defects initially. In an unprecedented step for a Japanese CEO, Toyota president Akio Toyoda, the grandson of the founder of the company, went to the United States early in 2010 to speak before Congress, Toyota workers, and dealers to apologize for Toyota's handling of the problems.[20]

In an example of a **material defect**, the toy manufacturer Fisher-Price discovered that 21 million toys contained excessive amounts of lead and could endanger the lives of the children using the toys. Just three years after that discovery, the company faced a design defect forcing a recall for toddler's tricycles and high chairs with protruding parts that caused injuries when children fell against them. In an example of a manufacturing defect, Fisher-Price recalled over three million toys due to choking hazards from small parts that fell off the toys.[21]

Laws in different states and countries determine how long a company is responsible for defects in their products. In the U.S., aircraft manufacturers are responsible for design and manufacturing defects for up to 18 years. Automobile and boat manufacturers have a five-year window of responsibility. If defects are discovered, recall warnings might be mandated by governments or done voluntarily by companies.

Companies have both a moral and a legal duty to warn users of these potential dangers. This is why nearly all directions for product assembly and use contain a "read me first" section dealing with warnings. The obligation to warn consumers about potential dangers continues after the initial sale. That is, liability can exist even after purchase if manufacturers discover a defect or misuse of the product later.[22]

What should a warning say to the consumer? Experts[23] identify the following:

- Note the severity of the potential danger (e.g., death)
- Note the nature of the hazard (e.g., poisoning)
- Communicate the consequences of the hazard (e.g., potential choking)
- Explain how to avoid the hazard (e.g., wear protective gloves)

In addition, there are several issues to consider when evaluating warnings for product use:[24]

- What is the likelihood that the product can cause harm? Products that are more dangerous require more attention to warnings.
- Whether there is a reasonable likelihood that the consumer will use the product in a way not identified in the labeling and if such use could cause harm to the consumer. In this case, companies should consider redesigning the product, if possible, to prevent such misuse.
- How serious is the potential harm? With greater potential harm, the obligation to provide warnings increases.
- What level of knowledge should the manufacturer expect from the users of a product? For example, a licensed pilot would be expected to have basic knowledge about dangers related to flying. People using fertilizers might not be aware of the potential dangers of exposure to the chemicals.
- Can the typical user of the product read and understand the warnings? Rather than technical language or translations into several languages, some companies will use pictorial warnings. IKEA provides directions on how to assemble its furniture, complete with safety warning information all through the pictures.

Perspectives on Product Liability

There are several perspectives regarding if or to what extent companies should assume liability for harm caused by the products they produce. These include the buyer beware view, contractual theory, due care, and strict liability.

Buyer Beware

The **buyer beware** perspective is sometimes called *caveat emptor*, which is Latin for "let the buyer beware." The legal definition is "A doctrine that often places on buyers the burden to reasonably examine property before purchase and take responsibility for its condition. Especially applicable to items that are not covered under a strict warranty."[25]

According to the buyer beware view, once a consumer purchases a product, the manufacturer has no responsibility for any risks associated with the product that they produced. Because it was a free market exchange, the purchaser and not the manufacturer must bear any costs of any injuries. It is the consumer's duty to research the product and the risks for harm prior to making the purchase. *The objection to this perspective is that consumers often do not have sufficient knowledge or expertise to identify any risks associated with a product.*

Contract View

According to the **contract view**, the relationship between the manufacturer and a consumer is based on a contract. The contract has both explicit (i.e., written) and implied claims regarding the product. The implicit or implied claims relate to the consumers' expectations regarding reliability (the probability that the product will function as expected), life of the product (expectations regarding the service life of the product), maintainability (the ease of keeping the product working), and product safety (the risk associated with using the product). There is an implied warranty that the product is fit for sale and is of acceptable quality for ordinary use.

The contract implies certain moral duties for the seller, including:

- Duty not to coerce—the buyer must enter the contract voluntarily
- Duty to comply with the terms of the contract regarding express and implied claims of reliability, product life, maintainability, and safety
- Duty not to misrepresent the product in any way
- Duty to disclose the nature of the product

As with the buyer beware approach to product safety, a problem with contract view is the assumption that consumers understand the products sufficiently to enter into a contract. For example, if you buy a car sold "as is" from a car dealer, there is an assumption that you understand automobiles sufficiently well to know that the car is safe to drive. In many instances, the buyer and seller are not equals in the knowledge required to understand the contract.

Due Care Theory

Due care theory addresses the weaknesses of the buyer beware approach by accepting that sellers and buyers do not have equality in knowledge and expertise regarding products. This is increasingly true, as products get more technologically complex. Thus, for example, few people have the engineering knowledge to assess all of the safety components of a modern automobile such as ABS braking, frame construction to absorb impacts, or the workings of airbags. As such, since manufacturers have much greater knowledge than their consumers do, they assume an obligation to take reasonable precautions that their products do not harm the buyers. The more powerful and knowledgeable have more duties.

Legal wording emphasizes the actions of an *ordinary* and *reasonable* person to look out for the safety of others. If a manufacturer fails to use due care, then he or she is liable for negligence. If one uses due care, then an injured party cannot prove negligence. The "reasonable person" who exercises due care is not negligent. The issue most courts face is how to determine what a reasonable and ordinary person would do. Due care can apply to others besides the manufacturer, including retailers and wholesalers.

Critics of the due care view note that it is difficult to determine when a company has shown sufficient "due care." There is also the issue of how the manufacturer can discover the problems with a product prior to its use if they followed all legal and industry safety standards. Can a manufacturer be negligent if they could not foresee that a product was dangerous or eventually misused in a way that was dangerous?

Consider the Business Ethics Insight on page 261, which shows how two boat manufacturers went beyond legal duties to protect their customers.

Strict Liability Theory

Under **strict liability**, if a product injures a user because it was defective, the manufacturer is responsible to compensate the user. This applies even if the manufacturers used due care in the production. That is, it applies even if a manufacturer was not negligent in producing the product based on the current knowledge at the time of production. For example, under strict liability, furnace manufacturers that built furnaces using asbestos insulation before it became known that asbestos was dangerous are still be held responsible for the sicknesses and deaths related to asbestos poisoning.

Many think that strict liability is not fair to companies and artificially increases costs to consumers, even though companies often exercise due care. If a product injured a member of your family, would you be willing to absolve the manufacturer from guilt if they designed and built the product to known safety standards but it still caused injury?

Exhibit 6.6 shows the major court decision in the U.S. supporting strict liability. Justice Traynor makes it clear that a company's liability for product defects goes beyond any warranties. Following this famous *Greenman v. Yuba Power Products* case, the California Supreme Court extended strict liability to all parties involved in the manufacturing, distribution, and sale of defective products.[26]

BUSINESS ETHICS INSIGHT

A Tale of Two Voluntary Recalls in the Practice of Due Care

In spite of the fact that neither company was required to do so under U.S. law, two major boat manufacturers inspected and repaired hundreds of boats in voluntary recall campaigns. The companies warned owners of the 31-foot to 33-foot Tiara and Pursuit models built by Tiara/S2 Yachts and owners of 36-foot Outlaw models built by Baja Marine Corp. that their boats may be unsafe to use.

As with many products, U.S. federal law requires builders to recall boats when they contain manufacturer-generated defects that "create a substantial risk of personal injury." The Tiara/S2 boats faced potential fires from possible fuel tank leaks. The Baja boats had potential stress cracks in the boat hulls.

By U.S. law, marine manufacturers are responsible for defects only up to five years from the date boat construction began. Agreeing to repair boats much older than five years, Tiara/S2 went far beyond what the law required. Although some of the Tiara/S2 boat owners were willing to sign waivers releasing Tiara/S2 from liability, a Tiara/S2 representative said, "We are not suggesting this approach, this recall is an effort to protect our customers. Any waiver of liability would not address the safety issues."

Baja's action was equally extraordinary, as the company offered to reinforce hulls on 36-foot Outlaws that might fail when owners replaced factory-installed engines with heavier and higher horsepower models that "encroach on the upper limits of what our boats were originally designed for."

Baja discovered the problems when company president Doug Smith repowered his boat with a larger engine and then developed cracks. "We went back and looked at the product line. The boats were within the design scope and within our safety factor. But we decided to increase our upper margin of safety," James O'Sullivan, Baja's customer service manager, told *BoatUS*. "While we cannot force a customer to have the procedure done . . . we do strongly recommend that the procedure be performed as soon as possible." Costing the company around $5,000 per boat in factory modifications, but free to boat owners, the company reinforced hull panels below the engine compartment.

Based on *BoatUS Magazine*, May 2000. http://my.boatus.com/consumer/TaleRecalls.asp.

One argument for strict liability is that by forcing producers to internalize all the costs of a product, manufacturers will then bear the full cost of production. Otherwise, manufacturers only cover their own production costs and not the costs to others from lost work, injury, or even death. Advocates argue that strict product liability gives manufacturers the incentive to maximize their efforts to produce the safest products possible to reduce the risks to consumers in order to lower their costs. Additionally,

Greenman v. Yuba Power Products
In *Greenman,* Traynor cited his own earlier concurrence in *Escola v. Coca-Cola Bottling Co.,* 24 Cal. 2d 453, 462 (1944) (Traynor, J., concurring) stating:
Even if there is no negligence, however, public policy demands that responsibility be fixed wherever it will most effectively reduce the hazards to life and health inherent in defective products that reach the market. It is evident that the manufacturer can anticipate some hazards and guard against the recurrence of others, as the public cannot. Those who suffer injury from defective products are unprepared to meet its consequences. The cost of an injury and the loss of time or health may be an overwhelming misfortune to the person injured, and a needless one, for the risk of injury can be insured by the manufacturer and distributed among the public as a cost of doing business. It is to the public interest to discourage the marketing of products having defects that are a menace to the public. If such products nevertheless find their way into the market it is to the public interest to place the responsibility for whatever injury they may cause upon the manufacturer, who, even if he is not negligent in the manufacture of the product, is responsible for its reaching the market. However intermittently such injuries may occur and however haphazardly they may strike, the risk of their occurrence is a constant risk and a general one. Against such a risk there should be general and constant protection and the manufacturer is best situated to afford such protection.

EXHIBIT 6.6—Strict Liability in U.S. Law—A Ruling by Justice Robert J. Traynor

if the companies were not responsible for the costs associated with injuries, then the consumer bears all those costs.

However, strict liability may raise the costs of products for everyone, since manufacturers must either pay liability insurance or pay any potential damages from their earnings, both of which prompt price increases. In more extreme cases, companies may stop producing the product entirely, as happened in the small plane aviation market in the U.S. as explained in the Business Ethics Insight on page 263. Some also argue that strict liability is unfair to manufacturers who exercise due care.[27] That is, manufacturers should not be at fault for things that are beyond their control, so they should not be penalized for non-preventable defects resulting in injuries. However, one might argue that even if the manufacturers used due care, there are some defects that were still preventable. While that may reduce the moral responsibility of the manufacturer, it still does not eliminate the fact that there was a failure to produce a product without defects when it was possible to do so. Hence, some would argue that the manufacturer still is accountable and thus obligated to compensate those who suffer injury.

The Business Ethics Insight below shows how the application of strict liability almost drove the general aviation companies out of business in the U.S. It also deals with the issue of how long companies should be responsible for their products. In the next section, you will see how privacy issues impact on the relationships between the customer and the company.

BUSINESS ETHICS INSIGHT

Downside of Strict Liability: How Long Should a Company be Liable? The Case of U.S. General Aviation

Spending over $20 million a year to defend product liability lawsuits, some that involved planes over 40 years old, and faced with soaring insurance costs, Cessna Aircraft Co. stopped producing propeller-driven airplanes in 1986. For a company that once produced about 6500 small aircraft per year to suddenly stop building was a major shock to the general aviation industry. Other small airplane manufacturers faced similar product liability challenges. In just four years' time, Beech Aircraft spent over $100 million in legal fees from 203 liability suits. Piper Aircraft Corp. was forced into bankruptcy around the same time.

By 1994, the U.S. light airplane manufacturers produced only 444 planes. However, this was a year of turnaround when Congress passed the General Aviation Revitalization Act. This limited product liability to 18 years from the date of production. The reasoning is that if a product demonstrates its safety over an extended period, then it is no longer reasonable to hold manufacturers liable for defects or failure. In 1994, Cessna went back to producing light aircraft. In 2011, they produced a fleet of six different style single-engine aircraft. Beech no longer produces small aircraft but Piper offers seven different versions of single-engine planes.

In legal terms, limiting the amount of time that a product is open to strict liability is called a **statute of repose**. The only national statute of repose in the U.S. is the General Aviation Revitalization Act. Some people in the U.S. support a national 15-year time span for product liability. Some U.S. states have other statutes dealing with product liability with statutes of repose ranging from 7 to 20 years. Some have none. Japan and the European Union have a ten-year statute of repose.

Perhaps leading to another setback for the small plane segment of the general aviation industry, recent court rulings have established precedents that challenge the oversight of the FAA in determining liability cases. For example, in a crash of a single-engine propeller aircraft a retired doctor was killed and his estate attributed the engine failure leading to the crash as resulting from a carburetor with manufacturing defects. The Washington State Supreme Court ruling in the case of *Estate of Becker v. Avco Corp.*, concluded that, in cases of product liability in the aviation industry, federal law does not preempt state laws. This allowed the suit to go forward and perhaps opens the industry to longer liability exposure than with Federal laws.

Based on www.globalsecurity.org/military/world/general-aviation.htm; www.cessna.com/single-engine/stationair.html. Epstein, Curt. 2017. "Courts say FAA not the final word in product liability." *General Aviation*, May 16.

In today's interlinked global economy products or their components can originate in any country. This creates potential problems when product safety standards may differ across borders and regulations differ regarding liability. In the Emerging Market Business Ethics Insight below you can see the complexities of importing rapidly evolving products from China into the U.S. creates challenges for companies in both countries.

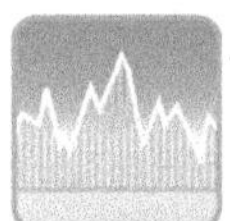

EMERGING MARKET BUSINESS ETHICS INSIGHT

The Challenge of Setting Standards for Emerging Market Imports: Hoverboards

A new product can spread widely in the United States before U.S. standard setters have a chance to provide safety guidance to protect consumers. This occurred briefly with Chinese hoverboards, a type of self-balancing two-wheeled skateboard. Between December 2015 and February 2016, the CPSC received 52 reports of hoverboards catching fire, resulting in more than $2 million in damage, "including the destruction of two homes and an automobile." The fires were widespread, affecting U.S. consumers in 24 different states. Many of these hoverboards were assembled from parts sourced from multiple factories in China, mostly in the industrial center of Shenzhen. Despite the hoverboards being a new product, hundreds of Chinese factories rapidly transitioned to manufacturing them for export. The first hoverboard patent was filed in February 2013 in the United States, and by one account the first hoverboard was marketed in China at a trade show in August 2014. By 2015 an estimated 1000 Chinese factories were manufacturing hoverboards, 4.5 million of which were exported to the United States that year. The speed with which these products entered wide-scale circulation threatened to outpace the development of applicable safety standards. Under U.S. law, the CPSC is required to use voluntary safety standards in most circumstances, and these voluntary standards are typically drafted by third-party standard-setting organizations. At times, setting effective standards can take several years. Without an effective safety standard, sellers, importers, and manufacturers lack clear guidelines to avert product safety risks. In the case of hoverboards, the CPSC and standard setters worked quickly to draft an appropriate standard, and online vendors rapidly removed hoverboards associated with safety hazards in the interim. As hoverboards entered the U.S. market, defects in components resulted in several fires. In November 2015, a house in Louisiana burned down after a hoverboard ignited. Within a month, Amazon pulled a number of hoverboard models from its marketplace and instructed hoverboard manufacturers to demonstrate that their products fulfilled existing safety standards for batteries and chargers. By February 2016, UL—a U.S.-based standard-setting organization—announced it had developed a preliminary standard for hoverboards and would accept certification for hoverboard providers. A few days later, the CPSC strongly urged importers to comply with this new standard, issuing a letter stating that noncompliant hoverboards would be considered defective and may be subject to detention or seizure as they entered the United States. While safety issues associated with hoverboards continued—more than 500,000 hoverboards were recalled in July 2016 over fire concerns—importers received an applicable safety standard shortly after reports of defective hoverboards first emerged. In the meantime, Chinese hoverboard manufacturing appears to have declined. In Shenzhen, one manufacturer reported that his orders fell by 50% following Amazon's safety requirements and cut his staff by 80 percent following the downturn.

Source: Snyder, Matt and Carfagno, Bart. 2017. *Chinese product safety: A persistent challenge to U.S. regulators and importers.* U.S.-China Economic and Security Review Commission, US Government Publishing Office. Pp. 9–10.

PRIVACY

Modern economies generate extensive personal information on consumers. Every click of a mouse, credit card transaction, application for credit, or visit to the doctor creates a store of personal information. Of course, most companies use this information for legitimate reasons that benefit the consumer. However, beyond clearly illegal and unethical use of personal information such as identify theft, there are many gray areas regarding the use of customer information that confront companies in our increasingly digital business world.

Calls for protection of privacy have existed for some time. Consider the call by Samuel Warren and former U.S. Supreme Court chief justice Brandeis in an 1890 *Harvard Law Review* article:

> Recent inventions and business methods call attention to the next step which must be taken for the protection of the person, and for securing to the individual what Judge Cooley calls the right "to be let alone" . . . the question whether our law will recognize and protect the right to privacy in this and in other respects must soon come before our courts for consideration. Of the desirability—indeed the necessity—of some such protection there can, it is believed, be no doubt.[28]

In spite of this early call, that still sounds remarkably current, there is not nation-level comprehensive legislation protecting consumer privacy in the U.S. Instead, privacy legislation exists in specific industries or for specific types of transactions as, for example, the health insurance industry (Health Insurance Portability and Accountability Act), credit reporting industry (Fair Credit Reporting Act), tele marketing (National Do Not Call Registry), and Children's Online Privacy Protection Act (COPPA). At the state level, laws vary widely, with California having the most comprehensive privacy protection.

The prime method of monitoring consumer privacy in the U.S. falls on the Federal Trade Commission (FTC). The approach, however, is indirect. The duty of the FTC is to protect consumers against unfair or deceptive acts or practices in the marketplace. To protect consumers' privacy, the FTC monitors the promises that companies make to consumers regarding consumer privacy protection. While probably not as effective as a comprehensive law, the Business Ethics Insight below shows how some penalties may make managers think twice when they do not live up to the promises made to their customers.

Unlike the U.S., consumer privacy laws in most countries, especially in the EU, Australia, New Zealand, and Canada, are more comprehensive. In Europe, privacy is considered a fundamental right, whereas in the U.S. there are competing views over who owns the information consumers provide to companies. As the Global Business Ethics Insight on page 268 shows, this difference in views regarding privacy has resulted in some mutual accommodation between the U.S. and the EU. With the increased ease of cross-border transactions, there is growing worldwide pressure to harmonize privacy standards.

BUSINESS ETHICS INSIGHT

Consequences of Failure to Protect Customer Privacy: Rite Aid Settled a U.S. Federal Trade Commission Case but Faced Continued Liabilities

Rite Aid operates the third largest pharmacy chain in the United States, with about 4900 retail pharmacies and an online pharmacy business. The FTC began its investigation following news reports about Rite Aid pharmacies using open dumpsters to discard trash that contained consumers' personal information such as pharmacy labels. At the same time, Health and Human Services began investigating the pharmacies' disposal of health information protected by the Health Insurance Portability and Accountability Act (HIPAA).

"Companies that say they will protect personal information shouldn't be tossing patient prescriptions and employment applications in an open dumpster," said Jon Leibowitz, Chairman of the FTC. "We hope other organizations will learn from the FTC's action against Rite Aid to take their obligation to protect consumers' personal information seriously."

According to the FTC's complaint, Rite Aid failed to use appropriate procedures in the following areas:

- Disposing of personal information
- Adequately training employees
- Assessing compliance with its disposal policies and procedures
- Employing a reasonable process for discovering and remedying risks to personal information.

Rite Aid made claims regarding its privacy policies such as,

> Rite Aid takes its responsibility for maintaining your protected health information in confidence very seriously . . . Although you have the right not to disclose your medical history, Rite Aid would like to assure you that we respect and protect your privacy.

The FTC alleged that the claim was deceptive and that Rite Aid's security practices were unfair.

Rite Aid Corporation agreed to settle FTC charges that it failed to protect the sensitive financial and medical information of its customers and employees, in violation of federal law. In a separate but related action, the company's pharmacy chain also agreed to pay $1 million to resolve Department of Health and Human Services (HHS) allegations that it failed to protect customers' sensitive health information.

The FTC settlement order required Rite Aid to establish a comprehensive information security program designed to protect the security, confidentiality, and integrity of the personal information it collects from consumers and employees. It also required the company to obtain audits, every two years for the next 20 years, to ensure that its security program meets the standards of the order. In addition, the order barred future misrepresentations of the company's security practices. The HHS settlement required Rite Aid pharmacies to establish policies and procedures for disposing of protected health information, create a training program for handling and disposing of patient information, conduct internal monitoring, and get an independent assessment of its compliance for three years. Rite Aid also paid HHS $1 million to settle the matter.

In spite of the heavy fines, Rite Aid has faced continuing challenges to preserve customer privacy. The company was fined an additional $1 million in 2015 for failing to train employees on best practices for data disposal and failing to have adequate policies to safeguard patient information. Two years later, hackers compromised its ecommerce site taking extensive customer credit card information.

Based on: Press Release, "Rite Aid settles FTC charges that it failed to protect medical and financial privacy of customers and employees." July 27, 2010 (FTC File No. 0723121). Davis, Jessica. 2017. "Rite Aid's ecommerce platform breached, personal info stolen." *Heathcare IT News*. May 22

Ethical Rationales for Consumer Privacy

Scholars have often debated the ethical rationales for keeping consumer information private.[29] Utilitarian theory offers support to a company perspective that the use of consumer information provides both the consumer and the company benefits because the company can better provide consumers with what they need and can be more efficient in doing so.

From the deontological viewpoint, Kant's[30] categorical imperative can support the gathering and use of consumer information if both sides accept equal rights and protections regarding the use of the information. This had led to the position that, as long as companies provide consumers with a detailed privacy protection policy statement and control over their information, the use of the information is ethical. Somewhat similarly, others argue that social contract theory[31] supports the idea of an equitable exchange between the consumer and the company. The consumer provides information in exchange for some benefit that the company provides by using this information. It is a social contract because there should be shared normative expectations regarding the use of the information.

Ethical perspectives concerning justice also apply to the use of consumer information. If consumers believe the company will use their personal information following practices that preserve their privacy, then the acquisition and use of the information is procedurally just. To be just from a distributive justice perspective, consumers must believe that what the company provides them in terms of products or services is a fair exchange for the personal information that they give to the company. When companies communicate their privacy policies to their customers and stick to those policies, they can build trust with the customer and appeal to interactional justice.

GLOBAL **BUSINESS ETHICS INSIGHT**

Privacy Views in Europe and the United States

In spite of some enforcement by the FTC to require companies to back up their privacy statements, European cultural norms regarding privacy and more stringent laws often shock U.S. companies doing business in Europe. Differing from the U.S., where privacy is a consumer protection issue, in the EU the privacy of personal data is a fundamental human right. The EU's approach to privacy originates from Europe's history and legal traditions. In Europe, protection of information privacy relies on comprehensive lawmaking that seeks to guard against future harms, particularly where social issues are concerned. Thus, for companies in Europe, protection of the personnel data is required and expected, whereas, in the U.S., with the exception of some specific areas such as banking, many U.S. companies act on the assumption that once they acquire the data they own it and can do what they want with it.

As noted by Indiana University associate professor Scott Shackelford, who teaches cybersecurity law, "[They have] this idea that privacy is something that's quite central, that it could be thought of in terms of if property rights," "Having privacy be the starting point and carving out free speech." In the U.S., free speech is paramount and protections secondary.

Since privacy protection is centralized in the EU, privacy laws tend to be more comprehensive, consumer friendly, and easier to understand. In contrast, numerous regulators protect U.S. data. FCC provides rules for data protection by ISPs. The Health Insurance Portability and Accountability Act rules health data. Children's privacy protection is in the domain of the Federal Trade Commission. States play in with their own rules as well. The multitude of players makes the regulations difficulty and inconsistent

However, to do business in Europe, U.S. companies must comply with EU standards. One system used by over 2000 firms is a self-certifying scheme called "Safe Harbor." To meet EU concerns, the U.S. Department of Commerce (DOC) drew up the Safe Harbor Privacy Principles to comply with the EU's standard of "adequate privacy protection," as required by the EU Directive. The European Commission approved those principles in 2000 and the Safe Harbor program went into effect that year.

Although voluntary, if companies become Safe Harbor certified and violate the terms of the certification, the FTC can put companies under increased scrutiny for up to 20 years and even give fines. However, some critics, such as Adam Levitin from Georgetown Law School, see little enforcement and perceive U.S. companies using the data as they wish. Similarly, Edward Janger from Brooklyn Law School noted that "Nobody from the air sector is in Safe Harbor: Delta (DAL), American Airlines (AMR), none of them are. When you give them the information in Europe, I am sure beyond any doubt that the information goes to Atlanta (U.S.)."

Based on Pop, Valentina. "U.S. firms get privacy lessons from Europe." *BusinessWeek*. www.businessweek.com/print/globalbiz/content/jul2010/; *The Economist*. 2010. "Legal confusion on internet privacy: Sharply differing attitudes towards privacy in Europe and America are a headache for the world's internet giants." June 17; U.S. Department of Commerce. www.export.gov/safeharbor/eu/eg_main_018474.asp; Wagner, Tony. 2017. "The main differences between internet privacy in the US and the EU." *Marketplace*. April 24.

Emerging Challenges

There are several issues related to the ease of gathering information, particularly with the use of modern technologies, which should concern companies with an ethical focus on their customers as stakeholders. One area, behavioral targeting, monitors your web-browsing behaviors. Companies like Amazon.com use this information to select advertisements and product offerings that match their information on your tastes. Companies that use these techniques argue that they can better provide their customers with the content that fits their needs so there is a benefit to the consumer. The challenge from an ethical point of view is that companies often get such information without the customers' knowledge and without the customers realizing how others could use the information. Even if the site has a privacy policy that covers such issues, critics argue that few customers actually read the policies but simply check the acknowledgment box and go on. If you intend to use the information for better customer service, could you argue that getting the information without customers' knowledge is ethical?

RFIDs, or **radio-frequency-identifiers**, are very tiny computer chips with miniature antennae embedded in tags attached to physical objects. The data can be sent to computers over a range of just a few feet, or much longer if there is power in the tag. While acknowledging the ethical use of these devices such as for tracking pharmaceuticals, supply chain tracking, and the tracking of toxic substances, the Privacy Rights Clearing House[32] sees several threats to privacy and civil liberties. For example, the tags can be hidden from the people using the tagged products, such as being sewn into clothing. The readers of the information also can be hidden. The bottom line is that, if the data associated with the movement and use of a product are linked with other personal data, companies can profile individuals without their knowledge.

The Privacy Rights Clearing House recommends that the following should be prohibited:

- Forcing or coercing customers into accepting RFID tags in the products they buy
- Preventing people from disabling RFID tags and readers on items in their possession
- Tracking individuals without their informed and written consent.

Cell phone location tracking represents a similar challenge to privacy. In the Business Ethics Insight below we can see some of the suggestions offered by the US FTC regarding location tracking.

BUSINESS ETHICS INSIGHT

The Privacy Implications of Mobile Data Collection: FTC Suggestion

The rapid growth of the mobile marketplace illustrates the need for companies to implement reasonable limits on the collection, transfer, and use of consumer data and to set policies for disposing of collected data. The unique features of a mobile phone—which is highly personal, almost always on, and travels with the consumer—have facilitated unprecedented levels of data collection. Recent news reports have confirmed the extent of this ubiquitous data collection. Researchers announced, for example, that Apple had been collecting geolocation data through its mobile devices over time, and storing unencrypted data files containing this information on consumers' computers and mobile devices. The *Wall Street Journal* has documented numerous companies gaining access to detailed information—such as age, gender, precise location, and the unique ID associated with a particular mobile device—that can then be used to track and predict consumer behavior.

Not surprisingly, consumers are concerned: for example, a recent Nielsen study found that a majority of smartphone app users worry about their privacy when it comes to sharing their location through a mobile device. The Commission calls on companies to limit collection to data they need for a requested service or transaction. For example, a wallpaper app or an app that tracks stock quotes does not need to collect location information. The extensive collection of consumer information—particularly location information—through mobile devices also heightens the need for companies to implement reasonable policies for purging data.

Without data retention and disposal policies specifically tied to the stated business purpose for the data collection, location information could be used to build detailed profiles of consumer movements over time that could be used in ways not anticipated by consumers. Location information is particularly useful for uniquely identifying (or re-identifying) individuals using disparate bits of data. For example, a consumer can use a mobile application on her cell phone to "check in" at a restaurant for the purpose of finding and connecting with friends who are nearby. The same consumer might not expect the application provider to retain a history of restaurants she visited over time. If the application provider were to share that information with third parties, it could reveal a predictive pattern of the consumer's movements thereby exposing the consumer to a risk of harm such as stalking. Taken together, the principles of reasonable collection limitation and disposal periods help to minimize the risks that information collected from or about consumers could be used in harmful or unexpected ways. With respect to the particular concerns of location data in the mobile context, the Commission calls on entities involved in the mobile ecosystem to work together to establish standards that address data collection, transfer, use, and disposal, particularly for location data. To the extent that location data in particular is collected and shared with third parties, entities should work to provide consumers with more prominent notice and choices about such practices.

Source: Excerpted from Federal Trade Commission. 2012. *Protecting consumer privacy in an era of change.* Pg. 33. www.ftc.gov/sites/default/files/documents/reports/federal-trade-commission-report-protecting-consumer-privacy-era-rapid-change-recommendations/120326privacyreport.pdf

Another area of sensitivity in the use of customer information focuses on children. In this U.S.-specific law, the Children's Online Privacy Protection Act (COPPA) focuses on companies that collect personal information from children under the age of 13.[33] The law requires operators to:

- Post a privacy policy on the homepage of the website and link to the privacy policy on every page where personal information is collected.
- Provide notice about the site's information collection practices to parents and obtain verifiable parental consent before collecting personal information from children.
- Give parents a choice regarding the disclosure of their child's personal information to third parties.
- Provide parents with access to their child's personal information and the opportunity to delete the child's personal information and opt out of future collection or use of the information.

- Note condition of a child's participation in a game, contest, or other activity on the child disclosing more personal information than is reasonably necessary to participate in that activity.
- Maintain the confidentiality, security, and integrity of personal information collected from children.

Exhibit 6.7 shows some general suggestions for managing consumer privacy information. They provide good guiding principles for companies wishing to develop ethical privacy practices.

Principles	Explanation
Notice/Awareness	Consumers should be given notice of an entity's information practices before any personal information is collected from them. • Identification of the entity collecting the data • Identification of the uses to which the data will be put • Identification of any potential recipients of the data • The nature of the data collected and the means by which it is collected • Whether the provision of the requested data is voluntary or required, and the consequences of a refusal to provide the requested information • The steps taken by the data collector to ensure the confidentiality, integrity and quality of the data.
Choice/Consent	Choice means giving consumers options as to how any personal information collected from them may be used. Specifically, choice relates to secondary uses of information—i.e., uses beyond those necessary to complete the contemplated transaction. Opt-in regimes require affirmative steps by the consumer to allow the collection and/or use of information; opt-out regimes require affirmative steps to prevent the collection and/or use of such information.
Access/Participation	Access refers to an individual's ability both to access data about him or herself—i.e., to view the data in an entity's files—and to contest the data's accuracy and completeness.
Integrity/Security	To assure data integrity, collectors must take reasonable steps, such as using only reputable sources of data and cross-referencing data against multiple sources, providing consumer access to data, and destroying untimely data or converting it to anonymous form.

EXHIBIT 6.7—U.S. Federal Trade Commission Privacy Principles

CHAPTER SUMMARY

In this chapter, you learned about three of the many major issues companies face as they deal with customers. The three key points of customer interface include marketing, product safety, and privacy.

In the marketing section, you learned that the basic 4Ps of marketing are product, price, promotion, and place. Each of these basic functions has their unique ethical challenges. Most issues dealing with products related to product safety and the chapter devoted a separate section to that issue.

With regard to price, the chapter introduced the concept of the "just price." All companies need to make a profit to survive. However, there are unethical pricing practices in pricing. One is the "bait-and-switch," where the customer is lured to the store with a cheap price and then offered a more expensive alternative. Another is "price gouging," where businesses take advantage of situations like natural disasters to raise prices when customers are desperately in need of their products.

With regard to advertising, you learned that, under U.S. law, advertisers must have evidence that supports both express *and* implied claims that advertisements make to consumers. If an advertisement makes health or safety claims, scientific evidence from studies evaluated by other professionals or scientists in the field must support the claims. Ads that fail this test are considered deceptive. Techniques used in deceptive advertising include ambiguity, concealed facts, and exaggeration.

Two areas of special concern in advertising are the use of sexuality and advertising to children. With regard to sexuality, it seems that moderate levels of sexual innuendo can attract attention and possibly increase sales. However, you also saw that sexuality in advertisements might not work in all cultural settings.

Advertising to children is one of the more controversial issues in the ethics of marketing. The debate over advertising to children focuses on four areas: at what age children recognize an advertisement as such; at what age children understand the intent of the advertisement; the effect of "pester power" to influence parents; and indirect effects from peer groups. Children less than ten years old seem to be able to identify ads and understand the intent and this ability increases with age. Advertisements do seem to result in appeals to parents to purchase products and, similarly, ads that influence peer groups work indirectly through peer pressure. Exhibit 6.4 gives a guide for ethical ads to children.

In the section on product safety you learned that, even if the safety of a product such as an automobile can be improved, it is seldom possible to make a perfect product and do it at prices that consumers can afford. Thus, since many if not most products we use can potentially cause harm, the basic question is: who has the responsibility for this harm? This section introduced you to various theories regarding how to determine product liability. These included the buyer beware view, contractual theory, due care, and strict liability. The most stringent is strict liability, in which the manufacturers are responsible for its products' safety regardless of reasonable efforts made to build a safe product and the customers' use of the product. A major issue here is how long liability should be maintained.

The chapter concluded with a section on consumer privacy. This is a growing area of ethical concern for businesses because the same technologies that make business transactions faster and easier also generate much personal information on customers. Unlike for the EU, you learned that the U.S. does not have a general privacy protection law, although there are several statutes that protect privacy in particular or with particular customers such as children. There remains a debate in the U.S. considering whether privacy is a fundamental right or whether businesses have a degree of ownership over personal information. This section concluded by giving you a general guideline for managing consumer information that came from principles suggested by the U.S. Federal Trade Commission.

NOTES

1 Zinkhan, G.M. & Williams, B.C. 2007. "The New American Marketing Association definition of marketing: An alternative assessment." *Journal of Public Policy & Marketing*, 26, 2, 284–288.
2 American Marketing Association. 2007. www.marketingpower.com/AboutAMA/Pages/DefinitionofMarketing.aspx.
3 Chartered Institute of Marketing (CIM). 2011. www.cim.co.uk/resources/glossary/home.
4 Wicks, A.R., Freeman, E., Werhane, P.H. & Martin, K.E. 2010. *Business ethics*. New York: Prentice Hall.
5 Bryant, C.X. 2004. *ACE Fitness Matters*. January/February.
6 Friedman, D.D. 1980. "In defense of Thomas Aquinas and the just price." *History of Political Economy*, 12, 234–242.
7 U.S. Department of Transportation. 2010. "DOT fines US airways for violation of price advertising rules." Press Release, DOT 44–10 March 8.
8 U.S. Federal Trade Commission. 1998. "Children's Online Privacy Protection Act of 1998." www.ftc.gov/privacy/privacyinitiatives/childrens.html.
9 International Chamber of Commerce. 2017. *Advertising and Marketing Communication Practice*. https://cdn.iccwbo.org/content/uploads/sites/3/2011/08/ICC-Consolidated-Code-of-Advertising-and-Marketing-2011-English.pdf
10 Shaw, W.H. 2008. *Business ethics*. Belmont, CA: Thomson.
11 Cowley, E. 2006. "Processing exaggerated advertising claims." *Journal of Business Research*, 59, 6, 728–734.
12 Beauchamp, T.L. 1984. "Manipulative advertising." *Business and Professional Ethics Journal*, 3, 1–22.
13 Reichert, T., Heckler, S.E. & Jackson, S. 2001. "The effects of sexual social marketing appeals on cognitive processing and persuasion." *Journal of Advertising*, 30, 1, 13–27 (at 13–14).
14 Levit, M. 2005. "Sex in advertising: Does it sell?" *Business: Advertising*, February 15.
15 Levit "Sex in advertising: Does it sell?"
16 Bushman, B.J. 2005. "Violence and sex in television programs do not sell products in advertisements." *Psychological Science*, 16, 9, 702–708; Prendergast, G. & Hwa, C.H. 2003. "An Asia perspective of offensive advertising on the web." *International Journal of Advertising*, 22, 393–411.
17 Jarlbro, G. 2001. *Children and television advertising: The players, the arguments and the research during the period 1994–2000*. Stockholm: Konsumentverket.
18 McDermott, L., O'Sullivan, T., Stead, M. & Hastings, G. 2006. "International food advertising, pester power and its effects." *International Journal of Advertising*, 25, 4, 513–539.
19 Jarlbro, *Children and television advertising*.
20 Associated Press. 2010. "Toyota's chief apologizes for global recalls." www.msnbc.msn.com/id/35254001/ns/business-autos/February 5; Vartabedian, Ralph & Bensinger, Ken. 2010. "Doubt cast on Toyota's decision to blame sudden acceleration on gas pedal defect." *Los Angeles Times*, January 30.
21 Birchall, J. 2010. "Mattel forced to recall 11m products." *Financial Times*, September 30, 20, 40.
22 Schwartz, V.E. 1998. "Continuing duty to warn: An opportunity for liability prevention or exposure." *Journal of Public Policy & Marketing*, 17, 124–126.

23 McAlpin, R.J. 2000. "Failure to warn: A product liability issue." Speech presented at Boating Week. 2000, Annual meeting of the Recreational Boat Builders Association, Orlando, FL. www.rbbi.com/folders/show/bw2000/sessions/failure.htm.

24 McAlpin, "Failure to warn: A product liability issue"; U.S. Food and Drug Administration. 2002. "Determination of intended use for 510(k) devices; Guidance for CDRH staff (update to K98-1)." December 3. www.fda.gov/downloads/MedicalDevices/DeviceRegulationandGuidance/GuidanceDocuments/ucm082166.pdf.

25 *Greenman v. Yuba Power Products*, 59 Cal. 2d 57 (1963).

26 *Elmore v. American Motors Corp.*, 70 Cal. 2d 578 (1969).

27 Piker, A. 1998. "Strict product liability and the unfairness objection." *Journal of Business Ethics*, 17, 885–893.

28 Warren, S. & Brandeis, L.D. 1980. "The right to privacy." *Harvard Law Review*, IV, 195–196.

29 Caudill, E.M. & Murphy, P.E. 2000. "Consumer online privacy: Legal and ethical issues." *Journal of Public Policy & Marketing*, 19, 1, 7–19; Lanier, Clinton D. & Saini, Amit. 2008. "Understanding consumer privacy: A review and future directions." *Academy of Marketing Science Review*, 12, 2. www.ams review.org/articles/lanier02–2008.pdf.

30 Kant, I. 1959. *Foundations of the metaphysics of morals*. Indianapolis: Bobbs-Merrill Company.

31 Dunfee, T.W., Smith, C.N. & Ross, W.T. 1999. "Social contracts and marketing ethics." *Journal of Marketing*, 63, 14–32.

32 Privacy Rights Clearing House. 2003. "RFID Position Statement of Consumer Privacy and Civil Liberties Organizations." www.privacyrights.org/ar/RFIDposition.htm.

33 U.S. Federal Trade Commission. 1998. "Children's Online Privacy Protection Act of 1998." www.ftc.gov/privacy/privacyinitiatives/childrens.html.

KEY TERMS

4Ps: product, price, promotion, and place.

Ambiguity in advertisements: advertisements with confusing wording that leads the consumer to make erroneous conclusions about the nature of the product.

Bait-and-switch: occurs when a product is advertised at a low price, but when the consumer comes in he or she finds, or is offered, only a higher priced version of the product.

Behavioral targeting: software that monitors web-browsing behaviors to track customer behaviors.

Buyer beware: a perspective that places the burden on the buyer for judging the value, safety, and characteristics of a product.

Concealing facts: advertisements that leave out pertinent information regarding their products.

Contract view: a perspective where the relationship between the manufacturer and a consumer is based on a contract.

Design defect: a potentially harmful characteristic of a product that is related to how the product is designed or manufactured.

Due care theory: manufacturers have an obligation to take reasonable precautions that their products do not harm the buyers.

Exaggeration: advertisements that overstate the benefits of a product.

Express claim: expected performance of a product is stated directly in an advertisement.

Failure to disclose the full price: when listed prices do not include other fees or charges that the consumer will have to pay.

Implied claim: expected performance of a product is stated indirectly or by inference in an advertisement.

Just price: attributed to St. Thomas Aquinas and suggests a seller should not raise prices because a buyer has a strong need for a product.

Marketing: usually the first level where the organization interacts with customers.

Material defect: a potentially harmful characteristic of a product due the materials used in production.

Predatory pricing: when a company lowers its prices so far below competitors' that it drives the competitors out of the market.

Price discrimination: when different groups are charged different prices.

Price fixing: when sellers agree with each other to sell at one price that is often above what they would have to do in a competitive market.

Price gouging: when sellers take advantage of situations like national disasters or shortages to raise prices.

Promotion: activities like advertising, sponsorships, coupons, and point-of-sale displays that make the customer aware of your product.

Puffery: an exaggeration so extreme that the assumption is that no reasonable person would believe the statement.

Radio-frequency-identifiers: computer chips with miniature antennae embedded in tags attached to physical objects and which send information to others.

Sexual appeals: messages in advertisements and promotions that contain sexual imagery.

Statute of repose: limiting the amount of time that a product is open to strict liability.

Strict liability: the manufacturer is responsible to compensate the user for defective or unsafe products that potentially cause harm even if due care was used in the production.

DISCUSSION QUESTIONS

1. How can you determine if a customer has a legitimate need for your product? Should you care if he/she is willing to buy?
2. Consider the concept of a "just price." Contrast that with pricing based on supply and demand. Make an ethical argument for both perspectives.
3. Discuss whether price gouging is wrong.
4. Identify advertisements that conceal facts. Discuss whether customers are likely deceived by these concealments.
5. Identify advertisements that are exaggerations. Discuss whether different customer groups might be likely not to realize that these ads are exaggerations.
6. Is sexual appeal in advertisements a form of sexual harassment? Discuss the types of sexual harassment and provide examples.

7. Identify what special provisions should be made when advertising to children. Give an ethical argument as to why these provisions are considered, at least by some, as necessary.
8. Consider the amount of time manufacturers might be liable for product defects (in the U.S., 5 years for automobiles and 18 years for aircraft). Use due care theory and strict liability theory to justify a time period.
9. Develop and augment that the protection of consumer information is or is not a fundamental right.
10. Given what we know about advertisements to children, do you think such ads should be banned?

INTERNET ACTIVITY

1. Go to the internet and search on advertising ethical codes. You will find many codes from different professional societies and different countries, including the Vatican.
2. Compare the codes by country. How are they different? How are they similar?
3. Prepare recommendations for multinational companies that might want to use the same advertising copy around the world. Will they find different standards? Could they offend local customers?

For more Internet Activities and resources, visit the Companion Website at www. routledge.com/cw/parboteeah.

WHAT WOULD YOU DO?

Product Safety in Brazil

Your U.S. company has started producing all-terrain vehicles (ATVs) in Brazil for selling in the South American market. The company's strategy is to build a presence and market share in Brazil before moving to other countries. In your first international assignment, the company has appointed you the manager of the manufacturing plant. The sales staff is Brazilian.

After a year on the job, the manufacturing plant is running smoothly and sales are starting to grow. You are confident that this assignment will be a major career boost and, when you return to the U.S., you will receive a substantial promotion and salary raise.

Late one afternoon, Marcus Alves, your head of marketing, comes to your office. He tells you how happy he is to work for the company but he is worried that sales growth is slowing and if that continues the company may abandon its Brazilian investment. He tells you, "The real problem is that prices are a bit too high for the

Brazilian market." He and the sales force have been discussing the problem and come up with an idea to cut manufacturing costs that can lower the price to a more affordable level.

Alves suggests that you abandon the four-wheel version of the ATV and produce a three-wheel version like the company did in the 1980s. You could save money by not having an extra wheel and the associated suspension, and the ATV would probably be lighter and go faster—something your target market of younger men would like.

You remind Alves that the industry stopped producing three-wheelers because they caused so many accidents and deaths. He counters, noting, "It's perfectly legal here in Brazil to sell these vehicles. All we would need to do is put a warning label and encourage people to wear helmets." You know that wearing helmets is not very popular among your customers, but he presses: "We need this to survive and people need the jobs."

What would you do? Do you manufacture the cheaper and affordable product or keep with the safety standards accepted in a much richer nation? What stakeholders are affected by your decision?

BRIEF CASE: BUSINESS ETHICS INSIGHT

Profits and People in the Drug Industry

Routinely, the drug industry reports the highest profit margins among all industries. A significant amount of this profit comes from the U.S., which is one of the few larger nations that does not regulate drug prices.

Particularly during economic downturns, shopping for prescription drugs in Canada has become popular for people living close to the border. The same multinational companies that sell in the U.S. make the drugs but the prices are much lower. The savings can be 25% to 80%. While it is technically legal to import prescription drugs into the U.S., the actual status of doing so is somewhat ambiguous, as the Federal Drug Administration has not implemented the law for fear of not controlling the quality of the drugs.

This has not stopped bus tours of seniors from buying drugs across the border and even some local governments working to make it easier. A recent *60 Minutes* report examined the program set up by former Springfield, MA mayor Michael Albano. This program works with a Canadian pharmacy to supply drugs to municipal workers in the city.

When the city of Springfield faced a budget deficit, Albano was forced to lay off firefighters, police officers, and teachers. Albano realized that the city could make substantial savings in healthcare costs if the 3000 city employees, retirees, and family members bought Canadian drugs rather than drugs from the local pharmacy. Noted Albano:

> We can save anywhere from $4 to $9 million on an annual basis if I get everybody enrolled and everybody goes to Canada. And that's a huge amount of money right now. If I can save $9 million for my city and put it back, redirect it back into police and fire and to public education, it'll make a world of difference. So it's a huge saving.

Albano practices what he preaches, as his son is diabetic and he buys insulin from the Canadian pharmacy as well.

Naturally, U.S. Americans buying in Canada is bad for the pharmaceutical companies' business, although good for local Canadian pharmacies that often make up to 30% of revenues from U.S. customers. However, Canadian pharmacists risk alienating their suppliers. As the pharmacist that supplies the Springfield workers noted, "We've had several letters from the big multinationals, certainly threatening to cut off the drug supply very explicitly if you are supplying medications to U.S. patients."

Why are drug prices so high? Perhaps the most compelling argument made by the big pharmaceuticals is that they must cover the high costs of research and development (R&D) to make major advances in developing new drugs. Not all drugs succeed, and even if they work wonders it takes years for a drug to receive governmental approval for human use.

Some question this argument. A recent Bank of America study found that many companies spend more on paying dividends to stockholders and buying back shares to increase the prices of their stocks. These activities benefit the stockholders and not the people who need the drugs. The Bank of America figures are telling. The world's largest drug firm, Pfizer, spent $22.2 billion on buybacks and dividends. This equaled 210% of the amount spent on R&D. Similarly, British drug giant GlaxoSmithKline spent 122% of its R&D spending on buybacks and dividends and Merck spent 143% of its R&D budget.

Another recent report by the consumer health organization Families USA also questions the claim that high drug prices are necessary to support R&D. This study found that drug companies spent more than twice as much on administration, advertising, and marketing than they did on R&D. Among the nine companies examined in the study, which included Merck, Pfizer, Bristol-Myers Squibb, Pharmacia, Abbott Laboratories, American Home Products, Eli Lilly, Schering-Plough, and Allergan, only Eli Lilly spent less than twice as much on marketing, advertising, and administration than on R&D. In the year of the study, six of these firms reported higher net profits than spending on R&D.

Not all of the press is negative on big pharmaceuticals. Historically, pharmaceutical companies have aggressively used patents to protect their intellectual property rights for their drug creations and prevent other companies from copying the drugs and producing generic versions for a much cheaper price. The rationale behind this also rests on the return on R&D to the company that makes the investment.

However, this has placed many of the pharmaceuticals in the ethical dilemma of not providing drugs to people in desperate need, especially those from the poorer nations. Healthcare activists have long argued that drug patents deny the poor essential medicines. Whether responding to external pressures or internally derived concern for people, many drug companies are now relaxing their patent restrictions. For example, GlaxoSmithKline (GSK), a British drug company, waived patent restrictions and now allows generic drug firms to copy its HIV drugs and sell them in poor countries. The Swiss company Novartis shares proprietary research in a partnership with the Institute for OneWorld Health, a non-profit research organization, to develop drugs for secretory diarrhea. Secretory diarrhea is a leading cause of death for children in poor countries. The institute also works with Roche, another Swiss company that waived patent restrictions to produce drugs targeted at common diseases in the poor nations.

Based on Off the Charts: Pay, Profits and Spending by Drug Companies. www.actupny.org/reports/drugcosts.html; www.cbsnews.com/stories/2004/03/12/60minutes/main605700.shtml; *The Economist*. "All together now, new initiatives to cure diseases of the poor world." July 16, 2009; Wagg, Oliver. 2004. "Drug companies: Consumers or shareholders?" *Ethical Corporation*, November 18, 2004.

BRIEF CASE QUESTIONS

1. The pharmaceutical industry presents a complex case on how to balance the interests of stakeholders: the stockholders of the companies and the people who need affordable drugs to survive and live decent lives. Take the position of the company and counter the arguments from the groups discussed in the case.
2. Should drug prices be regulated in a rich country such as the U.S.?
3. From a justice point of view, discuss the issue of whether it is fair for people to pay for drugs (or other fundamental necessities) based on their income.

LONG CASE: BUSINESS ETHICS

http://sevenpillarsinstitute.org/case-studies/mylans-epipen-pricing-scandal

MYLAN'S EPIPEN PRICING SCANDAL

September 14th, 2017 by Kara in Case Studies

By: Andreas Kanaris Miyashiro

Each year about 3.6 million Americans are prescribed EpiPen, the epinephrine auto-injector. The EpiPen is a life-saving treatment for anaphylactic reactions, which are caused by allergens such as nuts, seafood, and insect bites. A sharp increase in EpiPen's price between 2009 and 2016 caused outrage, and prompted debate over whether Mylan N.V, the owner of EpiPen, acted unethically. Beyond the behaviour of Mylan, EpiPen's price increases raise questions about the conditions of the U.S. pharmaceutical market, and whether existing regulations and laws are sufficient to protect consumers.

Epipen Price Increases

In 2007, Mylan N.V. acquired the right to market EpiPen as part of its acquisition of Merck KgaA. In 2009, Mylan began to steadily increase the price of EpiPen. In 2009, the wholesale price (the price which pharmacies paid) was $103.50 for a two-pack of autoinjectors. By July 2013 the price was up to $264.50, and it rose a further 75% to $461 by May of 2015. By May of 2016, the price rose again up to $608.61. Over a seven year period, the price of EpiPen had risen about 500% in total.

Mylan's Colossal Marketing Efforts

In tandem with these price increases, Mylan embarked on a strategy to cement the market dominance of EpiPen, while expanding the market for epinephrine as a whole. The first element of this strategy consisted of extensive marketing campaigns designed

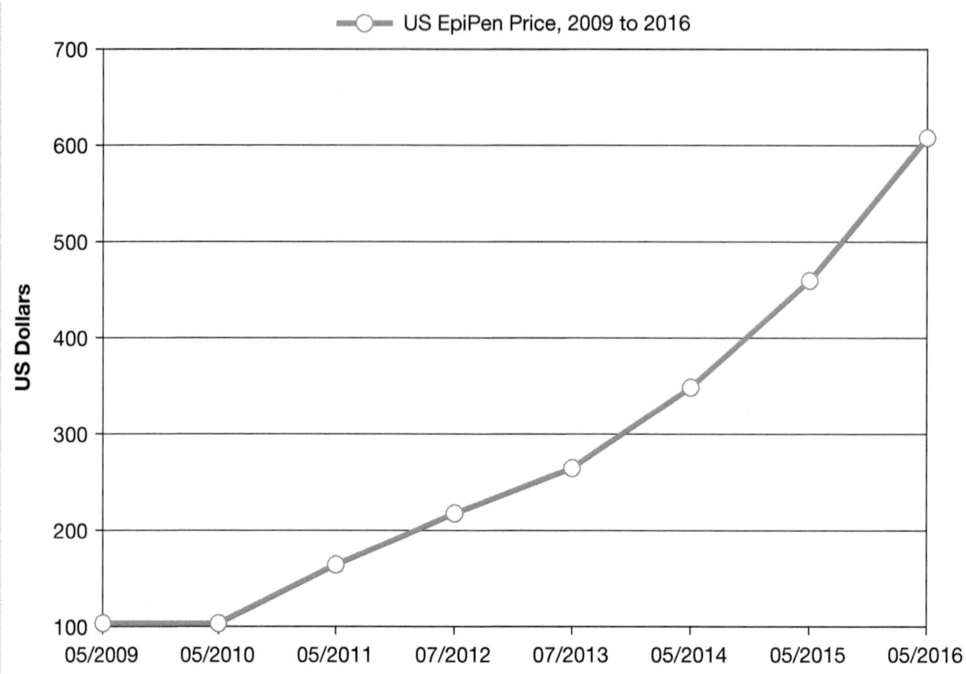

to raise awareness about the dangers of anaphylactic reactions. Mylan's marketing efforts included television advertising, as well as some other less traditional advertising approaches. In 2014, for example, Mylan struck a deal with Walt Disney Parks and Resorts which produced a website and several storybooks designed for families living with severe allergies distributed in 2015.

In addition, Mylan embarked on an extensive lobbying campaign. Mylan successfully lobbied the FDA in order to broaden the wording of the label of the drug, such that it could be prescribed to those who were "at risk" of experiencing an anaphylactic reaction, in addition to those who had experienced anaphylaxis in the past. The company also added lobbyists in 36 states between 2010 and 2014, in order to pressure lawmakers to require epinephrine be made available in public schools. The rate at which Mylan hired new lobbyists during this period was faster than any other U.S. company, according to the Center for Public Integrity. Increasingly, states have passed laws designed to encourage epinephrine injections to be made available in schools. In 2006, Nebraska became the first state to introduce a requirement that public schools must be able to provide epinephrine injections. Mylan's lobbying efforts helped to accelerate this trend. A further nine states have introduced similar requirements since 2006, some prompted by much publicised deaths as a result of anaphylaxis. Virginia's 2012 law, for example, followed 7-year-old Amarria Johnson's death at a Chesterfield County school from a reaction to peanuts. A further 38 states passed laws permitting epinephrine in schools during the same period. In 2013, President Obama signed off on a federal law, which provides financial incentives for states to require epinephrine treatments in schools.

The rate at which Mylan hired new lobbyists during this period was faster than any other U.S. company, according to the Center for Public Integrity.

Mylan's lobbying efforts helped to increase the availability of epinephrine in schools. Simultaneously, Mylan attempted to increase the number of EpiPens sold to schools by establishing the "Epipen4Schools" program in 2012. Schools that sign up to the program receive four free EpiPens. The scheme not only helps to increase the visibility of the EpiPen brand, but also has the potential to be lucrative for the company in the short term. Donations of EpiPens are tax deductible. Mylan is likely able to deduct the cost of producing each EpiPen which it donates plus 50% of the difference between the production cost and the sticker price. In addition, schools which signed up for the EpiPen4Schools program were offered discounted prices to buy more EpiPens, provided they signed an agreement to the effect that the schools would "not in the next 12 months purchase any products that are competitive to EpiPen® Auto-Injectors". This provision was discontinued in July, 2016, according to a statement Mylan gave to Congress. In the long term, Mylan's Epipen4Schools program was clearly designed to cement a strong consumer base for the EpiPen. Nicholson Price, an assistant professor at the University of Michigan Law School, describes the company's business model as giving customers "the first hit" for free.

Mylan's strategy to increase sales and market share of EpiPen proved highly effective between 2007 and 2016. The product gained market share, from about 90% in 2007 when Mylan first purchased the rights to produce EpiPen to around 95% in 2015 and early 2016. Annual prescriptions for EpiPen products more than doubled to 3.6 million during the same period, according to IMS Health data. In 2007, the total U.S. market for epinephrine was around $207 million a year. In 2015, and 2016, Mylan alone exceeded a billion dollars in EpiPen sales.

Controversy and Lawsuits in Response to Price Increases

In the summer of 2016, however, Mylan's fortunes began to turn. The last round of price increases, which saw the wholesale price of a two pack of auto injectors rise to about $608 drew widespread criticism from the public and lawmakers. Multiple congressional committees requested Mylan explain the rapid price increases, resulting in a hearing by the House Committee on Oversight and Government Reform in September of 2016. Heather Bresch, CEO of Mylan since January of 2011, faced harsh criticism during her testimony. Bresch was unable to answer questions about revenues and the company's patient assistance programs, but defended Mylan's business practices and refused to accept the assertion the company had raised the prices of EpiPen's to increase profits. Bresch insisted the price surge was a result of increased research and development costs, as well as the costs of Mylan's EpiPen4Schools program. In addition, she claimed that half of the wholesale price of EpiPens are received by middlemen such as insurance companies and pharmacy benefit managers, and that the U.S. healthcare system was partially to blame for rising costs.

In response to criticism about the price increases, Mylan announced it would reduce the price of EpiPen through increased financial assistance in the form of savings cards that would cover up to $300 of the cost for those who have private health insurance. In addition, Mylan raised the income threshold for families who are uninsured or underinsured to be eligible for free EpiPens from under $48,600 a year to under $97,200 a year. Despite the fact that the new savings cards allowed patients to eliminate up to $300 of co-pay in buying an EpiPen, critics have pointed out the scheme is not a substitute for lowering prices. Though the amount the patients pay in co-pay for EpiPen is significantly reduced in using the savings card, insurance companies continue to pay for the high remaining cost of the drug. This results in higher healthcare premiums. For this very reason, such savings cards cannot be used by patients covered by Medicaid. Discounts such as this are considered "kickbacks" which incentivise patients to buy pharmaceutical products, while leaving the government to pay for the remaining costs. As such, Harvard Medical School professor Aaron Kesselheim criticised the savings cards as a "classic public relations move" which fails to address the fundamental problem of high prices.

Lawsuit 1: Mylan Misclassified EpiPen as a generic drug

In September, 2016, increased scrutiny of Mylan's business practices led to questions being raised about the drug classification of EpiPen. Mylan misclassified EpiPen as a generic drug, in order to avoid the higher rebates drug companies must pay when they sell their brand-name products to state Medicaid programs. Pharmaceutical companies selling generic drugs pay rebates of 13% of the average manufacturer's price, while companies which sell brand-name drugs must offer discounts of 23% off either the average price, or the difference between the average price and the best price they have negotiated with any other American payer, depending on which option provides the bigger discount. Brand-name manufacturers must also pay further rebates if their products' prices rise faster than inflation.

Mylan misclassified EpiPen as a generic drug, in order to avoid the higher rebates drug companies must pay.

Patented drugs such as EpiPen are typically considered to be brand-name drugs, but Mylan classified the EpiPen as a generic on the basis that the active substance (epinephrine) used in EpiPens is common and widely used. This clearly was a misclassification, considering the extremely high market share which EpiPen enjoys, and the fact that Mylan owns a patent for EpiPen which will expire in 2025. The Department of Justice pursued legal action against Mylan in September of 2016. The case was resolved in a $465 million settlement in October. As part of the settlement, Mylan agreed to reclassify EpiPen as a branded drug.

Lawsuit 2: Antitrust violation

Also in September of 2016, New York attorney general Eric T. Schneiderman launched an antitrust investigation into Mylan, on the basis that the sales contracts with schools as part of the EpiPen4Schools program violated antitrust laws. The investigation is ongoing, but it seems likely that Mylan may eventually face consequences for the illegal contracts, which forced schools to refrain from buying EpiPen's competitors in order to buy EpiPens at discounted prices.

In December of 2016, Mylan again attempted to address criticisms of EpiPen's price by releasing a generic version of EpiPen with a list price of $300 for a two-pack, less than half the price of the brand-name version. A press release from Mylan stated this "unprecedented action, along with the enhancements we made to our patient access programs, will help patients and provide substantial savings to payors". It is highly unusual for a pharmaceutical company to release a generic competitor for its own brand name product. As well as serving as an attempt to quiet criticism of EpiPen's price, the move may have been motivated by Teva pharmaceutical's development of its own generic epinephrine auto-injector, expected to win FDA approval at some point in 2017. Mylan's release of its own generic device might have been an attempt to steal market share from Teva's product

Lawsuit 3: Class action based on RICO

In April of 2017, Mylan faced two new lawsuits related to their business practices in selling EpiPen. The first, filed April 3rd, was a class-action lawsuit filed by three EpiPen purchasers who claim that Mylan engaged in illegal schemes to dominate the market with Pharmacy Benefit Managers (PBMs). PBMs serve as intermediaries between insurance companies, pharmaceutical companies, and pharmacies. The plaintiffs claim that agreements reached between Mylan and a number of PBMs including CVS Caremark, Express Scripts Holding Co and OptumRX, were illegal under the Racketeer Influenced and Corrupt Organizations Act. Mylan allegedly offered the PBMs large rebates in exchange for favouring EpiPen over competitors.

Lawsuit 4: Anti-competitive acts

The second lawsuit, filed April 24th by pharmaceutical company Sanofi SA, also accused Mylan of illegally attempting to prevent competition for the EpiPen. Sanofi claims that Mylan offered rebates to PBMs, insurers, and state Medicaid agencies on the condition they would not reimburse patients to buy Sanofi's Auvi-Q rival auto-injector device. Sanofi seeks damages against Mylan for the hundreds of millions of dollars they may have lost in sales due to these illegal agreements. Any damages which Mylan pays to Sanofi will be tripled under U.S. antitrust law.

Determinants of EpiPen Pricing

A number of different factors interact in determining the price for a specific drug in a particular country. These include the market for the drug in question, the judgment and business practices of the manufacturer, and the conditions of the wider pharmaceutical market and healthcare system in the country of interest. Examining these factors in relation to the EpiPen can explain the dramatic increase in its price between 2009 and 2016.

Background on the Epinephrine Market

Epinephrine is a hormone used to treat anaphylaxis (severe allergic reactions) since 1977. Anaphylactic reactions can be deadly due to swelling and closing of the airways. Epinephrine injections, by triggering the "fight or flight" response, quickly causes patients' airways to open, preventing death from suffocation.

Marginal Costs

Epinephrine is widely used and very cheap to produce. It takes less than one U.S. dollar to manufacture one millilitre of epinephrine. A single EpiPen dispenses less than a third of that amount. What makes the EpiPen valuable is it quickly administers the correct dose of epinephrine, and is simple enough to operate that a person suffering from anaphylaxis can self-administer the treatment if necessary. Still, the manufacturing cost of EpiPen is estimated to be under $10 per two pack.

R&D Cost

The marginal costs of most drugs to manufacturers are typically low. More influential supply-side factors in determining drug pricing are research and development costs and marketing costs. Heather Bresch, in her September 2016 congressional hearing, testified that the price increases for EpiPen were in part due to research and development costs involved in improving the drug. Since purchasing EpiPen in 2007, Mylan has made incremental upgrades to the EpiPen, designed to make the drug easier to administer and clarify instructions about how to use the product. Daniel Kozarich, an expert on pricing, suggests that the EpiPen price increases up to 2013, by which time the price of a two-pack had risen to $264.50, could justifiably be explained as compensation for research and development costs. This cannot be said for the subsequent price increases between 2013 and 2016.

Marketing Cost

Mylan engaged in extensive marketing of the EpiPen, paying about $35 million for advertising in 2014, for example. Usually, such heavy marketing costs are reserved for new products, which are often advertised widely in order to introduce the drugs to the medical community. The amount Mylan spends in advertising, however, is dwarfed by its yearly sales of EpiPen, which exceeded $1 billion for the first time in 2015. Mylan's aggressive advertising efforts have proved very successful in expanding the size of the market for EpiPen, and cannot justify an over 500% increase in price during a seven year period.

"Willingness to Pay" and Pricing

While supply-side factors may have played a part in Mylan's determination to increase prices, demand-side factors may have been more influential. For the most part, drug prices in the U.S. predominantly rest on demand-side considerations. As William Comanor and Stuart Schweitzer, professors at the UCLA School of Public Health explain, the key factor in determining pharmaceutical prices is patients' "willingness to pay" for a given product.

The most important factor determining the magnitude of patients' "willingness to pay" for a product is the therapeutic advance it provides. New drugs with a significant therapeutic advantage over old ones are the subject of large amounts of demand, which warrant high prices. The EpiPen, however, has been on the market since 1987. Typically, innovative products such as the EpiPen offering a large therapeutic advance are introduced with high prices that decrease over time. This pricing strategy is referred to as "skimming". EpiPen's price increases under Mylan are unusual given that the product has been on the market for three decades.

A Lack of Competition

The high price of EpiPen can better be explained by the lack of competition the product faces. The amount of competition a particular drug faces in its specific category has a significant effect on price, as prescribing physicians must select between rival drugs. A 1998 study by Lu and Comanor finds that launch prices of pharmaceutical products are significantly lower when there are more branded rivals in direct competition with them.

During the period in which Mylan increased EpiPen prices, few direct competitors existed to threaten EpiPen's market dominance in the U.S. In the UK and other European countries, the EpiPen competes against the Jext auto injector from ALK pharma, and the Emerade auto injector from Valeant, among others. In contrast, prior to June of 2013, when the Adrenaclick autoinjector was reintroduced by Amedra, few direct competitors to the EpiPen existed in the U.S. Since its relaunch, the Adrenaclick has faced manufacturing constraints, which prevented it from gaining significant market share until recently. Auvi-Q, manufactured by French pharmaceutical Sanofi S.A., was designed to rival the EpiPen, but was on the market for only three years before Sanofi voluntarily recalled all Auvi-Q devices due to concerns the auto injectors were administering incorrect doses. The Auvi-Q is the most significant competitor to EpiPen worldwide, but its recall in the U.S. damaged its reputation. Since the beginning of 2017, EpiPen has lost a significant amount of market share in the U.S., partly to cheaper products such as the generic version of the Adrenaclick which costs only $110, but also to Mylan's own generic version of EpiPen. Between 2007 and 2016, EpiPen's market share in the U.S. hovered between 90 and 95%. Between January and March of 2017, EpiPen's market share in the U.S. has been only 71%, according to a study by AthenaInsight.

Fiona Scott Morton and Lysle T. Boller of the Yale School of Management comment on the subject of EpiPen's lack of competition that "there is a tension between imitating a reference product like EpiPen without imitating its injector". Generic applicants hoping to create a new version of a patented product face navigating through unclear FDA guidelines concerning how to avoid infringing on the existing patent. In the case of EpiPen, developing competitor drugs may have been particularly difficult due to the fact the patented element being the injector rather than epinephrine, which is an old generic. Any injector imitating EpiPen is likely to infringe on EpiPen's patent protection. A similar patent issued helped to facilitate the recent dramatic price increases of Evzio, an autoinjector for naloxone, used to treat opioid overdose. As with EpiPen, Evzio's patented element is the delivery device rather than the drug itself.

It should be noted that one factor which helped reduce competition for the EpiPen in the U.S. was Mylan's own business practices. Multiple lawsuits, such as the 2016 lawsuit regarding the EpiPen4Schools program, revealed Mylan may have violated antitrust laws by offering rebates and discounts to buyers such as insurance companies and schools, in exchange for agreements which would preclude those buyers from purchasing any of EpiPen's competitors.

The U.S. Healthcare System and EpiPen pricing

The list price of a two-pack of EpiPen is about $69 in the UK, about $100 in France, and about $200 in Germany. These prices are dramatically lower than the $609 list price of EpiPen in the U.S. As was mentioned previously, EpiPen prices in Europe are lower in part due to a larger number of direct competitors to the EpiPen there. But the most significant factor causing this price differentiation is the healthcare system in the U.S. The UK, France, and Germany all have different forms of universal healthcare systems, which severely restrict the price of pharmaceutical drugs.

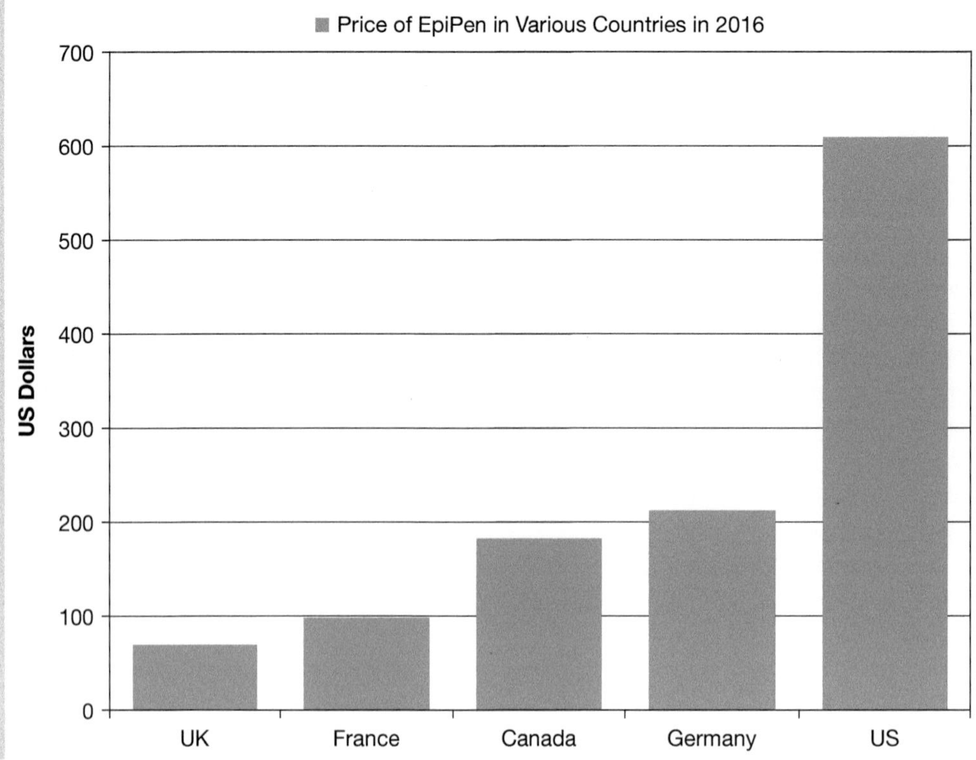

UK Pharmaceutical Price Controls

In the UK, there exists a long-held consensus among lawmakers that there is a need for price regulation of pharmaceuticals, as the supply of pharmaceuticals is viewed as non-competitive due to the patent system. Within the Medicines, Pharmacy, and Industrial (MPI) division of the UK Department of Health, the Pricing and Supply branch oversees drug price controls. The Pricing and Supply branch negotiates an agreement, called the Pharmaceutical Price Regulation Scheme (PPRS) with the pharmaceutical industry that sets a cap to profits which pharmaceutical companies can make on NHS business. Pharmaceutical companies are required to repay any amount that exceeds this fixed cap. This agreement is renegotiated every time the existing PPRS agreement expires, which typically occurs 4–5 years after they come into effect. PPRS agreements explicitly aim to create a balance between "[supporting] the NHS by ensuring that the branded medicines bill stays within affordable limits and [delivering] value for money" and "promoting a strong and profitable pharmaceutical industry that is both capable of and willing to invest in sustained research and development". The UK is a hub of research and development in the pharmaceutical sector, and has continued to attract investment, despite the decline in pharmaceutical research and development in Europe as a whole. PPRS agreements aim to control prices such that pharmaceutical companies' profits are largely in line with the profits of British industry in general, without damaging this important sector of the UK economy. Of course, the PPRS was implemented on the basis that the NHS is the sole healthcare provider for about 90% of the UK population. A system such as the one the PPRS sets out is not feasible in the U.S., where no universal public healthcare option exists.

The effects of the PPRS in relation to the cost of EpiPen are striking. The National Health Service (NHS), the public healthcare provider in the UK, pays £53 per two pack for EpiPen, then distributes them to patients who pay only £8.40.

A Lack of Price Controls in the U.S.

In the U.S., in contrast, a lack of price controls set by the government allows drugs to be sold at whatever prices pharmaceutical companies see fit. State Medicaid programs mandate that pharmaceutical companies sell these drugs at a rebate, which is higher or lower depending on whether the drugs in question are classed as innovators (brand-name drugs) or generics. However, even taking into account rebates, certain drugs such as EpiPen are sold to state Medicaid programs at far higher prices than they are sold to the NHS in the UK.

This does not necessarily mean all drug prices are much higher in the U.S. than they are in other countries. Reports by the U.S. Government Accountability Office (GAO) in 1992 and 1994 show that the cash prices for the same branded products are generally higher in the United States than elsewhere. However, the GAO reports, and other studies of a similar nature fail to account for a number of factors which obfuscate price comparisons.

One issue is the GAO report relies on established nominal prices of drugs. These prices do not take into account the rebates and discounts granted to large-scale buyers

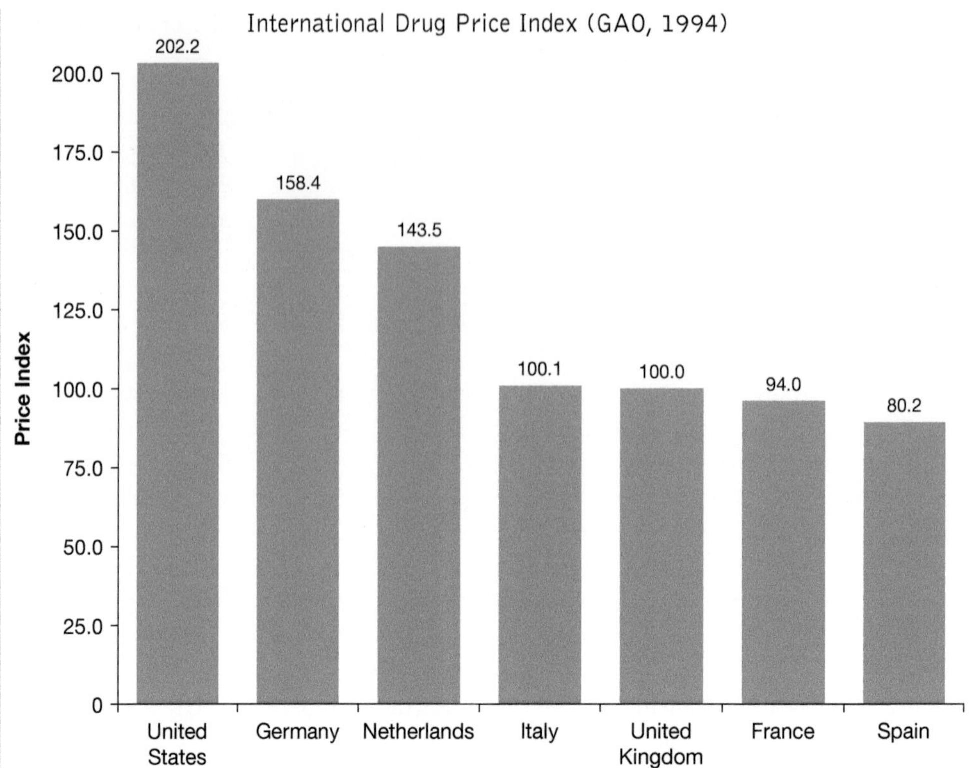

Source: Pharmaceutical Industry Branch, Department of Health, United Kingdom

of pharmaceutical products. This is a huge oversight, considering these bulk buyers comprise the largest segment of demand for pharmaceutical products in the U.S. Given the prices at which large-scale buyers buy drugs are not disclosed, it is difficult to estimate the magnitude of how this skews the GAO results.

Even more significantly, the GAO report fails to account for the influence of generic drugs in the U.S. pharmaceutical market. Generic drugs are more widely used in the U.S. than in most other countries, accounting for about half of the total sales in pharmaceutical products, and are also generally much cheaper than their branded counterparts. The generic version of the EpiPen introduced by Mylan costs about half the price of the branded version, for example. As such, it is insufficient to simply compare U.S. prices of popular branded drugs to those in other countries. The market share of generic drugs, and their prices should also be compared. William Comanor and Stuart Schweitzer, professors at the UCLA School of Public Health provide the following example to illustrate this point:

"Suppose that half of US prescriptions for Cimetidine, a popular H2 blocker for gastric reflux and ulcers, are filled by the generic version, the price of which is, say, $104 per hundred, while the price of the branded product, Tagamet, is $167. The average price is $135.50. Suppose further that the prices of both versions of the drug are lower in Canada, with a price of Tagamet of $150 and a generic price of $100. If the generic version's market share is only 20% in Canada, the average price there is $140, which is higher than the average US price, even though the prices charged for both products are lower in Canada."

It should be noted this argument is predicated on the idea that generic drugs are identically effective to branded drugs, which is not necessarily the case. Generic drugs must be bioequivalent to their branded counterparts under U.S. Food and Drug Administration (FDA) rules, and the FDA considers generic drugs therapeutically equivalent to brand-name drugs. However, the inactive ingredients in branded drugs may result in slightly different outcomes for patients than generic drugs in some cases. Furthermore, as was the case with the EpiPen until Mylan introduced its own generic version of the product, some pharmaceutical products do not have generic counterparts.

In sum, the problem of inflated pharmaceutical prices does not apply to all drugs in the U.S. Many drug prices are well regulated in the U.S. by market forces. The main conclusion from empirical studies comparing U.S. drug prices to drug prices in other countries is the U.S. system gives pharmaceutical companies license to sell certain drugs, most often brand-name drugs, at extremely inflated prices.

Many drug prices are well regulated in the U.S. by market forces. The main conclusion from empirical studies comparing U.S. drug prices to drug prices in other countries is the U.S. system gives pharmaceutical companies license to sell certain drugs, most often brand-name drugs, at extremely inflated prices.

PBMs and Pricing Opacity

Heather Bresch, during her December 2016 testimony to the House Oversight committee, claimed the "opaque and frustrating" healthcare system in the U.S. was partly to blame for price increases. Rather than a lack of regulation in the U.S. giving licence to companies to increase prices, the healthcare system actually forces companies such as Mylan to raise prices, according to Bresch.

There is some degree of truth to this assertion. Some commentators suggest the U.S. healthcare system suffers from a lack of transparency, which results in inflated pharmaceutical prices.

Pharmacy Benefit Managers (PBMs), the "middlemen" who bridge the gap between drug manufacturers, insurance companies, and pharmacies are one of the players who are most at fault for creating opacity in the U.S. health system.

Fundamentally, PBMs serve an important function in the U.S. health system. Their core purpose is to aid insurance companies, HMOs, and large employers who purchase drugs for their beneficiaries. PBMs help these large buyers to process claims, and make transactions between the various players involved in providing drugs to insured patients. The beneficiaries themselves buy drugs from local pharmacies. PBMs reimburse pharmacies for the cost of the drug, based on the price the pharmacy paid for the drug, and the size of the co-payment. The PBMs themselves receive payments both from the large-scale buyers of drugs such as insurance companies, but also from drug manufacturers who pay them rebates taken from the amount that they receive from pharmacies who sell their drugs. The drug manufacturers receive revenue equal to the

Prescription Drug Distribution Chain (Kaiser Foundation, 2005)

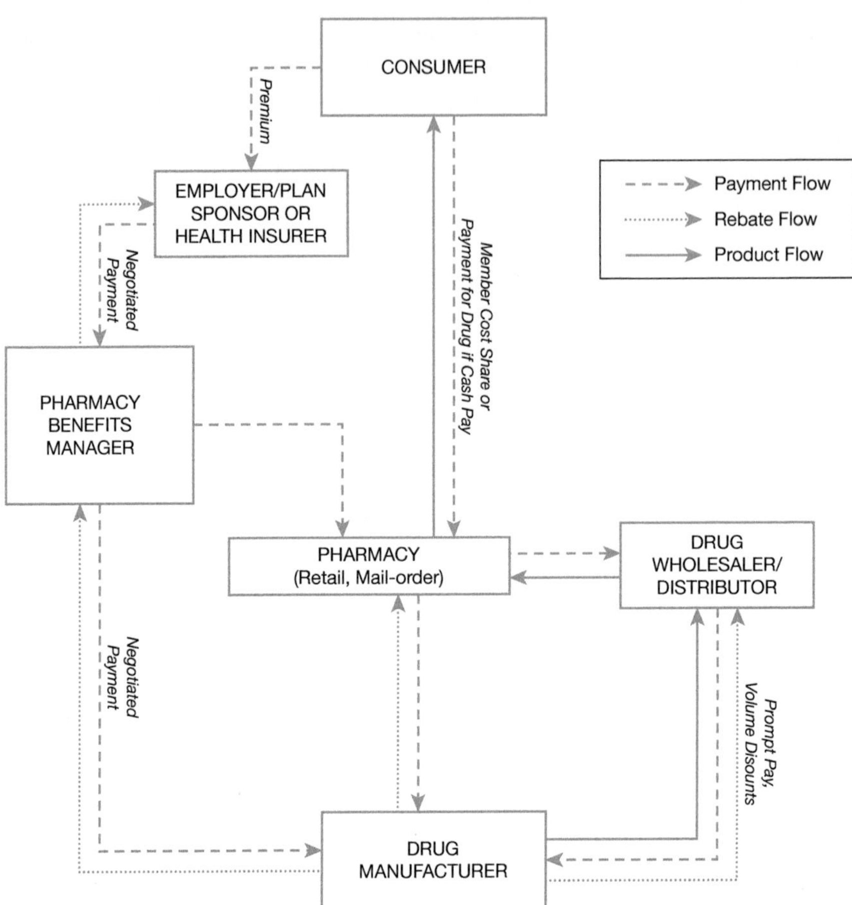

list price of drugs minus the rebates they provide to PBMs. PBMs negotiate rebates with manufacturers, meaning that various PBMs receive differential rebates when selling the same brands of drugs.

This system, working effectively, has a number of advantages. The rebates system permits manufacturers to charge different prices to different buyers and creates a complex system of differential pricing, responsive to differential demand. Large-scale buyers pay less than the full list price of drugs due to rebates. Patients receive drugs, and pay only the co-pay amount.

In addition, PBMs should have a beneficial effect on the demand side of the pharmaceutical market, as PBMs buy drugs in large quantities on behalf of insurance companies. Ideally, PBMs should augment the elasticity of demand, and improve competition in place of consumers, whose demand is inelastic and who are uninformed about competing products. On the other hand, if PBMs do not respond to price changes in an appropriate way, they risk distorting the market. If a rival company begins selling a drug, which is a close substitute for another drug at a lower price, demand for the rival's drug should rise accordingly. If PBMs, as large-scale buyers, fail to increase the amount of the rival drug that they purchase, there is a risk the rival company will not be able to generate sales and market share. The incentive to lower prices in the first place is removed, and pharmaceutical companies are likely to continue charging their existing customers high prices rather than attempt to increase sales by lowering prices. As such, PBMs have the capacity to distort the effects of competition.

The fundamental problem with the operation of PBMs currently is that the savings generated by rebates are not passed on directly to consumers. As Fiona Scott Morton and Lysle T. Boller of the Yale School of Management note, "rebates are never made public because they reflect the competitive advantage of both the PBM and the brand's manufacturer". As such, PBMs are able to profit from the discrepancies between the price at which the manufacturers sell them the drugs, and the prices at which pharmacies and insurance companies buy them. For example, if a manufacturer increases the price of a particular drug, the PBM might be paid a rebate for the extra cost. However, the insurance company purchasing the drugs eventually will not be aware of this additional rebate the PBM is receiving. The rebate simply becomes profit for the PBM.

As such, PBMs have strong incentives to buy and distribute drugs from companies offering them high rebates, rather than those who sell drugs at lower prices. Low prices save patients and insurance companies money, whereas high rebates result in higher profits for PBMs. PBMs' earnings would be significantly reduced if pharmaceutical companies curtail price hikes, as is illustrated by a 2013 Morgan Stanley report.

As a result, PBMs distort demand rather than improving its elasticity. PBMs facilitate high drug prices, encouraging pharmaceutical companies to raise prices but increase rebates. High prices are translated into higher premiums charged to consumers by insurance companies, but fall hardest on those without insurance, who face paying the full list price of expensive products such as EpiPen.

Bresch's comments have an element of truth in light of these facts. If EpiPen were to lower prices rather than reduce rebates to PBMs, they would risk losing sales given that PBMs prefer to purchase products with high prices. On the other hand, the buying practices of PBMs do not necessarily encourage price increases as they do not profit from price increases in themselves. Furthermore, Mylan may have entered into illegal, anticompetitive agreements with PBMs as is alleged by the class-action lawsuit filed in April 2017. The lawsuit raises the possibility that rather than suffering from the practices of PBMs, Mylan benefitted from them. Ultimately, Mylan is culpable for increasing prices.

Background on Mylan N.V.

Mylan N.V., an American generic and brand-name pharmaceuticals company, was founded in 1961. Initially, Mylan was a small generics-only drug company, but it expanded into the brand-name sector when it introduced a highly successful new formulation of the diuretic Dyazide in 1987.

Through a number of acquisitions, Mylan grew to be one of the largest pharmaceutical companies in the U.S., and one of the largest generic drug producers in the world. In 2007, Mylan made its most significant acquisition ever, purchasing Merck KGaA's generic's arm in a $6.6 billion deal. As part of the same deal, Mylan gained the right to produce and distribute EpiPen. According to a press release by Mylan, the acquisition had the potential to triple the company's revenue.

A History of Controversial Business Practice

The recent controversy surrounding Mylan's practices is unsurprising given Mylan's history of questionable business decisions:

- In December 1998, the FTC charged Mylan with restraint of trade, monopolisation and conspiracy to monopolise the markets as a result of their price increases for two widely-prescribed anti-anxiety drugs, lorazepam and clorazepate.
- In January 1998, Mylan raised the wholesale price of clorazepate from $11.36 to $377.00 per bottle of 500 tablets.
- In March of 1998, the wholesale price of lorazepam was increased from $7.30 for a bottle of 500 tablets to $190.00. According to the FTC, Mylan entered into anticompetitive agreements with ProFarmica, a company producing raw ingredients required to manufacture the two drugs. The agreements restricted the supply of these raw ingredients in order to facilitate Mylan's dramatic price increases. After 32 states joined the suit against Mylan, a $100 million settlement was reached in 2000.
- In October 2009, the US Justice Department brought a lawsuit against Mylan concerning false claims to State Medicaid programs. The plaintiffs claimed that Mylan had deliberately misclassified drugs (including nifedipine extended release tablets, flecainide acetate, selegiline HCL) sold to State Medicaid companies as generic drugs, when they should have been classified as innovator drugs. Mylan misclassified the drugs for the purpose of avoiding the higher rebates which generic drugs are subject to under state Medicaid programs. In October of 2009, the case was settled for $124 million.

What is striking about these cases of illegal misconduct is that they closely mirror misconduct that Mylan would later carry out in relation to EpiPen. The September 2016 lawsuit against Mylan, resulting in a $465 million settlement, was a result of Mylan illegally avoiding rebates to state Medicaid programs just as it had done in 2009. The three separate lawsuits Mylan has faced since the October 2016 settlement are all related to claims that Mylan violated antitrust laws in contracts selling EpiPen, the same crime Mylan was charged with in 1998. While illegal behaviour such as this is unfortunately common amongst pharmaceutical companies operating in the U.S., Mylan's repeat offences suggest the company has bred a culture of questionable business practices transcending changes in management over time. Studying Mylan's history of illegal and exploitative conduct, the company's decision to raise EpiPen prices to an unethical extent is unsurprising.

According to reporting by the *New York Times*, high level executives at Mylan operate on principles far removed from what Mylan's mission statement espouses. According to Mylan's website, management "[challenges] every member of every team to challenge the status quo" and the business model of the company puts "people and patients first, trusting that profits will follow". According to anonymous sources within the company who spoke to the *New York Times*, a number of mid-level executives began to grow concerned about EpiPen price increases in 2014, feeling the prices were reaching exploitative levels. When these concerns were aired to Robert Coury, Mylan's chairman, he replied that "anyone criticising Mylan, including its employees, ought to go copulate with themselves".

Ethics Analysis of Mylan N.V. Acts

As the analysis illustrates, there are a number of interrelated factors contributing to the high prices of pharmaceutical products in the U.S. These factors deserve to be the subjects of scrutiny, and inform attempts to reform the U.S. health market. However, the ultimate responsibility for drastic price increases lies with pharmaceutical companies.

Heather Bresch's Response to Criticism of Mylan

In her 2016 testimony to Congress, Heather Bresch argued Mylan was responsible for a "tremendous amount of good . . . for millions of patients in the U.S and around the world". She made a number of claims to prove this assertion.

Firstly, she argued Mylan was responsible, through its advertising and advocacy efforts, for dramatically increasing awareness and use of EpiPens. The cost of these efforts contributed to price increases. According to Bresch "the issue of EpiPens has two equally critical dimensions—price and access."

Secondly, Mylan had invested in research and development aimed at improving the EpiPen. This also contributed to price increases. The combined costs of research and development of EpiPen, plus advertising and lobbying costs amounted to $1 billion.

Thirdly, the opacity and complexity of the drug distribution chain in the U.S. resulted in higher prices.

Finally, Bresch claimed that Mylan only profited about $50 per EpiPen, or $100 per two pack in total. Furthermore, a new generic version of EpiPen was being developed which would be priced at $300, and new savings vouchers had been introduced which offered patients up to $300 off the price of their co-pay for EpiPen.

Refuting Bresch's Response

Bresch's response to criticism of EpiPen's price was disingenuous and misleading, for a number of reasons.

Overriding goal was to increase sales

Mylan's advertising and advocacy efforts were beneficial in that they successfully increased awareness of the dangers of anaphylaxis. However, they clearly were aimed at increasing EpiPen's sales rather than preventing harm. The strategies Mylan employed as part of this campaign demonstrate this. Mylan enticed schools in to signing anticompetitive agreements that precluded them from purchasing EpiPen's competitor products as part of the EpiPen4Schools program. Mylan's aim was not only to encourage schools to make epinephrin injections available, but also to ensure that schools would buy its product alone.

Mylan's advertising campaign also crossed ethical boundaries, deliberately misleading customers. In 2012, Mylan released an advertisement that implied that as long as anaphylaxis sufferers had an EpiPen on hand, they could eat whatever allergenic foods they wanted. Heather Bresch and other executives approved the ad, despite concerns being raised about its misleading message in a number of stages of the internal review process. Reportedly, Bresch suggested that it was best to be "bold" in advertising. Mylan pulled the ad subsequent to a record number of consumer complaints being sent to the FDA. The complaints claimed the ad overstated the efficacy of EpiPen.

In 2012, Mylan released an advertisement that implied that as long as anaphylaxis sufferers had an EpiPen on hand, they could eat whatever allergenic foods they wanted.

These details of Mylan's advertising and advocacy campaign illustrate that the overriding aim of the campaign was clearly to increase sales of EpiPen. The campaign may also have had altruistic motivations, as Bresch suggests, but these were a secondary objective.

In any case, Mylan's advertising and lobbying were highly successful in expanding the market for epinephrine auto injectors, increasing sales of EpiPen by over 400%. The increases in sales more than compensated for the costs of the campaign

R&D costs insufficient to explain price increase

Furthermore, the research and development costs of improving the EpiPen, as previously mentioned, can only reasonably be used to justify the price increases which occurred up to 2013. While Bresch claimed the combined cost of advertising, lobbying, research and development exceeded $1 billion, the House Oversight Committee commented that none of Bresch's financial data presented was substantiated. Bresch also claimed during the hearing that Mylan had saved the federal government $180 billion during its ownership of EpiPen. Bresch presented no evidence in support of this claim, and failed to even elaborate the reason why it might have been the case.

Bresch's claims about the amount of profit from each EpiPen were proved to be incorrect after subsequent analysis. Independent estimates suggest that Mylan profits $80 per EpiPen, and $160 per two-pack, 60% more profit than Bresch claimed in the hearing.

EpiPen price an outlier, even in the context of the U.S.

While Bresch's claims about the opacity and complexity of the U.S. health system have an element of truth, it is doubtful that the operation of PBMs could have necessitated price increases of the magnitude that Mylan carried out. PBMs were responsible for the price increases only insofar as they may have discouraged competition and enabled Mylan to increase prices without reducing sales. The ultimate responsibility for raising prices lies with Mylan, particularly considering Mylan may have entered into anti-competitive agreements with PBMs.

Insufficient response to price increases by Mylan

Furthermore, the discount vouchers and the generic version of EpiPen Mylan introduced in response to criticism were insufficient to solve the pricing problem. As previously mentioned, the savings cards are only available to families with private health insurance, and up to $97,200 a year combined income. Families with under $28,000 in income are typically eligible for Medicaid coverage. This leaves only a margin of $69,200 in income within which families are eligible for the savings card (excluding individuals covered by Medicare). Furthermore, many families and individuals who have income too high to be eligible for Medicaid or Obamacare feel they cannot afford private health insurance. In sum, the subset of patients eligible to use the savings card for EpiPen is small. In cases where patients are able to use the savings cards, insurance companies absorb most of the costs of the savings, leading to higher premiums.

The generic version of the EpiPen is perhaps a more effective measure to lift the financial burden on patients. However, many commentators suggest that Mylan's introduction of the generic EpiPen was a preemptive strategy to steal market share from Teva pharmaceuticals, which is set to release its own generic epinephrine autoinjector. It is also important to note that $300, the cost of the new generic, still represents a 200% markup of EpiPen's price in 2009.

Given that Bresch's explanations for the dramatic increases in EpiPen pricing do not withstand scrutiny, it seems clear that Mylan's motivation for the price increases was simply to increase profits. Having a near monopoly on the epinephrine auto-injector market, and knowing that demand for EpiPen is relatively inelastic given that the drug is an essential, life-saving treatment, executives at Mylan believed that they could raise prices without reducing sales. Clearly, Mylan's acts fall into the category of exploitative and unethical behaviour.

Conclusion and Policy Prescriptions

In light of Mylan's EpiPen price gouging, it is clear that there is a need for reform of the U.S. health system such that pharmaceutical companies are prevented from raising prices of essential medicines to exploitative levels.

Price Controls

Given the effectiveness of the PPRS in the UK, price-controls (or indirect price controls through laws which limit profits) are the most obvious solution. However, it is a matter of debate whether price controls would be beneficial overall in the context of the U.S. pharmaceutical market.

Detractors of pharmaceutical price controls argue that price controls might discourage valuable innovation in the U.S. pharmaceutical market. The pharmaceutical industry is particularly fast-moving, so it would be a difficult market for regulators to govern effectively. Regulators may struggle to regulate drugs because they might be uninformed about valuable research, be captured by the industry given the power of lobbyists in the U.S., or lack the resources to keep up with changes in science or the cost of production

"Reference pricing", a popular form of government price control utilised in Germany, Italy, and Spain among other countries, illustrates the difficulties regulators face in controlling pharmaceutical prices. In a reference pricing system, drugs are classified into therapeutic classes based on the way in which they attack diseases. Prices of drugs are capped based on their therapeutic class, Clearly, such a system might discourage innovations which offer therapeutic advances, as the classification system dis-incentives companies from formulating new drugs which are more effective but fall into the same therapeutic classes as existing drugs.

A study by Joseph Golec and John A. Vernon reach similar conclusions, finding that the U.S. would have never formulated 117 new medicines and would have lost 4368 research jobs had European-style price controls been implemented over a 19 year period.

In addition to disincentivising companies from innovating, price controls might restrict drug companies' financial ability to fund research and development. Ronald Vogel, researcher at the Center for Health Outcomes and PharmacoEconomic Research of the University of Arizona, finds that pharmaceutical price controls in European countries result in reduced research and development spending by drug companies. Vogel concludes that price controls "[reduce] the amount of profit available for further

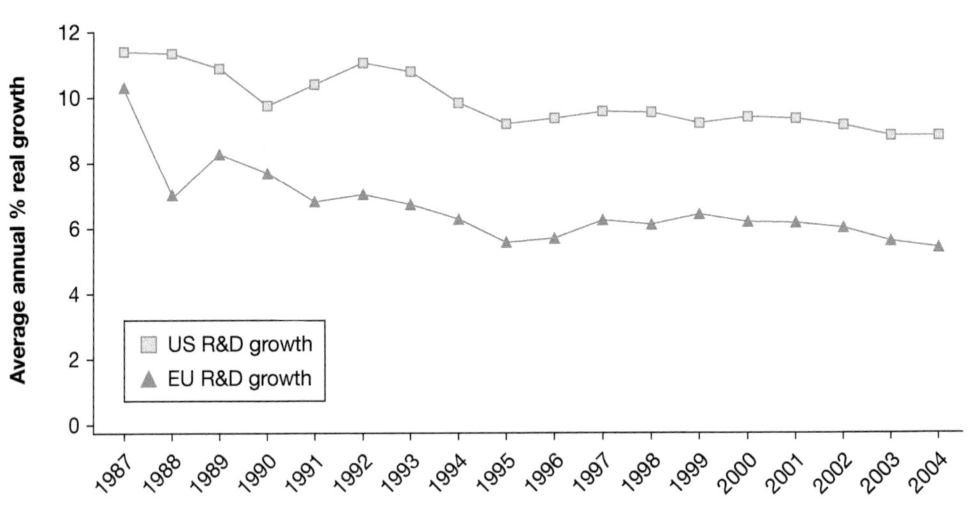

Average annual real growth in U.S. and EU pharmaceutical R&D spending between 1987 and 2004 (Golec and Vernon, 2010)

R&D, which is a detriment to consumers worldwide" and in effect invalidates the benefits of patent protection. A study by Joseph Golec and John A. Vernon reached similar conclusions, finding that the U.S. would have never formulated 117 new medicines and would have lost 4368 research jobs had European-style price controls been implemented over a 19-year period.

The cost of reducing development of new drugs is heavy. An econometric study by Frank Lichtenberg (2002) shows that between 1960 and 1997, every $1,345 spent on pharmaceutical research and development resulted in an additional U.S. life year (meaning a full healthy year of a person's life). The introduction of new drugs not only improves patient outcomes, but also significantly expands the number of patients who can be treated who suffer from a given condition.

The central question in the debate over whether price controls should be introduced into the U.S. drug market, then, is whether it is worth correcting the injustice of limited cases of price gouging at the cost of damaging patient outcomes on a somewhat wider scale. Some politicians, such as Democrats Hillary Clinton and Bernie Sanders, have voiced their support for price controls. The political will to create price control legislation does not yet exist on a large scale, however.

Targeted Price Negotiation

Considering the deleterious effects that wide ranging price controls could have, some analysts have suggested that limited, targeted price controls might prove more effective in controlling excessive prices while preserving innovation. Richard G. Frank, of Harvard Medical School, and Richard J. Zeckhauser, Harvard Kennedy School of Government, propose a framework for drug price negotiation designed to correct market imperfections related to "MISCs". MISCs are drugs subject to a combination of a monopoly and insurance subsidised consumption and can be identified by the following characteristics:

A) Being a unique product with few competitors
B) Likely to be paid for under the reinsurance benefit provided by Medicare
C) Represents a significant claim on spending by the Part D program of Medicare

In Zeckhauser and Frank's framework, drugs with the fulfilled criteria could be subject to a mandatory negotiated payment system, not dissimilar to the PPRS negotiation in the UK. The price negotiations would take into account a number of factors, such as the therapeutic advance offered by the drug, in calculating how much it should cost. The pricing regulations would be in effect until competitors entered the market. This particular framework is designed specifically for the market inefficiency resulting from high-cost drugs which are bought largely by State Medicare programs. The fact that Medicare buys MISCs in large quantities distorts the market, as several players in the process of distributing the drugs, including patients and doctors have no incentive to seek lower prices or adjust their buying practices because the price of the drugs are subsidised.

... companies such as Mylan holding virtual monopolies over segments of the market could be required to submit to price negotiation. Zeckhauser and Frank's

framework is designed to ensure that there continue to be strong incentives for companies to create new, innovative products.

It is reasonable to imagine that Zeckhauser and Frank's framework could be implemented on a larger scale, tailored to correct a wider number of market imperfections. For example, companies such as Mylan holding virtual monopolies over segments of the market could be required to submit to price negotiation. Zeckhauser and Frank's framework is designed to ensure that there continue to be strong incentives for companies to create new, innovative products. As such, a large-scale version of the framework could prove effective in regulating prices in a manner that does not have a significant impact on the creation of new drugs.

An Alternative to Price Controls

Even moderate forms of price controls such as those discussed above would likely be strongly opposed by the pharmaceutical industry, which has significant lobbying power in the U.S. An alternative approach to limiting pharmaceutical prices might encompass two dimensions: (1) encouraging competition, and (2) ensuring that competition is effective in regulating price.

As previously discussed, EpiPen's high price was in part a result of its lack of competitors in the U.S. Increased competition in certain sectors within the pharmaceutical market might help to prevent excessive price increases. Encouraging competition in the pharmaceutical market might involve a number of reforms. Instructing the FDA to use more resources in approving drugs, especially those in the biosimilar and generic categories, in order to prevent delays would be particularly beneficial.

As analysis of the practices of PBMs illustrates, competition does not always have the desired effect of decreasing prices in the U.S. drug market. As such, encouraging competition is insufficient to solve the pricing problem. Imperfections in the market, which prevent competition from having the desired effect could be corrected through a number of reforms. The issue of PBMs, for example, might be corrected by legislation mandating that rebate rates be published by PBMs. This would prevent the pricing opacity that encourages PBMs to buy products with higher rebates rather than those with lower prices.

Disadvantages to this alternative approach to limiting drug prices include its complexity, and also the fact that, since it is an indirect, "soft" approach to limiting prices, it may not be effective in every case. Inevitably, there would be cases of price gouging, even if such regulations were implemented.

A Need for Reform

Despite the numerous challenges that face lawmakers in preventing high drug prices, there is no doubt this is an area which urgently requires reform. Just as it is wrong to price gouge during a state of emergency when essential supplies are scarce, it is wrong that companies can exploit vulnerable populations who require drugs by raising prices to extreme levels. Public outrage and even lawsuits are insufficient to solving the pricing problem as EpiPen's case illustrates. Even in the face of reputational damage and numerous lawsuits, Mylan has not decreased the price of EpiPen.

In the absence of drug price reforms, it is important that lawmakers ensure as many Americans as is possible have health insurance. Those without health insurance are affected most deeply by drug price increases, often having no choice but to buy drugs such as EpiPen at their full list price. Recent Republican proposals for healthcare reform, which cut Medicaid and risk reducing the number of insured Americans by up to 22 million, are dangerous for this reason.

Bibliography

Bartolone, Pauline. "EpiPen's Dominance Driven By Competitors' Stumbles And Tragic Deaths." NPR, 7 Sept. 2016, www.npr.org/sections/health-shots/2016/09/07/492964464/epipen-s-dominance-driven-by-competitors-stumbles-and-tragic-deaths.

Comanor, William S., Schweitzer, Stuart O., Vernon, John A. & Manning, Richard L. "Determinants of Drug Prices and Expenditures." *Managerial and Decision Economics* 28.4_5 (2007): 357–370. Web.

Court, Emma. "Mylan's EpiPen Sales Have Taken a Hit." MarketWatch, 10 May 2017, www.marketwatch.com/story/mylans-epipen-sales-have-taken-a-hit-2017-05-10 .

"Follow the Pill: Understanding the U.S. Commercial Pharmaceutical Supply Chain." The Henry J. Kaiser Foundation, Mar. 2005. Kaiser Foundation.

Goldberg, Robert. "Race Against the Cure: The Health Hazards of Pharmaceutical Price Controls." Policy Review 68 (1994): 34. Web.

Golec, Joseph, and John Vernon. "Financial Effects of Pharmaceutical Price Regulation on R&D Spending by EU versus US Firms." *PharmacoEconomics* 28.8 (2010): 615–628. Web.

Greene, Jan. "EpiPen Controversy Reveals Complexity Behind Drug Price Tags." *Annals of Emergency Medicine* 69.1 (2017): A16–19. Web.

Johnson, Carolyn Y. "Why Mylan's 'Savings Card' Won't Make EpiPen Cheaper for All Patients." *The Washington Post*, WP Company, 25 Aug. 2016, www.washingtonpost.com/news/wonk/wp/2016/08/25/under-pressure-mylan-will-expand-patient-assistance-for-epipen/?utm_term .

Johnson, Carolyn Y. "EpiPen CEO to Defend Lifesaving Drug's Soaring Price in Front of Lawmakers." *The Washington Post*, WP Company, 21 Sept. 2016, www.washingtonpost.com/news/wonk/wp/2016/09/21/what-to-expect-when-congress-takes-on-epipen-maker-mylan/?utm_term=.9d182e90e904.

Johnson, Carolyn Y. & Catherine Ho. "How Mylan, the Maker of EpiPen, Became a Virtual Monopoly." *The Washington Post*, WP Company, 25 Aug. 2016, www.washingtonpost.com/business/economy/2016/08/25/7f83728a-6aee-11e6-ba32–5a4bf5aad4fa_story.html?utm_term=.c539c2d9306f .

Koons, Cynthia & Robert Langreth. "How Marketing Turned the EpiPen Into a Billion-Dollar Business." Bloomberg.com, Bloomberg, 23 Sept. 2015, www.bloomberg.com/news/articles/2015–09–23/how-marketing-turned-the-epipen-into-a-billion-dollar-business.

Larson, Erik & Jared S. Hopkins. "Mylan's EpiPen School Sales Trigger N.Y. Antitrust Probe." Bloomberg.com, Bloomberg, 6 Sept. 2016, www.bloomberg.com/news/articles/2016–09–06/n-y-s-schneiderman-launches-probe-into-mylan-epipen-sales.

Leonard, Kimberly. "Mylan's CEO Hit Over Multi-Million Dollar Salary Amid EpiPen Price Controversy." *U.S. News & World Report*, 21 Sept. 2016, www.usnews.com/news/articles/2016–09–21/mylan-head-defends-epipen-price-gouging-in-capitol-hearing.

Lichtenberg, Frank. "Sources of U.S. Longevity Increase, 1960–1997." NBER Working Paper Series (2002): 8755. Web.

Lopez, Linette. "These Companies You've Never Heard of Are about to Incite Another Massive Drug Price Outrage." Business Insider, Business Insider, 12 Sept. 2016, www.businessinsider.com/scrutiny-express-scripts-pbms-drug-price-fury-2016–9.

Lopez, Linette & Lydia Ramsey. "Congress Railed on the Maker of EpiPen." Business Insider, 21 Sept. 2016, www.businessinsider.com/mylan-ceo-heather-bresch-house-oversight-committee-hearing-epipen-2016–9.

Morton, Fiona Scott & Lysle Boller. "Enabling Competition in Pharmaceutical Markets." Brookings, 2 May 2017, www.brookings.edu/research/enabling-competition-in-pharmaceutical-markets/.

Relakis, Maniadakis, Kourlaba, Shen & Holtorf, Anke-Peggy. "Systematic Review on the Impacts of Strict Pharmaceutical Price Controls-PHP199." *Value in Health* 16.7 (2013): A486. Web.

Rosenthal, Elisabeth. "The Lesson of EpiPens: Why Drug Prices Spike, Again and Again." *The New York Times*, 2 Sept. 2016, www.nytimes.com/2016/09/04/opinion/sunday/the-lesson-of-epipens-why-drug-prices-spike-again-and-again.html.

Santerre, Rexford & John Vernon. "Assessing Consumer Gains from a Drug Price Control Policy in the U.S." NBER Working Paper Series (2005): 11139. Web.

Sedgley, Michael David. *An Analysis of the Government-industry Relationship in the British Pharmaceutical Price Regulation Scheme.* (2004). Print.

Tunney, Kelly. "How Many People Use EpiPens In America? Mylan's Price Increase Is Taking Advantage Of Its Users." Bustle, 26 Aug. 2016, www.bustle.com/articles/180800-how-many-people-use-epipens-in-america-mylans-price-increase-is-taking-advantage-of-its-users.

Tuttle, Brad. "EpiPen Prices: Mylan CEO Heather Bresch & Big Pharma Scandal | Money." *Time*, 21 Sept. 2016, www.time.com/money/4502891/epipen-pricing-scandal-big-pharma-politics/.

United States, Congress, House of Representatives Committee on Oversight and Government Reform. "Testimony of Mylan CEO Heather Bresch before the United States House of Representatives Committee on Oversight and Government Reform", 2016.

United States, Congress, Jagar, Sarah F. "Prescription Drugs: Prices and Regulation in Canada and Europe." Prescription Drugs: Prices and Regulation in Canada and Europe, GAO, 1994. GAO Archive.

Vogel, Ronald J. "Pharmaceutical Patents and Price Controls." *Clinical Therapeutics* 24.7 (2002): 1204–1222. Web.

LONG CASE QUESTIONS

1. Why *is* the EpiPen so expensive? How would you determine a "fair" price for EpiPen?
2. Should pharmaceutical companies be held to a different standard of fair pricing?
3. Reacting to the EpiPen controversy, Bresch said "No one's more frustrated than me." Do you find CEO Bresch's statement convincing?
4. What happens next for Mylan and CEO Bresch?
5. Who are EpiPens' stakeholders and what roles do they play in the pricing issues?
6. If you were CEO, would you make any changes to prices and how would you defend your decisions?
7. Should prices vary across countries? Why or why not?

Chapter 7

Primary Stakeholders:

Shareholders and Corporate Governance

LEARNING OBJECTIVES

After reading this chapter you should be able to:

- Understand the types of shareholders and agency theory
- Be aware of the importance of corporate governance
- Appreciate the role played by boards of directors and the steps needed to design an appropriate board
- Become aware of the controversial issues associated with executive compensation and the appropriate design of such compensation packages
- Understand the role of ownership structures in corporate governance
- Appreciate how national culture impacts corporate governance around the world
- Read about the future of corporate governance and shareholder rights

PREVIEW BUSINESS ETHICS INSIGHT

The Fall of Nortel

Nortel Network Corporation was a major player in the telecommunications industry in the 1990s. Headquartered in Canada, the company had capitalization in excess of C$350 billion in July 2000. Although a diversified company, Nortel focused primarily in the telecommunications industry. Using a very aggressive acquisition strategy, Nortel quickly grew worldwide acquiring companies linked to its business. Nortel was lauded for its performance and praised by analysts for its "solid sustainable growth." The CEO of Nortel was also praised for his visionary ideas and his deftness in growing Nortel. The company was seen as the pride of Canada as it continued its invincible ascent. Share prices of Nortel tripled in four years and were at a peak of C$200 in 2000.

However, reality soon hit Nortel as its fortune declined quickly in the early 2000s. Why did such a model of growth fall so fast? Why did the company's share fall from its high of C$200 to C$0.67? While thousands of workers were losing their jobs, Nortel was trying to find ways to prevent its UK subsidiary from taking its assets to pay for a shortfall in its pensions.

A look at the company's actions reveals many weaknesses that contributed to its dramatic downfall. However, a major contributing factor to the fall of Nortel was poor governance structure. First, Nortel suffered from overvaluation. Specifically, the company was manipulating accounting figures to inflate share prices way above their true underlying values. Furthermore, managers were smoothing earnings to provide a stable pattern of earnings for Nortel. A second major problem at Nortel was the weak role played by its board of directors. The board is typically put in place by shareholders to monitor the actions of management. Furthermore, it is expected that a board will have individuals with financial expertise to monitor the financials of the firm. Unfortunately, Nortel's board of directors did not have such financial expertise. Furthermore, many of the members of the board had multiple memberships on other boards. As a consequence, they neither had the time nor expertise to perform due diligence in approving Nortel's strategic actions. Third, another major factor that contributed to Nortel's decline was its ownership structure. Most companies rely on a combination of individual and institutional investors. However, a large proportion of Nortel's institutional investors were of the transient nature and were more interested in short-term earnings. To satisfy such short-term needs, the company management engaged in manipulation to continue providing the perception of growth at Nortel. Finally, **executive compensation** played a big role in Nortel's decline. A big component of the executives' compensation level was stock options. However, because the value of stock options is tied to the market share price of a company, managers with stock options have every incentive to maximize the short-term price of a company's share. This was also the case at Nortel, where management were overly optimistic about the company's health and engaged in steps to keep the share price of Nortel growing.

Nortel continues to be in the news today. The company was able to raise $7 billion from the sales of its patents and assets. However, U.S. bondholders and UK pensioners have taken other creditors of the company to court to dispute the amount of money they are receiving from the bankruptcy proceedings. The clear winners so far have been the lawyers and accountants navigating the complexities of Nortel's bankruptcy involving a clash of bondholders against creditors in three countries over two continents.

Based on Cohen, T. 2010a. "Regulator acts as recession hits pensions." *Financial Times*, February 23; Duffy, J. and Greene, T. 2009. "Nortel's fall took years to hit bottom." *Network World*, January 19, 26, 3; Fisher, D. 2017. "Nortel bankruptcy near $2 billion as creditors, pensioners fight over assets." *Fortune*, April 5, 14; Forgarty, T., Magnan, M.L., Markarain, G. and Bohdjalian, S. 2009. "Inside agency: The rise and fall of Nortel." *Journal of Business Ethics*, 84, 165–187.

The above Preview Business Ethics Insight shows the impact of managerial actions on investor well-being. This and other high-profile examples such as Enron, WorldCom, and countless other companies worldwide show the ethical landscape facing investors. Investors or shareholders invest money in companies hoping for a return on their investments in the form of dividends and increased share prices. Managers are hired by shareholders to take the necessary steps to ensure that such benefits are produced for shareholders. However, as the above case illustrates, managers may not always act in the best interest of shareholders. These examples illustrate cases of companies where managers engaged in self-interested behaviors that destroyed shareholder wealth.

In this chapter, we therefore examine the shareholder as a primary stakeholder and the relationship of the shareholder with the company. We will examine the role of shareholders and the responsibilities companies have toward them. You will also read about the many mechanisms that can be put in place to ensure that managers behave in the interests of shareholders. Finally, you will also learn some of the rights shareholders have today.

Next, we examine the relationship between the company and a shareholder by understanding agency theory.

TYPES OF SHAREHOLDERS AND AGENCY THEORY

Shareholders are legal owners of business corporations. As mentioned earlier, shareholders invest their money in businesses hoping for a return on their investment. They believe that such returns will be higher than if they invest their money in alternative forms of investment. As a result, companies can decide to pay part of their earnings back to shareholders in the form of dividends. However, shareholders also have a "residual claim on a firm's assets and earnings, meaning they get what's left after all other claimants—employees and their pension funds, suppliers, tax-collecting governments, debt holders, and preferred shareholders (if any exist) are paid.'[12] In other words, the shares of shareholders are worth the future cash flows after all those payments. Thus, shareholders buy stocks in a company if they believe that the future cash flows will be greater than the payments to lead to an increase in the share prices. If they sell the shares in the future at a much higher price, shareholders also make money.

There are two main types of shareholders: individual shareholders and large shareholders. **Individual shareholders** include regular persons buying and selling shares of any company. Such transactions are usually done through a stockbroker and are typically held in brokerage accounts.

While individual shareholders used to traditionally make up a large proportion of shareholders, the past decade has seen a dramatic growth of large shareholders.[3] **Large shareholders** are typically grouped as blockholders and institutional shareholders. Blockowners are "individuals or corporations that buy firms' shares directly, not through an investment entity."[4] In the U.S., blockholders are defined as any investor with more than 5% equity stake in a firm.[5] We will discuss blockholders in more depth later.

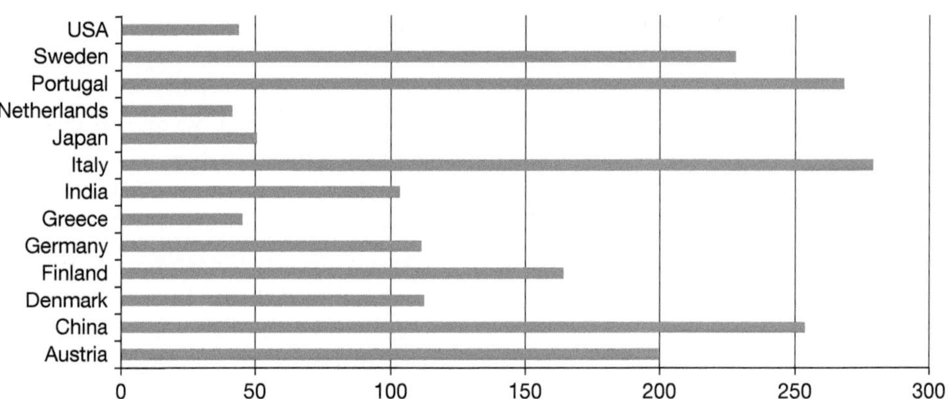

EXHIBIT 7.1—Growth of Institutional Investors Worldwide

In contrast, institutional investors are entities such as mutual funds, banks, pension funds, and insurance companies that invest money on other people's behalf. Extant research suggests that such institutional investors own around 65% of U.S. corporate equity. But is the importance of institutional shareholders only prevalent in the U.S.? Exhibit 7.1 shows the growth in institutional ownership in selected countries from 1995 to 2006.

As Exhibit 7.1 shows, the proportion of institutional investors has grown significantly worldwide. With blockholders, large shareholders constitute an important aspect of ownership structure worldwide. This has important implications for how companies are run. As you will see later, large shareholders can have significant influence on the way companies are run. Such shareholders can hold board of director seats and directly influence the company. However, other large shareholders can have indirect influence by threatening to liquidate their shares. Consider the following Business Ethics Brief.

Given the nature and variety of shareholders and the fact that managers are hired to run companies, the differences in interests between the two groups (shareholders and managers) leads to problematic issues. Specifically, agency theory provides some understanding of how these problems arise. **Agency theory** views the firm as a "legal entity that serves as a nexus for a complex set of contracts among disparate individuals."[6] The contract is often between principals engaging agents to perform some service on behalf of their agents. More specifically, shareholders (the principals) hire top managers and the CEO (the agents) to manage the company. This relationship between shareholders and top management represents the agency problem whereby the interests of the shareholders may not necessarily coincide with the interests of top managers.[7] In fact, for the example of German corporate environment discussed below, large shareholders could often act in their own interests thereby potentially hurting

BUSINESS ETHICS BRIEF

Blockholders in Germany

While the U.S. sees companies largely owned by small shareholders, the German corporate environment traditionally saw ownership in the form of large blockholders. In fact, the German ownership system was dominated by large investors including mostly large banks. Furthermore, many German companies are controlled by management boards that include representatives of the blockholders such as employees, banks and former top managers. This system therefore made it more likely that the interests of the owners (large shareholders) matched the interests of the management (as they also represent these large shareholders). As a result, German companies did not see as much of the problematic issues related to agency costs you will read about later. However, this system also resulted in large shareholders having a disproportionate influence on the direction any company took. As a consequence, large German shareholders such as banks and family owners could make decisions that would benefit themselves at the expense of smaller shareholders.

Based on Engelen, C. 2015. "The effects of managerial discretion on moral hazard related behavior: German evidence on agency costs." *Journal of Management Governance*, 19, 927–960.

the interests of dispersed smaller shareholders. In this case, agency costs arise because of the divergence in needs between large and small shareholders.[8]

According to Tosi,[9] owners of companies, specifically shareholders, face two problems with top management and the CEO. First, there is moral hazard whereby the top management does not put in the right effort or misuses the company resources for its own interests. Experts see the recent financial institution crash in the U.S. as an example of moral hazard. Most of these institutions (JP Morgan Chase, Morgan Stanley, Goldman Sachs, etc.) had top management supporting the peddling of complex and toxic securities. Executives at banks supported loans to individuals and companies who could barely provide assets to back these loans. The results of such moral hazard have been serious concerns about financial stability in the U.S. Additionally, because managers may not feel the effects of losses immediately, they are also more likely to spend scarce resources on pet projects or provide themselves with many perks.

Moral hazard is not solely a U.S. phenomenon. Consider the case of Satyam Computers, an Indian outsourcing company involved in computer systems for many *Fortune* 500 companies. The chairman and chief executive of the company admitted to committing a $1.47 billion fraud. Quarter after quarter, the chairman manipulated numbers to show a rosier picture at Satyam. He inflated profits, claimed cash reserves that did not exist, overstated the money it was owed. The scandal was revealed when he tried to buy two companies owned by his relatives. Shareholders were outraged, leading to a closer auditing of the company's finances and discovery of the elaborate scam. The results of such moral hazard have been catastrophic for both India and Satyam. India took a large hit because many large multinationals rely on Indian companies for computer services.[10] The reputation of these companies and India had been severely damaged.[11] However, Satyam also suffered because shareholders lost large sums of their investments, while Satyam is still struggling to overcome the scandal.

The effects of moral hazard can therefore be very catastrophic for both the company and its shareholders. As we saw in the Preview Business Ethics Insight, Nortel also suffered considerably because of moral hazard. However, owners can also face an additional problem from CEOs; namely, adverse selection. According to Tosi,[12] adverse selection is the misrepresentation by the CEO of his/her ability to do the work that he/she is being paid for. Consider the case of a firm hiring a new CEO. Generally, candidates for the CEO position may have more information about their true competencies than the company. They may therefore misrepresent that information to be able to get the job. However, as research shows, many companies eventually find out that the new CEO misrepresented himself/herself. This explains the very high rate of dismissal of new CEOs as their companies become aware of their misrepresentation.[13]

As the above discussion reveals, because of the nature of the modern corporations whereby ownership is separated from management, owners face significant problems. Such problems stem from information asymmetry whereby the CEO has private information that is not accessible to the owners. Furthermore, CEOs and top managers can engage in self-interested behaviors that hurt shareholders. However, because owners are not always aware of managers' actions and the outcomes of such actions, it is critical to have systems in place to align the interests of both owners and managers.

We do note that the above agency problems discussed above tend to be of relevance in a more Anglo or American environment. However, even in other parts of the world dominated by other ownership forms such as large shareholders or family firms, corporate governance is critical. We therefore look at corporate governance next and how its many aspects can solve the agency problem. We also discuss the specific issues related to family firms later.

CORPORATE GOVERNANCE

Corporate governance refers to the many mechanisms that can be used to align managements' interests with owners' interests. Specifically, corporate governance refers to the system that controls and directs companies' and top managements' actions. Consider the Strategic Business Ethics Insight below. It clearly shows the strategic importance of corporate governance, and companies need to ensure that appropriate governance systems are implemented. In the next few sections, we examine some of the key aspects of corporate governance.

The Strategic Business Ethics Insight below clearly shows the strategic importance of corporate governance, and companies need to ensure that appropriate governance

STRATEGIC BUSINESS ETHICS INSIGHT

Strategic Importance of Corporate Governance

Most companies and nations are now expected to have strong corporate governance in place to protect investors and others from corporate and top management misbehavior. This is especially critical given that these societies often have environments that may not always be protective of shareholders. Consider the many examples discussed earlier in this chapter. The U.S. banking industry has been very severely impacted by lack of good corporate governance and this has spilled into almost all industries, such as automotive and construction. Companies such as Satyam Computers in India and Nortel in Canada have both suffered financial consequences. Investors and societies have also suffered catastrophic consequences because of the lack of corporate governance. Corporate governance is thus a crucial factor in ensuring strategic success at the company level and survival of industries at the country level. However, beyond merely having a strong environment for investors, strong corporate governance can have other benefits.

Consider the strategic importance of corporate governance as provided by a large study of Chinese firms undertaken by Lu, Xu, and Liu.[14] In that study, the authors find that stronger corporate governance such as having more outsiders on the board of directors or appropriate executive compensation are both related to higher exports. This suggests that outside boards of directors have potentially better views of the importance of internationalization. Furthermore, when the interests of both executives and shareholders are aligned through an appropriate compensation scheme, CEOs are more likely to see the importance of exporting to grow the firm. This study also shows the importance of strong corporate governance in a firm's future strategic health by going international.

Another study also provides evidence of the importance of corporate governance in other emerging markets. In that study of 24 emerging market economies, the authors look at the impact of ownership structures and investment in research and development (R&D). They find that the more ownership is concentrated in a few hands, the less likely the firm is to invest in R&D. Given the importance of R&D to innovation, increased ownership suggests that owners are less likely to take risks. Conversely, if ownership of firms is dispersed among many smaller shareholders, investment in R&D is stronger. This effect is even stronger in emerging countries with stronger shareholder rights protection. This again underscores the importance of appropriate governance mechanisms.

Based on Lu, J., Xu, B. and Liu, X. 2009. "The effects of corporate governance and institutional environments on export behaviour in emerging economies." *Management International Review*, 49, 455–478; Rapp, M.S. and Udoieva, I.A. 2017. "Corporate governance and its impact on R&D investment in emerging markets." *Emerging Markets Finance & Trade*, 53, 2159–2178.

systems are implemented. Strong corporate governance not only provides an environment where investors can have trust in the capital market to invest with confidence. Furthermore, in addition to protecting investors, strong corporate governance has positive effects on R&D investment impact, internationalization efforts and even firm performance.[15]

Given the critical importance of corporate governance, in the next few sections we therefore discuss some of its key aspects.

Board of Directors

One of the key goals of corporate governance is how to solve the agency problem. Such problems arise because of the conflicts of interests between the principal (shareholders) and agents (top management). This separation of ownership and control often results in managers having increased power.

The **board of directors** is often seen as one of the primary mechanisms to monitor and control the conflict. A board of directors is expected to act in ways that put shareholder interests ahead of their own interests.[16] Thus, a board has a duty of loyalty to shareholders. In fact, many of the corporate governance problems mentioned in this chapter, such as Satyam Computers and Nortel, were the result of a board of directors not properly fulfilling its functions. A board of directors thus fulfills many functions and these functions include:[17]

- Review and provide guidance on all aspects of strategic management such as reviewing the corporate strategy, monitoring and implementing corporate performance, and providing guidance on major strategic decisions such as major capital expenditures, acquisitions of new companies, and divestitures.
- Provide guidance on tactical and operational planning such as annual budgets and business plans, setting goals in terms of performance objectives, and reviewing implementation.
- Act as advisors to top management and CEO and provide guidance with respect to the above strategic, tactical, and operation issues.
- Continuously monitor the company's other governance practices and make changes as needed.
- Provide human resource management expertise such as selection, recruitment, and performance appraisal of the CEO, top management, and other executives.
- Perform the important task of determining the executive's compensation and benefits package to align the package with the company's long-term interests.
- Assist in special investigations that question top management's integrity such as the recent investigation of the former CEO of Hewlett-Packard and sexual harassment or other major ethical violations on the part of the CEO or top managers.
- Have the appropriate financial and accounting expertise to ensure the accurateness and integrity of the company's financial and accounting reporting.
- Take steps to ensure that there is a transparent and formal mechanism to elect new board members.

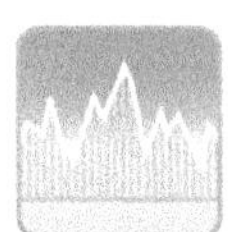

EMERGING MARKET BUSINESS ETHICS INSIGHT

Board Composition and Firm Performance in Malaysia and Nigeria

It is widely believed that having an independent board with an outside board of directors is beneficial for a company. Outside directors have fewer conflicts of interest with current management and are more likely to bring new expertise to the board. In an interesting study of 277 Malaysian firms, Ameer, Ramli and Zakaria examined the impact of the board of directors on firm performance.[18] The authors considered several types of directors. Specifically, they considered inside directors (those individuals who hold more than 5% of shares and who tend to be typically related to the founding family), non-independent directors (those individuals who are former employees of the company or any of its associated companies), outside directors (individuals who have no ties to the company but represent one of the major institutional shareholders), and foreign directors (directors who are foreign nationals).

Results reveal that companies with a high representation of outside directors or foreign directors tend to have better performance than those companies that have a majority of inside or non-independent directors. This result is even stronger when the majority of shareholders is made up of a combination of both independent and foreign directors. These results are therefore consistent with the view that outside directors represent a strong mechanism that can adequately solve the agency problems. In the case of Malaysia, foreign directors and those independent directors representing institutional investors are more likely to bring the outside expertise and due diligence required to ensure that management is on track.

Consider another study that was conducted in Nigeria. Because of poor corporate governance, the country saw the collapse of many banks in the early 2000s. As a result, the Nigerian government implemented many new corporate governance policies to increase confidence in its markets. Have these policies worked? A recent study provides evidence of the effectiveness of such policies. The study finds that aspects of corporate governance such as board independence, audit committee independence and financial expertise all had positive effects on desirable outcomes such as share prices, volume of trade, and earnings per share. The study showed that corporate governance was very beneficial in restoring confidence of investors in the market and protecting their interests.

Based on Ameer, R., Ramli, F. and Zakaria, H. 2010. "A new perspective on board composition and firm performance in an emerging market." *Corporate Governance*, 10, 5, 647–661; Ojeka, S.A., Iyoha, F.O., Ikpefan, O.A. and Osakwe, C. 2017. "Does the reformed code of corporate governance 2011 enhance the market performance of the firms in Nigeria?" *International Journal of Economic Perspectives*, 11, 1, 155–164.

- Take every step to make sure that decisions that affect shareholder welfare are made on the basis of due diligence of gathering and considering the required material information.
- Recent investigations also reveal that more boards of directors are playing a bigger role in risk management. Such roles involve understanding the many areas of risk for the company and the ways such risks can be minimized.
- Conduct regular self-evaluations to ensure that the board is meeting its obligations.

A board of director is, thus, a critical corporate governance mechanism to ensure that interests of shareholders are met. If the above functions are conducted properly, most companies and their shareholders should be protected from managerial mischief. However, the composition of the board is also a key aspect of the effectiveness of a board of directors. We next consider the many issues relevant to the effectiveness of a board of directors.

A first critical issue in board composition is **board independence**. Specifically, many countries now prescribe that a number of the members of a board of directors should be independent.[19] In the U.S., the Sarbanes-Oxley Act also mandates that a board should include a significant proportion of independent board members.[20] The expectations are that outside boards of directors are more likely to monitor management and represent shareholder interests. Because of their external nature, board members are less likely to be connected to the current firm's top management. This independence should therefore give such a board of directors a stronger ability to carefully monitor top management's actions without fear of hurting their relationships with the top management. Does the empirical evidence show that board independence is conducive to better protection of shareholder wealth? Consider the following Emerging Market Business Ethics Insight on page 311.

The Emerging Markets Business Ethics Insight clearly shows the benefits of board independence. However, a second critical aspect of a board of directors is the presence of **board diversity**. Most worldwide reforms in corporate governance now require that the different stakeholders are represented on a board of directors.[21] An important aspect of such calls for diversity has been to increase the number of women on such boards. In fact, a recent study of 4200 global companies found that only 9.4% of directors on these boards are women.[22] Furthermore, a recent study of the *Fortune* Global 200 companies shows that over 77.5% of these companies had at least one woman on their board of directors.[23] However, data from 2006 to 2009 shows that the percentage of women on a board of directors increased by only 1% to 12.2%. Thus, while there has been progress, men still hold 87.8% of board seats in the world's largest corporations.

A more recent study by the Credit Suisse Research Institute provides evidence of the presence of women on boards of directors worldwide.[24] Using data from 3400 companies worldwide, Exhibit 7.2 shows the percentage of women on boards in selected countries.

As Exhibit 7.2 shows, the trends worldwide do suggest that more women are increasingly being placed on boards of directors. Data from 2010 to 2015 shows growth for more countries. Furthermore, the global average growth is very steep,

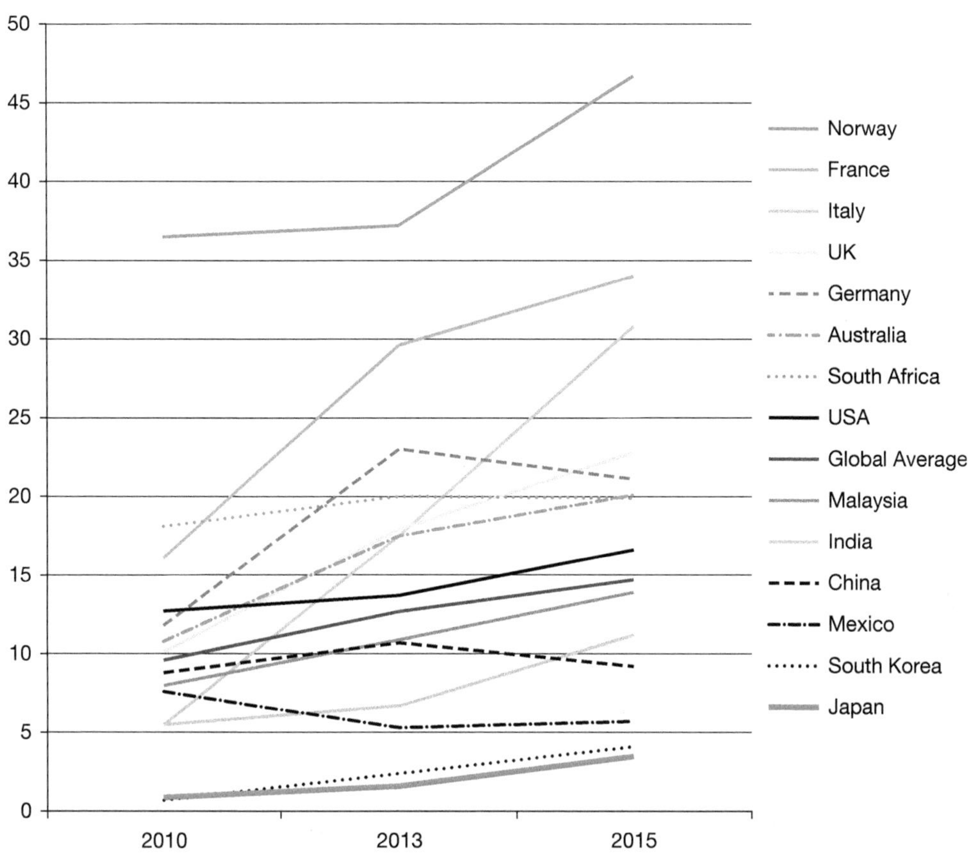

EXHIBIT 7.2—Highest Percentage of Women on Boards of Directors around the World

changing from 9.6% in 2010 to 14.7% in 2015. This change was much more pronounced for European countries where many countries have set specific quotas. However, Asian countries have seen the most progress.

Experts suggest that having women on a board of directors can be very beneficial for companies. It is generally believed that women tend to bring richer ideas to discussions and thus encourage better and more innovative management.[25] Women directors bring divergent experiences to boards and such experiences may help better understand different consumers. Furthermore, it is expected that women are more likely to carefully scrutinize management actions to ensure that the right actions are occurring. It is also generally accepted that the addition of women to a board of directors should positively affect firm performance. For instance, recent research done in Singapore suggests that companies that added women to their board of directors experienced higher performance.[26] The same study also found that investors reacted very positively when companies in Singapore announced the addition of women to their boards. Investors also believe that the addition of women will positively affect the long-term prospects of the company. But does this relationship hold worldwide? Consider the following Global Business Ethics Insight.

GLOBAL BUSINESS ETHICS INSIGHT

Board Diversity and Firm Performance Around the World

It is widely believed that having a diverse board with an outside board of directors is beneficial for a company. Studies conducted worldwide seem to confirm this belief. For instance, in a broad study using data from 8,876 public firms located in 47 countries, the researchers examined the impact of the presence of female directors on firm performance. They find overwhelming evidence that having female directors on the board contributes to higher firm performance. Additionally, the study also showed that such firms also enjoyed higher returns on assets. Furthermore, the authors also find that having external independent directors is not effective unless such boards have diversity. This also provides evidence of the importance of board diversity in enhancing other aspects of boards of directors.

In another study conducted in Turkey, researchers also showed the value of board diversity. In that study, the researchers examine the demographic diversity of the board in terms of age, gender, education, and nationality. Creating an index of demographic diversity by combining all of the above aspects, this study also finds that demographic diversity has an impact on firm performance.

Finally, the Credit Suisse study mentioned earlier also provides evidence of similar effects of the presence of women on boards of directors and corporate performance. Companies that had more than 15% of women on their boards had 50% higher profitability than those companies that had less than 10% of women.

Based on Ararat, M., Aksu, M. and Cetin, A.T. 2015. "How board diversity affects firm performance in emerging markets: Evidence on channels in controlled firms." *Corporate Governance: An International Review*, 23, 2, 83–103; Credit Suisse Research Institute. 2018. The CS Gender 3000: The Reward for Change. https://glg.it/assets/docs/csri-gender-3000.pdf; Tejersen, S., Couto, E.B. and Francisco, P.M. 2016. "Does the presence of independent and female directors impact board performance? A multi-country study of board diversity?" *Journal of Governance*, 20, 447–483.

A third critical aspect of the board of directors is **board size**. Board size is simply the number of members on the board of directors. Pozen mentions that the average board size for the Standard and Poor 500 companies is 11 members.[27] A large board size has many advantages. For example, as O'Connell and Cramer argue, a large board size provides wider expertise to a board of directors.[28] Furthermore, having a large board means having access to a wider network. Such access can also provide a board and its company with greater external linkages.

Despite these advantages, Pozen notes that many of the financial institutions that recently failed had very large boards.[29] For instance, Citigroup had 18 members. Having large boards does present some disadvantages.[30] First, large boards are more likely to have members engage in social loafing. In other words, some members may choose not to fully participate in board activities because they can "hide" behind the large number of members. Second, a large board may also result in higher levels of conflict. Such conflict may also make it more difficult for team members to develop the necessary cohesion they need to function effectively. Finally, large boards also make it much more difficult for team members to communicate and reach decisions. Larger sizes may make reaching consensus somewhat problematic.

Does board size thus negatively affect firm performance? In an interesting study, O'Connell and Cramer studied most of the Irish companies quoted on the Irish Stock Exchange.[31] They did indeed find that the larger the board size, the worse a company's performance. However, this negative impact is much smaller for smaller companies. This lends support to the notion that large board sizes do impact performance negatively because of the many disadvantages. For smaller firms, larger board sizes may be necessary for them to take advantage of the network afforded by larger boards.

Given the above-mentioned problems associated with larger boards, Pozen argues that research on group dynamics suggests that the best group size is around six or seven.[32] A group this size can work together such that individual members are accountable for their contributions to larger decisions and can therefore take personal responsibility for group decisions. Furthermore, this size makes it easier for teams to reach consensus in a reasonable amount of time. Thus, critical decisions can still be made.

A final and generally ignored aspect of a board is **board expertise**. For a board of directors to operate effectively, the board needs the necessary expertise to understand the industry the company is operating in to have the ability to make decisions of strategic importance. Experts argue that many boards actually lack members with the sufficient expertise to adequately understand the business.[33] This lack of expertise may be problematic.

Given the above issues, what issues should a company take to form the best board? The following lists some of the key considerations based on prior research:[34]

- Have a board with six to seven members. As argued earlier, larger boards have too many disadvantages that exceed the advantages brought by a larger group. A smaller size board has more chances at succeeding.
- Get the right mix by bringing in people with new expertise. It is important to have a strong balance of personalities and skills in the group. Furthermore, it is critical to have the right balance with independent directors to get outsiders' perspectives to objectively understand firm decisions. In fact, the earlier research about policy reforms in Nigeria also provided evidence of the utility of board expertise[35]. Such research showed that the board having the necessary audit financial expertise was related to a stronger environment for investors.
- Have board members with sufficient expertise so that they can adequately understand the industry and ask the right questions. Board members with expertise can provide insights into new areas or niches that are not apparent to current management.

- Have board members representing the stakeholders the company will serve. Have an adequate number of women on the board.
- Have board members with accounting and financial expertise. Decisions often involve understanding financial implications of what will be done. Someone with the expertise to understand cash-flow statements and other financial reports is critical.
- Explore new channels when recruiting new board members. A company should make use of its professional network to make sure that the right candidate is hired.
- Encourage board members to commit their time to making meetings work. The necessary time needs to be invested so that the board members can understand the business and how both internal and external factors are affecting the company. Such deep understanding of a company can only come with significant study.

The above list describes some of the characteristics of the board that enhance success. However, a company also has several responsibilities to ensure that the board works well. First, the company should provide the board with the right types of information in a timely manner. The board should be fully informed of the company's health and where the company is going in terms of its strategy. Second, the board responsibilities and roles should be clearly defined. Be sure that board members know their roles and how to communicate with each other. Finally, a company should play an active role in the process. Boards are not created to rubber-stamp decisions. Rather, they should be made up of bold people with an understanding of the industry and visionary ideas of where the company should be going.

Executive Compensation

Executive compensation, which refers to the pay, perks, and benefits given to top executives in a company, is a second important aspect of corporate governance. As argued earlier, investors give top executives of a company control over their assets in the form of investments. Top managers can take advantage of investors because of information asymmetry.[36] Specifically, top executives have access to information about the company's situation and direction that investors do not generally have access to. Executives can thus use this information asymmetry to manipulate stock prices to give investors a rosier picture of the company. Executive compensation is thus a mechanism whereby the interests of shareholders can be aligned with the interests of top executives.

Executive compensation remains one of the most controversial aspects of corporate governance. To give you an idea of average compensation around the world, Exhibit 7.3 shows the median compensation of top executives in companies by country.

To come up with the data for Exhibit 7.3, researchers examined data from the *Financial Times* Global Largest 200 companies.[37] As Exhibit 7.3 shows, Swiss companies pay the highest salaries. In contrast, Chinese companies pay the least compared to the

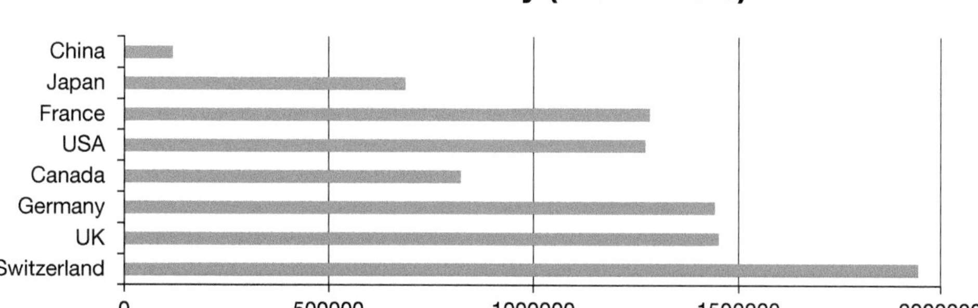

EXHIBIT 7.3—Median Compensation by Countries

other countries. Surprisingly, while there are often complaints that U.S. companies pay their CEOs too much, the U.S. companies on that list sit somewhere in the middle of all the countries. But the compensation data for many countries can be tricky. The U.S. pay plans for CEOs often include bonuses and other payments meant to reward short-term performance. This can add significantly to CEOs earnings. Later, you will see which companies pay the most bonuses.

Critics routinely argue that executives earn too much money. Consider, for instance, the Great Recession (2008–2012) led by the U.S. banking crises. Critics claimed that banking executives continued to receive very high bonuses despite accepting government bailouts. In fact, despite Exhibit 7.3, most experts agree that U.S. CEOs make much more than their foreign counterparts. Additionally, a recent study mentioned that the average U.S. CEO earned 475 times the average employee pay.[38] However, this ratio is much smaller in other nations.[39] For instance, CEOs in Japan earn 11 times the average employee. For European countries such as France, Germany, Belgium, and Italy, the ratio is less than 40 to 1. Finally, a CEO in the United Kingdom earns around 22 times the average employee.

There is clearly a big difference between CEO pay and the average worker in most societies. This is one of the most important criticisms leveled against companies regarding executive compensation. Are CEOs really worth 475 average U.S. employees? Furthermore, given the many recent scandals and the banking crises, many believe that the high levels of compensation led to such excesses. Specifically, such high pay has encouraged CEOs to take excessive risks to keep companies growing.[40]

At a strategic level, high CEO pay is also very damaging to a company's shareholders. As Strier argues, the high salaries paid to executives represent losses in the form of lost dividends and earnings for shareholders.[41] Furthermore, the high disparity between CEO and average employees may result in a decrease in employee morale and thereby employee productivity. While most employees are currently experiencing pay decreases and even layoffs, employees become very resentful when CEOs continue to be awarded large salaries and benefits. But how is CEO compensation determined? The following Business Ethics Brief provides some insights.

BUSINESS ETHICS BRIEF

CEO Compensation and Political Ideology of Boards

According to recent research, CEO compensation determination remains a mystery. Researchers have looked at traditional economic drivers of pay such as the size of the company, economic conditions and the type of industry companies are in. However, even after accounting for these factors, there still remain differences in CEO compensation. A recent study therefore took a more innovative approach and examined the political ideology of the board and how much CEOs are paid.

Comparing liberal boards (i.e., more sensitive to social justice issues, concern for the environment etc.) with more conservative boards (i.e., preference for free markets and private property), the researchers show that conservative boards tend to pay CEOs more than liberal boards. This is consistent with the belief that liberals tend to be more concerned about pay equality. However, the study of 4000 CEOs from 1998 to 2013 also shows that the relationship between CEO compensation and performance is actually stronger for more conservative boards. This is also consistent with expectations that more conservative boards are more concerned about market forces.

Based on Gupta, A. and Wowak, A.J. 2017. "The elephant (or donkey) in the boardroom: How board political ideology affects CEO pay." *Administrative Science Quarterly*, 62, 1–30.

However, despite these critics, some argue that high executive compensation is justified. For instance, Farid et al. mention that stock values have grown astronomically over the past 25 years, thereby justifying the increase in pay level to those who made such growth possible.[42] Furthermore, many argue that CEOs and top executives have rare skills and that they devote their entire lives to the company. These factors are also seen as justification for high pay. Additionally, a recent study of U.S. CEOs based on various aspects of CEO pay shows that most of the directors surveyed find the current level of CEO pay acceptable. Consider Exhibit 7.4 below.

As Exhibit 7.4 shows, the directors and other CEOs surveyed do not see any problems with the current CEO compensation level and also believe that CEO compensation is strongly linked to company performance. Furthermore, when asked about whether the government should intervene to reform CEO pay practices, a resounding 97% did not agree with the statement.

Nevertheless, to fully understand the criticisms against executive compensation, it is also important to note the other forms of CEO compensation. While most CEOs and executives earn a base salary, they also earn significant bonuses and other benefits, such as club memberships, use of corporate jets, and tax preparation. Exhibit 7.5 below shows the top 10 bonus payments top executives received in 2014/2015.

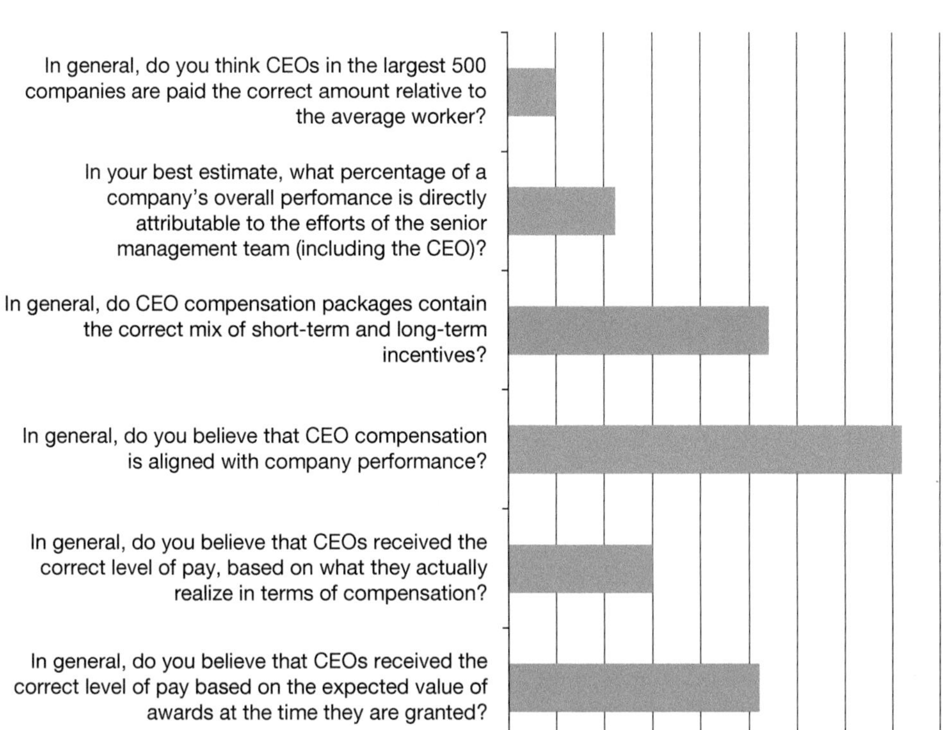

EXHIBIT 7.4—Directors' Agreement with Statement Pertaining to CEO Compensation

As Exhibit 7.5 shows, the U.S. companies dominate the list of top 10 bonus payments. This provides support for the contention that U.S. companies rely more on variable pay plans.[43] Furthermore, as the exhibit shows, CEOs earn significantly more above and beyond their base salary. Experts believe that such bonuses are some of the main factors behind CEOs' extremely risky actions. One of the dominant forms of compensation on top of base salary is stock options. **Stock options** are stocks awarded to the CEO, who then has the ability to sell the stock at a future date. However, many companies have allowed their CEOs to backdate these stock options to enable the CEO to make more money when they sell their stocks. In other words, when the companies grant stock options to their CEOs, they allow the CEO to backdate the price of the stock to a much lower price. In fact, Collins, Gong and Li report that the board of United Health allowed its former CEO to choose the day of the option grant and several stock options were dated back to the year's lowest price.[44] The CEO then sold the stocks at a much higher price and earned a significant profit.

It is widely believed that stock options provide corrupting incentives to encourage CEOs to manipulate accounting figures ("cook the books") in order to boost the

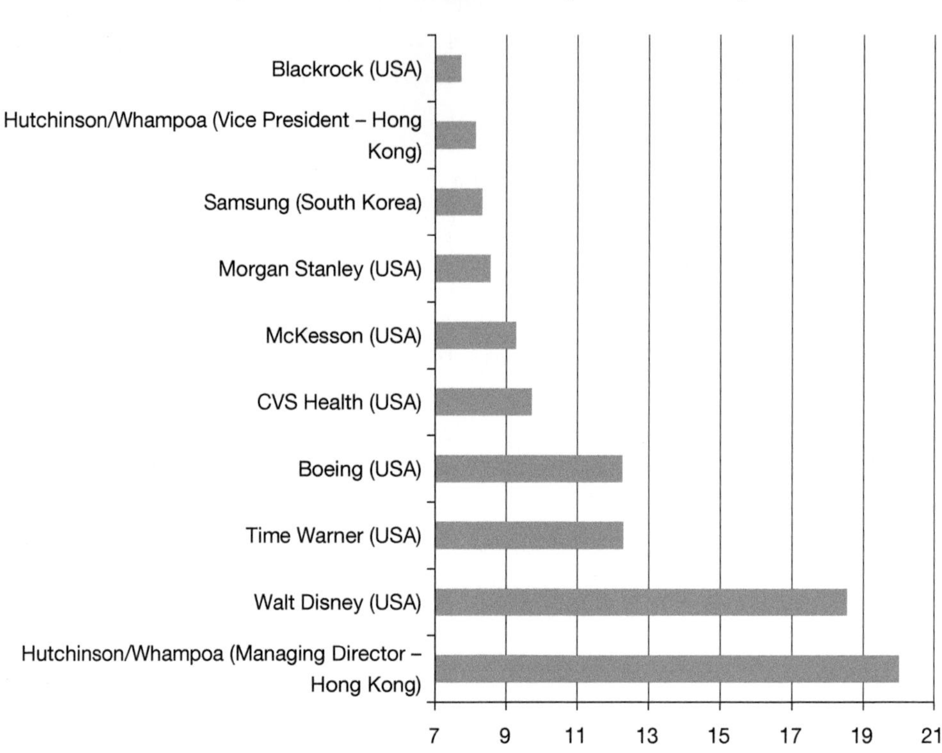

EXHIBIT 7.5—Top 10 Bonus Payments by Company

short-term price of stocks.[45] CEOs are thus encouraged to manipulate earnings, backdate options, and engage in unprofitable mergers. Such short-term actions are made at the expense of long-term profitability and growth. Although these actions may increase share price in the short term, they ultimately undermine shareholder wealth.

Executive compensation will continue receiving negative attention as critics continue decrying such excesses. For any multinational, it therefore becomes important to design a compensation package appropriate enough to retain the best CEOs but reasonable enough not to invite criticisms. However, such packages will likely remain very large relative to the average employee. Nevertheless, multinational companies will need to address a number of issues as they devise such packages. In fact, most countries are considering policies on executive compensation and these include:[46]

- Aligning COE incentives with long-term health and profitability of companies. Although this remains a difficult task, many companies are abandoning compensation practices that promote short-term gains. As an example, more companies are abandoning the use of stock options in favor of deferred stock units. Deferred stock units are said to align investor and CEO interests more because executives lose as much as investors if shares lose value. This loss is less apparent for stock options.

- Most compensation decisions are made by the board of directors. Boards of directors are therefore increasingly being asked to be fair, accountable, objective, and transparent about the determination of CEO and executive compensation. Experts agree that directors should be selected based on their loyalty to shareholders rather than the CEO.
- Become more aware of recent regulations. For instance, the U.S. saw the passing of the Dodd-Frank Act, which places many new boundaries on executive compensation. For instance, CEOs are increasingly being asked to hold on to their stocks until they retire. Many companies are adopting stock ownership guidelines for CEOs and executives to prevent focus on short-term gains. Furthermore, the Dodd-Frank Act contains "clawback" policies whereby executives are required to reimburse any compensation that was awarded as a result of erroneous financial results. The Australian government has also decided to toughen rules on executive pay. It proposed a number of new reforms that are expected to keep executives' salary in check. For instance, shareholders will now have more power to be able to vote on executive compensation. Furthermore, measures will be implemented to force executives to return bonuses if financial statements done when the bonuses were given were misleading. Finally, companies that do not do not respond to shareholder concerns regarding salaries are expected to be penalized.[47]
- Review perquisite policies of compensation packages. Because of shareholder and employee revolt, more companies are being asked to review their policies regarding generous perquisites provided to CEOs. Companies are finding it increasingly difficult to fund benefits such as expensive country club memberships and use of corporate jets when employees are being laid off. Even the European Union is taking a tough stance on executive pay, especially those of bankers.[48] The Committee of European Banking Supervisors helped draft new legislation. For instance, banks are now required to limit executive bonuses to only a maximum of 20% as upfront cash. Other rules are being implemented to make executives' pay more reasonable.
- Adjusting pay plans in response to changing conditions. Many compensation plans were relatively inflexible in that executives would get the agreed-upon pay despite poor performance.
- Give shareholders the means to vote on CEO and executive compensation. Shareholders should have some say in terms of generous compensation packages and the notoriously generous golden parachutes. This will then give shareholders an opportunity to express their approval (or disapproval) of a compensation plan.

Ownership Structure

While most of the corporate governance studies have focused on boards of directors and executive compensation as main corporate governance mechanisms, **ownership structure** is also an important mechanism to control managers. Ownership structure refers to the primary way that ownership of shares of the company is structured. One way the interests of shareholders and managers can be aligned is where shareholders become large owners of the company. According to Connelly et al., such shareholders will often become owners to achieve key financial objectives.[49] There are many different types of ownership structures and we therefore examine some of these critical forms of ownership and the likely impact on the company.

The first form of ownership structure is **blockholders**. As we discussed at the beginning of the chapter, blockholders are those shareholders that have more than 5% equity stake in a company. A review of corporate governance worldwide shows that there are three main types of blockholders: corporate blockholders, family blockholders, and state blockholders. All three forms of ownership are guided by the owner's desire to better monitor management. However, some blockholders can also get access to private benefits that may not always be available to minority shareholders.

According to Connelly et al., corporations often acquire significant ownership in a company and become **corporate blockholders** as a prior step to actual taking over a target company. Consider, for instance, the case of the French luxury company Louis Vuitton Hennessy Moët (LVHM), which recently acquired a 17% stake in Hermès, the famous French scarf maker. LVHM hopes to eventually acquire the company. However, a corporation may also buy a minority stake in another company before selling the shares. Both forms of ownership provide the target firm with fresh capital. Nevertheless, the target company may also be subjected to more control from the firm buying the shares. Thus, there is potential for resources to be diverted to benefit the company acquiring the shares. Consider the following Business Ethics Brief.

As the Brief shows, the fact that L'Oreal has a corporate blockholder in Nestlé means that its future is dependent on Nestlé. However, a second and very popular form of blockholder worldwide is the **family blockholder**, where a single family is a major owner of a company. While most share ownership in the Anglo countries such as the UK and the U.S. is more of the dispersed nature, whereby a large number of shareholders own small percentages of equity in a company, many European nations see a more dominant form of family ownership. A recent study reports that, while only 11% of firms in the U.S. are owned by families, ownership percentage is more than 35% in Europe, with a family ownership percentage of 43% in Germany and 68% in Italy.[50]

Family ownership modifies the corporate governance issues discussed earlier. While dispersed ownership in the U.S. and the UK means that the needs of shareholders and managers have to be aligned, family ownership poses a host of other problems.[51] Often, the family owners control managers through voting rights. Some family firms can also be managed by the family founders, thereby aligning interests of owners and managers. Furthermore, the family owners can use insider information to buy equity in other promising firms or redirect profits to their own affiliates.

The major challenge with regards to family ownership is the protection of minority shareholders. As Johnson et al. mention, minority shareholders often have no voting rights on how the company is managed and what strategic direction the company takes. Furthermore, majority shareholders have the ability to expropriate earnings through the form of profit reallocation, assets misuse, and selling parts of the firm to other firms at below market prices. Thus, the challenge for corporate governance with regards to family ownership is to ensure that the needs of the minority shareholders

BUSINESS ETHICS BRIEF

Death of Liliane Bettencourt and L'Oreal's Fate

In September of 2017, Liliane Bettencourt, the famous French heiress of the French cosmetics company L'Oreal, passed away. She held a controlling stake in the company. However, she was suffering from Alzheimer's disease before her death and many individuals took advantage of her. It is believed that politicians, lawyers, and friends stole millions of euros from her. This prompted her daughter to take control of the family assets including the stake in L'Oreal.

L'Oreal is currently facing some uncertainty. Although Ms. Bettencourt's daughter controls a third of the company, Nestlé holds a 23.2% stake in the company. Nestlé is therefore a major corporate blockholder of the company. Nestlé's shareholders want the company to sell its stake in L'Oreal as they don't believe the latter fits within the overall strategy of Nestlé. This pressure has increased because the maker of well-known brands such as Kit Kat and Nescafé has been fast losing market share to new rivals. However, the current CEO of Nestlé is not so sure that he wants to sell given the healthy returns L'Oreal has provided. In fact, given that Nestlé's major competitor recently acquired Carver Korea, a leading South Korean cosmetics company, Nestlé is more inclined to acquire L'Oreal.

Based on *The Economist*. 2017. "Nestlé and L'Oreal; Because it's worth it." September 30, 6061.

are not being subordinated to satisfy only majority shareholders. In fact, as discussed in the case of German corporate governance, large family blockholders can often favor long-term growth and firm survival coming at the expense of short-term cash flows to smaller dispersed shareholders.[52] As such, the influence and grip of a family on family-owned companies is very difficult to control and minority shareholders will often endure such control.[53]

Having families own companies can therefore be problematic. Consider the Emerging Market Business Ethics Insight below.

As the Emerging Market Business Ethics Insight shows, having family ownership can be problematic to minority owners. In this case, Mr. Ratan Tata, a member of the family, wielded disproportionate influence on Mr. Mistry. It is likely that the Tata family did not agree with some of the tough decisions that Mr. Mistry felt were necessary. This firing may therefore hurt the long-term prospects of the company. Mr. Mistry has also damaged Tata's reputation by revealing many questionable practices.

A third and final form of blockholder ownership is **state ownership**. State ownership is more popular in emerging nations, whereby the government owns a significant percentage of a company. Consider that China, for instance, has transitioned from socialism to capitalism by keeping ownership interests in many companies. This has allowed the government to keep control over key business areas in the country. However, developed nations like the U.S. and the UK have seen an increased growth in state ownership. Consider the U.S. government's decision to purchase shares of General Motors as a result of the financial crisis, thereby infusing some state ownership

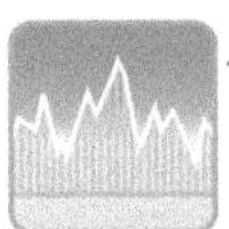

EMERGING MARKET BUSINESS ETHICS INSIGHT

Mr. Mistry and Tata

Founded in 1868, the Tata Group remains one of India's main multinational conglomerates. It has stakes in over 100 different businesses ranging from IT consulting, cars, hotels, and the manufacturing of steel. Tata Group is owned by the Tata family and has had five of the previous chairmen come from the Tata family. The fifth chairman, Mr. Mistry, was the first chairman who was not connected to the Tata family. Mr. Mistry was abruptly fired after only four years at the helm of the Tata Group.

Mr. Ratan Tata, the chairman after Mr. Mistry was fired, argued that Mr. Mistry was fired because he was not turning around companies quickly enough to make profits. Except for Tata Consultancy and Jaguar/Land Rover, most of the other 100 companies that Tata had stakes in were not making good returns. Mr. Mistry was seen as doing too little to boost profits.

Mr. Mistry claimed that he was not being given free reins to run the company. He considered himself a "lame duck" chairman whose decisions were always being second guessed by Mr. Ratan Tata. He also argued that the Tata Group invested in many new businesses that were not making money. While he wanted to sell some of these assets to turn the company around, the controlling family members did not want such sales to occur. Mr. Mistry claimed that projects such as the Tata Nano had to be closed down but that family members were interfering for emotional reasons.

The Tata Group is suffering from this incident. While it had taken a long time to cultivate a culture of consensus, the abrupt firing was a shock to many. Additionally, Mr. Mistry, whose family also owns a minority stake in Tata Group, is not going without a fight. He wrote a scathing letter to the company's board of directors mentioning the many questionable decisions. Furthermore, he has already hired a team of lawyers to sue Tata Group for his firing. He is also questioning the hiring of Mr. Natarajan Chandrasekaran, the person who replaced him as chairman of the Tata Group.

Based on Atkison, S. 2016. "Tata sacking: Cyrus Mistry was lame duck chairman." *BBC News*, October 26, www.bbc.com/news/business-37775458; *The Economist*. 2016. Tata Group; Misty exit, October 29, 57; *The Economist*. 2017. "Tata sons; Chandra's challenge." January 21, 57; Kripalini, M. 2009. "India Inc.'s murky accounting." *Bloomberg Business Week* online, January 15; Osawa, J. 2010. "Shake-up at Seiko reflects changing culture." *Wall Street Journal*, June 23, B1.

in GM. According to Johnson et al., the motivation for governments to become part owner of companies is driven by a desire to correct market failures.[54] Such failures may occur in industries that are deemed too big to fail (e.g., banking or automobile in the U.S.) or in industries that are characterized as monopolies.

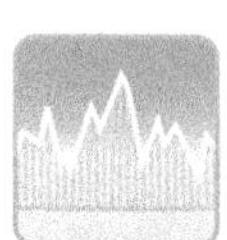

EMERGING MARKET BUSINESS ETHICS INSIGHT

State-owned Firms in India and China

India has over 244 state-owned enterprises that are involved in industries ranging from earth movers to hotels to textiles and fertilizer. These companies originate from India's socialist years (1997 until early 1990s) and were created to be involved in many of India's critical industries. One out of three of these companies do not make any profits. Such losses are due to many factors.

First, many of these companies are run by individuals who rose through the government bureaucracy. As a result, these individuals may not always have the expertise to run such companies. In fact, many of these companies have executives who are very conservative and cautious in approach. This means that significant opportunities that may require some risk-taking are ignored. Second, the government also guaranteed grants in some critical sectors such as oil and coal and these companies never had to become efficient to be able to tackle free markets. Third, many of these companies are mired in structures that make them less nimble than private companies. For instance, while companies such as Jet Airways have been able to experience dramatic profit, Air India has experienced losses despite a crash in fuel prices. Finally, some of these companies have also been involved in questionable decisions. Consider, for instance, the banking sector that accounts for 70% of India's banking system by assets. Many of these banks have made loans that are unlikely to be repaid. This is an issue that private lenders have managed to avoid.

China also has a large number of state-owned enterprises and many of them also experience less than profitable operations. The government has tasked a smaller number of bureaucrats to monitor these state-owned enterprises. Unfortunately, because of the small number of officials, the close monitoring of the assets of these enterprises and their managers is impossible. As a result, monitoring of top management tends to be weak and these government officials generally do not place emphasis on profit maximization. Consequently, these state-owned enterprises are less likely to be run efficiently and there is higher likelihood of managers using the enterprise for their own benefit.

Based on *The Economist*. 2017. "Indian state-owned companies; The everything makers." June 3, 57–58; Su, Z., Li, S.Y. and Li, L. 2010. "Ownership concentration and executive compensation in emerging economies: Evidence from China." *Corporate Governance*, 10, 3, 223–233.

Existing research suggests that state ownership generally results in problems for a company's well-being. Connelly et al. discuss current studies that show that state ownership typically faces soft budget constraints.[55] Furthermore, state-owned companies suffer from a lack of innovation and suffer from poor financial performance and corruption. Consider the Emerging Market Business Ethics Insight on page 325.

In addition to blockholders, another form of firm ownership that can be used for corporate governance purposes is **private equity**.[56] Private equity refers to the various forms of private funding that are available to companies that are not necessarily publicly traded. The forms of private equity vary greatly depending on the stages the company is at. Although there seems to be a number of types of private equity, Bruton, Filatotchev, Chahine and Wright distinguish between two main types of private equity; namely, the business angel and the venture capital.[57]

When a venture is too small or risky, there are often "business angels" who provide private equity funds. Business angels tend to know the entrepreneur personally and thus invest their own money in the company. They are more likely to invest on the basis of trust with the entrepreneur.[58] Furthermore, business angels are more patient investors who do not necessarily have a timeline determining when they take their investments out of the company.

In contrast, venture capitalists are those individuals who invest money in a company on behalf of other companies. While business angels tend to rely on informal monitoring methods, venture capitalists emphasize more formal contractual methods of monitoring. Furthermore, the primary motivation for such professional investors is mostly capital gains.[59] Bruton et al. also note that venture capitalists are both principals (they invest their money in companies and expect management to run the company efficiently) and agents (acting as agents of their investors).[60] As agents, they face pressures to make the appropriate exit from the company to gain as many returns as possible on their investments. However, they also face long-term pressures to raise future funds.

Given the differences between business angels and venture capitalists, the corporate governance is also based on what each form of private equity is trying to achieve. As such, because business angels are more often interested in the long-term success of the company, they are more likely to use their long-term commitment and trust as the basis to influence management of the company. In contrast, venture capitalists are more likely to place direct control on management because of a firm's dependence on such sources of funding. Venture capitalists thus rely on more formal forms of monitoring.

CORPORATE GOVERNANCE AND GLOBALIZATION

As multinationals continue their global expansion in trading with new countries, it will become more critical to understand corporate governance worldwide. Corporate governance will remain a key aspect of how companies need to be governed in order to run a company efficiently and effectively.[61] Furthermore, corporate governance will be used as the means to ensure that the needs of all stakeholders and shareholders are met. In this section, we examine how corporate governance differs worldwide.

Research has devoted significant attention to how countries differ on corporate governance.[62] However, a significant aspect of the research has been to examine how countries differ in terms of the structure and composition of the board of directors. Such an emphasis is not surprising given the critical role of the board of directors in corporate governance. In this context, research has examined how national culture impacts differences in boards of directors worldwide. National culture represents the beliefs, norms, and values of individuals within a country. Such values, norms, and beliefs are likely to affect how boards of directors are structured.

Hofstede argues that national culture can be represented by a number of ways in which countries are different.[63] According to Hofstede, power distance is an important aspect of national culture and refers to the degree to which a society accepts that power differences exist and that such power distance is distributed unequally. In such societies, people accept that there are individuals who have more power and authority and that these individuals have the right to exercise such authority.

In a large-scale study involving 399 multinational firms, Li and Harrison found that countries with high power distance are more likely to have a board of directors with consolidated leadership structures whereby the CEO is also the chair of the board.[64] This is consistent with the view that, in high power distance, few have authority and privileges that are accepted by others. Having a CEO who also serves as chairperson of the board is consistent with the CEO using his/her authority and stature on other board members. Furthermore, companies in high power distance societies are also more likely to have boards with a higher percentage of outsiders on the board of directors. This is also consistent with the view that there should be an appropriate display of power within companies. Having outside directors reflects the influence of powerful individuals outside a company.

Uncertainty avoidance is another cultural aspect that has been studied. Uncertainty avoidance reflects the degree to which individuals within a country are comfortable with ambiguity and uncertainty. In high uncertainty avoidance countries, people are less likely to be comfortable with uncertainty. Rules and procedures are thus relied upon to reduce uncertainty and unknown situations.

Research shows that countries high in uncertainty avoidance tend to have boards where the CEO also acts as the chairperson of the board.[65] This is consistent with the view that having a CEO acting as chairperson of the board reduces ambiguity about the position. Furthermore, high uncertainty avoidance is also linked to having more outsiders on the board of directors. This increase in outsiders provides the company with added expertise and capabilities to reduce risks and ambiguities.

Another important national culture aspect is individualism.[66] Countries that are high on individualism tend to value individual freedom. In contrast, countries that are low on individualism tend to place emphasis on interpersonal relationships and group affiliations are highly preferred.

Research shows that countries that are more individualistic tend to have smaller boards, the CEO acting as chairperson of the board of directors, and a smaller percentage of outsiders on the board of directors.[67] Such results are consistent with the view of individual freedom (one person as both CEO and chairperson of the board) and less emphasis on group affiliations (higher percentage of insiders).

Recent research also shows that both individualism and uncertainty avoidance have an impact on corporate governance[68]. In that study, the researchers argue that most cross-cultural studies have assumed that the only form of corporate governance is protection of investors through practices such as transparency and board independence (the Anglo-Saxon corporate governance model). However, as was argued earlier in this chapter, some societies may have other forms of corporate governance through large shareholder forms of ownership. In such cases, these companies may have

Cultural Dimension	Level	Example of Countries	Corporate Governance Findings for High Levels
Power Distance	High	Malaysia, Guatemala, Mexico, India	Consolidated leadership structure where CEO is also chair of board
		Singapore, Brazil, France, Hong Kong	Higher percentage of outside directors
	Low	Austria, Israel, Denmark, Ireland	
		Sweden, Norway, Finland	
Uncertainty Avoidance	High	Greece, Portugal, Guatemala	Consolidated leadership structure where CEO is also chair of board
		Uruguay, Spain, France, Chile, Israel	More outsiders on board of directors
	Low	Singapore, Jamaica, Denmark, India	
		Hong Kong, UK, USA, Canada	
Individualism	High	USA, Australia, UK, Canada	Smaller number of board members
		Italy, Belgium, France, Norway	Consolidated leadership structure
	Low	Ecuador, Peru, Taiwan, South Korea	
		Singapore, Chile, Hong Kong	
Masculinity	High	Japan, Austria, Italy, Mexico, UK	Consolidated leadership structure
		Germany, USA, Australia, Jamaica	Higher percentage of outside directors on board
			Larger size of board of directors
	Low	Sweden, Norway, Netherlands	
		Denmark, South Korea, Chile	

EXHIBIT 7.6—National Culture and Impact on Corporate Governance

shareholders that exert direct control over the company. As such, there seems to be two forms of trade-offs of corporate governance: how much of corporate governance is needed and which forms of corporate governance. Using data from over 16,000 firms years from 41 countries, the authors show that individualism has a positive impact on Anglo-Saxon forms of corporate governance while uncertainty avoidance has a negative impact on Anglo-Saxon forms of corporate governance.

Finally, another cultural aspect studied is masculinity. More masculine societies tend to embrace values that are stereotypically male. As such, more masculine societies tend to value aggressiveness, competition, ambition, assertiveness, and the acquisition of material goods. In contrast, less masculine societies tend to be more concerned about quality of life and harmonious interpersonal relationships.

In the study of a large number of multinationals, Li and Harrison (2008, 2010) show that countries with high masculinity tend to have a board of directors with a higher percentage of outside directors (i.e., reflecting of power and ambition), consolidated CEO and chairperson position (again reflecting values of personal dominance and aggressiveness), and larger board of directors (i.e., consistent with the view that larger shows more power and ambition).[69]

As the above shows, there are clearly differences in terms of corporate governance worldwide. As multinationals engage in more cross-border trade, they will have to understand such differences to operate effectively worldwide. Exhibit 7.6 shows examples of countries on the above discussed national culture aspects and the implications for the board.

THE FUTURE OF CORPORATE GOVERNANCE

Corporate governance will continue to grow in importance. As more of the emerging nations strive to present an environment conducive to business, there will be an increased reliance on corporate governance to demonstrate that such aims are being achieved. Consider, for example, that India has been implementing many new corporate governance policies to ensure that shareholders do not lose their investments because of managerial misbehavior. Similarly, countries with dominant family ownership structures are also implementing measures to ensure that the needs of minority shareholders are heard and respected.

The World Bank, through its "Doing Business project,"[70] strongly believes in the value of corporate governance in furthering entrepreneurship. The project was conceived to give an idea of the environment conducive to entrepreneurship in different societies. An important aspect of the World Bank project pertaining to corporate governance and hence investors is the **protection of minority investors**. Companies can often raise capital by selling shares to investors. In return, investors expect transparency and accountability from managers running the company. However, company insiders can often use such funds or corporate assets for their personal gains. As you saw earlier, concentrated ownership such as family ownership, for instance, makes it possible for controlling family shareholders to abuse company assets. Controlling shareholders can sell company assets at low prices, thereby hurting both the company's and the minority shareholders' financial health. In these cases, shareholder rights can be abused. This aspect of the World Bank project thus looks at the government regulation in place to ensure that such rights are respected.

Several regulatory aspects are seen to contribute to investor protection. First, governments can mandate transparency in related-party transactions. For instance, if a company decides to sell company assets to a related company, it is necessary that shareholders are made aware of such transactions. This index is referred to as the extent of disclosure index. Second, regulation pertaining to the ease with which shareholders

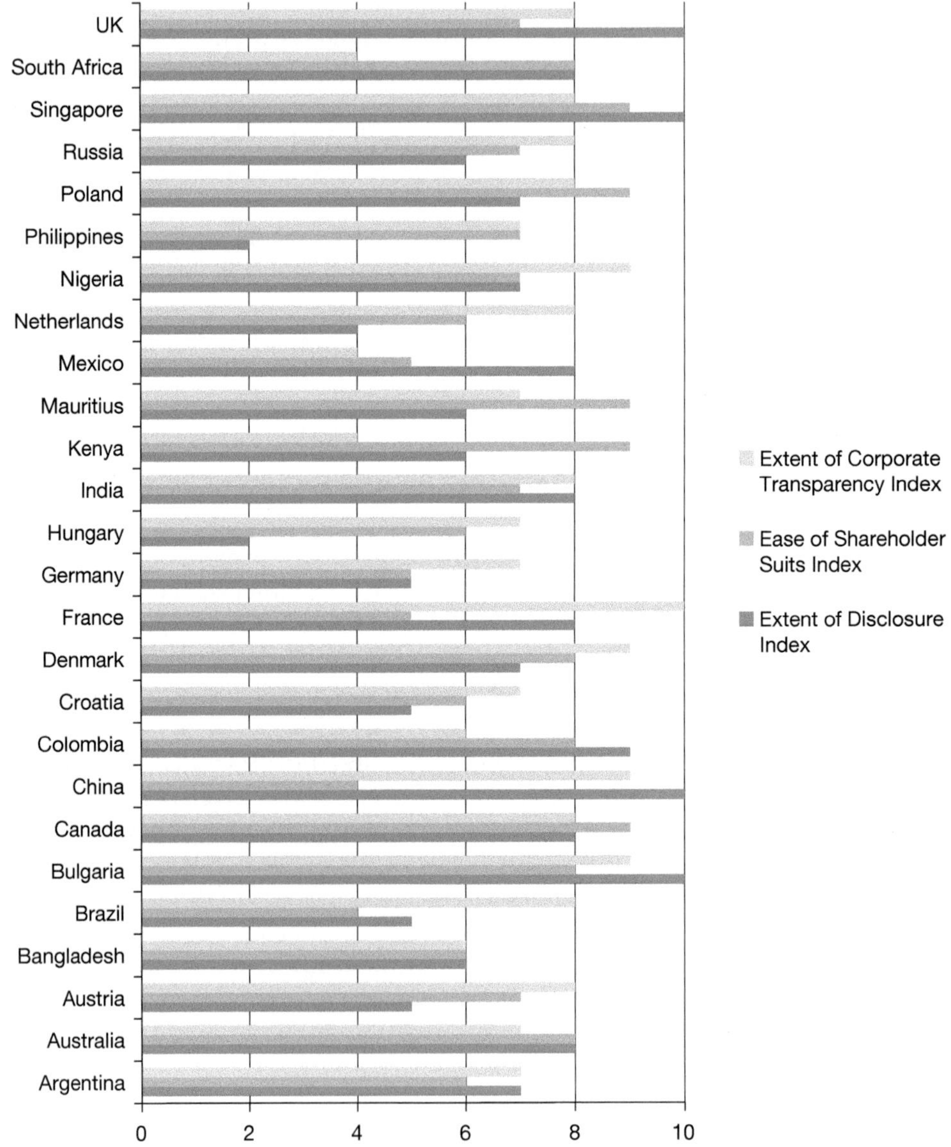

EXHIBIT 7.7—Minority Shareholders Indices

can sue companies for mismanagement is also seen as an important aspect of investor protection (i.e., ease of shareholder suits index). Minority shareholders should have access to a functioning legal system whereby they can defend their case and get retribution within a reasonable amount of time. Finally, governments can mandate protection of shareholders through transparency regarding corporate governance aspects such as executive compensation and annual meetings. This index is known as the extent of corporate transparency.

To give you further insights into these aspects, Exhibit 7.7 above shows these three indices for 25 selected countries. These indices range from 1 to 10 with 10 indicating the highest level.

In addition to the World Bank, the Organisation for Economic Co-operation and Development (OECD) also views corporate governance as critical. In fact, the OECD sees the failure of corporate governance as the root cause of the economic crisis in most Western societies. Implementing appropriate corporate governance measures is seen as a way to prevent such disasters occurring again. In fact, many countries have seen investors lose their investments as a result of management misbehavior. As a consequence, more countries are considering shareholders when they implement new corporate governance measures. It is therefore becoming more critical for multinationals to consider shareholder rights, which include the following:[71]

- Shareholders have the right to purchase shares. They should be able to secure registration for their shares. They should also be able to freely buy or sell such shares.
- Shareholders have the right to timely and accurate information from the company. Such information is necessary to allow shareholders to make informed decisions about what they want to do with their shares.
- Shareholders have the right to share in the profits of the corporation.
- Shareholders have the right to participate in key decisions related to new strategic directions of the company. Shareholders should be provided with accurate and timely information to help them make such decisions.
- Shareholders have the right to vote at board meetings. They should be informed of meeting times and agenda and be given the opportunity to voice their opinions on decisions being considered.
- Shareholders have the right in determining compensation packages for executives. They should be given the means to voice their opposition to compensation packages that they deem too excessive. In fact, more countries are now giving shareholders the right to also vote on compensation of the board of directors. Exhibit 7.8 shows selected countries and the rights shareholders now have.
- Shareholders have the right to participate in the nomination and election of board members. Information regarding new board election should be provided to shareholders in a timely manner.
- Recent regulation in the U.S. now allows large shareholders to nominate at least 25% of board members of a company. Such rights, known as proxy access, give large shareholders the right to have a say on who is nominated for board positions.
- Shareholders have the right to freely exercise their ownership rights. Such action should be facilitated by companies.

Country	Right to Vote On Renumeration of Board	Right to Vote On Renumeration of Management	Right to Vote On Stock and Option Plans
Austria	✓		✓
Denmark	✓		✓
France	✓		✓
Germany	✓		✓
Netherlands	✓		✓
Norway	✓	✓	✓
Sweden	✓		✓
Switzerland			
Canada			✓
USA			✓
Australia			
Japan			
UK			✓
Italy	✓	✓	✓

EXHIBIT 7.8—Selected Countries and Shareholder Rights

Finally, corporate governance is also seen by both investors and governments as a critical way to curb corruption. Companies with strong governance mechanisms are more likely to have systems in place to prevent misappropriation and misuse of assets. For instance, strong corporate governance can prevent corruption such as stock options backdating and self-dealings on the part of top executives.[72] Similarly, Halter et al. discuss how stockholders are now pushing for corporate governance in Brazilian firms.[73] Corruption is rife in Brazil and investors are wary of the risks of unethical behavior on the part of firms in which they own stocks. They are therefore pushing for more of these companies to adopt more ethical practices and implement strong corporate governance.

CHAPTER SUMMARY

In this chapter, you learned about shareholders as a primary stakeholder. You read about the types of shareholder. However, you were also exposed to agency theory and how the theory helps explain the problematic issues facing shareholders. Specifically, managers are hired to manage a firm by shareholders. Nevertheless, shareholders' and managers' interests may not diverge and managers can sometimes make self-interested decisions. Corporate governance is thus seen as a way to resolve this agency problem.

The first aspect of corporate governance discussed in this chapter is the board of directors. You learned about the critical role played by a board of directors and the many aspects of the board (board independence, board diversity, board size, and board expertise). Many experts see board diversity and specifically increasing women on such boards as a critical step to create the appropriate board. You also read about the issues that companies need to keep in mind when they design a board of directors.

The second critical aspect of corporate governance you learned about is executive compensation. You read about the controversial issues with executive compensation (high ratio of CEO salary to average worker, large benefits package, stock options, etc.) and the extent of these problems worldwide. You also learned about the arguments for and against high executive compensation. Finally, you read about some of the issues companies should keep in mind when designing top executives' compensation. As executive compensation gets more attention globally, these issues will have to be paid attention to.

A final critical aspect of corporate governance discussed is ownership concentration. You read about the different types of blockholders (corporate blockholder, family blockholder, and state blockholder). You also learned about the many problematic issues associated with the family blockholder (minority shareholder rights not respected) and state ownership (lack of innovation and corruption). Finally, you also learned about the importance of private equity as a form of ownership.

Given the importance of corporate governance worldwide, you also learned about the impact of culture on corporate governance. You read about the different forms of cultural dimensions such as uncertainty avoidance, individualism, and masculinity and how they affect corporate governance.

In the final part of the chapter, you read about the future of corporate governance. You learned about the sustained importance of corporate governance worldwide. As more emerging nations try to shape an environment conducive to business, more of them will rely on stronger corporate governance mechanisms. Furthermore, given that many shareholders were severely impacted by the last economic crisis, you also read about the many shareholder rights being enacted worldwide. Finally, you also learned about the importance of corporate governance to curb corruption worldwide.

NOTES

1 Martin, R. 2010. "The age of customer capitalism." *Harvard Business Review*, January–February, 58–65 (at 61).

2 Zhong, N., Wang, S. & Yang, R. 2017. "Does corporate governance enhance common interests of shareholders and primary stakeholders?" *Journal of Business Ethics*, 141, 411–431.

3 Johnson, R.A., Schnatterly, K., Johnson, S.G. & Chiu,S. 2010. "Institutional investors and institutional environment: A comparative analysis and review." *Journal of Management Studies*, 47, 8.

4 Pergola, T.M. & Verreault, D.A. 2009. "Motivations and potential monitoring effects of large shareholders." *Corporate Governance*, 9, 5, 551–563 (at 553).
5 Connelly, B.L, Hoskisson, R.E., Tihanyi, L. & Cresto, T. 2010. "Ownership as a form of corporate governance." *Journal of Management Studies*, 47, 8.
6 Fama, E.F. & Jensen, M.C. 1983. "Separation of ownership and control." *Journal of Law and Economics*, 26, 2, 301–325.
7 Nyberg, A.J., Fulmer, I.G., Gerhart, B. & Carpenter, M.A. 2010. "Agency theory revisited: CEO return and shareholder interest alignment." *Academy of Management Journal*, 53, 5, 1029–1049; Engelen, C. 2015. "The effects of managerial discretion on moral hazard related behavior: German evidence on agency costs." *Journal of Management Governance*, 19, 927–960.
8 Engelen, "The effects of managerial discretion."
9 Tosi, H.J. 2008. "Quo Vadis? Suggestions for future corporate governance research." *Journal of Management and Governance*, 12, 153–169.
10 Leahy, J. 2009. "$1bn fraud at India IT group." *Financial Times*, January 8, 13; Tripathi, S. 2009. "India faces an 'Enron moment'." *Wall Street Journal*, January 9, A11.
11 Morrow, R. 2009. "Satyam scandal leaves no place for India to hide." *Asiamoney*, February.
12 Tosi, "Quo Vadis?"
13 Zhang, Y. 2008. " Information asymmetry and the dismissal of newly appointed CEOs: An empirical investigation." *Strategic Management Journal*, 29, 859–872.
14 Lu, J., Xu, B. & Liu, X. 2009. "The effects of corporate governance and institutional environments on export behavior in emerging economies." *Management International Review*, 49, 455–478.
15 Ojeka, S.A., Iyoha, F.O., Ikpefan, O.A. & Osakwe, C. 2017. "Does the reformed code of corporate governance 2011 enhance the market performance of the firms in Nigeria?" *International Journal of Economic Perspectives*, 11, 1, 155–164.
16 Tejersen, S., Couto, E.B. & Francisco, P.M. 2016. "Does the presence of independent and female directors impact board performance? A multi-country study of board diversity." *Journal of Governance*, 20, 447–483.
17 Aguilar, M.K. 2010. "Special investigations 101: The board's role." *Compliance Week*, November, 48–49; Whitehouse, T. 2010. "Boards turn to self-evaluation to regain trust." *Compliance Week*, 49–50; Yammeesri, J. & Herath, S.K. 2010. "Board characteristics and corporate value: Evidence from Thailand." *Corporate Governance*, 10, 3, 279–292; Tejersen et al. "Does the presence of independent and female directors impact board performance?"
18 Ameer, R., Ramli, F. & Zakaria, H. 2010. "A new perspective on board composition and firm performance in an emerging market." *Corporate Governance*, 10, 5, 647–661.
19 Wagner, A.F. 2011. "Board independence and competence." *Journal of Financial Intermediation*, 20, 71–93.
20 Tejersen et al. "Does the presence of independent and female directors impact board performance?"
21 Francouer, C., Labelle, R. & Sinclair-Desgagne, B. 2008. "Gender diversity in corporate governance and top management." *Journal of Business Ethics*, 81, 83–95.
22 Governance Metrics International. 2010. "Women on boards." www.gmiratings.com.
23 GlobeWomen. 2010. www.globewomen.org.
24 Credit Suisse Research Institute. 2018. The CS Gender 3000: The Reward for Change. https://glg.it/assets/docs/csri-gender-3000.pdf
25 Governance Metrics International. "Women on boards."
26 Kang, E., Ding, D.K. & Charoenwong, C. 2010. "Investor reaction to women directors." *Journal of Business Research*, 63, 888–894.
27 Pozen, R.C. 2010. "The case for professional boards." *Harvard Business Review*, December.
28 O'Connell, V. & Cramer, N. 2010. "The relationship between firm performance and board characteristics in Ireland." *European Management Journal*, 28, 387–399.
29 Pozen, "The case for professional boards."
30 O'Connell & Cramer, "The relationship between firm performance"; Pozen, "The case for professional boards."

31 O'Connell & Cramer, "The relationship between firm performance."
32 Pozen, "The case for professional boards."
33 Pozen, "The case for professional boards."
34 Pozen, "The case for professional boards"; Ojeka et al. "Does the reformed code of corporate governance 2011 enhance the market performance of the firms in Nigeria?"
35 Ojeka et al. "Does the reformed code of corporate governance 2011 enhance the market performance of the firms in Nigeria?"
36 Ryan, L.V., Buchholtz, A.K. & Kolb, R.W. 2010. "New directions in corporate governance and finance: Implications for business ethics research." *Business Ethics Quarterly*, 20, 4, 673–694.
37 e-reward.co.uk. 2018. Worldwide executive compensation 2015: Survey of FT Global 200 Companies www.e-reward.co.uk/executive-pay/reports/worldwide-executive-compensation-2015-survey-of-global-ft-200-companies.
38 Strier, F. 2010. "Runway CEO pay? Blame the boards." *The IUP Journal of Corporate Governance*, 3, 8–27.
39 Strier, "Runway CEO pay?"; Martin, "The age of customer capitalism."
40 Farid, M., Conte, V. & Lazarus, H. 2011. "Toward a general model for executive compensation." *Journal of Management Development*, 30, 1, 61–74.
41 Strier, "Runway CEO pay?"
42 Farid et al., "Toward a general model for executive compensation."
43 e-reward.co.uk. 2018. Worldwide executive compensation 2015.
44 Collins, D.W., Gong, G. & Li, H. 2009. "Corporate governance and backdating of executive stock options." *Contemporary Accounting Research*, 26, 2, 403–445.
45 Strier, "Runway CEO pay?"
46 Chodhury, D.S. 2009. "Director compensation: The growing popularity of deferred stock units." *Ivey Business Journal* online, January/February; Lynn, D.M., Parris, B.C. & Thorpe A.D. 2010. "Revisiting your key corporate governance and disclosure policies." *Corporate Governance Advisor*, 18, 6; Ryan et al. "New directions in corporate governance and finance."
47 Curran, E. 2010. "Australia to toughen rules on executive pay." *Wall Street Journal* online, April 16.
48 Munoz, S.S. 2010. "Europeans stay tough on pay rules." *Wall Street Journal*, December 1, B3.
49 Connelly et al., "Ownership as a form of corporate governance."
50 Lazardies. T., Drimpetas, E. & Dimitrios, K. 2009. "Ownership structure in Greece: Impact of corporate governance." *IUP Journal of Corporate Governance*, 8, 3 & 4.
51 Johnson et al., "Institutional investors and institutional environment."
52 Engelen, "The effects of managerial discretion."
53 Johnson et al., "Institutional investors and institutional environment."
54 Johnson et al., "Institutional investors and institutional environment."
55 Connelly et al., "Ownership as a form of corporate governance."
56 Morrell, K. & Clark, I. 2010. "Private equity and the public good." *Journal of Business Ethics*, 96, 249–263.
57 Bruton, G.D., Filatotchev, I., Chahine, S. & Wright, M. 2010. "Governance, ownership structure, and performance of IPO firms: The impact of different types of private equity investors and institutional environments." *Strategic Management Journal*, 31, 491–509.
58 Bruton et al., "Governance, ownership structure, and performance of IPO firms."
59 Connelly et al., "Ownership as a form of corporate governance."
60 Bruton et al., "Governance, ownership structure, and performance of IPO firms."
61 Strange, R., Filatotchev, I., Buck, T. & Wright, M. 2009. "Corporate governance and international business." *Management International Review*, 49, 4, 395–407.
62 Griffin, D., Guedhami, O., Kwok. C.Y.K., Li, K. & Shao, L. 2017. "National culture: The missing country-level determinant of corporate governance." *Journal of International Business Studies*, 48, 740–762.
63 Hofstede, G. 1980. *Culture's consequences: International differences in work-related values*. Newbury Park, CA: Sage.

64 Li., J. & Harrison, J.R. 2008. "Corporate governance and national culture: A multi-country study." *Corporate Governance*, 8, 5, 607–621; Li., J. & Harrison, J.R. 2008. "National culture and the composition and leadership structure of boards of directors." *Journal of International Corporate Governance*, 16, 5, 375–385.
65 Li & Harrison, "Corporate governance and national culture"; Li & Harrison, "National culture."
66 Hofstede, *Culture's consequences*.
67 Li & Harrison, "Corporate governance and national culture"; Li & Harrison, "National culture."
68 Griffin et al. "National culture: The missing country-level determinant of corporate governance."
69 Li & Harrison, "Corporate governance and national culture"; Li & Harrison, "National culture."
70 World Bank. 2018. www.doingbusiness.org/~/media/WBG/DoingBusiness/Documents/Annual-Reports/English/DB2018-Full-Report.pdf
71 OECD. 2015. "G20/OECD principles of corporate governance", OECD Publishing, Paris. http://dx.doi.org/10.1787/9789264236882-en; Organisation for Economic Co-operation and Development (OECD). 2009. "Corporate governance and the financial crisis: Key findings and main messages." www.oecd.org; Ryan et al., "New directions in corporate governance and finance"; Steinberg, R.M. 2010. "Shareholders, be careful what you wish for." *Compliance Week*, December, 46–47.
72 Bishra, N.D. & Schipani, C.A. 2009. "Strengthening the ties that bind: Preventing corruption in the executive suite." *Journal of Business Ethics*, 88, 765–780.
73 Halter, M.V., Coutinho, M.C. & Halter, R.B. 2009. "Transparency to reduce corruption?" *Journal of Business Ethics*, 84, 375–385.

KEY TERMS

Agency theory: views the firm as a legal entity that serves as a nexus for a complex set of contracts among disparate individuals.

Blockholders: shareholders that have more than 5% equity stake in a company.

Board diversity: reforms in corporate governance that require that different stakeholders, especially women, are represented on a board of directors.

Board expertise: the necessary expertise needed by the board to understand the industry the company is operating in to have the ability to make decisions of strategic importance.

Board independence: prescription that a number of the members of a board of directors should be independent from the company.

Board of directors: often seen as one of the primary mechanisms to monitor and control the agency conflict.

Board size: the number of members on the board of directors.

Corporate blockholders: corporations with significant ownership in a company.

Corporate governance: the many mechanisms that can be used to align managements' interests with owners' interests.

Executive compensation: refers to the pay, perks, and benefits given to top executives in a company.

Family blockholder: single family is a major owner of a company.

Individual shareholders: include regular persons buying and selling shares of any company.

Large shareholders: blockholders and institutional shareholders that buy firms' shares directly, not through an investment entity.
Ownership structure: primary way ownership of shares of the company is structured.
Private equity: various forms of private funding that are available to companies that are not necessarily publicly traded.
Shareholders: legal owners of business corporations.
State ownership: government owns a significant percentage of a company.
Stock options: stocks awarded to the CEO, who then has the ability to sell the stock at a future date.

DISCUSSION QUESTIONS

1. Briefly define shareholders. What are the two different types of shareholders? Which type has more control on a company and why?
2. What is agency theory? Discuss the two problems faced by shareholders as they deal with top management.
3. What is corporate governance? What are some of the major benefits of having strong corporate governance systems?
4. What is a board of directors? Discuss five important roles played by a board of directors.
5. Discuss three key aspects of a board of directors. How does each of these aspects contribute to stronger company performance?
6. What are some of the key issues a company needs to consider when designing a board of directors? Be as specific as possible.
7. Why is executive compensation worldwide such a controversial issue? Discuss two arguments to support the high levels of executive compensation.
8. What is ownership concentration? Briefly discuss each of the three types of blockholders and the challenges they present for corporate governance.
9. How is corporate governance different worldwide? Be specific by discussing the link between national culture dimensions and how they affect corporate governance.
10. What are shareholder rights? Discuss five rights shareholders should have.

INTERNET ACTIVITY

1. Go to the Organisation for Economic Co-operation and Development website: www.oecd.org.
2. Find the general corporate governance report and the report for a specific region (e.g., Africa, Asia, or Latin America).
3. What do you learn about the importance of corporate governance from the general report?

4. Describe the situation in the region you researched. Why is corporate governance the way it is in that region?
5. Discuss some of the recommendations provided by the OECD to improve corporate governance in that region. Present some of your own recommendations to the class.

For more Internet Activities and resources, visit the Companion Website at www.routledge.com/cw/parboteeah.

WHAT WOULD YOU DO?

International Negotiations

You come to the U.S. to get your Bachelor's degree in International Business. After graduation, you get a job with a local company that is interested in expanding operations in your native country. You do very well during your first year and you are soon invited to meet with the CEO to discuss investment opportunities in your native country. You are very valuable to the company as you speak the local language and could also act as a trusted interpreter.

The CEO mentions that he has been approached by a company in your native country. The owner of that company is interested in selling the company. You therefore arrange for negotiations with the owner of the company. Your CEO and relevant personnel have done extensive research on the local company and strongly believe that acquisition would be very beneficial to your company. The local company has some technology that will allow your company to develop expertise in new areas.

Negotiations proceed smoothly and you have the impression that the deal will be concluded soon. However, the owner of the local company approaches you and mentions in your native language that he is willing to seal the deal if $1 million is transferred to a private bank account. He argues that he has run the family business for a long time and deserves an additional incentive compared to the other shareholders of his company. He also tells you that he will not sign unless he is given the money.

What would you do? Do you mention the $1 million to your CEO? Do you try to reason with the owner?

BRIEF CASE: BUSINESS ETHICS INSIGHT

The Olympus Scandal

On February 10, 2011, Olympus made a surprising announcement. Bypassing several domestic senior managers, the Japanese camera maker decided to appoint the 50-year-old Briton Michael Woodford as its company president. The outgoing president saw Woodford as the person who would be able to cut costs at Olympus and provide a more international perspective to the company. However, on October 14, 2011, Mr. Woodford was terminated at an Olympus board meeting. The board meeting only lasted ten minutes and Mr. Woodford was not even allowed to speak. One of his fellow board members even told him to "catch a bus to the airport"! Why did Olympus fire Mr. Woodford so soon after he was hired?

During his tenure, Mr. Woodford alleges that he discovered several irregularities and decided to investigate these issues. For example, he found that Olympus had paid over $2.88 billion for four small and midsize companies in businesses unrelated to their core camera business. Olympus predicted highly optimistic profits from these companies and ended up writing these companies off. However, most troubling was that Olympus paid about $2 billion for a UK company developing "non-invasive" surgical cameras. However, in making the deal, Mr. Woodford alleges that Olympus paid a $678 million fee to a financial advisor for help with the deal. Such a fee was seen as very unusual given that it represented almost seven times Olympus' profits in 2010. Furthermore, he believes that the money actually went to criminal organizations.

Major shareholders of Olympus are obviously very disturbed by these allegations. The value of the company has halved since the news broke out. Larger shareholders are demanding investigations into these acquisitions and why the company paid such high fees for these acquisitions. For instance, Nippon Life Insurance, Olympus' largest shareholder (with 8.3% shares) is requesting details about these deals. Such questioning is rare in the Japanese environment, where domestic investors are typically very passive.

Despite the scandal, many argue that the Japanese have been very sluggish in embracing progress in corporate governance. Olympus is still denying any wrongdoing and argues that they fired Mr. Woodford for his failure to master Japanese culture. Furthermore, the scandal was barely mentioned in Japan, and the Tokyo Stock Exchange has still not declared Olympus a candidate for delisting. As of October 25, 2011, none of the Japanese government officials have commented on the matter.

Based on *Financial Times*, 2011. "Olympus." Online edition, October 22; Inagaki, K. 2011. "Olympus is under pressure." *Wall Street Journal*, online, October 21; Soble, J., Soble, L. and Whipp, J. 2011. "A camera-maker obscurer: The Olympus affair." *Wall Street Journal* online, October 22.

BRIEF CASE QUESTIONS

1. Do you think that Olympus is justified in terminating Mr. Woodford? What other information do you need to make this determination?
2. Why do critics contend that the Japanese have been more reluctant to adopt progressive corporate governance practices? What Japanese cultural elements make such changes difficult?
3. Which elements of corporate governance were weak in this case and allowed the scandal to occur?
4. What changes would you suggest so that such corporate misbehavior does not occur again?

LONG CASE: BUSINESS ETHICS

SATYAM COMPUTER SERVICES LTD.: ACCOUNTING FRAUD IN INDIA

It was a warm day in Hyderabad, India. Ramalinga Raju sat in his corner office at Satyam's headquarters and looked around to see the company that he had built over the last 20 years. He remembered starting the company in 1987 with his brother, and the day in 1991 when he landed his first *Fortune* 500 client, John Deere & Co. He had singlehandedly turned Satyam from an unheard-of company to the fourth largest provider of information technology outsourcing in India. However, these were not happy thoughts. Raju watched the history of his career flash before his eyes because he knew that, once he mailed this letter, his career and reputation would be gone.

Raju knew this was the only thing that he could do. All of his attempts to cover up his transgressions had failed, foreign investors were dumping his stock, the Maytas deal had been effectively shelved, the Security and Exchange Board of India was conducting an investigation on his company, and Merrill Lynch had just snapped ties with Satyam, citing material accounting irregularities. So he put pen to paper and wrote down the story of how he managed to destroy a company that he himself had nurtured. Then he prepared himself for the worst.

Meanwhile, a first-year associate ran into Thomas Mathew's office at Pricewater-house-Coopers' (PwC) offices in India. The associate knew Mathew emphasized an open-door policy, but, as the head of PricewaterhouseCoopers' assurance wing, he at least expected people to knock. Mathew asked the associate what had happened, and she asked him if he had heard the news about Satyam. He replied no, even though he was vaguely familiar with the company, as it was one of his firm's largest clients. She then broke the news to him. Satyam's founder had admitted to orchestrating a massive accounting fraud, by which he overstated the company's cash balance by 45 billion Indian Rupees (US$1 billion) and, subsequently, its stock was in freefall.

Mathew knew this would be very bad for PwC, as Satyam's auditors they were responsible for detecting any material misstatements in the company's financial statements. Additionally, PwC had spent over a hundred years in the Indian financial services market, building the reputation it held today. He wondered what the backlash from this would be. Then the last, but most horrifying, thought ran through his mind. What would be the consequence that the partnership would have to face if its partners were involved in the scandal?

The account that had been overstated was cash. He knew that any auditor worth his salt could detect missing cash, because it was the only account for which two separate entities accounted for it: the bank and the company. He buried his head in his hands and thought hard. He tried to call his partners in charge of the Satyam audit, but their secretaries informed him that they had been arrested by the police.

The biggest financial fraud in the history of India had taken place. Some had likened it to the Enron scandal that happened in the United States in the early 2000s. Both the company Enron and its auditor Arthur Andersen no longer exist as a result of the fraud. Whether or not Satyam and PwC were walking a similar path was yet to be determined. However, one thing was certain: fraud had occurred and now both firms had to deal with it.

The History of Satyam

Satyam Computer Services Ltd. (NYSE:SAY) is a leading global business and information technology services company headquartered in Hyderabad, India. Satyam's core competencies are in consulting, systems integration, and outsourcing.[1]

As of 2008, Satyam serviced 690 clients, including 185 *Fortune* 500 companies, in 20 industries and more than 65 countries. Satyam employed more than 52,000 associates in engineering and product development, supply chain management, client relationship management, business process quality, business intelligence, enterprise integration and infrastructure management, among other key capabilities. Its revenues exceeded $2 billion, and Satyam became the first company to launch a secondary listing on Euronext Amsterdam under NYSE Euronext's new "Fast Path" process for cross listings in New York and Europe.[2]

Before 2008, Satyam's beginnings were quick and promising. On June 24, 1987, the company was incorporated as a Private Limited Company for providing software development and consultancy services to large corporations. The company was promoted by B. Rama Raju and B. Ramalinga Raju.[3] On August 26, 1991, Satyam was recognized as a public limited company after its Initial Public Offering; it was listed on the Bombay Stock Exchange (BSE). Also in 1991, Satyam obtained its first *Fortune* 500 customer in a software project with John Deere & Co.[4] By 1999, Satyam had established its presence in 30 countries. In the following year, the associate count within Satyam reached a new level at 10,000. In 2001, Satyam was listed on the New York Stock Exchange under the ticker symbol "SAY." Five years after listing on the NYSE, Satyam reported revenues that exceeded US$1 billion.[5]

The Founder of Satyam

Byrraju Ramalinga Raju, the founder and chairman of Satyam Computers, was born in West Godavari, India, in 1954. He received his Bachelor of Commerce from Andhra Loyola College at Vijayawada prior to receiving an MBA degree at Ohio University. He also attended the Owner/President course at Harvard. Before Raju founded Satyam, he had tried his hand in other businesses such as textiles and real estate.

Satyam was initially an IT company with only 20 employees. The IT projects performed at Satyam were for contracts obtained from mainly U.S. companies. Over time, Satyam quickly emerged as a multinational corporation with thousands of employees and a presence in many countries.[6]

During his time at Satyam, Raju received many awards and distinctions, the most recent of which was the Ernst & Young Entrepreneur of the Year 2007 award.[7] Raju was also a philanthropist: he helped create a foundation that assisted in the building of progressive and self-reliant rural communities,[8] and furthered the cause of several not-for-profit institutions.[9]

However, there was another side to Raju. After his arrest, some interesting facts came to light that displayed his greed. According to the Andhra Pradesh police, Raju owned more than 1,000 designer suits, 321 pairs of shoes, and 310 belts. His desire to lead a lavish lifestyle drove him to own "palatial mansions and villas" in 63 countries.[10] Raju was truly living the lifestyle that any billionaire could.

THE BACKGROUND OF PWC INDIA

PricewaterhouseCoopers is the largest professional services firm in the world and employs over 155,000 people in 153 countries.[11] It was formed in 1998 from a merger between Price Waterhouse and Coopers & Lybrand. Not only did both firms share similar origins, starting in London in the 1800s, but they each also had a history in client services that dated back to the nineteenth century.[12]

In the United States, PwC is the third largest privately owned organization. It operates as PricewaterhouseCoopers LLP. PwC is a Big Four auditor in the U.S., alongside KPMG, Ernst & Young, and Deloitte Touche Tohmatsu. Along with being the largest professional services firm, PwC generated $28.2 billion in total worldwide revenues for its fiscal year 2008. The firm's dominant practice is auditing, which accounted for nearly 50% of PwC's total worldwide revenues in 2008.[13]

Currently PwC offers industry-focused professional services that are grouped into three main service lines. These service lines are assurance, tax, and advisory. The assurance service line is focused on the audit of financial statements. The tax service line is concerned with tax planning and the compliance with local, national, and international tax laws. The advisory service line primarily handles consulting activities such as transaction services, mergers and acquisitions, performance improvement, business recovery services, and crisis management. Not only does PwC work with corporations and large business structures, but they also work with educational institutions, governments, non-profits, and international relief agencies to address their unique business issues.[14]

PwC's Indian arm operates under the name Price Waterhouse. Price Waterhouse is the largest professional services firm in the country, with nearly 4,000 professionals. It has had a long history of involvement in India and has been there for over 128 years. PwC's Indian operations began in 1880 in the city of Kolkata. Since then, Price Waterhouse has expanded its offices to Bangalore, Bhubaneshwar, Chennai, Ahmedabad, Hyderabad, Mumbai, Delhi NCR, and Pune.[15]

In recently published research, India's economy is expected to grow to almost 90% of the U.S. economy by 2050. Nonetheless, PwC is already seeing amazing growth in India. In 2007, PwC India's revenues went up 36% from the previous year. In 2008, PwC India's revenues went up 44%.[16] The rapid growth in India's economy is something that PwC is aware of. It would like to continue to be the dominant leader in the professional services industry there. Any opportunity to expand and grow PwC is an opportunity not to be missed.

The Background on Indian Business

India has long been known to be one of the most highly regulated economies in the world. With tariffs on imports over 32% and caps placed on foreign investments, the country was largely left out of participating in international trade. In 2002, the United States Secretary of Treasury, Paul O'Neill, stated, "India is rated among the most restrictive countries in the world in terms of its trade and investment rules."[17] The government of India, realizing a need for change, implemented various strategies by which it could open up the economy and liberalize trade. It effectively abolished the cap on direct foreign investment and drastically reduced tariffs on foreign goods coming into the country.[18] This was done in the hopes of a reciprocal response by foreign governments on Indian goods and services. The relaxed restrictions proved helpful to business in India, eventually leading to the information technology (IT) outsourcing industry's rapid growth. The major IT outsourcing companies in India are Wipro, Infosys Technologies, Tata Consultancy Services, and Satyam. The client list of these firms spans the breadth of *Fortune* 500 companies from General Electric to Lufthansa Airlines.

Satyam-Maytas Fiasco

On December 16, 2008, Satyam announced that it would acquire a 100% stake in Maytas Properties Ltd. and a 51% stake in Maytas Infra, both of which are companies that develop properties in smaller cities in India. ("Maytas" is also "Satyam" spelled backwards.) The Raju family was the controlling shareholder in both Maytas Properties and Maytas Infra. Satyam stated that it would purchase Maytas Properties for $1.3 billion and pay $300 million for its stake in Maytas Infra. This decision was made without seeking the approval of minority shareholders, who controlled over 90% of the voting shares in Satyam.[19]

Management's rationale for the deal was to de-risk the business model for the company in light of slowing demand for the company's IT services. However, the acquisition itself would have netted the Raju family $570 million. The deal would have also drained Satyam of its excess cash, which was $1.1 billion, and would have caused the company to take on $400 million in debt financing. Investors retaliated by dumping the stock, which lost over 30% of its value in a single day of trading on the Bombay Stock Exchange (BSE). The company immediately withdrew the deal; however, the damage had already been done as investors had lost their faith in management.[20]

The Security and Exchange Board of India Initiates an Inquiry

The Securities and Exchange Board of India (SEBI), the primary market regulator for the Indian capital markets, decided to investigate the corporate governance issues concerning the Satyam-Maytas deal. SEBI Chairman C.B. Bhave stated, "We do not want to react immediately to the incident (the acquisition bid that triggered investor outrage) . . . we will study issues involved and then come to a conclusion."[21]

World Bank Ban

On December 22, 2008, a story broke on Fox News that the international outsourcing giant Satyam had been banned from providing services to the World Bank.[22] The reason for the ban was first reported to be due to Satyam employees installing improper backdoor software programs that were used to snoop on the bank's activities. However, a bank official later clarified that the reason for the ban was actually due to Satyam providing "improper benefits to bank staff." Satyam's contract with the World Bank exceeded $100 million in value and was awarded by the then-chief information officer for the bank, Mr. Mohamed Vazir Muhsin. However, the internal anti-corruption unit of the bank started looking at Mr. Muhsin's dealings and found that he had "purchased shares of stock in companies that had then current or prospective business interests"[23] with his department, including Satyam. The bank also found "reasonably sufficient evidence showing that [Muhsin] purchased some of the shares of stock under preferential terms,"[24] as he blatantly awarded major contracts to Satyam. Satyam shares traded on the BSE lost 13% of their value, bringing them to their lowest point in over four and a half years.[25]

This was a major blow to Satyam. It had already been hurt by investor discontent arising from the failed Maytas deal. Additionally, this was a smear on the company itself as it had been shown to be unethical. Harshad Deshpande, an IT analyst, said, "Once a firm is declared unethical, everyone doubts its credibility. Other clients could take a fresh look at their contracts."[26] A Satyam spokesperson stated, "As a matter of company policy we normally do not comment on individual customers, contracts and relationships."[27] This did nothing to allay the fear of the market, and hence most analysts put a "Sell" recommendation on the stock. Satyam's stock continued its freefall, eventually shedding 69% of its value from its 52-week high.[28]

Merrill Lynch Resignation

In a bid to alleviate investor anger, Satyam hired DSP Merrill Lynch to explore strategic opportunities to enhance shareholder value. However, a week after being hired, the Merrill Lynch team found material accounting irregularities and resigned from the assignment. A spokesperson for DSP Merrill Lynch stated, "We, DSP Merrill Lynch Limited, have terminated our advisory engagement with Satyam Computer Services Ltd. for considering various strategic options on January 6, 2009 . . . In the course of such engagement, we came to understand that there were material accounting irregularities, which prompted our aforesaid decisions."[29]

The Letter

On January 7, 2009, Mr. Raju mailed a letter to the board members of Satyam, the Securities and Exchange Board of India, as well as the various stock exchanges at which Satyam traded, in which he detailed the massive fraud perpetrated by him. The letter states:

1. The Balance Sheet carries as of September 30, 2008
   a. Inflated (non-existent) cash and bank balances of Rs. 5,040 crore (as against Rs. 5361 crore reflected in the books)
   b. An accrued interest of Rs. 376 crore which is non-existent
   c. An understated liability of Rs. 1,230 crore on account of funds arranged by me
   d. An overstated debtors position of Rs. 490 crore (as against Rs. 2651 reflected in the books)[30]

The holes in the balance sheet were due to inflated profits recognized in the past several years. What began as a small gap between actual and reported performance soon swelled in size, and each failed attempt to cover up the scam resulted in a larger gap. In describing the scam, Raju stated, "It was like riding a tiger, not knowing how to get off without being eaten." He stated that "the aborted Satyam-Maytas deal was the last attempt to fill the fictitious assets with real ones." His final words in the letter were, "I am now prepared to subject myself to the laws of the land and face consequences thereof."[31]

Price Waterhouse's Involvement

Price Waterhouse had been the auditor for Satyam since 2000. Subramani Gopalakrishnan, Price Waterhouse's chief relationship partner, had signed off on all of the Satyam audits since 2000, except for the last one, which was signed off by Talluri Srinivas, the engagement leader.[32] After the news came out about the Satyam fraud, the board of directors at Satyam was replaced. The new board at Satyam dropped Price Waterhouse and appointed Deloitte and KPMG as its auditors. The two Price Waterhouse partners mentioned previously were arrested.

Since Raju's shocking disclosures, Price Waterhouse has come under close scrutiny. The market regulator Securities and Exchange Board of India (SEBI) and the Registrar of Companies (RoC) have launched a probe into Price Waterhouse. The Andhra Pradesh police have also conducted raids at Price Waterhouse's office in Hyderabad. Price Waterhouse is under as much scrutiny as Satyam.[33]

In a statement that was released, PwC said that there is "not an iota of material to link them with the accusations leveled against them."[34] S. Gopalakrishnan and T. Srinivas also initially denied allegations brought against them. These Price Waterhouse partners were both arrested and charged with cheating, forgery, criminal breach of trust, and criminal conspiracy under the Indian Penal Code (IPC).[35] Following their arrests, PwC International Chief Executive Sam DiPiazza flew to New Delhi to talk with Prem Chand Gupta, the government minister in charge of corporate affairs, to discuss the firm's involvement in the scandal.[36]

Although PwC claims its innocence, there are some that think that Price Waterhouse was not completely blameless. Satyam's CFO Vadlamani Srinivas, who was also arrested, blamed Price Waterhouse for not pointing out the deficiencies in the company's accounts. He further said that, as Satyam's auditors, Price Waterhouse normally shared its audit findings but failed to play its role.[37] In a recent report, T. Srinivas and S. Gopalakrishnan told police that the agenda used to be clear in the meetings, though the word "fudging" was not used. Everyone present was aware of the motive of the meetings, which was to falsify the accounts.[38] They also told the Crime Investigation Department (CID) that they approved the accounts of Satyam because of Raju's "towering presence" and did so without ever questioning him. "We did not dare raise questions when the client was a reputed company."[39]

The Institute of Chartered Accountants of India (ICAI), a sort of AICPA of India, announced that it would take six more months to determine the extent of the involvement of the company's auditor in the Satyam fraud. Uttam Prakash Aggarwal, President of ICAI, said that whether the auditors (Price Waterhouse) are guilty of falsifying accounts or not will become clear as soon as the investigation is completed. According to Amarjit Chopra, Chairman of the Accounting Standards Board at the ICAI, "If the government decides against giving any consultancy work to Price Waterhouse until the investigations are completed, then it [the firm] will have problems."[40]

In addition to Satyam dropping Price Waterhouse as its external auditor, two software firms—Infotech Enterprises and Applabs—are evaluating options to replace Price Waterhouse as their statutory auditors.[41] A senior official at Infotech Enterprises is quoted as saying: "Though [S. Gopalakrishnan's] involvement in the Satyam scandal is not yet proved, there's some amount of bad reputation and, certainly, no company would like to be associated with it for long." Meanwhile, Applabs, the world's third largest software testing company, will soon be replacing Price Waterhouse. "We are seriously looking at changing our auditors. We will soon start talking to other auditing firms," said Sashi Reddi, the founder and chairman at Applabs.[42]

It will be hard to believe that Price Waterhouse won't suffer a large loss of credibility from the Satyam scandal. Even if Price Waterhouse is proven innocent or that, at the very least, this fraud proves to be an isolated incident, the damage has already been done.

Indian Government Response

The financial crisis and tightened lending standards made it extremely difficult for Satyam to find liquidity. This put the company in a precarious situation, as it was quickly running out of cash. The corporate sector looked to the government to bail Satyam out, as they were the only ones who could raise the capital required in a short period of time. In response, Commerce Minister of India Kamal Nath stated, "We are considering all options and will soon announce definite steps to help the company overcome the current crisis as it is the question of saving jobs and an international brand."[43] These steps included dissolving Satyam's existing board of directors and appointing new candidates to these positions. The first thing the new government-appointed board did was to find sources of liquidity to meet approaching pay days for its staff both in India and overseas. However, a few days later Nath revealed that the government would not bail out Satyam. He also mentioned that even though there was a problem with liquidity, the company had engaged investment bankers to find the cash it needed to survive. He stated, "There is no question of bailing out Satyam. It has strong bankers who would look for investors."[44]

Conclusion

Satyam found itself in a precarious position. It had a global network of clients and a strategically sound business, but it was running out of cash. The government had appointed a Satyam veteran, A.S. Murthy, to the position of chief executive officer. As the new CEO, he promised to "restore Satyam to its well-deserved glory."[45] Satyam had managed to secure a loan for 6 billion rupees ($123 million) to fund its operations for the short term. However, clients were reconsidering renewing their contracts with Satyam, and this would put the long-term viability of the company in jeopardy. In the meantime, Satyam's bankers were looking for strategic partners to buy the ailing outsourcing giant. The government stated, "The next step of the government is to find out some suitable strategic investor who can take over the company."[46]

Halfway across the country, in Mumbai, Thomas Mathew knew that PwC's days in India might be numbered. Although he knew that he did not have anything to do with the Satyam scandal, he felt it was necessary to send an appropriate message to the rest of the firm. As he signed his own resignation letter as PwC India's audit head, he hoped that this act would help his fellow employees realize that personal accountability applies to everybody in an organization, even top management.

Notes

1 "Satyam: About us—About." Satyam Computer Services. 30 September 2008. www.satyam.com/about/about_us.asp.
2 "Satyam: About us—About." Satyam Computer Services.
3 "Satyam: About us—About." Satyam Computer Services.
4 "Company history—Satyam Computer Services." 2007. www.moneycontrol.com/stocks/company_info/company_history.php'sc_did=SCS.
5 "Satyam: About Us—About." Satyam Computer Services.
6 "Satyam stunner: Highs and lows of Raju's career." IBN. 7 January 2009. http://ibnlive.in.com/news/satyam-stunner-highs-and-lows-of-rajus-career/82183-7.html?from=rssfeed.
7 Seth, K. "Satyam's Raju is E&Y Entrepreneur of the year 2007." 21 September 2007. www.topnews.in/satyam-s-raju-e-y-entrepreneur-year-2007-26759.
8 Byrraju Foundation. www.byrrajufoundation.org/.

9 "EMRI looking for corporates, donors to replace Raju family." 2008. Headlines India. 19 January 2009. www.headlinesindia.com/business-news/satyam-fraud/emri-looking-for-corporates-donors-to-replace-raju-family-5422.html.

10 "Raju owned 321 shoes, 310 belts, 1000 suits." *Times of India*. 4 February 2009. http://timesofindia.indiatimes.com/articleshow/4073101.cms.

11 "Raju owned 321 shoes, 310 belts, 1000 suits." *Times of India*.

12 "PricewaterhouseCoopers Global home." PricewaterhouseCoopers.

13 "PricewaterhouseCoopers Global home." PricewaterhouseCoopers.

14 "PricewaterhouseCoopers Global home." PricewaterhouseCoopers.

15 "Empower poor." www.empowerpoor.com/pricewaterhousecoopers.asp.

16 "Empower poor."

17 "U.S. calls for reform in India." British Broadcasting Corporation. 22 November 2002. http://news.bbc.co.uk/2/hi/business/2501943.stm.

18 "U.S. calls for reform in India." British Broadcasting Corporation.

19 Aggarwal, A. "World Bank admits ban on Satyam for data theft." Merinews.com. 22 December 2008. www.merinews.com/catFull.jsp?articleID=154269.

20 Aggarwal, A. "World Bank admits ban on Satyam for data theft."

21 "Satyam fiasco puts Sebi on alert." *The Telegraph*. 19 December 2008. www.telegraphindia.com/1081220/jsp/business/story_10278343.jsp.

22 Behar, R. "World Bank admits top tech vendor debarred for 8 years." 24 December 2008. www.foxnews.com/story/0,2933,470964,00.html'sPage=fnc/world/unitednations.

23 "Satyam: Govt looking for strategic investor, Hindujas interested." *Economic Times*. 12 February 2009. http://economictimes.indiatimes.com/Infotech/Software/Satyam_Govt_looking_for_strategic_investor_Hindujas_interested/rssarticleshow/4120147.cms.

24 "Satyam: Govt looking for strategic investor, Hindujas interested." *Economic Times*.

25 Aggarwal, A. "World Bank admits ban on Satyam for data theft." Merinews.com.

26 "Satyam: Govt looking for strategic investor, Hindujas interested." *Economic Times*.

27 "Satyam: Govt looking for strategic investor, Hindujas interested." *Economic Times*.

28 Aggarwal, A. "World Bank admits ban on Satyam for data theft." Merinews.com.

29 "Merrill Lynch snaps ties with Satyam." *Financial Express*. 7 January 2009. www.financial express.com/news/merrill-lynch-snaps-ties-with-satyam/407864/.

30 Raju, R. "Satyam Raju letter." Scribd.com. 7 January 2009. www.scribd.com/doc/9812606/Satyam-Raju-Letter.

31 Raju, R. "Satyam Raju letter." Scribd.com.

32 "Satyam scandal casts shadow over PwC India." *Accountancy Age*. 5 February 2009 www.accountancyage.com/accountancyage/news/2235787/satyam-scandal-casts-shadow-pwc-4463639.

33 "Satyam scandal casts shadow over PwC India." *Accountancy Age*.

34 Chatterjee, S. "Price Waterhouse India partners to remain in custody (Update1)." CAclubindia. 3 February 2009. 6 May 2009 www.caclubindia.com/forum/messages/2009/2/24041_price_waterhouse_india_partners_to_remain_in_custody_updat.asp?quote=143753&.

35 "Two partners of PwC arrested, sent to judicial custody." Chennaionline News. 25 January 2009 http://news.chennaionline.com/newsitem.aspx?NEWSID=27acf181-f9dd-471d-9771-61c78a5c2579&CATEGORYNAME=NATL.

36 "Satyam scandal casts shadow over PwC India." *Accountancy Age*.

37 Kundu, S. "PwC dumped as Satyams auditors." *IT Examiner*. 22 February 2009. www.it examiner.com/pwc-dumped-as-satyams-auditors.aspx.

38 "Raju's agenda: Cook the books." *Times of India*. 8 February 2009. http://timesofindia.indiatimes.com/Home/Satyam-A-Big-Lie/Rajus-agenda-Cook-the-books/articleshow/4094116.cms.

39 "Raju's agenda: Cook the books." *Times of India*.

40 "ICAI wants 6 mths to determine PwC's involvement in Satyam." *Economic Times*. 13 February 2009. http://economictimes.indiatimes.com/News/News_By_Industry/Services/ICAI_wants_6_mths_to_determine_PwCs_involvement_in_Satyam/articleshow/4123010.cms.

41 "PWC finds itself in deep waters after Satyam fraud." *Express buzz*. 28 January 2009. www.expressbuzz.com/edition/story.aspx?Title=PWC+finds+itself+in+deep+waters+after+satyam+fraud&artid=5rR7aIxyTBQ=&SectionID=XT7e3Zkr/lw=&MainSectionID=XT7e3Zkr/lw=&SectionName= HFdYSiSIflu29kcfsoAfeg==&SEO=PwC,+S+Gopalakrishnan+and+Srinivas+Talluri.

42 "PWC finds itself in deep waters after Satyam fraud." *Express buzz*.

43 Simpkins, J. "Indian government ponders Satyam bailout to salvage corporate image." *Seeking Alpha*. 16 January 2009. http://seekingalpha.com/article/115111-indian-government-ponders-satyam bailout-to-salvage-corporate-image.

44 "Govt not to bail out Satyam, reiterates Kamal Nath." *Times of India*. 19 January 2009. http://timesofindia.indiatimes.com/No_question_of_bailing_out_Satyam_Kamal_Nath/articleshow/4001432.cms.

45 Kripalani, M. "Satyam's new CEO: Asset or liability." *Business Week*. 6 February 2009. www.businessweek.com/globalbiz/blog/eyeonasia/archives/2009/02/satyams_new_ceo.html?campaign_id=rss_daily.

46 "Satyam: Govt looking for strategic investor, Hindujas interested." *Economic Times*. 12 February 2009. http://economictimes.indiatimes.com/Infotech/Software/Satyam_Govt_looking_for_strategic_investor_Hindujas_interested/rssarticleshow/4120147.cms.

LONG CASE QUESTIONS

1. Although there weren't many options after the fraud had been committed, what could Satyam have done better to minimize the media attention?
2. In a unique crisis such as this, how did Satyam address the needs of its stakeholders? What could it have done better?
3. Both Satyam officials and Price Waterhouse officials have been blamed for the corporate scandal. In your assessment, who really deserves to take responsibility for the fraud?
4. What actions can Satyam take to regain the trust and confidence of its shareholders, clients, and the Indian government?

Chapter 8

Secondary Stakeholders:

Government, Media, and Non-Governmental Organizations

LEARNING OBJECTIVES

After reading this chapter you should be able to:

- Understand the government and how the government influences corporations
- Appreciate how companies influence the government through corporate political activity
- Appreciate the role played by the media as a secondary stakeholder
- Become aware of media analysis and its importance in managing the media
- Understand the critical role played by non-governmental organizations (NGOs) and the strategies they use to influence corporations
- Comprehend how NGOs can be managed and appreciate the role of cooperation with these NGOs

PREVIEW BUSINESS ETHICS INSIGHT

Nike and Sweatshops

In 2008, an Australian TV reporter posed as a fashion buyer to gain entry into a Nike Malaysian factory. The investigation into the factory, which employed mostly foreign migrants, showed horrific working conditions. Large numbers of workers were living in cramped and filthy rooms and sharing toilets that were in a very bad condition. Furthermore, these workers had to pay recruiting fees in order to get access to these jobs. Once they got to the Nike plant, their passports were seized so that they would not be able to escape. Additionally, their wages were being reduced to pay off the recruiting fees.

This case of the Nike Malaysian factory quickly reminded the public of similar ethical crises at Nike in the 1990s. Nike is widely known as the company that pioneered the outsourcing model whereby most of its products are contracted to manufacturers in developing nations. However, it was exposed in the early 1990s and quickly became the poster for sweatshops and corresponding bad working conditions. The media and non-governmental organizations exposed abuses such as child labor in Pakistan and these resulted in protests on university campuses and outside Nike stores. Nike remained the target of protests for most of the 1990s and quickly realized that such protests were taking their toll. In 1998, Nike reported a 50% decline in profit over the previous year.

In addition to the protests, Nike also attracted the attention of non-governmental organizations interested in improving working conditions. For instance, Oxfam, a non-governmental organization working on aid and development issues, started targeting Nike. Its Australian branch set up a Nike Watch campaign where it called for clothing and footwear companies (and specifically Nike) to help eradicate sweatshops and to improve labor conditions. This activity brought significant negative publicity to Nike.

When Nike first confronted the abuse reports in the 1990s, it initially rejected responsibility, arguing that the subcontractors are the ones responsible for the abuses. However, Nike quickly realized that it had to take responsibility to turn its tarnished image around. It implemented a number of steps such as the development of a code for its vendors, while also setting up a monitoring system. However, the broadcast on Australian TV in 2008 showed that Nike had still not addressed the issue completely. When faced with the new report, they quickly took responsibility by admitting a serious breach of its code. Furthermore, it reimbursed the workers and helped them relocate back to their home country if they wanted to. The company also set up meetings with its subcontractors to address labor regulation.

Nike has come a long way addressing sweatshop conditions. It now has a website dedicated to working conditions where it strives to be transparent about its list of factories, working conditions, and audit results. The company has also become a world leader in terms of sustainability and waste reduction. Additionally, in 2000, Nike adopted a lean manufacturing approach. In contrast to traditional manufacturing based on efficiency whereby workers become specialized at specific activities and mass produce at the lowest cost possible, lean manufacturing requires the workers to learn many different aspects of the production process and produce higher quality products in smaller batches. A study of Nike's lean factories show that standards have improved and compliance with labor regulations have also increased dramatically.

Based on Brenton, S. and Hacken, L. 2006. "Ethical consumerism: Are unethical labour practices important to consumers?" *Journal of Research for Consumers*, 11, 1–4; Distelhorst, G. 2016. "Can lean manufacturing put an end to sweatshops?" *Harvard Business Review*, May 26, 2–4; Drickhamer, D. 2002. "Under fire." *Industry Week*, 251, 5; Levenson, E. 2008. "Citizen Nike." *Fortune*, 158, 10, 165–170; Nike. 2018. https://help-en-us.nike.com/app/answer/article/supply-chain/a_id/20878/country/us.

The Preview Business Ethics Insight shows the experience of Nike as they dealt with groups such as the media and non-governmental organizations (NGOs). Both groups played an important role in educating consumers about the abuses occurring at Nike and other clothing and footwear giants. Both groups represent examples of key secondary stakeholders. Recall in Chapter 4 that **secondary stakeholders** were defined as those groups or entities that have an indirect impact on the company's survival and strategic activities. Thus, while secondary stakeholders may not necessarily have a direct impact on a company, they can still have a significant influence on how companies operate. For instance, Nike and most other clothing and footwear giants such as Puma and Reebok all responded by investing significantly in improving worker conditions. For many of these companies, secondary stakeholders had a significant impact on their bottom line and thus an important impact on their strategic health.

For a company to succeed and to gain a strategic competitive advantage, it needs to be able to strategically manage its secondary stakeholders. In this chapter, we therefore consider secondary stakeholders in depth. While there are a number of entities or groups that may have indirect influences on a company, we discuss three secondary stakeholders that seem most critical for companies. First, you will read about the role of the government as a secondary stakeholder. You will learn about the regulative power of governments and what companies can do to deal with such regulation. Governments play critical roles as secondary stakeholders and we devote a significant portion of this chapter to the government. Second, we will learn about the media and its impact on companies as secondary stakeholders. Third, and finally, you will learn about NGOs and their roles in effective business ethics functioning.

GOVERNMENT REGULATION

The government is one of the most important secondary stakeholders. **Governments** are considered as regulative institutions that can constrain and regularize behaviors and actions through its capacity to establish rules, to inspect and review conformity, and to manipulate consequences to reinforce behaviors. In other words, governments through **regulation** can create laws and regulations to force companies to behave in ways that are more ethical. Furthermore, governments can punish companies that deviate from respecting such norms.

Why is regulation necessary? Many argue that the recent economic crisis worldwide is the result of too much deregulation. The government is seen as an important antidote to markets that seemed to have promoted greed and unethical behaviors.[1] Markets may not always function as effectively as required and governments will need to intervene to influence the market forces in positive ways. Furthermore, company actions can also result in negative externalities such as pollution, which is then borne by consumers and societies. Governmental regulation can help prevent the impact of such negative externalities on other stakeholders.

An examination of the business ethics literature shows that the government can regulate companies in two ways. First, government regulation itself can create the conditions that make competition possible whereby companies can expect to be dealt with ethically. It seems feasible to assume that to encourage ethical behavior companies must first be presented with an environment that promotes ethics. For instance, the government can create rules and regulations to ensure that contracts are thoroughly enforced. In this case, government regulation pertains to making sure that companies can expect to be treated ethically by both the government and other entities. Second, the government can also create regulation to force companies to behave ethically or to engage in corporate social responsibility. We consider both aspects next.

The government has therefore a key role in creating an environment where companies can operate ethically. Consider the following Emerging Market Business Ethics Insight.

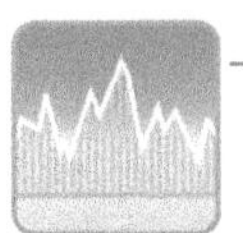

EMERGING MARKET BUSINESS ETHICS INSIGHT

Role of Governments in Different Emerging Markets

Samsung, the South Korean consumer electronics conglomerate, has been engulfed in a scandal over the last year. A major reason for this scandal is that the Korean government revealed that Samsung paid around $28 million to a fund linked to former President Park. It is alleged that the former president forced many South Korean conglomerates such as Samsung and Lotte to pay into funds that were then siphoned for personal use. In return for such payment, these companies avoided other headaches such as tax audits. To find more information, Samsung has now been the subject of at least three raids. Prosecutors continue to gather information on this case.

The above shows the role of the government in enforcing ethics. In another example, China views the media as an important tool for political control. Flow of information is constrained, as the Chinese Communist Party believes that such information should be controlled. Foreign companies operating in China have therefore had to consider the ethical dilemmas of operating in such an environment. Consider the case of Yahoo!. They entered the Chinese market in 1999 and, unlike other companies such as Google or Microsoft, they kept personal information of their members inside China. In doing so, they had to abide by the Chinese "Public Pledge on Self-Discipline for the Chinese Internet Industry." The pledge meant that Yahoo! basically agreed to have their data monitored. Furthermore, signing the pledge also means that Yahoo! needs to censor electronic communication if such communication could jeopardize state security.

Yahoo! came under intense criticism when it gave information about two Chinese citizens to the Chinese government. Both individuals were arrested, prosecuted, and sentenced to prison for e-mailing pro-democracy views from their accounts. Although Yahoo! has strict policies regarding privacy of its users, it had no choice but to divulge such information to the Chinese government.

Finally, consider the case of New Delhi, India's capital city. It has one of the highest pollution indices and has double the annual average of Beijing in terms of PM 2.5, a toxic fine dust. However, despite such pollution, the government has not been able to implement new policies to curb pollution. An important reason for such difficulties is that the local government does not have the same clout as in other cities. Most of the authority on policy matters in New Delhi comes from the national government. Additionally, different Indian states have disagreed on the source of the pollution. Some of the state officials have argued that the pollution comes from necessary agricultural fires in surrounding Indian states. However, one minister in the national government has claimed that such pollution is home produced while others have suggested that the large number of diesel engines on New Delhi's roads are to blame. Such disagreements have led to paralysis whereby no effective measures to curb pollution have yet been implemented.

Based on Dean, J. 2010. "Ethical conflicts for firms in China." *Wall Street Journal* online, January 13, A6; *The Economist.* 2017. "Pollution in India; Worse than Beijing." November 12, 38; *The Economist.* Samsung; Ponying up?" November 26, 60; Venezia, G. and Venezia, C.C. 2010. "Yahoo! And the Chinese dissidents: A case study of trust, values, and clashing cultures." *Journal of Business Case Studies*, 6, 2.

As the Emerging Market Business Ethics Insight shows, governments in emerging markets have significant but varying impact on the environment facing any organization. While free-flowing information and individual privacy are ethical ideals in most societies, the Chinese government sees such information flow as a threat to their stability. Multinationals operating in China thus have to consider whether they want to deal with such an environment. Similarly, in the case of Samsung, the government has shown that it has the ability to go after ethical transgressions and many of the companies are now paying the price for their behaviors. In contrast, the local and national governments in India have been unable to reach agreements on the causes of pollution and have been very limited in their ability to implement legislation to curb pollution.

What other aspects of the ethical environment should multinationals consider? The World Bank Doing Business project,[2] which studies business environments worldwide, provides some insights into ethical aspects of the business environment. As you saw in Chapter 7 on shareholders and corporate governance, the project was conceived to give an idea of the environment conducive to entrepreneurship in different societies. While the project considers nine areas, two of these are directly pertinent to government regulation promoting an ethical environment. We therefore focus on these two areas here.

The first aspect of government regulation pertaining to the creation of an ethical environment is the registration of property. **Registration of property** refers to the "full sequence of procedures necessary for a business to purchase a property from another business and transfer the title to the buyer's name."[3] The ability to have formal property rights is a key aspect determining a company's ability to do business ethically. Formal property ownership enables a company to use such assets as guarantees for loans and other financial funds to facilitate economic growth. Furthermore, formal property rights allow companies to rightfully own property. However, if the environment in a country only allows informal property ownership, companies will not easily be able to use such property as a guarantee to access more finance to experience further growth. In such societies, companies will not have the ability to grow and flourish as they should.

The World Bank notes that registration of property is especially critical for women starting their own businesses. In many developing countries, women are important sources of income for their families. However, if registration of property is very difficult, these women will often face insurmountable barriers in trying to access loans to start their businesses. In some economies, women often do not have the same rights as men with regards to mortgaging a property or even owning a property.

Given the above, a multinational should strive to operate in nations that make property registration possible. Exhibit 8.1 shows the averages for selected countries on three aspects of registration of property; namely, the number of procedures, the time it takes to register the property, and the cost of registration as a percentage of the value of the property. Multinationals can use such guides for location decisions. As Exhibit 8.1 shows, some of the emerging market countries such as Brazil, Kenya, Nigeria, and the Philippines have some of the highest number of procedures to register property. In contrast, countries such as the Netherlands, Denmark, and Australia show the lowest number of days it takes to register property.

Finally, a second aspect of the Doing Business project that sheds light on the ethicality of a business environment is **enforcement of contract**. If parties engage in contracts, they expect that the terms and conditions of the contract will be respected. Business transactions that take place between entities that do not fully know each other rely on the assumption that the parties will deliver on the agreed-upon aspects of contracts. Companies will thus less likely be able to engage in transaction with others if they do not feel that there are sufficient regulations to enforce contracts.

The World Bank project suggests that contract disputes have increased dramatically as a result of the economic crisis. Many large creditors such as utility companies have filed suits to try to recover money they are owed. Having an efficient system to ensure that such contract disputes are resolved is thus critical.

What contributes to adequate contract enforcement? The World Bank examines three indicators; namely, the time it takes to resolve a contract dispute and the cost of the dispute as a percentage of the claim. Exhibit 8.2 shows the averages for selected countries on these aspects.

Similar to other exhibits, the data shows that the richer societies in the OECD group tend to have a better ethical environment. On all three aspects, the OECD has, on average, the smallest indicator. Furthermore, African nations tend to show some of the highest levels on these indicators, reflecting the less ethical environment.

The above regulatory aspects deal with the creation and enforcement of an environment where a company is confident that it will be dealt with in an ethical manner by

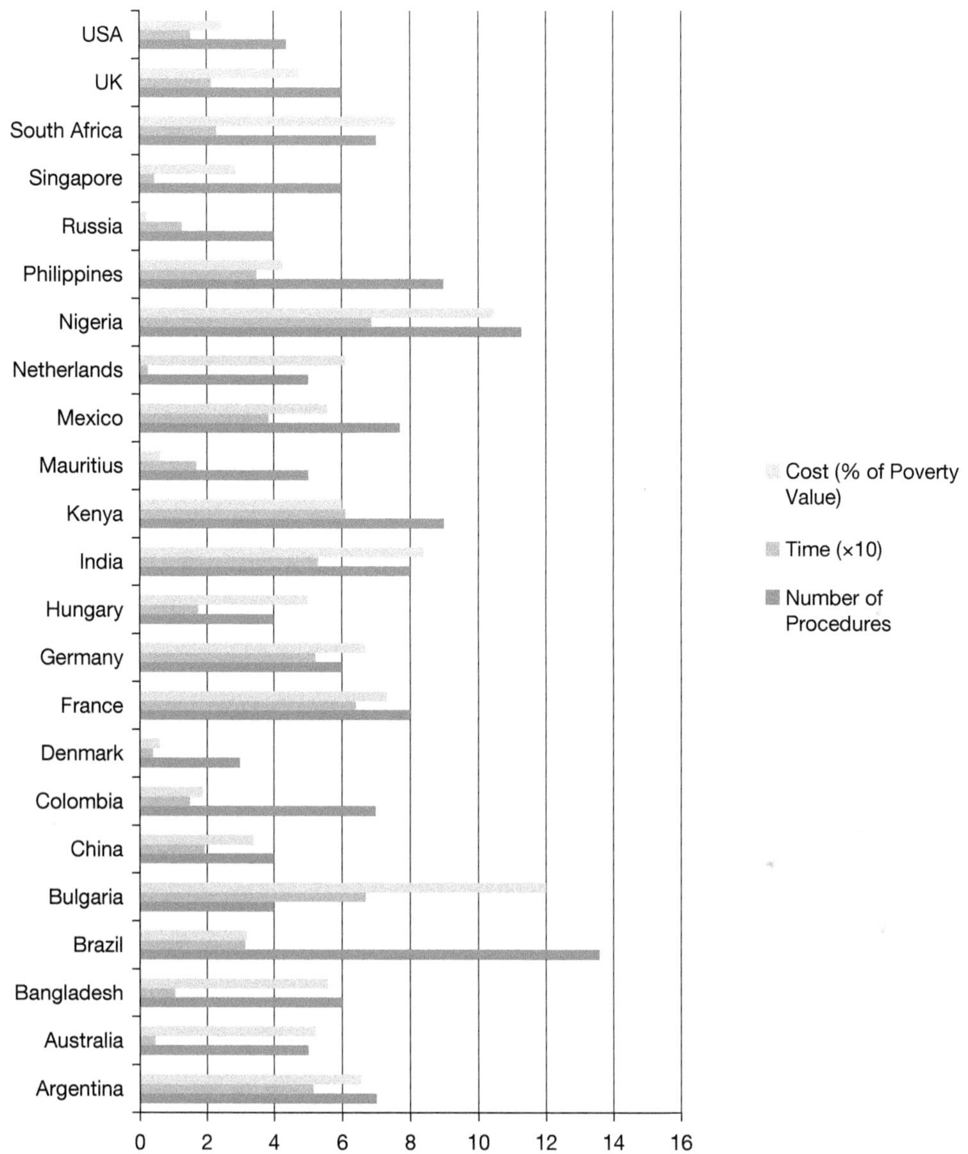

EXHIBIT 8.1—Property Registration around the World

both the government and other entities. However, government regulation can also take the form whereby they create rules and regulations to force companies to be ethical. For example, many of the recent U.S. legislations, such as the Sarbanes-Oxley Act and the Volcker Rule, were created to make it illegal for companies when they behave unethically.

Governments can regulate so that businesses behave in more ethical ways. Lawrence and Weber argue that there are two types of government regulation; namely, economic and social regulation.[4] Economic regulations are aimed at the modification of the free

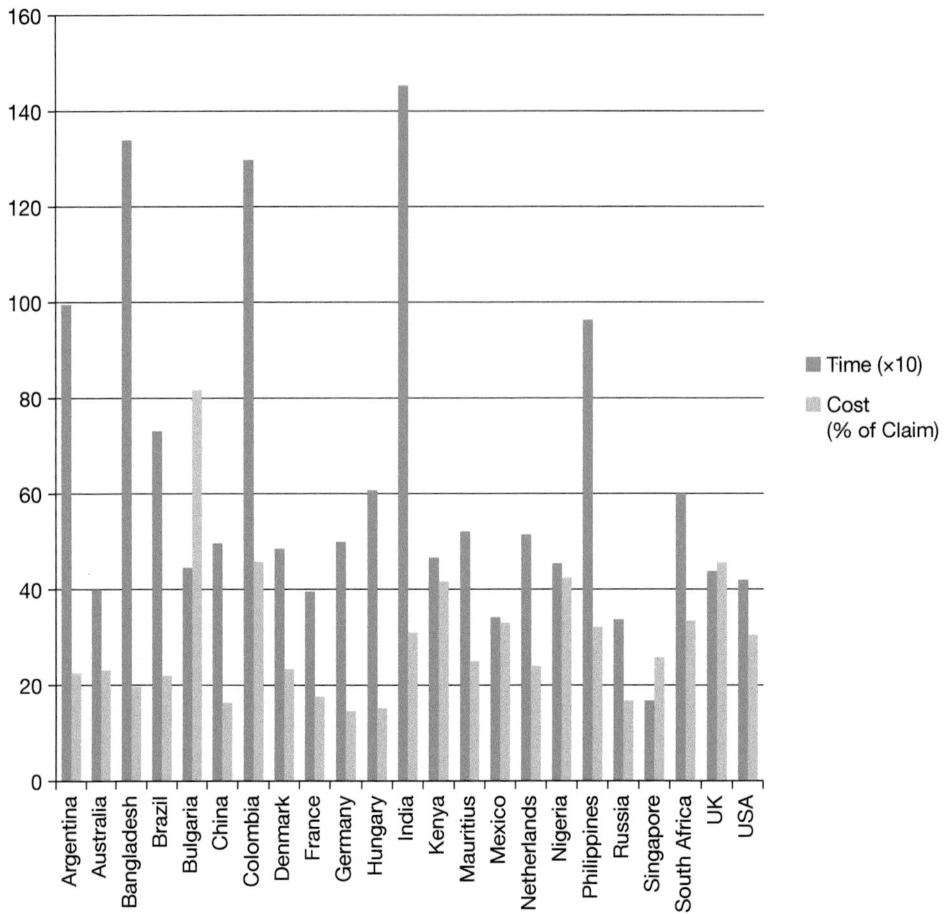

EXHIBIT 8.2—Regional Averages in Enforcing Contracts

market to counter some negative aspects of the market. The aim of such economic regulation is to tackle market failures that occur, such as when firms have monopolistic power or when some consequences of company actions are thought to be undesirable. For instance, if firms have monopolistic power, they can restrict output and increase prices. Similarly, sometimes firms' activities can result in negative consequences, such as air or water pollution. In both cases, the government can step in and impose regulation to correct such market failures.

Steiner and Steiner argue that most regulation in the U.S. was historically economic in nature.[5] For instance, the late 1800s and early 1900s saw the public asking for more regulation of big businesses in the U.S. Such demands resulted in legislations such as railroad regulations and anti-trust laws. Such new economic regulation in the U.S. continued well into the 1950s. The 1960s to the present saw a severe decline in economic regulations.

Although there was a considerable decline in economic regulation after the 1950s, a significant economic regulation was passed in 2002. The Sarbanes-Oxley Act (SOX)

SARBANES-OXLEY MAIN RULES
■ Chief Executive Officers and Chief Financial Officers need to certify financial reports
■ Financial statements should fairly represent financial conditions of company
■ Pro Forma financial statements cannot contain fraudulent statements or misleading information
■ Filing schedules should be done in a more timely fashion
■ Internal controls need to be audited and documented
■ Auditors are prohibited from providing non-audit consulting services to their customers
■ Off-balance-sheets items need to be properly disclosed
■ Board of directors need to include independent members
■ Companies should not destroy, alter, or fabricate evidence when investigated for abuse
■ Whistle-blowers should be protected from company retaliation

EXHIBIT 8.3—Sarbanes-Oxley Act Summary

was passed in 2002 as a result of the accounting scandals at companies such as Enron and WorldCom. The act was passed mostly to improve financial reporting to ensure that accounting practices were being rigorously followed. Such measures also aimed at restoring investor confidence in such reports. Among the many new conditions, SOX now requires that both CEOs and Chief Financial Officers certify financial reports to ensure honest and transparent reporting. Furthermore, SOX requires that internal controls are audited and documented. Exhibit 8.3 summarizes some of the main aspects of SOX.

A second form of regulation grew worldwide after the decline of economic regulation; namely, social regulation. Social regulations are aimed at improving the lives of individuals in society. As such, social regulations have social goals such as protection of consumers, providing employees with a safe and healthy work environment, and providing workers with equal opportunity at work. In contrast to economic regulations more focused on correcting problems associated with the proper functioning of the market, social regulation emphasizes the improvement of the quality of life of individuals as members of society, employees, consumers, etc. To give further insights on social regulation, Exhibit 8.4 summarizes some of the recent social regulation coming from the European Union.

Exhibit 8.4 shows the many social regulations that the European Union has implemented. Taken together, the government has significant clout in terms of forcing companies to abide by such rules and regulations. But it is important to note that governments can also influence without regulation. Consider the following Global Business Ethics Insight.

Consumers	• Consumers have the right to a safe product. A safe product is one that causes no harm when used the way it is supposed to be used. • Manufacturers should provide consumers with information so that they can assess the inherent threat of using a product. • Consumers should not be subject to misleading advertising. Advertising is misleading if it fails to provide a minimum standard of information to consumers prior to purchase. • Commercial practices such as pyramid schemes, bait advertising, or use of advertorial (advertising disguised as editorial) are prohibited.
Employees	• Employees cannot be discriminated on the basis of their disability, age, sexual orientation, religion, or beliefs. • Employers need to consult with authorities at the national level in case of mass layoffs. Reasons for the layoff, the length of the layoffs, the decision criteria for layoffs, and the compensations for the layoffs need to be presented. • Both men and women should be treated equally in all respects and specifically with regards to pay. • Employees have the right to a safe and healthy work environment.
Environment	• Member states should assess the level of pollution in their air. Measures need to be taken to ensure "Pure Air for Europe." • Member states agree to require car manufacturers to reduce carbon emissions progressively. For instance, 100% of cars in 2015 can only produce 130g of carbon dioxide per kilometer. • All member states will take every step necessary to measure noise levels across their boundaries. Steps need to be implemented to reduce or manage noise levels.
Human Rights	• All member states should enforce human rights based on six main principles, namely 1) dignity (the right to dignity and right to life), 2) freedoms (right to liberty and security, right to private life and family, right to safeguard of private data), 3) equality (equality before the laws, non-discrimination, right of the child), 4) solidarity (right of workers to engage in collective bargaining, fair and just working conditions, protections against unjustified firing), 5) citizens' right (right to vote, right to good administration, right to information), and 6) justice (right to fair trial, presumption of innocence, right not to be punished twice for the same offence).
The Information Society	• Members will strive to increase media literacy. Media literacy refers to the ability of citizens to access, understand, and critically assess media content. • Members should ensure that their citizens have equal access to computers, telephones, televisions, online administration, online shopping, call centers, self-service terminals, and automatic teller machines. • All member states should work towards the creation of a single market in creative content online. For instance, one of the aims is the creation of a single market for online music, films, and games.

EXHIBIT 8.4—European Union Social Regulation

GLOBAL BUSINESS ETHICS INSIGHT

Non-regulative Government Influence

Corporate social responsibility (CSR), which will be discussed in Chapter 13, suggests that companies have the duty to balance the interests of stakeholders while also keeping in mind the impact of their actions on the environment. The European Union started encouraging companies to take a proactive stance on CSR in 2001 when it published *Corporate Social Responsibility. A Business Contribution to Sustainable Development.* This report was the result of intense public consultation in the European Union and was written to provide some form of common grounds for CSR implementation in the European Union countries. Many companies located in the European Union then started implementing CSR programs. In fact a recent study showed that 90% of European companies on the *Fortune* Global 250 published sustainability reports. This suggests that the value placed on CSR by the European Union encouraged most companies to adopt such CSR practices.

Further evidence of this voluntary approach is evidenced by a more recent study. This study found that governmental non-regulatory guidelines and support of specific ethical activities resulted in more companies adopting such practices. For example, in a study of Danish companies overseas, voluntary guidelines advanced by the government resulted in less corruption. Voluntary initiatives in the UK focused on individuals with disabilities were also adopted by many multinationals. In Australia, the government is supporting an industry-led plan to promote a national e-waste program. Additionally, governments can also promote adherence to some regulations by providing regulatory reliefs. For instance, multinationals in Europe are adopting the voluntary European Eco-Management Audit Scheme knowing that they can get access to other benefits such as subsidies for green technology, preferential treatment with permits etc.

Based on Dentchev, N.A., van Balen, M. and Haezendonck, E. 2015. "On voluntarism and the role of governments in CSR: Towards a contingency approach," *Business Ethics: A European Review*, 24, 2, 378–397; Liederkerke, L.V. and Dubbink, W. 2008. "Twenty years of European business ethics—past developments and future concerns." *Journal of Business Ethics*, 82, 273–280.

But do companies always respond to such regulation? In the next section, we examine company reactions to regulations.

GOVERNMENT REGULATION AND COMPANY POLITICAL ACTIVITY

When government regulations are enacted, companies have two main choices. They can either abide by the new regulations or they can find ways to make the regulation less effective or delay the implementation of the new rules. If the company accepts the new regulation, they are effectively behaving legitimately to avoid prosecution. Institutional theory argues that the government is a key constituent in modern society forcing companies to adopt government mandate as a way to seek legitimacy.[6] In this respect, legitimacy refers to conduct of behavior in a manner that is consistent with widely held values and norms.

Why do companies seek legitimacy by adopting government mandates? From a strategic management perspective, legitimacy is critical. First, such behaviors reduce the need for managers to decide what is appropriate. As government regulations are adopted by more companies, they become institutionalized and taken for granted. Such norms reduce the need for managers to engage in complex decision-making processes. Second and most importantly, legitimacy shows that a company is abiding by governmental rules and regulations. This provides continued support from key stakeholders while also providing access to valued resources from key constituents. Legitimacy thus facilitates company survival. However, there are clearly limits to legitimacy. In some cases, companies may actively find ways to either change regulations or delay the implementation of new regulation. Next we look at corporate public activity.

Corporate public activity (CPA) refers to the attempt by a company to influence or manage the political entities and the government.[7] CPA includes non market activities such as lobbying, campaign contributions, operation of a government relations office, commenting on proposed regulation and contributions to industry trade groups.[8] The aim of such activities is to influence policymakers and regulators. Consider the following Global Business Ethics Insight.

GLOBAL BUSINESS ETHICS INSIGHT

Fiji and CPA of Food Industry

Fiji is an island country in the South Pacific region. It is considered one of the most economically developed economies in the Pacific because of the abundance of its natural resources and a strong tourism sector. Unfortunately, similar to many other high-income countries, Fiji's high mortality rate is largely due to non-communicable diseases linked to poor diets and high obesity rates. An important factor contributing to such diets is the increased availability of unhealthy processed food products. Given that this situation is now considered a public crisis, the Fijian government has been examining ways to implement public policy to fight such obesity. However, a recent study shows that the Fijian food industry is engaging in significant CPA to prevent any potential regulation. Interviews with key stakeholders and examination of public documents show some of the ways the food companies are using CPA.

The study found that the food industry relies on several key strategies to try to influence public policy in its favor. First, the companies rely on an informational and messaging strategy using several approaches such as lobbying where public representatives are contacted directly and the views of the industry position on issues are made known. The food industry also regularly promotes deregulation and reminds public representatives of the economic importance of the industry and the industry's need to feed families. An important component of the messaging of the industry with regards to economic importance has been to remind the government of the contribution to the tax base and the possibility of the companies leaving the country in the face of regulation. Additionally, the industry has also shaped the discussion around public health policy by partnering with the government to promote the view that parents are ultimately responsible for diets and that physical activity should be encouraged. Additionally, some companies also provide educational materials to schools and actively promote their products as being healthy. Such strategies have aimed at shifting the blame for the crisis.

A second important CPA activity was for the industry to build relationships with key stakeholders. For instance, many companies are involved in the local communities through events and other programs (e.g., the Coca-Cola Games, which is an annual secondary school athletics competition or Chow Games, a primary school competition held by FMF foods, a local company). Such events enable the companies to develop stronger relationships with their customers. Furthermore, the industry also has strong relationships with the media. Journalists are routinely invited to events held by the industry. Through such relationships, the industry gets portrayed positively. It is also important to note that one of the major Fijian newspapers is owned by C.J. Patel, also a player in the food industry. Finally, the industry has also partnered with the government to help fight non communicable diseases linked to obesity. Such partnerships have resulted in initiatives such as the Free Milk program and others to promote a healthier diet.

Based on Mialon, M., Swinburn, B., Wate, J., Tukana, I. and Sacks, G. 2016. "Analysis of the corporate political activity of major food industry actors in Fiji." *Globalization and Health*, 12, 18, 1–14.

As you can see from the above Global Business Ethics Insight, companies have different strategies to engage in CPA through nonmarket actions. However, companies can also engage through CPA using market actions.[9] Activities such as mergers and acquisitions as well as the relocation of production are market examples of what companies can do to sway policies in their favor. Many companies have threatened to move production elsewhere to get better tax benefits.

Companies thus engage in CPA for many reasons. First, they engage in CPA to influence legislation pertaining to their operations. For instance, lobbying is often seen as influencing the government to take into account company private interests while making public interest regulation.[10] As you saw earlier, the Fijian food industry has lobbied to communicate the economic importance of the industry.

Second, companies also engage in CPA to get access to governmental resources. Consider, for instance, that in Chapter 7 on corporate governance we considered the role of the government in state-owned companies. In such cases, the company can often derive significant funds from the government. Furthermore, in many countries, governments are significant business actors providing the opportunity to companies to make sales. The decision to award business to companies is usually made by specific government officials.[11] Thus, CPA may be a direct way to influence these government officials.

A final reason why companies engage in CPA is to positively affect its performance. Ties with the government provide a firm with the ability to ward off future negative attention while also providing access to government resources. However, research has shown mixed results in that respect. A recent review does provide support for a positive link with performance. In a large-scale compilation of 78 studies, Lux et al. show that CPA indeed leads to higher firm performance.[12] Okhmatovskiy's study provides a more refined look at the relationship between government ties and firm performance.[13] Rather than merely looking at the direct ties with the government, Okhmatovskiy studied around 600 Russian banks and found that indirect connect with the government through ties with state-owned businesses resulted in higher firm performance. However, in this sample, direct ties with the government do not help performance. Finally, more recently, research has examined 93 studies and finds that CPA has a weak effect on corporate performance.[14] Furthermore, the study showed that CPA has also very weak effects on influencing public policy.

In this section, you learned about the importance of the government as a secondary stakeholder. In the face of the recent economic crises, many have argued that the government should play an even bigger role in the future. This suggests that companies will have to contend with more expanded government influence in the future in devising their strategies. Furthermore, many of the emerging markets also have dominant governments that have significant influence on the business environment. As Google have found, it became difficult for them to operate freely once they decided to not abide by Chinese rules and regulations governing the internet. Astute companies intent on taking advantage of such emerging markets will face a definite dilemma as they decide between abandoning such markets or entering these markets and violating their own mission. This also suggests that governments will remain critical in the future.

THE MEDIA

The **media**, referring to the many avenues of information such as newspapers, television, and the internet, is also a powerful secondary stakeholder. Most people rely on the media to get information about companies and it is powerful because of such reach and prominence.[15] Furthermore, Donlon goes as far as claiming that the media has often created "headline-grabbing" cases that have brought down companies.[16] How companies and industries are perceived by the public thus becomes an important aspect of how these companies are viewed. In this section, we therefore consider media influence. We also note that internet media such as social media is also a powerful media form. However, we will cover internet and social media ethics in Chapter 9.

How powerful is the media? Consider the Strategic Business Ethics Insight below.

STRATEGIC BUSINESS ETHICS INSIGHT

Power of the Media

The U.S. pharmaceutical industry is undoubtedly a very vital industry. It has significant economic impact for the U.S. economy. Furthermore, it has significant impact on the well-being and health of people at all levels. The industry continues to invest in research and development to develop new drugs to address new ailments to help people to live longer, healthier, and more productive lives. However, despite this importance, the pharmaceutical industry continues to be viewed very negatively in the U.S. An analysis of media portrayal of the industry in newspapers provides evidence of such a claim. In an interesting study of the top five U.S. newspapers, the authors of the study examined a number of attributes of the portrayal of the industry in these newspapers. For example, they examined the nature of both headlines and the content of the articles about the industry. The authors classified the headline as negative, positive, or neutral toward the industry. They also considered whether the article's content took a positive, negative, or neutral position toward the industry.

Results of the study showed that 2004 and 2005 headlines and articles viewed the industry overwhelmingly as either negative or neutral. In 2004, only 18.1% of headlines were positive while only 9.2% of headlines were considered positive in 2005. As far as the articles are concerned, only 20% of articles were positive in 2004 and only 19.2% of articles were positive in 2005. These results clearly supported the industry's perception that they are unfairly portrayed negatively.

Is the portrayal of the industry really negative? The industry has certainly engaged in many unethical practices such as pricing issues, gift-giving, sales, and marketing practices. In the U.S., the industry has been criticized for high prices given the high costs of drugs. However, the industry also engages in positive actions but such actions do not get much press coverage. Consider that Merck's drug safety issues related to Vioxx received much more press coverage than its efforts to provide HIV treatment for patients in sub-Saharan Africa.

Based on *The Economist*. 2017. "The pharma business; A better pill from China." March 18, 68; Sillup, P.G. 2008. "Ethical issues in the pharmaceutical industry: An analysis of U.S. newspapers." *International Journal of Pharmaceutical and Healthcare Marketing*, 2, 3.

As the Strategic Business Ethics Insight shows, the media can have a powerful impact on how companies and industries are perceived. This can have long-term effects on the survival of the industry. No one disputes the notion that the pharmaceutical industry has engaged in unethical behaviors. However, the study does put in question whether the industry has received fair coverage of issues.

Recent research in the political arena has some implications for how businesses are portrayed.[17] For instance, in election coverage, it is found that the media is more likely to focus on campaign controversies. Rather than provide a balanced view of candidates, the media is more likely to create or emphasize controversial issues in such campaigns. Why this focus on controversy? Ridout and Smith argue that commercial pressures often compel the media to focus on the sensational rather than the routine. To attract large audiences to allow media companies to get more advertising funds, the media is more likely to focus on the sensation to attract attention. This is also true for businesses whereby the media is more likely to focus on a sensational story about the unethical behaviors of executives at a specific company rather than the charitable work of another company.

Understanding how the media influences the public is thus very critical. Andina-Diaz argues that the "media hold great power, as they transmit information to the public and are free to highlight certain news items and ignore others, setting the agenda of public life and creating consensus or disagreement on certain issues."[18] While the influence of the media has been the subject of a large body of literature, we focus only on those that are relevant to business ethics. In that context, Barber and Axinn (2004) provide some understanding of how the media can influence the public about businesses.[19] First, the media can affect the public's attitudes and behaviors simply by increasing knowledge about business ethics issues. Through simple reporting of organizational wrongdoing to the public, the media can become the main publicizer of ethical transgressions.[20] However, as Andina-Diaz suggests, such information may sometimes reinforce people's already existing attitudes.[21] For example, if the public believes that businesses are unethical, they may be receptive to new information to confirm such pre-existing attitudes. Second, the media can also influence the public as the public identifies with the television or radio personalities communicating the message. For instance, people may be more likely to change their attitudes regarding global warming if such messages are coming from a known celebrity dedicated to environmental awareness. Third, the media can also shape discussions and public opinion through framing. Consider the following Business Ethics Brief.

Clearly the media affect how the public perceives businesses or specific companies. The way newspapers framed the diesel scandal can influence public perception about who is responsible for the scandal. However, the mechanisms discussed mostly show direct effects of the media. The literature on the media also shows that indirect influences are also possible. One of the most prominent theories explaining indirect effects of the media is known as the "third-person" effect.[22] The third-person effect basically implies that people exposed to media generally think that such messages have much greater influence on others than themselves. However, such messages are likely to affect the person receiving the message. For example, it has been shown that

BUSINESS ETHICS BRIEF

The Volkswagen Diesel Scandal and Framing in the Media

The media has a strong role to play in revealing organizational wrongdoing. As mentioned earlier, the media can play a strong role revealing unethical corporate behaviors. However, how stories are framed plays a big role in terms of how others perceive stories. Such framing can be very powerful as it can change the public's opinion on organizational wrongdoing. Consider the case of Volkswagen and the diesel scandal. In September 2015, the company was accused of tampering with engine controls in its diesel engines to emit lower nitrogen oxide levels. Investigations revealed that Volkswagen was manipulating laboratory tests to show levels of pollution 40 times lower than in the real world.

The framing of the issue, or the way the media anchors an example of wrongdoing, has an important influence on how any case of wrongdoing can be perceived. In an interesting study of four major newspapers in Germany, framing reveals how the media help project the scandal. All four major newspapers revealed that Volkswagen was indeed responsible for manipulating the software for laboratory testing purposes. However, the responsibility for the scandal was different for different newspapers. For instance, one newspaper blamed the CEO and high-level executives as being the culprits. As high-level employees, they should be responsible for such wrongdoing despite not being directly implicated. Another newspaper blamed the industry arguing that other competitors were also likely involved in similar practices. Furthermore, another newspaper blamed a few rogue employees. However, in that case, the newspaper suggested that the wrongdoing of a few employees should not discount the good work done by the 600,000 other employees of Volkswagen. In this case, the blame is not on Volkswagen but rather on a few rebel employees.

Based on Clemente, M. and Gabbioneta, C. 2017. "How does the media frame corporate scandals? The case of German newspapers and the Volkwagen diesel scandal. *Journal of Management Inquiry*, 26, 3, 287–302.

teenagers are more likely to smoke when they felt that pro-smoking media messages influenced their peers. Similarly, doctors were less likely to prescribe direct-to-consumer drugs when they perceived that direct-to-consumer drug advertising adversely affects their clients. When applied to business ethics, the third-person effects occurs when, for instance, someone watches the news and learns about a company that deceived a customer and that person decides not to patronize the company for fear that the company will also deceive him/her. This could be clearly the case here for the Volkswagen scandal. Someone could read the newspaper and attribute blame to Volkswagen sharing such news with others thereby influencing others.

Media Analysis and Business Ethics

The preceding paragraphs show that the media can be very powerful. Although the media may sometimes unfairly portray businesses, it is still an important source of information for most people. While research shows that companies often survive public revelations of ethical wrongdoing, experts argue that it is important to carefully monitor the media.[23] A company's reputation is an extremely important asset. Over time, media coverage often defines what people believe about companies.[24] If such beliefs project a bad company reputation and unethical activities, such effects can have very adverse effects on the company. Furthermore, the media provides the information that the public uses to decide whether they can trust a company.[25] Trust is also a critical aspect of a company's survival. In fact, the earlier discussed example of Volkswagen showed that it suffered significant loss of trust because of the media portrayal of the scandal.[26]

Despite the importance of understanding the media, fairly recent research suggests that not all companies routinely conduct media analysis. Consider Exhibit 8.5. As it shows, only 27% of companies in this sample conduct any form of formal media analysis. However, such **media analysis** when companies "routinely scan the media to discover what is being said about them" is extremely critical.[27] Media analysis can help companies assess the way the company is being portrayed in the media and address inconsistencies. Media analysis can also help a company understand what its competitors are doing. From a strategic management standpoint, media analysis of competitors can become an important source of competitive intelligence.[28]

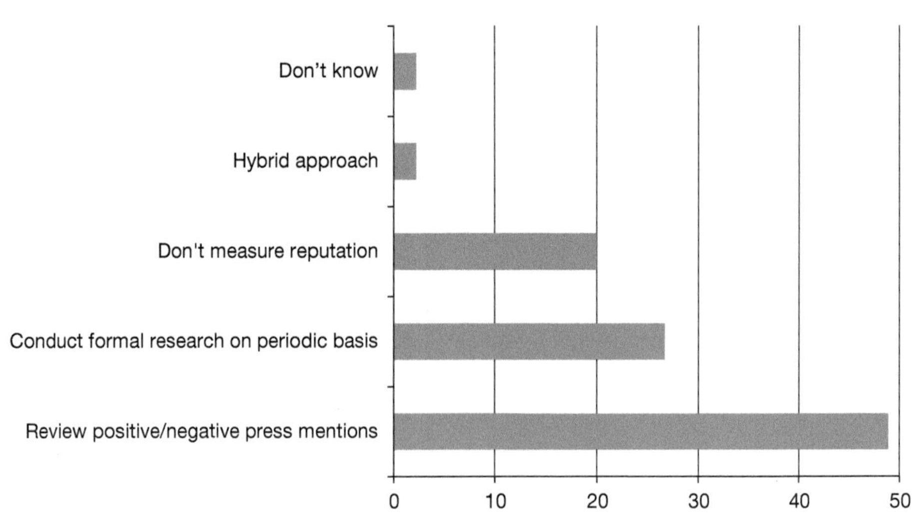

EXHIBIT 8.5—Percentage of Companies Conducting Media Analysis

Media analysis is typically done by third-party firms specializing in scouring the media for company coverage. As we will see later in Chapter 9, companies also now spend significant resources to understand what is being said about them on social media such as Facebook and Twitter. Furthermore, the high speed of information flow on social networks and other forms of social media suggests that companies need to also respond quickly to damaging information.

According to Dowling and Weeks, media analysis typically takes place in three forms.[29] First, media analysis can be of the **salience and sentiment analysis** form. Salience is measured by the number of times a company is mentioned in selected outlets. This can also take a more refined form if the prestige of the media is also taken into consideration. Sentiment analysis refers to whether the company is being portrayed in a positive, neutral, or negative way. Such salience and sentiment analysis can thus provide some idea of how the company is generally viewed. Tagging such analysis with events in the company can also reveal the impact of such events on the media.

Consider a recent study of small nanotechnology firms in the U.S. The media mention of 22 small nanotechnology firms were analyzed.[30] Results of that study found that small nanotechnology firms are often held in high esteem by the media. The study found that these companies were often portrayed as being innovators, strong leaders and as showing strong long-term potential. Such results are very beneficial for such companies as they strive for increased funding and growth. But does such positive media salience and sentiment matter? Consider the following Strategic Business Ethics Insight.

STRATEGIC BUSINESS ETHICS INSIGHT

Media Salience and Organizational Outcomes

Does media mention affect companies? Several recent studies shed some light on the issue and provides evidence that media salience does have some significant impact on firm performance as well as media reputation. In an interesting study of firms listed on the Taiwan Stock Exchange, researchers examined how media coverage affects media reputation. Media reputation refers to the degree to which the public recognizes and pays attention to any company. The media have a significant role in alerting the public to the existence of a company while also endorsing a firm's public relations efforts. The researchers found that media coverage and news sentiment are indeed related to a company's media reputation. Additionally, companies that had stronger media attention tended to do better than those that had less attention. Furthermore, previous media reputation also resulted in stronger performance.

A second study of firms in the UK examined how a firm's media reputation is linked to the firm's willingness to offer credit to its customers. The authors argue that companies will often offer credit to customers as a way to combat lack of knowledge of product quality before purchase. If customers are offered credit, they are more likely to be willing to buy the product and the credit becomes some form of insurance against product malfunctioning. The study found that the stronger a firm's media reputation, the less likely it is to offer trade credit to its customers. Firms that have more positive mentions in the media are less likely to need to provide guarantees to their customers about the quality of their products. As such, given the cost of trade credit to any company, such results also shows that media reputation from positive mentions in the media can be economically beneficial.

Based on Van den Bogaerd, M. and Aerts, W. 2014. "Media reputation of a firm and extent of trade credit supply." *Corporate Reputation Review,* 17, 28–45; Wei, Y., Hsu, Y. Lu, Y. and Huang, C. 2016. "The impact of media reputation on firm performance and market returns." *Journal of Management and Business Research,* 33, 4, 587–616.

As the above shows, media mention and the consequent media reputation matters to companies. However, a second form of media analysis is the **theme and contradiction analysis**. In such cases, the media can be analyzed to determine whether ongoing media coverage is portraying the company under some specific theme. For instance, Dowling and Weeks argue that the recent themes behind media coverage of the computer giant Apple has been decreasing customer satisfaction as the company keeps growing and seems less responsive to customer needs.[31] Uncovering this theme has enabled Apple to devise a concerted public relations strategy to address problematic issues. Additionally, contradiction analysis refers to the comparison of media portrayal of issues with what the company is itself saying. For example, the banking industry is currently fighting contradictions in that, while they say they are responding to foreclosures by being more careful about which homes are being foreclosed, media coverage seems to show recklessness with regards to foreclosure decisions.

Finally, media analysis can also take form of **problem and solution analysis**. Specifically, the above two forms of analysis can provide a company with many aspects of its media portrayal such as what is being said, whether the information is being portrayed positively or negatively, what themes are being reported, and how the company compares to rivals. This information can then be used to address issues that are seen as problems. According to Dowling and Weeks, from a strategic management standpoint, such media analysis should encourage companies to do the following:[32]

- *Reinforcing strong company messages*. A company should link its strengths to ongoing messages in the media. Consider how the U.S. company GE has shifted the company theme from being profit motivated to being a green company with the consistent "eco-imagination" advertising theme. Such consistency helps build new themes for companies.
- *Addressing negative information*. If a company is being portrayed in an unfairly negative way, the reasons for such portrayal should first be analyzed. It is possible that there are real problems behind such portrayals. A company should then address these issues and slowly communicate the new information to the media. For example, in

the case of Volkswagen discussed earlier, the CEO quickly took responsibility for the crisis and discussed the ensuing loss of trust.[33] This is in contrast to other companies such as Toyota that initially denied the braking scandal.

- *Appreciating mixed messages*. A company should carefully analyze why it is being portrayed in both negative and positive messages. Careful analysis of the negatives may sometimes reveal important ethical areas that need to be addressed. It is therefore important for companies to address such contradictions.
- *Understanding missing messages*. A company also needs to consider whether some core company message is missing when conducting a theme analysis. For instance, if a company has embarked recently on a new environmental mission and finds that this has not been covered in the media, a more concerted effort is needed to get this message out. Similarly, if new ethical initiatives are not covered in much depth, it is important for a company to address such gaps.

The above discusses some of the more obvious steps a company can take after a media analysis. It is important that the right messages be consistently communicated to the media. Such consistency in communication is important to project the required ethical image. Furthermore, much of this can take place in a concerted public relations campaign. We discuss public relations later in the chapter.

NON-GOVERNMENTAL ORGANIZATIONS

The final secondary but influential stakeholders we consider in this chapter are **non-governmental organizations** (or NGOs). As the power of multinationals and companies have grown worldwide, NGOs have emerged as important counterbalances to such power.[34] For example, as we saw with the Preview Business Ethics Insight at the beginning of this chapter, many NGOs kept strong pressure on Nike to address labor and other human rights. Without such consistent and strong NGO attention, Nike would probably not have responded quickly to the labor abuses. NGOs such as the Fair Labor Association and the Social Accountability International have all emerged as organizations dedicated to fighting sweatshop conditions for workers.[35]

"NGOs" is an umbrella term that includes "special interest groups, activist groups, social movement organizations, charities, religious groups, protest groups, and other non-profit groups"[36] organized around and committed to specific shared beliefs or principles. Exhibit 8.6 shows some of the more popular NGOs and the causes they believe in.

As Exhibit 8.6 shows, NGOs are organized around issues such as child labor, sweatshops, human rights, sustainable development, oil pollution, fair trade, and attention to future generations.[37] In such cases, NGOs are known as "social purpose" NGOs that are typically confronting organizations to tackle these issues.[38] Such NGOs are also known as "non-membership" organizations, whereby the interests of the members are represented by other individuals who contribute time and money. In contrast, there are NGOs that are known as "membership NGOs" that represent the interests of their members. Such NGOs are trade associations, industry groups, and

Organization	Description and Causes
Amnesty International	Founded in 1961, it is an organization with around 3 million members from around 150 countries Works to end abuses of human rights and protect human rights according to Universal Declaration of Human Rights See www.amnesty.org for more detail
Conservation International	Founded in 1987 with around 900 employees in more than 30 offices globally Uses a strong foundation in science to influence global development and to demonstrate that inherently caring for and valuing nature is critical to humankind See www.conservation.org for more detail
Fair Labor Association	Founded in 1999, the Fair Labor Association is a collaborative effort of socially responsible companies, universities, and civic society organizations Dedicated to ending sweatshop conditions and improving workers' rights and working conditions worldwide See www.fairlabor.org for more detail
Greenpeace International	Founded in 1971 and now has offices in more than 30 countries with funding coming from around 2.8 million members worldwide Main mission is to campaign and fight for the earth by addressing threat of global warming, destruction of ancient forests, deterioration of oceans, and threat of nuclear disaster See www.greenpeace.org for more detail
Oxfam International	Founded in 1995 by a group of independent NGOs and is now a confederation of 14 organizations working in 99 countries Works with over 3,000 local organizations to work with people living in poverty to exercise their human rights and assert their dignity as human beings. Main mission is to find solutions for poverty and injustice worldwide See www.oxfam.org for more detail
Transparency International	Founded in 1993 and is a global network of more than 90 locally established chapters Dedicated to fighting corruption by bringing awareness of corruption, reducing apathy and tolerance of corruption, and implementing actions to end corruption globally See www.transparency.org for more detail
Social Accountability International	Founded in 1997 and is a global NGO dedicated to advancing human rights in workplaces Established SA 8000 standard that measures performance in 8 social areas including child labor, health and safety of employees, working hours, renumeration, discrimination etc. See www.sa-intl.org/ for more detail

EXHIBIT 8.6—Popular NGOs and their Causes

STRATEGIC BUSINESS ETHICS INSIGHT

NGOs and Influence

NGOs have had a major influence on how multinationals have operated in the last few decades. Consider, for instance, that many experts agree that the push for corporate social responsibility (CSR) has been mainly due to the strong and consistent pressures from NGOs. For example, in a study of the progression and adoption of CSR in Spain, Arenas et al. argue clearly that although NGOs are sometimes controversial, they played a big role in forcing Spanish companies to adopt CSR policies.[39] Furthermore, Sobczak and Martins illustrate the critical role of NGOs in CSR discourses in countries such as France and Brazil.[40] Such critical roles of NGOs in CSR are not surprising given the important role they played in keeping climate change prominent in discussions. Carpenter shows how the various climate conferences started seeing more and more NGOs with specific goals in mind.[41] As worldwide negotiations for the Kyoto Protocol continued, such negotiations had to increasingly contend with more powerful NGOs. Additionally, although the Fair Labor Association and Social Accountability International may not have the desired effects on working conditions, they have still focused attention on such issues.

Another area where NGOs have had lots of influence is through NGOs geared towards microfinance to the "bottom of the pyramid" customers. Microfinance institutions are NGOs and banks that provide loans to the poorest in order to help these individuals get out of poverty. Dr. Mohammad Yunus is credited with starting the first microfinance institution when he founded Grameen Bank in Bangladesh. He discovered that the traditional banks were ignoring the poorest but that small loans to these groups could help them become entrepreneurs and help them escape poverty. This has resulted in thousands of small NGOs worldwide with the aim to help people get out of poverty. A recent study also suggests that the microfinance institutions can also help societies develop more ethical contexts.

Based on Chakrabarty, S. and Bass, A.E. 2014. "Institutionalizing ethics in institutional voids: Building positive ethical strength to serve women microfinance borrowers in negative contexts." *Journal of Business Ethics*, 119, 529–542; Arenas, D., Lozano, J.M. and Albareda, L. 2009. "The role of NGOs in CSR: Mutual perceptions among stakeholders." *Journal of Business Ethics*, 88, 175–197; Sethi, S.P. and Rovenpor, J.L. 2016. "The role of NGOs in ameliorating sweatshop-like conditions in the global supply chain: The case of Fair Labor Association (FLA), and Social Accountability International (SAI)." *Business and Society Review*, 121, 1, 5–36; Sobczak, A. and Martins, L.C. 2010. "The impact and interplay of national and global CSR discourses: Insights from France and Brazil." *Corporate Governance*, 10, 4, 445–455.

labor unions. It is also important to note that the size and structure of NGOs can vary greatly. Some NGOs are smaller, informal, but very dynamic grassroot type organizations. Other NGOs can have very formal structures and be larger and more mature organizations.

How influential are NGOs on companies and business ethics? Consider the Strategic Business Ethics Insight on the previous page.

It provides some insights of the influence of NGOs on the business ethics environment. However, recent research shows that NGOs can have impact on specific companies. In a longitudinal study, Skippari and Pajunen show how the Finnish multinational Metsä-Botnia was unable to make foreign direct investments in Uruguay because they ignored the demands of NGOs.[42] Botnia wanted to make a pulp mill investment in Uruguay. However, although their assessment showed that the mill would not have had much environmental impact and would contribute to the economy, activist groups soon started opposing the mill. People from regions affected by the mill formed NGOs. At the national level, activist groups also started raising concerns about the groups. Because it strongly believed in its assessments, Botnia proceeded with the mill project. However, this resulted in more conflicts with the NGOs. At some point, the conflicts were so out of hand that it made reconciliation impossible. Botnia later agreed that they should have listened to the NGOs' demands.

Similar to other stakeholders, NGOs also need to be appropriately managed. However, to understand how NGOs needs and demands can be satisfied, it is important to understand the various strategies they use to influence companies. We examine these issues next.

NGO Strategies

While there seem to be wide variations in terms of what NGOs can do, most experts agree that NGOs' strategies can range on a continuum from **active cooperation** and engagement to confrontation with threats and other adversarial behaviors. NGOs that cooperate typically assume that the multinational that they are working with will adopt some form of voluntary code of conduct.[43] In a study of Spanish firms and their interactions with NGOs, Valor and Merino provide evidence of cooperative strategies used by NGOs.[44] Their findings show that in the Spanish environment both companies and NGOs are actively seeking each other to establish partnerships. In fact, while there is evidence that many companies will seek NGOs to partner with, the findings also show that NGOs are equally likely to seek firms to work with. In seeking such companies, an NGO may identify key areas that a company must attend to. Such cooperation and engagement often results in a win–win relationship for both companies and NGOs.

However, NGOs can also adopt a **confrontational strategy**. In such cases, the NGOs assume that the offending multinationals are less likely to make changes to improve the cause they believe in. They therefore believe that being confrontational will likely affect the financial interests of the offending multinational and bring changes. In pursuing a confrontational strategy, NGOs may rely on symbolic damage strategies such as negative publicity or material damage strategies such as boycotts. In extreme cases, NGOs may also resort to vandalism and other property destruction strategies.

The above discusses some of the more direct ways that NGOs can interact with companies. However, Fassin argues that NGOs can also influence companies indirectly.[45] In such cases, NGOs can try to influence the company by targeting other stakeholders of the company and the media. Specifically, NGOs can indirectly influence the company by operating at three levels. First, NGOs can target primary stakeholders such as customers and employees. For example, consumers may be asked to boycott a specific company because of unethical practices. Second, NGOs can indirectly target companies by shaping public opinion. In such cases, the media can be used to change public opinion about a company. Letter-writing campaigns, denunciation campaigns, and other moral stigmatization tactics are the likely means. Consider the following Emerging Market Business Ethics Insight.

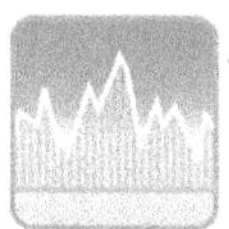

EMERGING MARKET BUSINESS ETHICS INSIGHT

NGOs, the Media, and Workplaces Practices in Bangladesh

NGOs use a variety of means to influence companies. An interesting study of local and international NGOs in Bangladesh shows some of the ways that NGOs can use indirect means to influence multinationals. In this study, the researchers first interviewed senior officials from these NGOs on their objectives. Overwhelmingly, the authors found that these NGOs "stated that they particularly focus on influencing the workplace policies of multinational clothing and retail companies sourcing products from suppliers in developing countries." Specifically, these NGOs were all toiling to create awareness surrounding work conditions as well as improving the working conditions of workers in Bangladesh's factories.

The study also interviewed the NGOs' senior officials about what they considered the most effective strategy in achieving their aims. Most individuals interviewed argued that they saw the media as the most important ally that allowed them to achieve their goals. The interviewees agreed that the media had the power to influence the global community and consumers by making them aware of the plight of workers in the industry. For example, after the fire accident in the Bangladeshi city of Dhaka, thousands of workers demonstrated to demand punishment for the suppliers as well as the multinationals sourcing from such suppliers. Coverage of these demonstrations by CNN and the BBC revealed the true conditions facing workers, which is now leading to changes. As such, multinational managers have no choice but to respond to these accusations as they don't want the media attention to influence customer perception negatively.

Based on Deegan, C. and Islam, M.A. 2014. "An exploration of NGO and media efforts to influence workplace practices and associated accountability within global supply chains." *British Accounting Review*, 46, 397–415.

The above clearly shows how NGOs can effectively influence companies through the media. However, a third and final method NGOs can influence companies indirectly by targeting regulators and lawmakers. Lobbying, discussed earlier, is a typical way that NGOs can use to encourage regulators to pass new laws and regulations to make specific company actions illegal.

Although NGOs play an important role to counterbalance company actions on society, it is important to note that they may not always be effective and may sometimes engage in questionable practices. In a study of various cases of NGO practices, Fassin and others[46] have found evidence of the following questionable practices:

- *Distorted communication*. In some cases, NGOs may rely on unchecked information or distort information to make their point. If the media publicizes such information, it may sometimes be more difficult to correct errors.
- *Arbitrary attacks*. Because of their size and clout, multinationals may sometimes be arbitrarily targeted for attack campaigns. Consider that, for instance, the oil company Total was attacked by environmentalists when there was an oil disaster in Brittany in 1999. Although the responsibility for the disaster was largely attributed to the transport companies, Total was blamed for a lack of judgment in choosing companies to transport their products.
- *Conflicts of interest*. NGOs may not always fight for all stakeholders involved. In fact, some industry and trade groups may fight for specific stakeholders. For instance, consider that when Dow Corning was faced with the breast implant scandal whereby silicon was leaking into women's bodies, one of its unlikely defendants was an NGO representing plastic surgeons. It defended the practice as necessary for women.
- *Fraud*. NGOs exist because of the funding they received from various sources. Fassin notes that there are numerous cases of NGOs receiving multiple sources of funding for the same project.[47] Furthermore, some NGOs have submitted duplicate invoices for the same project and received funding multiple times from sources such as the World Bank and the European Union.
- *Lack of independence*. Many NGOs' goals is to improve worker conditions, an issue that may sometimes conflict with a company's profit maximization efforts. However, NGOs may find it difficult to achieve such goals if they are not truly independent from the companies they are monitoring. Consider, for example, the in-depth examination of both the Fair Labor Association and Social Accountability International, two NGOs emphasizing improving conditions in supply chains and eliminating sweatshop conditions. The Fair Labor Association has many corporate members on its board thereby comprising its activities. As an example, the factory monitoring process is not necessarily transparent and the frequency of such visits is very limited. Similarly, Social Accountability International has been more focused on raising revenues thereby becoming unwilling to displease potential buyers through the application of rigorous standards. Such lack of independence has therefore compromised the effectiveness of both companies.

Despite these questionable practices, NGOs play an important role in today's business environment. In the final section of this chapter, we examine how companies can manage NGOs.

NGO Management

NGOs, similar to most other stakeholders, have to be managed. The many cases discussed in this chapter show that they can have significant influence on a company. For instance, the Preview Business Ethics Insight discussed at the beginning of the chapter showed how Nike received significant negative publicity that eventually affected their profitability. They gradually had to address the NGOs' demand for better work conditions. Furthermore, the Metsä-Botnia case discussed earlier and their ignorance of the demands of the NGOs resulted in irreversible damage that doomed the pulp mill project. It is therefore important that the presence and actions of NGOs be analyzed and be managed.

How should NGOs be managed? The techniques and tools discussed in Chapter 4 are very useful here. A multinational should conduct the many steps discussed in that chapter. Specifically, a company is expected to conduct stakeholder identification (which NGOs currently have impact for the company), stakeholder prioritization (which stakeholders have a combination of power, legitimacy, and urgency), stakeholder visualization and mapping (which stakeholders have the most power and urgency), stakeholder engagement (how to engage NGOs through dialogue and cooperation), and stakeholder monitoring (the nature of NGO actions). More extensive detail on these issues can be found in Chapter 4.

One of the key steps of the stakeholder analysis that experts suggest companies should adopt is stakeholder engagement. Valor and Merino go as far as arguing that most NGOs now have gone from confrontation to cooperation with the firms they target.[48] NGOs are now seen as becoming more practical and flexible and less ideological. NGOs also seem to be more willing to work with the companies they target to find solutions to problems. NGOs see such a path as a better way to become more credible among policymakers, while also improving their reputations. Most multinationals are therefore well advised to adopt a more cooperative posture when interacting with NGOs. The final Strategic Business Ethics Insight below shows some of the benefits when companies and NGOs cooperate.

STRATEGIC BUSINESS ETHICS INSIGHT

NGOs and Cooperation

For decades, companies and NGOs operated mostly in conflict with each other. The influential scholar C.K. Prahalad termed this as "co-existence." However, companies are now facing new challenges and, as they strive to embark on corporate social and environmental responsibility, they are now increasingly partnering with NGOs. This new era termed "co-creation" signals a new direction for company–NGO relationships. Consider the case of Danone and work with NGOs in developing countries to better understand the low-income but economically viable consumers in such countries. Similarly, FedEx partnered with Environmental Defense Fund, an NGO based in Washington, DC, to launch its hybrid electric truck fleets. Both forms of cooperation resulted in significant strategic advantage for the company involved.

Perez-Aleman and Sandilands' study of cooperation between Starbucks and NGOs also shows how cooperation and engagement can be beneficial to affected stakeholders.[49] As early as 1994, NGOs started targeting Starbucks to pressure the company to set standards for the wages, benefits, housing, and health of its coffee suppliers. Although it initially resisted such NGO activism, it eventually started partnering with the various NGOs representing suppliers. Specifically, the relationship it built with the Conservation International NGO (see description in Exhibit 8.6) resulted in significant improvement in the lives of its suppliers worldwide. The partnership helped Starbucks identify problematic areas with its suppliers worldwide. In partnership with these NGOs, Starbucks developed solutions and a code of standards as it interacts with its suppliers. For instance, its suppliers must show how much of the money they are spending actually goes to farmers. Starbucks now purchases a high percentage of its coffee from sustainable and fair trade suppliers.

Companies are thus finding significant benefits when partnering with NGOs. Danone, for instance, was able to learn about the four billion people who are considered low income and earn less than $2 a day. By better understanding these individuals, Danone has been better able to devise products to satisfy their needs. Besides such marketing benefits, companies are improving their reputation while also earning improved returns in their research and development. In the process, companies are helping these NGOs better fulfill their missions.

Based on Auriac, J. 2010. "Corporate social innovation." *Organisation for Economic Co-operation and Development*, May, 279; Perez-Aleman, P. and Sandilands, M. 2008. "Building value at the top and the bottom of the global supply chain: MNC-NGO partnerships." *California Management Review*, 51, 1, 24–49.

CHAPTER SUMMARY

In this chapter, you learned about three critical secondary stakeholders. For a company to survive, it has to adequately analyze its environment. Secondary stakeholders are extremely important elements of a company's strategic environment. While there are many stakeholders that can potentially influence a company's strategy indirectly, we emphasized three important secondary stakeholders.

First, you read about the government as an influential secondary stakeholder. You learned about the role of the government in both creating an environment leading to ethics and to enacting of rules and regulations to reinforce ethical behavior. You read about the World Bank Doing Business project and the various indicators of the extent of ethicality of the business environment. However, you also learned about the types of government regulation; namely, social and economic regulation. Furthermore, you learned how companies can react to the government either by adopting the rules or regulations or delay such rules through corporate political activity.

The second secondary stakeholder you learned about is the media. You read about the important influence the media plays on companies. You also learned about the direct influence the media have on public perception of companies. However, you also read about the "third-person" effect and the indirect ways the media can influence public perception of companies. To adequately manage the media, you also learned about media analysis and the strategic importance of the various steps inherent in media analysis. You also read about the various possible options available to companies based on media analysis.

Finally, you also read about non-governmental organizations (NGOs) as critical secondary stakeholders. You learned about the various strategies NGOs can use to influence companies. You read about the continuum ranging from active cooperation to open confrontation and the assumptions behind adoption of such strategies. However, you also read about questionable NGO practices such as misinformation, conflicts of interest, and fraud. Similar to other secondary stakeholders, you learned about NGO management. You also learned about the importance and benefits of multinationals to actively cooperate and engage with NGOs.

NOTES

1 Verschoor, C.C. 2009. "Can government manage more ethically than capitalism?" *Strategic Finance*, October, 91, 4, 14.
2 World Bank. 2018. www.doingbusiness.org/~/media/WBG/DoingBusiness/Documents/Annual-Reports/English/DB2018-Full-Report.pdf
3 World Bank. 2018. www.doingbusiness.org/~/media/WBG/DoingBusiness/Documents/Annual-Reports/English/DB2018-Full-Report.pdf
4 Lawrence, A.T. & Weber, J. 2011. *Business & society: Stakeholders, ethics, public policy*. New York: McGraw-Hill Publishing.
5 Steiner, G.A. & Steiner, J.F. 2010. *Business, government and society: A managerial perspective, text and cases*. 12th ed. New York: McGraw-Hill.
6 DiMaggio, P.J. & Powell, W. 1983. "The iron cage revisited: Institutional isomorphism and collective rationality in organizational fields." *American Sociological Review*, 48, 147–160.
7 Lux, S., Crook, T.R. & Woehr, D. 2011. "Mixing business with politics: A meta-analysis of the antecedents and outcomes of corporate political activity." *Journal of Management*, 37, 1, 223–247.
8 Funk, R.J. & Hirschman, D. 2017. "Beyond nonmarket strategy: Market actions as corporate political activity." *Academy of Management Review*, 42, 1, 32–52.
9 Funk & Hirschman, "Beyond nonmarket strategy."
10 Scheppers, S. 2010. "Business-government relations: Beyond lobbying." *Corporate Governance*, 10, 4, 475–483.
11 Okhmatovskiy, I. 2010. "Performance implications of ties to the government and SOEs: A political embeddedness perspective." *Journal of Management Studies*, 47, 6.
12 Lux et al., "Mixing business with politics."
13 Okhmatovskiy, "Performance implications of ties to the government and SOEs."
14 Hadani, M., Bonardi, J. & Dahan, N.M. 2017. "Corporate political activity, public policy uncertainty, and firm outcomes: A meta-analysis." *Strategic Organization*, 15, 3, 338–366.

15 Dowling, G. & Weeks, W. 2008. "What the media is really telling you about your brand." *MIT Sloan Management Review*, 49, 3.
16 Donlon, J.P. 2009. "The criminalization of corporate conduct." *Chief Executive*, 241.
17 Ridout, T.N. & Smith, G.R. 2008. "Free advertising: How the media amplify campaign messages." *Political Research Quarterly*, 61, 4, 598–608.
18 Andina-Diaz, A. 2007. "Reinforcement vs. change: The political influence of the media." *Public Choice*, 131, 65–81 (at 65).
19 Barber. J.S. & Axinn, W.G. 2004. "New ideas and fertility limitation: The role of mass media." *Journal of Marriage and Family*, 66, 5, 1180–1200.
20 Clemente, M. & Gabbioneta, C. 2017. "How does the media frame corporate scandals? The case of German newspapers and the Volkswagen diesel scandal." *Journal of Management Inquiry*, 26, 3, 287–302.
21 Andina-Diaz, "Reinforcement vs. change."
22 Tal-Or, N., Cohen, J., Tsfati, Y. & Gunther, C.A. 2010. "Testing casual direction in the influence of presumed media influence." *Communication Research*, 37.
23 Reuber, R.A. & Fischer, E. 2010. "Organizations behaving badly: When are discreditable actions likely to damage organizational reputation?" *Journal of Business Ethics*, 93, 39–50.
24 Dowling, G. & Weeks, W. 2011. "Media analysis: What is it worth?" *Journal of Business Strategy*, 32, 1, 26–33.
25 Ingenhoff, D. & Sommer, K. 2010. "Trust in companies and CEOs: A comparative study of the main influences." *Journal of Business Ethics*, 95, 339–355.
26 Clemente & Gabbioneta "How does the media frame corporate scandals?"
27 Dowling & Weeks, "Media analysis: What is it worth?"
28 Cullen, J. 2003. "A rounded picture: Using media framing as a tool for competitive intelligence and business research." *Business Information Review*, 20, 2, 88–94.
29 Dowling & Weeks, "Media analysis: What is it worth?"
30 Huang-Horowitz, N.C. "The media reputation of small firms: Exploring the applicability of existing reputation measures." *Corporate Reputation Review*, 19, 2, 127–139.
31 Dowling & Weeks, "Media analysis: What is it worth?"
32 Dowling & Weeks, "Media analysis: What is it worth?"
33 Clemente & Gabbioneta "How does the media frame corporate scandals?"
34 Fassin, Y. 2009. "Inconsistencies in activists' behaviours and the ethics of NGOs." *Journal of Business Ethics*, 90, 503–521.
35 Sethi, S.P. & Rovenpor, J.L. 2016. "The role of NGOs in ameliorating sweatshop-like conditions in the global supply chain: The case of Fair Labor Association (FLA), and Social Accountability International (SAI)." *Business and Society Review*, 121, 1, 5–36.
36 Fassin, "Inconsistencies in activists' behaviours," 503.
37 Arenas, D., Lozano, J.M. & Albareda, L. 2009. "The role of NGOs in CSR: Mutual perceptions among stakeholders." *Journal of Business Ethics*, 88, 175–197; Fassin, "Inconsistencies in activists' behaviours."
38 Arenas et al., "The role of NGOs in CSR."
39 Arenas et al., "The role of NGOs in CSR."
40 Sobczak, A. & Martins, L.C. 2010. "The impact and interplay of national and global CSR discourses: Insights from France and Brazil." *Corporate Governance*, 10, 4, 445–455.
41 Carpenter, C. 2001. "Business, green groups & the media: The role of non-governmental organizations in the climate change debate." *International Affairs*, 77, 2, 313–328.
42 Skippari, M. & Pajunen, K. 2010. "MNE-NGO—host government relationships in escalation of an FDI conflict." *Business & Society*, 49, 619.
43 Fassin, "Inconsistencies in activists' behaviours"; Burchell, J. & Cook, J. 2013. "Sleeping with the enemy? Strategic transformations in business-NGO relationships through stakeholder dialogue." *Journal of Business Ethics*, 113, 505–518.
44 Valor, C. & Merino, A. 2009. "Relationship of business and NGOs: An empirical analysis of strategies and mediators of their private relationship." *Business Ethics: A European Review*, 18, 2.

45 Fassin, "Inconsistencies in activists' behaviours."
46 Sethi & Rovenpor "The role of NGOs in ameliorating sweatshop-like conditions."
47 Fassin, "Inconsistencies in activists' behaviours."
48 Valor & Merino, "Relationship of business and NGOs."
49 Aleman, P.P. & Sandilands, M. 2008. "Building value at the top and the bottom of the global supply chain: MNC-NGO partnerships." *California Management Review*, 51, 1, 24–49.

KEY TERMS

Corporate public activity: attempt by a company to influence or manage the political entities and the government.
Enforcement of contract: expectation that the terms and conditions of a contract will be respected.
Governments: institutions that can constrain and regularize behaviors and actions through its capacity to establish rules, to inspect and review conformity, and to manipulate consequences to reinforce behaviors.
Media: many avenues of information such as newspapers, television, and the internet.
Media analysis: routine scan of media to discover what is being said about companies.
NGO active cooperation: engage with stakeholders to develop solutions.
NGO confrontational strategy: reliance on symbolic damage strategies such as negative publicity or material damage strategies such as boycotts.
Non-governmental organizations: umbrella term that includes special interest groups, activist groups, social movement organizations, charities, religious groups, protest groups, and other non-profit groups.
Problem and solution analysis: using information from salience/sentiment analysis and theme/contradiction analysis to formulate solutions to ongoing problems.
Protection of investors: expectations investors have of transparency and accountability from managers running the company.
Registration of property: procedures necessary for a business to purchase a property from another business and transfer the title to the buyer's name.
Regulation: laws and regulations to force companies to behave in ways that are more ethical.
Salience and sentiment analysis: the number of times companies are mentioned and whether they are portrayed positively or negatively.
Secondary stakeholders: those groups or entities that have an indirect impact on the company's survival and strategic activities.
Theme and contradiction analysis: analysis of media to determine whether ongoing media coverage is portraying the company under some specific theme.

DISCUSSION QUESTIONS

1. What are secondary stakeholders? How do they differ from primary stakeholders? How do they influence companies? Be specific with examples.
2. Discuss the role of the government as a secondary stakeholder. What are the various ways they can influence companies?
3. What is legitimacy in reference to the government as a secondary stakeholder? How can companies achieve legitimacy?
4. What is corporate political activity? Describe the various forms of corporate political activity. What purposes does corporate political activity serve?
5. Briefly define the media. How do the media influence perception of companies? Be specific about both direct and indirect influences.
6. Describe the various activities involved in a media analysis. Discuss the possible responses to the results of a media analysis.
7. Discuss the salience and sentiment media analyses. How are the salience and sentiment analyses different from themes and contradiction media analyses? How can the results of the above analyses be used for the problems and solutions media analyses?
8. What are NGOs? Discuss some of the strategies NGOs can use to influence companies.
9. Discuss some of the questionable practices NGOs sometimes engage in. Be specific with examples.
10. Why are more companies now cooperating with NGOs? What are the benefits of such NGO engagement and cooperation?

INTERNET ACTIVITY

1. Go to the World Bank website: www.worldbank.org.
2. Find the Doing Business Project Report for 2018.
3. What are the ten indicators of the Doing Business project? Which of these indicators are also relevant to ethics? Do you think that paying taxes should also be included in the ethics environment?
4. Research the "Enforcing Contracts" report. What are some of the major trends worldwide regarding contract enforcement? Which regions have the highest contract enforcement? Why?
5. Research the "Protecting Investors" report. What are the major trends? Which regions have made the most progress protecting their investors?

For more Internet Activities and resources, visit the Companion Website at www.routledge.com/cw/parboteeah.

WHAT WOULD YOU DO?

The Non-Governmental Organization

You start a Bachelor's degree in Business Administration at a prestigious university. However, you have always been very environmentally conscious and you are dismayed to find that so many companies end up being strong polluters of the environment. You are also unhappy with current environmental regulations being weakened in most parts of the country. You therefore become very frustrated with the field of business administration and vow to change things.

After graduation, you join a well-known non-governmental organization (NGO). The NGO's main aim is to scrutinize practices of multinationals with regards to the environment. The NGO will then publicize the actions of offending multinationals. However, similar to employment in many NGOs, you find that you are not getting paid as much as you could if you were in the private sector. You also know that there is lots of uncertainty regarding your position. Your position could easily be cut if the NGO does not get similar levels of donation.

You have been working very hard on a large multinational that is headquartered in your town. You discover that the multinational has a very poor environmental record and that they have engaged in many practices locally that have resulted in severe pollution. Before such actions are publicized, the NGO will typically share the findings with the company. This is done to give a chance to the offending organization to respond to such allegations.

You are asked to share your findings with the company. You arrange a meeting with the CEO to share these results. The CEO is actually very appreciative of your work and the findings. She asks you about your role in the NGO and about your educational qualifications. The CEO then proceeds to ask you to work for them. She assures you that they want to be more environmentally sensitive. She also believes that the company needs someone like you to determine what changes will need to occur and where.

What do you do? You have vowed to never work for a large corporation. However, you also know that the pay will be much better and you will have a more stable job. But if you take the job, you feel that you will be selling out your friends at the NGO. Do you still go along and take the job? Why or why not?

* * *

BRIEF CASE: BUSINESS ETHICS INSIGHT

Mercedes in China

As the Chinese enjoy increasing affluence, Mercedes-Benz cars are becoming important status symbols and signifiers of luxury. High-powered executives see Mercedes-Benz as the car of choice, while the average Chinese views the car as a glamorous vehicle. Mercedes-Benz vehicles are often sought to lead wedding processions. It is therefore not surprising to find that Mercedes-Benz has the highest sales figure among both domestic and international luxury car brands.

In 2002, Mercedes-Benz faced a major media nightmare that threatened to destabilize its image of luxury in China. The major incident that led to this nightmare was a press conference with around 50 journalists. During the press conference, six young individuals proceeded to destroy a Mercedes-Benz car with a sledgehammer. The car was completely decimated in less than ten minutes. Over the next months, Mercedes had to deal with the impact of the media repeatedly showing the event.

Why did the six individuals decide to destroy the car? A close examination of events leading to the destruction sheds some insight. The conflict between Mercedes-Benz and its Chinese consumers started when management of the Wuhan Wild Animals Zoo discovered numerous defects and other reliability issues in their newly purchased Mercedes-Benz vehicles. To repair the vehicles, the cars had to be towed to Beijing. There, they allegedly faced significant delays in the repair. Furthermore, Mercedes-Benz refused to cover the repairs, although these individuals had spent over $100,000 for each vehicle. Their frustrations continued after they met with further reticence on the part of Mercedes-Benz in assuming responsibility for the defects. Rather than trying to fix the problems, Mercedes-Benz blamed the problems on consumers, arguing that the cars were not being maintained as needed and the quality of gas not being adequate to run the high-powered engines.

This case illustrates the dangers of not properly addressing customer needs in an emerging market. The widely publicized initial demolition led to similar stunts across China. These led to more unrest as more consumers confronted the company with similar grievances. Furthermore, the media continued their sensational coverage of the various events giving consumers a voice. Soon Mercedes-Benz was being seen as an arrogant company having double standards with regards to how they treated their consumers worldwide. Chinese consumers were frustrated that they were not being treated similarly to consumers in Western countries. Fueled by the media, this resulted in further controversy and outrage, seen as an affront to Chinese cultural identity.

Based on Tan, J. and Tan. A.E. 2009. "Managing public relations in an emerging economy: The case of Mercedes in China." *Journal of Business Ethics*, 86, 257–266.

BRIEF CASE QUESTIONS

1. What are some of the major factors that led to this media nightmare for Mercedes?
2. Why did the news spread so rapidly? Why did other consumers start engaging in similar demonstrations?
3. Do Western companies approach emerging market consumers with arrogance? Why or why not?
4. What should Mercedes do to ensure that similar events do not occur in the future? Illustrate with concepts discussed in the chapter.

LONG CASE: BUSINESS ETHICS

IBS Center for Management Research

IKEA IN RUSSIA—ETHICAL DILEMMAS

This case was written by Namratha V. Prasad, under the direction of G.V. Muralidhara, IBS Hyderabad. It was compiled from published sources, and is intended to be used as a basis for class discussion rather than to illustrate either effective or ineffective handling of a management situation.

> *"IKEA consistently combats corruption. All of our divisions operate completely transparently. The company has adopted a strict code of conduct and its provisions are binding not only for rank-and-file employees and executives, but also for business partners. These regulations are uniform throughout the world and Russia is no exclusion."*[1]
>
> – IKEA's Press Release following investigation of bribery cases against former employees of IKEA Russia, in July 2012

> *"People in the West know astonishingly little about Russia. Those who call themselves Russia experts usually don't understand the first thing about it. People who say they don't know much about Russia come much closer to understanding it."*[2]
>
> – Lennart Dahlgren, Former Russia Country Manager for IKEA, in February 2011

www.icmrindia.org

Introduction

In July 2012, a Turkish national, Okan Yunalan (Yunalan), who acted as an intermediary for Carl Ola Ingvaldsson (Ingvaldsson), former Head of the Leasing Department in IKEA's Russian subsidiary (IKEA MOS), to extract a bribe, was sentenced to five years in a high-security prison. Yunalan was found guilty of large-scale extortion after he demanded 6.5 million rubles (US$225,000) from a company that sought to lease two premises at IKEA's Mega shopping complex in Tyoply Stan, a suburb in Moscow. Ingvaldsson and another accomplice managed to leave the country and Russia was seeking their extradition.

IKEA stated that it welcomed the investigation by Russian authorities into the incident and would cooperate fully with them. This was not the first instance of corruption seeping into its Russian operations negating its tough stance against the all-pervasive corrupt business environment in Russia.[3] IKEA was known for its uncompromising attitude toward corruption but it had not always been successful in ensuring that its employees adhered to its ethical standards.

The same year, the company came under the scanner of global environmental agencies when an investigative report revealed that it was utilizing ill-defined Russian logging rules to cut down old growth forests.[4] This raised questions about its claims of being an ecologically sensitive company that believed in sustainable logging practices.

It was in the late 1990s that IKEA decided to enter the Russian market as part of its global expansion strategy. From its early days, the company had displayed a non-tolerance for corruption. This standpoint meant that it had to face several setbacks when setting up stores, inaugurating them, and even while advertising for them. However, there were also instances of support from authorities, whether local or federal, and of difficulties being smoothed out, which enabled the company to get things done faster than in any other country in the world.

Over the years, the company expanded and experienced success with its stores in Russia. Some of them, in fact, became the top grossers in the world for IKEA. It was also in Russia that the company introduced its successful new business model, wherein its furniture stores were operated not as standalone stores but as part of large shopping and entertainment complexes.

Though the company continuously faced and overcame the serious hurdles caused by the corrupt bureaucratic system, it finally decided to halt all expansion in Russia in 2009. The decision came in the wake of permission being denied to setup two if its stores, allegedly after it refused to pay bribes to safety inspectors. However, the top Russian ministry officials convinced the company to go ahead with its expansion in 2011.

As of 2012, with 14 existing stores (**See Exhibit I for more Information about Russia's IKEA Stores**), the company's expansion plan in Russia was on track, and it had plans to open several new stores and even a retail bank.

Background Note

IKEA, founded in Sweden, was the most successful entrepreneurial venture of its founder Ingvar Kamprad (Kamprad). Kamprad was just a boy in the 1920s, when he began selling matches. He later graduated to selling flower seeds, greeting cards, Christmas tree decorations, pencils, and then ball-point pens.

In 1943, Kamprad set up a business with money given by his father. He called it IKEA (representing his own initials (I.K.), in addition to the first letter of his farm, Elmtaryd (E), and the village where he spent his childhood Agunnaryd (A)). IKEA started out selling products such as pens, wallets, picture frames, table runners, watches, jewelry, and nylon stockings, at discounted prices. In 1948, furniture made by local manufacturers was also sold through the business.

Over the years, the company took to advertising its products by various methods, including through catalogs. In 1953, the first IKEA furniture showroom was opened in Älmhult, Sweden. In 1956, the company took to designing its own furniture, adopting flat packaging and enabling self-assembly of the furniture. In the early 1960s, the "IKEA Concepts"[5] of form, function, and price were created, with furniture designed accordingly.

Over the next three decades, the company launched some highly successful products such as the POÄNG armchair, the SKOPA chair, the ÖGLA chair, the BILLY Bookcases, the KLIPPAN sofa, the LACK table, the MOMENT, sofa and the STOCKHOLM furnishings. IKEA gradually expanded its footprint across Europe and North America, opening stores in Norway (1963), Denmark (1969), Switzerland (1973), Germany (1974), Australia (1975), Canada (1976), Austria (1977), the Netherlands (1979), France (1981), Belgium (1984), the U.S. (1985), the UK (1987), and Italy (1989).

In 1982, the Stitchting INGKA Foundation, based in the Netherlands, became the owner of the newly formed "The IKEA Group". In 1984, the customer club, "IKEA Family", was launched. In 1991, the company started the industrial group, Swedwood, to produce wood-based furniture and wooden components. In addition, IKEA purchased several sawmills and production plants.

In 1997, IKEA launched its website, www.ikea.com. The same year, the company also launched Children's IKEA, with the focus on providing home furnishing solutions to cater to families having young children. In 2000, IKEA launched e-shopping in Sweden and Denmark. Over a period of time, it began providing this facility in several other countries.

The company continued its global expansion endeavor, opening stores in Hungary (1990), the Czech Republic, Poland (1991), Spain (1996), China (1998), Russia (2000), Portugal (2004), and Japan (2006). The company also entered into several partnerships to execute numerous social and environmental projects.

The company's business concept in all its markets was to offer furniture of simple designs at affordable prices. Though the company designed its own furniture and other items, it manufactured only a minimal portion; most of the supplies were made through a global network of contract manufacturers (a significant quota of these were located in emerging markets). The company's business strategy could be summed up as cheap labor, combined with expedient retail pricing.

With regard to human resources, IKEA claimed that it gave precedence to values and beliefs over skills, academics, or work experience in all of its standard jobs interviews. Prospective employees were expected to even take a culture quiz to determine if they fit in with the corporate culture.

IKEA strove hard to project itself as an environmentally conscious, ethical company. It took measures to ensure that the materials it used were sustainably sourced and the labor it employed met international labor regulations. By 2012, it hoped to fully implement the "IKEA Way", a roster of rules and regulations for its suppliers. It was also against child labor being used at its supplier's operations. The idea behind these rules was to provide the world with a clear picture on the origin, volume, and kind of wood used in IKEA's products.

Over the years, IKEA won several awards for its ethical practices. As of 2010, it had been recognized by the Ethisphere Institute[6] as one of the "World's Most Ethical Companies" in specialty retail for four consecutive years.

As of 2012, IKEA had 338 stores in 40 countries. Of IKEA's revenues, 80% came from Europe and the company had future plans to expand into Asian markets, especially India. By the end of the decade, IKEA expected to increase the number of its stores by 50% (to 500 stores) and to double its sales figures and customer numbers. IKEA was judged the "2012 World Retail Congress International Retailer of the Year" because of its superiority as compared to its peers in global profitability, branding, and strategizing.

Foray into Russia

Kamprad had been quite keen to do business in Russia since the 1960's, when it was still the Soviet Union.[7] However, he was unable to do so for quite a few decades for several reasons. IKEA's first attempt to begin Russian operations was stalled due to the collapse of the Soviet Union in 1991. A later attempt failed due to the "Russian constitutional crisis of 1993"[8] and the country's subsequent unfavorable economic scenario.

In 1998, Lennart Dahlgren (Dahlgren), a prominent IKEA employee, who was on the verge of retirement, was asked to oversee the setting up of IKEA's operations in Russia. Dahlgren stated that he, like many others in the West, had harbored several negative opinions about Russia, including the thought that the country was teeming with poor people. He quickly abandoned this view and came to realize that there was a large retail opportunity waiting to be tapped. In the early 2000s, a market report from A.T. Kearney, a global market consulting firm, stated that in terms of retail expansion, Russia was the top country in the world. The report further said, "With a growth rate of 30 percent for retail sales from 1999 to 2003 and a relatively sparse retail network to serve its growing market, Russia is full of promise."[9]

In time, Dahlgren also realized that Russia had a highly corrupt bureaucracy, which demanded bribes for getting anything done. However, in concurrence with IKEA's policy of zero tolerance of corruption, Dahlgren decided that he would not give in to the corrupt system. On the issue of companies dealing with corruption in Russia, Dahlgren said, "Companies interested in Russia should be absolutely up-front and honest in their dealings. When a foreign company pays bribes, there is no end to demands for bribes. In turn, foreign companies should feel an urgency to report corruption."[10]

Dahlgren entered into discussions with the Mayor of Moscow, Yuri Luzhkov (Luzhkov), with regard to the opening of the first IKEA store in that city. However, IKEA's endeavor to open a store in Moscow's prosperous Kutuzovsky Prospekt[11] fell through when it became a victim of vicious slander. Later, Luzhkov suggested that IKEA set up its store in a recently constructed building complex. But IKEA found the building impractical for setting up its store.

After some deliberation, IKEA came across a site it found suitable for setting up the store and approached Luzhkov to get a lease on the site. But the city authorities asked for sky high land lease rates that the company deemed to be economically unfeasible. Dahlgren said, "Buying land on these terms would make it impossible to keep low prices on products."[12]

Consequently, IKEA decided to move the project to a suburb 12 miles north of Moscow called Khimki, whose Mayor displayed a friendlier demeanor toward the setting up of the store. As soon as the construction of the Khimki store began, the "Russian Financial Crisis" or the "Ruble Crisis", broke out. The crisis was the result of the Russian Government's default on domestic debt and devaluation of the Ruble. The crisis period caused a jump in food prices and a break-out of mass protests. Millions lost their life savings. In spite of the setback it faced as a result of the crisis, the company continued with the construction of the store.

Opening of the Stores

In March 2000, IKEA's first store in Russia was opened at Khimki. The inaugural day drew a large crowd of 40,000 shoppers. People waited for an hour to get into the store and all the roads leading to it were backed up with traffic for miles around.

Analysts believed that by the time IKEA opened its first store there was a lot of pent up demand in Russia, especially from the middle class. It was a time of transition in the country, with the rising middle class looking to abandon the old world Soviet-era furniture in favor of the modern Scandinavian furniture showcased by IKEA.

At a time when furniture stores in Russia offered only two extreme choices, pricey furniture for the affluent and cheap stuff for the other classes, IKEA's offering of simple, sturdy furniture at affordable rates created quite a stir. Many of the shoppers expressed disbelief over the pricing of IKEA's items, with some of them even wondering whether they were priced in US dollars rather than Russian Rubles. Speaking on this issue, Dahlgren said, "We spent the first weekend writing the word 'ruble' on all the price tags."[13]

In contrast to other stores in Russia, IKEA laid emphasis on customer service. It had a highly selective process of recruitment, with its initial 440 employees picked from a total of 16,000 applicants. Moreover, the Store Supervisors, whom it termed the "Core Employees", were provided training at IKEA stores in other countries. Through its stores, IKEA also offered several other amenities such as free shuttle services from select places, a playroom for children and coffee to customers who came in early.

The store continued to be popular, with 100,000 visiting it even after a month. Within a year, IKEA opened another store in the Moscow region. The Russian IKEA stores were similar in size, structure, and style to their counterparts in other parts of the world. In the first year of operations, IKEA reported sales of more than US$100 million in Russia, three times more than what the company had expected. IKEA's Khimki store became one of its top 10 grossing stores in the whole world. The rousing response to the store's opening encouraged IKEA to formulate ambitious plans of expansion.

In addition, IKEA tested its new business model for the first time in Russia. The company observed that the land value of the areas surrounding its new stores greatly appreciated in value over a period of time. It decided to take advantage of this by trying to develop the areas around its stores into commercial complexes.

The company had a land lease for its store's sites extending for a period of 98 years, with the option to purchase it, if Russia ever allowed it. This gave it sufficient leeway to make use of the excess land to increase its business prospects. IKEA invited other stores selling electronics, hardware, and clothes, most of whom were leading international brands, to set up operations in its store sites. It also set up areas for leisure such as movie theaters, ice rinks, and play areas in these complexes. Apart from that, the company created comfort zones which housed cafés, restaurants, childcare facilities, and baby care rooms.

This initiative enabled certain IKEA stores in Russia to be operated as enormous shopping and entertainment complexes, unlike in other countries where they were standalone furniture stores. Over the years, IKEA's new division called the "Mega Mall", which was set up to manage these complexes, made more money than the standalone retail business.

However, the company did struggle to make profits in Russia until the mid-2000s. The main reasons for this were the high startup costs and the steep 25% tariff imposed on imported furniture. IKEA got only 13% of the furniture it sold at its stores locally made. Dahlgren was of the opinion that the company needed to produce 30% of its furniture locally in order to make its operations profitable.

Accordingly in April 2002, IKEA started production at its first Russian factory, in the vicinity of St. Petersburg. Built at a cost of US$15 million, the facility employed 250 people. Apart from opening a production facility, the company provided its local suppliers with credit of US$400 million to purchase equipment and arrange for credit. Russia had about 25% of the world's hardwood supply and the company's efforts to develop its production facilities there were expected to make Russia a major supplier for the company for its global operations.

A Growth Story Marred by Problems

However, it was not all smooth sailing for IKEA in its expansion plans. The business environment in Russia dictated that IKEA constantly faced problems with regard to its stores from government officials in the fire, health and safety, electricity, tax, customs, and other related departments. These officials reportedly discovered problems with IKEA stores, especially during critical times such as store openings. Analysts observed that IKEA would then be provided pointers by the same authorities to overcome these serious issues by way of some monetary payment or engaging a party recommended by them to rectify the problem.

A few weeks before the opening of its first store, IKEA was asked by the local utility department officials to pay a bribe to get an electricity connection for its stores. In order to counter this demand, IKEA decided to hire large diesel generators to power its stores. This became a standard practice for the company for most of its stores in Russia.

IKEA's earlier decision to move out of Moscow didn't go down well with the city authorities, causing them to hold a grudge against IKEA for a long time. When the company finally opened its first store, the Moscow City authorities did not give it permission to advertise the store in the Moscow metro. Dahlgren stated that the municipal authorities refused citing certain scientific studies which showed that people who used the underground had damaged psyches, thereby making IKEA's ads potentially harmful.

Later, when the company wanted to build an off-ramp over Leningrad Highway to ease traffic and enable customers to reach the Khimki store without hardship, Moscow put obstacles in its way. IKEA had not realized that the Leningrad Highway was controlled by Moscow City, rather than Khimki. Though IKEA had completed all formalities necessary to gain the necessary construction permits, once the construction began, the proceedings were halted by Luzhkov and his team. They refused to grant permission for construction of the off-ramp stating that it would thwart the view of a historic place called the Tank Trap monument, which depicted the place where the Red Army[14] obstructed the march of the German Nazi forces during World War II.[15]

The off-ramp stood half-constructed for about a year, causing hardship to customers and traffic snarls on the Leningrad Highway. Later, the company received permission to build the bridge after Kamprad appealed to Vladimir Putin[16] and the 200 other store owners in the complex protested against authorities on the issue.

However, IKEA did make certain compromises with regard to the construction. It agreed to get the off-ramp built by the company endorsed by the municipal authorities of Moscow. This cost the company in terms of cost and time, as it had to pay US$5 million more than the estimated cost. Besides, the off-ramp's construction took three times longer than necessary.

In 2003, the company planned to build a US$40 million warehouse in the Solnechnogorsky district of the Moscow region. Things worked out smoothly for the company as long as Deputy Governor Mikhail Men, who was well-disposed toward the company, was in office. Once he was discharged, the company began facing problems with authorities. Dahlgren accused Vladimir Popov, who was District Head at that time, of using the police to halt work at the warehouse. IKEA was given the go-ahead to continue work only after it donated US$30 million as aid to elderly people and hired a contractor endorsed by the regional government.

In December 2004, IKEA was all set to inaugurate the "Mega Mall" at Khimki, just outside of Moscow. The US$250 million store was one of the biggest in Europe with large boutiques, ice halls, children's play area, and cinema multiplex. The construction of the store began with the blessings of the Mayor of Khimki. However, when he was replaced with Vladimir Strelchenko (Strelchenko), an ex-military officer who showed marked indifference toward Western investors, the store's inauguration faced a major setback.

Officials stalled the store's opening saying that the road to the store ran over a gas pipe, making it dangerous. Therefore, the company was ordered to build a new roadway. It was another matter that the pipeline in question also passed underneath a heavily used six-lane highway and a crucial railroad. Dahlgren stated that the company had agreed to construct a number of pressure reducers over the gas pipes, but the real reason the opening was stopped was because they had refused to pay bribes.

Dahlgren described the prevention of the store opening as "sabotage against Russia"[17] and raised his voice about the corruption dogging Russia, something which had never been done earlier by any official of a company doing business in Russia. He said, "Like all Western companies in Russia we're subject to blackmail, sabotage, and pressure for bribes. In many cases we're totally in the hands of local chieftains. IKEA is big in Russia and doesn't pay bribes."[18]

Dahlgren announced that the inauguration on December 10, 2004, would go ahead as scheduled. Though police forces blocked the store, Dahlgren and his team, along with the Swedish Ambassador to Russia held a grand opening ceremony. This incident drew the attention of the worldwide media and IKEA's plight gained it a lot of sympathy. At the same time, the Khimki municipal authorities drew harsh criticism. Strelchenko's superiors were worried about the incident and its possible ill-effects on Russia's reputation. They then put pressure on him to give the go-ahead for the mall's opening.

Even though Kamprad made several attempts to meet the political leadership of Russia, he was not able to meet either Putin or his successor Dmitry Medvedev.[19] In one such attempt in 2005 in which Dahlgren strove to arrange a meeting between Kamprad and Putin, he was told by a senior government official that it would cost US$5–10 million. Dahlgren said, "I sensed that it would be better not to get into that discussion any deeper."[20]

A Stop to Everything?

Fortunately for IKEA, it did not face only problems in Russia. There were instances when support from the authorities made things smoother. In 2005, IKEA opened another store called the "Mega Kazan" in the Kazan region, 500 miles east of Moscow. The store was built in partnership with Ramstore hypermarket.[21] Mega Kazan went on to become the largest regional mall in Russia. Dahlgren said that the authorities in Kazan were very cooperative, which caused the store to be opened in record time. He said, "It took less than a year between the first meeting with Kazan's mayor and the store's opening—a record impossible to break anywhere in the world."[22]

Over a period of time, IKEA became the largest foreign retailer in Russia. The company invested US$4 billion in Russia over a period of 10 years, making it the country's sole largest foreign investor. It opened 14 stores and three manufacturing facilities, along with one distribution center. Company officials stated that IKEA's success was attracting other world retailers to set up their operations in Russia. The popularity of IKEA and its impact on the younger generation caused Russia's yuppies[23] to be named the "IKEA Generation". IKEA's Managing Director, Per Wendschlag said, "We are one of the top-selling IKEA countries in the world. The potential with 141 million people who are interested in consuming and furnishing their homes is big."[24]

However, despite its runaway success, IKEA put a freeze on its expansion in June 2009, after officials refused to give it permission to open two of its stores in the central cities of Samara and Ufa. According to Kirill Kabanov, Head of the NGO National Anti-Corruption Committee in Moscow, the reason for the non-opening of the stores was IKEA's refusal to give bribes to safety inspectors. Officials refused to give approval in Samara stating that the walls of the store were not in a condition to withstand hurricane-force winds, notwithstanding the fact that such weather conditions had never been experienced in that region.

A company official stated that the municipal authorities had recommended that IKEA use the services of a local construction company to "quickly help"[25] fix the construction deficiencies. Gigibulla Khasaev, Economic Development Minister for the Samara region, however, stated that the company's allegations were untrue and that IKEA was publicizing its complaints to divert attention from its substandard construction. He added, "To say the government is creating artificial barriers is an invention."[26]

IKEA stated that it was tired of being conned out of its money and was halting expansion. Kamprad claimed that the company had been swindled to the tune of US$ 190 million because of the failure of Russian authorities to provide electricity to its stores as promised. However, some incidents seemed to indicate that certain IKEA officials were bowing down to the all-encompassing corruption in Russia.

In 2009, IKEA discovered that the key executive responsible for renting the diesel generators had hyped up the rental charges in collaboration with the generator rental company, causing the company a loss of several million dollars.

In February 2010, IKEA fired two of its executives Per Kaufmann, a Director for IKEA in Eastern Europe, and Stefan Gross, a Director for IKEA's shopping mall business in Russia, for turning a blind eye to corruption.

Though they had not committed any personal indiscretion, their decision to overlook a corrupt transaction between a subcontractor of IKEA and an electricity company official in order to resolve a power-supply issue at IKEA's St. Petersburg mall, did somewhat dent IKEA's reputation for non-tolerance of corruption. Speaking on this issue, Kamprad said, "The documented mess in our Russian shopping center company is completely unacceptable. I have been too optimistic. It is shocking and deplorable that we have wandered off course."[27]

In April 2011, the Ministry of Economic Development of Russia got in touch with IKEA's senior leadership and persuaded them to carry on with their expansion plans in the country. Minister Elvira Nabiullina who met company executives claimed that

IKEA had agreed not only to open new stores, but also to enhance its local manufacturing capability. Analysts felt that the company's meeting with the Russian senior ministry demonstrated a strategy of building relationships with authorities at the federal, rather than local level.

Apart from the rising cases of corruption being detected among its ranks, IKEA's image took a further beating when reports on its alleged unethical logging practices surfaced. In early 2012, Swedish public service television came out with an investigative report that proclaimed that IKEA's subsidiary Swedwood cut down several hundred acres of old growth forests every year. This revelation caused various global conservation groups to condemn IKEA's logging practices. IKEA refuted the allegations and claimed that it was logging wood according to local guidelines.

However, analysts pointed out that IKEA was adhering to local guidelines that were highly questionable. Viktor Säfve, Chairman of Swedish NGO "Protect the Forest", said, "This all comes down to a question of credibility and we believe that they are cheating their customers by claiming that the wood they use is sustainably sourced. The wood they are cutting down in Russia is from a high conservation area and we have the evidence to prove it. They are hiding behind flawed and criticized FSC accreditation."[28,29] Analysts felt that IKEA should show greater responsibility in sourcing wood without taking advantage of defunct environmental guidelines in countries such as Russia and China, in which it mostly logged wood.

The Road Ahead

As of 2012, Russia was IKEA's primary target for expansion. Out of its three top globally performing stores, two were located in Russia. Apart from that, the country's extensive boreal or taiga forest belt was a source of high-quality timber. The company was also in the process of executing new business plans, such as the initiative to open a bank.

IKEA's journey reflected the fact that even though Russia was one of the fastest emerging markets of the world, and a part of the BRIC (Brazil, Russia, India and China), it was one of the toughest in which to do business.

Analysts said that the major stumbling block for business was the country's corrupt systems at both the regional and national levels. In Transparency International's[30] 2011 Corruption Perceptions Index, Russia was placed at 143rd position, on par with notorious nations such as Nigeria and Belarus. As per the cables published by Wikileaks,[31] it was estimated that bribery in Russia was worth US$300 billion per annum. Analysts opined that bribery was like another taxation system in the country, which benefited the political elite including the police and the Federal Security Service (FSB).[32]

Over the years, IKEA's clash with government officials across various store locations over corruption continued, prompting the Russian Government to come out with several promises that it would eradicate corruption. Speaking on this issue, Dahlgren said, "Officials regularly make public statements about increasing the war on corruption, bureaucracy, and abuse of office. But we did not notice any positive changes over all this time. While some legislation has changed for the better, the authorities have not."[33]

Political observers were of the opinion that unless Russia brought about major changes in its political system such as permitting the formation of a free press and allowing a genuine opposition to exist, which could then criticize government drafts, corruption and bribery would remain omnipresent. Speaking on this issue, Evgeny Kovrov, a Researcher at Retail Consultancy Magazin Magazinov, said, "Investors need dozens and dozens of approvals from an incredible number of agencies. That provides for unlimited corruption opportunities."[34]

On the other hand, analysts felt that corruption was an institutional problem and not a transactional issue. They agreed that multinationals took measures to ensure compliance of their conduct with their Code of Conduct, regulations prevalent in their home country, and internationally relevant rules and regulations. However, they felt that this was not enough to address a systemic problem like corruption, particularly in emerging nations. They were of the opinion that companies through "Business Associations" and "Chambers of Commerce" should develop a collective voice and strive for concrete steps to eradicate corruption.

As in Russia, IKEA passed through ethical minefields in certain other countries in which it had operations. In May 2012, it came to light that IKEA France had been spying on staff and disgruntled customers in that country over a long period of time. The company had reportedly employed private detectives and gained access to police files illegally to gain information about them. To make amends, IKEA fired several key executives, including the country head.

In September 2012, a report released by research company, Ernst & Young claimed that East German political prisoners had been forced to manufacture products for an IKEA supplier for a period of 30 years. Speaking on this issue, Jeanette Skjelmose, IKEA's Sustainability Manager, said, "We deeply regret that this could happen. At the time, we did not yet have the well-organized control system we have today and clearly did not do enough to prevent this type of production method."[35]

It was obvious that IKEA's various global operations were floundering in their attempts to adhere to its own ethical standards. Speaking about the difficulty in maintaining the unique corporate culture and ethical stance across geographies, Christopher Bartlett, an emeritus professor at Harvard Business School said, "In any company that is as large and diverse as Ikea it does become a challenge [to maintain the culture].There is often a tension between the corporate culture and a national culture."[36]

* * *

Exhibit I: Russia's IKEA Stores

Store Location	Opened	Store Location	Opened
Moscow Khimki	2000	Yekaterinburg	2006
Moscow Teply Stan	2001	Novosibirsk	2007
St Petersburg Dybenko	2003	Rostov-on-Don	2007
Kazan	2004	Adygea Adygea-Kuban	2008
Moscow Belaya Dacha	2005	Omsk	2009
Nizhniy Novgorod	2006	Samara	2009
St Petersburg Parnas	2006	Ufa	2010

Source: www.ikea.com

Chapter 8: Long Case Notes

1 "IKEA Cooperates with Investigation in Cases against Executives," www.rapsinews.com, July 18, 2012.
2 Svetlana Smetanina, "Addicted to Russia," http://rbth.ru, February 23, 2011.
3 Augusto Come, "Corruption, Corruption, Corruption," www.opendemocracy.net, November 29, 2012.
4 Old growth forests are those that have been left undisturbed for about 300 to 600 years, resulting in them exhibiting unique ecological features.
5 IKEA believed in the practice of providing its products at prices which made them affordable to everyone. It was this belief that dictated the way it sourced its raw materials (maximizing their use), its production processes (cost effective and innovative) and its retail practices (reasonable pricing).
6 The research-based Ethisphere Institute based in New York is concerned with the creation, advancement, and sharing of best practices in business ethics, corporate social responsibility, anti-corruption, and sustainability. It publishes a quarterly called the "Ethisphere Magazine".
7 The Soviet Union or USSR (Union of Soviet Socialist Republics) was in existence between 1922 and 1991. It constituted 15 socialist states, which were ruled collectively by the Communist Party.
8 The Russian constitutional crisis of 1993 occurred when a war erupted between the Russian President, Boris Yeltsin, and the Russian Parliament. The conflict that was spread over a period of 10 days gave rise to the deadliest street battle ever witnessed in Moscow. The issue was later resolved through the use of military force.
9 Curt Hazlett, "Russia is an Alluring but Sometimes Scary Place for Western Retailers," www.icsc.org, May 2005.
10 Lennart Dahlgren, "The Basics of Doing Business in Russia," http://blogs.hbr.org, October 25, 2010.
11 Kutuzovsky Prospekt is one of the key streets in Moscow. It is flanked by expensive residential areas.
12 Maria Antonova, "Ex-IKEA Boss Bares Russia's 'Chaotic Reality'", www.sptimes.ru, March 26, 2010.
13 Colin McMahon, "Russians Flock to Ikea as Store Battles Moscow," http://articles.chicagotribune.com, May 16, 2000.
14 Red Army or "The Workers' and Peasants' Red Army" were the Soviet Union's communist war group, who were active during the time of the Russian Civil War (1918–1922). Later, it became the national army of the USSR.
15 World War II occurred during the period 1939–1945. Several major nations participated in it and it was considered to be the deadliest war in human history, due to the large number of human casualties and the use of nuclear weapons.

16 Vladimir Putin has been the President of Russia since May 7, 2012. Previously, he had served as President from 2000 to 2008. He had also served as Prime Minister of Russia for the periods 1999–2000 and 2008–2012.

17 Curt Hazlett, "Russia is an Alluring but Sometimes Scary Place for Western Retailers," www.icsc.org, May 2005.

18 Andrew Osborn, "In Fear of His Life: Ikea's Man in Moscow Tells of Threats and Bribes," www.independent.co.uk, December 15, 2004.

19 Dmitry Medvedev has been the Prime Minister of Russia since May 8, 2012. Previously, he had been President of Russia from 2008 to 2012.

20 Maria Antonova, "Ex-IKEA Boss Bares Russia's 'Chaotic Reality'", www.sptimes.ru, March 26, 2010.

21 Ramstore Hypermarkets are owned by Turkish retail giant, MigrosTürkTicaret A.Ş. There are about a dozen Ramstore hypermarkets in Russia.

22 Maria Antonova, "Ex-IKEA Boss Bares Russia's 'Chaotic Reality'", www.sptimes.ru, March 26, 2010.

23 Yuppie stands for "young urban professional" or "young upwardly-mobile professional" and generally refers to the earning members of the upper middle class or upper class, in their 20s and 30s.

24 "IKEA's Freeze Curtails Medvedev's Goal," www.themoscowtimes.com, March 15, 2011.

25 "Why IKEA Is Fed Up with Russia," www.businessweek.com, July 2, 2009.

26 "Why IKEA Is Fed Up with Russia," www.businessweek.com, July 2, 2009.

27 "Ikea Owner 'Distressed' Over Russian Expansion," www.thelocal.se, December 11, 2010.

28 FSC (Forest Stewardship Council) includes some of the world's leading environmental NGOs who develop "Principles and Criteria"—the highest standards of forest management which are environmentally appropriate, socially beneficial and economically viable.

29 Annie Kelly, "Ikea to go 'Forest Positive' – But Serious Challenges Lie Ahead," www.guardian.co.uk, December 14, 2012.

30 Transparency International is an international organization that measures corruption and publishes a comparative listing of corruption worldwide.

31 Wikileaks is a non-profit organization which has been publishing secret and classified documents through its website launched in 2006.

32 The Federal Security Service of the Russian Federation (FSB) is the successor to Soviet Committee of State Security (KGB). It is the primary domestic security agency of the Russian Federation whose responsibilities include ensuring security and gathering intelligence.

33 Maria Antonova, "Ex-IKEA Boss Bares Russia's 'Chaotic Reality'", www.sptimes.ru, March 26, 2010.

34 "Why IKEA Is Fed Up with Russia," www.businessweek.com, July 2, 2009.

35 "Ikea 'regrets' forced labor use in East Germany," www.telegraph.co.uk, November 16, 2012.

36 Richard Milne, "Ikea: Against the Grain," www.ft.com, November 13, 2012.

Suggested Readings and References

1. Anna Ringstrom, "One Size Doesn't Fit All: IKEA Goes Local for India, China," http://in.reuters.com, March 7, 2013.
2. "Ikea Announces Global Expansion Plans," www.oregonlive.com, January 23, 2013.
3. "IKEA Shopping Malls as Expansion Opportunity for Retailers," www.property-magazine.eu, November 22, 2012.
4. Mark Bergen, "IKEA in India: Heading into Untapped Retail Terrain," www.forbes.com, November 21, 2012.
5. Fiona Briggs, "Ikea's Mega Shopping Malls Are Gateway for Western Retailers to Enter Russia," http://retailtimes.co.uk, November 20, 2012.
6. Ben Quinn, "Ikea Apologizes over Removal of Women from Saudi Arabia Catalogue," www.guardian.co.uk, October 2, 2012.

7. Mark J. Miller, "Ikea Looks to Asia for Growth, as Russia's Old Growth (Trees) Cause Concerns," www.brandchannel.com, June 12, 2012.
8. Matt Hickman, "IKEA under Fire for Clearing Ancient Russian Forest," www.forbes.com, June 6, 2012.
9. "IKEA Sacks Four French Managers over Spying Scandal," www.telegraph.co.uk, May 18, 2012.
10. "IKEA to Open Bank in Russia," http://en.rian.ru, April 27, 2012.
11. Svetlana Smetanina, "Living in Russia as a Foreigner: The Memoirs of Former Ikea Boss Reveal an Unusual Truth," www.telegraph.co.uk, April 27, 2011.
12. Henry Meyer, "Corruption Halts IKEA in Russia," www.theage.com.au, March 7, 2011.
13. Henry Meyer, "Russia Repels Retailers as Ikea Halt Curtails Medvedev Goal," www.bloomberg.com, March 2, 2011.
14. "The Secret of IKEA's Success," www.economist.com, February 24, 2011.
15. Vivian Tse, "Ikea Owner 'Distressed' Over Russian Expansion," www.thelocal.se, December 11, 2010.
16. Jesse Heath, "IKEA in Russia: Now 'Everything Is Possible' ... For A Price," www.opendemocracy.net, February 22, 2010.
17. "Growing IKEA Russia Corruption Scandal – Two Execs Fired," http://therussiamonitor.com, February 15, 2010.
18. Andrew E. Kramer, "Ikea Tries to Build Public Case against Russian Corruption," www.nytimes.com, September 11, 2009.
19. "What Ikea's Decision to Halt Expansion in Russia Says about Corruption," www.goodhonestdollar.com, July 6, 2009.
20. Nataliya Vasilyeva, "Red Tape Stalls Ikea Russian Expansion," www.thestar.com, June 12, 2009.
21. www.ikea.com/ru/
22. eng.megamall.ru/company/Russia
23. www.ikea.com
24. www.retailbusinessrussia.com
25. www.pwc.com

LONG CASE QUESTIONS

1. What are the various external factors that a company must take into account while devising a market strategy for a new country? Discuss these factors in the Russian context and in the actions taken by IKEA.
2. What are some of the specific ethical dilemmas faced by IKEA because of the Russian government? How did IKEA's stance on corruption prove problematic for them?
3. What is the impact of strong and cooperative political machinery on the business prospects of an emerging market? In this context, discuss IKEA's experiences in Russia.
4. What are the strategies to be undertaken by a company to grow its business in an emerging market? What should IKEA's strategy be going forward with respect to the ethical dilemmas presented by the Russian government?

Part II: Comprehensive Case

BRISTOL-MYERS SQUIBB: PATENTS, PROFITS, AND PUBLIC SCRUTINY

Abstract

This case discusses challenges faced by Bristol-Myers Squibb during the tenure of former CEO Peter Dolan, including an accounting scandal and a patent protection dispute involving Plavix, a drug that contributes 30% of the company's global revenue.

"All The World's A Stage"

Bob Zito let out a deep breath as he hung up the phone in his office. It was 11:07am on Saturday morning, and the weather was perfect for the first college football game day of the season. He opened his office window to let in the brisk autumn air of September 2, 2006, and tried to relax for the first time in what felt like weeks. His corporate counsel had called to tell him that the U.S. District Court for the Southern District of New York had just granted Bristol-Myers Squibb a preliminary injunction against the Canadian generic drug producer Apotex.

Zito leaned back in his chair, thankful for the breathing space. In the past month alone, Apotex's generic version of Bristol-Myers' Plavix had siphoned off almost 75 percent of the $4 billion annual market for the blockbuster blood thinner. Many pharmacies had already stocked up multiple months' worth of the product, but this injunction would prevent Apotex from shipping any more of the generic until the patent-protection question was resolved.

Zito was grateful for the temporary respite, which he hoped to use to construct and implement a corporate communication strategy to help the embattled pharmaceutical giant. Such a strategy would have to be comprehensive and incredibly detailed, addressing the widely-publicized Apotex negotiation scandal, the potential loss of patent protection (and revenues) for the company's best-selling drug, and the looming dismissal of Bristol-Myers' CEO, while simultaneously steering attention away from the company's past ethical troubles. Zito opened his laptop and checked the time. With a sigh, he resigned himself to the fact that he wasn't likely to make it home in time to watch the game.

The History of Bristol-Myers Squibb

Bristol-Myers Squibb is the leading worldwide provider of anti-cancer therapies, as well as a leader in the discovery and development of innovative treatments to fight heart disease, stroke, and infectious diseases including HIV/AIDS. Its areas of specialization include most of the pharmaceutical spectrum, from oncology to cardiovascular disease to infectious diseases (including HIV/AIDS) and mental illness. The company enjoys a distinguished history: in the early 1960s Bristol-Myers produced its first anti-cancer medicine (still in use today), while the 1980s witnessed Squibb market the first of an important new class of medications, called ACE inhibitors, for the treatment of hypertension. In 1989 these two companies joined forces in one of the largest mergers in corporate history. During the 1990s, Bristol-Myers Squibb brought to market the first medicine specifically designed for the treatment of HIV/AIDS, as well as a breakthrough therapy "hailed as the most important cancer medication in 20 years."[1]

Bristol-Myers

In 1887, William McLaren Bristol and John Ripley Myers invested $5,000 into a failing drug manufacturing firm located in Clinton, New York. The company was officially incorporated on December 13, 1887, and in May 1898 changed its name to the Bristol, Myers Company (a hyphen would replace the comma when the company became a corporation in 1899).

The partners strove to grow the business in a challenging environment, maintaining two rules above all: an insistence on high quality products and the maintenance of the firm's good financial standing at all costs. With these two priorities in mind, Bristol-Myers became profitable for the first time in 1900, and from 1903 to 1905 saw a tenfold increase in sales. Bristol-Myers was transformed from a regional to a national company, soon to become an international one. With the company's products being sold in 26 countries, gross profits topped $1 million for the first time in 1924. At the same time, "the shares held by John Myers's heirs became available for sale, triggering a series of moves that in 1929 turned Bristol-Myers into a publicly held company, listed on the New York Stock Exchange."[2] Subsequent business decisions saw Bristol-Myers take over smaller, well-managed pharmaceutical firms in a strategy of growth through judicious acquisition that has continued to this day.[3]

Squibb

Edward Robinson Squibb founded his pharmaceutical company in 1858, headquartered in Brooklyn, New York. He dedicated Squibb to the production of "consistently pure medicines", a cause that claimed his lifelong interest. In 1906, six years after Edward Squibb's death, Congress passed the Pure Food and Drugs Act. As related in company lore, the law still stands as the triumph of his lifelong crusade for safe, reliable pharmaceutical products.[4] In 1921, Squibb adopted a slogan that reflected the ideals of its founder: "The priceless ingredient in every product is the honor and integrity of its maker." The company enjoyed respectable growth, and the company expanded into South America and Europe. Squibb International was incorporated in 1946, and built manufacturing facilities in Mexico, Italy and Argentina. Squibb researchers made a significant breakthrough in 1975 with the creation of Capoten®, the first of a brand-new class of antihypertensive agents called ACE inhibitors.

Bristol-Myers Squibb (BMS)

Bristol-Myers merged with Squibb in 1989, creating a global leader in the healthcare industry. The merger created what was then the world's second-largest pharmaceutical enterprise. BMS core products include: Videx (1991), Monopril (1991) and Pravachol (1991, expanded usage granted in 1995 by the FDA), TAXOL Injection (1991), Glucophage (1993), Avapro (1997), Plavix (1997), Excedrin (1998), Sustiva capsules (2001), Coumadin Crystalline (2001), Abilify (2002), Reyataz (2004), Orencia (2005), EMSAM transdermal (2006), SPRYCEL (2006), and ATRIPLA (2006). Bristol-Myers Squibb received the National Medal of Technology in December 1998, an award widely respected as America's highest honor for technological innovation. The company received outstanding recognition "for extending and enhancing human life through innovative pharmaceutical research and development, and for redefining the science of clinical study through groundbreaking and hugely complex clinical trials that are recognized models in the industry."[5]BMS attempts to act as a good global corporate citizen and live the ideals of its founders through its outreach programs.

In 1999, the company announced Secure the Future, a $100 million commitment to advance HIV/AIDS research and community outreach programs in five southern African countries. In 2000, BMS and four other pharmaceutical companies and international agencies joined the UNAIDS "Drug ACCESS Initiative," which aims to make antiretroviral medicines and therapies widely available in African countries that have developed a coherent national AIDS strategy. As part of the program, the company offered to lower the prices of HIV/AIDS medicines in those countries by 90 percent.

More recently, Bristol-Myers Squibb took its access efforts a step further, offering HIV/AIDS drugs below cost in Africa. The company is also ensuring that its patents do not prevent inexpensive HIV/AIDS therapy in Africa.[6] BMS had 2005 revenues of approximately $19 billion, with profits of $3 billion. This is a -7.6% decrease and 25.6% increase, respectively, on 2004 results.[7] R&D expenditures in 2005 were $2.7 billion, up 10% from 2004. This included $2.5 billion in payments for in-licensing and development programs. The first quarter of 2006 saw $750 million spent on R&D, up 22% from the previous year.

BMS is determined to retain its position as a leader in drug development. Current strategies include: in-house development and collaboration, the acquisition of smaller dynamic pharmaceutical companies, the divestiture of non-core assets (including the May 2005 sale of BMS' Oncology Therapeutics Network distribution business, as well as the divestiture of the U.S. and Canadian Consumer Medicines business to Novartis).

BMS' forecast for the future is cautiously optimistic. New BMS blockbuster drugs may strengthen the company's financial position. In the first half of 2003 two major drugs were approved: Abilify, an antipsychotic, and Reyataz, the first once-daily protease inhibitor for the treatment of HIV/AIDS. The FDA also granted limited clearance to Erbitux, the sidelined cancer drug that BMS developed in conjunction with ImClone. Analysts at SunTrust Robinson Humphrey estimated that Erbitux sales could peak at more than $700 million. These promising drugs signal a potential new beginning for the company. Morningstar projects an average revenue growth rate of 3 percent through 2007. However, generic challengers continue to enter the market at a steady pace, and there is the constant threat of competition from the large drug developers (Merck, Novartis, and Pfizer) in BMS's core territories. If the first quarter is a trend indicator, 2006 will be more profitable for BMS: the company reported a 34% increase in first-quarter profit to $714 million, helped by higher sales of heart and blood-pressure drugs, and a $200 million gain from the sale of assets. Erbitux sales were $413 million for the year up 58%. Plavix, Abilify, and Reyataz sales were up 15%, 54% and 68% respectively – definitely a bright spot for the company. Nevertheless, revenues were up only 3% to $4.7 billion, while the average U.S. pharmaceutical industry revenues rose 7% to $2.1 billion.[8] In February 2001, *Fortune* magazine named Bristol-Myers Squibb "America's Most Admired Pharmaceutical Company." One month later, Peter R. Dolan, a 13-year veteran of the company, succeeded Charles A. Heimbold, Jr., as chief executive officer.[9]

Peter R. Dolan

Peter R. Dolan was born on January 6, 1956, in Salem, Massachusetts. He received his BA from Tufts University in 1978, and his MBA from Dartmouth College in 1980. He began his career at General Foods from 1983–1987, but by 1988 had transferred to Bristol-Myers Squibb as Vice-President of Marketing.

Dolan served as president of the Mead Johnson Nutritional Group from 1995–1996. Under his direction, the company opened related manufacturing facilities in four countries and international sales climbed to 40 percent of the corporation's revenue by 1996.

Dolan was named CEO in February 2001 and made Chairman of the Board in 2002. He was infamous within the company for setting "Big Hairy Audacious Goals", such as his 2001 promise to double BMS revenues within five years. He would come to regret that particular statement, as 2002 sales totaled $18.1 billion, down 1% from 2000.

Robert Zito and BMS Corporate Communications

Robert T. Zito joined Bristol-Myers Squibb as Chief Communications Officer (CCO) in June 2004. Zito received his BA in English from Fairfield University and is a 1998 Ellis Island Medal of Honor recipient.[10] He is responsible for implementing external and internal communications initiatives, as well as developing a long-term corporate strategic communications plan for BMS. He oversees all aspects of communication and public relations for the company, including corporate brand management, advertising, media relations, employee and policy communications, executive prep and communications, creative services and community affairs.[11]

Before accepting his current position with BMS, Zito was the EVP of Communications at the New York Stock Exchange, where he was responsible for developing and building the NYSE's brand. He has also worked as VP of Corporate Communications at Sony (North America), VP of CN Communications, and as an account executive at the public relations firm of Hill and Knowlton.[12]

What is Plavix?

Plavix was an FDA-approved anti-platelet daily medication that reduced the risk of heart attack, stroke or vascular death in patients with established peripheral arterial disease (PAD).[13] The drug had also been shown to reduce occurrences of peripheral artery disease and stroke. Plavix was brought to market through a partnership between Bristol-Myers Squibb and French drug maker Sanofi-Aventis, the world's third largest pharmaceutical company and the largest in Europe.

Plavix Function

Clot formation is a natural defense mechanism of the body that protects excessive bleeding in the case of an injury. When the skin is cut, particles in human blood called platelets bond together to form a clot. Clot formation can also be triggered by the rupture of plaque, which is a buildup of cholesterol and other materials in the walls of the arteries. When platelets clump together on or near the plaque, they can form a clot that may limit or completely stop the flow of blood to various parts of the body. If a clot forms in an artery leading to the heart, heart-related chest pain or a heart attack may occur. If a clot forms in an artery leading to the brain, it can cause a stroke. Plavix prevents platelets from sticking together and forming clots, which keeps blood flowing and helps protect against future heart attack or stroke.

Plavix Revenues

Plavix 2005 global sales were $5.9 billion, up more than 15% from 2004.[14] According to Pharmaceutical Business Revenue and Data Monitor, sales were expected to peak at $6 billion in 2011, when the Plavix patent was expected to expire. Bristol-Myers Squibb total 2005 revenues were $19.2 billion; Plavix sales thus represented 30% of the company's total revenues.

Pharmaceutical Industry

The global pharmaceutical sales market in 2005 was $565 billion, growing at an estimated 7% per year.[15] Generic competition is currently the principal threat to branded drug makers. Between 2006 and 2010, at least 70 innovative brand-name drugs are expected to go off-patent in the United States. Nineteen of these drugs are "blockbusters," meaning that they have annual sales of more than $1-billion. This accounts for $45 billion in revenues, or roughly 8% of the global market.[16]

Generic Drug Competition

A generic drug may be comparable to a brand name drug in dosage form, strength, performance characteristics and intended use. Brand name drug patents are usually protected for 20 years from the date of the patent submission.[17] The patent protects the drug manufacturer that incurred the costs of researching, developing and marketing the drug. Once a drug's patent has expired, any other drug company may release a generic version. Generic drugs tend to be drastically cheaper than brand-name drugs, with prices ranging from 20–70 percent of the brand-name version.

FDA Approval: Brand Name and Generic Drugs

All new drugs must be approved for human use by the United States Food and Drug Administration. The approval process includes laboratory, animal and human testing. Human testing is completed in three phases and may include data collected from thousands of patients. It is not uncommon for a drug to take as long as eight years to be approved.[18] Generic drugs must also obtain FDA approval. However, generic drugs may take advantage of an abbreviated process wherein they do not have to submit the generic drug for animal or human tests, as the drug's safety and effectiveness were already established in the initial clinical trials.

Accounting Irregularities: Dolan's Troubles Begin

On March 10, 2003, just over two years after Dolan took over as CEO, Bristol-Myers Squibb announced that it had overstated sales by $2.5 billion over a three-year period. The earnings overstatement was due to Bristol-Myers employing a "channel surfing" scheme in which the company used financial incentives that rewarded wholesalers for buying and holding larger prescription drug inventories. The scheme resulted in wholesalers acquiring almost $2 billion in excess inventories. Bristol-Myers eventually admitted that the incentives were designed to help the company meet its quarterly sales projections.[19]

Bristol's accounting troubles continued when former CFO Frederick S. Schiff and former executive vice president Richard J. Lane were indicted and charged with securities fraud for artificially inflating sales through the channel surfing scheme. Schiff and Lane were also charged with signing inaccurate SEC filings and purposely misleading investors through press releases and conference calls that masked the increasing wholesaler drug inventories. Both were asked to leave in 2001.

At the end of the scandal, Bristol-Myers Squibb reduced net sales figures by $1.4 billion for 2001, $678-million for 2000, and $376 million for 1999.[20] A total of $839 million was paid to shareholders harmed by BMS' fraudulent conduct.[21] The Department of Justice agreed to dismiss criminal complaints against the company if it cooperated with the legal investigation, admitted wrongdoing, and adopted strict internal compliance controls.

Plavix Generic Drug Agreement

In July 2006, BMS announced that the U.S. Justice Department was investigating the company's March 2006 agreement with Canadian generic drug manufacturer Apotex. The agreement was intended to delay Apotex's release of an inexpensive generic version of Plavix. The investigation led FBI agents to search Dolan's office in New York the day before the announcement was made.

Under the terms of Bristol-Myers' ill-conceived agreement with Apotex, BMS offered Apotex $40 million to halt production of the generic Plavix until June 1, 2011. This date was five months before the Plavix patent was set to expire.[22] Bristol-Myers also agreed not to release its own non-branded Plavix until six months after Apotex began to sell its generic version of the blood thinner. When asked to approve the agreement, the U.S. Federal Trade Commission and state Attorneys General objected to these provisions. They labeled the Bristol-Myers concession anti-competitive because it assured that Apotex would be the sole market vendor of cheap, generic Plavix for at least six months.[23] Bristol-Myers Squibb agreed to remove the anti-competitive provision from the contract. Nevertheless, the Federal Trade Commission began questioning Apotex regarding the revised agreement. During these questioning sessions, Apotex told the federal regulators that Bristol-Myers had given Apotex private assurance that it would not release a general version of Plavix to the market.[24] These statements, which contradicted statements made by Bristol-Myers to the FTC, led the Federal Trade Commission to pursue a criminal investigation into the rejected contract.

When the agreement did not receive approval, Apotex quickly introduced its generic version of Plavix (which had obtained FDA approval earlier that year), and the drug became universally available in August 2006. While Plavix cost about $4 per dose in the U.S., Apotex priced the generic version at an estimated 10 to 20 percent discount.[25] Apotex's generic Plavix quickly gained 75% market share of new prescriptions.[26] Within the month, Bristol-Myers Squibb was able to get a United States District Judge to order a temporary injunction halting further sales of the generic Plavix. However, the judge did not order a recall of generic Plavix. The District Court set January 22, 2007 as the start of the patent trial. The Court required Bristol-Myers and Sanofi-Aventis (BMS' Plavix development partner) to post a $400 million bond to the court. The bond provided security to Apotex in the event that the Court ruled that Apotex had the legal right to sell its generic version of Plavix.

After only one month of generic Plavix competition, BMS was forced to reduce its 2006 earnings forecast by 25%. Bristol-Myers' reduced per share earnings estimate was below the company dividend, meaning that Bristol would be paying more to shareholders than it actually earned.[27] Citing the threat of generic competition, Moody's Investor Services downgraded Bristol-Myers' debt from A1 to A2. The BMS Board stated that it still intended to declare its regular 28 cents per share quarterly dividend, but some analysts predicted that the lost Plavix sales would force Bristol-

Myers to slash the dividend in half. In sum, over the five years of Dolan's tenure, the stock price of Bristol-Myers Squibb had declined by over 60%.[28]

The Board Decides to Act

On September 12, 2006, CEO Peter Dolan and General Counsel Richard K. Willard were dismissed by the Bristol-Myers board. Dolan was replaced on an interim basis by James M. Cornelius, a Bristol-Myers director and former executive at Guidant Corporation. The board maintained that it would search both internally and externally for a permanent replacement, but Dolan's firing increased Wall Street speculation that Bristol-Myers would be acquired.

The Uncertain Path Ahead for Bristol-Myers Squibb

As Dolan's rocky tenure came to a close, CCO Zito wondered what he needed to communicate to stakeholders to overcome Bristol-Myers' poor financial projections questionable practices over the past five years. With the threat of acquisition looming larger, Zito began to brainstorm, crafting a communications strategy that would help retain investor, employee and customer confidence in the pharmaceutical giant.

With the January 22, 2007 patent trial date approaching rapidly, Zito also knew he had to consider if and how corporate communication could help Bristol-Myers win its patent dispute with Apotex. If Bristol-Myers lost the legal case, it risked losing 30% of its revenues and would forfeit its share of the $400 million bond set by the U.S. District Court.

Acknowledgment

"Bristol-Myers Squibb: Patents, Profits, and Public Scrutiny." This case was prepared by Research Assistants Meghan Carter, Matt McHale, and Tom Triscari under the direction of James S. O'Rourke, Teaching Professor of Management, as the basis for class discussion rather than to illustrate either effective or ineffective handling of an administrative situation. Information was gathered from corporate as well as public sources.

Part II Comprehensive Case Notes

1 BMS Official Site: Company History. Last updated: August 2006. Website: www.bms.com/aboutbms/content/data/ourhis.html

2 Ibid.

3 Ibid.

4 Ibid.

5 Ibid.

6 Paraphrased from: Bristol-Myers Squibb Homepage. Last updated: August 2006. Website: www.bms.com/aboutbms/content/data/ourhis.html
7 CNN Money.com, *Fortune* 500 2006 rankings.
8 Website: www.contractpharma.com/articles/2006/07/bristol-myers-squibb.php
9 Quote from BMS Official Site: Company History. Last updated: August 2006. Website: www.bms.com/aboutbms/content/data/ourhis.html
10 Biography of Robert Zito. Last updated 2006. Website: www.bms.com/news/pressroom/content/data/zito.pdf
11 Ibid.
12 Adapted from Ibid.
13 Plavix Website (Bristol-Myers Squibb). Last updated: 2006. Website: www.plavix.com
14 S&P Market Insight: Pharmaceuticals Industry Survey
15 Ibid.
16 Medco Health Solutions Inc. & S&P Market Insight
17 Generic Drugs: Questions & Answers. Website: www.fda.gov/cder/consumerinfo/generics_q&a.htm.
18 "Solving The Drug Patent Problem." Last updated: May 2, 2002. Website: www.forbes.com/2002/05/02/0502patents.html.
19 "Bitter Pill? Bristol-Myers Squibb Off by $900 Million." Last updated: March 11, 2003. Website: www.cfo.com/printable/article.cfm/3008682?f=options
20 Ibid.
21 "Bristol's Former CFO Indicted." Last updated: June 17, 2005. Website: www.cfo.com/article.cfm/4096065?f=related
22 "Bristol stock hurt by generic Plavix." Last updated: August 8, 2006. Website: http://money.cnn.com/2006/08/08/news/companies/plavix/index.htm?postversion=2006080812
23 "Bristol-Myers Probed For Deceiving U.S. Regulators." Last updated: July 29, 2006. Website: www.investmentsmagazine.com/ManageArticle.asp?C=160&A=17351
24 Ibid.
25 "Battle over a Blood Thinner Goes to Court." Last updated: August 18, 2006. Website: www.npr.org/templates/story/story.php?storyId=5673477
26 "Bristol-Myers Ousts CEO Dolan, Willard." Last updated: September 12, 2006. Website: www.wtopnews.com/?nid=111&pid=0&sid=909672&page=2
27 "Bristol-Myers Chief Fired Over Patent Dispute." Last updated: September 12, 2006. Website: www.nytimes.com/2006/09/12/business/13bristolcnd.html?pagewanted=1&ei=5088&en=829899f21a96a8a2& ex=1315713600&partner=rssnyt&emc=rss
28 "Bristol-Myers CEO Forced Out." Last updated: September 12, 2006. Website: http://news.yahoo.com/s/nm/20060912/bs_nm/bristolmyers_dc

COMPREHENSIVE CASE QUESTIONS

1. What are the critical issues facing Bristol-Myers Squibb in this case?
2. Who are the key stakeholders in this case? How would a patent case verdict for or against Bristol-Myers Squibb affect the stakeholders?
3. What messages does Zito need to communicate to the stakeholder groups? How should he deliver his message to them?
4. Does Bristol-Myers Squibb need to retain an external firm to help it craft an effective public response to Dolan's firing or the patent dispute?

5. What other actions (if any) should the board take in response to the accounting and patent protection scandals?
6. What mistakes did Dolan make while negotiating with Apotex? What else could he have done to protect the Plavix patent?
7. Can corporate communication play a role in helping Bristol-Myers Squibb win the upcoming patent protection trial? What can Zito and his team do?

Part III

The Environment

Chapter 9

Information Technology and Ethics

LEARNING OBJECTIVES

After reading this chapter you should be able to:

- Understand how the use of information technology is bringing about important ethical implications
- Learn about the various forms of social media and the ethical implications of such social media for company stakeholders
- Become aware of the need for properly managing the ethical implications of social media
- Understand the growth of e-commerce worldwide and the consequent ethical implications such as e-commerce privacy, e-commerce security, and e-commerce trust
- Learn about other IT ethical issues such as those occurring in global e-commerce and the global digital divide
- Become aware of the amount of waste created by IT and the steps companies can take to minimize the impact of such waste

PREVIEW BUSINESS ETHICS INSIGHT

IT and Business Ethics

The use of information technology is raising many new ethical issues for companies and employees worldwide. Consider the following short cases:

- A few weeks before a Canadian Mazda car dealership became unionized, two employees started posting disparaging comments about their employer and supervisor. One of the employees posted hostile comments about his supervisor, while the other employee started posting profanities about the company. The second employee went as far as advising his Facebook friends not to patronize the car dealership. Both employees were then fired. The company argued that their comments created a hostile work environment while also damaging the company's reputation and business interests.

- Beginning with when they were created, social media platforms such as Facebook and Twitter were not held responsible for the criminal activities that took place on their platforms. These companies were regarded more as telecom companies. However, more governments are now making these internet companies responsible for postings on their platforms. For instance, social media companies will be required to remove hateful or other inaccurate messages within 24 hours of being posted. Violators run the risk of large fines if they do not obey such directives. In the UK, firms will be encouraged to block objectionable content as soon as they appear.
- Retailers are now making increasing use of tracking technologies to follow customers in a store. They can track movement of customers by tracking the smartphones of the owners. Retailers gain from such monitoring because they can figure out where most of the traffic within a store is occurring for better advertisement placement. Additionally, if companies can merge such tracking with personal information, it will be possible for retailers to offer customized deals to entice a customer to shop.
- While multinationals have benefitted tremendously from information technologies, the data that they are collecting and storing has become desirable objects for hackers. There are now more cyberattacks on companies now and cybercrime costs the global economy between $450 and $600 billion a year. Cyberattacks will continue to become ever more frequent and multinationals will be more pressed to safeguard their data.

Based on Crawshaw, C. 2010. "Status update: 'You're fired.'" *Canadian HR Reporter*, 23, 21; Derousseau, R. 2017. "A big payoff for cybercop stocks." *Fortune*, September 1, 28–31; *The Economist*. 2017. "The global techlash; Chaining giants." August 12, 46–47; *The Economist*. 2017. "Retailing; Following the fashion." December 24, 87.

The Preview Business Ethics Insight above shows four short cases of the ethical issues presented by new **information technologies (IT)**. The internet and new forms of social media have brought a host of new ethical dilemmas that companies have to contend with. Companies are finding that using such new technologies can be very rewarding. However, the misuse of such technologies can also be very damaging, as such misuse gets communicated to thousands of individuals over the internet. Additionally, IT is allowing massive amounts of data collection. Such data collection also means that multinationals are under increased pressure to safeguard such data. Such issues are also posing ethical issues for companies.

To understand the implications of IT, it is first necessary to examine how information gathering and storing has changed. Information collection is not new. According to

Beauchamp et al., governments and private agencies have always been involved in collecting data and keeping such records.[1] However, IT has brought a number of changes that make data gathering and storing different. First, data can now be collected and stored on a very large scale. While data collected in the past was limited to physical paper storage, IT developments have made data storing and gathering extremely cheap. For example, a computer can easily store the web navigation of any individual. Second, the types of information that are being collected have also changed. As you will see later, companies now routinely scan their employees' e-mails and online activities and take actions on those. Such information can now be easily collected. Finally, it is also easy for companies to exchange information. Customer information collected by one company can easily be shared with other companies without the customers' knowledge and marketing decisions made on such information.

As more companies exchange information about transactions with their business partners, employees, customers, and other stakeholders, many more ethical issues are arising.[2] Today, most companies have to contend with IT ethical concerns such as confidence in customer online transactions, safeguarding threats to data integrity, safeguarding employee and customer privacy, while also protecting sensitive proprietary organizational information. Properly managing ethical aspects of IT is therefore becoming a critical aspect of any company's ethical program. This chapter will therefore examine the ethical aspects of IT.

From a strategic standpoint, it is also becoming more critical for companies to manage their IT ethics. Consider the case of Ms. Dawanmarie Souza, an employee of a Connecticut-based ambulance services company who was asked by her supervisor to prepare an investigative report concerning a customer complaint about her work.[3] Before preparing the report, she requested but was denied union representation. When she got home, she posted a negative comment about her supervisor on the popular social media outlet Facebook. When she posted the comments, her coworkers responded in supportive fashion, leading to even more negative comments about the supervisor. However, when she went back to work, she was suspended and eventually terminated. However, after the company fired the employee, the National Labor Review Board filed a complaint against the company, arguing that the employee's Facebook postings are protected by the National Labor Relations Act. The company was also told that their social media policies were too restrictive, as they violated the law. The company had to therefore settle with the employee. The cases also show the potential damage to a company's strategic health if they do not properly understand the ethical implications of their IT operations. Improper action can result in devastating losses that can put the company's reputation and financial health in danger. However, if properly implemented, IT ethical programs can also be a source of competitive advantage.

Given the above, we examine the ethical implications of IT for a multinational. We first discuss the ethical implications of social media. The explosion in use of social media has led to new ethical dilemmas for companies. We also look at the growth of e-commerce and the many ethical issues (consumer privacy, e-commerce trust) associated with such growth. Finally, we examine IT in a globalized world and the many ethical issues such aspects take. Specifically, we look at the ethics of operating e-commerce globally, the global digital divide, and the waste created by the use of IT.

SOCIAL MEDIA AND ETHICS

"**Social media**" is the popular term that refers to the advanced internet technology and applications that have largely enabled collaboration among internet users. Social media sites all form part of the new Web 2.0 phenomena. Unlike the Web 1.0, whereby few entities had control on the construction of websites and flow of information.

Web 2.0 is user-generated, allowing millions of individuals to interact. An important aspect of Web 2.0 is online social networking that allows the creation of virtual communities "which have opened up possibilities for rich, online human-to-human interactions unprecedented in the history of Internet communication."[4] Much of Web 2.0 is thus based on exchange of personal information online. Examples of social media platforms include blogging, YouTube, Facebook, LinkedIn, Wikipedia, Twitter, and Yammer. Exhibit 9.1 shows some of the more popular social media websites and how they are used.

Why should companies be concerned about the ethical implications of social media? Consider the following Strategic Business Ethics Insight.

As the Strategic Business Ethics Insight shows, social media is critical for companies. Adequate use of social media can build a stronger brand and help address the needs of stakeholders in a more ethical manner. This need is even more critical considering that few companies devote attention to social media.[5] However, as the above shows, data collection and storing raises two other critical issues, namely privacy and transparency.

Social Media	Functions
Blogs	Blogs refer to a combination of the terms "web" and "log." Blogs give readers the ability to leave comments in an interactive format in response to other people's comments.
Video sharing sites	YouTube and others give users the ability to easily post videos for viewing by web users.
Social networks	Websites such as Facebook and LinkedIn give users the ability to connect and share personal information.
Wikis	Wikis are sites that allow the easy creation and editing of webpages. For example, Wikipedia allows users to post and update information about a large number of topics.
Augmented reality	Technology that blends the virtual world with reality.
Micro-blogging	Sites such as Twitter that allow people to share information based on a number of limited characters.
Massively multi-player online role-playing game	Site that allows a large number of users to interact in a virtual world. An example is World of Warcraft.
WikiLeaks	Host of websites that leak information about governments or companies.

EXHIBIT 9.1—Examples of Social Media

STRATEGIC **BUSINESS ETHICS INSIGHT**

Ethical Implications of Social Media

Some of the short cases discussed in the Preview Business Ethics Insight at the beginning of the chapter show that it is strategically important for companies to properly understand the ethical implications of social media for their operations. Failure to do so can result in serious damages that can hurt a company's finances and reputation. Recovering from such mistakes can be very difficult.

When properly managed, social media can have important benefits for companies. Companies such as Comcast and Zappos are well known for engaging customers on Twitter. Furthermore, Zappos is known to respond to complaints posted on Twitter quickly. In another example, Southwest Airlines was able to respond quickly to complaints when Kevin Smith, the film director, complained that he was not allowed to board a Southwest flight because of his weight. Monsoon, a fashion retailer, used social media to fight inaccurate information about its supply chain. When stories came out about alleged use of child labor in its supply chain, it quickly used Twitter and its Facebook page to fight such false information.

Recent studies of companies also show that companies are keenly aware of the importance of social media to their business. For instance, a review of such research suggested that 86% of the companies viewed social media as gaining critical importance within three years. Additionally, consumers are also going online worldwide at a fast pace. Consider that it is estimated that there will be 225 million users of social media in 2018. Rural India is also seeing growth averaging 100%. And consumers are also likely to rely on each other regarding company and product reputation rather than company backed media.

Social media is also enabling companies to gather massive amounts of information. However, collection of such data is raising many new ethical questions. Companies need to collect such data appropriately while also making such data accessible only to appropriate individuals. Additionally, such data collection is raising issues of privacy whereby the ownership and control of such data is relevant. Many countries are now starting to implement regulations to address such issues.

Based on Baker, R. 2010. "Monsoon uses social media to fight claims." *Marketing Week*, November 25, 4; Brandel, M. 2010. "Are you listening?" *Computerworld*, July 12, 44, 13, 13; *The Economist*. 2017. "The Dodd-Frank of data." *The World in 2018*, 123–124; Kaul, A. and Chaudhri, V. "Social media: The new mantra for managing reputation." *Vikalpa*, October–December, 40, 455–460; Mishra, S. 2015. "Saying 'sorry': The role of apology in online crisis communication in India." *Vikalpa*, October–December, 40, 466–469.

Privacy refers to the ability of individuals to control or restrict access to information about them. This is considered a fundamental human right.[6] In fact, in an influential paper, Rachels argues that privacy is extremely important because it allows people to maintain the diversity of relationships they value.[7] For instance, people at work should only act professionally and provide information that is professionally relevant. What the person does in his/her private life may not necessarily be relevant to the work environment. However, if information about different relationships is revealed (e.g., information about the person's partying habits), privacy of the individual is breached. Consider, for instance, when posted party pictures from Facebook are used to decide whether someone should be hired or promoted. Should such information be relevant to human resource management decisions? Should such activities be used in, for example, promotion decisions?

Mooradian argues that computers have greatly modified people's privacy.[8] To appreciate the issue of privacy with regards to social media, Mooradian distinguishes among three forms of information; namely, institution specific personal information such as medical and financial information, socially sensitive personal information such as embarrassing information, and biographical personal information such as mundane facts about who a person is, etc. Mooradian further argues that there is ample regulation in the U.S. to limit access to institutional specific personal information. However, most access to biographical information remains virtually unregulated, whereby companies can easily access and use such information.

Mooradian continues by suggesting that most aspects of social media rely a lot on biographical personal information. For instance, blogging is a medium where people routinely disclose very personal aspects of their information. Furthermore, bloggers need to understand that blogs tend to be accessible to the public and their personal information is thus accessible to millions of internet users. Similarly, social networks provide users with pages where very personal information can be listed. In both cases, companies can have easy access to significant amounts of information and make use of such information.

It is clear from the above that social media use is affecting privacy of individuals. Most people using apps will typically agree to various conditions that are set out in long contracts. These regulations also often ask users to give up their privacy. Companies then use the data they have gathered to improve products or to find other meaningful intelligence that can be used to improve a company's performance.

Given the above and the cases discussed earlier, social networks present significant ethical risks to companies. Such risks exist for many stakeholders. However, it is most pronounced for employees. Companies therefore need to implement privacy policies for employees to avoid potential ethical risks and consequent legal repercussions of such risks. As we saw earlier, breaching social media ethics can result in unnecessary negative publicity and legal costs as companies are sued by employees. To address ethical implications for employee use of social media, experts suggest the following:[9]

- Employees should be made aware that companies constantly monitor their social media postings for legitimate and business reasons. Because such information is publicly available, employees should not expect privacy. However, companies should not access other sources of information that may not be publicly available as this would violate privacy laws.

- Monitoring social media to ensure that employees are not creating social media communication that is supposed to represent the company. Employees should also be warned to properly inform viewers that postings represent their own views rather than the company's views. Furthermore, to avoid potential conflicts, employees should be encouraged to disclose their employment with the company when commenting on the company's products or services.
- Inform employees that all communications they make are public. Such communications should thus be made in good taste, representing the company values. For instance, employees should be encouraged to avoid insulting coworkers or others or denigrating competitors. As such, employees should be informed that general policies regarding employee communication apply to social media too. As such, employees should refrain from harassment or discrimination. However, employees should also know that their rights to expression about discussion regarding their terms and conditions of employment and unionization is protected by law and that they have the ability to discuss such issues. Consider the Business Ethics Brief below.
- Employees should also be encouraged to avoid posting sensitive information. Experts suggest avoiding identification and discussion of others such as competitors or coworkers. Employees should make sure that posted materials are not copyrighted. It is important for employees to know that posted information is often impossible to delete and all efforts should be made to protect such information.

BUSINESS ETHICS BRIEF

Justine Sacco and the Twitter Disaster

In December 2013, Justine Sacco, PR Manager of InterActive Corp (IAC) tweeted a 12-word comment about her upcoming trip to Africa. Her tweet read "Going to Africa. Hope I don't get Aids. Just kidding. I'm White." She only had 170 followers and did not think twice about the tweet. After she made the tweet, she boarded a flight to Cape Town from New York. When she landed in New York, her tweet was one of the top trending tweets. During her flight, a technology blogger had shared her tweet across the internet. Not surprisingly, the tweet was viewed as being racist and the hashtag #hasjustinelanded had become one of the most trending tweets. When she landed at the airport in Cape Town, she found that she was fired by her company. IAC is the parent company of many leading companies on the internet (e.g., Vimeo, OkCupid etc.) and they had no tolerance for such a tweet that were against company values.

Based on Pridmore, J. 2015. "Employee social media monitoring: Corporate reputation and new workplace surveillance practices." *Vikalpa*, October–December, 472–475.

- Employees should be discouraged from using social media during work times. Furthermore, to avoid potential ethical conflicts, employees should be warned of the potential risks of "friending" subordinates or supervisors. Some companies are going as far as prohibiting such relationships.

However, social media is not impacting only employees. In fact, having a social media strategy is critical as social media allows other stakeholders to have a voice that can be damaging to a company.[10] Companies no longer have total control of information being posted online or shared by consumers and other stakeholders. Because of easy accessibility through the internet, stakeholders can easily post information that may not always be accurate. Companies therefore have a critical role in clarifying information or correcting information. Consider the following Emerging Market Business Ethics Insight.

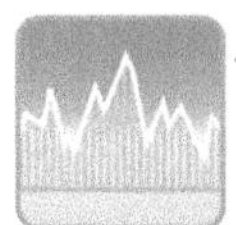

EMERGING MARKET BUSINESS ETHICS INSIGHT

Flipkart and Social Media Crisis

Flipkart is India's largest online retailer. It currently has over 100 million users and over 100 thousand sellers. It was created in 2007 and is the marketplace for over 80 million products distributed over more than 80 categories. As such, it sells a variety of products including baby care, books, laptops, smartphones etc. A LinkedIn survey also showed that it ranks #1 among companies that Indians want to work for.

It faced a crisis when it organized a "Big Billion Day Sale" the day when people shop for gifts for the well-known Hindu holiday Diwali. Many people complained that some products were priced as much as possible to give the impression of deep discounts in the case of other products. Furthermore, many products on sale seemed to be out of stock as soon as the sale started. Additionally, the company's website ran into technical difficulties and many shoppers were unable to make the purchases they wanted. Because of all these difficulties, they faced significant criticisms from their customers. Many took to social media to blame the company for not being prepared for such a sale.

Flipkart's response to the crisis is now seen as a textbook example of how companies should address such social media criticisms. The next day the company co-founders sent an e-mail (and Tweet) apologizing for the hassles shoppers had endured. Additionally, they also shared the lessons they had learned from the experience. They used the word "sorry" twice and promised to address any concerns that arose because of the scandal. Most importantly, the company was very specific about how it would make sure to address any problems that arose because of the crisis.

What did Flipkart do right? First, it responded to the crisis in very timely fashion. This showed that the company was attentive to consumer needs. Second, the apology came from the CEO. Indian consumers were not used to receiving apologies from company leaders and this had an impact. Third, Flipkart was very specific about how it would ensure that the problem would not happen again. It clearly described the steps it would take to prevent similar future crises. Finally, Flipkart also showed that apologies should first appear where the crisis erupted. Rather than having a press conference, it apologized first on Twitter and then sent a more detailed apology e-mail afterwards.

Based on Mishra, S. 2015. "Saying 'sorry': The role of apology in online crisis communication in India." *Vikalpa*, October–December, 40, 466–469.

As the above Emerging Market Business Ethics Insight shows, companies can use the power of social media to manage their reputation. However, in addition to the employee social media ethical issues discussed above, most experts agree that another critical aspect of social media ethics is **information transparency**.[11] In fact, some have even argued that "transparency, as opposed to privacy, is the new ethical issue of the century."[12] Information transparency refers to the process of making information explicitly and openly available to concerned stakeholders. For example, as Turilli and Floridi argue, transparency for green and socially ethical banks has meant that these banks had to disclose information related to their investments and the way they treat customers.[13]

Vaccaro and Madsen suggest that companies need to take a corporate approach to information transparency.[14] Specifically, they argue that more companies will be required to provide access to information as they deal with their stakeholders. As such, information transparency will become increasingly important as more companies try to gain trust and collaborate with their stakeholders. In fact, we saw in Chapter 7 how many multinationals are now becoming more transparent about their suppliers to show their commitment to improving labor conditions of their suppliers. Such efforts have been necessary to build collaborative efforts with stakeholders such as non-governmental organizations.

How can companies use social media and IT to implement information transparency policies? Vaccaro and Madsen suggest three potential avenues. First, the internet and social media can be used as a repository of critical information. Stakeholders can then easily get access to information regarding their need in the level of detail and in the format they prefer. Second, transparency can also take the form of information-sharing and exchanges. Consider the case of Johnson & Johnson, which has a presence on Twitter, YouTube, and Facebook. They use all three formats to share information and to get customer feedback on products.[15] Finally, companies can also use both of the above to find better ways to improve their information transparency for the future.

It is likely that company use of social media will continue its growth in the near future. Similar to policies governing employees with regards to social media, it is also important for companies to develop programs to address social media use with regards to other stakeholders visiting a company's various social media websites. Experts suggest the following:[16]

- Most experts agree that companies need to be transparent and truthful. Using social media to influence public opinion about the company or its products can backfire. Companies need to disclose information about itself in a truthful and honest manner.
- Companies need to clearly inform users of how collected data is being used. How such data will be shared with other companies or sold to other entities needs to be clearly explained to both customers and others who surf a company's website.
- Social media communication should be timely. For instance, the growth of microblogging use such as Twitter has grown considerably. Customers expect that companies will respond quickly to their voiced concerns. If companies wait too long to respond to such concerns, these comments can quickly become mainstream issues. Consider the case of Domino's Pizza and the employee video that showed a distasteful look at how pizza is made. Domino's Pizza waited for more than 24 hours to respond to complaints on social media and faced a significant public relations nightmare.
- Implement policies to govern the use of all social media. For instance, Johnson & Johnson has created strict policies regarding live tweeting. While live tweeting can add to a company's efforts during a live event, such efforts can also be disastrous if not done properly. Experts suggest that all tweets be reviewed by the legal department to ensure that they comply with existing rules and regulations. Care must be taken when responding to customer tweets to ensure that information is protected when needed but also divulged in an honest manner. Tweets should also provide links to relevant information on the company's website.
- Finally, it is important for company employees to be respectful and tactful when responding to customer or other stakeholder complaints. Rather than negate such complaints or berate those posting such comments, it is more advisable to consider and respond to such complaints in a respectful manner.

ELECTRONIC COMMERCE AND ETHICS

Electronic commerce (e-commerce) refers to the selling and trading of goods and services over the internet. E-commerce can occur when companies buy products from online-only companies such as Amazon.com or from companies that also have brick-and-mortar outlets (e.g., Best Buy) and have the products delivered by mail. However, e-commerce can also take place fully online, such as when a customer buys software online. Most online transactions occur either in the B2B form (business-to-business representing selling among businesses) or in the B2C form (business-to-consumers).

Electronic commerce also brings a host of ethical implications for companies. However, to appreciate the necessity of addressing the ethical implications of e-commerce, it is first important to note the explosive growth of e-commerce both in the U.S. and worldwide. Consider the Global Business Ethics Insight on the facing page.

As the Global Business Ethics Insight shows, e-commerce is predicted to grow dramatically in the future. To give you further insights on this growth, Exhibit 9.2 shows the estimated growth of e-commerce sales worldwide.

GLOBAL BUSINESS ETHICS INSIGHT

E-Commerce Activity Worldwide

The growth of e-commerce is predicted to continue growing dramatically in the near future. Consider the following:

- A recent study provides some evidence of the importance of e-commerce in the U.S. In that survey of 1164 business owners, they found that 34% sold through their own websites. 25% of the owners sold through Facebook while 16% sold through Amazon. When coupled with data that suggests that 67% of millennials, 56% of Gen Xers and 41% of baby boomers prefer to shop online than in-store, the data suggest that e-commerce will continue exploding in growth.
- Other data from Statista, an online repository of databases, shows that global retail e-commerce is predicted to grow to US$4479 billion in 2021. This is an increase of around 235% from 2014 levels. This growth has been fairly steady since
- In 2016, China had the highest business-to-customer e-commerce (US$975 billion). This was followed by the U.S. ($US648 billion), and the UK ($US192.5 billion). It is important to note that the emerging markets of India, South Korea, and Russia feature on the list of the top 10 countries with the largest business to customer markets.
- China will continue leading retail e-commerce sales. In fact, the growth of such sales will be the highest among all countries. In 2014, e-commerce sales in China was $US473 billion and it is predicted to grow to $US1973 billion in 2019. This is an increase of 317%. In contrast, the growth of retail e-commerce sales in the U.S. is predicted to increase only by 79% to $US535 billion in 2019.
- Other regions will continue seeing explosive growth. For example, a recent McKinsey report suggests that Africa will see tremendous growth over the next decade. While the internet penetration rate (% of people with access to the internet) was 16% in 2013, it is predicted to exceed 50% in 2025. Most importantly, the number of internet users will grow from 167 million users in 2013 to over 600 million users in 2025. Additionally, it is estimated that annual e-commerce sales will increase by 317% to $US75 billion. The internet will also reach more rural African consumers as 360 million individuals have smartphones.
- Experts also predict that Latin America will continue to see tremendous growth in e-commerce. While the internet penetration rate is currently only 62%, business to consumer e-commerce will continue growing steadily.

Based on Manyika, J, Cabral, A, Moodley, L., Moraje, S. Yeboah-Amankwah, S., Chui, M. and Anthonyrajah, J. 2018. "Lions go digital: The internet's transformative potential in Africa." www.mckinsey.com/industries/high-tech/our-insights/lions-go-digital-the-internets-transformative-potential-in-africa; Statista. 2018. www.statista.com.

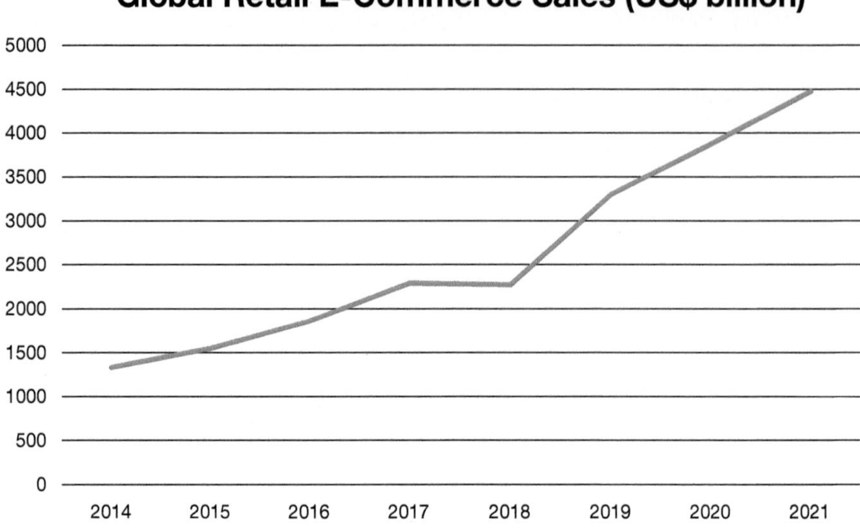

EXHIBIT 9.2—E-Commerce Sales (2014–2021)

As Exhibit 9.2 shows, the growth of e-commerce sales is predicted to be steady. Coupled with the data presented in the Global Business Ethics Insight, whether companies are operating in developed, emerging, or developing nations, they will have to contend with increased e-commerce. It will therefore become critical for multinationals to increasingly consider the ethical implications of their e-commerce operations. We consider three main interrelated areas in this section of the chapter; namely, e-commerce customer privacy, e-commerce security, and e-commerce trust.

CUSTOMER PRIVACY

In the section on social media, we discussed the privacy implications for employees. E-commerce also poses important ethical implications for **customer privacy**, the expectations that customers can protect their personal information. Why are consumers worried about privacy? While most individuals assume that surfing the web is anonymous, marketers are routinely watching every click an individual makes, every site that person visits, while also scanning every e-mail that is being written. Through such collected information, it is possible for web watchers to discover who a web user is, what the web user's interests are, and where they live. Furthermore, the seamless integration of global positioning system (GPS) technology also means that web watchers can know the exact location of any individual at any point. This has offered tremendous potential to marketers, as they engage in behavioral targeting whereby they monitor individual web surfing and provide more targeted advertising based on this information.

Pollach argues that customers are especially at risk for violation of privacy issues.[17] Consider that most online transactions require data that identifies the individual making the purchase. Use of a credit card implies disclosing information such as the buyer's home address, etc. However, through the collection of IP addresses, a company can easily match the web surfing information discussed above with the more personal information about purchases. By combining such data, companies can have access to very personal user profile.

Companies are now also increasingly relying on data mining companies to detect patterns in the data. For instance, Chiang discusses the case of Palantir, a company that created software that can integrate data from various sources and then create filters or other mapping processes for end-users.[18] For instance, data mining makes it possible for a bank to notice that many of its loans are not paid on time from customers in a specific geographic area. Is it ethical for the bank to then use this information to justify charging customers from the specific geographic area higher rates of interest?

The ethical implications of such data collection thus relates to how companies make use of the data.[19] For example, they can use the data to recognize their users and facilitate e-commerce transactions. However, companies can also share such information with other companies or use the information to send marketing e-mails or banner advertisements to users. Furthermore, because of the ease of the movement of data and access to such data, companies can either buy or sell such information. For instance, consider Facebook's recent decision to suspend some application developers from using its website. The developed "apps" which let users share information were also collecting identifiable information about Facebook users and selling such information to data brokers. Facebook found such activity in violation of its policies.

It is also important to note that privacy is viewed very differently globally. What is acceptable and legal in the U.S. may not necessarily be acceptable in other parts of the world. Consider the Global Business Ethics Insight below and the case of privacy in the European Union.

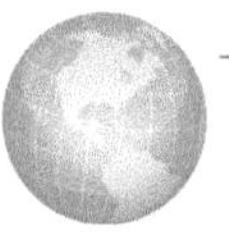

GLOBAL BUSINESS ETHICS INSIGHT

Privacy in the European Union

The earlier paragraphs discussing potential data that can be collected on the web suggest that companies run the risk of violating privacy laws regarding customers. In Europe, privacy and ownership of one's data is considered a basic human right. However, many people give up privacy by agreeing to extensive and complicated contracts when they use apps. However, the European Union is taking a very stringent stance to protect customer privacy. As such, they recently agreed on the General Data Protection Regulation (GDPR) aiming to regulate consumer privacy.

The regulation wants to put individual users back in charge. For instance, companies will need to clearly specify what type of data they are collecting.

Blanket statements such as "data will be used to improve services" will no longer be acceptable. Additionally, individual users will have the ability to request the type of data that has been collected on them. The new law will allow users to also ask that data be corrected or deleted as needed. The GDPR has put very strict fines in place. If companies are guilty of privacy violations, they will be fined 4% of their annual sales up to 20 million Euros.

Not surprisingly, many multinationals are very wary of this new regulation. Smaller companies complain that this new regulation will be very burdensome and may lead to bankruptcy. Larger companies also complain that they will not have access to big data to develop new services. Some argue that this will put European companies at a disadvantage. Additionally, the regulation does not apply only to Europe. If data about European citizens are being housed and analyzed in other countries, they will still be subject to the regulation. Some therefore argue that the regulation may also stifle innovation as a result of such overregulation.

Based on *The Economist.* 2017. "The Dodd-Frank of data." *The World in 2018,* 123–124.

Privacy therefore becomes more critical in the light of the above as it is important for companies to address consumer privacy. Experts suggest that customers should be made aware of the types of data that a company is collecting and how such data will be used. Companies should inform customers whether collected data is also being sold or shared with other companies. Furthermore, as the above Global Business Ethics

Internal	External
Physical protection of data	Privacy newsletter for customers
Privacy policy	Resources for parental guidance and child safety
Privacy employee training	Guidance for customers
Privacy board	Privacy e-mail address
Disciplinary action for privacy breach	Privacy blog
Employee monitoring	Involve stakeholders in design of privacy policy
Privacy office	Working with industry, government, and trade group
Privacy hotline	Publishing privacy research papers
Online reporting of privacy statements	Supporting IS education
Regular review of privacy policy	Working with NGOs and think tanks
Internal privacy campaign	Privacy seal
Privacy newsletter for employees	Compliance and exceeding privacy laws
Online privacy resources for employees	Self-regulation

EXHIBIT 9.3—Content of Corporate Privacy Programs

Insight shows, privacy is not viewed similarly worldwide. Companies are therefore strongly advised to respect local laws and traditions when implementing policies regarding customer privacy.

What are some of the ways companies address privacy issues? Exhibit 9.3 provides further insights into the content of corporate privacy programs.

E-commerce Security

E-commerce security refers to the degree to which stakeholders feel that the data collected online by companies is safe. For instance, data collected for e-commerce transactions involve very personal information such as credit card information, home addresses, and phone numbers. The degree to which a company can ensure that such information is kept safe and private reflects the company's effort at e-commerce security.

Gordon and Loeb provide some insights into the many components of e-commerce security.[20] A company needs to be concerned about 1) **confidentiality** (making sure that private information is protected and such information is not made available to unauthorized parties), 2) **availability** (ensuring that information is made available in a timely manner to authorized users), 3) **integrity** (protecting and ensuring that data collected is accurate, reliable, and truthful), 4) **authentication** (ensuring that those who are using the data are really who they claim to be), and 5) **non-repudiation** (making sure that authorized users are not denied access to data).

E-commerce security is becoming increasingly important as the amount of online fraud grows. Consider the following Business Ethics Insight.

BUSINESS ETHICS INSIGHT

E-commerce Security

As more companies collect data and become connected and interwoven with the internet, they are increasingly subjected to cyberattacks. Consider the case of the WannaCry ransomware program that hit companies in May and June 2017. They attacked corporate servers worldwide and infected hundreds of thousands of corporate computers. In many cases, the cyber hackers take a corporate IT system hostage and demand a ransom payment from the victims. If they do not pay, the cyber hackers can inflict significant damage on such systems. Unfortunately, cyberattacks have now become a sad reality of corporate life.

Cyberattacks have significant consequences for companies. First, companies incur significant costs trying to implement corrective measures. For instance, it is estimated that it cost Target over $60 million to address the theft of over 40 million credit card details from its servers. Additionally, it is estimated that it will cost them over $200 million to address future lawsuits and other long-term upgrades to ensure that such incidents don't occur again in the future. In fact, it is also estimated that cybercrime now costs the global economy between $450 billion and $600 billion annually.

Second, research also shows that companies suffer long-term share value falls as a result of cyberattacks. Consider that the global food company Mondelez International and pharmaceutical giant Merck have both not recovered from the cyberattacks they suffered during the summer of 2017. Such research shows that there are both immediate damage as well as long-term falls in company valuation. Clearly, investors are very wary of companies that are victims of cyberattacks.

Finally, cyberattacks can be very damaging to a company's reputation. As many multinationals have found, it takes years to build reputations. However, such reputations can be destroyed overnight as a result of cyberattacks. In addition, companies can also lose customer trust as they do not always address cyberattacks in a timely fashion.

Based on Derousseau, R. 2017. "A big payoff for cybercop stocks." *Fortune*, September 1, 28–31.

The above provides some evidence as to why companies need to pay stronger attention to e-commerce security. However, another academic study shows that e-commerce security breaches at companies can be strategically damaging to a company. Yayla and Hu examined stock market reactions to information-security breaches.[21] The researchers found that both traditional brick-and-mortar stores and pure e-commerce companies experienced negative market reactions. However, the effect was much stronger for pure e-commerce companies. Furthermore, the study shows that denial of service attacks where access to a website is denied tends to have the most negative impact on market reactions. The study shows that information security breach thus has important strategic implications for companies, as such breaches can have a damaging impact on the company's share prices and financial health.

E-commerce security breaches can thus be very disastrous for companies. Exhibit 9.4 shows some of the costs associated with information breaches.

As Exhibit 9.4 shows, e-commerce security breaches can be very costly for companies. It is therefore critical to first identify the types of e-commerce and information security breaches to be able to address such breaches. Yayla and Hu's study provides some insights into the many forms of e-commerce security breaches.[22] At a basic level, e-commerce security breaches occur when unauthorized users gain access to customer, company, or employee data. These breaches can be disastrous, as the fraudsters can use such information for personal gain. Customer information can be used for illegal online purchases while company data can reveal proprietary information. However, e-commerce security breaches can also occur when unauthorized individuals either deny access to a company's website (denial of service attacks) or find ways to alter a company's website. Both breaches can result in a significant public relations nightmare.

Security Breaches Description	Cost
Denial of service attack where web server or order processing slows down	Loss of revenue
Virus attacks shut down e-mail or networks and employees must spend time to restore system	Loss of productivity
Virus attack damages hardware or file servers	Cost of replacing software or hardware
Denial of service attack or virus lead to customers not trusting company's ability to protect data	Loss of revenue, customer trust, and loyalty
Virus attack encourages customers to switch to competitors	Loss of revenue and loss of competitive advantage
Security breaches cause investors to sell shares or stop buying shares	Loss of investor confidence

EXHIBIT 9.4—E-Commerce Security Breaches and Costs

To ensure e-commerce security, companies are now strongly advised to take a strategic approach to data management. Simply using firewalls or anti-virus programs is no longer sufficient. Companies need to implement an overall program starting with an inventory of collected data. Experts thus suggest the following:[23]

- Conducting an inventory of data and keeping only data that is needed—companies need to know what data has been collected and where such information is stored. Companies often collect more data than is needed. In the current world of information overload, it is important for companies to decide what information they really need to collect. Furthermore, once data is no longer needed, it is important to purge the data. The less data a company has at any point in time, the less disastrous the potential for information leaks.
- Protect the data—efforts have to be taken to ensure that the data is protected. Firewalls and anti-virus programs need to be implemented. However, recent evidence suggests that companies have a variety of approaches to protect data. Content management systems allow a company to control acquisition of data, to classify the data, and to control who has access to such data. Data loss prevention takes a different approach to protecting data. Such systems are placed on the boundary of a firm's network to monitor outgoing data. If the system detects sensitive information is being leaked, it can block such information from leaving the organization. Finally, network forensics systems examine a company's digital operations and report any suspicious activity or patterns that diverge from the past. Companies need to thus decide on which of the three approaches works best for their situation.
- Control access to data—data access also needs to be controlled. It is critical for the company to determine which employees will have access to which types of data. Key aspects of data access control such as user account management (providing appropriate user identity and password), password management (creation and protection of passwords), data encryption (protection of data flowing through the

company's network), user access policies (policies governing responsibility of user are needed), and monitoring access have to be dealt with. Furthermore, the physical aspects of the data, such as tapes, etc., need to be controlled. For instance, data needs to be in a secure building so that the data is not easily accessible to all.
- Create data management policies and train employees on such policies—while data leakages can occur because of malicious activities, some data leakage can also occur inadvertently because of the increased exchanges of data outside of the company's confines. Employee collaboration software, mobile devices, video teleconferencing, and online chats are all examples of data exchanges and sharing that occur outside of the boundaries of the organization. Employees should thus be reminded of their responsibilities when using data outside of the company. Appropriate precautions should be taken to avoid leakages. For instance, it may be possible for employees to download critical data on their smartphones. Policies have to be enacted to ensure that such data is safeguarded, especially when the employee loses the smartphone. Companies may also decide to implement policies whereby no company data is allowed to be downloaded on a smartphone.
- Create a contingency plan—companies should have systems in place to enable them to deal with any e-commerce security breaches. A sound incident management system needs to be in place, as such breaches need to be dealt with in a very timely manner.

It is also important to note that many multinationals are not relying on expert cybersecurity firms to address their e-commerce security needs.[24] Cyber hackers have become increasingly sophisticated whereby multinationals seldom have the resources and expertise to keep a cyber-security team in-house. According to recent research, expenses on cybersecurity firms are expected to jump from $86 billion in 2017 to around $108 billion in 2020.

E-commerce trust

A final ethical aspect of e-commerce we consider in this chapter is **e-commerce trust (e-trust)**. E-trust refers to the confidence that a buyer has that an online transaction will occur according to expectations.[25] For instance, if someone decides to buy a product from Amazon.com from a third party vendor, e-trust refers to the expectation that the buyer will receive the product after payment. McCole, Ramsey and Williams[26] argue that there are three main components of e-trust: namely, 1) trust in the internet—the perceived ability of the internet to perform what it is supposed to perform such as speed and integrity of the system, 2) trust in the vendor—trust in the company selling the products, and 3) trust in other parties, such as third parties certifying that a vendor has pledged integrity and honesty.

Why is e-trust important? Most experts agree that customers will not engage in online commercial transactions with a company unless they have trust.[27] Furthermore, in the light of the many new potential e-commerce problematic issues that companies are facing today (i.e., information breaches, denial of service attacks, identity theft, etc.), it is important for stakeholders to perceive a company as trustworthy in order to entice the stakeholder to develop a relationship with the company. From a strategic standpoint, e-trust is thus very critical as it forms the backbone of business-to-consumer trade. Consider the following Emerging Market Business Ethics Insight.

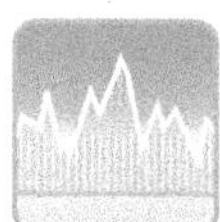

EMERGING MARKET **BUSINESS ETHICS INSIGHT**

E-trust in Emerging Markets

As mentioned earlier, many emerging markets will continue seeing individuals having access to the internet. However, because e-commerce is relatively new in these countries, e-commerce adoption will be heavily dependent on customers' trust. Consider the recent study of e-commerce adoption in Turkey. In that study, the researchers found that trust was one of the most important factors determining consumers' e-commerce adoption. However, e-trust was not the only factor that encouraged e-commerce adoption. The Turkish consumers also mentioned trust in the products and services as a determining factor as to whether they decide to use e-commerce as a means of purchase. As such, multinationals interested in selling products through online means in such markets will need to find ways to develop trust in e-commerce as well as the goods and services being sold.

In another study of the case of Nigeria, the authors argue similarly that trust is extremely critical if e-commerce adoption is to be encouraged. Consumers in such markets are often reluctant to purchase through online means because they do not trust the system and they also want to try products before purchase. Furthermore, e-trust is also non-existent for companies. In fact, even companies are often reluctant to sell their products online because they also do not trust the system. As a result, the authors argue that both companies and governments need to implement the necessary policies and infrastructure to build trust in consumers. Necessary regulations also need to be adopted so that the average customer can trust that if they buy something, they will receive the product in good order.

Based on Basarir-Ozel, B. and Mardikyan, S. 2017. "Factors affecting e-commerce adoption: A case of Turkey." *International Journal of Management Science and Information Technology*, 23, 1–11; Uwemi, S., Khan, H.U. and Fournier-Bonnila, S.D. 2016. "Challenges of e-commerce in developing countries: Nigeria as case study." Proceedings of the North East Decision Sciences Institute Conference.

As the above shows, e-trust is extremely critical in most markets. However, such factors are even more critical in emerging markets.[28] As discussed earlier, most emerging markets are experiencing dramatic growth in internet access but many represent untapped e-commerce markets. As such, multinationals are well advised to develop systems to promote trust in such countries. E-trust is also very important because increased e-commerce is often associated with larger national revenues. Local companies can quickly get access to new markets domestically. However, such companies, whether small or big, can also experience growth in international markets as they take advantage of such markets.

Given the above, it is important for multinationals to develop e-trust. Recent research provides evidence of some of the factors that promote e-trust in a company. Academic research done through a wide review of all of the studies conducted on understanding factors leading to e-trust (also known as a meta-analysis) suggests that the following main factors promote e-trust. The factors are organized in order of importance:[29]

- Perceived service quality—how much do consumers like using a website and do they feel that their needs are being met?
- Perceived privacy—does the company address all privacy concerns and do they meet all regulations to properly manage personal data?
- Perceived reputation—is the company perceived as being honest and do they deliver on their promises?
- Perceived usefulness—how much is the technology viewed as being useful in making the online transaction.

Other research has also indicated that the following factors are critical:[30]

- Disposition to trust—some people seem more likely to trust than others.
- Perceived security protection—how much security is perceived?
- Previous transaction experience—the more buyers have engaged in online transactions before, the more likely they are to e-trust.
- Familiarity—are users familiar with aspects of the website? The higher the familiarity, the higher the e-trust.
- Referral and word-of-mouth—what are others saying about transactions with the company? Positive word-of-mouth engenders e-trust.
- Trusted third parties—is there an organization that provides a privacy seal to reduce fear about online security and privacy? Privacy or other seals encourages e-trust.
- Social influence—users are more likely to trust a company if their friends or family have engaged in a transaction with the company before.
- Structural assurance—the basic internet structure needs to function as expected. Companies therefore need to provide technological safeguards such as data encryption, etc.

Recent research by Yang, Lin, Chandlrees, Lin and Chao provides some evidence that the perceived ethics of shopping websites also contributes to ethics.[31] In that study, the researchers found that individuals were more likely to trust a website if the website maintains a good ethical performance. To be perceived as being ethical, a company needs to clearly practice posted privacy policies while also describing products and services in an appropriate way. This research provides evidence of the connection between perception of ethics of online companies and trust in the company.

More practical research provides further evidence of the importance of the above factors in promoting e-trust.[32] The study found that the most important factor is whether the company is well known or not. Some 84% of respondents suggested that they are more likely to give personal data to a company they already know, as they are confident that such companies will protect their data. The next most important factor promoting e-trust is whether the company has websites with very obvious security features. In total, 81% of surveyed customers indicated that they are more likely to give personal information to companies that have such websites.

Building e-trust is thus a critical aspect of a company's strategic health. Online transactions tend not to require the same investments as typical brick-and-mortar stores and are thus more efficient. Companies that want to succeed will therefore be increasingly pressured to grow their online sales and increase e-trust. One of the most critical aspects of e-trust is providing users with the guarantee that their data will be safe with the company. As such, protecting data privacy and building e-security are all intertwined. The many steps discussed earlier to protect customer privacy and strengthen e-security apply here too. Companies need to ensure that they are perceived as having a strong reputation through transparency and the ethics of their online transactions.

OTHER IT ETHICS ISSUES

In the final section of this chapter, we examine three remaining IT ethics issues. First, we look at global e-commerce and the consequent ethical issues arising from such operations. We emphasize ethical issues related to operating in a specific culture. Second, we also examine the global digital divide and the role multinationals are playing in addressing this divide. Finally, we also discuss the amount of waste generated by IT operations and what responsible companies are doing to address such issues.

Ethics and Global E-commerce and the Global Digital Divide

The inherent features of the internet make it possible for companies to easily have a global presence. However, operating globally is fraught with ethical dilemmas. Consider our earlier consideration of how privacy may not be viewed similarly worldwide. To avoid ethical violations, companies need to ensure that they operate within acceptable limits. Consider the case of Yahoo!, which was forced to give names of individuals voicing pro-democracy views on its Chinese website. While Google has refused to behave similarly, Yahoo! had decided to embrace Chinese demands as a condition of doing business there. Yahoo! has received a significant public backlash for its role in helping the Chinese government arrest those voicing pro-democracy views. Yahoo! had to choose between enforcing its own privacy rules in the U.S. or those enforced by the Chinese government. Most experts agree that China offers significant potential as the number of citizens having access to the internet and disposable income grows. Yahoo! therefore decided to respect the local laws at the expense of its reputation in the Western world.

Operating globally in an IT environment thus poses significant risks. A company cannot be viewed as ethical if it breaches local culture or norms. As you will see in Chapter 11 on global ethics, companies can approach operations in other countries either through a universal lens (doing the same thing in all countries) or a relativist approach (responding to local conditions). Current research reports significant differences in cross-cultural aspects of IT that necessitate a relativist approach. We discuss the many IT aspects that differ by culture.

Similar to online retailing within local contexts, companies need to be trusted in order to encourage users to engage in transactions with them.[33] A critical component of the trust will emerge from the user's interaction with a company's website. However, most research has assumed that online trust is built similarly across cultures. Nevertheless, research by Sia et al. shows that online trust varies by culture. In that research, the authors examine two of the most important ways companies build trust; namely, **reputable website affiliation** (unknown website affiliating itself with a more reputable website to build online trust) and **peer endorsement** (existing customers providing feedback encouraging new customers to trust the website). They find that individualistic cultures such as the U.S. are more likely to build trust through reputable website affiliation. This is underscored by further research that suggests that people in more individualistic cultures tend to be more trusting of each other.[34] However, in contrast, in more collectivistic cultures such as Hong Kong and South Korea, where the needs and values of the group takes precedence over the individual, peer endorsement is much more critical. This is mostly because more collectivistic societies base their trust on relationships as they are more likely to respect the views of the peers.[35] This research suggests that companies need to adopt the appropriate web strategies based on the culture to be viewed as ethical and trusted.

Further current research suggests that companies need to provide consumers with website elements that are consistent with local norms and culture.[36] For example, at a basic level, websites should not offend local norms. Culturally inappropriate images should not be displayed on a company's local websites. However, cultural customization goes beyond merely adapting physical imaging. There are many other subtle aspects that need to be catered to.

Wurtz provides some interesting insights into the other many factors that contribute to a culturally appropriate website.[37] In that study, she examines the websites of McDonald's in the 119 countries they operated in at the time of study. To examine the cultural appropriateness of the various websites, she examines differences between high-context (e.g., Japan, Arab countries, Greece, Spain, Italy) and low-context cultures (e.g., German-speaking countries, Scandinavian countries, the U.S.). People in high-context cultures communicate extensively using non-verbals such as body language, silence, and gestures. In contrast, people in low-context cultures tend to communicate more directly and explicitly.

Wurtz finds that McDonald's websites in high-context cultures tend to have much more animation. This is consistent with the notion that high-context communication is much more complex than low-context communication. High levels of animation indicate preference for the situation to play a role in the communicated message. Additionally, high-context websites are more likely to have embedded links whereby website surfers are more likely to try to find information. In contrast, low-context cultures feature much more explicit information on the home page. Furthermore, Wurtz found that McDonald's websites in more collectivistic countries are more likely to feature families or friends or other activities spent with others. In contrast, more individualistic websites feature individuals engaging in activities such as listening to music or relaxing.

The above clearly shows that some form of cultural customization is indeed necessary to ensure that a company does not break local norms and views as unethical. While it is outside of the scope of this chapter to discuss all culture customization aspects (see Singh et al., for example, on how to customize 36 aspects of websites to make them culturally appropriate[38]), companies will need to understand whether their e-commerce policies and practices are consistent with local norms. Issues such as privacy, appropriateness of a website, and safeguarding data will all have to be dealt with. However, one of the other key issues that multinationals have to contend with in the global e-commerce environment is the global digital divide.

The **digital divide** refers to the "gap between the more privileged who have access and the less privileged who do not have access to information and communication technology."[39] As the internet and communication technology continues to play an increasingly important role both in terms of economic development and human interaction, countries and companies are increasingly focused on reducing the digital divide. Consider the following Business Ethics Insight.

BUSINESS ETHICS INSIGHT

Using Technology to Reduce Inequality

Development in information technologies have given people worldwide increased access to bank accounts. According to estimates, those who don't have access to bank accounts (the unbanked) have been reduced from 2.5 billion to around 2 billion individuals (around 38% of the world's population). Experts agree that having access to a bank account is extremely critical for people with low income or variable incomes. Groups such as the poor, immigrants, and refugees tend to benefit from having access to financial services. Additionally, even if they are included in the banking services, it doesn't mean that they can be fully engaged. As such, many new forms of information technologies are helping such disadvantaged groups.

Consider the case of M-Pesa, a mobile-money service used by many Africans. Such mobile technologies have allowed more people to get access to financial services from institutions other than traditional banks. Another example is Monese, a start-up that was created in London. It allows customers to create online bank accounts using a mobile phone and allows users to gain access to a debit card and other financial services in exchange for a monthly fee. This has provided a bank account to immigrants who find it difficult to open such an account with traditional banks that requests that these immigrants provide physical evidence of documents. MONI, another Finnish start-up, provides limited banking services to refugees who often have difficulty providing all of the rigid documentation requirements needed by traditional banks to open bank accounts.

The rapid development in IT has also allowed other ways to help disadvantaged groups. Because of the recent mortgage crisis in the U.S., banks have been relying on ever more rigid algorithms to determine credit worthiness. Big data management now enables companies to provide more accurate ways to determine credit worthiness in the absence of voluminous data. Digital technologies are also allowing traditional banks to find ways to become more efficient while also reaching a wider group of customers.

Based on *The Economist*. 2017. "Technology and financial inclusion; Underserved and overlooked." September 9, 57–58.

As the above shows, having appropriate access to the internet and adequate IT can be very beneficial. In fact, disadvantaged groups are often the most vulnerable and can greatly improve their standard of living if they have access to IT services. However, most experts agree that access to internet technologies is also beneficial to societies as it has a strong link with economic development.[40] The internet provides the infrastructure that is minimizing costs and uncertainty of distribution of goods and services in most societies. For instance, a farmer in rural India can quickly access the internet to check the prices of agricultural products before deciding on pricing. However, the internet is also playing a societal function in terms of the strengthening of civil societies. The internet provides access to information regarding constitutional rights, social movements, etc. that plays a key role in terms of democratic societal functioning.[41]

Recent research suggests that the digital divide between countries is narrowing. Exhibit 9.5 gives an indication of the digital divide by region. It shows the percentage of the population who have access to the internet.

As Exhibit 9.5 shows, the digital divide is a challenge today. Despite the progress in IT worldwide, the data shows significant access differences between low income and high income countries. Consider that over 80% of the population use the internet in high income societies whereas only 12.5% use the internet in low income countries. It is also important to note that many regions have made significant progress in terms of reducing the digital divide as the East Asian, Latin American, and North African regions show that more than 40% of the population are internet users. However, the South Asian and Sub-Saharan regions have a much lower percentage of population using the internet.

Given the above, it is important for multinationals to play a key role in reducing the digital divide. While governments typically provide the internet backbone, research by Chen, Lin and Lai (2010) of China's urban–rural digital divide suggest that users may not always take advantage of infrastructure because of limited internet literacy

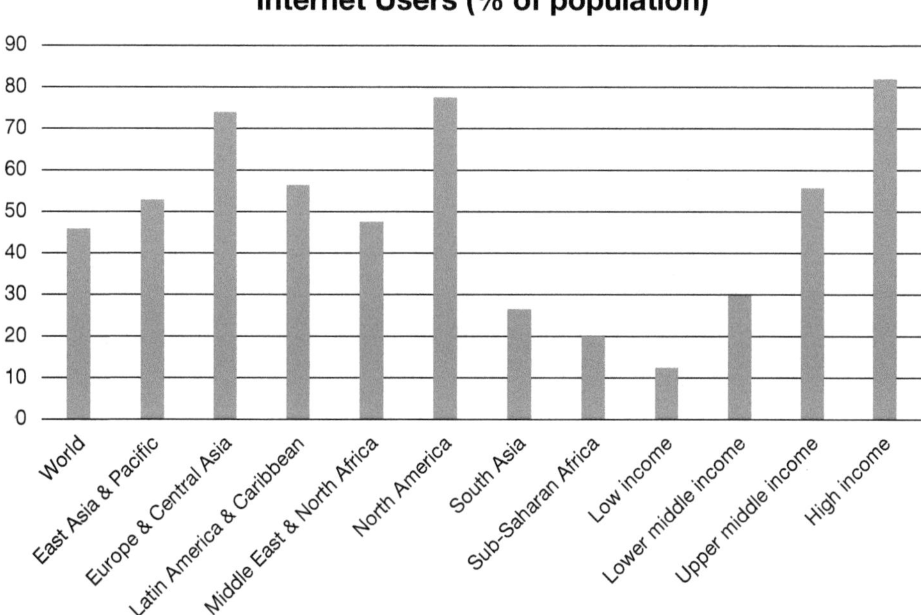

EXHIBIT 9.5—Internet Users (Percentage of Population)

Source: Based on World Bank. 2018. "World Development Indicators: The information society." http://wdi.worldbank.org/table/5.12#

skills and computer skills.[42] Multinationals are thus well advised to provide opportunities for their employees to get internet-related training. Furthermore, multinationals may have a critical role to play in less developed societies by also providing the equipment to reduce the global digital divide. For instance, computer equipment can be donated to local community centers to ensure that disadvantaged locals have access to some minimal internet access. Additionally, Wresch's essay suggests that multinationals can play a big role in encouraging the creation of local websites.[43] Local websites can be an important repository of locally relevant medical information. Furthermore, the worldwide access to locally created websites can make such countries visible. The web is now dominated by websites from mostly Western countries, thus dominating the web culture.

Electronic Waste

In the final section of this chapter, we examine electronic waste or e-waste. **E-waste** refers to the waste stream that occurs as a result of a company's use of information technology. A major reason behind the sustained growth of e-waste is the constant availability of new products with better design and technology. Furthermore, products are becoming obsolete faster. Additionally, as more individuals worldwide have access to IT, the amount of waste generated from these devices will continue contributing

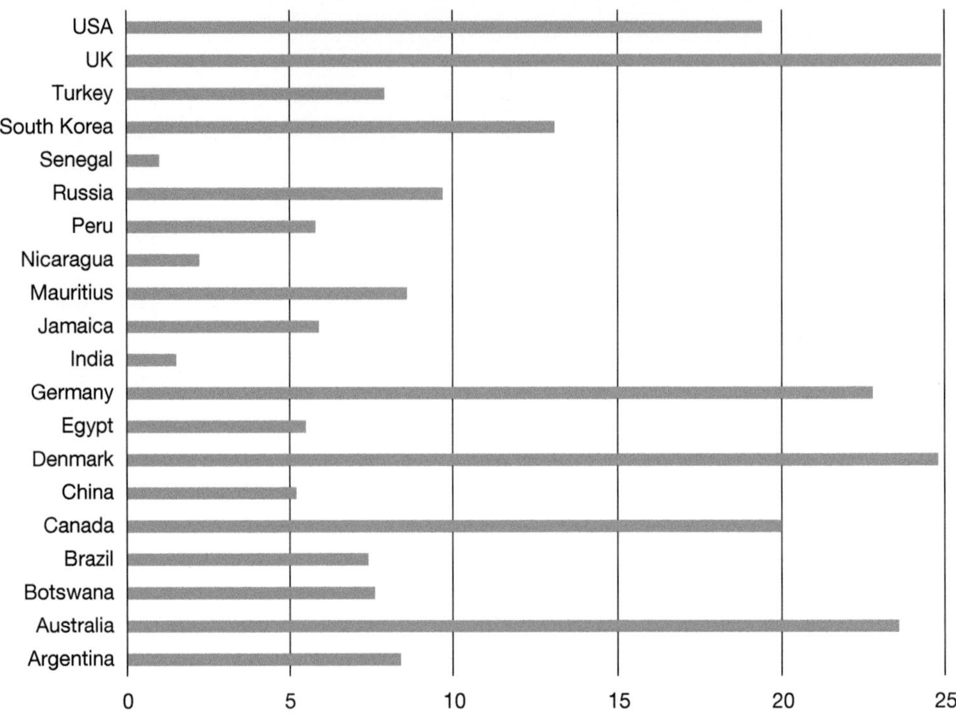

EXHIBIT 9.6—Domestic E-Waste (kilogram per inhabitant)

ETHICS SUSTAINABILITY INSIGHT

E-waste and the Environment

As more people have access to the internet but also have rising disposable incomes worldwide, more will purchase products that generate e-waste. Such products include smartphones, laptops, fridges and TVs. When these products reach the ends of their lives, they are discarded. However, these discarded products contain many toxic chemicals that pose considerable environmental and health risks, especially if treated inadequately. Additionally, countries are not doing an adequate job assessing the level of waste to know what policies to implement. Additionally, an important aspect of e-waste is what is done with the large amount of e-waste generated annually. Countries may not have adequate recycling programs in place to deal with such e-waste.

Consider that over 80,000 Indian workers in the informal sector collect and dismantle the e-waste. In the process, these workers are exposed to a host of toxic by-products as they do most of the work by hand and do not have the necessary safety equipment. Most IT equipment includes known carcinogenic and toxic elements such as lead, mercury, and cadmium. As these workers handle the e-waste, they are thus being exposed to toxic products that are known to cause brain damage in children, kidney damage, and even abnormal hormonal function. Furthermore, the informal nature of the work means that no effort is being made to protect the environment. The recycling process involves the disposal of these toxic products in the environment. For example, the disposal of used circuit boards, which are often melted in open fires, releases toxic flames in the environment.

An added aspect of e-waste that produces another ethical dimension to the problem is that most e-waste generated in the developed world is exported to developing nations for recycling. For instance, a recent report suggests that 80% of collected e-waste in the U.S. is exported. As the pace of e-waste grows in both Europe and the U.S., e-waste exports to less developed countries will mean that poor workers are being exposed to toxic materials in very dangerous environments and significant harm is being done to the environment.

Based on Baldé, C.P., Forti V., Gray, V., Kuehr, R. and Stegmann, P. 2017. "The Global E-waste Monitor – 2017." United Nations University (UNU), International Telecommunication Union (ITU) & International Solid Waste Association (ISWA), Bonn/Geneva/ Vienna; Rahman, N. and Akhter, S. 2010. "Incorporating sustainability into information technology management." *International Journal of Technology Management & Sustainable Development*, 9, 2, 95–111; Sohrabji, S. 2010. "End of life." *India-West, San Leandro*, 35, 19, A1, 5.

to many challenges. Finally, other factors contributing to e-waste are that many individuals now own more than one piece of electronics while growth of disposable income in emerging markets will continue fueling growth. According to recent estimates, global e-waste was 44.7 metric tons in 2016 and is expected to climb to 52.2 metric tons in 2021.[44]

How much waste is generated per inhabitant worldwide? Consider Exhibit 9.6 above.

As Exhibit 9.6 shows, the more developed nations tend to generate more e-waste because more individuals in these societies have personal electronics. However, experts agree that emerging markets will continue seeing growth as more individuals have access to such electronics. This means that efforts to control e-waste will become ever more critical. But why should companies be concerned about e-waste? Consider the above Ethics Sustainability Insight.

As it shows, it is very critical for multinationals to manage their IT operations in order to reduce the environmental and human impact of their IT operations. More experts are encouraging companies to engage in green IT initiatives to achieve such goals.[45] Such efforts seem to be geared either toward reduction of energy use or more efficient use of existing equipment. These include:[46]

- More companies are experimenting with ways to reduce their IT-related energy use. For instance, techniques such as virtualization, cloud computing, and PC power management software are common techniques. Virtualization involves running multiple computers on a single computer. This reduces the need for hardware while also reducing the need for energy. Furthermore, the use of cloud computing involves placing data on the web as opposed to on in-house servers. For instance, companies that have moved their e-mail services to cloud computers save by eliminating the need for servers. Finally, companies are also purchasing software that lets companies control and reduce energy use centrally on their network. By optimizing energy use, companies can enjoy energy savings without loss of productivity.

- Companies are also analyzing their data to maintain only the needed data. Redundant data is being eliminated, while redundant databases are being combined. Such efforts reduce the need for servers that consume large amounts of energy to run and to be kept cool.
- Companies are also finding ways to extend the lifecycle of the products they use. More companies are participating in renewing, reusing, and refurbishing personal computers. Furthermore, computer makers are increasingly considering personal computers that are easily upgradable with interchangeable parts, etc.
- More companies are considering the recycling options when making purchase decisions. One of the more recent developments in design is the cradle-to-cradle approach. Such products are designed to allow products to be produced waste-free. Thus, products can be designed so that all the types of materials used can be separated and recycled at all stages of the products' lifecycles. The cradle-to-cradle approach thus reduces the need for critical landfill space.
- Green IT initiatives also include companies managing the IT recycling process. Companies keep track of recycling rates of their own products. Furthermore, when making purchase decisions, companies can only purchase those products that have a minimum use of other recycled materials.
- Countries are also working to implement legislation to encourage recycling programs. A big part of such legislation will be to ensure that multinationals are held responsible for the e-waste generated as the result of the use of their products. As such, multinationals are also well advised to continue cooperating with the appropriate authorities to ensure that they contribute effectively to support recycling programs.
- Finally, multinationals can also implement marketing campaigns to encourage their customers to recycle their discarded products. Research conducted in China[47] and Malaysia[48] showed that residents of these societies were more likely to be receptive to e-waste if they are aware of the beneficial consequences of e-waste recycling to the environment. Residents aware of the implications of their actions were more likely to be receptive to e-waste recycling. People who had a positive attitude towards recycling were also more receptive to recycling. Additionally, if multinationals can advertise and do other campaigns to encourage norms of recycling, residents will be more likely to be receptive to e-waste recycling.

* * *

CHAPTER SUMMARY

In this chapter, you learned about IT and the ethical implications of IT. As more companies rely on IT for most aspects of their operations and as IT becomes ever present in most aspects of people's lives, the ethical aspects of IT will become more critical. Furthermore, the ease and scale of information collection has changed dramatically. Understanding and managing IT ethics will therefore become more critical.

First, you read about the types of social media and the ethical implications of such social media. You learned about the importance of managing social media and the inherent privacy issues raised by social media. The social media section also discussed some of the best practices regarding how companies can manage their social media for employees. Furthermore, prescriptions for social media were discussed for other stakeholders.

In the second part of the chapter, you read about electronic commerce and the tremendous global growth in e-commerce. You learned about a number of e-commerce ethical issues such as customer privacy, e-commerce security, and e-commerce trust. You read about the many steps companies can take to boost these three aspects of e-commerce.

In the final part of the chapter, you learned about a number of remaining IT ethical issues. First, you learned about the importance of access to IT and the role of such access in furthering both personal and economic growth. You read about the global digital divide and the role multinationals can play in addressing such a divide. You also learned that the global digital divide exists for small and medium companies and can actually have negative implications for the strategic health of such companies.

A second critical aspect discussed in the last part of the chapter is e-waste. As hardware becomes cheaper and lifecycles of such hardware become shorter, e-waste is growing at a dizzying rate every year. The ethical implications of such e-waste pertain to the appropriate disposal and recycling of such waste. Most of the e-waste generated in the Western world ends up being processed by workers in very poor conditions in less developed nations. Reducing and managing e-waste is therefore a critical consideration for most multinationals today.

NOTES

1 Beauchamp, T.L., Bowie, N.L. & Arnold, D.G. 2010. *Ethical theory and business*. Harlow, UK.: Pearson Publishing.
2 Sipior, J.C. 2007. "Ethically responsible organizational privacy protection." *Information Resource Management Journal*, 20, 3, i–iii.
3 Aguilar, M.K. 2011. "Facebook firing tests social media policies." *Compliance Week*, 35, 71.
4 Grabner-Krauter, S. 2009. "Web 2.0 social networks: The role of trust." *Journal of Business Ethics*, 90, 4, 505–522 (at 505).
5 Aguilar, M.K. 2009. "How companies are coping with social media." *Compliance Week*, 56, 57, 71.
6 *The Economist*. 2017. "The Dodd-Frank of data. "*The World in 2018*, 123–124.

7 Rachels, J. 1975. "Why privacy is important." *Philosophy and Public Affairs*, 4, 323–333.

8 Mooradian, N. 2009. "The importance of privacy revisited." *Ethics Information Technology*, 11, 163–174.

9 Aguilar, "How companies are coping with social media"; Aguilar, "Facebook firing tests social media policies."; Palm, E. 2009. "Securing privacy at work: The importance of contextualized consent." *Ethics Information Technology*, 11, 233–241.

10 Kaul, A. & Chaudhri, V. "Social media: The new mantra for managing reputation." *Vikalpa*, October–December, 40, 455–460.

11 Turilli, M. & Floridi, L. 2010. "The ethics of information transparency." *Ethics Information Technology*, 11, 105–112.

12 Vaccaro, A. & Madsen, P. 2009. "Corporate dynamic transparency: The new ICT-driven ethics?" *Ethics Information Technology*, 11, 113–122 (at 113).

13 Turilli & Floridi, "The ethics of information transparency."

14 Vaccaro & Madsen, "Corporate dynamic transparency."

15 Aguilar, M.K. 2010. "Compliance and social media: Yes, it can be done." *Compliance Week*, 50–51.

16 Aguilar, "How companies are coping with social media"; Brandel, M. 2010. "Are you listening?" *Computerworld*, July 12, 44, 13, 13; Kaplan, A.M. & Haenlein, M. 2011. "The early bird catches the news: Nine things you should know about micro-blogging." *Business Horizons*, 54, 105–113; Mishra, S. 2015. "Saying 'sorry': The role of apology in online crisis communication in India." *Vikalpa*, October–December, 40, 466–469.

17 Pollach, I. 2011. "Online privacy as a corporate social responsibility: An empirical study." *Business Ethics*, 20, 1, 88–102.

18 Chiang, O. 2011. "Super crunchers." March 14, Forbes.com.

19 *The Economist*. 2017. "The Dodd-Frank of data."; Pollach, "Online privacy as a corporate social responsibility."

20 Gordon, L.A. & Loeb, M.P. 2006. "Budgeting process for information security expenditures." *Communication of the ACM*, 49, 1, 121–125.

21 Yayla, A.A. & Hu, Q. 2011. "The impact of information security events on the stock value of firms: The effect of contingency factors." *Journal of Information Technology*, 26, 60–77.

22 Yayla & Hu, "The impact of information security events on the stock value of firms."

23 Anderson, S. & McClendon, T. 2011. "Data, data everywhere." *Risk Manager's Forum*, February, 30; *The Economist*. 2011. "The leaky corporation: Companies and information." *The Economist*, February 26, 398, 8722, 75; Nash, K.S. 2011. "Forget WikiLeaks: Your CEO may be paranoid about Wikileaks, but his mobile device and cloud computing are the real threats to corporate security." *CIO*, 24, 10; Stelter, L. 2011. "Physically protecting data." *Security Systems News*, 14, 1, 15.

24 Derousseau, R. 2017. "A big payoffs for cybercop stocks." *Fortune*, September 1, 28–31.

25 Kim, Y. & Peterson, R.A. 2017. A meta-analysis of online trust relationship in e-commerce." *Journal of Interactive Marketing*, 38, 44–54.

26 McCole, P., Ramsey, E. & Williams, J. 2010. "Trust considerations on attitudes towards online purchasing: The moderating effect of privacy and security concerns." *Journal of Business Research*, 63, 1018–1024.

27 McCole et al., "Trust considerations on attitudes towards online purchasing."

28 Uwemi, S., Khan, H.U. & Fournier-Bonnila, S.D. 2016. "Challenges of e-commerce in developing countries: Nigeria as case study." Proceedings of the North East Decision Sciences Institute Conference.

29 Kim, Y. & Peterson, R.A. 2017. A meta-analysis of online trust relationship in e-commerce." *Journal of Interactive Marketing*, 38, 44–54.

30 Kim, Y.H., Kim, D.J. & Hwang, Y. 2009. "Exploring online transaction self efficacy in trust building in B2C e-commerce." *Journal of Organizational and End User Computing*, 21, 1, 37–59; Sinclaire, J.K., Simon J.C. & Wilkes, R.B. 2010. "A prediction model for initial trust formation in electronic commerce." *International Business Research*, 3, 4, 17–27.

31 Yang, M., Lin, B., Chandlrees, N., Lin, B. & Chao, H. 2009. "The effect of preceived ethical performance of shopping websites on consumer trust." *Journal of Computer Information Systems*, 50, 1, 15–24.

32 Kim, Y. & Peterson, R.A. 2017. A meta-analysis of online trust relationship in e-commerce;" Mortimer, R. 2010. "Customer data: Only trust can overcome data privacy fears." *Marketing Week*, 26.
33 Sia, C.L., Lim, K.H., Leung, K., Lee, M.K.O., Huang, W.W. & Benbasat, I. 2009. "Web strategies to promote internet shopping: Is cultural-customization needed?" *MIS Quarterly*, 33, 3, 491–512.
34 Abyda, A. 2017. "Importance of consumer trust in e-commerce." *Middle East Journal of Business*, 12, 20–24.
35 Abyda, "Importance of consumer trust in e-commerce."
36 Cyr, D., Head, M., Larios, H. & Pan, B. 2009. "Exploring human images in website design: A multi-method approach." *MIS Quarterly*, 33, 3, 539–566; Singh, N., Zhao, H.X. & Hu, S. 2003. "Cultural adaptation on the Web: A study of American companies' domestic and Chinese websites." *Journal of Global Information Management*, 11, 3, 63–81.
37 Wurtz, E. 2005. "A cross-cultural analysis of websites from high-context cultures and low-context cultures." *Journal of Computer-Mediated Communication*, 11, 13–40.
38 Singh et al., "Cultural adaptation on the Web."
39 Huang, C. & Chen, H. 2010. "Global digital divide: A dynamic analysis based on the bass model." *Journal of Public Policy and Marketing*, 29, 2, 248–264 (at 248).
40 Chen, D., Lin, Z. & Lai, F. 2010. "Crossing the chasm—Understanding China's rural digital divide." *Journal of Global Information Technology Management*, 13, 2, 4–34.
41 Robinson, K.K. & Crenshaw, E.M. 2010. "Reevaluating the global digital divide: Socio-demographic and conflict barriers to the internet revolution." *Sociological Inquiry*, 80, 1, 34–62.
42 Chen et al., "Crossing the chasm."
43 Wresch, W. 2009. "Progress on the global digital divide: An ethical perspective based on Amartya Sen's capabilities model." *Ethics Information Technology*, 11, 255–263.
44 Baldé, C.P., Forti V., Gray, V., Kuehr, R. & Stegmann, P. 2017. "The Global E-waste Monitor – 2017." United Nations University (UNU), International Telecommunication Union (ITU) & International Solid Waste Association (ISWA), Bonn/Geneva/Vienna.
45 Jain, R.P., Benbunan-Fich, R. & Mohan, K. 2011. "Assessing green IT initiatives using the balanced scorecard." *IT Pro*, January/February, 26–32.
46 Baldé et al. "The Global E-waste Monitor – 2017"; Jain, R.P. et al., "Assessing green IT initiatives"; Rahman, N. & Akhter, S. 2010. "Incorporating sustainability into information technology management." *International Journal of Technology Management & Sustainable Development*, 9, 2, 95–111.
47 Wang, Z., Guo, D. & Wang, X. 2016. "Determinants of residents' e-waste recycling behavior intentions: Evidence from China." *Journal of Cleaner Production*, 137, 850–860.
48 Tan, C.H., Ramayah, T., Yeap, J.A.L. & Ooi, S.K. 2017. "Examining residents' receptiveness towards E-waste recycling in Penang, Malaysia." *Global Business and Management Research: An International Journal*, 9, 374–390.

KEY TERMS

Authentication: ensuring that those who are using the data are really who they claim to be.

Availability: ensuring that information is made available in a timely manner to authorized users.

Confidentiality: ensuring that private information is protected and such information is not made available to unauthorized parties.

Customer privacy: the expectations that customers can protect their personal information.

Digital divide: gap between the more privileged who have access, and the less privileged who do not have access, to information and communication technology.

E-commerce security: refers to the degree to which stakeholders feel that the data collected online by companies is safe.

E-commerce trust (e-trust): refers to the confidence that a buyer has that an online transaction will occur according to expectations.

E-waste: waste stream that occurs as a result of a company's use of information technology.

Electronic commerce (e-commerce): refers to the selling and trading of goods and services over the internet.

Information technologies (IT): refers to the internet and new forms of social media.

Information transparency: process of making information explicitly and openly available to concerned stakeholders.

Integrity: protecting and ensuring that data collected is accurate, reliable, and truthful.

Non-repudiation: making sure that authorized users are not denied access to data.

Peer endorsement: where existing customers provide feedback to encourage new customers to trust the website.

Privacy: ability of individuals to control or restrict access to information about them.

Reputable website affiliation: where an unknown website affiliates itself with a more reputable website to build online trust.

Social media: popular term that refers to the advanced internet technology and applications that have largely enabled collaboration among internet users.

DISCUSSION QUESTIONS

1. What are some of the major changes that have occurred over the past decade regarding how information is collected? What are some of the ethical implications of these new data collection procedures?
2. What is social media? What are some of the main ethical issues companies face as they deal with social media?
3. What is privacy? Why is privacy important? What can companies do to protect employee privacy?
4. What is customer privacy? How does IT put customer privacy in danger? What can companies do to protect customer privacy?
5. Discuss the five components of e-commerce security; namely, confidentiality, availability, integrity, authentication, and non-repudiation. Give examples of how each of the five components is breached.
6. What are some of the key aspects of e-commerce security? What are some of the costs of e-commerce security breaches? What can companies do to protect their e-commerce security?
7. What is e-commerce trust? Why is e-commerce trust important? What are some of the major factors encouraging e-commerce trust?
8. What is the global digital divide? Why is reduction of the global digital divide important? What can multinationals do to reduce the divide?

9. What is electronic waste? Why is e-waste predicted to grow significantly in the future?
10. What are some of the ethical implications of e-waste? What can companies do to reduce e-waste?

INTERNET ACTIVITY

1. Go to the World Internet Usage Statistics Website: www.internet worldstats.com.
2. Review the data for the different regions of the world.
3. Which region of the world is experiencing most growth in internet usage? What are the factors that explain such growth?
4. Review the top 20 countries with the highest number of internet users. Which countries are on the list? Which country has the highest penetration rate? What led to such high penetration rates in that country?
5. Review broadband internet statistics. Which countries have the highest penetration rate using broadband? Why is broadband penetration considered a better indicator of internet penetration?

For more Internet Activities and resources, visit the Companion Website at www.routledge.com/cw/parboteeah.

WHAT WOULD YOU DO?

The IT Job

You complete a Bachelor's degree in Information Technology. After graduating, you get a job with a local company. Your main responsibility will be to manage the servers holding critical data and e-mails for the company. You start the job and feel very satisfied with the work. The company is moderate in size and you have the opportunity to learn most aspects of the company. You also like the company culture, as the latter values integrity, strong work ethic, but also a balance of work and family.

After several months on the job, you are asked to meet with the CEO. During the meeting, she mentions that she has read recently about software that allows the company to monitor productivity and the extent to which employees are accessing non-work sites such as Facebook and news sites. You are asked to investigate the possibility of installing such software.

During the conversation, you also find that the CEO also suspects some employees of unethical behavior. While you don't know the nature of the unethical behavior, the CEO asks you to provide access to these employees' e-mails. You personally know many of these employees.

What would you do? Do you go along with the software monitoring employee use of the internet? Do you also provide access to these employees' e-mails? Why or why not?

BRIEF CASE: BUSINESS ETHICS INSIGHT

Alibaba.com and Online Fraud

Alibaba.com, founded in 1998, is the leading business-to-business retailer in China. It acts primarily as a directory of sellers offering products in bulk to other businesses. Alibaba.com was the first company created by well-known Chinese entrepreneur and former English teacher Jack Ma. After Mr. Ma created Alibaba.com, he went on to create Taobao, China's largest online retail website. A recent report suggests that Taobao accounts for 75% of all online transactions in China.

In early 2011, Alibaba.com had to face a major scandal. Investigation of the scandal started when an employee noticed suspicious activity and reported the activity to the company. An internal staff investigation revealed that over 2,300 sellers had committed fraud on the site, sometimes with the help of Alibaba.com staff. Would-be suppliers are required to provide business registration documents in order to set up a store front on the site. However, around 100 internal Alibaba.com staff helped around 2,300 sellers to evade such business verification paperwork. With the help of the staff, these vendors were able to bypass the verification process and became listed on Alibaba.com. In some cases, these companies also provided fake paperwork that the staff accepted. The result was that many companies became listed despite any lack of authentication. Unfortunately, the result was that many buyers were tricked into doing business with fraudulent companies. Furthermore, many of these buyers ended up paying for products they did not receive.

Jack Ma is obviously very disturbed by the scandal. Like many of his companies, he places much premium on values such as "integrity," "ethics," "commitment," and "passion." This scandal has led a major blow to the company's credibility as a reliable source of goods. Furthermore, the scandal is ill timed as Alibaba.com is now facing an ever-increasing base of aggressive competitors. Mr. Ma has vowed to improve internal fraud detection processes. In addition, two of the senior executives of the company have accepted responsibility for the scandal, although they were not directly involved in such systematic breakdown. One of these executives, Mr. Wei, was a major force behind the company's long-term strategy and was instrumental in boosting Alibaba.com as the leading place for online business-to-business transactions.

Based on Chao, L. 2011. "Alibaba starts to repair reputation." *Wall Street Journal*, online edition, February 23; Chao, L. and Lee, Y. 2011. "Alibaba.com CEO resigns in wake of fraud by sellers." *Wall Street Journal*, online edition, February 21.

BRIEF CASE QUESTIONS

1. What are some of the factors that led to this scandal? What aspects of the online environment explain the scandal?
2. Do you think the company was justified in accepting the resignation of key executives such as Mr. Wei? Do you think people should be allowed to resign although they are not personally aware of unethical behaviors on the part of their subordinates?
3. What changes would you recommend to Alibaba.com internal processes to make sure that such fraud does not occur again in the future?
4. What should Mr. Ma do to restore confidence in Alibaba.com?

LONG CASE: BUSINESS ETHICS

ARTHUR W. PAGE SOCIETY

WALKING THE "ENCRYPTION TIGHTROPE": GETTING TO THE CORE OF APPLE'S PRIVACY AND SECURITY BATTLE WITH THE FBI

Graphic Source: Raza, 2016

Abstract

Following the December 2015 San Bernardino shooting, the FBI asked Apple to provide access to the perpetrator's iPhone, forcing Apple to stand its ground on protecting consumer privacy. Agreeing to provide access would jeopardize its consumers' privacy by creating a "backdoor" into the iPhone which Apple deemed unacceptable. Apple's decision was met with praise and criticism by the public and other technology companies. Finally, the FBI used a third party to hack the iPhone. Although consumer privacy was eventually compromised, Apple's response set a precedent and started an important dialogue across the business world about customer privacy and security.

Overview: Taking a Bite Out of The Apple

In December of 2015, a married couple named Syed Rizwan Farook and Tashfeen Malik burst through the doors of Farook's office holiday party in San Bernardino, CA. The couple had spent months planning a terrorist attack that came to fruition when they opened fire on Farook's co-workers killing 14 and injuring 22. Police were called to the scene, engaging in a gunfight with the perpetrators, killing Farook and Malik. After the incident, investigators searched the couple's home finding large amounts of ammunition, weapons and pipe bombs (Mozingo, 2015).

During the investigation, the FBI requested data from Farook's iPhone that might contain valuable information about the attack. Apple provided the data that had been backed up on iCloud, however, Farook had not backed up his phone for several weeks before the attack. Although the FBI had Farook's password protected-phone in their

THE SUN

A TRAGIC TOLL

New to Medicare?

The New York Times

ARMS STOCKPILE IS FOUND IN HOME OF TWO SUSPECTS

The Washington Post

14 slain at California office party

Report details Secret Service lapses

Source: Newseum, 2015

February 16, 2016

A Message to Our Customers

The United States government has demanded that Apple take an unprecedented step which threatens the security of our customers. We oppose this order, which has implications far beyond the legal case at hand.

This moment calls for public discussion, and we want our customers and people around the country to understand what is at stake.

Answers to your questions about privacy and security ›

Source: Apple, 2016

possession, the phone's operating system was setup to automatically erase all local data after too many incorrect password attempts to unlock the phone. Because no one knew Farook's password, this left the FBI with few options for unlocking the phone and accessing the data.

The FBI then turned to Apple again, requesting that the company unlock Farook's phone, specifically asking Apple to create a custom version of iOS for Farook's phone, also known as a "backdoor" in. This would allow someone to connect an external computer to the phone and unlock the device by "brute force." Apple's CEO, Tim Cook, refused to meet this demand, due to the customer privacy and safety concerns that would arise from the creation of this software.

In a public letter to Apple's customers, Cook called this request, "an unprecedented use of the All Writs Act of 1789 to justify an expansion of its authority (Apple, 2016)." Apple appealed the request because it believed that the creation of this "backdoor" to the iPhone was too dangerous. Apple argued that if it were to create the software for this case, it would be providing a way for hackers to unlock other Apple devices (Crovitz, 2016).

This case is relevant to multiple corporate communication areas including data privacy, government relations and issues management. Because Apple is such a well-known company, when it declined to decrypt the iPhone its decision and justification was extremely public and put the company at risk for alienating certain stakeholder groups. As a result, Apple had to figure out how to navigate and explain the ethical and legal ramifications of its decision to all its stakeholders as its decision was heavily debated within the court of public opinion.

Furthermore, this public battle between the FBI and Apple brought the tension between national security and individual and corporations' rights to the forefront. It raised issues of privacy and national security, of freedom of speech, and even foreign policy considerations with respect to repressive regimes and those governments hoping to track journalists' sources.

Lastly, this case is an important milestone in the evolution of the digital world and technology. Apple's argument about potential government misuse or criminal appropriation, and the government's counter that the tradeoff with privacy in certain cases is needed to fight terrorists, will help decide how *all* companies balance safety and security in the future against a suspicion about government intrusion into peoples' daily lives.

Company Background: Getting "Siri"ous

History of Apple

Founded by Steve Jobs, Steve Wozniak and Ronald Wayne in 1976, Apple has been at the forefront of technological innovation for the last four decades. Apple is the world's largest technological company in terms of total assets, and the largest information technology company in terms of revenue (Chen, 2015). Since its genesis, Apple has set the standard for functional, innovative and user-friendly consumer software and electronics. The company has had its ups and downs, including the death of Steve Jobs in 2011. Through it all, one thing that has been consistent is Apple's authority in the technology industry. Apple has been called groundbreaking, brilliant and a company that leads by example (Bajarin, 2012).

Although Apple has a strict customer privacy policy, the 2016 incident is not the first time the company has faced privacy concerns. The initiation of the iCloud in 2011 caused consumer concern amongst Apple's customers. Speculations were made that iCloud played a part in the leaking of private celebrity photos. This caused Apple to work on its security issues and protect its customer's privacy (Timberg, 2014). Now Apple has a strong customer privacy policy that it refuses to compromise.

Mission Statement

Apple has never formally published a mission statement, however, the statement found at the bottom of all of its most recent press releases, is viewed by many as Apple's version of a "Mission Statement". The statement is as follows:

> *"Apple revolutionized personal technology with the introduction of the Macintosh in 1984. Today, Apple leads the world in innovation with iPhone, iPad, Mac, Apple Watch and Apple TV. Apple's four software platforms—iOS, macOS, watchOS and tvOS—provide seamless experiences across all Apple devices and empower people with breakthrough services including the App Store, Apple Music, Apple Pay and iCloud. Apple's 100,000 employees are dedicated to making the best products on earth, and to leaving the world better than we found it."*

"Core" Values

Although Apple does not expressly publish a mission statement, it lists six core company values on its website. Each value is discussed in detail and Apple's site provides multiple examples of how it incorporates its values into everything they do and create as a company.

Apple's Values:

- **Accessibility**
- **Education**
- **Environment**
- **Inclusion and Diversity**
- **Supplier Responsibility**
- **Privacy:** Apple knows the importance of consumer trust. Privacy is one of Apple's core values, taken into consideration when creating Apple products. Because the company respects its customer's privacy, Apple products have been designed to provide maximum security to its customers' data (Apple Inc., 2016). The software, hardware and services of an iOS device are built to work together to encrypt data and keep it safe on the iCloud server. Apple does not have a backdoor for this server and no one other than Apple has access to this server (Apple Inc., 2016). These stringent security policies are the reason that Syed Farook's iPhone could not be unlocked. The data on Farook's phone had not synchronized with iCloud and incorrect passcode attempts would have completely erased it.

Corporate Reputation

According to the Arthur W. Page Society, all actions of an organization are a reflection of its defined character. The beliefs and the actions of the company towards its stakeholders help in building its character. The perception of this character is the measure of its reputation. Thus, reputation is the non-financial component of a company on which the other financial factors depend (Ragas & Culp, 2014, p. 28). A successful organization with a good reputation is reflected not only by its profits but

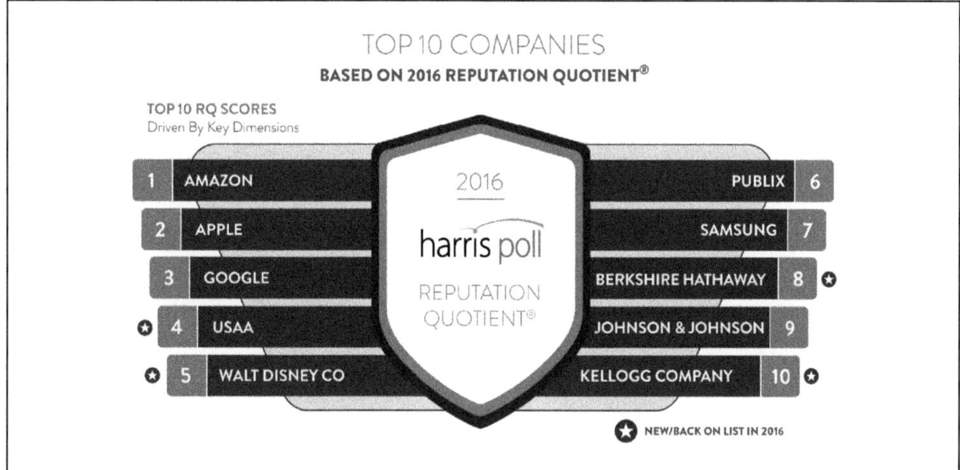

Source: Harris Poll RQ®, 2016

also by its services towards its stakeholders (Arthur W. Page Society, 2012).

Apple has worked hard to establish and maintain strong relationships and trust with its customers. This effort, combined with Apple's high quality products, has established a very strong corporate reputation. A poll, conducted by Morning Consult, of 1,935 Americans on February 24 and 25, 2016, showed that 54% of respondents trusted Apple with their data and personal information. In the same poll question, Apple was more trusted by respondents than other technology companies, including Uber, Facebook and Google (O'Neill, 2016). Apple earned a reputation quotient of 83.03 from the 2016 Harris Poll RQ® (Reputation Quotient), which was the second highest reputation score among the general public (Harris Poll, 2016).

Finally, Apple has held the number one spot on *Fortune*'s *World's Most Admired Companies Top 50 All-Stars* list for the past nine years (*Fortune*, 2016).

Corporate Character

A company defines its Corporate Character on the basis of its "mission, purpose, values, culture, business model, strategy, operations, and brand". This creates a company's brand identity which is relatable to its customers and is represented consistently through all its communications (Arthur W. Page Society, 2012, p. 5). A company should maintain this corporate character all throughout its hierarchy levels by adhering to its core purpose, values, and culture, leading to a consistent message of corporate character to all the stakeholders.

As indicated by its high reputation rankings, Apple generally communicates its corporate character effectively to its customers. The message is that Apple is innovative, high quality and trustworthy. These values have created something that many companies want, but few achieve such a high degree of brand loyalty (Smith, 2014). This case served as a high-profile test of Apple's corporate character and reputation during a complex, high-profile situation.

Situation Analysis

Over the years, Apple has become a leader in the technology world. The company is credited with redefining product categories, such as the MP3 player and smartphone, and forging new territory with technological innovation and exceptional design. Each time Apple introduced a new product, both consumers and other tech manufacturers followed, embracing Apple's vision of each new device and the software that accompanied it (Bolluyt, 2015).

Furthermore, Apple and its CEO, Tim Cook, have become more outspoken on their stance regarding societal issues, making Apple and Cook leaders not just in business, but also in terms of corporate social responsibility. After Steve Jobs stepped down as CEO, Cook began making Apple more transparent publishing an annual report on suppliers and working conditions for more than a million factory workers. Speaking on behalf of Apple, he has also taken aggressive positions on social and legal issues, pushing a once secretive company into the center spotlight of some highly charged issues (Benner & Perlroth, 2016).

More specifically, privacy has been a priority for Apple and Tim Cook for a long time. At a tech conference in 2010, he said Apple "has always had a very different view of privacy than some of our colleagues in the Valley" (Benner & Perlroth, 2016). Those views on privacy toughened over the years as customers globally began entrusting more personal data to Apple's iPhones and the number of requests from government officials worldwide asking the company to unlock smartphones rose.

After a while, Cook and other Apple executives committed not only to lock up customer data, but to do so in a way that would put the keys into the hands of the customer, not the company. By the time Apple released a new mobile operating system, iOS7, in September 2013, the company was encrypting all third-party data stored on customers' phones by default (Benner & Perlroth, 2016).

Legal Precedence and Implications

Apple's stance on privacy and security comes from a long-held, business-based decision to protect its brand with customers who prize the data protection built into iPhones. In a New York legal dispute with prosecutors in 2015, Apple argued, "forcing Apple to extract data . . . absent clear legal authority to do so, could threaten the trust between Apple and its customers and substantially tarnish the Apple brand" (Harris, Shane 2016).

The 2016 court's order to create a new technological method that would allow government officials to override login safeguards built into Apple's latest phones was completely unprecedented. Not only had something of this magnitude never been requested of a technology company by the U.S. government, no government had ever made a demand of such substance. Furthermore, if Apple obliged to this order, it would have set a legal standard for the U.S. government and other foreign governments to make similar requests of Apple and other technology companies and in future legal cases.

Timeline

- **December 2, 2015:** Shooting occurs in San Bernardino, California killing 14 and wounding 22.
- **February 16, 2016:** The Federal Bureau of Investigation (FBI) issues a court order to Apple to unlock the phone of Syed Farook, the terrorist involved in the shooting attacks in San Bernardino (Source: Weise, 2016).
  Apple responds to the FBI's request by issuing a statement on their website saying they "oppose this order, which has implications far beyond the legal case at hand" (Source: Apple, 2016).
- **February 17, 2016:** Josh Earnst, a spokesperson for the White House, responds to Apple claiming that the FBI was not asking them to create this backdoor encryption but merely have them open the single phone of the terrorist (Source: *Apple vs FBI*, 2016).
- **February 18, 2016:** Apple is told they have until February 26, 2016 to reply to the court order to unlock the phone.

Twitter founder, Jack Dorsey, tweets from his account in support of Tim Cook, Apple's CEO, on his decision to not unlock the phone. Facebook also releases a statement supporting Apple (Source: *Apple vs FBI*, 2016).

- **February 19, 2016:** Donald Trump gives his opinion on the *Apple vs. FBI* case during a campaign rally in South Carolina. Trump urges his supporters to boycott Apple until they help unlock the phone.
  The Department of Justice files a motion against Apple asking them to comply with the FBI and unlock the phone (Source: *Apple vs FBI*, 2016).
- **February 24, 2016:** Apple CEO Tim Cook is interviewed by ABC's David Muir. Cooks speaks of his concerns for safety and privacy involving a backdoor access to the iPhone. Cook reiterates that Apple has cooperated with the FBI but will continue to put its customers' safety first (Source: *Apple vs FBI*, 2016).

Source: *ABC News*, 2016

- **February 25, 2016:** Apple files a motion to vacate the previously issued court order, stating that the FBI is "attempting to expand the use of All Rights Act" (Source: *Apple vs FBI*, 2016).
- **February 26, 2016:** Major tech companies, including Google, Facebook, and Twitter, issue statements saying they will file friend of the court briefs in support of Apple (Source: Weise, 2016).
- **February 29, 2016:** Judge James Orenstein of the US District Court of the Eastern District of New York rules against the Department of Justice's request to sidestep a passcode on the iPhone of a criminal involved in a drug case (Source: *Apple vs FBI*, 2016).
- **March 1, 2016:** A court hearing labeled "The Encryption Tightrope: Balancing Americans' Security and Privacy," is held in front of the House Judiciary committee involving representatives from both Apple and the FBI (Source: Tepper, 2016).

March 3, 2016

Facebook and Industry Peers Support Apple in Amicus Brief

"Forcing engineers to build security vulnerabilities into products to allow extraordinary government access is an unprecedented legal step that would weaken security for everyone. We are proud to join our peers today in urging the court to reject the government's demands," – Colin Stretch, Facebook General Counsel

Source: Facebook, 2016

- **March 3, 2016:** 17 major tech companies publicize their support for Apple in their decision. Some big names providing support are Amazon, Facebook, Cisco, Microsoft, Mozilla, Yahoo and Google (Source: Weise, 2016).
- **March 10, 2016:** The Justice Department replies to Apple's motion to vacate the court order stating that the FBI's request was "modest" as they only wanted to open the phone of the terrorist and that was it (Source: Weise, 2016).
- **March 15, 2016:** Apple responds to Justice Department comment stating that the government is forcing Apple to assist them without having the official authority to do so (Source: Weise, 2016).
- **March 21, 2016:** While at a launch event for the new iPhone SE, CEO Tim Cook speaks out about Apple's stance on privacy with regards to their dispute with the FBI. Cook states, "We owe it to our customers and we owe it to our country. This is an issue that affects all of us and we will not shrink from our responsibility" (Source: *Apple vs FBI*, 2016).

Source: Goldman, 2016

- **March 28, 2016:** The Justice Department announces they have unlocked the terrorist's iPhone using a third party. The Justice Department says it will not release how this was accomplished (Source: Weise, 2016).
- **March 29, 2016:** At 4:44pm Pacific time, Judge Sheri Pym withdraws the case against Apple that began on February 16, 2016 and the case comes to an end (Source: Weise, 2016).

Response: How the (Apple) Pie was Sliced

Public Response

When the news broke, the public immediately began to take sides. The Pew Research Center surveyed the general American public and asked their opinions of the case. The results indicate that, of those surveyed, 51% believe Apple should help the FBI unlock the phone, while 38% support Apple's stance of not unlocking the phone (Maniam, 2016). In a national online poll conducted by Reuters/Ipsos, results showed again that the public was pretty divided on who's side to take with about 45% agreeing with Apple's opposition and 35% disagreeing.

About half say Apple should unlock terror suspect's iPhone; 38% disagree

In response to court order tied to ongoing FBI investigation of San Bernardino attacks, Apple…

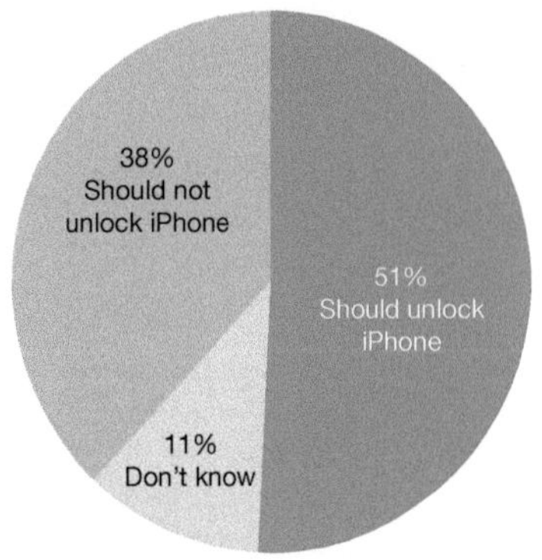

Sources: Maniam, 2016 and Bedford, 2016

People also responded online via social media with their opinions about the case and showed up at Apple stores across the country to show support for Apple's stance and protest the FBI's demand.

Lastly, one of the most notable public responses came from Salihin Kondoker, a Muslim man and the husband of one of the San Bernardino shooting victims. Kondoker submitted a letter to the judge in support of Apple's position. In the letter, he says, "I believe privacy is important and Apple should stay firm in their decision. Neither I, nor my wife, want to raise our children in a world where privacy is the tradeoff for security. I believe this case will have a huge impact all over the world" (Kondoker, 2016).

Social Media Response

The story trended on multiple social media channels throughout its duration. Zignal Labs, a social media analytics company, measured and tracked the online chatter at multiple points during the case. Zignal Labs took a 24-hour snapshot of the conversation on Twitter after Tim Cook responded to the court's demand with his public letter. During this time, the case's mention volume averaged in at around 7,115 mentions an hour, with nearly 172,000 per day. They also created a word cloud to visually represent what people were talking about most in regards to the case (Dietrich, 2016).

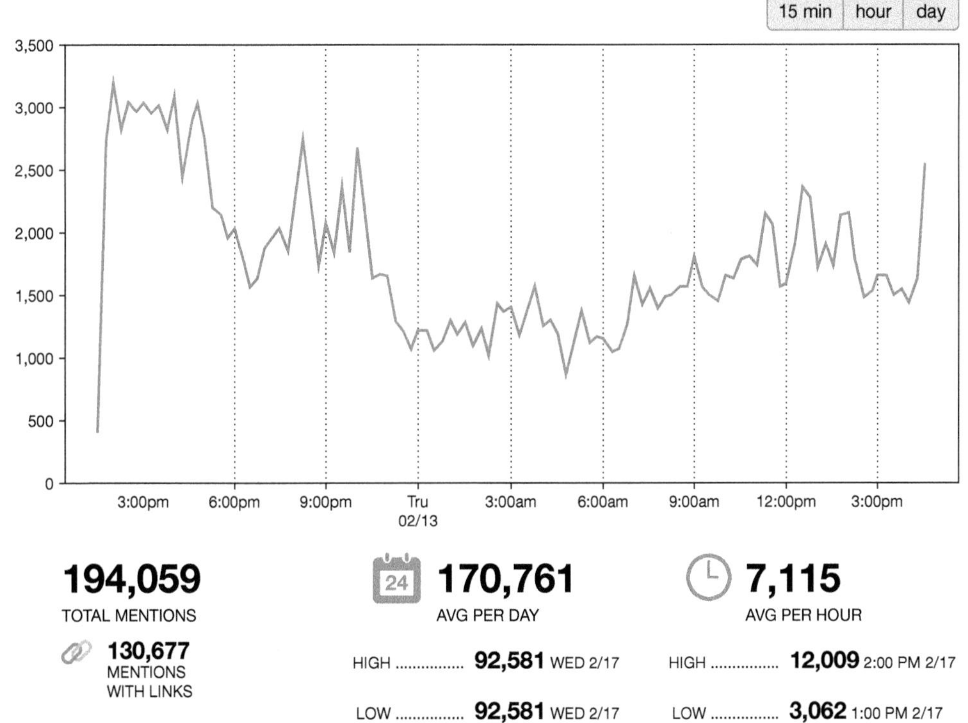

Source: Hughes, 2016

News Media Response

News media and blogs around the world immediately began covering the *Apple v. FBI* case as soon as the federal court ordered Apple to assist in unlocking the iPhone. Every major news outlet and news blog seemed to be covering the story including, BBC, *TechCrunch*, the *Washington Post*, *New York Times*, *CNBC*, NPR, *TIME Magazine*, *Last Week Tonight with John Oliver* and *Wired*, to name a few. Steady media coverage continued to analyze the FBI's demand and Apple's response through

Source: Dietrich, 2016

The New York Times

TECHNOLOGY

Explaining Apple's Fight With the F.B.I.

By MIKE ISAAC FEB. 17, 2016

Source: Isaac, 2016

September 2016, long after the FBI could unlock the iPhone, through an unnamed third-party, and after they dropped their demand on March 28, 2016.

Many news outlets remained neutral in their reporting and attempted to explain the nuances of the FBI's demand and why Apple was opposing it. As the case developed, media also reported on who was taking whose side from influential opinion makers, to large corporations, like Amazon, to the 2016 Presidential candidates. Multiple news outlets also published op-ed articles with authors either siding with the FBI or Apple and political cartoons depicting the situation.

On February 18, 2016, *The Washington Post* published an op-ed article written by Bruce Schneier, a security technologist and lecturer at the Kennedy School of Government at Harvard University, titled: "Why You Should Side with Apple, not the FBI, in the San Bernardino iPhone Case." Finally, many media outlets polled readers to see which party readers sided with to gauge public opinion on topics including privacy rights, security and government access.

At the start of this incident, Apple CEO, Tim Cook, did not hold a formal press conference, but rather wrote a personal response to the motion, via a message to Apple customers which was posted on its website, about his stance on the case and explaining why Apple would not create the "backdoor" the FBI requested of them. At the same time that Apple posted the customer letter, it created an FAQ section on its website that addressed privacy and security questions more in depth (Apple, 2016).

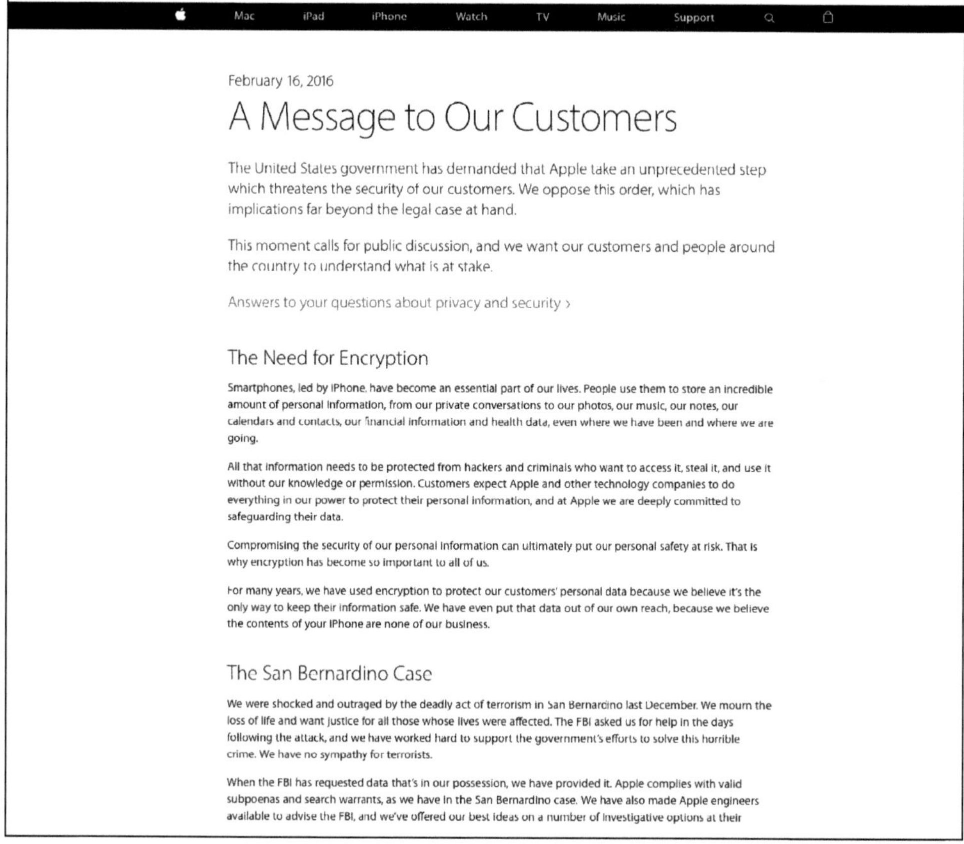

Mac iPad iPhone Watch TV Music Support

February 16, 2016

A Message to Our Customers

The United States government has demanded that Apple take an unprecedented step which threatens the security of our customers. We oppose this order, which has implications far beyond the legal case at hand.

This moment calls for public discussion, and we want our customers and people around the country to understand what is at stake.

Answers to your questions about privacy and security ›

The Need for Encryption

Smartphones, led by iPhone, have become an essential part of our lives. People use them to store an incredible amount of personal information, from our private conversations to our photos, our music, our notes, our calendars and contacts, our financial information and health data, even where we have been and where we are going.

All that information needs to be protected from hackers and criminals who want to access it, steal it, and use it without our knowledge or permission. Customers expect Apple and other technology companies to do everything in our power to protect their personal information, and at Apple we are deeply committed to safeguarding their data.

Compromising the security of our personal information can ultimately put our personal safety at risk. That is why encryption has become so important to all of us.

For many years, we have used encryption to protect our customers' personal data because we believe it's the only way to keep their information safe. We have even put that data out of our own reach, because we believe the contents of your iPhone are none of our business.

The San Bernardino Case

We were shocked and outraged by the deadly act of terrorism in San Bernardino last December. We mourn the loss of life and want justice for all those whose lives were affected. The FBI asked us for help in the days following the attack, and we have worked hard to support the government's efforts to solve this horrible crime. We have no sympathy for terrorists.

When the FBI has requested data that's in our possession, we have provided it. Apple complies with valid subpoenas and search warrants, as we have in the San Bernardino case. We have also made Apple engineers available to advise the FBI, and we've offered our best ideas on a number of investigative options at their

Source: Apple, 2016

As far as speaking directly with the media, Tim Cook sat down with David Muir from *ABC World News* for his first exclusive press interview regarding the case. Only a small portion of the interview aired on TV on February 24, 2016. However, the

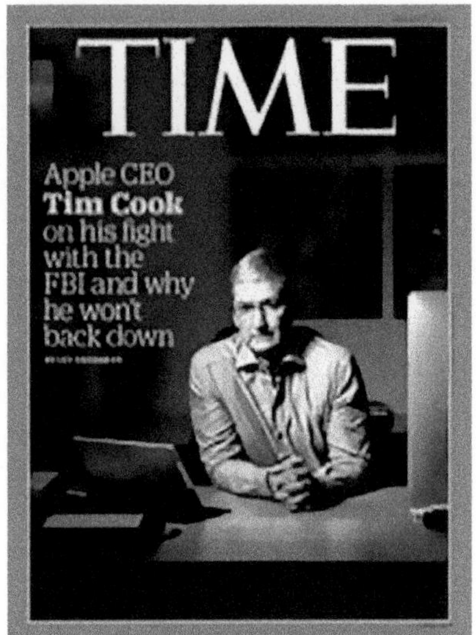

Source: *TIME*, 2016

full-length interview was made available online the same day and picked up and shared by multiple news outlets and blogs. On March 10, Tim Cook sat down with *TIME*'s Nancy Gibbs and Lev Grossman to discuss Apple's rapidly escalating fight with the FBI over encryption. That interview transcript was made available on *TIME*'s website March 17, 2016 and finally, on March 28, 2016, the same day the FBI dropped its demand, *TIME Magazine* released a cover story about the interview and the case in its entirety. Also just before the court dropped its demand, on March 21, 2016, Apple held a press conference. During the conference, Cook talked about the ongoing conflict with the FBI by saying, "We have a responsibility to protect your data and your privacy. We will not shrink from this responsibility" (Dillet, 2016).

Response by Silicon Valley

Much like the rest of the country, technology companies were divided on the issue. Technology giants Amazon, Box, Cisco Systems, Evernote, Nest, Pinterest, Snapchat, Whatsapp, Yahoo, Mozilla, Dropbox, Facebook, Google and Microsoft backed Apple, submitting amicus briefs supporting Apple's decision.

On the other end of the issue, tech companies AirBnB, Atlassian PTY, Ltd., Automattic Inc., CloudFlare Inc., Ebay Inc., GitHub Inc., Kickstarter, PBC, LinkedIn Corporation, MapBox Inc., A Medium Corporation, Meetup Inc., Squarespace Inc., Twilio Inc., Twitter Inc., and Wickr Inc. sided with the government, submitting amicus briefs opposing Apple's decision (Roth, 2016).

Some companies also wrote blog posts and took to social media to express opinions on the controversial topic. For example, Box tweeted about its joint amicus brief.

Although these companies publicly opposed Apple's decision, the briefs voiced the idea that the All Writs Act, under which the government had requested information

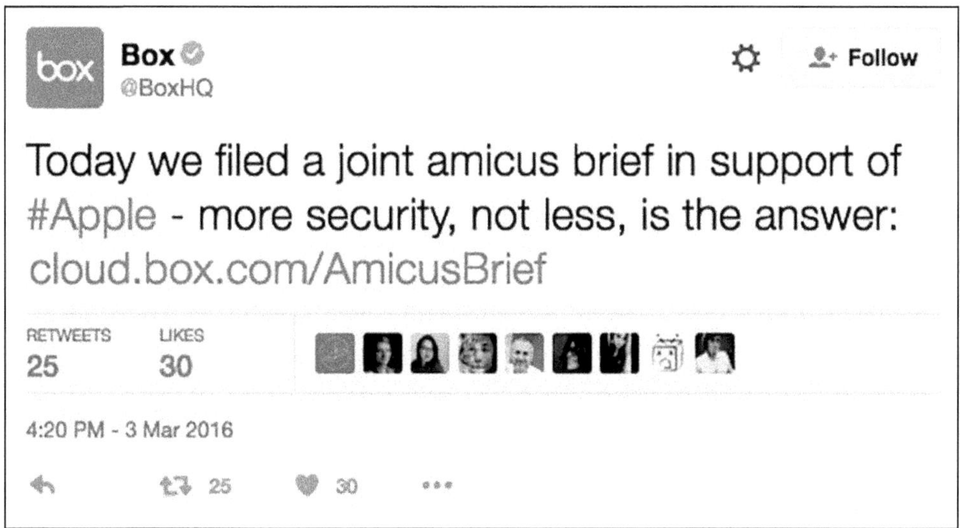

Source: Box, 2016

from Apple, was unbound by legal limits (Deluca, 2016). Ultimately, these opposing companies believe that Apple should have accepted the FBI's request, while still acknowledging that the government could have used a better strategy to request this information.

Business Performance: Will One Bad Apple Spoil the Whole Bunch?

Financial Impact

Prior to the San Bernardino shooting, Apple's stock had been sufficiently lower than previous years (Source: Thielman, Neate, Hern, 2016). 2016 was the first year that Apple had seen a sufficient dip in its stock in years. While this case affected Apple and its customers, many other factors came into play during 2016 that affected Apple's stock price.

According to Apple's second quarter 2016 financial report, quarterly revenue was $50.6 billion, which was down from the prior year's revenue of $58 billion (Source: Apple Reports Second Quarter Earnings, 2016). Apple briefed investors prior to releasing its quarterly report that revenue and sales would be down. iPhone sales were down from the previous year and Apple attributed this to no new iPhone releases in 2015 and customers purchasing their phones at that time rather than in 2016. "The total tally for the device was $32.9 billion from 51.2 million phones sold; the previous year Apple brought in $40.3 billion from 61.2 million phones" (Source: Thielman, Neate, Hern, 2016). Apple did not make as much money on the iPhone in 2016, resulting in a decline in revenue.

While the sales of the iPhone declined in 2016, there is no clear evidence to indicate that it was directly correlated to the ongoing FBI case. Before the San Bernardino

Apple's annual sales fall for first time since 2001

by Seth Fiegerman

Apple's 15-year streak is officially over.

Apple (AAPL, Tech30) just posted its first annual sales decline since 2001, the year it launched the iPod and kicked off a tremendous run of groundbreaking products.

The tech company revealed Tuesday that annual sales fell to $216 billion in the 2016 fiscal year ending September 30, from a record $234 billion in 2015.

The sales decline is closely connected to the falling sales for the iPhone, which remains Apple's largest source of revenue.

Source: Fiegerman, 2016

Source: Yahoo! Finance, 2016

shooting, Apple had been struggling to generate revenue growth in the face of maturing product lines, such as the iPhone.

When the case first began on February 16, 2016 and Tim Cook released his statement online about why Apple would not help, Apple's stock closed the day at $96.64 per share. When the FBI and Apple met on March 1, 2016, to discuss the case in front of the House Judiciary Committee, Apple shares closed at $100.53 per share. This was an increase from February 16th when the case began. On March 29, 2016, the case officially closed after the FBI was able to unlock the phone the day before. On this day, Apple's stock closed at $107.68 per share making it its highest close since the case began (Source: Apple Reports Second Quarter Earnings, 2016).

Throughout the case, Apple's stock continued to rise, further showing that this issue cannot directly correlate to the lower than normal stock prices seen in early 2016. This dip could be correlated to a mix of different factors, such as a new iPhone release the year prior, international sales lower than normal, etc. With many factors impacting the company's stock price, we cannot attribute causation to just one. After the case, Apple shares continued to rise (*New York Times*, 2016).

Reputation Impact

Although the iPhone was ultimately unlocked by an unknown third-party, the fact that Apple stuck to its core value of privacy in all of its responses throughout the 43 days strengthens Apple's reputation as a defender of privacy, and its claim that strong encryption isn't a security disaster (Grossman, 2016).

Over the past couple of decades, Apple has become one of the most admired and valuable companies in the world. Even though much of the public was split over Apple's decision of whether Apple should comply with the FBI's orders to unlock the iPhone or not, Apple has long ranked among the most reputable companies worldwide (Harris Poll Reputation Quotient, 2016). Reputation rankings for 2017 (post this incident) seem likely to continue this trend.

Looking Ahead: Apple-y Ever After

As we move further into the age of big data, customer data privacy and security will be a challenge for all companies. Cybersecurity, hacks, breaches and requests by government entities is the new reality that all companies, and, by extension all Chief Communications Officers and Corporate Communication Departments, must be prepared to address and expertly navigate.

When pushed, Apple reverted to its core principle of privacy to create a strong, clear message on where it stands in this broader discussion. On June 13, 2016, Apple reaffirmed its commitment to encryption by announcing it was applying "differential privacy" research to keep users' information private, a move that bolster's the company's standing as a leader in digital privacy. Executives at Apple's annual developer conference in San Francisco also emphasized the company's commitment to using encryption by default to protect customer's data. Furthermore, privacy researcher

Aaron Roth said the move reaffirmed Apple's status as the "clear privacy leader among technology companies today" (Drange, 2016).

References: Isn't There an App for That?

Apple Inc. (n.d.). *Apple Values.* Retrieved from: www.apple.com

Apple Inc. (2016, May). *iOS Security.* Retrieved from: www.apple.com/business/docs/iOS_Security_Guide.pdf

Apple Inc. (n.d.). *Privacy.* Retrieved from: www.apple.com/privacy/government-information-requests/

Apple Inc. (2016). Retrieved from https://finance.yahoo.com/chart/AAPL#eyJtdWx0aUNvbG9yTGluZSI6ZmFsc2UsImxpbmVXaWR0aCI6IjIiLCJib2xsaW5nZXJVcHBlckNvbG9yIjoiI2UyMDA4MSIsImJvbGxpbmdlckxvd2VyQ29sb3IiOiIjOTU1MmZmIiwibWZpTGluZUNvbG9yIjoiIzQ1ZTNmZiIsIm1hY2REaXZlcmdlbmNlQ29sb3IiOiIjZm Y3YjEyIiwibWFjZE1hY2RDb2xvciI6IiM3ODdkODIiLCJtYWNkU2lnbmFsQ29sb3IiOiIjMDAwMDAwIiwicnNpTGluZUNvbG9yIjoiI2ZmYjcwMCIsInN0b2NoS0xpbmVDb2xvciI6IiNmZmI3MDAiLCJzdG9ja ERMaW5lQ29sb3IiOiIjNDVlM2ZmIiwicmFuZ2UiOiJ5dGQifQ==

Apple Inc. (2016) *Supplier Responsibility 2016 Progress Report.* Retrieved from http://images.apple.com/supplier-responsibility/pdf/Apple_SR_2016_Progress_Report.pdf

Apple Reports Second Quarter Results. (2016, April 26). Retrieved from www.apple.com/pr/library/2016/04/26Apple-Reports-Second-Quarter-Results.html

Apple vs. FBI: A Timeline of the Legal Battle. (2016, March 28). Retrieved from www.graphiq.com/vlp/DW36cJUvtj?utm_source=viz&utm_medium=viz.referral&utm_campaign=viz.ref&utm_viz_id=DW36cJUvtj&utm_pubreferrer=www.foxnews.com/tech/2016/03/29/fbi-breaks-into-san-bernardino-gunmans-iphone-without-apples-help-ending-court-case.html&vlp_ver=2#0-Apple-vs-FBI-a-Timeline-of-the-Legal-Battle

Arthur W. Page Society (2012). *Building belief: A new model for activating corporate culture & authentic advocacy.* Retrieved from: www.awpagesociety.com/wpcontent/uploads/2012/03/Building-Belief-New-Model-for-Corp-Comms-2012.pdf

Bajarin, T. (2012, May 7). 6 Reasons Why Apple Is Successful. Retrieved January 9, 2017, from http://techland.time.com/2012/05/07/six-reasons-why-apple-is-successful/

Bedford, K. (2016, February 24). *Demonstrators rally outside Apple store in Boston* [Photograph found in Boston, MA]. In *Boston Globe.* Retrieved November 20, 2016, from www.bostonglobe.com/metro/2016/02/23/demonstrators-rally-outside-apple-store-boston/fyy2bsnMjxuyszSShr9xaP/story.html (Originally photographed 2016, February 24)

Benner, K. & Perlroth, N. (2016, February 18). How Tim Cook, in iPhone Battle, Became a Bulwark for Digital Privacy. Retrieved November 20, 2016, from www.nytimes.com/2016/02/19/technology/how-tim-cook-became-a-bulwark-for-digital-privacy.html

Bolluyt, J. (2015, June 20). Apple: 5 Ways It's Gone From Industry Leader to Follower. Retrieved November 20, 2016, from www.cheatsheet.com/technology/apple/apple-5-ways-its-gone-from-industry-leader-to-follower.html/?a=viewall

Chen, L. (2015, May 11). The World's Largest Tech Companies: Apple Beats Samsung, Microsoft, Google. Retrieved October 17, 2016, from www.forbes.com/sites/liyanchen/2015/05/11/the-worlds-largest-tech-companies-apple-beats-samsung-microsoft-google/#77efae0c415a

Coldewey, D. (2016, April 15). Apple Tells NY Judge FBI has "Utterly Failed" to Prove it Needs Help Unlocking iPhones. Retrieved November 6, 2016, from https://techcrunch.com/2016/04/15/apple-tells-ny-judge-fbi-has-utterly-failed-to-prove-it-needs-help-unlocking-iphones/

Cook, T. (2016, February 16). A Message to Our Customers [Letter written February 16, 2016 to Apple Customers]. In *Apple.* Retrieved November 6, 2016, from www.apple.com/customer-letter/

Cook, T. (2016, February 24). Exclusive: Apple CEO Tim Cook Sits Down With David Muir (Extended Interview) [Interview by D. Muir]. In *ABC News*. Retrieved November 6, 2016, from http://abcnews.go.com/WNT/video/exclusive-apple-ceo-tim-cook-sits-david-muir-37174976

Cook, T. (2016, March 17). Here's the Full Transcript of *TIME*'s Interview With Apple CEO Tim Cook [Interview by N. Gibbs & L. Grossman]. In *TIME*. Retrieved November 6, 2016, from http://time.com/4261796/tim-cook-transcript/

Crovitz, L.G. (2016, February 19). The FBI vs. Apple—*WSJ*—www.wsj.com/articles/the-fbi-vs-apple-1455840721. Retrieved November 6, 2016, from http://grabpage.info/t/www.wsj.com/articles/the-fbi-vs-apple-1455840721

Customer Letter—FAQ—Apple. (2016, February 16). Retrieved November 6, 2016, from www.apple.com/customer-letter/answers/

Deluca, M. (2016, March 03). Tech vs. the Feds: Apple Allies Rally in Flurry of New Court Filings. Retrieved November 6, 2016, from www.nbcnews.com/tech/tech-news/apple-allies-expected-form-ranks-flurry-court-filings-n530987

Dietrich, G. (2016, March 10). Privacy, Security, Transparency, and Crisis Management. Retrieved November 20, 2016, from http://explore.zignallabs.com/h/i/222559635-privacy-security-transparency-and-crisis-management/239301

Dillet, R. (2016, March 21). Apple's Tim Cook on iPhone Unlocking Case: "We Will Not Shrink from this Responsibility" Retrieved November 6, 2016, from https://techcrunch.com/2016/03/21/apples-tim-cook-on-iphone-unlocking-case-we-will-not-shrink-from-this-responsibility/

Drange, M. (2016, June 13). Apple Reaffirms Commitment To Encryption. Retrieved November 21, 2016, from www.forbes.com/sites/mattdrange/2016/06/13/apple-to-strengthen-privacy/#b8292b36b075

Encryption: Last Week Tonight with John Oliver [Television series episode]. (2016, March 13). In *Last Week Tonight with John Oliver*. New York City, NY: HBO.

Facebook and Industry Peers Support Apple in Amicus Brief | Facebook Newsroom. (2016, March 3). Retrieved November 20, 2016, from http://newsroom.fb.com/news/h/facebook-and-industry-peers-support-apple-in-amicus-brief/

Fiegerman, S. (2016, October 25). Apple's Annual Sales Fall for First Time Since 2001—Oct. 25, 2016—http://money.cnn.com/2016/10/25/technology/apple-earnings-decline/index.html. Retrieved November 20, 2016, from http://grabpage.info/t/money.cnn.com/2016/10/25/technology/apple-earnings-decline/index.html

Finkle, J. (2016, February 24). Solid Support for Apple in iPhone Encryption Fight: Poll. Retrieved November 6, 2016, from Solid support for Apple in iPhone encryption fight: poll

Fortune. (2016).*The World's Most Admired Companies for 2016*. Retrieved November 6, 2016, from http://fortune.com/worlds-most-admired-companies/

Goldman, D. (2016, February 16). Tim Cook Says the FBI Wants Apple to "Hack" Your iPhone. Retrieved November 20, 2016, from http://money.cnn.com/2016/02/17/technology/fbi-apple-hack-iphone/index.html

Grossman, L. (2016, March 28). Inside Apple CEO Tim Cook's Fight With the FBI. *TIME, 187*(11). Retrieved November 6, 2016, from http://time.com/4262480/tim-cook-apple-fbi-2/

Harris Poll. (2016, February). *The Harris Poll Releases Annual Reputation Rankings for The 100 Most Visible Companies in the U.S.* Retrieved from: www.theharrispoll.com/business/Reputation-Rankings-Most-Visible-Companies.html

Harris, Shane. "Apple Unlocked IPhones for the Feds 70 Times Before." *The Daily Beast*. The Daily Beast Company, Feb. 17, 2016. Web. Nov. 20, 2016.

Hughes, G. (2016, February 22). Social Media's Response to *Apple vs. The FBI*. Retrieved November 20, 2016, from www.convinceandconvert.com/realtime-today/social-medias-response-to-apple-vs-the-fbi/

Isaac, M. (2016, February 17). Explaining Apple's Fight With the F.B.I.—*The New York Times*. Retrieved November 6, 2016, from www.nytimes.com/2016/02/18/technology/explaining-apples-fight-with-the-fbi.html

Kharpal, A. (2016, March 29). *Apple vs FBI*: All You Need to Know. Retrieved November 6, 2016, from www.cnbc.com/2016/03/29/apple-vs-fbi-all-you-need-to-know.html

Kokalitcheva, K. (2016, March 22). Apple's Fight With the FBI Isn't Keeping People From Wanting an iPhone. Retrieved November 20, 2016, from http://fortune.com/2016/03/22/poll-apple-fbi-iphone/

Kondoker, S. 2016. Letter to Honorable Judge Sheri Pym]. In *Apple*. Retrieved November 20, 2016, from http://images.apple.com/pr/pdf/Letter_from_Salihin_Kondoker.pdf

La Monica, P. (2016, February 24). Apple's stock has Worms but FBI Isn't One of Them. Retrieved November 20, 2016, from http://money.cnn.com/2016/02/24/investing/apple-stock-fbi-iphone/index.htm

Lee, D. (2016, February 18). Apple v. The FBI—A Plain English Guide. Retrieved November 6, 2016, from www.bbc.com/news/technology-35601035

Madigan, M. (2016, March 22). Amazon, Box, Cisco, Dropbox, Evernote, Facebook, Google . . . Retrieved November 6, 2016, from http://images.apple.com/pr/pdf/Amazon_Cisco_Dropbox_Evernote_Facebook_Google_Micros oft_Mozilla_Nest_Pinterest_Slack_Snapchat_WhatsApp_and_Yahoo.pdf

Maniam, S. (2016, February 22). More Support for Justice Department Than for Apple in Dispute Over Unlocking iPhone. Retrieved November 20, 2016, from www.people-press.org/2016/02/22/more-support-for-justice-department-than-for-apple-in-dispute-over-unlocking-iphone/

Mozingo, J. (2015, December 9). San Bernardino Shooting Update. Retrieved November 6, 2016, from www.latimes.com/local/lanow/la-me-ln-san-bernardino-shooting-live-updates-htmlstory.html

Newseum: San Bernardino Shooting. (2015, December 3). Retrieved from www.newseum.org/todays frontpages/?tfp_display=archive-summary

O'Neill, P.H. (2016, February 26). Americans trust Apple but remain divided on unlocking iPhone for FBI, new poll finds. Retrieved November 06, 2016, from www.dailydot.com/layer8/apple-tim-cook-fbi-iphone-unlock-encryption-morning-consult-poll/

Ragas, M.W. & Culp, R. (2014). *Business Essentials for Strategic Communicators: Creating Shared Value for the Organization and its Stakeholders.* New York: Palgrave Macmillan.

Raza, O. (2016, February 29). [Apple Arm Wrestling FBI]. Retrieved November 13, 2016, from www.technewstoday.com/28776-apple-vs-fbi-national-security-justice-or-mass-surveillance/

Roth, J.C. (2016, March 3). Retrieved November 6, 2016, from http://images.apple.com/pr/pdf/Airbnb_Atlassian_Automattic_CloudFlare_eBay_GitHub_Kickstarter_LinkedIn_Mapbox_Medium_Meetup_Reddit_Square_Squarespace_Twilio_Twitter_and_ Wickr.pdf

Schneier, B. (2016, February 18). Why You Should Side with Apple, Not the FBI, in the San Bernardino iPhone Case [Editorial]. *Washington Post.* Retrieved November 6, 2016, from www.washingtonpost.com/posteverything/wp/2016/02/18/why-you-should-side-with-apple-not-the-fbi-in-the-san-bernardino-iphone-case/

Selyukh, A. (2016, March 29). *Apple v. The FBI*: The Unanswered Questions and Unsettled Issues. Retrieved November 6, 2016, from www.npr.org/sections/alltechconsidered/2016/03/29/472141323/apple-vs-the-fbi-the-unanswered-questions-and-unsettled-issues

Smith, D. (2014, July 14). Loyalty To Apple's iPhone is Strongest of Any Phone, and It's Getting Stronger. Retrieved November 6, 2016, from www.businessinsider.com/chart-of-the-day-iphone-owners-are-more-loyal-than-ever-2014-7

Taking a bite at the Apple. (2016, February 27). *The Economist.* Retrieved November 6, 2016, from www.economist.com/news/science-and-technology/21693564-fbis-legal-battle-maker-iphones-escalation

Tepper, F. (2016, February 20). *Apple v. the FBI*: Everything You Need to Know. Retrieved from https://techcrunch.com/timeline/a-timeline-of-apples-iphone-unlocking-fight-with-the-fbi/slide/18/

Thielman, S., Neate, R. & Hern, A. (2016). Decline in iPhone Sales Leads to First Revenue Decline in 13 Years for Apple. Retrieved November 20, 2016, from www.theguardian.com/technology/2016/apr/26/apple-iphone-first-revenue-decline-13-years

Timberg, C. (2014, November 4). Apple Users Raise Privacy Concerns after Hard-drive Files Uploaded to Servers. Retrieved November 6, 2016, from www.theguardian.com/technology/2014/nov/04/apple-data-privacy-icloud

Weise, E. (2016, March 30). Apple v. FBI Timeline: 43 Days that Rocked Tech. Retrieved from www.usatoday.com/story/tech/news/2016/03/15/apple-v-fbi-timeline/81827400/

Welch, C. (2016, February 24). Watch Tim Cook's Full 30-minute Interview on Apple's Fight with the FBI. Retrieved November 6, 2016, from www.theverge.com/2016/2/24/11110802/apple-tim-cook-full-interview-fbi-iphone-encryption

Zetter, K. (2016, February 19). DoJ Files Motion to Force Apple to Hack iPhone in San Bernardino Case. Retrieved November 6, 2016, from

LONG CASE QUESTIONS

1. What are some of the main ethical issues in this case? Which ones relate to IT and privacy?
2. Do you think it was appropriate for Apple to stick to its decision of protecting its customers' privacy? How do you balance societal needs versus customer values?
3. What were some of the consequences of these actions on Apple? Overall, was it a good move?
4. What should multinationals do in the future to address ethical issues related to IT?

Chapter 10

The Environment and Sustainability

LEARNING OBJECTIVES

After reading this chapter you should be able to:

- Understand what sustainability is
- Learn about the arguments for and against sustainability from a company perspective
- Become aware of the environment and key aspects of environmental degradation
- Learn about the many steps that lead to the successful sustainable company
- Become aware of the many benefits accruing to companies that are sustainable

PREVIEW BUSINESS ETHICS INSIGHT

Plastic Food Packaging

According to the United Nation's Food and Agriculture program, around 33% of the food produced worldwide does not make it to the end consumers' plate. This issue is even more pronounced for people living in poorer countries where harvested foods can end up as waste as difficult road conditions makes transport to consumers difficult. Additionally, bad storage can also mean that perishable foods quickly deteriorate and have to be thrown away. The situation in more developed nations is not much better. In such places, supermarkets and other grocery stores routinely throw away food that is not purchased. Because of safety regulations, most food is placed on shelves for a period of time. However, after the expiration of that date, the food is considered unsafe and has to be disposed of.

The costs of such waste are significant. For poorer nations, wasted food means hungry people go without food although they could be fed. In more developed nations, produced foods incur use of significant amounts of water, fertilizer, and land. Such waste means that the environment is being damaged for no good use. Experts also agree that meat products cost a lot to produce given the significant carbon emissions associated with meat products. And given the significant threat due to climate change and the associated growing pollution worldwide, finding ways to reduce food waste is quickly becoming a priority.

One of the new ways companies are finding ways to reduce waste is through vacuum packaging. While the green movement has generally shunned the use of plastics, the vacuum packing process has shown to be an important step in reducing food waste. Vacuum packing allows grocery stores to keep products on the shelf longer. For instance, vacuum packed meat can stay on shelves twice as long as meat placed in regular packing. Sainsbury, a major British supermarket, which now vacuum packs all of its meat, has seen waste reduced by half. Many other companies are following suit with the goal of reducing such waste.

Based on *The Economist.* 2017. "Retailing and the environment." December 17, 58–59; *The Economist.* 2017. "Climate change; No cooling." April 22, 37–38; *The Economist.* "Pollution in India; Worse than Beijing." November 12, 38.

The Preview Business Ethics Insight above highlights the importance of sustainability and environmental responsibility to companies today. **Sustainability** "refers to capacity of healthy ecosystems to continue functioning indefinitely"[1] or "economic development that meets the needs of the present generation without compromising the ability of future generations to meet their needs."[2] A core aspect of sustainability is the ability to make judicious use of current resources to ensure that such resources are available in the future. In the case of companies involved in the food industry, finding ways to reduce waste is a critical aspect that has far reaching implications for both the companies and the environment.

As the world faces climate change, air and water pollution, and other environmental changes, sustainability is becoming more critical. **Sustainable or environmentally responsible organizations** are seen as those that are gradually modifying their operations in order to have less impact on the environment while also making better use of resources. But do companies have a special obligation to the environment? In an important piece, Bowie argues that companies have no special obligations to protect the environment above and beyond what the law prescribes.[3] This view is consistent with the view that the only responsibility for companies is to pursue profits while respecting the law. He argues that the only moral obligation of companies is to ensure that they do not intervene in the political arena to help defeat or weaken environmental laws. However, as long as a company is obeying the law, it has no special moral obligation to protect the environment. Furthermore, Bowie argues that businesses can only help solve environmental problems if they have the expertise to do so. In reality, most companies are not necessarily experts in the environment and should focus mostly on respecting the appropriate laws and avoiding negligent behaviors. Additionally, Bowie argues that customers are the ones that are responsible for environmental protection by paying higher prices if they want more environmentally conscious products.

Many experts have since argued that Bowie's views are based on erroneous assumptions. According to Desjardins,[4] Bowie's solution for environmental damage is either consumer action or legislation. However, Desjardins argues that the consumerist culture is placing severe pressures on the earth's biospheres. As the new economies of China, India, and others continue to grow, the earth will not be able to sustain the carbon dioxide emission that could potentially come from these new customers. Furthermore, not all societies have democratic institutions to enact laws to pressure companies to be more environmentally sensitive. Additionally, Desjardins argues that a business case can be made for sustainability. Contrary to the view that sustainability always incurs expense, Desjardins suggests that sustainability can actually be profitable for a company. For instance, even companies like WalMart see sustainability as going beyond mere window dressing. Consider the following Ethics Sustainability Insight.

ETHICS SUSTAINABILITY INSIGHT

WalMart and Sustainability

WalMart is not seen as a model environmentally friendly company. It is known for its size, achieving a billion dollars of sales per day. It has a global workforce of more than two million employees and is located in around 28 countries today. Many are therefore surprised to hear that WalMart has actually been a world leader among the *Fortune* 500 companies pushing for sustainability and environmental responsibility. It has pioneered a number of environmental standards that have become targets in many industries. Because of its size, it has the ability to influence many of its partners to become more environmentally friendly.

To embark on its sustainability mission, WalMart started working with many of the world's leading environmental organizations. It brought in organizations such as Rocky Mountain Institute, Patagonia, and Seventh Generation, and even hired a former president of the Sierra Club to help the company improve its environmental performance. These individuals and organizations helped WalMart set industry-wide standards for sustainability.

WalMart also created a questionnaire that was sent out to thousands of its suppliers. Through the questionnaire, WalMart surveyed its suppliers' every aspect of operations from energy use to level of waste. With such information, WalMart has created a "sustainable product index" that puts a green ranking on all of the products they carry. WalMart is pushing its suppliers to continue modifying their operations to improve on that index.

Today, WalMart continues its efforts to be sustainable. Consider the warehouse that was recently opened in Balzac, Canada. While the building is the typical large WalMart building, it has many features that reduce both waste and energy use. For example, the building is equipped with LED lighting using less energy while also lasting longer than fluorescent or other bulbs. Most of the lights are motion activated. This leads to huge savings as most warehouses have lights that are either on or off all the time. Lighting often makes up around 75% to 90% of a warehouse's costs. The doors leading to freezers have special air curtains to prevent the cold air from rushing outside to the warmer temperatures. The doors on the loading docks have motion sensors that open only when the trucks are parked on the loading bays. This also saves energy as it prevents chilled air from escaping. The building also has two wind turbines and solar panels that are used to heat the water the warehouse needs. The vehicles used in the building are also very environmentally friendly as they are all powered by hydrogen.

WalMart is also encouraging the sale of products that are considered sustainable. Consider the case of Magic Dirt, a potting soil product that is produced after food and dairy waste products are treated to make biogas. Through an innovative technology, the treatment process results in a fiber-like material that is seen as much more sustainable than other alternative potting products such as peat moss. The CEO of the company making Magic Dirt recalls how when he met with the CEO of WalMart, the latter was very interested in knowing how they made sure that end customers were aware of their sustainability story. Today, WalMart has helped Magic Dirt become a successful company as the products are now being sold in its stores.

Based on Goldstein, N. 2017. "Selling your sustainability story." *BioCyle*, March/April, 58, 3, 31–34; Turner, C. 2010. "How WalMart is saving the world." *Canadian Business*, November 23–December 6, 83, 20, 44–49; Dutton, G. "Sustainable warehousing." *World Trade 100*, November, 28–34; Spicer, A. and Hyatt, D. 2017. "Walmart's emergent low-cost sustainable product strategy." *California Management Review*, 59, 2, 116–141; *WalMart*. 2018. https://corporate.walmart.com/.

Similar to WalMart's view that sustainability can be profitable, most experts currently side with the latter view. Sustainability and environmental responsibility are among the most important goals as perceived by top executives in companies.[5] Recent surveys across industries (i.e., automobiles, commodities, construction, financial services, etc.) suggest that most see sustainability as critical to achieving sustainable

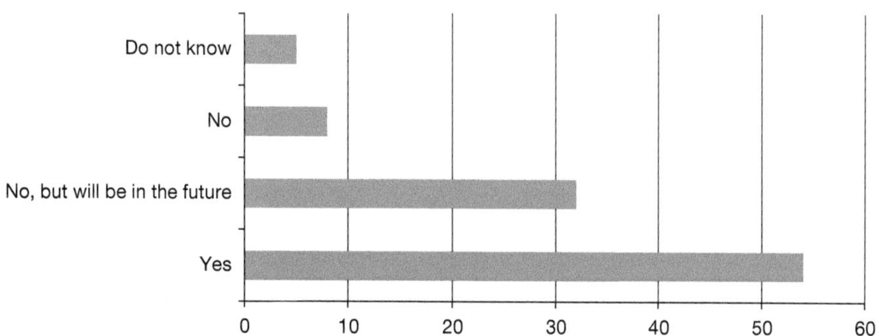

EXHIBIT 10.1—Sustainability Strategies and Competitive Advantage across Industries

competitive advantage. Exhibit 10.1 shows the percentage of respondents who agreed with the statement "Is pursuing sustainability-related strategies necessary to be competitive?"

Additionally, even country leaders see sustainability as extremely critical. Consider the case of China.[6] While a decade ago, the country saw climate change as a way for Western countries to impose policies to slow down the economy, China now sees climate change as a key reason why they should pursue sustainability efforts. As you will read later, climate change is causing many changes that are being seen as dangerous by both the government and the public.

Given the critical importance of sustainability, this chapter will therefore discuss the key aspects related to sustainability. First, we discuss issues such as air pollution, land pollution, and water pollution. We also discuss water issues, as many are predicting that water will become increasingly scarce in the future and needs to be managed. Second, we discuss the many aspects of the model sustainable company. We use a strategic approach and discuss the many aspects of the successful companies pursuing strategic environmental sustainability. In the final section of the chapter, we discuss the many benefits companies can reap from sustainability.

ENVIRONMENTAL DEGRADATION

One of the most important reasons why multinationals are getting so much attention for their environmental performance is because of the impact they have on the environment. Companies are important contributors to many aspects of environmental degradation. In this section of the chapter, we look at aspects of environmental degradation, specifically air pollution, land pollution, and water pollution. We also address critical water issues.

Air Pollution

Air pollution occurs when the release of materials to the atmosphere cannot be safely disposed of by natural processes. While some air pollution is caused by natural events such as forest fires and volcano eruptions, most air pollution is caused by human activity. Furthermore, companies contribute significantly to air pollution. A recent study of 230 of Standard and Poor's 500 companies showed that these companies released around 1.4 billion metric tons of carbon dioxide or 30% of all carbon dioxide from industrial sources in the U.S.[7]

What contributes to air pollution? The most recent effort to examine air pollution worldwide suggests common **air pollutants** such as particulate matter (small particles that occur because of dusty industries and smoke) and the degree to which populations are exposed to such matter, how much solid fuel such as coal, wood, and kerosene are used indoors and the average concentration of nitrogen oxide (a highly reactive gas that comes mostly from vehicle emissions in the atmosphere). The Environmental Protection Agency (EPA), which regulates environmental quality in the U.S., lists other common air pollutants.[8] In addition to particulate matter and nitrogen oxide, they also list ozone, lead, carbon monoxide, sulfur dioxide. Ozone refers to the combination of three atoms of oxygen that occurs in the atmosphere. At high levels in the atmosphere, ozone is considered beneficial as it protects the earth from the sun's rays. However, ozone occurring at lower levels due to vehicle and industrial emissions is very harmful as it is a primary factor for smog. Carbon monoxide is an extremely dangerous odorless gas that comes mainly from vehicle emissions. Sulfur dioxide refers to the group of highly reactive gases that come mainly from power plants using fossil fuels. In contrast, nitrogen oxide is also a highly reactive gas coming from vehicle emissions. Finally, lead is a metal that is found naturally in the environment. Most lead came historically from vehicle emissions but has reduced considerably with the EPA's efforts to remove lead from gasoline.

The major concern regarding air pollutants is that they contribute to major health problems. Consider the Emerging Market Business Ethics Insight on the facing page.

As you can see from the Emerging Market Business Ethics Insight, reduction of air pollution is critical given the many health effects of air pollution. High levels of ground ozone have been linked to various respiratory ailments. High exposure to particulate matter has also been linked to respiratory ailments, as well as heart disease, such as irregular heartbeat and heart attacks. Carbon monoxide is an extremely dangerous gas that reduces the ability of the body to deliver oxygen to the heart and the brain. High levels of carbon monoxide are often fatal. To give you more insights into the health effects of these pollutants, Exhibit 10.2 shows the sources of the various types of pollutants and their likely health effects.

As Exhibit 10.2 shows, the common air pollutants can be very harmful to humans. Presence of the six pollutants can result in significant health problems ranging from respiratory difficulties to heart disease. However, another area of concern is acid rain. **Acid rain** occurs when both sulfur dioxide and nitrogen oxide combine with air vapor in the atmosphere and return to earth in the form of acid rain. Acid rain has also been

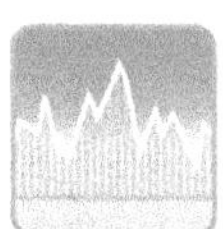

EMERGING MARKET BUSINESS ETHICS INSIGHT

Air Pollution in Nepal

The Environmental Performance Index has been computed regularly to rank countries based on key environmental issues. Nepal places 177th out of 180 based on air quality issues. This therefore suggests that air pollution is a major problem in Nepal. However, this ranking is not too surprising. First, regulation in Nepal regarding vehicle emission is not as strict as in other countries. The Kathmandu valley is rapidly urbanizing and the growth in number of cars etc. is contributing to pollution. Additionally, the major cities have older vehicles that are not properly maintained and such vehicles are major contributors to pollution. Furthermore, Nepal has cement and brick kiln factories in suburban areas that are also major contributors to air pollution. Finally, recent surveys indicate that around three-quarters of all Nepalese households use solid fuel such as charcoal and wood as a source of energy to cook. Such factors also contribute to pollution.

The impact of such pollution is clear. While there have not been any direct studies examining the impact of air pollution in health, data from hospitals in Nepal suggests that air pollution is having a devastating impact on the population. For instance, one of the top reasons why outpatients consulted with Nepalese health services was because of upper and lower tract respiratory infections. These are well-known health effects of air pollution. Additionally, chronic obstructive pulmonary disease (COPD) is now one of the leading causes of mortality in Nepal. Compared to 2010, authorities estimate that deaths due to COPD have increased by 43% and it is now the second leading reason for death. COPD has also been linked to air pollution. Finally, cardiovascular disease is very high in Nepal. This will likely be aggravated by the rise of air pollution in the country.

Based on Kurmi, O., Regmi, P.R. and Pant, P.R. 2016. "Implication of air pollution on health effects in Nepal: Lessons from global research." *Nepal Journal of Epidemiology*, 6,1, 525–527; Environmental Performance Index. 2018. http://epi.yale.edu/

shown to be a pollutant, contributing to acidification of lakes while also contributing to degradation of buildings.

Another important issue that is contributing to the discussion of air pollution is **greenhouse gases**. According to scientific evidence, life on earth is possible through energy from the sun. The earth absorbs energy from the sun and also radiates some energy back to space. However, the presence of greenhouse gases in the atmosphere traps the energy going to space. Such energy is then radiated back to earth, keeping the earth warmer. Without such greenhouse gases, the earth would be around 60°F colder, making life on earth impossible. Unfortunately, recent human activity has

Pollutants	Sources	Health Effects
Ozone	Emissions from industrial facilities, motor vehicle exhaust, gasoline vapors, and other chemical solvents	People with lung problems, children, and older adults are affected when breathing unhealthy levels of ozone. These include: • Wheezing and breathing difficulties when exercising or outdoors • Airway irritation and coughing when breathing deeply • Permanent lung damage with repeated exposure
Particulate matter	Found near dusty roadways, smog, and haze	• Irritation of the airways, coughing, difficulty breathing • Decreased lung function and aggravated asthma • Cardiovascular disease and non-fatal heart attacks • Premature death of individuals with heart or lung disease
Carbon monoxide	Emitted from combustion processes	• Reduces oxygen-carrying capacity of blood to organs • Causes harmful effects when less oxygen carried to organs such as brain and heart • Is particularly harmful to people with heart disease • Causes death at extremely high levels
Nitrogen oxides	Major sources are emissions from cars, trucks and buses, power plants, and off-road equipment	• Airway inflammation in healthy people • Increased respiratory problems in people with asthma • Breathing elevated levels of nitrogen oxides is linked with emergency room visits for respiratory issues • Specially harmful to children, older adults, and adults with respiratory disease
Sulfur dioxide	Major sources are from fossil fuel combustion at power plants and other industrial facilities	• Adverse respiratory effects including bronchoconstriction and increased asthma symptoms • Interacts with other small particles in the air and can cause lung damage and premature death for those with heart disease
Lead	Major sources used to be car emissions. Most are found now near lead smelters	• When ingested, is distributed in the body and accumulates in bones • Affects the nervous system, kidney function, immune system, reproductive and developmental systems, and the cardiovascular system

EXHIBIT 10.2—Pollutant Types, Sources, and Health Effects

increased the level of greenhouse gases dramatically through the increased use of fossil fuels such as gas, coal, oil, and others. These activities release both carbon dioxide and methane which are known to contribute to greenhouse gases. The enhanced greenhouse gases are believed to be contributing to the global climate change.

While there are still political debates about whether climate change is actually occurring or not, scientific evidence shows that the earth is indeed becoming warmer. Furthermore, the consequences of the climate change for the earth are both direct and indirect. According to the EPA, the direct effects of climate change for individuals include more heatwaves and fewer cold weather spells.[9] This can affect people, directly causing deaths among the elderly. Heatwaves can also make smog more dangerous. In fact, as you saw earlier, in China,[10] climate change is seen as the reason for rising sea levels, droughts in the northern part, and floods in the southern part of China. Additionally, global warming has also meant lack of rain and wind in Eastern China. Such changes are also resulting in atmospheric stagnation that is preventing clearing of pollutants.

The dangerous indirect effects of climate change include more extreme weather events. Data now shows more extreme hurricanes and extreme heat and floods. Furthermore, some areas are expected to experience more droughts. Climate change is also expected to result in changes to the earth's ecosystem thus affecting some species.

Given the dire consequences of climate change for the earth, most companies are being pressured to reduce their emission of greenhouse gases. As discussed earlier, companies contribute significantly to emission of greenhouse gases.[11] Such emissions occur directly as a result of the company's fuel combustion or use of other industrial processes that emit carbon dioxide. However, carbon emissions can also occur indirectly through purchasing electricity made from fossil fuels or from other suppliers that provide goods and services to the company. Furthermore, as you read earlier, the example of WalMart shows how they implemented measures to reduce greenhouse gases.

Given the relatively high contribution of companies to overall carbon emissions, many countries are experimenting with regulation to reduce such emissions. One such mechanism is the cap-and-trade method where the government will impose a limit on carbon emissions while also allowing companies to trade such allowances. In the U.S., a recent attempt to impose cap-and-trade legislation failed.[12] The legislation, known as the Waxman-Markley Bill, would have proposed a target of greenhouse gas reduction of 17% from 2005 to 2020. However, critics have argued that the U.S. economy is heavily dependent on fossil fuels and such rules would result in severe loss of jobs.[13] In contrast, the European Union has implemented the European Trading System to cap the greenhouse emissions of aircraft operators as they produce 50% of greenhouse emissions. It is expected that such a cap-and-trade system will be expanded to most sectors.[14]

To give you an idea of air pollution worldwide, Exhibit 10.3 below shows the top and bottom ten countries on the overall Air Quality Score based on the Environmental Performance Index rankings. A score of 100 indicates the lowest air pollution.

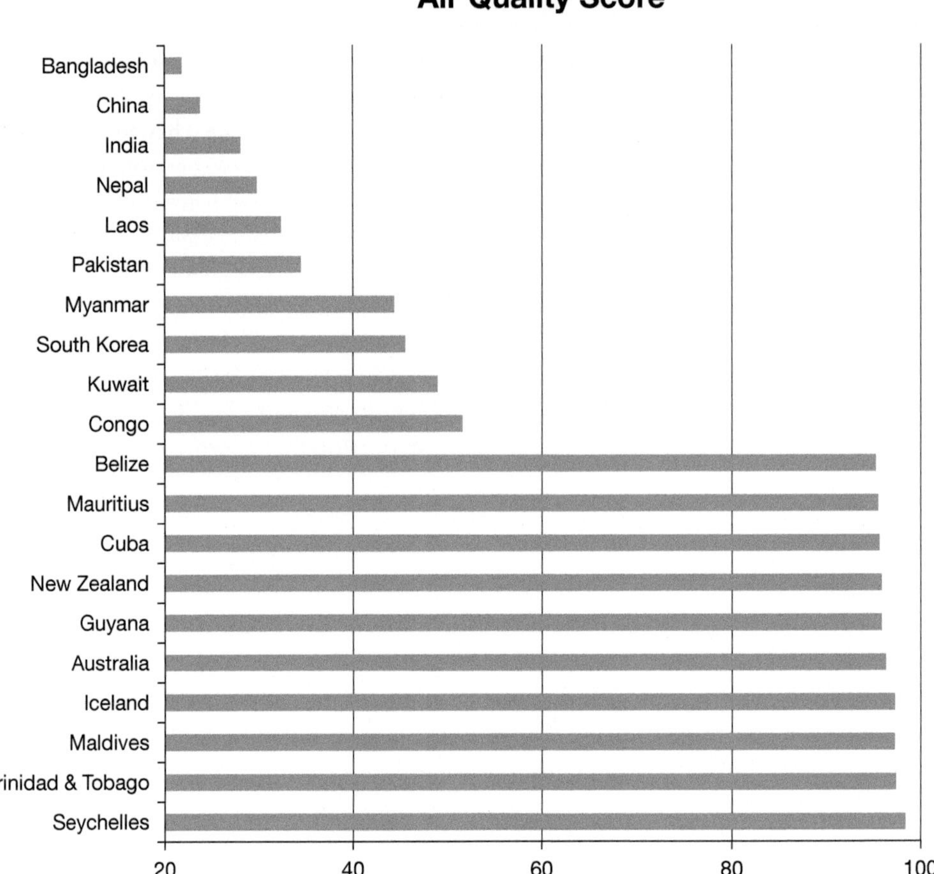

EXHIBIT 10.3—Air Quality Score

Source: Based on EPA. 2018. https://epa.gov

As the exhibit shows, key emerging markets such as India, China, and South Korea have all experienced dramatic growth in the last few decades. Unfortunately, such growth has also been accompanied by high levels of pollution. Another aspect of pollution that societies are concerned about is land pollution, which we discuss next.

Land Pollution

Another important aspect of environmental degradation is land pollution. **Land pollution** refers to the contamination that occurs when toxic waste and other waste material that do not belong on land are disposed of on land. Such materials then are either consumed by plants or animals, which are then consumed by humans. Land pollution also occurs when toxic materials seep into the ground and affect the soil. Such pollution can affect individuals living in the area of the polluted land for decades.

Land pollution occurs because of many factors. For example, the growth in the use of fertilizers, pesticides, and insecticides to satisfy human demand for food has resulted in both land and plant absorption of such material. Human consumption of such plants can result in birth defects and other disease. Heavy metals can also cause land pollution. Such heavy metals (e.g., cadmium) are often dumped on land in industrial waste. However, these metals can be consumed by animals and plants and consequently get consumed by humans. Gradual increase of heavy metals in humans can eventually result in various forms of illnesses and cancer.

Another big factor resulting in land pollution is disposal of garbage. As many societies such as India, China, and Russia experience rapid economic growth, there is a consequent growth in waste. As more individuals in industrialized societies experience higher purchasing power, they are able to consume various new types of products.[15] However, as these products become obsolete and as more products are designed with shorter life spans, disposal of such products is adding to more complex and heterogeneous waste. Consider the Global Business Ethics Insight below.

***GLOBAL* BUSINESS ETHICS INSIGHT**

Sustainable Landfilling in Malaysia

Malaysia is a relatively small nation with significant population density. Furthermore, as the standard of living has been growing, more individuals have the means to consume a wide range of products. Unfortunately, disposal of waste created by increased use of these products has not been very efficient. Consider that Malaysia generates more than 30,000 tons of waste daily. Furthermore, this waste is expected to grow from year to year.

Malaysia had a fairly low population density in the 1970s and landfill use was not a problem. Additionally, most of the landfills were of the most basic classes, whereby the landfill was simply fenced and perimeter drains installed. However, as the demand on such waste facilities has increased, use of these facilities has resulted in serious environmental damage as the waste seeps into the streams and other water areas. Organic waste such as food waste accounts for a very large percentage of all waste generated in Malaysia. Such waste is also a major culprit in gas emissions at such landfills. Furthermore, Malaysia has very little regulation regarding waste disposal. As a result, both households and companies have disposed of waste without concern for the environment. Consider the case of illegal dumping at many landfill sites. Malaysian companies have routinely dumped toxic and other caustic materials at these illegal dumpsites.

Malaysia has therefore recently enacted legislation to manage waste disposal. However, they have faced significant barriers in ensuring that the law is followed. For instance, recent reports suggest that the Malaysian general population have not had very positive attitudes toward these new environmental efforts.

Furthermore, the lack of financial assistance from the government means that only few landfills have the financial means to operate at sustainable levels. Nevertheless, recent surveys suggest that Malaysia recognizes landfills as a major contributor to environmental degradation. For example, there is strong desire by the government to support anaerobic recycling of organic waste, a major contributor of waste in most landfills. Although the use of biogas is in its infancy in Malaysia, many local governments are examining such recycling programs seriously.

Based on Agamuthu, P. and Fauziah, S.H. 2011 "Challenges and issues in moving toward sustainable landfilling in a transitory country." *Waste Management and Research*, 29, 1, 13–19; Badgie, D., Samah, M.A.A., Manaf, L.A. and Muda, A.B. 2012. "Assessment of munipal solid waste composition in Malaysia: Management, practice, and challenges." *Polish Journal of Environmental Studies*, 21, 3, 539–547; Khairuddin, N., Manaf, L.A., Hassan, M.A., Halimoon, N. and Karim, W.A.W.A. 2015. "Biogas harvesting from organic fraction of municipal solid waste as a renewable energy resource in Malaysia: A review." *Polish Journal of Environmental Studies*, 24, 4, 1477–1490.

As the Global Business Ethics Insight shows, garbage disposal is also a significant contributor to land pollution. For instance, as we saw in Chapter 9 on Information Technology, disposal of electronic waste in less developed societies often put low paid workers' health at risk while also damaging the land. Some of the types of garbage generated by high-income countries may often pollute land in poorer countries.

Weber, Watson, Forter and Oliaei also discuss another aspect of landfill use that may become problematic in the long term.[16] Persistent organic pollutants (POPs) are chemical products such as polychlorinated biphenyls (commonly known as PCBs) and hexachlorocyclohexane (HCH) that are increasingly being produced. Such POPs are commonly used in a wide variety of consumer goods. However, as these consumer goods are disposed of at landfills, the POPs they contain tend to degrade very slowly. As the number of products containing POPs grows at landfills, POPs concentration will likely grow. Degradation of concentrated levels of POPs will likely build up in the food chain as animals and plants are exposed to POPs. This will also eventually affect humans.

In sum, similar to air pollution, companies are often significant contributors to land pollution in terms of both the way their operations pollute the land and the amount of waste they generate that ends up in landfills. Additionally, multinationals are also often criticized for taking advantage of poor or non-existent regulations to dump their waste. Consider the case of Shell in Nigeria, which is often blamed for poor operations and significant damage to the land.[17] Shell's poorly run and sometimes sabotaged oil extraction in the Niger Delta has resulted in significant damage to the land and waterways around their operations. This has negatively impacted the communities surrounding their operations. Many fishing communities have been decimated, while some residents of the local communities are suffering. Companies will therefore have to play an important role in reducing land pollution.

Water Pollution

Water pollution refers to the contamination of water sources such as lakes, streams, wells, and oceans by substances that are harmful to living organisms. Water is one of the most critical resources that sustain life. Humans need access to clean water for drinking on a daily basis. Lacking such access, humans eventually get sick and die. In fact, it is reported that around 5000 children die daily due to dirty water, while it is estimated that around 1.8 million individuals die annually from diarrheal diseases linked to lack of access to clean water.[18] More recent research suggests that unsafe water is responsible for 2% of global deaths.[19] Ensuring that water is accessible and not polluted is therefore a critical endeavor.

Similar to other forms of pollution, companies contribute significantly to water pollution. This is especially salient for companies operating in new markets such as China and India. Consider the case of China where environmental regulation is very weak and companies routinely pollute water sources. A prominent Chinese environmental organization released a list of multinationals that are believed to be contributing to water pollution. This list includes companies such as PepsiCo, DuPont, Nestlé, and even Suzuki. More recent incidents also show that local companies are contributing to water pollution. For instance, in 2010, the Zijin Mining Company accidentally released 2.4 million gallons of acidic waste water in the Ting River in Fujian. Around 2000 tons of fish perished and 60,000 individuals lost their source of safe water. A chemical spill near the city of Jilin resulted in around 3000 barrels dumped in the Songhua river. The situation is so dire that it is reported that around 40% of surface water is so polluted that it is unusable.

The above reveals a major problem facing most societies as they deal with water issues. Water pollution is clearly a major issue that many societies are facing.[20] Facing weak regulations, companies routinely dump pollutants that affect water sources. However, another water-related problem facing most societies today is scarcity of water. While experts generally agree that the earth is not necessarily running out of water, water remains scarce for a sizable proportion of the world's population.[21] Companies are therefore already playing a critical role in promoting water conservation.

Another critical aspect related to water is the presence of wastewater treatment facilities. Many rural areas in the world do not have properly functioning sewer systems. Unfortunately, this means that common pollutants, bacteria and viruses tend to disperse in the water supply. This results in access to unsafe drinking water which sickens and kills many children worldwide. Countries therefore need to ensure that they have the right waste water treatment and other systems in place to ensure that their population have access to safe drinking water.

The many factors above contribute to severe scarcity of water. Consider the following most important water-related statistics:[22]

- Although the earth is covered with water, less than 3% of the water is fresh and drinkable. The rest is seawater and undrinkable. Of the 3%, 2.5% is frozen, thereby providing less than 0.5% for human use.

- There is high inequality regarding water distribution. Fewer than ten countries (Brazil, Canada, China, Colombia, Democratic Republic of Congo, Indonesia, India, Russia, and the U.S.) have 60% of the world's access to freshwater. There is also wide variation in water consumption.
- 1.8 million individuals die yearly from diarrhea and other water-related illnesses because of lack of access to safe water. Around 8% of the world's population does not have easy access to clean water.
- Humans are putting incredible stress on water supply because of excessive use of water as well as pollution and inefficient use of such water. Furthermore, around one-fifth of the world's population live in areas where water is scarce.
- A recent study forecasts that demand for water in 2030 will grow from 4500 billion cubic meters today to around 6900 million cubic meters. This represents a 40% jump above our current water reserves.
- More than 80% of the world's discharged wastewater is not treated and gets released into the environment. Furthermore, around 8% of the world's countries have no wastewater treatment plants.
- Over 90% of usable water is used in agriculture in developing nations. However, after agriculture, industry is the next biggest user of water.
- Waterways are routinely used for waste disposal. Although nature can often break down some waste quantities, current levels suggest that the water ecosystems are severely threatened.

Given the above dire statistics regarding water, more companies will be asked to play a critical role in preserving water in the future. In fact, one of the most important water initiatives taken by companies recently is known as the "CEO Water Mandate." As part of the United Nations Global Compact (see Chapter 1), companies are now launching initiatives to help face the water challenges.[23] Business leaders met and developed six key areas that companies can voluntary adapt to. These include: 1) direct operations (conduct water footprint to assess water use and find ways to reduce such water use), 2) supply chain water management (find ways to work with others in the supply chain to improve water use), 3) collective action (work with local and national organizations to address water challenges), 4) public policy (working with governments to influence water policy), 5) community engagement (work with local communities to improve water use), and 6) transparency (be truthful about water use and strategies). More companies are joining this initiative, recognizing the urgency and extent of the water challenges facing the world today.

To give you further insights into water access and sanitation, Exhibit 10.4 below shows the top and bottom ten countries on the water and sanitation score as computed by the Environmental Performance Index project. Exhibit 10.4 also includes data for the U.S. and several emerging markets such as India, China, and Mexico. Higher scores mean that the country has access to excellent water quality.

Exhibit 10.4 shows that most of the countries affected by water issues are also poor. Inadequate water quality is very devastating for any society. As such, the above sections on environmental degradation show the extent of challenges facing companies today.

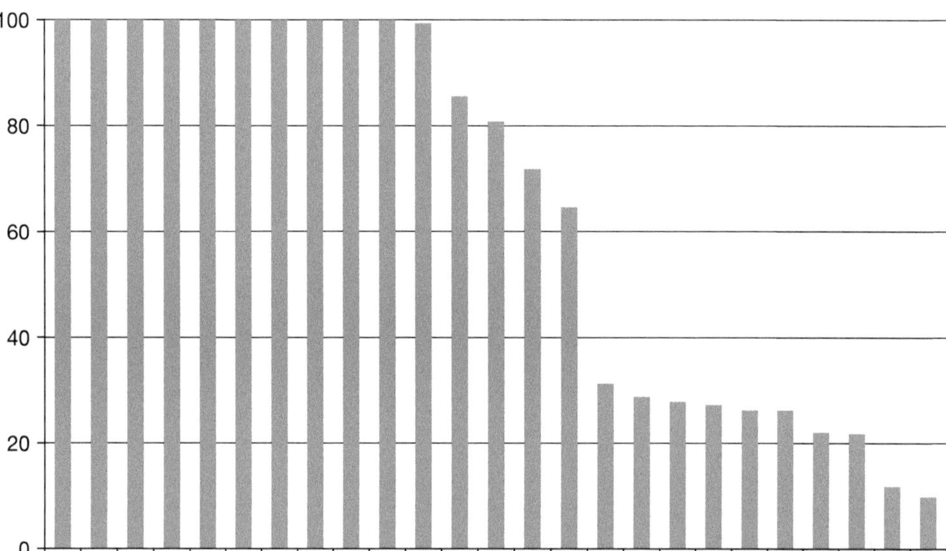

EXHIBIT 10.4—Water and Sanitation Score For Selected Countries

Source: Based on http://archive.epi.yale.edu/epi/issue-ranking/water-and-sanitation

Many companies are important contributors to such degradation. They will therefore be required to play an important role in helping address such challenges. Next, we consider how to build the sustainable company.

BUILDING THE ENVIRONMENTALLY SUSTAINABLE COMPANY: A STRATEGIC APPROACH

The above sections of this chapter provide strong evidence of the need for companies to become more environmentally sensitive in the future. In this section, we discuss the many steps companies can take to become more environmentally sensitive. In doing so, we propose a strategic framework consistent with the theme of this text.

Top Management Support

Extant research suggests that **top management support** is extremely critical in implementing sustainability.[24] Without such support, it is unlikely that employees and others will buy into the effort. Most examples of successful environmental organizations tout leaders who were willing to engage employees and support the initiatives that will make sustainability a priority. Consider the following Business Ethics Brief.

BUSINESS ETHICS BRIEF

Top Managers and Sustainability

There is ample evidence that sustainability efforts at many successful companies started with determined top managers willing to champion sustainability causes. As you read earlier, WalMart is a sustainability champion. However, WalMart's sustainability efforts began with an influential speech by the CEO Lee Scott. In that speech, he acknowledged the size of WalMart and the ability to use that size to positively impact the world. Similarly, consider the case of CEO of PepsiCo, Indra Nooyi. Even before she became CEO, she was an avid supporter of PepsiCo's green efforts. Executives remember how she loosened capital expenditure requirements to fund water- and heat-related conservation projects at an important meeting early in her career at PepsiCo. However, when she became CEO, she pushed for a new visionary strategy called "Performance with Purpose." The strategy basically links all green efforts in the company to the bottom line. This strategy has resulted in most employees participating in efforts to help PepsiCo become greener.

But do CEOs worldwide share this view of the importance of sustainability? The most recent CEO study is that conducted by Accenture examining the United Nations Global Compact (see Chapter 1). The study included surveys of over 1000 CEOs worldwide in companies from around 150 countries and 30 different industries. The study suggests that CEOs are convinced about seeing sustainability and solving societal problems as a key to sustainable competitive advantage. In the past, sustainability was not necessarily seen as the way to be more competitive. However, the recent study suggests that CEOs see sustainability as the way forward. Of those questioned, 80% of those CEOs believe that sustainability is the key differentiator in their industries while 89% agree that sustainability is making important differences in their industries. This study therefore suggests that sustainability is critical to most CEOs.

Based on Accenture. 2018. The UN Global Compact-Accenture Strategy CEO Study – www.accenture.com/us-en/insight-un-global-compact-ceo-study; Morris, B. 2008. "The Pepsi challenge." *Fortune*, March 3, 54–66; Spicer, A. and Hyatt, D. 2017. "Walmart's emergent low-cost sustainable product strategy." *California Management Review*, 59, 2, 116–141.

The Business Ethics Brief clearly shows that not only is top management commitment critical to implementing sustainability initiatives but most CEOs see the value of sustainability. In fact, recent research conducted in England suggests that the top management mindset regarding sustainability is often a key barrier as to why sustainability efforts are not always successful. In interviews with executives from a variety of industries such as telecoms, food wholesaling, and banking, they found evidence of different types of top management sustainability mindsets.[25] Understanding the mindset of top management will provide important clues as to potential success of sustainability efforts.

According to Ahern,[26] there are four top management mindsets regarding sustainability. The first type known as the "**corporate conventionality**" mindset places strong emphasis on profit making. This type of mindset suggests that top management is unlikely to see much benefit from sustainability initiatives. Rather, these executives believe that the company's sole focus is to make profits and, if the company goes bankrupt because of sustainability efforts, the company does not really serve any purpose. A second type of mindset is the "**new sustainability paradigm**" view. Such executives see the need for a new way of measuring the success of sustainability efforts. However, these executives do not necessarily believe that sustainability can be profitable for the company. Rather, they see such efforts as not profitable for shareholders. The last two types tend to be more sympathetic to sustainability. Specifically, the third type, known as "**reconciliation**," believes that it is possible to reconcile sustainability with profitability. Such managers believe that sustainability can be profitable and beneficial to the organization despite the difficulties of getting there. Finally, the "**pragmatism**" mindset suggests that these executives take a more pragmatic view of sustainability. These executives are often involved in implementation of sustainability initiatives.

While the above research about mindsets is mostly practical, a lesson for most companies is that top management can have better appreciation for sustainability efforts if they move beyond understanding performance outcomes merely in terms of financial indicators. Specifically, those top managers comfortable with sustainability understand that sustainability cannot always be measured in terms of its impact on profits. Profits remain an adequate measure of success for shareholders. However, comprehensively understanding the impact of sustainability often means understanding the impact of actions on both social and environmental performance. As we will see later, measuring the impact of sustainability efforts in terms of social and environmental outcomes implies departure from conventional thinking regarding how project success is measured.

Another critical aspect of top management support is the role of top financial executives in ensuring that sustainability efforts go as planned. Consider, for instance, some of the "biodiversity" offsets that are being proposed where companies can counterbalance the environmental impact of one business activity in a region by preserving natural habitat in another area. Shell is currently engaged in this approach, where it is preserving antelopes and other natural habitat in one area of Qatar while developing a new natural gas facility in another.[27] Properly evaluating the trade-offs of such a project will require top financial executives with the ability to properly evaluate such a project. Financial executives need to have the skills to evaluate sustainability initiatives, set budgets, and track progress of such initiatives. Ultimately, the company will need the skills of someone who can effectively communicate the impact of such sustainability initiatives in terms of their impact on the environment.

The above suggests that companies will need to reconcile financial aspects of the organization with sustainability objectives. Fortunately, the Accenture study described earlier suggests that CEOs worldwide understand the financial implications of their sustainability efforts. Exhibit 10.5 shows the degree of agreement with statements pertaining to financial and investor aspects.

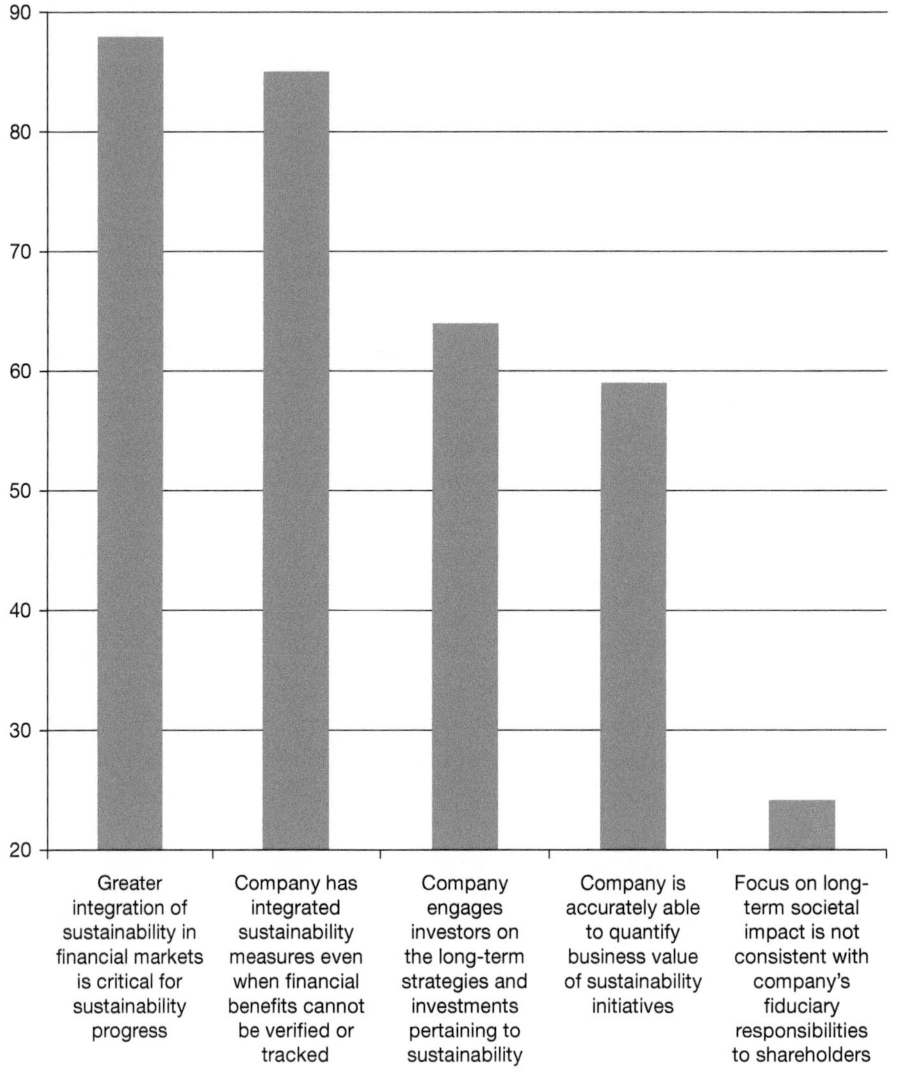

EXHIBIT 10.5—Sustainability and Financial Issues

Source: Accenture. 2018. The UN Global Compact-Accenture Strategy CEO Study www.accenture.com/us-en/insight-un-global-compact-ceo-study

Assessing Current Sustainability Situation

Once a company has the necessary support from top managerial levels, it is important to start assessing where the company stands with regards to the sustainability. This is conceptually similar to asking the "Where are we now?" question typical of strategic management practice. In this phase, the company examines the many aspects related to its business. Careful examination of the many areas will reveal potential avenues to implement sustainability initiatives.

Experts agree that one way that companies initially examine their activities to implement sustainability initiatives is by focusing on waste reduction and resource efficiencies.[28] Rather than embark immediately on full-fledged sustainability, companies will often adopt "low hanging fruits" that are easy to implement. For instance, for WalMart, understanding how to deal with its waste was a big factor to drive sustainability in the organization. It discovered that it was paying tens of millions of dollars to use 10-ton semi-compactors in order to get rid of the trash generated from its 4400 locations. This realization led to the decision to start finding ways to reduce the amount of trash it was generating.

In assessing the current level, it is important to understand the types of companies engaged in sustainability. A recent report suggests that companies can be of the **embracer types** where such companies fully embrace sustainability efforts.[29] However, some companies are **cautious adopters** where they see sustainability as limited to those activities that are linked to short-term efficiency. Embracer types are more likely to see the business case for sustainability and see sustainability as key to competitive advantage. As such, they are more likely to see and implement a stronger link between sustainability and profit and market share. In contrast, cautious adopters are less likely to take leaps of faith if they do not see properly quantified benefits of sustainability. Cautious adopters are obviously less enthusiastic of sustainability initiatives if they cannot see the monetized benefits of sustainability.

Either type of company will likely determine the extent to which assessment of the current situation is approached. Cautious adopters are more likely to adopt the "low hanging fruits," as these efforts are more easily quantifiable. However, embracers are more likely to look at the organization more strategically to find ways to make the company become more sustainable. For instance, WalMart embarked on its sustainability journey by working closely with consultants and outside experts to help it identify areas where sustainability initiatives could be implemented. These outside experts helped WalMart systematically analyze its operations to become more sustainable.

One of the many ways companies are analyzing the ways they can embrace sustainability is through the use of renewable power. Consider the following Global Business Ethics Insight.

As the Global Business Ethics Insight shows, many global multinationals are resorting to using renewable energy as one of the ways to implement sustainability. One of the more systematic ways to understand a company's operations related to sustainability is by conducting a value chain analysis. According to strategic management experts Gamble and Thompson Jr., the **value chain** of a company consists of the various

GLOBAL BUSINESS ETHICS INSIGHT

Global Multinationals and Renewable Energy

Multinationals worldwide are examining ways they can adopt new sustainability initiatives. Many of these initiatives have included energy-efficient initiatives like the ones you read earlier. However, many global multinationals are increasingly seeing the power of renewable energy sources as a way to reduce their carbon emissions. Many of these companies are therefore playing an important role by investing in new wind and solar power projects worldwide. These projects have enabled these companies to show their commitment to sustainability.

Consider the case of AnheuserBusch-InBev, the Belgian-based largest beer brewer in the world. Refrigeration accounts for a significant part of its energy use and amounts to around 10% of its cost. The company's chief sustainability officer has set a goal of using 100% renewable energy by the year 2025. One of the ways it is increasing its use of renewable energy is by getting such sources of energy from utilities involved in the production of wind energy. For example, Iberdola, one of the world's largest utility companies, is now building a wind farm in Mexico. This plant will provide clean energy for AnheuserBusch-InBev's operations by 2019.

This push for renewable energy is also resulting in innovation. One of the challenges of energy sourcing from wind or solar origins is that the supply can be intermittent. A possible solution is to store the energy in batteries. However, Iberdola is experimenting with other approaches as the company's head doesn't believe customers will always go for expensive batteries. His company is now pumping water up hilltops. The water can then be used to generate hydroelectricity by letting the water run downhill. Energy can thus be generated when needed and not necessarily when natural wind or solar power is available.

Based on *The Economist*. 2017. "Business and clean energy; We've got the power." June 10, 63-65; *The Economist*. 2017. "Iberdola; The storage question." June 10, 64.

activities that a company performs internally to create value for consumers.[30] Value chain analysis provides a systematic method to identify the many activities that are necessary to create the final product. To understand the value chain concept, Exhibit 10.6 shows the typical value chain and an illustrative example for the popular clothing retailer Gap.

As Exhibit 10.6 shows, the value chain consists of both primary activities and support activities. **Primary activities** are those activities directly linked to creating the product. Primary activities include:

- *Supply chain management*. The many activities and costs incurred in securing the raw materials and other energy requirements needed for production. This aspect may not be as relevant for Gap as they outsource most production. However, finding

Primary Activities

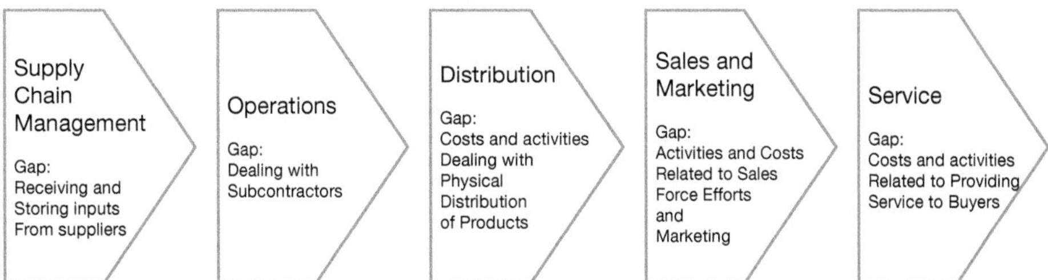

Support Activities and Costs

Product R&D, Technology and Systems Development
Gap – Product R&D, computer systems to run company, telecommunication systems

Human Resource Management
Gap – Costs associated with training, recruiting and compensation of employees

General Administration
Gap – Costs associated with general management, finance, accounting etc.

EXHIBIT 10.6—Value Chain and Example of Value Chain for Gap

ways to work with these external contractors has been a critical aspect of Gap's sustainability strategy.

- *Operations*. This pertains to the many activities and costs that are necessary to convert the raw materials into finished products. While this may not be a critical activity for Gap, it is a critical aspect for other companies such as Procter & Gamble and others.
- *Distribution*. This pertains to the many costs and activities that are involved in physically distributing the products to buyers. For Gap, this involves the shipping and trucking of the clothing items to its stores.
- *Sales and marketing*. The activities and costs involved in the marketing and sales of the product. For Gap, this involves the advertising and other sales training their sales people receive.
- *Service*. The activities and costs associated with providing after-sales service to buyers. For Gap, this would involve the many activities related to returns.

The value chain also consists of **support activities** that are provided to support the primary activities. These include:

- *Product research and development, technology and systems development*. These include the costs and activities related to R&D as well as the development of appropriate information systems to support primary activities. For Gap, this would involve the use of computers for data analysis processes to determine buyer patterns.

- *Human resource management*. The activities and costs related to the hiring and firing of employees. For Gap, this would relate to training and other activities provided to support its workforce.
- *General administration*. These are activities and costs associated with the general management of the company. For Gap, this would involve the costs associated with activities such as finance, accounting, general management, and other management functions needed to adequately manage the company.

The value chain is thus a very systematic way in which companies can analyze their activities to determine where sustainability initiatives can be implemented. However, it should be noted that the value chain will differ by industry. For instance, a manufacturer will most likely be concerned about primary activities such as supply chain

***GLOBAL* BUSINESS ETHICS INSIGHT**

Volkswagen and Sustainability

Despite its recent ethical nightmare related to its diesel vehicles, for the German automotive company Volkswagen, the supply chain aspect of its value chain is a very important aspect of its operations. Volkswagen has therefore taken many initiatives to reduce the environmental impact of its supply chain. By carefully analyzing its value chain activities, it determined areas where sustainability initiatives could take place. For instance, it not only has sustainability requirements for its suppliers but also provides them with environmental and sustainability training. Furthermore, it is very aware of the potential for the high environmental impact of its logistics. As such, the company is now aiming to reduce reliance on road transport to the more efficient rail and sea transport. The company has also developed software to ensure that fewer empty containers are being used during transport. Additionally, through analysis of its internal supply chain, it is now analyzing its in-house logistics to reduce the use of packaging and plastics when spare parts are moved to locations. Volkswagen has also implemented many initiatives aimed at the reduction of water use and air emissions. Furthermore, it has developed an extensive recycling system to go beyond manufacturing. It is aiming to recycle 95% of vehicles at the end of their lives to reduce the pressure on landfills, where a significant percentage of old cars end up.

Similarly, WalMart is also taking steps to analyze its value chain to reduce carbon emissions. Its recent 'Gigaton' project will involve understanding its value chain and those of its suppliers to collectively reduce 1 billion tons of carbon emissions in its operations by 2030.

Based on *The Economist*. 2017. "Business and clean energy; We've got the power." June 10, 63–65; Nunes, B. and Bennett, D. 2010. "Green operations initiatives in the automotive industry." *Benchmarking: An International Journal*, 17, 3, 396–420.

management and distribution. In contrast, a hotel chain is more concerned about primary activities such as sales and marketing.

Despite the differences by industry, the value chain is a critical mechanism to help a company understand the activities that contribute to environmental degradation. Consider the Global Business Ethics Insight on the previous page.

As you can see from the Global Business Ethics Insight, properly analyzing a company's value chain is critical to implement sustainability initiatives. By focusing only on some of its core aspects, Volkswagen was able to determine which areas to address.

Setting Sustainability Goals

An important aspect of a strategic approach to sustainability is to set **sustainability goals**. This is important as it will provide the focus for the company's sustainability efforts. Such goals will influence how new activities take shape in the company. It is likely that embracers are more likely to set sustainability goals for the whole organization, while cautious adopters may focus more on specific areas or set goals mostly focused on cost reductions. Consider, for instance, the case of Burt's Bees, the manufacturer of personal care products. Being a sustainability embracer, it has set an ambitious goal of "zero waste, zero carbon company, operating on 100% renewable energy" by the year 2020.[31] Additionally, many of the world's leading companies, for example, have signed the famous Paris climate accord (see Chapter 1) and have pledged to reduce carbon emissions by 26% by 2025. Companies such as Amazon, Target, Twitter and WalMart are also working hard to find ways to achieve such goals.

From a strategic standpoint, an important aspect of a company's sustainability effort is the setting of its strategic vision. The **strategic vision** describes a company's aspirations about "where it is going," thus helping steer the company in that direction. Setting a strategic vision is a logical outcome of assessing where the company first stands on sustainability. By understanding the current situation, a company can then decide to what extent it will address sustainability issues. As such, it is likely that most embracers will incorporate sustainability at the strategic vision level to ensure that such efforts influence every aspect of a company's operations. However, cautious adopters may be less likely to set goals at the strategic vision level. In such cases, sustainability goals may be set at lower levels of the organization.

For sustainability goals to work, they must cascade down the organization and influence what each worker is doing. Consider, for example, that Burt's Bees provides paid time for its employees to volunteer for sustainability and other causes. In an effort to achieve its zero waste goal, it holds an annual dumpster dive where employees will go through the trash the company has generated to identify missed recycling opportunities. When the program started in 2007, Burt's Bees was generating around 40 tons of waste on a monthly basis. However, through the annual dumpster dive efforts, it reduced its waste to zero in 2009.

However, to set goals, companies need to be able to measure their sustainability efforts. **Measurable sustainability goals** provide a company with the needed benchmarks to determine whether it is successful in its sustainability efforts.[32] Measurement also creates awareness around key issues and focuses energies toward improving such issues. The measurement process should also logically evolve from the value chain analysis. For each set of activities, the company can assess the level of energy consumption, water use, and waste created. Furthermore, companies can assess the level of land resources use.[33] These sustainability goals can then become benchmarks that the company can use to assess whether it is successful in its sustainability efforts.

Which sustainability goals should a company adopt? The types of goals adopted will likely depend on whether the company is an embracer or a cautious adopter. Embracers are more likely to adopt goals that cover the company's activities comprehensively. In contrast, cautious adopters may pick specific activities to achieve efficiencies or reduce waste. Furthermore, there are several organizations that provide guidance regarding sustainability. For instance, the International Organization for Standardization (ISO) provides very specific guidance regarding particular environmental indicators, thereby

Category	Examples
Materials	• Materials used by weight or volume • Percentage of materials used that are recycled
Energy	• Direct and indirect energy consumption • Energy saved due to conservation and efficiency measures • Energy sourced from alternative or other sources of energy
Water	• Total water use by source • Percentage of water recycled and reused • Rain water harvested • Existence of water treatment plan
Biodiversity	• Percentage of land owned, used, or managed in or near protected lands with high biodiversity • Habitats protected or restored • Strategies in place to manage impact of activities on biodiversity
Emissions	• Direct and indirect greenhouse gas emissions by weight or volume • Significant pollutant emissions by weight or volume • Emissions of ozone-depleting materials by weight or volume
Waste	• Total weight of waste by type and disposal method • Total water discharge by quality and destination • Total number and volume of significant spills
Products and Services	• Initiatives to reduce environmental impact of products • Percentage of products sold and packaging materials reclaimed or recycled • Energy efficiency of products purchased
Compliance	• Amount of fines and number of non-monetary sanctions for breaking laws and regulations
Transport	• Impact of transporting materials • Impact of transporting organizational members

EXHIBIT 10.7—Sustainability Goals

allowing companies to gauge their progress on environmental goals. Similarly, the Global Reporting Initiative (GRI) provides guidance regarding specific sustainability goals.

To get a better understanding of sustainability goals, Exhibit 10.7 shows some of the environmental measures as used by the Global Reporting Initiative and also by a recent review of the literature.[34]

Corporate Social Responsibility (CSR) Reporting

Another important component of any sustainability efforts is reporting. **Corporate social responsibility (CSR) reporting** refers to the efforts by a company to report its sustainability efforts and the progress made on such efforts. Reporting is essential as it can provide the justification for sustainability choices while also addressing stakeholder concerns.[35] While companies have often voluntarily provided information about their social and environmental efforts, companies in the European Union will soon be required to provide such information. This European Union Mandate will require the 6000 European companies with more than 500 employees to report and explain their sustainability performance.[36]

What do companies report in their CSR reports? Many of the sustainability goals discussed in Exhibit 10.7 can be included in the CSR reports. However, the European Union mandate requires large European companies to report the detail on their policies on issues such as their sustainability policy and the social impact of their environmental and social policies.[37] The mandate also requires such multinationals to provide detail on the working conditions of their employees, their respect of human rights and information on their anti-bribery and anti-corruption efforts.

Many companies are engaging in CSR reporting to ensure that stakeholders are aware of their sustainability efforts.[38] In some cases, such efforts may result in lower cost of capital as companies reduce the lack of information regarding their practices. Additionally, some companies engage in CSR reporting as a way to self-regulate and to provide the critical information through voluntary disclosures. CSR reporting can also be a way for companies to build trust with the public.[39] For example, in the face of the financial crisis in the finance industry, CSR reports are ways for such companies to document their efforts to be more ethical and sustainable. Finally, companies also engage in CSR reporting as a way to counteract potential government regulation. Complying with laws can often be costly. By voluntarily disclosing CSR reports, companies can show their sustainability efforts to ward off governmental intervention.

CSR reporting has grown in importance over the last decade.[40] This importance has grown both for developed countries as well as emerging markets. Consider the following Global Business Ethics Insight.

As the Global Business Ethics Insight shows, more Chinese companies have released CSR reports. Additionally, most societies now expect some degree of CSR reporting from their companies. As such, there has also been significant interest to also understand which companies are more likely to produce CSR reports. A recent review of studies suggests some of the reasons why companies disclose their CSR efforts.[41]

GLOBAL BUSINESS ETHICS INSIGHT

CSR Reporting in China

Prior to 2008, very few companies issued CSR reports in China. However, in 2008, the Shanghai and Shenzen stock exchanges started requiring companies in some sectors to report their CSR activities. This resulted in a dramatic jump of CSR reports from less than 100 for publicly listed firms in China in 2007 to over 500 in 2011. However, such requirements were mostly voluntary and the government did not impose penalties on those companies that did not disclose their report. As a result, the quality and timing of reports have varied tremendously.

A recent study provides some insights on the variation of quality of CSR reports in China. The authors examined a sample of 584 firms that issues CSR reports and found that those companies that had government linkages but were also pressured domestically had lower quality reports that were released quicker. Specifically, the researchers argue that local provincial companies may put conflicting demands on companies as they emphasize rapid growth that is typically incompatible with CSR. In contrast, the central government has more ethical goals in requiring CSR reporting and this places pressure on companies to report CSR. As a result of these tensions, the researchers find that such companies try to satisfy both local and central governments by quickly releasing CSR reports that are of lower quality.

Another review also suggests that those Chinese companies that release CSR reports are typically ones that are in high-profile industries or have high performance or high levels of internationalization. In contrast, companies in less competitive industries do not have as strong incentives to release their CSR reports.

Based on Luo, R.X, Wang, D. and Zhang, J. 2017. "Whose call to answer: Institutional complexity and firms' CSR reporting." *Academy of Management Journal*, 60, 1, 321–344; Norohona, C., Tou, S, Cynthia, M.I. and Guan, J.J. 2013. "Corporate social responsibility reporting in China: An overview and comparison with major trends." *Corporate Social Responsibility and Environmental Management*, 20, 29–42.

In more developed countries, company characteristics such as size and industry types are more likely to encourage companies to publish CSR reports. Additionally, the desire for companies to respond to stakeholders such as regulators, shareholders, investors, and the media makes it more likely for companies to issue CSR reports. In contrast, companies in developing nations are more likely to publish CSR reports as a way to respond to the needs of strong external stakeholders such as foreign investors, international buyers and international regulators such as the media.

Other Success Factors

The above provided a strategic oversight of a successful sustainability program in a company. However, best practices suggest that a number of other factors contribute to success. These include:[42]

- Be a first mover. Surveys of successful companies attest to the need of being first movers. By being a first mover, a company can more quickly navigate the challenges associated with implementation of sustainability. Such knowledge can be very helpful as competitors attempt to mimic sustainability efforts.
- Balance visionary thinking with "low hanging fruits." While a long-term strategic view is necessary if a company is serious about sustainability, experts suggest that short-term projects with tangible benefits be integrated within the long-term plans of the company. Short-term projects can provide evidence of quick success that will convince skeptics about the benefits of sustainability.
- Balance between top-down and bottom-up. While CEO and top management support and communication regarding sustainability are important, experts also agree that employees need to be involved in the process. They are often more aware of places where sustainability steps can be taken. Involving workers also makes it more likely that they will embrace sustainability.
- Make the link between sustainability and innovation. Many multinationals are realizing that sustainability can be the path to competitive advantage and innovation. Consider the case of a European manufacturing company that produces corn-based ethanol. Unfortunately, production of corn-based ethanol is not as sustainable because the process diverts corn from the food supply. The company therefore partnered with another company to produce cellulosic ethanol from corn stover, all of the waste that is left behind after corn is harvested. Because of its strong sustainability goals, it has been able to enter the market producing cellulosic ethanol. This has enabled the company to develop new technology that can now be sold to other companies.
- Devise and measure intangible benefits. As you may have realized, sustainability often involves benefits that may not always be tangible. It is therefore critical for companies to develop measures for those intangible benefits. For instance, Unilever's efforts to develop products that use less water may not provide direct benefits. However, the ability to evaluate the goodwill and other benefits from such an action needs to be developed in order to adequately quantify the benefits of sustainability. To give you further insights into intangible benefits, Exhibit 10.8 shows the potential intangible benefits of sustainability based on different stakeholders.
- Educating consumers. Successful companies are also keen on educating their customers about the benefits of sustainability. For instance, WalMart is now only stocking fluorescent bulbs and educating its consumers about the benefits of such bulbs compared with traditional bulbs. Unilever is also encouraging its consumers to use products that are better for the environment.
- Role of human resource management (HRM) department. Experts agree that the HRM department has a critical role to play to build a sustainability culture. HRM

can play a critical role in hiring those employees who are more likely to embrace sustainability. However, HRM also has an important role in educating existing employees about the importance of sustainability and how such efforts can benefit the wider society.

Stakeholder	Intangible Benefits	Potential Way to Assess Benefits
Consumers	• Stronger brand • Stronger customer loyalty	• Stronger sales and market share • Increase in sales and repeat sales
Employees	• More satisfied and happier employees • Ability to attract top talent	• Stronger productivity • Lower turnover • Higher productivity and returns on employee training
Shareholders	• Stronger relationship with shareholders	• Fewer lawsuits • Higher share prices
Society and community	• Better relationship with public • Better relationship with community	• More positive mention in media • More publicity • Lower costs of operations • Easier expansion efforts
Other companies	• Improved business alliances relations	• Lower costs of negotiations • More successful alliances

EXHIBIT 10.8—Intangible Sustainability Benefits

Source: Based on Kreiss, C., Nasr, N. and Kasmanian, R. 2016. "Making the business case for sustainability: How to account for intangible benefits—A case study approach." *Environmental Quality Management*, Fall, 5–24.

BENEFITS OF SUSTAINABILITY

In the preceding section, we discussed the many steps to build the successful sustainable organization. But why should companies engage in operations that may be costly? Unfortunately, companies are important contributors to the many environmental problems we are facing and should therefore play a critical role in implementing changes to address such issues. Large multinationals have specially been targets for such calls and have been criticized for their lack of concern for the impact of their activities. This is exemplified in cases such as Shell Nigeria or, more recently, British Petroleum (BP), which have both been under tremendous pressure to improve their environmental performance. However, as we see below, **sustainability benefits** include many key advantages for companies.

An important benefit of sustainability today is avoiding the public relations nightmare that can occur when damages to the environment occur. Consider, again, the case of BP. While it took many years for the company to build its seemingly environmentally friendly image, the oil spill revealed the weaknesses of its environmental policies. BP had to face significant consumer backlash in many countries. It now has to toil in order to rebuild its reputation.

A related benefit of sustainability is avoiding fines and other legal costs associated with violating regulations. Most societies now have significant regulation enforcing environmental sustainability. Companies that break such environmental laws are often fined and may have to endure frequent inspections to satisfy regulators. Furthermore, companies that choose to fight the fines usually incur substantial legal costs as they endure years in the courtroom. Being environmental thus avoids incurring such costs.

An important benefit of sustainability is cost reduction. As the many examples have shown, sustainability has the potential to save significantly from the green warehouse. Pursuing sustainability efforts enables a company to identify areas where waste can be reduced and resources used more efficiently. In fact, the traditional view is that greening is costly and unprofitable for companies.[43] However, recent experiences at major companies such as Dow Chemical and United Technologies show that investments in green technology can help reduce costs and improve profits. In fact, Hopkins reports that some green investment can have a payback period as short as two to three years. This is much shorter than the typical payback period expected for technology investment.

Furthermore, although sustainability can have a clear impact on the ability of companies to lower costs, sustainability efforts can also result in higher revenues. Research suggests that customers are more likely to purchase from companies that they perceive as being more sustainable relative to companies that have less perception of sustainability.[44] Additionally, research shows that customers tend to be more loyal to companies that have sustainable practices. Furthermore, as discussed earlier, this can also be the key to innovation and sustainable competitive advantage.[45] Companies that embrace sustainability can benefit from such efforts.

Another important benefit of sustainability is improved relationships with stakeholders and improved brand reputation. As more multinationals are scrutinized for their practices, adopting sustainable practices can provide a positive perception to stakeholders. For instance, as we saw in the chapter on secondary stakeholders, actively engaging stakeholders such as non-governmental organizations can provide companies with the ability to proactively deal with potential future environmental problems. Furthermore, sustainability projects a positive image in the community the company is located in. Such an image can help the company develop a better relationship with the local community. Wexler argues that sustainable companies can have a positive influence on their industries.[46] Consider the case of Levi's, which partnered with other companies like IKEA and Marks and Spencer. By partnering with these companies and demanding more sustainable cotton (reduced water use, reduced pesticide, and improved working conditions), Levi's is influencing the cotton industry to become more sustainable.

Another benefit of sustainability is enhanced relationships with employees. Employees are more likely to feel committed and engaged with companies that demonstrate concern for the earth and the environment. Consider the case of Burt's Bees, maker of natural personal care products, which has made sustainability its core reason for existence.[47] On an annual basis, employees gather to go through the trash to come up with more ways to reduce waste. Such concern for the environment has resulted in increased engagement with the company. Furthermore, such enthusiasm for sustainability has translated into further ideas for Burt's Bees to become more sustainable and profitable. Furthermore, employees have started changing their behaviors to reduce waste.

A final benefit of sustainability is enhanced relationships with shareholders. There is more evidence that investors are increasingly paying attention to environmental performance. Any impending environmental disaster is likely to send share prices tumbling. In contrast, companies that have engaged in sustainable paths have had more stable share prices.

From a strategic management standpoint, achieving the above advantages can also lead to increased competitive advantage. Pursuing sustainability can be a good source of innovation as companies not only discover new ways of doing things but also new markets. Through cost reductions and better resource use, a company can become a cost leader in the market. Such efforts can thus provide important sources of competitive advantage.

To better appreciate these benefits, Exhibit 10.9 shows the percentage of executives who agreed with the importance of different sustainability objectives. As Exhibit 10.9 shows, the executives see reduced incidence of noncompliance with laws as a key benefit. However, most importantly, 49% of executives also see sustainability as the key to achieving sustainable competitive advantage.

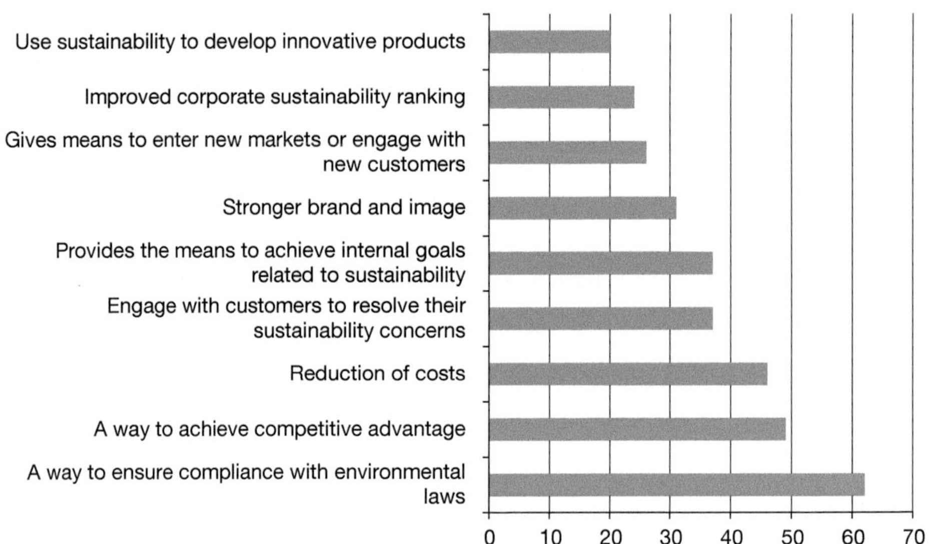

EXHIBIT 10.9—Benefits of Sustainability

Source: Based on Metz, P., Burek, S., Hultgren, T.R., Kogan, S. and Schwartz, L. 2016. "The path to sustainability-driven innovation." *Research-Technology Management*, May–June, 50–60.

CHAPTER SUMMARY

In this chapter, you read about the importance of sustainability for companies. You learned about the many changes that are occurring that makes addressing sustainability issues critical. You read about the many forms of environmental degradation including air pollution, land pollution, and water pollution. You also became aware of how multinationals are important contributors to such problems and should therefore play important roles in addressing such problems.

In the second part of the chapter, you read about the many steps to a successful sustainability program. You learned about the importance of top management support and financial executives. You read about assessment of current sustainability efforts as well as the need to measure and set sustainability goals. You also became aware of the need to provide feedback while also reading about several other key factors that ensure success.

In the final part of the chapter, you read about the many benefits of sustainability. You learned about the cost benefits as well as avoiding significant fines and costs because of regulation. You also read about how sustainability can benefit a company by improving relationships with stakeholders. Sustainability efforts can demonstrate caring for the community and other stakeholders thus improving relationships with such stakeholders. Sustainability can also improve relationships with shareholders, as many shareholders now pay attention to the sustainability records of the company they invest in. Finally, you learned that sustainability efforts can lead to improved competitive advantage.

NOTES

1 Unruh, G. 2008. "The biosphere rules." *Harvard Business Review*, 86, 2, 111–117 (at 111).
2 Epstein, M.J. 2008. *Making sustainability work*. Sheffield, UK: Greenleaf Publishing, p. 20.
3 Bowie, N. 1990. "Morality, money, and motor cars." In W.M. Hoffman, R. Frederick & E.S. Petry (Eds.), *Business ethics, and the global environment*. New York: Quorum Books, pp. 89–97.
4 Desjardins, J.R. 2007. "Sustainability: Business's new environmental obligation." In *Business, ethics, and the environment: Imagining a sustainable future*. Upper Saddle River, NJ: Prentice Hall.
5 Thomason, B. & Marquis, M. 2010. "Leadership and the first and last mile of sustainability." http://iveybusinessjournal.com.
6 *The Economist*. 2017. "Climate change; No cooling." April 22, 37–38.
7 Trucost. 2009. "Carbon risks and opportunities in the S&P 500." www.trucost.com/published research/6/carbon-risks-and-opportunities-in-the-sp-500.
8 EPA. 2018. www.epa.gov.
9 EPA, www.epa.gov.
10 *The Economist*. 2017. "Climate change; no cooling."
11 Trucost. "Carbon risks and opportunities in the S&P 500."
12 Power, S. 2011. "Senate halts efforts to cap CO_2 emissions." *Wall Street Journal*, July 23, http://online.wsj.com/article/SB10001424052748703467304575383373600358634.html.
13 Power, "Senate halts efforts to cap CO_2 emissions."

14 https://ec.europa.eu/clima/sites/clima/files/docs/ets_handbook_en.pdf
15 Agamuthu, P. & Fauziah, S.H. 2011 "Challenges and issues in moving towards sustainable landfilling in a transitory country." *Waste Management and Research*, 29, 1, 13–19.
16 Weber, R., Watson, A., Forter, M. & Oliaei, F. 2011. "Persistent organic pollutants and landfills—A review of past experiences and future challenges." *Waste Management & Research*, 29, 1, 107–121.
17 Warder, A. 2009. "Delivering the Delta from the spills of Shell." *Women in Action*, 2, 33–35.
18 World Business Council for Sustainable Development. 2009. "Water: Facts and trends." www.wbcsd.org.
19 Environmental Performance Index. 2018. http://epi.yale.edu
20 Spencer, J. 2007. "Ravaged rivers. China pays steep price as textile booms." *Wall Street Journal*, August 22, A1.
21 World Business Council for Sustainable Development. "Water: Facts and trends."
22 World Business Council for Sustainable Development. "Water: Facts and trends"; United Nations Global Compact. 2010. www.unglobalcompact.org; Environmental Performance Index. 2018. http://epi.yale.edu.
23 United Nations Global Compact. www.unglobalcompact.org.
24 Epstein, *Making sustainability work*, p. 20.
25 Ahern, G. 2009. "Improving environmental sustainability in ten multinationals." *Corporate Finance Review*, 13, 6, 27–31.
26 Ahern, "Improving environmental sustainability."
27 Etzion, D. 2009. "Creating a better environment for finance." *MIT Sloan Management Review*, Summer, 50, 4, 21–22.
28 *MIT Sloan Management Review*. 2011. "Sustainability: The 'embracers' seize advantage: The survey." Winter, 23–27
29 *MIT Sloan Management Review*. "Sustainability."
30 Gamble, J.E. & Thompson, Jr. 2011. *Essentials of strategic management*. New York: McGraw-Hill.
31 Thomason & Marquis, "Leadership."
32 Mata-Lima et al., "Measuring an organization's performance."
33 Shaw, S., Grant, D.B. & Mangan, J. 2010. "Developing environmental supply chain performance measures." *Benchmarking: An International Journal*, 17, 3, 320–339.
34 Mata-Lima et al. "Measuring an organization's performance."
35 Thomason & Marquis, "Leadership."
36 https://ec.europa.eu/info/business-economy-euro/company-reporting-and-auditing/company-reporting/non-financial-reporting_en
37 Voyles, B. 2015. "EU firms face CSR reporting mandate in 2016." *Compliance Week*, June, 52–53.
38 Luo, R.X, Wang, D. & Zhang, J. 2017. "Whose call to answer: Institutional complexity and firms' CSR reporting." *Academy of Management Journal*, 60, 1, 321–344.
39 Sethi, S.P., Martell, T.F. & Demir, M. 2017. "An evaluation of the quality of corporate social responsibility reports by some of the world's largest financial institutions." *Journal of Business Ethics*, 140, 787–805.
40 Malik, M. 2015. "Value-enhancing capabilities of CSR: A brief review of contemporary literature." *Journal of Business Ethics*, 127, 419–438.
41 Ali, W., Frynas, J.G. & Mahmood, Z. 2017. "Determinants of corporate social responsibility (CSR) disclosure in developed and developing countries: A literature review." *Corporate Social Responsibility and Environmental Management*, 24, 273–294.
42 Metz, P., Burek, S., Hultgren, T.R., Kogan, S. & Schwartz, L. 2016. "The path to sustainability-driven innovation." *Research-Technology Management*, May–June, 50–60; *MIT Sloan Management Review*. "Sustainability"; Thomason & Marquis, "Leadership"; Sroufe, R., Liebowitz, J. & Sivasubramaniam, N. 2010. "HR's role in creating a sustainability culture: What are we waiting for?" *People and Strategy*, 33, 1, 34–42.
43 Hopkins, M.S. 2009. "8 reasons sustainability will change management." *MIT Sloan Management Review*, 51, 1, 27–29.

44 Manget, J., Roche, C. & Munnich, F. 2009. "Capturing the green advantage." *MIT Sloan Management Review*, online edition, http://sloanreview.mit.edu/special-report/for-real-not-just-for-show/.
45 Metz et al., "The path to sustainability-driven innovation."
46 Wexler, E. 2010. "Talking 'bout my (green) reputation." *Strategy*, May 1, 13.
47 Thomason & Marquis, "Leadership."

KEY TERMS

Acid rain: occurs when both sulfur dioxide and nitrogen oxide combine with air vapor in the atmosphere and return to earth in the form of acid rain.

Air pollutants: The six materials (particulate matter, nitrogen oxide, ozone, lead, carbon monoxide, sulfur dioxide) that contribute to air pollution.

Air pollution: when the release of materials into the atmosphere cannot be safely disposed of by natural processes.

Cautious adopters: sustainability is limited to those activities that are linked to short-term efficiency.

Corporate conventionality: mindset places strong emphasis on profit making.

Embracer types: where such companies fully embrace sustainability efforts.

Greenhouse gases: gases in the atmosphere that trap heat.

Land pollution: contamination that occurs when toxic waste and other waste material that do not belong on land are disposed of on land.

Measurable sustainability goals: provides a company with the needed benchmarks to determine whether it is successful in its sustainability efforts.

New sustainability paradigm: executives with this view see the need for a new way of measuring the success of sustainability efforts.

Pragmatism: mindset suggests that these executives take a more pragmatic view of sustainability.

Primary activities: those activities that are directly linked to creating the product.

Reconciliation: executives with this view believe that it is possible to reconcile sustainability with profitability.

Strategic vision: describes a company's aspirations about "where it is going," thus helping steer the company in that direction.

Support activities: activities that are provided to support the primary activities.

Sustainability: capacity of healthy ecosystems to continue functioning indefinitely.

Sustainability benefits: the many advantages companies enjoy as a result of their sustainability efforts.

Sustainability feedback: feedback regarding sustainability provided to all concerned parties regarding the company's progress toward achieving sustainability goals.

Sustainability goals: sustainability targets that companies set to achieve.

Sustainability reporting: efforts by the company to report its sustainability efforts and the progress made on such efforts.

Sustainable or environmentally responsible organizations: those companies that are gradually modifying their operations in order to have less impact on the environment while also making better use of resources.

Top management support: support for sustainability from top management.
Value chain: the various activities that a company performs internally to create value for consumers.
Water pollution: contamination of water sources such as lakes, streams, wells, and oceans by substances that are harmful to living organisms.

DISCUSSION QUESTIONS

1. What is sustainability? Do companies have any special obligations to the environment? Why or why not?
2. Defend the argument that companies have no special obligations to the environment.
3. What is air pollution? What are the six forms of pollutants? What types of dangers do these pollutants cause?
4. What is land pollution? What are the factors contributing to land pollution?
5. Why is it critical to address water pollution issues? How does the United Nations Global Compact help address such challenges?
6. What are some of the critical factors in building the environmentally sustainable organization? Which factor is most important? Why?
7. What is the value chain? What are the key components of the value chain? How can the value chain help companies assess their sustainability efforts?
8. What are the four top management mindsets regarding sustainability? What are the implications of such mindsets for the company?
9. What are sustainability goals? Why are measuring and setting sustainability goals critical in building the sustainable company?
10. Discuss five important benefits of sustainability.

INTERNET ACTIVITY

1. Go to the International Standards Organization website: www.iso.org.
2. Review ISO 14000: the environmental management aspect of ISO.
3. Describe the ISO 14000 standards. What are some of the major features of the ISO 14000?
4. What are some of the major areas that the ISO 14000 covers?
5. How can a company get the ISO 14000 certification? What steps are needed to get such certification?
6. Discuss some of the advantages of companies receiving the ISO 14000 certification.

For more Internet Activities and resources, visit the Companion Website at www.routledge.com/cw/parboteeah.

WHAT WOULD YOU DO?

Environmental Management

You are hired by a multinational as an environmental manager. Your task is to review the company's efforts toward sustainability and to provide suggestions on improvement. You conduct a sustainability analysis and quickly come up with many "low hanging fruit" suggestions. For example, you suggest that water taps in the company's stores be replaced with more efficient taps that can reduce water consumption for the company. You also embark on an energy-saving campaign whereby employees are encouraged to turn off lights and laptops when not in use. You also suggest a bike incentive program to encourage workers to use their bikes to come to work. Furthermore, you implement a new software program that facilitates car pooling among workers.

As you start considering more involved and drastic measures, you learn about a new packaging material that could result in significant carbon emission reduction for the company. The new material is lighter and is also better for the environment. However, you also learn that this new material could be more costly than the one you currently use. Furthermore, you recall reading about the fast-food company McDonald's efforts to change from polystyrene (foam) packaging to paper packaging and the resulting challenges, as it turned out that paper takes more energy to produce and is much harder to recycle than foam. Despite these misgivings, you believe that the new material will also endear the multinational to environmental groups.

What do you do? Do you recommend the new packaging? How do you take into account the costs of the new material and unanticipated challenges associated with the use of the new material?

BRIEF CASE: BUSINESS ETHICS INSIGHT

Unilever and Sustainability

Unilever is a successful global Anglo-Dutch multinational selling products in over 180 countries. Famous brands of the company include Dove, Lux, Pond's, and Lipton. Unilever has also been a strong supporter of sustainability. In fact, the CEO recently announced that Unilever has ambitious growth plans. However, the company has set numerous goals to ensure that such growth does not come at the expense of the world's scarce resources. The company recently released its "Sustainable Living Plan" whereby it has set goals of halving its environmental footprint by 2020. To achieve this goal, Unilever has conducted a value chain of its activities. It has also analyzed 1,651 products and their use in

14 countries to determine the environmental impact of these products. Based on these analyses, it has developed key areas and has set goals based on these areas.

The first area that Unilever has set goals for is to halve greenhouse gases by 2020. Through a comprehensive analysis, Unilever developed a carbon dioxide emission per consumer use based on its products. It also discovered that most of its carbon emissions came from consumers' use of hot water when using their products. To achieve its goals, Unilever is working to reduce the carbon emissions of its factories that produce the products. However, it is also working to produce products that need less energy to be used. Furthermore, it is encouraging consumers to do their part for the environment. For instance, it is now encouraging consumers to do their laundry using colder water.

Another key area for Unilever is halving the waste with the disposal of its products. It measures waste based on the waste per consumer use in terms of packaging and product leftovers. To address this goal, it has implemented a number of steps aiming at reducing packaging, reusing, and recycling, while also reducing waste from its manufacturing process. To give you further insights on Unilever's overall sustainability goals, and the consequent metrics and sub-goals, Exhibit 10.10 illustrates Unilever's goals and how they connect across the organization.

BRIEF CASE QUESTIONS

1. What are some of the main components of Unilever's sustainability goals? How will the company achieve its main sustainability goals?
2. Discuss how the various goals are related.
3. Why do you think Unilever places so much emphasis on consumer education? Do you think they will be successful in these efforts?
4. Draw a tentative value chain for Unilever. Are there other areas they could address to achieve their sustainability goals?
5. What are some benefits Unilever is achieving through its sustainability efforts?

Unilever Overall Goal: Halve the Environmental Footprint of Making and Using Unilever Products by the Year 2020

Greenhouse Gas Sub-goals: Aim to halve the gas impact of products across the lifecycle by 2020	**Water Use Sub-goals:** Halve the water associated with consumer use of products by 2020	**Waste Sub-goals:** Halve waste associated with disposal of products by 2020
How will Unilever achieve sub-goals?		
Develop products that will use less water and energy	Focus on countries where water scarcity is a problem	Reduce size of packaging
Convince 20 million consumers to cut their shower time by 1 minute	Work with farmers to ensure water is being used sustainably	Use lightweight materials for packaging
Develop laundry products that use minimal energy	Use drip irrigation and low-pressure irrigation whenever appropriate	Eliminate unnecessary packaging
Move to concentrated products to minimize packaging, etc.	Harvest water during rainy season for use later	Reuse as much of packaging coming into factories
Double use of sustainable energy in manufacturing facilities	Reformulate all products so that they require less water	Encourage reuse of primary products packaging
Newly built factories will aim at half the emissions of old ones	Inform consumers of most efficient way to use products	Educate consumers about the benefits of packaging reuse
Use lower-emission vehicles for transportation	Educate consumers of the benefits of reduced water footprint	Increase use of recycled material to the maximum extent possible
Use rail or ship as more efficient transportation	Persuade consumers to take shorter and less intense showers	Use materials that best fit end-of-life material treatment facilities
Use freezer cabinets that use climate-friendly refrigerants	Continue identifying ways to reduce water consumption during manufacturing process	Encourage consumers to get recyclable material to recycling centers

EXHIBIT 10.10—Sustainability Goals at Unilever

Based on www.sustainable-living.unilever.com.

BP'S DEEPWATER HORIZON OIL SPILL CRISIS AND ITS RECOVERY THROUGH TEAM USA OLYMPIC SPONSORSHIP

An Analysis of Reputation Management and Corporate Sponsorships

Arthur W. Page Society 2015 Case Study Competition
January 16, 2015

Situational Overview

On April 20, 2010, the Deepwater Horizon oil rig exploded, triggering what is considered the biggest marine oil spill in the petroleum industry.[1] The oil spill would claim eleven lives. BP's brand perception immediately plummeted, and there was an outcry from a wide range of people—everyone from environmentalists to grassroots activists to students and their consumers took issue with BP.

"We've never had a spill of this magnitude in the deep ocean," said Ian R. MacDonald, a professor of oceanography at Florida State University. "These things reverberate through the ecosystem."[2]

Zygmunt Plater, an attorney who headed the legal team for the state-appointed Alaska Oil Spill Commission that investigated the 1989 spill, said he felt a "horrible, sickening feeling" upon learning about the 2010 Gulf disaster.[3]

In an interview with TODAY's Matt Lauer, President Obama said, "[Tony Hayward, BP's CEO] wouldn't be working for me after any of those statements," referring to controversial comments that appeared to be downplaying the Gulf oil spill.[4]

By June 2010, 81% of American consumers viewed BP in a negative light.[5]

BP's share price dropped down by 55%—from $59.48 a share in April 2010 to $27 a share in June 2010.[6]

At this juncture, BP could have easily collapsed as a company, especially considering its previous controversial oil spills. Qualitative market evaluations have stated that in an industry with high public mistrust overall—due to factors ranging from resentment towards wealthy oil families, boom-and-bust cycles, significant performance problems such as oil spills, perception as non environment-friendly, and lack of public understanding of gas price fluctuations[7]—a performance issue of this magnitude could tip public opinion to the point of being boycotted, causing significant loss of revenue and business sustainability.

In the face of these odds, BP managed to not only recover, but also boost its public perception through efforts to clean up the oil spill, public relations campaigns that showcased its Gulf recovery efforts, and an Olympics sponsorship and associated campaign. During the 2012 London Olympics, BP had the second largest increase of brand perception among all Olympic sponsors, going from –5.9 (prior to the Olympics) to +2.6 (after the Olympics).[8]

BP's sponsorship selection and its strategic campaign highlighting Team USA during the Olympics produced tangible results for the brand, which demonstrates the value of thoughtful corporate sponsorship for the market as a whole. Though it also brings up ethical questions about brand affiliation—for BP, the Olympics organization, and the sponsored athletes—on the whole, it showcases the value of thoughtful brand reputation management and crisis communications.

BP Company Background

In order to better understand why the Deepwater Horizon oil spill impacted BP significantly, BP's history must first be examined. BP has a history of being environmentally friendly and among its peers in the petroleum industry, it was the only one to speak out against global warming. Its core values and mission were strong. So, where did it go wrong?

BP plc—former name, British Petroleum—started in 1908 when William Knox D'Arcy and his surveyors struck oil in Persia. The British government became the company's major stakeholder on the eve of World War I, seeing a necessity for mobilizing Britain's fleet. The company saw continued profits through the 1920s and 30s as Western society increasingly moved towards automobiles and petroleum-powered power plants. During World War II, the refinery worked with the Allied troops. Post 1975, BP began expanding further, building up holdings in the North Sea, near the UK, and Papua, eastern Indonesia.

BP started creating a presence in the United States in the 1980s and 90s.[9]

BP and Initial Move Towards Focus on Safety and Environmental Awareness via CEO John Browne

"BP is committed to . . . a balance between the needs of development and environmental protection . . . we believe we can contribute to achievement of the right balance."[10]
—John Browne
Former CEO of BP, in a speech at Stanford University

John Browne, BP's controversial CEO, set the stage for BP to develop as an environmentally responsible "green" company. His focus on corporate social responsibility sought to establish BP as a "green" petroleum company, and that set him—and BP—apart among industry peers. He instituted several changes for BP over the years, which won him a great deal of both applause and criticism.

After taking over in 1995, he began focusing on cutting costs, one of the areas which would be blamed in the future for BP's negative incidents (e.g., explosion in Texas refinery).[11] He wanted BP to grow in size and brokered several important deals such as the BP-Amoco merger, and buying ARCO, Vastar, Burmah Castrol, and Veba.[12] He further negotiated and created a presence within China, Azerbaijan, and Russia. All these efforts paid off—BP more than doubled its annual revenues and became the largest oil producer in the U.S.[13]

Early on, Browne made an effort to align BP with environmental sustainability. He branded it as the first "green" oil company and in 1997, he did something most other oil companies at the time were not doing: he acknowledged evidence of global warming. He invested billions in alternative fuels and launched a $200 million rebranding campaign. At this point, British Petroleum also legally renamed itself and adopted the slogan, "Beyond Petroleum."[14] Browne was honored with an Earth Day award from the United Nations, 18 honorary degrees, and was named Britain's "most admired" CEO. He was even knighted by Queen Elizabeth.

During years when BP saw disastrous incidents and had to rethink their safety strategy, Browne continued to work towards implementing safety regulations and ensuring that BP would not undergo future disasters. In 2007, he was forced to resign when a small lie during a court battle with regards to his personal life was revealed.[15] Browne's protégé, Tony Hayward, took over as CEO.

Current Corporate Philosophy

Among others, one of BP's core values is safety. Since BP highlights this as a core value, it becomes more problematic that BP has encountered numerous safety issues.

What we stand for

We care deeply about how we deliver energy to the world.

Above everything, that starts with safety and excellence in our operations. This is fundamental to our success. Our approach is built on respect, being consistent and having the courage to do the right thing. We believe success comes from the energy of our people. We have a determination to learn and to do things better. We depend upon developing and deploying the best technology, and building long-lasting relationships. We are committed to making a real difference in providing the energy the world needs today, and in the changing world of tomorrow. We work as one team. We are BP.

BP states that it provides essential sources of energy to people. The company strives to be a safety leader, a good corporate citizen, and a great employer. The company has five core values that it expresses as what it stands for: Safety, Respect, Excellence, Courage, and One Team.[16] BP also internally recognizes team members through The Helios Awards—a platform whereby teams around the world can share their challenges and achievements.[17]

Notable Controversies

"It was a big blast then, a big spill now, and either way nobody at BP's being held accountable. This is business as usual for BP."[18]
—David Senko
Manager of construction at the Texas site during the BP explosion, speaking about similarities between the 2005 explosion and the 2010 Deepwater Horizon oil spill

BP's Deepwater Horizon oil spill is the most notable crisis it has had, but there are previous problems as well that could be called harbingers for what was to come. Many reports and communications, such as those obtained by the House Energy and Commerce Committee, make it appear that BP's culture involves cutting costs to maximize profits, compromising safety in the process—and that this has not changed over the years.[19] Regardless of whether or not this surmise is true, it is important to understand how BP's prior incidents and the negative backlash surrounding them informed public perception during the Deepwater Horizon crisis.

Explosion in BP Refinery in Texas (2005)

An explosion in a BP refinery in Texas killed 15 workers.[20] Another 180 people were injured in the blast.[21] The official report from the U.S. Chemical Safety and Hazard Investigation Board claimed that BP used inadequate methods to measure safety conditions. It also stated that despite previous fatalities at the Texas City refinery (23 deaths in the 30 years prior to the 2005 incident), BP did not take effective steps.[22] A three-month investigation by *60 Minutes* also corroborated with this assessment—investigators stated that in their opinion, the incident was a failure on BP's part to protect the health and safety of its workers. The investigation also stated that it found evidence that BP ignored warnings about issues with its Texas City refinery. Post the incident, BP CEO John Browne stated there would be "no stone left unturned" to investigate what happened and correct any safety issues.[23]

Oil Spill in Alaska (2006)

In 2006, over 250,000 gallons of oil spilled through corroded sections of the BP pipeline in Alaska across the North Slope. This led to a partial shutdown of the company's Prudhoe Bay field. It also created a costly cleanup. It was alleged that cost-cutting measures instituted by BP executives had led to poor maintenance, which resulted in the incident.[24]

Deepwater Horizon Oil Spill (2010)

On April 20, 2010, the BP-leased Deepwater Horizon drilling rig exploded off the coast of Louisiana, killing 11 workers and releasing more than 200 million gallons of oil.[25] This oil spill has been called by some the "worst in history."[26]

There was a high cost to this oil spill, both in terms of revenue loss and public perception. The loss of stock value was estimated at $70 billion by June 2010. BP lost its position from Interbrand's Top 100 brands. The company's dividend was estimated to be 65% lower in 2011. Add on legal fees, reparation costs, approximately $25–30 million for each state tourism board affected, a 10% rise in upstream production costs, and the $20 billion claims fund, and we see that BP suffered significant monetary losses due to the incident.[27]

BP also immediately became the target of public outcry and social media backlash, ranging from negative public opinion on social media sites, anti-BP groups being created on social media channels (e.g., the Boycott BP Facebook group, which gained approximately 100,000 fans in about a month after the oil spill),[28] activists and environmentalists calling out for action against BP, and former BP employees publicly issuing statements that they had seen this coming.

By June 2010, BP was encountering an onslaught of attacks in the digital world. Over 350 Facebook groups had been created to protest BP. The WaveMetrix social media tracker showed that BP had been criticized for their initial response to the crisis. Within the blog universe, negative sentiment about BP went from 24% in March to 51% in May. Tweets increased from approximately 2,200 to 19,900 per day, which highlights the leap in what people felt they had to say to BP.[29]

At this juncture, if BP had not mobilized a social media strategy in a timely and effective fashion, the avalanche of negative sentiment could easily have overpowered the brand irreparably.

Among efforts to clean up the Gulf, BP began to use social media effectively in order to keep the public updated on what they were doing and create a two-way conversation with consumers.

Some key elements of their social media strategy included:

- Creating a section on their corporate site which discusses the oil spill and BP's efforts to manage it and restore the Gulf
- Creating relationships with local bloggers who could report how the spill was affecting the area
- Using their Facebook page to keep the public updated every day on what was happening within the Gulf, and also giving people the ability to comment and give their opinions on BP's efforts. They also regularly posted videos and photos, attempting to show people the reality of what was happening in the Gulf.
- Ramping up updates on BP_America Twitter handle (before the oil crisis, only 12 tweets had been posted with that handle).[30] Following the crisis, BP included important contact information, tweeted daily on their progress within the Gulf, and answered people's questions. They also began to more regularly use the Twitter handle, @Oil_Spill_2010 (later renamed @Restore_TheGulf), to provide timely updates and add links to non BP-controlled materials.[31]

- Creating a channel on YouTube to share videos about different areas that had been affected by the spill and BP's efforts to restore the Gulf
- Using their Flickr page to show images of the Gulf
- Running a live stream[32]

(See Appendix A for samples of BP's media outreach)

BP's social media work got traction; however, several public-relations gaffes caught up to BP's CEO, Tony Hayward, and he resigned in July 2010. He was succeeded by Bob Dudley, who was the managing director at the time.[33]

Public Reaction—Two Sides to Every Coin

BP Gulf Recovery Campaign and Environmentalists'/Scientists' Statements

> "I think the environmental impact of this disaster is likely to be very, very modest. It is impossible to say and we will mount, as part of the aftermath, a very detailed environmental assessment as we go forward. We're going to do that with some of the science institutions in the US."[34]
> —Tony Hayward
> *Former CEO of BP, May 18, 2010*

> "The oil spill is to the Gulf what smoking is to a human," he said. "You're still able to function overall, but not nearly as well."[35]
> —Doug Inkley
> *Senior scientist with the National Wildlife Federation*

After the Gulf Coast oil spill, BP set aside $500 million for independent scientific research into the spill.[36] About 20 months after the spill, they also created a public relations campaign highlighting the ways in which the Gulf region had recovered. "I'm glad to report that all beaches and waters are open for everyone to enjoy," BP representative, Iris Cross, said in one TV spot. "And the economy is showing progress, with many areas on the Gulf Coast having their best tourism season in years."[37]

Ogilvy, the agency that helped support BP's crisis communications during the Gulf of Mexico oil spill, worked on ensuring that its social media presence ran effectively, managing user comments and publishing third-party content to provide insight into the situation. Ogilvy stated that the campaign's achievements ranged from ensuring transparency by creating a pie chart showcasing the percentage of comments deleted and why they were deleted, to using content metrics and community insights to "co-narrate—giving [BP's] fans control over the types of stories they hear, facts they discover, and employees they meet."[38]

Aside from their Facebook focus, the team also used Twitter and YouTube to create a narrative of BP's support of the U.S. and the energy industry. Especially noteworthy is that the personalized responses to fans created a shift in positive sentiment, with an increase of over 3% from September to November 2012.[39]

While some have called BP's ad campaign "propaganda," others have more forgivingly stated that the campaign is overly optimistic. Some examples of the counter-movement that occurred in response to the Gulf oil spill are Greenpeace's "new logo for BP" contest, where Greenpeace invited people to redesign BP's logo in order to make a statement about the environmental implications, and a website that allows people to visualize the oil spill by placing the oil field over their home on a map.

(See Appendix B for examples of the counter-BP graphics and website)

Many have noted that scientists and environmentalists are also guilty of "spinning" the incident, and that their claims that the oil spill had completely devastated the Gulf were also—in many ways—equally untrue. Oceanographer and former director of the Dauphin Island Sea Lab in Alabama stated, "The beaches are people-safe, there's no doubt about that."[40]

On the whole, while BP's efforts to restore the Gulf and showcase its work were positive steps forward in restoring its brand, its overall reputation and public perception was still significantly low. Additional efforts to repair the damage done to its brand were needed.

Overview—The Importance of Corporate Sponsorship

> "Sponsorship is an important tool of marketing communication that seeks to achieve favourable publicity for a company and/or its brands . . . via the support of an activity not directly linked to the company's normal business. It is an indirect form of promotion . . . a large amount of sponsorship aims to project a sponsor's corporate image to an audience."[41]
>
> —Roger Bennett
>
> *British-American journalist, author, radio presenter and filmmaker – he has written about sports, music, and culture for the* New York Times, ESPN: The Magazine, *and* Time, *among others*

Corporate sponsorships can potentially augment brand reputation and create positive publicity—but how much must the sponsorship align with the brand's image and values? How does the sponsorship impact the brand being sponsored? Historically, we have seen many instances of sponsorships that have hit the mark and also many that have caused significant problems for the brand and the associated sponsored organization.

Sponsorship has traditionally been a fast growing form of marketing.[42] Sponsorship was still seeing steady growth in the market during 2014, but corporate interest in other marketing alternatives such as digital media has trimmed sponsorship spending somewhat. Forecasts are advising sponsors to consider their role in driving digital, social, and mobile interest for their partners.[43] In light of this, it is more important than ever to consider how to best delegate sponsorship budgets and ensure that the sponsorship has the desired impact for brand reputation management and public brand perception—both of which not only drive revenue, but also become critical elements when a company is dealing with a crisis situation.

BP, Corporate Social Responsibility, and Sponsorship Initiatives

"To BP, working responsibly means seeking to have positive impacts on the communities in which we operate."
—BP Sustainability Review Report, 2013

Corporate social responsibility (CSR) affects brand perception and consumer behavior in a significant way—people want to increasingly put their money towards causes they care about, and they notice when a company stands out. In a survey conducted by Do Well Do Good LLC at the end of 2011, it was found that 71% of Americans would pay an extra $2.28 for a $10 product if the product supported a cause. 56% of Americans would travel an extra 1–10 minutes to buy a cause-supporting product. 60% of consumers would switch to a competitor if they thought a brand was harming the environment.[44]

It is also important to understand that the top three ways through which people form perceptions about whether or not a company is environmentally responsible are: news and media reports, personal experiences with the brand, and advertisements/branding campaigns. People judge whether a company is socially responsible through the same three areas, albeit in a different rank order. A recent 2014 survey spanning 23 countries confirmed this information, and further demonstrated that 45% of consumers were unable or unwilling to name a socially responsible company.[45]

In the light of these facts, it's more important than ever for a company to define what its corporate social responsibility is, how CSR fits into the company's overall business goals, and how it aligns with the company's core values.

Despite significant incidents in BP's history that have raised questions about BP's corporate social responsibility, BP has also been the recipient of several CSR awards. In a 2006 survey of 510 American adults, BP was voted the most "green" in the petroleum-and-energy category, outranking competitors such as Exxon Mobil, Chevron, Royal Dutch Shell, and Chevron Texaco.[46] In 2007, BP was given the #1 ranking on lists of the world's most responsible companies by both *Fortune* and AccountAbility. In 2008, BP still ranked #9. Even after the Deepwater Horizon oil spill, in May 2010, BP was named a runner-up for the "Openness and Honesty" category at the Corporate Register's 2010 CR Reporting Awards.[47]

BP has also maintained a strong presence within the sponsorship arena, keeping to its focus on community. In its 2013 Sustainability Review, BP reported that it had spent $78.8m on community investment, and planned to continue to support community development programs and update its framework for managing social investment.[48] BP has sponsored Warrior Games, its sponsorship in 2014 making it the fourth consecutive event. The Warrior Games is a sporting event for wounded, ill, or injured U.S. military veterans and active-duty service members, and BP has stated that its Games sponsorship showcases the company's commitment to America and highlights its core values. "We look forward to cheering on these passionate and remarkable athletes," said John Mingé, chairman and president of BP America. "[They] are the embodiment of BP's values of excellence, courage, and teamwork."[49] In conjunction with this sponsorship, BP also has a Wellness Warrior Challenge program, which is a wellness initiative set up for BP employees who are aligned with the Warrior Games.

BP has also been committed to U.S. Paralympics, earning a Paralympic Amazing Impact Award in 2013 from the United States Olympic Committee. Since 2011, BP-branded retailers in 13 states donated more than $700,000 to their local Paralympic Sport Clubs.[50]

BP is also involved with arts sponsorships, supporting institutions such as the British Museum, the National Portrait Gallery, the Royal Opera House, and Tate Britain. In 2011, BP pledged £10m for these sponsorships for the next five years.[51]

BP's sponsorship initiatives have been met with a degree of opposition from those who feel that the partnerships are not ethically sound or problematic in other ways (e.g., artists who dislike BP's inroads into the artistic community, activists who oppose BP's involvement in athletic events, etc.). However, BP's partners have retained the partnerships and have publicly spoken out with support for BP's work and continued alliance.

BP and Team USA Olympics Sponsorship

> "We're grateful for BP's commitment to America's elite athletes and to honoring Ted Stevens, a champion of Olympic and Paralympic sport in the U.S."[52]
> —Scott Blackmun
> *United States Olympics Committee, speaking about their continued BP partnership and BP's contribution of $1m to a new Ted Stevens Sports Services Center at the U.S. Olympics Training Center, Nov 2013*

At the Vancouver 2010 Winter Olympics, BP announced its long-term sponsorship with the United States Olympic Committee (USOC) and Team USA, which would extend through the 2016 Summer Games. Sixty-four days later, BP's Gulf of Mexico oil spill occurred. By June 2010, BP had 81% of American consumers viewing it negatively.[53]

The timing of the two collided so closely that BP's Olympics sponsorship now brought about loaded questions: Is the focus on Team USA a deflection from the real issue? Is BP a sponsor that the Olympics should even have? How do the Olympics fit in with BP's mission, vision, and values? What does this sponsorship say about the big picture of the relationship between sponsors and athletics?

The Team USA page states: "For nearly 150 years, BP and its heritage companies have been committed to supporting the American people, economy and energy industry. In honor of BP's deep ties to the U.S., we proudly announced our sponsorship of the United States Olympic Committee (USOC) and Team USA during the Vancouver 2010 Olympic Winter Games. And we've since extended our sponsorship through the 2016 Games in Rio de Janeiro."[54]

Together with Ogilvy, BP created an integrated paid, owned, and earned program centered on Facebook, which provided fans with unprecedented access to each athlete's personal stories and inspirations. Fans were given a medium through which they could communicate and engage with both the athletes and other fans, which created a circle of community engagement.[55]

Facebook was used extensively to create a more personalized, emotional bond. BP featured content from various events (e.g., internal employee functions, U.S. Olympic Trials, live updates of race results, etc.). Relationships with popular magazines further added to both campaign buzz and community engagement. For instance, collaboration with *Time* magazine yielded a *Time* app, which gave fans the opportunity to send athletes "good luck" messages before the Olympics. *Sports Illustrated* provided fans with the chance to put their own pictures on its cover.[56]

The campaign was a success. One of the primary goals of the campaign was to raise visibility of BP's relationship with the USOC. By the end of the Olympic Games, BP surpassed the initial goal of 15%, reaching 23% among the campaign's target audience. This surpassed other major USOC sponsors, including Citibank (14%), BMW (7%) and Dow Chemical (5%). Also, BP had the second largest increase of brand perception among all Olympic sponsors going from –5.9 to +2.6.[57]

On Facebook specifically, BP's following grew to over 300,000 fans. As of July 2012, during the Olympics, Facebook post comments were 74% positive in support of BP's commitment to U.S. athletes. BP also found itself receiving a high engagement rate overall during the Olympics. According to a third-party source (AlchemySocial), BP was one of the most popular brands engaging on Facebook during the Olympics, receiving the most "likes" and "comments" of any single Olympic-related Facebook post with 93,000+ likes, 2,000+ comments and 1,300+ shares.[58]

Timeline of BP Response to Gulf Oil Spill & Team USA Campaign

(Timeline created with data from various sources—sources are listed in endnotes)

Gulf Recovery Campaign[59]	Team USA Campaign
2010	
February	
	2.16.10 – BP Announces Partnership with USOC & Team USA[60]
4.20.10 – Deepwater Horizon Oil Spill	
April	
4.27.10 First Tweet from BP_America after oil spill[61]	
4.29.10 First Tweet from @Oil_Spill_2010[62]	BP remained committed to its Team USA sponsorship, post Deepwater Horizon[63]
May	
5.02.10 First post on Facebook about the oil spill[64]	
5.18.10 BP announces the launch of its new blog site	
5.20.10 Live feed put into place	
5.26.10 Link to anti-BP blog posted by accident	

June	
6.19.10 Special section for suggestions posted on website	
6.28.10 Deep Water Horizon Response widget becomes available	
July	
7.06.10 Administration launches new, streamlined oil spill response website & changes feed to @RestoretheGulf	
7.15.10 Update claiming no oil flowing into the Gulf	
August	
September	
9.19.10 BP seals the ruptured well. Well is declared "dead"	
2011	
	BP extends its partnership with the USOC as its official energy partner through 2016[65]
2012	
	BP and Ogilvy (PR Agency) create an integrated paid, owned, and earned program centered on Facebook[66]
	7.16.12–7.20.12 (1 week prior to Olympics) BP brand perception is -5.9, the lowest perception score of all major Olympic sponsors[67]
	8.3.12 After the Olympic period, 7/27–8/3, BP's brand perception score rises to 2.6. This is one of the biggest positive shifts in brand perception among the Olympic sponsors[68]

Public Response towards BP and the Olympics Committee

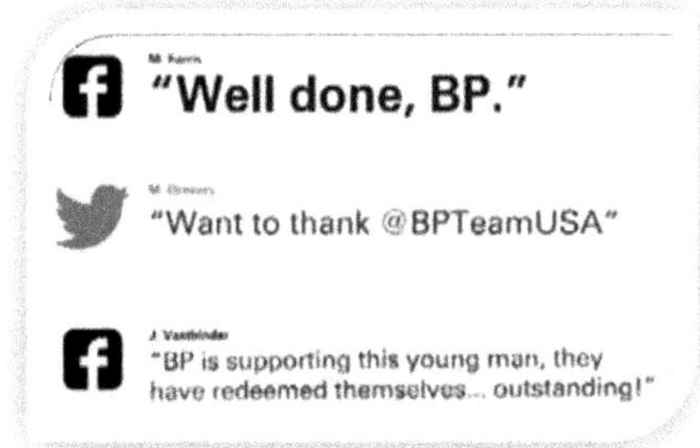

The results of the campaign showed an incredible raise in overall brand perception. However, there were still vocal detractors as well.

Some environmental groups, protesting against BP's involvement in the Olympics, encouraged "brand piracy." In order to show their resentment, they vandalized BP's billboards by splashing them with oil-black paint. One activist group splattered each panel on a massive, six-panel billboard on London's Cromwell Road, for instance, signing it with their website url—f-ingthefuture.org. The name is a play on the Olympics slogan, "Fueling the future."[69] **(See Appendix C for examples of vandalized billboards)**

Another activist group, Campaign for a Sustainable Olympics (Camsol), created a hoax London Olympics website and posted a story stating that BP had been removed as a partner.[70] Camsol even convinced a local London radio station, LBC, and *City AM*, a free morning newspaper, that their fake website was real. Other grassroots groups worked with the protest group Occupy London to arrange sit-ins that aimed to stop construction of key buildings. One example is that Occupy protestors and activists attempted to thwart the building of temporary basketball courts that were going to be used as training centers for Olympic teams—four activists were arrested at the site.[71] A "die-in" was also staged in front of the International Olympic Committee inspection, which gained significant attention.[72]

Meredith Alexander, formerly a member of the London Olympic Games' sustainability commission, spearheaded a campaign called Greenwash Gold 2012, which criticized BP along with other Olympic sponsors such as Dow and Rio Tinto.[73]

Communications: Strong Elements

Strong Across-the-Board Social Media Response –

> "I'd have to give it an A+"
> —Larry Smith
> *Institute for Crisis Management*

Post the oil spill debacle—and an initial 7-day silence in the digital world—BP dived headfirst into its social media strategy. Its cross-channel strategy, consistent updates, and efforts to include non-BP material in posts and tweets all speak to the strength of BP's social media response. Apart from usual staples like Facebook and Twitter, BP also engaged sites such as YouTube and Flickr to further demonstrate the state of the Gulf and how its recovery efforts were making a difference.[74]

Strong Sponsorship Alignment & Intelligent Campaign Surrounding It –
Even before the oil spill, BP had aligned itself with the Olympics and Team USA. This was an intelligent move on BP's part—and so was the campaign built around Team USA.

Communications: What Left More to be Desired

Delayed Initial Response –

> "People aren't waiting for Walter Cronkite to tell them what to think. They're talking with each other online. It's too late for companies if they don't use social media right away when a crisis strikes."[75]
> —Patrick Kerley
> *Senior digital strategist at Levick Strategic Communications, a PR and crisis communication firm*

Though BP's communications team was likely using that time to determine what their social media response would be, in crisis situations, each day can make a big difference. A gap of seven days—though miniscule under regular circumstances—can become a significant problem in the aftermath of a crisis. Also, it sets a negative first impression in the public's mind—they feel that the company is being unduly negligent about a situation, when that may not necessarily be the case.

Lack of Ownership of Situation –

> "It wasn't our accident, but we are absolutely responsible for the oil, for cleaning it up."[76]
> —Tony Hayward
> *Former BP CEO, on the* Today *show*

Though what BP said is not false—the oil rig did belong to the drilling contractor, Transocean Ltd.—taking this approach makes the public feel like the company is deflecting blame.

Lack of Proactive Social Media Engagement –

> "Companies have to realize that they need to be proactive and generate a social media audience in peace time . . . When crisis time comes around, then people would know where to go to get information. So now when people go to social media, they find joke sites and parody accounts. It's because BP was nowhere to be found [before]."[77]
> —Patrick Kerley
> *Senior digital strategist at Levick Strategic Communications, a PR and crisis communication firm*

Though BP did a good job creating a swift social media strategy and implementing it, BP could have done a better job of being consistent with social media before the oil spill crisis. Because BP had not been actively engaged with its consumers beforehand, spoof or fake Twitter handles and Facebook pages (e.g., #BPGlobalPR) confused more people than they would have otherwise.

Former CEO, Tony Hayward's PR Errors –

> "There's no one who wants this thing over more than I do. You know, I'd like my life back."[78]
> —Tony Hayward
> *Former BP CEO*

Much of the criticism about BP's PR efforts was directed at Tony Hayward, whose verbal gaffes were blasted in the media repeatedly. One theory that has been circulated about why he continued to make insensitive remarks is that because BP had cut the public-relations budget to save money, he was relegated to listening to outside consultants for the oil spill crisis. During a crisis of this magnitude, it would have benefitted him to be able to use a more solid in-house public relations team that had already been tried and tested.

Brand Implications—BP

On the whole, BP has successfully recovered from the oil spill crisis and has regained its position in the public eye. Through open communication, strategic social media efforts, and an extremely strong sponsorship choice, BP was able to reinstate its brand perception.

In the future, ideally, BP will learn from its mistakes and take precautions so that similar events do not happen. However, if BP does undergo another crisis, it can take best practices from the 2010 oil spill and the biggest mistakes made during this crisis in order to better inform future decisions.

Brand Implications—Olympics

The Olympics committee has stood behind its choice for BP as one of their sponsors, despite activist resentment and protests leading up to the Olympics. Jacques Rogge, the International Olympics Committee (IOC) president, defended the choice saying that all sponsors were subjected to an in-depth audit before acceptance. "Before accepting a new company, they are vetted in detail by independent advisers," Rogge said. "Look at BP. They had an oil spill. But they took corrective measures and did everything they had to do."[79]

Brand Implications—Athletes (Personal Brand)

> "Being affiliated with BP has given me greater national recognition and legitimacy in the US sports world, as well as a greater reach to inspire others."
> —Kikkan Randall
> *Four-times Olympian, member of BP's Team USA*
> Original interview conducted by author over e-mail on 12/29/14

BP's sponsorship has further implications for the athletes who received money from them. BP's sponsorship through the U.S. Olympic Committee is worth between $10 million and $15 million, which represents about 6–7 percent of the federation's sponsorship revenue. The London 2012 Olympic organization sponsorship was valued at around $58 million.[80] In today's world, athletes are increasingly judged on their actions and their partnerships. Agent Evan Morgenstein has stated that he received a number of calls from athletes he represents who were concerned about their connection to BP. Morgenstein did not reveal which clients specifically made those comments, but his clients include Olympic swimmers Dara Torres, Amanda Beard, Aaron Peirsol and Eric Shanteau. "In the end, it's not about the $15 million," Morgenstein said. "It's about the brand. They [in the Olympic movement] talk about branding all the time and the value of the rings."[81]

Despite fears, most public response for the athletes themselves has been positive. As stated before, the campaign on Facebook showed us that a high percentage (74%) of post comments were positive in support of BP's commitment to U.S. athletes. Many athletes are also very thankful for BP's support and sponsorship. "The BP Team USA sponsorship has been one of the most impressive and enjoyable sponsorship programs I have ever experienced in my career," stated four-time Olympian Kikkan Randall. "Not only has it been an opportunity for financial support, which is most common, the BP Team USA program has provided so many additional elements. Support for my family to be at the Olympics in Sochi with me, a donation to a charity of my choice and a fuel card have all been special perks. But most importantly, the very personable approach and caring support from the BP Team have been above and beyond most normal sponsorship programs." **(Full transcript of author's original interview with Kikkan Randall is included in Appendix D)**

Concluding Thoughts—With An Eye to the Future

> "I can't think of another company that has faced as big a crisis as BP recently, or at least since the advent of social media. This situation with BP could end up being very instructive for companies needing to handle problems like this in the future – either in a positive or negative way." [82]
>
> —Dan Olds
>
> *Analyst, The Gabriel Consulting Group*

BP's crisis and subsequent crisis management shines light on which elements helped the company survive a negative event of this magnitude, and also showcases what other companies should keep in mind with regards to their sponsorship choices and crisis strategies.

Whether or not BP is deserving of having been "forgiven" in the public eye, the shift in public opinion and perception is sharp enough that it presents an extremely valuable case study for other companies to learn by.

Appendix A—Samples of BP's Media Outreach

Sources: Facebook[83] (see endnote for full URL) and Slideshare[84] (see endnote for full URL)

facebook

2010

BP America
Dec 17, 2010 ·
Get on-the-ground updates from Mike Utsler, COO of BP's Gulf Coast Restoration Organization, as he oversees response operations along the Gulf. Visit http://twitter.com/BP_America to see his latest tweet.

28 · Share

BP America
Dec 16, 2010 via Hootsuite ·
(Calendar) Ring in the New Year on Alabama's Gulf Coast! Gulf Shores and Orange Beach are offering parties for every taste to help you start 2011 right.

Gulf Shores AL – Gulf Shores Calendar things to do – Gulf Shores events
Tired of lounging lazily on the beach in Gulf Shores, AL? Shake off the sand, throw on a pair of...

7 · Share

BP America
Dec 14, 2010 ·
Get on-the-ground updates from Mike Utsler, COO of BP's Gulf Coast Restoration Organization, as he oversees response operations along the Gulf. Visit http://twitter.com/BP_America to see his latest tweet.

twitter — Home Profile Find People Settings Help Sign out

(Video) "Most of [Gulf] Coast in great shape," says environmental prof. "We've got to show people": http://bit.ly/amqcDV

Reply Retweet

BP_America
Official BP

Appendix B—Examples of Counter-BP Graphics and Website

(Images taken from https://csrcsr.wordpress.com/category/bp-case-study/, tweet taken from a fake Twitter account created called "BPGlobalPR" via www.businessinsider.com/fake-bp-pr-tweets-2010-5#-3—and website image pulled from www.ifitweremyhome.com/disasters/bp)

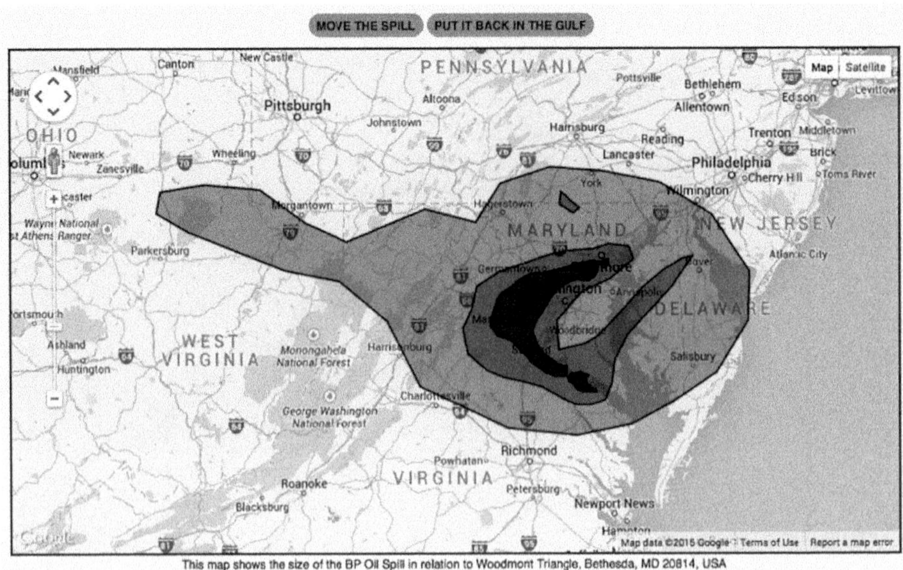

This map shows the size of the BP Oil Spill in relation to Woodmont Triangle, Bethesda, MD 20814, USA

Appendix C—Examples of Vandalized BP London Olympics Billboards

(Images taken from www.buzzfeed.com/copyranter/huge-bp-london-olympics-billboard-gets-vandalized)

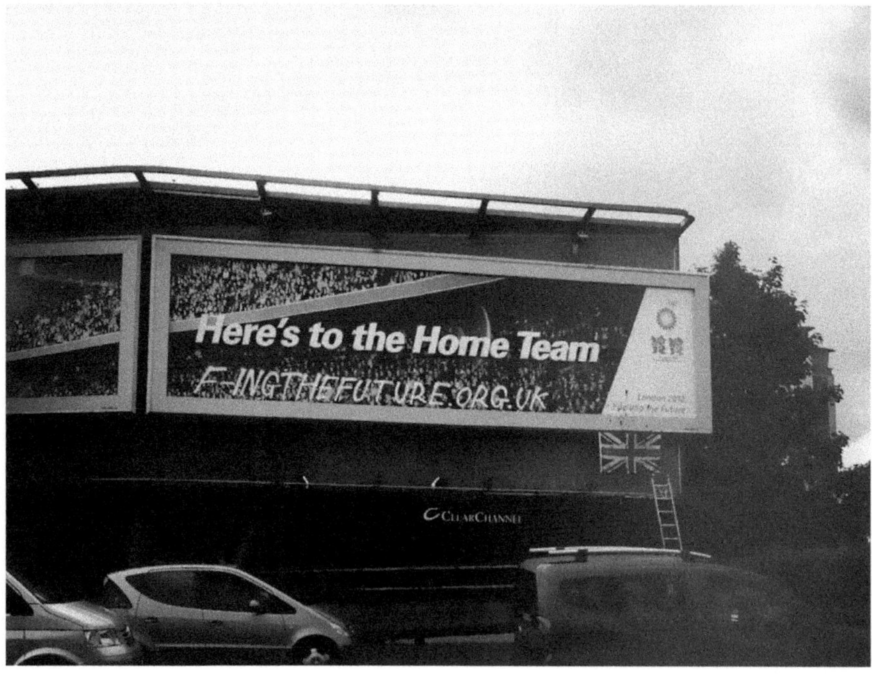

Appendix D: Transcript of Interview with Kikkan Randall, 4-time Olympian (member of BP's sponsored Team USA)

(Original interview, conducted by author over e-mail on 12/29/14)

Could you describe your athletic career briefly? (E.g., What inspires you, what you most value in your career, where you see yourself in the future) From the age of 5, I have aspired to be an Olympian and one of the best ski racers in the world. I have been a full-time cross country ski racer for the past 15 years, representing the United States at four Olympic Games and seven World Championships. I was the first U.S. woman to win a World Cup, a World Championship medal, a World Cup Overall Discipline Title and be top 10 in the Olympics in cross-country skiing. My most valued accomplishments are my World Championships gold medal we won in the team sprint in 2013 and my 3 overall World Cup sprint titles. I absolutely love the lifestyle of being a top international ski racer and I would love to continue competing through the 2018 Olympics where I will continue to chase a first Olympic medal for U.S. women's cross country.

What role do athletic sponsors play in your career? The support from my sponsors has been absolutely crucial for my career. Their support has allowed me to focus on training full-time and has helped me get access to the necessary training, competitions and resources I need to keep improving and be competitive at the highest international level.

How do you feel about the BP Team USA sponsorship? (E.g., How was the experience, how did it affect your career) The BP Team USA sponsorship has been one of the most impressive and enjoyable sponsorship programs I have ever experienced in my career. Not only has it been an opportunity for financial support, which is most common, the BP Team USA program has provided so many additional elements. Support for my family to be at the Olympics in Sochi with me, a donation to a charity of my choice and a fuel card have all been special perks. But most importantly, the very personable approach and caring support from the BP Team have been above and beyond most normal sponsorship programs.

Are there communications on BP's part that you were especially interested in? (E.g., Did you follow their Facebook page, Twitter, etc.) It has definitely been fun to learn more about BP as a company and what they're doing all over the world. I also really enjoyed getting to meet the other athletes in the BP TEAM USA program and have enjoyed following their careers as well. Social media has been an easy way to learn and follow along. Their activity on social media has also been very helpful for me to be able to share my story and be a role model to inspire others to chase dreams and live healthy.

Do you feel that being affiliated with BP adversely affects your career or future in any way? Do you feel that being affiliated with BP positively affects your career or future in any way? Of course there have been a few people that commented on my affiliation with BP in a negative way, tied mostly to the oil spill in the Gulf. But for every negative response received there have been many more positive comments and overall the affiliation with BP has been positive for my career. Being affiliated with BP has given me greater national recognition and legitimacy in the U.S. sports world, as well as a greater reach to inspire others.

What are some best practices or lessons learned that other companies could learn about sponsorship, based on your experience? One of the elements of the BP TEAM USA sponsorship program that has stood out to me the most is how personal the relationship has been and how much the BP team seems to genuinely care about me as an athlete and as a person. That BP took the time to get to know me and my family and made the relationship so personable, really made me excited about representing their company.

Are there any best practices or lessons learned that other athletes could learn about sponsorship, based on your experience? It's not enough to just be results on a page. As an athlete, you have to think of yourself as a business and really understand the "product" you are able to offer. The more dimensions you have to your character and the better you are able to interact with the community, the more value you will provide to a sponsor.

References

1 Robertson, C. & Krauss, C. (2010, August 2). Gulf Spill Is the Largest of Its Kind, Scientists Say. Retrieved December 5, 2014, from www.nytimes.com/2010/08/03/us/03spill.html?_r=2&fta=y&

2 Robertson, C. & Krauss, C. (2010, August 2). Gulf Spill Is the Largest of Its Kind, Scientists Say. Retrieved December 5, 2014, from www.nytimes.com/2010/08/03/us/03spill.html?_r=2&fta=y&

3 Schwartz, N. (2010, May 25). Exxon Valdez veterans see parallels in BP's spill. Retrieved December 7, 2014, from www.newsminer.com/news/alaska_news/exxon-valdez-veterans-see-parallels-in-bp-s-spill/article_4b8dfb9d-e74a-50b2-bb71-5df2def3f9d8.html

4 I would have fired BP chief by now, Obama says. (2010, June 9). Retrieved December 10, 2014, from www.nbcnews.com/id/37566848/ns/disaster_in_the_gulf/t/i-would-have-fired-bp-chief-now-obama-says/

5 Who's Hot on Facebook Studio. (2013, January 30). Retrieved December 10, 2014, from https://social.ogilvy.com/whos-hot-on-facebook-studio/

6 Chamberlin, A. (2014, September 10). BP lost 55% shareholder value after the Deepwater Horizon incident. Retrieved December 10, 2014, from http://finance.yahoo.com/news/bp-lost-55-shareholder-value-225105539.html

7 Edman, S. (2013). "Public Perception of the Oil and Gas Industry." *The Way Ahead*, 9(2), 15–17. Retrieved December 8, 2014, from www.spe.org/twa/print/archives/2013/2013v9n2/08_Pillars_FINAL.pdf

8 BP Team USA: Using Social to Win Gold—Shorty Awards for Brands, Agencies, and Organizations. (2012, January 1). Retrieved December 9, 2014, from http://industry.shortyawards.com/nominee/5th_annual/BR/bp-team-usa-using-social-to-win-gold

9 Tharoor, I. (2010, June 2). A Brief History of BP. Retrieved December 8, 2014, from http://content.time.com/time/magazine/article/0,9171,1993882,00.html

10 Browne, J. (n.d.). Climate Change Speech By John Browne, Group Chief Executive, British Petroleum (BP America), Stanford University, 19 May 1997. Retrieved December 11, 2014, from http://dieoff.com/page106.htm

11 Elkind, P., Whitford, D. & Burke, D. (2011, January 24). BP: "An accident waiting to happen". Retrieved December 11, 2014, from http://fortune.com/2011/01/24/bp-an-accident-waiting-to-happen/

12 Elkind, P., Whitford, D. & Burke, D. (2011, January 24). BP: "An accident waiting to happen". Retrieved December 11, 2014, from http://fortune.com/2011/01/24/bp-an-accident-waiting-to-happen/
13 Elkind, P., Whitford, D. & Burke, D. (2011, January 24). BP: "An accident waiting to happen". Retrieved December 11, 2014, from http://fortune.com/2011/01/24/bp-an-accident-waiting-to-happen/
14 Elkind, P., Whitford, D. & Burke, D. (2011, January 24). BP: "An accident waiting to happen". Retrieved December 11, 2014, from http://fortune.com/2011/01/24/bp-an-accident-waiting-to-happen/
15 Elkind, P., Whitford, D. & Burke, D. (2011, January 24). BP: "An accident waiting to happen". Retrieved December 11, 2014, from http://fortune.com/2011/01/24/bp-an-accident-waiting-to-happen/
16 Our Values. (n.d.). Retrieved December 9, 2014, from www.bp.com/en/global/corporate/about-bp/company-information/our-values.html
17 The Helios Awards. (n.d.). Retrieved December 9, 2014, from www.bp.com/en/global/corporate/about-bp/company-information/our-values/the-helios-awards.html
18 Carroll, J., Calkins, L. & Efstathiou Jr., J. (2010, November 8). BP May Pay Billions for "Missed Signals" That Led to Disaster. Retrieved December 13, 2014, from www.bloomberg.com/apps/news?pid=newsarchive&sid=a4T48F1NIIbY
19 Knutson, R. (2010, July 2). Blast at BP Texas Refinery in '05 Foreshadowed Gulf Disaster. Retrieved December 14, 2014, from www.propublica.org/article/blast-at-bp-texas-refinery-in-05-foreshadowed-gulf-disaster
20 Tharoor, I. (2010, June 2). A Brief History of BP. Retrieved December 8, 2014, from http://content.time.com/time/magazine/article/0,9171,1993882,00.html
21 Investigation Report—Refinery Explosion and Fire. (2007, March 20). Retrieved December 14, 2014, from www.csb.gov/assets/1/19/csbfinalreportbp.pdf
22 Investigation Report—Refinery Explosion and Fire. (2007, March 20). Retrieved December 14, 2014, from www.csb.gov/assets/1/19/csbfinalreportbp.pdf
23 Elkind, P., Whitford, D. & Burke, D. (2011, January 24). BP: "An accident waiting to happen". Retrieved December 11, 2014, from http://fortune.com/2011/01/24/bp-an-accident-waiting-to-happen/
24 Tharoor, I. (2010, June 2). A Brief History of BP. Retrieved December 8, 2014, from http://content.time.com/time/magazine/article/0,9171,1993882,00.html
25 Zelman, J. (2012, January 8). BP Ad Campaign Following Gulf Oil Spill Deemed "Propaganda" By Some. Retrieved December 11, 2014, from www.huffingtonpost.com/2012/01/08/bp-ad-campaign-gulf-oil-_n_1192600.html
26 Tharoor, I. (2010, June 2). A Brief History of BP. Retrieved December 8, 2014, from http://content.time.com/time/magazine/article/0,9171,1993882,00.html
27 Natividad, A. (2010, December 12). BP vs The Internet. Retrieved December 11, 2014, from www.slideshare.net/luckthelady/bp-vs-the-internet
28 BP Facing Social Media Backlash. (2010, May 25). Retrieved December 12, 2014, from http://digitalimpactblog.iirusa.com/2010/05/bp-facing-social-media-backlash.html
29 Bulman, L. (2010, June 9). BP Responds to Oil Spill Backlash. Retrieved December 11, 2014, from http://wave.wavemetrix.com/content/bp-responds-oil-spill-backlash-00098
30 Walton, L., Cooley, S. & Nicholson, J. (2012, March 8). "A Great Day for Oiled Pelicans:" BP, Twitter, and the Deep Water Horizon Crisis Response. Retrieved December 14, 2014, from www.instituteforpr.org/wp-content/uploads/BP-Twitter-The-Deep-Water-Horizon.pdf
31 Walton, L., Cooley, S. & Nicholson, J. (n.d.). "A Great Day for Oiled Pelicans:" BP, Twitter, and the Deep Water Horizon Crisis Response. Retrieved December 14, 2014, from www.prsa.org/intelligence/prjournal/documents/2012waltoncooleynicholson.pdf
32 Lee, J. (2010, July 1). BP, Crisis Communications and Social Media. Retrieved December 15, 2014, from www.bruceclay.com/blog/bp-crisis-communications-and-social-media/
33 "Timeline: BP's Deepwater Horizon Disaster and the Oil Spill in the Gulf of Mexico". (2010). *Engineering and Technology Magazine*, 5(8). Retrieved December 15, 2014, from http://eandt.theiet.org/magazine/2010/08/oil-spill-latest.cfm?origin=EtOtherStories

34 BP Boss Tony Hayward's Gaffes. (2010, June 20). Retrieved December 15, 2014, from www.bbc.com/news/10360084
35 Fowler, T. (2012, April 12). Experts Weigh Spill's Lasting Effects. Retrieved December 16, 2014, from www.wsj.com/articles/SB10001424052702303624004577339943866694420
36 Zelman, J. (2012, January 8). BP Ad Campaign Following Gulf Oil Spill Deemed 'Propaganda' By Some. Retrieved December 11, 2014, from www.huffingtonpost.com/2012/01/08/bp-ad-campaign-gulf-oil-_n_1192600.html
37 Zelman, J. (2012, January 8). BP Ad Campaign Following Gulf Oil Spill Deemed "Propaganda" By Some. Retrieved December 11, 2014, from www.huffingtonpost.com/2012/01/08/bp-ad-campaign-gulf-oil-_n_1192600.html
38 Who's Hot on Facebook Studio. (2013, January 30). Retrieved December 10, 2014, from https://social.ogilvy.com/whos-hot-on-facebook-studio/
39 Who's Hot on Facebook Studio. (2013, January 30). Retrieved December 10, 2014, from https://social.ogilvy.com/whos-hot-on-facebook-studio/
40 Zelman, J. (2012, January 8). BP Ad Campaign Following Gulf Oil Spill Deemed "Propaganda" By Some. Retrieved December 11, 2014, from www.huffingtonpost.com/2012/01/08/bp-ad-campaign-gulf-oil-_n_1192600.html
41 Bennett, R. (1999). "Sports Sponsorship, Spectator Recall And False Consensus". *European Journal of Marketing*, 33(3/4), 291–313. Retrieved December 16, 2014, from www.emeraldinsight.com/doi/abs/10.1108/03090569910253071
42 2013 Sponsorship Outlook: Spending Increase Is Double-edged Sword. (2013, January 7). Retrieved December 16, 2014, from www.sponsorship.com/iegsr/2013/01/07/2013-Sponsorship-Outlook—Spending-Increase-Is-Dou.aspx
43 2013 Sponsorship Outlook: Spending Increase Is Double-edged Sword. (2013, January 7). Retrieved December 16, 2014, from www.sponsorship.com/iegsr/2013/01/07/2013-Sponsorship-Outlook—Spending-Increase-Is-Dou.aspx
44 Second Annual Report on Cause Marketing. Rep. 2012. Web. Retrieved December 17, 2014, from http://dowelldogood.net/wp-content/uploads/2011/11/Second-Annual-Report-on-Cause-Marketing-FINAL.pdf
45 Malmqvist, T. (2014, August 15). What Responsible Company? Almost Half of Consumers Can't Name One. Retrieved December 20, 2014, from www.greenbiz.com/blog/2014/08/15/what-responsible-company-almost-half-consumers-cant-name-one
46 McCarthy, C. (2006, July 7). Study: BP, Toyota Top Green Energy, Auto Brands. Retrieved December 20, 2014, from http://news.cnet.com/Study-BP,-Toyota-top-green-energy,-auto-brands/2100–1030_3–6091611.html
47 Newsdeck, E. (2010, August 2). Beyond Petroleum: Why the CSR Community Collaborated in Creating the BP Oil Disaster. Retrieved December 20, 2014, from www.ethicalcorp.com/communications-reporting/beyond-petroleum-why-csr-community-collaborated-creating-bp-oil-disaster
48 Sustainability Review 2013. (2013, January 1). Retrieved December 22, 2014, from www.bp.com/content/dam/bp/pdf/sustainability/group-reports/BP_Sustainability_Review_2013.pdf
49 BP: Highlights Commitment to US Military Veterans with Sponsorship of 2014 Warrior Games. (2014, September 25). Retrieved December 22, 2014, from www.4-traders.com/BP-PLC-9590188/news/BP—Highlights-Commitment-to-US-Military-Veterans-with-Sponsorship-of-2014-Warrior-Games-19102704/
50 BP: Highlights Commitment to US Military Veterans with Sponsorship of 2014 Warrior Games. (2014, September 25). Retrieved December 22, 2014, from www.4-traders.com/BP-PLC-9590188/news/BP—Highlights-Commitment-to-US-Military-Veterans-with-Sponsorship-of-2014-Warrior-Games-19102704/
51 BP Pledges £10m Art Sponsorship. (2011, December 19). Retrieved December 22, 2014, from www.bbc.com/news/entertainment-arts-16243960
52 BP To Contribute $1 Million To U.S. Olympic Training Center And Paralympic Programs. (2013, November 13). Retrieved December 22, 2014, from www.teamusa.org/News/2013/November/13/BP-To-Contribute-1-Million-To-US-Olympic-Training-Center-And-Paralympic-Programs

53 Who's Hot on Facebook Studio. (2013, January 30). Retrieved December 10, 2014, from https://social.ogilvy.com/whos-hot-on-facebook-studio/
54 Team USA. (n.d.). Retrieved December 9, 2014, from www.bp.com/en/global/corporate/about-bp/company-information/bp-and-london-2012/team-usa.html
55 BP Team USA: Using Social to Win Gold—Shorty Awards for Brands, Agencies, and Organizations. (2012, January 1). Retrieved December 9, 2014, from http://industry.shortyawards.com/nominee/5th_annual/BR/bp-team-usa-using-social-to-win-gold
56 BP Team USA: Using Social to Win Gold—Shorty Awards for Brands, Agencies, and Organizations. (2012, January 1). Retrieved December 9, 2014, from http://industry.shortyawards.com/nominee/5th_annual/BR/bp-team-usa-using-social-to-win-gold
57 BP Team USA: Using Social to Win Gold—Shorty Awards for Brands, Agencies, and Organizations. (2012, January 1). Retrieved December 9, 2014, from http://industry.shortyawards.com/nominee/5th_annual/BR/bp-team-usa-using-social-to-win-gold
58 BP Team USA: Using Social to Win Gold—Shorty Awards for Brands, Agencies, and Organizations. (2012, January 1). Retrieved December 9, 2014, from http://industry.shortyawards.com/nominee/5th_annual/BR/bp-team-usa-using-social-to-win-gold
59 Walton, L., Cooley, S. & Nicholson, J. (2012, March 8). "A Great Day for Oiled Pelicans:" BP, Twitter, and the Deep Water Horizon Crisis Response. Retrieved December 14, 2014, from www.instituteforpr.org/wp-content/uploads/BP-Twitter-The-Deep-Water-Horizon.pdf
60 Wolaver, N. (2010, February 25). Pumped About New USOC Sponsor. Retrieved December 23, 2014, from http://olympicringsandotherthings.blogspot.com/2010_02_01_archive.html
61 Lee, J. (2010, July 1). BP, Crisis Communications and Social Media. Retrieved December 15, 2014, from www.bruceclay.com/blog/bp-crisis-communications-and-social-media/
62 Walton, L., Cooley, S. & Nicholson, J. (2012, March 8). "A Great Day for Oiled Pelicans:" BP, Twitter, and the Deep Water Horizon Crisis Response. Retrieved December 14, 2014, from www.instituteforpr.org/wp-content/uploads/BP-Twitter-The-Deep-Water-Horizon.pdf
63 How did BP Connect Facebook Fans Directly with Team USA? (n.d.). Retrieved December 11, 2014, from https://social.ogilvy.com/expertise/cases/10700–2/
64 Lee, J. (2010, July 1). BP, Crisis Communications and Social Media. Retrieved December 15, 2014, from www.bruceclay.com/blog/bp-crisis-communications-and-social-media/
65 BP America Supports Six US Olympic and Paralympic Hopefuls in Their Quest for Gold at the Sochi 2014 Olympic and Paralympic Winter Games. (2013, September 9). Retrieved December 23, 2014, from www.bp.com/en/global/corporate/press/press-releases/bp-america-supports-6-us-olympic-hopefuls-sochi-2014.html
66 BP Team USA: Using Social to Win Gold—Shorty Awards for Brands, Agencies, and Organizations. (2012, January 1). Retrieved December 9, 2014, from http://industry.shortyawards.com/nominee/5th_annual/BR/bp-team-usa-using-social-to-win-gold
67 Marzilli, T. (2012, August 8). Winning Olympic Sponsors. Retrieved December 23, 2014, from www.brandindex.com/article/winning-olympic-sponsors
68 Marzilli, T. (2012, August 8). Winning Olympic Sponsors. Retrieved December 23, 2014, from www.brandindex.com/article/winning-olympic-sponsors
69 Levy, G. (2012, July 6). BP Olympics Ads Splashed with Oil. Retrieved December 24, 2014, from www.upi.com/blog/2012/07/06/BP-Olympics-ads-splashed-with-oil/7771341589244/
70 Magnay, J. (2012, April 11). London 2012 Olympics: Anti-BP Activists Carry Out Sponsor Sacking Hoax as Protests Grow. Retrieved December 24, 2014, from www.telegraph.co.uk/sport/olympics/9198561/London-2012-Olympics-Anti-BP-activists-carry-out-sponsor-sacking-hoax-as-protests-grow.html
71 Magnay, J. (2012, April 11). London 2012 Olympics: Anti-BP Activists Carry Out Sponsor Sacking Hoax as Protests Grow. Retrieved December 24, 2014, from www.telegraph.co.uk/sport/olympics/9198561/London-2012-Olympics-Anti-BP-activists-carry-out-sponsor-sacking-hoax-as-protests-grow.html
72 Magnay, J. (2012, April 11). London 2012 Olympics: Anti-BP Activists Carry Out Sponsor Sacking Hoax as Protests Grow. Retrieved December 24, 2014, from /www.telegraph.co.uk/sport/olympics/

9198561/London-2012-Olympics-Anti-BP-activists-carry-out-sponsor-sacking-hoax-as-protests-grow.html

73 Greenwash Gold 2012 Medals Awarded. (2012, January 1). Retrieved December 18, 2014, from www.greenwashgold.org/

74 Lee, J. (2010, July 1). BP, Crisis Communications and Social Media. Retrieved December 15, 2014, from www.bruceclay.com/blog/bp-crisis-communications-and-social-media/

75 Gaudin, S. (2010, June 15). BP, in Crisis Mode, Misses Social Networking Target. Retrieved December 30, 2014, from www.computerworld.com/article/2518975/web-apps/bp—in-crisis-mode—misses-social-networking-target.html

76 Beam, C. (2010, May 5). How BP is Handling its P.R. Disaster. Retrieved January 2, 2015, from www.slate.com/articles/news_and_politics/politics/2010/05/oil_slick.html

77 Gaudin, S. (2010, June 15). BP, in Crisis Mode, Misses Social Networking Target. Retrieved December 30, 2014, from www.computerworld.com/article/2518975/web-apps/bp—in-crisis-mode—misses-social-networking-target.html

78 Shogren, E. (2011, April 21). BP: A Textbook Example Of How Not To Handle PR. Retrieved January 2, 2015, from /www.npr.org/2011/04/21/135575238/bp-a-textbook-example-of-how-not-to-handle-pr

79 Dow, BP, Rio Tinto Must Jump Reputation Hurdles at Olympics. (2012, July 3). Retrieved December 12, 2014, from www.greenbiz.com/blog/2012/07/03/dow-bp-rio-tinto-must-jump-reputation-hurdles-olympics

80 USOC Says BP Sponsorship Still Solid. (2010, June 6). Retrieved December 28, 2014, from http://sports.espn.go.com/oly/news/story?id=5257596

81 USOC Says BP Sponsorship Still Solid. (2010, June 6). Retrieved December 28, 2014, from http://sports.espn.go.com/oly/news/story?id=5257596

82 Gaudin, S. (2010, June 15). BP, in Crisis Mode, Misses Social Networking Target. Retrieved December 30, 2014, from www.computerworld.com/article/2518975/web-apps/bp—in-crisis-mode—misses-social-networking-target.html

83 BP America. (2010, December 1). Retrieved December 12, 2014, from https://m.facebook.com/BPAmerica?v=timeline&timecutoff=1416844799§ionLoadingID=m_timeline_loading_div_1293868799_1262332800_8_&timeend=1293868799×tart=1262332800&tm=AQA1oD03l4wffxU-

84 Natividad, A. (2010, December 12). BP vs The Internet. Retrieved December 11, 2014, from www.slideshare.net/luckthelady/bp-vs-the-internet

LONG CASE QUESTIONS

1. What are some of the major environmental disasters BP has been responsible for?
2. What are some of the factors that caused these disasters?
3. Do you think that it is ethical for BP to use sponsorship to improve its brand image? Why or why not?
4. What should BP do to make sure environmental disasters don't occur again in the future?

Chapter 11

Global Ethics

LEARNING OBJECTIVES

After reading this chapter you should be able to:

- Understand what global business ethics is
- Understand why there are differences in ethics worldwide
- Be aware of the approaches to global ethics
- Appreciate the key ethical issues facing multinationals today
- Understand what companies can do to address global ethical issues

PREVIEW BUSINESS ETHICS INSIGHT

Multinational Ethical Scandals

Ethical scandals among multinationals abound. For instance, in the 1990s, Nike was criticized by activists for its harsh labor practices. Stories surfaced of child labor in Pakistan and workers working in very inhumane conditions in many of its plants. Even the founder acknowledged in 1998 that Nike was synonymous with slave wages, forced overtime, and abuse. Nike then started implementing many measures to become more socially responsible. But did things change? The answer emerged with a broadcast aired on an Australian channel. Posing as a fashion buyer, an Australian reporter got access to a Nike plant operating in Malaysia. The reporter was shocked to find workers living in extremely bad conditions. They had to work for very long hours with very little pay. Worst of all, many of them were Bangladeshi and came to Malaysia for employment. However, as soon as they arrived, their passports were confiscated and they had to work long hours to pay for recruiting fees. The broadcast showed that Nike has seemingly not addressed the earlier labor problems. In fact, the 2008 broadcast made it seem like no progress had been made regarding the worker issues.

More recently, the major meat producers in Brazil came under fire. They were accused of colluding with officials and engaging in many unethical practices. These practices ranged from repacking meat past its due date, using soy bean in turkey ham instead of turkey, and using potentially harmful additives. These companies were accused of bribing official food inspectors so that they would ignore these ethical infractions. While these practices took place in Brazil, the fallout for the industry globally has been very damaging. Although more investigations revealed that only a small fraction of Brazilian meat producers were involved in the scandal, China, Chile, South Korea and the European Union said they would ban meat imports from Brazil. Both China and Chile have banned all meat from Brazil while the European Union has banned meat from the affected producers.

In Japan, Kobe steel, one of Kobe's oldest firms, admitted to adding iron powder to large quantities of several materials such as aluminum and copper. They falsified data by claiming that the materials had levels of stiffness that such material did not really have. Although no deaths had yet been reported as a result of use of these materials, Kobe's customers include many household names such as Boeing, Ford and GM as well as many well-known Japanese companies such as Toyota and Nissan. These customers are now rushing to test the safety of the products that they made from Kobe Steel material. The consequences for Kobe Steel have also been damaging. Their market value fell by a third. Additionally, it is likely that replacing the faulty material will cost the company a significant amount of money.

Based on *The Economist*. 2017. "Kobe Steel; Base metal." October 14, 59–60; *The Economist*. 2017. "Food suppliers; Another grilling for Brazil." March 25, 58–59; Levenson, E. 2008. "Citizen Nike." *Fortune*, 158, 10, 165–170.

The Preview Business Ethics Insight above shows that it is extremely critical for companies to manage their ethics worldwide. Consider the case of Nike and the workers in the plants in Malaysia. While Nike was not directly employing these workers, the media blamed Nike for the horrible working conditions. Is Nike to blame if their subcontractors decide to have bad working conditions for workers? How can they counteract weak government regulations in most of the emerging countries (Vietnam, China, Indonesia and Thailand) where most of their shoes are made? The constant attention paid to Nike and the bad publicity with such reports suggests that multinationals have to strive very hard to be ethical. Nike admits that it is their responsibility to monitor and ensure that their suppliers have humane working conditions.

Both the Brazilian meat producers and the Kobe Steel examples discussed in the Preview Business Ethics Insight provide more evidence of the need for large multinationals to behave ethically. In both cases, by committing unethical behavior, these multinationals have attracted negative publicity. Additionally, they have both suffered major consequences. The Brazilian meat producers have had to contend with meat banning from countries that buy a third of their product. Such actions will likely have a very damaging impact on the industry. Kobe Steel will also likely suffer as a result of their data falsification. In addition to having to deal with tough economic conditions in the steel industry, the company will have to deal with the consequences of negative publicity and lack of consumer trust. Additionally, the recalls of the faulty material will take a long time to fix and will likely cost the company significantly.

WHAT IS GLOBAL BUSINESS ETHICS?

In Chapter 1, we defined business ethics as the principles and standards that guide business. However, when applied to the global environment, **global business ethics** apply to the myriads of ethical issues any company faces when operating in the global environment. Companies have to deal with questions such as "Should we bribe knowing that we would not get the contract without bribes?" or "Should we locate a plant in a country because of cheap labor?" or "Should we dump wastes in the local river knowing that such actions are illegal in the home country?" Answering such questions provides insights into how multinationals approach ethics.

Why should companies be concerned with global ethics? In Chapter 1, we saw the many benefits pertaining to companies that pursue ethical goals domestically. Many of these benefits also accrue to companies pursuing ethics globally. However, as we saw from the Preview Business Ethics Insight above, large multinationals are constantly scrutinized for their ethical practices. Any ethical violations can be quickly reported and these companies can suffer serious reputational damage. Because of their size and extent of operations, global multinationals are often the subject of criticism. Consider Exhibit 11.1, where we compare some of the world's largest multinationals' revenues with selected countries' gross domestic product.

As Exhibit 11.1 shows, there are many multinationals that are larger than some countries. Such large firms have access to vast financial, capital, and human resources, and such access provides power that limits the ability of the developing countries' governments to regulate these companies. In some cases, the governments of developing countries are not willing to regulate because they are competing for foreign investment. Because of their power and clout, the actions of these companies are often carefully watched. Multinationals are thus well advised to implement proactive ethical programs to ward off such scrutiny.

Furthermore, in Chapter 1, we discussed the many reasons why domestic companies should be ethical. However, society also expects multinationals to display high levels of ethics. Part of these expectations comes from the power yielded by multinationals. In fact, there is strong evidence that multinationals have significant political power that can have significant influence on officials. Consider Rolls-Royce, the famed British

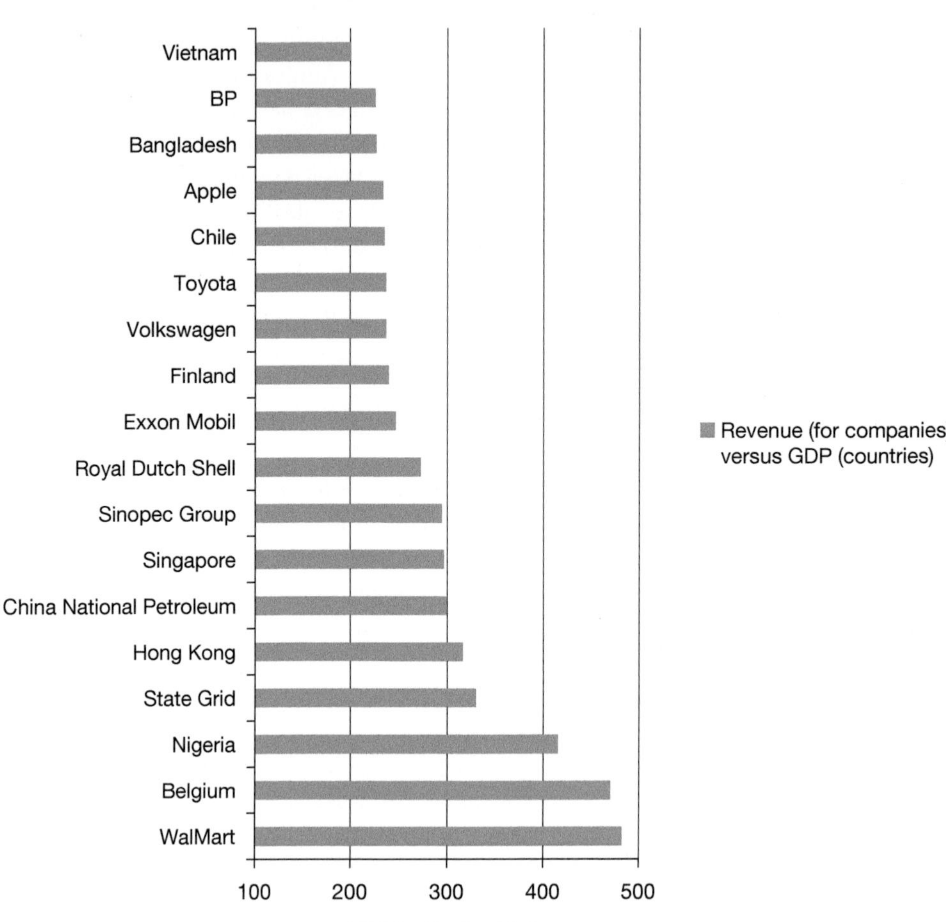

EXHIBIT 11.1—Largest Multinational Revenue vs. Country Gross Domestic Product

airplane engine producer. In January 2017, it agreed to pay US$809 million to settle claims that it had bribed officials in many countries to sell its engines.[1] It admitted that it bribed officials in at least seven countries over the last decade. The bribes of officials included giving officials money, paying for hotel stays and even giving one official a Rolls-Royce car. In return, these officials would make engine sale decisions that ended up benefitting Rolls-Royce.

As the above shows, multinationals have strong political power that has attracted intense attention from the public and the media. Multinationals are expected to use such power wisely if they do not want to suffer negative backlashes. Rolls-Royce is now paying the price for these ethical scandals. But multinationals in some societies now have to fear backlash from the public. Consider the following Emerging Market Business Ethics Insight.

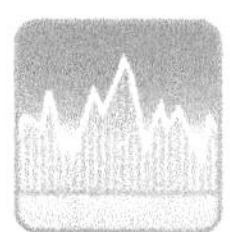

EMERGING MARKET BUSINESS ETHICS INSIGHT

Corruption in Russia

Alexei Navalny, currently the opposition leader and aiming to run in Russia's 2018 election, is a staunch corruption fighter. After graduating with a Masters in securities and stock exchanges, he became a full-time stock trader. Back in 2007, he decided to invest in Rosnef, Gazprom and Transneft, three of Russia's largest gas producers. Despite high gas prices and ample supply, Mr. Navalny was very surprised at the low returns on his investment. During his research, he was surprised to find that Transneft had donated $300 million to U.S.-based charities. When he started contacting the biggest charities in Russia, none mentioned that they received any charity from the company. Additionally, when he asked Transneft for the names of the U.S. charities they donated to, Transneft refused. Over the following decade, Mr. Navalny continued hounding many state owned companies to reveal aspects of operations that seemed unethical. He also started publishing his findings on his own website and he got an international following from such actions. His anti-corruption efforts have led to cancellations of many suspicious bids. Additionally, such scrutiny of companies led others to provide tips about suspicious decisions.

As a result of the success of his work, Mr. Navalny became unable to tackle all of the tips he was receiving. He therefore created RosPil, a website dedicated to fight corruption. He invited people to submit tips regarding corruption. Because his staff is limited, he started crowdsourcing tips to an army of volunteers made up of lawyers, engineers, accountants and economists. If tips are deemed to have merit, these are then released to the volunteers who take on the task of further investigations and filing lawsuits with the court system. Because Rospil is such a decentralized network of these volunteers, the Russian government has been unable to close the website. The effort is paying off as Russian officials are much more careful about their actions.

Based on *BBC News*. 2017. "Alexei Navalny: Russia's vociferous opposition leader." February 8, www.bbc.com/news/world-europe-16057045; Healy, P.M. and Ramanna, K. 2013. "When the crowd fights corruption." *Harvard Business Review*, January-February, 122–128.

As the above shows, Russian multinationals are increasingly being scrutinized for their unethical behavior. Furthermore, because of internet technologies, stories of misbehavior can be quickly spread to reach millions of individuals. Such efforts can have an important impact on reduction of corruption. In fact, a non-profit in India has also set up a similar website where private citizens can report bribery or corruption (see 2018, http://ipaidabribe.com). This site has also made unethical behavior more transparent and encouraged officials as well as multinationals to behave more ethically.

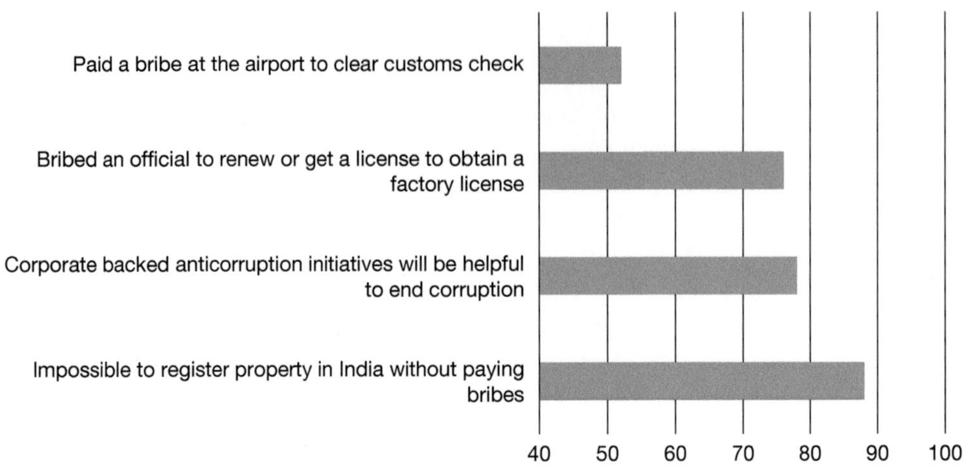

EXHIBIT 11.2—Response to Several Bribery-Related Questions

To give you further insights on the extent of corruption in Indian society, Exhibit 11.2 reveals the percentage of individuals who responded to several bribery-related questions.

Clearly, corruption is problematic in both Russia and China and more multinationals and officials are responding because of the increased transparency. However, another reason why multinationals are expected to be more ethical is the increasing similarity of ethical practices or **convergence**. Experts believe that many management practices, including those related to ethics, are becoming more similar.

Many forces are pressuring this need for convergence. For example, agreements among countries, such as regional trade agreements and membership in the WTO, provide supranational regulatory environments that affect ethical practices. Cross-border competition, trade, mergers and acquisitions provide more opportunities to learn about and copy successful managerial practices from anywhere in the world. Furthermore, other factors such as global customers and products and growing levels of economic development are all creating the pressures for convergence.

This chapter will therefore provide you with a solid background in global ethics. To understand global ethics, we must first determine if ethics is approached differently around the world. In doing so, we examine the nature of these differences. For instance, why are people more likely to tolerate bribery in some cultures than others? After we discuss the nature of such differences, you will read about ethical approaches adopted by multinationals. Finally, the chapter will consider some of the most pressing global ethical issues and conclude with what multinationals can do to build their global ethics program.

WHAT IS THE NATURE OF DIFFERENCES IN ETHICS?

In the Preview Business Ethics Insight above, you read about the ethical scandals at Nike. However, although Nike had implemented strong policies aiming at monitoring suppliers, the 2008 scandal shows that it is difficult to be able to monitor all suppliers. In fact, Levenson argues that many of Nike's plants are in emerging countries with weak governments.[2] In the absence of strong regulation, companies need to be even more forceful to ensure that the suppliers abide by ethical regulations. This implies that it is critical to understand whether ethics are viewed differently and the nature of such differences. For instance, why would any society allow its workers to work in harsh conditions? Why do some societies tolerate and participate in bribery? Consider again, for instance, the case of the Brazilian meat producers and the fact that many officials allowed themselves to be bribed. These examples suggest that there are varying degrees of what are considered unethical behaviors. In this part, we discuss the extent and nature of such differences.

What is the nature of differences in ethics **cross-nationally**? Many aspects of ethics have been studied in various nations. One of the most widespread surveys of ethics worldwide is undertaken by the InterConsortium for Political and Social Research. In their last World Values Survey, respondents from over 40 nations were asked the degree to which they justify unethically suspect behaviors, such as claiming government benefits to which they are not entitled, cheating on their taxes, or accepting stolen property. Exhibit 11.3 shows the scores for selected countries.

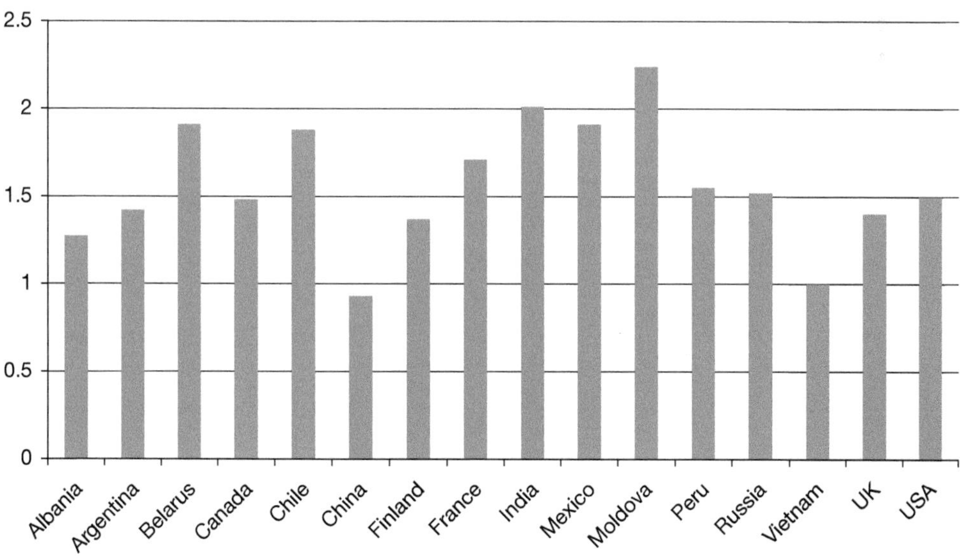

EXHIBIT 11.3—Justification of Ethically Suspect Behaviors for Selected Countries

Source: Based on World Values Survey, 2018. www.worldvaluessurvey.org/wvs.jsp

The exhibit shows that there are indeed differences between societies regarding how much people justify ethically suspect behaviors. How can these differences be explained? Cullen, Parboteeah and Hoegl argue that national cultural differences (differences in what people think is the right way to do things) and social institutions (differences in educational systems, religion, etc.) are likely to encourage people to break norms and thereby justify ethically suspect behaviors.[3] Societies with national cultural dimensions such as values of high achievement (i.e., people value achievement), high individualism (i.e., people value their own personal freedom), high universalism (i.e., people are more ambitious because they expect to be treated fairly), and high pecuniary materialism (i.e., people have high materialist tendencies) are likely to have a greater number of people engaging in deviant acts such as crime, as these cultural dimensions are more likely to encourage people to be ambitious and want to achieve. In the process, they are more likely to break norms. In addition to these national cultural values, the authors specified that societies with relatively high levels of industrialization, capitalist systems, low degrees of family breakdown and easily accessible education should encourage more deviance. Testing their theory on 3450 managers from 28 countries, the researchers found support for most of their hypotheses.

The above study shows that national cultural and social institutional differences explain the degree to which people are willing to tolerate unethical behaviors. Other studies have focused on alternative aspects of business ethics. Recall that in Chapter 1 we discussed that there are differences in corruption levels worldwide. As the Global Business Ethics Insight shows, understanding corruption and the nature of differences cross-culturally is important. Seleim and Bontis provide some understanding of how culture affects corruption.[4] They use the Corruption Perception Index (as reported in Chapter 1) and examine how national culture dimensions influence the index for 62 countries. They find that specific cultural values such as uncertainty avoidance (the degree to which people prefer certainty and order in their lives), individualism (the degree to which people are focused on themselves) and future orientation (the degree to which people are focused on the future) all promote higher corruption. In contrast, cultural dimensions such as gender egalitarianism (degree to which people promote gender equality in a society) is related to less corruption.

A more recent study investigating 98 countries provides similar results.[5] However, this new study relied on another national culture model based on Hofstede's work. This study shows that power distance (the degree to which people accept that there are power differences in society) has a positive effect on corruption. This is not surprising given that high power distance societies such as Russia, Saudi Arabia and Iraq tend to have higher inequality. Such societies do tend to have higher corruption relative to other countries such as Austria, New Zealand and Denmark that have low power distance. In contrast to the earlier study, societies with high individualism tend to have more law abiding citizens and therefore lower corruption. Finally, this study also looked at long-term orientation (degree to which societies look to maintaining links with the past to deal with current challenges) and found that such societies tend to have lower corruption. This is also not surprising as short-term oriented societies tend to have individuals more focused on gains in the short term (e.g., Honduras,

Nigeria and Ghana with the highest short-term orientation) and corruption tends to be higher.

The studies provide some explanations of the nature of differences among countries on ethics. As the studies show, both culture and social institutions such as industrialization, economic development, degree of wealth and religion have important influences on how people perceive ethics. Such findings are critical for multinational managers as they work to reduce unethical behavior. Specifically, managers making location decisions can assess the emphasis on cultural dimensions to gauge the degree to which unethical behavior will be tolerated. Research has shown overwhelmingly that some cultural dimensions such as high masculinity (people are more focused on work than quality of life), achievement and performance orientation (degree to which people are focused on achievement and performance in a society) and uncertainty avoidance are all related to higher corruption. Managers can assess these cultural dimensions and determine people's approach ethics. Furthermore, managers can often use only their own knowledge of a country's social institutions and culture to make inferences about which ethical issues are important and how they are best managed.

In addition to differences in the ways of tolerating or engaging in unethical behavior, the methods people and multinationals use to approach or resolve ethical dilemmas is worth exploring. Specifically, the concepts of ethical relativism and ethical universalism are important. Next, we discuss these concepts.

Ethical relativism is an ethical viewpoint based on the assumption that there are no objective and universal moral standards. Rather, the relativist sees morality as subjective and moral standards as different between cultures or groups within a single culture. For example, if the people in one country believe that abortion is morally wrong, then for the relativist abortion is morally wrong. If, on the other hand, people in another country believe that abortion is morally correct, then for the relativist abortion is correct. For multinational companies, ethical relativism means that managers need only follow local ethical conventions. Thus, for example, if bribery is an accepted way of doing business in a country, then it is okay for a multinational manager to follow local examples, even if it would be illegal at home. The opposite of ethical relativism is **ethical universalism**, which holds that basic moral principles transcend cultural and national boundaries. All cultures, for example, have rules that prohibit murder, at least of their own people. In such cases, the multinational manager will follow moral standards coming from the headquarters.

Why is it important to understand these ethical positions? Consider the following Global Business Ethics Insight.

As the Global Business Ethics Insight shows, understanding ethical relativism and countries where it is followed is important. In other cases, ethical universalism should prevail. For the multinational company, however, there are problems following either approach. Some argue that a universalist approach may be insensitive and, as we see above, may go against well-established cultural norms. Other ethicists argue that cultural relativism cannot be applied to ethics. Thomas Donaldson, a famed business ethicist, argues that multinational companies have a higher moral responsibility than ethical relativism.[6] He argues that the extreme form of ethical relativism, namely

GLOBAL BUSINESS ETHICS INSIGHT

Ethical Relativism Worldwide

There is strong evidence to suggest that following ethical relativism principles may be the only way to do business in certain countries. Consider the impact of religion on business ethics rules in some countries. Islam, currently the world's second largest religion, with adherents in Africa, the Middle East, China, Malaysia and the Far East, provides many ethical guidelines for business operations. For instance, Islam prohibits paying of interest. In other cases, Islam also prohibits the employment of women or encourages segregation based on gender. Multinationals may sometimes have to be cautious about posting women in such societies.

Hinduism, the religious traditions followed by around 760 million people in countries such as India, Nepal and Sri Lanka, also provides moral guidelines for businesses. For Hindus, the caste system whereby people at birth are segregated into occupational groups is sacred. Often, multinationals have to consider whether they can have a person from a lower caste lead others from higher castes. While the caste system may be disappearing, it is still an important aspect of the ethical environment in India.

Besides religion, other aspects of the business environment may be indirectly affected by religion. Consider the case of *guanxi* prevalent in many of the Pacific Rim countries such as China and Taiwan. *Guanxis* generally refer to the social networks or relationships that companies in these countries develop to do business. *Guanxi* is based on the patient development of relationships between businesses to reach a point where businesses trust each other completely and have faith that businesses will look out for each other and reciprocate on favors. *Guanxi* has been a feature of Chinese society for more than 2500 years and evolved from Confucianism and the latter's emphasis on harmony, loyalty, benevolence and trust.

Many experts agree that having the right *guanxi* is essential for any multinational doing business in the Pacific Rim region. However, companies from Western societies have often argued that such arrangements lead to unethical behaviors, bribery and corruption. In fact, *guanxis* have been getting negative publicity. In the absence of a good legal infrastructure, *guanxis* can sometimes lead to unethical behaviors because members within the same network engage in under-the-table dealings and give preferential treatment to each other.

Based on Huang, W., Hunag, C. and Dubinsky, A.J. 2015. "The impact of Guanxi on ethical perceptions: The case of Taiwanese salespeople." *Journal of Business-to-business Marketing*, 21, 1–17; Hwang, D., Golemon, P., Chen, Y., Wang, T-S. and Hung, W.-S. 2009. "Guanxi and business ethics in Confucian society today: An empirical case study in Taiwan." *Journal of Business Ethics*, 89, 235–250.

convenient relativism, can occur when companies use the logic of ethical relativism to behave any way they please, using differences in cultures as an excuse. However, such approaches may backfire.

In sum, in this section we argued that it is necessary to understand the differences in ethics worldwide and the nature of these differences. Multinationals can use such understanding to refine their approaches to ethics in different societies. Next, we consider some of the major international ethics issues facing multinationals.

KEY GLOBAL ETHICAL ISSUES

In Chapter 1, you read about the many ethical issues facing the domestic company. When applied to the global level, companies also face many ethical issues. Exhibit 11.4 illustrates the many issues facing any company operating in the international environment today based on how stakeholders are affected.

While the global company faces a range of ethical issues in the international environment, two of the most important global ethical issues are labor issues and bribery. We consider these two in depth.

Employees	• Discrimination, diversity, and sexual harassment • Working conditions • Gender equality • Compensation
Shareholders	• Shareholder interests • Transparency in accounting • Transparency in shareholder communications • Executive salaries and compensation • Corporate governance
Government	• Respecting rules and regulations • Practices in foreign nations with weak governments • Lobbying
Country	• Respecting local laws • Influence on political climate • Bribery and corruption • Lobbying and other influence

EXHIBIT 11.4—Global Ethical Issues

Labor Issues

It is undeniable that many companies choose to source to other countries to benefit from lower labor costs. Low wages, weak unions, and corrupt governments often encourage Western-based multinationals to have their products manufactured in developing countries in both Asia and Latin America.[7] However, this approach has also resulted in **labor issues** and many ethical dilemmas that have brought attention to multinationals. For instance, is it wrong to pay market wages to individuals in developing nations when such wages amount to a pittance locally? How should a company deal with child labor when children in these societies have no alternative? Should companies pay the same wage to women as men when there is a plentiful supply of female workers? Addressing these challenges has been the focus of many companies in the retail sector.

One of the major labor issues facing multinationals is **women workers and their rights**. Women workers provide the bulk of labor in developing nations in export-oriented sectors, often in factories in export processing zones or in agriculture. However, in most cases, women workers are paid very low wages for insecure work in poor working conditions.[8] Furthermore, women are often paid lower wages than men. Additionally, fieldwork has shown that women work in such factories that often reflect patriarchal subordination. Men typically tend to be disproportionately represented in the managerial level relative to women. Women are also considered flexible labor and can easily be fired if they become pregnant or sick. Finally, women may also have to juggle both unpaid domestic work with paid work.

The current research suggests that how women are treated is mainly dependent on how gender roles are viewed. In that respect, the World Values Survey has collected valuable data to understand how the role of women is viewed in different societies. Some societies have very traditional views of gender roles where women are expected to stay at home and take care of children. In other societies, people share less traditional views where both men and women are expected to share in household chores.[9] Exhibit 11.5 shows country scores of traditional gender roles in selected countries. This was assessed by asking respondents the degree to which they believed that university education is more important for boys than girls.

Clearly, there are important differences regarding gender roles around the world. Some countries, such as Bangladesh and India, perceive women's role as very traditional. Countries such as Sweden have more modern views. Multinationals can rely on such scores to determine how to address women's ethical labor issues. For instance, when operating in societies with more traditional gender roles, multinationals must take more deliberate efforts to facilitate entry of women in the workforce. Stronger efforts must be exerted to provide mechanisms to change such traditional views. Multinationals should provide fair wages and also ensure that women have equal rights to men in terms of promotion and success at work.

Although such industrialization has had negative effects on women, there is also evidence that entering the workforce has been beneficial for women. Prieto-Carron reviews work suggesting that, despite the bad working conditions, women often benefit from having access to such jobs.[10] Employment alternatives for these women workers are often worse than the factory jobs and wages for such jobs still tend to be higher than in other sectors. Furthermore, being employed means that women have access to other female companies and the opportunity to be financially independent. Jobs also mean the ability to achieve greater equality in the household and more personal freedom. Finally, recent evidence suggests that women's employment allows them to organize collectively to better their working conditions.

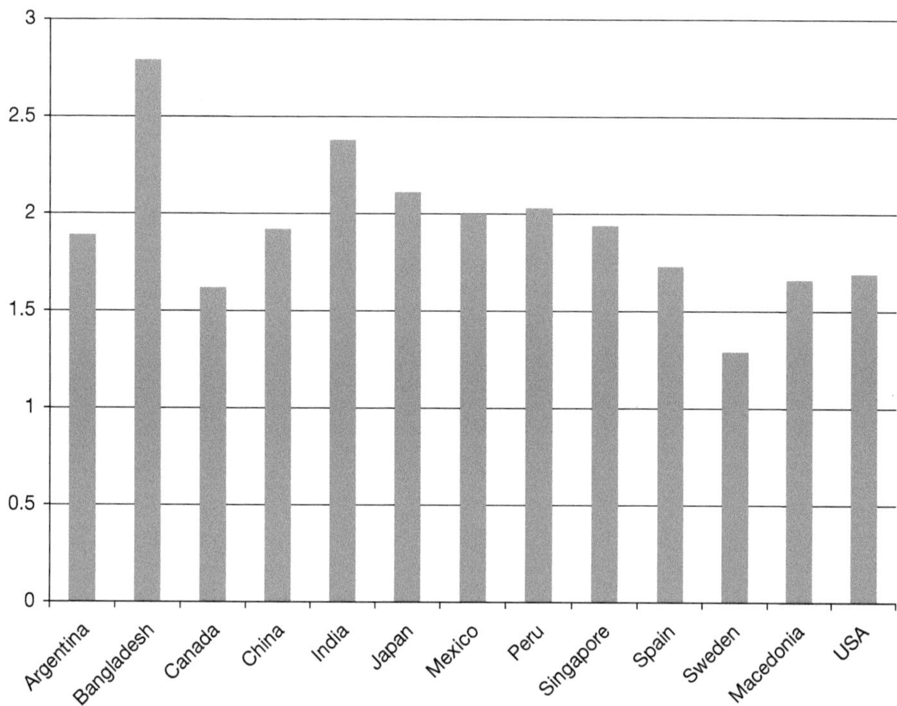

EXHIBIT 11.5—Traditional Gender Roles

Despite the benefits, it will take time before women workers' conditions are significantly improved. Multinationals will thus need to continue working hard to improve women's working conditions and facilitate their entry into the workforce. Next we discuss another important aspect of the labor ethical issues.

A related labor force issue is **child labor**, the practice of employing children.[11] Even companies such as Apple and Nike have occasionally been hit with allegations of child labor. Gap, the retailing giant, was also accused of using children in India to manufacture clothing for GapKids.[12] Critics condemn such companies for supporting exploitation of children. These children often work in very poor conditions and are paid very low wages. Such practices are threats to these children's development and their health and safety. As such, various organizations and child advocates are working tirelessly to convince governments and multinationals to aggressively address child labor and to ban such employment.

While most multinationals are working hard to ban child employment, some argue that child labor is not necessarily as simple as it seems. For instance, French suggests that such views ignore the complex environment such children employees face.[13] For instance, children sometimes have to work to help their families cope with poverty. If these children do not work, they may not have the means to get access to education. Second, it is also typically assumed that work is devastating to children. However, there is some evidence that child labor can provide children with psychosocial benefits and provide some education that a formal education system does not provide.

GLOBAL BUSINESS ETHICS INSIGHT

Expatriate Safety

Expatriate safety is becoming a core issue for many multinationals. Consider the potential for violence and unrest in many countries where expatriates are posted. For instance, Mexico has seen over 5400 people slain in the drug-fueled war in 2008. Many companies lost employees and others could not account for their foreign employees for days. Yet another critical safety issue in India is the potential for kidnappings. Executives for companies such as Adobe and Satyam have all been kidnapped in high-risk areas. Others have been blackmailed or forced to withdraw money from ATMs in high-risk countries. Another case involves an expatriate's child who had powdered lime thrown in her eyes. The child was taken to the hospital and discharged quickly.

International non-governmental organizations (NGOs) in the international aid and development sectors are also very likely to have employees in difficult situations. These expatriates are often likely to work in vulnerable situations whereby the NGO has limited control on the environment in the country they are operating in. In such cases, these NGOs also have to ensure that they provide adequate protection for these valuable expatriates.

How responsible are multinationals for their expatriates' safety? Most companies are actually legally responsible to ensure their employees' safety. For instance, a company in the U.S. faces significant liability if it does not implement risk management plans. Employers are responsible for providing employees with the education and means to protect themselves against such situations in remote or dangerous locations. The situation is similar for NGOs. They need to make sure they have systems in place to ensure the safety of their workers.

How can multinationals prepare for such situations? Various companies provide intelligence services documenting difficulties in particular countries. Such reports can document potential risks in dangerous locations and also provide some ideas for preventive strategies. Other companies purchase annual membership for emergency medical services in situations where employees have to be returned home for emergency medical care. Recent research on NGOs suggests that they incorporate many practices through the human resource management department emphasizing safety and security of their expatriates. In doing so, they promoted a culture focused on keeping everyone safe.

Based on Fee, A. and McGrath-Champ, S. 2017. "The role of human resources in protecting expatriates: Insights from the international aid and development sector." *International Journal of Human Resource Management*, 28, 1960–1985; Lorenzo, O., Esqueda, P. and Larson, J. 2010. "Safety and ethics in the global workplace: Asymmetries in culture and infrastructure." *Journal of Business Ethics*, 92, 87–106.

Despite these benefits, the reality is that children do work in less regulated and less visible areas of most economies. As such, rather than take a more complex look at child labor, many multinationals have created codes of conduct that ban any form of child labor. This universal position makes more sense given how vulnerable children are. Next, we consider worker safety.

Another critical labor issue that multinationals have to contend with is **work safety**, pertaining to the many steps multinationals take to ensure that their workers operate in an environment free of harm. Such safety can take many dimensions. First, multinationals have become more concerned about the safety of their workers in foreign plants. For instance, there is increased pressure for multinationals in the retail sector, such as Gap and Levi Strauss, to ensure that their employees work in safe conditions. A second key aspect is safety issues faced by expatriates. Consider the Global Business Ethics Insight on the facing page.

Next, we discuss the issue of bribery.

Bribery

One of the most pressing global ethics issues facing most multinationals is bribery. As you saw in Chapter 1, bribery and corruption occur to some varying degrees in most societies. In that context, corruption is the "misuse of entrusted power for private gain" (see www.transparency.org). Corruption occurs when someone receives a bribe and does something that they are legally prohibited from doing. **Bribery** also refers to gifts or payments to someone to expedite a government action or to gain some business advantages. Furthermore, as both Exhibits 1.1 and Exhibit 1.2 from Chapter 1 showed, there are significant differences in corruption worldwide. Earlier in this chapter, we discussed the nature of these differences.

Why should companies be concerned with bribery and ethics? There seem to be two major reasons for concern for ethics. First, companies put themselves at serious financial risk if they engage in bribery. In the U.S., the Foreign Corrupt Practices Act (FCPA) prohibits bribery and companies are fined for such violations. Exhibit 11.6 below shows some of the more recent fines paid by selected global companies as a result of settlements or fines imposed because of the FCPA in 2016 and 2017.

As the Global Business Ethics Insight shows, one important reason for multinationals to implement anti-bribery measures is to avoid the potential of future fines. The U.S. government has been particularly aggressive enforcing FCPA guidelines over the last five years. As the exhibit shows, fines have ranged from as high as almost a billion US dollars to a few million. In all cases, the companies involved receive bad publicity and scrutiny because of such fines. Additionally, such infractions also involved large legal fees as companies hire lawyers to settle such cases.

Recent research provides a startling view of how bribery can have devastating effects on the firm. In that study, Fisman and Svensson examine the impact of bribery on firm growth.[14] They argue that bribery is detrimental to the firm because it diverts scarce resources away from critical business growth and innovation. The researchers find that increases in bribery in firms indeed resulted in lower annual growth rates for the firms.

Year	Company	Nationality of Company	Type of Infraction	Fine (US$million)
2017	Telia	Sweden	Violation of FCPA to win business in Uzbekistan	$965
2017	Halliburton	USA	Payment to company in Angola to win oil-related services contract	$29.2
2017	SQM	Chile	Improper payment to Chilean political figures	$30
2017	Biomet	Poland	Bribery violations in Mexico and Brazil	$30
2016	Braskem S.A.	Brazil	Illicit payment to Brazilian government officials to get business	$957
2016	Las Vegas Sands	USA	Millions of dollars of payment to consultant facilitating business in China and Macao	$9
2016	JP Morgan	USA	Bribed government officials by offering jobs and internships to family and friends of these officials	$264
2016	GlaxoSmithKline	UK	Pay-to-prescribe schemes in China to increase sales	$20
2016	AstraZeneca	UK	Improper payments to officials in China and Russia	$5
2016	VimpelCom	Holland	Violation of FCPA to win business in Uzbekistan	$795

EXHIBIT 11.6—Fines Paid By Multinationals

Source: Based on SEC, 2018. www.sec.gov/spotlight/fcpa/fcpa-cases.shtml

In fact, the researchers found that a 1% increase in rate of bribery results in a 3.3% drop in the annual company growth rate. Thus, these results also suggest that bribery not only increases the potential of fines that can bankrupt a company but also reduces growth rate.

The above pertained to the impact of bribery on the company. However, many studies have also shown the devastating effects of bribery on societies. Bribery, in contrast to taxes, represents private goods that benefit a few government officials at the expense of the wider society. Blackburn and Forgues-Puccio further provide a good review of studies that have examined the negative effects of bribery and corruption on countries.[15] Some studies have shown that bribery has negative effects on country growth rate. Rather than investing in development, bribes go directly to the private individuals who are being bribed. Consider the Emerging Market Business Ethics Insight below.

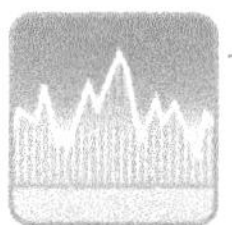

***EMERGING MARKET* BUSINESS ETHICS INSIGHT**

Corruption Worldwide

The many examples you have read in this chapter so far show the damaging effects of corruption. In India, corruption of officials means that people are not all being treated fairly. Those with the means to bribe can get their way while those who do not have the financial means to bribe get left behind. In Russia, corruption has meant that government funds are being misappropriated by private individuals. Such funds are being diverted from critical uses and are instead being used to enrich those in power and to further grow inequality in society.

A recent article documents the effects of corruption in Mexico. In 2010, the construction project of the "Estela de Lutz," a 104-meter tower, was meant to celebrate the 200th anniversary of Mexico's independence from Spain. However, the project was inaugurated two years later and ended up costing more than three times the original estimates. Investigations revealed that many officials were bribed and involved in fraud leading to costs running over. While the federal government could have used the money for other projects, they ended up footing the bill. The Balderos metro station is another example of where corruption can have bad consequences for society. In this case, one of the lines was built so poorly that it had to be closed for a period of time. This also meant that scarce public funds had to be devoted to fixing problems that should not have occurred to begin with. In yet another case, the institute of social security, Mexico's third largest buyer of goods and services were paying suppliers over 33% more because suppliers had colluded. In this case too, the public ended up suffering as scarce public funds are being diverted to pay for mistakes.

Based on *The Economist*. 2017. "Corruption in Mexico; The backhander bus." March 4, 26–27.

The above provides evidence of the damage bribery can do to society. The World Bank (www.worldbank.org) also argues that bribery often creates obstacles to doing business. As multinationals consider foreign investment decisions, they may be dissuaded because of bribery demands. Such decisions thus reduce the flow of foreign investment, thereby hurting a nation's growth. Thus, bribery may also become an important obstacle to doing business. Corruption and bribery may also discourage entrepreneurship because of the inherent obstacle creation. Furthermore, bribery may cause misallocation of public expenditure. Bribery may often encourage officials to favor specific pet projects or divert resources from more necessary projects.

Compte, Lambert-Mogiliansky and Verdier also suggest that companies typically make up for bribery by increasing the contract price by the amount of the bribe.[16] As such, many developing countries suffer because they are charged higher prices. However, companies also routinely use poorer-quality products or materials to make up for the bribe, thus putting out inferior products. Furthermore, corruption can result in collusion among firms, resulting in even higher prices. As a result, corruption and bribery usually result in higher public spending, lower-quality projects, undermined competition, and the inefficient allocation of resources.

Despite the evidence that bribery is devastating for many nations, it is nevertheless important to note that not all societies are affected similarly. For instance, as Blackburn and Forgues-Puccio report, many countries such as China, Indonesia, South Korea and Thailand have a reputation of being more corrupt but have yet enjoyed considerable economic growth.[17] However, the authors show that in such countries government bureaucrats tend to be more organized in corruption networks. In contrast, in countries where bureaucrats are less organized in networks, they are more likely to seek bribes to maximize their own income without regard to the effect of such bribes on other officials. In contrast, well-organized networks act as monopolies that minimize the extent of bribery while maximizing the provision of public goods. Thus, such networks have less damaging effects on the country's growth.

Given the widely acknowledged disadvantages associated with bribery, it is not surprising to note that many organizations worldwide are attempting to eradicate it. One of the more well-known efforts is led by the Organisation for Economic Co-operation and Development (OECD). The OECD is an association of 30 of the world's largest economies in terms of gross domestic product, including countries such as Belgium, Canada, Ireland, South Korea, New Zealand, Spain, the UK and the U.S. It was originally created in 1960 with 20 members and added ten new members over time.

The OECD members have ratified guidelines to combat bribery (OECD 2018, www.oecd.org). Specifically, the members agree to take measures to make bribery a criminal offence. Furthermore, members are expected to provide legal assistance to each other to prosecute nationals who are engaged in bribery. Additionally, members are also expected to collaborate to prevent or tackle money laundering related to bribery. Members have to provide mutual legal assistance and can be asked to extradite foreign officials for prosecution.

In addition to providing clear guidelines regarding the eradication of bribery, the OECD has also enacted regulations to address bribery in companies. As such,

Enterprises should not, directly or indirectly, offer, promise, or demand a bribe or other undue advantage to obtain or retain business or other improper advantage. Nor should enterprises be solicited or expected to render a bribe or other under advantage. In particular, enterprises should:	
1.	Not offer, nor give in to demands, to pay public officials or the employees of business partners any portion of a contract payment. They should not use subcontracts, purchase orders or consulting agreements as means of channeling payments to public officials, to employees of business partners or their relatives or business associates.
2.	Ensure that remuneration of agents is appropriate and for legitimate services only. Where relevant, a list of agents employed in connection with transactions with public bodies and state-owned enterprises should be kept and made available to competent authorities.
3.	Enhance the transparency of their activities in the fight against bribery and extortion. Measures could include making public commitments against bribery and extortion and disclosing the management systems the company has adopted in order to honor these commitments. The enterprise should also foster openness and dialogue with the public so as to promote its awareness of and cooperation with the fight against bribery and extortion.
4.	Promote employee awareness of and compliance with company policies against bribery and extortion through appropriate dissemination of these policies and through training programs and disciplinary procedures.
5.	Adopt management control systems that discourage bribery and corrupt practices, and adopt financial and tax accounting and auditing practices that prevent the establishment of "off the books" or secret accounts or the creation of documents that do not properly and fairly record the transactions to which they relate.
6.	Not make illegal contributions to candidates for public office or to political parties or to other political organizations. Contributions should fully comply with public disclosure requirements and should be reported to senior management.

EXHIBIT 11.7—OECD Bribery Guidelines for Multinationals, 2018.

www.oecd.org/daf/inv/mne/48004323.pdf

multinationals operating in OECD and other countries are expected to have adequate accounting practices and internal controls and audits to ensure that they are complying with anti-bribery laws. In fact, the OECD has also proposed six guidelines that multinationals are widely expected to follow. Exhibit 11.7 shows these guidelines.

While the OECD guidelines were ratified in May 1997, the U.S. made bribery illegal in 1977. In that year, in response to widespread allegations of bribery in various agencies, President Carter passed the Foreign Corrupt Practices Act (FCPA). The FCPA forbids U.S. companies from making or offering payments or gifts to foreign government officials for the sake of gaining or retaining business. However, not all forms of payment are forbidden by the FCPA. Payments made under duress to avoid injury or violence are acceptable. For example, in an unstable political environment, a company may pay local officials "bribes" to avoid harassment of its employees. Furthermore, similar to the OECD guidelines, small payments that are needed for officials to do their legitimate and routine jobs are legal. For instance, small payments to induce officials to do their functions, such as issuing licenses or permits, are legal.

The FCPA has a tricky component known as the reason-to-know provision. This provision means that a firm is liable for bribes or questionable payments made by agents hired by the firm, even if members of the firm did not actually make the payments or see them being made. To take advantage of a local person's knowledge of "how to get things done" in a country, U.S. multinational managers often use local people as agents to conduct business. If it is common knowledge that these agents use part of their fees to bribe local officials to commit illegal acts, then the U.S. firm is breaking the law. If, however, the U.S. firm has no knowledge of the behavior of the agent and no reason to expect illegal behavior by the agent, then the firm has no liability under the FCPA.

One of the toughest anti-bribery legislations ever enacted is the UK Bribery Act.[18] This legislation outlaws any form of bribery. This is evidenced by some of the key differences between the U.S. FCPA and the UK Bribery Act.[19] For instance, while the FCPA prohibits bribery to foreign officials, the UK Bribery Act prohibits bribery to anyone. Additionally, while the FCPA legislates giving bribery, the UK anti-bribery legislation makes it illegal to receive bribes. The UK anti-bribery Act thus ensures that both givers and receivers of bribes are held liable.

As the above shows, bribery is an unethical behavior that most societies take seriously. However, as Exhibit 11.4 shows, there are many ethical issues that a multinational has to contend with. You learned about two of the most pressing of these ethical issues. Next, we discuss how multinationals can approach ethics.

MULTINATIONAL ETHICS: GOING LOCAL OR GLOBAL?

As we discussed in the opening paragraphs of this chapter, multinationals are constantly faced with ethical decisions. Such ethical decisions can sometimes result in cross-cultural ethical conflicts in which the company's business practices may be different from the host country's accepted business practices. For instance, if sweatshops are accepted business practices in some societies, should a multinational engage in such practices although it has specific policies prohibiting such practices? Because multinationals face constant scrutiny for such practices, they need to make the right decisions in these situations.[20] Specifically, these multinational managers frequently need to decide which set of business practices should prevail when cross-cultural conflicts occur. In this section, we consider the various approaches available to multinationals to make such decisions.

Several approaches rooted in ethical universalism whereby multinationals are expected to follow universal principles have been proposed. For instance, Donaldson offers an approach where the ethical decisions are made based on fundamental international rights.[21] Specifically, he argues that three moral languages of avoiding harm, rights, and duties, and the social contract, should guide multinational companies. He thus advocates prescriptive ethics for multinationals; that is, multinational companies should engage in business practices that avoid negative consequences to their stakeholders (e.g., employees, the local environment). Donaldson believes that these moral languages are the most appropriate for managing ethical behaviors among culturally heterogeneous multinationals; that is, regardless of their national culture, companies can agree with their stakeholders on the basic rules of moral behavior.

A more recent universalist approach is the **Integrated Social Contracts Theory**.[22] In this approach, multinationals are expected to make decisions that recognize universally binding ethical practices known as "hypernorms." They argue that **hypernorms** are norms that are accepted by all cultures and organizations irrespective of local cultures. Examples include the freedom of speech or freedom of association. In turn, business practices such as bribery or censoring of the internet violate such hypernorms. Multinationals are therefore advised to base their decisions on whether such decisions violate hypernorms. One source of such hypernorms is the United Nations Global Compact, providing guidelines addressing many areas of operations. Exhibit 11.8 shows some elements of the Global Compact.

Wood, Logsdon, Lewellyn and Davenport propose a similar universalist approach.[23] However, instead of focusing on transnational rights or hypernorms, Wood et al. argue that multinationals should use their core values as the fundamental principles on which local ethical decisions can be made. This approach focuses on aiding the company in adjusting its practices to reflect local culture. However, when such adaptations are needed, there is strong emphasis on ensuring that these local adaptations are accommodated in such a way that the adaptations contribute to the company's culture. Thus, this approach focuses more on the company values rather than the local values.

Human Rights	• Principle 1: Businesses should support and respect the protection of internationally proclaimed human rights; and • Principle 2: make sure that they are not complicit in human rights abuses.
Labor Standards	• Principle 3: Businesses should uphold the freedom of association and the effective recognition of the right to collective bargaining; • Principle 4: the elimination of all forms of forced and compulsory labor; • Principle 5: the effective abolition of child labor; and • Principle 6: the elimination of discrimination in respect of employment and occupation.
Environment	• Principle 7: Businesses should support a precautionary approach to environmental challenges; • Principle 8: undertake initiatives to promote greater environmental responsibility; and • Principle 9: encourage the development and diffusion of environmentally friendly technologies.
Anti-Corruption	• Principle 10: Businesses should work against corruption in all its forms, including extortion and bribery.

EXHIBIT 11.8—United Nations Global Compact

While the above approaches provide some insights into ethical decision-making, multinationals may not always be able to follow universal approaches. In some cases, it is critical to respect local norms. For instance, Google decided to accept the Chinese requests of censoring the internet in order to be able to operate in China and take advantage of the potential offered by the Chinese market. In such cases, multinationals may need to assess their decisions to determine whether they want to implement such decisions. In that respect, Hamilton, Knouse and Hill offer an ethical decision-making approach, referred to as the **HKH**, based on key questions.[24] They propose three possible outcomes: do business the firm's way, do business the host's way, or leave the country altogether. We discuss this approach next and which outcomes to adopt based on these questions.

The first step of the decision-making process in the HKH model is to determine whether the decision being pondered is actually a questionable practice. In such cases, the multinational has to determine whether the practice represents a conflict between the company's own values and the host country's accepted business practices. For instance, consider the case of Google's decision to do business in China. At the outset, there was a definite conflict between their corporate values (freedom of expression and "do no evil") and the Chinese demands for censorship. This gap between the company's business practices and the country's requests suggests that a questionable practice does exist.

In the second step of the model, the multinational needs to ask whether the questionable practice breaks any laws or regulations. This is critical as it allows the company to determine the legality of any decision. Furthermore, the multinational needs to consider whether the practice breaks both home and the host country's laws. For instance, in the case of bribery, a U.S. multinational needs to be aware that bribery is illegal under the Foreign Corrupt Practices Act. However, laws in the host country must also be considered. If the questionable practice breaks any laws, the multinational should rightly decide not to engage in the questionable practice. However, if no laws or regulations are broken, the multinational needs to subject the practice to the next question.

In the third step of the HKH model, the multinational needs to consider whether the questionable practice is simply a cultural difference or could represent a potential ethics problem. It is critical to make the distinction so that the multinational can determine whether they can adopt the host business practices as an acceptable way to do business. According to Hamilton et al., one way to determine whether a questionable practice represents a cultural difference is whether the practice in question does not harm anyone and represents a valid way for the culture to achieve an important cultural goal.[25] However, a questionable practice represents an ethics issue if the practice violates acceptable ethical practices such as those represented by hypernorms. For instance, if the behavior violates human rights, then it poses an ethical issue to the multinational. Thus, by assessing whether the questionable practice represents a genuine cultural difference or an ethics issue, the multinational can decide on the appropriate response.

After a multinational has determined whether a questionable practice represents a cultural difference or an ethics issue, the multinational needs to determine whether the practice violates any of its core values or some industry code of conduct. For example, if it is determined that a practice represents a cultural difference, it is also important to determine whether the practice goes against some corporate values. Consider the decision of promoting a woman manager in Saudi Arabia. While this practice is reflective of cultural differences due to the influence of Islam on the workplace, a multinational cannot simply decide to not promote the woman because it runs the risk of violating a cultural difference. It is critical for the multinational to also consider whether the practice is consistent with its own corporate culture or other aspects of the industry culture. Thus, if the questionable practice represents a cultural difference that does not violate any codes of conduct, the multinational can adopt the host's way of doing business. This principle would apply even if the questionable practice is a potential ethics issue. However, if the questionable practice violates industry codes of conduct or its own core values, the multinational needs to subject the practice to the next step.

In the fifth step of the HKH model, a multinational needs to determine whether it has leverage to do business its own way. Leverage refers to the ability of the multinational to have clout based on its reputation or ability to provide jobs or train

BUSINESS ETHICS INSIGHT

Google in China

It is widely claimed that Google entered the Chinese market for 400 million reasons—equivalent to the number of potential customers Google could reach in China. It therefore initially decided to abide by the Chinese requests to censor its search sites so that those websites with offending material to the government would not be available. Google accepted requests counter to its corporate values in order to secure access to the market.

However, some events led Google to abandon its Chinese presence in 2010. There have been claims that its e-mail system was hacked in order to get access to the e-mails of individuals linked to opposition to the government. Furthermore, its search results were being subject to strong censorship and the state-controlled press has become extremely hostile to Google. In the end, the government censorship proved too much.

Why did Google decide to leave China? Part of the reason is because of Google's leverage in China. Google found that most of its revenues came from Chinese companies advertising on its Chinese website. Furthermore, many of these companies have enjoyed increased revenues because of such advertising. Thus, if Google leaves, many of these companies will still need to advertise on Google's website if they want to get exposure. Google therefore has strong leverage, as it sees that China and Chinese companies have more to lose if it leaves the country.

Additionally, in 2017, Google made the decision to go back to China. It now no longer wants to be in the "search" business. Rather, Google is now betting on its Artificial Intelligence (AI) business. The AI sector presents lots of opportunities for Google to provide services to the many Chinese companies. And China remains one of the largest homogenous markets.

Based on Bergen, M. and Ramli, D. 2017. "Google has a new plan for China (And it's not about search)." Bloomberg, October, 31, www.bloomberg.com/news/articles/2017-10-30/google-plots-grassroots-path-into-china-through-ai-investments; *The Economist*. 2010. "Google ponders leaving China." March 2010.

employees in the host country. A company that has strong leverage is more likely to be able to do business its own way in the host country. Consider the Business Ethics Insight above.

The Business Ethics Insight shows how Google used its leverage to make the decision to leave China. Multinationals can also make similar decisions. For example, if they have significant leverage, they could decide to do business their own way even if such decisions are counter to local cultural norms. This assumes that the multinational's way is ethically superior relative to the local way of doing business. However, if the multinational finds that it has no leverage to enforce its own way of doing things, the best option is to leave the host.

The HKH approach thus provides insights into the key questions multinationals need to ask before they decide whether they want to adopt their own way of doing business or follow the host's way.

Next, we consider some of the major aspects of a multinational's ethics program.

WHAT CAN MULTINATIONALS DO TO BECOME MORE ETHICAL?

In Chapter 12, you will learn about how companies can become more ethical. You will read about the many aspects that need to be implemented to build an ethical culture (e.g., codes of ethics, ethics training, presence of ethics officers, ethics measurement and monitoring). We will not repeat these aspects here. However, because of the global nature of the environment facing them, multinationals face some unique conditions compared to domestic-only firms. While it may seem easier to build an ethical culture for domestic firms, a multinational has to face multiple national cultures that may not view ethics similarly. As we saw earlier in this chapter, some societies tend to have higher tolerances for unethical behavior. What can a multinational do to ensure that it is behaving ethically worldwide? In this chapter, we consider two key aspects of a multinational ethics program; namely, code of ethics and whistle-blowing programs.

Code of Ethics

One of the key aspects of any multinational's ethics program is a code of ethics. The **code of ethics** is a formalized public statement that articulates the rules and regulations that will guide organizational practices with ethical consequences.[26] A code of ethics is a guide that governs both present and future employee behaviors as these employees interact with each other and with their stakeholders. A code of ethics implicitly assumes that the multinational will use universalistic standards that transcend the local cultural norms.

While you will read about the importance of codes of ethics in building the socially responsible firm in Chapter 12, a code of ethics is also extremely critical for multinationals. As multinationals get more media exposure, they are becoming increasingly responsible and visible when they break ethical norms in other societies. As we saw in the opening Preview Business Ethics Insight, Nike suffered a significant publicity backlash after it was revealed that its subcontractor had employees working in very poor conditions. A code of ethics thus allows a multinational to specify conditions and rules that all employees and stakeholders should follow worldwide. Furthermore, because of their size, multinationals cannot rely on their corporate cultures to ensure that similar behaviors are occurring worldwide. It therefore becomes important to specify appropriate behaviors worldwide in the code of ethics to ensure that all employees behave similarly. How critical is a code of ethics? Consider the Business Ethics Insight below.

BUSINESS ETHICS INSIGHT

Code of Ethics at GE

GE is a global company engaged in a variety of industries ranging from finance and media, global infrastructure to jet engines. It operates in more than 170 countries, employing around 295,000 employees worldwide. GE is very dedicated to being a responsible global corporate citizen and sees a global code of ethics as critical to achieve that goal. It has developed a set of global standards that is more rigorous than the financial and legal requirements in place in any particular country. Although there are wide variations in terms of local conditions, GE sees the global code of ethics as a simpler way to ensure that its employees are all aware and can follow the values that the company stands for. For instance, GE has global standards specifying how to prevent money laundering and standards expected of their suppliers regarding worker exploitation and the environment.

How has GE been able to develop these global standards? First, GE has made the development of standards a corporate activity. It has a set of dedicated corporate officers who regularly review key activities to determine which activities need new standards. Second, it also involves experts at all levels. These experts review potential new laws and regulations to determine whether new standards are needed. As such, it can stay ahead of potential new regulations and even foresee potential areas where unethical behavior is likely.

GE makes sure it lives by these standards. For example, it will regularly terminate senior managers for failing to abide by company rules. This was the case with a senior manager who failed to properly conduct due diligence on suppliers in an emerging nation. GE terminated the manager, although that individual had rare extensive knowledge and experience in a difficult market. Furthermore, GE has also terminated senior leaders who failed to create the right culture. In several cases, the senior leaders were not personally aware of the failings of their subordinates (e.g., an employee agreeing to falsify supplier documents for a customer). However, they were deemed responsible for creating the right culture and were fired.

In contrast to other multinationals, GE has considerably simplified its code of conduct. Rather than burden employees with a long list of rules and regulations, GE has four simple principles that aim to build a culture of integrity. Employees are encouraged to apply these principles to all areas of their work life thereby inculcating key ethical values.

Based on General Electric. 2018. *Integrity and Compliance* www.gesustainability.com/how-ge-works/integrity-compliance/#letter; Heineman, B.W. 2007. "Avoiding integrity landmines." *Harvard Business Review*, April, 100–108, www.ge.com.

Given the importance of codes of ethics, what is the nature of such codes? Stohl, Stohl and Popova provide some interesting insights on global codes of ethics.[27] They studied the code of ethics of 157 corporations of the Global *Fortune* 500 list. They classify codes of ethics as **first generation** (focus on the legal responsibility of the company), **second generation** (focus is on the responsibility to stakeholders), and **third generation** (focus on responsibilities grounded in the wider interconnected environment). Not surprisingly, they find that codes of ethics are becoming a more widespread aspect of a company's communication feature across regions and industries. However, findings also reveal that third generations are becoming more widespread, as over three-quarters of the companies studied had such codes that transcend profit motives. Furthermore, the authors found that only companies located in the European Union show a stronger degree for concern for the global environment and their ability to respond to such challenges.

Despite the popularity of codes of ethics, it is important to note that imposing the universalism inherent in such codes may be problematic in some countries. Talaulicar documents such challenges in the case of two U.S. multinationals implementing the U.S. codes of ethics in Germany.[28] The first example details WalMart's efforts to implement its statement of ethics in Germany. However, the law allows most German companies to establish work councils that are granted certain rights guaranteeing the welfare of its workers. By imposing the statement of ethics, the workers felt that

WalMart violated their rights, as they were not consulted in determining these rights. WalMart fought these claims several times in court but was found to have indeed violated these rights. However, although WalMart could have appealed, the subsequent appeals were not heard, as WalMart sold its German stores in 2006 and exited the market. Similarly, Honeywell's implementation of its code of business conduct met similar resistance. The German courts argued that workers' co-determination rights are violated in some cases when foreign codes of ethics are unilaterally imposed without giving workers some voice in the matter.

As the above shows, multinationals have to be aware of cultural constraints when implementing in foreign locales. However, codes of ethics will likely remain as one of the key aspects of building a global ethical culture. Next, we discuss whistle-blowing.

Whistle-blowing

A code of ethics regulates ethical behavior through control. In contrast, **whistle-blowing programs** shift ethics monitoring to employees. This is based on the assumption that employees know the most about unethical behavior and should therefore be involved in any ethics program. As such, ethics hotlines have become important mechanisms to reduce the probability of unethical behaviors. By providing employees with the means to report on the ethical violations, multinationals expect to detect such behaviors before it is too late. Prominent multinationals such as British Petroleum (Open Talk), Philips (Ethics Line) and P&G (Alert Line) all make use of ethics hotlines to reduce unethical behavior. Furthermore, Vodafone has gone one step further and has an online whistle-blowing system in addition to the traditional ethics hotline to detect ethical violations.

Multinationals are increasingly adopting ethics hotlines for many reasons.[29] First, because of their size, multinationals find it difficult to use only internal controls to control ethical behavior. By providing employees the opportunity to report violations, a multinational hopes to increase the likelihood of reducing unethical behavior. Second, there have been many new legal developments that now require companies to have ethics hotlines. For example, new European Union regulations require companies to have such mechanisms. Third, as we have discussed numerous times in this chapter, multinationals often face multiple cultural norms and rules. By including an ethics hotline, it can determine the potential to encounter conflicts in implementing its own corporate values with respect to local cultural norms.

How prevalent are whistle-blowing programs? Caldenon et al. provide some insights into ethics hotlines worldwide.[30] They reviewed the ethics policies of the 150 transnational companies on the United Nations Conference on Trade and Development (UNCTAD) ranking. The ranking includes both the top 50 financial transnational and top 100 non-financial transnational companies from a wide variety of locations, including the NAFTA region, Europe and Asia, and a variety of industries ranging from media to finance to telecommunications. The authors carefully studied the website of each company to gauge their ethics policies.

Results show that ethics hotlines are becoming very prevalent: 101 of the 150 firms showed that they had some form of ethics hotline. The researchers also reviewed the terminology that was used to indicate the existence of these hotlines. It is widely assumed that employees can gauge the importance of an ethics program through the language that is used. Results show that around 57% of the firms use the term "hotlines" to denote some form of reactive response to ethics violations. However, for the 43% of firms not using the word "hotline," the ethics whistle-blowing program is described in terms of corporate values such as "helpline." Furthermore, the authors show that there are wide variations regarding which employees are required to report wrongdoing if they observe such behaviors. Firms located in North America are more likely to require their employees report ethical wrongdoing compared with firms located in Europe. Finally, the authors also reviewed the mechanisms through which hotlines are implemented. They find that a majority of companies use a combination of both traditional systems such as mail and phone and new technologies such as e-mail and web. Furthermore, the findings show that financial firms are less likely to use new technologies such as e-mail to implement their hotlines. Exhibit 11.9 provides overall detail on these results.

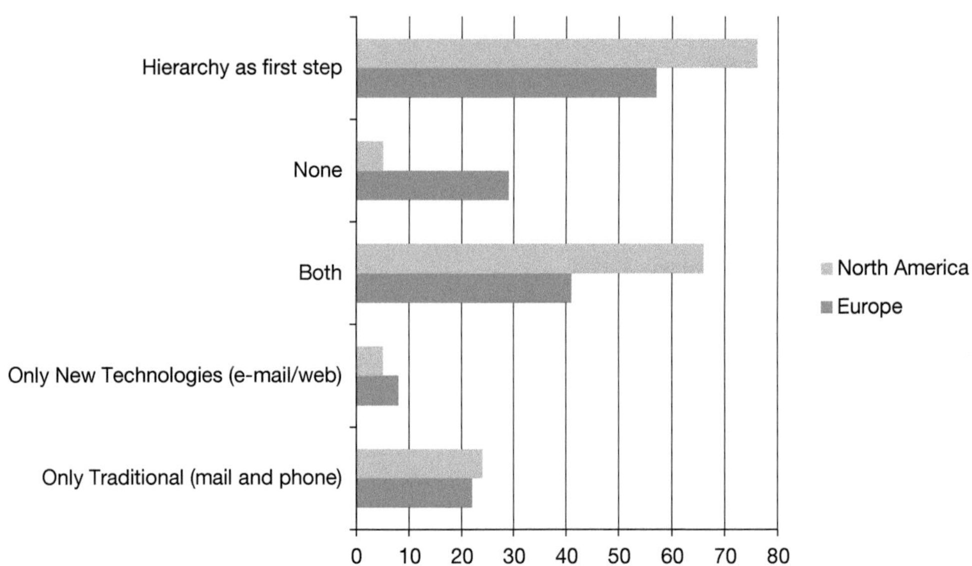

EXHIBIT 11.9—Ethics Hotlines Implementation Mechanism

As the above shows, ethics hotlines and whistle-blowing programs are very prevalent and likely to become more widespread in the future. We will revisit this issue again in Chapter 12 as we discuss some of the ethics hotlines' best practices.

Ethics Training

A final aspect of making a multinational more ethical is a training program. As you will see in Chapter 12, any multinational must ensure that employees are aware of all aspects of ethics in the company. For instance, if the company has a code of conduct, it must ensure that employees are aware of the content of the code. To do so, employees must be trained to understand the key principles behind such codes and ensure that employees are all on the same wavelength regarding these principles. As such, the training program can play a critical role in ensuring that employees are adequately informed of and socialized in the values and principles the company wants to live by.

What objectives do companies want to achieve when conducting training programs? A recent study of global companies based in the U.S. reveals some interesting insights.[31] The author surveyed the responsible ethics officers of 71 multinationals that are based in the U.S. Exhibit 11.10 below shows the key goals of ethics training.

As Exhibit 11.10 shows, it is not surprising that the goal of ethics training of many multinationals is to make their employees more aware of ethics when these employees are confronted with situations that have ethical implications. Training also plays another awareness function as companies make their employees aware of the standards they need to abide by. It is also important to note that only half of the surveyed companies view ethics training as a way of minimizing lawsuits. If companies want to achieve an ethical culture, they will likely need to see ethics more as a way to get their employees to be ethical for the right reasons.

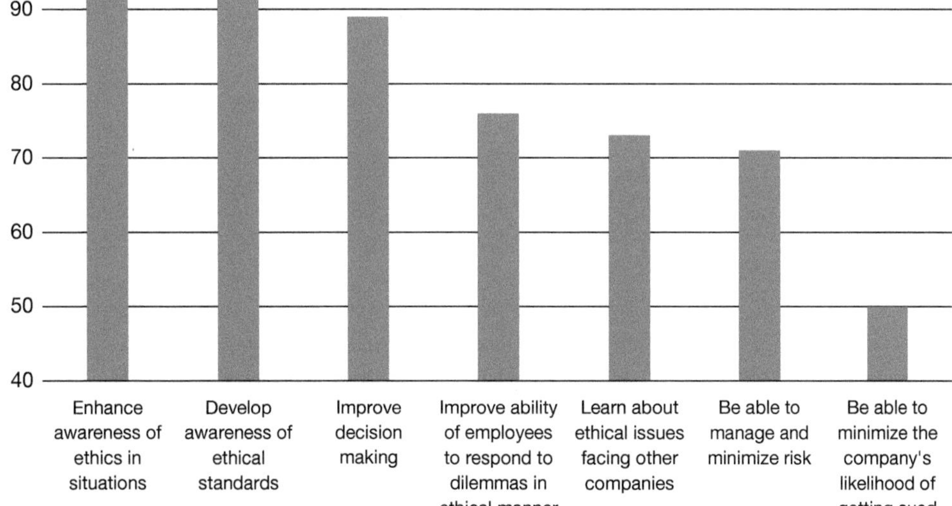

EXHIBIT 11.10—Goals of Ethics Training (% of Firms)

The survey also revealed some areas of concern for multinationals. Below we discuss some of these areas of concern and provide some helpful suggestions for multinationals.[32]

- Lack of resources: Many of the surveyed ethics officers stated that they did not have adequate resources to provide ethics training. If multinationals want ethics training to be effective, they need to provide the necessary resources to ensure that training can be adequately provided to all employees.
- Keeping the training fresh, relevant and appropriate given the diversity of employees: Surveyed ethics officers also complained that it is difficult to keep training fresh given that many of the ethical issues tend to be obvious. Many multinationals report some cultural conflict given the acceptance of some unethical practices (e.g., hiring of family members) in other countries. Given these challenges, it is important for companies to emphasize the reasoning behind the training so that employees are more likely to buy such training. Involvement of employees to help design the training program may also help.
- Training is often short and infrequent: Many ethics officers often complain that ethics training is often too short or infrequent thereby hurting the effectiveness of such training. Multinationals are encouraged to give ethics training its importance by ensuring that employees are trained in depth and regularly.
- Training mode of delivery not effective: Many multinationals relied on online or other forms of technology-enhanced training. However, these forms were not viewed as seriously by employees. Additionally, simply training through lectures is also not seen as effective. Multinationals are therefore strongly advised to use combinations of online, lectures and experiential based activities to make the training more effective. A combination of pedagogical approaches is likely to be seen as more authentic.
- Weak or inexistent assessment of ethics training effectiveness: Many of the ethics officers also complained that there was no strong way to measure the effectiveness of training. Many companies had weak metrics. Multinationals should therefore develop stronger training effectiveness measures. Wider organizational measures of ethics effectiveness tied to revenues or other monetary approaches will also likely be seen as a stronger basis for training.

CHAPTER SUMMARY

In this chapter, you learned about the many ethical aspects facing multinationals. You first read about the various factors determining why ethics differ between countries. You learned that national culture plays an important role in determining how people view ethics in a society. You also read about social institutions such as education and religion and how they also affect the way societies view ethics. The section also discussed the approaches to ethics for multinationals. Some multinationals respect local norms in their ethical decisions and follow ethical relativism. However, others are more likely to adopt a universalist approach and apply the same ethical standards worldwide.

The chapter discussed two of the key ethical issues facing multinationals: labor issues and bribery. You read about the many facets of labor issues such as women workers and child labor. You learned that such issues are not always as black and white as portrayed. For instance, child labor does provide some benefits to children workers. Furthermore, you read about safety issues as related to employees worldwide. The chapter also discussed bribery and the many devastating effects of bribery on societies. Furthermore, you also learned about the many factors motivating multinationals to fight bribery. Important regulations regarding bribery were also discussed.

In the last section of the chapter, you read about the many aspects of an ethical multinational. You read about an approach that provides answers to one of the key ethical questions for multinationals: whether to adopt home ethical country standards or to follow local norms and values. Furthermore, you learned about two unique aspects regarding a multinational's approach to ethics. You read about codes of ethics and the importance of such codes. You also learned about the difficulties of implementing global ethical standards worldwide. In the final section, you read about whistle-blowing and the usefulness of whistle-blowing programs for multinationals. Recent research on the use of ethics hotlines in some of the world's largest multinationals was also reviewed.

NOTES

1 *The Economist*. 2017. "Rolls Royce; Weathering the storm." January 21, 54–55.
2 Levenson, E. 2008. "Citizen Nike." *Fortune*, 158, 10, 165–170.
3 Cullen, J.B., Parboteeah, K.P. & Hoegl, M. 2004. "Cross-national differences in managers' willingness to justify ethically suspect behaviors: A test of institutional anomie theory." *Academy of Management Journal*, 47, 3, 411–421.
4 Seleim, A. & Bontis, N. 2009. "The relationship between culture and corruption: A cross-national study." *Journal of Intellectual Capital*, 10, 1, 165–184.
5 Achim, M.V. 2016. "Cultural dimension of corruption: A cross country survey." *International Advances in Economic Research*, 22, 333–345.
6 Donaldson, T. 1989. "The ethics of international business." In *Ethics and governance*, New York: Oxford University Press, 39–43.
7 French, L. 2010. "Children's labor market involvement, household work, and welfare: A Brazilian case study." *Journal of Business Ethics*, 92, 63–78.
8 Prieto-Carron, M. 2008. "Women workers, industrialization, global supply chains and corporate codes of conduct." *Journal of Business Ethics*, 83, 5–17.
9 Parboteeah, K.P., Hoegl, M. & Cullen, J.B. 2008. "Managers' gender role attitudes: A country institutional profile approach." *Journal of International Business Studies*, 39, 795–813.
10 Prieto-Carron, "Women workers."
11 Berlan, A. 2016. "Whose business is it anyway: Children and corporate social responsibility in the international business agenda." *Children & Society*, 30, 159–168.
12 Gupta, S., Pirsch, J. & Girard, T. 2010. "An empirical examination of a multinational ethical dilemma: The issue of child labor." *Journal of Global Marketing*, 23, 288–305.

13 French, "Children's labor market involvement."
14 Fisman, R. & Svensson, 2007. "Are corruption and taxation really harmful to growth? Firm level evidence." *Journal of Development Economics*, 83, 1, 63–75.
15 Blackburn, K. & Forgues-Puccio, G. 2009. "Why is corruption less harmful in some countries than in others?" *Journal of Economic Behavior & Organization*, 72, 797–810.
16 Compte, O., Lambert-Mogiliansky, A. & Verdier, T. 2005. "Corruption and competition in procurement auctions." *RAND Journal of Economics*, 35, 1, 1–15.
17 Blackburn & Forgues-Puccio, "Why is corruption less harmful in some countries?"
18 www.gov.uk/anti-bribery-policy
19 The UK Bribery Act and US FCPA: Key Differences. 2018. www.acc.com/legalresources/quickcounsel/UKBAFCPA.cfm
20 Hamilton, B., Knouse, S. & Hill, V. 2009. "Google in China: A manager-friendly heuristic model for resolving cross-cultural ethical conflicts." *Journal of Business Ethics*, 86, 143–157.
21 Donaldson, "The ethics of international business."
22 Donaldson, T. & Dunfee, T.W. 1999. *Ties that bind: A social contracts approach to business ethics*. Boston, MA: Harvard Business School Press.
23 Wood, D.J., Logsdon, J.M., Lewellyn, P.G. & Davenport, K. 2006. *Global business citizenship: A transformative framework for ethics and sustainable capitalism*. Armonk, NY: M.E. Sharpe Co.
24 Hamilton et al., "Google in China."
25 Hamilton et al., "Google in China."
26 Stohl, C., Stohl, M. & Popova, L. 2009. "A new generation of corporate codes of ethics." *Journal of Business Ethics*, 90, 607–622.
27 Stohl et al., "A new generation of corporate codes of ethics."
28 Talaulicar, T. 2009. "Barriers against globalizing corporate ethics: An analysis of legal disputes on implementing U.S. codes of ethics in Germany." *Journal of Business Ethics*, 84, 349–360.
29 Calderon, R., Alvarez-Arce, J., Rodriguez-Tejedo, I. & Salvatierra, S. 2009. "Ethics hotlines in transnational companies: A comparative study." *Journal of Business Ethics*, 88, 199–210.
30 Calderon et al., "Ethics hotlines in transnational companies."
31 Weber, J. 2015. "Investigating and assessing the quality of employee ethics training programs among US-based global organizations." *Journal of Business Ethics*, 129, 27–42.
32 Weber, "Investigating and assessing the quality of employee ethics training programs."

KEY TERMS

Bribery: refers to gifts or payments to someone to expedite a government action or to gain some business advantages.

Child labor: the practice of employing children.

Code of ethics: a formalized public statement that articulates the rules and regulations that will guide organizational practices with ethical consequences.

Convergence: belief that many management practices including those related to ethics, are becoming more similar.

Cross-national ethics: the differences that exist between countries when considering ethical issues.

Ethical relativism: ethical viewpoint based on the assumption that there are no objective and universal moral standards.

Ethical universalism: approach based on the notion that basic moral principles transcend cultural and national boundaries.

First generation code of ethics: focus on the legal responsibility of the company.

Global business ethics: apply to the myriad of ethical issues any company faces when operating in the global environment.

HKH: ethical decision-making approach based on key questions.

Hypernorms: norms that are accepted by all cultures and organizations irrespective of local cultures.

Integrated Social Contracts Theory: in this approach, multinationals are expected to make decisions that recognize universally binding ethical practices known as "hypernorms."

Labor issues: the many ethical dilemmas pertaining to labor.

Second generation code of ethics: focus is on the responsibility to stakeholders.

Third generation code of ethics: focus on responsibilities grounded in the wider interconnected environment.

Whistle-blowing programs: shifts ethics monitoring to employees by providing the means to report ethical violations.

Women workers and their rights: key ethical issues pertaining to the employment of women by multinationals.

Work safety: steps multinationals take to ensure that their workers operate in an environment free of harm.

DISCUSSION QUESTIONS

1. What is global business ethics? How is global ethics different from domestic ethics?
2. Discuss some of the factors explaining why global ethics differ worldwide. Explain the cultural and social institutional approach.
3. What are some of the ways multinationals approach ethical decision-making? What are some of the dangers of a relativist approach?
4. What are some of the key ethical issues facing multinationals?
5. What are some of the major challenges facing women workers worldwide? Why do such challenges exist?
6. What is bribery? How is bribery different worldwide? What are some disadvantages of bribery for both multinationals and the societies they operate in?
7. Discuss the key steps in deciding whether a universalist approach or a relativist approach should be used. What important questions does a multinational need to ask?
8. What is a code of ethics? How prevalent are codes of ethics worldwide?
9. What is whistle-blowing? Why do multinationals need a whistle-blowing program?
10. Discuss recent research regarding adopting of ethics hotlines in multinationals worldwide. What are some major lessons?

INTERNET ACTIVITY

1. Go to the Vodafone website: www.vodafone.com.
2. Review the company's corporate responsibility program.
3. What are some of the major elements of Vodafone's effort to implement a global ethical program?
4. Which important stakeholder areas do Vodafone address? What are the important requirements for each area?
5. What lessons do Vodafone provide for multinationals? Is it possible for a multinational to adopt global ethical standards?

For more Internet Activities and resources, visit the Companion Website at www.routledge.com/cw/parboteeah.

WHAT WOULD YOU DO?

A Job in Saudi Arabia

You finish your degree in business administration and are hired to work in the marketing department of a multinational. You perform extremely well two years into the job. Your work ethic and performance stand out among those who were hired at the same time as you. You are personally commended by your supervisor and others at the executive level. You are at a crossroads and need to make the next move to continue your ascent in the company.

You chat with numerous individuals and with your mentor and learn that most successful employees had to work for a few years in a foreign subsidiary of the company. You learn that your company is seriously considering entry into Saudi Arabia. Any employee who can take charge and make the subsidiary successful in Saudi Arabia will likely do very well in the company.

You are seriously considering taking the position. However, as a woman, you know that the work environment in Saudi Arabia for women is not necessarily ideal. You talk to others who have worked there and find that business is divided along gender lines and that it is sometimes tough for women to do business. However, you also hear from others that such attitudes are changing and that women can also be successful in Saudi Arabia.

What do you do? Do you take the challenge and work hard to overcome such attitudes? Or do you seek a global posting in a subsidiary where women are more easily accepted? Why?

BRIEF CASE: BUSINESS ETHICS INSIGHT

Ernst Lieb and Mercedes-Benz

In September 2006, Daimler appointed Ernst Lieb, a German national, to the post of CEO for Mercedes-Benz USA. Prior to coming to the U.S., Mr. Lieb was head of then Daimler Chrysler Australia/Pacific after being CEO of Mercedes Canada. Mr. Lieb was hired to bolster Mercedes cars in the U.S. Upon his arrival, he travelled the U.S. and listened to customers and dealers. He encouraged customers to discuss their problems with him. Dealers were also amazed that he was willing to listen and talk with them for hours. Because most dealers liked him, he was able to push most dealers to adopt a new controversial facilities improvement for the Mercedes dealerships. As of October 2011, he was able to get 300 out of 355 Mercedes-Benz dealerships to adopt new standards or build new stores, spending a combined $1.4 billion since 2008.

According to most dealers, Mr. Lieb was the best thing that happened to Mercedes-Benz USA. Through his leadership, Mercedes-Benz was able to close the gap with its main rival, BMW. While BMW outsold Mercedes by around 40,000 units in 2007, the gap was only around 3738 vehicles in 2010. Many experts predicted that the gap would get even smaller. Furthermore, Mr. Lieb was the major force behind the push for the C-class compact vehicles as well as the C-class coupes. These moves have been hailed as major successes for Mercedes-Benz USA.

However, despite these successes, the automotive community was shocked to hear that Mr. Lieb was fired in October 2011. While Daimler has yet to comment on the matter, the media suggests that Mr. Lieb was fired for repeatedly violating Daimler ethical rules. In one report, Mr. Lieb is accused of taking a personal trip to Australia at company expense. He is also alleged to have used company funds for private expenditures, such as golf club fees as well as building his house in New York. After Daimler had paid $185 million fines to the Department of Justice, Chairman Dieter Zetsche instituted a zero tolerance policy for ethical violations. Mr. Lieb probably violated this policy.

Based on Kurylko, D.T. 2011. "Leib's fall stuns Mercedes-Benz dealers." *Automotive News*, October 24, 86, 6487; Roberts, G. 2011. "Lieb firing reasons emerge in media." *Just-auto Global News*, online edition, October 20; Schulz, J. 2011. "Mercedes fires chief and cancels dealer meeting." *New York Times* online, October 31.

BRIEF CASE QUESTIONS

1. Do you think Daimler is justified in firing Mr. Lieb given his success in the U.S.?
2. What message does the firing send to Mercedes-Benz USA employees and other stakeholders?
3. Mr. Lieb was well liked by most Mercedes-Benz dealers in the U.S. and they were shocked by his firing. What should Daimler do to calm dealer anger?
4. Was there some other way Daimler could have dealt with this issue?

LONG CASE: BUSINESS ETHICS

THE NEED FOR CULTURAL INTELLIGENCE

An Analysis of Asiana Airlines' response to the Crash Landing of Flight 214

Case Study Competition

On July 6, 2013, Asiana Airlines' Flight 214 crashed while attempting to land at the San Francisco International Airport. This case addresses the crisis communication efforts Asiana undertook with key stakeholders in the U.S. in the wake of the crash. It assesses the social and traditional media communication activities of Asiana in the U.S. and how cross-cultural norms affected perceptions of this communication. The crash demonstrates the need for corporate communication professionals at multinational companies to have cross-cultural competence and training. More precisely, the case considers the theory of cultural intelligence, which is defined as the ability to recognize and comprehend different beliefs, practices, attitudes, and behaviors of a group and then apply that certain cultural knowledge to attain your goals—whether those goals are political, business or otherwise. The case is ultimately valuable to all global companies building their cross-cultural acumen.

II. Case Study

A. Overview

On July 6, 2013, 291 passengers boarded a Boeing 777 on Asiana Airlines' Flight 214 without a worry in sight. Passengers were flying from Incheon, South Korea to San Francisco, California. What was thought to be a regular sunny day turned into everyone's nightmare. At 11:27 a.m., the flight crashed while attempting to land at the San Francisco International Airport. Out of 291 passengers, there were three fatalities and over 180 injured.

Passengers and witnesses alike were shaken. According to passenger Lee Jang Hyung, who was flying with his wife, baby, and parents-in-law, "Suddenly, the plane's tail part hit the ground and the aircraft bounced upwards and then bam, it hit the ground again. This time it felt like the entire plane hit parallel, but tilted to the left. That pressure was huge. Very strong. I saw luggage fall from the top. And the plane gradually stopped. Until then, there was no warning," Hyung said. Hyung called it a close call and is grateful that his family survived.

Timeline of Events as Flight 214 Makes Final Approach[i]

11:27 a.m.

- *8 seconds before impact*—Call in cockpit for increased speed (Flight 214 travelling at 112 knots at 125 feet above the ground)
- *3 seconds before impact*—Engines at 50% power and engine power increasing (Flight 214 travelling at 103 knots)

- *1.5 seconds before impact*—No distress calls are made asking air traffic control to abort the landing. From cockpit recordings, the pilot is heard saying "go around."

11:30 a.m.—Emergency exit slides are deployed.

11:35 a.m.

- Rescue crews race to the aircraft.
- It is noticed that at two of the exits, emergency exit slides incorrectly inflated inside the aircraft which pinned some of the flight attendants to the wall inside.

1:00 p.m.

- Injured passengers and crew are taken to the hospital, while the critically injured are taken sooner.
- "The most critically injured people came right away. Some of them had burns, they had fractures, they had internal injuries, internal bleeding, also head injuries . . . we also saw spinal injuries," said San Francisco General Hospital and Trauma Center spokeswoman Rachael Kagan.

4.18 p.m.

- The first two fatalities are confirmed: Wang Linjia and Ye Mengyuan (both 16-year-old students from China). Mother is seen crying over two daughters.

7:47 p.m.

- All passengers and crew are accounted for and NTSB (National Transportation Safety Board) launches full safety investigation.

The Cause

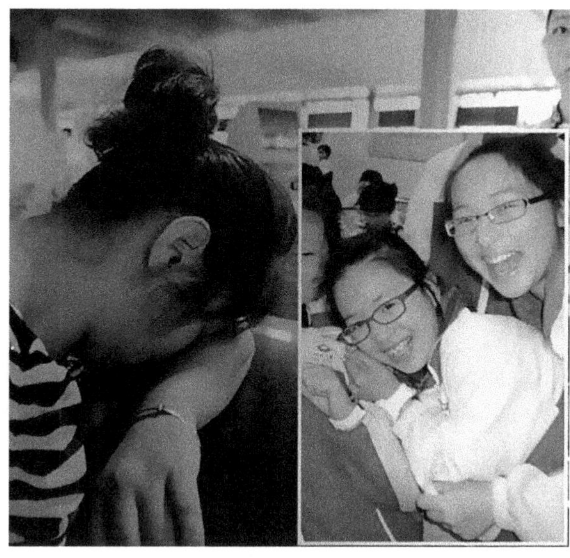

Immediately following the crash landing, individuals, news outlets, and key stakeholders like the NTSB scrambled to find the cause of the crash. There was much speculation around the actual cause.

Initially, mechanical error was rumored to be the cause. The *Huffington Post* reported that the key device control called the automatic throttle might have malfunctioned, which might not have sent enough power to the engine to abort the landing.[ii] Since then, the NTSB has ruled out mechanical error. However, most of the speculation placed blame on the pilots. Fatigue was ruled out immediately, which left many news outlets and individuals on social media turning to the pilots' experience. According to the *Wall Street Journal*, many have argued that the pilots lacked manual flying skills.[iii] Pilot Lee Kang Kuk had only 43 hours of flight experience with a Boeing 777, which is the equivalent of nine flights. When the plane crashed, Lee Kang Kuk was flying under the supervision of Pilot Lee Jeong-min, who is considered a veteran pilot. There is speculation that the pilots ignored warning signals in the cockpit.[iv] Airline officials have refuted the allegation that the pilots were not experienced enough, stating that the pilots have had thousands of hours of prior training.[v] There have also been differences between the pilots' recollection of the crash and the cockpit recordings. Whatever the reason of the crash, what is known is that there was not enough power available to abort the landing.[vi] What really happened then, you ask?

While the official NTSB investigation can take six to nine months to determine the result of the crash, there are a few things known. In the final moments of the regular 11-hour flight, Flight 214 experienced what is called a "hard landing" that turned out to be short of the actual landing strip. The aircraft was traveling below landing speed and was too low as it approached the threshold. The plane was roughly 80 feet away from the runway when it crashed. A piece of the tail clipped the seawall at the end of the runway, which caused the Boeing 777 to hit the tarmac hard.[vii] Within 90 seconds, a blaze ignited close to the bay waters and debris scattered immediately **(See Appendix A)**. According to NTSB Chairman Deborah Hersman, the most seriously injured passengers were sitting in the rear of the aircraft. Two of the fatalities occurred from the actual flight. The third fatality, according to San Francisco Police Officer Albie Esparza, was completely covered in flame-retardant foam when a fire truck ran over the student as it was trying to fight the fire. An autopsy-report done by San Mateo County Coroner Robert Foucrault confirmed death by injuries consistent with the fire truck.[viii] At the end of the day, much is still left to be determined, as the NTSB is still reviewing cockpit recordings, the aircraft mechanics, and testimonials from survivors.

On December 11, 2013, the NTSB announced that the hearing has adjourned however the investigation remains ongoing. According to the information the NTSB released that same day, the veteran pilot, Lee Kang Kuk had momentarily adjusted the power without realizing the plane's computers then assumed he wanted the engine to remain at idle. According to NTSB documents, in some combinations of auto-throttle and autopilot settings, such as during Flight 214's approach to SFO, the system becomes dormant.[ix]

The two pilots, Lee Kang Kuk and Lee Jeong-min, still work for the airline however they have not flown since the accident. On January 1, 2014, Kim Soo Cheon took over as CEO. A spokesperson for the airline said that the "personnel change has nothing to do with the accident."[x] To strengthen pilot training the airline has hired Akiyoshi Yamamura, a veteran Japanese pilot and safety expert, as Chief Safety and Security Manager. This is Asiana's first foreign hire in its 25-year history.[xi]

B. A History of Asiana Airlines

Asiana Airlines Company Background

Asiana Airlines, Inc. is one of South Korea's two major airlines, along with Korean Air. Asiana Airlines, the smaller of the two airlines, was founded on February 17, 1988 and is headquartered in Seoul, South Korea. The company has a fleet of 80 aircraft as of April 2013. Asiana serves 12 cities on 14 routes domestically, 24 countries and 73 cities on 93 routes internationally. The company provides service routes for international cargo to 14 countries and 29 cities on 27 routes.[xii] As of August 2013, the airline staffs 10,381 employees and maintains an average of 15 million passengers annually. The airlines domestic hub is located at Gimpo International Airport and its international hub at Incheon International Airport, which is 43 miles from central Seoul. Asiana Airlines is also one of the 13 primary sponsors of the South Korean national football team.

Korean Air, which was privatized in 1969, monopolized the South Korean airline industry until Asiana was founded in 1988. Asiana Airlines, originally known as Seoul Air International, was not formed to promote liberalized market conditions but rather because of the pressure from potential shareholders along with chaebols, family controlled industrial conglomerates in South Korea, that wanted to compete.[xiii] Asiana Airline's parent company is Kumho Asiana Group. According to an article in the *Journal of Air Transport Management*, the Park family closely holds the "Kumho Chaebol."[xiv] Kumho Asiana Group was founded by Park In-cheon in 1946 and currently, the Chairman of the group is Park Sam-Koo.[xv]

Asiana Airlines Corporate Philosophy

Asiana Airlines' corporate philosophy appears on the company website as follows:

> "*The highest value of Asiana Airlines is to achieve customer satisfaction with the maximum safety and service. As an international airline, we will provide the greatest flight service for each one of our customers in the safest way. Asiana Airlines' goal of a beautiful future through thorough customer satisfaction management will continue.*" [xvi]

According to Star Alliance, a global grouping of carriers, Asiana Airlines adopted the term "uncompromising safety" as its mission statement with the aim of guiding every thought and action of its employees.[xvii] To maintain this promise, Star Alliance goes on to explain that Asiana upholds the most modern fleet worldwide and that the airline was the first in the world to be granted ISO 9002 certification on aircraft maintenance, which means that that airline meets a certain criteria for quality assurance in production, installation, and servicing. [xviii]

In February, just four months before the fatal crash at SFO, Asiana Airlines celebrated its 25th anniversary and its 10th anniversary of joining the Star Alliance, the largest airline code-share alliance in the world, which allows passengers to accumulate airline miles.[xix] Last year, *Business Traveler* magazine called Asiana Airlines the "Best Overall Airline in the World."[xx] Consulting service Skytrax, based in the United Kingdom, awarded Asiana "Airline of the Year" in 2010.[xxi]

For the third quarter, Asiana reported its first profit in 2013. The July–September quarter earnings of $82.8 billion won ($77.8 million) were up 3.3% over the year earlier. But, the third-quarter operating income plunged 42% to $63.4 billion won while sales dropped 3% to $1.52 trillion won.[xxii] Asiana Airlines makes more than half of its revenue from overseas flights.[xxiii] However, this year the company's passenger business was hit by lower demand for flights from Japan to South Korea because of the weaker yen and bombast from North Korea threatening nuclear war. Asiana Airlines remained in the red for the first nine months of this year, with a net loss totaling $45.6 billion won.[xxiv] This is unrelated to the plunge following the Flight 214 crash.

Past Crises

The company has experienced two other major fatal crashes in its 25-year history. Asiana Airlines' first major incident was in 1993 when Flight 733—a Boeing 737–500—crashed in poor weather while approaching Mokpo airport in South Korea, killing 68 out of 116 occupants, including two crew members. In July 2011, a cargo plane—a Boeing 747–400F—slammed into the East China Sea, killing the only two people on board. The plane crashed due to a reported in-flight fire en route from Seoul's Incheon International Airport to Shanghai Pudong International Airport in China.[xxv]

Korean Air also experienced numerous accidents during this period of time. In 1997, a Korean Air flight crashed while approaching Guam Island during a rainstorm killing 228 people. In April 1999, a Korean Air flight crashed after takeoff from Shanghai killing 8 people, and another crash in December 1999 after takeoff from London

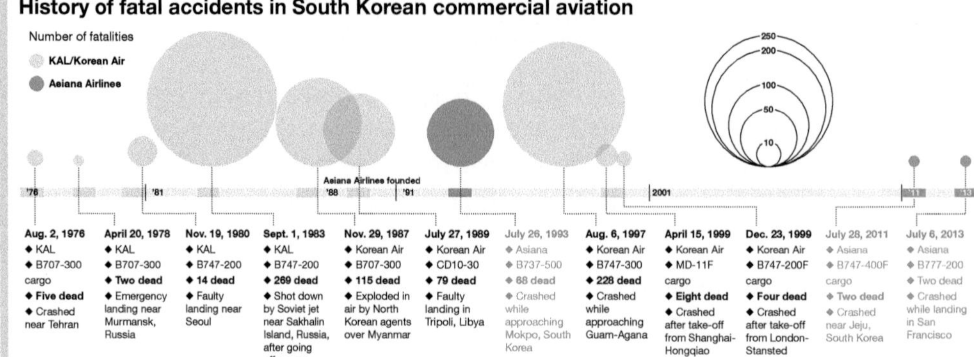

Photo Source: *Wall Street Journal,* "Asiana's Response to San Francisco Plane Crash Draws Notice."

killing four. Korean Air experienced a third crash in 1999, which was not fatal, when the jet skidded off the runway while landing in Pohang, South Korea.[xxvi]

After these crashes and fatal accidents in South Korean commercial aviation, the Federal Aviation Administration downgraded South Korea's safety system's ratings in 2001, saying the country's aviation authority did not comply with the International Civil Aviation Organization's standards. After changes were made, the restrictions were lifted in December of that year.[xxvii]

C. Crisis Communication Strategy

With much information still to be determined, it is important to address the crisis communication efforts with Asiana Airlines' key stakeholders in the United States: the media/general public, victims/families, and employees.

Within a minute of the crash, Krista Seiden, who was boarding another plane, posted a photo on Twitter of the incident. Less than 20 minutes later, a stream of journalists started using the live feed on Twitter to get immediate updates on what happened. Journalists from places like Bloomberg News and NPR made multiple attempts via Twitter to ask for an interview with Krista. Within a day of the incident, Krista's photo and tweets were quoted in thousands of articles. Krista was not the only person posting photos via social media.[xxviii]

Some of the passengers used social media to get word out that they were alive and to report on the crash. A passenger named David Eun posted the first photo via Twitter less than a few hours after the incident. David stated, "I just crash landed at SFO. Tail ripped off. Most everyone seems fine. I'm ok. Surreal . . ."[xxix] People flocked to social media outlets to find information about Flight 214. According to the *Wall Street Journal,* David Eun's tweets prompted a flood of well-wishes and questions.[xxx] Hashtags such as #SFOcrash were utilized. People went to social media to find news updates and some also acted as news reporters themselves. Everyone was searching for information.

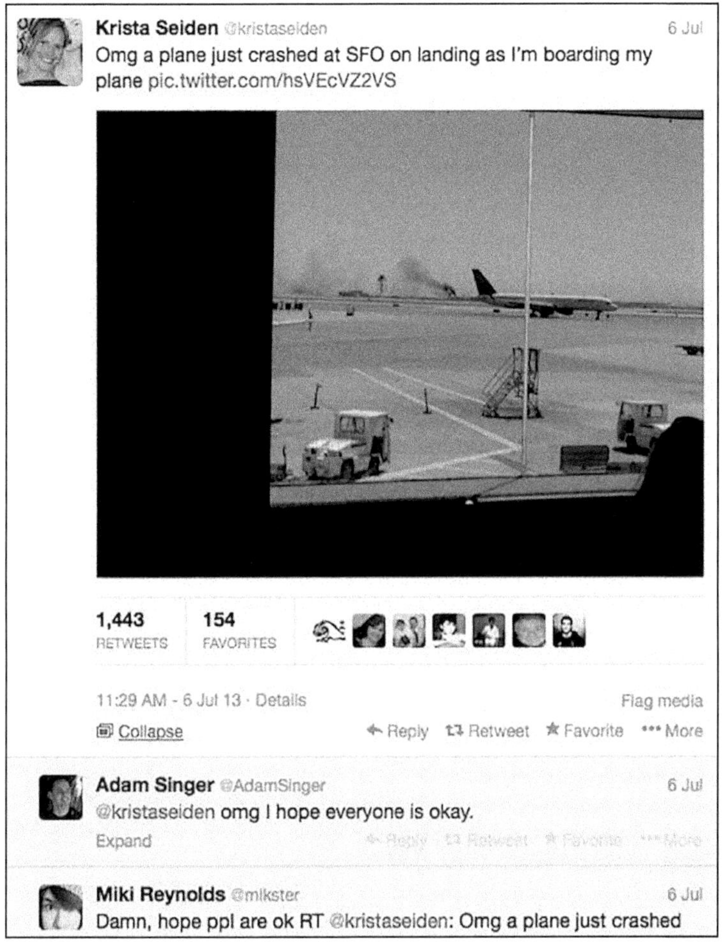

Krista Seiden @kristaseiden
6 Jul
Omg a plane just crashed at SFO on landing as I'm boarding my plane pic.twitter.com/hsVEcVZ2VS
1,443 RETWEETS
154 FAVORITES
11:29 AM - 6 Jul 13 · Details
Flag media
Collapse
Reply
Retweet
Favorite
More
Adam Singer @AdamSinger
6 Jul
@kristaseiden omg I hope everyone is okay.
Expand
Miki Reynolds @mikster
6 Jul
Damn, hope ppl are ok RT @kristaseiden: Omg a plane just crashed

What was lacking was information from credible organizations such as Asiana Airlines, NTSB, or Boeing.

Communication to Media/General Public

Response finally came a little after 1 p.m. PT. Boeing and the NTSB were the first entities to respond via Twitter. The entities recognized the situation and informed viewers that they were gathering information. By approximately 3:50 p.m., the NTSB held a press conference while also doing continuous update with photos to Twitter. In less than an hour after this, the White House released a statement stating, "[Obama's] thoughts and prayers go out to the families who lost a loved one and all those affected by the crash."[xxxi] At this time, everyone was still turning to Asiana Airlines' social media feeds for a live update.

Around this same time as the White House Statement, Asiana Airlines finally joins in on the action. Asiana Airlines released its first statement via Twitter giving its thoughts and prayers to the passengers and crew on the flight. Seven hours after the flight, Asiana releases a press statement via Twitter, Facebook, Google+, and the

company website **(See Appendix B)**. The press release states that Asiana Airlines is working to determine the cause of the incident and that the airline is cooperating with government agencies during the investigation. The release finishes with Asiana Airlines claiming that nothing else can be confirmed at that point in time. Since then, four additional press releases were posted for the general public and media to view. Asiana Airlines did not respond to any comments posted via social media and declined any media attention outside of Korea. On social media, since July 13th, Asiana Airlines has returned back to its regular communication strategy, which consists of many consistent customer service support and promotion on flights, contests, and new technology. The CEO of the airlines has since then stated his plans to improve the training for its pilots, but has not given specifics as to what those plans are due to the ongoing investigation at this point. Besides the changes made to personnel, communication is forthcoming on the airlines' plan of attack moving forward.

Communication to the Victims/Families

Asiana Airlines' crisis communication strategy in the following days replicated the slow response rate of day one. The airline created a toll-free emergency hotline for passengers and families to find out updates. However, the hotline was not put up on Asiana Airlines' website until nine hours after the crash landing. According to the *Wall Street Journal*, "It took three days for Asiana Airlines to dispatch its chief executive and a team of staffers to Saturday's plane-crash site at San Francisco International Airport, where the executive was set to apologize, meet with federal officials and call for a thorough investigation."[xxxii] Asiana Airlines has also rejected offers to form a communication team in the United States to help respond to questions

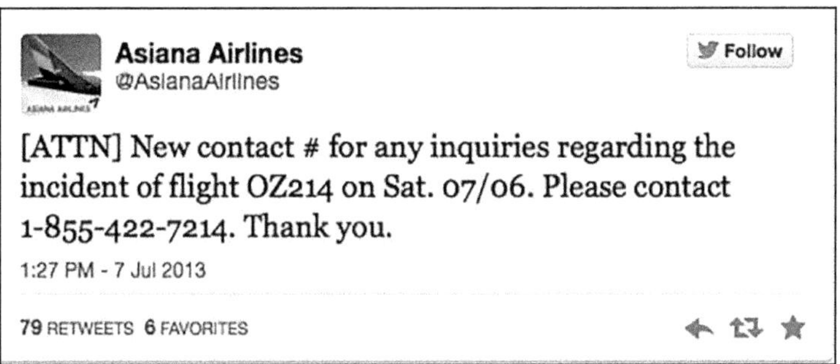

from families or the media. When the airlines hotline was flooded with calls, Asiana Airlines had to set up additional lines to call. According to *CBS News*, the Associated Press said that Asiana Airlines originally "posted an automated reservations number and, changed the number several times in the following days."[xxxiii] From July 6th through July 13th, five press releases had been posted on the company website. The releases provide Asiana Airlines' condolences, emergency hotline information, and brief information as to how the airline is servicing the victims. The latest press release offers the airlines' condolences for the first two fatalities of the crash **(See Appendix C).** CEO, Yoon Young-Doo is noted saying:

> *"My deepest condolences go out to the grieving family and loved ones of this passenger and to all those who have been affected by this regretful situation. We will devote all attention and efforts to support the families of the victims and expedited recoveries for the other injured passengers."*[xxxiv]

The Facebook and Twitter posts on Asiana Airlines' page reiterates hotline contact information and directs viewers to the company website to view the press releases **(See Appendix D).** Visible information regarding Flight 214 concludes after July 13th.

Other communication and services were provided to the victims and families of the crash, but many news outlets or even the airlines did not promote this information. Necessary airfare and lodging was provided to passengers and families with the support of United Continental Holdings Inc., who opened its airport lounges and helped provide emergency assistance. The airline relied heavily on United in the aftermath. United even sent representatives to hospitals to act as liaisons to those injured.[xxxv] Temporary passports were also provided to passengers who lost theirs in the crash. In some cases, family members of the extremely injured were flown to the United States. The airlines worked to provide medical, lodging, meals, translation, and transportation services to families.[xxxvi] Financially, the airline provided a great deal of support.

Communication to the Employees

Information available about communication related to employees in the crash and on employees actions following the crash is very miniscule. Besides an initial tweet offering the airlines' thoughts and prayers to the passengers and crew, the employees affected are not mentioned. There is also no mention of a settlement. However, there are a number of statements from the airlines defending the pilots' experience when it is questioned. Other than diffusing rumors, not much praise or information is given on the employees' actions taken following the crash. The press releases acknowledge the number of crewmembers on board the aircraft at the time of the crash. At the July 9th press conference, Asiana Airlines communicated that employees were working around the clock to assist passengers and that more employees would be on-site soon to provide aid. The communication regarding employees comes off with a sense of urgency. It gives the impression that the airline and its employees will "spare no efforts" to help the passengers. However, it does not provide information as to how the affected crewmembers responded during the crash or how support will be given to them.

D. Stakeholder Response in the United States

The United States did not respond well to Asiana Airlines' crisis communication strategy to the crash landing for a number of reasons. First, upon his arrival in the U.S., Asiana's President and CEO, Yoon Young-Doo, declined to speak to the South Korean and U.S. reporters who mobbed him at the airport, and no one spoke on his behalf, giving the impression he had something to hide. According to Glenn F. Bunting, who runs G.F. Bunting, a San Francisco-based strategic communications company that specializes in crisis management, there is a need for the media spokesperson, in this case the CEO, to assure the public that everything is going to be okay and that the airline is safe.[xxxvii] Jonathan Bernstein, a U.S.-based consultant and crisis manager, compared Asiana's response to that of JetBlue Airways Corp., which came under fire in 2007 for keeping passengers on the tarmac during rough weather. Jetblue's then-CEO, David Neeleman, "got out there," Mr. Bernstein said. "He put a face, a real human compassionate face on the crisis, and I think Asiana needs to find someone who can speak for them like that."[xxxviii] In this case, Asiana failed to address the needs and concerns of its stakeholders in the United States. Some argued that Asiana Airlines took "an inordinate amount of time" to respond to the crisis.[xxxix] On the other hand, a number of organizations like the SFO, NTSB, Boeing, and other influential journalists were praised for the constant and immediate updates posted on their social media sites regarding Flight 214.

While Asiana Airlines' communication with society did occur in less than 24 hours, its communication was scrutinized because Asiana Airlines' response came after other organizations had already provided multiple updates. Mary Kirby, a social media savvy Facebook user, posted:

> *"The fact that Asiana Airlines has not yet made a statement on Twitter or Facebook about the 777 crash at the SFO is unacceptable."*[xl]

Within a day, Asiana Airlines' "Facebook fan engagement increased by 50%, while Twitter followers grew by 4,000 . . ."[xli] However, as previously stated, Asiana Airlines did not utilize this reach a great deal to get information out about the crash landing. Asiana Airlines did not respond to comments or concerns on any social media account. Asiana Airlines was also scrutinized for the delay in dispatching the CEO to speak to the media and visit the location of the incident. In a country where companies have crisis communication plans already prepared, many felt that Asiana Airlines' response was extremely slow. As said in the *Wall Street Journal*, Asiana Airlines' approach "is foreign to many U.S.-based crisis managers, who help clients develop elaborate plans and targeted messaging far in advance of potential problems.[xlii]

What concerned Americans characterized as a lack of immediate action on Asiana Airlines' part, only further developed into frustration. Asiana Airlines communication even after its initial response was looked at negatively for the lack of posts. For example, Asiana Airlines only posted ten times on Facebook, and most of it leads people to the website to view press conference information or the emergency hotline number. With this, the airlines declined to speak to any media journalists outside of Korea immediately following the crash. There was instant media backlash from many influential journalists and a large amount of bloggers in the United States.

The victims/families were also not thrilled with the airline. Families were completely dependent on the airline following the incident and complaints started to arise. Haijun Xu, a passenger on Flight 214, was told by Asiana to not speak with the media. His daughter cried, "We did not get any help except the $400 emergency fee" that would cover the basics such as food. While the family was provided lodging, the family was forced to sleep three people to a bed due to the amount of lodging space provided to them.[xliii] Many families like the Xus have decided to sue Asiana Airlines. The Aviation Disaster Family Assistance Act was passed in 1996. The law requires carriers—now, both foreign and domestic— to regularly file with the NTSB detailed plans for assisting families of those injured or killed in plane crashes.[xliv] Federal agents are now investigating whether or not the airline met its legal obligation to support the passengers and families of Flight 214.

E. Cross-Cultural Communication

There is undoubtedly room for improvement when it comes to Asiana Airlines' focus on providing reassurance to nervous flyers in the aftermath of a fatal plane crash. In the hours after the crash, Asiana was slow to respond to the overwhelming need for information at the rate at which the United States is accustomed. Why did the airline provide such a perplexing response, based on U.S. norms, to Flight 214's crash?

Directly after the accident and while still in Korea, Asiana's President and CEO Yoon Young-Doo made several public apologies, along with statements about the experience of the plane's pilots. Yoon Young-Doo held a news conference in Seoul with several board members present explaining what the company knew, offering condolences for the victims, and defending the airlines' pilots and planes.[xlv] However, the Seoul-based airline issued few statements in the U.S. and declined to arrange for any media representatives outside of Korea. The carrier said it has received offers from stateside communications companies eager to help manage the crisis and had an uninterested response.

> *"It's not the proper time to manage the company's image," said an Asiana representative in Korea, when asked about the company's response to outside assistance.*[xlvi]

Jee-eun Song studies South Korean culture as a lecturer in Asian studies at UC Berkeley and told *San Jose Mercury News* that Asiana officials may have thought its initial apology to victims and families in South Korea would "cover them in San Francisco in the days following the crash."[xlvii]

On July 12, the Fox affiliate in Oakland, KTVU, reported on an anonymous tip, which turned out to be an embarrassing gaffe. The KTVU anchor identified the pilots in its noon broadcast over the weekend as "Sum Ting Wong," "Wi Tu Lo," "Ho Lee Fuk," and "Bang Ding Ow"—obvious racially insensitive names. They cited the NTSB as their source. It turns out an NTSB intern answered the phone when KTVU called and mistakenly confirmed the fake pilot names.[xlviii] Asiana threatened to sue the television station after the false report but dropped those plans a few days later. Several critics of Asiana Airlines' crisis management found the company's uproar towards KTVU out of place. The airline should have been concentrating on the passengers of Flight 214 and its other nervous travelers, but the airlines focus seemed to be on the Bay Area television station that fell victim to a humorless prank.[xlix]

Business Insider reported that the airline also attempted to silence the passengers of Flight 214.[l] The Xu family, previously referred to, was among those passengers and featured in a story on *CBS This Morning.* In the interview that took place at the hotel room the family was provided, the Xu family told the CBS reporter that the airline told them not to speak with media. The CBS reporter had to tape this interview with his smartphone because airline security called the police when they spotted his camera crew in the hotel lobby. The journalist was eventually allowed upstairs but constrained to using his iPhone's camera.[li]

Asiana Airlines' crisis communication tactics in the aftermath of Flight 214 may seem strange and its priorities out of place. But, perhaps Asiana's response is not as strange as it is just different from the U.S. norm. Simply saying, Korean corporate culture contrasts with several corporate practices in the Western world. Koreans responded well to the efforts Asiana took.

South Korean Corporate Culture

James Chung, chief partner at Strategy Salad, a crisis communications firm based in Seoul said that "Few big Korean companies take outside counseling if a crisis happens." That contrasts with common practice in the U.S., where crisis managers help clients develop on plans and messages for dealing with problems far in advance. South Korea's top managers hesitate to use outside counsel because they think it could interfere with management and decision-making processes. Chung told the *Wall Street Journal*, "They think 'Why do we need outside help when we have strong internal public relations?'".[lii]

South Korea's corporate culture, like the Korean economic boom of the last few decades, is much-studied. Part of it has to do with the way South Korea's economy grew: with a heavy guiding hand from the state.[liii] The government helped a number of once-small companies consolidate into massive conglomerates known as chaebols, which are often family-run and have since accumulated tremendous political and economic power. According to a 2005 article on chaebols in the *Journal of Consumer Psychology*, "Korean consumers have a strong attachment to chaebols with which they associate quality and, in turn, trust," with the chaebols serving as a kind of extension of Confucian ideals of the family.[liv] Thus, Asiana is treated as a family business by its employees and South Korean consumers. That sense of family loyalty may be why South Koreans were eager to defend or sympathize with Asiana after the crash.[lv]

The "Kumho Chaebol", also known as the Kumho Asiana Group, owns Asiana Airlines.[lvi] In efforts of upholding quality and trust associated with chaebols, Yoon and the board's first response to the public was a press conference where they offered a solemn apology to the victims and defending the pilots. Initially, Asiana Airlines may have resisted the public's demand for information out of respect for the victims. To a U.S. audience, this may have seemed like a muted response.

III. Cultural Intelligence?

Asiana Airlines must alter its tactical view on cultural intelligence if they hope to survive in this global economy. Cultural intelligence is defined as one's ability to function in places that are characterized by cultural diversity. Cultural intelligence is the ability to build relationships with different cultures and respond effectively to them, which Asiana Airlines failed to do with people in the United States. This case displays the importance of cross-cultural sensitivity and the need for preparedness during a crisis in our global economy. Cross-cultural challenges have become increasingly more common and thus more important to look into for large corporations. This is due in large part to globalization and cross-national business. Stakeholder differentiation across countries in this crisis would have allowed the airlines to create an altered response to the United States and avoided such backlash.

In order to possess this idea of cultural intelligence, Asiana Airlines must first accept and adapt to new media. With more and more people using social media on desktops and on mobile devices, access to news has become instant. Social media has become so crucial to communication teams that employers have started recruiting job seekers highly experienced with social media. In 2012 alone, "over 43% of people aged 20–29 spent more than 10 hours a week on social media sites."[lvii] This has only increased in the past year. Social media has an influence on what people think and what they view. This case has offered an in-depth look into the rising importance of social media in the United States and the need for crisis communication teams. Asiana

Airlines failed to realize the vital role social media played in Americans' perception of the airlines response to the crash.

Asiana Airlines is now seeing the results of its crisis communication response. The stock price took a big hit. Within a day, Asiana Airlines' stock price dropped by 5.8% and within a month, it dropped by 6.64%.[lviii] The company reached an all-time low on April 12, 2013 and is still struggling to bring back the stock to what it used to be. The impact of the communication will not only affect the shareholder value.

There is also now a lack of trust with the airline and an image concern in the United States. Asiana Airlines' code, OZ, embodies the airlines mission statement: "uncompromising safety." However, the airlines reputation has taken a hit as many have decided to switch carriers due to the airlines inability to live up to its mission. According to Bloomberg News, one frequent flyer of the airline stated that she will switch to Korean Air due to safety concerns for her children.[lix] This is the second crash since 2011. Moving forward, Asiana Airlines is faced with the task of repairing and restoring the credibility the airline once had as being one of the safest airlines to fly with.

Nonetheless, Asiana Airlines is not the only company to avoid adapting to different cultures. There is a great need for more research on cross-cultural corporate communication. Literature on cross-cultural communication is miniscule all-around. The crisis will serve as a teaching example for the future and shed light on the need for cultural intelligence.

* * *

IV. Appendices

Appendix A[lx]

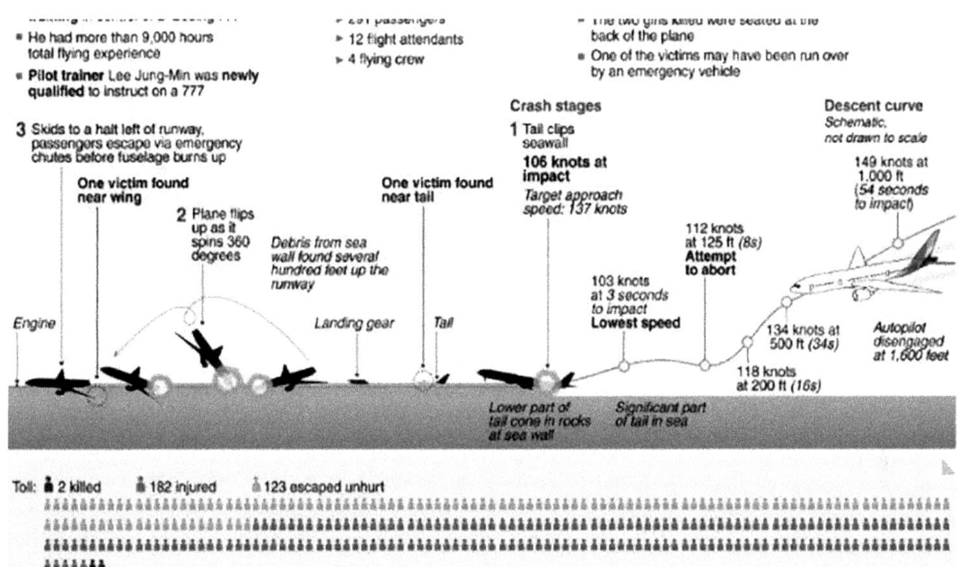
He had more than 9,000 hours total flying experience
Pilot trainer Lee Jung-Min was newly qualified to instruct on a 777
12 flight attendants
4 flying crew
back of the plane
One of the victims may have been run over by an emergency vehicle
Crash stages
Descent curve
Schematic, not drawn to scale
3 Skids to a halt left of runway, passengers escape via emergency chutes before fuselage burns up
One victim found near wing
2 Plane flips up as it spins 360 degrees
Debris from sea wall found several hundred feet up the runway
One victim found near tail
1 Tail clips seawall
106 knots at impact
Target approach speed: 137 knots
149 knots at 1,000 ft (54 seconds to impact)
112 knots at 125 ft (8s)
Attempt to abort
103 knots at 3 seconds to impact
Lowest speed
134 knots at 500 ft (34s)
Autopilot disengaged at 1,600 feet
118 knots at 200 ft (16s)
Engine
Landing gear
Tail
Lower part of tail cone in rocks at sea wall
Significant part of tail in sea
Toll: 2 killed 182 injured 123 escaped unhurt

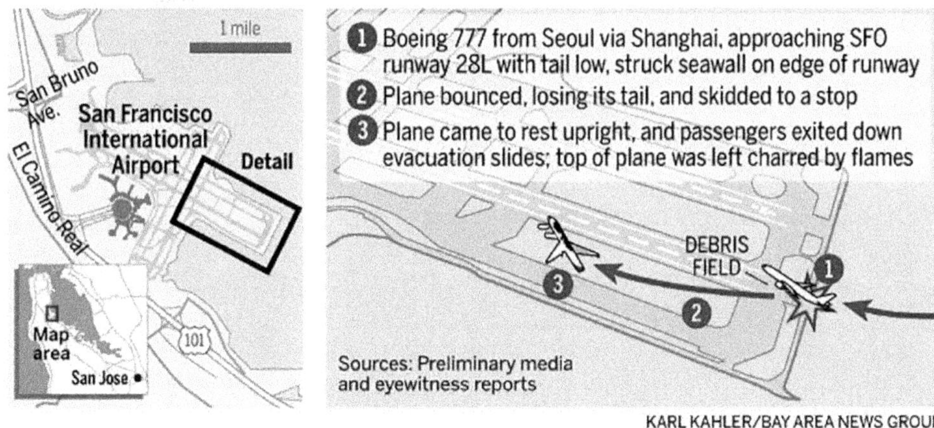
How it happened
1 mile
San Bruno Ave.
El Camino Real
San Francisco International Airport
Detail
Map area
San Jose
101
1 Boeing 777 from Seoul via Shanghai, approaching SFO runway 28L with tail low, struck seawall on edge of runway
2 Plane bounced, losing its tail, and skidded to a stop
3 Plane came to rest upright, and passengers exited down evacuation slides; top of plane was left charred by flames
DEBRIS FIELD
Sources: Preliminary media and eyewitness reports
KARL KAHLER/BAY AREA NEWS GROUP

Appendix B – Released via Social Media[xi]

ASIANA AIRLINES
Shared publicly · Jul 6, 2013 #SFO

Press Release for Incident Involving Asiana Flight OZ 214 (July 7, 2013 06:30 KOR.Time)

The following information has been confirmed.

Asiana Airlines flight OZ214 (Aircraft Registration HL7742) departed Incheon International Airport on July 6, 2013 at 16:35 (Korea time) bound for San Francisco. On July 6, 2013 at 11:28 (Local time) an accident occurred as OZ214 was making a landing on San Francisco International Airport's runway 28.

There were a total of 291 passengers (19 business class, 272 travel class) and 16 cabin crew aboard. The majority of the passengers were comprised of 77 Korean citizens, 141 Chinese citizens, 61 US citizens, 1 Japanese citizen, etc. for a total of 291 people.

Asiana Airlines is currently investigating the specific cause of the incident as well as any injuries that may have been sustained to passengers as a result. Asiana Airlines will continue to cooperate fully with the investigation of all associated government agencies and to facilitate this cooperation has established an emergency response center at its headquarters.

At this point no additional information has been confirmed. New developments will be announced as more information becomes available. .

■ Asiana Airlines Emergency Response Center: Asiana Town Operational Command Center, Seoul
■ Press Center: Asiana Town, Training Center Room #101, Seoul
(Dongwon Kim : 82-11-498-5921 / Gyeongtaek Park : 82-17-721-1236)

#SFO #asianaairlines #OZ214 #sanfrancisco

Show less

+82 47

Appendix C – Asiana Airlines' Press Releases

| Press Release

Press Release for Incident Involving Asiana Flight HL7742 - July 7, 2013 06:30 (Kor. Time) 2013-07-07 10:02

The following information has been confirmed.

Asiana Airlines flight HL7742 departed Incheon International Airport on July 6, 2013 at 16:35 (Korea ti me) bound for San Francisco. Only July 7, 2013 at 11:28 (Local time) an accident occurred as HL774 2 was making a landing on San Francisco International Airport's runway 28.

There were a total of 291 passengers (19 business class, 272 travel class) and 16 cabin crew aboard. The majority of the passengers were comprised of 77 Korean citizens, 141 Chinese citizens, 61 US cit izens, 1 Japanese citizen, etc. for a total of 291 people.

Asiana Airlines is currently investigating the specific cause of the incident as well as any injuries that may have been sustained to passengers as a result. Asiana Airlines will continue to cooperate fully wi th the investigation of all associated government agencies and to facilitate this cooperation has establi shed an emergency response center at its headquarters.

At this point no additional information has been confirmed. New developments will be announced as more information becomes available.

List

| Press Release

Official Asiana Statement from HL7742 Incident Press Conference 2013-07-07 16:31

We at Asiana Airlines would like express our utmost sympathy and regret for the distress experienced by the pas sengers of HL7742 and their families as a result of this accident. We apologize most deeply.

Asiana Airlines flightHL7742departed Incheon International Airport on July 6, 2013 at 16:35 (Korea time) boun d for San Francisco. On July 6, 2013 at 11:27 (Local time) an accident occurred asHL7742landed on San Franci sco International Airport's runway 28.

A total of 291 passengers were aboard the aircraft. (77 Koreans, 141 Chinese, 64 Americans, 3 Indians, 3 Canad ians, 1 French, 1 Japanese and 1 Vietnamese)

Asiana Airlines has established emergency response centers to ascertain the cause of this crash and to look after injured passengers and contact their families. Asiana continues to actively cooperate with all Korean and US go vernmental institutions in the ongoing investigation.

List

| Press Release

Statement from July 8th Press Conference on HL7742 Incident 2013-07-08 15:42

Asiana would like to provide a brief update regarding the status ofHL7742.

The special charter flight dispatched by Asiana Airlines yesterday at 13:33 (Korea Time) carrying twelve suppor t staff, eight government inspectors and members of the Korean media has arrived on location in San Francisco. Its passengers have begun supporting the victims and their families and assisting in the investigation.

Asiana Airlines is providing airfare and lodging for families of the passengers. In the event that the number of fa mily members seeking support increases, Asiana is also preparing to operate additional charter flights.

Two Korean family members departed for the United States yesterday. Another four are expected to depart toda y followed by an additional four on Wednesday. Asiana Airlines is also supporting twelve Chinese family memb ers and six Chinese government officials, who will depart from Shanghai for the United States (via Incheon) tod ay.

48 injured persons are being treated at local hospitals in the San Francisco area. Each hospital is staffed with ded icated personnel and transportation to provide the utmost support for the victims and their families.

Asiana Airlines will continue to exert great effort in providing assistance and on the ongoing investigation.

.

| Press Release

Statement from July 9th Press Conference regarding the HL7742 Incident 2013-07-09 18:01

Asiana Airlines would like to provide a brief update on the status of the HL7742 incident.

Asiana Airlines is putting forth great effort to assist the families of the passengers on flightHL7742. As of this a fternoon, family members of 6 passengers have departed for San Francisco, and families of another 4 Korean pa ssengers are scheduled to depart at 5:25pm local time. Furthermore, 5 more families will be departing tomorro w and 2 more on the 12th.

With regard to the Chinese passengers, one of our employees is escorting 12 family members and 6 government officials from Shanghai. The group departed last night and is on their way to San Francisco via Incheon. We w ould like to take this moment to again express our deep regret and offer our most sincere condolences.

In San Francisco, Asiana employees in coordination with United Airlines employees are devoting all their energ y in providing on-site assistance and aid. Asiana will be dispatching 13 more employees to ensure a more smoot h operation.

Moreover, 5 Korean passengers who were on flight HL7742 is scheduled to return this evening at 5:28pm. We will spare no efforts in providing assistance that the passengers may need. President & CEO, Young-Doo Yoon will also be traveling to San Francisco this afternoon to get a better understanding of the situation and to provide any additional assistance needed.

Asiana Airlines will continue to exert great effort in providing assistance and on the ongoing investigation

Press Release

Asiana Laments Loss of Third Passenger 2013-07-13 13:56

According to San Francisco General Hospital, another passenger who was aboard flight HL7742 has passed away this morning after having been hospitalized in critical condition following the accident.

The hospital is respecting the wishes of the girl's parents that no further information be publicly released at this time. With this regretful loss of life, the death toll of the recent Asiana crash landing has risen to 3.

Asiana Airlines President and CEO, Young-Doo Yoon expressed his deepest sympathies by saying, "My deepest condolences go out to the grieving family and loved ones of this passenger and to all those who have been affected by this regretful incident. We will devote all attention and efforts to support the families of the victims and expedited recoveries for the other injured passengers".

Asiana will continue to provide updated information as soon as it becomes available.

List

Appendix D – Asiana Airlines' Communication via Twitter and Facebook

Asiana Airlines
July 7

[ATTN] We have a new contact number for any inquiries regarding the incident of flight OZ214 on Saturday, July 6th.

Please contact 1-855-422-7214 for better assistance.

Thank you for your continued support, patience and understanding at this time.

Like · Comment · Share 362 71 31

Asiana Airlines changed their cover photo.
July 8

For up-to-date press release and further information regarding Flight OZ214, please refer to the links below:

English: http://j.mp/12xnzyX
Korean: http://j.mp/12Q22At
Chinese: http://j.mp/12RTWf6

For phone inquiries in the US, please contact the following hotline: 1-855-422-7214.

Thank you for your continued support, condolences, encouragement, and concerns during these trying times.

Information for Incident Involving Asiana Flight OZ 214

ASIANA AIRLINES

Like · Comment · Share 463 38 22

Asiana Airlines @AsianaAirlines 11 Jul
US toll-free number will be changed. US: 855-422-7214 (until July 12,2013) → 866-528-8241 (Starting July 13,2013)
Expand Reply Retweet Favorite More

Asiana Airlines @AsianaAirlines 10 Jul
We have additional toll-free numbers for passengers and family: US: 866-528-8241 / KR: 080-233-4000 / CN: 400-650-8905
Expand Reply Retweet Favorite More

Asiana Airlines @AsianaAirlines 9 Jul
Updated statements from 7/9/13 Press Conf. available: bit.ly/13zqpdk, Google+ bit.ly/172eUlp #SFO #AsianaAirlines #OZ214
Expand Reply Retweet Favorite More

Asiana Airlines @AsianaAirlines 8 Jul
New updates from Press Conference listed on our website: bit.ly/18JsOhl // Or read it on Google+ bit.ly/11wU6dE
Expand Reply Retweet Favorite More

Asiana Airlines @AsianaAirlines 8 Jul
Statement from the July 8th Press Conference on OZ214 Accident: j.mp/12xnzyX
Expand Reply Retweet Favorite More

V. References

i Artria, Gred. (2013). "Asiana Airlines San Francisco Plane Crash Interactive Timeline." *ABC News.* Retrieved from http://abcnews.go.com/US/fullpage/asiana-airlines-san-francisco-plane-crash-interactive-timeline-19615893 (accessed October 22, 2013).

ii Lowy, Joan. (2013)."Mechanical Failure May Have Caused Asiana Airlines Crash." *Huffington Post.* Retrieved on www.huffingtonpost.com/2013/10/09/asiana-crash-cause_n_4074196.html (accessed October 22, 2013).

iii *Wall Street Journal.* http://online.wsj.com/news/articles/SB10001424127887323664204578608040691727544 (accessed October 26, 2013).

iv Via Good Morning America. (7/7/13). *ABC News.* Retrieved on http://abcnews.go.com/US/san-francisco-plane-crash-pilot-43-hours-flying/story?id=19598352&page=2 (accessed October 22, 2013).

v *Wall Street Journal.* "The Crash of Flight 214: Pilots' Experience, Training Are Questioned — Safety Board Assessing How the Crew Allowed Jet's Speed to Drop to Dangerous Level, and Why Warnings Weren't Heeded." [New York, N.Y.].

vi Pasztor, Andy & Ostrower, Jon. *Wall Street Journal.* (7/11/13). "The Crash of Flight 214: Pilots' Recollections Differ From Cockpit Recordings". *Wall Street Journal,* Eastern edition [New York, N.Y]: A.4.

vii McCown, Brigham. (7/ 7/13). "Asiana 214 Crashes At San Francisco, What Happened?" *Forbes.* Retrieved from www.forbes.com/sites/brighammccown/2013/07/07/asiana-214-crashes-at-san-francisco-what-happened (accessed October 22, 2013).

viii Harless, William. (7/19/13). "Emergency Vehicle Killed Asiana Airlines Plane-Crash Victim; Ye Meng Yuan Died of Multiple Blunt Injuries." *Wall Street Journal* (Online) [New York, N.Y]: n/a.

ix Bloomberg News. (2013). www.bloomberg.com/news/2013–12–11/asiana-pilot-set-throttles-he-didn-t-understand-to-idle.html (accessed January 3, 2014).

x Park, Kyunghee. (2013). Asiana Names CEO Five Months After San Francisco Crash. Bloomberg News. www.bloomberg.com/news/2013–12–24/asiana-names-ceo-five-months-after-san-francisco-crash.html (Retrieved on January 4, 2014).

xi Nam, In-Soo. (2013). Asiana Seeks to Boost Safety Record with Foreign Hire. *Wall Street Journal: Asia.* http://blogs.wsj.com/korearealtime/2013/12/06/asiana-seeks-to-boost-safety-record-with-foreign-hire/ (accessed January 4, 2014) .

xii Asiana Airlines: Sustainability Report (2013) https://flyasiana.com/download_file/ASIANA_AIRLINES_SR_2012_Eng_low.pdf

xiii Kim, Jongseok (1997). Findlay, Christopher and Sien Chia, Karmjit Singh, ed. *Asia Pacific Air Transport: Challenges and Policy Reforms.* Singapore: Institute of Southeast Asian Studies. pp. 74–104. ISBN 978–981–230004–1 (accessed February, 15 2013).

xiv Carney, Michael & Dostaler, Isabelle. "Airline Ownership and Control: A Corporate Governance Perspective." *Journal of Air Transport Management.* 12 (2006): 63–75.

xv Kumho Asiana Group. (2013). "About Kumho Asiana." www.kumhoasiana.com/eng/group/history.asp (accessed November 17, 2013).

xvi Asiana Airlines. http://us.flyasiana.com/Global/US/en/main (accessed October 27, 2013).

xvii Star Alliance. (2013). "Member Airlines" www.staralliance.com/en/about/airlines/asiana_airlines/# (accessed November 17, 2013).

xviii The 9000 Store. (2013). http://the9000store.com/what-is-iso-9002.aspx (accessed November 17, 2013).

xix Star Alliance. (2013). "Asiana Airlines Celebrates 10th Anniversary with Star Alliance" www.staralliancee mployees.com/news/latest-news/news-details/browse/10/article/asiana-airlines-celebrates-10th-anniversary-within-star-

xx *Business Traveler.* (2013). www.businesstravelerusa.com/archive/december-2012-january-2013/special-reports/2012-worlda-s-best-in-business-travel (accessed November 11, 2013).

xxi Web Jet. www.webjet.com/sale/asiana-bangkok/ (Accessed November 11, 2013).

xxii *USA Today.* www.usatoday.com/story/todayinthesky/2013/11/11/asianas-q3-profit-is-airlines-first-of-2013/3490429/ (accessed November 4, 2013).

xxiii Associated Press. (2013). http://bigstory.ap.org/article/asiana-posts-1st-profit-3-quarters (accessed October 29, 2013).

xxiv Yahoo! Finance. (2013). http://finance.yahoo.com/news/asiana-posts-1st-profit-3–045525825.html (accessed October 30, 2013).

xxv Aviation Safety Network. (2013). *Flight Safety Foundation.* Retrieved from http://aviation-safety.net/database/operator/airline.php?var=6453 (accessed October 22, 2013).

xxvi Bloomberg. 2013. "Asiana Air Crash Adds Pressure on Korea Safety Regulations" www.bloomberg.com/news/2013–07–07/asiana-air-crash-may-bring-new-safety-regulations-in-south-korea.html (accessed November 4, 2013).

xxvii Yahoo News. (2013). http://news.yahoo.com/asiana-airlines-crash-unlikely-scare-away-customers-190422517.html (accessed October 29, 2013).

xxviii Simplyflying. (2013). "Crisis Management 2.0 Asiana Airlines OZ214 Case Study and Analysis." Retrieved from www.slideshare.net/shanxz/asiana-flight-214-crash-in-sfo-crises-management-case-study-and-analysis (accessed October 22, 2013).

xxix Bloggerchica. (2013). "How Social Media Broke the Story of the SFO Plane Crash." Retrieved from http://bloggerchica.com/how-social-media-broke-the-story-of-the-sfo-plane-crash/ (accessed October 22, 2013).

xxx Clark, Don. (7/8/13). "The Crash of Flight 214: Survivor Updates In 140 Characters." *Wall Street Journal.* Eastern edition [New York, N.Y]: A.7.

xxxi ABC Channel 7. (7/6/13). "Asiana Airlines Flight 214 Crashes at SFO." Retrieved from http://abclocal.go.com/kgo/story?id=9164032 (accessed October 22, 2013).

xxxii Carey, Susan, Feintzeig, Rachel & Kong, Kanga. (7/10/13). "Asiana's Response to San Francisco Plane Crash Draws Notice; Delay in Dispatching CEO, Refusal to Use Outside Communications Signal a Departure." *Wall Street Journal* (Online) [New York, N.Y].

xxxiii "The Crash of Asiana Flight 214: Special Coverage of the Fatal Accident at San Francisco International Airport." *CBS News.* Retrieved from www.cbsnews.com/2718–201_162–2226/the-crash-of-asiana-flight-214/ (accessed October 22, 2013).

xxxiv Asiana Airlines. "Asiana Laments Loss of Third Passenger." Retrieved from http://us.flyasiana.com/Global/US/en/homepage?fid=ABOUT14000&cmd=NEWSVIEW&seq=2402 (accessed on November 12, 2013).

xxxv Carey, Susan, Feintzeig, Rachel & Kong, Kanga. (7/9/13). "Asiana's Response to San Francisco Plane Crash Draws Notice." *Wall Street Journal.* Retrieved from http://online.wsj.com/news/articles/SB10001424127887324507404578595730188554270) (accessed November 12, 2013).

xxxvi (7/8/13). "Asiana Airlines Flying in Victims' Families From Overseas." *KTVU.* www.ktvu.com/news/news/local/asiana-airlines-flying-victims-families-overseas/nYjRr/ (accessed October 22, 2013).

xxxvii Nakaso, Dan. (7/16/13). "Asiana Airlines' perplexing Response to Flight 214 Crash." *San Jose Mercury News.* Retrieved from www.mercurynews.com/ci_23671823/asiana-airlines-perplexing-response-flight-214-crash (accessed November 12, 2013).

xxxviii Carey, Susan, Feintzeig, Rachel & Kong, Kanga. (7/9/13). "Asiana's Response to San Francisco Plane Crash Draws Notice." *Wall Street Journal.* Retrieved from http://online.wsj.com/news/articles/SB10001424127887324507404578595730188554270) (accessed November 12, 2013).

xxxix Carey, Susan, Feintzeig, Rachel & Kong, Kanga. (7/10/13). "Asiana's Response to San Francisco Plane Crash Draws Notice; Delay in Dispatching CEO, Refusal to Use Outside Communications Signal a Departure." *Wall Street Journal* (Online) [New York, N.Y].

xl Mary Kirby. In Facebook. (accessed November 11, 2013).

xli Nigam, Shashank. 2013. "COPING WITH TRAGEDY." *Airline Business* 29, no. 9: 59. Business Source Complete, EBSCOhost (accessed October 22, 2013).

xlii Carey, Susan, Feintzeig, Rachel & Kong, Kanga. (7/10/13). "Asiana's Response to San Francisco Plane Crash Draws Notice; Delay in Dispatching CEO, Refusal to Use Outside Communications Signal a Departure." *Wall Street Journal* (Online) [New York, N.Y].

xliii "The Crash of Asiana Flight 214: Special Coverage of the Fatal Accident at San Francisco International Airport." *CBS News.* Retrieved from www.cbsnews.com/2718–201_162–2226/the-crash-of-asiana-flight-214/ (accessed October 22, 2013).

xliv "Aviation Disaster Family Assistance." *National Transportation Safety Board*. Retrieved from www.ntsb.gov/tda/ops.html (accessed November 12, 2013).

xlv The *Washington Post*. (2013). www.washingtonpost.com/blogs/worldviews/wp/2013/07/08/asiana-airlines-president-bows-in-apology-for-crash-a-show-of-koreas-very-different-corporate-culture/ (accessed November 12, 2013).

xlvi Carey, Susan, Feintzeig, Rachel & Kong, Kanga. (7/9/13). "Asiana's Response to San Francisco Plane Crash Draws Notice." *Wall Street Journal*. Retrieved from http://online.wsj.com/news/articles/SB10001424127887324507404578595730188554270) (accessed November 12, 2013).

xlvii Nakaso. "Asiana Airlines' Perplexing Response to Flight 214 Crash." *San Jose Mercury News*. Retrieved from www.mercurynews.com/ci_23671823/asiana-airlines-perplexing-response-flight-214-crash (accessed November 12, 2013).

xlviii *Huffington Post*. 2013. "KTVU Reports Racist Joke as Names of Asiana 214 Pilots" www.huffingtonpost.com/2013/07/12/asiana-pilots-fake-names-racist_n_3588569.html (accessed November 4, 2013).

xlix Nakaso, Dan. (7/16/13). "Asiana Airlines' Perplexing Response to Flight 214 Crash." *San Jose Mercury News*. Retrieved from www.mercurynews.com/ci_23671823/asiana-airlines-perplexing-response-flight-214-crash (accessed November 12, 2013).

l Business Insider. (2013). "Asiana Airlines Needs Serious Help with Crisis Management." www.businessinsider.com/asiana-airlines-accident-response-continues-to-be-just-plane-stupid-2013-7 (accessed November 17, 2013).

li *CBS News*. (2013). "Asiana Crash Victim: 'We Didn't Get Any Help' From Airline.'" www.cbsnews.com/8301–505263_162–57594106/asiana-crash-victims-we-didnt-get-any-help-from-airline/ (accessed November 17, 2013).

lii Gale, Alastair. (7/10/13). "Why Asiana Has a PR Problem." *Wall Street Journal*. Retrieved from http://blogs.wsj.com/korearealtime/2013/07/10/why-asiana-has-a-pr-problem/ (accessed October 22, 2013).

liii The *Washington Post*. (2013). www.washingtonpost.com/blogs/worldviews/wp/2013/07/08/asiana-airlines-president-bows-in-apology-for-crash-a-show-of-koreas-very-different-corporate-culture/ (accessed November 12, 2013).

liv Sung, Yongjun. "Brand Personality Structure in Korea and the United States: Implications for Global Marketing Strategy." *University of Georgia*. Retrieved from http://athenaeum.libs.uga.edu/bitstream/handle/10724/6767/sung_yongjun_200308_ma.pdf?sequence=1 (accessed November 12, 2013): pg 48.

lv H. Jay. (7/8/13). "Korea Responds to Asiana Airlines Crash." *Korea Bang*. Retrieved from www.koreabang.com/?p=15510 (accessed November 12, 2013).

lvi Carney, Michael & Dostaler, Isabelle. "Airline Ownership and Control: A Corporate Governance Perspective." *Journal of Air Transport Management*. 12 (2006): 63–75.

lvii Bosari, Jessica. (8/8/12). "The Developing Role of Social Media in the Modern Business." *Forbes*. www.forbes.com/sites/moneywisewomen/2012/08/08/the-developing-role-of-social-media-in-the-modern-business-world/ (accessed November, 18, 2013).

lviii Yahoo! Finance. (accessed November 12, 2013).

lix Park, Kyunghee. (7/10/13). "Asiana Tarnished by Crash with Passengers Warming to Korean Air". Retrieved from www.bloomberg.com/news/2013-07-09/asiana-tarnished-by-crash-with-passengers-warming-to-korean-air.html (accessed November 12, 2013).

lx Ha-Won, Jung. (7/9/13). "Asiana Chief Defends 'very experienced' Crash Pilots. *Fox News*. Retrieved from www.foxnews.com/world/2013/07/09/asiana-chief-defends-very-experienced-crash-pilots/ (accessed November 12, 2013).

lxi Asiana Airlines. In Facebook. Retrieved from https://plus.google.com/u/0/114095967881168349734/posts/YiszZ5TSwMZ) (accessed November 12, 2013).

LONG CASE QUESTIONS

1. What are some of the main factors that led to the crash?
2. How did Asiana Airlines address the crisis after the crash? How did Asiana Airlines address the crash in the U.S.? Was the approach appropriate?
3. How did the way Asiana Airlines handle the crisis show its inability to attend to cross-cultural differences in preferred communication styles? How critical is it for multinationals to carefully consider the cross-cultural implications of their ethical actions?
4. How should Asiana Airlines have ideally handled the situation? What is the role of cultural intelligence in handling crises?

Part III: Comprehensive Case

WHY WAS THE SNOW POLLUTED? A BLIND SPOT FOR THE JAPANESE TOP MILK PRODUCT COMPANY, SNOW BRAND

Introduction

Tetsuro Ishikawa, the president of Snow Brand at that time, had to raise his voice. He shouted at the Osaka plant manager at the press conference. "You, is that true?"

On July 1, 2000, Snow Brand Milk Products Co. Ltd., the top company in the Japanese milk product industry, held its fourth press conference about the food poisoning it caused on June 27. This was President Ishikawa's first appearance in public and he apologized for the failure along with accounting for the cause. He mentioned part of the production process was contaminated with the *Staphylococcus aureus* toxin but the reason for it was unclear. However, on this occasion, the Osaka plant manager exposed the fact that contamination was due to the negligence of routine cleaning which had already been found on June 29, two days after the poisoning happened. Neither the president nor the public relations manager who attended the press conference knew about the larger picture or the incident.

History of Snow Brand

Snow Brand started in 1925 as a sales guild for dairy products in Hokkaido, the northernmost part of Japan. A big earthquake occurred two years before, in 1923, and it led to a supply shortage, and a large number of foreign-made dairy products flowed into Japan due to the abolishment of tariffs by the government. The origin of Snow Brand was to help dairy farmers in Hokkaido suffering from a fall in milk prices to become independent. Snow Brand's crystal mark (logo), a logo familiar to the Japanese public, was designed in 1926. The mark symbolizes stark white and purity, and the Pole Star in the center of the mark signifies Hokkaido. Torizo Korosawa, one of Snow Brand's founders, advocated *Kendo-Kenmin*, which means "dairy fertilizes earth and enriches people." This "spirit of establishment" has been the base of the corporate philosophy of Snow Brand.

After several changes to its name and organization, Snow Brand Milk Products Co., Ltd. was incorporated in 1950 and its business grew. However, Snow Brand caused a serious food-poisoning case in 1955. Over 1,900 students in nine elementary schools in Tokyo came down with food poisoning after drinking skim milk made at Snow Brand's Yakumo Plant in Hokkaido. *Hemolytic staphylococcus* was breeding in a portion of fresh milk made at the Yakumo Plant where germicidal treatment had been held up because of mechanical troubles and a power outage. Snow Brand's employees' response to the food poisoning was prompt and appropriate. Mitsugi Sato, the president at the time, immediately directed employees to stop distribution and ordered a recall of the products, published an apology in the newspapers, and took the lead in an investigation into the causes at the plant. In addition, he made apology visits to many of those who had been poisoned, to business partners, and to the dairy farmers. Other plants were also rechecked and drastic measures for preventing a recurrence of food poisoning were worked out. For example, departmental self-dependence of hygiene management and examination and reinforcement of the inspection process were implemented. Sato issued a document titled as "Announcement to all employees" regarding the Yakumo case and distributed it to all employees. It included these statements, "It takes long time to gain credit and no time to lose it. Additionally, we cannot buy credit" and "It is only quality improvement that can result in regaining the honor lost due to quality contamination."[1] It was also handed out to new employees from 1956 until 1985 during their hygienic management training.

After the food poisoning incident, Snow Brand afterwards started to pursue quality and credibility by developing technical capabilities and expansion of its plants by bringing the nationwide market into view. However, it also resulted in increasing the distance between Snow Brand and dairy farmers in Hokkaido who had been working together toward the progress of dairy food product manufacturing in Hokkaido. Before the 1960s in Japan, sales outlets of dairy food manufacturers that offered home delivery service supported the milk industry since milk is perishable and could not suitably be shipped in the distribution channel like other common foods. When Snow Brand expanded its market nationwide, its competitors had already set up their distribution networks. Snow Brand's weak distribution network allowed it to ride the wave of marketing revolution by moving into supermarkets without disturbing the existing distribution channels. By taking the largest share in the supermarket and convenience store channels, combined with technological advancements, Snow Brand became the leading company in the market. Specifically, the outstanding technology of Snow Brand generated high-quality dairy food products and it succeeded in building an excellent brand image along with the perception of snow's purity and fertile farmland in Hokkaido. Snow Brand remained at the top of the dairy food product industry for years. Nevertheless, the company had to deal with price competition, international trends toward free trade, and increased demand for freshness by consumers.

Milk in the Japanese Market

Milk has a special status in the Japanese product market. Because of its historical and social background, people from various age groups drink milk on a daily basis. Many consumers believe that milk is nutritious and healthy.[2] At the time of the food poisoning incident by Snow Brand, consumers did not imagine that milk could be bad for them.

Milk was introduced in Japan in the seventh century. Since only the aristocracy drank milk mainly for medical purposes, milk did not appear in the Japanese mass market till 1863. In 1871, the media reported that the Emperor drank milk twice a day; therefore, drinking milk became popular. In 1954, after World War II, the school lunch program was officially regulated by the government. Most Japanese children suffered from malnutrition at the time. Based on this program, all children in mandatory education schools were provided with lunches. The Japanese government included powdered milk into the school lunch program, provided by the U.S. government. In 1963, the school lunch program now included real daily milk and it became the fundamental drink for all children. The product volume of milk increased by 1,822% between 1948 and 1964. After they graduated from their mandatory schools, they continued to drink milk at home to maintain a healthy and balanced diet. The consumer milk market increased. The Japanese government also encouraged drinking milk by protecting the milk industry.[3] In 1985, product volumes of milk exceeded 4 million kiloliters, and then it grew to 5 million kiloliters in 1994[4] (see Exhibit 1). After that, as demands for milk based on the school lunch program declined because of low birthrates, the product volume was decreased. However, in the twentieth century, many people still include milk in their dairy diet.[5]

Sequence of the Food Poisoning Event

The Snow Brand Company received the first report about food poisoning on the morning of June 27, 2000. The West Japan Branch got a phone call from a consumer whose children showed significant symptoms after they drank Snow Brand's low-fat milk at dinner on June 26. An employee of the company immediately visited the consumer's house and asked several questions. The employee did not think that Snow Brand milk was the source of the children's symptoms. He told the consumer that the company had received no similar reports. However, the employee, just in case, took the remaining milk cartons from the house to have them inspected.[6]

Osaka City Hall also received several reports from local public health centers about food poisoning symptoms, which were possibly caused by Snow Brand's low-fat milk. Based on a previous experience with a food poisoning outbreak caused by O-157 bacteria in 1996, officials from City Hall responded to the situation promptly and conducted an on-site investigation at Snow Brand's Osaka Plant on the afternoon of June 28. While conducting their inspection, City Hall continued to receive complaints from consumers about possible food poisoning from Snow Brand milk. At 11 p.m. on June 28, employees at Osaka City Hall asked a representative of the Snow Brand West Japan Branch to conduct a recall of its products and make a public announcement to tell consumers about the food poisoning immediately; however, the Osaka plant manager thought that seven complaints out of hundreds of thousands of products was usual. He believed that a public announcement would just confuse the consumers.[7]

On the 28th, Snow Brand also held a general stockholder meeting at its headquarters in Sapporo, with the executives and many of the directors at this meeting. They were not told about the possible food poisoning and the inspection of the Osaka Plant by Osaka City Hall until 1 a.m. on June 29. At 8 a.m., Snow Brand's executives finally decided to voluntarily recall the products in Western Japan, but did not make a public announcement. Tetsuro Ishikawa, the president of Snow Brand who used to be the financial director of the company, was informed about the recall one hour later. After the stockholder meeting, Ishikawa visited several stockholders in Sapporo; therefore, he was not included in the decision-making process. When the decision to make a public announcement was made, it was already 2 p.m.

At 4 p.m., Osaka City Hall held a press conference to report the food poisoning by Snow Brand's milk. At 9:45 p.m., the general manager of the Snow Brand West Japan Branch called a press conference to explain its product recall. Approximately 58 hours had passed since the first phone call reached Snow Brand.[8]

On July 1, the number of food poisoning cases had risen to 6,121 in eight of the 47 prefectures (a prefecture is similar to one state in the United States) in Western Japan. Snow Brand milk Products Company held two press conferences on July 1, 2000. The president, Ishikawa, attended the second press conference along with the Osaka plant manager to apologize to the public. In that conference, the plant manager disclosed that there were contaminants in the valves of the milk products line when the equipment was checked on June 29. Ishikawa shouted at him, "Is that true?" The director of the public relations department also shouted at the plant manager in a loud voice, "Is it a fact or your guess?" Moreover, the contamination of the valves for the milk products line was confirmed before the first press conference that day; however, that fact was not reported at the conference. The Osaka Plant was shut down the same day.[9]

On July 4, the number of cases reported was 9,394. Snow Brand published its official announcement in newspapers, but the manufacture date of possible poisoned products was mistakenly reported in the announcement. In another press conference, held on the 4th, a managing director replied to the questions about that mistake about the product date. "There is chaos in the company. It is very difficult to manage accurate information." In addition, it was found that two other milk products caused the food poisoning as well. First, Snow Brand denied that, but the inspection by Osaka City Hall confirmed the product lines for those two products were contaminated. Osaka City Hall ordered Snow Brand to recall those two products and strongly recommended a voluntary recall of all of the products, 56 items, produced at the Osaka Plant. During the press conference, media reporters asked Ishikawa many questions. He replied saying, "I do not know details about the manufacturing. I feel displeased because information did not reach me." Then, finally, Ishikawa shouted at the reporters, "I have not slept!!" His comments were aired on nationwide television.[10]

Osaka Prefecture Police conducted an investigation on the grounds of professional negligence resulting in food poisoning. A police executive commented, "Each person at Snow Brand told a different story. It seems that they do not share information among the plant, the branch and the headquarters. Accurate information from the production front-line may not be reported to the executives."[11]

On July 5, the number of cases finally exceeded 10,000. The next day, Ishikawa announced his resignation. During the press conference, he said, "I sincerely apologize that Snow Brand jeopardized its consumers and society," and "this incident happened because of our overconfidence in our policy and product quality." Ishikawa replied to the questions about the crisis management of Snow Brand by saying, "We have a crisis management manual, but in reality, it was difficult to follow the situation based on the manual." He also admitted that part of the reason may have been due to the company's conceit as the top selling brand. On the other hand, he insisted that the problem was only at the Osaka plant, and did not affect all Snow Brand plants and products. Ishikawa asserted, "We are sure about the quality of our other products."[12]

On July 10, however, Osaka City Hall confirmed that Snow Brand's Osaka Plant recycled its returned and outdated products to manufacture new products. Although technically this practice was not the source of the food poisoning, this finding damaged the entire image of Snow Brand's products.[13]

On July 11, at 11 p.m., Snow Brand announced its decision to voluntarily shut down its 21 plants nationwide. In dual press conferences, originally scheduled for 5 p.m. and conducted at 11 p.m. at the Western Japan Branch and Snow Brand headquarters in Tokyo,[14] reporters' questions were answered. However, at the conference in the West Japan Branch, a spokesperson from Snow Brand replied to questions suggesting that reporters ask for details from the headquarters in Tokyo. On the other hand, at the Tokyo headquarter's conference, a spokesperson suggested that reporters ask for details from the Western Japan Branch. Criticism by the media heated up because of Snow Brand's disorganized media relations.[15]

In addition, since the media could not get a timely response from the company or even fundamental explanation, the reporters tried to collect information from other sources, such as those who had been poisoned, Osaka City Hall or the Osaka Prefecture Police. Both accurate and inaccurate information was reported by the media and led to employee confusion regarding the internal communication from the company.[16] As a result, the employees of Snow Brand did not have the same level of information as the consumers, retailers and media.[17] The tone of media coverage changed. It became sloppy, careless, and insincere. The media started to report the organizational problems of the company, not just the technical mistakes of the company.[18]

On August 4, Kouhei Nishi, who had worked in the company's sales department, became the president. In a press conference, he explained the company's rebuilding plan. Nishi used a different approach with the media and included many visual aids to explain the plans well to the media.[19]

Despite Snow Brand's hopes, on August 18, Osaka City Hall pointed out that one of the sources of the food poisoning came from the Taiki Plant in Hokkaido. City Hall officials concluded that the contaminated milk products were manufactured with powdered milk made at the Taiki Plant. The Taiki Plant was the flagship plant of Snow Brand. The next day, the Hokkaido government conducted an on-site inspection of the Taiki Plant. The inspectors found that there was an electric power outage accident on March 31, 2000, because freezing snow fell on the electric powerhouse for the plant. During the electric outage, raw milk material for the powdered skim milk remained on the line for three hours. At the time, *staphylococcus aureus* bacteria proliferated, and enterotoxin grew in the milk. However, the plant produced powdered milk as usual after the electric outage. Although plant workers found that the high bacterial count exceeded the company's own safety standards during the quality examination, the plant employees shipped the powdered milk to the Osaka Plant. It is common knowledge for someone who has studied food sanitation that *staphylococcus aureus* bacteria could proliferate during an electric outage in food plants, but the staff of the Taiki plant had not realized that risky connection between the electric outage and the proliferation of *staphylococcus aureus* bacteria until the Hokkaido government and the Hokkaido Prefecture Police confirmed the linkage. On August 23, Snow Brand held a press conference and admitted the contamination of the powdered milk made in the Taiki Plant. Hokkaido Prefecture Police had started an investigation of the Taiki Plant on the grounds of professional negligence resulting in milk poisoning.[20]

On September 26, Snow Brand submitted its business reconstruction plan, but the company was forced to revise the plan several times. Snow Brand's fiscal earnings were expected to show a deficit on March 31, 2001. The number of food poisoning cases was 13,000 in 15 prefectures. Snow Brand's milk poisoning incident was recorded as the worst case of food poisoning in Japanese history.[21] (See Chart 1 and Exhibit 2.)

Problems

Business Problem—Snow Brand as a Gigantic Top Brand

Snow Brand was a giant in the Japanese Milk Product Market. Although the market was very competitive, the brand image of Snow Brand was well established, and it strongly supported the company's sales. The brand image was composed of two main factors: a high level of manufacturing control process and its birthplace, Hokkaido.

Marketing research shows Snow Brand's high level of manufacturing control processes. The product blind recall survey by Hokuren, which is an association of Hokkaido Agricultural Cooperatives, indicated that Snow Brand placed second in any area in Japan. In each area, the first-place company varied, but Snow Brand always came in second. A director of Hokuren pointed out that this stability was the strength of Snow Brand. He insisted that it was very hard for the milk product companies to provide such a high-quality product in such a wide area. An executive of Meiji, one of Snow Brand's competitors, observed that 70% of respondents in a marketing survey indicated that Snow Brand milk was the best when they knew the product's name. On the other hand, 70% of respondents indicated that the Meiji product was the best when they did not know the product's name.[22]

Another component of Snow Brand's strong brand equity was its birthplace, Hokkaido. In contemporary Japanese society, Hokkaido is regarded as a beautiful, broad, exotic northern place, which is one of the largest Japanese islands. Hokkaido was famous for its agriculture and fisheries. Hokkaido is also a very popular destination for domestic tourists. Like Florida in the United States, Hokkaido has a high recognition factor. Since the livestock industry is one of the representative industries of Hokkaido, milk products made in Hokkaido or the companies from Hokkaido are attractive to consumers in nationwide markets. As explained in the previous section, Snow Brand was born in Hokkaido, and that fact is widely recognized by consumers. Snow Brand utilized the brand equity of Hokkaido well to strengthen its marketing position.

Snow Brand became a giant brand; however, the company suffered from several problems because of its strong brand equity.

Competition as a Top Brand

Snow Brand owned its distribution company and earned a good reputation through good responses and flexibility in the market. Utilizing that distribution system, Snow Brand established its channels in supermarkets.[23] In the 1970s, milk products companies jumped into tough competition to gain shares of distribution channels in supermarkets, when the number of supermarkets bloomed. After successfully winning the competition, Snow Brand rapidly increased its sales. In 1996, the share of distribution channels for milk products held by Snow Brand was 82.3% for supermarkets, 8.6% for retailers which mainly delivered products door to door, and 9.1% for school lunch programs. Among the top three makers of milk products, Snow Brand, Meiji, and Morinaga, Snow Brand was slightly higher in terms of sales volume supported by its sales in supermarkets. On the other hand, maintaining its share of sales in price-competitive mass merchandise channels put a lot of pressures on Snow Brand. It is necessary for manufacturers to keep providing an enormous volume of products and discounting the trade price to maintain an advantage over the competition. Without following a low margin, high volume policy, Snow Brand could not maintain its share on shelves at supermarkets. This policy overwhelmed the production process. In 1999, Snow Brand fell into second place in the milk market. It was the first time in history for Snow Brand to be beaten by its competitors. Snow Brand became very aggressive in order to regain the top position, and the quality control was gradually forgotten.[24]

Inertia at the Top

In 1999, Snow Brand was the largest milk product company in the industry, with 6,678 employees. Snow Brand had been the long-term defending champion in the market, even though the competition was tough.[25] This may have fueled overly optimistic thinking among its employees regarding the business. Many of the employees were aware of the company's history, but did not understand the challenge of starting a business in the market. They just knew their company was a strong establishment with a beautiful brand image and well-known products. Arrogance in the company could be one of the reasons why Snow Brand ignored the most fundamental rules for food product safety.[26]

Communication Problem

Physical Factors

It is said that the delay of the initial response to this milk poisoning was due to the absence of executives who were attending a shareholders' meeting in Sapporo (the capital of Hokkaido) on June 28, the day after the occurrence of the event. According to the Public Communication Division, at that time Snow Brand had four branches (Hokkaido, Eastern Japan, Central Japan, and Western Japan) and six regional offices (Hokkaido, Tohoku, Kanto, Chubu, Kansai, and Kyushu) belonging to each branch. For instance, the Western branch contained two regional offices (Kansai and Kyushu) and two quality assurance centers (Kansai and Kyushu); moreover, the Kansai regional office had area marketing and sales divisions with respect to each market: milk, dairy food, frozen food, ice cream, and baby food. Each regional office had a customer service division responsible for certain areas. At the time of the incident, information channels were extremely complicated within the company. An official at the Osaka City Public Health Office stated that "We couldn't understand which office was in charge because of getting faxes from both the Tokyo headquarters and the Western Branch."[27] Takafumi Isomura, Mayor of Osaka City at that time, complained that Snow Brand's announcements were incoherent.[28] For example, when the press required Snow Brand to hold a news conference, the responses of Snow Brand were: "We can't figure out whether the skim milk was made in the Taiki Plant [Tokyo headquarters]" or "We cannot deal with the issue of Taiki Plant since it is under the control of the dairy production division at the Tokyo headquarters [Western Branch]."[29] When the president of Snow Brand at the time, Tetsuro Ishikawa, was informed of the valve contamination in the Osaka Plant at the press conference, this was clear evidence of the confusion in the information channels (see Exhibits 3 and 4).

Structural Factors

Generally in Japan, personnel are moved between divisions every two to four years in order to foster executive trainees as generalists in business. The Japanese tradition of lifelong employment allows for this rotation system. For example, it is not unusual for cadres to transfer from sales to public relations, and then to the legal section. New recruits who are expected to be executives in the future are also required to train for approximately six months, which allows them to understand the overall business. For instance, a newspaper writer would receive on-the-job training and would be expected to deliver the newspaper. In this way, cadres get to grasp their company's main and related business, to share the basic knowledge about them, and to build a personal connection for information exchange within their organization. This rotation system contributed to the high growth of Japanese companies after World War II. However, this system has disadvantages. It is difficult to train specialists and thus the management cannot obtain professional advice.[30] Therefore some Japanese firms have begun to train professionals due to the competition in the global market. At Snow Brand, according to a former employee, personnel exchanges between different departments were seldom done because of the rationale that the staff should display its originality in each profession.[31] This may result in overvalue of an employees' profession, ignorance of their outside domain within the company, and loss of organizational flexibility. While generalist-oriented personnel strategy anticipates sharing information through experience and networking, specialist-oriented strategy needs more internal communication, such as training, education, and information exchange, for figuring out the organization and sharing of knowledge and information.

Some point out the lack of sales experience of President Ishikawa, whose only experience was in financial affairs, as the reason for a sequence of failures in response to the food poisoning. In 1986, Snow Brand also stopped the tradition of handing out Sato's "Announcement to all employees" to newcomers. Consequently, "the lessons of Yakumo" were not utilized and all of Snow Brand's employees became overconfident and dependent on technology. After the 2000 food poisoning incident, Snow Brand decided to start dairy practical training for new employees because it realized that employees needed to have basic knowledge related to hygiene management and production processes.[32]

Cultural Factors

The fundamental causes of the food poisoning incident were that the plant manager and manufacturing chief in the Taiki Plant did not follow basic food safety rules established by the company and shirked the responsibility of disposing of the tainted dry milk. This led to the reuse of the tainted dry milk, covering-up of the facts, and intentional record alteration. The media leveled accusations against Snow Brand for its lack of flexibility due to its corporate culture. Favors were exchanged between the employees to improve their communication. The lack of flexibility and the exchanging of favors which created a better working environment may be related to Japanese general cultural aspects, such as collectivism, high levels of Uncertainty Avoidance, tendency of large Power Distance and emphasis on harmonization.[33] Then, emphasizing of using non-verbal communication, people encouraged maintaining harmonious interpersonal relations and group solidarity and discouraged self-assertions.[34] Warnings, concerns, or negative comments against the organization are perceived as a violation of harmonization, and this superior manner results in organizational inflexibility. The behavior of the staff in the Taiki Plant previously mentioned can be considered part of Uncertainty Avoidance. Favor exchanging is what has become of collectivism where a group is given priority over an individual. Although they normally do not emerge, these organizational dispositions of Snow Brand seriously affect its business once a problem happens.

It would be fair to say that the food poisoning would not have spread and the number of people poisoned could have been minimized if Snow Brand's communication process worked. What were the fundamental mistakes in terms of its communication? What kind of organizational culture should the company have? What did the company not prepare for the crisis?

APPENDIX

CHART 1—Sequence of the food poisoning event

2000 June 27	a.m.	• First phone call from a victim's family reached Snow Brand Western Japan Branch • Osaka City Hall received several reports about food poisoning
June 28	a.m.	• Snow Brand general stockholders meeting at Sapporo, Hokkaido
	p.m.	• On-site investigation of Osaka Plant by Osaka City Hall
	evening	• Osaka City Hall asked Snow Brand to conduct a recall
June 29	8 a.m.	• The recall of the production was decided in Sapporo
	2 p.m.	• Executives decide to make a public announcement
	4 p.m.	• Press conference by Osaka City Hall to report the food poisoning case of Snow Brand
	9:45 p.m.	• Press conference by Snow Brand Western Japan Branch
July 1	a.m.	• Snow Brand confirmed the existence of contaminated valve in Osaka plant on June 29, but did not report it at the first press conference
	p.m.	• The CEO, Ishikawa, attended the second press conference of the day • Osaka Plant was shut down • 6,121 victims were reported
July 4		• Snow Brand published an official announcement in the newspapers • All products made by the Osaka Plant were recalled • 9,394 victims were reported
July 5		• Number of victims exceeded 10,000
July 6		• The CEO, Ishikawa, resigned
July 11		• Snow Brand announced 21 plants nationwide were shut down
Aug. 4		• The new CEO, Nishi, takes over. He held a press conference and explained the rebuilding plan of the company
Aug. 18		• Taiki plant in Hokkaido was pointed out as one source for food poisoning
Aug. 19		• Hokkaido government and Prefecture Police conducted an on-site investigation of Taiki Plant
Aug. 23		• Snow Brand admitted contaminated skim milk was shipped from Taiki Plant before the food poisoning outbreak
Sep. 26		• Snow Brand released the business reconstruction plan
2001 March 31		• Snow Brand reported fiscal deficit

EXHIBIT 1—Drinking Milk Product Volume

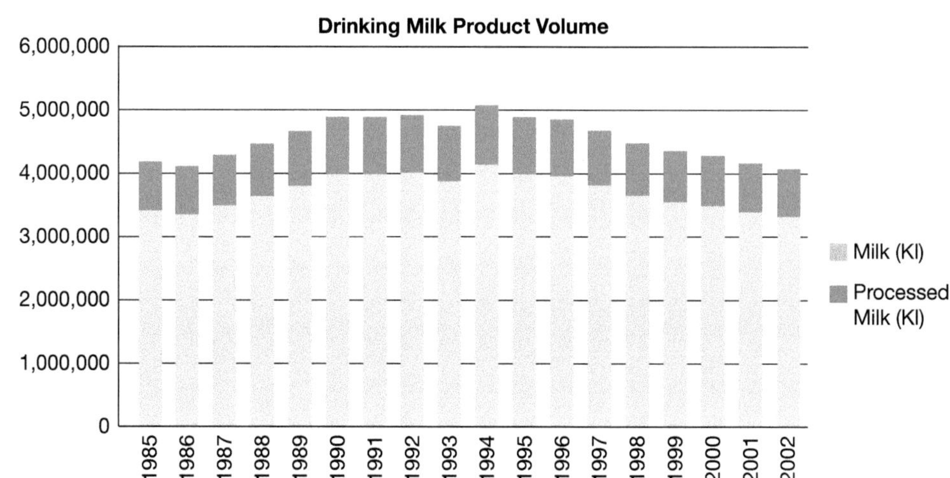

Source: Ministry of Agriculture, Forestry and Fisheries of Japan, 2003. *Gyunyu Nyuseihin Toukei* [Milk product statistics]. Retrieved January 1, 2004, from www.maff.go.jp/www/info/bun05.html.

EXHIBIT 2—Snow Brand Stock Price and Volume

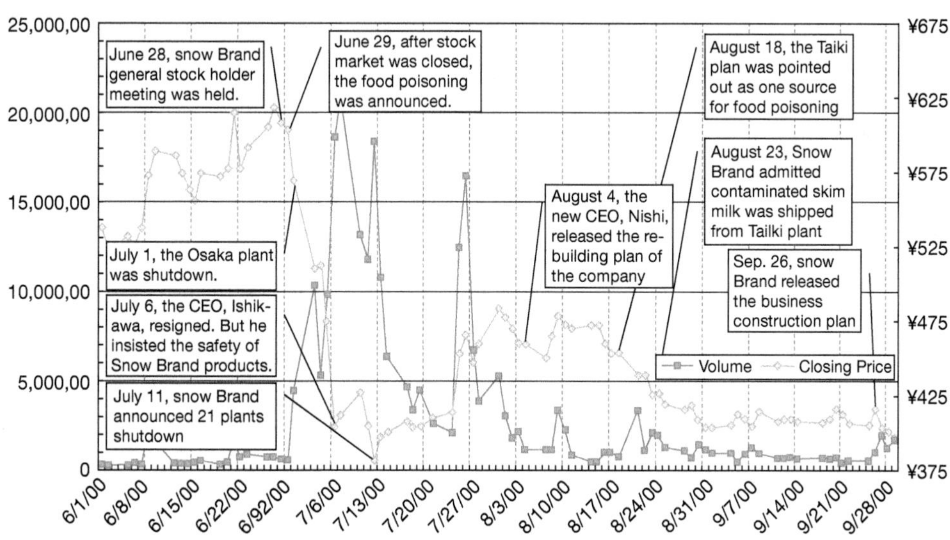

Source: Toyo Keizai Inc., 2003. *Kigyu JhoHo 2262, Yukijirushi* [Corporate Information 2262, Snow Brand]. Retrieved January 1, 2004, from http://profile.yahoo.co.jp/biz/independent/2262.html.

EXHIBIT 3—Snow Brand Organizational Structure

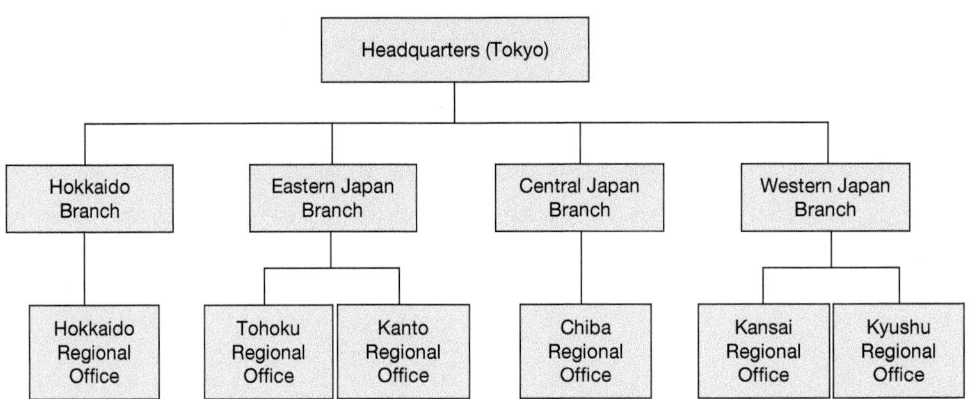

Source: Snow Brand Public Communication Department.

EXHIBIT 4—Japan Map

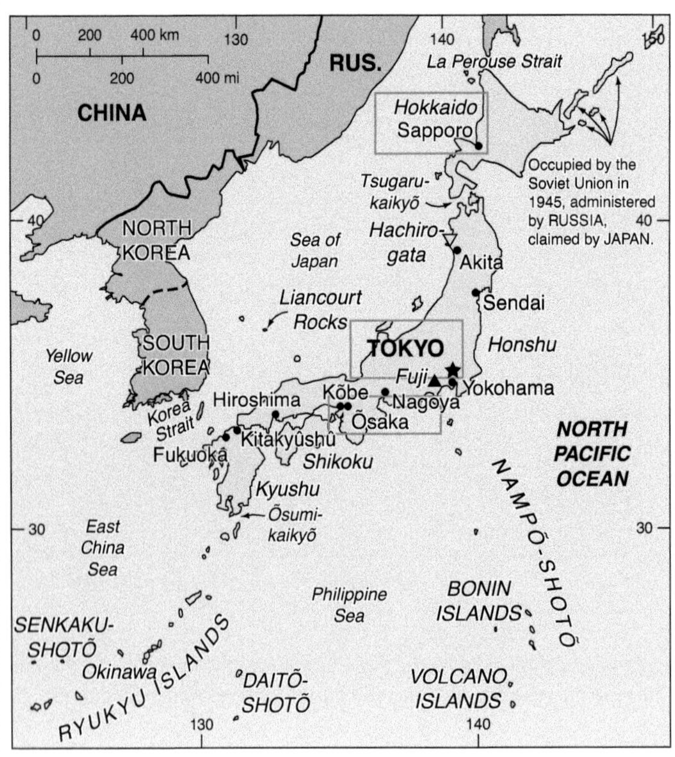

EXHIBIT 5—Financial Highlights (Consolidated)—Snow Brand Milk Products Co., Ltd., and its Consolidated Subsidiaries

(Millions of Yen)	Years ended March 31				
	2003	2002	2001	2000	1999
Net Sales	727,071	1,164,716	1,140,763	1,287,769	1,263,727
Cost of Sales	584,170	929,072	914,475	980,912	958,383
Net Income (Loss)	−27,091	−71,741	−52,925	−28,545	3,079
Total Assets	284,910	581,356	567,914	576,766	543,122
Stockholders' Equity	34,396	30,371	64,506	118,608	139,807
Number of Employees	4,591	12,404	15,326	15,127	15,343

Notes: Snow Brand Milk Products Co., Ltd. conducted a stock binding (reverse stock split), binding two shares into one share of common stock, on August 1, 2002. The following per share figures are computed as if the stock binding (reverse stock split) had been conducted on April 1.

Source: Snow Brand Milk Product Co., Ltd. (2003). Annual Report 2003. Retrieved January 1, 2003, from www.snowbrand.co.jp/ir/index.htm.

Notes

1 Sankei Shimbun Shuzaihan. (2002). *Brand wa naze ochitaka: Yukijirushi, Sogo, Mitsubishi Jidousha, jiken no shinso* [Why did the brand reach the bottom?: The truth of Snow Brand, Sogo, and Mitsubishi Motors Cases]. Tokyo: Kadokawa-shoten, pp. 44 and 45.
2 Milk Museum, *Statistics and history of milk* by Naraken Nyu Gyou Shogyou Kumiai. Retrieved January 1, 2004, from www.asm.ne.jp/~milknara/milktown/museum/museum.htm.
3 Milk Museum, *Statistics and history of milk.*
4 The Ministry of Agriculture, Forestry and Fisheries of Japan. (2003). *Gyunyu Nyuseihin Toukei* [Milk product statistics]. Retrieved January 1, 2004, from www.maff.go.jp/www/info/bun05.html
5 Milk Museum, *Statistics and history of milk.*
6 Hokkaido Shinbun Shuzaihan. (2002). *Kensho, "Yukijirushi" houkai: sonotoki, naniga okottaka* [Investigation of Snow Brand's disruption: What happened at that time]. Tokyo: Kodansha; Sankei Shimbun Shuzaihan. *Brand wa naze ochitaka.*
7 Hokkaido Shinbun Shuzaihan. *Kensho, "Yukijirushi" houkai*; Sankei Shimbun Shuzaihan. *Brand wa naze ochitaka.*
8 Hokkaido Shinbun Shuzaihan. *Kensho, "Yukijirushi" houkai*; Sankei Shimbun Shuzaihan. *Brand wa naze ochitaka.*
9 Hokkaido Shinbun Shuzaihan. *Kensho, "Yukijirushi" houkai*; Sankei Shimbun Shuzaihan. *Brand wa naze ochitaka.*
10 Hokkaido Shinbun Shuzaihan. *Kensho, "Yukijirushi" houkai*; Sankei Shimbun Shuzaihan. *Brand wa naze ochitaka.*
11 Hokkaido Shinbun Shuzaihan. *Kensho, "Yukijirushi" houkai*; Sankei Shimbun Shuzaihan. *Brand wa naze ochitaka.*
12 Hokkaido Shinbun Shuzaihan. *Kensho, "Yukijirushi" houkai*; Sankei Shimbun Shuzaihan. *Brand wa naze ochitaka.*
13 Hokkaido Shinbun Shuzaihan. *Kensho, "Yukijirushi" houkai*; Sankei Shimbun Shuzaihan. *Brand wa naze ochitaka.*
14 Hokkaido Shinbun Shuzaihan. *Kensho, "Yukijirushi" houkai.*
15 Ono, T. (2001). *Naze Fushoji wa Okoruka* [Why do scandals happen?]. *Jissen Kigyo Kouhou* [Practice: Corporate Public Relations], pp. 39–51. Hyogo, Japan: Kwansei Gakuin University Press.
16 Ono, T. *Naze Fushoji wa Okoruka.*

17 Takahashi, J. (2000, September 18). *Yukijirushi Shain no Atsuku Nagai Natsu* [A long, tough summer for Snow Brand employees]. *Asahi Shimbun Weekly AERA*, 30–33.
18 Ono, T. *Naze Fushoji wa Okoruka.*
19 Sankei Shimbun Shuzaihan. *Brand wa naze ochitaka.*
20 Hokkaido Shinbun Shuzaihan. *Kensho, "Yukijirushi" houkai*; Sankei Shimbun Shuzaihan. *Brand wa naze ochitaka.*
21 Hokkaido Shinbun Shuzaihan. *Kensho, "Yukijirushi" houkai*; Sankei Shimbun Shuzaihan. *Brand wa naze ochitaka.*
22 Sankei Shimbun Shuzaihan. *Brand wa naze ochitaka.*
23 Kaneda, S. (2000, June 7). *Yukijirushi Shokuchudoku jiken wa "Kozo fushoku" da* [The food poisoning by Snow Brand is because of the company's structural decay]. *Nikkei Business*, 8–10.
24 Hokkaido Shinbun Shuzaihan. *Kensho, "Yukijirushi" houkai*; Sankei Shimbun Shuzaihan. *Brand wa naze ochitaka.*
25 Inoshita, K. & Hasegawa, T. (2000, August 5). *Sochiki wo Ohu Kinou Fuzen. Kyoko no Brand "Yukijirushi"* [A functional disorder over companies. A fictitious brand "Snow Brand"]. *Shukan Toyo Keizai*, 62–68.
26 Sankei Shimbun Shuzaihan. *Brand wa naze ochitaka.*
27 Inoshita & Hasegawa. *Sochiki wo Ohu Kinou Fuzen*, p. 63.
28 Hokkaido Shinbun Shuzaihan. *Kensho, "Yukijirushi" houkai.*
29 Sankei Shimbun Shuzaihan. *Brand wa naze ochitaka*, p. 23.
30 Inoue, T. (2003). An overview of public relations in Japan and the self-correction concept. In K. Sriramesh & D. Vercic (Eds.), *The global public relations handbook: Theory, research and practice*, pp. 68–85. Mahwah, NJ: Lawrence Erlbaum Associates.
31 Sankei Shimbun Shuzaihan. *Brand wa naze ochitaka.*
32 Sankei Shimbun Shuzaihan. *Brand wa naze ochitaka.*
33 Hofstede, G. (2001). *Culture's consequences, comparing values, behaviors, institutions, and organizations across nations* (2nd ed.). Thousand Oaks, CA: Sage Publications.
34 *Japan: An Illustrated Encyclopedia.* (1996). Keys to the Japanese Hearts and Soul. Tokyo: Kodansha International.

COMPREHENSIVE CASE QUESTIONS

1. Why do you think it took Snow Brand executives so long to recall their poisoned milk?
2. What actions would you take if you had discovered contamination in the values of the milk product line?
3. What pressures do workers face that might encourage them to continue to produce a product when they knew it exceeded the company's safety levels for bacteria and fail to report it?
4. What would you recommend to Snow Brand regarding how to rebuild their reputation after this product failure?
5. Did Snow Brand suffer from an ethical problem or an organizational problem? Explain your answer.
6. The case attributes part of the failure of Snow Brand to respond to the contamination crisis as originating from Japanese culture. What is your assessment of this position? Do you see any parallels with other recalls for Japanese companies, such as the recent recalls by Toyota?

Part III: Comprehensive Case

AIRBNB: SCALING SAFETY WITH RAPID GROWTH

The Lopez Incident

When 19-year-old Jacob Lopez traveled overseas to Madrid in July 2015, he anticipated an enjoyable trip and planned to stay at an Airbnb property. His decision to book an Airbnb in Madrid stemmed mainly from his great experience at an Airbnb property in Brazil just a year prior.[1,2]

Lopez arrived in Madrid on July 4th and met his host, a transsexual, at the subway near the property. The male transformed to female walked with Lopez to the apartment and, upon arrival, locked the main door to the unit. Then, according to Lopez, the woman ordered him to perform a series of sexual acts. Lopez initially refused to obey. Scared for his life after the host began to hint that she would harm him if he did not comply and realizing that she had severed the Internet lines to hinder his ability to reach out for assistance, Lopez texted his mother, Micaela Giles. Giles immediately phoned Airbnb from the family's Massachusetts home for help. However, Airbnb personnel indicated that an address to the property could not be provided as Giles was not the registered guest. Personnel went on to say that Giles would need to ask the Madrid police to call Airbnb directly for the address to be released. Giles hung up the phone and repeatedly attempted to call the Madrid police. Each time she rang authorities, she was led through a series of prompts in Spanish only to have her calls continuously dropped. After several attempts, Giles tried to call Airbnb again, but was unable to connect to the company's emergency hotline.

Eventually, Lopez was able to escape by telling the host that he had to meet friends who knew where he was and who would call the police if he did not show up to join them. According to Lopez, the host sexually assaulted him prior to his escape. When questioned, the host indicated that the sexual actions were consensual. Lopez has undergone extensive counseling to overcome the trauma resulting from the situation.[3]

Airbnb Company Overview

In 2007, two twenty-something entrepreneurs, Brian Chesky and Joe Gebbia, saw a need in a century-old industry. These two recognized that the lodging and hospitality business had not tapped into the sharing economy. Doing so could provide convenient and economical options for consumers. So, with a website entitled, airbedandbreakfast.com, the duo launched their idea.[4] Chesky and Gebbia decided to pair the debut of their start-up with a local San Francisco design conference in hopes of garnering more attention. For $80 a night, the friends rented air mattresses in their shared apartment and reached out to members of the city's designer population to do the same. Gaining the interest of only three guests and three hosts, the first attempt was an overall failure.[5] But Chesky and Gebbia did not stop there. Instead, they paralleled their second attempt with an even bigger event, the 2008 Democratic National Convention in Denver, Colorado. At this time, Nathan Blecharczyk, Gebbia's former and technologically savvy roommate, joined the team. The three were able to secure a steady revenue. However, when elections came to an end, revenue dropped significantly.[6]

At the advice of an established entrepreneur, the three took their gig to New York City, an area overpopulated with tourists and desperate for economical lodging options. This environment paired with an increasingly "open" society in which members were quickly becoming more willing to share due to social media expansion, proved to be the perfect springboard for the startup.[7]

Not long after its debut, Air Bed and Breakfast, or more commonly referred to as Airbnb, transformed into a global billion-dollar company. The entity's affiliated transactional process is fairly straightforward. Airbnb hosts post pictures of their property on the company's website and online community members can search the site to find lodging. Property prices range from less than $50 to more than $1,000 a night and guests can choose between renting an entire home or apartment, a private room, or a shared room.[8]

Airbnb prides itself in fostering a community feel amongst guests and hosts. Chesky sums it up as follows, "Airbnb is about so much more than just renting space. It's about people and experiences. At the end of the day, what we're trying to do is bring the world together.

You're not getting a room, you're getting a sense of belonging."[9] Airbnb's business model provides assets to both hosts and guests. Hosts are able to earn supplemental income, sometimes enough to cover the cost of their own rent or other property-related expenses, and guests have access to relatively low-cost accommodations that they can book efficiently.

Today, a small team of Airbnb executives manage the company. These key staff members include Chief Executive Officer, Chief Technology Officer, Chief Product Officer, Chief Financial Officer, Head of Global Hospitality, Head of Global Policy and Government Affairs, and Chief Business Affairs and Legal Officer.[10]

Airbnb's Business Model

Airbnb is among the fastest growing accommodation companies in the world. In December 2014, Chesky shared some news via Twitter: "Airbnb now has 1 million homes on its platform, and is adding more than 20,000 new ones each week".[11] Equally as impressive, the company's growth stemmed from a small workforce of approximately 1,600 employees globally.[12] Airbnb deliberately runs a lean operation, but what is most compelling about the company is that it does not own real estate. Unlike traditional hotel companies, which own and profit from physical real estate, Airbnb is purely in the business of connecting people with other people and, by doing so, people with places.

The company's core focus is connecting cost-focused travelers to homeowners that provide lodging solutions in desirable sections of cities that hotels traditionally underserve. Many users are repeat customers highlighting the fact that the service enables travelers to live like the locals. In essence, Airbnb provides unique travel experiences as well as quick, affordable, and safe accommodation for travelers.

Airbnb's business model is straightforward. Users fall into one of two classifications: hosts or guests. Hosts represent the asset owners who list their homes and apartments on the platform. In effect, hosts provide the supply of listings that are available to customers on the Airbnb digital platform. Guests reflect the demand on the platform, representing customers that are seeking to rent listings in cities around the world.

Airbnb's two main customer segments are personal travelers and business travelers, with personal travelers comprising the majority share of its users.[13] Airbnb approaches customer acquisition through two core sales channels—online advertising and word-of-mouth.[14]

According to Kenontech.com, a blog that highlights startups, "Airbnb is very aggressive with its online marketing and ads can be found through an extensive network of affiliate sites and as part of search results on major search engines."[15] Kenontech.com goes on to state that the second sales channel, which emphasizes a word-of-mouth approach, stems from the founders' belief that "if they provided their users with a great experience there would be a high probability that their users would spread the word."[16]

Furthermore, the company generates revenue from two main sources, commission from renters and commission from homeowners. Commission rates are maintained at a minimum to keep users from moving the transaction offline. Airbnb charges hosts a 3% host service fee for each booking completed on its platform. Withdrawn from the host payout, this fee covers the cost of processing guest payments.[17] Airbnb also charges a guest service fee when a customer's reservation is confirmed. The current guest service fee is a variable fee that ranges between 6–12% of the reservation subtotal (before fees and taxes). The higher the subtotal, the lower the percentage, allowing users to save money when booking large reservations.[18] Below is a useful calculation the company provides on its website to explain the host service fee structure.

Example: 4-night reservation at a listing with a nightly rate of $100 and $50 cleaning fee

- Subtotal: (4 nights x $100) + $50 cleaning fee = $450
- Host Payout: $450—(3% _ $450) = $436.50
- $450—$436.50 = $14
- Host Service Fee to Airbnb = $14 (*rounded up to nearest dollar amount*)[19]

The Nature of the Sharing Economy

The sharing economy renders the ability for anyone with an asset, whether it is a car, a home, or extra space in his or her driveway, to capitalize monetarily on that asset through simply renting it.[20] The nature of the sharing economy facilitates peer-to-peer business transactions. By way of a digital clearinghouse, companies such as Parking Panda and On the Spot allow consumers to find a parking space before they even enter a garage. Via Uber or Lyft's electronic platform, the consumer can summon a personal driver with just a couple of clicks.[21] As for finding a deal on overnight accommodations in an instant? Airbnb allows travelers to forego a call to the Holiday Inn by renting another consumer's bedroom for $50 a night or, if one prefers a more glamorous option, renting a beachside mansion for a $1,000 a night by simply perusing the company's website.[22]

All members of the sharing economy share three main attributes:

1. Rely on recent technological advances to satisfy established consumer demands in innovative ways.
2. Enter space with well-established companies and disrupt current competitive landscape.
3. Function in interstitial areas of the law due to the timing of emergence.[23]

Rapid Growth of Airbnb

Since 2008, Airbnb has enjoyed unmatched growth in the accommodations industry compared to its peers. According to the *Wall Street Journal*, which reported Airbnb's most recent valuation in June of 2015, the company has a valuation of $25 billion and 2015 revenues were projected to reach $900 million.[24] By comparison, Marriot, which manages more than 4,000 hotels and last year reached $13.8 billion in revenue, is valued at $21 billion.[25] In only a few years, Airbnb grew from a small start-up to an established company with a market value larger than many of its traditional hotel competitors. Furthermore, Airbnb's valuation is also approximately twice the size as rival travel site Expedia and more than five times the size as HomeAway, Airbnb's closest online competitor (see Figure 1).

Analysts contend Airbnb commands a premium valuation given the company's accelerated growth rate over the last few years. Airbnb's $900 million in projected revenue for 2015 was 360% of the company's revenue in 2013, which totaled $250 million. From 2014 to 2015, the company had an estimated revenue growth of 113% year-over-year.[26] Airbnb's next closest competitor for year-over-year growth was HomeAway at 24% and Expedia at 20%.

Traditional Hotels like Marriot continue to grow at more conservative rates hovering between 5-10% (see Figure 2).

Beyond revenue and valuation, Airbnb is quickly becoming a mainstream lodging brand recognized among travelers. And as brand recognition increases, interest in the company will only continue to grow. According to equity research firm CB Insights, the term "Airbnb" recently surpassed "Marriot" in Google search popularity for the first year ever in 2015.[27] Analysts remain bullish that Airbnb's online dominance will only continue to grow, further enhancing its competitive position among its primary rivals in the lodging industry (see Figure 3).

With many promising growth metrics, institutional investors continue to flock to Airbnb as a secure investment opportunity with a bright future. The Dow Jones Venture Source, an online database that tracks company performance of privately held ventured-backed companies, currently ranks Airbnb as the third most valuable private start-up in the world, trailing only Uber and Xiaomi.[28] Airbnb maintains a stable roster of investors from some of the most prominent financial services companies in the world. Notable companies include Sequoia Capital, Andreessen Horowitz, Tiger Global Management, TPG Growth, T. Rowe Price, and Fidelity Investments.[29] What is clear is that the company is well capitalized and positioned to grow.

What remains fairly uncertain to some is the company's ability to sustainably handle this growth moving forward.

Political and Regulatory Environment

On September 2, 2014, an independent city-wide poll from Quinnipiac University asked, "Do you think New York City residents should be permitted to rent rooms in their homes for a few days at a time to strangers, similar to a hotel, or should this practice be banned?"[30] The results of this poll showed a sound majority of voters, 56%, in favor of allowing short-term rentals to strangers. Only 36% of New York voters wanted to ban the use of short-term rentals.[31]

And approximately one year later in November 2015, Airbnb commissioned a survey to gauge how New York residents perceived the company to determine whether people viewed their rental service in a favorable or unfavorable way. David Bender Research, which polled more than 400 respondents over an 11-day period, conducted the survey and the following findings were determined:

- 65% believed Airbnb should be legal in New York
- 22% believed Airbnb should be illegal in New York
- 5% answered they view Airbnb "very unfavorable"
- 10% answered they view Airbnb "somewhat unfavorable"
- 25% answered they view Airbnb "somewhat favorable"
- 12% answered they view Airbnb "very favorable"
- 48% of voters had "No Opinion" of Airbnb[32]

While Airbnb maintains sound consumer support in many of the cities where it operates, the company is no stranger to political and regulatory controversy. Over the last two years, the company has been embroiled in high-profile political battles with regulators in some of its most lucrative markets, including San Francisco and New York City. In November of 2015, San Francisco voters headed to the polls to vote on Proposition F, which was commonly known as the "Airbnb Initiative."

Proposition F was a ballot initiative drafted by city officials in an effort to toughen regulations on short-term rental apartments and homes in the city of San Francisco.[33] A political initiative capable of reducing short-term listings and revenue for Airbnb, Proposition F presented the first significant instance in which Airbnb faced an organized political effort to regulate the company's business model in its own backyard—San Francisco. Numerous Airbnb opponents, including hotel industry backed opposition, affirmed Airbnb was operating under interstitial areas of law and urged regulators to codify clear rules that would regulate online rental platforms to a similar standard that traditional hotels must comply with under the law.

Proposition F attempted to enact the following key rules for Airbnb and other short-term rental platforms. If the proposition passed by a majority vote, each company, and their rental hosts, would be required to comply with the following rules:

- A 75-day imposed limit over the course of a year on all forms of short-term rentals where the host is not present during the stay. Hosts prohibited from listing a unit if it exceeded the 75-day limit.
- Require hosts and rental platforms to submit quarterly reports to the San Francisco Planning Department detailing which nights the unit was rented out and which nights the host occupied the unit
- Insert Legal Standing provisions enabling permanent residents and nonprofit housing groups the right to sue hosts and rental platforms for violating the rules.

"On November 4, 2015, San Francisco voters handed a victory to Airbnb and city residents who wanted to turn their homes into vacation rentals."[34] Proposition F lost by a vote of 55 percent to 45 percent. Airbnb outspent its opposition by a factor of 16 to 1, spending $8 million dollars to defeat the measure. In comparison, Unite Here, a hotel workers' union, raised only $482,000 in support of the measure. In the wake of Airbnb's victory, Christopher Nulty, a spokesman for the company, released the following statement, "Voters stood up for working families' right to share their homes and opposed an extreme, hotel-industry-backed measure."[35]

Terms of Service and User Liability

As opposition groups across the country remain committed to portraying Airbnb as unsafe and preoccupied with evading sensible regulations, Brian Chesky, CEO and Cofounder of Airbnb, provides his viewpoint as it relates to the sharing economy. Chesky asserts, "There were laws created for businesses, and there were laws for people. What the sharing economy did was create a third category: people as businesses."[36] Regulators in cities across the world, in particular where Airbnb operates, continue to grapple with the new business model that has risen from the sharing economy. While consumers continue to lend support to Airbnb and similar sharing economy services, questions still remain on where liabilities rest in this new way of doing business. Do liabilities rest with the users of the service or the company facilitating the service?

Airbnb's Terms of Service agreement clearly defines which party assumes liability and how Airbnb approaches risk management and legal strategy. Airbnb operates in hundreds of countries, territories, and cities across the world. Naturally, this diverse geographical presence makes it inherently difficult to inform users of all the applicable public safety, housing, and zoning laws that might apply to them as hosts or guests. Instead of opting to educate all users of the relevant housing and safety laws that apply to them in their respective territories, Airbnb chooses to place all legal responsibility on the user through their terms of service agreement.

Airbnb's Terms of Service states, "Please read these terms of service carefully as they contain important information regarding your legal rights, remedies, and obligation." Airbnb's Terms of Service is over 16,000 words in length.[37] In comparison, Marriott's Terms of Use for the United States and Canada is just under 2,500 words,[38] Uber's Terms are under 5,000 words,[39] and Homeaway, an Airbnb competitor which owns more than five other rental companies, has a Terms page on their website that totals just under 13,500 words.[40] As of February 14, 2016, Airbnb's Terms of Service were last edited on July 6, 2015, two days after the Lopez incident.

Airbnb states that it has no control over the conduct of its hosts, guests, or any other user of the site. The company disclaims all liability in this regard to the maximum extent permitted by the law. Airbnb states that it does not control the content contained in any of its listings and the condition, legality, or suitability of any accommodations. Furthermore, Airbnb states that all bookings are made and accepted at the member's own risk. The Terms of Service agreement also states that Airbnb does not act as an insurer. However, as of May 2012, Airbnb offers a Host Protection program or Host Guarantee, in which hosts are covered up to $1 million for damage and injuries. Airbnb's website states that the Host Guarantee does not cover cash and securities, pets, personal liability, or common areas.[41] Furthermore, the insurance is "secondary," meaning only after a host exhausts his or her personal insurance coverage does the Airbnb policy take effect.[42]

Members of Airbnb are sometimes listed as "verified" or "connected" which simply indicates that they went through the verification process. Per the Terms of Service, this is not a guarantee of the member's identity or whether they are trustworthy, safe, or suitable. Members are encouraged to use their own judgment when accepting and selecting hosts and guests.

Airbnb's preferred strategy of informing users of their legal responsibilities through the Terms of Service agreement does not come without contention between users and the company. Many users confirm they do not read the Terms of Service agreement and the company is aware of this significant caveat.

In September 2012, Nigel Warren, a New York City resident, illegally rented out his bedroom for $100 a night while he was away in Colorado for a three-night trip. Upon his return from Colorado, Nigel was contacted by his landlord who had been cited for five violations for operating as an "illegal transient hotel."[43] The fines, if enforced, would have amounted to $40,000 in punitive damages. Fortunately for Mr. Warren and his landlord, the city dropped the sizable fines due to an administrative error on their part.

Due to his experience, Mr. Warren posed a pressing question that many stakeholders wish the company would more thoroughly address. Acknowledging that Airbnb knows within reason that many of its hosts who live in large cities are violating rules, he wondered, "why not warn people more explicitly about the kind of trouble they could find themselves in? By ignoring local laws, you (Airbnb) are making casualties of the very people you need to make your site a success."[44]

Airbnb's Safety Tips

Tips for Guests

Clicking on the link "Trust and Safety" at the bottom of Airbnb's homepage directs one to another page where there is a link entitled "I'm a guest. What are some safety tips I can follow?" Airbnb suggests reading the reviews of other guests to ensure the host is reputable. If the guest is skeptical about the host after reading the review, they are encouraged to use their intuition and not book their stay with that host. Guests can also ask hosts to complete "profile verifications" before booking with them. Airbnb suggests that guests talk to the host and start a conversation about the upcoming stay. It also recommends traveler's insurance and reminds guests to call the local police or emergency services immediately if personal safety is threatened.[45]

Tips for Hosts

Above the link for guest safety tips, customers can learn about how to stay safe as a host. Airbnb encourages hosts to read reviews of the guests and to use common sense when accepting a guest's request to stay at their listing. Hosts can require guests to complete verifications before they book, such as Verified ID. With Verified ID, guests might be asked to upload their government-issued ID, link their Airbnb account with their page on another social media site (i.e. Facebook), or upload an Airbnb profile photo. Airbnb also asks hosts to call the local police or emergency services if their personal safety is threatened. Airbnb suggests that hosts designate a safe location in case of an emergency. Hosts can also notify their neighbors that they are hosting an Airbnb guest as a precautionary measure.[46]

Other Incidents Leading Up to July 2015

Incident 1

In June of 2011, an Airbnb host, who identified herself as "EJ," reported that the person who rented her apartment trashed it and stole jewelry, cash, and electronics. EJ wrote about this incident on her personal blog. Airbnb initially responded by trying to persuade EJ to remove her blog post and neglected to help her recover from the damages. Following the incident, Chesky stated in a blog on Airbnb's website on August 1, 2011 that he hopes "this can be a valuable lesson to other businesses about what not to do in a time of crisis. With regards to EJ, we let her down, and for that we are very sorry. We should have responded faster, communicated more sensitively, and taken more decisive action to make sure she felt safe and secure. But we weren't prepared for the crisis and we dropped the ball. Now we're dealing with the consequences." Following the response Airbnb said they would provide a $50,000 insurance guarantee for any loss or damages at the property of an Airbnb host. Since the incident the policy has increased to $1 million but is secondary to the host's personal insurance. Also, Airbnb planned to launch a 24/7 hotline for its users to report problems. Finally,

Chesky offered his own e-mail address in case customers had trouble getting in contact with an Airbnb representative.[47]

Incident 2

A couple rented an Airbnb property in the Hamptons (New York) in June 2014. Following Airbnb's safety tips, the couple read the reviews of the host and, because of the positive nature of the reviews, decided to book the stay. Before arriving at the home and exchanging keys with the host, the couple texted the host to let him know the timing of their arrival and asked a few questions about items in the house and where to pick up the keys. The host was reportedly friendly and responsive. Later that night at 2:45 AM, the male guest received a text from the host that read, "Do you want to try." Shortly after, the host let himself into the locked house with another set of keys and appeared to be inebriated. The host then asked the male guest, "The girlfriend, she's cool, right?" The male guest calmly asked the host to leave, but not before the host picked up the guest's keys and wallet. The male guest asked the host to put the items down and the host did so before departing. Shortly thereafter, the terrified couple left the home. The female guest tried to call the 24-hour emergency line, but could not reach an Airbnb representative after waiting on the line for 45 minutes. The couple then filed a complaint and received a response that Airbnb would be forwarding the case to their Trip Experience Team.

The couple drove back to Manhattan where they found a hotel to stay at for $350. That Monday, the couple contacted Airbnb by phone twice, but no one returned their calls. Only after Business Insider reached out to Airbnb for comment on the incident did Airbnb take down the host's listing and ban him from the site permanently. They refunded the couple's stay, apologized for the delay, and gave them a $500 credit to try Airbnb again. A spokesperson for Airbnb commented about the incident in a Business Insider article, "We deeply regret that this matter was not handled properly and our response fell well short of the standards we set for ourselves. This behavior is totally unacceptable and the host has been permanently removed from Airbnb."[48]

In September 2015, the couple ventured back onto Airbnb's site and found that the same property where the incident occurred was relisted on the site under a different name. Nick Papas, an Airbnb spokesman, commented in another Business Insider article, "We have technological tools and procedures that help ensure bad actors don't try to come back to our community. In this case, one investigator didn't properly employ these tools. We've since addressed this issue and we are implementing procedures to ensure it doesn't happen again.

We will also make it clear to the host that he is not welcome and has no place in the Airbnb community."[49]

Response to Lopez Incident

The onus was left to Lopez's mother to rescue her son. At the time of the incident, Airbnb's policy was to withhold the location of the guest if anyone other than the guest were to ask and would not report a crime unless contacted by the guest. Lopez's mother called the Madrid police department, but was unsuccessful in her attempts. Even if she was able to reach someone in Madrid, the inefficiency of Airbnb's protocol would likely not have allowed for police to reach her son in time. Nick Papas commented in a *New York Times* article, "We realize we can learn a lot from this incident and we can do better. We are clarifying our policies so that our team will always contact law enforcement if we are made aware of an emergency situation in progress. Safety is our No. 1 priority, and we want to get our hosts and guests as much help as possible."[50]

As reported on July 13, 2015, Belinda Johnson was promoted to Airbnb's Chief Business Affairs and Legal Officer. In this role, she is responsible for legal, civic partnerships, public policy, social and philanthropic initiatives, and communication and she "will become more of the face and the voice of the company."[51]

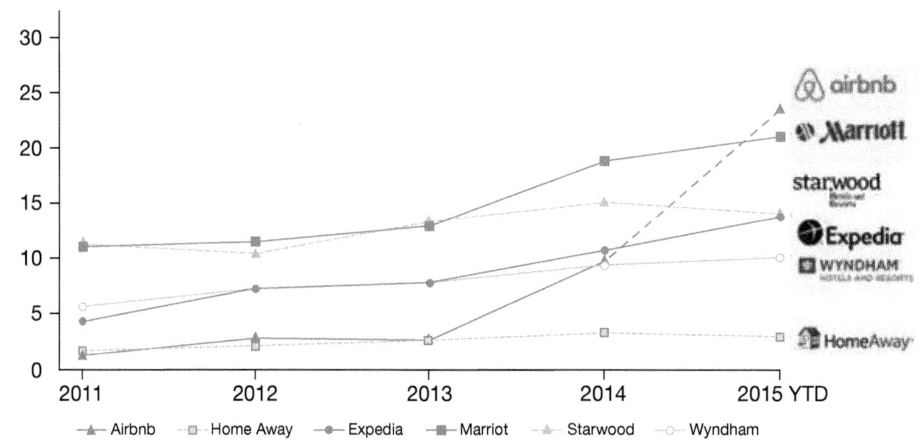

FIGURE 1—AirBnB vs. Public Competitors: Valuations Over Time ($B): 2011–2015 YTD (6.18.2015)

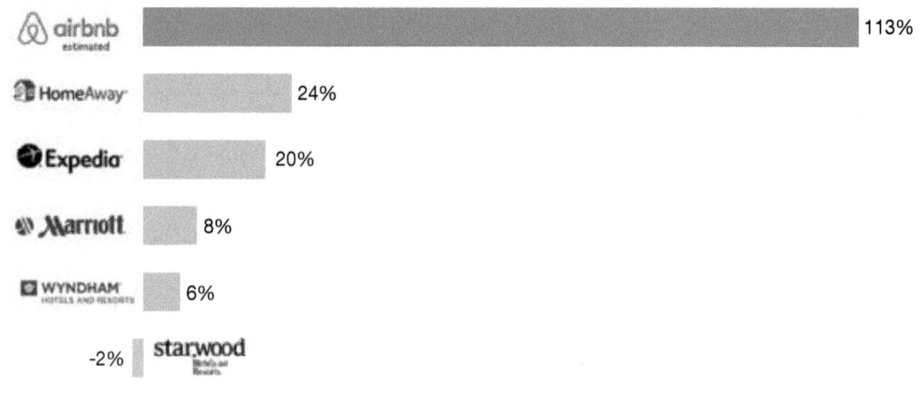

FIGURE 2—AirBnB vs. Public Competitors: Revenue Growth 2014 vs. 2015

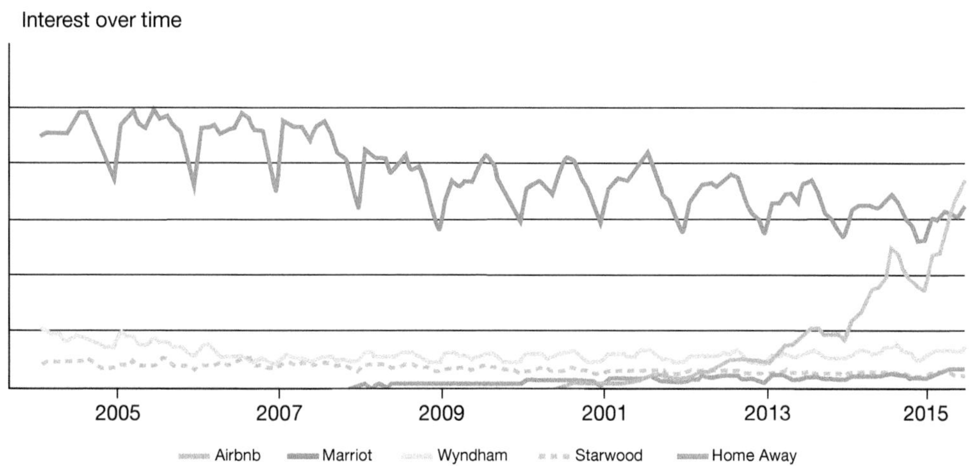

FIGURE 3—Google Search Popularity (2015)

References

1 Stump, Scott. "Airbnb Horror Story Reveals Safety Issues for Lodging Site," Web. <www.today.com/money/airbnb-horror-story-reveals-safety-issues-lodging-site-t39091>

2 Gander, Kashmira. "Airbnb Safety: Sexual Assault Allegations Against Host in Madrid Raise Questions About Website's Responsibilities," *Independent.* August 16, 2015. Accessed February 2016. <www.independent.co.uk/travel/news-and-advice/airbnb-safety-sexual-assault-allegations-against-host-in-madrid-raise-questions-about-websites-10457992.html>

3 Lieber, Ron. "A Warning for Hosts of Airbnb Travelers," *New York Times.* November 30, 2012. Accessed February 2016. <www.nytimes.com/2012/12/01/your-money/a-warning-for-airbnb-hosts-who-may-be-breaking-the-law.html?_r=1>

4 Helm, Burt. "Airbnb is Inc.'s 2014 Company of the Year," Web. <www.inc.com/magazine/201412/burt-helm/airbnb-company-of-the-year-2014.html>

5 Ibid.

6 Ibid.

7 Ibid.

8 Airbnb. "About Us," Accessed February 2016. Web. <www.airbnb.com/about/about-us>

9 Helm, Burt, "Airbnb is Inc.'s 2014 Company of the Year." Web. <www.inc.com/magazine/201412/burt-helm/airbnb-company-of-the-year-2014.html>

10 *Bloomberg Business.* Accessed February 2016. Web. <www.bloomberg.com/research/stocks/private/people.asp?privcapId=115705393>

11 Griswold, Allison. "Airbnb's Latest Milestone: 1 Million Homes, and Hardly Anyone Noticed," December 8, 2014. Accessed April 2016. <www.slate.com/blogs/moneybox/2014/12/08/airbnb_has_1_million_homes_brian_chesky_announces_milestone_and_almost_no.html>

12 Polletti, Therese. "What Really Keeps Airbnb CEO, Brian Chesky, Up At Night," February 2015. Web. <www.marketwatch.com/story/what-really-keeps-airbnbs-ceo-up-at-night-2015–02–13 >

13 Osterwalder, Alexander. "Dissecting Airbnb's Business Model Case," February 2014. Web. <www.kenontek.com/2014/02/09/dissecting-airbnbs-business-model-canvas/>

14 Ibid.

15 Ibid.

16 Ibid.

17 Airbnb. "What Are Host Service Fees," Accessed February 2016. Web. <www.airbnb.com/help/article/63/what-are-host-service-fees>

18 Airbnb. "What Are Guest Service Fees," Accessed February 2016. Web. <www.airbnb.com/help/article/104/what-are-guest-service-fees>

19 Airbnb. "What Are Host Service Fees," Accessed February 2016. Web. <www.airbnb.com/help/article/63/what-are-host-service-fees>

20 Kokalitcheva, Kia. "Who's Liable When an Airbnb Stay or Uber Ride Ends Badly?" November 10, 2015. Accessed February 2016. <http://fortune.com/2015/11/10/sharing-economy-safety-liability/>

21 Geron, Tomio. *Forbes*. January 23, 2013. Accessed February 2016. <www.forbes.com/sites/tomiogeron/2013/01/23/airbnb-and-the-unstoppable-rise-of-the-share-economy#73ff0df56>

22 Millette, Eric. "Airbnb and the Unstoppable Rise of the Share Economy," *Forbes*. Feb. 11, 2013.

23 Kaplan, Roberta & Nadler, Michael. "Airbnb: A Case Study in Occupancy Regulation and Taxation," *The University of Chicago Law Review*. 2015.

24 Winkler, Rolfe & Macmillan , Douglas. "The Secret Math of Airbnb's 24 Billion Valuation," *Wall Street Journal*. June 17, 2015. Accessed February 2016. <www.wsj.com/articles/the-secret-math-of-airbnbs-24-billion-valuation-1434568517>

25 Ibid.

26 Krishnan, Nikhil. "Why That Crazy-High Aibnb Valuation Is Fair," Linkedin. June 24, 2015. Accessed February 2016. <www.linkedin.com/pulse/why-crazy-high-airbnb-valuation-fair-nikhil-krishnan>

27 Ibid.

28 Austin, Scott, Canipe, Chris & Slobin, Sarah. "The Billion Dollar Start Up Club," *Wall Street Journal*. February 18, 2015. Accessed February 2016. <http://graphics.wsj.com/billion-dollar-club/>

29 Ibid.

30 Fischer, Ben. "Q-Poll Doesn't Quite Say What Airbnb Wants It To Say," *Biz Journals*. September 2, 2014. Accessed February 2016. <www.bizjournals.com/newyork/blog/techflash/2014/09/q-poll-doesnt-quite-say-what-airbnb-wants-it-to.html>

31 Ibid.

32 Noto, Anthony. "Poll: Majority of New Yorkers View Airbnb in Positive Light," *Biz Journals*. November 5, 2015. Accessed February 2016. <www.bizjournals.com/newyork/news/2015/11/05/majority-of-new-yorkers-view-airbnb-in.html>

33 Lien, Tracey. "Everything You Need To Know About San Francisco's Airbnb Ballot Measure," *Los Angeles Times*. October 30, 2015. Accessed February 2016. <www.latimes.com/business/technology/la-fi-tn-airbnb-prop-f-san-francisco-20151029-htmlstory.html>

34 Said, Carolyn. "Prop F: S.F. Voters Reject Measure to Restrict Airbnb Rentals," SF Gate. November 4, 2015. Accessed February 2016. <www.sfgate.com/bayarea/article/Prop-F-Measure-to-restrict-Airbnb-rentals-6609176.php>

35 Ibid.

36 Kaplan, Roberta & Nadler, Michael. "Airbnb: A Case Study in Occupancy Regulation and Taxation," *The University of Chicago Law Review*. 2015. Accessed February 2016. <https://lawreview.uchicago.edu/page/airbnb-case-study-occupancy-regulation-and-taxation>

37 "Airbnb Terms of Service." Accessed February 2016. Web. <www.airbnb.com/terms>

38 "Marriott Terms of Use for United States & Canada," Accessed February 2016. Web. <www.marriott.com/about/terms-of-use.mi>

39 "Uber Terms and Conditions." Accessed February 2016. Web. <www.uber.com/legal/usa/terms>

40 "Homeaway Terms and Conditions." Accessed February 2016. Web. <www.homeaway.com/info/about-us/legal/terms-conditions>

41 "Airbnb Host Guarantee Terms and Conditions." Accessed February 2016. Web. <www.airbnb.com/terms/host_guarantee>

42 Lieber, Ron. "A Liability Risk for Airbnb Hosts," *New York Times*. December 5, 2014. Accessed February 2016. <www.nytimes.com/2014/12/06/your-money/airbnb-offers-homeowner-liability-coverage-but-hosts-still-have-risks.html>

43 Lieber, Ron. "A Warning for Hosts of Airbnb Travelers," *New York Times*. November 30, 2012. Accessed February 2016. <www.nytimes.com/2012/12/01/your-money/a-warning-for-airbnb-hosts-who-may-be-breaking-the-law.html?_r=1>

44 Ibid.

45 "Airbnb Trust and Safety," Accessed February 2016. Web. <www.airbnb.com/help/article/241/i-m-a-guest—what-are-some-safety-tips-i-can-follow>

46 Ibid.

47 Olivarez-Giles, Nathan. "Airbnb Offers $50,000 Insurance Policy after User's 'Nightmare'," *Los Angeles Times*. August 1, 2011. Accessed February 2016. <http://latimesblogs.latimes.com/technology/2011/08/airbnb-insurance-guarantee.html>

48 Bort, Julie. "An Airbnb Host Got Drunk And Let Himself Into The House While A Business Insider Employee Was Sleeping," Business Insider. June 24, 2014. Accessed February 2016. <www.businessinsider.com/bi-employee-has-airbnb-horror-story-2014–6>

49 Bort, Julie. "Banned Airbnb Host Who Entered The House While His Guests Were Sleeping Was Back On Airbnb," Business Insider. October 6, 2014. Accessed February 2016. <www.businessinsider.com/banned-airbnb-host-was-back-on-the-site-2014–10>

50 Lieber, Ron. "Airbnb Horror Story Points to Need for Precautions." *New York Times*. August 14, 2015. Accessed February 2016. <www.nytimes.com/2015/08/15/your-money/airbnb-horror-story-points-to-need-for-precautions.html>

51 Bellstrom, Kristen. "Exclusive: Meet Airbnb's Highest Ranking Female Exec Ever." *Fortune*. July 13, 2015. Accessed February 2016. <http://fortune.com/2015/07/13/airbnb-belinda-johnson-promotion/>

Part IV

Building the Ethical Company

Chapter 12

Building Ethics at the Corporate Level

Managing the Ethical Climate

LEARNING OBJECTIVES

After reading this chapter you should be able to:

- Understand the concept of ethical climate as a type of work climate
- Identify the different types of ethical climates and be able to explain how each type works
- Understand how ethical climates affect ethical decision-making and behaviors in organizations
- Explain the differences between the general organizational culture and the ethical climate
- Know how to create and maintain different ethical climate types
- Understand how to identify the ethical climate in your organization

PREVIEW BUSINESS ETHICS INSIGHT

Caring Climates: Salesforce and Synovus

How do companies promote a caring climate? A caring ethical climate is when a company values the welfare of people, both inside and outside the organization, more than other organizational objectives. Here you see two companies, Salesforce and Synovus, that have similar ethical climates.

Salesforce is an information technology company selling customer relationship management tools. How does Salesforce show its caring climate? Below are just a few examples.

Volunteering is important and the company gives all employees seven paid days off to volunteer. As part of its Global Volunteer Week employees work at over 1200 nonprofits worldwide. By March of last year, the company easily passed its goal to provide 17,000 volunteer hours to the nonprofits.

A survey of the employees found:

- 97% feel good about the ways we contribute to the community.
- 96% report that they are proud to tell others I work here.
- 96% believe that management is honest and ethical in its business practices.
- 95% people care about each other here.

Consider the following quotes to get a feeling for the ethical climate at Salesforce:

> This is an extraordinarily special place that really cares about its employees, customers, and community. We are strongly encouraged to give back. I have done everything from volunteering in a soup kitchen, to working at a children's hospital in Morocco—all supported by the company. Most importantly, I look forward to coming to work every day, working with our wonderful community, and doing satisfying, challenging work.

> The thing I think that most separates [Salesforce] from other companies is the focus on giving back. Personally, it provides me with a greater sense of purpose when I come in each day.

For over 20 years, Synovus, a financial holding company, has been on *Fortune*'s "100 Best Companies to Work for" list. Synovus has over 13,000 employees in 700 locations throughout the U.S. yet they manage to create a team feeling that makes work have a family atmosphere. Creating this climate starts at the top with Senior Vice President Marty Grueber, who is responsible for external community involvement and for the quality of the work lives of team members. Symbolizing this team climate is the Synovus motto: "It's a team and we love each other." Consider these values from their website:

Putting People First. Passion. Humility. Values. Family: These are not just words to us, but a way of life at Synovus. We call it the "Culture of the Heart," and we believe it is the key to being a great company. It's a special spirit and a way of work that leads each of us to do great things each day.

People First: People are our top priority. This is what makes the Synovus family special. It is what makes us a great place to work. Our number one responsibility is for our team members. If we take care of our people, our people will take care of the business.

Based on: http://fortune.com/2017/02/09/best-workplaces-giving-back. *People's 50 Companies that care 2017: People partners with great place to work® to identify the top U.S. companies caring for their communities, their employees, and the world* http://reviews.greatplacetowork.com/salesforce?utm_source=fortune&utm_medium=referral&utm_content=reviews-link&utm_campaign=2017-Care-list. GeorgiaTrend, *2016 Best places to work* www.georgiatrend.com/July-2016/2016-Best-Places-to-Work/. www.synovus.com/about-us/news/2016/2016-07-01-georgia-trend-best-places-to-work.

The Preview Business Ethics Insight above shows how companies can create different types of climates or cultures that influence ethical decision-making. For Salesforce and Synovus, it is clear that people in the company are expected to have a high concern for others. The leadership supports this view and the employees react with loyalty to the company. The Preview Business Ethics Insight also shows how critical it is for companies to encourage an organizational culture that emphasizes caring.

Given the importance of ethical climate and culture, in this chapter we will learn about both. First, you will learn about ethical climate and the various types of climates found in companies. Each type provides the members of the organization guides on how to make ethical decisions. Second, you will also read about organizational culture and how it differs from ethical climates. You will also become aware of the many ways of promoting the right types of ethical culture in the organization.

AN OVERVIEW OF ETHICAL CLIMATE

An Ethical Climate Model

Ethical climate is a type of work climate. **Work climates** represent the shared perceptions of procedures, policies and practices, both formal and informal, of the organization.[1] Researchers have identified an assortment of work climate such as climates for innovation,[2] creativity,[3] and warmth and support.[4] Ethical climate is a work climate that reflects the organizational procedures, policies, and practices with moral consequences.

The **ethical climate** represents what organizational members believe are the forms of ethical reasoning or behavior and the expected standards or norms for ethical decision-making within the company.[5] That is, the ethical climate tells you what constitutes right behavior, and thus becomes a psychological mechanism through which ethical issues are managed. Ethical climate not only influences which moral criteria members use to understand, weigh and resolve ethical dilemmas but also tells organization members which stakeholders to consider in ethical decision-making.[6] As such, the ethical climate in your organization is part of the organizational culture that represents how people in the organization believe ethical decisions are made and how ethical decisions should be made.

Formally, ethical climate is defined as "the shared perception of what is considered correct behavior in the organization, and how ethical situations should be handled in the organization."[7] It is important to remember that the idea of an ethical climate as used here is not what an employee believes is ethical for him/herself but what is expected of them by the organization—the leadership, colleagues and friends. Thus, climate represents shared norms and values of what you "should" do and what you are expected to do in your organization when confronted with an ethical dilemma.

An ethical climate can differ by team, department, or the whole organization. Sport teams and social organizations also have ethical climates. Think about the organizations where you have worked or joined. To get a picture of an ethical climate you can consider questions like the following:

- What behaviors do organizational members believe are ethical in the company?
- What issues do people consider relevant to guide their ethical decision-making?
- What criteria do people use to understand and resolve these issues?
- How similar are the organizational members in their behaviors and decision-making styles related to ethics.

Ethical Climate Types

An organization's ethical climate is more complex than a single perspective on how to behave ethically in the organization. Rather, an ethical climate can be mapped into a variety of different sub-dimensions, the mixture of which is unique to each organization.

Over 30 years ago, Victor and Cullen introduced what is perhaps the most famous model of the types of ethical climate. Since then it has been the dominant way researchers have looked at ethical climate. Exhibit 12.1 shows a diagram of the types of ethical climates based on their work and the numerous research studies done since the model was developed.[8] These ethical climates represent the different ways employees identify the forms of reasoning they are expected to use in organizational decision-making.

To understand how Exhibit 12.1 maps ethical climate types you need to look at each axis. In the vertical axis, you see the ethical criteria that help guide possible ethical decision-making in the organization. These very much match the major ethical theories of egoism, benevolence and deontology (principle). Basically, these criteria mean that, when faced with an ethical issue, you can take into account what is good for one's self (egoism), take into account what is good for others (benevolence), and take into

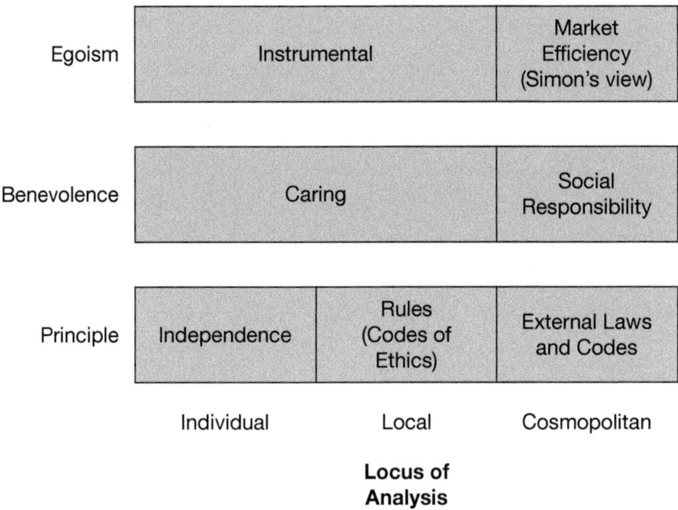

EXHIBIT 12.1—Ethical Climate Types

account rules of behavior (principles). The horizontal axis further defines the ethical climate types by identifying the groups that are considered when making ethical decisions in the organization. Using the ethical criteria, people can make ethical decisions taking a personal perspective (individual), a local perspective (such as the team or the company), or an external perspective, what we call the cosmopolitan. Next, we describe each climate type in a little more detail.

Principled climates occur when the organization has norms that encourage people to make ethical decisions based on a set of standards. In terms of the reference level, people in some organizations may make ethical decisions based on external codes such as a professional code of conduct. For example, you can see the classic ethical code of physicians, called the Hippocratic Oath, in the Business Ethics Insight on page 624. Although the Hippocratic Oath has evolved to deal with modern medicine, it still provides guiding principles for those who work in the medical profession. So, for example, the ethical climate of a hospital may be represented by values from the Hippocratic Oath or its more modern renditions. Other cosmopolitan principles that may guide ethical decision-making in organizations might include following national law or religious laws such as the Muslim *Sharia* or the Christian Bible. Consider the Business Ethics Insight on page 624.

To the degree that a hospital, for example, has expectations that physicians follow codes like the Hippocratic Oath, this would represent a principled ethical climate based on **law and code**.

Companies also develop their own **ethical codes** of conduct in an attempt to identify the ethical principles that are used to guide the ethical decision-making within their organizations. In this sense, for a local principled ethical climate, people are expected to follow the company's code of conduct. For example, with regard to bribery, if the code says one cannot take a gift worth more than $10, the "right" thing to do when offered something more expensive by a possible supplier is to refuse the gift. Codes of conduct increasingly being implemented by organizations in the contemporary corporate landscape appeal primarily to this dimension of ethical climate, which we call the rules of ethical climate.

Professor Charles Kerns categorizes company ethical codes into three types:[9]

- Type 1. **Inspirational–Idealistic** codes focus on broad virtuous themes such as "Be honest," "Show integrity in all matters," "Practice wise decision-making." They do not identify specific behaviors or situations but instead give broad guiding principles that can be applied when faced with an ethical dilemma. Perhaps the most famous of this type of principle guide is the Johnson & Johnson Credo shown in Exhibit 12.2.
- Type 2. **Regulatory** codes of conduct specify how to behave in specific situations. This is what Kerns calls a "do and don't" approach. The Coca-Cola code shown in Exhibit 12.3 represents this type of code.
- Type 3. **Educational/Learning-Oriented** codes of conduct are something of a cross between the inspirational–idealistic code and the regulatory codes. It suggests guides for decision-making and behavioral reactions when faced with ethically challenging situations.

Codes of ethical conduct help establish the local principled ethical climate in organizations. However, without managerial leadership, example-setting and enforcement they will not be very effective in creating a principled ethical climate.

The last principal ethical climate, called **independent**, has norms that support ethical decision-making based on personal morality. In this sense, each individual is expected to behave in a way that he or she personally considers ethical. Organizations that promote this type of climate often attempt to recruit people who are similar in terms of what they believe are the correct ways to behave ethically.

BUSINESS ETHICS INSIGHT

Hippocratic Oath: Ethical Principles for a Physician's Work

I swear by Apollo the Physician and Asclepius and Hygieia and Panaceia and all the gods, and goddesses, making them my witnesses, that I will fulfill according to my ability and judgment this oath and this covenant:

To hold him who has taught me this art as equal to my parents and to live my life in partnership with him, and if he is in need of money to give him a share of mine, and to regard his offspring as equal to my brothers in male lineage and to teach them this art—if they desire to learn it—without fee and covenant; to give a share of precepts and oral instruction and all the other learning to my sons and to the sons of him who has instructed me and to pupils who have signed the covenant and have taken the oath according to medical law, but to no one else.

I will apply dietic measures for the benefit of the sick according to my ability and judgment; I will keep them from harm and injustice.

I will neither give a deadly drug to anybody if asked for it, nor will I make a suggestion to this effect. In purity and holiness I will guard my life and my art.

I will not use the knife, not even on sufferers from stone, but will withdraw in favor of such men as are engaged in this work.

Whatever houses I may visit, I will come for the benefit of the sick, remaining free of all intentional injustice, of all mischief and in particular of sexual relations with both female and male persons, be they free or slaves.

What I may see or hear in the course of treatment or even outside of the treatment in regard to the life of men, which on no account one must spread abroad, I will keep myself holding such things shameful to be spoken about.

If I fulfill this oath and do not violate it, may it be granted to me to enjoy life and art, being honored with fame among all men for all time to come; if I transgress it and swear falsely, may the opposite of all this be my lot.

Based on Translation from the Greek by Ludwig Edelstein. From *The Hippocratic Oath: Text, translation, and interpretation, by Ludwig Edelstein.* Baltimore, MD: Johns Hopkins Press, 1943. www.pbs.org/wgbh/nova/doctors/oath_classical.html.

Caring climates, as shown in our Preview Business Ethics Insight, occur when the organization has norms that encourage people to make ethical decisions based on looking out for the welfare of others, particularly for team members and those within the company as well as caring for the community and society in general. In most organizations with caring climates, people believe that the right thing to do is to look out for the welfare of friends and co-workers. The Preview Business Ethics Insight showed two companies that are dominated by caring climates that encourage caring both within and outside the organization. In addition, recent research[10] suggests that organizations with more caring cosmopolitan climates—that is, those with norms and values for caring directed outside their organization—are more likely to see social responsibility as something done to benefit people rather than help make the organization more profitable.

Our Credo

We believe our first responsibility is to the doctors, nurses and patients, to mothers and fathers and all others who use our products and services, in meeting their needs everything we do must be of high quality. We must constantly strive to reduce our costs in order to maintain reasonable prices. Customers' orders must be serviced promptly and accurately. Our suppliers and distributors must have an opportunity to make a fair profit.

We are responsible to our employees, the men and women who work with us throughout the world. Everyone must be considered as an individual. We must respect their dignity and recognize their merit. They must have a sense of security in their jobs. Compensation must be fair and adequate, and working conditions clean, orderly and safe. We must be mindful of ways to help our employees fulfill their family responsibilities. Employees must feel free to make suggestions and complaints. There must be equal opportunity for employment, development and advancement for those qualified. We must provide competent management, and their actions must be just and ethical.

We are responsible to the communities in which we live and work and to the world community as well. We must be good citizens—support good works and charities and bear our fair share of taxes. We must encourage civic improvements and better health and education. We must maintain in good order the property we are privileged to use, protecting the environment and natural resources.

Our final responsibility is to our stockholders. Business must make a sound profit. We must experiment with new ideas. Research must be carried on, innovative programs developed and mistakes paid for. New equipment must be purchased, new facilities provided and new products launched. Reserves must be created to provide for adverse times. When we operate according to these principles, the stockholders should realize a fair return.

EXHIBIT 12.2—Johnson & Johnson Credo

- **Acting with Integrity Around the Globe**
  Integrity is fundamental to The Coca-Cola Company. Along with our other values of leadership, passion, accountability, collaboration, diversity and quality, it is a pillar of our 2020 Vision.
- **What Is Expected of Everyone**
  Comply with the Code and the Law. Understand the Code. Comply with the Code and the law wherever you are. Use good judgment and avoid even the appearance of improper behavior. Consider Your Actions, and Ask for Guidance
- **When Written Approval Is Required**
  Certain actions referenced in the Code—specifically, use of Company assets outside of your employment and certain conflict of interest situations—require prior written approval from your Local Ethics Officer.
- **Raising Concerns**
  We all have an obligation to uphold the ethical standards of The Coca-Cola Company. If you observe behavior that concerns you, or that may represent a violation of our Code, raise the issue promptly. Doing so will allow the Company an opportunity to deal with the issue and correct it, ideally before it becomes a violation of law or a risk to health, security or the Company's reputation.
- **Business and Financial Records**
  Ensure the accuracy of all Company business and financial records. These include not only financial accounts, but other records such as quality reports, time records, expense reports and submissions such as benefits claim forms and résumés.
- **Company Assets**
  Protect the Company's assets, and use those assets in the manner intended. Do not use Company assets for your personal benefit or the benefit of anyone other than the Company.
- **Use of Information**
  Safeguard the Company's nonpublic information, which includes everything from contracts and pricing information to marketing plans, technical specifications and employee information.
- **Conflict of Interest**
  Act in the best interest of The Coca-Cola Company while performing your job for the Company. A conflict of interest arises when your personal activities and relationships interfere, or appear to interfere, with your ability to act in the best interest of the Company.
- **Gifts, Meals and Entertainment**
  Do not accept gifts, meals or entertainment, or any other favor, from customers or suppliers if doing so might compromise, or appear to compromise, your ability to make objective business decisions in the best interest of The Coca-Cola Company.
- **Dealing with Governments**
  In general, do not offer anything to a government official—directly or indirectly—in return for favorable treatment. You must obtain prior approval from Company legal counsel before providing anything of value to a government official.
- **Dealing with Customers, Suppliers and Consumers**
  The Company values its partnerships with customers, suppliers and consumers. Treat these partners in the same manner we expect to be treated.
- **Dealing with Competitors**
  Take care in dealing with competitors, and gathering information about competitors. Various laws govern these sensitive relationships.

EXHIBIT 12.3—Coca-Cola's Code of Business Conduct

Source: Excerpts from The Coca-Cola Company. *Code of Business Conduct,* May 2016

BUSINESS ETHICS INSIGHT

Malden Mills: Too Much of a Caring Ethical Climate; any Regrets?

Malden Mills, a family-run and -operated company in Malden, Massachusetts, grew by 200% in the 1980s and 1990s as Polarfleece, a 100% polyester, capable of wicking moisture away from the body while still providing warmth, drove up sales. As Polarfleece became a popular fabric for high-performance athletic and aerobic apparel, outerwear producers such as L.L. Bean, Eddie Bauer and Patagonia flooded Malden with orders. The product was even adapted for military use. *Time* magazine named Polartec, the trade name for Polarfleece, as one of the greatest inventions of the twentieth century.

At a time when the textile industry in New England was in sharp decline, Malden Mills was booming. While outdated factories and increased labor costs led many companies to abandon the area and relocate to lower-cost countries, Malden had over 2000 employees and contributed approximately $100 million a year into the local economy.

Unfortunately, on December 11, 1995, while owner Aaron Feuerstein was celebrating his 70th birthday with family and friends at a Boston restaurant, a devastating fire destroyed much of the factory and injured 33 employees. The explosion-sparked fire destroyed three of the company's nine buildings and caused an estimated $500 million in damages. The fire was not only a disaster for Malden but it was also a potential disaster for an entire community.

Many predicted that Aaron Feuerstein would take the $300 million insurance money and relocate or dissolve the business. This was an opportunity to follow the industry to lower-cost areas with cheaper labor or for the 70-year-old Feuerstein just to retire. Feuerstein shocked many when he immediately vowed to rebuild and announced just three nights later that Malden Mills would reopen on January 2. Moreover, he intended to pay all employees their regular salaries (at a cost of $1.5 million per week) for the next 30 days, possibly longer, and that he would continue health benefits for 90 days. This choice gained him international and national recognition for putting employees first.

It cost Feuerstein $25 million to keep his employees on the payroll. In spite of Malden's continued support of health benefits and exoneration from blame, the injured employees also sued the company and Feuerstein settled for an undisclosed amount. Rebuilding a state-of-the-art plant, the first new textile mill in New England in more than 100 years, cost an additional $100 million. This was all too much for Malden. By 2001, Feuerstein was forced to file for bankruptcy due to the cost of financing the rebuilding project. He struggled until 2003 to maintain family control of his company. Although he failed, he told reporters,

> we insist the business must be profitable . . . But we also insist a business must have responsibility for its workers, for the community and the

environment. It has a social obligation to figure out a strategy, which will be able to permit workers to make a living wage. There's a responsibility to the workforce, to this community.

By July 2004, Aaron Feuerstein, at 78, was fired as Malden Mills' CEO by the new owners.

More than a decade after he was fired, on his 90th birthday in 2015 Mr. Feuerstein, who still lives alone and is self-sufficient, responded emphatically "The answer is yes," when asked if he would do it again. Not only did he run a caring company he demonstrated a type of principled moral reasoning but keeping to his beliefs. A devout Jew, Mr. Feuerstein is often called a "mensch," meaning a person of honor and strong character in Yiddish.

Based on Tennant, Paul, "Despite bankruptcy, former Malden Mills owner glad he saved jobs after historic fire," www.pressherald.com, December 11, 2015. www.fundinguniverse.com/company-histories/Malden-Mills-Industries-Inc-Company-History, html; *Boston Globe*, December 12, 13, 14, 1995; September 14, 2003; January 29 and July 27, 2004; *Lawrence Eagle Tribune*, November 15, 2001; *Forward*, "Fabled mill owner works to manufacture a miracle," July 25, 2003; Diesenhouse, Susan, "A textile maker thrives by breaking all the rules," *New York Times*, July 24, 1994: Herszenhorn, David M., "A plume of hope rises from factory ashes . . ." *New York Times*, December 16, 1995; Teal, Thomas, "Not a fool; Not a saint," *Fortune*, November 11, 1996; Owens, Mitchell, "A mill community comes back to life," *New York Times*, December 26, 1996: Rotenier, Nancy, "The golden fleece," *Forbes*, May 24, 1993; Lee, Melissa, "Malden looks spiffy in New England textile gloom," *Wall Street Journal*, November 10, 1995: Goldberg, Carey, "A promise is kept," *New York Times*, September 16, 1997.

The Business Ethics Insight above discusses Malden Mills and its CEO owner Aaron Feuerstein. Mr. Feuerstein had perhaps what is considered the most classic example of the caring organization as he held to those expectations of caring under the most trying times by keeping his employees on the payroll even after his factory was destroyed by fire. However, perhaps because he failed to keep an eye on the bottom line, Malden Mills eventually was forced into bankruptcy and employees and other stakeholders eventually lost out. After reading the Business Ethics Insight, how do you react to Mr. Feuerstein's approach to his organization?

Organizations having an **instrumental ethical climate** see their organizational unit as having norms and expectations that encourage ethical decision-making from an egoistic perspective. What is more, the actor perceives that self-interest guides behavior, even to the possible detriment of others. One believes that decisions are made that serve the organization's interests or provide personal benefits.[11] Even when considered in a variety of contexts, studies consistently show that instrumental climates are the least preferred.[12]

Instrumental ethical climates occur when the organization has norms that encourage people to define right and wrong in terms of the consequences to one's self. Thus, when faced with an ethical dilemma people are expected to make decisions based on what best serves self-interest. Researchers have found that, within organizations, one's self most often means the organization rather than the individual. As such, an instrumental ethical climate often means what you are expected to do is to look out for what is best for company profit.

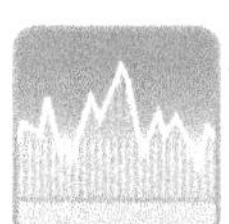

EMERGING MARKET BUSINESS ETHICS INSIGHT

Cost versus Safety in the Indian Auto Industry: Does History Repeat Itself

India has among the highest number of road accidents in the world. One possible reason is that many of the top selling cars are unsafe, at least according to ratings from the UK-based Global New Car Assessment Programme.

But there is a trade-off. Indian manufacturing companies argue that adding such safety protections such as airbags and anti-lock braking systems to their smaller less expensive cars will increase costs and reduce sales. RC Bhargava, chairman of Maruti Suzuki, captured the issue noting, "The growth of manufacturing will be impacted if the government decides to mandate these features across Indian car models."

Ford produced the Pinto in the 1970s in response to rising fuel prices and competition from fuel efficient Japanese auto manufacturers. The charge from then Ford CEO, Lee Iacocca was clear—we need a competitive fuel-efficient car now. The pressure to move fast resulted in a design flaw where the fuel tank, located in the rear, could explode with a rear end collision. The first reaction was to recall the car and fix the problem as it only cost $11 a car for the necessary repairs. However, the smart financial analysts at Ford scurried to their calculators. What did Ford do? They opted for the economically rational decision. A cost-benefit analysis showed that the cost of repairs ($137 million) exceeded the predicted cost of settlements for deaths and injuries ($50 million). The conclusion was that it made financial sense to allow a small number of people die in a car with a known design flaw.

According to Luis Miranda, a famous Indian business executive,

> the case in India sounds remarkably similar to the Ford Pinto case in the US. The argument by the Indian car manufacturing industry today is the same – the cost of lives is less than the cost of improving the safety standards of small cars in India. The Pinto story became a symbol of the cold-hearted profit maximization attitude of companies. Unfortunately, after 40 years we hear a repeat in India.

Miranda cautions Indian auto manufacturers to learn from the Pinto experience in the U.S.

Based on: Miranda, Luis. 2014. "Is the Indian auto industry ethically blind? The case of airbag costs vs passenger safety." *Forbes, India*. November 25, 2014 www.forbesindia.com/blog/author/luis.miranda/

An instrumental climate is actually close to what the Nobel-Prize-winning economist Milton Friedman argued: the only moral obligation of business is to make a profit and the only constraint is to obey the law.[13] Although on first glance such an ethical climate may seem inherently unethical, free market economists such as Friedman argue that, when acting under the rule of law, companies acting in their own self-interest create an efficient economic system. The market selects out the best companies that survive and profit, and everyone is better off. The Emerging Market Business Ethics Insight above gives some insights about the dangers of such an approach.

BUSINESS ETHICS INSIGHT

Wells Fargo's Instrumental Ethical Climate

Founded in 1852 as a stagecoach express, Wells Fargo eventually became one of the largest banks in the United States.

In 2015, the industry was rocked by a major scandalous revelation.

In an effort to have customers buy additional Wells Fargo products (called "cross-selling"), between 2011 and 2015 and possibly before, Wells Fargo employees opened more than 1.5 million unauthorized deposit accounts and over 550,000 credit card accounts. The payoff was that Wells Fargo collected over 2.6 million dollars in fees on accounts, most of which the customers did not know they had. Some customers even had to deal with collection agencies that attempted to collect on the fees for these unknown accounts. To open the accounts, some Wells Fargo employees assigned bogus pins to customers without their knowledge and then used the pins to enroll customers unknowingly in other Wells Fargo products. After an *LA Times* investigation discovered these offenses, several state and national regulatory boards investigated. This led to Wells Fargo paying US$185 million in fines and the firing of over 5300 employees. Eventually, the CEO and several top executives were forced out.

How could this come about for a company that claims, "We place customers at the center of everything we do. We want to exceed customer expectations and build relationships that last a lifetime," as one of its primary values?

As the scandal became public, it became apparent that intense pressure on employees to meet or exceed unrealistic sales quotas pushed employees to succeed at any cost. Starting at the top, CEO John Stumpf, pointed out repeatedly that Wells Fargo's cross-selling success was a driver of stock prices. "Eight is great," where every customer has at least eight Wells Fargo products was the mantra for Stumpf.

The sales pressure became so strong that it was a called a breeding ground for unethical behavior. Examples of practices in the company included such things as hourly tracking of sales and a heavily bonus-based compensation system. Other organizational culture rituals increased the pressure as well. One was the practice of "running the gantlet." Dressed in themed costumes, district managers formed a gautlet and subordinate managers ran individually down the line to report their sales numbers on whiteboards. One regional sales manager used "morning huddles" to discuss sales reports as well as pressuring district managers to call branches multiple times a day to get reports on sales figures. Retail scorecards, also apparently "generated significant sales pressure." One practice, called "Jump into January" was a sales campaign to kick off each year with high sales was described by some as "a breeding ground for bad behavior."

A high-level report later commissioned by Wells Fargo to assess how this scandal happened concluded: "Even when challenged by their regional leaders, the senior leadership of . . . failed to appreciate or accept that their sales goals were too high and becoming increasingly untenable."

It was convenient instead to blame the problem of low quality and unauthorized accounts and other employee misconduct on individual wrongdoers.

Effect was confused with cause. When Wells Fargo did identify misconduct, its solution generally was to terminate the offending employee without considering causes for the offending conduct or determining whether there were responsible individuals who, while they might not have directed the specific misconduct, contributed to the environment that increased the chances of its occurrence.

Based on: Frost, Wilfred. 2017. "Wells Fargo report gives inside look at the culture that crushed the bank's reputation." April 10, 2017, CNBC.com. McLean, Bethany. 2017. "How Wells Fargo's cutthroat corporate culture allegedly drove bankers to fraud." *Vanity Fair* Summer 2017. www.wellsfargo.com/about/corporate/vision-and-values/

However, an instrumental climate comes with risks. Consider the Business Ethics Insight above, which looks at some of instrumental climate characteristics of Wells Fargo and the consequences of such a climate leading to ethics failure.

As the Business Ethics Insight shows, an instrumental ethical climate comes with severe risks to the company. Because of the emphasis on the self, such climates can encourage very self-interested behaviors that may hurt the organization. Later, you will see that different ethical climate types can have widely different consequences for companies. Think about what you would have done if you worked for Wells Fargo.

Although the ethical climate has received significant attention within mostly Western nations, is it relevant in a global environment? Exhibit 12.4 shows the list of countries that ethical climates have been studied in and some of the findings.

As Exhibit 12.4 shows, clearly the ethical climate is relevant in the global environment. The exhibit confirms the universal nature of these climate types, as many of the same findings in the U.S. or Europe have been reproduced in other countries, such as Nigeria and Singapore. This also confirms the utility of ethical climates for multinationals as they operate worldwide.

Next, we look at organizational culture.

Country	Summary of Findings
Belgium	Ethical climates have organizational influences
Canada	Existence of ethical climates in non-profit organizations
China	Ethical climates affect personal ethical decisions
Denmark	Concept of ethical climates validated in Danish sample
Hong Kong	Ethical climates affected organizational citizenship behaviors
India	Ethical climates affect manager manipulative behaviors
Israel	Ethical climates affect employee work misconduct
Japan	Comparison of ethical climates between USA and Japan
Mexico	Ethical climates influence commitment to companies
Nigeria	Ethical climates exist in Nigerian banks
Philippines	National and professional culture influence ethical climates
Russia	Ethical climates affect success and ethical behavior
Singapore	Ethical climates affect job satisfaction
South Korea	Ethical climates affect job satisfaction and commitment
Taiwan	Ethical climates affect job satisfaction
Turkey	Ethical climates affect both commitment and bullying

EXHIBIT 12.4—Ethical Climates in the Global Environment

ORGANIZATIONAL CLIMATES AND ETHICAL CULTURE

As you saw in the opening pages of this chapter, the organizational culture is a critical aspect of a company's long-term survival. **Organizational culture** refers to the general beliefs and views of how things are done in an organization. Organizational climates, including ethical climates, are reflections of the basic organizational culture. **Ethical culture** refers more specifically to the norms and values that guide organizational members when faced with ethical dilemmas. Cultural norms and values related to ethics are reflected in the ethical climate or the employees' shared perceptions of how to deal with ethical dilemmas. The degree to which employees agree on their perceptions of the ethical climate indicates the strength of the ethical culture and how likely it is that the ethical culture will affect behaviors. The relationship between organizational culture and ethical climate is shown in Exhibit 12.5.

Organizational cultures are very important for understanding ethics in companies. Organizational cultures often define what is right and wrong in companies and such aspects clearly govern how people behave in organizations. Furthermore, companies can impart employees with the essential moral principles and values that are conducive to ethics. Consider the Strategic Business Ethics Insight on the facing page.

As the Strategic Business Ethics Insight shows, having organizational culture that fits the challenges in your industry is extremely important. Without the right elements,

Organization Culture
- Based on anthropological theory
- Focuses on formal and informal control systems and how those systems teach values and impact behavior
- Expressed in such things as company jargon, symbols, critical incidents, office lore, reward and punishment systems
- Affects many aspects of organizational climate (e.g. safety climate) as well as ethical climate

Ethical climate
- Based on psychological theory
- Focuses on the existence and impact of the organization's "personality" regarding how to act ethically
- Includes collective perceptions regarding the norms and values for ethical decision-making criteria
- Answers the question of "what should we do" when confronted with an ethical dilemma

EXHIBIT 12.5—The Relationship between Organizational Culture and Ethical Climate

STRATEGIC BUSINESS ETHICS INSIGHT

Johnson & Johnson: Challenges for its Ethical Culture

Johnson & Johnson (J&J) used to be seen as the model iconic U.S. company that most parents trust enough to give J&J products to their children. This had been a strategic aspect of doing business for J&J for decades. For instance, in 1982, facing a catastrophe where seven people died from using extra-strength Tylenol, J&J quickly tackled the crisis. Although someone laced the Tylenol with cyanide, J&J took responsibility for the crisis and quickly recalled the medicine and devised tamper-proof packaging. Furthermore, the company CEO made several TV appearances to reassure the public and its customers about the safety of their products. Although the recall cost J&J over $100 million, it quickly recovered and continued making a safety and ethical culture as the cornerstone of their strategy and competitive advantage.

Unfortunately for J&J, many changes occurred in the past decade and these changes have quickly demolished J&J's ethical culture. First, like most companies, J&J faced serious cost-cutting. This was manifested in the laying off of experienced staff in favor of new employees in the safety department. This quickly led to changes that affected the safety culture at J&J. Employees would routinely ignore safety concerns and pass drugs that had red flags. Second, facing serious competition, J&J acquired Pfizer's consumer division, makers of products such as Listerine, Sudafed, etc. This merger also meant that several key positions such as quality and R&D had to be centralized to achieve cost savings. This also led to J&J staffers losing their independence and pride. Furthermore, consumer executives at Pfizer were requesting ill-advised operation reductions that hurt J&J's safety culture. Third, J&J had to also lay off around 4000 employees across the company in 2007. This meant that seasoned floor employees left with their expertise. Such layoffs resulted in a dilution of the company's ethical culture and increased safety concerns on the floor. Finally, instead of its usual approach to recalls, J&J started engaging in unusual recall operations that led to admonishment from the FDA. For instance, in 2009, it was reported that J&J relied on contractors who acted as regular customers to purchase all of the Motrin they could find. Rather than recall the products publicly, the company decided to do a quiet recall.

The troubles continue for J&J suggesting they have not recovered to the state of the ethical culture they had in the early 1980s. Suits are common in the pharmaceutical industry and companies must move fast and truthfully to mitigate damages. In 2018, the company expected to face at least 17 trials in state and federal courts related to five J&J products purported to cause injuries or death. In 2017, J&J already faced losses from verdicts against the company over ovarian cancer.

Based on Kimes, M. 2010. "Why J&J's headache won't go away." *Fortune*, September 6, 101–108. Cronin Fisk, Margaret and Feeley, Jef. 2017. "The lawsuits keep coming for Johnson & Johnson." *Bloomberg Business Week*, March 9. www.bloomberg.com/news/articles/2017-03-09/the-lawsuits-keep-coming-for-johnson-johnson

a company will likely fail. Furthermore, in the case of Johnson & Johnson above, they allowed an excellent organizational culture that emphasized ethics to slowly erode. In that context, recent research suggests that a variety of ethical cultures can exist in different companies. Some types of cultures have helped organizational leaders and members to overcome ethical challenges, while other types of cultures have supported actions of questionable legal and ethical behaviors.[14]

In the case of J&J discussed above, the ethical culture emphasized safety for decades. However, as the emphasis on safety declined, J&J's ethical culture also declined.

What are the components of an ethical culture? Researchers argue that ethical cultures have two main components.[15] The formal components include elements such as the mission and vision, codes of conduct, and the socialization process that new and existing employees go through. However, the informal components are usually harder to observe. These include such aspects such as beliefs in heroes, myths, and stories discussed in the organization about how ethical dilemmas should be dealt with.

Extant evidence suggests that both formal and informal aspects of the ethical culture are important. For example, the formal component of an ethical organization will socialize members in the need of being ethical. Such companies are likely to emphasize key aspects of stakeholder ethics such as health and safety of employees, safe products and community involvement. These companies are also more likely to focus on fairness. However, as examples of companies such as Wells Fargo have shown, the informal aspects of ethical culture are also important to promote ethics. Although Wells Fargo had all the key elements of the formal aspect of an ethical culture, such as a strong code of conduct and employee training, it still experienced significant ethical disasters that led to the downfall of the company. Thus, the informal aspects are also very important.

The researchers also mention that companies with strong informal ethical culture aspects are more likely to have organizational rituals that emphasize ethical behavior.[16] Furthermore, such companies are also more likely to have top executives and other leaders who talk about ethics regularly. When facing situations and dilemmas, such companies are more likely to engage in ethics-oriented conversations to help find solutions.

The above clearly shows that both formal and informal aspects of ethical cultures are critical. How can companies build their culture? Edgar Schein, a leading organizational culture expert, has identified several steps that managers can use to create their organizational cultures and hence their ethical climates.[17] These include:

- *What managers pay attention to, measure, and control.* What managers pay attention to communicates to the people in the organization the beliefs and values that dominate the leadership. This is not necessarily done formally. Employees notice comments made and casual questions and remarks. For example, if the management team pays attention to individual achievement and individual and unit competition, the ethical climate that results will likely reflect more egoistic norms and values. Conversely, if managers pay more attention to following the law, the ethical climate will more likely reflect a law and code orientation.
- *Manager reactions to critical incidents and organizational crises.* At some point in its life every organization will face a crisis. This might be, for example, a failed product, a natural disaster, a product recall, or a severe drop in demand. How managers deal with crises goes a long way to showing the dominant values of the leadership and the organization. Because crises heighten anxiety, they often help encourage culture change or are very important in the development of a new culture. Consider the Global Business Ethics Insight below regarding Toyota CEO Akio Toyoda's response to the recalls Toyota faced when accelerators stuck in some of its models.
- *Observed resource allocation and criteria for resource allocation.* In all organizations, there are public goals (what is stated publicly) and what are called operational goals (what is the organization's real concerns). One way to tell the operative goals and policies of an organization is what projects, people, units, etc. get resources. This communicates to the people in the organization "what really counts." For example, if donating time to community organizations gets recognized and rewarded, it signals that external caring is part of the organization's culture and ethical climate.

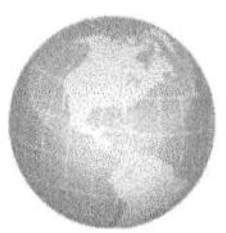

GLOBAL BUSINESS ETHICS INSIGHT

Toyota's CEO Apologizes: A Critical Incident for Toyota?

Toyota CEO Akio Toyoda is the grandson of the car company's founder. He has publicly criticized Toyota's prioritization of profits during the last decade, perhaps seeing the ethical climate of Toyota becoming more instrumental. After Toyota's major recall crisis in late 2010, where a defect found in eight of its models involving a sticky gas pedal led to massive recalls throughout the world, his first public statement was to say, "I am deeply sorry" in an interview with the Japanese television network NHK. He went on to say, "Truly we think of our customers as a priority and we guarantee their safety." Later, while testifying in front of a U.S. government committee, he apologized again. Prior to his testimony the company released the statement:

[In] the past few months, our customers have started to feel uncertain about the safety of Toyota's vehicles, and I take full responsibility for that. Today, I would like to explain to the American people, as well as our customers in the U.S. and around the world, how seriously Toyota takes the quality and safety of its vehicles.

Toyoda, a trained test driver, also went on to note:

I drove the vehicles in the accelerator pedal recall as well as the Prius, comparing the vehicles before and after the remedy in various environmental settings. I believe that only by examining the problems onsite can one make decisions from the customer perspective. One cannot rely on reports or data in a meeting room.

This is a critical incident in the history of Toyota that may foster the creation of a more caring climate for customers as stakeholders. However, some skeptics see apologizing as just a reflection of Japanese culture. When a leader apologizes, he takes responsibility for the action and does not blame others. Such apologies are considered a virtue. However, an apology to a foreign government may be more than a ritual and still affect the Toyota climate for years ahead. As Japan's *Asahi Shimbun* newspaper noted in an editorial, Toyoda's testimony in the U.S. "not only determines Toyota's fate, but may affect all Japanese companies and consumer confidence in their products. President Toyoda has a heavy load on his shoulders."

Based on http://abcnews.go.com/Blotter/toyota-ceo-apologizes-deeply/story?id=9700622; pressroom.toyota.com; miamiherald.com.

Additionally, how managers make the decisions to allocate resources communicates which stakeholders are important. If only stockholders count, then the organization will likely have a more instrumental ethical climate.

- *Deliberate role modeling, teaching, and coaching*. How managers behave communicates values and assumptions to others in the organization. It is often not what managers say but what they do that sends the most powerful messages. Professors Sims and Brinkmann described the organizational culture of the now defunct Enron as "the ultimate contradiction between words and deeds, between a deceiving glossy facade and a rotten structure behind." As in the more recent case for Wells Fargo discussed above, Enron executives created an organizational culture with an instrumental organizational climate where profits (the bottom line) were valued over ethical behavior and doing what is right.[18]
- *Observed criteria for allocation of rewards and status*. Employees learn a lot about the organizational culture from their personal experiences in the organization. Performance appraisals, promotions (or lack of them), raises and informal discussions with superiors send strong messages to employees regarding organizational values. What is rewarded or punished sends a message about organizational values.
- *Observed criteria for recruitment, selection*. Beyond formal qualifications, organizations usually strive to hire people who "fit"; that is, those who have similar values and beliefs. Current employees see the criteria used for recruitment and eventual selection. These observations communicate to them if the culture is changing or maintaining. For example, a disproportionate hiring of men might communicate that female employees have less value. Or, more positively, a firm that recruits college graduates with some experience in philanthropic work communicates that caring is important.

COMMUNICATING THE DESIRED ETHICAL CLIMATE AND CULTURES IN YOUR ORGANIZATION

Schein's model tells us generally how organizational cultures get formed and changed. Many of his ideas can be applied to managing your organization's ethical climate as well. As such, we now need to look specifically at what strategies you can use to build and strengthen the ethical climate culture in your organizational culture.[19] Here are some practical suggestions:

- *Walk the walk*. When subordinates see managers demonstrate high ethical integrity, it sends a positive message to all employees about the importance of organizational values.
- *Keep people in the loop*. Keeping employees informed about what goes on in the organization builds trust in the openness and fairness of the organization's value system.
- *Encourage thoughtful dissent*. When employees can disagree with management they are more likely to identify potential ethical problems. Research shows that

empowerment of subordinates by management increases the existence of caring climates and reduces the existence of egoistic climates.[20]

- *Show them that you care.* Research shows that caring organizations are less likely to have ethical problems, and also have more committed employees.
- *Don't sweep problems under the rug.* Ethical issues and problems should be addressed directly and consistently with the organization's values. Employees must see that management deals effectively with ethical issues.
- *Celebrate the successes.* More than talk or formal statements, the recognition and rewards for ethical behavior build a stronger climate that supports the organizational value system. Managers can make this happen by recognizing the ethical heroes as well as the business superstars.
- *Be fair.* Ethical standards must be applied consistently to all levels of management and employees.
- *Make the tough calls.* It is not always easy to uphold organizational values. Managers must make tough calls like firing an unethical person or dropping an otherwise good supplier for ethical violations such as child labor.
- *Get the right people on the bus and keep them.* Research shows that ethical climate and culture affect the ethical behaviors and commitment of managers and employees. As with organizational culture in general, managers need to create and sustain an ethical culture and climate by selecting people who match the organization's values and by making ethics a condition for retention.
- *Communicate ethical expectations.* Create a code of ethics to reduce ethical ambiguities and lay out the principal dimensions of your ethical climate. This is a formal way of stating the organization's primary values and the ethical rules to follow. Research shows that, when leaders communicate, they are more likely to develop a principled ethical climate.[21]
- *Offer ethics training.* Use seminars, workshops, and external ethical training programs to reinforce and clarify what is in the code and what is in the unwritten normative expectations in the organization.

The above shows the many steps and actions companies can undertake to build the right type of ethical climate. But how can companies maintain an ethical culture when they operate worldwide in countries that may have different norms and cultures? The Global Business Ethics Insight on the facing page shows how GE maintains an ethical culture in the global marketplace.

The Global Business Ethics Insight clearly shows some of the steps that are needed to promote a strong ethical culture. To summarize, Exhibit 12.6 (page 640) shows the key steps of building an ethical culture.

It is important to note that different types of ethical cultures may also exist in companies. It is often argued that there are two types of ethical cultures: a **compliance-based culture** and a **values-based culture**.[22] This framework was later empirically verified.[23] A compliance program usually emphasizes the law and prevention, detection, and punishment of violations of the relevant laws. In contrast, a values-based program stresses organizational values that are consistent with ethical ideals. In values-based companies, employees become committed to ethical aspirations.

BUSINESS ETHICS INSIGHT

Ethical Culture at GE

GE is a U.S. company involved across many industries, such as the medical field, aviation, locomotives, and alternative energy. It has operations in over 100 countries and more than half of its sales now coming from outside of the U.S. In the face of such global operations, whereby cultural norms predict different levels of ethical behavior, GE has been able to maintain a fairly uniform culture of ethics and integrity in all of its subsidiaries. How has GE been able to maintain such a uniform culture worldwide?

First, GE demonstrates committed leadership to the ideals of integrity and an ethical culture. Although it seems a cliché to suggest that leaders should show by example, GE overemphasizes this aspect. In fact, GE actually fired a top manager with significant local experience for willingly violating company codes. GE was willing to forgo the extensive experience offered by the manager to show the importance of an ethical culture. However, most surprising was when GE fired some top executives for ethical violations by their subordinates. Although these managers were not aware of these ethical transgressions, GE placed the responsibility on the manager.

Second, GE will always strive to stay ahead of global standards. By regularly assessing its environment, GE is proactive by anticipating potential future regulations and rules. Such actions also show commitment to the ethical culture.

Third, GE understands that it cannot maintain a strong ethical culture unless employees are involved. As such, GE devotes significant resources to educate and train the workers. GE ensures that many aspects of its ethical code and rules are directly applicable to the lowest employee. By making ethics relevant to all workers, GE can ensure that employees are aware of how ethics impact their actions. Furthermore, employees are trained regularly worldwide on the global ethical code. Furthermore, GE acknowledges that the employee often knows best about maintaining ethics. Thus, employees are given voices through many channels. Employees are thus free to voice their ethical concerns but can also contribute to ethics discussions.

Finally, GE strives to develop global standards that transcend the standards in any specific country. GE understands that global ethical standards are necessary even if such standards are in violation of local norms. For instance, GE has some of the most rigorous non-discrimination rules in its subsidiaries worldwide.

GE is one of only 13 companies that Ethisphere has listed as one of "the world's most ethical companies" since it starting the listings in 2006.

Based on www.ge.com and Heineman, B.W. 2007. "Avoiding integrity landmines." *Harvard Business Review*, April, 100–108. Casler, Kristin. 2015. "How Dell and GE embed a culture of compliance." *Corporate Law Advisory*. www.lexisnexis.com/communities/corporatecounsel newsletter/b/newsletter/archive/2015/11/10/how-dell-and-ge-embed-a-culture-of-compliance. aspx. Kauflin, Jeff. 2017. "The world's most ethical companies 2017." *Forbes*. March. www. forbes.com/sites/jeffkauflin/#789eb76863ae

Key Policies and Practices to Build and Maintain an Ethical Culture
• Formalize policy identifying ethical conduct such as a code of ethics or code of conduct
• Demonstrate consistent and committed leadership to ethics issues
• Provide employees with training regarding all aspects of ethics
• Make information accessible and available
• Provide access to advice when employees face ethical dilemmas
• Provide employees with the means to report ethical misconduct
• Appoint an employee ombudsperson to act on behalf of employees
• Have a process to investigate and discipline employees for ethical violations
• Make ethics part of the regular employee assessment and performance appraisal
• Strive to stay ahead of rules and regulations
• Punish employees when necessary but also reward employees for ethical behaviors
• Build ethical standards in day-to-day operations—make ethics part of everyday life and relevant for employees
• Hold key executives and senior managers as responsible as lower-level employees

EXHIBIT 12.6—Key Policies and Practices to Build and Maintain an Ethical Culture

Research on the two types of ethical culture suggests that a values-based ethical culture is much more effective. A compliance-based culture is much more rooted in respect of the law and its implementation relies on employees focusing on obeying the laws for fear of punishment. However, in contrast, a values-based culture emphasizes self-governance and belief in better ethical ideals. Thus, a values-based culture seems more likely to encourage ethical behavior, as employees believe in the ideals of the culture as opposed to behaving in ways to avoid punishment.

In a study of several corporations, Treviño et al. find support for the effectiveness of the values-based ethical culture.[24] In contrast to compliance cultures, the researchers find that companies with values-based cultures have fewer unethical behaviors and were more aware of ethical issues. Furthermore, employees were more likely to ask for advice in such companies when faced with an ethical dilemma. Finally, values-based cultures are also more likely to encourage report of ethical violations. However, despite these advantages, the researchers also suggest that compliance-based cultures have advantages in that it emphasizes respect of the laws.

WHAT DO WE KNOW ABOUT THE EFFECTS OF DIFFERENT CLIMATE TYPES?

As with outcomes related to ethical culture, we also have substantial research regarding the effects of ethical climates. For both ethical cultures and climates, perhaps the most important research finding is that employees are more ethical in those organizations where the ethical climate and culture encourage ethical behavior.[25] In addition, there are other benefits for organizations with strong ethical values including higher

DYSFUNCTIONAL BEHAVIORS	
Study Participants	**Findings**
207 marketing professionals	Individuals operating under rules climates were less likely to engage in questionable selling practices even when they themselves did not feel that the practices were unethical. Individuals operating under caring climates were more likely to engage in questionable selling practices when they felt that the practices were unethical.
201 full-time employees	Instrumental climates were positively associated with bullying behaviors; rules, caring, and law and code climates were negatively associated with bullying behaviors.
243 managers	Differ in terms of their moral reasoning in principled climates as compared to managers in benevolent climates.
202 university alumni	A higher frequency of unethical behavior was found in egoistic climates as compared to benevolent and principled climates. A higher frequency of unethical behavior was found in companies without a code of conduct.
97 full-time employees	A negative relationship was found between benevolent climates and organizational misconduct. Frequency of misbehavior reported by managers was negatively related to rules, instrumental, and caring climates.
ETHICAL BEHAVIORS	
206 managers	People operating under caring climates perceived a positive association between success and ethical behavior; the opposite was true for people under instrumental climates.
103 nurses	Independence climates had a significant positive association with ethical behavior.
241 employees	Law and code and independence climates were associated with ethical behavior. There was an equal likelihood of people in instrumental climates either paying or not paying a bribe.
109 employees	Instrumental and independence climates were associated with negative extra-role behaviors; caring and law and code climates were associated with positive extra-role behaviors.
237 manufacturing employees	Principled climates and benevolent climates were negatively associated with injuries, and principled climates were positively associated with safety-enhancing behaviors.
198 police officers and 184 civilians	Friendship or team ethical climates had positive associations with willingness to engage in whistle blowing.
174 marketing executives	Egoistic climates were associated with lower risk-taking propensity; benevolent climates were associated with higher risk-taking propensity.
264 state government project team members	Rules climates were associated with less frequent misreporting; instrumental climates were associated with more frequent misreporting.
525 retail store employees	Instrumental climates were positively associated with unethical behaviors; independence, caring, law and code, and rules climates were negatively associated with unethical behaviors.

EXHIBIT 12.7—What Managers Need to Know: The Effects of Ethical Climates on Ethical and Dysfunctional Organizational Behaviors

commitment, job satisfaction and employee performance. Numerous studies[26] link ethical culture and climate to lower rates of observed misconduct, exposure to situations facilitating misconduct, and pressure to compromise standards. Employees in such organizations also show more satisfaction with management's responses to incidents of misconduct and report that they are more prepared to handle potentially unethical situations.

More specifically, affective responses to the organization, such as organizational commitment and job satisfaction, are positively related to the existence of caring climates and negatively related to the existence of instrumental climates. Organizational climates that originate from externally based rules such as professional or religious codes also seem to produce positive relationships with organizational outcomes.

Past research generally indicates that caring, law and code, rules, and independence climates reduce organizational misbehaviors such as stealing and sabotage. This contrasts with the negative effects stemming from perceptions of instrumental ethical climates. Importantly, when rules climates are perceived, these perceptions seem to serve as effective control mechanisms that limit unethical behaviors but do not successfully produce attachment to the organization such as more commitment.[27]

Exhibit 12.7 shows a summary of findings for how ethical climates affect an array of important organizational outcomes.

THOUGHTS ON A POSITIVE WORK CLIMATE

A new philosophical approach to the work environment is emerging that represents a type of ethical climate supportive of human flourishing. The **positive work climate** perspective argues that work climates create emotional reactions for employees. If these emotions are predominantly positive, then people will flourish.

Härtel notes that a positive work climate exists when employees perceive "the workplace environment as positive, respectful, inclusive and psychologically safe; leaders and co-workers as trustworthy, fair and diversity open; and policies and decision-making as interactionally, procedurally and distributively just."[28] The research on positive work climates, although recent, is showing that the climate characteristics noted above tend to help people develop an emotional attachment to their organization and, in turn, this results in greater organizational performance.[29] Similar to what we know about caring ethical climates, people are more likely to identify with the organization and relate better with co-workers, ultimately benefiting the company.

DISCOVERING YOUR ETHICAL CLIMATE

As new employees in an organization, it is often a good idea to learn the ethical climate norms and expectations as quickly as possible. This has two benefits. First, you can avoid making mistakes that violate local norms and more quickly fit in with your work environment. Second, and perhaps more important, is that you can assess your fit with the ethical environment. The question pertains to how closely your personal moral beliefs match the expectations from the organization. The famous organizational culture expert Edgar Schein[30] suggests you can understand climate by following the steps below.

1. Observe behavior, language, customs and traditions. Try to understand how these affect ethical decision-making.
2. Understand group norms, standards and values. Tightly knit groups will often have clear expectations of those who join their team.
3. Observe the published, publicly announced values and formal philosophies such as in the mission statement. These are often in the codes of conduct and mission statements.
4. Learn the informal rules of the game, the unwritten expectations of how things are done around here. Eventually, employees learn the informal organization, which may differ radically from official statements. One way of speeding up this process is seeking a mentor, or someone more experienced in the organization, to give you insider hints.
5. Look for stores or symbols that reinforce organizational norms and values. Most people in organizations can report critical incidents or local folklore that helped define the organizations' values.

CHAPTER SUMMARY

This chapter began with an overview of the ethical climate model and its relationship to the more general concept of work climate. The ethical climate is a type of work climate. The ethical climate represents what organizational members believe are the forms of ethical reasoning or behavior and the expected standards or norms for ethical decision-making within the company.[31] You can determine the ethical climate of your organization or department by looking at such things as what criteria people use to understand and resolve ethical issues.

Ethical climate is not a single component of the organization, but there are several climate types identified by the ethical climate model. Past research has refined these climate types and the important ones are considered in the chapter. Principled climates occur when the organization has norms that encourage people to make ethical decisions based on a set of standards. Some organizations may make ethical decisions based on external codes such as a professional code of conduct. For example, you can see the classic ethical code of physicians, called the Hippocratic Oath. In other organizations, people look to their company's code of conduct to guide their ethical behaviors and decision-making. You saw two examples in the Johnson & Johnson Credo and the Coca-Cola Code, shown in Exhibits 12.2 and 12.3. Organizations can also have a principled ethical climate, called the independent, where each individual is expected to behave in a way that he or she personally considers ethical.

Caring climates occur when the organization has norms that encourage people to make ethical decisions based on looking out for the welfare of others, particularly for team members and those within the company. In most organizations with caring climates, people believe that the right thing to do is to look out for the welfare of friends and co-workers. The Preview Ethics Insight (pages 619 and 620) showed two companies that are dominated by caring climates. The Business Ethics Insight for Malden Mills (pages 627 and 628) gave an example of a situation where perhaps caring went too far and the owner lost sight of the need for economic performance to ensure organization survival.

Organizations having an *instrumental* ethical climate see their organizational unit as having norms and expectations that encourage ethical decision-making from an egoistic perspective. Instrumental ethical climates occur when the organization has norms that encourage people to define right and wrong in terms of the consequences to oneself. Thus, when faced with an ethical dilemma, people are expected to make decisions based on what best serves self-interest. Even when considered in a variety of contexts, studies consistently show that instrumental climates are the least preferred.

Organizational culture and climate are closely related ways to view the informal side of an organization. Basically, organizational climates, including ethical climates, are reflections of the basic organizational culture. Because ethical climate is a reflection of the ethical side of the local culture, the chapter reviewed basic principles of how cultures evolve and change, building on the idea of the leading organizational culture expert Edgar Schein.[32] Schein identifies several factors that help leaders build and maintain a culture. These include: what managers pay attention to, measure, and control; manager's reactions to critical incidents and organizational crises; observed resource allocation and criteria for resource allocation; deliberate role modeling, teaching, and coaching; observed criteria for allocation of rewards and status; observed criteria for recruitment, selection; and communicating the desired ethical climate in your organizational culture. The chapter also provided you with a list of practical suggestions for building the type of ethical climate desired by the owners and managers of the organization.

The chapter provided a summary of the basic findings from scientific research regarding the effects of ethical climates on organizations. Importantly, we know that employees are more ethical in those organizations where the ethical climate and culture encourage ethical behavior.[33] Also, affective responses to the organization such as organizational commitment and job satisfaction are positively related to perceptions of caring climates and negatively related with perceptions of instrumental climates. Research indicates that caring, law and code, rules, and independence climates reduce organizational misbehaviors such as stealing and sabotage, whereas instrumental ethical climates may encourage these behaviors.[34]

This chapter introduced a new concept of positive work climates that is based on the philosophy that positive emotions can be created by the climate and that these are beneficial both to individuals and to organizations. Finally, the chapter concluded with some hints to help you identify your own ethical climates when you enter new organizations.

NOTES

1 Reichers, A.E. & Schneider, B. 1990. "Climates and culture: An evolution of constructs." In B. Schneider (Ed.), *Organizational climate and culture*. San Francisco: Jossey-Bass, 5–39; Schneider, B. 1975. "Organizational climate: an essay." *Personnel Psychology*, 36, 447–479.
2 Klein, K.J. & Sorra, S. 1996. "The challenge of innovation management." *Academy of Management Review*, 21, 1055–1080.
3 Mumford, M.D., Scott, G., Gaddis, B. & Strange, J.M. 2002. "Leading creative people: Orchestrating expertise and relationships." *Leadership Quarterly*, 13, 705–750.
4 Field, R.H. & Abelson, M.A. 1982. "Climate: A reconceptualization and proposed model." *Human Relations*, 35, 181–201.
5 Cullen, J.B., Parboteeah, K.P. & Victor, B. 2003. "The effects of ethical climates on organizational commitment: A two-study analysis." *Journal of Business Ethics*, 46, 127–141.
6 Cullen, J.B. Victor, B. & Stephens. C. 1989. "An ethical weather report: Assessing the organization's ethical climate." *Organizational Dynamics*, 18, 50–60.
7 Victor, B. & Cullen, J.B. 1987. "The organizational bases of ethical climate." *Administrative Science Quarterly*, 33, 101–125.
8 Dugan-Martin, K. & Cullen, J.B. 2006. "Continuities and extension of ethical climate theory: A meta-analytic review." *Journal of Business Ethics*, 69, 175–194.
9 Kerns, C.D. 2003. "Creating and sustaining an ethical workplace culture: The values–attitude–behavior chain." *Graziadio Business Review*, 6, 3.
10 Ubius, U. & Alas. R. 2009. "Organizational cultural types as predicators of corporate social responsibility." *Inzinerine Ekonomika-Engineering Economics*, 1, 90–99.
11 Wimbush, J.C. & Shepard, J.M. 1994. "Toward an understanding of ethical climate: Its relationship to ethical behavior and supervisory influence." *Journal of Business Ethics*, 13, 637–647.
12 Erondu, E.A., Sharland, A. & Okpara, J.O. 2004. "Corporate ethics in Nigeria: A test of the concept of ethical climate." *Journal of Business Ethics*, 51, 349–357.
13 Friedman, M. 1970. "The social responsibility of business is to increase its profits." *New York Times Magazine*, September 13.
14 Ardichvili, A. & Jondle, D. 2009. "Integrative literature review: Ethical business cultures: A literature review and implications for HRD." *Human Resource Development Review*, 8, 223–244.
15 Ardichvili & Jondle. "Integrative literature review."
16 Ardichvili & Jondle. "Integrative literature review."
17 Schein, Edgar H. 2010. *Organizational Culture*. San Francisco, CA: Wiley.
18 Sims, R.R. & Brinkmann, J. 2003. "Enron ethics (or: Culture matters more than codes)." *Journal of Business Ethics*, 45, 3, 243–256 (at 243).
19 Ethics Resource Center. 2008. *Ethical culture building: A modern business imperative*. Washington, DC: Ethics Resource Center; Robbins, S.P. & Judge, T.A. 2009. *Organizational behavior*. 13th ed. Upper Saddle River, NJ: Pearson Education, Inc.
20 Parboteeah, K., Praveen, Chen, Hsien Chun, Lin, Ying-Tzu, Chen, I-Heng, Y-Plee, Amber & Chung, An Yi. 2010. "Establishing organizational ethical climates: How do managerial practices work?" *Journal of Business Ethics*, 97, 4, 535–541.
21 Parboteeah et al. "Establishing organizational ethical climates."
22 Paine, L.S. 1994. "Managing for organizational integrity." *Harvard Business Review*, March/April, 106–117.
23 Treviño, L.K., Weaver, G.R., Gibson, D.G. & Toffler, B.L. 1999. "Managing ethics and legal compliance: What works and what hurts." *California Management Review*, 41, 2, 131–151.
24 Treviño et al., "Managing ethics and legal compliance."
25 Ethics Resource Center. *Ethical culture building*; Dugan-Martin & Cullen, "Continuities and extension of ethical climate theory."

26 Ethics Resource Center. 2005. *National business ethics survey*. Washington, DC: ERC; Ethics Resource Center. *Ethical culture building*; Treviño et al., "Managing ethics and legal compliance"; Treviño, L.K., Butterfield, K.D. & McCabe, D.L. 2001. "The ethical context in organizations: Influences on employee attitudes and behaviors." *Research in Ethical Issues in Organizations*, 3, 301–337.
27 Dugan-Martin & Cullen. "Continuities and extension of ethical climate theory."
28 Härtel, C.E.J. 2008. "How to build a healthy emotional culture and avoid a toxic culture." In C.L. Cooper & N.M. Ashkanasy (Eds.), *Research companion to emotion in organizations*. Cheltenham, UK: Edwin Elgar, pp. 575–588 (at 584).
29 Wilderom, Celeste P.M. 2011. "Toward positive work climate and cultures." In N.M. Ashkanasy, C.P.M Wilderom & M.F. Peterson (Eds.), *The handbook of organizational culture and climate*. Los Angeles, CA: Sage, pp. 79–84; Härtel, Charmine E.J. & Ashkanasy, Neal M. 2011. "Healthy human cultures as positive work environments." In N.M. Ashkanasy et al., *The handbook of organizational culture and climate*, pp. 85–100.
30 Schein, Edgar H. 2010. *Organizational culture*. San Francisco, CA: Wiley.
31 Cullen et al., "The effects of ethical climates."
32 Schein, *Organizational culture*.
33 Ethics Resource Center. *Ethical culture building*; Dugan-Martin & Cullen, "Continuities and extension of ethical climate theory."
34 Dugan-Martin & Cullen. "Continuities and extension of ethical climate theory."

KEY TERMS

Caring ethical climate: has norms values that encourage people to make ethical decisions based on looking out for the welfare of others.

Compliance-based culture: usually emphasizes the law and prevention, detection, and punishment of violations of the relevant laws.

Educational/learning-oriented codes: suggest general guidelines for decision-making and behavioral reactions when faced with ethically challenging situations.

Ethical climate: represents what organizational members believe are the forms of ethical reasoning or behavior and the expected standards or norms for ethical decision-making within the company.

Ethical codes: documents that identify the ethical principles used to guide the ethical decision-making within an organization.

Ethical culture: refers to the norms and values that guide organizational members when faced with ethical dilemmas.

Independent ethical climate: has norms and values that support ethical decision-making based on personal morality.

Inspirational–idealistic codes: focus on broad virtuous themes such as "Be honest."

Instrumental ethical climate: has norms and values that encourage ethical decision-making that serve the organization's interests or provide personal benefits.

Law and code: a type of principled ethical climate that emphasizes ethical decision-making based on laws or other written codes.

Organizational culture: refers to the general beliefs and views of how things are done in an organization.

Positive work climate: a view that work climates create emotional reactions for employees.

Principled climates: occur when the organization has norms and values that encourage people to make ethical decisions based on a set of standards.

Regulatory codes: specify how to behave in specific situations, typically with a "do and don't" approach.

Values-based culture: stresses organizational values that are consistent with ethical ideals.

Work climates: represent the shared perceptions of procedures, policies, and practices, both formal and informal, of the organization.

DISCUSSION QUESTIONS

1. Ethical climate is one type of work climate. How might other climates such as the climate for safety influence the ethical context of an organization?
2. Consider how organizations communicate their ethical climates to employees. How is this done and what makes it more or less effective?
3. Describe a principle ethical climate.
4. Give examples of a principle ethical climate that has influenced your participation in an organization or group.
5. Describe a caring ethical climate.
6. Give examples of a caring ethical climate that has influenced your participation in an organization or group.
7. Describe an instrumental ethical climate.
8. Give examples of an instrumental ethical climate that has influenced your participation in an organization or group.
9. Discuss the relationship between ethical climate and organization culture.
10. Consider all the ethical climate types and discuss the risks and benefits associated with each type. Risks might include ethical issues as well as general performance issues.

INTERNET ACTIVITY

1. Search the internet for company codes of conduct and find four different codes.
2. Re-examine Professor Kerns type of codes (in this chapter): inspirational/idealistic, regulatory, and educational/learning.
3. Assign each code to a type, or perhaps more than one.
4. Be ready to discuss what type of code seems to have the greater impact.
5. Google your example companies to see how they have handled any ethical dilemma.

6. Find recent examples of companies with ethical failures and excellence in CSR activities. From the popular press articles on these companies, analyze how their ethical climates and cultures led to their current situations.

For more Internet Activities and resources, visit the Companion Website at www.routledge.com/cw/parboteeah.

WHAT WOULD YOU DO?

My First Company

January 1, 2020 turned out to be one of the best days of your life. After years of savings and sacrifice, as well as some investments that paid off nicely, you purchased a successful BMW car dealership. Prior to making the purchase, you carefully studied the performance of the company over the last five years. Even during tough economic times, they made money selling new and used cars and in providing service. The building was only three years old and the location was great. "I made a great choice," you thought.

A month later you were not so comfortable with your new company. In spite of the economy improving, sales were flat and two of your best sales people quit unexpectedly. What was wrong? Being a "numbers" person, you knew the sales staff did very well, with high commissions on expensive cars. The company also had a great benefits package. You decided to discuss the problem with the sales manager, Frank Whidbey. Frank had been selling cars nearly all of his life and everyone seemed to like him, customers and fellow works alike.

"Frank, what's going on here? This does not seem to be the company I bought." Frank hesitated with your opening question. "Ms. Brooks, things have been changing around here since before you took over," he said.

After a couple of hours of discussion, you began to get a picture of the problem. During a slow period of sales due to general economic conditions and the end of the model year, the previous management had reduced base salaries and increased commissions to motivate more sales. Competition among the sales people soared and the relationships among the sales team began to change. Frank noted,

> Previously, the sales people would cover for each other. If you were not on the floor and the customers were looking for you, the person doing the showing would make sure you got your commission. We had a climate where everyone looked out for each other and you knew that you would get your fair share. However, a couple of new sales people really took to the new high commission approach and began taking some of the returning customers away from the old-timers. This did not go over well.

In thinking back to your old business ethics course, you remember the idea of an ethical climate. You now see that changing the compensation scheme was a critical incident that turned a once caring climate into an instrumental climate. You are losing people that fit with the old climate and it seems to be affecting sales. "Maybe I should just hire all extremely competitive people and use that as a motivator to succeed, and everyone will understand how the game is played now," you think. "Maybe I should work to rebuild the caring climate that worked so well in the past."

What are you going to do?

BRIEF CASE: BUSINESS ETHICS INSIGHT

The Zappos Caring Culture and Climate

Zappos was founded in 1999 as an online shoe store. Since then it has expanded its product offerings to clothing and accessories. Zappos' headquarters is in Las Vegas, Nevada, and it employs approximately 2000 people. The company is an example of a caring organizational culture and climate, with core values focusing on the happiness of both its employees and its customers.

CEO Tony Hsieh, a Harvard-educated computer scientist, sees culture as a driving force in his company. He notes, "If you get the culture right, then most of the other stuff, like great customer service or building a brand will just happen naturally." Working with his employees Hsieh developed a list of ten core values that drive the company. Even though he first thought that codifying the core values was too "corporate," he realized that the values could be a rallying point for his employees to deliver superior and ethical customer service. Ultimately, Hsieh believes that core values are more than a vague sense of cultural expectations. To be effective, companies must have "committable" core values. "By committable, you must be willing to hire and fire based on them," he notes.

The ten core values are:

1. Deliver WOW Through Service.
2. Embrace and Drive Change.
3. Create Fun and a Little Weirdness.
4. Be Adventurous, Creative, and Open-Minded.
5. Pursue Growth and Learning.
6. Build Open and Honest Relationships with Communication.
7. Build a Positive Team and Family Spirit.
8. Do More with Less.
9. Be Passionate and Determined.
10. Be Humble.

To reinforce the cultural values, every year, Zappos employees contribute to a "Culture Book." Employees share their thoughts, stories, and photos that identify their personal experiences about what Zappos' culture means to them. Readers of the book note such cultural key words as *fun, family, smile, proud, weird, thank you*, and *I heart Zappos*. The nearly 500-page Culture Book comes out every year and Hsieh provides free copies to anyone who asks.

For Hsieh, the true test of commitment to an organizational culture is whether a company is willing to hire and fire based on cultural fit. As Hsieh notes, "It doesn't so much matter *what* your culture is, so long as you commit to it." As such, all job candidates have an interview with the HR department that focuses only on cultural fit. The HR department uses a series of interview questions to probe an applicant's views regarding the ten core values. To screen for creativity and individuality, the Zappos HR department uses interview questions such as: "How weird are you?" "What's your theme song?" "What two people would you most like to invite to dinner?" According to Hsieh, "We've actually passed on a lot of really talented people that we know would make an impact to our top or bottom line . . . but if you know they're not a culture fit we won't hire them." Even if someone is doing a good job, the company will fire them if they do not fit with the culture. "We do our best to hire positive people and put them in an environment where the positive thinking is reinforced," says Hsieh.

Once through the selection process, all new Zappos employees have five weeks of training. Regardless of level, everyone gets the same training as the call center employees. The curriculum includes company history and customer service training followed by taking real calls from real customers beginning at 7 a.m. Be late or call in sick and you are not Zappos material.

Perhaps the most unusual cultural reinforcing technique is that, when training is complete, all new hires are offered $4000 to quit! Zappos tells the new employees, "We will pay for the training you've received, and give you an additional $4000 if you quit right now." Hsieh explains it this way: "We don't want employees that are just there for a pay check. We want employees who are there because the culture is the right fit for them."

For Zappos employees, building a strong caring culture is a daily event. There is the free lunch in the cafeteria, regular happy hours, a nap room, profit sharing, and paid-in full healthcare. There is even a full-time life coach that the employees can consult for confidential advice on just about anything. There is only one requirement to use the coach: employees must sit on a red velvet throne. Zappos managers also spend 10% to 20% of their time with team members outside the office. This builds team commitment to each other and the company. And one does not need to be a boss to pass out rewards—any employee can give a $50 bonus to other employee for good work.

Like most companies, Zappos has faced business events that challenge some of its fundamental cultural values. Two critical incidents show how it responded.

On May 21, 2010 a computer glitch on a Zappos website set the price of every product to $49.95. It took six hours to fix the error and by then Zappos had lost nearly $1.6 million in revenue. Rather than try to cancel these incorrect sales, Zappos made the announcement that they would honor these sales even though the prices were wrong. In spite of such a large loss Zappos remained true to its caring culture that focuses on customers.

A recession economy challenged the caring culture of Zappos when employees are involved: how would they lay people off? Their venture capital backer, Sequoia Capital, demanded that its portfolio companies, including Zappos, cut costs. In 2007, in spite of the economy, Zappos was profitable with a positive cashflow. Still, Hsieh knew he had to act and the top management team identified 124 employees out of 1500 that they would lay off.

Zappos' reaction was to make a bad situation as positive as possible. Said Hsieh: "The motivation was, let's take care of our employees who got us this far." Long-term employees who were laid off received four weeks of pay for every year of service. Those with less than two years of service were paid through the end of the year. All laid-off employees received six months of paid health coverage.

Based on Burkus, David. 2011. "A tale of two cultures: Why culture trumps core values in building ethical organizations." *Journal of Values Based Leadership*, 4, Winter/Spring. http://money.cnn.com/2009/01/15/news/companies/Zappos_best_companies_obrien.fortune/index.htm; http://experiencematters.wordpress.com/2008/05/28/discussing-zappos-culture-with-tony-hsieh/; www.innovationexcellence.com/blog/2011/06/17/culture-is-king-atzappos/; www.readwriteweb.com/archives/zappos_ceo_talks_culture_fit_a.php

BRIEF CASE QUESTIONS

1. The Zappos culture seems to work well for a small company. How would you transfer such cultural values to a larger organization?
2. A charismatic leader such as Tony Hsieh can be the driver of an organizational culture and climate. Discuss how future managers might continue the cultural traditions of this company.
3. It is difficult to quantify the results of a company that has a caring approach to customers and employees. How would you respond to a critic that notes that Zappos sells good products at good prices and many of the culturally supporting "extras" are just a waste of money?

LONG CASE: BUSINESS ETHICS

'BAD APPLE' BEHAVIOR OR A SPOILED BARREL: AN ANALYSIS OF WELLS FARGO'S CRISIS RESPONSE TO ALLEGED CULTURE FLAWS

Submitted to the 2017 Arthur W. Page Society and Institute for Public Relations Case Study Competition

Source: Erik M./Pacific/Barcroft Images

Abstract

Who's held accountable when deceptive practices are revealed in a company's operations—those conducting the unethical behavior or company leadership? Wells Fargo continues to publicly grapple with this question as it mitigates damages from a fraudulent account scandal. Initial leadership response seemingly laid blame on a few "bad apples," but former employees pointed to a cross-sell-driven culture breeding bad behavior. The disparity between these viewpoints resulted in a controversy that gained intense stakeholder attention. This case study examines Wells Fargo's crisis response to the scandal, as well as impacts to its financials, reputation and character.

Table of Contents

Overview

> "If any of these things transpired, it's distressing and it's not who Wells Fargo is . . ."
>
> – *Wells Fargo statement to NPR, October 2016*

On May 5, 2015, the Los Angeles City Attorney filed a lawsuit against Wells Fargo for allegedly opening accounts *without* customer authorization. Sixteen months later, Wells Fargo announced it would pay $185 million in fines and $5 million in customer remediation for fraudulent account activities occurring between 2011 and 2015. The news media, customers and policymakers immediately sought answers for how Wells Fargo, America's "Main Street bank," allowed this to happen. Early comments from company leadership, including the CEO and CFO, seemed to blame the activities on a few "bad apples" who did not reflect the company's broader culture. Former employees countered the "bad apple" claims with vivid accounts of a high pressure, cross-sell-driven work environment breeding unethical behavior (Arnold, 2016, para. 1). The stark contrast between Wells Fargo's preached "culture of caring" and the deceptive actions of 5,300 employees left stakeholders wondering whether company leadership recognized the potential cultural challenges and knew what actions were needed in order to right the ship.

While reading this case study, remember that the challenges discussed do not solely apply to Wells Fargo and the highly scrutinized banking industry. A broad range of organizations, from car manufacturers to government departments (Picoult, 2016, para. 6), have and will continue to be confronted by empowered stakeholder groups for alleged deceptive business practices. To best manage growing stakeholder demands for corporate authenticity, company and communications leadership must be prepared to defend who a company is *and* how it acts.

Company Background

1. Wells Fargo History

Wells Fargo & Company (NYSE: WFC) is a financial services company headquartered in San Francisco, CA. American businessmen Henry Wells and William G. Fargo founded Wells, Fargo & Company on March 18, 1852, in New York City. Wells and Fargo sought to capitalize on the California Gold Rush by providing banking and express services in the west (*Encyclopedia Britannica*, para. 1). As explained by the company, "[i]n the boom and bust economy of the 1850s, Wells Fargo earned a reputation of trust by dealing rapidly and responsibly with people's money" (2016b, para. 3). Wells Fargo also operated and owned the largest stagecoach empire in the world from 1852 to 1918 (Wells Fargo & Company, 2016b). The company continues to be linked with the stagecoach emblem, signifying its heritage and the small-town values that built the business.

Wells Fargo has since grown to become the third largest bank in the United States by assets. It was ranked no. 27 on *Fortune*'s 2016 list of America's largest corporations by revenue. The company is divided into four primary business segments—wholesale banking, brokerage and retirement, community banking and consumer lending —and offers approximately 90 separate lines of business (Carlozo, 2015). According to the company's September 2015 earnings report, the community banking division led all other divisions, producing $13.6 billion or 62 percent of total company revenues (CSI Market, 2016).

Wells Fargo's community banking division currently operates more than 8,000 retail banking locations across the United States, making the division the face of Wells Fargo.

Wells Fargo's success captured the attention of Berkshire Hathaway's Warren Buffett and in 1990 he announced to shareholders that he would be investing $290 million in the bank (Gandel, 2014). From 1990 to 2015, Berkshire Hathaway continued to accumulate shares in Wells Fargo, which culminated in a 10% ownership stake as of March 2016. In a February 2016 interview with *CNBC*, Buffett called

Community	III. Quarter (Sep. 30, 2015)	II. Quarter (June 30, 2015)	I. Quarter (March 31, 2015)	IV. Quarter (Dec. 31, 2014)	III. Quarter (Sep. 30, 2014)
Revenues (in millions $)	**13,618.0**	**12,661.0**	**12,784.0**	**12,835.0**	**12,828.0**
% of total Revenues	62.25%	59.39%	60.08%	50.02%	60.47%

Source: CSI Market

Wells Fargo "a terrific operation" and said the company CEO John Stumpf had done a "fabulous job" (Stempel, 2016). As far back as 2009, Buffett explained to *Fortune*'s Adam Lashinsky that "those guys [Wells Fargo] have gone their own way. That doesn't mean that everything they've done has been right. But they've never felt compelled to do anything because other banks were doing it" (2009b, para. 1). The company's innovative approach to business focuses on consumers and midsize businesses, in addition to cross-selling products and services. Lashinsky elucidated upon the bank's approach, noting, "Wells relentlessly cross-sells everything, including credit cards and mortgages (to consumers) and treasury-management services and insurance (to businesses). Wells persuades each retail customer to buy an average of almost six products, roughly twice the level of a decade ago" (2009a, para. 9).

2. Corporate Reputation

Wells Fargo is known as America's "Main Street bank" in contrast to its "Wall Street bank" competitors. During the 2008 recession, when many banks struggled with the financial crisis, Wells Fargo emerged comparatively unscathed (*The Economist*, 2013). The bank's stability amidst crisis further bolstered its image and reaffirmed the approval of major investors like Berkshire Hathaway's Warren Buffett. Wells Fargo ranked no. 74 in reputation out of the top 100 most visible U.S. companies among the public in the 2015 Harris Poll Reputation Quotient—well ahead of its major competitors JP Morgan, Citigroup and Bank of America. The company has also consistently appeared on *Fortune*'s Most Admired Companies list—the "definitive report card on corporate reputations" (*Fortune*, 2016)—ranking 25 in 2016, 22 in 2015 and 35 in 2014. Further evidence of Wells Fargo's broad recognition as one of the top banks in North America, *Global Finance* named it as the "Best Developed Market Bank" on its 2016 list.

3. Corporate Culture

Heralded as a business built on relationships and trust, Wells Fargo employees, directors and executive officers are expected to follow its *Code of Ethics*, which stresses individual accountability and seeking out guidance in situations of doubt. Actions are also to be guided by the company's vision to satisfy customer's financial needs and help them succeed financially. Wells Fargo's "culture of caring" asserts that "success depends on how much we care for each other, our customers, our communities, and

> The *reason* we wake up in the morning is to help our customers succeed financially and to satisfy their financial needs, and the *result* is that we make money. It's never the other way around.

Source: The Vision and Values of Wells Fargo

our stockholders" (Wells Fargo & Company, 2016a, para. 4). The company's focus on people is further reflected in its brand and slogan, "Together we'll go far," which emphasizes strong relationships. Wells Fargo also promotes a "One Wells Fargo" mindset, meaning "we [Wells Fargo] show our customers we know them at every moment of the relationship by making it easy for them to do business, providing guidance to them, and ensuring they feel valued" (Wells Fargo & Company, 2016a, para. 9).

Fraudulent Account Activity Timeline (2011 to 2016)

Between 2011 and 2015, Wells Fargo employees reportedly opened two million fraudulent debit and credit card accounts *without* customer knowledge. Roughly 5,300 Wells Fargo staff members were terminated over this same span of time for "sales-related misconduct" (Stumpf, 2016b, p. 3). In comparing those terminated to Wells Fargo's total retail bank branch workforce, the company fired approximately *one percent* of employees each year for performing unethical banking practices.

Dec. 21, 2013	The *Los Angeles Times* publishes a report on Wells Fargo's alleged pressure-cooker work environment and unethical employee behavior.
May 5, 2015	The Office of Los Angeles City Attorney Mike Feuer sues Wells Fargo for allegedly opening fraudulent accounts without customer knowledge (see Appendix A).
Sept. 8, 2016	Wells Fargo announces an agreement to pay $100 million to the Consumer Financial Protection Bureau (CFPB), $35 million to the Office of the Comptroller of the Currency, $50 million to the City and County of Los Angeles and $5 million for customer remediation tied to allegations of staff opening unauthorized accounts (see Appendix B).
Sept. 20, 2016	Wells Fargo CEO John Stumpf testifies before the U.S. Senate Banking Committee on Banking, Housing, and Urban Affairs.
Sept. 26, 2016	Wells Fargo stock price hits a 31-month low.
Sept. 27, 2016	Stumpf forfeits $41 million in salary and stock, and will not receive salary while Wells Fargo's board investigates the unauthorized account allegations.
Sept. 29, 2016	Stumpf testifies before the U.S. House of Representatives Committee on Financial Services.
Oct. 1, 2016	Wells Fargo eliminates sales goals for retail banking business.
Oct. 12, 2016	Wells Fargo announces Stumpf's retirement and the subsequent promotion of former Wells Fargo President and Chief Operating Officer Tim Sloan to CEO.
Oct. 24, 2016	Wells Fargo launches "Commitment" television ad campaign.
Oct. 25, 2016	Sloan issues a company-wide address apologizing to team members and emphasizing focus on restoring trust in Wells Fargo (2016, para. 6).
Dec. 1, 2016	Wells Fargo announces its Board of Directors amended company by-laws to require the separation of the chairman and CEO roles.

Wells Fargo's Actions and Response

In a December 2013 *Los Angeles Times* article, Wells Fargo spokesman Oscar Suris countered claims of a supposed pressure-cooker work environment and scandalous sales tactics by explaining the company's strong stance on ethics and following the law. Reinforcing the seriousness of the matter, he said, "when we find lapses, we do something about it, including firing people" (Reckard, 2013, para. 21). The company also shared that it would create an Ethics Program Office to help ensure the bank's broad population understood its ethics policies (para. 22). Three years later, Wells Fargo would again have to reinforce its stance on ethics as well as the actions the company would take to right wrongdoing.

On September 8, 2016, Wells Fargo issued a press release stating that Wells Fargo Bank reached a settlement of $185 million with the Consumer Financial Protection Bureau (CFPB), the Office of the Comptroller, and the City and County of Los Angeles regarding accusations of customers receiving "products and services they did not request" (2016c, para. 1). The release outlined a series of actions taken by Wells Fargo, including third-party account reviews, customer refunds, employee terminations, training updates, and process changes to ensure customers are aware of new account activity. The official company statement referred to the settlement as a step toward "putting this matter behind us" (2016c, para. 4). The same day, Wells Fargo sent an e-mail to employees from CEO John Stumpf in which he shared much of the same information, but also reaffirmed the expectation that team members "adhere to the highest possible standards of ethics and business conduct" (2016a, para. 7).

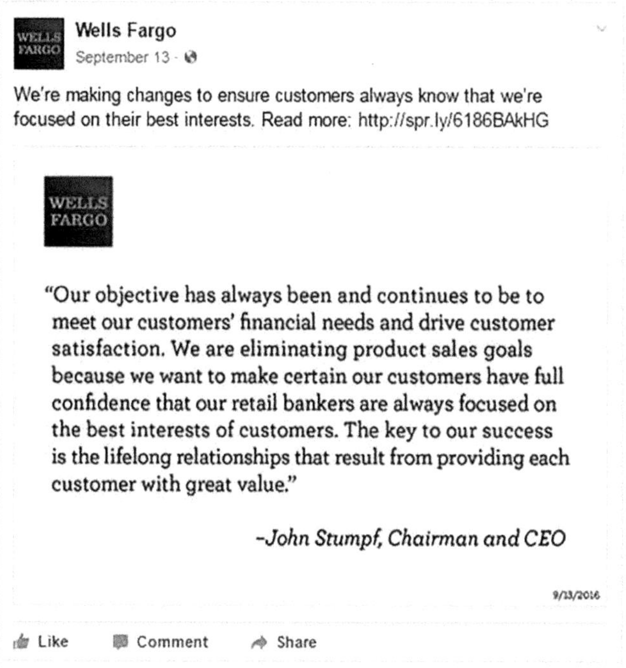

Source: Wells Fargo Facebook Page

On September 13, 2016, Wells Fargo issued a press release regarding intent to eliminate sales goals in its retail banking business. The change would be completed by January 1, 2017, to further ensure team members act in the best interest of customers. Wells Fargo's CFO, John Shrewsberry, shared this news at the Barclays Global Financial Services Conference 2016 and also commented on how the fraudulent account activity was predominantly carried out by a group "at the lower end of the performance scale where people apparently were making bad choices to hang on to their job" (Marino, 2016, para. 2). Stumpf also commented on the isolated group, stating, "the 1 (percent) that did it wrong, who we fired, terminated, in no way reflects our culture nor reflects the great work the other vast majority of the people do" (Glazer & Rexrode, 2016, para. 17).

A week later Wells Fargo issued a statement outlining Stumpf's commitment to regaining the trust of customers, team members and the American people (2016d, para. 7). The release included multiple quotes from Stumpf's earlier testimony before the U.S. Senate Banking Committee. In his testimony, Stumpf claimed responsibility for the fraudulent account activity while also clarifying that Wells Fargo never encouraged team members "to provide products and services to customers they did not want or need" (2016b, p. 1). He explained how the unethical behavior did not reflect the business culture nor strategy as cross-selling is only successful when products are wanted and used. Stumpf went on to recite a series of actions taken between 2011 and 2016 to weed out unethical behavior, such as proactive monitoring, training updates, changing incentive compensation, downplaying sales goals, and establishing a new oversight office and compliance program (2016b, p. 2–4).

On September 29, 2016, Wells Fargo announced the company was escalating the timeline for ending product sales goals to October 1, 2016. Stumpf shared this update

Source: Wells Fargo Twitter Page

in his next testimony before the U.S. House of Representatives Committee on Financial Services. In early October, Wells Fargo issued media statements noting regret for the loss of business with the Chicago City Council and the City of Seattle. The company also commented on losing business in Ohio, stating the company "values the State of Ohio's business and will fight to earn it back" (Egan, 2016d, para. 5).

In the wake of continued scrutiny, Wells Fargo announced that Stumpf would step down and the company's President and COO Tim Sloan would assume the role of CEO, effective October 12, 2016. An article detailing Sloan's experience and leadership style was posted on the company's online journal the next week. The brief introduction was followed by the posting of a company-wide announcement on October 25, 2016, in which Sloan confronted the company's many challenges and the long road ahead to recovery. He referenced a "wide array of actions to address sales practices issues" (2016, para. 29), including new leadership and performance plans as well as Ethics Line process reviews. Further, independent culture experts will be consulted to identify weaknesses and team members will be surveyed to better understand their perspective of the company (2016, para. 30). Also released in late October, Wells Fargo launched a 30 second television ad featuring the iconic stagecoach and reinforcing its commitment to make things right. The company's YouTube posting of the video encourages visitors to click through to a Wells Fargo webpage titled "We're building a better Wells Fargo."

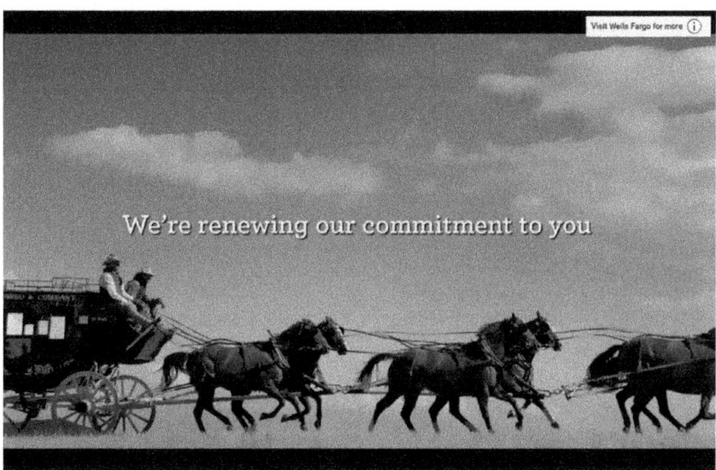

Source: Wells Fargo YouTube Page

Cultural Disconnect

1. Employee Response in the Media

Testifying before the U.S. Senate, Wells Fargo CEO John Stumpf spoke to the company's broad reach and population, noting how "one in every 600 working adults is a member of the Wells Fargo team" (2016b, p. 1). According to Glassdoor.com, a job site featuring company reviews from employees, Wells Fargo employees rate the company 3.4 out of 5 and approximately 65% would recommend working there to a friend (Wells Fargo Reviews, n.d.). The company is also a three-time award winner for strong employee engagement, and it's been consistently applauded for efforts in diversity and LGBT employment. However, the former employee accounts flooding the media after the company's September 8, 2016, announcement generally neglect to note these accomplishments. Rather, they portray a tense, high-pressure work environment driven by impractical sales quotas.

In a 2013 *Los Angeles Times* article, former employees explained how "top Wells Fargo executives exhort employees to shoot for the 'Great 8'—an average of eight financial products per household" (Reckard, para. 37). Varied personal accounts emphasize how supervisors as well as their direct reports would often work unpaid overtime to try to achieve high sales goals. Former employees claimed that those who fell short of the goals risked being chastised in coaching sessions or fired for poor performance. Employees shared how they talked family and customers into unnecessary products and services, and, in some instances, escalated to opening accounts without customer knowledge.

The former staff members quoted in more recent articles from the *Los Angeles Times*, the *New York Times*, *CNN Money* and NPR span the country, reinforcing the far reach of the alleged unethical banking practices. Dennise C., a former teller and banker in Houston, recounted to the *New York Times* how she transferred multiple times hoping the environment would be different at another Wells Fargo branch, but it was the "same story" (Cowley, 2016, para. 20). In addition to transfer attempts, several former employees said they tried to alert Human Resources and/or call an ethics hotline to disclose the unethical banking practices. Bill Bado, a former Wells Fargo banker in Pennsylvania, told *CNN Money* that he was terminated eight days after sending an e-mail to Human Resources (Egan, 2016c, para. 6). The article goes on to cite a former Wells Fargo HR team member who claims there was a "method" to "fire employees 'in retaliation for shining light' on sales issues" (para. 11).

Source: *CNN Money*

Some former employees described difficulty in finding a new job post-termination from Wells Fargo. For Bado, "it put a permanent stain on his securities license, scaring off other prospective bank employers" (Egan, 2016c, para. 25). A former employee recalled a coaching session in which branch management allegedly made such a threat, telling her "if you're bringing down the team then you will be fired and it will be on your permanent record" (Arnold, 2016, para. 18). Some employees claimed that they developed physical reactions, such as stomach aches, chest pains and panic attacks. For example, Angie Payden, a former Wells Fargo banker in Wisconsin, told the *New York Times* she became addicted to drinking hand sanitizer to cope with the pressure (Cowley, 2016, para. 10–11).

Several of the media outlets sharing the employee accounts sought comment from Wells Fargo. For the *New York Times*, the company refused to comment on individual accounts, but reiterated ongoing efforts to promote a customer-focused culture and alleviate pressures to sell unwanted products (Cowley, 2016, para. 3). A step further in NPR, Wells Fargo stated, "if any of these things transpired, it's distressing and it's not who Wells Fargo is" (Arnold, 2016, para. 35). A stronger response came in the form of a company-wide address from newly appointed CEO Tim Sloan on October 25, 2016. Sloan apologized to staff "for the pain you have experienced as team members as a result of our company's failures" (2016, para. 2). He acknowledged problems within the corporate culture and the need for employees to feel safe discussing these issues openly. Directly referencing the previous "bad apple"comments, he noted the company's failure to "acknowledge the role leadership played" (para. 27).

2. *Corporate Values and Character*

Republican Senator David Vitter asked John Stumpf if it was normal "for one percent of a business unit to be fired over fraud" (Oran, 2016, para. 15). In other words, is the work culture healthy if a small percent of your workforce consistently acts counter to company values? Former IBM Chairman Lou Gerstner penned a commentary on the clear disconnect between values and action occurring at Wells Fargo and, more broadly, across the corporate world. Gerstner noted how companies rely on a list of values to define their culture; however, "people do not do what you expect but what you *inspect*" (2016, para. 5). Cultures are created through employee interpretations of both leadership action and work systems that reinforce company priorities, like compensation and recognition. On the company's website, Wells Fargo defines culture "as understanding our vision and values so well that you instinctively know what you need to do when you come to work each day" (2016a, para. 1). While company leadership and communications may have consistently shared "customer-first" value statements and ethics policies, a high sales quota environment could have conceivably communicated a different set of priorities.

Better Banking Project founder Susan Ochs also commented on culture influences and Wells Fargo's alleged leadership blind spot, stating Stumpf "called this an operations and compliance issue, perhaps not realizing that both of those functions influence corporate culture" (2016, para. 11). In contrast, new CEO Tim Sloan recognized the need to fix culture issues in his company-wide address (2016, para. 9). He has also noted the importance of *behavior*, referencing leading by example and reinforcing customer focus as part of his leadership style in Wells Fargo's online journal (Randolph, 2016, para. 12). Among these shifts, Sloan affirmed that the company values will not change, stating, "Our failures are not the result of our values. I suspect they are the result of some of us forgetting to be guided by them" (2016, para. 36).

Connecting company values to employee behavior is central to the concept of corporate character. The Arthur W. Page Society defines corporate character as "the definition and alignment of mission, purpose, values, culture, business model, strategy, operations and brand to create the unique, differentiating identity of the enterprise" (2012b, para. 3). Inconsistencies in any of these elements weaken corporate character and may impact perceptions of authenticity and trustworthiness. Strong character is especially important in today's world of empowered stakeholders who demand greater transparency and honesty (Arthur W. Page Society, 2012b, para. 23). For Wells Fargo, unethical employee behavior questions whether the "Main Street bank" is actually more akin to traditional "Wall Street banks." Passionate responses from the public and various stakeholder groups illustrate a strong sense of betrayal, which may have a long-term impact on Wells Fargo's reputation and customer relationships.

Public Response

1. *Media Response*

Following Wells Fargo's announcement of the $185 million agreement, national news sources were immediately consumed with the reasons why. Major business news sources such as the *Wall Street Journal*, Bloomberg and the *Financial Times* reported daily on the progression of the Wells Fargo scandal. Coverage was further fueled as Wells

Source: Mike Luckovich, *Atlanta Journal-Constitution*

Fargo confirmed they had terminated 5,300 employees for unethical banking practices. Reporters, such as *CNN Money*'s Matthew Egan, called the scandal "shocking" (2016a, para. 6) and painted a disparaging picture of Wells Fargo in the press. News coverage did not slow as the days and weeks progressed, especially as pressure from the U.S. Congress escalated and former CEO John Stumpf seemed to blame the account openings on individual employees rather than the bank's culture (Glazer & Rexrode, 2016). Contradictory accounts from former employees surfaced to combat Stumpf's statements and media coverage shifted to a focus on Wells Fargo's corporate culture.

2. Policymaker Response

For weeks following the announcement of the settlement, Wells Fargo, and, more specifically CEO John Stumpf, was villainized in the media and interrogated by policymakers. Most notably, U.S. Sen. Elizabeth Warren (D-MA), who has historically challenged big banks, stood out as the main opponent of Stumpf in a series of Senate hearings (Egan, 2016b). Warren demanded Stumpf's resignation and questioned his leadership abilities, asking "If you [Stumpf] have no opinions on the most massive fraud that's hit this bank since the beginning of time, how can it be that you get to continue to collect a paycheck" (Egan, 2016b, para.11). Following Stumpf's retirement, Warren continues to criticize Wells Fargo for requiring "customers affected by its unauthorized accounts scandal to go through arbitration rather than allowing them to sue" (Barlyn, 2016, para. 1).

Shareholder Response

Notable shareholders, such as Berkshire Hathaway's Warren Buffett, were initially reluctant to comment on Wells Fargo and the fraudulent accounts. When Buffett's silence finally broke, he labeled the scandal as a "terrible mistake," yet asserted that Wells Fargo is "still a great bank" and decided against selling any shares (Aitken, 2016, para. 1). In contrast, other investors filed a class-action suit against the bank in September 2016 claiming Wells Fargo misled investors regarding its sales practices and resulting financial performance. Furthermore, certain religious organizations made headlines when they publicly condemned the bank and filed a shareholder resolution to fully review business standards (Bryan, 2016). In response to shareholder concerns, Wells Fargo's Board of Directors amended the company by-laws to require the separation of the Board Chairman and company CEO roles.

Impact on Financials and Reputation

Although Wells Fargo announced it would pay $185 million in fines and $5 million in customer remediation, the larger financial detriment was the loss in future business. Several states decided to suspend business with Wells Fargo for one year to hold the company accountable for its perceived lack of ethical standards. California, Massachusetts, Illinois and Ohio sanctioned the company for a culture "compromised by greed," in the words of U.S. Sen. John Kasich (R-OH) (Egan, 2016d, para. 2).

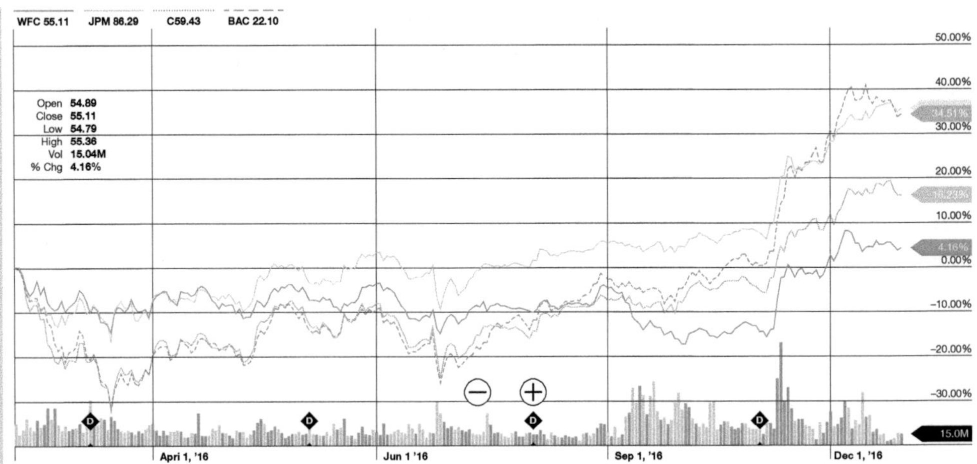

Source: Yahoo! Finance

According to *CNN Money*, the loss of business from Illinois alone will cost the bank millions in fees (Lobosco, 2016). Moreover, the spate of negative news sent shares of Wells Fargo plummeting down to a two-and-a-half year low on September 26, 2016 (Egan & Gogoi, 2016).

In addition to financial losses, Wells Fargo's reputation took a hit as the scandal garnered national coverage. Initial outcry was reported in national media outlets ranging from major television networks to social media channels such as Twitter and Facebook. As the story developed and former employees came forward with accusations of unrealistic goals and intense pressure to perform, Wells Fargo continued to lose esteem in the public eye. According to a study completed by management consulting company cg42, negative perceptions of the brand rose to 52% from 15% and 54% of customers said they would *not* bank with Wells Fargo compared with 22% before the fraudulent account scandal (2016). Further, in September 2016, JPMorgan claimed the title of World's Most Valuable Bank, which had been held by Wells Fargo since 2015 when it surpassed the market value of The Industrial & Commercial Bank of China (Lorenzetti, 2015).

With negative perceptions of the bank rising, one major concern is how the scandal will affect new customer accounts and, perhaps more importantly, Wells Fargo's ability to retain customers. cg42's research states "[w]hile only 3% of Wells Fargo's customers report being affected by the scandal, a full 30% claim they are actively exploring alternatives and 14% have already made the decision to switch banks as a result of the scandal. This represents $212B of deposits and $8B of revenues at risk" (2016, p. 3). Increased scrutiny of the bank also prompted additional investigations into Wells Fargo's business practices by FINRA, the Department of Justice and the SEC, which may result in a regulatory downgrade by the Office of the Comptroller of the Currency (Glazer & Witkowski, 2016). Consequently, the fraudulent account scandal may have initially cost the company $190 million in fines and remediation, but the true loss is yet to be fully realized as reputation damages continue to play out.

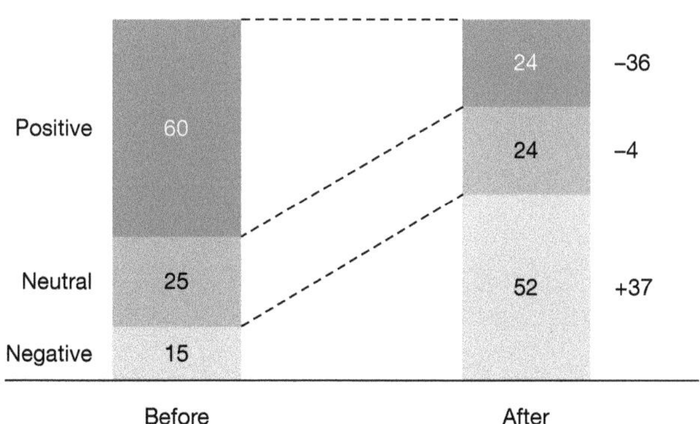

Source: cg42

Wells Fargo's Challenges

Following years of alleged fraudulent activity, Wells Fargo generated a relatively modest $2.6 million in fees from the creation of unauthorized accounts. To further clarify, *Fox Business* reporter Steve Tobak said the fees amount to approximately $1.30 for the average consumer (2016). Several recent bank scandals exceed these financial returns, and yet, the Wells Fargo scandal generated headline after headline. Sheelah Kolhatkar, staff writer for *The New Yorker*, hypothesized why the Wells Fargo scandal was so highly publicized, noting "Unlike the Libor scandal, in which global interest rates were manipulated, or the creation of credit derivatives by people who knew they were likely to fail, the creation of bogus accounts at Wells Fargo required no special math or financial-modelling skills" (2016, para. 2). She also highlighted how easy it is for people to empathize with the deceived customer and the terminated lower level employee. To put it simply, the Wells Fargo scandal is highly accessible

Source: Twitter

and relatable for a broad range of people, which spells trouble for the company's once strong reputation.

Wells Fargo is countering such perceptions of Wall Street banking practices and employee victimization by promoting its commitment to making things right and implementing a series of initiatives, such as surveying employees, consulting culture experts and doubling down on core company values. Wells Fargo CEO Tim Sloan acknowledged that it will be a long road to not only fix the corporate culture but also strengthen character and regain trust. Banking experts and consultants agree the fix initiative will require a substantial investment, noting how "Executives will have to dismantle and rebuild systems of sales incentives and performance management that date back two decades" (Freed & Reckard, 2016, para. 4). Dov Siedman, CEO of LRN, a company that advises organizations on ethics and regulatory compliance, also commented on Wells Fargo's need to restructure and the broader applicability of employee incentive issues. He explained that the Wells Fargo scandal is "no different than a pharmaceutical giant whose people are more interested in selling pills, as opposed to truly making patients healthy" (Simon, Warren & Siedman, 2016, para. 13).

Whether it is pills or financial products, companies rely on quotas and goals to help drive the business forward. However, do the sales tactics and compensation structures support the company's purpose and values? Are employee success measures helping shape a healthy corporate culture? These are the types of questions Wells Fargo, and organizations across industries, must ask to evaluate whether daily frontline operations truly align with the company's purpose, vision and values.

Communications teams play a critical role in promoting company direction and employee expectations. Further, communications may have responsibilities for monitoring and shaping the work culture. Therefore communications leadership must consistently evaluate the connections between company identity and operations to validate direction as well as reinforce consistency with both internal and external audiences. When operational inconsistencies draw stakeholder scrutiny, communications leadership should also be prepared to manage the narrative. Following Wells Fargo's September 8, 2016, announcement, the company's "Main Street bank" narrative began to crack under allegations of greed and abuse. The company responded with increased communications, greater transparency and a commitment campaign to minimize damages. As Wells Fargo navigates the long road to recovery, communications will continue to play a pivotal role in engaging concerned stakeholders, promoting company improvements and again solidifying the company's once reputable narrative.

* * *

APPENDIX A

FOR IMMEDIATE RELEASE
CONTACT: Frank Mateljan
(213) 978-8340 (office)
(213) 479-5675 (mobile)

From the Office of the City Attorney
Mike Feuer

Suite 800, City Hall East
Los Angeles, CA 90012

Phone: 213-978-8340 Fax: 213-978-2093
Web: http://www.atty.lacity.org, Twitter: @CityAttorneyLA

PRESS RELEASE

May 5, 2015

CITY ATTORNEY FEUER FILES LAWSUIT AGAINST WELLS FARGO FOR ALLEGEDLY OPENING UNAUTHORIZED CUSTOMER ACCOUNTS

Complaint Also Alleges Wells Failed to Notify Customers of Unauthorized Use of Personal Information

LOS ANGELES – City Attorney Mike Feuer today announced that his office has filed a civil lawsuit against Wells Fargo, alleging the company has victimized consumers by opening customer accounts, and issuing credit cards, without authorization--then failing to inform customers of the alleged misuse of their personal information or refund fees for unwanted services.

"Consumers should be entitled to expect that major financial institutions will treat them fairly," said Feuer. "Our lawsuit alleges that in Wells Fargo's push for growth the bank often elevated profit over its customers' legal rights."

The complaint alleges Wells Fargo's business model imposed unrealistic sales quotas that, among other things, have driven employees to engage in unlawful activity including opening fee-generating customer accounts and adding unwanted secondary accounts to primary accounts without permission. These practices allegedly have led to significant hardship and financial loss to consumers, including having money withdrawn from customer's authorized accounts to pay for fees assessed by Wells Fargo on unauthorized accounts and derogatory notes on credit reports when unauthorized fees went unpaid, causing some customers to purchase identity theft protection.

Furthermore, the complaint alleges that Wells Fargo failed to properly inform customers of misuse of their personal information and failed to refund unauthorized fees.

Feuer is seeking Wells Fargo customers' help asking them to review their own accounts and answer the following:

- Have unauthorized savings and checking accounts been opened in your name?
- Have accounts you've closed stayed open?
- Have you received debit or credit cards you didn't request?
- Has a line of credit been opened that you didn't ask for?
- Have you been charged fees for any of these unauthorized activities?

Wells Fargo customers finding discrepancies can call the City Attorney's dedicated hotline: 213-978-3393.

-more-

APPENDIX B

Wells Fargo Issues Statement on Agreements Related to Sales Practices

SAN FRANCISCO—(BUSINESS WIRE)—Wells Fargo Bank, N.A., a subsidiary of Wells Fargo & Company (NYSE:WFC), reached agreements with the Consumer Financial Protection Bureau, the Office of the Comptroller of the Currency, and the Office of the Los Angeles City Attorney, regarding allegations that some of its retail customers received products and services they did not request.

The amount of the settlements, which Wells Fargo had fully accrued for at June 30, 2016, totaled $185 million, plus $5 million in customer remediation.

The company issued the following statement related to today's news:

"Wells Fargo reached these agreements consistent with our commitment to customers and in the interest of putting this matter behind us. Wells Fargo is committed to putting our customers' interests first 100 percent of the time, and we regret and take responsibility for any instances where customers may have received a product that they did not request.

Our commitment to addressing the concerns covered by these agreements has included:

- An extensive review by a third party consulting firm going back into 2011, which we completed prior to these settlements. The review included consumer and small business retail banking deposit accounts and unsecured credit cards opened during the period reviewed.
- As a result of this review, $2.6 million has been refunded to customers for any fees associated with products customers received that they may not have requested. Accounts refunded represented a fraction of one percent of the accounts reviewed, and refunds averaged $25.
- Disciplinary actions, including terminations of managers and team members who acted counter to our values.
- Investments in enhanced team-member training and monitoring and controls.
- Strengthened performance measures that are tied to customer satisfaction, loyalty and ethics.
- Sending customers a confirming e-mail within one hour of opening any deposit account, and sending an application acknowledgement and decision status letter after submitting an application for a credit card."

In addition, as noted in a message emailed to all Wells Fargo team members today, the company said "Our entire culture is centered on doing what is right for our customers. However, at Wells Fargo, when we make mistakes, we are open about it, we take responsibility, and we take action. Today's agreements are consistent with these beliefs." Customers can visit wellsfargo.com/commitment to view their accounts, and for information about this announcement.

About Wells Fargo

Wells Fargo & Company (NYSE: WFC) is a diversified, community-based financial services company with $1.9 trillion in assets. Founded in 1852 and headquartered in San Francisco, Wells Fargo provides banking, insurance, investments, mortgage, and consumer and commercial finance through more than 8,600 locations, 13,000 ATMs, the internet (wellsfargo.com) and mobile banking, and has offices in 36 countries and territories to support customers who conduct business in the global economy. With approximately 268,000 team members, Wells Fargo serves one in three households in the United States. Wells Fargo & Company was ranked No. 27 on Fortune's 2016 rankings of America's largest corporations. Wells Fargo's vision is to satisfy our customers' financial needs and help them succeed financially. Wells Fargo perspectives are also available at Wells Fargo Blogs and Wells Fargo Stories.

References

Aitken, R. (2016, November 13). Berkshire Hathaway's Buffett Says Wells Fargo's A "Great Bank," Holding Stock. *Forbes*. Retrieved from www.forbes.com/sites/rogeraitken/2016/11/13/berkshire-hathaways-buffett-says-wells-fargos-a-great-bank-holding-stock/#7021d8e65739

Arnold, C. (2016, October 4). Former Wells Fargo Employees Describe Toxic Sales Culture, Even At HQ. NPR. Retrieved from www.npr.org/2016/10/04/496508361/former-wells-fargo-employees-describe-toxic-sales-culture-even-at-hq

Arthur W. Page Society. (2012a). Building Belief: A New Model for Activating Corporate Character and Authentic Advocacy. Retrieved from www.awpagesociety.com/thought-leadership/building-belief

Arthur W. Page Society. (2012b). Building Belief: A New Model for Activating Corporate Character and Authentic Advocacy. Executive Summary. Retrieved from www.awpagesociety.com/attachments/390013a47e275312f1c81dcbf15314a10eaf02ca/store/fe2f00efbd50caa148a5f4d29146f3f9a6e1c1b0b21a0ea818a46e48aa8c/Building-Belief_Executive-Summary.pdf

Barlyn, S. (2016, November 29). Warren Slams Wells Fargo Over Arbitration Position. *Reuters*. Retrieved from www.reuters.com/article/us-wells-fargo-accounts-arbitration-idUSKBN13N2GA

Bryan, B. (2016, October 10). Things are Getting so Bad for Wells Fargo Even Catholic Nuns are Dumping the Bank. Business Insider. Retrieved from www.businessinsider.com/wells-fargo-interfaith-center-on-corporate-responsibility-nuns-condemn-2016–10

Carlozo, L. (2015, July 24). Why Wells Fargo is the Best Bank Stock Today. *U.S. News*. Retrieved from http://money.usnews.com/money/personal-finance/mutual-funds/articles/2015/07/24/why-Wells-fargo-is-the-best-bank-stock-today

cg42. (2016, October). Wells Fargo Mini Study. Retrieved from http://cg42.com/pdf/cg42-Wells-Fargo-Mini-Study.pdf

CNN Money. Retrieved from http://money.cnn.com/2016/09/08/investing/wells-fargo-created-phony-accounts-bank-fees/

Cowley, S. (2016, October 20). Voices from Wells Fargo: "I Thought I Was Having a Heart Attack." *The New York Times*. Retrieved from www.nytimes.com/2016/10/21/business/dealbook/voices-from-wells-fargo-i-thought-i-was-having-a-heart-attack.html

CSI Market. (2016). Wells Fargo & Company Segments. Retrieved from http://csimarket.com/stocks/segments.php?code=WFC

Egan, M. (2016a, September 9). 5,300 Wells Fargo Employees Fired Over 2 Million Phony Accounts. *Money*. Retrieved from http://money.cnn.com/2016/09/20/investing/wells-fargo-elizabeth-warren-resign-criminal-investigation/index.html?iid=EL

Egan, M. (2016b, September 21). Elizabeth Warren's Epic Takedown of Wells Fargo CEO. *CNN*

Egan, M. (2016c, September 21). I Called the Wells Fargo Ethics Line and Was Fired. *CNN Money*. Retrieved from http://money.cnn.com/2016/09/21/investing/wells-fargo-fired-workers-retaliation-fake-accounts/

Egan, M. (2016d, October 4). John Kasich Bans Wells Fargo from Lucrative Ohio Deals. *CNN Money*. Retrieved from http://money.cnn.com/2016/10/14/investing/wells-fargo-kasich-fake-accounts/index.html?category=investing

Egan, M. & Gogoi, P. (2016, October 1). Wells Fargo's September from Hell. *CNN Money*. Retrieved from http://money.cnn.com/2016/10/01/investing/wells-fargo-fake-account-scandal-september-2016/index.html?iid=EL

Freed, D. & Reckard, E. (2016, October 12). Wells Fargo Faces Costly Overhaul of Bankrupt Sales Culture. *Reuters*. Retrieved from www.reuters.com/article/us-wells-fargo-accounts-profits-analysis-idUSKCN12C0E3

Gandel, S. (2014, October 31). Warren Buffett's 6 Best Investments of all Time. *Fortune*. Retrieved from http://fortune.com/2014/10/31/warren-buffett-best-investments/?iid=sr-link10

Gerstner, L. (2016, October 2). The Culture Ate Our Corporate Reputation. *Wall Street Journal*. Retrieved from www.wsj.com/articles/the-culture-ate-our-corporate-reputation-1475445084

Glazer, E. & Rexrode, C. (2016, September 13). Wells Fargo CEO Defends Bank Culture, Lays Blame With Bad Employees. *Wall Street Journal*. Retrieved from www.wsj.com/articles/wells-fargo-ceo-defends-bank-culture-lays-blame-with-bad-employees-1473784452

Glazer, E. & Witkowski, R. (2016, December 9). Wells Fargo Likely Faces Regulatory Downgrade Harming Its Prospects. *Wall Street Journal*. Retrieved from www.wsj.com/articles/wells-fargo-likely-faces-regulatory-downgrade-harming-its-prospects-1481293662

Global Finance. (2016, March 14). *Global Finance* Names the World's Best Developed Market Banks 2016. [Press release]. Retrieved from https://d2tyltutevw8th.cloudfront.net/media/document/worlds-best-developed-markets-banks-2016–1458080129.pdf

Kolhatkar, S. (2016, October 4). Wells Fargo and a New Age of Banking Scandals. *The New Yorker*. Retrieved from www.newyorker.com/business/currency/wells-fargo-and-a-new-age-of-banking-scandals

Lashinsky, A. (2009a, April 20). Riders on the Storm. *Fortune*. Retrieved from http://archive.fortune.com/2009/04/19/news/companies/lashinsky_wells.fortune/index.htm?postv ersion=2009042011

Lashinsky, A. (2009b, April 24). Warren Buffett on Wells Fargo. *Fortune*. Retrieved from http://archive.fortune.com/2009/04/19/news/companies/lashinsky_buffett.fortune/index.htm

Lobosco, K. (2016, October 3). Illinois Yanks Billions of Banking Biz from Wells Fargo. *CNN Money*. Retrieved from http://money.cnn.com/2016/10/03/investing/wells-fargo-illinois-moratorium/

Lorenzetti, L. (2015, July 23). This is the Most Valuable Bank in the World. *Fortune*. Retrieved from http://fortune.com/2015/07/23/wells-fargo-worlds-most-valuable-bank/?iid=sr-link2

Marino, J. (2016, September 13). Wells Fargo CFO Blames Unauthorized Accounts on Under-performers. *CNBC*. Retrieved from www.cnbc.com/2016/09/13/wells-fargo-cfo-blames-reason-for-bank-fine-on-under-performers.html

Ochs, S. (2016, October 6). The Leadership Blind Spots at Wells Fargo. *Harvard Business Review*. Retrieved from https://hbr.org/2016/10/the-leadership-blind-spots-at-wells-fargo

Oran, O. (2016, September 28). "Wells Fargo scandal Reignites Debate about Big Bank Culture." *Reuters*. Retrieved from www.reuters.com/article/us-wells-fargo-accounts-culture-analysis-idUSKCN11Y1S1

Picoult, J. (2016, October 8). What Went Awry at Wells Fargo? The Beaten Path of a Toxic Culture. *New York Times*. Retrieved from www.nytimes.com/2016/10/09/jobs/what-went-awry-at-wells-fargo-the-beaten-path-of-a-toxic-culture.html?_r=1

Randolph, A. (2016, October 17). Getting to Know Tim Sloan. *Wells Fargo Stories*. Retrieved from https://stories.wf.com/getting-know-tim-sloan/

Reckard, E.S. (2013, December 21). Wells Fargo's Pressure-cooker Sales Culture Comes at a Cost. *Los Angeles Times*. Retrieved from www.latimes.com/business/la-fi-wells-fargo-sale-pressure-20131222-story.html

Simon, S., Warren, E. & Siedman, D. (2016, September 24). Wells Fargo Case Prompts Questions Of Corporate Ethics Reform. NPR Weekend Edition Saturday. Podcast retrieved from www.npr.org/2016/09/24/495295116/wells-fargo-case-prompts-questions-of-corporate-ethics-reform

Sloan, T. (2016, October 25). Sloan: "My Primary Objective is to Restore Trust." *Wells Fargo Stories*. Retrieved from https://stories.wf.com/companywide-address-ceo-tim-sloan/

Stempel, J. (2016, March 28). Buffett Boosts Berkshire's Wells Fargo Stake to 10 Percent. *Reuters*. Retrieved from www.reuters.com/article/us-berkshire-wellsfargo-idUSKCN0WU1T1

Stumpf, J. (2016a, September 8). Perspective on Sept. 8 Settlement Announcement: A Message from John Stumpf, Chairman and CEO of Wells Fargo & Company. *Wells Fargo Stories*. Retrieved from https://stories.wf.com/perspective-todays-settlement-announcement/?cid=adv_prsrls_1609_102495

Stumpf, J. (2016b, September 20). Testimony for the U.S. Senate Committee on Banking, Housing, and Urban Affairs. Retrieved from www.wellsfargomedia.com/assets/pdf/about/corporate/john-stumpf-written-statement.pdf

Tobak, S. (2016, September 22). In Defense of John Stumpf and Wells Fargo. *Fox Business*. Retrieved from www.foxbusiness.com/features/2016/09/22/in-defense-john-stumpf-and-wells-fargo.html

Wells Fargo. (n.d.). In *Encyclopedia Britannica* online. Retrieved from www.britannica.com/topic/Wells-Fargo-American-corporation

Wells Fargo & Company. (2016a). Our Culture. Retrieved from www.wellsfargo.com/about/corporate/vision-and-values/our-culture

Wells Fargo & Company. (2016b). History of Wells Fargo. Retrieved from www.wellsfargo.com/about/corporate/history/

Wells Fargo & Company. (2016c, September 8). Wells Fargo Issues Statement on Agreements Related to Sales Practices [Press release]. Retrieved from www.wellsfargo.com/about/press/2016/sales-practices-agreements_0908.content

Wells Fargo & Company. (2016d, September 20). Wells Fargo Chairman and CEO John Stumpf Outlines a Series of New Actions to Strengthen Culture and Rebuild Trust of Customers and Team Members at Senate Banking Committee Hearing. [Press release]. Retrieved from www.wellsfargo.com/about/press/2016/new-actions-strengthen-culture_0920.content

Wells Fargo & Company. (2016e, November 15). Wells Fargo Commitment Campaign. [Video]. Retrieved from www.youtube.com/watch?v=uh3zleQY-QY

Wells Fargo Reviews. (n.d.). Retrieved November 14, 2016, from glassdoor.com: www.glassdoor.com/Reviews/Wells-Fargo-Reviews-E8876.htm

Wells Fargo: Riding High. (2013, September 14). *The Economist*. Retrieved from www.economist.com/news/finance-and-economics/21586295-big-winner-financial-crisis-riding-high

World's Most Admired Companies. (2016). *Fortune*. Retrieved from http://fortune.com/worlds-most-admired-companies/

LONG CASE QUESTIONS

1. Has Wells Fargo grown too large to enforce corporate governance or internal controls? What effect has the organization's size and complexity had on the continued problems?
2. Was Wells Fargo's fraudulent activity an individual employee problem or a broader cultural problem?
3. How does a company verify or ensure employee behavior aligns with company purpose and values?
4. If you were Wells Fargo's CO during the scandal, what would your crisis response action plan be?
5. In a crisis response situation, what is the role of the CEO? Should the CEO assume responsibility for unethical behavior carried out by 'lower-level' employees?
6. Do you believe it is possible to enforce an ethics program to redesign and ethical climate or culture with this or any other organization?
7. What effect will the new plans have on Wells Fargo's investors? What can Wells Fargo do to mitigate negative responses?
8. Who are the critical stakeholders? How should the new leadership handle the stakeholders' responses and concerns?

Chapter 13

Corporate Social Responsibility

LEARNING OBJECTIVES

After reading this chapter you should be able to:

- Understand the development of corporate social responsibility during the last few decades
- Understand the arguments that support more social responsive businesses than those that counter this position
- Become aware of the basic models of corporate social responsibility
- Understand the fundamental premises of strategic social responsibility
- Become aware of the social responsibility reporting options

PREVIEW BUSINESS ETHICS INSIGHT

LEGO Takes Top CSR Honors

The Boston-based management consulting firm, Reputation Institute (RI), produces an annual CSR ranking from its tracking of social responsibility reputations derived from consumers' perceptions of company governance, positive influence on society and treatment of employees. The recent study used respondents from 15 countries resulting in 170,000 company ratings. Coming out on top in 2017 was the Danish toy maker LEGO, up from 5th place the year before. Reputation Research's Chief Research Officer Stephen Hahn-Griffiths noted that LEGO "has embraced corporate social responsibility from top to bottom" was recently ranked as having the best CSR reputation on safeguarding the environment, helping worthy causes, conducting business impartially, acting transparently, and generally behaving ethically. Below we note just two examples of LEGO's CSR activities.

An example of the Danish toy company's push for sustainability includes the LEGO Group's effort to shrink packing box sizes to save cardboard that resulted in a reduction of approximately 7000 tons of cardboard. Further, the smaller boxes also gained the Forest Stewardship Council® (FSC®) certification. FSC® certification requires that wood-based packaging comes from sustainable sources such that tree harvesting will not exceed what the forest can reproduce. Getting the FSC® logo also guarantees the protection of animal and plant life and fair working conditions for forestry workers.

By 2015, LEGO reached its goal to use 100% Forest Stewardship Council-certified paper and packaging in all operations. Jørgen Vig Knudstorp, President and Chief Executive Officer of the LEGO Group noted:

> Reducing our box size makes sense for shoppers, retailers, our business and most importantly the environment. The new boxes and our commitment to 100% FSC®-certified paper are examples of our dedication to constant improvement. We believe we share responsibility for our planet, the wider community, and the generations to come.

In another example of corporate social responsibility, LEGO collaborates with its suppliers with the goal to reduce total emissions. Recently, they reduced emissions by 10,000 tons, which is like taking 2000 cars off the streets.

Recognizing LEGO's actions, the World Wildlife Fund (WWF) Group, one of the largest conservation organizations in the world, named LEGO as a "Climate Savers Partner." LEGO is the only toy company in the world to get such a distinction. LEGO Group's CEO Jørgen Vig Knudstorp notes:

Partnering with WWF is an important step in our efforts to get the best out of our sustainability initiatives. We are proud to contribute to WWF's overall vision of 100% renewable energy by 2050 and already know they have played a part in the targets we have set – and how we can achieve them.

Based on: Strauss, Karsten. 2017. "The 10 companies with the best CSR reputations in 2017." *Forbes*, September 17. www.lego.com/en-us/aboutus/responsibility

This chapter considers the broad issue of **corporate social responsibility** (CSR). Up to this point, you have seen how the various stakeholders come into play when managers consider ethical issues. Here we broaden our focus to consider generally the degree to which companies should or perhaps must go beyond the requirements of running an economically viable business within the constraints of the law. We will consider various definitions of CSR below. However, common themes focus on how companies can protect the environment and enhance the well-being of their stakeholders, all while maintaining an economically viable business. The Preview Business Ethics Insight above gives a perspective on how LEGO prioritizes CSR as a core value.

At LEGO, there is hardly any activity in the company that is not influenced by a concern for CSR. Moreover, consumers recognize this and likely reward LEGO for its efforts.

A BRIEF HISTORY OF CORPORATE SOCIAL RESPONSIBILITY

Some scholars trace the "modern" era of corporate social responsibility to the 1960s.[1] However, others see the genesis of CSR, at least as a formal issue, to a debate in the *Harvard Law Review* during the 1930s between Columbia Professor Adolf A. Berle and Harvard Professor E. Merrick Dodd. Berle contended that managers are only responsible to shareholders, while Dodd countered that managers have wider responsibilities and "that the powers of corporate management are held in trust for the entire community." Providing an intellectual basis for what we now know as CSR, Dodd went on to note that the modern firm is "permitted and encouraged by the law primarily because it is of service to the community rather than because it is a source of profit to its owner."[2] Although CSR is on firm grounds throughout the world, this debate has not ended.

One can set the debate for the need for CSR in the context of Adam Smith's classical economic theory. For Smith, the maximum benefits for society are achieved in an unfettered market where people and organizations act in self-interest. The "**invisible hand**" allows the best organizations to flourish because competition favors those who produce the best products at the best prices as consumers also seek their own self-interest in buying those products. As Smith notes in the often-quoted statement below:

> It is not from the benevolence of the butcher, the brewer, or the baker, that we expect our dinner, but from their regard to their own interest. We address ourselves, not to their humanity but to their self-love, and never talk to them of our own necessities but of their advantages.[3]

The Industrial Revolution seemed to support Smith's ideas, as many people took jobs in newly created factories, often achieving a better standard of living. However, large organizations now held greater power than ever before and their founders and owners became some of the richest people in the world. The landscape of a laissez-faire economy often encouraged severe and often cutthroat competition among organizations that led to little or no concern for the company's impact on employees, the community, or the larger society.

Paradoxically, many of these same industrialists that ran these companies that exploited workers and local communities were also among the world's greatest philanthropists. Although sometimes referred to as robber barons, the very wealthy of this era gave millions of dollars to charity and educational institutions. Many of the foundations they, and later their families, established are still engaged in philanthropy today. You will recognize some of the names as, for example, John D. Rockefeller, Leland Stanford, Cornelius Vanderbilt, and Andrew Carnegie. However, this was not CSR. If philanthropy occurred, it was done by individuals for their own reasons and not as a representative of a company.

With the start of the twentieth century, criticism of big business increased. More people began to believe that the big corporations were too powerful and used business practices that were anti-social and anti-competitive. As a result, the government responded with laws and regulations that limited the power of large corporations and served to protect employees, consumers, and society at large. Between 1900 and 1960, in response to changes in prevailing cultural values and perhaps the threat of increased regulations, business leaders gradually accepted that corporations have additional responsibilities beyond making a profit and obeying the law.

The 1960s and 1970s continued a cultural shift in the expectations for business in most countries. Movements related to civil rights, consumerism, and environmentalism changed the context for doing business and therefore society's expectations for business responsibilities. Such shifts in expectations resulted in growing legal constraints on business in areas related to equal employment opportunity, product safety, worker safety, and the environment. In the 1970s, social legislation in the United States sent an increasingly strong message to the corporate world that the playing field was changing. Creation of the Environmental Protection Agency (EPA), the Equal Employment Opportunity Commission (EEOC), Occupational Safety and Health Administration (OSHA), and the Consumer Product Safety Commission (CPSC) elevated the influence of many stakeholders in the corporate world. However, going beyond legal compliance and based on the premise that those with greater power have greater responsibilities, most of the developed world called on businesses to become proactive. Increasingly, it became an expectation that it is not sufficient to avoid causing social problems but it is also necessary to help solve social problems.[4] Today this is even more apparent, as you will see later in the chapter when we discuss the rising pressure for CSR performance measurement, reporting, and engagement with stakeholders.

In the U.S., the first legal precedent for the dominance of the stockholder as the prime stakeholder was the influential 1919 case of ***Dodge v. Ford***.[5] Despite its name, the case had nothing to do with competition between automakers. At that time Ford was slowly lowering the price of his cars from $900 to $360. He also decided that he could no longer pay special dividends. He needed to offset the losses from cutting prices and he intended to increase wages and expand production capacity. Ford defended his decision altruistically based on his broader social goals: "to employ still more men, to spread the benefits of this industrial system to the greatest possible number, to help them build up their lives and their homes." He also noted that he had paid out considerable dividends to the shareholders, giving them substantial profits, and they should be content with lower dividends now.

The Dodge brothers (10% owners of Ford and a competitor company) sued, claiming that Ford had no right to use stockholder equity (their money) for his own philanthropic ends. The Michigan Supreme Court sided with the Dodges saying that the corporation exists for the benefit of stockholders. Corporate boards only have flexibility in how they choose to achieve those ends. They left open the idea that a certain amount of philanthropic giving might benefit the company. However, the case largely established the belief in the U.S. that corporations have prime, if not sole, responsibilities to shareholders.[6]

At least in the U.S., the switch from stockholder dominance to corporate philanthropy began with ***Smith v. Barlow***,[7] a landmark court decision in 1953. A.P. Smith Manufacturing Company, a manufacturer of valves and fire hydrants, was sued by a stockholder for donating $1500 to Princeton University under the premise that this was not in the best interest of the stockholders. In *Smith v. Barlow*, the court upheld the contribution as legal ruling against the stockholders. The court ruled that the stockholders,

> whose private interests rest entirely upon the well-being of the corporation, ought not to be permitted to close their eyes to present-day realities and thwart the long-visioned corporate action in recognizing and voluntarily discharging its high obligations as a constituent of our modern social structure.

After this case, the dominant model of CSR was corporate philanthropy. Donations to worthy causes such as universities and social services were considered beneficial for the health of society. Associated with this philanthropy was a notion that it should "come from the heart" and not necessarily benefit the company.[8]

Sometimes considered the "father" of CSR, Howard Bowen offered an early definition of CSR that showed movement away from a purely philanthropic position:

> It [CSR] refers to the obligations of businessmen [sic] to pursue those policies, to make those decisions or to follow those lines of action which are desirable in terms of the objectives and values of our society.[9]

During the 1960s and 1970s, the concept of CSR broadened both in practice and in academic thinking.[10] Although over a decade before R. Edward Freeman's classic *Strategic Management: A Stakeholder Approach*, Harold Johnson introduced an array of stakeholders into his 1971 definition of CSR:

> A socially responsible firm is one whose managerial staff balances a multiplicity of interests. Instead of striving only for larger profits for its stockholders, a responsible enterprise also takes into account employees, suppliers, dealers, local communities, and the nation.[11]

The idea of the duties and obligations to stakeholders is now entrenched in both practitioner and academic thinking about CSR.

One way of thinking about CSR, born in the 1970s, but still popular today is the CSR pyramid developed by Archie Carroll.[12] His pyramid is shown in Exhibit 13.1.

For Carroll, there are four essential responsibilities of a business. These include **economic**, **legal**, **ethical**, and **philanthropic**. He accepts that the principal role of a business is to produce goods or services that people need and to make an acceptable profit in the process. Without a surviving and profitable business, all other responsibilities are moot. Businesses must conform to laws and regulations as part of the social contract between business and society that allows them to operate. This is now often called a **license to operate**. Although the legal requirements of business operations

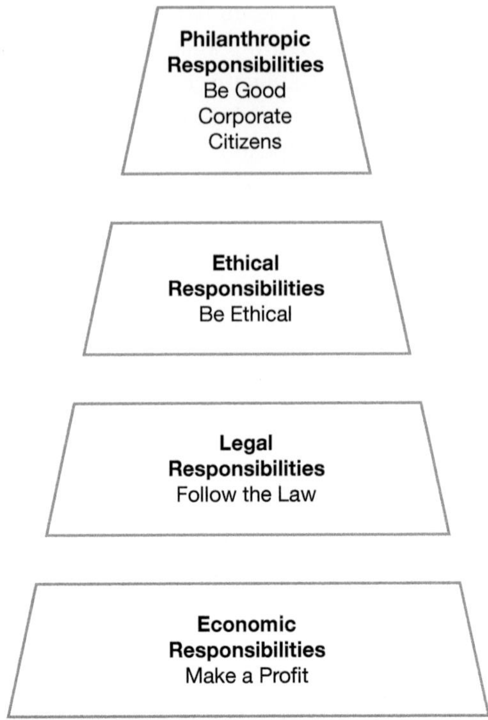

EXHIBIT 13.1—Carroll's Pyramid of CSR

may control activities and practices with ethical consequences, such as regulations regarding product safety and consumer protection, businesses must conform to the ethical expectations of society that are not codified into law. These ethical expectations reflect what the organizational stakeholders—stockholders, consumers, employees, and the greater community—consider fair, just, and beneficial to society at large. These obligations rest on moral reasoning based principles such as rights and justice and utilitarian logic.

Such ethical expectations often precede formal codification into laws, as changing societal values often drive later legislation. You will see later in this chapter how the formal reporting of CSR performance is gradually moving beyond voluntary and is required in some form in many parts of the world.

At the top of the pyramid is a philanthropic responsibility. This is the responsibility to be good corporate citizens and engage in activities that promote human welfare and goodwill. Contributions to the arts and education fall into this category. What distinguishes philanthropic from ethical responsibility is that philanthropy is not a moral obligation. Stakeholders typically do not see the firm as immoral if it does not engage in philanthropy.

Carroll cautions that the components of the pyramid are not mutually exclusive. In fact, they are in a dynamic tension, with the most critical being between the economic versus the other components. However, it is an oversimplification to view CSR as a concern for profits versus concern for society. The pyramid provides a metaphor to look

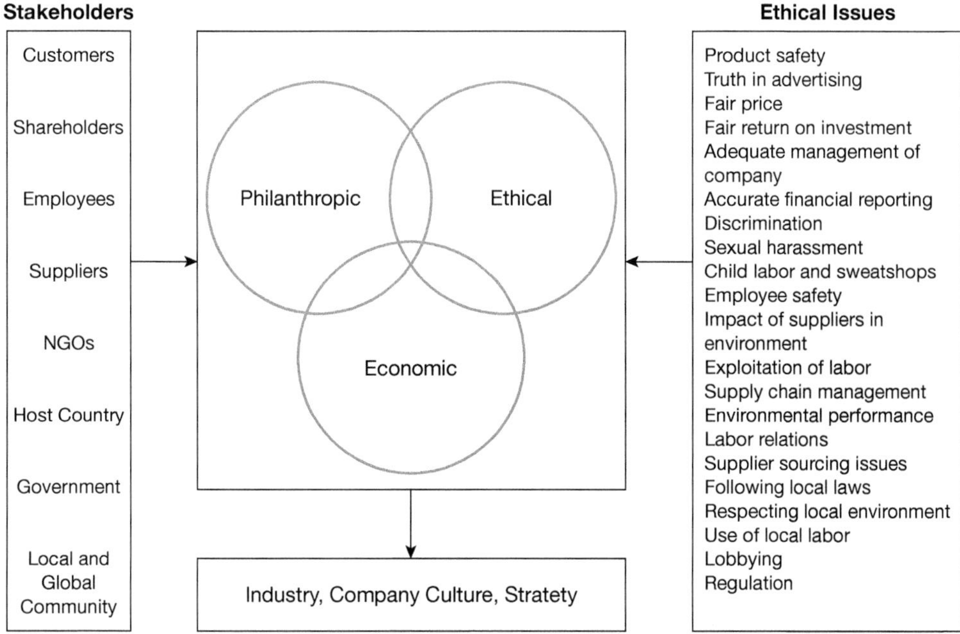

EXHIBIT 13.2—Tensions, Stakeholders, and Issues in the CSR Responsibility Mix

at the issues and tensions and Carroll's research shows that many companies organize their CSR efforts around such issues. To emphasize how the core areas of CSR work not necessarily as a pyramid, Carroll has viewed these areas in the perspective of a Venn diagram, with issues and stakeholders pressing for the dominance of one CSR focus over another. A visual representation of this is shown in Exhibit 13.2.

In spite of some CSR advocates such as Carroll giving economic performance and profits a major position in thinking about CSR, during this early rise in CSR interest and activities many business leaders and academics feared that the movement would lead to increased involvement of the government in private decisions.[13] Nobel laureate **Milton Friedman** is probably the most famous critic. His five-page article in the September 13, 1970, issue of the *New York Times Magazine*, "The Social Responsibility of Business is to Increase its Profits," remains to this day the rallying point of those who see CSR as an affront to shareholder rights. For Friedman, there is only one purpose of the corporation:

> There is one and only one social responsibility of business—to use its resources and engage in activities designed to increase its profits so long as it stays within the rules of the game, which is to say, engages in open and free competition without deception or fraud.[14]

Otherwise, he reasoned, managers are deciding how to spend other people's money. It is better that shareholders get their just share of the profits and decide for themselves as individuals whether to give to charity or support other causes.

GLOBAL BUSINESS ETHICS INSIGHT

International Reactions to Friedman's Position

Edelman, a U.S. public relations firm that specializes in and measures consumer trust of business, recently conducted a survey of people's reaction to the statement, "The social responsibility of business is to increase its profits." The survey focused on what Edelman calls the "informed public." These are people who are university educated and in the top quarter of the wage earners in their age groups and countries. The survey covered 23 countries. The chart below shows the percentage of people agreeing with the Friedman position from a selection of those countries.

The emerging markets lean in Friedman's direction, with India, Indonesia, Mexico and Poland nearing the top of the list. The recently emerged markets of Singapore and South Korea are also firmly behind the role of the corporation as being to make profits. However, China and Brazil are closer to the social democracies of Europe, which tend to be pro-CSR. Sweden differs from other social democratic countries, with nearly 60% of the well informed supporting Friedman. *The Economist* speculates that "perhaps people feel little need for CSR when the government cares for them from cradle to grave."

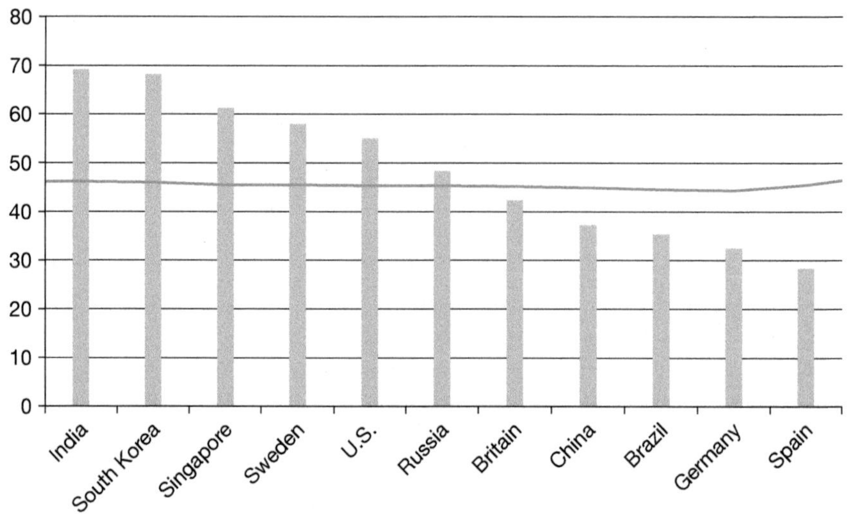

Percentage Agreeing: Social Responsibility of Business is to Increase Profits

Based on Edelman. 2011. Trust Barometer, www.edelman.com/p/6-a-m/trust-transformed-results-of-the-2011-edelman-trust-barometer/; *The Economist*. 2011. "Milton Friedman goes on tour: A survey of attitudes to business turns up some intriguing national differences." January 27.

Although the increased concern for social responsibility issues is accepted as legitimate in most large multinational corporations around the world, the Global Business Ethics Insight above suggests that Friedman's position on the role of the corporation still resonates with some people from different areas of the world.

Much of the contemporary view of CSR supports Carroll's thinking, reflecting a mix of economic and socially responsive actions. Perhaps the major shift in orientation in the recent decade is the specific concern for environmental sustainability and corruption. While sustainability might be subsumed under the general concern for society, it is now a cornerstone of most CSR initiatives in organizations.

A currently popular way of looking at the mix of the components of CSR is called the **triple bottom line (TBL)**, consisting of social, economic, and environmental sustainability. It is also known as "people, planet, and profit." TBL was popularized by John Elkington in his 1998 book *Cannibals with Forks: The Triple Bottom Line of 21st Century Business*. The Global Reporting Initiative, which we consider below, uses a TBL approach to identify CSR issues and measures of performance.

The TBL is a stakeholder approach to CSR that seeks to balance the needs of all. Like Carroll's pyramid and his representation of the areas of CSR from a competition perspective rather than a hierarchy, TBL also contains a concern for philanthropy and going beyond ethical and legal requirements. In the people sector, there is a focus on issues such as fair wages, child labor, occupational health and safety, training, and equal opportunity. There is also a focus on community engagement, such as support for education and the protection of indigenous people.

Planet represents environmental stewardship and sustainable environmental practices. The objective is to reduce the environmental impact in the lifecycle of use. Reduced raw material, energy and water are combined with lower emissions, waste and efficient transport of the products to customers. It is often easier to quantify financial returns from environmental savings in waste reduction and energy use.

Profit represents not only standard economic returns to stockholders but also a concern for the benefits of others such as using local suppliers or indirect economic benefits for the local community. Innovation is also part of the economic returns.

The TBL model is summarized in Exhibit 13.3.

The Emerging Market Business Ethics Insight below for Tata Steel gives an example of a firm whose CSR activities resemble aspects of the TBL model.

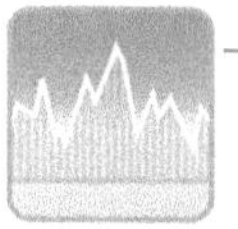

EMERGING MARKET BUSINESS ETHICS INSIGHT

Tata Steel's Company Town: "We also make Steel"

A company town is usually in a remote area where a business needs workers. To attract the needed labor the company builds its own town, giving workers a place to live. The company typically owns the real estate, utilities, hospitals and small businesses such as grocery stores. In the early 1900s, company towns were common in the West. The U.S. had more than 3000 and the Cadbury's built them in England. For the most part, companies built company towns to solve a practical problem. In the U.S., the vital resources for the mining and lumber industries were in remote places, so it was the only way to get workers.

Some company towns were little better than the gulags, the forced labor camps of the former Soviet Union. The housing was inadequate and often people had to spend most of their earnings at the company-owned store to survive. They were often in debt to the company, making it difficult for them to leave. Basically, this was a mechanism to get labor at the lowest price possible. In contrast, other company towns represented the Utopian spirit of the times. Henry Kaiser, the shipping magnate, and Milton Hershey, of chocolate fame, provided their company towns with decent housing, schools, libraries and hospitals.

Although company towns have long since faded away in the West, new company towns are being created or making comebacks in the developing world. Jamshedpur, the headquarters location for Tata Steel in India, was built at the turn of the century to solve the same practical problem faced by the U.S. industrialists. The coal and iron ore necessary to make steel were in the middle of an isolated forest. However, Jamsetji Tata, the founder of the town and the Tata Group, had other goals than just the practical need for workers. He wanted a model town with good schools, sports facilities, and modern amenities.

Although Tata Steel is now a global force in the steel industry, it has not broken its ties with the town. Far from that, it has modernized and expanded its relationship. As *The Economist* notes, "The Western doctrine of 'corporate social responsibility' (CSR) has also given the founder's very Victorian vision a new lease of life." Tata provides the town a 900-bed hospital. It owns the local newspaper and the town zoo. Its subsidiary, Jusco, delivers the utilities. Many workers have company houses and company cars. The company also has 250 employees who engage in rural outreach, teaching local tribespeople how to create irrigation systems and grow crops as well as giving health advice. The local sports facility, open to all, is a Tata Steel property. It also serves as a national center for various sports academies.

How central are these CSR activities to the Tata Steel culture? Telling is a phrase in its advertisement: "We also make steel."

Tata Steel is not alone in the Indian conglomerate that not only includes steel but also chemicals, power and automobiles. Recently, three of its business units were ranked as the top organizations in the *2017 Responsible Business Ranking* released by Futurescape. The ranking was based on four factors including Governance, Disclosure, Stakeholders and Sustainability.

Based on *The Economist*. 2011. "Company towns: The universal provider." June 19; *The Economist*. 2010. "Monuments to power: The politics and culture of urban development." October 14. Kumar, Rusen. 2017. "Three Tata companies top in 2017 Responsible Business Rankings." *India CSR Network*. September 25.

A slightly different way of looking at the relationship between business and society is through the concept of **corporate citizenship**. Although the idea of corporate citizenship is not new, it has gained in use and prominence during the last decade.

What is corporate citizenship? There are three basic views.[15] The "limited view" is similar to Carroll's philanthropic CSR that you read about above. A good corporate citizen is a company that gives back to the community as a voluntary action. The focus is on the close environment of the firm, such as supporting local sports teams.

The "equivalent view" of corporate citizenship is very similar to Carroll's view of CSR focusing on legal, ethical, and discretionary responsibilities of business. The "extended view" of corporate citizenship focuses on the role of the corporation as an entity that is independent of the owners and managers and can in many ways be treated like another human being. In this view, the corporation not only has responsibilities to act within the law and within moral expectations, but it also has rights. The corporation has social rights to choose to provide or not to provide individuals with additional social services. The corporation has civil rights to act freely similar to those of other citizens. Finally, the corporation has political rights to participate in the political process and influence its environment, again similar to other citizens.

Why another term for many of the same issues we see in CSR? Professors Matten, Crane, and Chapple argue that much of the language of CSR, particularly the concepts

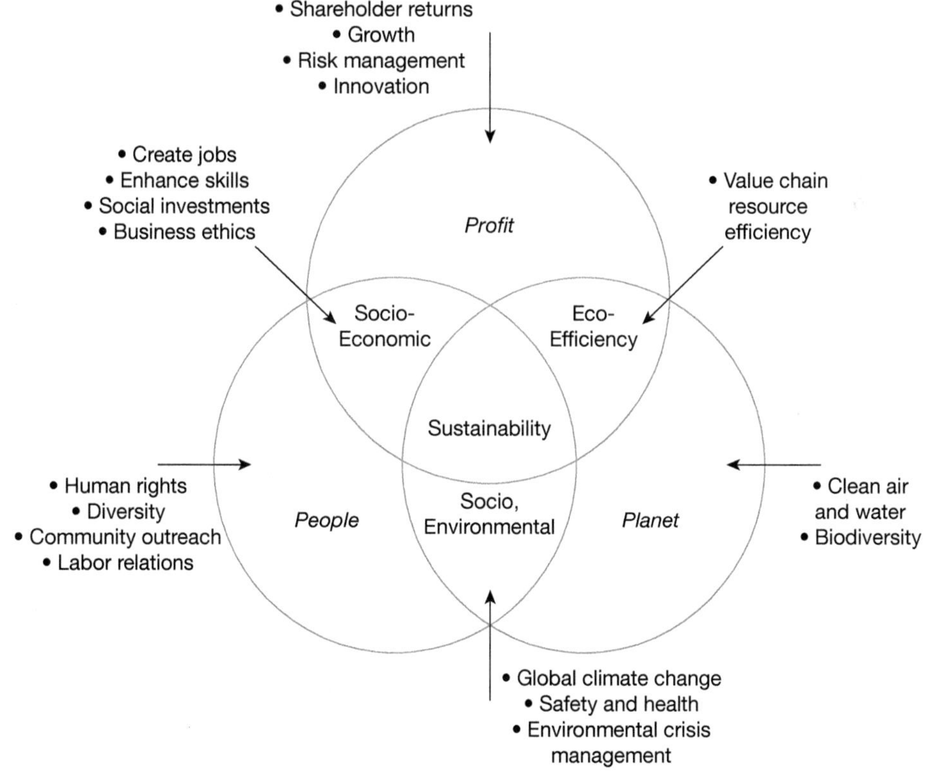

EXHIBIT 13.3—The Triple Bottom Model

of "ethics" and "responsibility," are not part of the language of business and thus may not be completely accepted.[16] Managers, they argue, can be more comfortable with the idea of "citizenship" where corporations can take their rightful place in society.

Regardless of the approach taken to identify CSR issues, an increasingly popular position is to view CSR as a potential asset. The next section gives an overview of strategic CSR and some ideas of how this can be implemented.

STRATEGIC CSR

Strategic CSR rests on the assumption that "doing good" can be good for a business as well as for society. With strategic CSR, corporations attend to their stakeholders because managers believe it is in the best interest of the company.[17] Is strategic CSR different?

In looking at the evidence of how CSR in general affects company performance, the results are inconclusive.[18] Some research shows that companies engaged in CSR do prosper in the long run, while other studies have found negative or no relationship.[19] Making assessment more difficult, CSR often leads to qualitative outcomes that may help a company but may not be quantifiable, such as employee morale, corporate image, reputation, public relations, goodwill, and popular opinion.[20] Such benefits might not produce immediate financial returns. Although broadly targeted quantitative studies of corporations show no systematic relationships with CSR activities, there is ample anecdotal evidence from individual firms that benefited from CSR. Highly successful corporations that also lead on CSR include the Body Shop, Ben & Jerry's, and Tom's of Maine.[21]

Some anecdotal examples of the benefits of strategic CSR include:[22]

- Positive consumer responses and growth in market share. Aravind Eye Hospitals in India charge just $50 a patient for cataract surgeries to target patients that cannot afford a more traditional price. They do over 200,000 surgeries a year, resulting in a $46.5 million profit.
- Organizational learning. To help inner-city children learn via technology, Bell Atlantic developed Project Explore in Union City, New Jersey. This led to innovations in networking technology that created Infospeed DSL. This new product more than covered the costs of the project.
- Committed and engaged employees. Research shows that employees who come into direct contact with those who benefit from their efforts work better, harder, and are less likely to turnover.
- Investor relations. Investors are paying attention. Increasing at nearly 20% a year, the amount of money dedicated to socially responsible investing has increased yearly.

The examples such as those above suggest that CSR may benefit an array of stakeholders while still contributing to the bottom line. But companies need to find ways to integrate CSR into their business models. Consequently, because of the somewhat uncertain relationship between CSR and organization performance, strategic experts, such as Michael Porter of Harvard University, have begun to develop insights into how CSR could be better linked to competitive advantage and be truly strategic. Professor Porter and his colleague Mark Kramer identified many of these issues in an important article published in the *Harvard Business Review*. Below we will consider some of the highlights of their insights.[23]

CSR is Here and Going to Stay

For business leaders in most every country, CSR either is, or is becoming, a significant priority. Nearly every major stakeholder, including governments, NGO activists, employees, and local communities, demands that corporations consider social responsibility in the business decisions. Consequently, in the current global marketplace, it is an "inescapable priority" that businesses engage in some level of social responsibility in such areas of environmentalism, social accountability to the larger society, and employee health and safety. In a recent McKinsey report,[24] 95% of the CEOs surveyed "believe that society has higher expectations for business to take on public responsibilities than it had five years ago." As a result, the majority of their firms report adding environmental, social, and governance into their core strategies. Although pressures from an array of stakeholders play an important role in these actions, more CEOs see these new demands not only as motivation to address global problems but also as an opportunity to gain competitive advantages.

Although Porter and Kramer recognize that many companies are already improving the environmental and social consequences of their business activities, they see two reasons why many companies have not been as productive as they should be. First, there has been a tendency to pit business against society when it is more productive to realize that the two are interdependent. Businesses need societies with well-educated and healthy workers and a sustainable environment. Society needs businesses to go beyond a self-centered look on profits and participate in making the world better. Second, many businesses think of CSR in a general way, with various check-offs, rather than thinking strategically. So how can businesses overcome these problems?

One of the first suggestions is to find ways to use CSR to do things differently than competitors. Managers need to look at CSR as a strategic tool to lower costs or better serve customers' needs. Porter and Kramer caution against simply throwing money at good causes but, instead, strategically picking areas that align with their expertise. Toyota, for example, is known for innovation in car production and design. Being one of the first to market a hybrid gasoline/electric car, Toyota designed the Prius to meet customer needs for a highly efficient automobile. At the same time, its hybrid engine emits only 10% of the pollutants from a typical internal combustion engine, resulting in environmental benefits to society. Because this is such a differentiated product, Toyota can charge, and customers are willing to pay a higher price than for a more conventional car.

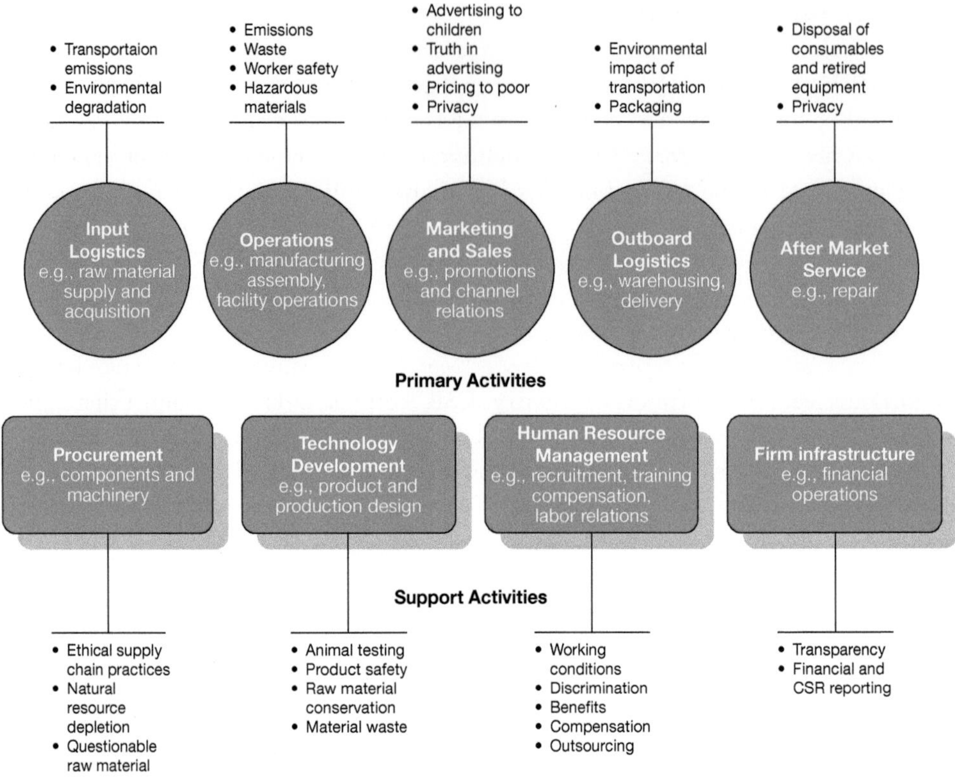

EXHIBIT 13.4—Building CRS Considerations into Porter's Value Chain

Porter and Kramer suggest one way to identify potential areas of strategic CSR competitive advantages is to map the impact of the company's value chain. A value chain shows all of the activities a company uses to do business. In looking at these activities, managers can assess positive and negative social impacts from their business operations. The next step is to make plans to mitigate potential negative outcomes and to identify areas upon which to build strategic advantages.

Exhibit 13.4 shows the value chain and illustrates potential CSR opportunities and threats linked to each component. The value chain begins with inbound logistics, such as getting parts or raw material into the organization. In an example below, you will see that Starbucks found an economic and socially responsible mechanism to support local farmers while ensuring a supply of high-quality coffee. In the operations component of the value chain, there are often many economically beneficial opportunities to cut costs while also benefiting society such as reducing waste. Consider the example of Hydro in the next section as a company that has made recycling a critical part of their production process a part of their competitive advantage.

In the next section, we expand the view of strategic CSR to identify several guiding principles that managers use to build a competitive advantage.

STRATEGIC CSR PRINCIPLES

Professor Peter Heslin and strategy consultant Jeann Ochoa studied numerous companies to identify seven exemplary strategic CSR principles.[25] They note that not all organizations are excellent at all strategic principles but some excel at some. However, they found many companies that successfully use these strategic CSR principles to build CSR into their value chains. Below, we describe these principles and some organizations that seem to follow them well.

- *Cultivate needed talent.* Marriott International and Microsoft use CSR initiatives to attract and maintain a superior workforce. Marriott's "Pathways to Independence" program focuses on welfare recipients to teach them life skills and job skills. The curriculum includes such job skills as how to search for a job and how to interview. Life skills include developing a household budget. Graduates are offered jobs at Marriott. Marriott benefits by getting a diverse group of eager employees initially at entry-level jobs but also with potential career paths leading to management. Turnover for these employees is 50% less than other employees.

Like Marriott, Microsoft has also used CSR activities to improve the quality of its workforce and those of its suppliers and customers. Microsoft donated $47 million to the American Association of Community Colleges to improve IT curricula and faculty skills at community colleges. To improve diversity in the IT workforce, Microsoft also donated $75 million in software, reference materials, and training materials to the 39 United Negro College Fund member institutions. What is their benefit? In the company's own words,

> UNC:Microsoft strives to be the leader in attracting minorities and women to careers in technology. We believe that diverse ideas and representation add value to our corporate community and to our products. We are committed to working with colleges and universities to help students achieve the knowledge and necessary skills to thrive in this competitive industry.[26]

- *Develop new markets.* The Dutch multinational Philips is a leading producer of electronic, lighting, and medical products. Philips specializes in finding innovative ways to penetrate markets in the developing world. For example, to deliver high-quality healthcare to rural communities in India, Philips uses traveling medical vans. These vans use satellite technology to link up with high-quality medical facilities in urban areas. This allows patients in isolated villages to get high-quality care.

Whole Foods Market is the largest natural and organic food supermarket. With a business model that promotes organic farming, Whole Foods not only contributes to sustainable agriculture but also benefits farm workers, who avoid exposure to chemicals that are commonly used in large industrial companies. Whole Foods gives 5% of its total net profits to non-profit organizations and provides time off for employees to perform community service. Traditionally rated as one of the best companies to work for, Whole Foods has an enthusiastic workforce that helps them support a differentiation strategy aimed at a socially conscious consumer who is willing to pay a higher price for its organic products.

- *Protect labor welfare*. Protecting the rights and working conditions of the labor force is a continuing CSR issue. This has been an especially troublesome issue for the companies in the garment industries, particularly with regard to child labor and sweatshops. Levi Strauss found an innovative way to deal with the child labor issue. Their first reaction to dealing with the fallout from using children under 15 in some of their factories was to consider firing all underage employees. However, when they considered the labor market in Bangladesh, they discovered that many of the children made significant contributions to the family's income and some were even the sole providers. Their solution: send all underage children back to school with paid wages and, on completion, give them a guaranteed job.

Starbucks takes an aggressive approach to CSR in its supply chain, noting

> we work on-the-ground with farmers to help improve coffee quality and invest in loan programs for coffee-growing communities. It's not just the right thing to do, it's the right thing to do for our business. By helping to sustain coffee farmers and strengthen their communities, we ensure a healthy supply of high-quality coffee for the future.[27]

To implement this CSR strategy, Starbucks established Farmer Support Centers in Costa Rica and Rwanda. These centers provide local farmers with resources and expertise to help lower their costs of production, reduce fungus infections, improve coffee quality, and increase the production of premium coffee. Starbucks also funds organizations that make loans to coffee growers. They have given over $15 million to farmer loan funds. The loans allow the farmers to counter pressures to sell their coffee early at a low price and wait to sell their crops at the best time to get the right price.

- *Reduce your environmental footprint*. Ethel M Chocolates, known nationally for its gourmet chocolates, attracts 700,000 visitors a year. It tours not only the factory but also the Living Machine. Designed and built by Living Technologies of Burlington, Vermont, the Living Machine is a water recycling plant used to purify Ethel M's wastewater. The treatment plant uses no chemicals. Instead, it mimics nature's natural water purification process using artificial wetlands with live bacteria, algae, protozoa, snails, fish and plants to eliminate pollutants from the water. The treated water ends up in an open pond after a day of travel through the artificial wetlands. The treated wastewater is clean enough for air-conditioning systems, irrigation and vehicle washing.[28] Not only are there environment benefits but the company also gets positive outcomes by cultivating its reputation and sales as a Las Vegas attraction.

The Norwegian multinational aluminum company Hydro operates in 40 countries. Hydro has 19 plants for recycling scrap aluminum in Asia, America, and Europe. In 2010 Hydro produced more than a million tons of aluminum, of which 260,000 tons were recycled. By 2020 the company expects to recycle around one million tons.

Rather than traditional mining, they call this recycling effort "urban mining." That is, the source of raw materials tends to be in urban centers.[29]

Recycling requires only 5% of the energy used to produce new aluminum. Roland Scharf-Bergmann, head of Hydro's Recycling unit, notes:

> Scrap has become a strategic raw material in regions like Europe, but also across the globe. We know that China views scrap as strategic, so we can expect China to grow their investment in recycling as well as scrap imports significantly.

Scharf-Bergmann said

> Hydro's role in the future will be to take our share of the market as a leading integrated producer over the whole value chain. Our position in the market, combined with commercial and technological competence, will provide us with growth opportunities in recycling to help us improving our carbon footprint.[30]

Hydro is one example of how an environmentally friendly strategy can become a core strategy of the company.

• *Profit from by-products.* Shaw Industries, a flooring company in Georgia, uses what it calls a "cradle-to-cradle" production process so that carpets can be collected and returned to manufacturing, with the raw material used to produce the original product again and again. Shaw invests heavily in technologies that it hopes will move all of its products to a cradle-to-cradle future. One innovation is the use Nylon 6 fiber. It is the only residential carpet fiber capable of repeated recycling back into the raw material to make new carpet. Shaw views this manufacturing process as a mimic of natural cycles of renewal, such as occurs with natural products returned to the earth for decomposition to make fertilizers in a cycle of renewal. Shaw recycles carpets of Type 6 nylon at its Evergreen Nylon Recycling facility in Augusta, Georgia. The company believes that cradle-to-cradle is the path to true sustainability.[31] Shaw saves customers money by taking carpets back and giving credit for the use of the raw material.

Manildra is an international producer of grains and starches used for industrial purposes. They have made a business using waste products from grain processing. For example, they make ethanol and agricultural feed from "waste starch." They profit from what otherwise would be discarded and the environment benefits with less waste. Such innovation marries environmental benefits with a sound business model.

• *Involve customers.* Hewlett-Packard's (HP) "Planet Partners Return & Recycling Program" involves customers by allowing them to return and recycle (usually free) products such as computer hardware, batteries and printing cartridges. HP also gives customers the opportunity to get the fair market value of aging technology. HP Financial Services pays customers for qualified computer equipment they no longer want or need. HP benefits by refurbishing and reselling the products. If customers prefer, HP's donate program makes it easy to donate their used computer equipment to charity. In the U.S., HP coordinates this program with the National Cristina Foundation (NCF).[32] The Cristina Foundation is a non-profit organization that matches donated computer equipment with needy schools and non-profit organizations around the world.

Patagonia, a privately owned leading manufacturer of outdoor clothing and equipment, engages customers to be environmentally sensitive though its website and catalogue. The catalogue is approximately 45% social message and 55% product content. The message content contains articles related to environment and social issue. Some of the content comes from Patagonia customers. Environmentalism is a prominent tab on its website, positioned next to the product ordering tab. On face value, one might think that devoting website and catalogue space to CSR issues might hurt sales. However, Patagonia discovered that reducing message content actually reduced sales.

- *Develop a green supply chain*. A number of companies have shown that there is proof of the link between improved environmental performance and financial gains. Companies have looked to their supply chain and seen areas where improvements in the way they operate can produce profits. In one example, Shanghai General Motors (SGM) recently partnered with the World Environment Center (WEC) for a "Greening the Supply Chain Initiative." This program targeted 125 suppliers of the 50/50 joint venture between General Motors and Shanghai Automotive Industry Corp. This joint venture is one of China's largest vehicle producers. The 125 suppliers invested about $21 million in 498 projects focusing on reducing energy use, water consumption and waste. The results not only improved the local environment, it generated an expected annual cost saving of approximately $19 million. Some projects were profitable in the first year. The environmental performance included a reduction of 55,400 tons of greenhouse gas emissions, equivalent to the annual emissions produced by more than 35,000 passenger vehicles. Annually, water consumption dropped by more than 282 million gallons. Liquid waste dropped 36 million gallons and solid waste by more than 9,300 tons.

WEC President and CEO Terry F. Yosie in a statement said:

> By managing sustainable development initiatives through a business process, SGM has improved the energy and environmental performance across its supply chain, built stronger customer-supplier relationships and increased its ability to adapt to evolving governmental requirements.[33]

By automating its supply chain transactions with trading partners, Burton Snowboards, the world's leading snowboard company, significantly reduced its paper usage by substituting electronic transactions. Less postage, paper and envelopes also reduced costs. In total, Burton saved approximately 4 tons of wood use, 30 million BTUs (British Thermal Units), 5882 lb CO_2, 22,219 gallons wastewater, and 1909 lb solid waste in one year of the new automated system's use. Buoyed with the success, Burton plans further reductions in the company's environmental impact through greater use of B2B automation and other paper-reducing initiatives. Goals include saving an additional 40 tons of wood use, 350 million BTUs, 65,000 lb CO_2, 250,000 gallons wastewater, and 20,000 lb solid waste. Burton's success demonstrates that green IT in the supply chain directly impacts both the bottom line and the environment.[34]

In the changing CSR environment for corporations, one issue that more firms address each year is how to report and audit their CSR performance to their stakeholders. The next section gives an overview of CRS reporting and detail on three of the most used systems.

REPORTING CSR

Corporations are required to produce annual reports on their economic performance for their stockholders. As owners, investors can use this information to consider whether to invest more or less in the company. Increasingly, however, corporations are facing growing institutional pressure to also produce **social performance reports**. In some countries, such as the UK and Denmark, this pressure is legal. For example, as an early mover, in 2008, the Danish parliament passed a bill that makes it mandatory for the 1100 largest businesses to report on CSR in their annual reports. Although reporting is required, CSR is not mandatory but the goal of mandatory reporting is to motivate Danish businesses to take an active position on CSR. Thus, businesses are required to report their CSR practices or state that they do not engage in CSR.

More recently, an October 2014 the EU mandated that publically owned companies with more than 500 employees to report on their environmental, social and employees' concerns, and their measures to respect human rights and fight corruption. The law took effect in 2018 with companies required to publish CSR reports for their CSR performance in 2017. Most EU member nations incorporated the directive into national law in anticipation of the law coming into effect in 2018. EU Commission guidelines are available here: http://dqs-cfs.com/2017/07/csr-reporting-requirements-guidelines-published-european-commission/).[35]

When not required by legal constraints, there are additional pressures on companies to report on their social responsibility activities. One of the more important relates to the trend for socially responsible investing. Increasingly, investors are considering a company's CSR activities as a factor in choosing where to invest their money. According to a recent survey by KPMG the worldwide demand for accountability and transparency is at an all-time high, resulting in the demands for a more complete picture of companies including not only financial information but also information on risk management and value-creation in the social and environmental areas.[36]

Periodically KPMG surveys the top 250 companies from Global *Fortune* 500 and the largest 100 companies from 49 countries. Based on their most recent 2017 survey, KPMG concluded that CSR reporting is becoming entrenched at least among the dominant multinational companies. Over 90% of the Global 250 now issue reports as

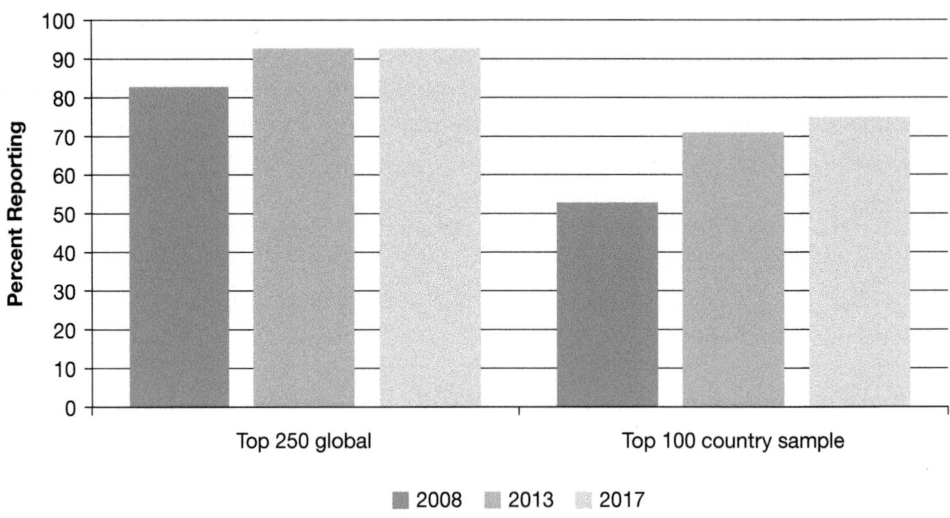

EXHIBIT 13.5—Percentage of Companies using CSR Reporting: A Global Sample

Source: Adapted from KPMG *International Survey of Corporate Responsibility Reporting,* 2017.

do 75% of the larger companies is most nations.[37] Exhibit 13.5 shows the data for these companies.

In addition to the KPMG, other recent research found that increasing government regulation accounts for the largest proportion of social reporting worldwide as governments in over 80% of the countries studied have some form of regulatory sustainability reporting required. While mandatory reporting dominates growth in voluntary reporting is also a factor with a third of the companies studied reporting voluntary reporting. Mandatory reporting often originates from stock exchanges and financial market regulators and accounted for one third of reporting instruments identified.[38]

For all companies that issue reports, KPMG identifies the following benefits:[39]

- *Differentiation*: allows a company to stand out in the marketplace based on CSR strategies and commitments
- *A license to operate*: gives a company a moral position to operate with the public and specific stakeholders
- *Attracting favorable financing*: as financial markets demand more information on environmental and social performance, those who report CSR activities have an advantage
- *Innovation*: CSR encourage innovation through a better understanding of stakeholder needs and possible risks
- *Attracting and retaining employees*: in a time of high employee expectations, social performance makes a company more competitive for the best talent
- *Enhancing reputation*: reporting shows that a company is truthful in reporting information of tough issues.

Recent research found that increasing government regulation accounts for the largest proportion of social reporting worldwide as governments in over 80% of the countries studied have some form of regulatory sustainability reporting required. While mandatory reporting dominates growth, the growth in voluntary reporting is also a factor with a third of the companies studied reporting voluntary reporting. Mandatory reporting often originates from stock exchanges and financial market regulators and accounted for one third of reporting instruments identified.

What Is in a CSR Report?

CSR reporting is still in development and the choice of what is reported, how it is reported, and how the report is verified are still open to debate. A recent 64-country review[40] of mandatory and voluntary CSR reporting standards by the joint efforts of KPMG Advisory N.V., United Nations Environment Program, Global Reporting Initiative, and the Unit for Corporate Governance in Africa found "an increasingly dense network of national and international standards for sustainability reporting." Depending on the country, there is a complex mix of mandatory and voluntary standards. What the study found in the 64 countries included:[41]

- a total of 400 country standards and/or laws with some form of sustainability-related reporting requirement or guidance
- approximately two-thirds (65%) of these standards able to be classified as mandatory and one third (35%) as voluntary
- 61% of the instruments identified focus on reporting on specific environmental or social topics.
- large listed companies are the focus of almost one-third of existing reporting instruments. However, two-thirds of the instruments found apply to all companies including some state-owned.
- for the large listed companies, approximately three-quarters of the reporting requirements were introduced by financial market regulators and stock exchanges.

We can conclude from the recent trends that CSR measurement and reporting is becoming a requirement driven by both legislative actions and society's expectations. As such, it will be ever more incumbent on future managers to be aware of mandatory and expected standards and how they fit strategically into one's company and industry.

Broadly, CSR reporting falls into two modes. One focuses primarily on sustainability issues and such reports are often mandatory to comply with stock exchange or government regulatory agencies. The other types of reports are broadly focused including not only sustainability issues but also issues related to broader environmental concerns as well as social and governance issues. Such reports tend to be more often voluntary but may meet sustainability reporting requirements as well. There are many available guides provide reporting formats for reporting CSR activities that include but are not limited to:

- *GRI*. Global Reporting Initiative's Sustainability Reporting Guidelines set out the principles and Performance Indicators that organizations can use to measure and report their economic, environmental, and social performance.
- *CDP*. Focuses primarily on sustainability issues regarding emissions but also includes issues related to water and forestry.
- *AA1000*. AccountAbility's AA1000 series are principles-based standards to help organizations become more accountable, responsible, and sustainable.
- *Good Corporation's Standard*. Developed in association with the Institute of Business Ethics, this reporting format covers 62 areas of management practice focusing on six stakeholders: employees; customers; suppliers and subcontractors; community and environment; shareholders or other providers of finance; and management commitment.
- *SA8000*. Social Accountability International's standard SA8000 focuses on certifying labor practices for companies and those of their suppliers and vendors. It is based on the principles of international human rights norms as described in International Labor Organization conventions, the United Nations Convention on the Rights of the Child, and the Universal Declaration of Human Rights.
- *ISO 14000*. ISO 14001:2004 gives generic requirements for an environmental management system. When used as a basis for a CSR report, it provides a common reference for communicating about environmental management issues between organizations and their customers, regulators, the public, and other stakeholders.
- *COP (Communication on Progress)*. A COP report describes the company's implementation of the United Nations Global Compact's ten universal principles.

Companies may use one or more of the above guides to track and measure their CSR performance and to produce CSR reports. However, the most popular general CSR guidelines are based on the **Global Reporting Initiative (GRI)** and the **Communication on Progress (COP)** for the **UN's Global Compact**'s ten principles. The most popular for sustainability monitoring is the **CDP (formerly the Carbon Disclosure Project**). We will discuss those CSR monitoring and reporting formats in more detail below, as you will likely use one or more of them in your organizations.

The CDP, formally called the Carbon Disclosure Project, is a reporting framework that allows companies to measure and disclose their Greenhouse Gas (GHG), water and supply chain performance. As such, the CDP's primarily emphasizes protection of natural resources (forests and water) and mitigating the negative outcomes from climate change. It is the most popular framework for reporting sustainability performance. With over 5000 businesses as well as additional governmental units reporting, CDP claims to have the most comprehensive collection of self-reported environmental data in the world. With offices in over 50 countries, the CDP is likely the world leader in driving environmental disclosures. The reports are used by investors and regulators to assess the sustainability performance of companies.[42] Why engage in CDP reporting. Anne Shiraishi from *GreenBiz* argues:[43]

- **Investors want it**
  Research by Goldman Sachs found that publicly traded stocks of sustainability reporters outperformed that of non-reporters. Such disclosures are becoming a requirement for listing on some stock exchanges.
- **Stakeholders demand it**
  Disclosing to CDP communicates to stakeholders that your firm takes a serious approach to the relevant environmental challenges to your business and industry.
- **It is becoming the defacto norm**
  More than 5000 organizations now report CDP, which includes over 85 percent of the Global 500.
- **It will make you rethink your business**
  Research shows that sustainability disclosures identify risks, expose new ways to cut costs, help identify new products and service offerings.
- **Benchmarks matter to see where you stand**
  The CDP framework provides a proven mechanism for a company's sustainability disclosures with the added benefit of seeing how you match up with your peer group.

The Global Reporting Initiative (GRI) is the most recognized global standard for CSR reporting. The GRI provides principles and indicators that companies can use to identify and measure economic, environmental, and social performance. The most recent generation of the guidelines were released in 2016 and are available from their website: www.globalreporting.org. Exhibit 13.6 provides a copy of the indicators that companies can use as measures.[44]

The GRI also has industry-specific supplements that provide indicators specific to the needs in areas such as Electric Utilities, Financial Services, Mining and Metals, NGOs, Food Processing, Airport Operators, and Construction and Real Estate. According to the GRI, using their GRI Framework can demonstrate organizational commitment to CSR, provide measures of organizational performance with respect to laws, norms, standards and voluntary initiatives, and allow companies to track organizational performance over time.[45] The reasons organizations need such CSR measurement and tracking include:[46]

- Measuring CSR performance allows organizations to identify opportunities to improve operations and avoid risks to the long-term value of their organization.
- Measuring CSR performance indicates an ability to manage CSR impacts that help organizations preserve and increase their value.
- Investors and analysts gain insights into organizational performance and risks beyond that indicated by financial data.
- Transparency increases trust—stakeholders can respond to comparable and standardized information.
- Organizations can mitigate negative impacts in social, environmental, and governance areas.

An overview of the GRI standards is reported in Exhibit 13.6.

EXHIBIT 13.6—The Global Reporting Initiative Performance Indicators

Indicator	Disclosure	Indicator	Disclosure
Economic performance		Investment and procurement practices	
EC1	Direct economic value generated and distributed, including revenues, operating costs, employee compensation, donations and other community investments, retained earnings, and payments to capital providers and governments.	HR1	Percentage and total number of significant investment agreements and contracts that include clauses incorporating human rights concerns, or that have undergone human rights screening.
EC2	Financial implications and other risks and opportunities for the organization's activities due to climate change.	HR2	Percentage of significant suppliers, contractors and other business partners that have undergone human rights screening, and actions taken.
EC3	Coverage of the organization's defined benefit plan obligations.	HR3	Total hours of employee training on policies and procedures concerning aspects of human rights that are relevant to operations, including the percentage of employees trained.
EC4	Significant financial assistance received from government.	Non-discrimination	
Market presence		HR4	Total number of incidents of discrimination and corrective actions taken.
EC5	Range of ratios of standard entry level wage by gender compared to local minimum wage at significant locations of operation.	Freedom of association and collective bargaining	
EC6	Policy, practices, and proportion of spending on locally-based suppliers at significant locations of operation.	HR5	Operations and significant suppliers identified in which the right to exercise freedom of association and collective bargaining may be violated or at significant risk, and actions taken to support these rights.
EC7	Procedures for local hiring and proportion of senior management hired from the local community at significant locations of operation.	Child labor	
Indirect economic impacts		HR6	Operations and significant suppliers identified as having significant risk for incidents of child labor, and measures taken to contribute to the effective abolition of child labor.
EC8	Development and impact of infrastructure investments and services provided primarily for public benefit through commercial, in-kind, or pro bono engagement.	Prevention of forced and compulsory labor	

Indicator	Disclosure	Indicator	Disclosure
EC9	Understanding and describing significant indirect economic impacts, including the extent of impacts.	HR7	Operations and significant suppliers identified as having significant risk for incidents of forced or compulsory labor, and measures to contribute to the elimination of all forms of forced or compulsory labor.
		Security practices	
		HR8	Percentage of security personnel trained in the organization's policies or procedures concerning aspects of human rights that are relevant to operations.
Materials		Indigenous rights	
EN1	Materials used by weight or volume.	HR9	Total number of incidents of violations involving rights of indigenous people and actions taken.
EN2	Percentage of materials used that are recycled input materials.	Assessment	
Energy		HR10	Percentage and total number of operations that have been subject to human rights reviews and/or impact assessments.
EN3	Direct energy consumption by primary energy source.	Remediation	
EN4	Indirect energy consumption by primary source.	HR11	Number of grievances related to human rights filed, addressed and resolved through formal grievance mechanisms.
EN5	Energy saved due to conservation and efficiency improvements.	Local communities	
EN6	Initiatives to provide energy-efficient or renewable energy based products and services, and reductions in energy requirements as a result of these initiatives.	SO1	Percentage of operations with implemented local community engagement, impact assessments, and development programs.
EN7	Initiatives to reduce indirect energy consumption and reductions achieved.	SO9	Operations with significant potential or actual negative impacts on local communities.
Water		SO10	Prevention and mitigation measures implemented in operations with significant potential or actual negative impacts on local communities.
EN8	Total water withdrawal by source.	Corruption	
EN9	Water sources significantly affected by withdrawal of water.	SO2	Percentage and total number of business units analyzed for risks related to corruption.

EXHIBIT 13.6—*continued*

Indicator	Disclosure	Indicator	Disclosure
EN10	Percentage and total volume of water recycled and reused.	SO3	Percentage of employees trained in organization's anti-corruption policies and procedures.
Biodiversity		SO4	Actions taken in response to incidents of corruption.
EN11	Location and size of land owned, leased, managed in, or adjacent to, protected areas and areas of high biodiversity value outside protected areas.	Public policy	
EN12	Description of significant impacts of activities, products, and services on biodiversity in protected areas and areas of high biodiversity value outside protected areas.	SO5	Public policy positions and participation in public policy development and lobbying.
EN13	Habitats protected or restored.	SO6	Total value of financial and in-kind contributions to political parties, politicians, and related institutions by country.
EN14	Strategies, current actions, and future plans for managing impacts on biodiversity.	Anti-competitive behavior	
EN15	Number of IUCN Red List species and national conservation list species with habitats in areas affected by operations, by level of extinction risk.	SO7	Total number of legal actions for anti-competitive behavior, anti-trust, and monopoly practices and their outcomes.
Emissions, effluents and waste		Compliance	
EN16	Total direct and indirect greenhouse gas emissions by weight.	SO8	Monetary value of significant fines and total number of non-monetary sanctions for non-compliance with laws and regulations.
EN17	Other relevant indirect greenhouse gas emissions by weight.	Customer health and safety	
EN18	Initiatives to reduce greenhouse gas emissions and reductions achieved.	PR1	Life cycle stages in which health and safety impacts of products and services are assessed for improvement, and percentage of significant products and services categories subject to such procedures.
EN19	Emissions of ozone-depleting substances by weight.	PR2	Total number of incidents of non-compliance with regulations and voluntary codes concerning health and safety impacts of products and services during their life cycle, by type of outcomes.
EN20	NOx, SOx, and other significant air emissions by type and weight.	Product and service labelling	
EN21	Total water discharge by quality and destination.	PR3	Type of product and service information required by procedures, and percentage of significant products and services subject to such information requirements.

Indicator	Disclosure	Indicator	Disclosure
EN22	Total weight of waste by type and disposal method.	PR4	Total number of incidents of non-compliance with regulations and voluntary codes concerning product and service information and labeling, by type of outcomes.
EN23	Total number and volume of significant spills.	PR5	Practices related to customer satisfaction, including results of surveys measuring customer satisfaction.
EN24	Weight of transported, imported, exported, or treated waste deemed hazardous under the terms of the Basel Convention Annex I, II, III, and VIII, and percentage of transported waste shipped internationally.	Marketing communications	
EN25	Identity, size, protected status, and biodiversity value of water bodies and related habitats significantly affected by the reporting organization's discharges of water and runoff.	PR6	Programs for adherence to laws, standards, and voluntary codes related to marketing communications, including advertising, promotion, and sponsorship.
Products and services		PR7	Total number of incidents of non-compliance with regulations and voluntary codes concerning marketing communications, including advertising, promotion, and sponsorship by type of outcomes.
EN26	Initiatives to mitigate environmental impacts of products and services, and extent of impact mitigation.	Customer privacy	
EN27	Percentage of products sold and their packaging materials that are reclaimed by category.	PR8	Total number of substantiated complaints regarding breaches of customer privacy and losses of customer data.
Compliance		Compliance	
EN28	Monetary value of significant fines and total number of non-monetary sanctions for non-compliance with environmental laws and regulations.	PR9	Monetary value of significant fines for non-compliance with laws and regulations concerning the provision and use of products and services.
Transport			
EN29	Significant environmental impacts of transporting products and other goods and materials used for the organization's operations, and transporting members of the workforce.		
Overall			
EN30	Total environmental protection expenditures and investments by type.		

Source: www.globalreporting.org/resourcelibrary/G3-1-Index-and-Checklist.xls

Recognizing the synergy between the sophisticated measurements and reporting format of the GRI and the Global Compact as the world's largest corporate responsibility platform, the UN's Global Compact and GRI signed an agreement in May 2010 to align their work in advancing corporate responsibility. As part of the agreement, GRI integrates the Global Compact's ten principles into its Sustainability Reporting Guidelines. In turn, the Global Compact adopted the GRI guidelines as their recommended reporting framework for businesses.[47] This is a natural alliance, as many businesses have adopted the GRI guidelines to report on the performance measurement required by the Compact's Communication on Progress.

The UN's Global Compact is based on the following ten principles in the areas of human rights, labor, the environment, and anti-corruption:[48]

Human Rights

- *Principle 1*: Businesses should support and respect the protection of internationally proclaimed human rights; and
- *Principle 2*: make sure that they are not complicit in human rights abuses.

Labor

- *Principle 3*: Businesses should uphold the freedom of association and the effective recognition of the right to collective bargaining;
- *Principle 4*: the elimination of all forms of forced and compulsory labor;
- *Principle 5*: the effective abolition of child labor; and
- *Principle 6*: the elimination of discrimination in respect of employment and occupation.

Environment

- *Principle 7*: Businesses should support a precautionary approach to environmental challenges;
- *Principle 8*: undertake initiatives to promote greater environmental responsibility; and
- *Principle 9*: encourage the development and diffusion of environmentally friendly technologies.

Anti-corruption

- *Principle 10*: Businesses should work against corruption in all its forms, including extortion and bribery.

Joining the Global Compact initiative is voluntary but, once a company commits to join, it agrees to integrate the principles into its business operations and communicate annually on progress. Business participants are required to submit an annual Communication on Progress (COP) and to share the COP widely with their stakeholders. The COP must contain the following elements: a statement by the CEO expressing continued support for the UN Global Compact, a description of practical actions the company has taken to implement the principles, and a demonstration of how outcomes are measured. The Strategic Business Ethics Insight below shows excerpts from COPs from various companies demonstrating their compliance. By 2018, over 8000 businesses were actively involved in the Global Compact. Other governmental and other non-government organizations also participate. The Strategic Business Ethics Insight shows examples of companies reporting on the three elements of the COP.

STRATEGIC BUSINESS ETHICS INSIGHT

Elements of the COP for the UN's Global Compact

Example CEO Statement of Support

The Coca-Cola Bottling Company of Ghana—*2014 COP*

The Coca-Cola Bottling Company of Ghana Limited, incorporating the principles of the Global Compact into our business means ensuring sustainability for our numerous stakeholders such as our consumers, customers, regulators, shareholders and our communities. It also means finding new ways to support the principles and updating our current practices that support the principles. As such, we as a company have the intention of implementing a new sustainability program called the Source Water Protection Plan (SWPP). On the people front, for the first time this year, the company gave out Christmas baskets or goodies to outsourced or third-party employees in addition to our permanent employees. Our relationship with our communities and the planet through our corporate social responsibility is still going strong. Schools and hospitals facilities were rehabilitated in line with our strategies to enhance education and better health for the deprived in society. And at the workplace, there has been a consistent approach in ensuring gender equality by way of recruitment and promotion. We continue to have a mutual relationship with all our Local Unions, labor regulatory authorities and agencies in promoting the human and labor rights of all. With all these strategies and activities in place, The Coca-Cola Bottling Company of Ghana continues to imbibe the ten principles of the Global Compact into its business to ensure that sustainability is achieved for all. Xavier Selga, Managing Director / Chief Operating Officer.

Example of Implementation

Talal Abu-Ghazaleh & Co. International (Egypt)—*2015 COP*

Upon joining the UN Global Compact, TAG-Org made compliance with UN human rights' principles a requirement for all suppliers and business partners. An addendum on the importance of supporting the Universal Declaration of Human Rights was incorporated into the TAGCO standard audit outline. TAG-Org completed an internal evaluation of our organization-wide exposure to human rights issues and concerns; it was determined that despite limited direct links to significant human rights issues, we can provide constructive support for this principle through express affirmations of our support across our extensive communication and public relations networks and by focusing on one of our group's longtime strengths, advocacy and education.

Example of Outcome Measurement

Martha Tilaar Group (Indonesia)—*2011 COP*

In our company, the minimum age of workers is 18 years old as shown by the data below. The company also has equal opportunity for men and women. Data reported include:

Age	Non-management		Management	
	2009	2010	2009	2010
Less than 18 years old	0	0	0	0
18–20 years old	0	0	8	10
21 and above	584	603	110	100
Gender	2009		2010	
	MGT	Non-MGT	MGT	Non-MGT
Women	65	279	64	280
Men	63	305	64	370

Source: www.unglobalcompact.org/participation/report/cop/create-and-submit/active/168941

One area where reporting CSR performance remains weak is in assurance. **Assurance** is the auditing function to validate that what a company reports in its CSR report is true and accurate. Financial statements require audits but this aspect of social responsibility reporting is still in a growth, however with an increasing number of firms using external audits of their CSR reports. However, even if reports are not audited, companies are not out of sight and there are a growing number of CSR rankings that evaluate companies on CSR performance. One popular ranking for U.S. companies is shown in Exhibit 13.7. Similar to ranking of colleges and universities, there is not complete agreement on the methodology or accuracy of these rankings.[49] Nevertheless, they represent a source of information to stakeholders regarding a company's CSR activities.

Overall Rank	Company	Financial Rank	Environment Rank	Climate Change Rank	Human Rights Rank	Employee Relations Rank	Corporate Governance Rank	Philanthropy Rank
1	Hasbro, Inc.	64	5	1	4	8	81	3
2	Intel Corp.	111	12	23	6	6	45	12
3	Microsoft Corporation	68	1	88	1	14	16	1
4	Altria Group Inc.	42	74	13	33	13	191	10
5	Campbell Soup Co.	121	46	33	59	31	13	27
6	Cisco Systems Inc.	142	8	36	25	7	147	96
7	Accenture plc	83	40	17	83	46	82	17
8	Hormel Foods Corp.	22	85	76	6	25	8	113
9	Lockheed Martin Corp.	36	13	40	16	81	179	73
10	Ecolab, Inc.	350	15	2	33	21	160	7
11	Abbott Laboratories	365	3	7	59	19	87	30
12	Clorox	284	27	10	33	64	99	53
13	S&P Global Inc.	120	75	38	83	57	34	70
14	DXC Technology	38	67	45	83	42	294	15
15	Texas Instruments Inc.	47	19	120	83	82	88	55
16	Johnson Controls Int'l plc	393	6	6	6	54	279	44
17	NVIDIA Corp.	1	117	16	212	30	24	72
18	Adobe Systems Inc.	429	51	26	83	12	74	26
19	General Mills, Inc.	246	31	5	1	102	420	8
20	Bristol-Myers Squibb Co.	326	32	82	33	63	26	90

EXHIBIT 13.7—Top 20 of *Corporate Responsibility Magazine*'s 100 Best Corporate Citizens in the United States

Source: Based on *CR Magazine*, 2017. CR's 100 Best Corporate Citizens 2017.

CHAPTER SUMMARY

The chapter began with a Preview Business Ethics Insight on LEGO. LEGO recently ranked highest on CSR reputation based on safeguarding the environment, helping worthy causes, conducting business impartially, acting transparently and generally behaving ethically. LEGO has a particularly outstanding record for sustainability activities. An example of the Danish toy company's push for sustainability includes the LEGO Group's effort to shrink packing box sizes to save cardboard that resulted in a reduction of approximately 7000 tons of cardboard.

The brief history of CSR traced the intellectual history of the CSR debate from the writings of the classical economist Adam Smith to the current triple bottom line approach to CSR. In the U.S., two landmark court decisions influenced both academic and practitioner thinking about CSR. In the U.S., the first legal precedent for the dominance of the stockholder as the prime stakeholder was the influential 1919 case of *Dodge v. Ford.* Later, the switch from stockholder dominance to corporate philanthropy began with *Smith v. Barlow,* a landmark court decision in 1953 that allowed A.P. Smith Manufacturing Company to donate $1500 to Princeton University. In *Smith v. Barlow,* the court upheld the contribution as a legal ruling against the stockholders. The court ruled that the stockholders

> whose private interests rest entirely upon the well-being of the corporation, ought not to be permitted to close their eyes to present-day realities and thwart the long-visioned corporate action in recognizing and voluntarily discharging its high obligations as a constituent of our modern social structure.

With the start of the twentieth century, criticism of big business increased. More people began to believe that the big corporations were too powerful and used business practices that were anti-social and anti-competitive. As a result, the government responded with laws and regulations that limited the power of large corporations and served to protect employees, consumers, and society at large. The 1960s and 1970s continued a cultural shift in the expectations for business in most countries. Movements related to civil rights, consumerism and environmentalism changed the context for doing business and therefore society's expectations for business responsibilities. However, going beyond legal compliance and based on the premise that those with greater power have greater responsibilities, most of the developed world called on businesses to become proactive. Increasingly, it became an expectation that it is not sufficient to avoid causing social problems but it is also necessary to help solve social problems.

During the 1960s and 1970s, the concept of CSR broadened both in practice and in academic thinking. Of particular importance was the clarification of the concept of stakeholders, suggesting that companies have responsibilities to take into account how their actions affect not only stockholders but also employees, suppliers, dealers, local communities, and the nation. The idea of the duties and obligations to stake holders is now entrenched in both practitioner and academic thinking about CSR.

Archie Carroll introduced the concept of the pyramid of CSR in the 1970s and this is still a popular way that management scholars and practitioners look at CSR. For Carroll, there are four essential responsibilities of a business. These include economic, legal, ethical, and philanthropic. The idea of the pyramid evolved to take into account stakeholders and the tensions among their interests.

Although the acceptance of CSR as a corporate obligation grew considerably in the late twentieth century, there remain critics. The most famous to this day is still Nobel laureate Milton Friedman, who argued that there is only one purpose of the corporation:

> There is one and only one social responsibility of business—to use its resources and engage in activities designed to increase its profits so long as it stays within the rules of the game, which is to say, engages in open and free competition without deception or fraud.

The TBL is a stakeholder approach to CSR that seeks to balance the needs of all. It is also known as "people, planet, and profit." Like Carroll's pyramid and his representation of the areas of CSR from a competition perspective rather than a hierarchy, TBL also contains a concern for philanthropy that goes beyond ethical and legal requirements. In the people sector, there is a focus on issues such as fair wages, child labor, occupational health and safety, training and equal opportunity. There is also a focus on community engagement, such as support for education and the protection of indigenous people. Planet represents environmental stewardship and sustainable environmental practices. Profit represents not only standard economic returns to stockholders but also a concern for the benefits of others, such as using local suppliers or indirect economic benefits for the local community.

Taking a more practitioner point of view, the two concluding sections of this chapter considered strategic CSR and the practicalities of reporting CSR performance. Strategic CSR rests on the assumption that "doing good" can be good for a business as well as for society. With strategic CSR, corporations attend to their stakeholders because managers believe it is in the best interest of the company.

Strategic management experts Michael Porter of Harvard University and his colleague Mark Kramer identified many of these issues related to strategic CSR in an important article published in the *Harvard Business Review.* Although Porter and Kramer recognize that many companies are already improving the environmental and social consequences of their business activities, they see two reasons why many companies have not been as productive as they should be. First, there has been a tendency to pit business against society when it is more productive to realize that the two are interdependent. Businesses need societies with well-educated and healthy workers and a sustainable environment. Society needs businesses to go beyond a self-centered look on profits and participate in making the world better. Second, many businesses think of CSR in a general way with various check-offs rather than thinking strategically.

Porter and Kramer caution against simply throwing money at good causes but, instead, strategically picking areas that align with their expertise. Managers need to look at CSR as a strategic tool to lower costs or better serve customers' needs. Porter and Kramer suggest one way to identify potential areas of strategic CSR competitive advantages is to map the impact of the company's value chain.

All publically owned corporations are required to produce annual reports on their economic performance for their stockholders. Investors can use this information to consider whether to invest more or less in the company. Increasingly, however, corporations are facing institutional pressures to also report on their social performance. Based on their most recent 2017 survey of the top 250 companies from Global *Fortune* 500 and the largest 100 companies from 49 countries, KPMG concluded that CSR reporting is becoming entrenched at least among the dominant multinational companies. Over 90% of the Global 250 now issue reports as do 75% of the larger companies in most nations.

CSR reporting is still in development and the choice of what is reported, how it is reported, and how the report is verified is still open to debate. Depending on the country, there is a complex mix of mandatory and voluntary standards. However, we can conclude from the recent trends that CSR measurement and reporting is becoming a requirement driven by both legislative actions and society's expectations. As such, it will be ever more incumbent on future managers to be aware of mandatory and expected standards and how they fit strategically into one's company and industry.

The UN's Global Compact is based on ten principles in the areas of human rights, labor, the environment, and anti-corruption. Joining the Global Compact initiative is voluntary, but once a company commits to join, it agrees to integrate the principles into its business operations and communicate annually on progress. Business participants are required to submit an annual Communication on Progress (COP) and to share the COP widely with their stakeholders.

The Global Reporting Initiative (GRI) is the most recognized global standard for general CSR reporting. The GRI provides principles and indicators that companies can use to identify and measure economic, environmental, and social performance. The third generation of the guidelines was released in 2016.

Recognizing the synergy between the sophisticated measurements and reporting format of the GRI and the Global Compact as the world's largest corporate responsibility platform, the UN Global Compact and GRI signed an agreement in May 2010 to align their work in advancing corporate responsibility. As part of the agreement, GRI integrated the Global Compact's ten principles into its Sustainability Reporting Guidelines. In turn, the Global Compact adopted the GRI Guidelines as their recommended reporting framework for businesses.

The CDP, formally called the Carbon Disclosure Project, is a reporting framework that allows companies to measure and disclose their Greenhouse Gas (GHG), water and supply chain performance. As such, the CDP's primarily emphasizes protection of natural resources (forests and water) and mitigating the negative outcomes from climate change. It is the most popular framework for reporting sustainability performance.

NOTES

1 Carroll, A.B. 1999. "Corporate social responsibility: Evolution of a definitional construct." *Business & Society*, 38, 268–295.
2 As quoted in Cochran, P.L. 2007. "The evolution of corporate social responsibility." *Business Horizons*, 50, 449–454.
3 Smith, A. 1982. "The theory of moral sentiments," in D.D. Raphael & A.L. Macfie (Eds.), *Glasgow edition of the works and correspondence of Adam Smith*, Vol. I, Indianapolis: Liberty Fund, pp. 26–27. http://oll.libertyfund.org/title/192, accessed June 29, 2011.
4 Barnett, T. 2011. "Corporate responsibility. Reference for business." *Encyclopedia of Business*, 2nd edn. www.referenceforbusiness.com.
5 270 Fed. Appx. 200, 2008 U.S. App.
6 Hood, J. 1998. "Do corporations have social responsibilities? Free enterprise creates unique problem-solving opportunities." *Freeman*, 48.
7 13 N.J. 145, 98 A.2d 581, 1953 N.J. 39 A.L.R.2d 1179.
8 Cochran. "The evolution of corporate social responsibility."
9 Bowen, H.R. 1953. *Social responsibilities of the businessman*. New York: Harper & Row, p. 6.
10 Rahman, S. 2011. "Evaluations of definitions: Ten dimensions of corporate social responsibility." *World Review of Business Research*, 1, 166–176.
11 Johnson, H.L. 1971. *Business in contemporary society: Framework and issues*. Belmont, CA: Wadsworth, p. 50.
12 Carroll, A.B. 1979. "A three-dimensional model of corporate performance." *Academy of Management Review*, 4, 497–505; Carroll, A.B. 1991. "The pyramid of corporate social responsibility: Toward the moral management of organizational stakeholders." *Business Horizons*, July.
13 Hood, J. 1998. "Do corporations have social responsibilities?"
14 Friedman, M. 1970. *New York Times Magazine*, September 1970.
15 Matten, D. & Crane, A. 2005. "Corporate citizenship: Towards an extended theoretical conceptualization." *Academy of Management Review*, 30, 166–179.
16 Matten, D., Crane, A. & Chapple, W. 2003. "Behind the mask: Revealing the true face of corporate citizenship." *Journal of Business Ethics*, 45, 1/2, 109–120.
17 Goodpaster, K.E. 1996. "Business ethics and stakeholder analysis." In Rae, S. B. & Wong, K.L. (Eds.), *Beyond integrity: A Judeo-Christian approach,* Grand Rapids, MI: Zondervan Publishing House, pp. 246–254.
18 McWilliams, A. & Siegel, D. 2001. "Corporate social responsibility: A theory of the firm perspective." *Academy of Management Review*, 26, 117–127; Treviño, L.K. & Nelson, K.A. 1999. *Managing business ethics: Straight talk about how to do it right*, 2nd edn, New York: J. Wiley & Sons.
19 Verschoor, C.C. & Murphy, E.A. 2002. "The financial performance of large U.S. firms and those with global prominence: How do the best corporate citizens rate?" *Business and Society Review*, 107, 371–380.
20 Miller, F.D. & Ahrens, J. 1993. "The social responsibility of corporations." In T.I. White (Ed.), *Business ethics: A philosophical reader,* Upper Saddle River, NJ: Prentice-Hall, pp. 187–204.
21 Boatright, J.R. 2000. "Globalization and the ethics of business." *Business Ethics Quarterly*, 10, 1–6; Smith, N.C. 2003. "Corporate social responsibility: Whether or how?" *California Management Review*, 45, 52–76.
22 Heslin, P.A. & Ochoa, J.D. 2008. "Understanding and developing strategic corporate social responsibility." *Organizational Dynamics*, 37, 125–144.
23 Porter, M.E. & Kramer, M.R. 2006. "Strategy and society: The link between competitive advantage and corporate social responsibility." *Harvard Business Review*, December, 76–93.
24 Bielak, D., Nonini, S.M.J. & Oppenheim, J.M. 2007. "CEOs on strategy and social issues." *McKinsey Quarterly*, October, 1–8.

25 Heslin & Ochoa, "Understanding and developing strategic corporate social responsibility."
26 www.microsoft.com/about/diversity/en/us/programs/college.aspx# Higher Education Support.
27 www.starbucks.com/responsibility/sourcing/farmer-support.
28 www.chocolateeuphoria.com/ethelmchocolates/livingmachine.html.
29 www.hydro.com/en/Our-future/Technology/Recycling/.
30 www.hydro.com/en/Press-room/News/Archive/2010/11/Strong-growth-expected-in-global-aluminium-recycling/.
31 www.shawfloors.com/Environmental/RecyclingDetail.
32 www.hp.com/hpinfo/globalcitizenship/environment/recycling/unwanted-hardware.html.
33 GreenBiz Staff. 2010. "Shanghai GM green supply chain program saved $19M in 2009." June 16. www.greenbiz.com/news/2010/06/16/shanghai-gm-supply-chain-program-saved-19m-2009.
34 www.greensupplychain.com/burton-riding_the_green_supply_chain_wave.html.
35 http://eur-lex.europa.eu/legal-content/EN/TXT/?uri=CELEX:52017XC0705(01).
36 KPMG International Survey of Corporate Responsibility Reporting 2008.
37 KPMG International Survey of Corporate Responsibility Reporting 2017.
38 www.sustainability-reports.com/new-trend-report-about-sustainability-reporting-instruments/ New trend report about Sustainability Reporting Instruments. May 2016.
39 KPMG International Survey of Corporate Responsibility Reporting 2008, p. 10.
40 KPMG Advisory N.V., United Nations Environment Program, Global Reporting Initiative, and the Unit for Corporate Governance in Africa. 2016. *Carrots and sticks—Promoting transparency and sustainability: An update on trends in voluntary and mandatory approaches to sustainability reporting.*
41 KPMG Advisory N.V. et al., *Carrots and sticks,* p. 4.
42 www.cdp.net/en/info/about-us https://guidance.cdp.net/en/guidance?cid=2&ctype=theme&idtype=ThemeID&incchild=1µsite=0&otype=Questionnaire&tags=TAG-597%2CTAG-604%2CTAG-600.
43 Anne Shiraishi. June, 2014. "Six reasons your firm should report to CDP." www.greenbiz.com/blog/2014/06/06/6-reasons-your-company-should-report-cdp.
44 www.globalreporting.org/standards/getting-started-with-the-gri-standards/www.globalreporting.org/standards/.
45 www.globalreporting.org/information/about-gri/what-is-GRI/Pages/default.aspx.
46 www.globalreporting.org/network/report-or-explain/Pages/default.aspx.
47 www.globalreporting.org/information/news-and-press-center/newsarchive/Pages/default.aspx.
48 www.unglobalcompact.org/docs/publications/UN_Global_Compact_Guide_to_Corporate_Sustainability.pdf.
49 Arena, C. 2010. "Are corporate social responsibility rankings irresponsible?" *Christian Science Monitor*, March 17. www.csmonitor.com/Business/Case-in-Point/2010/0317/Are-corporate-social-responsibility-rankings-irresponsible.

KEY TERMS

Assurance: the auditing function to validate the accuracy of a company's CSR report.

Communication on Progress (COP): the reporting procedures for showing compliance to the Global Compact—must contain the following elements: a statement by the CEO expressing continued support for the UN Global Compact, a description of practical actions the company has taken to implement the principles, and a demonstration of how outcomes are measured.

Corporate citizenship: voluntarily giving back to the community with an increased focus on the close environment of the firm; an increased focus on legal, ethical and discretionary responsibilities of business; a focus on the rights of the firm to be a social actor and participate politically.

Corporate social responsibility: activities when companies go beyond the requirements of running an economically viable business within the constraints of the law to protect the environment and enhance the well-being of their stakeholders.

Dodge v. Ford: the first legal precedent in the U.S. for the dominance of the stockholder as the prime stakeholder.

Economic responsibility: the role of a business to produce goods or services that people need and to make an acceptable profit in the process.

Ethical responsibility: obligation to conform to the ethical expectations of society that are not codified into law.

Global Reporting Initiative (GRI): provides principles and indicators that companies can use to identify and measure economic, environmental, and social performance.

Integrated reports: reports built into annual reports, which traditionally have focused only on financial performance.

Invisible hand: the control by market forces where competition favors those who produce the best products at the best prices as consumers also seek their own self-interest in buying those products or services.

Legal responsibility: obligation to conform to laws and regulations with ethical consequences such as regulations regarding product safety and consumer protection.

License to operate: the social contract between businesses and society that allows them to operate.

Milton Friedman: a critic of CSR who wrote the now famous article in the *New York Times Magazine*, "The Social Responsibility of Business is to Increase its Profits."

Philanthropic responsibility: the responsibility to be good corporate citizens and engage in activities that promote human welfare and goodwill.

Smith v. Barlow: the U.S. court decision that weakened the legal position of stockholder dominance and allowed more corporate philanthropy.

Social performance reports: similar to annual reports on economic performance, they report on CSR performance.

Strategic CSR: corporations attend to their stakeholders because managers believe it is in the best interest of the company; rests on the assumption that "doing good" can be good for a business as well as for society.

Triple bottom line (TBL): the addition of social and environmental sustainability performance to economic performance, also known as "people, planet, and profit."

UN's Global Compact: ten principles in the areas of human rights, labor, the environment, and anti-corruption that guide social performance for signatories.

DISCUSSION QUESTIONS

1 Discuss the legal evolution of CSR.
2 Write two or three definitions of CSR and discuss the underlying assumptions of each.
3 Compare and contrast Friedman's view of the legitimacy of CSR with Carroll's perspective. How do they differ and overlap?
4 Compare and contrast the differences between the two models for looking at Carroll's dimensions of CSR. Which makes most sense? Should economic considerations be a foundation or does a competing values view make more sense?
5 With the continuing move of formally optional CSR actions into the framework of legal requirements, discuss the future of CSR. Will governments mandate what is now optional?
6 Discuss the dimensions of the Triple Bottom Line. How does this perspective relate to Carroll's earlier view?
7 What are the challenges of implementing a TBL strategy?
8 In strategic CSR, companies search for ways to meet the bottom line while being socially responsible in ways that benefit the company. Is this really CSR?
9 Discuss why U.S. firms seem less likely to adopt GRI reporting standards than European firms.
10 What are the major weaknesses of the current reporting practices in CSR?

INTERNET ACTIVITY

1 Go to the internet and find the CSR reports for four companies in two different countries (two from each country). Try to stay in one industry so the companies will face similar CSR challenges.
2 Compare the reports by country. How are they different? How are they similar? Are different issues more important in different countries?
3 Analyze the reports in terms of how well they present the companies' CSR position in a believable manner. Identify aspects of the reports that can be verified.

For more Internet Activities and resources, visit the Companion Website at www.routledge.com/cw/parboteeah.

WHAT WOULD YOU DO?

CSR at Dixie Manufacturing Company

Dixie Manufacturing Company (DMC), located in Tuscaloosa, Alabama, is a small manufacturing company of fewer than 50 employees that produces medical instruments such as scalpels, periodontal scalers and curettes (the tools dentists use to scrape your teeth) for the medical community.

You recently graduated from the University of Alabama and have been working for DMC in the marketing group for six months. Yesterday, George Day, the CEO, called you and asked what you know about CSR. He said,

> You're a recent college grad and probably had some courses in business ethics and corporate social responsibility. When most of the senior managers were in college no one worried about these issues. So, I am going to rely on you to help us out.

DMC has no formal code of conduct or CSR policies. They sponsor a local little league team and are pretty generous to the students from the University of Alabama who come by each semester asking for donations. You have noticed that most people think that is pretty good and DMC has little to worry about. However, Day tells you, "I want an outline of a CSR plan in a couple of weeks, as times are changing."

DMC is in a competitive industry and you have heard rumors that some manufacturing might move to Mexico to cut costs. However, some in the plant say that will not work because DMC will not be able to match the quality and reliability of the current plant, where most of the workers have over ten years of experience and on-the-job training is really successful. An alternative is layoffs, yet many of the older workers produce some of the less profitable products, so it would be difficult to take seniority into account.

What will you do first? Who are the stakeholders that you must consider in your plan? If DMC faces a financial crisis now, do you think it is too late to build a viable CSR strategy?

BRIEF CASE: BUSINESS ETHICS INSIGHT

Novo Nordisk, the CSR Superstar

Novo Nordisk is a Danish pharmaceutical firm specializing in diabetes care with over 30,000 employees worldwide. Novo Nordisk has production facilities in 7 countries, offices in 74 countries, and sells its products in 180 countries. In 2010, *Fortune* ranked Novo Nordisk one of the top 25 best companies to work for.

Novo Nordisk is a CSR superstar. Awards for superior CSR around the world abound. Here is just a sampling of their 2011 accolades.

- Sixth Golden Bee International CSR Forum in Beijing—the Harmonious Contributors Award for sustainability commitment and achievements. The Award recognizing companies in areas of customer focus, employee care, and responsible purchasing.
- 2010 TakeAction! award, given to the most impressive employee volunteer activity of the year—employees from Novo Nordisk Pakistan recognized for their rapid response to last year's devastating floods in Pakistan.
- Annual report recognition—two awards for best integrated financial and social reporting, CorporateRegister, a worldwide resource for corporate responsibility reporting, and Justmeans, a corporate social responsibility news service.
- Gold Class in the Sustainability Yearbook 2011, Sustainability Asset Management (SAM) has awarded Novo Nordisk the Gold Class distinction, recognizing the company's strong performance on economic, environmental, and social issues that focus on long-term value creation.
- 2011 Global 100 Most Sustainable Corporations—ranked 16th, up 33 positions.

The company did not become a CSR superstar overnight. They have been working for more than a decade to move from a view of CSR as simply risk management toward what they call "a more opportunity-driven perspective." To achieve their CSR goals Novo Nordisk adopted the triple bottom line approach, striving to conduct all activities "in a financially, environmentally and socially responsible way." Their approach is to integrate TBL into all business activities.

The statement of their commitment to TBL is part of their Articles of Association. More importantly, perhaps, TBL is integrated into their corporate governance structures, management tools, and individual performance assessments. As part of their organizational culture, they note, "the principle of 'preserving the planet while improving the quality of life for its current and future inhabitants' resonates well with Novo Nordisk's business rationale." They are confident, and the external observations seem to confirm, that the TBL allows them to make decisions that balance financial growth with CSR focusing on shareholder returns and stakeholder interests.

In following TBL, Novo Nordisk identifies specific areas that are particularly relevant to the company and the pharmaceutical industry in which they operate. A short overview of the TBL areas shows the degree of integration of TBL into their organizational policies and culture.

Environmental Responsibility

The company has a general concern for environmental sustainability but specific concerns related to issues such as animal experimentation and safety issues regarding the use of genetic engineering.

- *Animal welfare.* Live animal experimentation is necessary for the discovery, development, and production of pharmaceutical and medical products. Also, it is often required by regulatory authorities in different countries. Novo Nordisk is pledged to reduce and or replace live animal experiments and seeks to develop alternative experiments for drug release that regulatory authorities will accept.
- *Environmental management.* The company uses an extremely thorough assessment of its environmental impact with a lifecycle approach monitoring inputs (raw materials, packaging, water, energy) and outputs (emission to the air, liquid and solid waste).
- *Climate change.* Novo Nordisk goes beyond compliance in reducing CO_2 emissions. As a signatory of the Climate Savers agreement, Novo Nordisk has set an ambitious target to achieve a reduction of 10% of its CO_2 emissions by 2014.

Social Responsibility

Novo Nordisk identifies key stakeholders as the people whose healthcare needs they serve and their employees. They also consider the impact of their business on the global society and the local community.

- *Access to health.* Novo Nordisk's strategy for improved access to diabetes care follows the recommendations of the World Health Organization. One of their many strategies is a tiered pricing system for the developed and developing world to allow low-cost access to diabetes drugs in poorer countries.
- *Diversity.* Novo Nordisk has numerous policies and structures to maximize diversity and gender equity. This is not just an HR issue, as they require all senior vice presidents to develop action plans to identify and address diversity issues.
- *Employee volunteering.* The company's TakeAction! program encourages employees to engage in voluntary activities during working hours and integrate the company's triple bottom line approach into their own work lives. Such activities help meet social and/or environmental objectives in the communities in which the company operates.
- *Health and safety.* Historically, the company's health and safety practices were compliance-based, following local standards related to local legislation. As a multinational company, they realized they needed a more globally standardized approach. Novo Nordisk now has the Occupational Health and Safety Management System that identifies the roles and responsibilities for health and safety work, including (but not limited to) safety training of personnel, efforts to identify and document risk factors, and actions to minimize these risks.
- *Human rights.* As a signatory to the United Nations' Global Compact, Novo Nordisk is committed to supporting and respecting human rights throughout

its operations and has agreed to report annually how it accomplishes these goals.

- *Workplace quality*. Included in the assessment of workplace quality are the wages and benefits offered to employees, quality of management practices, corporate culture, training and educational opportunities, talent development, appropriate shift lengths, the levels of job stress, and the physical attributes of the workplace.

Economic Viability

To Novo Nordisk, economically viability includes making a profit for the company's shareholders, educating employees, and investing in the growth of the business.

- *Economic footprint*. Broadly, Novo Nordisk's economic footprint includes interactions with stakeholders through the sales of products and services, payments to suppliers, remuneration of employees, dividend and interest to investors and funders, taxes paid to the public sector, and profits generated for future growth of the company. Novo Nordisk also impacts society by using sustainable business practices, providing healthcare knowledge and products. They have several programs that target developing nations that provide jobs and access to healthcare.
- *Financial performance*. Novo Nordisk is a very successful firm. Operating profit growth in 2010 was 27%. Operating profit margin was 31%. From 2006 to 2010, the average operating profit growth was 19% on an average margin of 26%. The main insulin products command nearly 50% of the market.

Conclusion

In summary, for Novo Nordisk, the triple bottom line strategy serves as an integrated CSR management tool. It is not a stagnant system and the company identifies six processes that facilitate organizational learning and innovation in the CSR area:

- monitoring issues and spotting trends that may affect the future business
- engaging with stakeholders to reconcile dilemmas and find common ground for more sustainable solutions
- building relationships with key stakeholders in the global and local communities of which Novo Nordisk is a part
- driving and embedding long-term thinking and the triple bottom line mindset throughout the company
- accounting for the company's performance and conveying Novo Nordisk's positions, objectives, and goals to audiences with an interest in the company
- translating and integrating the triple bottom line approach into all business processes to obtain sustainable competitive advantages in the marketplace.

Source: Adapted from www.novonordisk.com/.

BRIEF CASE QUESTIONS

1 Novo Nordisk is a very rich company. Some would argue that this company can heavily engage in CSR activities because of its affluence and this is not what most companies can do. Discuss and assess this position.

2 Novo Nordisk is a model of TBL operations. Benchmark a company you know against this performance.

3 If one looks at the company's website, the CSR philosophy seems strongly driven by the Danish approach to a social democracy. The U.S. subsidiary seems to have more of a legal compliance level of CSR. Investigate and discuss if you perceive this to be true and, if so, why or why not.

LONG CASE: BUSINESS ETHICS

http://sevenpillarsinstitute.org/case-studies/the-ethics-of-executive-compensation-a-matter-of-duty

THE ETHICS OF EXECUTIVE COMPENSATION: A MATTER OF DUTY

June 15th, 2015 by Kara in Case Studies

© Scott Adams, Inc./Dist. by UFS, Inc.

By: Aidan Balnaves-James

It is well known that executive compensation growth beats average worker salary growth. By a wide margin. The outperformance contributes to increasingly pronounced levels of income inequality. Subjective peer group referents and benchmarking, combined with ineffectual regulatory instruments, account for much of this trend, despite public anger and media scrutiny. Excessively high executive compensation linked to operational goals, induces unnecessary risk-taking and increased probability of unethical, possibly unlawful behavior. Applying deontological ethics and the concept of fiduciary duty affirms that the current structure and levels of executive compensation is indeed, unjustified.

The Purpose and Composition of Executive Compensation

Executive compensation is a form of monetary incentive for talented individuals to maximize a firm's value (Moriarty 2009, p. 237). Executive compensation should be structured to remove conflicts of interest between executives and shareholders occurring in the principle-agent dynamic. An initial separation of management control and ownership between shareholders as principles and executives as agents establishes divergent interests. Rational agents will pursue personal utility maximization. Therefore, executives may act to the possible detriment of the shareholders' interests (Matsumura and Shin 2005, p. 102; Lin, Kuo and Wang 2013. p. 28). Three potential conflicts of interest exist in such cases: (1) exorbitant use of perquisites by executives; (2) executive aversion to certain risks as a result of the inability to diversify such risk and (3) a deficit of attention to long-term investments and corporate goals (Matsumura and Shin 2005 pp. 102–103).

Contemporary executive compensation packages generally comprise a combination of base salary, bonuses, restricted stock, stock options, perquisites and long-term incentive plans (Jarque and Muth 2013, p. 254; Valenti 2013, p. 2). Bonuses, stock options and restricted stock function, attempt to converge the interests of executives with shareholders. These compensation features act as incentives for executives to engage in potentially risky, profit-maximizing activities, which benefit shareholders when ventures are successful (Winkelvoss, Amoruso and Duchac 2013, pp.12–13). As executives cannot diversify risk across firms, a sufficiently high level of these forms of compensation is required to attract talented candidates (Jarque and Muth 2013, p. 256).

Rising Executive Compensation Levels: Empirical Data

Executive pay has continued to rise considerably since the 1960s, as the following points demonstrate:

- The Economic Policy Institute calculates CEO compensation grew by 937 percent between 1978 and 2013, compared to 10.2 percent for a "typical employee's" compensation (Mishel and Davis 2014).
- In the U.S., the average CEO-to-worker compensation ratio increased from 20 to 1 in 1965 to 295.9 to 1 in 2013 (Mishel and Davis 2014).
- In 2013, the average compensation for the CEOs of the top 350 U.S. firms, including realized stock options exercised, was calculated at $15.2 million (Mishel and Davis).

- The median total realized compensation for CEOs, from Standard and Poor's top 500 companies in 2010, recorded a 35 percent increase from 2009 (Murphy 2012, p. 11).
- From Standard and Poor's top 250 companies, Bloomberg calculated the highest ratio of CEO-to-average-worker compensation was 1795 to 1, accorded to Ron Johnston, former CEO of JC Penney Co., totalling $53.3 million at the end FY 2012. At No. 250, the ratio was 173 to 1, accorded to William Sullivan, CEO of Agilent Technologies Inc., equalling $10.1 million (Blair Smith and Kuntz 2013).

Why Does Executive Pay Continue to Rise?

A compensation committee of independent directors is generally responsible for assessing and formulating CEO and executive compensation in public companies (Bender 2012, p. 320). There are multiple factors accounting for rising compensation levels despite a climate of public displeasure. This article proposes two major determinants. Firstly, the cogent theoretical framework of 'leapfrogging' is a prominent contributor to a generalised increase in executive compensation (DiPrete, Eirich and Pittinsky 2010). Secondly, ineffective regulatory tools account for the continued upsurge in the face of public vexation. While other considerations, such as a lack of direct shareholder involvement in negotiation procedures are problematic, the primary focus is on governmental responses to public demands.

1. Efficient Contracting, Rent Extraction or Leapfrogging?

The two predominant sets of paradigms to account for the systemic growth in executive pay are the managerial power theories and efficient contracting theories (Murphy 2012, p. 35). Managerial power theories postulate CEOs and senior executives exert power over the board of directors and compensation committees in extracting rent. Efficient contracting theories maintain executive compensation is a function of market forces (DiPrete, Eirich and Pittinsky 2010, pp. 1671–1672; Murphy 2012, p. 35).

"Leapfrogging" theory provides a compelling explanation to account for the fluid interaction of micro and macro-level forces and key elements of both aforementioned theories (DiPrete, Eirich and Pittinsky 2010). Leapfrogging refers to the process in which a few CEOs during each year, "leapfrog" their peers by getting enormous raises that have little to do with the performance of their companies. Other companies then use the oversized pay of the leapfroggers in subsequent benchmarks. This process ultimately pushes up pay for everyone through a contagion effect. The selection of peer groups of executives for comparing compensation schemes by committees is not an objective endeavour, but a subjective assessment. Established periodic benchmarking of compensation in firms occurs through peer group analysis. Particularly noteworthy is the "aspirational" selection of those in higher status. This leads to increases in compensation for individual executives and facilitates system-wide upswings in executive pay (DiPrete, Eirich and Pittinsky 2010, pp. 1671, 1685–1686). "*Counterfactual analysis . . . says that c caused e, where c and e are individual events, means that e depended counterfactually on c . . . if c had not occurred, e would not have occurred"* (Bennett 1987, p. 368). Research on compensation practices supports leapfrogging theory with counterfactual analysis of statistics from Standard and Poor's Execucomp database (DiPrete, Eirich and Pittinsky 2010, pp. 1686–1705).

2. Ineffectual regulation

Public anger has intensified concerning perceived excessive compensation in the face of increasing income inequality and economic downturn, particularly since the global financial crisis (GFC). News articles such as "CEO pay rises at double the rate of workers" (Srinivas 2014) or "91 BBC executives who are paid more than the Prime Minister" (Infante, Steere, Robinson and Creighton 2014) are frequent and elicit public fury. Opinion polls lean in favour of limiting executive pay. *A Gallup poll conducted in June 2009 found 59 percent of Americans support federal government intervention in restraining executive compensation* (Jones 2009).

Despite negative public opinion, the upward trend of executive compensation has not abated. Implemented reforms have been unavailing or symbolic, or they have brought about unintended consequences (Suárez 2014, p. 73; Murphy 2012, p. 11). In the United States, executive pay has been subject to a plethora of legislative and regulatory reforms since the Great Depression (Murphy 2012 p. 11). For example, in 1993 the implemented restraint of a $1 million tax deductible for non-performance linked to the compensation of senior executives led to increases in many executive salaries to $1 million. In addition, the legislation facilitated the increased use of options as a form of remuneration, since options are assessed related to performance (Murphy 2012, pp. 24–25; *The Economist* 2009). Mandatory disclosure of compensation practices in public companies has not led to a subsidence of executive pay growth, despite extensive disclosure requirements in the U.S. (Suárez 2014, p. 90). These include mandated disclosures in proxy statements, disclosures of perquisites, provision of details regarding share options granted in summary compensation tables, and the recent Dodd-Frank Act (Murphy 2012, pp. 12–17). The supposition that disclosing the rules could successfully pressure executives and directors to limit compensation to improve the corporate image has not actualized (Suárez 2014, pp. 89–90).

Pay restrictions following the GFC are a case in point. In 2009, the Obama administration applied restrictions to executive compensation in institutions receiving financial assistance as a result of the GFC. Executives in institutions that accepted extraordinary assistance were subject to a $500,000 salary limit (Weisman and Lublin 2009). "Golden parachute" changes in control-agreement payouts were curtailed and restricted stock prohibited from being sold so long as the institution received government assistance (Suárez 2014, p. 87; Weisman and Lublin 2009). However, direct regulations in particular institutions may reduce the supply of talented individuals, who transfer to organizations offering greater incentives (Kaplan 2010, p. 42). Regarding the banks that were in the Troubled Assets Relief Program, directly regulating executive bonuses provided incentives for self-maximizing individuals to seek executive positions at firms offering more lucrative compensation (Borland 2013, pp. 91–93). Compensation may also be increased through other mechanisms, such as income and fringe benefits (Borland 2013, p. 93). Thus, as these regulations applied only to recipients of government assistance, executive compensation has continued to rise.

Justified Remuneration or Excessive?

The Defence of Current Compensation Schemes

Proponents of current systems and levels of compensation think it is right that directors, elected by shareholders, set compensation packages according to market rates. This ensures skilled executives are employed, whose work ensures all stakeholders benefit (Perel 2003, pp. 386–387). These executives add market value to the firm and increase returns to shareholders (Kay and Robinson 1994, p.26). For example, when Roberto Goizueta presided as CEO and chairman of Coca Cola, more than $50 billion was added in market value to the corporation. Goizueta was awarded $1 million in restricted stock (Kay and Robinson 1994, p. 26).

The use of pay-for-performance measures, such as restricted stock, stock options and bonuses, links executive remuneration to corporate profitability. This (faulty) connection is said to align the interests of principles and agents (Lin, Kuo and Wang 2013, p. 28). Correlation is evident between corporate profitability, share prices and increasing or decreasing levels of compensation (Kay and Robinson 1994, p. 26). For example, executive compensation at recipient institutions of the Troubled Assets Relief Program decreased during the Great Recession, demonstrating linkage between corporate performance and executive pay (Winkelvoss, Amoruso and Duchac 2013, pp. 14–21).

The Critique of Current Compensation Schemes

Executive compensation should be structured to attract talented managerial candidates and align the interests of executives and shareholders. Public corporations are complex entities that benefit society in their generation of wealth for shareholders, provision of employment, and production of goods and services for consumption. A sufficiently high compensation for CEOs and senior executives is therefore, justified. The question, however, is whether current levels are excessive, and whether the structure of executive pay is advantageous for stakeholders, particularly shareholders, and strategic business interests. There are cogent reasons for concluding this is not the case, as well as concerns of distributive justice. There are other criticisms, such as the perceived complicity of directors and compensation committees in facilitating excessive increases in executive pay (Perel 2003, p. 383). In such cases, critics call for greater shareholder control, such as binding shareholder votes and special committees, as opposed to the non-binding shareholder vote implemented under President Obama (Kothari 2010, p. 66; Suárez 2014, p. 87).

Measurements of performance derived from operational indicators exacerbate the pressure for executives to take action to maximize short-term profitability that may be antithetical to long-term survival and growth (Kothari 2010 pp. 55–57). While not explicitly tied to compensation, excessive greed in aim of short-term shareholder wealth has arguably been an underlying factor behind the GFC (Yahanpath 2011). More specifically, stock options as a large proportion of executive compensation can result in excessive risk-taking and unethical behavior (Purcell 2011, p. 7; Perel 2003, pp. 383). Inevitably, this detracts from the wellbeing of other stakeholders.

High proportions of pay linked to equity levels, such as options and restricted stock, can encourage manipulation of short-term corporate data to ensure high earnings. In 2009, bonds were repackaged in order to augment the perceived performance of particular financial institutions (Kothari 2010, p. 59). In a study of unethical financial restatements, the proportion of share options comprising CEO compensation positively affected the likelihood of such an occurrence (Harris and Bromiley 2007, pp. 356, 362–363). Perhaps, the application of behavioral economics alongside conventional utility maximization finance theory may improve compensation schemes (Harris and Bromiley 2007, p. 352). Unethical behavior is not assured or inherent, but current schemes are flawed in their incentive design. The costs of unethical activity and failures of excessive risk-taking are placed heavily on all stakeholders and are damaging to the long-term interests of shareholders.

High compensation even in cases of substandard performance or operational failure reinforces such financially damaging behavior. Many executive compensation schemes are structured so that unsuccessful ventures still result in large payouts. These include "golden parachute" severance schemes. Successful but excessive risk-taking grants managers prodigious rewards, which in turn are the impetus for such conduct (Blinder 2009).

An analysis of 903 U.S. corporations between 2007 and 2010 finds the number of high-compensating, low-performing firms rose at a substantial rate (Lin, Kuo and Wang 2013, pp. 38–39). The provision of large executive pay packages despite poor performance and in some cases unethical behavior inherently damages the linkage of interests between shareholders and management that incentive programs are supposed to provide.

Distributive Justice

Distributive justice is also critically levelled at current amounts of executive compensation. Distributive justice examines the dispersion of material and immaterial resources, including social, economic and cultural capital in a society, and the rationales for certain inequalities (Calhoun 2002; Blackburn 2014). Income inequality is increasing across the developed world, demonstrated through increases in the Gini coefficient, a numerical indicator between 0 and 1 reflecting the distribution of wealth in a society. (The higher the coefficient, the more unequal the distribution (Bernanke, Olekalns and Frank 2011, pp. 178–179).) From 1995 to 2011, the U.S. Gini coefficient increased from 0.36 to 0.39. In the OECD the coefficient increased from 0.30 to

0.32 during the same time period (OECD 2014). The increasing disparity between CEO compensation and that of average workers may be counted as a contributing factor (Neeley and Boyd 2010, p. 546).

Perceptions of injustice regarding excessive compensation practices can have adverse effects on employee performance, commitment, morale and organizational citizenship behavior (Neeley and Boyd 2010, pp. 548–554). Criticisms were targeted at the CEO of government-owned Australia Post, Ahmed Fahour, who earned AU$4.8 million in 2013 as 900 administration workers were sacked in 2014. By comparison, the Australian Prime Minister's pay is AU$507,000 (Bourke 2014). Research of low to senior management and executives in 122 firms found that relative inequity in annual compensation between the CEO and lower management increased the probability of turnover (Wade, O'Reilly and Pollock 2006, pp. 532, 540). This adverse effect of pay inequity negatively impacts company performance and is antithetical to the shareholders' interests.

The Ethics of Executive Compensation

There are multiple ethical issues with executive compensation. These include whether such compensation is excessive compared against provision of service and whether the compensation process is compromised by inadequately transparent negotiation (Perel 2003, p. 381; Moriarty 2009, p. 235). We analyse these issues using a deontological approach.

Deontology concerns the moral duties that apply to us. Accordingly there are acts we are obligated to perform or to refrain from performing (McNaughton and Rawling 1998, 2011) to comply with such duties. Thus, business activity should be pursued within self-imposed moral boundaries (Micewski and Troy 2007).

According to the deontological theory, the principle of fiduciary duty is a moral principle we are obliged to follow. We can therefore, examine the ethics of compensation using this principle. The principle-agent relationship, which is central to executive compensation, generates fiduciary duties for executives and directors to shareholders. A fiduciary duty is embodied in a relationship of trust, where the agent owes allegiance, obedience and fidelity to the principle (Strudler 2009, p. 395). A primary fiduciary duty of a CEO or executive must be acting in the best interests of the shareholders, for acting against the best interests of the shareholders would violate the fidelity owed. Directors, as elected representatives of shareholders, must also hold a similar fiduciary duty (Demosthenous 2000). Therefore, in relation to executive compensation, directors, CEOs and senior executives have a fiduciary duty to negotiate and accept a compensation package that is in the best interests of the shareholders (Moriarty 2009, pp. 236–238).

This includes short- and long-term interests. Growth in the share price will increase utility for shareholders, directors and executives in the short term. However, when this activity, such as excessive risk-taking and unethical, potentially unlawful behavior like financial misrepresentation, comes at the expense of long-term corporate viability, those operational decisions ultimately go against the strategic interests of shareholders.

If all executives and directors acted against the interests of the shareholders, the institutional structure of modern corporate business would be fundamentally compromised and unsustainable. Shareholders, as rational agents, would not invest in public companies, knowing the agent would act in a manner incompatible with their interests.

A particular fiduciary duty of CEOs is to accept no more than the minimum compensation necessary to ensure productive and effective performance in the best interests of shareholders (Moriarty 2009, p. 235). This is logically sound, for if a CEO or executive accepts more than the minimum, they are effectively detracting from the profitability of the business by increasing costs (Moriarty 2009, pp. 236–238). It should be noted that "minimum" does not mean "minute". The minimum level can be any amount. Theoretically, this particular fiduciary duty could extend to directors and members of compensation committees. However the virtual impossibility of anyone other than the executive in question correctly determining the minimum level renders it infeasible. However, as representatives of shareholders, directors do have a moral duty to ensure decisions enhance operational and strategic corporate value. Given this duty, they must also ensure the structure and amount of compensation guarantees this. As any amount above the "minimum effective compensation" detracts from the firm's value, the duty of directors and executives precludes exorbitant compensation (Moriarty 2009, pp. 236–238).

Current compensation schemes would be morally permissible if the voluntary actions of awarding such compensation harmonizes with the voluntary actions of all stakeholders, providing justice is upheld (Micewski and Troy 2007, p. 22). However, high amounts of compensation linked to operational goals can encourage unethical behavior to ensure continued pay levels and employment (Perel 2003, pp. 384, 386). Research linking high use of equity-associated pay, such as share options and restricted stock, to unethical behavior such as financial misrepresentation (Harris and Bromiley 2007) indicates structuring executive compensation in this way is not beneficial to long-term corporate interests. An excessive propensity for risk-taking and other detrimental actions to the strategic interests of the firm prevent harmonization of the actions of managers, directors and shareholders and thus may be declared unjust (Micewski and Troy 2007, p. 22). Therefore, excessively high CEO and senior executive compensation does not accord with the fiduciary duty owed to shareholders.

More articles on Executive compensation can be found at the High Pay Centre website.

Bibliography

Bender, R 2012, "Executive Compensation Consultants", in R S Thomas and J G Hill (ed.), *Research Handbook on Executive Pay*, Edward Elgar Publishing Limited, Cheltenham

Bennett, J 1987, "Event Causation: The Counterfactual Analysis", *Philosophical Perspectives*, vol. 1, *Metaphysics*, pp. 367–386

Bernanke, B, Olekalns, N, Frank, R 2011, *Principles of Macroeconomics*, McGraw-Hill Australia, North Ryde

Blackburn, S 2014, *The Oxford Dictionary of Philosophy*, (2nd revised ed.), first published in print 2008, first published online 2008, current online version as of 2014, accessed 8 January 2015 from <www.oxfordreference.com>

Blair Smith, E, Kuntz, P 2013, "Top CEO Pay Ratios", Bloomberg, published 30 April 2013, accessed 5 December 2014, < http://go.bloomberg.com/multimedia/ceo-pay-ratio/>

Blinder, A S 2009, "Crazy Compensation and the Crisis", *Wall Street Journal*, published/updated 28 May 2009, accessed 10 December 2014, <www.wsj.com/articles/SB124346974150760597>

Borland, J 2013, *Microeconomics: Case Studies and Applications*, 2nd edn, Cengage Learning, South Melbourne

Bourke, L 2014, "Critics of Australia Post's Decision to Sack 900 Staff Questioning CEO Ahmed Fahour's $4.8 Million Salary", *Australian Broadcasting Corporation*, published 11 June 2014, accessed 9 December 2014, <www.abc.net.au/news/2014–06–11/critics-question-australia-post-ceos-multi-million-dollar-salary/5514682>

Calhoun, C (ed.) 2002, *Dictionary of the Social Sciences*, Oxford University Press, published in print 2002, published online 2002, accessed 8 January 2015 from <www.oxfordreference.com>

Demosthenous, M 2000, "The Social Responsibility of Business: A Review", *Flinders University School of Commerce Research Paper Series*, accessed 13 December 2012, <www.flinders.edu.au/sabs/business-files/research/papers/2000/00–08.doc>

DiPrete, T A, Eirich, G M, Pittinsky, M 2010, "Compensation Benchmarking, Leapfrogs, and the Surge in Executive Pay", *American Journal of Sociology*, vol. 115, no. 6, pp. 1671–1712

Harris, J, Bromiley, P 2007, "Incentives to Cheat: The Influence of Executive Compensation and Firm Performance on Financial Misrepresentation", *Organization Science*, vol. 18, no. 3, pp. 350–367

Infante, F, Steere, T, Robinson, M, Creighton, S 2014,"Revealed: The 91 BBC Executives who are Paid More than the Prime Minister and 11 Bosses Get More Than Double His Salary", *Daily Mail*, published 2 December 2014, accessed 6 December 2014, <www.dailymail.co.uk/news/article-2856908/The-91-BBC-executives-paid-Prime-Minister-Eleven-including-Director-General-BBC-One-controller-head-radio-earn-100–000-Cameron.html>

Jarque, A, Muth, J 2013, "Evaluating Executive Compensation Packages", *Economic Quarterly*, vol. 99, no. 4, pp. 251–285

Jones, J M 2009, "Most Americans Favour Gov't. Action to Limit Executive Pay", *Gallup*, published 16 June 2009, accessed 6 December 2014, <www.gallup.com/poll/120872/americans-favor-gov-action-limit-executive-pay.aspx>

Kaplan, S 2010, "Should Bankers Get Their Bonuses?", *Finance and Development*, vol. 47, no. 1, pp. 42–43

Kay, I T, Robinson, R F 1994, "Misguided Attacks on Executive Pay Hurt Shareholders", *Compensation and Benefits Review*, vol. 26, no. 1, pp. 25–33

Kothari, V B 2010, *Executive Greed*, Palgrave Macmillan, New York

Lin, D, Kuo, H-C, Wang, L-H 2013, "Chief Executive Compensation: An Empirical Study of Fat Cat CEOs", *The International Journal of Business and Finance Research*, vol. 7, no. 2, pp. 27–42

Matsumura, E M, Shin, J Y 2005, "Corporate Governance Reform and CEO Compensation: Intended and Unintended Consequences", *Journal of Business Ethics*, vol. 62, no. 2, pp. 101–113

McNaughton, D, Rawling, P 2011, "Deontological Ethics", in E. Craig (ed.), *Routledge Encyclopaedia of Philosophy*, Routledge, London, accessed 11 December 2014, <www.rep.routledge.com/article/L015>

McNaughton, D, Rawling, P 1998 "On Defending Deontological Ethics", Ratio, vol. 11, no. 1, pp. 37–54.

Micewski, E R, Troy, C 2007, "Business Ethics: Deontology Revisited", *Journal of Business Ethics*, vol. 72, no. 1, pp. 17–25

Mishel, L, Davis, A 2014, "CEO Pay Continues to Rise as Typical Workers Are Paid Less", *Economic Policy Institute*, published 12 June 2014, accessed 12 December 2014, <www.epi.org/publication/ceo-pay-continues-to-rise/>

Moriarty, J 2009, "How Much Compensation can CEOs Permissibly Accept?", *Business Ethics Quarterly*, vol. 19, no. 2, pp. 235–250

Murphy, K J 2012, "The Politics of Pay: A Legislative History of Executive Compensation", in R S Thomas, J G Hill (ed.), *Research Handbook on Executive Pay*, Edward Elgar Publishing Limited, Cheltenham

Neeley, C R, Boyd, N G 2010, "The Influence of Executive Compensation on Employee Behaviors Through Precipitating Events", *Journal of Managerial Issues*, vol. 22, no. 4, pp. 546–559

Organisation for Economic Co-operation and Development (OECD) 2014, *OECD Income Distribution Database: Gini, Poverty, Income, Methods and Concepts*, accessed 8 December 2014, <www.oecd.org/social/income-distribution-database.htm>

Perel, M 2003, "An Ethical Perspective on CEO Compensation", *Journal of Business Ethics*, vol. 48, no. 4, pp. 381–391

Purcell, N 2011, "Heads I Win, Tails You Lose-The Need to Reform Executive Compensation", *Journal of International Business Ethics*, vol. 4, no. 1, pp. 3–9

Srinivas, S 2014, "CEO Pay Rises at Double the Rate of Workers", *The Guardian*, published 6 December 2014, accessed 6 December 2014, <www.theguardian.com/money/2014/dec/05/save-jobs-numbers-companies-big-salaries-perks-executives>

Stanford Encyclopaedia of Philosophy (SEP) 2004, 2008, "Kant's Moral Philosophy", *Stanford Encyclopaedia of Philosophy*, published 23 February 2004, substantively revised 6 April 2008, accessed 12 December 2014, <http://plato.stanford.edu/entries/kant-moral/#CatHypImp>

Stanford Encyclopaedia of Philosophy (SEP) 2007, 2012, "Deontological Ethics", *Stanford Encyclopaedia of Philosophy*, published 21 November 2007, substantively revised 12 December 2012, accessed 11 December 2014, <http://plato.stanford.edu/entries/ethics-deontological/>

Strudler, A 2009, "The Moral Problem in Insider Trading", in G G Brenkert, T L Beauchamp (eds.), *The Oxford Handbook of Business Ethics*, Oxford University Press, New York

Suárez, S L 2014, "Symbolic Politics and the Regulation of Executive Compensation: A Comparison of the Great Depression and the Great Recession", *Politics and Society*, vol. 42, no. 1, pp. 73–105

The Economist 2009, "Attacking the Corporate Gravy Train", *The Economist*, published 28 May 2009, accessed 7 December 2014, <www.economist.com/node/13726705>

Valenti, A 2013, "Trends in Executive Compensation: CEO and CFO Pay from 2006 through 2011", *Journal of Human Resources Management Research*, vol. 2013, pp. 1–10

Wade, J B, O'Reilly, C A, III, Pollock, T G 2006, "Overpaid CEOs and Underpaid Managers: Fairness and Executive Compensation", *Organization Science*, vol. 17, no. 5, pp. 527–544

Weisman, J, Lublin, J S 2009, " Obama Lays Out Limits on Executive Pay", *Wall Street Journal*, published 5 February 2009, accessed 7 December 2014, <http://online.wsj.com/articles/SB123375514020647787>

Winkelvoss, C M, Amoruso, A J, Duchac, J 2013, "Executive Compensation at Banks Receiving Federal Assistance Under the Troubled Asset Relief Program (TARP)", *Allied Academics International Conference, Academy of Legal, Ethical and Regulatory Issues, Proceedings*, vol. 17, no. 2, pp. 11–22

Yahanpath, N 2011, "A Brief Review of the Role of Shareholder Wealth Maximisation and Other Factors Contributing to the Global Financial Crisis", *Qualitative Research in Financial Markets*, vol. 3, no. 1, pp. 64–77

In-text Hyperlinks

The Economist, "Economics A-Z Terms Beginning With R", *The Economist*, accessed 7 January 2015, <www.economist.com/economics-a-to-z/r#node-21529810>

Cartoon: http://dilbert.com

LONG CASE QUESTIONS

1. The fiduciary responsibility of CEOs is to manage the company in the interest of the shareholders. How might a CEO determine if she is drawing a salary in excess of her contributions to the company and thus misusing shareholder monies?
2. Contrast the view of high CEO salaries as rent extraction versus the view as salary as efficient contracting.
3. While it seems logical that attempts to converge CEO interests with shareholder interest such as using stock options as compensation, research has shown that there are often unintended consequences such as risky strategies for short term benefits and unethical behaviors (e.g., manipulation of financial reporting). Would you favor eliminating such compensation policies?
4. European CEO generally make less than their US counterparts. Many Europeans see the vast differences in CEO salary and that of the average worker as unethical. What might cause this difference?
5. College football coaches often make more money than anyone else in their university, including the president. Is it or it is not an ethical use of a university's resources to pay millions of dollars for a form of entertainment? Could one argue that the money might be better spent on financial aid for poor students and better resources for the educational mission of the university?

Part IV: Comprehensive Case

GENERAL MOTORS' CORPORATE CULTURE CRISIS: AN ASSESSMENT OF THE IGNITION SWITCH RECALL

GM's Failed Corporate Culture Source: Tulsa World

Arthur W. Page Society
2015 Case Study Competition
January 16, 2015

Table of Contents

1. Overview

Warnings about defective devices and automotive industry recalls appear in the news regularly. These recalls often stem from technical, production and development issues. When an automotive company learns that its products could cause its customers harm, the required action is to report it to the National Highway Traffic Safety Administration (NHTSA) and take measures to remedy the problem. Sometimes, however, employees do not understand, or even know about, the issue, or in some cases, choose to hide the truth. Whatever the reason, when a recall comes to light, the company is supposed to act.

The 2014 General Motors (GM) ignition switch recall took the company into crisis communications mode. Unveiled at the beginning of the 2014 calendar year, the recall uncovered a large, long running internal cultural problem at GM, where employees were not encouraged to speak up and were instead meant to focus on the bottom line.

On February 13, 2014, headlines across the nation announced the recall of nearly 800,000 GM vehicles, 31 vehicle accidents and 13 deaths. The giant automaker admitted that the switch, when bumped or when key chains hung too heavy, could cause a car's engine to stall and its airbags to malfunction.

More recalls followed shortly after the February announcement, bringing the total number of recalled ignition switch vehicles to 2.6 million. To date, GM has verified more than 2,000 compensation claims for the victims of the faulty switch, of which

100 have been deemed eligible for compensation, 42 for deaths (Muller, D., 2014). The internal investigation revealed that GM was aware of the switch defect since the early 2000s, but had not taken any responsibility for it.

During the first 10 months of her tenure, Mary Barra, the company's first female CEO, took actions to try and open up the lines of communication between employees and management, and comply with all investigations into the dormant ignition switch problem. Barra ordered an internal investigation into her company, appeared before Congress four times and confessed the mistakes of what the "old" GM had done. Additionally, she said she terminated 15 employees and began to implement new corporate culture initiatives (Stock, 2014).

2. Introduction to General Motors and Cultural Change

2.1 General Motors History

For more than 100 years, GM has played a pivotal role in the global auto industry, from the first Buick horseless carriages to technological advancements such as the Chevrolet Volt. The company manufactures vehicles in 37 countries worldwide, across 13 different brands, including Chevrolet, Buick, GMC and Cadillac (Twentyman, 2014).

William Durant founded the company in 1902. In 1908, GM acquired Oldsmobile, and in 1909, the automaker bought Cadillac, Elmore and Oakland. By 1911, GM had entered the foreign market and began exporting vehicles outside of the United States and Canada. In the early 1930s, GM bought railcar builder companies, such as Yellow Coach Company and the Electro-Motive Corporation. For the following two decades, America saw the company's engine powering locomotives travel across the country. For a significant part of its history, General Motors was the largest company in the United States and the largest single employer in the world. However, the economic slide in the early 2000s took a toll on GM, and the U.S. government stepped in to prevent the company's total collapse (GM Lifestyle, 2014).

Today, GM manufactures and markets new cars and trucks, and offers worldwide special features including OnStar vehicle protection, special services and parts, accessories, maintenance, XM satellite radio and more (Bloomberg, 2014). As of November 2014, GM had a market capitalization of $51.62 billion, revenue for the first three quarters of 2014 of $116.3 billion and it employs 219,000 people in 35 countries (Yahoo! Finance, 2014). The automaker is headquartered in Detroit, Michigan.

2.2 The Challenges of Culture Change

GM is not the first company facing the repercussions of a cultural crisis. In today's fast shifting world, some big corporations are stuck in their old mindset. For more than a decade, the ignition switch problem was known by some of GM's inside people. However, no one seemed to speak up or take appropriate action to remedy the problem until accidents happened and lives were lost (Business Insider, 2015).

Multiple *Fortune* 500 corporations face the problem of employees not evolving or becoming accustomed to cultural change as quickly as they would need to stay ahead of the competition. According to Himsel (2014, para. 7), "we are programmed not to change [. . .] we are wired to survive, so we hang on to what has worked in the past." Resistance to change is natural. Employees feel comfortable in their set mind-sets, routines and a culture that works for them. When facing a threat, or something unfamiliar, the brain goes into a defense mode (Black & Gregersen, 2003).

Most organizational culture evolutions take longer than most CEOs expect, on average about five years. To grow for the future, management might find it difficult to open up to a new corporate culture (Himsel, 2014). The enthusiastic leader driving the current change can overestimate the power of change initiatives, meanwhile underestimating the power of their entrenched cultures. Many companies have gotten caught in the whirlpool of their cultural norms. Xerox, Kodak and IBM are some examples of large organizations that launched major change programs only to realize their old cultural beliefs fought to reassert themselves (Himsel, 2014).

3. GM's Culture Crisis

3.1 GM's Old Corporate Culture

When the recall of GM vehicles for faulty ignition switches came to light in February 2014, there were already more than 10 years of silence surrounding it. While speculation grew that executives had tried to cover up the ignition switch issue, some believed the problem went unanswered largely because no one truly understood the issue, a reflection of a much larger underlying problem found within the company's very core: *its culture.*

Resulting from the economic recession of 2000 and intense cost-cutting measures, GM became a practitioner of cost culture (Himsel, 2014). GM was restructuring, shrinking and cutting costs out for the survival of the company. It was then followed by years of an "organizational culture that prized cost over quality, hesitating to pass along bad news and possibly condoned a cover-up," (Himsel, 2014, para. 2). Fletcher and Mufson (2014, A01) point out that "the problem [was] a corporate culture reluctant to pass along bad news. When GM was struggling to cut costs and buff its image, a recall of its popular small cars would have been a terrible setback."

The quiet, cost-driven culture potentially caused employees who knew about the ignition problem to fail to speak up. This pattern of silence could have contributed to the company's eventual bankruptcy and federal bailout in 2009 (Fletcher, 2014b).

According to Stock (2014, para. 2), Barra said "the faulty parts and fatal accidents that went on for almost a decade were born of bureaucratic bumbling and 'individuals seemingly looking for reasons not to act,' rather than any sort of executive cover-up or risky attempt to avoid extra expenses." Shepardson and Burden (2014, para. 3) outline that "GM has been criticized for decades as insular, slow to take responsibility for problems, hesitant to deliver bad news to superiors and reluctant to fire poorly performing executives."

The Valukas report, an in-depth report that summarized the investigation of former United States attorney Anton Valukas into the company's handling of the ignition switch recall, introduces the concept of a GM "nod culture." Executives and managers in charge would all nod to changes in meetings, but never actually take the action to do it, based on "managers being afraid or unwilling to report problems to other departments or senior executives" (George, 2014, para. 5).

3.2 Ignition Switch Recalls—Tipping Point of a Culture Crisis

According to Fletcher (2014b), GM had problems with the ignition switch because the part never met GM specifications. The problem began in 2004 as a faulty ignition switch lacking torque. Considering lead-time, cost and effectiveness, GM decided against fixing it. Instead, GM advised its customers not to use heavy key chains that could pull the ignition switch out of its running position (Fletcher & Mufson, 2014). Initially, lead engineer Ray DeGiorgio reportedly pushed against efforts to address the switch's torque problem, which he did not know posed a danger to drivers by disabling the airbags.

In 2006, DeGiorgio approved a new design for the part without documenting the change or alerting executives, who could have then ordered a recall (Fletcher & Mufson, 2014). By the time engineers wised up to the gravity of defect, the recession was in full swing and GM was heading toward bankruptcy.

According to Isidore and Wallace (2014), not all the blame in this case can be put on GM. An NHTSA defects assessment panel in 2007 was dismissed because overall rates of crashes and injury due to non-airbag deployment were similar to others in the industry.

4. Ignition Recall Timeline 2001 to 2014

2001—During pre-production testing, GM engineers experience problems with ignition switches—a mechanism that is supposed to hold the ignition key in place. According to GM, an internal report indicates the problem was solved when the switch was redesigned (Valdes-Depena & Yellin, 2014).

Source: CBS

2003—A GM service technician reports that additional weight of keys had worn out the ignition switch on a Saturn Ion (Valdes-Depena & Yellin, 2014).

2004—Test driving Chevy Cobalts reveals the engine shuts down when the ignition switch is jostled (Gutierrez, 2014).

2005—Engineers suggest fixing the ignition switch, but the fix was deemed too costly at less than $1 per car. Instead of reengineering the part, a key insert was made. A bulletin was sent to dealers, but less than 500 drivers received them (Gutierrez, 2014).

2006—The company that manufactured the switch proposes a design change. A GM engineer signs off on the alterations and the new part goes into production. However, the part number is not changed, so most of the automaker's employees are not aware of the fix (Valdes-Depena & Yellin, 2014).

2007—GM begins installing the new, redesigned switch on 2007 model year cars (Valdes-Depena & Yellin, 2014). An NHTSA official tries to open an investigation following airbag non-deployment accidents involving GM vehicles. However, there was not enough evidence to warrant an official investigation (Isidore & Wallace, 2014).

2009—GM files for bankruptcy protection (Isidore, 2009).

2010—The NHTSA proposes another investigation, but again there is not enough evidence.

2012—GM engineers notice that crashes involving the ignition switch were of 2007 and earlier model year vehicles (Valdes-Dapena & Yellin, 2014).

2014

January 15—Mary Barra is announced as the company's first female CEO (Smith, 2013).

February 13—GM announces the recall of 778,562 small cars due to a problem with the ignition switch that, when bumped, turns the car's engine off and disables the airbags. As many as 13 people have died (Bennett, 2014d).

March

- GM hires Anton Valukas, U.S. attorney, to lead internal investigation of the ignition switch recall (Bennett, 2014d).
- The Department of Justice and U.S. Congress committees launch investigations. GM announces new safety chief Jeff Boyer (Hirsch, 2014).
- Barra meets privately with families of ignition switch accident victims (Bennett, 2014d).
- The ignition switch recall now covers 2.6 million vehicles sold worldwide (Valdes-Dapena & Yellin, 2014).

April 1–2—Barra appears before the House Energy and Commerce Subcommittee and announces GM has hired Kenneth Feinberg as the compensation lawyer for victims and their families, placing no cap on the compensation fund (Valdes-Dapena & Yellin, 2014).

April 10—GM creates Speak Up For Safety program, encouraging employees to come forward with safety issues and make suggestions. The program is meant to break down the walls that stood in the way of open communications between employees and upper management in the past (General Motors, 2014c).

May 16—GM agrees to pay a $35 million fine to Department of Transportation, the highest possible civil penalty, to settle the federal probe (Bennett, 2014d).

June 5—Barra announces the findings of the Valukas Report to employees at a Global Town Hall Meeting. She also announces she has fired 15 employees and disciplined five more (General Motors, 2014b).

November 17—Of 21,000 claims to date, 33 death claims and 39 injury claims have been deemed eligible for compensation, according to Kenneth Feinberg (Belvedere, 2014).

December 15, 2014—Of 2,326 claims to date, 100 have been deemed eligible for compensation, including 42 deaths and 58 injuries (Muller, D., 2014).

5. The "New GM"

5.1 Mary Barra—Woman with a Mission: Fixing a Leaking Boat

Mary Barra, who officially became GM's CEO January 15, 2014, says she is adamant about changing GM for the better. She restructured the company by terminating people associated with the ignition switch scandal, appointed a new Vice President of Global Vehicle Safety and hired external investigators to look into the problem. She has been cooperative with government investigations and has launched communication initiatives to promote a new corporate culture (General Motors, 2014b).

Source: Mark Lennihan, AP

5.2 Internal Investigation

GM hired Anton Valukas, former U.S. Attorney, to lead the internal probe into the ignition switch recall, to get to the bottom of why it took the company so long to recall the affected vehicles. His 315 page report, released June 5, 2014, covered interviews with 230 witnesses over seven months, revealing that the cost associated with fixing the ignition switch in 2005 would have cost GM $400,000 (Kaptik, 2014).

Valukas' report concluded that GM's ignition switch problem was an issue tied to a culture where employees should have been able to fix this problem, not a deliberate cover-up tied to top executives. Employees failed to take responsibility or treat instances like this one with urgency. Outside investigators misdiagnosed the severity of the issue, and information within the company had nowhere to go (Fletcher, 2014b).

5.3 Barra's Public Remarks

Barra initially appeared before the House Energy and Commerce Subcommittee April 1–2, 2014, saying that "whatever mistakes were made in the past, we will not shirk from our responsibilities now and in the future. Today's GM will do the right thing" (General Motors, 2014b, para. 4). She emphasized that GM customers and safety are the center focus of today's GM. Barra summarized her approach to dealing with the ignition switch recall and addressed her vision for the future of her company and its culture.

She held an in-person Global Town Hall meeting in Michigan on June 5, 2014, which was broadcast to employees not in attendance (General Motors, 2014b). She pledged to do the right thing and take responsibility for the families of the victims and prevent anything like this from happening again. She announced Valukas' report findings, and said that while she was saddened, "this is about our responsibility to act with integrity, honor and a commitment to excellence" (General Motors, 2014b, para. 9). She vowed to use the report as a template to strengthen the company, and that, instead of forgetting this happened, would use it as a reminder to never let it happen again.

5.4 Embracing a New Safety Centric Culture

In the face of GM's old culture, where no one spoke up for fear of disrupting the flow of the company, Barra says she is taking matters into her own hands. She is starting over, promising to shift the focus of the company from one on cost, to one on customer safety (Himsel, 2014). She has restructured the decision-making process for safety issues so that they can be heard by the highest levels of the company (General Motors, 2014b).

Since the 1970s, GM's culture has been like a sponge. You press on it, and it indents. Then, once you're finished, it simply bounces back to its previous shape (Maynard, 2014b). Barra, like her predecessors, says she is determined to keep that rebound from happening again. Barra says she has laid out the changes the company is making to overhaul its bureaucratic culture (Maynard, 2014b).

5.5 New Core Values and the Speak Up For Safety Program

According to an interview between Barra and Forbes reporter Joann Muller (2014), GM rolled out its three core values in 2013—the Customer is Our Compass,

Relationships Matter and Individual Excellence is Crucial. Barra said "We're now getting an opportunity to accelerate the adoption of these values because they're seeing from [us] that we mean it" (Muller, J., 2014, para. 10). Barra said she wants her employees to hear her, so that they believe her, and will follow her example to be open and to communicate.

In April 2014, Barra started Speak Up For Safety. The new program encourages employees to share ideas on improving customer safety, and to come forward when they see something that could be fixed (General Motors, 2014c). This program is meant to further establish GM as a company that embraces a culture "where safety and quality come first" (General Motors, 2014c, para. 2).

5.6 The Challenges for the New Culture

Culture change is about behavior and consequences. While some employees understand the importance of a company's culture, others get by with a values drift, where they either don't know what the top position is striving for or ignore their directives (Maynard, 2014a).

This long-standing culture shaped the DNA of GM and will take time to repair (Maynard, 2014a). GM will have to prove that going forward without falling back into the habits of employees stuck in the culture for the past several decades. "'Like its hometown, GM is burdened by legitimate suspicions it cannot change, cannot slay the demons of its past to become a functioning member of corporate America not wedded to the worst habits of a golden era now long gone,' said *Detroit News* columnist Daniel Howes. 'Switchgate,' despite all the new GM rhetoric, only reinforces suspicions compounded by the fact that most of Barra's leadership team are products of 'old' GM' (Maynard, 2014a, para. 7).

With so much riding on resolving Switchgate, Barra cannot risk that GM's cultural sponge will simply go back to its "old" GM shape. To succeed, she will have to "put her fingers in the holes, rip it into pieces, and then knit together what she wants GM to be" (Maynard, 2014a, para. 16). Maynard (2014a, para. 18) states that former U.S. Safety Chief Joan Claybrook believes Barra has a historic chance to make that happen. "'I think she has the richest opportunity of any CEO in America because this company needs her badly,' said Claybrook on public radio's The Diane Rehm Show. 'They need her to perform. And she can then use that power and authority that she now has to reorganize General Motors.'"

6. Public Response to the Ignition Switch Recall and GM's Culture Crisis

6.1. GM Uses Social Media to Manage Customers and Its Reputation

GM must balance its day-to-day business with its image and communication with consumers on its social media channels. This is where customers' perceptions of a brand are shaped by what the company does and what people are saying about the company. GM's Facebook and Twitter sites are playing a major role in helping GM to regain customers' trust and confidence. As Barra pointed out in an October 2014 interview, "every chance to connect with customers is an opportunity to build a stronger relationship" (Twentyman, 2014, para. 4).

The automaker is primarily using traditional methods, such as letters to customers, blogs, a call center and the media to get its recall message out. A video message from Barra has received wide play on GM's websites and elsewhere. Additionally, social media sites have become an important tool for the company to reveal its commitment to making things right, even as it tries to show off its newest car models and exert enthusiasm among customers unaffected by the recall. "'We're trying to help customers out, but we are also trying to stay true to what the majority of customers are looking for,' said Phil Colley, a social media strategist at the company" (Goel, 2014, para. 12).

The opening of GM's Social Command Center at its Detroit, Michigan headquarters in April 2013 had plenty of social muscle to flex when it come to building those connections online. According to Rebecca Harris, the company's senior manager for global social media strategy, there are 500 employees whose job consist of engaging with customers across 400 social media channels, from Twitter and Facebook to specialist forums for motoring enthusiasts (Twentyman, 2014). In the U.S. alone, GM operates 20 different Facebook pages. Harris says, "from an engagement and sentiment perspective, we (in social media) can absolutely help with corporate reputation" (Twentyman, 2014, para. 7).

At less than two years old, the Social Command Center is already attracting a great deal of senior management attention. It has been reported that Barra herself is regularly provided with reports that keep her updated on GM's social media responses, as well as to her public statements (Twentyman, 2014). Barra says social media will

Employees in General Motors' Social Command Center in Detroit face a wall of monitors, keeping an eye out for product problems and people in need of a part or a dealership.

Source: *Automotive News*

be one of the ways customers will provide driving directions so GM can navigate the road to recovery (Twentyman, 2014).

6.2. Media Response to Barra's Appointment to CEO

After Barra testified before the House Energy and Commerce Subcommittee in April 2014, she became the subject in the opening skit on NBC's "Saturday Night Live." The short sketch poked fun on Barra answering questions from Congress and not having any real answers for them. Her responses repeatedly stated, "we're looking into it" and "that is part of the investigation."

After much speculation that Mary Barra was appointed as CEO for the automaker because of her gender, NBC's Matt Lauer asked Barra on the "Today" show in June 2014 whether she thought she got the job because she is a woman and a mother (Breitman, 2014). Barra is the first female CEO of GM and a mother of two who has been with the carmaker since 1980. She dismissed the speculation, saying that she believes she was selected as the new CEO based on her qualifications (Breitman, 2014).

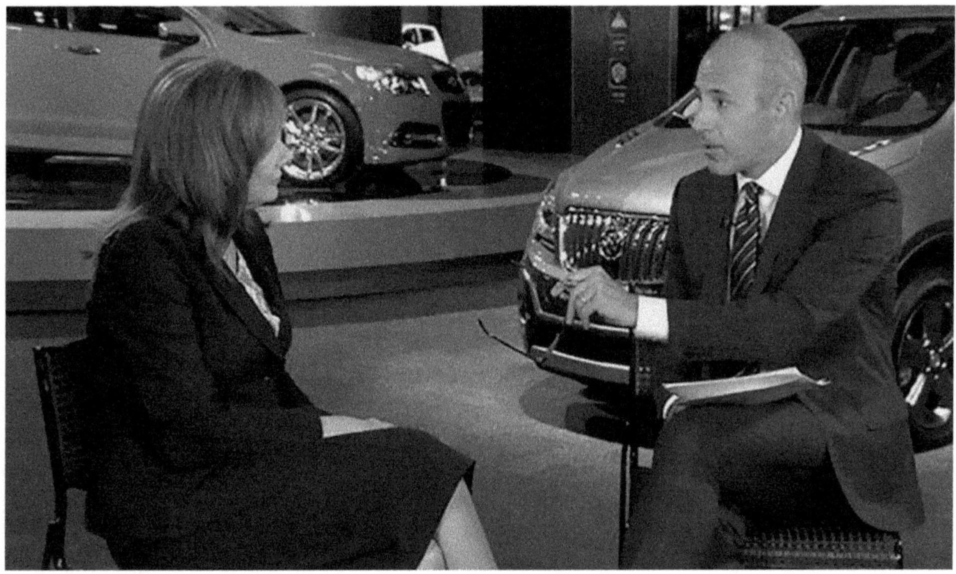

Source: NBC

7. Financial Impact

According to each company's first three 2014 quarterly financial press releases, GM's net revenue surpassed those of competitors Ford and Chrysler, signaling that the recall did not play a significant role on its sales. This is a shift from 2013, when GM lagged significantly behind Ford for the calendar year.

Since February 2014, GM has spent $2.7 billion to cover expenses linked to the ignition switch recall, including $1.3 billion from its first quarter of 2014 earnings,

$.2 billion in restructuring costs, an uncapped compensation program for the victims of the faulty switch (General Motors, 2014d) and $1.2 billion from its second quarter of 2014 (General Motors, 2014e). All the while, GM's vehicle sales increased its second and third quarters of 2014 compared to 2013 (General Motors, 2014d, 2014e).

GM opened 2014 with a share price of $40.95. While it fluctuated between $38 and $33, October 2014 marked a significant decrease in stock value, and at the end of the month, GM shares were worth $31.40. After news broke that the ignition switch death toll had risen to 27, GM hit an all-year low of $29.69 on October 15. Likewise, GM stock dropped to $30.73 on December 16 after the death toll was verified at 42. GM closed 2014 with a share price of $34.91 (Yahoo! Finance, n.d.).

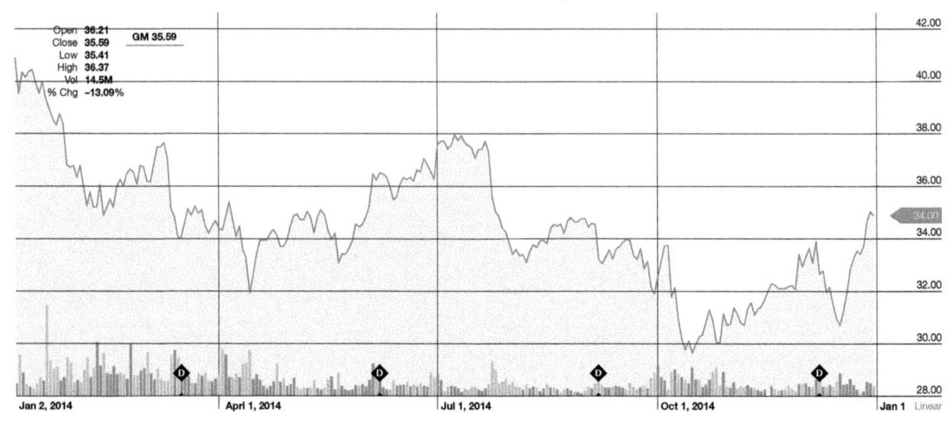

Source: Yahoo! Finance

GM's stock peaked around Barra's public appearances in March 2014 at $37.69, and it steadily climbed after she held a Global Town Hall meeting in June 2014, hovering between $36.50 and $38. In March 2014, Barra announced that GM would set aside $300 million for costs related to the recall, and shares rose 1.6 percent that day, signifying that customers responded positively to Barra's messages (Bennett, 2014b). This correlation between Barra's announcement and the increase in shares is an important indicator to the overall sales and long run success of company. This recall is an early test of her leadership and her ability to make changes to a bureaucracy ruled by committees (Bennett, 2014b).

8. Summary—GM's Challenge

GM's major challenge has not only been dealing with the recall of 2.6 million vehicles, which does a certain amount to tarnish the reputation of any automotive company, but also the way the company owns up to the accusations that employees knew about the problem well before anything was substantially done about it. Over the course of 10 years, several members of the GM staff, across all levels, had an opportunity to speak up, and stand up, to fix a then-minor problem. No one seemed to take the time to consider all the options surrounding the ignition switch.

With the implementation of a new CEO, GM has the opportunity to make amends and turn around its practices in communications, or lack thereof. By refusing to stay quiet or to sugarcoat new information, Barra is leading by example that being honest is the direction she wants her company to head. She beefed up the safety department, hiring a new vice president as a means to ensure something like this never happens again. Barra hired an outside investigator to look into the issues of why GM took so long to come forward with this information and why GM did not take the appropriate measures in the first place. Furthermore, she hired a compensation lawyer to ensure the victims and their families got some justice. Barra discharged multiple colleagues in the best interest of moving the company forward. She created a program to encourage employees to follow her lead and to be more open. She says she is doing all she can to keep her company successful and her customers safe. Barra will have to practice what she preaches if she wants to keep this momentum going and successfully change a culture that has been unable to do so in the past.

II. Resources

Belvedere, M. (2014, November 17). 33 death claims OK'd in GM ignition fund: Feinberg. *CNBC.* Retrieved from www.cnbc.com/id/102190563#

Bennett, J. (2014a, May 6). General Motors offers new discount to owners of recalled cars; move is a sign auto maker is using recall as opportunity to sell new vehicles. *Wall Street Journal.* Retrieved from www.wsj.com/articles/SB10001424052702303417104579546170924474550

Bennett, J. (2014b, March 17). General Motors recalls 1.7 million more vehicles; auto maker plans $300 million charge to cover ignition-switch fix, new recalls. *Wall Street Journal.* Retrieved from www.wsj.com/articles/SB10001424052702303563304579445180043774l5\

Bennett, J. (2014c, November 11). GM's Ammann drives for change. *Wall Street Journal.* Retrieved from http://online.wsj.com/articles/gms-ammann-pushes-for-change-1415751611

Bennett, J. (2014d, June 10). GM developing financial fallout estimate. *Wall Street Journal.* Retrieved from http://online.wsj.com/articles/gm-to-give-ignition-switch-financial-fallout-estimate-in-august-1402407999

Breitman K. (2014, June 26). Matt Lauer defends GM mom question. *Politico.* Retrieved from www.politico.com/story/2014/06/matt-lauer-mary-barra-108346.html

Brody, R. (2014 June 5). Is GM doing enough about its recall delays. *U.S. News.* Retrieved from www.usnews.com/opinion/articles/2014/06/05/are-gm-and-mary-barra-doing-enough-about-recall-delays

Business Insider. (2015, January 1). GM adds another 92,000 cars to its ignition switch recall. Retrieved from www.businessinsider.com/afp-gm-adds-another-92000-vehicles-to-ignition-switch-recall-2015-1

Chicago Tribune. (2015, January). GM ignition switch recall timeline. Retrieved from www.chicagotribune.com/classified/automotive/chi-gm-ignition-switch-recall-timeline-htmlstory.html

Fletcher, M. (2014a, June 5). GM CEO: 15 fired over ignition switch recalls; probe shows pattern of failures, no coverup. *Washington Post.* Retrieved from www.washingtonpost.com/business/economy/gm-ceo-15-fired-over-ignition-switch-recalls-probe-shows-pattern-of-failures-no-coverup/2014/06/05/2dc575bc-ecb8-11e3-9f5c-9075d5508f0a_story.html

Fletcher, M. (2014b, June 6). GM: Faulty ignitions were not covered up. *Washington Post.* pp. A01.

Fletcher, M. & Mufson, S. (2014, March 31). GM's culture is blamed in safety recall. *Washington Post.* pp. A01.

Geier, B. (2014, August 1) General Motors posts its best July since 2007. *Fortune.* Retrieved from http://fortune.com/2014/08/01/general-motors-posts-its-best-july-sales-since-2007/

General Motors. (2014a, March 31). CEO Mary Barra's written Congressional testimony now available [Press release]. Retrieved from http://media.gm.com/media/us/en/gm/news.detail.html/content/Pages/news/us/en/2014/ma r/0331-barra-written-testimony.html

General Motors. (2014b, June 5). GM CEO Mary Barra's remarks to employees on Valukas Report findings [Press release]. Retrieved from http://media.gm.com/media/us/en/gm/news.detail.html/content/Pages/news/us/en/2014/Jun/060514-mary-remarks.html

General Motors. (2014c, April 10). GM Creates Speak Up For Safety Program for employees [Press Release]. Retrieved from http://media.gm.com/media/us/en/gm/news.detail.html/content/Pages/news/us/en/2014/Apr/0410-speakup.html

General Motors. (2014d, April 24). GM reports first quarter net income of $.1 billion [Press release]. Retrieved from http://media.gm.com/content/dam/Media/gmcom/investor/2014/apr/q1-2014-earnings/GM-2014-Q1-Press-Release.pdf

General Motors. (2014e, July 24). GM reports second quarter net income of $.2 billion [Press release]. Retrieved from http://media.gm.com/content/dam/Media/gmcom/investor/2014/jul/2nd-qtr/GM-2014-Q2-Press-Release.pdf

General Motors. (2014f, October 23). GM reports third quarter net income of $1.4 billion [Press release]. Retrieved from http://media.gm.com/content/dam/Media/gmcom/investor/2014/oct/third-qtr/GM-2014-Q3-Press-Release.pdf

George, P. (2014, June 18). Stop blaming GM's 'culture' and start blaming people. Jalopnik. Retrieved from http://jalopnik.com/stop-blaming-gms-culture-and-start-blaming-people-1592657410

GM Lifestyle. (2014). The history of General Motors. Retrieved from www.gmlifestyle.biz/the-history-of-general-motors.php

Goel, V. (2014, March 23). G.M. uses social media to manage customers and its reputation. *New York Times.* Retrieved from www.nytimes.com/2014/03/24/business/after-huge-recall-gm-speaks-to-customers-through-social-media.html

Gress, J. (2014, November 17). GM ignition-switch claims deadline extended to Jan. 31. *Reuters.* Retrieved from www.reuters.com/article/2014/11/17/us-general-motors-recall-extension-idUSKCN0J10B120141117

Gutierrez, G. (2014, March 13). GM chose not to implement a fix for ignition problem. *NBC News.* Retrieved from www.nbcnews.com/storyline/gm-recall/gm-chose-not-implement-fix-ignition-problem-n51731

Himsel, D. (2014, May 16). General Motors, Avon, and the devastating power of entrenched corporate culture. *Forbes.* Retrieved from www.forbes.com/sites/forbesleadershipforum/2014/05/16/general-motors-avon-and-the-devastating-power-of-entrenched-corporate-culture/

Hirsch, J. (2014, March 18). GM appoints safety chief to deal with mounting recall crisis. *Los Angeles Times.* Retrieved from www.latimes.com/business/autos/la-fi-hy-gm-appoints-recall-safety-chief-20140318-story.html#axzz30DR26qas

Isidore, C. (2009, June 2). Will the GM bankruptcy work? *CNN Money.* Retrieved from http://money.cnn.com/2009/06/02/news/companies/gm_will_it_work/index.htm

Isidore, C. (2014, October 23). After six months of recall costs, GM making money again. *CNN Money.* Retrieved from http://money.cnn.com/2014/10/23/news/companies/gm-earnings/

Isidore, C. & Wallace, G. (2014, March 31). Documents show GM, regulators dropped ball before fatal crashes. *CNN Money.* Retrieved from http://money.cnn.com/2014/03/30/autos/general-motors-recall-documents/index.html

Kaptik, A. (2014, June 5). GM's Valukas Report. *Wall Street Journal.* Retrieved from http://blogs.wsj.com/briefly/2014/06/05/gms-valukas-report-the-numbers/

Koenig, B. (2014, June 10). A (partial) list of people who had a chance to change GM's culture. *Forbes.* Retrieved from www.forbes.com/sites/billkoenig/2014/06/10/a-partial-list-of-people-who-had-a-chance-to-change-gms-culture/2/

Maynard, M. (2014a, June 17). As Mary Barra returns to D.C., can GM's culture really change? *Forbes.* www.forbes.com/sites/michelinemaynard/2014/06/17/as-mary-barra-returns-to-d-c-can-gms-culture-really-change/

Maynard, M. (2014b, April 2). Is GM CEO Mary Barra being thrown under the bus? *Forbes.* Retrieved from www.forbes.com/sites/michelinemaynard/2014/04/02/is-gm-ceo-mary-barra-being-thrown-under-the-bus/

Maynard, M. (2014c, June 5)."The GM nod" and other cultural flaws exposed by the ignition defect report. *Forbes.* Retrieved from www.forbes.com/sites/michelinemaynard/2014/06/05/ignition-switch-report-spares-ceo-barra-but-exposes-gms-culture/

McGregor, J. (2014a, June 10). How jargon hurt the culture at GM. *Washington Post.* Retrieved from www.washingtonpost.com/blogs/on-leadership/wp/2014/06/10/how-jargon-hurt-the-culture-at-gm/

McGregor, J. (2014b, June 5). What GM could do to change its culture. *Washington Post.* Retrieved from www.washingtonpost.com/blogs/on-leadership/wp/2014/06/05/what-gm-could-do-to-change-its-culture/

Muller, D. (2014, December 15). Approved death claims related to GM ignition switch recall rise to 42. *M Live.* Retrieved from www.mlive.com/auto/index.ssf/2014/12/approved_death_claims_related_5.html

Muller, J. (2014, May 29). Exclusive Q&A: GM CEO Mary Barra on crisis management, culture change and the future of GM. *Forbes.* Retrieved from www.forbes.com/sites/joannmuller/2014/05/29/exclusive-qa-gm-ceo-mary-barra-on-crisis-management-culture-change-and-the-future-of-gm/

Shepardson, D. & Burden, M. (2014, October 28). GM's Barra: It's time to get candid. *Detroit News.* Retrieved from www.detroitnews.com/story/business/autos/general-motors/2014/10/28/gm-barra-candid/18040051/

Smith, A. (2013, October 10). GM names Mary Barra as CEO. *CNN Money.* Retrieved from http://money.cnn.com/2013/12/10/news/companies/gm-ceo-mary-barra/

Stock, K. (2014 June 5). GM's Mary Barra fires 15, says more recalls are coming. *Bloomberg Businessweek.* Retrieved from www.businessweek.com/articles/2014-06-05/gms-mary-barra-fires-15-says-more-recalls-are-coming

Twentyman, J. (2014, October 17). Using social media to drive change at General Motors. *Diginomica.* Retrieved from http://diginomica.com/2014/10/17/using-social-media-drive-change-general-motors/

Valdes-Dapena, P. (2010, April 21). GM pays off its bailout loans. *CNN Money.* Retrieved from http://money.cnn.com/2010/04/21/autos/gm_loan_repayment/index.htm

Valdes-Dapena, P. & Yellin, T. (2014, March 19). GM: Steps to a recall nightmare. *CNN Money.* Retrieved from http://money.cnn.com/infographic/pf/autos/gm-recall-timeline/

WXYZ Detroit. (2014, April 6). *Saturday Night Live* pokes fun at General Motors CEO Mary Barra. Retrieved from www.wxyz.com/news/region/detroit/gm-ceo-mary-barra-made-fun-of-during-opening-skit-on-saturday-night-live

Yahoo! Finance. (2014). Retrieved November 22, 2014 from http://finance.yahoo.com/echarts?s=GM+Interactive#{%22range%22%3A{%22start%22%3A%222014-01-01T18%3A00%3A00.000Z%22%2C%22end%22%3A%222014-11-23T18%3A00%3A00.000Z%22}%2C%22scale%22%3A%22linear%22}

Permissions

1 "The Volkswagen emissions scandal" by Cameron Cutro (author), Elizabeth Bird (author) and Professor Luann J. Lynch, Almand R. Coleman Professor of Business Administration. It was written as a basis for class discussion rather than to illustrate effective or ineffective handling of an administrative situation. Copyright 2016 by the University of Virginia Darden School Foundation, Charlottesville, VA. All rights reserved.

2 "Which Kaptein to choose? The Havøysund fleet question" by Gregory B. Fairchild, Isidore Horween Research Associate Professor of Business Administration; Bidhan L. Parmar, Associate Professor of Business Administration; Jared D. Harris, Samuel L. Slover Research Chair in Business Administration; and Jenny Mead, Senior Researcher. It was written as a basis for class discussion rather than to illustrate effective or ineffective handling of an administrative situation. Copyright 2018 by the University of Virginia Darden School Foundation, Charlottesville, VA. All rights reserved.

3 "Philosophical foundations of impact investing" by Georgette Fernandez Laris. Used by permission of Dr. Kara Tan Bhala, President and Founder, Seven Pillars Institute for Global Finance and Ethics.

4 "Starbucks Corporation: Tax avoidance controversies in the U.K." by Jack Gay (author) and Scott Manwaring (author) and James O'Rourke (faculty advisor). First prize winner 2015 Arthur W. Page Society Case Study Competition. Used by permission of Professor James O'Rourke, Teaching Professor of Management, University of Notre Dame. Copyright Eugene D. Fanning Center for Business Communication, University of Notre Dame. All rights reserved. No part of this publication may be reproduced, stored in a retrieval system, used in a spreadsheet, or transmitted in any form by any means—electronic, mechanical, photocopying, recording, or otherwise—without permission.

5 "China and Corruption: The Case of GlaxoSmithKline" by Conner Lee. Used by permission of Dr. Kara Tan Bhala, President and Founder, Seven Pillars Institute for Global Finance and Ethics.

6 "A sexual harassment complaint and the fallout." This case was written by Syeda Maseeha Qumer and Debapratim Purkayastha (IBS Hyderabad), and Vijaya

Narapareddy (faculty advisor, Daniels College of Business, University of Denver). It was compiled from published sources, and is intended to be used as a basis for class discussion rather than to illustrate either effective or ineffective handling of a management situation. Copyright 2017, IBS Center for Management Research. All rights reserved.

7 "Mylan's EpiPen Pricing Scandal" by Andreas Kanaris Miyashiro. Used by permission of Dr. Kara Tan Bhala, President and Founder, Seven Pillars Institute for Global Finance and Ethics.

8 "Satyam Computer Services Ltd.: Accounting scandal in India." This case was prepared by Research Assistants Michael Barton and Parag Bhutta under the direction of James S. O'Rourke, Teaching Professor of Management, as the basis for class discussion rather than to illustrate either effective or ineffective handling of an administrative situation. Information was gathered from corporate as well as public sources. Copyright 2005 Eugene D. Fanning Center for Business Communication, University of Notre Dame. All rights reserved. No part of this publication may be reproduced, stored in a retrieval system, used in a spreadsheet, or transmitted in any form by any means—electronic, mechanical, photocopying, recording, or otherwise—without permission.

9 "IKEA in Russia—ethical dilemmas." This case was written by Namratha V. Prasad, under the direction of G.V. Muralidhara, IBS Hyderabad. It was compiled from published sources, and is intended to be used as a basis for class discussion rather than to illustrate either effective or ineffective handling of a management situation. Copyright 2013, IBS Center for Management Research. All rights reserved.

10 "Bristol-Myers Squibb: Patents, Profits, and Public Scrutiny." This case was prepared by Research Assistants Meghan Carter, Matt McHale, and Tom Triscari under the direction of James S. O'Rourke, Teaching Professor of Management, as the basis for class discussion rather than to illustrate either effective or ineffective handling of an administrative situation. Information was gathered from corporate as well as public sources. Copyright 2005 Eugene D. Fanning Center for Business Communication, University of Notre Dame. All rights reserved. No part of this publication may be reproduced, stored in a retrieval system, used in a spreadsheet, or transmitted in any form by any means—electronic, mechanical, photocopying, recording, or otherwise—without permission.

11 "Walking the 'encryption tightrope': Getting to the core of Apple's privacy and security battle with the FBI" by Brooke Lichtman (author), Jaymie Polet (author), Bria Smith (author), Rubai Soni (author) under the supervision of Professor Matt Ragas (De Paul University). Grand prize winner 2017 Arthur W. Page Society Case Study Competition. Used by permission of Professor Matt Ragas, Professor of Communication, DePaul University.

12 "BP's Deepwater Horizon oil spill crisis and its recovery through Team USA Olympic sponsorship an analysis of reputation management and corporate sponsorships" by Neha Jain (author) under supervision of faculty advisor John Trybus. Third prize winner 2015 Arthur W. Page Society Case Study Competition. Used by permission of Professor John Trybus, Managing Director and Adjunct Professor Georgetown University's Center for Social Impact Communication.

13 "The Need for Cultural Intelligence: An Analysis of Asiana Airlines' Response to the Crash Landing of Flight 214" by Dionne Gomez and Erin Reed (author) under the supervision of Professor Matt Ragas (De Paul University). First prize winner 2014 Arthur W. Page Society Case Study Competition. Used by permission of Professor Matt Ragas, Professor of Communication, DePaul University.

14 "Why was the snow polluted?: A blind spot for the Japanese top milk product company, Snow Brand" by Dr. Brenda J. Wrigley, APR, Professor, Curry College, Milton, MA, Shizuko Ota and Akie Kikuchi, Alumnae, Michigan State University.

15 "Airbnb: Scaling safety with rapid growth" by Matthew Beck (author), Will Foster (author) and Claire Kenney (author) under supervision of faculty advisor: Dr. James S. O'Rourke. Third prize winner 2015 Arthur W. Page Society Case Study Competition. Used by permission of Professor James O'Rourke, Teaching Professor of Management, University of Notre Dame. Copyright Eugene D. Fanning Center for Business Communication, University of Notre Dame. All rights reserved. No part of this publication may be reproduced, stored in a retrieval system, used in a spreadsheet, or transmitted in any form by any means—electronic, mechanical, photocopying, recording, or otherwise—without permission.

16 "'Bad Apple' behavior or a spoiled barrel: An analysis of Wells Fargo's crisis response to alleged culture flaws" by Eva Marne (author) and Haleigh Stern (author) under supervision of Faculty Advisor: Dr. Matt Ragas, DePaul University. First prize winner 2017 Arthur W. Page Society Case Study Competition. Used by permission of Professor Matt Ragas, Professor of Communication, DePaul University.

17 "The ethics of executive compensation: A matter of duty" by Aidan Balnaves-James. Used by permission of Dr. Kara Tan Bhala, President and Founder, Seven Pillars Institute for Global Finance and Ethics.

18 "General Motors' corporate culture crisis: An assessment of the ignition switch recall by Alie Kuopus (Author), Sue Nicole Susenburger (author) and Lily Kim (author) under the supervision of Professor Matt Ragas (De Paul University). First prize winner 2015 Arthur W. Page Society Case Study Competition. Used by permission of Professor Matt Ragas, Professor of Communication, DePaul University.

Index